HUGMAN'S CRICKET ANNUAL 1990

Out at last. Mark Taylor, the batting hero of the 1989 Test series, is stumped by Russell off Cook for 219 at Trent Bridge in the sixth Test. Adrian Murrell

Compiled by Peter Arnold and Peter Wynne-Thomas

Edited by Barry J. Hugman

HUGMAN'S SPORTING PUBLICATIONS LIMITED

First published in Great Britain in 1990 by
Hugman's Sporting Publications Ltd
24 Notting Hill Gate
London W11 3JQ

British Library Cataloguing in Publication Data
Hugman, Barry J. (Barry John)
Hugman's Cricket Annual 1990

ISBN 1 872290 04 3

Typeset by Area Graphics Ltd, Arden Press Way, Letchworth, Hertfordshire SG6 1LH
Printed in Great Britain by The Bath Press, Avon

Contents

Introduction

The compilers of this new Cricket Yearbook have no desire to put the bible of cricket, *Wisden Cricketers' Almanack*, out of business. That would be rather presumptuous, considering *Wisden* has 126 years start.

All we wish to do is to produce an annual which gives the keen follower of the game all he needs in order to savour in future the significant events of the season.

We therefore include the scorecards of all the first-class matches, county by county. We present them in a manner which makes for the easiest comprehension of the progress of a game, i.e. in one column, the first innings at the top, and proceeding to the fourth innings at the bottom. And a short note of any interesting facts of the match are attached. The scorecards are set out in the section of the home team, which also includes potted scores for the away matches.

Each of the one-day matches of the season also have their scorecards included in the same way. The county sections also include a team photograph and short biographies of the players. Thus a reader looking up a particular match can also discover the ages, etc of the players, and find a picture of them.

Because the big matches of any cricket year are still the Test matches, there is a chapter on the winter season 1988–89, in which are given accounts of international cricket between all the Test-playing countries. Test match scorecards are given in full, but such is the proliferation of one-day tournaments all round the world these days that overseas one-day internationals are merely noted, and the full scorecards are not given.

All of these chapters are illustrated, some in colour. So far as photographs are concerned, twelve are full-page colour shots of the selected best team of the 1989 season, plus the 12th man.

However since this is also a serious annual of statistics, generous details of matches concerning the Universities, the Minor Counties, Scotland, Ireland and the first-class counties' second eleven competition are included. All first-class matches are given their full scorecards.

The first-class averages for the 1989 season are included, as are averages elsewhere, e.g. for the individual counties, and for the Test series.

On the grounds, still, of giving the reader what he wants, an alphabetical list is included of all the major cricket books published during the year, with publishers and prices, and a one-line appraisal of each. There are almost 100 titles in the 1989 list. Obituaries are also included, plus the fixtures for 1990.

We hope that the book is as free from error as possible, and in this regard we record our thanks to David Baggett and Steve Langbridge, who did sterling work in checking the proofs of countless scorecards.

Peter Arnold
Peter Wynne-Thomas
January 1990

Robin Smith (centre) was among the runs with 143 in the fourth test against Australia at Old Trafford.

Allsport/Adrian Murrell

Diary of the 1989 Season

The following is a month by month review of the 1989 season, mainly in relation to news stories and the progress of the domestic cricketing trophies, since the Australian tour is dealt with separately.

November 1988–March 1989

In the close season, during which attempts failed to arrange a replacement tour for England after the scheduled tour of India was called off, the news was mostly of retirements. Keith Fletcher, the Essex captain who became the first to win all four of the major domestic competitions, retired in order to captain the second XI.

C.J. 'Jack' Richards, Surrey's Cornish-born wicket-keeper, and the second Cornishman to play Test cricket for England, was dismissed by Surrey with a year of his contract to run. The reason was said to be personality clashes between him and the new Surrey captain Ian Greig. Richards had finished top of the Surrey batting averages in 1988, and had played for England eight times since 1986–87, scoring a century in his second Test.

One who would be making a debut in County cricket in 1989 was Transvaal's opening batsman Jimmy Cook, who was signed as their overseas player by Somerset.

The new season would see a switch of counties by England bowler Philip DeFreitas, who had experienced some well-publicised differences with colleagues in the Leicestershire dressing-room. He switched his allegiance to Lancashire. Another former England player, batsman Chris Tavaré, decided to sign a one-year contract with Somerset. He had been unhappy at Kent since being deposed as captain and replaced by Chris Cowdrey in 1985. He was later appointed Somerset vice-captain. David Graveney, the Gloucestershire captain, was similarly deposed with little justification in 1988, but agreed to play on in 1989 under new skipper Bill Athey.

West Indians featured in the plans of two counties. Glamorgan signed a two-year contract with the ex-Somerset player Viv Richards, but it was announced that the injured Richards would not be eligible before 1 July – in the event he was missing all season. However, one purpose of the signing was to have Richards available in 1990, when Ravi Shastri, Glamorgan's current overseas player, would probably be in the Indian party touring England. Middlesex also signed a two-year contract with experienced Test opener Desmond Haynes.

The winter meeting of the TCCB voted against a recommendation of their executive committee to reduce the seven-year qualification period which players from non-Test-playing countries had to serve before becoming eligible for England. This had been reduced from ten years in 1987, and the recommendation was to reduce it further to four years. The obvious beneficiary would have been Graeme Hick, the Zimbabwe-born Worcestershire batsman, who could have played for England immediately had the resolution been passed, but who must continue to wait until 1991 for Test match eligibility.

The International Cricket Conference meeting on 23 and 24 January dealt with the question of players with links with South Africa. The 25 participating countries agreed that cricketers who played or coached in South Africa after 31 March 1989 would be banned from international cricket for four years. The ban would not be retrospective. It meant that all those players qualified for England who earned a living by playing or coaching in South Africa in the winter season would have to assess their prospects of selection for international teams and decide whether such prospects were sufficient for them to give up their winter earnings.

No sooner had the meeting ended than there was speculation as to how many players would prefer to play in South Africa in 1989–90 rather than to go on the scheduled tour of the West Indies, and Jack Bannister, the secretary of the Cricketers Association, said that already eight of England's senior squad would prefer South Africa.

At the TCCB's spring meeting in March, a new chairman of Test selectors was chosen to replace Peter May, who had resigned some months earlier. Ted Dexter was named chairman of a new 'England Committee', also comprising Mickey Stewart, the England manager, and *ex officio* members in the TCCB's chief executive and cricket committee chairman, currently Alan Smith and Ossie Wheatley. The old selection panel was dispensed with, so Fred Titmus and Phil Sharpe lost their selectorial responsibilities.

The new committee announced David Gower's appointment as captain for all the summer's Test matches, and named a 19-man training squad, whose first session was held at Lord's on 13, 14 April.

April

The new season got under way in mid-April. Early announcements came from the sponsors. Cornhill Insurance committed themselves to £852,000 for the Test series. Britannic Assurance announced that the 1989 Championship winners would receive £37,000, an increase of £2,000 from 1989, while there would be similar increases in all the other awards, including 30 school awards. Benson and Hedges, National Westminster Bank and Refuge Assurance all announced that the winners of their competitions would receive £22,000, with pro-rata payments for runners-up, etc. In addition, the winners of the Refuge Assurance Cup would received £5,500. For the tourist's games, the Australian brewers Castlemaine announced the 'XXXX County Challenge' prize fund of £25,000 for awards for outstanding performances by the tourists and home players in the county matches. The Counties 2nd XI Championship was renamed the Rapid Cricketline Championship after TCCB signed a £1,000,000 sponsorship deal lasting three years with bookmaker William Hill, whose telephone update service on first-class matches carried TCCB endorsement as the 'official TCCB service'. MCC broke a 202-year old tradition by signing a £30,000 sponsorship deal with the brewers Bass, which would provide prize money for various MCC matches.

On the cricket field, many of the early matches were drawn, including Champion County (Worcestershire) v MCC at Lord's (scorecard reproduced here), during which there was a minute's silence before the second day in memory of the victims of the soccer tragedy at Hillsborough the previous day.

The Britannic Assurance Championship got under way on 20 April. In the four-day games, Northants survived at Derby to draw with their last pair at the wicket. Peter Roebuck made the first Championship century for Somerset against Hampshire at Southampton, where Jimmy Cook scored 85 and 44 not out on his debut. David Gower made an auspicious start by getting his highest score with 228 at Leicester against Glamorgan. During the innings he scored his 20,000th first-class run.

At Lord's, where Middlesex played Yorkshire, there was a minute's silence before the game in memory of Wilf Slack, their opening batsman who had died in The Gambia in January. With plenty of rain about, there was only one winning side in the first round of matches: the Champions Worcestershire, who beat Nottinghamshire at Trent Bridge by seven wickets.

The first Sunday of the Refuge Assurance League, 23 April, saw four matches abandoned without results, including that at Derby, where snow prevented play.

The Benson and Hedges Cup got under way on 25 April, and there was an immediate surprise result, when the Combined Universities team registered their first win for five years. In a match reduced to 37 overs they scored 116 and then restricted Surrey to 107 for nine. Off-spinner James Boiling, 21 years old, took three wickets for 9 in eight overs to win the match award – ironically he is on Surrey's books.

In the second round of Championship games, rain washed out the first day in half the games.

Graeme Hick playing towards third man. Hick was the outstanding batsman of the 1988 season, and he began 1989 in tremendous style with 173 not out for Worcestershire against the MCC at Lord's. It was to be his highest score of the season.

Allsport/Adrian Murrell

MCC v WORCESTERSHIRE (Lord's)
April 15, 16, 17, 18
Drawn.

Worcestershire 1st Innings					
T.S. Curtis	c Russell b Medlycott				92
J. Lord	c Russell b Fraser				80
G.A. Hick	not out				173
D.B. d'Oliveira	c Parker b Agnew				38
*P.A. Neale	not out				50
I.T. Botham					
†S.J. Rhodes					
P.J. Newport					
R.K. Illingworth					
N.V. Radford					
G.R. Dilley					
Extras	b 3, lb 21, nb 17				41
Total (3 wkts dec)					474
177, 205, 310					
Lawrence	31	6	82	0	
Agnew	33	9	100	1	
Fraser	38	10	64	1	
Medlycott	32	5	141	1	
Cowdrey	15	1	54	0	
Barnett	2	0	9	0	
MCC 1st Innings					
K.J. Barnett	c Botham b Newport				39
J.D. Carr	c Botham b Illingworth				64
*P.W.G. Parker	b Radford				12
R.A. Smith	b Botham				56
A.J. Lamb	not out				67
C.S. Cowdrey	not out				12
K.T. Medlycott					
J.P. Agnew					
†R.C. Russell					
A.R.C. Fraser					
D.V. Lawrence					
Extras	b 2, lb 12, w 4, nb 13				31
Total (4 wkts)					281
57, 123, 139, 209					
Dilley	16	6	58	0	
Radford	17	6	60	1	
Newport	17	1	75	1	
Botham	20	5	36	1	
Illingworth	16	3	36	1	
Curtis	1	0	2	0	

Umpires: D.J. Constant and J.H. Hampshire
Toss: Worcestershire.
The first day was mainly taken up with some mundane batting from Curtis and Lord, the county ending at 256–2. Hick 35* overnight reached 173 at tea on the second day, rain then ending play. His innings lasted 330 minutes. No play was possible on Monday and this made Tuesday play rather meaningless.

BENSON AND HEDGES CUP
Qualifying Groups

GROUP A	*P*	*W*	*L*	*NR*	*Pts*	*Rate*
ESSEX	4	4	0	0	8	65.73
KENT	4	2	2	0	4	57.95
Sussex	4	2	2	0	4	57.40
Hampshire	4	1	3	0	2	70.91
Glamorgan	4	1	3	0	2	48.13
GROUP B						
GLOUCESTERSHIRE	4	4	0	0	8	67.79
COMBINED UNIVERSITIES	4	2	2	0	4	62.11
Middlesex	4	2	2	0	4	58.99
Worcestershire	4	1	3	0	2	57.22
Surrey	4	1	3	0	2	49.17
GROUP C						
SOMERSET	4	4	0	0	8	61.86
NOTTINGHAMSHIRE	4	3	1	0	6	55.96
Yorkshire	4	2	2	0	4	51.91
Derbyshire	4	1	3	0	2	56.11
Minor Counties	4	0	4	0	0	50.75
GROUP D						
NORTHAMPTONSHIRE	4	3	0	1	7	69.86
LANCASHIRE	4	3	1	0	6	61.33
Leicestershire	4	2	1	1	5	65.75
Warwickshire	4	1	3	0	2	64.79
Scotland	4	0	4	0	0	45.00

Allan Lamb, the captain of Northants, who began the season well, making 148 in 149 balls (100 in 81 balls) in a one-wicket victory over Leicestershire, but was to suffer a succession of unrelated injuries during the season which kept him out of several games.

Allsport/Ben Radford

There were two results, Essex beating Middlesex and Northants beating Gloucestershire. Essex won in a day and a half, Pringle taking five wickets in each innings as Middlesex made 129 and 85. Warwickshire drew with Worcestershire with the scores level, but as Warwickshire had six wickets to fall, they earned eight extra points. Lancashire captain David Hughes was critical of Notts in the match at Old Trafford. Having set them 268 to win in 55 overs he saw Broad and Robinson make no attempt, ending at 147 for no wicket.

There were results in all Sunday League games on the last day of April and the season was well and truly launched.

May

There were plenty of good performances in the first Championship matches of May, perhaps the best being that of Notts' Franklyn Stephenson at Headingley. Stephenson seems to like playing against Yorkshire, and his seven for 38 and six for 37 gave him his best figures for both an innings and a match. Notts won by ten wickets, after being dismissed for 86 in their first innings. The match was over half an hour after lunch on the second day, it being scheduled to last four.

Essex had an overwhelming win over Derbyshire, by an innings and 212 runs after losing only three wickets themselves. Derbyshire performed the rare feat in a completed match of taking no points. At the other extreme, Northants beat Leicestershire by one wicket. Lamb made a century in 81 balls, although there was no hurry, as victory was obtained with a day to spare.

Surrey's new recruit from Queensland, left-arm fast-medium Dirk Tazelaar, was banned from further bowling in the first innings against Middlesex at Lord's for running down the pitch. A happier event was Rodney Ontong's return for Glamorgan at Cardiff to play his first first-class match since a bad road accident nine months earlier.

In the middle of May, David Bairstow of Yorkshire caught Northamptonshire's Geoff Cook to record his 1,072nd first-class dismissal, passing the record for Yorkshire wicket-keepers established by Jimmy Binks. Ian Bishop of Trinidad made his debut for Derbyshire in a match against Leicestershire, but was on the losing side, the bowling honours being taken by Leicestershire's Antiguan, Winston Benjamin, whose first-innings six for 26 was his best bowling and shot Derbyshire out for 57.

In an extraordinary Championship match at Bristol, 24 wickets fell on the first day, 20 May: Essex 178 and 18 for four, Gloucestershire 80. Essex won in two days. The series of games beginning on 20 May were the first three-day Championship games of the season. Five of the six produced a result, but eight of the remaining 11 three-day games played in May finished as draws.

There was more good bowling in the match between Glamorgan and Northants at Swansea, but again not from the distinguished West Indian debutant. Test bowler Curtly Ambrose of the Leeward Islands made his Northants debut. In a match of incidents Northants fast bowler Greg Thomas, playing against his old colleagues, was reprimanded by umpire David Evans for dissent, and Wayne Larkins was given out 'hit wicket' when his helmet fell on the stumps. The good bowling came when Northants were asked to score 305 in 73 overs. Steven Watkin took four wickets without conceding a run to have them 1 for four. His final figures were six for 42 as Northants were out for 60.

In the last round of Championship matches in May it was the turn of the batsmen to do well as the summer settled down to one of good weather, and at Cardiff there was no joy for Watkin or any bowlers as Chris Broad of Notts made a century in each innings (132 and 113) in a high scoring draw.

At the end of May, Lancashire, having played seven matches, led the Championship with 89 points. The counties doing best, however, were Northants, Essex and Middlesex, who had 77, 77 and 75 points respectively from five games. These were the only four counties with three wins. Hampshire and Worcestershire had won twice, while the counties who had yet to register a win were Warwickshire, Sussex, Kent, Yorkshire and Gloucestershire.

The Benson and Hedges Cup reached the quarter final stage on 31 May. There was a high scoring game on 9 May when Hampshire and Glamorgan shared 576 runs while only five wickets fell: Glamorgan won by eight wickets despite Robin Smith's 155 not out. Hugh Morris replied with 143 not out. The main interest in the competition lay in the progress of Combined Universities, however. On 11 May they beat the County Champions, Worcestershire, by scoring 217 for five. On 13 May they lost by seven wickets after a curious last over. Universities made 223 for seven, and the scoreboard showed Gloucestershire 223 for six, as Jack Russell blocked the first four balls of the over in an attempt to win on the 'fewer wickets lost' principle. However, umpire Evans then pointed out that the board was wrong, and that seven wickets were down, whereupon Russell hit the four that won the match. Nevertheless Combined Universities became the first of the 'lower ranking' sides to reach a Benson and Hedges quarter-final. The final tables are reproduced on page 7.

In the quarter-finals on 31 May, Essex beat Lancashire by three wickets, scoring 250 for seven. Brian Hardie (65) and Mark Waugh (93) set up the win with a third-wicket partnership of 158. Neil Foster took nought for 67 in 11 overs; Mike Watkinson one for 68 in nine.

In an excellent match at Bristol, Chris Broad (106) scored a third century in five days as Notts beat Gloucestershire by only five runs, Gloucestershire's last wicket falling in the last over. Broad had to take over Franklyn Stephenson's bowling after he broke down with a hamstring strain in his third over.

Eddie Hemmings turns John Lever to leg in the Benson and Hedges Cup Final at Lord's. This Final was to provide the most exciting finish of the one-day competitions, when Hemmings, a few minutes later, needing a boundary off the last ball, managed to squeeze Lever past point for four runs.

Patrick Eagar

Combined Universities effort only just failed against Somerset after Cook (61) and Roebuck (102) had put on 109 for Somerset's first wicket. Chasing 252, Nasser Hussain (118) and J.I. Longley added 114 for the fourth wicket in 17 overs. Needing nine from the last over with four wickets in hand, Universities scored only five and lost three wickets, ending at 249 for nine.

Kent beat Northants in the other quarter-final by 21 runs after Curtly Ambrose took one for 66, including 11 no-balls in Kent's 208 for eight.

The unhappy Surrey made news again near the end of May when they sacked their West Indian fast bowler Sylvester Clarke in his 11th season with them. Clarke failed to attend a team meeting and next day arrived late for a Sunday league match, not for the first time, and was dismissed for 'persistent breaches of the terms and conditions of his contract'.

At the end of May, the Refuge Assurance League was led by Essex with six wins from six matches. Lancashire, having suffered a 'no result' were two points behind. Then came Surrey, Northants, Middlesex and Hampshire.

June

Bad weather early in June led to the first batch of Championship games being drawn, although Surrey's last pair, Tony Murphy and Mark Frost, had to survive ten overs for the draw – neither scored a run. At Worcester, Ian Botham top-edged a delivery from Steve Barwick into his face, and fractured his cheek bone in three places. The injury caused him to miss the first Test.

With many delays about, the next group of Championship games contained some contrived results. At Cardiff, Glamorgan forfeited their first innings, and Somerset their second, but Glamorgan's last-wicket pair then held on for four overs for the draw. At Tunbridge Wells and Leicester, the sides batting second (Sussex and Leicestershire) both declared when well behind. Sussex went on to beat Kent, but Leicestershire lost to Yorkshire – both finishes were close, but did not necessarily bear any relation to the relative strengths of the sides.

Tim Robinson and Paul Pollard could count themselves unlucky to be on the losing side in a match with Kent at Trent Bridge. Robinson made a century in each innings (128 and 146 not out), while Pollard made 83 and 131. They shared opening stands of 222 and 286, the first instance of two 200-plus opening stands in England (the only other instance being in Auckland in 1948–49, B. Sutcliffe and D.D. Taylor, 220 and 286). Kent needed 311 in 54 overs to win, and got them with eight balls to spare.

Industry won Essex a match against Hampshire at Ilford. They actually managed 22 overs in the last hour, and took the final wicket to give themselves victory with the first ball of the 22nd. In the same series of games, Somerset's Jimmy Cook became the first batsman to 1,000 runs when he reached 12 against Gloucestershire, remarkable in that Somerset were all out for 73 against Courtney Walsh, who took seven for 19. Cook added to his aggregate with 147 in the second innings, but Gloucestershire won by eight wickets. At Edgbaston, where Warwickshire and Glamorgan drew, Warwickshire's Andy Moles, with 130 not out and 46 not out, was on the field for the entire match.

Surrey's signing from Australia, Dirk Tazelaar, was forced to go home with a back injury after playing only four first-class matches for his new county. Glamorgan's fast bowler Steve Watkin had better luck – he was Britannic Assurance Championship player of the month for his 29 wickets. Essex were team of the month.

Essex led the table at the end of the month with 140 points from nine unbeaten matches. Their six wins were two more than any other county, some of whom had played ten or 11 matches. Northants and Middlesex with four wins were second and third, with Lancashire, Hampshire and Champions Worcestershire, each with three wins, next.

The Benson and Hedges semi-finals were played on 14 June. At Trent Bridge, Broad (66) and Pollard (77) began Notts' innings with a stand of 141, and with Robinson, dropping himself in the order, making 80, Notts reached 296 for six, too many for Kent, who were bowled out for 227. At Taunton, Essex made only three fewer than Notts, with 293 for five, but Somerset made a great effort, led by Tavaré, who made 104 not out. Somerset needed ten from Lever's last over, and were all out for 289. Derek Pringle, coming from the first Test where he took one for plenty, was the butt of the crowd and made a rude gesture to them after Essex's win, for which the TCCB fined him £150 and warned him about his future behaviour.

The NatWest Trophy first round held no real surprises, although the apparently unbeatable Essex were knocked out – by Somerset, gaining revenge at Taunton for the Benson and Hedges defeat. Tavaré made another century, and with Peter Roebuck, who also made a hundred, added 195 for the third wicket.

The Refuge Assurance League provided some nostalgia for Surrey supporters when because of injury Surrey were forced to play coach Geoff Arnold, whose previous appearance for them had been 12 years before. As steady as ever, he took one for 7 in six overs against Northants in a lost cause. On the same day Gatting broke his left thumb against Leicestershire and missed the first Test (Botham's injury occurred next day). Glamorgan's Steve Barwick had a strange match against Worcestershire, for whom he had taken six for 40 the previous day in the Championship game. He made his highest Sunday score of 48 not out, but conceded 75 runs with no reward in eight overs. Botham scored 70, and next day Barwick fractured Botham's cheek. Such are the day to day fortunes of cricketers.

Near the end of June Curtly Ambrose had another odd day. After Northants had been shot out for 81 (Lawrie Taylor five for 20), he began Leicestershire's innings with five wides.

Essex led the table at the end of June, as they did

Ricardo Ellcock of Middlesex bowling in the NatWest Final. Although he did not shine in this match, Ellcock impressed the selectors sufficiently during the summer to get himself on the boat to the West Indies as one of the winter touring party.

Patrick Eagar

the Championship. Eight wins and one defeat kept them two points clear of Lancashire, with their one no result. Hampshire, Surrey and Yorkshire laboured at least eight points behind.

July

The first round of Championship games in July produced a couple of quick wins and some contrived finishes. One man happy with his first-class debut was Leicestershire's wicket-keeper Paul Nixon, who took seven catches against Warwickshire. Not happy were the entire Middlesex side, routed for 43 in their second innings against Lancashire at Lord's. DeFreitas took seven for 21.

With some rain about, there were more contrived results in the matches beginning 8 July. Essex, Hampshire and Worcestershire won well, but must have been disappointed to see Gloucestershire, Middlesex and Yorkshire also win after convenient declarations – at Middlesbrough, Yorkshire and Sussex each forfeited an innings.

In the matches of 19 July, Essex beat Kent by an innings and six runs in two days at Southend, and the pitch consultant, Harry Brind, was called in to examine the quality of the wicket. He was also needed at Headingley after Middlesex, needing 75, got them after being 34 for seven.

There was an extraordinary match at Trent Bridge, when Somerset's Jimmy Cook scored 120 not out and 131 not out, becoming the fifth player in history to carry his bat in both completed innings of a match, and the second to achieve it with two centuries (C.J.B. Wood, Leicestershire v

Yorkshire in 1911 being the other). Cook's scores were made out of totals of 186 and 218. In the second innings, Somerset's last seven batsmen contributed three runs. Cook made over 60 per cent of his side's runs in each innings. His outstanding feat was in vain, as Somerset lost by an innings and 67 runs!

In the next series of matches the Southend pitch again was inspected after Essex beat Yorkshire by three wickets. Harry Brind was accompanied by the TCCB pitches committee, and the result was that 25 points were deducted from Essex's total on the grounds that the pitch was 'clearly unsuitable for first-class cricket'. Essex were the first to pay such a forfeit under the TCCB's plan to improve the standard of pitches. There was no reflection on Essex, as they had no control over the pitch, which was prepared by the local council.

Somerset's Cook was in the headlines again at Taunton with his fourth consecutive first-class century (148), a Somerset record. He had batted for 14 hours and 21 minutes between dismissals, scoring 399 runs.

The Cardiff pitch came under inspection in the matches beginning 26 July, but no action was taken. At Portsmouth, Gloucestershire were dismissed in their second innings by Hampshire for 48, with Cardigan Connor producing his career-best bowling performance with seven for 31. At Uxbridge Essex gained a first-innings lead of 195 over Middlesex, but Haynes (143 not out) and Gatting (158 not out) shared an unbroken third-wicket stand of 319 to force the draw. Cook made a second innings 130 for Somerset against Sussex at Hove to register his fifth century in six innings.

The last Championship games of the month, beginning on 29 July, were highlighted by a great bowling performance by Franklyn Stephenson for Notts against Essex at Trent Bridge. He took seven for 59 and eight for 47 (15 for 106 in the match) to record the best match figures in England since 1972 (Bob Massie) and the best in the Championship since 1967 (Tom Cartwright).

Jimmy Cook was an obvious choice for the Britannic Assurance player of the month award, and Worcestershire were the team winners. On a sadder note Glamorgan's former captain, Rodney Ontong, was forced to retire after his car accident the previous August. He topped 14,000 runs and 800 first-class wickets.

On 2 August, Worcestershire headed the Championship, by virtue of Essex losing 25 points over the Southend pitch. They led Essex by seven

BENSON AND HEDGES CUP FINAL
ESSEX v NOTTINGHAMSHIRE
Lord's, July 15
Nottinghamshire won by 3 wkts

Essex		
*G.A. Gooch	b Afford	48
B.R. Hardie	b Stephenson	0
A.W. Lilley	not out	95
M.E. Waugh	c Robinson b Evans	41
P.J. Prichard	lbw b Cooper	1
J.P. Stephenson	run out	9
D.R. Pringle	run out	15
†M.A. Garnham	c Johnson b Evans	0
N.A. Foster	not out	2
G. Miller		
J.K. Lever		
Extras	b 1, lb 26, w 4, nb 1	32
Total (7 wkts, 55 ov)		243

4, 74, 156, 162, 185, 220, 235

Stephenson	11	0	61	1
Cooper	11	3	30	1
Evans	11	0	28	2
Afford	11	0	50	1
Hemmings	11	0	47	0

Nottinghamshire		
B.C. Broad	c Garnham b Lever	6
P.R. Pollard	lbw b Lever	2
*R.T. Robinson	run out	86
P. Johnson	b Foster	54
D.W. Randall	c Waugh b Pringle	49
F.D. Stephenson	c Gooch b Miller	0
K.P. Evans	run out	26
†B.N. French	not out	8
E.E. Hemmings	not out	6
K.E. Cooper		
J.A. Afford		
Extras	b 1, lb 3, w 2, nb 1	7
Total (7 wkts, 55 ov)		244

5, 17, 149, 162, 221, 234

Lever	11	2	43	2
Foster	11	1	40	1
Gooch	11	0	57	0
Pringle	11	1	38	1
Miller	9	0	50	1
Stephenson	2	0	12	0

Umpires: K.E. Palmer and D.R. Shepherd
Toss: Essex. Gold: R.T. Robinson

NATWEST TROPHY FINAL
MIDDLESEX v WARWICKSHIRE
Lord's, September 2
Warwickshire won by 4 wkts

Middlesex		
J.D. Carr	c Humpage b Reeve	17
D.L. Haynes	b N.M.K. Smith	50
*M.W. Gatting	b Munton	1
M.R. Ramprakash	b Donald	24
M.A. Roseberry	c Asif Din b Small	26
†P.R. Downton	not out	43
J.E. Emburey	not out	21
S.P. Hughes		
A.R.C. Fraser		
N.G. Cowans		
R.M. Ellcock		
Extras	lb 16, w 9, nb 3	28
Total (5 wkts 60 ov)		210

40, 41, 98, 111, 148

Donald	12	1	41	1
Small	12	3	35	1
Reeve	12	4	27	1
Munton	11	3	37	1
P.A. Smith	4	0	21	0
N.M.K. Smith	9	0	33	1

Warwickshire		
A.J. Moles	b Fraser	10
*T.A. Lloyd	b Emburey	34
A.I. Kallicharran	c Downton b Fraser	0
†G.W. Humpage	c Gatting b Cowans	36
P.A. Smith	b Carr	24
D.A. Reeve	run out	42
M. Asif Din	not out	34
N.M.K. Smith	not out	15
G.C. Small		
A.A. Donald		
T.A. Munton		
Extras	b 4, lb 7, w 5	16
Total (6 wkts, 59.4 ov)		211

6, 26, 66, 99, 122, 191

Ellcock	10	1	45	0
Cowans	12	4	23	1
Fraser	12	3	30	2
Hughes	10.4	4	45	0
Emburey	12	2	46	1
Carr	3	0	11	1

Umpires: H.D. Bird and N.T. Plews
Toss: Middlesex. MofM: D.A. Reeve

REFUGE ASSURANCE CUP FINAL
ESSEX v NOTTINGHAMSHIRE
Edgbaston, September 17
Essex won by 5 runs

Essex		
*G.A. Gooch	b Pick	31
B.R. Hardie	b Saxelby	18
M.E. Waugh	b Hemmings	4
P.R. Prichard	run out	56
N. Hussain	run out	32
J.P. Stephenson	not out	2
†M.A. Garnham		
D.R. Pringle		
G. Miller		
N.A. Foster		
J.H. Childs		
Extras	b 1, lb 13, w 3	17
Total (5 wkts, 40 ov)		160

52, 59, 75, 158, 160

Cooper	8	2	34	0
Pick	8	2	26	1
Stephenson	8	1	37	0
Saxelby	8	1	25	1
Hemmings	8	2	24	1

Nottinghamshire		
B.C. Broad	b Miller	39
P. Pollard	lbw b Gooch	12
*R.T. Robinson	c Hussain b Pringle	22
D.W. Randall	c Childs	14
P. Johnson	st Garnham b Childs	1
F.D. Stephenson	c and b Gooch	16
E.E. Hemmings	c Waugh b Pringle	24
†C.W. Scott	c Garnham b Foster	1
K.E. Cooper	lbw b Pringle	10
K. Saxelby	c and b Pringle	5
R.A. Pick	not out	1
Extras	lb 8, w 3	10
Total (39.4 ov)		155

35, 69, 81, 90, 95, 118, 131, 147, 154

Foster	8	0	48	1
Pringle	7.4	0	20	4
Miller	8	0	20	1
Gooch	8	1	34	2
Childs	8	0	26	2

Umpires: J.W. Holder and B.J. Meyer
Toss: Nottinghamshire. MofM: P.J. Prichard

points. Middlesex were 32 points behind Essex, with Northants, Lancashire and Hampshire next. It looked like a two-horse race.

The second round of the NatWest Trophy saw an exciting win by Lancashire at Bristol, where they beat Gloucestershire by one wicket with Paul Allott hitting the last ball of the match for six (two were required). At Taunton, where Northants beat Somerset, the home bowler Adrian Jones was reported for swearing after an umpire's decision – he was fined £150 and warned by the TCCB.

The attraction of the Refuge Assurance League was shown at Scarborough on 16 July, where Yorkshire beat their record Sunday receipts by taking £23,544 from a crowd of 10,000, who saw a very exciting match in which Worcestershire's captain Phil Neale scored a four off the last ball for a six-wicket win. At Heanor the following week both Kim Barnett and John Morris scored exactly 100 not out, adding an unbeaten 182, a record Derbyshire stand for any wicket on a Sunday, to beat Glamorgan by nine wickets.

On the last day of the month Essex still led the table by two points from Lancashire, but had now played a game more, suffering two defeats to Lancashire's one. Worcestershire, who had had a good month, were creeping up, but were still eight points behind Lancashire, while Surrey and Nottinghamshire followed.

The Benson and Hedges Final was played at Lord's on 15 July (score card reproduced here), and it provided fluctuating fortunes and an exciting finish, with Notts needing four off the last ball, bowled by John Lever in his last big final. Eddie Hemmings, at 40 four days older than Lever, managed to drive the ball past point, and 39-year-old Hardie chased it to the boundary. The ball and Notts won.

August/September

There was an important Championship clash early in August when Worcestershire were the visitors at Colchester. Worcestershire had much the better of it, dismissing Essex for 208 and scoring 447 for nine declared themselves. Essex achieved the draw at 323 for nine. Graeme Hick recorded his best bowling in both match and innings with five for 52 and five for 131.

In their next matches, Essex beat Northants in a contrived finish, Northants declaring behind and Essex forfeiting second innings, while Worcestershire outplayed Somerset to win by nine wickets. Worcestershire then comprehensively beat Hampshire by an innings and 91 runs, while Essex hung in with a seven-wicket win over Lancashire. Needing 77 in 14 overs they got there with 13 balls to spare.

At Chesterfield, in an exciting match with Derbyshire, Lancashire's keeper Warren Hegg made 11 catches (seven in the first innings) to equal the world record (jointly held by A. Long, R.W. Marsh and D.L. Bairstow).

There was trouble at Trent Bridge in the local 'derby' with Derbyshire. The pitch was reported to Lord's at lunch on the first day, during which 19

Paul Prichard of Essex was the Man of the Match in the last one-day final of the season, the Refuge Assurance Cup. Prichard made 56 in Essex's five-run victory over Notts, a consolation trophy for a side which had lost the Championship because of a penalty imposed for a sub-standard pitch.

Patrick Eagar

wickets fell. On the second day Chris Broad ostentatiously shook hands with the fielder after being caught at short leg after he and Pollard had each been hit by Michael Holding. Play was stopped for 90 minutes and resumed on a different strip. Holding, who was retiring at the end of the season, refused to take any further part on principle. He was later reprimanded by Derbyshire. Notts, who won, lost 25 points, the second penalty imposed for a sub-standard pitch. On this score, Essex, the earlier sufferers, announced that they had reached agreement with Southend Borough Council whereby in future the county club would prepare the pitches there.

After Hegg becoming the fourth wicket-keeper in history to take 11 catches in a match, the fifth instance was recorded only 11 days later. Surrey's Alex Stewart achieved the feat (six and five) against Leicestershire at Leicester.

The last first-class match played at Priory Meadow, Hastings, ended on 22 August, when Middlesex beat Sussex by nine wickets. The ground, in a prime site in the centre of the town, was scheduled to be 'redeveloped' as a shopping centre.

The next set of Championship matches proved decisive. Worcestershire beat Somerset at Worcester by five wickets in a contrived finish. Declaring behind, they were set 300 in 57 overs. Graeme Hick scored 136 not out, scoring his second 50 in 20 balls, and Worcestershire won with five balls to spare. Essex, at Northampton, after leading by 97 on first innings, set the home side a target of 264 in 73 overs, and lost by four wickets.

The last matches of August clinched it for Worcestershire. They beat Gloucestershire at Worcester by 131 runs with a day to spare, and although Essex scrambled home by two wickets

John Lever of Essex retired at the end of the 1989 season after an exemplary career. He reserved his best performance of the season for his last match: seven for 48 against Surrey.

Allsport/Adrian Murrell

HOLLAND v ENGLAND (Amstelveen)

August 16

Holland won by three runs

Holland		
E. Gouka	b Pringle	18
P. Holland	c Capel b Base	0
R.E. Lifman	c Bailey b Pringle	18
N. Clarke	c Medlycott b Base	77
R. Lefebvre	c Hussain b Medlycott	7
R. Gomes	c Roebuck b Thomas	18
S.W. Lubbers	c Capel b Thomas	6
F. Aponso	not out	12
C. Ruskamp	not out	5
F. Jansen		
P. Edwards		
Extras	b 1, lb 8, w 4, nb 2	15
Total (7 wkts, 40 ov)		176

2, 29, 57, 106, 137, 151, 159

Thomas	8	2	32	2
Base	8	1	22	2
Pringle	8	0	35	2
Capel	4	0	23	0
Medlycott	7	0	32	1
Watkinson	5	1	23	0

England		
*P.M. Roebuck	c Gomes b Aponso	19
J.P. Stephenson	b Lubbers	43
R.J. Bailey	not out	68
†A.J. Stewart	c Gomes b Lubbers	0
N. Hussain	b Edwards	21
D.J. Capel	c Holland b Jansen	5
M. Watkinson	c Raskamp b Jansen	0
D.R. Pringle	c Gomes b Aponso	1
K.T. Medlycott	not out	2
S.J. Base		
J.G Thomas		
Extras	b 4, lb 4, w 4, nb 2	14
Total (7 wkts, 40 ov)		173

46, 101, 101, 145, 159, 162, 165

Jansen	8	1	25	2
Edwards	8	0	41	1
Aponso	8	0	44	2
Lubbers	8	0	33	2
Lefebvre	8	1	22	0

The Dutch side was rather cosmopolitan in composition with only six natives and three West Indians, a New Zealander and a Sri Lankan, nevertheless the defeat of the 'young' England side came as rather a shock. Clarke from Barbados attacked the English bowling with vigour and made easily the highest score for his side. Very good bowling and tight fielding made sure the English team just failed to reach the 177 required, though they had only needed 50 off the final 10 overs.

HOLLAND v ENGLAND (Amstelveen)

August 17

England won by 98 runs

England		
*P.M. Roebuck	c Jansen b Aponso	60
J.P. Stephenson	b Lefebvre	121
R.J. Bailey	run out	18
†A.J. Stewart	c Lefebvre b Lubbers	5
N. Hussain	c Gomes b Lubbers	11
M. Watkinson	b Lubbers	6
D.R. Pringle	not out	24
D.J. Capel	run out	2
K.T. Medlycott	not out	0
S.L. Watkin		
S.J. Base		
Extras	b 2, lb 6, w 4, nb 2	14
Total (7 wkts, 55 ov)		261

112, 156, 179, 214, 231, 244, 261

Jansen	11	0	82	0
Lefebvre	11	1	32	1
Aponso	11	0	38	1
Coster	11	0	48	0
Lubbers	11	0	53	3

Holland		
R. Vos	lbw b Watkin	10
F. Aponso	c Capel b Medlycott	9
R.E. Lifman	c Stewart b Capel	12
N. Clarke	b Capel	12
R. Lefebvre	c Bailey b Base	11
R. Gomes	c Roebuck b Pringle	22
R. Holland	b Pringle	5
S.W. Lubbers	c Base b Medlycott	32
C. Ruskamp	not out	21
F. Jansen	b Capel	0
J. Coster	run out	6
Extras	lb 5, w 9, nb 9	23
Total (48.3 ov)		163

22, 22, 41, 53, 87, 92, 101, 154, 154

Base	8	3	12	1
Watkin	9	0	37	1
Medlycott	8.3	1	25	2
Capel	7	0	39	3
Roebuck	2	0	10	0
Pringle	8	1	23	2
Watkinson	6	0	12	0

The English opening pair put on 112 at four runs an over before they were parted, but none of the other visiting batsmen made much of a show. The Dutch side never kept up with the clock and England had a firm grip on the game long before the closing overs.

WORLD XI v MCC XI (Scarborough)

August 30, 31, September 1

Word XI won by 257 runs

World XI 1st Innings		
Mudassar Nazar	c Bailey b Pringle	34
C.A. Best	c Knight b Watkin	100
C.G. Greenidge	c Knight b Hemmings	25
*M.D. Crowe	not out	138
R.J. Shastri	c Bailey b Hemmings	40
†P.J.L. Dujon	not out	42
R.A. Harper		
†D.L. Bairstow		
S.J. O'Donnell		
Wasim Akram		
Maninder Singh		
Extras	b 4, lb 7, nb 7	18
Total (4 wkts dec)		398

85, 138, 174, 285

Watkin	14	3	52	1
Pringle	16	0	91	1
Christie	13	2	64	0
Hemmings	26	4	101	2
Knight	14	3	79	0

MCC XI 1st Innings		
W. Larkins	c Harper b O'Donnell	108
M. Robinson	c Harper b Wasim Akram	2
H. Morris	c Mudassar b Wasim Akram	28
R.J. Bailey	retired hurt	1
D.W. Randall	lbw b Wasim Akram	0
R. Knight	c Crowe b O'Donnell	11
†N.D. Burns	not out	58
M.W. Pringle	c sub b Shastri	53
E.E. Hemmings	b Harper	53
S.L. Watkin	c Shastri b Harper	3
P. Christie		
Extras	b 8, lb 2, w 2, nb 4	16
Total (8 wkts dec)		333

Wasim Akram	15	6	26	3
O'Donnell	19	3	81	2
Harper	29	9	86	2
Maninder Singh	15	1	94	0
Shastri	6	0	36	1

World XI 2nd Innings		
Mudassar Nazar	c Larkins b Christie	27
C.A. Best	c Burns b Christie	39
C.G. Greenidge	c Randall b Watkin	5
R.A. Harper	b Hemmings	27
†D.L. Bairstow	c Burns b Christie	28
S.J. O'Donnell	c Morris b Pringle	96
†P.J. L. Dujon	c Burns b Pringle	24
Wasim Akram	not out	14
Extras	lb 11, nb 1	12
Total (7 wkts dec)		273

Watkin	21	4	70	1
Pringle	18	2	103	2
Christie	14	3	57	3
Hemmings	12	4	32	1

MCC XI 2nd Innings		
D.W. Randall	c Shastri b Wasim Akram	10
W. Larkins	c Shastri b Harper	29
H. Morris	c Greenidge b Harper	24
M. Robinson	b Wasim Akram	0
R. Knight	not out	6
M.W. Pringle	lbw b Wasim Akram	0
E.E. Hemmings	b Wasim Akram	1
S.L. Watkin	lbw b Wasim Akram	0
P. Christie	b Wasim Akram	0
R.J. Bailey	absent injured	0
Extras	b 1, lb 2, w 1, nb 7	11
Total		81

Wasim Akram	17.4	5	42	7
O'Donnell	3	0	11	0
Mudassar Nazar	4	2	13	0
Harper	10	5	12	2

Toss: World XI

Best of Barbados hit a hundred off 119 balls on the opening day and Crowe hit his off 122. By the close MCC were 63–1. Larkins fought back on the second day, hitting 16 fours in his 108, the middle failed, but the later batsmen did well enough to allow a declaration and over 400 runs were made in the day. MCC were set 339 to win, but with Wasim Akram in fine form, the batting fell apart giving the World XI an easy win.

against Surrey, and each county had another match to play, Worcestershire could not now be caught.

As it happened, Essex won the last match convincingly by ten wickets at Leicester, with Gooch and Gower, the newly appointed and deposed captains of England, each getting a century. Worcestershire's last match was in the middle of September, when rain prevented any Championship results and Worcestershire could gain only four points at Pontypridd, with virtually the last three days washed out. So they won the Championship by six points only, and Essex's forfeiture of 25 points proved to be crucial.

The NatWest quarter-finals and semi-finals were played in August. In the former, Middlesex beat Sussex (Gatting 132 not out), Warwickshire beat Northants, Hampshire beat Surrey and Worcestershire beat Lancashire. In the semi-finals, Middlesex beat Hampshire at Southampton by three runs, and Warwickshire beat Worcestershire at Edgbaston by 100 runs. Warwickshire won the Trophy at Lord's on 2 September (the score-card is reproduced on page 10) with a four-wicket win, a six in the final over by Neil Smith being virtually the shot which settled it.

In the Refuge Assurance League, the important match between Lancashire and Essex at Old Trafford ended as a 'no result' because of rain – Essex, who were in the better position, were upset at the non-resumption of play. It meant Lancashire needed to win one of their last two games to take the title. They failed to do it against Yorkshire, whose win at Old Trafford was their first over Lancashire on Sunday since 1976, but came good against Surrey with a three-wicket win in the last over. As it happened, the win was unnecessary, as Essex lost their last match, and Lancashire's margin was six points.

The Refuge Assurance Cup, a knock-out competition for the top four teams in the Refuge Assurance League, saw Lancashire lose by five wickets to Notts at Old Trafford in one semi-final, while Essex went to Worcester and beat Worcestershire easily by 101 runs. The final was at Edgbaston on 18 September (scorecard reproduced on page 10). Essex won by five runs after being on top virtually throughout and finally salvaged something from a disappointing season.

Various touring parties were announced during the final months of the season. A number of 'rebel' players decided to tour South Africa under the management of David Graveney and the captaincy of Mike Gatting. Two black players were in the original party announced, Roland Butcher and Phil DeFreitas, but on second thoughts they withdrew later.

On 11 and 17 August an England side led by Peter Roebuck played two one-day games in Holland against a Dutch side, winning one and losing one (scorecards reproduced here).

England announced the party to tour West Indies. Graham Gooch was named as captain, and the big surprises were the omission altogether of the captain for the summer series, David Gower, and of Ian Botham, whose availability had been checked upon. Most the players on this tour were to take part in the Nehru Cup Tournament in India. Mark Nicholas was chosen to lead an 'A' side on a tour of Zimbabwe. The composition of the sides and their performances in 1989–90 will be discussed in next year's Yearbook.

Two distinguished former England cricketers retired at the end of the 1989 season, Essex's John Lever and Somerset's Vic Marks.

BRITANNIC ASSURANCE CHAMPIONSHIP
Final Table 1989

		M	W	L	D	Bt	Bl	Pts
1	Worcestershire (1)	22	12	3	7	44	83	319
2	Essex (3)	22	13	2	7	59	71	313
3	Middlesex (8)	22	9	2	11	50	72	266
4	Lancashire (9)	22	8	5	9	57	65	260
5	Northamptonshire (12)	22	7	8	7	47	63	222
6	Hampshire (15)	22	6	8	8	55	65	216
7	Derbyshire (14)	22	6	6	10	45	75	216
8	Warwickshire (6)	22	5	4	13	44	75	207
9	Gloucestershire (10)	22	6	11	5	38	70	204
10	Sussex (16)	22	4	4	14	60	68	192
11	Nottinghamshire (5)	22	6	6	10	54	65	190
12	Surrey (4)	22	4	7	11	50	69	183
13	Leicestershire (7)	22	4	8	10	43	74	181
14	Somerset (11)	22	4	6	12	50	54	168
15	Kent (2)	22	3	8	11	53	53	154
16	Yorkshire (13)	22	3	9	10	41	60	149
17	Glamorgan (17)	22	3	6	13	38	59	145

REFUGE ASSURANCE LEAGUE
Final Table 1989

		P	W	L	T	NR	Pts
1	Lancashire (3)	16	12	2	0	2	52
2	Worcestershire (1)	16	11	4	0	1	46
3	Essex (6)	16	11	4	0	1	46
4	Nottinghamshire (17)	16	9	6	0	1	38
5	Derbyshire (12)	16	9	6	0	1	38
6	Surrey (5)	16	9	7	0	0	36
7	Hampshire (9)	16	8	6	1	1	36
8	Northants (14)	16	8	6	0	2	36
9	Middlesex (4)	16	8	7	1	0	34
10	Somerset (12)	16	7	8	1	0	30
11	Kent (7)	16	7	9	0	0	28
12	Yorkshire (8)	16	7	9	0	0	28
13	Sussex (14)	16	6	8	1	1	28
14	Warwickshire (10)	16	5	10	0	1	22
15	Leicestershire (14)	16	5	10	0	1	22
16	Gloucestershire (2)	16	3	13	0	0	12
17	Glamorgan (5)	16	2	12	0	2	12

Mike Gatting batting in a Test match against Pakistan. After a Test career which latterly had some remarkable ups and downs, from the England captaincy to an ignoble sacking, he seemed to remove himself from the Test arena, possibly for good, by his decision to captain a rebel tour to South Africa in the 1989–90 winter season.

Allsport

Test Matches and One-Day Internationals

The Australian tour was anticipated with great excitement on both sides of the world, although neither side had enjoyed much recent success. Both sides, however, seemed to have reasons for optimism. Australia were coming to an end of a rebuilding phase, and England, having missed out on a winter's tour, were looking to their players to be refreshed and eager for the fray.

England, having appointed a team manager, Mickey Stewart, a few seasons earlier, rearranged their whole international structure in the close season. Ted Dexter was confirmed as the new chairman of selectors in succession to Peter May at the TCCB's spring meeting at Lord's in March. Dexter's title was announced as Chairman of the England Committee, and he was the first chairman to be paid for his services. The previous selectors, Fred Titmus and Phil Sharpe, lost their positions, and Dexter was joined on the new committee by Mickey Stewart and the *ex officio* members Alan Smith, the TCCB's chief executive, and Ossie Wheatley, the cricket committee chairman.

A former captain of England himself, Dexter was an inspirational cricketer and his early comments seemed to confirm he would be an inspirational chairman, not afraid to take decisions, or to discuss them with the press and fans. The general consensus was that there would be a more positive and dynamic lead coming from the top in English selectional affairs, and this welcome sign was confirmed with an early appointment of a captain for the series.

For various reasons, not all cricketing ones, England had fielded no fewer than four captains during the disastrous series against West Indies in 1988: Mike Gatting, John Emburey, Chris Cowdrey and Graham Gooch. Gooch was the incumbent, having taken over the job for the final Test. The new selectors gave most attention to Gooch, Gatting, dismissed from the job the previous year after a tabloid story concerning an encounter with a waitress, and David Gower, the skipper whom Gatting had replaced in 1986, during a losing series with India.

The triumvirate who were supposed to put English cricket back on top in 1989, but who, for one reason or another, failed completely. David Gower, who was appointed captain for the whole series, but who was not even to be in the party for the following winter tour, Mickey Stewart, the manager, and Ted Dexter, the newly appointed chairman of the cricket committee, virtually the chief selector, who at the end of the season claimed to be unaware of any errors he might have made.

Allsport

Gower won the nomination, after curiously being interviewed by the new powers-that-be. Whether or not Dexter discovered anything he did not previously know about Gower, he announced the decision with great certainty, and everybody was impressed with the new enthusiasm which he seemed to be bringing into the Test scene. Gower, with his undoubted flair, was perhaps the obvious 'golden boy' to lead England with this new spirit of optimism about, and as he had thrillingly led the side to victory over Australia on their previous visit in 1985, his appointment was greeted with general satisfaction. It seemed the cavalier approach was the one to be adopted, and Englishmen looked forward to a good series and were reasonably confident of a good result.

The Australian selection committee, manager Lawrie Sawle, coach Bobby Simpson, Jim Higgs and John Benaud, on the other hand, had aroused controversy with their choice. The selection of Allan Border as captain did not excite much comment, since he was the outstanding candidate, having been the skipper and most successful cricketer since the 1984–85 season. The main batsmen, too, more or less picked themselves. So far as the openers were concerned, there seemed an embarrassment of riches, since the long-established and successful partnership of David Boon and Geoff Marsh seemed likely to be broken with the emergence of the New South Wales left-hander Mark Taylor. But even this seemed to be a bonus, because Boon would make an aggressive and experienced number 3. Dean Jones and Steve Waugh completed a strong line-up of six likely batsmen for the international matches.

It was when the selection committee got down to the fast bowlers that controversy arose. Bruce Reid, who had looked likely to be Australia's leading fast bowler was ruled out of the tour after having to undergo major surgery to his back. On the previous Australia tour to Pakistan he had bowled splendidly, but his back had begun to trouble him and he had not taken part in the domestic season. Terry Alderman, Geoff Lawson and Carl Rackemann were selected as the spearhead of the Test team, Alderman and

Rackemann being two bowlers who were now back in the fold having earlier been banned for going on Kim Hughes' rebel South African tour. Most Australians thought that the New South Wales left-armer Mike Whitney should have been the other paceman selected, since he had topped the wicket-taking table in the Australian season with 58 wickets. However Whitney was overlooked, the first leading wicket-taker not to be chosen for an Ashes tour since the Second World War (apart from two not available). Since Whitney had nine wickets in the Adelaide Test against the West Indies, most people assumed that he had missed out solely on account of his age. At 30, he was younger than Alderman (32) and Lawson (31), but with Rackemann 28, another 30-year-old would have made the fast bowling squad fairly old, so the selectors gave the final places to the inspirational Merv Hughes (27) and the surprise choice, the uncapped Greg Campbell (25), of Tasmania.

Tim May, of South Australia, was the first-choice off-spinner, while Trevor Hohns, of Queensland, a leg-spinner, was chosen to make his first tour aged 35. He was the oldest member of the party. Ian Healy was the first-choice wicket-keeper, and Tim Zoehrer was given the second spot. The party of 17 was completed by the selection of the all-rounder Mike Veletta.

Only Border, Lawson and Boon had been on the 1985 tour. Alderman, however, who was not available in 1985, had taken an Australian record of 42 Ashes wickets in the 1981 series, and clearly was ideal for English conditions. The full party was: A.R. Border (Queensland, captain), G.R. Marsh (West Australia, vice-captain), T.M. Alderman (West Australia), D.C. Boon (Tasmania), G.D. Campbell (Tasmania), I.A. Healy (Queensland), T.V. Hohns (Queensland), M.G. Hughes (Victoria), D.M. Jones (Victoria), G.F. Lawson (New South Wales), T.B.A. May (South Australia), T.M. Moody (West Australia), C.G. Rackemann (Queensland), M.A. Taylor (New South Wales), M.R.J. Veletta (West Australia), S.R. Waugh (New South Wales), T.J. Zoehrer (West Australia).

Texaco Trophy

David Gower won the toss in the first one-day international at Old Trafford, and contrary to the usual preferred tactic these days, decided to bat. Gower opened himself with Gooch, and won the first round of exchanges between the sides by playing a delightful knock in his 100th one-day international innings (in his 103rd match). After hitting Lawson for six he helped put up 50 in 10 overs before being caught behind for 36 out of 55. Gooch went on to top-score with 52, but only Lamb and Robin Smith, who each scored 35, did much before DeFreitas and Emburey scrambled a few at the end: 231 for nine did not seem an outstanding total.

It seemed much better when Foster and DeFreitas were launching their opening spell. Boon, Jones and Border were all dismissed with only 17 on the board, whereupon Marsh decided to play sheet anchor. At tea, after 25 overs, he had made only 13 runs, while Australia had advanced to 51 for three. When Marsh was out, and Waugh followed, there was never a chance that Australia would approach England's total. When they were all out for 136, they were 96 runs short of the target, and would have had to score them at 12 per over.

Allan Lamb receiving the Man of the Match award after the second Texaco Trophy match, in which he scored 100 not out in 105 balls. The match was tied. Lamb looked to be England's soundest batsman for the Test series, but because of injury he played in one only, scoring a century. England's only consolation for his absence was the outstanding success of his replacement, Robin Smith.

Allsport/Adrian Murrell

The second match at Trent Bridge was again played in excellent weather and it produced plenty of drama, with the match evenly poised throughout the last hour or two.

England again won the toss and batted, but this time did not get away to so quick a start. After 45 minutes Gooch was out for 10, with the total only 30, and this was to be the pattern of England's innings, with batsmen playing themselves in and then getting themselves out when they should have been accelerating. The one glorious exception was Lamb, who reached exactly 100 not out from only 105 deliveries. Unfortunately for England, Botham was run out when poised to launch an attack. When the last over began Lamb was 91 not out, and not on strike, but a bonus of a no-ball from Alderman helped him to three figures. Pringle (25 not out) had helped him add 88, including 53 from the last five overs. But 226 for five was a lower total than in the first match.

It was Australia's turn to make the dynamic start, with Boon and Marsh having 56 on the board after only 15 overs. Boon was then out, but the middle order kept them well ahead of the clock and they were proceeding nicely until two run-outs brought about a change in fortunes. Moody, who had come in and hit a six, was then run out when starting too late for a run to Gower, whose weak, injury-affected, throwing arm was to cause him trouble throughout the year. Then Healy got into two minds over a third run and ended falling over; Waugh had to run back but was beaten by a throw to wicket-keeper Rhodes which he promptly transferred to the bowler's end.

There was an amusing incident when Jones came on as a runner for Healy, who had supposedly injured a leg, but when Healy *and* the runner had sprinted a quick two, Jones was good-naturedly required to get back in the pavilion.

Healy was still there when the last over started, Australia now requiring seven to win. DeFreitas began the over with a wide, then Healy and May each took a single from each of the next four balls. Two to get in two balls; then DeFreitas made amends for his wide by bowling May. The last ball went through to keeper Rhodes standing back, but Healy, the non-striker, rushed through for the single as Rhodes threw at the stumps. The match was therefore a tie.

England had lost fewer wickets than Australia in the tied match, and according to the rules, should the series also be tied, this would count as a win for England. This unfortunate rule meant that England had won the Texaco Trophy, irrespective of what happened at Lord's, which robbed the match of a little of its excitement. However, Australia were anxious to win it and put themselves back into shape for the Tests, and in the event the match provided the best batting of the series, apart from Lamb's century at Trent Bridge.

Gower again won the toss and batted, and he and Gooch excelled, racing to 123 before Gower was caught for 61. Gooch had the benefit of a mistaken run-out decision and went on to make the highest individual score in England–Australia one-dayers of 136. Luckily for Australia Lamb was out first ball, although nobody could have hit the ball harder than Smith and Botham, who succeeded him. Four wickets tumbled in the final scramble for runs, so the total of 278 for seven, although it looked formidable, might have been even better.

Boon looked as if he was attempting to get them all on his own, but at 24 he was lbw, having made 19 of them. Marsh and Jones carried the innings to tea, surviving a burst of excitement just before the break when a shapely streaker ran from the nursery end diagonally right across the ground to the Warner Stand, wearing only a wristwatch. Having performed a cartwheel near the press box she was escorted away to a police caution.

Jones, perhaps still unnerved, was out soon after tea, but Border and Marsh took the score to 197 before Border was bowled, by which time the springboard was primed for Australia to make a dash for victory. Marsh continued to play at a solid rate, while Waugh began to gather runs quickly. With 35 needed from the last four overs, the match was still evenly poised. Waugh hit two sixes in Foster's next over, and in the penultimate over hit him hard and high again – this time Gooch caught it in the deep. But Australia were left with only five to get from the final over and new batsman Moody got them with three balls to spare for a six-wicket win.

First Test, Headingley

Both sides were affected by injury as they went into the first Test at Headingley. Ian Botham, looking forward to a return to Test cricket, had to withdraw after suffering a triple depressed fracture of the cheekbone. The injury came when he top-edged a ball from Glamorgan's Stephen Barwick into his face in a match at Worcester only three days before the Test. Mike Gatting withdrew when breaking his left thumb in taking a catch in the Refuge Assurance League the previous Sunday, and Graham Dilley was also out injured. Australia were without Carl Rackemann who, after a fall at Hove, needed an operation on his left knee. He was to miss the whole series.

Australia went into the Test with five fast or medium-paced bowlers: Lawson, Alderman, Hughes, Waugh and Greg Campbell, who was making his Test debut. England fielded four medium-to-fast bowlers in DeFreitas, Foster, Newport and Pringle, with Gooch as a possible fifth. The only spinners on view were the very occasional ones of Barnett for England and Border for Australia – and indeed this was the first post-war Ashes Test in which neither side had fielded a front-line spinner.

The choice of bowlers was no doubt helped by the reputation of the Headingley wicket, which in recent seasons had been ideal for the seamers. However groundsman Keith Boyce had produced a new wicket which he promised would be a good Test Match batting strip, and before the end both sides might have rued the lack of a quality spinner.

TEXACO TROPHY: FIRST MATCH

Old Trafford, May 25

England won by 95 runs

ENGLAND			*Mins*	*Balls*	*4s*
G.A. Gooch	c Jones b Border	52	*134*	*111*	*4*
*D.I. Gower	c Healy b Rackemann	36	*49*	*33*	*5**
M.W. Gatting	c Boon b Waugh	3	*20*	*12*	–
A.J. Lamb	b Lawson	35	*80*	*59*	–
R.A. Smith	c & b Alderman	35	*41*	*40*	*4*
I.T. Botham	c Boon b Lawson	4	*9*	*12*	–
D.R. Pringle	lbw b Waugh	9	*40*	*18*	–
†S.J. Rhodes	b Lawson	8	*16*	*16*	–
P.A.J. DeFreitas	not out	17	*33*	*20*	–
J.E. Emburey	b Rackemann	10	*14*	*11*	–
N.A. Foster	not out	5	*4*	*3*	–
Extras	(lbw 12, w 3, nb 2)	17			
Total	(55 overs) (9 wkts)	231		**plus one six*	
55, 70, 125, 161, 167, 179, 190, 203, 220					

Alderman	11	2	38	1
Lawson	11	1	48	3
Rackemann	10	1	33	2
Waugh	11	1	45	2
Moody	8	–	37	–
Border	4	–	18	1

AUSTRALIA			*Mins*	*Balls*	*4s*
G.R. Marsh	c Rhodes b Emburey	17	*101*	*78*	*1*
D.C. Boon	b DeFreitas	5	*15*	*9*	–
D.M. Jones	c Rhodes b Foster	4	*15*	*15*	*1*
*A.R. Border	b Foster	4	*7*	*6*	*1*
S.R. Waugh	c Smith b DeFreitas	35	*81*	*74*	*2*
T.M. Moody	b Emburey	24	*43*	*38*	–
M.R.J. Veletta	lbw b Pringle	17	*32*	*31*	*1*
†I.A. Healy	c Emburey b Foster	10	*22*	*20*	*1*
G.F. Lawson	c DeFreitas b Emburey	0	*2*	*1*	–
C.G. Rackemann	b Botham	6	*20*	*9*	–
T.M. Alderman	not out	0	*2*	*2*	–
Extras	(b 1, lb 9, w 4)	14			
Total	(47.1 overs)	136			
8, 13, 17, 64, 85, 115, 119, 120, 136					

Foster	10	3	29	3
DeFreitas	8	3	19	2
Pringle	8	2	19	1
Botham	10.1	1	28	1
Emburey	11	–	31	3

Man of the Match: P.A.J. DeFreitas
Umpires: J.W. Holder and N.T. Plews
Toss: England

The pitch and the weather persuaded Gower to put Australia in when winning the toss. The weather was cloudy, and Headingley wickets in such conditions on the first morning had in the past proved to be at their trickiest.

As it happened the bad light curtailed play in the first session and the Aussie openers Taylor and Marsh needed to navigate only some 80 minutes play to achieve the first objective of lunch unparted. In some ways the first session set up the whole series for Australia. Batting was not easy, and neither batsman was error free, but they stayed together to lunch at 44 for no wicket.

England's chances were at their best in the half-hour or so after lunch. Marsh was lbw for the first ball, bowled by DeFreitas, and Boon lasted for 28 minutes for 9 runs before being caught behind off Foster. Border then joined Taylor, who was looking more and more solid, and the two left-handers stayed together until well after tea.

Batting became easier as the light improved, and England were relieved when Border got underneath a ball from DeFreitas and was caught by Foster from a mistimed pull. His 66 had occupied 140 minutes, and had put Australia in a strong position.

Dean Jones, who had recovered from an early season break of the cheekbone, was not inclined to

Graham Gooch scored 136 in the third Texaco Trophy match and was England's Man of the Series. He did not have a good Test series, but was subsequently chosen as England's new captain to lead his country in the West Indies during the winter.

Allsport/Ben Radford

TEXACO TROPHY: SECOND MATCH

Trent Bridge, May 27

Match tied

ENGLAND			*Mins*	*Balls*	*4s*
G.A. Gooch	c Jones b Alderman	10	*45*	*35*	–
*D.I. Gower	b Waugh	28	*88*	*59*	*3*
M.W. Gatting	b May	37	*104*	*76*	*3*
A.J. Lamb	not out	100	*140*	*105*	*9*
R.A. Smith	st Healy b May	3	*6*	*9*	–
I.T. Botham	run out	8	*17*	*15*	–
D.R. Pringle	not out	25	*51*	*32*	*2*
†S.J. Rhodes					
P.A.J. DeFreitas					
J.E. Emburey					
N.A. Foster					
Extras	(lb 14, w 1)	15			
Total	(55 overs) (5 wkts)	226			

30, 57, 119, 123, 138

Alderman	9	2	38	1
Lawson	11	–	47	–
Rackemann	11	1	37	–
Waugh	11	1	47	1
May	11	1	35	2
Moody	2	–	8	–

AUSTRALIA			*Mins*	*Balls*	*4s*
D.C. Boon	b Botham	28	*61*	*35*	*2*
G.R. Marsh	lbw b Emburey	34	*91*	*87*	*3*
D.M. Jones	b Emburey	29	*52*	*47*	*3*
*A.R. Border	c Rhodes b Pringle	39	*65*	*58*	*3*
S.R. Waugh	run out	43	*79*	*61*	*5*
T.M. Moody	run out	10	*12*	*7*	–*
†I.A. Healy	not out	26	*50*	*28*	–
G.F. Lawson	c Gooch b Foster	1	*12*	*5*	–
T.B.A. May	b DeFreitas	2	*8*	*3*	–
C.G. Rackemann	not out	0	*1*	*1*	–
T.M. Alderman					
Extras	(b 1, lb 6, w 7)	14			
Total	(55 overs) (8 wkts)	226	**plus one six*		

59, 81, 116, 153, 174, 205, 218, 225

Foster	11	–	44	1
DeFreitas	11	2	48	1
Pringle	11	1	38	1
Botham	11	–	42	1
Emburey	11	–	47	2

Man of the Match: A.J. Lamb
Umpires: H.D. Bird and J.H. Hampshire
Toss: England

TEXACO TROPHY: THIRD MATCH

Lord's, May 29

Australia won by 6 wickets

ENGLAND			*Mins*	*Balls*	*4s*
G.A. Gooch	b Alderman	136	*229*	*162*	*11*
*D.I. Gower	c Veletta b Moody	61	*127*	*100*	*6*
M.W. Gatting	run out	18	*46*	*31*	*2*
A.J. Lamb	lbw b Alderman	0	*3*	*1*	–
R.A. Smith	b Rackemann	21	*37*	*22*	*1*
I.T. Botham	not out	25	*21*	*11*	*3**
P.A.J. DeFreitas	c Rackemann b Alderman	0	*2*	*2*	–
D.R. Pringle	run out	0	*2*	*1*	–
†S.J. Rhodes	not out	1	*3*	*1*	–
J.E. Emburey					
N.A. Foster					
Extras	(lbw 14, w 2)	16			
Total	(55 overs) (7 wkts)	278	**plus one six*		

123, 180, 182, 239, 266, 266, 268

Alderman	11	2	36	3
Rackemann	11	–	56	1
Lawson	11	–	48	–
Waugh	11	–	70	–
May	6	–	33	–
Moody	5	–	21	1

AUSTRALIA			*Mins*	*Balls*	*4s*
G.R. Marsh	not out	111	*217*	*162*	*7**
D.C. Boon	lbw b Foster	19	*21*	*17*	*3*
D.M. Jones	c Gower b Emburey	27	*71*	*67*	*2*
*A.R. Border	b Pringle	53	*70*	*46*	*5*
S.R. Waugh	c Gooch b Foster	35	*41*	*32*	*0†*
T.M. Moody	not out	6	*6*	*4*	–
†M.R.J. Veletta					
T.B.A. May					
G.F. Lawson					
C.G. Rackemann					
T.M. Alderman					
Extras	(lb 18, w 9, nb 1)	28	**plus one six*		
Total	(54.3 overs) (4 wkts)	279	*†plus two sixes*		

24, 84, 197, 268

DeFreitas	11	1	50	–
Foster	11	–	57	2
Botham	11	–	43	–
Pringle	10.3	–	50	1
Emburey	11	–	61	1

Man of the Match: G.R. Marsh
Men of the Series: G.A. Gooch and S.R. Waugh
Umpires: B.J. Meyer and D.R. Shepherd
Toss: England

take any chances and he and Taylor batted out the first day at 207 for three. Taylor spent the night on 96, having been dropped at 89 by Gower at third slip off Foster, England's most effective bowler. The first day had clearly been Australia's, after they had been put in to bat.

The second morning was again overcast, but it was bright enough for Taylor, who soon became the 16th Australian to complete a century in his first Ashes Test. He continued solidly, seeing off the second new ball, until he surprisingly missed a straight one from Foster and was lbw. Waugh came in and, despite looking a little uncertain at first, began to get the scoreboard moving, and Jones, wearing a helmet, took confidence and blossomed into his strokes. By lunch they had taken the score to 327 for four, 120 runs having come in the pre-lunch period, and England's second line of seamers, Pringle and Newport, began to look a little ordinary.

After lunch, Waugh and Jones really flourished, until finally Jones was the second to be caught behind by Russell. He made 79 and he and Waugh had added 138 at better than a run a minute. Between lunch and tea Australia scored 114 runs. Healy did not last long, but Waugh reached an impressive maiden Test century in his 27th Test. His obvious pleasure was reasonable considering he had twice reached the nineties against West Indies.

The third session of the day saw the most runs as Waugh, taking a fresh wind in best Bradman fashion after reaching three figures, continued to batter the boundary boards with his drives and Merv Hughes came in to launch a less orthodox assault, which included an involuntary letting go of the bat and making the square-leg umpire jump. At the close these two were still together at 580 for six.

Border continued to bat on on Saturday, intent on trying to win by forcing the follow-on. Hughes became Russell's third victim for 79, his seventh-wicket stand with Waugh realising 149, 16 short of the record for an Ashes series, set by Clem Hill and Hugh Trumble in 1897–98. Border declared when the total reached 601 for seven, Waugh being 177 not out. The only English player to take much pleasure from this score was Russell, since it was the highest Test total in England not to contain a bye.

England began the task of scoring 402 to avoid the follow-on, upon which the game seemed to hinge. Gooch began circumspectly for him, and batted two minutes short of an hour before falling lbw to Alderman, whose habit of bowling from close to the stumps, and therefore often pitching in

FIRST TEST MATCH

Headingley, Leeds, June 8, 9, 10, 12, 13

Australia won by 210 runs

AUSTRALIA			*Mins*	*Balls*	*4s*			*Mins*	*Balls*	*4s*
G.R. Marsh	lbw b DeFreitas	16	*80*	*63*	*1*	(2) c Russell b Foster	6	*22*	*22*	–
M.A. Taylor	lbw b Foster	136	*392*	*315*	*16*	(1) c Broad b Pringle	60	*121*	*112*	*8*
D.C. Boon	c Russell b Foster	9	*28*	*24*	*1*	lbw b DeFreitas	43	*138*	*95*	*6*
*A.R. Border	c Foster b DeFreitas	66	*140*	*118*	*9**	not out	60	*96*	*76*	*8*
D.M. Jones	c Russell b Newport	79	*265*	*172*	*7*	not out	40	*55*	*34*	*3*
S.R. Waugh	not out	177	*308*	*242*	*24*					
†I.A. Healy	c & b Newport	16	*37*	*31*	*2*					
M.G. Hughes	c Russell b Foster	71	*132*	*105*	*6†*					
G.F. Lawson	not out	10	*11*	*13*	*1*					
G.D. Campbell										
T.M. Alderman			**plus 1 × 5, 1 × 6*							
Extras	(lb 13, w 1, nb 7)	21	*†plus 2 × 6*			(b 2, lb 5, w 9, nb 5)	21			
Total	(178.3 overs) (7 wkts dec)	601				(54.5 overs) (3 wkts dec)	230			
	44, 57, 174, 273, 411, 441, 588					14, 97, 129				

DeFreitas	45.3	8	140	2	Foster	19	4	65	1
Foster	46	14	109	3	DeFreitas	18	2	76	1
Newport	49	5	153	2	Pringle	12.5	1	60	1
Pringle	33	5	123	–	Newport	5	2	22	–
Gooch	9	1	31	–					
Barnett	6	–	32	–					

ENGLAND			*Mins*	*Balls*	*4s*			*Mins*	*Balls*	*4s*
G.A. Gooch	lbw b Alderman	13	*58*	*46*	*2*	lbw b Hughes	68	*175*	*118*	*10*
B.C. Broad	b Hughes	37	*107*	*74*	*5*	lbw b Alderman	7	*18*	*12*	*1*
K.J. Barnett	lbw b Alderman	80	*164*	*118*	*10*	c Taylor b Alderman	34	*51*	*46*	*7*
A.J. Lamb	c Boon b Alderman	125	*279*	*205*	*24*	c Boon b Alderman	4	*8*	*6*	*1*
*D.I. Gower	c Healy b Lawson	26	*59*	*38*	*5*	c Healy b Lawson	34	*51*	*44*	*6*
R.A. Smith	lbw b Alderman	66	*189*	*132*	*8*	c Border b Lawson	0	*5*	*3*	–
D.R. Pringle	lbw b Campbell	6	*14*	*15*	*1*	c Border b Alderman	0	*38*	*27*	–
P.J. Newport	c Boon b Lawson	36	*107*	*73*	*3*	c Marsh b Alderman	8	*39*	*27*	*1*
†R.C. Russell	c Marsh b Lawson	15	*52*	*33*	*3*	c Healy b Hughes	2	*26*	*22*	–
P.A.J. DeFreitas	lbw b Alderman	1	*9*	*6*	–	b Hughes	21	*25*	*17*	*3*
N.A. Foster	not out	2	*5*	*5*	–	not out	1	*18*	*16*	–
Extras	(b 5, lb 7, w 1, nb 10)	23				(b 4, lb 3, nb 5)	12			
Total	(121.5 overs)	430					191			
						(55.2 overs)				
	35, 81, 195, 243, 323, 338, 392, 421, 424					17, 67, 77, 134, 153, 153, 166, 170				

Alderman	37	7	107	5	Alderman	20	7	44	5
Lawson	34.5	6	105	3	Lawson	11	2	58	2
Campbell	14	2	82	1	Campbell	10	–	42	–
Hughes	28	7	92	1	Hughes	9.2	2	36	3
Waugh	6	2	27	–	Border	5	3	4	–
Border	2	1	5	–					

Man of the Match: T.M. Alderman
Umpires: J.W Holder and D.R. Shepherd
Toss: England

the line between the wickets, was to earn him many lbw victims in the series. The score was only 35, but Barnett began confidently and he and Broad looked in no difficulty until Hughes deceived Broad with a very much slower ball which was almost a donkey drop. Broad appeared bewildered as the ball hit the base of the wicket, and it was 81 for two.

Barnett was proceeding quite brilliantly, hitting the ball all round the wicket, and Lamb, who came in ahead of Gower, was on his best imperturbable run-gathering form and the two produced some of the best batting of the series. The century partnership came at one-day speed, and another session or two of these would have inspired thoughts of a possible win, but soon after tea Barnett was the victim of a very close lbw decision, and departed with 80 runs at four-an-over pace.

Captain Gower decided to calm things down but, though not producing the same sort of fireworks as Barnett, was actually proceeding at an identical rate until he was hit painfully on the arm by Hughes. Next over he glanced too close to the keeper, and Healy took an excellent catch. At 243 for four, the game was in the balance, but the two South Africans, Lamb and Robin Smith, took the score to 280 by the close, and almost certain safety. Lamb had reached a glorious century with a cover-drive and Smith, standing in for the injured Gatting, refused to be intimidated by Hughes, who

Kim Barnett, making his Ashes debut in the first Test, was impressive in his usual aggressive manner, but he was injured in the third Test and dropped afterwards having shown fallibility against the Aussie pace and swing bowlers.

Allsport/Ben Radford

SECOND TEST MATCH

Lord's, June 22, 23, 24, 26, 27

Australia won by 6 wickets

ENGLAND			*Mins*	*Balls*	*4s*			*Mins*	*Balls*	*4s*
G.A. Gooch	c Healy b Waugh	60	*167*	*123*	*9*	lbw b Alderman	0	*2*	*3*	–
B.C. Broad	lbw b Alderman	18	*54*	*45*	*3*	b Lawson	20	*44*	*30*	*4*
K.J. Barnett	c Boon b Hughes	14	*30*	*24*	*2*	c Jones b Alderman	3	*31*	*21*	–
M.W. Gatting	c Boon b Hughes	0	*6*	*1*	–	lbw b Alderman	22	*114*	*82*	*4*
*D.I. Gower	b Lawson	57	*105*	*62*	*8*	c Border b Hughes	106	*268*	*198*	*16*
R.A. Smith	c Hohns b Lawson	32	*52*	*36*	*6*	b Alderman	96	*269*	*206*	*16*
J.E. Emburey	b Alderman	0	*3*	*2*	–	(8) not out	36	*137*	*96*	*4*
†R.C. Russell	not out	64	*160*	*115*	*9*	(7) c Boon b Lawson	29	*71*	*65*	*4*
N.A. Foster	c Jones b Hughes	16	*56*	*51*	*3*	lbw b Alderman	4	*3*	*2*	*1*
P.W. Jarvis	c Marsh b Hughes	6	*16*	*14*	*1*	lbw b Alderman	5	*19*	*16*	–
G.R. Dilley	c Border b Alderman	7	*69*	*51*	–	c Boon b Hughes	24	*81*	*64*	*3*
Extras	(lb 9, nb 3)	12				(b 6, lb 6, nb 2)	14			
Total	(86.5 overs)	286				(130 overs)	359			
	31, 52, 58, 131, 180, 185, 191, 237, 253					0, 18, 28, 84, 223, 274, 300, 304, 314				

Alderman	20.5	4	60	3	Alderman	38	6	128	6
Lawson	27	8	88	2	Lawson	39	10	99	2
Hughes	23	6	71	4	Hughes	24	8	44	2
Waugh	9	3	49	1	Border	9	3	23	–
Hohns	7	3	9	–	Hohns	13	6	33	–
					Waugh	7	2	20	–

AUSTRALIA			*Mins*	*Balls*	*4s*			*Mins*	*Balls*	*4s*
G.R. Marsh	c Russell b Dilley	3	*19*	*14*	–	(2) b Dilley	1	*17*	*12*	–
M.A. Taylor	lbw b Foster	62	*223*	*162*	*8*	(1) c Gooch b Foster	27	*78*	*61*	*2*
D.C. Boon	c Gooch b Dilley	94	*253*	*189*	*12*	not out	58	*157*	*121*	*6*
*A.R. Border	c Smith b Emburey	35	*81*	*62*	*5*	c sub b Foster	1	*15*	*9*	–
D.M. Jones	lbw b Foster	27	*46*	*40*	*1*	c Russell b Foster	0	*8*	*4*	–
S.R. Waugh	not out	152	*329*	*249*	*17*	not out	21	*69*	*40*	*2*
†I.A. Healy	c Russell b Jarvis	3	*39*	*30*	–					
M.G. Hughes	c Gooch b Foster	30	*71*	*52*	*4*					
T.V. Hohns	b Emburey	21	*52*	*38*	*3*					
G.F. Lawson	c Broad b Emburey	74	*107*	*94*	*11*					
T.M. Alderman	lbw b Emburey	8	*36*	*39*	*1*					
Extras	(lb 11, nb 8)	19				(b 3, lb 4, nb 4)	11			
Total	(158 overs)	528				(40.2 overs) (4 wkts)	119			
	6, 151, 192, 221, 235, 265, 331, 381, 511					9, 51, 61, 67				

Dilley	34	3	141	2	Dilley	10	2	27	1
Foster	45	7	129	3	Foster	18	3	39	3
Jarvis	31	3	150	1	Emburey	3	–	8	–
Emburey	42	12	88	4	Jarvis	9.2	–	38	–
Gooch	6	2	9	–					

Man of the Match: S.R. Waugh

Umpires: H.D. Bird and N.T. Plews

Toss: England

England's best player in the 1989 series might have been said to be Mr Raine, who earned a draw at Edgbaston. This is the scene outside the ground after heavy rain had begun on the second day.

Patrick Eagar

seemed to be waging a personal war against him. He seemed almost to relish the bouncers, glares and occasional remarks.

Lamb and Smith continued in sparkling form on Monday until Lamb was unsettled by the new ball. Without apparently offering a false stroke in scoring 96 of his 125 in fours, Lamb was finally caught off bat and pad prodding at Lawson. The proportion of boundaries in his innings was the highest in any previous Ashes century at 76.8 per cent – a remarkable statistic when innings of Bradman, Trumper, Botham and others are recalled.

Pringle was soon the innings' third lbw victim (and Campbell's first Test wicket), but Newport and Smith took England to the brink of saving the follow-on before Smith was lbw for 66. England finally reached 430 at the frenetic pace of 3.52 runs an over – faster than Australia's rate. Alderman took five for 107 – four of them lbw.

With a day and a half left, and with a lead of 171, Border decided there was still a chance of victory, and the Australian batsmen began quickly, despite Marsh soon being caught behind. Taylor and Boon added 93 before Taylor was caught for 60 out of 97. Boon left at 129, and Border and Jones were really pushing the score along when, much to Border's obvious disappointment, slight rain deprived him of three overs play.

After only ten overs on the final morning, however, 158 for three became 230 for three declared, 101 runs having been added by Jones and his captain in two sessions in under an hour. Some of the bowling looked very ragged.

England had a minimum 83 overs, weather permitting, to bat out for a draw.

Broad soon went, lbw to Alderman, but Gooch was batting well in sober, responsible mood and Barnett began in the brisk fashion of the first innings. There seemed little danger, but the afternoon session was to scupper England. Barnett received a lifter from Alderman and Lamb faced only six balls before becoming for a second time a bat-pad victim. Gower stayed with Gooch while 56 were added, of which he claimed 34 in 51 minutes – exactly the same figures as Barnett. He and Barnett had scored at practically the same rate as each other throughout the match (about 4.25 an over – very fast, but England were seeking the draw). Smith faced three balls and failed to score.

Gooch, after nearly three hours resistance, was lbw to a big swinger from Hughes, and Pringle followed at the same score – his duck concealing a 38-minute defiance. Six wickets had fallen in the afternoon session. After tea, the tail did not look like saving the game, and Australia won by 210 runs with 27.4 overs to spare. Alderman's first-ever ten wickets in a Test won him the Man of the Match award.

Second Test, Lord's

Australia brought in a leg-spinner, Hohns, for Campbell at Lord's, a change which was to be their only one of the series. Lamb was injured, so Gatting returned to the England batting. Among the bowlers, who had generally been regarded as the main weaknesses at Headingley, only Foster kept his place. Graham Dilley, Paul Jarvis and spinner John Emburey came in for DeFreitas, Newport and Pringle.

Gower again won the toss and this time batted, his decision to put Australia in at Headingley having received plenty of criticism. This time the first day pitch allied to cloud cover did its work, and England lost three wickets in the pre-lunch period. Broad was lbw to Alderman after getting 18 in 54 minutes and then Barnett, after half-an-hour of trying to get going, was caught off bat and pad by Boon off Hughes. Gatting came in and having watched at one end for an over was also caught by Boon prodding. So England were 52 for three after an hour and a half. Gower, on 7, hooked high and Jones spilled a straightforward catch on the long leg boundary.

England, and Gower in particular, continued to bat as if attack were the best form of defence. At lunch Gower and Gooch had taken the score to 88, and the afternoon session was to bring 124 runs. But wickets went with the boundaries. At 131 Gooch's responsible knock of 60 ended when he was caught behind by Healy. Gower and Smith were undeterred, but at 180 Gower chopped Lawson on to his stumps, having scored 57 in only 62 balls. It was a decisive blow. Emburey was bowled second ball and Smith holed out at mid-on for 32 in 36 balls.

After tea Russell accumulated steadily to reach 64 not out, while the tail-enders sensibly kept an end going as well as they could. The last wicket added 33 runs in 69 minutes, but England were still all out for 286, leaving time for an over at Australia – rather reckless batting for a five-day match.

Australia showed how it should be done next day, despite Marsh soon being caught by a diving Russell. Taylor and Boon dug in and batted until half-an-hour before tea, reaching their fifties in the same over. Taylor was the first to go, and immediately after tea Boon steered the ball to slip when 94 and with a century apparently in his grasp.

England had one of their best sessions after tea, Border mishitting a sweep, Jones falling lbw and Healy nicking one to the keeper. Hughes saw out the day with Waugh, and Australia finished ten behind with four wickets left.

Early wickets for England on the Saturday would have seen a finely balanced match, but Hughes proved he is no mean batsman by scoring 30 and helping Australia to a lead of 45 before he was out. Hohns stayed nearly to lunch, adding 50 with Waugh.

The afternoon session was a devastating one for England, as Waugh, with classical driving, and Lawson, with a mixture of good shots and rustic thumps, took the attack apart. Gower came in for some press criticism later for his handling of the bowlers. By the time Emburey had claimed Lawson (for 74) and Alderman (after 36 minutes), Australia had made 528, and Waugh was 152 not out, having made 329 in two innings without being dismissed. The last four wickets had added 263 runs.

Having expected to go in to knock off a few runs deficit, Gooch and Broad went to the wicket in the evening facing arrears of 242. Gooch was lbw to Alderman on the third ball of the innings, and half-an-hour later Barnett was caught. When Lawson bowled Broad England were 28 for three; Gatting and Gower took the score to 58 by the close, 309 runs being scored in the day.

Gower was for once not his serene self at that evening's press conference, and stormed out after a tense few minutes, but next day he regained his usual charm and batted as only he can. Gatting soon went, in his patent fashion, shouldering arms and lbw to Alderman, but Smith was excellent support for the captain. They added 139 before Gower received a nasty lifter from Hughes and was grabbed at short leg.

Russell was promoted to number 7, and made 29 before caught off bat and pad, and Smith was bowled by Alderman with the new ball when 96. Foster and Jarvis were both lbw to Alderman, and England ended Monday on 322 for nine, 80 ahead.

The weather was Australia's only worry on the last day. Emburey and Dilley resisted for 16 overs, giving Australia a target of 118 as rain approached. But the rain fell in the lunch interval, and there was nothing but sunshine as Australia approached the target – not exactly serenely. Marsh was out for 1, and when between the totals of 51 and 67 Taylor, Border and Jones went, there were tiny thoughts of 1981. But Boon was solid and Waugh came next, Australia winning by six wickets and Waugh hoisting his undefeated aggregate to 350.

Only Hutton's one-innings 364 in 1938 was a larger unbeaten aggregate in Ashes matches.

Third Test, Edgbaston

Australia were unchanged for the third Test, but England, having made changes, were forced into others by injury. In the end the team showed four changes from Lord's. Botham and Lamb were

THIRD TEST MATCH

Edgbaston, Birmingham, 6, 7, 8, 10, 11 July

Match drawn

AUSTRALIA			*Mins*	*Balls*	*4s*			*Mins*	*Balls*	*4s*
G.R. Marsh	lbw b Botham	42	*145*	*134*	*2*	(2) b Jarvis	42	*111*	*86*	*4*
M.A. Taylor	st Russell b Emburey	43	*135*	*99*	*5*	(1) c Botham b Gooch	51	*172*	*148*	*4*
D.C. Boon	run out	38	*134*	*111*	*5*	not out	22	*116*	*112*	*1*
*A.R. Border	b Emburey	8	*17*	*21*	*1*					
D.M. Jones	c sub b Fraser	157	*327*	*293*	*17*					
S.R. Waugh	b Fraser	43	*78*	*54*	*6*					
†I.A. Healy	b Fraser	2	*16*	*12*	–	(4) not out	33	*55*	*46*	*3*
M.G. Hughes	c Botham b Dilley	2	*19*	*16*	–					
T.V. Hohns	c Gooch b Dilley	40	*119*	*99*	*4*					
G.F. Lawson	b Fraser	12	*34*	*28*	*2*					
T.M. Alderman	not out	0	*9*	*8*	–					
Extras	(lb 20, nb 17)	37				(b 4, lb 4, nb 2)	10			
Total	(142 overs)	424				(65 overs) (2 wkts)	158			
	88, 94, 105, 201, 272, 289, 299, 391, 421					81, 109				

Dilley	31	3	123	2	Dilley	10	4	27	–
Jarvis	23	4	82	–	Fraser	12	–	29	–
Fraser	33	8	63	4	Emburey	20	8	37	–
Botham	26	5	75	1	Jarvis	6	1	20	1
Emburey	29	5	61	2	Curtis	3	–	7	–
					Gooch	14	5	30	1

ENGLAND			*Mins*	*Balls*	*4s*
G.A. Gooch	lbw b Lawson	8	*41*	*33*	*1*
T.S. Curtis	lbw b Hughes	41	*121*	*81*	*7*
*D.I. Gower	lbw b Alderman	8	*27*	*26*	*1*
C.J. Tavaré	c Taylor b Alderman	2	*10*	*9*	–
K.J. Barnett	c Healy b Waugh	10	*31*	*21*	*2*
I.T. Botham	b Hughes	46	*154*	*110*	*6*
†R.C. Russell	c Taylor b Hohns	42	*156*	*131*	*3*
J.E. Emburey	c Boon b Lawson	26	*76*	*58*	*5*
A.R.C. Fraser	run out	12	*24*	*29*	*1*
G.R. Dilley	not out	11	*85*	*63*	*1*
P.W. Jarvis	lbw b Alderman	22	*39*	*31*	*2*
Extras	(b 1, lb 2, nb 11)	14			
Total	(96.3 overs)	242			
	17, 42, 47, 75, 75, 171, 171, 185, 215				

Alderman	26.3	6	61	3
Lawson	21	4	54	2
Waugh	11	3	38	1
Hughes	22	4	68	2
Hohns	16	8	18	1

Man of the Match: D.M. Jones
Umpires: H.D. Bird and J.W. Holder
Toss: Australia

selected to return after injury, and Broad and Jarvis were dropped, implying that Angus Fraser, of the 12 picked for Lord's would make his Test debut. However, Lamb and Smith dropped out with injury and Tim Curtis and Chris Tavaré were picked to replace them. Then Gatting returned to London the day before the match because of family bereavement, and Foster withdrew with a blistered finger. Jarvis was recalled.

Border won the toss after nine consecutive losses to Gower, and decided to bat. With thunderstorms around the country, Edgbaston remained hot and humid, and Taylor and Marsh did their first job by batting through to lunch. England bowled well, and the miracle-worker Botham, returning to Tests, bowled his 8,000th ball after being on 7,999 for 22 months. It rapped Taylor on the pads, but the umpire said 'not out' – the first serious threat to the great man's divinity.

Taylor was first out, stumped off Emburey for 34, and ten minutes later Marsh was lbw to Botham. Border scored only 8 (the seventh was his 8,000th Test run) and Australia were 105 for three. Boon and Jones were consolidating when Jones' straight drive was deflected by Jarvis onto the wicket and Boon, backing up, was unluckily run out.

A storm ended play at 232 for four, with Waugh having passed Hutton's aggregate 364 by three. Play did not start next day until 4.30, and Australia advanced to 294 for six before bad light ended the day. Waugh was finally out for 43 (his sequence ending at 393), bowled by Fraser, who also took his second Test wicket by bowling Healy. Jones, however, batting without a helmet, had reached 101. Rain and drizzle again held up play on Saturday till 3.30. Australia advanced to 391 for seven, Jones 141 not out. Russell, who again was not to allow a bye, must have been sorry to see Emburey's throw from third man proceed to the long-on boundary, giving Australia a remarkable seven leg-byes.

The sunshine, which apart from Edgbaston blessed the whole summer, returned on Monday, and Australia batted on to end their innings at 424. Jones made a gritty 157.

England, with no prospect of winning, and now finding the four-day-old pitch playing tricks, were soon in depressing straits. Gooch was lbw to a ball which didn't rise, and Gower was also lbw – both scored 8. Tavaré snicked to slip for 2, and Curtis, having batted two hours for 41, was also lbw playing across Hughes. Barnett, with a groin strain which necessitated a runner, was caught behind, and England were 75 for five.

Botham and Russell then got their heads down, and each batted for over 2½ hours. They added 96 before both were out at 171 to spinner Hohns.

England began the last day 40 runs short of avoiding the follow-on, and Fraser was foolishly

FOURTH TEST MATCH

Old Trafford, Manchester, July 27, 28, 29, 31, August 1

Australia won by 9 wickets

ENGLAND			*Mins*	*Balls*	*4s*			*Mins*	*Balls*	*4s*
G.A. Gooch	b Lawson	11	*50*	*32*	*1*	c Alderman b Lawson	13	*51*	*23*	*2*
T.S. Curtis	b Lawson	22	*136*	*103*	*4*	c Boon b Alderman	0	*6*	*2*	–
R.T. Robinson	lbw b Lawson	0	*15*	*9*	–	lbw b Lawson	12	*31*	*28*	*1*
R.A. Smith	c Hohns b Hughes	143	*355*	*285*	*15*	c Healy b Alderman	1	*5*	*8*	–
*D.I. Gower	lbw b Hohns	35	*86*	*51*	*6*	c Marsh b Lawson	15	*67*	*40*	*1*
I.T. Botham	b Hohns	0	*7*	*6*	–	lbw b Alderman	4	*24*	*23*	–
†R.C. Russell	lbw b Lawson	1	*12*	*11*	–	not out	128	*353*	*293*	*14*
J.E. Emburey	lbw b Hohns	5	*38*	*34*	*1*	b Alderman	64	*221*	*183*	*10*
N.A. Foster	c Border b Lawson	39	*100*	*68*	*4**	b Alderman	6	*39*	*28*	–
A.R.C. Fraser	lbw b Lawson	2	*16*	*9*	–	c Marsh b Hohns	3	*39*	*32*	–
N.G.B. Cook	not out	0	*15*	*10*	–	c Healy b Hughes	5	*10*	*11*	*1*
Extras	(lb 2)	2				(lb 6, w 2, nb 5)	13			
Total	(103 overs)	260	**plus 1 six*			(110.4 overs)	264			
23, 23, 57, 132, 140, 147, 158, 232, 252						10, 25, 27, 28, 38, 59, 201, 223, 255				

Alderman	25	13	49	–	Lawson	31	8	81	3
Lawson	33	11	72	6	Alderman	27	7	66	5
Hughes	17	6	55	1	Hohns	26	15	37	1
Hohns	22	7	59	3	Hughes	14.4	2	45	1
Waugh	6	1	23	–	Border	8	2	12	–
					Waugh	4	–	17	–

AUSTRALIA			*Mins*	*Balls*	*4s*			*Mins*	*Balls*	*4s*
M.A. Taylor	st Russell b Emburey	85	*179*	*180*	*10*	(2) not out	37	*112*	*83*	*4*
G.R. Marsh	c Russell b Botham	47	*156*	*100*	*5*	(1) c Robinson b Emburey	31	*95*	*94*	*1*
D.C. Boon	b Fraser	12	*40*	*40*	*2*	not out	10	*15*	*23*	–
*A.R. Border	c Russell b Foster	80	*312*	*266*	*10*					
D.M. Jones	b Botham	69	*173*	*141*	*7**					
S.R. Waugh	c Curtis b Fraser	92	*203*	*174*	*7*					
†I.A. Healy	lbw b Foster	0	*1*	*1*	–					
T.V. Hohns	c Gower b Cook	17	*62*	*64*	*2*					
M.G. Hughes	b Cook	3	*9*	*6*	–					
G.F. Lawson	b Fraser	17	*29*	*31*	*3*					
T.M. Alderman	not out	6	*22*	*12*	–					
Extras	(b 5, lb 7, w 1, nb 6)	19				(nb 3)	3			
Total	(167.5 overs)	447	**plus 1 six*			(32.5 overs) (1 wkt)	81			
135, 143, 154, 274, 362, 362, 413, 423, 423						62				

Foster	34	12	74	2	Foster	5	2	5	–
Fraser	36.5	4	95	3	Fraser	10	–	28	–
Emburey	45	9	118	1	Emburey	13	3	30	1
Cook	28	6	85	2	Cook	4.5	–	18	–
Botham	24	6	63	2					

Man of the Match: G.F. Lawson
Umpires: J.H. Hampshire and B.J. Meyer
Toss: England

run out in the first over, leaving the score 185 for eight. Emburey and Dilley took the score to within 10 of the target, and amid great excitement (which said something for English fans' need for anything to cheer) last man Jarvis drove the runs which saved the follow-on. Australia made 158 for two in the time remaining.

Fourth Test, Old Trafford

Two up with three to play meant no changes for Australia – two down meant four more changes for England. Barnett, Tavaré, Dilley and Jarvis were out (Dilley was injured again), Smith and Foster returned after injury and Tim Robinson and left-arm spinner Nick Cook came into the side.

With the heatwave temporarily disappearing again, England won the toss and batted on a coldish, grey day. Lawson bowled well and after 50 minutes bowled Gooch. There were only 23 runs on the board, and there were still only 23 runs scored when Lawson got Robinson lbw 15 minutes later. Curtis and Smith dug in and lunch was reached at 48 for two, two runs having come in an hour at one stage. It was the opposite approach to the first day's batting at Lord's.

Curtis' 2¼-hour innings ended after lunch for only 11, and Smith and Gower set themselves to get some runs. They made 75 before Gower made a mess of a pull against spinner Hohns after making 35 and it was 132 for four. Botham's new fallibility was highlighted when an intended six off Hohns found the ball sliding under his bat and he was out for nought. Russell and Emburey were both lbw and suddenly England were 158 for seven.

Smith then found a partner in Foster, who hit a solid 39 before being out next morning. With Fraser and Cook, Smith added 28 for the last two wickets, being last out for 143, his first Test century. England made 260, the last three wickets having added 102.

The total was soon put into perspective as Taylor and Marsh made the first century opening stand of the series. When Marsh was out for 47 Australia were 135, and although Taylor and Boon followed fairly quickly, Border and Jones took the score to 218 for three at the close.

Botham, whose bowling seemed to have been forgotten by Gower, dismissed Jones next morning for 69, but this brought in Waugh. Border, who clearly saw the Ashes as a reward for keeping up the pressure, played the anchor role in a partnership with Waugh which took Australia to 351 for four at tea. Eleven runs later, however, a surprising lapse saw his effort of over five hours end for 80. Healy was lbw to Foster first ball, but Waugh prevented a hat-trick on the first ball of

Jack Russell provided some much-needed fight during the fourth Test during which the news broke of the forthcoming tour of South Africa. With many of his team-mates thereby ruling themselves out of Test cricket Russell knuckled down with a defiant 128 not out. He ducks a bouncer from Steve Waugh.

Allsport/Adrian Murrell

Foster's next over. Hohns and Hughes departed and then Waugh, surprisingly, mishooked Fraser and was caught for 92, a rash stroke which immediately reduced his average to 242.50. Australia's innings lasted till Monday morning when they were out for 447.

There were now rumours about an English rebel tour of South Africa in the winter – a tour which would eliminate many of the season's Test players from future Tests, including three in the current side. It was also known that Botham had received a threat to his life and that an unfortunate gesture by Gower to the crowd had been recorded by TV. England's morale was at its lowest, and the batting reflected this.

Soon after lunch all six main batsmen were out for 59. Lawson and Alderman had claimed three each – only Gower had stayed for over an hour. Russell and Emburey fought hard to take the score to 123 for six at tea, when it poured with rain and play ended for the day.

Before play began on the last morning the South African tour was announced, and all could see the reason for England's apparent lack of spirit the previous day. There was no lack of it on the last morning, however, when Russell, England's greatest, almost only, success of the series, and Emburey, one of the rebels and so presumably playing in his last Test, showed some defiance. Just before lunch they avoided the innings defeat and, with rain about and the stand well into its fourth hour, the Australians were getting decidedly anxious.

However, the new ball finally disposed of Emburey for 64, after a seventh-wicket stand of 142. Russell was far from finished, though, and added 22 in 39 minutes with Foster, and 32 in another 39 minutes with Fraser. Ten minutes later, when Cook was out, Russell stood at 128 not out in seven minutes short of six hours, and Australia needed 78 to regain the Ashes.

Symbolically the sun came out as they set about the task, and Taylor and Marsh looked as if they might score them together. However Marsh was out at 62 (Emburey's 138th and probably last Test wicket) and Boon scored the winning run. It was the first time Australia had regained the Ashes in England for 55 years. It was Australia's 100th victory over England. It was a happy day for all Australians.

Fifth Test, Trent Bridge

England omitted the South African signatories for the Trent Bridge Test and Gooch asked for a rest to rediscover his confidence. The selectors included five names new to the series in the selected 12. Of these the 21-year-old Lancashire batsman Michael Atherton and Derbyshire's 26-year-old Jamaican-born fast bowler Devon

FIFTH TEST MATCH
Trent Bridge, Nottingham, August 10, 11, 12, 14, 15
Australia won by an innings and 180 runs

AUSTRALIA			*Mins*	*Balls*	*4s*
G.R. Marsh	c Botham b Cook	138	*426*	*382*	*15*
M.A. Taylor	st Russell b Cook	219	*554*	*461*	*23*
D.C. Boon	st Russell b Cook	73	*210*	*183*	*9*
*A.R. Border	not out	65	*221*	*143*	*7*
D.M. Jones	c Gower b Fraser	22	*51*	*44*	*3*
S.R. Waugh	c Gower b Malcolm	0	*13*	*8*	–
†I.A. Healy	b Fraser	5	*12*	*7*	–
T.V. Hohns	not out	19	*52*	*45*	*2*
M.G. Hughes					
G.F. Lawson					
T.M. Alderman					
Extras	(b 6, lb 23, w 3, nb 29)	61			
Total	(206.3 overs) (6 wkts dec)	602			

329, 430, 502, 543, 553, 560

Fraser	52.3	18	108	2
Malcolm	44	2	166	1
Botham	30	4	103	–
Hemmings	33	9	81	–
Cook	40	10	91	3
Atherton	7	–	24	–

ENGLAND			*Mins*	*Balls*	*4s*			*Mins*	*Balls*	*4s*
T.S. Curtis	lbw b Alderman	2	*25*	*16*	–	(2) lbw b Alderman	6	*20*	*10*	*1*
M.D. Moxon	c Waugh b Alderman	0	*2*	*3*	–	(5) b Alderman	18	*69*	*48*	*3*
M.A. Atherton	lbw b Alderman	0	*1*	*2*	–	c & b Hohns	47	*172*	*127*	*3*
R.A. Smith	c Healy b Alderman	101	*205*	*150*	*16*	b Hughes	26	*62*	*44*	*4*
*D.I. Gower	c Healy b Lawson	11	*31*	*25*	–	(1) b Lawson	5	*6*	*5*	*1*
†R.C. Russell	c Healy b Lawson	20	*91*	*63*	*1*	b Lawson	1	*16*	*14*	–
E.E. Hemmings	b Alderman	38	*101*	*83*	*5*	lbw b Hughes	35	*58*	*48*	*5*
A.R.C. Fraser	b Hohns	29	*85*	*55*	*3*	b Hohns	1	*15*	*9*	–
I.T. Botham	c Waugh b Hohns	12	*54*	*49*	*1*	absent hurt	–			
N.G.B. Cook	not out	2	*22*	*15*	–	(9) not out	7	*41*	*27*	–
D.E. Malcolm	c Healy b Hughes	9	*11*	*15*	*0**	(10) b Hughes	5	*5*	*9*	*1*
Extras	(lb 18, nb 13)	31				(b 3, lb 6, w 1, nb 6)	16			
Total	(76.5 overs)	255	**plus 1 six*			(55.3 overs)	167			

1, 1, 14, 37, 119, 172, 214, 234, 244 — 5, 13, 67, 106, 114, 120, 123, 160

Alderman	19	2	69	5
Lawson	21	5	57	2
Hohns	18	8	48	2
Hughes	7.5	–	40	1
Waugh	13	4	23	–

Alderman	16	6	32	2
Lawson	15	3	51	2
Hughes	12.3	1	46	3
Hohns	12	3	29	2

Man of the Match: M.A. Taylor
Umpires: N.T. Plews and D.R Shepherd
Toss: Australia

Malcolm, who played in spectacles, were new to Test cricket. Recalled from previous seasons were Martyn Moxon, Gladstone Small and Eddie Hemmings. Two days before the Test Small withdrew with injury, and Greg Thomas was named as his replacement, but on the morning of the match Thomas was the one omitted. Australia did not need to make any changes and, since the side could hardly be more successful, they did not make any.

Actually, the side *could* be more successful, and set about proving it on the first day. In fact only Taylor and Marsh needed to be more successful, for they were the only two players required. Opening the innings after Border had won the toss they remained together all day.

England bowled well at first, and the two had plenty of uncomfortable moments, particularly against Malcolm. But they safely reached lunch at 88, and by tea were looking to be fixtures at 192. Record books were being reached for when the two went out to bat after tea, and soon they passed Australia's highest opening stand in England (201) then their highest in Ashes matches (244), both held by Bill Lawry and the current tour coach Bobby Simpson. The highest Test opening stand in England (268 byHobbs and Sutcliffe) was passed, and at close the pair had reached 301.

Next morning the overall record opening stand in Ashes matches was passed (323 by Hobbs and Rhodes) and then suddenly Marsh was gone, edging Cook to slip; 329 for one. Boon settled into his place, and Taylor went on, passing 200 for the first time in his career. After being missed at 152, he was eventually stumped off Cook for 219; 430 for two. Boon was missed twice, the second miss dislocating Botham's finger, before departing for 73, another stumping off Cook. Jones and Waugh (for a duck) were dismissed before the close at 560 for five.

Border batted on on Saturday, not very quickly considering the score, and finally declared at 602 for six. There were 61 extras, a new Ashes record. Border's 65 not out took his aggregate Test runs to 8,146, moving him past Boycott into second place behind Gavaskar on the all-time list.

Once again England began batting in the depressing situation of having only a draw to play for. Curtis and Moxon opened, and Moxon was caught off Alderman for a duck. In his first Test Atherton was leg before second ball: 1 for two after five balls. Curtis scored 2 and Gower 11 before Smith and Russell (20) made a little stand of 82. Hemmings helped Smith add 53 during which Smith pulled a ball hard on to Boon's helmet at forward short leg. The helmet was knocked off and Boon was forced to retire, undoubtedly lucky that the damage was not more serious. Smith hammered his old adversary Hughes for five fours in ten balls, reached a century, and then touched Alderman's first delivery with the new ball to the keeper. After Hemmings went Fraser and a one-handed Botham tried to resist, and the innings did manage to last out the day, but 11 balls on Monday were enough for the side to be out for 255 – 347 behind.

Border enforced the follow on, and Gower went in at number 1, hitting the first ball for four. The change of order looked like an impulsive gesture of defiance, but Gower pointed out that, with Botham incapacitated, he wanted Moxon to provide some solid middle-order batting. It did not work because Gower was bowled by Lawson without offering a stroke in the second over and Curtis soon followed – like so many others, lbw to Alderman. Atherton offered most resistance with 47 in nearly three hours, and Hemmings made 35, which was popular with the local fans, but not with some Aussies, who thought he should have walked when the umpires turned down an appeal for a catch by Waugh in the slips.

It was over soon after tea, with England out for 167 and having to accept defeat by an innings and 180 runs.

Geoff Marsh and Mark Taylor walking out at Trent Bridge to continue their partnership in the fifth Test. They batted all the first day to make 301, and were not parted until they had passed the record opening stand in Ashes matches, previously held by Jack Hobbs and Wilfred Rhodes.

Allsport/Adrian Murrell

Sixth Test, the Oval

Australia were again pleased to announce an unchanged side for the Oval, while England had their worst selectorial problems yet. Gower did not resign, as some of the newspapers suggested he should, and 12 other names were added to his by the selectors. Botham's finger kept him out of consideration, and Capel replaced him. Small returned from injury, Gooch from introspection, and two more players new to Test cricket were selected in John Stephenson and Nasser Hussain, two Essex batsmen who were both graduates of Durham University. Curtis and Moxon were omitted. This was just the preliminary basis for the merry-go-round, however. Malcolm declared himself injured and was replaced by Greg Thomas, until Greg Thomas revealed that he was joining the South African rebels. DeFreitas, who had now announced that he would, after all, not be in the South African party, was selected, but then he, too, cried off with an injury. Fraser then announced he was unfit, so Kent's 6ft 6in pace bowler Alan Igglesden and Derek Pringle were added to the party. On the morning of the match, it was the oldest and the youngest of the party, Hussain and Hemmings, who were omitted. Stephenson and Igglesden thus earned first caps. Of the first Test team, only Gower and Russell had retained their places throughout.

Australia won the toss and batted, and the familiar figures of Marsh and Taylor faced the less familiar Small and Igglesden. At 48 Small had Marsh caught by Igglesden for 17, but Taylor and Boon settled in until Taylor surprisingly gave Igglesden his first Test victim by edging to the keeper at 130. Boon went 19 runs later, but that was the total of England's success on the first day, which closed at 325 for three. Jones had already come to an excellent century, scored in only 119 balls, and he and Border had added 135 in the final session.

Next day the two were out within two runs of each other, Waugh for once (or twice, actually) failed, and it was left to Healy, Hohns and Hughes to get the total up to 468.

Gooch and Stephenson comprised the fifth opening pair Alderman had faced in this summer's Tests, but the results were depressingly familiar from England's point of view. From the third ball Gooch was adjudged lbw for the fifth time in his eight innings, and England were 1 for one. Bad light and rain then ended play.

Stephenson and Atherton on the Saturday took the score to 28, when Atherton was out, and then Hughes took up his personal campaign with Smith, who seemed to be winning comfortably, especially when umpire Bird cautioned Hughes for his string of bouncers. Lawson unkindly ended the fun by bowling Smith. Stephenson, Capel and Russell then fell to Alderman and England at lunch were 98 for six. Bad light and rain came to England's rescue 14 runs later, but nobody in the England camp could have enjoyed Sunday.

Actually, Monday was a better day for the home side. Gower reached 79 handsomely, then Pringle and Small put up a little stand. At 201 for eight, however, the follow-on looked assured. But Cook, taking his promotion up the order to number 10 seriously, joined Small in one of England's grittiest stands of the summer. They took the score past the

SIXTH TEST MATCH
The Oval, August 24, 25, 26, 28, 29
Match drawn

AUSTRALIA			*Mins*	*Balls*	*4s*			*Mins*	*Balls*	*4s*
G.R. Marsh	c Igglesden b Small	17	*79*	*62*	*2*	(2) lbw b Igglesden	4	*16*	*13*	–
M.A. Taylor	c Russell b Igglesden	71	*163*	*125*	*4*	(1) c Russell b Small	48	*153*	*120*	*7*
D.C. Boon	c Atherton b Small	46	*124*	*90*	*6*	run out	37	*140*	*107*	*4*
*A.R. Border	c Russell b Capel	76	*245*	*156*	*11*	not out	51	*108*	*74*	*5*
D.M. Jones	c Gower b Small	122	*213*	*180*	*17*	b Capel	50	*79*	*69*	*4*
S.R. Waugh	b Igglesden	14	*44*	*28*	*1*	not out	7	*12*	*12*	–
†I.A. Healy	c Russell b Pringle	44	*57*	*44*	*6*					
T.V. Hohns	c Russell b Pringle	30	*97*	*62*	*4*					
M.G. Hughes	lbw b Pringle	21	*45*	*42*	*3*					
G.F. Lawson	b Pringle	2	*9*	*8*	–					
T.M. Alderman	not out	6	*16*	*10*	*1*					
Extras	(b 1, lb 9, nb 9)	19				(b 2, lb 7, nb 13)	22			
Total	(132.3 overs)	468				(63 overs) (4 wkts dec)	219			
48, 130, 149, 345, 347, 386, 409, 447, 453						7, 100, 101, 189				

Small	40	8	141	3	Small	20	4	57	1
Igglesden	24	2	91	2	Igglesden	13	1	55	1
Pringle	24.3	6	70	4	Capel	8	–	35	1
Capel	16	2	66	1	Pringle	16	–	53	–
Cook	25	5	78	–	Cook	6	2	10	–
Atherton	1	–	10	–					
Gooch	2	1	2	–					

ENGLAND			*Mins*	*Balls*	*4s*			*Mins*	*Balls*	*4s*
G.A. Gooch	lbw b Alderman	0	*3*	*3*	–	c & b Alderman	10	*54*	*34*	–
J.P. Stephenson	c Waugh b Alderman	25	*122*	*66*	*2*	lbw b Alderman	11	*31*	*23*	*1*
M.A. Atherton	c Healy b Hughes	12	*50*	*34*	*2*	b Lawson	14	*64*	*47*	*2*
R.A. Smith	b Lawson	11	*19*	*19*	*2*	not out	77	*143*	*99*	*11*
*D.I. Gower	c Healy b Alderman	79	*164*	*120*	*11**	c Waugh b Lawson	7	*23*	*24*	–
D.J. Capel	lbw b Alderman	4	*2*	*3*	*1*	c Taylor b Hohns	17	*66*	*50*	*2*
†R.C. Russell	c Healy b Alderman	12	*17*	*30*	*2*	not out	0	*9*	*6*	–
D.R. Pringle	c Taylor b Hohns	27	*147*	*90*	–					
G.C. Small	c Jones b Lawson	59	*136*	*97*	*8*					
N.G.B. Cook	c Jones b Lawson	31	*123*	*102*	*2*					
A.P. Igglesden	not out	2	*38*	*23*	–					
Extras	(b 2, lb 7, w 1, nb 13)	23				(lb 1, w 1, nb 5)	7			
Total	(92.1 overs)	285	**plus 1 five*			(46.1 overs) (5 wkts)	143			
1, 28, 47, 80, 84, 98, 169, 201, 274						20, 27, 51, 67, 138				

Alderman	27	7	66	5	Alderman	13	3	30	2
Lawson	29.1	9	85	3	Lawson	15.1	2	41	2
Hughes	23	3	84	1	Hughes	8	2	34	–
Hohns	10	1	30	1	Hohns	10	2	37	1
Waugh	3	–	11	–					

Man of the Match: D.M. Jones
Men of the Series: T.M. Alderman and R.C. Russell
Umpires: H.D. Bird and K.E. Palmer
Toss: Australia

ENGLAND v AUSTRALIA 1989
Test match averages

ENGLAND

Batting and Fielding	*M*	*I*	*NO*	*Runs*	*HS*	*Avge*	*100*	*50*	*Ct*	*St*
R.A. Smith	5	10	1	553	143	61.44	2	3	1	–
R.C. Russell	6	11	3	314	128*	39.25	1	1	14	4
D.I. Gower	6	11	–	383	106	34.82	1	2	4	–
J.E, Emburey	3	5	1	131	64	32.75	–	1	–	–
K.J. Barnett	3	5	–	141	80	28.20	–	1	–	–
N.G.B. Cook	3	5	3	45	31	22.50	–	–	–	–
G.R. Dilley	2	3	1	42	23	21.00	–	–	–	–
B.C. Broad	2	4	–	82	37	20.50	–	–	2	–
G.A. Gooch	5	9	–	183	68	20.33	–	2	4	–
M.A. Atherton	2	4	–	73	47	1.25	–	–	1	–
N.A. Foster	3	6	2	68	39	17.00	–	–	1	–
I.T. Botham	3	4	–	62	46	15.50	–	–	3	–
T.S. Curtis	3	5	–	71	41	14.20	–	–	1	–
P.W. Jarvis	2	3	–	33	22	11.00	–	–	–	–
D.R. Pringle	2	3	–	33	27	11.00	–	–	–	–
A.R.C. Fraser	3	5	–	47	29	9.40	–	–	–	–

Played in one match: D.J. Capel 4, 17; P.A.J. DeFreitas 1, 21; M.W. Gatting 0, 22; E.E. Hemmings 38, 35; A.P. Igglesden 2* (1 ct); A.J. Lamb 125, 4; D.E. Malcolm 9, 5; M.D. Moxon 0, 18; P.J. Newport 36, 8 (1 ct); R.T. Robinson 0, 12 (1 ct); G.C. Small 59; J.P. Stephenson 25, 11; C.J. Tavaré 2.

Bowling	*Overs*	*Mdns*	*Runs*	*Wkts*	*Avge*	*BB*	*5i*	*10m*
N.A. Foster	167	42	421	12	35.08	3-39	–	–
A.R.C. Fraser	144.2	30	323	9	35.89	4-63	–	–
J.E. Emburey	152	37	342	8	42.75	4-88	–	–
A.P. Igglesden	37	3	146	3	48.67	2-91	–	–
G.C. Small	60	12	198	4	49.50	3-141	–	–
N.G.B. Cook	103.5	23	282	5	56.40	3-91	–	–
D.R. Pringle	86.2	12	306	5	61.20	4-70	–	–
G.R. Dilley	85	12	318	5	63.60	2-123	–	–
P.A.J. DeFreitas	63.3	10	216	3	72.00	2-140	–	–
I.T. Botham	80	15	241	3	80.33	2-63	–	–

Also bowled: M.A. Atherton 8-0-34-0, K.J. Barnett 6-0-32-0, D.J. Capel 24-2-101-2, T.S. Curtis 3-0-7-0-, G.A. Gooch 31-9-72-1, E.E. Hemmings 33-9-81-0, P.W. Jarvis 69.2-2-8-290-2, D.E. Malcolm 44-2-166-1, P.J. Newport 44-7-175-2.

AUSTRALIA

Batting and Fielding	*M*	*I*	*NO*	*Runs*	*HS*	*Avge*	*100*	*50*	*Ct*	*St*
S.R. Waugh	6	8	4	506	177*	126.50	2	1	4	–
M.A. Taylor	6	11	1	839	219	83.90	2	5	5	–
A.R. Border	6	9	3	442	80	73.67	–	6	5	–
D.M. Jones	6	9	1	566	157	70.75	2	3	4	–
D.C. Boon	6	11	3	442	94	55.25	–	3	9	–
T.V. Hohns	5	5	1	127	40	31.75	–	–	3	–
G.R. Marsh	6	11	–	347	138	31.55	1	–	5	–
G.F. Lawson	6	5	1	115	74	28.75	–	1	–	–
M.G. Hughes	6	5	–	127	71	25.40	–	1	–	–
T.M. Alderman	6	4	3	20	8	20.00	–	–	2	–
I.A. Healy	6	7	1	103	44	17.17	–	–	14	–

Played in one match: G.D. Campbell (did not bat).

Bowling	*Overs*	*Mdns*	*Runs*	*Wkts*	*Avge*	*BB*	*5i*	*10m*
T.M. Alderman	269.2	68	712	41	17.37	6-128	6	1
T.V. Hohns	134	53	300	11	27.27	3-59	–	–
G.F. Lawson	277.1	68	791	29	27.28	6-72	1	–
M.G. Hughes	189.2	41	615	19	32.37	4-71	–	–

Also bowled: A.R. Border 24-9-44-0, G.D. Campbell 24-0-124-1, S.R. Waugh 57-15-208-2.

Allan Border batting against Lavinia, Duchess of Norfolk's XI at Arundel Castle in a tour warm-up. He could not have expected then that he would lead his side to a 4–0 Test series victory.

Allsport/Adrian Murrell

total required and had added 73 before Small (59) finally relaxed and holed out at cover. When Cook followed, England had reduced the deficit to 183.

England's bowling was refreshingly tight for the rest of the day, and Australia were kept to 87 for one in 35 hours, so beginning the last day 270 ahead. Border was obliged to bat on, and actually did so till lunch, which might have been a little too long if he wanted the win. Boon was run out from a no-ball. Border and Jones both completed 50s in quick time, but perhaps the most significant figure was Taylor's 48. He had not failed once in ten innings and his aggregate of 839 runs in the series was the third-highest recorded in Tests, the two above him being true greats; Bradman and Hammond.

Border's declaration at 219 for four left England a possible 67 overs to bat, so a target of 403 was somewhat over-cautious. England did not negotiate the overs without alarms, although Smith hit a typically powerful 77 not out and a final 143 for five does not sound too threatening, but play was limited to only 46.1 overs due to bad light.

So Australia won the series 4-0. The Men of the Series were Alderman (41 wickets) and Russell (great wicket-keeping and brave batting). Taylor and Border must have been equally as pleased as these two. For Border, too often the captain of losing teams through no fault of his own, the emphatic victory was particularly sweet – indeed he called it the highlight of his career.

The highly sucessful touring party, which notched up Australia's 100th Test match victory over England. From left, back: M. Walsh (scorer), M.R.J. Veletta, M.A. Taylor, M.G. Hughes, T.M. Alderman, T.M. Moody, C.G. Rackemann, G.F. Lawson, T.B.A. May, G.D. Campbell, T.V. Hohns, R.B. Simpson (coach). Seated: T.J. Zoehrer, D.C. Boon, G.R. Marsh (vice-captain) L.M. Sawle (manager), A.R. Border (captain), D.M. Jones, S.R. Waugh, I.A. Healy

Patrick Eagar

Other Tour Matches

Terence Michael ALDERMAN (W Australia); *b* Subiaco 12.6.1956; RHB RFM
Although he made his Test debut in 1981 on the tour to England that summer, and was the outstanding bowler of the season with 42 Test wickets, Alderman had only appeared in 24 Tests when he arrived in England for the 1989 tour. The reason for his paucity of Test caps was his decision to tour South Africa with the 1985–86 Australians and he resumed his Test career only in 1988–89. In the interval however he had played both for Kent and Gloucestershire in the County Championship. In 1989 he took 41 Test wickets at 17 runs each – this compares most favourably with his 1981 record, since his victims cost 21 runs each that summer.

The fact that six times he captured five wickets in an innings in the 1989 Tests shows how much was owed to him.

David Clarence BOON (Tasmania); *b* Launceston 29.12.1960; RHB RM
After opening the Australian batting in the three one-day internationals, Boon moved to first wicket down for the six Test matches of 1989. He batted consistently, failing to score a century in any of the Tests, but still averaging 55. His first-class record last summer shows very little change from his first visit in 1985, but his Test figures are a vast improvement.

First Match v LEAGUE CRICKET CONFERENCE
At West Bromwich, May 5
Won by 165 runs

Australians		
*G.R. Marsh	c Moseley b McMillan	101
M.A. Taylor	c McMillan b Trotter	23
D.M. Jones	c Samarasekera b Moseley	170
T.M. Moody	not out	7
M.R. Veletta	not out	2
S.R. Waugh		
†I.A. Healy		
T.V. Hohns		
C.G. Rackemann		
G.D. Campbell		
M.G. Hughes		
Extras	b 6, lb 10, w 3, nb 4	23
Total (3 wkts, 55 ov)		326

65, 299, 318

Moseley	11	1	27	1
Trotter	11	1	30	1
Manider Singh	10	0	88	0
O'Donnell	10	0	53	0
McMillan	11	0	72	1
Samarasekera	2	0	40	0

League Cricket Conference		
*B. Knowles	b Hughes	7
J. Foster	c Healy b Hughes	0
M.A.R. Samarasekera	b Campbell	0
P.R. Oliver	lbw b Waugh	31
M. Ingham	not out	56
B.M. McMillan	c Waugh b Rackemann	2
S.P. O'Donnell	not out	52
E.A. Moseley		
†D. Borthwick		
K. Trotter		
Maninder Singh		
Extras	lb 7, w 4, nb 2	13
Total (5 wkts, 55 ov)		161

2, 7, 9, 48, 55

Hughes	11	4	39	2
Campbell	7	0	27	1
Rackemann	11	3	35	1
Waugh	7	0	17	1
Hohns	11	3	18	0
Moody	8	1	18	0

Umpires: B. Turner and J. Potts
Toss: Australians
A brilliant second wicket stand of 234 in 29 overs provided the Australians with a large total. Jones hit out in a amazing fashion with 11 sixes and 9 fours – he hit 29 off one over from Samarasekera, including four sixes out of the ground. The League side began their reply very feebly and the competitve element of the game thus disappeared quickly, but in the closing stages Simon O'Donnell put up some resistance.

Second Match v LAVINIA, DUCHESS OF NORFOLK'S XI
At Arundel Castle, May 7
Won by 120 runs

Australians		
D.C. Boon	retired hurt	114
M.A. Taylor	lbw b Agnew	3
T.M. Moody	b Waller	72
*A.R. Border	c Boon b Needham	66
M.R.J. Veletta	c Whitticase b Parsons	8
S.R. Waugh	not out	44
†T.J. Zoehrer	c Willey b Taylor	1
M.G. Hughes	c Agnew b Taylor	1
G.F. Lawson	not out	2
T.B.A. May		
T.M. Alderman		
Extras	b 1, lb 1, nb 1	3
Total (6 wkts, 50 ov)		314

29, 177, 238, 272, 278, 283

Agnew	8	0	38	1
Taylor	9	0	42	2
Parsons	7	0	49	1
Willey	7	0	56	0
Waller	10	0	66	1
Needham	9	0	61	1

Lavinia, Duchess of Norfolk's XI		
P. Willey	c Boon b May	39
M.P. Speight	b Hughes	55
*D.I. Gower	lbw b Hughes	9
T.J. Boon	c Moody b Waugh	37
A. Needham	c Hughes b Waugh	8
†P. Whitticase	not out	26
C.T. Radley	not out	13
G.J. Parsons		
L.B. Taylor		
J.P. Agnew		
C.E. Waller		
Extras	b 1, lb 4, w 1, nb 1	7
Total (5 wkts, 50 ov)		194

88, 101, 106, 142, 159

Alderman	6	1	17	0
Lawson	9	0	23	0
Waugh	9	1	52	2
Hughes	10	2	23	2
May	10	2	43	1
Border	4	0	26	0
Veletta	2	0	5	0

Umpires: C. Cook and J.G. Langridge
Toss: Australians
Boon hit 114 before lunch with 2 sixes and 10 fours, then retired. Moody hit 66 off 72 balls. The home team never matched the scoring rate of the tourists and it was clear after 20 overs that Australia would win by a fair margin, the interest therefore faded. 11,000 spectators, a record for the ground, enjoyed a pleasant day.

Allan Robert BORDER (Queensland); *b* Cremorne, NSW 27.7.1955; LHB SLA
Captain of Australia in 39 consecutive Tests when he arrived for the 1989 tour, Border added a further six to this unparallelled record during the summer. He was the outstanding batsman on the 1985 visit and though eclipsed by Taylor in 1989, he was utterly reliable and his wicket still the most difficult to obtain. He had had rather a moderate season in Australia in 1988–89 and some critics wondered how he would fare in England, but he did all that could be expected of him as both batsman and captain, and after the miserable defeats he suffered in 1985, success in 1989 was sweet.

Gregory Dale CAMPBELL (Tasmania); *b* Launceston 10.3.1964; RHB RM
When Rackemann broke down just prior to the First Test, having appeared in all three one-day games, Campbell took his place at Headingley, this being the Tasmanian's Test debut. It was to prove his only appearance in the series, for he was displaced by Hohns in the next match.

The surprise selection for the tour, Campbell had played just one first-class game in 1986–87, not at all in 1987–88, but performed well for Tasmania in 1988–89. His role in 1989 was that of an 'also-ran', but he bowled usefully in the first-class matches, taking 30 wickets.

Ian Andrew HEALY (Queensland); *b* Spring Hill 30.4.1964; RHB WKT
Before the tour began it was thought that the wicket-keeping honours might go either way. When it was over, Healy had been chosen for all six Tests and the only time he missed out was in the third one-day international, when Veletta rather than Zoehrer took his place. Healy made his Test debut in September 1988 and now seems to have taken a permanent place in the Australian squad. He is also a useful batsman, though his talent in that direction was hardly needed on this tour.

Trevor Victor HOHNS (Queensland); *b* Brisbane 23.1.1954; LHB LB
The oldest member of the touring side, but curiously one of the least known, mainly because he was banned from Test cricket, having decided to tour South Africa. He made his first-class debut as far back as 1972–73 though his Test debut was not until 1988–89 v West Indies. His bowling in two matches against the Caribbean side was good enough to earn selection for England. He played in five Tests last summer, the only spinner used regularly by Australia and rather oddly his record in the Tests proved better than in the ordinary first-class games. He is no mug with the bat and a useful man to come in at number 8.

Third Match v SUSSEX
On the County Ground, Hove, May 9
Lost by 4 wickets

Australians		
M.A. Taylor	c Moores b Pigott	0
M.R.J. Veletta	c Moores b Pigott	2
S.R. Waugh	c Parker c Babington	86
D.M. Jones	lbw b Clarke	19
*G.R. Marsh	run out	0
†T.J. Zoehrer	b C.M. Wells	11
T.V. Hohns	b Babington	6
T.B.A. May	lbw b Dodemaide	9
G.D. Campbell	c Moores b Dodemaide	2
T.M. Alderman	b C.M. Wells	2
C.G. Rackemann	not out	1
Extras	b 2, lb 3, w 4, nb 7	16
Total (44.3 ov)		154

0, 22, 44, 67, 89, 106, 114, 125, 150

Pigott	9	3	20	2
Dodemaide	11	0	59	2
C.M. Wells	9	1	25	2
Babington	8.3	0	30	2
Clarke	7	1	15	1

Sussex		
A.M. Green	c Veletta b Rackemann	0
D.M. Smith	lbw b Waugh	22
*P.W.G. Parker	lbw b Rackemann	48
A.P. Wells	c Taylor b Rackemann	17
C.M. Wells	run out	1
I.J. Gould	c Taylor b May	12
A.I.C. Dodemaide	not out	17
A.C.S. Pigott	not out	28
†P. Moores		
A.R. Clarke		
A.M. Babington		
Extras	b 5, lb 4, w 1, nb 3	13
Total (6 wkts, 47.5 ov)		158

1, 40, 93, 100, 104, 114

Alderman	11	3	25	0
Rackemann	11	0	30	3
Campbell	8.5	1	35	0
Waugh	4	0	17	1
May	11	3	33	1
Hohns	2	0	9	0

Umpires: P.B. Wight and R. Julian
Toss: Australians
The tourists were soon in trouble with Taylor and Veletta dismissed and Jones retired hurt with 5. Waugh however batted well and Jones returned in an attempt to help Waugh to a century, but he was soon removed by Clarke. Sussex kept up with the clock and Pigott and Dodemaide made certain of victory.

Mervyn Gregory HUGHES (Victoria); *b* Eurora 23.11.1961; RHB RFM
An aggressive fast bowler who had built up a certain reputation through the press long before his arrival, Hughes played in all six Tests but he did not command the respect of English batsmen in the way achieved by Alderman and Lawson, and this is reflected in his Test record of 19 wickets at 32 runs each. He did not appear in any of the one-day internationals, despite the fact that he had been a regular in the 1988–89 Benson & Hedges Series. As a tail end batsman, Hughes could hit the ball very hard.

Dean Mervyn JONES (Victoria); *b* Coburg 24.3.1961; RHB RM
Although his record was not quite the equal of Taylor and Border in the 1989 Tests, he did so well in other first-class games that he ended the season as the leading batsman in England, way out in front of his rivals. Batting at number 5 he scores runs in a most stylish manner and by the end of the summer he had topped 2,000 with an average approaching 50 in 27 Tests.

Geoffrey Francis LAWSON (New South Wales); *b* Wagga Wagga 7.12.1957; RHB RFM
In 1985 he formed with McDermott the Australian attack against England and returned home with a bloody nose, his wickets costing 37 runs each. Last season partnered by Alderman he proved much more effective and his wickets cost 11 runs less. His best match was the fourth Test at Old Trafford when he took the first three wickets cheaply on the first morning and in all had nine victims in the match. He had had some problems with a back injury, but bowling slower than formerly he seems to have overcome the problem without it effecting his ability to take wickets.

Fourth Match v MCC
At Lords, May 11
Won by 101 runs

Australians		
D.C. Boon	c Fraser b Cowdrey	166
G.R. Marsh	c Ellison b Cowdrey	102
T.M. Moody	c Marks b Cowdrey	14
M.G. Hughes	c Carr b Cowdrey	6
*A.R. Border	not out	1
M.R.J. Veletta	not out	1
S.R. Waugh		
†I.A. Healy		
G.F. Lawson		
G.D. Campbell		
T.M. Aldermann		
Extras	b 1, lb 9, w 7, nb 2	19
Total (4 wkts, 55 ov)		309

277, 295, 307, 307

Ellison	11	1	61	0
Fraser	11	1	53	0
Watkinsoin	11	2	46	0
Cowdrey	11	0	60	4
Marks	8	0	63	0
Carr	3	0	16	0

MCC		
G.D. Mendis	c Veletta b Campbell	52
J.D. Carr	lbw b Alderman	23
*M.W. Gatting	c sub b Hughes	86
N.H. Fairbrother	b Campbell	0
M.R. Ramprakash	lbw b Waugh	1
C.S. Cowdrey	c Healy b Hughes	5
M. Watkinson	b Waugh	5
†P.R. Downton	b Lawson	15
V.J. Marks	b Waugh	0
R.M. Ellison	not out	2
A.R.C. Fraser	c Hughes b Lawson	0
Extras	b 2, lb 6, w 5, nb 6	19
Total (48.5 ov)		208

43, 141, 141, 145, 180, 180, 192, 192, 202

Alderman	8	0	41	1
Hughes	11	1	37	2
Campbell	11	0	47	2
Lawson	7.5	1	37	2
Waugh	11	1	38	3

Umpires: H.D. Bird and K.E. Palmer
Toss: Australians. MofM: D.C. Boon
Sponsored by Bass, this game was dominated by the first wicket stand of Boon and Waugh, worth 277. In effect they beat MCC on their own and gave their wickets away. Gatting batted well for the home side, but this fixture, once regarded like a Test Trial was a pale shadow of its former self.

Fifth Match v WORCESTERSHIRE
At New Road, Worcester, May 13, 14
Lost by 3 wkts

Australians 1st Innings		
G.R. Marsh	c Rhodes b Radford	21
M.A. Taylor	c Rhodes b Pridgeon	6
T.M. Moody	c Rhodes b Newport	9
*A.R. Border	c Hick b Newport	8
M.R.J. Veletta	c Radford b Newport	0
S.R. Waugh	c Rhodes b Newport	0
†I.A. Healy	not out	25
T.V. Hohns	lbw b Newport	3
G.F. Lawson	c Illingworth b Radford	8
M.G. Hughes	lbw b Radford	2
T.M. Alderman	c Pridgeon b Newport	6
Extras	lb 8, nb 7	15
Total		103

10, 34, 56, 56. 56, 64, 67, 82, 89

Radford	11	2	32	3
Pridgeon	9	1	20	1
Newport	10.5	2	43	6

Worcestershire 1st Innings		
T.S. Curtis	c Healy b Hughes	46
G.J. Lord	c Border b Alderman	0
G.A. Hick	c Marsh b Waugh	13
D.B. d'Oliveira	c Healy b Waugh	1
*I.T. Botham	c Taylor b Alderman	39
S.J. O'Shaughnessy	b Lawson	4
†S.J. Rhodes	c Taylor b Lawson	18
P.J. Newport	b Alderman	3
R.K. Illingworth	c Border b Alderman	0
N.V. Radford	not out	6
A.P. Pridgeon	c Taylor b Lawson	0
Extras	b 3, lb 6, w 5, nb 2	16
Total		146

7, 66, 68, 68, 104, 124, 132, 132, 146

Alderman	14	4	33	4
Lawson	14.4	1	50	3
Hughes	11	4	31	1
Waugh	6	1	23	2

Australians 2nd Innings		
M.A. Taylor	c d'Oliveira b Newport	11
G.R. Marsh	c Hick b Newport	0
T.M. Moody	c Botham b Newport	9
*A.R. Border	b Newport	48
M.R.J. Veletta	c Rhodes b Newport	2
S.R. Waugh	lbw b Botham	63
†I.A. Healy	b Radford	26
T.V. Hohns	c Rhodes b Radford	6
G.F. Lawson	b Radford	17
M.G. Hughes	c Botham b Radford	3
T.M. Alderman	not out	3
Extras	b 4, lb 7, w 3, nb 3	17
Total		205

6, 17, 27, 33, 130, 169, 169, 198, 202

Radford	28.2	8	58	4
Newport	27	4	84	5
Botham	10	3	18	1
Pridgeon	9	2	34	0

Worcestershire 2nd Innings		
T.S. Curtis	lbw b Alderman	8
G.J. Lord	lbw b Lawson	12
G.A. Hick	c Border b Waugh	43
D.B. d'Oliveira	c Veletta b Waugh	4
*I.T. Botham	c Healy b Alderman	42
S.J. O'Shaughnessy	lbw b Alderman	7
†S.J. Rhodes	b Alderman	16
P.J. Newport	not out	5
R.K. Illingworth	not out	12
Extras	b 3, lb 7, nb 4	14
Total (7 wkts)		163

20, 22, 65, 86, 109, 142, 145

Alderman	17	4	61	4
Lawson	18.4	6	44	1
Waugh	6	0	25	2
Hughes	4	1	23	0

Umpires: J.W. Holder and D.R. Shepherd
Toss: Australians
Newport exploited a helpful wicket to dismiss the tourists for 103, then it was the turn of Alderman and Lawson, though Curtis batted well for his 46 and provided the county with a lead on first innings. When rain ended play on Saturday the Australians were 51–4, with Newport picking up all four wickets. On Sunday the tourists were all out soon after lunch and Worcestershire went on to victory amid growing criticism of the New Road wicket. The Australians refused to play an additional One-Day game on Monday stating that the wickets at Worcester were not good enough.

Sixth Match v SOMERSET
At Taunton May 17, 18, 19
Drawn

Australians 1st Innings		
G.R. Marsh	c Burns b Jones	10
M.A. Taylor	c Burns b Rose	97
D.C. Boon	c Burns b Unwin	61
T.M. Moody	c Bartlett b Unwin	17
*A.R. Border	c Burns b Unwin	0
M.R.J. Veletta	c Burns b Mallender	46
†T.J. Zoehrer	lbw b Jones	48
T.B.A. May	not out	13
G.D. Campbell	b Mallender	10
M.G. Hughes	not out	21
C.G. Rackemann		
Extras	lb 7, w 1, nb 8	16
Total (8 wkts dec)		339

32, 142, 174, 177, 203, 290, 294, 315

Jones	21	2	83	2
Mallender	20	5	55	2
Foster	16	2	49	0
Rose	16	5	45	1
Unwin	24	5	73	3
Roebuck	7	1	27	0

Somerset 1st Innings		
S.J. Cook	c Veletta b Rackemann	11
P.M. Roebuck	c Boon b Hughes	13
R.J. Bartlett	c Taylor b Rackemann	0
*C.J. Tavare	c Veletta b Rackemann	6
R.J. Harden	c Border b May	45
†N.D. Burns	run out	27
G.D. Rose	c Boon b Hughes	0
N.A. Mallender	c Boon b May	0
A.N. Jones	c Taylor b May	15
P.D. Unwin	not out	4
D.J. Foster	b Campbell	6
Extras	b 2, lb 6, w 2, nb 3	13
Total		140

19, 19, 25, 48, 108, 112, 112, 112, 133

Rackemann	13	3	33	3
Campbell	9.4	1	25	1
May	28	15	48	3
Hughes	16	7	26	2

Australians 2nd Innings		
M.A. Taylor	c Bartlett b Roebuck	58
G.R. Marsh	c Jones b Unwin	57
M.G. Hughes	not out	15
C.G. Rackemann	c Roebuck b Unwin	0
T.M. Moody	not out	2
Extras	b 4, lb 7, nb 1	12
Total (3 wkts dec)		144

119, 129, 134

Jones	5	0	15	0
Mallender	6	1	25	0
Rose	6	1	18	0
Unwin	12	1	43	2
Foster	4	0	17	0
Roebuck	4	1	15	1

Somerset 2nd Innings		
S.J. Cook	lbw b Hughes	57
P.M. Roebuck	not out	100
R.J. Bartlett	c Campbell b Border	18
*C.J. Tavare	b Hughes	43
R.J. Harden	not out	4
Extras	b 1, lb 4, w 2, nb 6	13
Total (3 wkts)		235

111, 154, 230

Rackemann	14	6	29	0
Campbell	12	5	26	0
Hughes	15	4	44	2
May	21	5	63	0
Border	25	8	55	1
Moody	7	2	13	0

Umpires: D.J. Constant and N.J. Kitchen
Toss: Somerset
After Boon and Taylor had added a well made 110 for the second wicket, the tourists suffered a mini-collapse due to some good bowling by Unwin, the New Zealand spinner. The later batsmen however rallied the side and stumps were drawn at 339–8. Border declared overnight and the county batted poorly on the second day. Ignoring the follow on option, the Australians took some batting practice and reached 144–3 by the close. The county had the whole of the last day to make 344. Cook and Roebuck provided Somerset with a sound opening, but later the scoring rate dropped and Roebuck was quite content to bat out for a draw and his century – in 5½ hours.

Seventh Match v MIDDLESEX
At Lord's, May 20, 21, 22,
Won by 3 wkts

Middlesex 1st Innings

J.D. Carr	b Moody	22
D.L. Haynes	lbw b Alderman	13
*M.W. Gatting	lbw b Lawson	65
R.O. Butcher	c Alderman b Rackemann	31
M.R. Ramprakash	not out	46
†P.R. Downton	lbw b Lawson	8
J.E. Emburey	c Veletta b Alderman	4
N.F. Williams	lbw b Rackemann	28
S.P. Hughes	b Rackemann	0
A.R.C. Fraser	lbw b Rackemann	0
N.G. Cowans	b Hohns	17
Extras	lb 8, w 1, nb 2	11
Total		245

17, 60, 112, 142, 154, 162, 216, 216, 216

Alderman	15	6	31	2
Lawson	22	5	59	2
Rackemann	21	5	85	4
Moody	6	1	10	1
Hohns	17.5	5	52	1

Australians 1st Innings

G.R. Marsh	not out	100
M.A. Taylor	c Ramprakash b Williams	35
D.C. Boon	c Ramprakash b Hughes	20
T.M. Moody	not out	60
*A.R. Border		
M.R.J. Veletta		
†I.A. Healy		
T.V. Hohns		
G.F. Lawson		
T.M. Alderman		
C.G. Rackemann		
Extras	b 4, lb 11, w 2, nb 1	18
Total (2 wkts dec)		233

67, 111

Cowans	14	3	40	0
Fraser	17	4	42	0
Hughes	11	5	41	1
Emburey	20	7	49	0
Williams	12	1	35	1
Gatting	4	0	11	0

Middlesex 2nd Innings

J.D. Carr	b Lawson	13
D.L. Haynes	c Boon b Alderman	12
*M.W. Gatting	b Lawson	79
R.O. Butcher	lbw b Alderman	21
M.R. Ramprakash	c Healy b Alderman	33
†P.R. Downton	c Taylor b Lawson	6
N.F. Williams	not out	36
J.E. Emburey	b Lawson	0
S.P. Hughes	ht wkt b Lawson	5
A.R.C. Fraser	lbw b Hohns	3
N.G. Cowans	b Rackemann	0
Extras	b 4, lb 10, nb 5	19
Total		227

26, 26, 76, 159, 177, 177, 177, 204, 226

Alderman	21	2	73	3
Lawson	19	7	48	5
Moody	3	1	3	0
Rackemann	11.5	1	39	1
Hohns	13	3	36	1
Border	3	0	14	0

Australians 2nd Innings

D.C. Boon	b Fraser	86
M.R.J. Veletta	lbw b Cowans	7
*A.R. Border	b Fraser	77
†I.A. Healy	c Downton b Fraser	2
T.V. Hohns	c Downton b Fraser	7
M.A. Taylor	st Downton b Emburey	24
T.M. Moody	c Butcher b Emburey	7
G.R. Marsh	not out	12
G.F. Lawson	not out	5
Extras	b 5, lb 7, nb 4	16
Total (7 wkts)		243

17, 163, 169, 190, 191, 201, 234

Cowans	13	2	35	1
Fraser	30.3	5	89	4
Williams	8	1	23	0
Emburey	21	4	84	2

Umpires: H.D. Bird and B.J. Meyer
Toss: Middlesex

Gatting spent three hours scoring 65, as he and his colleagues were tied down by the Australian bowlers on the first day, which ended with Australians 37–0. On Sunday, Marsh was dropped twice, but completed a century, at which juncture Border declared. Gatting then batted well and was 78 not out when play ended, Middlesex being 157–3. The captain's innings ended quickly on the third morning and 70 runs saw the loss of the last seven wickets.

Eighth Match v YORKSHIRE
At Headingley, May 23
Won by 109 runs

Australians

D.C. Boon	b Sidebottom	172
G.R. Marsh	c and b Pickles	14
D.M. Jones	not out	89
S.R. Waugh	b Jarvis	13
†T.J. Zoehrer	not out	1
*A.R. Border		
T.M. Moody		
T.V. Hohns		
G.D. Campbell		
M.G. Hughes		
C.G. Rackemann		
Extras	lb 3, w 3, nb 2	8
Total (3 wkts, 55 ov)		297

66, 250, 283

Sidebottom	11	1	64	1
Jarvis	11	1	62	1
Pickles	11	2	48	1
Carrick	11	1	47	0
Hartley	4	1	31	0
Byas	3	0	18	0
Moxon	4	0	24	0

Yorkshire

M.D. Moxon	b Hohns	55
A.A. Metcalfe	b Hughes	2
R.J. Blakey	c Zoehrer b Campbell	2
K. Sharp	b Rackemann	6
D. Byas	c Zoehrer b Moody	13
†D.L. Bairstow	c Moody b Waugh	46
S.N. Hartley	c Marsh b Moody	5
*P. Carrick	c Zoehrer b Waugh	17
A. Sidebottom	b Waugh	2
P.W. Jarvis	c Zoehrer b Jones	15
C.S. Pickles	not out	5
Extras	b 5, lb 1, w 1, nb 13	20
Total (38.2 ov)		188

11, 16, 23, 86, 90, 105, 144, 163, 179

Campbell	8	2	14	1
Hughes	6	0	11	1
Rackemann	6	0	31	1
Waugh	9	1	41	3
Moody	8	2	23	2
Hohns	11	0	62	1
Jones	0.2	0	0	1

Umpires: N.T. Plews and J.H. Hampshire
Toss: Australians

Boon hit 21 fours and three sixes off 157 balls after rain had delayed the start of this match by 45 minutes. He reached his 100 in 133 minutes, whilst Marsh and Jones played supporting roles. Moxon hit a sound 55 and Bairstow a rapid 46, but otherwise the county reply was rather inept.

David Boon, 102 runs in boundaries in a one-day defeat of Yorkshire. Allsport/Adrian Murrell

Ninth Match v ENGLAND
At Old Trafford, May 25
Lost by 95 runs (see scorecard page 16)

Tenth Match v ENGLAND
At Trent Bridge, May 27
Tied (see scorecard page 17)

Eleventh Match v ENGLAND
At Lord's, May 29
Won by 6 wkts (see scorecard page 17)

Twelfth Match v WARWICKSHIRE
At Edgbaston, May 31, June 1, 2
Drawn.

Australians 1st Innings

D.C. Boon	lbw b Merrick	0
M.A. Taylor	st Humpage b Pierson	30
D.M. Jones	c sub b Asif Din	248
T.M. Moody	not out	144
*A.R. Border		
†T.J. Zoehrer		
T.V. Hohns		
T.B.A. May		
M.G. Hughes		
G.C. Campbell		
G.F. Lawson		
Extras	lb 14, nb 8	22
Total (3 wkts dec)		444

0, 95, 444

Merrick	22	4	107	1
Benjamin	14	2	81	0
Munton	21	6	85	0
Pierson	27	5	98	1
Twose	3	0	23	0
Asif Din	6.4	0	36	1

Warwickshire 1st Innings

A.J. Moles	lbw b Hughes	14
J.D. Ratcliffe	b Hughes	6
Asif Din	b Hohns	50
A.R.K. Pierson	c Zoehrer b Campbell	4
*T.A. Lloyd	c Campbell b Lawson	22
†G.W. Humpage	c Hohns	58
D.A. Banks	c Lawson b Campbell	28
R.G. Twose	c sub b Hohns	17
T.A. Merrick	c Campbell	0
J.E. Benjamin	not out	8
T.A. Munton	b Hohns	3
Extras	b 10, lb 10, w 1, nb 4	25
Total		235

20, 23, 33, 97, 131, 182, 220, 220, 231

Hughes	19	5	62	2
Campbell	18	4	41	3
Hohns	27.3	4	87	4
Lawson	7	1	20	1
Border	6	3	5	0

Australians 2nd Innings

M.A. Taylor	c Moles b Munton	67
†T.J. Zoehrer	lbw b Bejamin	0
*A.R. Border	c Moles b Munton	69
T.V. Hohns	b Asif Din	14
M.G. Hughes	not out	27
G.D. Campbell	not out	8
Extras	lb 10	10
Total (4 wkts dec)		195

4, 134, 153, 173

Merrick	8	0	23	0
Benjamin	7	1	31	1
Pierson	22	7	51	0
Munton	21	7	60	2
Asif Din	3	0	20	1

Warwickshire 2nd Innings

A.J. Moles	lbw c Campbell	9
J.D. Ratcliffe	c Moody b Hohns	17
Asif Din	lbw b Lawson	38
D.A Banks	not out	18
R.G. Twose	not out	15
Extras	lb 7, nb 1	8
Total (3 wkts)		105

15, 66, 84

Hughes	5	3	8	0
Campbell	7	3	15	1
Hohns	14	2	45	1
Lawson	11	3	30	1

Umpires: R. Palmer and N.T. Plews

Jones broke several records on the first day as he made 248 off 284 balls with 12 sixes and a partnership of 349 in 63 overs with Moody. Warwickshire ended the day 28–2. On the second morning with Boon and May injured and the other tourists elsewhere, the Australians took the field with two Warwickshire men as substitutes. The county batsmen however looked out of depth and Hohns and Campbell picked up wickets. Australia began the last day at 112–1 and surprisingly batted on for 90 minutes. Warwickshire had no hope of winning so rain at teatime was a relief to all.

Thirteenth Match v DERBYSHIRE

At Derby, June 3, 4, 5

Won by 11 runs

Australians 1st Innings

G.R. Marsh	c Maher b Base	34
M.A. Taylor	c Bowler b Malcolm	5
D.C. Boon	c Bowler b Base	34
S.R. Waugh	c Maher b Mortensen	14
*A.R. Border	b Base	17
T.M. Moody	c Roberts b Base	0
T.V. Hohns	b Malcolm	11
†I.A. Healy	c Roberts b Mortensen	30
G.D. Campbell	c Barnett b Mortensen	31
C.G. Rackemann	not out	0
T.M. Alderman	lbw b Mortensen	0
Extras	b 6, lb 11, w 5, nb 2	24
Total		200

18, 74, 79, 92, 93, 123, 137, 193, 200

Bishop	14	2	44	0
Malcolm	13	2	50	2
Mortensen	12.4	0	40	4
Base	12	0	49	4

Derbyshire 1st Innings

*K.J. Barnett	c Taylor b Campbell	76
P.D. Bowler	lbw b Alderman	4
†B.J.M. Maher	c Boon b Waugh	17
J.E. Morris	c Healy b Rackemann	7
B. Roberts	run out	31
S.C. Goldsmith	c Healy b Campbell	31
R. Sharma	c Alderman b Waugh	28
I.R. Bishop	c Moody b Alderman	4
O.H. Mortensen	c Border b Alderman	0
S.J. Base	c Healy b Rackemann	7
D.E. Malcolm	not out	4
Extras	b 5, lb 2, w 1, nb 11	19
Total		228

31, 106, 110, 129, 181, 182, 188, 198, 224

Alderman	18	6	38	3
Rackemann	17	2	60	2
Waugh	11.2	2	35	2
Campbell	18	3	70	2
Moody	5	1	18	0

Australians 2nd Innings

G.R. Marsh	b Malcolm	27
M.A. Taylor	c Morris b Base	28
D.C. Boon	c sub b Malcolm	6
S.R. Waugh	c Bishop b Base	9
*A.R. Border	c Roberts b Mortensen	5
T.M. Moody	c Maher b Bishop	34
†I.A. Healy	c Maher b Malcolm	39
T.V. Hohns	b Malcolm	11
G.D. Campbell	c Maher b Malcolm	11
C.G. Rackemann	b Bishop	5
T.M. Alderman	not out	5
Extras	lb 5, w 3, nb 1	9
Total		180

41, 47, 64, 77, 78, 149, 153, 159, 164

Bishop	15	4	32	3
Malcolm	18.3	1	68	4
Base	13	3	41	2
Mortensen	8	0	34	1

Derbyshire 2nd Innings

*K.J. Barnett	b Campbell	23
P.D. Bowler	c Healy b Campbell	9
†B.J.M. Maher	c Taylor b Alderman	0
J.E. Morris	c Taylor Campbell	34
B. Roberts	c Border b Alderman	1
S.C. Goldsmith	c Border b Alderman	0
R. Sharma	not out	37
I.R. Bishop	b Alderman	10
O.H. Mortensen	c Taylor b Rackemann	1
S.J. Base	c Taylor b Rackemann	6
D.E. Malcolm	c Healy b Rackemann	4
Extras	b 4, lb 7, w 2, nb 3	16
Total		141

31, 32, 34, 35, 35, 90, 122, 129, 137

Alderman	21	5	32	4
Rackemann	13	3	36	3
Campbell	16	1	44	3
Waugh	13	5	18	0

Umpires: J.H. Hampshire and K.E. Palmer
Toss: Derbyshire

On a wicket assisting the seamers, the touring side were not at home and with Border ignoring a delivery which bowled him, it was left to Healy and Campbell to produce a useful 8th wicket stand and a reasonable total. Barnett was in his best form when the county batted; he reached 50 off 58 balls and the total was 153–4 at stumps. Malcolm looked impressive on the second day as the Australians again appeared fragile. The county needed 153 to win, but were 63–5 at the close. Sharma survived a dropped catch on the last day, but he ran out of partners as the county failed to reach their target.

Fourteenth Match v ENGLAND

At Headingley, June 8, 9, 10, 12, 13

Won by 210 runs (see scorecard page 18)

Fifteenth Match v LANCASHIRE

At Old Trafford, June 14, 15, 16

Won by 9 wkts

Lancashire 1st Innings

G.D. Mendis	c Zoehrer b Waugh	25
N.J. Speak	c Marsh b Waugh	26
A.N. Hayhurst	c Zoehrer b Campbell	40
*N.H. Fairbrother	c Moody b Lawson	49
T.E. Jesty	c Zoehrer b Lawson	0
Wasim Akram	c and b Lawson	0
†W.K. Hegg	c Moody b Lawson	0
J.D. Fitton	c and b May	2
I. Folley	b Campbell	8
P.J. Martin	c Jones b May	16
B.P. Patterson	not out	4
Extras	b 1, lb 7, nb 6	14
Total		184

54, 55, 136, 136, 136, 144, 154, 156, 166

Lawson	17	2	44	4
Campbell	12	2	48	2
Waugh	9	2	28	2
May	15.3	6	29	2
Hohns	8	3	27	0

Australians 1st Innings

*G.R. Marsh	b Patterson	46
M.R.J. Veletta	c Speak b Patterson	0
D.C. Boon	c Hegg b Patterson	0
T.M. Moody	b Fitton	74
D.M. Jones	c Hegg b Martin	59
S.R. Waugh	c Fitton b Folley	42
†T.J. Zoehrer	b Folley	30
T.V. Hohns	c Folley b Patterson	12
T.B.A. May	not out	0
G.D. Campbell	b Wasim Akram	0
G.F. Lawson	c Hegg b Wasim Akram	0
Extras	b 3, lb 11, nb 11	25
Total		288

1, 1, 128, 147, 227, 266, 285, 285, 288

Patterson	16	4	48	4
Martin	17	3	46	1
Hayhurst	5	1	14	0
Wasim Akram	12.3	2	35	2
Fitton	18	2	59	1
Folley	17	3	72	2

Lancashire 2nd Innings

G.D. Mendis	c Zoehrer b Campbell	28
N.J. Speak	b Lawson	12
A.N. Hayhurst	b Campbell	13
*N.H. Fairbrother	c Zoehrer b Lawson	2
T.E. Jesty	c Moody b Campbell	12
Wasim Akram	c Valetta b Campbell	2
†W.K. Hegg	c and b Hohns	23
J.D. Fitton	c Hohns b Waugh	44
I. Folley	c Marsh b Campbell	27
P.J. Martin	c Hohns b Lawson	4
B.P. Patterson	not out	1
Extras	lb 8, nb 9	17
Total		185

39, 43, 46, 60, 64, 94, 101, 172, 179

Lawson	18	4	48	3
Campbell	20.2	4	54	5
May	12	3	32	0
Hohns	9	2	30	1
Waugh	5	1	13	1

Australians 2nd Innings

G.R. Marsh	not out	27
M.R.J. Veletta	c Martin b Wasim Akram	22
D.C. Boon	not out	23
Extras	w 5, nb 7	12
Total (1 wkt)		84

51

Patterson	4	0	16	0
Martin	4	0	15	0
Wasim Akram	8	2	21	1
Fitton	3.3	1	13	0
Folley	4	0	19	0

Umpires: D.G.L. Evans and A.A. Jones
Toss: Lancashire

The county side rested Fowler, Allott and DeFreitas and thus were no match for the tourists. Lawson bowled well on the first day, reducing Lancashire from 136–2 to 184 all out. Patterson took two cheap wickets in return, but Marsh and Moody changed the situation and the Australians were 137–3 by the close. A lead of 104 was gained on the second day and then Campbell and Lawson took wickets on a regular basis to reduce Lancashire to 172–8.

Sixteenth Match v NORTHAMPTONSHIRE

At Northampton, June 17, 18, 19

Won by 272 runs

Australians 1st Innings

G.R. Marsh	c Lamb b Penberthy	32
M.A. Taylor	c Noon b Penberthy	28
D.C. Boon	b Cook	54
*A.R. Border	st Noon b Cook	135
D.M. Jones	c sub b Penberthy	7
S.R. Waugh	lbw b Cook	13
†I.A. Healy	c Larkins b Cook	20
M.G. Hughes	b Cook	12
T.B.A. May	c Cook b Bailey	4
G.D. Campbell	c Felton b Bailey	2
T.M. Alderman	not out	4
Extras	lb 9, nb 9	18
Total		329

62, 77, 204, 217, 254, 299, 319, 320, 324

Davis	11	1	45	0
Walker	11	0	64	0
Robinson	16	2	39	0
Penberthy	15	1	56	3
Cook	30	8	76	5
Bailey	15.2	4	40	2

Northamptonshire 1st Innings

A. Fordham	lbw b Alderman	4
W. Larkins	c Taylor b Waugh	84
N.A. Felton	c Healy b Hughes	26
R.J. Bailey	c Healy b Hughes	2
A.L. Penberthy	c Boon b Hughes	0
†W.M. Noon	c Marsh b Hughes	0
N.G.B. Cook	b Hughes	2
W.W. Davis	c Marsh b Waugh	24
A. Walker	not out	14
M.A. Robinson	c Alderman b May	1
*A.J. Lamb	absent hurt	–
Extras	b 9, lb 9, w 1, nb 4	23
Total		180

4, 66, 78, 82, 82, 88, 125, 161

Alderman	10	2	35	1
Campbell	3	0	15	0
Hughes	11	2	37	5
May	15.3	1	35	1
Waugh	11	1	40	2

Australians 2nd Innings

G.R. Marsh	lbw b Walker	9
M.A. Taylor	c Penberthy b Robinson	69
D.C. Boon	c Noon b Robinson	22
†I.A. Healy	c Noon b Davis	39
D.M. Jones	not out	68
S.R. Waugh	b Davis	2
M.G. Hughes	not out	12
Extras	lb 4, nb 4	8
Total (5 wkts dec)		229

30, 99, 110, 197, 209

Davis	9	1	29	2
Walker	17	1	57	1
Penberthy	10	0	28	0
Bailey	8	0	29	0
Cook	14	3	43	0
Robinson	8	1	33	2
Fordham	1	0	6	0

Northamptonshire 2nd Innings

A. Fordham	lbw b Alderman	0
W. Larkins	c Hughes b Campbell	21
N.A. Felton	lbw b Alderman	1
R.J. Bailey	b May	17
A.L. Penberthy	lbw b Alderman	0
†W.M. Noon	lbw b Hughes	37
N.G.B. Cook	lbw b Waugh	14
W.W. Davis	b Waugh	0
A. Walker	not out	0
M.A. Robinson	b Waugh	0
*A.J. Lamb	absent hurt	–
Extras	b 5, lb 10, nb 1	16
Total		106

8, 22, 24, 24, 53, 104, 106, 106

Alderman	6	3	10	3
Campbell	8	1	31	1
May	6	1	17	1
Hughes	8	2	23	1
Waugh	4.5	1	10	3

Umpires: R.A. White and D.O Oslear
Toss: Australians

An injured finger prevented Lamb from batting in either innings and this took the spine out of the county side, only Larkins making much impact. Penberthy and Noon made their fc debuts for the county, Penberthy obtaining a wicket with his first ball. Northants were 28–1 at the start of the second day and by its end the Australians were 331 runs ahead with seven second innings wickets in hand. The match finished before tea on the last day.

Seventeenth Match v ENGLAND
At Lord's, June 22, 23, 24, 26, 27
Won by 6 wkts *(see scorecard page 19)*

Eighteenth Match v COMBINED OXFORD & CAMBRIDGE UNIV.
In The Parks, June 28
Won by 99 runs

Australians		
*G.R. Marsh	c Crawley b Hester	73
M.R.J. Veletta	c Edwards c Crawley	42
M.A. Taylor	b Pyman	33
T.M. Moody	not out	47
D.M. Jones	c Atkinson b Pyman	9
†I.A. Healy	run out	1
T.J. Zoehrer		
T.V. Hohns		
M.G. Hughes		
G.D. Campbell		
C.G. Rackemann		
Extras	lb 5, w 5	10
Total (5 wkts, 35 ov)		215

105, 153, 160, 197, 215

Henderson	6	0	39	0
Hester	7	1	47	1
Crawley	7	0	27	1
Edwards	6	0	41	0
Atherton	2	0	21	0
Pyman	7	0	35	2

Combined Universities		
S.P. James	not out	43
R. Heap	c Marsh b Campbell	4
M.A. Atherton	c Rackemann b Hohns	20
D.A. Hagan	b Hohns	16
J.C.M. Atkinson	c and b Hohns	0
*M.A. Crawley	not out	13
†R.J. Turner		
I.M. Henderson		
R.A. Pyman		
E.D. Hester		
P.G. Edwards		
Extras	b 4, lb 11, w 5	20
Total (4 wkts, 35 ov)		116

17, 53, 86, 86

Campbell	6	0	26	1
Rackemann	7	1	15	0
Moody	7	1	20	0
Hohns	7	0	14	3
Hughes	6	0	19	0
Veletta	1	0	2	0
Taylor	1	0	5	0

Umpires: J.H. Harris and M.J. Kitchen
Toss: Australians
This game was originally a 55-over match, but after 17 overs rain stopped play and on the resumption a fresh contest of 35-overs each was started and proved an easy win for the tourists.

Geoffrey Robert MARSH (W Australia); *b* Northam 31.12.1958; RHB
Vice-captain of the touring side, Marsh had been the regular opening partner with Boon for Several Test series, having made his debut for Australia in 1985-86. He is a determined batsman with notable successes in one-day internationals and in the third one-day game at Lord's he made an unbeaten 111, providing his side with their single victory in the series and himself with the Man of the Match award. He also scored one Test hundred in 1989, sharing with Taylor a record Ashes opening stand.

Timothy Brian Alexander MAY (S Australia); *b* North Adelaide 26.1.1962; RHB OB
He gained a place in the Australian touring side at the expense of Peter Taylor, the spinner who burst onto the Test scene when England last toured 'down under'. May had played in seven Tests before coming to England, but he was not required in the series last summer. He remained with Campbell as a useful bowler against the counties.

Thomas Masson MOODY (W Australia); *b* Adelaide 2.10.1965; RHB RM
Moody had not played in Test cricket when he arrived in England and he also missed out this time, though he was chosen for all three one-day matches. When it came to the Tests he had to make way for Taylor and so after the end of May his efforts were confined to county games. He was regarded as rather fortunate to have gained selection for the tour.

Nineteenth Match v GLAMORGAN
At Neath, July 1, 2, 3
Drawn.

Australians 1st Innings		
M.R.J. Veletta	not out	134
G.R. Marsh	c Maynard b Barwick	21
D.M. Jones	lbw b Watkin	37
T.M. Moody	lbw b Smith	29
*A.R. Border	c Maynard b Watkin	91
S.R. Waugh	not out	34
†I.A Healy		
M.G. Hughes		
T.B.A. May		
T.V. Hohns		
C.G. Rackemann		
Extras	b 4, lb 12, w 4, nb 7	27
Total (4 wkts dec)		373

45, 117, 168, 319

Watkin	24	5	81	2
Dennis	28	8	69	0
Barwick	16	2	41	1
Shastri	4	0	20	0
Smith	18	3	75	1
Cann	4	1	22	0
Holmes	12	0	49	0

Glamorgan 1st Innings		
A.R. Butcher	b May	54
*H. Morris	c Border b Hohns	94
M.J. Cann	c Healy b Rackemann	3
M.P. Maynard	b Waugh	42
R.J. Shastri	st Healy b Hohns	10
G.C. Holmes	not out	26
I. Smith	not out	61
†C.P. Metson		
S.J. Dennis		
S.L. Watkin		
S.R. Barwick		
Extras	lb 9, nb 2,	11
Total (5 wkts dec)		301

107, 128, 184, 204, 211

Hughes	15	5	42	0
Rackemann	15	1	67	1
Waugh	21	3	61	1
Moody	4	0	17	0
May	16	5	61	1
Hohns	20	6	44	2

Australians 2nd Innings		
M.R.J. Veletta	c Maynard b Smith	83
G.R. Marsh	c Holmes b Dennis	33
D.M. Jones	c Smith b Shastri	56
†I.A. Healy	c Metson b Dennis	13
T.V. Hohns	b Smith	15
T.B.A. May	not out	10
Extras	b 1, lb 3, nb 2	6
Total (5 wkts dec)		216

61, 156, 182, 196, 196

Watkin	14	2	36	0
Dennis	25	4	65	2
Smith	18.2	2	66	2
Cann	1	0	8	0
Holmes	6	0	21	0
Shastri	2	0	16	1

Glamorgan 2nd Innings		
A.R. Butcher	c Veletta b Waugh	14
*H. Morris	b Moody	5
M.J. Cann	b Waugh	5
M.P. Maynard	c and b Rackemann	26
G.C. Holmes	lbw b Waugh	0
I. Smith	not out	38
R.J. Shastri	not out	44
Extras	lb 1, nb 2	3
Total (5 wkts)		135

18, 20, 30, 30, 66

Waugh	10	2	32	3
Moody	9	2	32	1
Rackemann	9	1	31	1
May	9	2	39	0

Umpires: B. Leadbeater and K.J. Lyons
On Saturday the tourists hit a satisfactory 373–4 with Veletta reaching his first hundred of the season. Border declared first thing on Sunday morning and the Welsh county were given a sound start by Butcher and Morris. Smith then played an attractive innings which was cut short when Morris declared. The Australians began the last day at 56–0 and then set Glamorgan 289 off 46 overs. Wickets fell quickly until Shastri and Smith took root and batted out time.

Twentieth Match v ENGLAND
At Edgbaston, July 6, 7, 8, 10, 11
Drawn. *(See scorecard page 21)*

Twenty-first Match v SCOTLAND
At Hamilton Crescent, Glasgow, July 15
Won by 97 runs.

Australians		
D.C. Boon	c Govan b Brown	19
M.R.J. Veletta	c Haggo b Brown	101
T.M. Moody	b Moir	101
D.M. Jones	b Moir	36
†T.J. Zoehrer	lbw b Moir	2
*A.R. Border	b Moir	4
S.R. Waugh	not out	23
M.G. Hughes	b Moir	0
T.B.A. May	not out	7
G.D. Campbell		
C.G. Rackemann		
Extras	b 4, lb 5, nb 5	14
Total (7 wkts, 55 ov)		307

38, 212, 258, 265, 274, 287, 287

Moir	11	3	33	5
Brown	11	0	68	2
Goram	6	0	30	0
Smith	11	0	53	0
Henry	11	0	70	0
Govan	5	0	44	0

Scotland		
I.L. Philips	lbw b May	24
B.M. Patterson	lbw b May	70
*R.G. Swan	c Jones b Border	8
A.L. Goram	b May	4
O. Henry	lbw b Moody	3
M.J. Smith	st Zoehrer b Boon	24
D.L. Snodgrass	c Jones b Campbell	3
D.R. Brown	b Campbell	2
J.W. Govan	not out	32
†D.J. Haggo	st Zoehrer b Veletta	7
D.J. Moir	not out	14
Extras	lb 14, w 4, nb 1	19
Total (9 wkts, 55 ov)		210

98, 105, 115, 118, 134, 152, 156, 157, 184

Rackemann	10	2	48	0
Campbell	8	0	30	2
Waugh	2	0	17	0
Hughes	9	1	23	0
May	11	1	21	3
Moody	6	2	15	1
Border	3	0	8	1
Jones	2	0	5	0
Boon	2	0	7	1
Veletta	2	0	22	1

Umpires: P. Brown and A. Woods
Toss: Australians
In this holiday fixture, the home side were beaten but not disgraced by the tourists. The main talking point was the appearance of the Scottish goalkeeper, Goram, in defiance of his soccer bosses.

Carl Grey RACKEMANN (Queensland); *b* Brisbane 3.6.1960; RHB RF
Banned from official Tests when he chose to tour South Africa, Rackemann was regarded as Australia's fastest bowler, but his career has been hampered by injury and some journalists forecast that he would not survive an English season. In fact he broke down after the one-day series and did not appear in any Tests, though he did play in some of the later county games.

Mark Antony TAYLOR (New South Wales); *b* Leeton 27.10.1964; LHB
Having had an outstanding season in Australia in 1988-89, when he hit 1,241 runs and made his Test debut against West Indies (though only making 67 runs in four innings), Taylor came to England as the team's most promising young player. He fulfilled that promise twice over. His aggregate of 839 runs in the Test series was the third highest ever recorded in matches between the two countries, exceeded only by Bradman and Hammond. His most celebrated innings of the tour occurred at Trent Bridge when he and Marsh became the first batsmen in Test cricket in England to bat through a full day's play and their stand of 329 was also a new record for the series.

Michael Robert John VELETTA (W Australia); *b* Subiaco 30.10.1963; RHB
Although he has scored plenty of runs in Sheffield Shield matches and also been effective in one-day cricket, Veletta when he arrived in England had a poor Test record with only 198 runs in seven matches. He appeared in two of the one-day internationals of 1989, but was not selected for the first three Tests, then having scored 101 against Scotland, broke a finger in the next game and was not seen again in a first-class match.

Twenty-second Match v MINOR COUNTIES
At Trowbridge, July 17
Won by 27 runs

Australians		
*G.R. Marsh	c Evans b Taylor	110
M.R.J. Veletta	retired hurt	3
M.A. Taylor	c Folland b Conn	11
T.M. Moody	c Greensword b Conn	1
D.C. Boon	c Priestley b Taylor	61
†I.A. Healy	not out	25
T.V. Hohns	not out	2
T.M. Alderman		
G.D. Campbell		
G.F. Lawson		
C.G. Rackemann		
Extras	b 1, lb 4, w 9, nb 2	16
Total (4 wkts, 55 ov)		229

37, 41, 187, 211

Green	11	1	46	0
Taylor	11	2	50	2
Conn	11	1	34	2
Greensword	11	4	22	0
Evans	7	0	50	0
Plumb	4	1	22	0

Minor Counties		
*S.G. Plumb	lbw b Alderman	0
G.K. Brown	b Hohns	31
N.A. Folland	b Campbell	51
I. Cockbain	b Rackemann	28
T.A. Lester	not out	37
†N. Priestley	b Campbell	1
S. Greenword	hit wkt b Campbell	17
R.A. Evans	b Lawson	10
I.E. Conn	b Lawson	0
R.C. Green	b Alderman	3
M.R. Taylor	c Alderman b Lawson	7
Extras	lb 10, w 2, nb 5	17
Total (54 ov)		202

6, 84, 115, 131, 132, 156, 178, 178, 183

Alderman	10	1	43	2
Lawson	10	1	30	3
Hohns	11	1	30	1
Rackemann	11	0	35	1
Campbell	11	2	45	3
Moody	1	0	9	0

Umpires: P. Adams and D.J. Halfyard
Toss: Australians
The tourists had the misfortune to suffer an injury to Veletta, who retired with a broken finger and the score was only 50 after 25 overs. Marsh was joined by Boon and after lunch they raised the tempo. The Minor Counties kept up with the required scoring rate and it appeared as if they might win, but the later batsmen all failed.

Stephen Rodger WAUGH (New South Wales); *b* Canterbury, NSW 2.6.1965; RHB RMF
On his arrival in England Waugh had appeared in 26 Tests for Australia, but never scored a century. He made good this deficiency at the expense of England, making two hundreds and topping the Test averages, though aided by not outs. Coming in at number 6 in a year when Australian batsmen thrived, Waugh was not really tested to the full. He did have the satisfaction of completing 1,000 first-class runs, but his eight not outs put him second to Jones in the overall table. Of course he had had a brilliant season with Somerset in 1988 and this meant he was thoroughly at home on English wickets – a great help on a first tour. His bowling was used occasionally but was not up to Test standard.

Timothy Joseph ZOEHRER (W Australia); *b* Armadale 25.9.1961; RHB WK
Having made his Test debut in 1985–86 and played in ten Tests, Zoehrer lost his place in the Australian side. He had had a brilliant season in Sheffield Shield cricket prior to coming to England, but he failed to dislodge Healy. He kept well in county games and also scored runs freely, but he can be rather brash and this has counted against him.

Twenty-third Match v HAMPSHIRE
At Southampton, July 19, 20, 21
Drawn.

Australians 1st Innings		
*G.R. Marsh	c Parks b Jefferies	15
M.A. Taylor	run out	46
D.C. Boon	c Terry b James	103
S.R. Waugh	c and b Andrew	112
T.M. Moody	c R.A. Smith b Nicholas	7
†T.J. Zoehrer	b Andrew	42
T.V. Hohns	not out	2
T.B.A. May		
G.D. Campbell		
G.F. Lawson		
C.G. Rackemann		
Extras	b 1, lb 9, nb 6	16
Total (6 wkts dec)		343

22, 124, 242, 261, 324, 343

Andrew	14.5	3	60	2
Jefferies	15	2	59	1
Connor	15	2	51	0
Maru	21	2	85	0
James	14	4	39	1
Nicholas	9	0	39	1

Hampshire 1st Innings		
V.P. Terry	lbw b Lawson	19
C.L. Smith	c Boon b May	32
K.D. James	c Boon b May	5
R.A. Smith	c Zoehrer b Rackemann	9
*M.C.J. Nicholas	not out	102
J.R. Wood	c Zoehrer b Waugh	65
†R.J. Parks	c Marsh b Waugh	0
S.T. Jefferies	not out	28
R.J. Maru		
C.A. Connor		
S.J.W. Andrew		
Extras	b 7, lb 6, nb 2	15
Total (6 wks dec)		275

56, 56, 71, 77, 220, 220

Lawson	21	8	55	1
Rackemann	20	4	79	1
May	24	10	52	2
Waugh	7	1	28	2
Hohns	13	7	23	0
Campbell	7	2	25	0

Australians 2nd Innings		
*G.R. Marsh	c R.A. Smith b Andrew	5
M.A. Taylor	lbw b Maru	38
D.C. Boon	c and b Jefferies	24
S.R. Waugh	lbw b Maru	67
T.M. Moody	c and b Maru	5
†T.J. Zoehrer	c James b Maru	1
T.V. Hohns	not out	58
T.B.A. May	lbw b James	7
G.D. Campbell	c Nicholas b Maru	15
G.F. Lawson	c Parks b Connor	7
C.G. Rackemann	c Nicholas b Connor	11
Extras	lb 5, nb 3	8
Total		246

29, 57, 115, 145, 147, 147, 168, 189, 212

Andrew	10	0	68	1
Connor	14.1	1	68	2
Maru	23	10	44	5
C.L.Smith	2	0	3	0
Jefferies	11	1	26	1
James	9	0	32	1

Hampshire 2nd Innings		
V.P. Terry	not out	28
C.L. Smith	not out	49
Extras	b 4	4
Total (0 wkt)		81

Lawson	6	3	13	0
Campbell	6	2	8	0
Rackemann	10	1	29	0
May	3	0	4	0
Hohns	10	3	15	0
Waugh	3	2	8	0

Umpires: V.A. Holder and D.S. Thompsett
Toss: Australians
Waugh hit 112 off 146 deliveries, but Boon was more circumspect, however the pair enabled Marsh to declare and the county were 33 without loss at the close. Nicholas, together with the young left-hand batsman Wood, saved Hampshire from collapse on Thursday and on reaching his 100, with 18 boundaries, Nicholas closed the county's innings 68 in arrears. This did not inspire the tourists and on the final day the game drifted to a draw, though Waugh woke up spectators with 67 in an hour.

Twenty-fourth Match v GLOUCESTERSHIRE
At Bristol, July 22, 23
Won by an innings and 146 runs

Gloucestershire 1st innings		
A.J. Wright	b Aldermann	0
I.P. Butcher	lbw b Alderman	0
J.W. Lloyds	c Border b Hughes	46
*C.W.J. Athey	c Marsh b Campbell	34
K.M. Curran	c Healey b Campbell	46
M.W. Alleyne	b Lawson	22
†R.C. Russell	lbw b Alderman	16
V.S. Greene	c Healy b Alderman	4
M.C.J. Ball	b Campbell	4
D.A. Graveney	not out	1
K.B.S. Jarvis	b Campbell	0
Extras	b 12, lb 7, nb 8	27
Total		200

1, 11, 78, 108, 137, 188, 188, 193, 197

Alderman	13	3	39	4
Lawson	13	3	55	1
Campbell	13.1	4	47	4
Hughes	10	1	33	1
Hohns	6	3	7	0

Australians 1st Innings		
M.A. Taylor	lbw b Greene	141
G.R. Marsh	lbw b Greene	5
D.C. Boon	c Athey b Graveney	16
*A.R. Border	c and b Ball	25
D.M. Jones	not out	167
†I.A. Healy	c Lloyds b Jarvis	21
T.V. Hohns	lbw b Greene	2
M.G. Hughes	c Athey b Jarvis	14
G.D.Campbell	c Athey b Jarvis	3
G.F. Lawson	c Wright b Graveney	22
T.M. Alderman	st Russell b Lloyds	0
Extras	b 2, lb 9, w 3, nb 8	22
Total		438

28, 54, 101, 328, 353, 385, 389, 437

Greene	20	1	65	2
Jarvis	25	7	77	3
Alleyne	13	2	60	1
Athey	9	3	27	0
Graveney	26	3	112	2
Ball	15	1	64	1
Lloyds	4.2	0	22	1

Gloucestershire 2nd innings		
A.J. Wright	lbw b Lawson	21
I.P. Butcher	c Taylor b Alderman	8
J.W. Lloyds	c Boon b Lawson	36
*C.W.J. Athey	c Boon b Lawson	0
K.M. Curran	c Taylor b Lawson	4
M.W. Alleyne	c Healy b Lawson	0
†R.C. Russell	c Boon b Lawson	9
V.S. Greene	lbw b Campbell	1
M.C.J. Ball	b Hohns	4
D.A. Graveney	not out	1
K.B.S. Jarvis	lbw b Campbell	0
Extras	nb 8	8
Total		92

15, 54, 58, 72, 72, 81, 87, 87, 91

Alderman	7	0	31	1
Lawson	13	5	30	6
Hughes	6	1	26	0
Campbell	2	1	1	2
Hohns	1	0	4	1

Umpires: J.H. Harris and B. Dudleston.
After a very poor start the county recovered somewhat, but at the close of the first day the Australians had made 142–3 off 48 overs, with Taylor 69 not out and were therefore in a strong position. On Sunday both Taylor and Jones, the latter being in 272 minutes, reached well made hundreds. When the county batted a second time, Lawson bowled unchanged taking six for 30 and the entire innings lasted only 142 minutes, the game being completed inside two days.

Twenty-fifth Match v ENGLAND
At Old Trafford, July 27, 28, 29, 31, August 1
Won by 9 wkts *(see scorecard page 22)*

Twenty-sixth Match v NOTTINGHAMSHIRE

At Trent Bridge, August 2, 3, 4
Won by 196 runs

Australians 1st Innings

*G.R. Marsh	c Newell b Cooper	16
M.A. Taylor	c French b Millns	33
D.C. Boon	c Johnson b Millns	76
D.M. Jones	b Hemmings	82
T.M. Moody	c Newell b Hemmings	7
S.R. Waugh	not out	46
†T.J. Zoehrer	run out	0
M.G. Hughes	b Millns	0
T.B.A. May	c Robinson b Millns	1
G.D. Campbell	lbw b Cooper	7
C.G. Rackemann	b Cooper	2
Extras	lb 12, nb 2	14
Total		284

55, 55, 210, 226, 228, 228, 228, 242, 266

Stephenson	10	4	16	0
Millns	25	5	86	4
Cooper	17.3	7	47	3
Hemmings	17	4	48	2
Afford	13	2	75	0

Nottinghamshire 1st Innings

P.R. Pollard	c Zoehrer b Hughes	35
M. Newell	b Hughes	12
*R.T. Robinson	c Zoehrer b Rackemann	37
P. Johnson	c Zoehrer b Hughes	0
D.W. Randall	c Rackemann b Hughes	0
†B.N. French	c Zoehrer b May	20
F.D. Stephenson	b May	47
E.E. Hemmings	lbw b Rackemann	4
K.E. Cooper	c Zoehrer b Hughes	9
D.J. Millns	not out	7
J.A. Afford	c Boon b May	9
Extras	b 1, lb 10, w 1, nb 3	15
Total		195

44, 67, 67, 67, 116, 117, 149, 179, 179

Hughes	20	8	38	5
Campbell	12	2	34	0
May	16	6	40	3
Waugh	5	2	13	0
Rackemann	11	3	59	2

Australians 2nd Innings

*G.R. Marsh	lbw b Stephenson	66
M.A Taylor	lbw b Cooper	30
D.C. Boon	not out	102
D.M. Jones	st French b Afford	22
T.M. Moody	st French b Afford	11
S.R. Waugh	not out	13
Extras	b 6, lb 5	11
Total (4 wkts dec)		255

73, 120, 165, 205

Stephenson	10	3	12	1
Millns	14	2	53	0
Cooper	9	2	25	1
Hemmings	20.4	3	86	0
Afford	19	4	68	2

Nottinghamshire 2nd Innings

P.R. Pollard	c Jones b Rackemann	11
M. Newell	lbw b Hughes	4
D.W. Randall	c sub b May	48
P. Johnson	c Taylor b Rackemann	23
*R.T. Robinson	b May	5
†B.N. French	c Taylor b May	9
F.D. Stephenson	c Taylor b Rackemann	13
E.E. Hemmings	c Zoehrer b Rackemann	6
K.E. Cooper	c Marsh b Rackemann	10
D.J. Millns	c sub b May	9
J.A. Afford	not out	3
Extras	b 4, lb 1, nb 2	7
Total		148

15, 27, 86, 89, 102, 103, 117, 126, 135

Rackemann	18	3	65	5
Campbell	10.4	1	43	4
Hughes	9	4	35	1

Umpires: D.J. Contant and K. Taylor
Toss: Australians

Aided by three dropped catches, the tourists reached 210–2, but, apart from a brief sparkle by Waugh who was left stranded, the rest of the batting collapsed and Notts were 21–0 off 12 overs at the close. A very belligerent 47 by Stephenson was the only worthwhile innings by the home side on the second day and when play ended the Australians were in complete control being 158–2. Marsh declared on Friday setting Notts a remote 345 off 74 overs. The response was very feeble with just a bright 48 from Randall to cheer home supporters.

Twenty-seventh Match v LEICESTERSHIRE

At Leicester, August 5, 6, 7
Won by 9 wkts.

Leicestershire 1st Innings

N.E Briers	c Healy b Rackemann	15
T.J. Boon	c Moody b Rackemann	14
*D.I. Gower	c Moody b Lawson	9
J.J. Whitaker	b Lawson	6
L. Potter	c Healy b Rackemann	41
P.N. Hepworth	c Marsh b Hohns	6
W.K.M. Benjamin	lbw b Rackemann	0
†P.A. Nixon	b May	24
J.P. Agnew	c Border b Lawson	30
P.M. Such	b May	1
L.B. Taylor	not out	0
Extras	b 1, lb 4, nb 6	11
Total		157

27, 39, 45, 49, 62, 63, 117, 156, 157

Lawson	15	5	38	4
Hughes	14	3	48	0
Rackemann	10	2	19	3
Hohns	18	9	26	1
May	10.1	2	21	2

Australians 1st Innings

G.R. Marsh	c Whitaker b Taylor	22
M.A. Taylor	lbw b Benjamin	70
T.M. Moody	c Boon b Benjamin	6
*A.R. Border	b Benjamin	0
S.R. Waugh	b Agnew	7
†I.A. Healy	not out	73
T.V. Hohns	c Nixon b Benjamin	95
M.G. Hughes	lbw b Benjamin	7
T.B.A. May	c Potter b Benjamin	0
G.F. Lawson	b Benjamin	0
C.G. Rackemann	b Agnew	4
Extras	b 4, lb 15, nb 2	21
Total		305

50, 88, 88, 109, 139, 285, 300, 300, 300

Benjamin	23	6	54	7
Agnew	23	3	64	2
Taylor	14	1	49	1
Such	24	4	77	0
Potter	10	0	42	0

Leicestershire 2nd Innings

N.E Briers	b Rackemann	41
T.J. Boon	c Healy b Rackemann	20
*D.I. Gower	st Healy b May	46
J.J. Whitaker	lbw b Lawson	17
L. Potter	b Lawson	18
P.N. Hepworth	c Healy b Hughes	9
W.K.M. Benjamin	b May	14
†P.A. Nixon	lbw b Hohns	17
J.P. Agnew	c Lawson b Hohns	39
P.M. Such	b Hohns	0
L.B. Taylor	not out	2
Extras	b 2, lb 10, nb 8	20
Total		243

Lawson	17	9	30	2
Rackemann	11	2	41	2
May	29	7	79	2
Hughes	9	2	18	1
Border	3	0	14	0
Hohns	5.2	0	49	3

Australians 2nd Innings

G.R. Marsh	not out	27
T.M. Moody	c Potter b Taylor	36
*A.R Border	not out	22
Extras	b 8, lb 5, nb 1	14
Total (1 wkt)		99

52

Benjamin	6	3	7	0
Agnew	7	0	39	0
Taylor	7	1	31	1
Such	6	0	9	0
Boon	0.5	0	0	0

Umpires: J.D. Bond and P.J. Eele
Toss: Leicestershire

Gower decided to bat on winning the toss, but neither he nor his side prospered and at the close of the first day the tourists were 105–3 with Taylor 58 not out. On Sunday Hohns and Healy added 146 for the 6th wicket, but either side of this stand, Benjamin confused the batsmen and performed the hat-trick when he dismissed Hughes, May and Lawson. The county were 133–2 at the start of play on Monday, but 110 runs later they were all out and the Australians soon knocked off the runs required for victory.

Twenty-eighth Match v ENGLAND

At Trent Bridge, August 10, 11, 12, 14
Won by an inns and 180 runs (see scorecard page 24)

Twenty-ninth Match v KENT

At Canterbury, August 16, 17, 18
Drawn.

Australians 1st Innings

M.A. Taylor	c Farbrace b Kelleher	14
*G.R. Marsh	lbw b Kelleher	2
D.C. Boon	c Farbrace b Ealham	86
T.M. Moody	b Kelleher	14
D.M. Jones	c Kelleher b Davis	128
S.R. Waugh	b Kelleher	1
†T.J. Zoehrer	st Farbrace b Dobson	32
T.V. Hohns	not out	39
T.B.A. May	c Davis b Dobson	24
G.D. Campbell	not out	0
C.G. Rackemann		
Extras	lb 8, nb 8	16
Total (8 wkts dec)		356

17, 18, 35, 218, 228, 281, 311, 353

Kelleher	26.1	7	82	4
Ealham	24	5	92	1
Fleming	19	3	55	0
Davis	21	3	75	1
Dobson	12	0	44	2

Kent 1st Innings

S.G. Hinks	b May	85
*M.R. Benson	lbw b Rackemann	3
R.F. Pienaar	c Taylor b Rackemann	0
T.R. Ward	c Zoehrer b Waugh	32
J.I. Longley	c Hohns b Campbell	10
M.V. Fleming	b Campbell	7
M.C. Dobson	lbw b Campbell	2
†P. Farbrace	lbw b May	35
M.A. Ealham	c Boon b May	7
D.J.M. Kelleher	c Hohns b Campbell	8
R.P. Davis	not out	0
Extras	lb 1, nb 1	2
Total		191

7, 11, 63, 82, 98, 106, 173, 178, 191

Rackemann	10	3	39	2
Campbell	23.1	5	78	4
Waugh	7	1	29	1
May	15	5	40	3
Hohns	2	1	4	0

Kent 2nd Innings

S.G. Hinks	c Zoehrer b Moody	16
*M.R. Benson	c Waugh b Campbell	106
R.P. Davis	c Taylor b May	11
R.F. Pienaar	b May	7
T.R. Ward	c Marsh b Moody	36
J.I. Longley	lbw b Moody	0
M.V. Fleming	lbw b Moody	0
M.C. Dobson	c Waugh b Rackemann	33
†P. Farbrace	c Moody b Rackemann	1
M.A. Ealham	not out	4
D.J.M. Kelleher	not out	12
Extras	b 4, lb 6, nb 1	11
Total (9 wkts)		237

42, 63, 81, 149, 149, 149, 217, 219, 219

Campbell	18	7	46	1
Rackemann	20	7	36	2
Moody	21	11	30	4
May	29	10	42	2
Hohns	23	7	60	0
Jones	1	0	13	0

Umpires: B. Hassan and K. Taylor
Toss: Kent

A well earned century on the last day by Benson saved Kent from what appeared to be inevitable defeat. At the close of the second day Kent required 123 with nine wickets in hand to save an innings defeat, but Benson survived 330 minutes for his 106 and the game was drawn. On the first day the tourists hit up 353–8, Jones, in brilliant form, hit 100 in 137 balls with 17 fours. Play had just started on the second day, with the Australians adding three runs, when rain arrived. During the enforced interval Marsh declared, then Kent, apart from Hinks, collapsed and they were invited to follow on.

Thirtieth Match v ESSEX
At Chelmsford, August 19, 20, 21
Won by 150 runs

Australians 1st Innings

D.C. Boon	c Hardie b Childs	151
†T.J. Zoehrer	c Waugh b Lever	13
T.M. Moody	b Shahid	80
S.R. Waugh	lbw b Childs	1
*A.R. Border	st Garnham b Shahid	40
D.M. Jones	st Garnham b Childs	70
I.A. Healy	not out	.6
M.G. Hughes	c Garnham b Waugh	6
T.B.A. May		
G.F. Lawson		
G.D. Campbell		
Extras	b 1, lb 4, w 4, nb 11	20
Total (7 wkts dec)		387

21, 188, 189, 237, 370, 376 387

Lever	17	4	43	1
Topley	12	1	40	0
Waugh	20	3	68	1
Stephenson	5	0	30	0
Gooch	7	0	49	0
Childs	18	2	69	3
Shahid	14	2	83	2

Essex 1st Innings

*G.A. Gooch	c Border b Hughes	58
J.P. Stephenson	lbw b Lawson	3
Nadeem Shahid	b Lawson	0
P.J. Prichard	c Healy b Lawson	86
M.E. Waugh	not out	100
N. Hussain	c Border b Hughes	14
B.R. Hardie	c Border b Zoehrer	9
†M.A. Garnham	not out	1
T.D. Topley		
J.H. Childs		
J.K. Lever		
Extras	b 6, lb 8, nb 5	19
Total (6 wkts dec)		290

36, 36, 110, 200, 232, 287

Lawson	18	6	52	3
Hughes	20	4	69	2
Campbell	14	3	51	0
May	11	2	45	0
Moody	8	1	28	0
Border	7	1	22	0
Zoehrer	3	0	9	1
Boon	1	1	0	0

Australians 2nd Innings

†T.J. Zoehrer	lbw b Shahid	93
I.A. Healy	b Waugh	45
S.R. Waugh	not out	100
T.M. Moody	not out	13
Extras	b 5, lb 1, nb 1	7
Total (2 wkts dec)		258

89, 220

Lever	13	1	56	0
Topley	11	2	48	0
Waugh	7	0	40	1
Childs	12	1	53	0
Shahid	9.1	1	53	1
Stephenson	1	0	2	0

Essex 2nd Innings

*G.A. Gooch	b Lawson	21
J.P. Stephenson	b Hughes	3
B.R. Hardie	b Hughes	8
N. Hussain	b Hughes	31
P.J. Prichard	lbw b Lawson	52
M.E. Waugh	c Jones b Hughes	57
†M.A. Garnham	lbw b Lawson	1
Nadeem Shahid	c Jones b May	10
T.D. Topley	c Lawson b Hughes	9
J.K. Lever	c Campbell b May	0
J.H. Childs	not out	1
Extras	b 4, lb 6, nb 2	12
Total		205

20, 34, 40, 87, 169, 175, 193, 193, 193

Lawson	15	4	40	3
Hughes	17.4	5	64	5
Campbell	7	0	41	0
May	17	5	50	2

Umpires: A.G.T. Whitehead and M.J. Harris
Toss: Australians
The curiosity of this match was the double feat of the Waugh twins, both of whom scored exactly 100 not out. The tourists had all the best of the first day, scoring 287–7 and then taking 2 Essex wickets for 43. On Sunday Mark Waugh and Prichard enabled the county to get back into the game and Gooch declared 97 runs in arrears. The Australians were 130–1 at the close. Essex were set 356 to win on the last day and Prichard and Mark Waugh again batted well, but Australia won without too much difficulty.

Thirty-first v ENGLAND
At the Oval, August 24, 25, 26, 28, 29
Drawn. *(See scorecard page 26)*

Dean Jones (left), who headed the tourists' batting averages, seen during his innings of 157 in the third Test at Edgbaston. Terry Alderman (right) headed the tourists' bowling averages in both Test and all matches. He is seen bowling in the first innings of the fifth Test at Trent Bridge, one of the six occasions in the series when he claimed five wickets in an innings.

Allsport/Adrian Murrell

AUSTRALIANS FIRST CLASS AVERAGES 1989

Batting

	M	I	NO	Runs	HS	Avge	100	50
D.M. Jones	14	20	3	1510	248	88.82	5	8
S.R. Waugh	16	24	8	1030	177*	64.38	4	3
M.A. Taylor	17	30	1	1669	219	57.55	3	10
D.C. Boon	17	28	5	1306	151	56.78	3	8
A.R. Border	16	22	4	979	135	54.39	1	9
M.R.J. Valetta	5	8	1	294	134*	42.00	1	1
T.M. Moody	12	20	4	564	144*	35.25	1	3
G.R. Marsh	18	33	4	934	138	32.21	2	2
I.A. Healy	14	19	4	442	73*	29.47	–	1
T.J. Zoehrer	7	9	0	259	93	28.78	–	1
T.V. Hohns	15	18	4	393	95	28.07	–	2
M.G. Hughes	15	16	4	246	71	20.50	–	1
G.F. Lawson	14	12	2	174	74	17.40	–	1
T.B.A. May	10	8	3	59	24	11.80	–	–
G.D. Campbell	11	10	2	87	31	10.88	–	–
T.M. Alderman	11	10	6	38	8	9.50	–	–
C.G. Rackemann	8	6	1	22	11	4.40	–	–

Bowling

	O	M	R	W	Avge	BB	5i
T.A. Alderman	411.2	104	1095	70	15.64	6/128	6
G.F. Lawson	522.3	140	1447	69	20.97	6/30	3
C.G. Rackemann	223.5	47	747	32	23.34	5/65	1
S.R. Waugh	176.1	39	571	23	24.83	3/10	–
T.M. Moody	63	19	151	6	25.16	4/30	–
M.G. Hughes	399	102	1242	47	26.43	5/37	3
T.B.A. May	287.5	86	740	28	26.43	4/43	–
G.D. Campbell	250.2	50	824	30	27.47	5/54	1
T.V. Hohns	321.4	108	809	26	31.12	4/87	–

Also bowled: A.R. Border 68–21–154–1; D.M. Jones 1–0–13–0; T.J. Zoehrer 5–0–9–1; D.C. Boon 1–1–0–0.

Team of the Year

The compilers have chosen what is in their view the best team from cricketers playing regularly in the English season of 1989, ie the county players, including overseas players, and the Australian tourists. The selection is based on form shown during the season and not on their overall form during their careers.

Although most teams in recent seasons have been packed with fast bowlers, it was thought that a balanced side should be picked, with two openers, four middle-order batsmen, one or two of whom might bowl in an emergency, a wicket-keeper, two opening bowlers plus a medium-fast change bowler, and a slow bowler. A 12th man was also selected. A genuine all-rounder would have been chosen had one been available, but with Ian Botham not fully re-establishing himself at Test level due to injuries, it was not felt that any of sufficient stature played in 1989.

The chosen team, pictures of whom follow in the next 12 pages, are as follows.

Mark Taylor (Australia) established himself in the Australian Test side in the last two matches of the tour of West Indies in 1988–89. He split the established opening pair of Geoff Marsh and David Boon, Boon moving down to number 3. He scored only 77 in his first four innings, in the fifth Test having the rare distinction of being run out in both innings. But he was first choice for the Test matches when the Australians arrived in England and had a spectacularly successful series. His aggregate for the Tests was 839, the third highest ever in a series, after Bradman and Hammond. His average was 83.90.

A left-hander, Taylor got Australia off to many good starts with partner Marsh, twice they passed 100 and three other times they passed 50. Their highest partnership was 329 at Trent Bridge, the highest first-wicket partnership in Ashes history. They batted throughout the first day for 301 runs, and Taylor eventually reached 219.

Jimmy Cook (Somerset) was born in Johannesburg on 31 July 1953 and made his debut for Transvaal on Boxing Day 1972. He top-scored, but it was not until the late 1970s that he was promoted to open the innings, and made himself a permanent fixture. He and Henry Fotheringham became a prolific opening pair. In 1982–83 and 1983–84 Cook exceeded 1,000 runs in the South African season, one of only six batsmen ever to do so. Only Barry Richards scored more in a season and only Richards and Pollock have been as prolific as him in South Africa. The 6ft 1in (1.85m) opening bat did not fancy continuous county cricket but, at the age of 36, he decided to play for Somerset for the 1989 season. He was immediately successful, being the first in the country to pass both 1,000 and 2,000 runs. He had a purple patch in July with four consecutive first-class centuries and ended the season with 2,241 runs, the only batsman to pass 2,000. His average of 60.57 put him third in the national list. His eight centuries and 16 scores over 50 were both the best in the country.

Graeme Hick (Worcestershire) did not have such an outstanding season as in 1988, when he scored his amazing 2,713 runs, including an innings of 405 not out, but he did enough to demonstrate that he was in the top rank of batsmen, scoring his runs when they were most needed, and at the speed required. He was eighth in the averages with 57.00.

Dean Jones (Australia) another batsman from the touring side to be included, was only fourth in the Test averages at 70.75, but his aggregate of 566 stood second only to Taylor. He demonstrated fully what a fine attacking batsman he can be, an impression which was confirmed in the tourists' matches outside the Tests. On the tour as a whole he made 1,510 runs, including the highest score of the season, 248, at an average of 88.82, which was 24 ahead of the next batsman. He maintains a Test average of 50.28.

Allan Border (Australia) as the leader of the victorious Ashes-winning side (by a margin of 4–0), must be chosen as the skipper. He led his side with verve and made 979 runs on the tour at an average of 54.39. His average in the Tests was 73.67. During a highly successful series he moved himself into second place in the all-time Test aggregates with 8,273 runs, average 53.37. He would be an additional asset to the side as a second left-hand batsman.

Steve Waugh (Australia) the fourth tourist to make the side, began the Test series with scores of 177 not out, 152 not out, 21 not out and 43 – a total of 393 before being dismissed – an Ashes record sequence. He proved a resolute batsman at number six, and although the Aussies were markedly superior, his runs were far from being easy ones from tired bowling. At Lord's in particular, his 152 not out came at a time when England might have got back into the series. He played for Somerset in 1988, and finished third in the national averages with 1,314 runs at 73.00. In 1989 he went one better, finishing second with 1,030 runs at 64.38. He was classified as an all-rounder but his bowling has subsided as his batting has flourished, and he is only marginally an all-rounder now. His 1,605 Test runs have been made at an average of 40.12, while his 42 wickets have cost 42.40 each. By virtue of four not outs, he topped the Australian Test averages at 126.50. He was the third Australian to pass 500 runs in the series.

Jack Russell (Gloucestershire) had long been acknowledged as perhaps the best keeper in England (one or two others might challenge that) but his Test opportunities had been limited by a presumed lack of batting skill (despite the fact that before 1989 his highest first-class score, 94, had come in his only Test, against Sri Lanka. He was picked for the first Test against Australia and proved to be England's outstanding success. Only he and Gower played in all six Tests. Russell not only kept wicket superbly, but proved to be no mean batsman, especially in a crisis, where his application and concentration were lessons for many others. He improved upon his highest score by making 128 not out in a vain effort to save the game at Old Trafford, and finished second in the England averages at 39.25. His aggregate of 314 was beaten only by Smith and Gower for England.

Malcolm Marshall (Hampshire) has been one of the world's leading bowlers for many seasons, and as he bowled for Hampshire with no lessening of his powers in 1989 he is an automatic choice as principal strike bowler. He headed the first-class averages in 1988 and finished third in 1989 with 64 wickets at 16.67. In the winter he passed 300 Test wickets and, with 326, is now comfortably top of the West Indies' aggregates. Although the Test series was one-sided, it is not exaggerating to say that Marshall could probably have turned it round if loaned to England.

Terry Alderman (Australia) was the bowler who *did* win the Test series, and what's more, with 41 wickets he became the only bowler to reach 40 wickets in two Test series. Ideally suited to English conditions, he bowls straight from close to the stumps and either gets lbw decisions or moves the ball just enough to cause edges or misdirected drives. His Test wickets were taken at 17.36 each, and he took only 29 wickets outside Tests. His 70 wickets were taken at an average of 15.64, putting him top of the national averages.

Angus Fraser (Middlesex) made his Test debut in 1989 and was far from disgraced in a beaten side. Medium-fast right arm, he could progress in the direction of Alec Bedser and Maurice Tate. In three Tests, he took nine wickets at 35.88. He was 13th in the national averages with 92 wickets at 20.23. Bowlers above him who might have been given preference include Warwickshire's South African, Allan Donald, Lancashire's Pakistani, Wasim Akram, Leicestershire's Antiguan, Winston Benjamin, Notts' Barbadian all-rounder Franklyn Stephenson, or Essex's Derek Pringle, while Australian tourist Geoff Lawson might have claims, but with Marshall providing explosive power, Fraser's honest steadiness might be the best foil.

Nick Cook (Northamptonshire) might be surprised to find himself included, having come into the Test side for three Tests and captured five wickets at 56.50, but he has the best claims to the slow-bowling slot. Apart from Hick, who is already in the team, he was the top slow bowler in the national averages, just above Worcestershire's Richard Illingworth. The tourists's leg-breaker, Trevor Hohns, and Notts' off-breaker, Eddie Hemmings, were behind in both average and aggregate.

Robin Smith (Hampshire) who regained his place in England's Test team in 1989, was one of the few successes the home side could claim. Coming in because Lamb was injured, he played in the last five Tests, and scored 553 runs at 61.44, including two centuries. He proved an aggressive batsman who could dominate an attack, and at the same time show that he could fight a good rearguard action. He is selected as 12th man.

Mark Taylor (New South Wales and Australia).

Allsport/Adrian Murrell

Jimmy Cook (Transvaal and Somerset).

Allsport/Adrian Murrell

Graeme Hick (Worcestershire).

Allsport/Adrian Murrell

Dean Jones (Victoria and Australia).

Allsport/Adrian Murrell

Allan Border (Queensland and Australia)

Allsport/Ben Radford

Steve Waugh (New South Wales and Australia).

Allsport/Adrian Murrell

Jack Russell (Gloucestershire and England).

Allsport/Ben Radford

Malcolm Marshall (Barbados, Hampshire and West Indies).

Allsport/Adrian Murrell

Terry Alderman (Western Australia and Australia).

Allsport/Ben Radford

Angus Fraser (Middlesex and England).

Allsport/Adrian Murrell

Nick Cook (Northamptonshire and England).

Allsport/Adrian Murrell

Robin Smith (Hampshire and England).

Allsport/Adrian Murrell

Derbyshire

President: The Duke of Devonshire
Chairman: C.N. Middleton
Chief Executive: R.J. Lark, County Ground, Nottingham Road, Derby, DE2 6DA. *Tel:* 0332 383221
Coach: P.E. Russell
Captain: K.J. Barnett
Foundation of Present Club: November 1870 in Derby
First First-Class Match: Lancashire v Derbyshire (Old Trafford) May 1871
County Champions: 1936
Gillette/NatWest Trophy: Winners 1981
Benson & Hedges Cup: Losing finalists 1978, 1988
Sunday League Champions: Nil (best position 3rd in 1970)
Refuge Cup: Nil

Summary of Results in 1989
Britannic Assurance County Championship: Played 22, Won 6, Lost 6, Drawn 10, Position 6th equal
NatWest Bank Trophy: Lost in second round
Benson & Hedges Cup: Did not qualify for knock-out section
Refuge Assurance Sunday League: Played 16, Won 9, Lost 6, No Result 1, Position 5th
Refuge Assurance Cup: Did not qualify

From left, back: *F.A. Griffith, K.M. Krikken, T.J.G. O'Gorman, D.E. Malcolm, S.J. Base, D. Hallack, M. Wakefield, C.J. Adams.* Centre: *J.D. Brown (Director of Coaching), S.W. Tacey (Scorer), M. Jean-Jacques, R. Sharma, A.E. Warner, P.D. Bowler, M. Beardshall, S.C. Goldsmith, I. Edwards (Secretary).* Front: *B. Roberts, P.G. Newman, J.E. Morris, A. Hill, K.J. Barnett (Captain), P.E. Russell (Coach), B.J.M. Maher, O.H. Mortensen, R.J. Lark (Chief Executive).* Allsport

Occupying sixth place in the Championship with six wins, the county returned an identical record to the one they recorded in 1987, having fallen to 14th place with only four wins in between.

The bowling showed a great improvement on 1988. Malcolm, though ineffective when given a chance with England, took 37 Championship wickets in comparison with 50 the previous year, but they cost him ten runs less per victim, and Base, who arrived from South Wales in 1988, surprised the casual observer, his bowling figures for last summer being a total contrast to his first summer. Mortensen again topped the table, though he was more expensive. Newman's bowling was far less effective and it was announced that he would retire from county cricket.

With the New Zealander, Wright, having left the county and Barnett and Bowler not producing as many runs as in 1988, the batting was not so reliable. However Morris improved and headed the batting averages with over 1,500 Championship runs. The fact that he was 28th in the overall first-class table is a clear indication of Derbyshire's relative batting weakness.

The lack of local-bred talent is a point which continues to alarm traditionalists in the county – there are fewer Derbyshire-born players on the county circuit today than from any other first-class shire. The return of Miller to his home after his days with Essex is a small crumb of comfort.

Of the other players currently appearing for the county, O'Gorman, grandson of the music hall star, hit hundreds against Northants and Gloucestershire and looks promising; Goldsmith, who came from Kent in 1988, suffered from a knee injury, but should be fit for 1990. The veteran West Indian, Holding, was still feared by opposing batsmen, even if his final figures were modest. He has announced his retirement and will be replaced by Kuiper, the South African. Gladwin joined the Club early in the summer, having been with Essex, and hit a Championship hundred.

The county found little joy in the one-day competitions, except for the Sunday League, in which they moved up to fifth place.

ONE DAY AWAY MATCHES

The full scorecard of each of Derbyshire's away matches will be found in the sections for the respective home teams.

Refuge Assurance League

Leicester: April 30
Derbys 187–6 (40 ov) beat Leics 105 (31.5 ov) by 82 runs. Derbys 4pts, Leics 0pts.

Chelmsford: May 7
Essex 154–8 (40 ov) beat Derbys 153–8 (40 ov) by one run. Essex 4pts, Derbys 0pts.

Worcester: June 11
Worcs 207–6 (40 ov) beat Derbys 177–9 (40 ov) by 30 runs. Worcs 4pts, Derbys 0pts.

Trent Bridge: June 25
Notts 170–8 (39 ov) beat Derbys 128 (35.3 ov) by 42 runs. Notts 4pts, Derbys 0pts.

Lord's: July 9
Derbys 148–7 (40 ov) lost to Middx 89–4 (23.4) on faster scoring rate. Middx 4pts, Derbys 0pts.

Canterbury: July 16
Derbys 164 (37.4 ov) beat Kent 139 (38.3 ov) by 25 runs. Derbys 4pts, Kent 0pts.

Cheltenham: August 13
Gloucs 127 (40 ov) lost to Derbys 130–6 (28.2 ov) by 4 wkts. Derbys 4pts, Gloucs 0pts.

Edgbaston: August 20
Warwicks 192–7 (40 ov) lost to Derbys 195–5 (37.2 ov) (J.E. Morris 112*) by 5 wkts. Derbys 4pts, Warwicks 0pts.

Benson and Hedges Cup

Trent Bridge: May 2
Derbys 178–9 (55 ov) lost to Notts 179–5 (51.1 ov) by 5 wkts. Notts 2pts, Derbys 0pts.

Headingley: May 13
Yorks 208–5 (55 ov) beat Derbys 201–6 (55 ov) (K.J. Barnett 101) by 7 runs. Yorks 2pts, Derbys 0pts.

NatWest Bank Trophy

Worcester: July 12
Worcs 278–7 (60 ov) beat Derbys 240 (56 ov) by 38 runs.

REFUGE ASSURANCE LEAGUE

v NORTHAMPTONSHIRE (Derby)

April 23
Match Abandoned. No play. Derbys 2pts, Northants 2 pts

v LANCASHIRE (Leek)

May 14
Lost by 23 runs. Lancs 4pts, Derbys 0pts

Lancashire		
G. Fowler	b Base	35
A.N. Hayhurst	c Goldsmith b Warner	22
N.H. Fairbrother	c Newman b Warner	31
T.E. Jesty	b Newman	17
M. Watkinson	run out	44
Wasim Akram	b Mortensen	0
P.A.J. DeFreitas	c Maher b Mortensen	0
*D.P. Hughes	run out	8
I.D. Austin	not out	7
P.J.W. Allott	not out	2
†W.K. Hegg		
Extras	lb 5, w 5	10
Total (8 wkts, 40 ov)		176

65, 69, 111, 125, 125, 125, 165, 169

Mortensen	8	2	19	2
Newman	8	1	51	1
Holding	8	0	41	0
Base	8	0	31	1
Warner	8	0	29	2

Derbyshire		
*K.J. Barnett	c Hegg b DeFreitas	11
P.D. Bowler	c Hegg b Watkinson	35
J.E. Morris	b Wasim Akram	32
B. Roberts	lbw b Wasim Akram	0
S.C. Goldsmith	c Jesty b Austin	14
†B.J.M. Maher	c Hegg b Austin	11
M.A. Holding	c Fowler b Allott	0
P.G. Newman	c Hegg b Austin	8
A.E. Warner	c DeFreitas b Austin	11
S.J. Base	not out	6
O.H. Mortensen	not out	6
Extras	lb 10, w 9	19
Total (9 wkts, 40 ov)		153

44, 52, 54, 72, 109, 117, 121, 140, 141

Allott	8	2	36	1
DeFreitas	8	0	26	1
Wasim Akram	8	0	18	2
Watkinson	8	0	35	1
Austin	8	0	28	4

Umpires: K.J. Lyons and A.G.T. Whitehead
Toss: Derbyshire
In bitter weather, Lancashire made a solid start, but later Watkinson hit 44 off 33 balls and as Barnett went cheaply, Derbyshire were unable to muster enough runs to reach the visitors' total.

PLAYERS

Christopher John ADAMS *b* 6.5.1970 Whitwell; middle order right hand batsman; debut 1988; appeared in 7 Championship matches last season

Kim John BARNETT *b* 17.7.1960 Stoke-on-Trent; Opening right hand batsman; occasional leg-breaks; debut 1979; England Test debut 1988; played in 3 Tests in 1989; county captain since 1983; chosen for tour to South Africa 1989–90

Simon John BASE *b* 2.1.1960 Maidstone; Lower order right hand batsman; right arm medium fast bowler; debut 1988; previously played for Glamorgan 1986–87

Ian Raphael BISHOP *b* 24.10.1967 Port-of-Spain; lower order right hand batsman; aggressive right arm fast bowler; debut May 1989; also plays for Trinidad; toured England with 1988 West Indians, but did not appear in Tests; West Indies Test Debut v India 1988–89

Peter Duncan BOWLER *b* 30.7.1963 Plymouth; Opening right-hand batsman; debut 1988; previously played for Leics 1986 and created new record by scoring 100s on his debut for both Leics and Derbys; capped for Derbys July 30, 1989

Adrian Mark BROWN *b* 6.11.1964 Heanor; left hand batsman; debut 1985; re-appeared in 1989 in 2 matches; son of Derbys coaching organiser

Christopher GLADWIN *b* 10.5.1962 East Ham; middle order left hand batsman; debut May 1989; previously played for Essex 1981–87

Steven Clive GOLDSMITH *b* 19.12.1964 Ashford, Kent; right hand batsman; debut 1988; previously played for Kent 1987; scored 1,000 runs in first season with Derbyshire; but not so successful last summmer

Frank Alexander GRIFFITH *b* 15.8.1968 Whipps Cross, Essex; right hand batsman; right arm medium pace bowler; debut 1988

Michael Anthony HOLDING *b* 16.2.1954 Kingston, Jamaica; one of the outstanding right arm fast bowlers of his generation; played in 60 Tests and 102 One Day Internationals for West Indies; taking 249 Test wickets (av 23.68) and 140 One Day International wickets (av 21–46) retired from Test cricket in 1987 and from county cricket in Sept 1989; debut for Derbys 1983; appeared for Lancashire in 1981

Martin JEAN-JACQUES *b* 2.7.1960 Soufriere, Dominica; lower order right hand batsman; right arm medium fast bowler; debut 1986; played in only 5 Champhionship matches in 1989

Ole Mortensen, top of the bowling averages.

Allsport/Michael King

Karl Matthew KRIKKEN *b* 9.4.1969 Bolton; son of old Lancs/Worcs player; right hand batsman; wicketkeeper; debut for Derbys July 1989; but played in Sunday League match in 1987

Bernard Joseph Michael MAHER *b* 11.2.1958 Hillingdon, Middx; opening right hand batsman; wicketkeeper; debut 1981

Devon Eugene MALCOLM *b* 22.2.1963 Lively right arm fast bowler; lower order right hand batsman; debut 1984; surprise choice for England in 1989 Test at Trent Bridge; selected for England tour to West Indies

John Edward MORRIS *b* 1.4.1964 Crewe; attractive right hand batsman; debut 1982; after a moderate season in 1988; outstanding Derbyshire batsman last summer

Ole Henrek MORTENSEN *b* 29.1.1958 Vejle, Denmark; very effective right arm fast medium bowler; lower order right hand batsman; debut 1983

Paul Geoffrey NEWMAN *b* 10.1.1959 Evington; right arm fast medium bowler; lower order right hand batsman; had a poor season with the ball in 1989

Timothy Joseph Gerard O'GORMAN *b* 15.5.1967 Woking; grandson of old Surrey cricketer; promising right hand batsman; scored two Championship 100s in 1989; debut 1987

Ian REDPATH *b* 12.9.1965 Basildon; right hand batsman; made debut for Derbyshire last July; previously played for Essex

Bruce ROBERTS *b* 30.5.1962 Lusaka, N Rhodesia; middle order right hand batsman; debut 1984; also plays for Transvaal; not so successful during the last two seasons

Rajeshwar (Reg) SHARMA *b* 27.1.1962 Nairobi; Useful all-rounder; right hand batsman; off break or medium pace bowler; debut 1985

Allan Esmond WARNER *b* 12.5.1957 Birmingham; right arm fast medium bowler; fair right hand batsman; debut 1985; previously with Worcestershire 1982–1984

REFUGE ASSURANCE LEAGUE

v SUSSEX (Derby)

June 18

Won by 3 wkts. Derbys 4pts, Sussex 0pts

Sussex		
D.M. Smith	c Sharma b Newman	9
K. Greenfield	c Maher b Mortensen	16
A.P. Wells	c Maher b Mortensen	5
*C.M. Wells	b Mortensen	3
I.J. Gould	c Maher b Base	5
A.I.C. Dodemaide	c Newman b Griffith	21
A.C.S. Pigott	c Maher b Base	46
†P. Moores	b Griffith	0
I.D.K. Salisbury	not out	7
A.R. Clarke	b Holding	1
A.M. Babington	b Base	0
Extras	lb 8, w 4, nb 5	17
Total (37.4 ov)		130

13, 28, 34, 39, 42, 105, 106, 128, 129

Newman	8	1	25	1
Mortsensen	8	2	16	3
Holding	7	1	11	1
Base	7.4	0	29	3
Griffith	7	0	41	2

Derbyshire		
*K.J. Barnett	c Greenfield b Clarke	13
P.D. Bowler	not out	55
J.E. Morris	run out	1
R. Sharma	c Pigott b C.M. Wells	28
B. Roberts	run out	16
†B.J.M. Maher	lbw b Pigott	0
F.A. Griffith	b Pigott	0
M.A. Holding	st Moores b Salisbury	5
P.G. Newman	not out	0
O.H. Mortensen		
S.J. Base		
Extras	b 4, lb 8, w 3, nb 1	16
Total (7 wkts, 39 ov)		134

30, 32, 76, 112, 112, 112, 122

Pigott	8	1	21	2
Dodemaide	7	1	21	0
Babington	6	1	25	0
Clarke	8	2	18	1
Salisbury	6	0	28	1
C.M. Wells	4	0	9	1

Umpires: J.H. Harris and P.B. Wight

Toss: Sussex

On a green wicket Sussex fell to 42–5, before Pigott lashed out at some short pitched bowling. Derbyshire made hard work of their modest target and only a sound innings from Bowler brought victory with an over to spare.

v SOMERSET (Derby)

July 2

Won by 5 wkts. Derbys 4pts, Somerset 0pts

Somerset		
P.M. Roebuck	run out	1
S.J. Cook	lbw b Mortensen	10
C.J. Tavare	lbw b Mortensen	11
J.G. Wyatt	b Base	24
R.J. Harden	b Base	10
*V.J. Marks	run out	40
†N.D. Burns	not out	38
A.N. Jones	not out	4
M.W. Cleal		
H.R.J. Trump		
D.J. Foster		
Extras	lb 8, w 7, nb 2	17
Total (6 wkts, 40 ov)		155

3, 25, 32, 61, 82, 142

Mortensen	8	3	11	2
Newman	8	1	45	0
Holding	8	2	26	0
Base	8	0	28	2
Warner	8	0	37	0

Derbyshire		
*K.J. Barnett	c Wyatt b Roebuck	49
P.D. Bowler	run out	64
J.E. Morris	lbw b Roebuck	7
R. Sharma	c Wyatt b Roebuck	15
C.J. Adams	run out	0
M.A. Holding	not out	18
†B.J.M. Maher	not out	0
A.E. Warner		
P.G. Newman		
O.H. Mortensen		
S.J. Base		
Extras	b 1, lb 5, w 2	8
Total (5 wkts, 38.5 ov)		161

103, 123, 137, 137, 143

Jones	6.5	0	37	0
Foster	5	0	20	0
Trump	8	0	19	0
Cleal	5	0	24	0
Marks	8	0	32	0
Roebuck	6	0	23	3

Umpires: J.C. Balderstone and B.J. Meyer

Toss: Somerset

With Roebuck running himself out and Mortensen baffling Cook and Tavare, Somerset owed all to 60 in 10 overs by Marks and Burns. In contrast Derbyshire made a fine start and although Roebuck picked up 3 quick wickets, the home side won with 7 deliveries unbowled.

v GLAMORGAN (Heanor)

July 23

Won by 9 wkts. Derbys 4pts, Glamorgan 0pts

Glamorgan		
*A.R. Butcher	lbw b Holding	39
G.C. Holmes	lbw b Base	31
A. Dale	not out	67
M.P. Maynard	retired hurt	61
H. Morris	c Morris b Holding	6
I. Smith	not out	25
M.J. Cann		
†C.P. Metson		
K.A. Somaia		
S.J. Dennis		
S.L. Watkin		
Extras	b 2, lb 7, w 4, nb 1	14
Total (3 wkts, 40 ov)		243

73, 73, 188

Sharma	4	0	24	0
Malcolm	8	0	35	0
Base	8	0	52	1
Holding	8	0	33	2
Warner	8	0	55	0
Griffiths	4	0	35	0

Derbyshire		
*K.J. Barnett	not out	100
P.D. Bowler	c Metson b Dale	36
J.E. Morris	not out	100
R. Sharma		
B. Roberts		
†B.J.M. Maher		
F.A. Griffiths		
A.E. Warner		
M.A. Holding		
S.J. Base		
D.E. Malcolm		
Extras	lb 8, w 1	9
Total (1 wkt, 36 ov)		245

63

Dennis	8	0	42	0
Smith	6	0	26	0
Watkin	7	0	35	0
Dale	5	0	43	1
Holmes	6	0	55	0
Somaia	4	0	36	0

Umpires: D.R. Shepherd and B. Leadbeater

Toss: Derbyshire

Barnett and John Morris found no difficulty in the Glamorgan attack. Their partnership of 182 in 20 overs was a new county record and Morris hit the fastest Sunday 100 so far this season off 61 balls. Morris's knock contained 4 sixes and 11 fours.

John Morris, top of the Championship batting, driving against Hampshire in the Benson and Hedges final at Lord's in 1987. Allsport/Adrian Murrell

REFUGE ASSURANCE LEAGUE

v SURREY (Derby)

July 30

Won by 4 wkts. Derbys 4pts, Surrey 0pts

Surrey		
G.S. Clinton	lbw b Malcolm	1
D.J. Bicknell	c Sharma b Warner	24
†A.J. Stewart	lbw b Base	17
G.P. Thorpe	c Maher b Warner	3
D.M. Ward	b Holding	18
*I.A. Greig	b Base	1
K.T. Medlycott	c Base b Malcolm	23
M.A. Feltham	c Barnett b Malcolm	13
C.K. Bullen	c Maher b Malcolm	8
M.P. Bicknell	c Holding b Base	7
A.J. Murphy	not out	1
Extras	lb 5, w 3, nb 1	9
Total (39.4 ov)		125

20, 46, 50, 50, 52, 85, 101, 115, 120

Malcolm	8	0	21	4
Mortensen	8	0	29	0
Holding	8	0	24	1
Warner	8	0	22	2
Base	7.4	0	24	3

Derbyshire		
*K.J. Barnett	b Murphy	14
P.D. Bowler	lbw b Greig	22
R. Sharma	c Stewart b M.P. Bicknell	0
T.J.G. O'Gorman	not out	35
C.J. Adams	b M.P. Bicknell	1
M.A. Holding	c Bullen b M.P. Bicknell	1
†B.J.M. Maher	lbw b Thorpe	5
A.E Warner	not out	31
D.E. Malcolm		
S.J. Base		
O.H. Mortensen		
Extras	lb 12, w 6	18
Total (6 wkts, 32.5 ov)		127

24, 31, 39, 40, 50, 68

Murphy	8	3	22	1
M.P. Bicknell	8	2	14	3
Feltham	6	0	27	0
Greig	8	0	33	1
Thorpe	2	0	13	1
Bullen	0.5	0	6	0

Umpires: J.D. Bond and D.J. Constant
Toss: Derbyshire
Malcolm, who received his county cap during the match together with Bowler, dismissed Surrey cheaply on a wicket that helped the seamers. Derbyshire, in reply, looked doomed until Warner joined O'Gorman and the pair virtually doubled the score, winning the game by a fair margin.

v HAMPSHIRE (Derby)

August 6

Lost by 4 wkts. Hants 4pts, Derbys 0pts

Derbyshire		
*K.J. Barnett	b Bakker	2
P.D. Bowler	b Bakker	71
J.E.Morris	c Terry b James	0
R. Sharma	c Smith b James	5
T.J.G. O'Gorman	c and b James	0
M.A. Holding	c Jefferies b Connor	1
†B.J.M. Maher	c Parks b Jefferies	7
A.E. Warner	b Bakker	40
D.E. Malcolm	b Bakker	0
S.J. Base	b Bakker	3
O.H. Mortensen	not out	2
Extras	lb 11, nb 3, w 3	17
Total (40 ov)		148

7, 8, 22, 24, 25, 61, 127, 127, 139

James	8	1	17	3
Bakker	7	0	17	5
Connor	8	2	25	1
Jefferies	8	2	41	1
Nicholas	1	0	4	0
Maru	8	0	33	0

Hampshire		
*M.C.J. Nicholas	run out	7
C.L. Smith	c Sharma b Mortensen	4
R.A. Smith	c Maher b Mortensen	13
D.R. Turner	lbw b Base	3
V.P. Terry	c Barnett b Base	47
K.D. James	not out	39
S.T. Jefferies	b Base	7
†R.J. Parks	not out	6
R.J Maru		
C.A. Connor		
P.J. Bakker		
Extras	b 1, lb 9, w 10, n 3	23
Total (6 wkts, 39.2 ov)		149

9, 28, 30, 37, 132, 140

Malcolm	8	0	34	0
Mortensen	8	2	14	2
Holding	8	1	22	0
Base	7.2	0	37	3
Warner	8	0	32	0

Umpires: N.T. Plews and J.H. Hampshire
Toss: Derbyshire
Bakker and James reduced Derbyshire to 25 for 5, before Bowler and Warner managed to stabilise the home batting. Both Bakker and Bowler produced their best Sunday League figures. Hampshire also made a poor start, Terry and James however added 95 for the 5th wicket and Hampshire won in the 40th over.

v YORKSHIRE (Chesterfield)

August 27

Won by 7 wkts. Derbys 4pts, Yorks 0pts

Yorkshire		
M.D. Moxon	c and b Base	35
A.A. Metcalfe	c Bowler b Base	0
†R.J. Blakey	c Bowler b Warner	17
J.D. Love	run out	27
P.E. Robinson	not out	39
D. Byas	b Base	0
N.G. Nicholson	lbw b Mortensen	0
*P. Carrick	c and b Sharma	11
C.S. Pickles	lbw b Sharma	0
A. Sidebottom	not out	9
P.W. Jarvis		
Extras	b 1, lb 2, w 6	9
Total (8 wkts, 40 ov)		147

3, 27, 87, 93, 93, 94, 107, 107

Base	8	1	17	3
Mortensen	8	1	25	1
Warner	8	0	34	1
Holding	8	2	15	0
Roberts	3	0	20	0
Sharma	5	0	33	2

Derbyshire		
*K.J. Barnett	c Love b Pickles	13
†P.D Bowler	not out	66
J.E. Morris	c Byas b Pickles	7
B. Roberts	b Byas	10
T.J.G. O'Gorman	not out	46
S.J. Base		
O.H. Mortensen		
A.E. Warner		
R. Sharma		
M.A. Holding		
C.J. Adams		
Extras	lb 3, w 2, nb 1	6
Total (3 wkts, 37.5 ov)		148

16, 37, 57

Jarvis	8	2	18	0
Sidebottom	8	2	28	0
Pickles	7	1	27	2
Moxon	4.4	0	23	0
Byas	6.1	0	28	1
Carrick	4	0	21	0

Umpires: K.J. Lyons and R.A. White
Toss: Derbyshire
Some excellent bowling by Base severely restricted the Yorkshire batsmen and though Robinson survived until the end, he was unable to speed up the scoring rate. In contrast Bowler and later O'Gorman found batting much easier and finished off the game with a stand of 91.

BRITANNIC ASSURANCE COUNTY CHAMPIONSHIP AVERAGES 1989

Batting	*M*	*I*	*NO*	*Runs*	*HS*	*Avge*	*100*	*50*
J.E. Morris	21	40	4	1555	156	43.19	4	8
T.J.G. O'Gorman	8	14	2	462	124	38.50	2	–
K.J. Barnett	16	28	1	965	118	35.74	2	6
D.E. Malcolm	9	10	5	152	51	30.40	–	1
P.D. Bowler	22	43	1	1167	106	27.79	1	10
A.M. Brown	2	4	–	109	65	27.25	–	1
C.J. Adams	7	11	1	261	79	26.10	–	1
R. Sharma	19	34	4	669	77	22.30	–	3
I. Redpath	3	6	2	88	43*	22.00	–	–
B. Roberts	13	24	1	485	102	21.09	1	2
K.M. Krikken	4	8	3	88	37	17.60	–	–
B.J.M. Maher	20	36	5	506	97	16.32	–	2
C. Gladwin	4	8	–	127	59	15.88	–	1
A.E. Warner	14	22	6	246	46	15.38	–	–
P.G. Newman	14	23	3	306	86*	15.30	–	2
S.C. Goldsmith	9	17	–	252	88	14.82	–	1
S.J. Base	14	21	6	156	32*	10.40	–	–
I.R. Bishop	11	18	2	166	28*	10.38	–	–
F.A. Griffith	5	10	–	102	30	10.20	–	–
M.A. Holding	10	13	4	90	34	10.00	–	–
O.H. Mortensen	12	17	8	78	20*	8.67	–	–
M. Jean-Jacques	5	8	1	34	16*	4.86	–	–

Bowling	*O*	*M*	*R*	*W*	*Avge*	*BB*	*5i*	*10m*
O.H. Mortensen	314	64	804	38	21.16	6-38	2	–
D.E. Malcolm	207.2	32	789	37	21.32	4-69	–	–
I.R. Bishop	308	60	844	38	22.21	6-67	1	–
A.E. Warner	325.1	78	806	35	23.03	4-18	–	–
M. Jean-Jacques	90.2	11	359	15	23.93	4-84	–	–
K.J. Barnett	94.2	22	245	10	24.50	4-36	–	–
S.J. Base	376.5	64	1340	51	26.27	7-60	2	1
R. Sharma	174.5	43	513	18	28.50	5-60	1	–
F.A. Griffith	41	6	152	5	30.40	2-18	–	–
M.A. Holding	258.1	46	863	28	30.82	6-57	1	1
P.G. Newman	326.5	72	988	27	36.59	5-45	1	–

Also bowled: P.D. Bowler 32-5-138-3; K.M. Krikken 6-0-40-0; B.J.M. Maher 12-0-81-1; J.E. Morris 10-2-38-0; I. Redpath 5-2-11-0; B. Roberts 9-0-30-0.

Centuries

4 J.E. Morris: 127 v Somerset (Derby); 134 v Glamorgan (Derby); 121 v Glos (Cheltenham; 156 v Notts (Derby).

2 K.J. Barnett: 118 v Somerset (Derby); 106 v Hants (Derby). T.J.G. O'Gorman: 113* v Northants (Northampton); 124 v Glos (Cheltenham).

1 P.D. Bowler: 106 v Surrey (Derby). B. Roberts: 102 v Kent (Dartford).

BENSON AND HEDGES CUP

v SOMERSET (Derby)

April 25, 26

Lost by 7 wkts. Somerset 2pts, Derbys 0pts

Derbyshire		
*K.J. Barnett	c Hardy b Jones	0
P.D. Bowler	c Burns b Foster	17
†B.J.M. Maher	b Mallender	27
J.E. Morris	c Marks b Foster	0
B. Roberts	c Burns b Mallender	20
S.C. Goldsmith	c Cook b Jones	13
R. Sharma	c Roebuck b Mallender	0
P.G. Newman	not out	26
M.A. Holding	c Hardy b Rose	12
S.J. Base	run out	4
O.H. Mortensen	c Bartlett b Rose	1
Extras	b 6, lb 15, w 1	21
Total (54.2 ov)		141

0, 29, 29, 67, 70, 70, 93, 111, 134

Jones	11	3	25	2
Mallender	11	0	27	3
Rose	10.2	1	19	2
Foster	11	2	32	2
Marks	11	3	18	0

Somerset		
S.J. Cook	lbw b Base	27
P.M. Roebuck	c Maher b Roberts	65
J.J.E. Hardy	c Maher b Holding	12
C.J. Tavare	not out	17
R.J. Bartlett	not out	4
†N.D. Burns		
*V.J. Marks		
G.D. Rose		
N.A. Mallender		
A.N. Jones		
D.J. Foster		
Extras	lb 11, w 4, nb 2,	17
Total (3 wkts, 51.2 ov)		142

48, 96, 123

Holding	11	3	25	1
Mortensen	11	1	19	0
Newman	11	3	17	0
Base	11	0	48	1
Sharma	2.2	0	12	0
Roberts	5	2	10	1

Umpires: H.D. Bird and K.J. Lyons
Toss: Somerset. Gold: P.M. Roebuck
Owing to a wet ground play did not begin until late in the afternoon on the first day, and then Barnett was out first ball. Derbys had struggled to 134–9 when play ended for the day. Somerset also found runs hard to come by, but Roebuck held steadfast, being at the crease 45 overs for 65. Somerset won with 3.4 overs in hand.

v MINOR COUNTIES (Derby)

May 11

Won by 7 wkts. Derbys 2pts, Minor Counties 0pts

Minor Counties		
S.R. Atkinson	lbw b Mortensen	5
G.K. Brown	c Maher b Holding	4
N.A. Folland	c Holding b Warner	29
P.R. Oliver	c Roberts b Holding	0
*S.G. Plumb	c Holding b Mortensen	3
S. Greensword	c Maher b Base	39
D.A. Hale	c Maher b Newman	6
†A.R. Fothergill	c Goldsmith b Warner	4
R.A. Evans	not out	28
I.E. Conn	lbw b Warner	0
N.R. Taylor	b Holding	14
Extras	b 1, lb 3, w 9, nb 4	17
Total (44.4 ov)		149

11, 11, 13, 25, 69, 76, 81, 116, 117

Holding	6.4	1	17	3
Mortensen	11	6	21	2
Base	8	1	47	1
Newman	8	3	30	1
Warner	11	1	30	3

Derbyshire		
*K.J. Barnett	c Plumb	75
P.D. Bowler	lbw b Taylor	8
†B.J.M. Maher	not out	42
P.G. Newman	c Evans b Hale	11
A.E. Warner	not out	5
J.E. Morris		
B. Roberts		
S.C. Goldsmith		
M.A. Holding		
S.J. Base		
O.H. Mortensen		
Extras	lb 5, w 2, nb 2	9
Total (3 wkts, 34 ov)		150

38, 124, 138

Taylor	11	2	24	1
Hale	5	0	36	2
Conn	11	2	44	0
Evans	6	0	39	0
Plumb	1	0	2	0

Umpires: J.C. Balderstone and J.W. Holder
Toss: Derbyshire. Gold: K.J. Barnett
The Minor Counties fell to 25–4, but Greensword held firm and a respectable total was attained. With Barnett in splendid form Derbyshire found the Minors bowling of little consequence and the runs came in 34 overs.

NATWEST BANK TROPHY

v IRELAND (Derby)

June 28, 29

Won by 63 runs.

Derbyshire		
*K.J. Barnett	run out	16
P.D. Bowler	c Jackson b Jeffrey	8
J.E. Morris	lbw b Nelson	4
R. Sharma	c Warke b Garth	10
C. Gladwin	lbw b Jeffrey	8
B. Roberts	lbw b Nelson	13
†B.J.M. Maher	c Harrison b Halliday	14
P.G. Newman	c Warke b Thompson	4
M.A Holding	b Halliday	32
O.H. Mortensen	not out	4
D.E. Malcolm	b Lewis	4
Extras	lb 10, w 17, nb 1	28
Total (56.1 ov)		145

18, 23, 34, 43, 66, 69, 85, 130, 135

Nelson	12	3	19	2
Jeffrey	10	0	44	2
Garth	5	1	8	1
Thompson	12	2	32	1
Lewis	10.1	2	21	1
Halliday	7	2	11	2

Ireland		
S.J.S. Warke	c Holding b Mortensen	2
M.F. Cohen	b Holding	7
D.A. Lewis	lbw b Mortensen	2
J.D. Garth	c Maher b Mortensen	0
G.D. Harrison	lbw b Mortensen	1
M.A. Nulty	c Sharma b Mortensen	8
N.E. Thompson	b Malcolm	12
*†T.B. Jackson	b Malcolm	16
M. Halliday	c Sharma b Mortensen	2
A.N. Nelson	not out	9
A.S. Jeffrey	b Sharma	15
Extras	lb 3, w 3, nb 2	8
Total (31.4 ov)		82

9, 9, 12, 12, 13, 33, 37, 54, 56

Holding	9	1	29	1
Mortensen	12	6	14	6
Malcolm	7	1	18	2
Newman	3	0	18	0
Sharma	0.4	0	0	1

Umpires: B. Dudleston and C.T. Spencer
Toss: Ireland. MofM: O.H. Mortensen
Rain allowed only 21 overs on the first day during which Deryshire struggled to 66–5. Unfortunately for Ireland Holding was dropped early on the second day and then Mortensen completely overwhelmed the Irish batsmen, so the county escaped a humiliating defeat.

Away Matches

The full scorecard of each of Derbyshire's away matches will be found in the sections for the respective home teams.

Chelmsford: May 4, 5, 6
Derbys 113 (T.D. Topley 5–30) and 197 lost to Essex 522–3d (G.A. Gooch 148, A.W. Lilley 113*) by an inns and 212 runs. Essex 24pts, Derbys 0pts.

Dartford: May 20, 21, 22
Derbys 416 (B. Roberts 102) and 87–2 beat Kent 210 and 292 by 8 wkts. Derbys 23pts, Kent 5pts.

Headingley: May 24, 25, 26
Derbys 178 (A. Sidebottom 5–40) and 189–7 drew with Yorks 313. Yorks 8pts, Derbys 4pts.

Nuneaton: June 7, 8, 9
Warwicks 155 (O.H. Mortensen 6–38) and 199–6d drew with Derbys 135 and 212–8 (A.R.K. Pierson 6–82) Warwicks 5pts, Derbys 4pts.

Worcester: June 10, 12, 13
Worcs 220 and 227–8d beat Derbys 157 (G.R. Dilley 5–42) and 145 (N.V. Radford 6–59) by 145 runs. Worcs 22pts, Derbys 5pts.

Lord's July 8, 10, 11
Middx 223 and 215–2d (I.J.F. Hutchinson 106) beat Derbys 177–5d and 191 (P.C.R. Tufnell 5–78) by 70 runs. Middx 20pts, Derbys 5pts.

Northampton: July 26, 27, 28
Northants 283 (R.J. Bailey 116, O.H. Mortensen 6–105) and 165 lost to Derbys 420 (T.J.G. O'Gorman 113*) and 29–2 by 8 wkts. Derbys 24pts, Northants 6pts.

Cheltenham: August 12, 14, 15
Derbys 448–9d (J.E. Morris 121, T.J.G. O'Gorman 124) drew with Gloucs 175–6. Derbys 6pts, Gloucs 2pts.

Trent Bridge: August 19, 21
Notts 185 and 114 beat Derbys 165 and 64 (E.E. Hemmings 5–20) by 70 runs. Notts 21pts, Derbys 5pts.

Leicester: August 29, 30, 31
Derbys 204 (W.K.M. Benjamin 5–51) and 78 (W.K.M. Benjamin 5–25, C.C. Lewis 5–40) lost to Leics 241 (I.R. Bishop 6–67) and 42–0 by 10 wkts. Leics 22pts, Derbys 6pts.

Old Trafford: Sept 13, 14, 15, 16
Derbys 292 and 209–6d drew with Lancs 251–9d and 53–2. Derbys 7pts, Lancs 7pts.

v NORTHAMPTONSHIRE (Derby)

April 20, 21, 22, 24
Drawn. Derbys 5pts, Northants 5pts

Derbyshire 1st Innings

*K.J. Barnett	c Ripley b Davis	36
P.D. Bowler	b Davis	4
†B.J.M. Maher	c Ripley b Davis	15
J.E. Morris	c Thomas b Robinson	13
B. Roberts	c Ripley b Thomas	30
S.C. Goldsmith	c Ripley b Robinson	4
R. Sharma	c Lamb b Thomas	17
P.G. Newman	c Lamb b Thomas	0
A.E. Warner	c Capel	17
S.J. Base	b Davis	14
O.H. Mortensen	not out	20
Extras	b 1, lb 3, nb 9	13
Total (72. 1 ov)		183

10, 51, 74, 98, 103, 127, 127, 148, 148

Davis	19.1	4	43	4
Thomas	16	1	53	3
Robinson	18	6	44	2
Capel	19	9	39	1

Northamptonshire 1st Innings

G. Cook	b Base	53
W. Larkins	c Barnett b Newman	15
R.J. Bailey	c Bowler b Mortensen	0
*A.J. Lamb	c Roberts b Newman	6
D.J. Capel	b Base	24
R.G. Williams	c Roberts b Base	8
†D. Ripley	not out	27
J.G. Thomas	c Goldsmith b Base	9
N.G.B. Cook	c Sharma b Newman	5
W.W. Davis	b Newman	4
M.A. Robinson	c Roberts b Newman	0
Extras	b 1, lb 9	10
Total (84.5 ov)		161

33, 36, 51, 88, 103, 108, 126, 133, 149

Newman	28.5	8	45	5
Mortensen	18	6	34	1
Base	24	3	61	4
Warner	14	5	11	0

Derbyshire 2nd Innings

*K.J. Barnett	b Davis	74
P.D. Bowler	b Capel	35
†B.J.M. Maher	c Williams b Capel	18
J.E. Morris	run out	13
S.J. Base	c Ripley b Capel	0
B. Roberts	c Lamb b Capel	0
S.C. Goldsmith	c and b Capel	11
R. Sharma	c Larkins b Davis	11
P.G. Newman	c and b Robinson	13
A.E. Warner	lbw b Davis	3
O.H. Mortensen	not out	12
Extras	b 2, lb 16, nb 8	26
Total		216

110, 140, 145, 145, 145, 167, 174, 183, 187

Davis	23	3	76	3
Thomas	16	3	43	0
Capel	23	8	53	5
Robinson	17.3	4	26	1

Northamptonshire 2nd Innings

G. Cook	run out	27
W. Larkins	b Base	11
R.J. Bailey	c and b Mortensen	9
*A.J. Lamb	b Base	22
D.J. Capel	c Warner b Mortensen	6
R.G. Williams	c Maher b Warner	28
†D. Ripley	b Newman	24
J.G. Thomas	c Mortensen b Newman	7
W.W. Davis	not out	27
N.G.B. Cook	c Roberts b Mortensen	3
M.A. Robinson	not out	0
Extras	lb 11, w 1, nb 1	13
Total (9 wkts)		177

32, 47, 52, 74, 80, 136, 145, 149, 177

Newman	11	4	31	2
Mortensen	21	4	52	3
Base	19	4	61	2
Warner	8	1	22	1

Umpires: H.D. Bird and K.J. Lyons
Toss: Derbyshire.
In damp conditions runs came slowly on the first day and by the close Northants were 45–2 off 30 overs. The pattern remained unchanged on the second day, until Barnett hit 74 out of 110 before being bowled by a shooter. Derbyshire then lost four more wickets and were 146–5 at stumps. Rain reduced playing time on Saturday and on Monday Northants wanted 192 to win with 8 wickets in hand. Rain and snow prevented play resuming until 4.00 pm and in bitter conditions the visitors just avoided defeat.

v LEICESTERSHIRE (Chesterfield)

May 17, 18, 19
Lost by 9 wkts. Leics 23pts, Derbys 4pts

Leicestershire 1st Innings

T.J. Boon	b Warner	27
N.E. Briers	c and b Mortensen	73
*D.I. Gower	b Warner	14
P. Willey	c Newman b Bishop	10
J.J. Whitaker	c Maher b Newman	5
L. Potter	c Roberts b Mortensen	41
C.C. Lewis	c Maher b Mortensen	0
†P. Whitticase	c Mortensen b Base	15
W.K.M. Benjamin	b Bowler	37
G.J.P. Parsons	not out	33
J.P. Agnew	c Base b Bowler	0
Extras	b 4, lb 7, w 2, nb 6	19
Total (92 ov)		274

43, 73, 95, 104, 176, 176, 189, 198, 272

Bishop	17	4	54	1
Mortensen	26	4	71	3
Warner	19	3	53	2
Base	14	2	38	1
Newman	14	2	46	1
Bowler	2	1	1	2

Derbyshire 1st Innings

*K.J. Barnett	b Agnew	9
P.D. Bowler	c Lewis b Benjamin	0
†B.J.M. Maher	b Agnew	6
J.E. Morris	c Whitticase b Benjamin	0
B. Roberts	c Whitticase b Benjamin	2
S.J. Base	b Benjamin	4
S.C. Goldsmith	hit wkt b Benjamin	24
P.G. Newman	b Benjamin	4
I.R. Bishop	lbw b Agnew	4
A.E. Warner	not out	1
O.H. Mortensen	c Whitaker b Agnew	0
Extras	nb 3	3
Total (25.2 ov)		57

9, 15, 15, 17, 17, 22, 44, 52, 56

Benjamin	13	5	26	6
Agnew	12.2	2	31	4

Derbyshire 2nd Innings

*K.J. Barnett	c and b Benjamin	16
P.D. Bowler	c Whitaker b Lewis	16
†B.J.M. Maher	c Boon b Parsons	15
J.E. Morris	lbw b Benjamin	77
B. Roberts	c Lewis b Parsons	25
S.C. Goldsmith	c Boon b Lewis	4
P.G. Newman	c Whitticase b Lewis	0
I.R. Bishop	c Whitticase b Benjamin	20
A.E. Warner	c Willey b Lewis	29
S.J. Base	b Lewis	0
O.H. Mortensen	not out	0
Extras	b 1, lb 13, nb 12	26
Total		228

31, 56, 60, 14, 154, 159, 182,224, 228

Benjamin	21	9	49	3
Agnew	10	2	44	0
Parsons	13	2	43	2
Lewis	20.5	6	69	5
Willey	4	2	9	0

Leicestershire 2nd Innings

T.J. Boon	c Roberts b Bishop	9
N.E. Briers	not out	3
*D.I. Gower	not out	0
Extras		0
Total (1 wkt)		12

10

Bishop	4	2	6	1
Warner	3.1	1	6	0

Umpires: J.D. Bond and A.G.T. Whitehead
Toss: Leicestershire
The first day belonged to Benjamin who with Parsons added 74 for the 9th wicket after the middle batting had failed and then in the 15 overs allowed to Derbyshire at the end of the day reduced them to 31 for 6. Benjamin finished with a career best 6–26 on the second morning, but when Derbyshire followed on they were saved from a two day defeat by rain and a stout innings from Morris. The game was completed in 95 minutes on the final day.

v SUSSEX (Derby)
June 17, 19, 20
Drawn. Derbys 6pts, Sussex 6pts

Derbyshire 1st Innings

*K.J. Barnett	c and b Dodemaide	14
P.D. Bowler	b C.M. Wells	48
J.E. Morris	c Moores b Dodemaide	67
R. Sharma	c Pigott b Dodemaide	19
C. Gladwin	c Gould b Kimber	21
B. Roberts	b Dodemaide	1
†B.J.M. Maher	c Dodemaide b Salisbury	97
P.G. Newman	lbw b Dodemaide	27
I.R. Bishop	b Pigott	8
O.H. Mortensen	c Moores b Pigott	5
D.E. Malcolm	not out	13
Extras	b 5, lb 12, nb 5	22
Total (100 ov: 272–6)		342

19, 127, 137, 170, 178, 182, 274, 285, 309

Pigott	30	7	83	2
Dodemaide	41	8	112	5
C.M. Wells	24	6	59	1
Kimber	15	2	45	1
Salisbury	12	3	26	1

Sussex 1st Innings

N.J. Lenham	b Mortensen	62
D.M. Smith	c Gladwin b Bishop	34
K. Greenfield	c Newman b Malcolm	0
A.P. Wells	b Malcolm	60
*C.M. Wells	c Sharma b Newman	58
I.J. Gould	c Roberts b Bishop	62
A.I.C. Dodemaide	run out	29
†P. Moores	c Sharma b Barnett	29
A.C.S. Pigott	b Malcolm	30
S.J.S. Kimber	c Maher b Malcoln	25
I.D.K. Salisbury	not out	4
Extras	b 9, lb 9, w 3, nb 3	24
Total (100 ov: 371–8)		417

49, 60, 123, 200, 271, 294, 341, 363, 407

Bishop	25	3	86	2
Malcolm	18.1	2	94	4
Mortensen	13	2	31	1
Barnett	11	2	35	1
Newman	24	5	85	1
Sharma	19	3	68	0

Derbyshire 2nd Innings

*K.J. Barnett	c Salisbury b Kimber	86
P.D. Bowler	c Smith b Pigott	12
J.E. Morris	b Dodemaide	4
R. Sharma	c Smith b Dodemaide	17
C. Gladwin	c Greenfield b Salisbury	59
B. Roberts	c Moores b Pigott	11
†B.J.M. Maher	not out	15
P.G. Newman	c Dodemaide b Pigott	2
I.R. Bishop	b Pigott	0
O.H. Mortensen	c Greenfield b Salisbury	0
D.E. Malcolm	not out	0
Extra	b 8, lb 3, w 3, nb 3	17
Total (9 wkts dec)		223

32, 45, 72, 169, 197, 199, 213, 217, 221

Pigott	21	6	69	4
Dodemaide	19	4	64	2
C.M. Wells	4	2	5	0
Salisbury	20	6	58	2
Kimber	4	1	14	1
Smith	1	0	2	0

Umpires: J.H. Harris and P.B. Wight
Toss: Sussex
Derbyshire with the aid of Morris and Maher scored a slow 295–8 on the first day. In contrast Sussex scored at breakneck speed on Monday and had reached 246–7 off 97 overs by the close, helped by some rather inaccurate bowling from Malcolm and Bishop. On the last day, Barnett was dropped early in his innings and then held his side together, ending the match when 5 of the last 20 overs had been delivered.

v SOMERSET (Derby)
July 1, 3, 4,
Drawn. Derbys 6pts, Somerset 2pts

Derbyshire 1st Innings

*K.J. Barnett	c Cleal b Marks	118
P.D. Bowler	c Harden b Jones	54
J.E. Morris	c Roebuck b Cleal	127
R. Sharma	c and b Trump	70
I. Redpath	lbw b Marks	4
K.M. Krikken	b Marks	10
A.E. Warner	lbw b Trump	10
M.A. Holding	c Cleal b Trump	4
†B.J.M. Maher	not out	9
S.J. Base	b Trump	10
O.H. Mortsensen		
Extras	b 9, lb 15, nb 4	28
Total (100 ov: 302–2) (9 wkts dec)		444

179, 223, 376, 393, 401, 412, 416, 429, 444

Jones	25	5	55	1
Foster	22	1	97	0
Cleal	17	3	56	1
Trump	32.2	12	80	4
Marks	41	12	115	3
Roebuck	6	3	17	0

Somerset 1st Innings

P.M. Roebuck	lbw b Holding	7
S.J. Cook	lbw b Mortensen	44
J.J.E. Hardy	c Bowler b Warner	35
C.J. Tavare	b Base	28
R.J. Harden	lbw b Base	34
†N.D. Burns	not out	38
*V.J. Marks	not out	23
M.W. Cleal		
A.M. Jones		
D.J. Foster		
H.R.J. Trump		
Extras	b 4, lb 4, nb 14	22
Total (5 wkts dec, 78 ov)		231

42, 96, 101, 145, 190

Holding	18	3	61	1
Mortensen	21	1	56	1
Warner	13	1	41	1
Base	14	4	40	2
Sharma	10	3	23	0
Barnett	2	0	2	0

Derbyshire 2nd Innings

K.M. Krikken	c Burns b Jones	1
P.D. Bowler	c Tavare b Marks	33
I. Redpath	not out	43
†B.J.M. Maher	not out	2
Extras	lb 7, nb 1	8
Total (2 wkts dec)		87

1, 75

Jones	4	2	2	1
Foster	5	0	10	0
Cleal	5	0	17	0
Trump	13	2	28	0
Marks	10	3	11	1
Harden	2	0	6	0
Hardy	1.4	0	6	0

Somerset 2nd Innings

P.M. Roebuck	lbw b Warner	54
S.J. Cook	c Sharma b Holding	85
J.J.E. Hardy	b Holding	29
C.J. Tavare	c Maher b Holding	5
R.J. Harden	b Mortensen	7
†N.D. Burns	b Mortensen	10
*V.J. Marks	not out	14
M.W. Cleal	b Base	16
H.R.J. Trump	not out	0
Extras	b 2, lb 8, w 1, nb 9	20
Total (7 wkts)		240

110, 173, 185, 196, 200, 215, 236

Holding	17	3	64	3
Mortensen	16	3	46	2
Base	13	3	47	1
Warner	12	0	42	1
Barnett	12	2	31	0

Umpires: J.C. Balderstone and B.J. Meyer
Toss: Derbyshire.
Barnett and Bowler began the match with a splendid partnership of 179, the Derby captain making 118 in 209 minutes. The later stages of Saturday were then brightened by an innings of 93* by Morris. On Monday Derbyshire took their score from 329–2 to 444–9 and then declared. Somerset replied with 231–5 and Marks then closed the inings first thing on Tuesdsay. His side were invited to make 301 off 70 overs and looked well placed at 173–1. Holding then captured 3 wickets and effectively ended their hopes. Cook became the first batsman to reach 2,000 runs in all competitions in 1989.

v ESSEX (Derby)
July 5, 6, 7
Drawn. Essex 7pts, Derbys 5pts

Derbyshire 1st Innings

†B.J.M. Maher	b Childs	8
P.D. Bowler	c Hussain b Childs	26
J.E. Morris	c Pringle b Topley	93
R. Sharma	c Prichard b Childs	29
C. Gladwin	b Childs	0
I. Redpath	lbw b Pringle	0
K.M. Krikken	c Garnham b Topley	1
*P.G. Newman	c Hussain b Topley	4
A.E. Warner	lbw b Topley	0
I.R. Bishop	b Childs	0
D.E. Malcolm	not out	10
Extras	b 9, lb 8, nb 3	20
Total (85.2 ov)		191

46, 51, 140, 140, 142, 152, 166, 170, 171

Lever	10	3	18	0
Pringle	22	7	62	1
Childs	32	15	47	5
Topley	21.2	8	47	4

Essex 1st Innings

B.R. Hardie	c Maher b Newman	1
J.P. Stephenson	b Sharma	93
A.W. Lilley	c Sharma b Newman	11
M.E. Waugh	st Maher b Sharma	26
T.D. Topley	c Newman b Malcolm	0
P.J. Prichard	c Warner b Malcolm	1
N. Hussain	c Gladwin b Warner	28
†M.A. Garnham	c Bowler b Sharma	43
*D.R. Pringle	c and b Sharma	17
J.K. Lever	c and b Sharma	27
J.H. Childs	not out	7
Extras	b 5, lb 28, nb 6	39
Total (88.3 ov)		293

1, 17, 64, 69, 71, 138, 165, 194, 282

Bishop	21	3	52	0
Newman	19	5	55	2
Malcolm	16	3	48	2
Warner	17	7	45	1
Sharma	15.3	4	60	5

Derbyshire 2nd Innings

†B.J.M. Maher	c Hardie b Lever	3
P.D. Bowler	not out	56
J.E. Morris	b Topley	29
R. Sharma	c Hussain b Pringle	24
C. Gladwin	lbw b Childs	1
I. Redpath	c Waugh b Pringle	0
K.M. Krikken	not out	1
Extras		0
Total (5 wkts)		114

19, 60, 89, 105, 110

Lever	8	1	33	1
Pringle	18	5	42	2
Childs	18.5	12	11	1
Topley	10	1	28	1

Umpires: J.C. Balderstone and B. Hassan
Toss: Derbyshire
On a wicket which suited the pace bowlers, Morris batted 205 minutes for his 93 with 17 fours, while the rest of the Derbyshire side struggled. Essex also looked uncomfortable and were 64–3 off 21 overs at the close. Stephenson aided by Lever put on 88 for the 9th wicket, thus providing Essex with an unexpectedly large lead. Derbyshire were still one run in arrears with 7 wickets in hand at stumps. On the last day rain prevented a resumption until mid-afternoon and then after about an hour returned to end the match.

v GLAMORGAN (Derby)

July 22, 24, 25

Won by 9 wkts. Derbys 23pts, Glamorgan 4pts

Glamorgan 1st Innings

*A.R. Butcher	c Barnett b Malcolm	37
H. Morris	lbw b Holding	26
M.J. Cann	c Newman b Holding	1
M.P. Maynard	c and b Holding	3
A. Dale	c Maher b Holding	4
G.C. Holmes	b Malcolm	6
K.A.Somaia	c Holding b Warner	6
†C.P. Metson	c Bowler b Holding	40
S.J. Dennis	c Maher b Holding	38
S.L. Watkin	c Barnett b Malcolm	7
S.R. Barwick	not out	0
Extras	lb 9, nb 14	23
Total (72.1 ov)		191

61, 65, 75, 85, 89, 93, 112, 164, 191, 236, 237

Malcolm	18	6	37	3
Base	11	1	40	0
Holding	15.1	3	57	6
Newman	13	2	25	0
Warner	15	6	23	1

Derbyshire 1st Innings

*K.J. Barnett	lbw b Dennis	1
P.D. Bowler	b Barwick	53
J.E. Morris	b Somaia	134
R. Sharma	b Barwick	10
B. Roberts	c Metson b Dennis	40
†B.J.M. Maher	lbw b Holmes	22
P.G. Newman	c Butcher b Somaia	5
A.E. Warner	not out	17
S.J. Base	run out	2
M.A. Holding	b Holmes	8
D.E. Malcolm	b Holmes	25
Extras	lb 16, w 1, nb 4	21
Total (100 ov: 291–8)		338

2, 127, 157, 230, 273, 281, 283, 291, 300

Watkin	19	2	62	0
Dennis	26	10	65	2
Barwick	25	4	72	2
Somaia	20	6	69	2
Dale	7	1	26	0
Holmes	10.4	2	28	3

Glamorgan 2nd Innings

*A.R. Butcher	b Warner	43
H. Morris	c sub b Base	37
M.J. Cann	b Holding	40
†C.P. Metson	c Maher b Holding	8
M.P. Maynard	lbw b Base	21
A. Dale	not out	41
G.C. Holmes	lbw b Base	21
K.A. Somaia	b Holding	6
S.J. Dennis	c Newman b Holding	5
S.L. Watkin	c Maher b Malcolm	3
S.R. Barwick	lbw b Malcolm	0
Extras	b 5, lb 6, nb 5	16
Total		241

65, 99, 128, 134, 156, 191, 220, 234, 241

Malcolm	21.5	9	55	2
Base	18	4	59	3
Warner	17	5	40	1
Holding	23	6	66	4
Barnett	3	0	10	0

Derbyshire 2nd Innings

*K.J. Barnett	not out	51
P.D. Bowler	lbw b Holmes	17
J.E. Morris	not out	16
Extras	lb 6, w 2, nb 5	13
Total (1 wkt)		97

53

Watkin	5	0	24	0
Dennis	5	2	19	0
Barwick	9.5	5	26	0
Holmes	9	1	22	1

Umpires: B. Leadbeater and D.R. Shepherd
Toss: Derbyshire

Put in to bat, the visitors were overwhelmed by Holding and Derbyshire were 89–1 with Morris 56* by the close of the first day. Morris went on to 134 on Monday, but in very hot conditions Derbyshire failed to obtain full batting points, Maher making 22 off 75 balls. Glamorgan began the last day at 101–2, but with Holding still very effective, Derbyshire only required 97 in the last innings and Barnett made certain of victory.

v SURREY (Derby)

July 29, 31, Aug 1

Won by 9 wkts. Derbys 24pts, Surrey 4pts

Derbyshire 1st Innings

*K.J. Barnett	c Stewart b Frost	50
P.D. Bowler	b Murphy	106
R. Sharma	c Stewart b Feltham	23
C.J. Adams	c Stewart b Murphy	25
T.J.G. O'Gorman	lbw b Murphy	4
†B.J.M. Maher	lbw b Greig	11
P.G. Newman	lbw b Greig	0
A.E. Warner	b Murphy	0
I.R. Bishop	b Murphy	25
D.E. Malcolm	c Alikhan b Murphy	51
O.H. Mortensen	not out	2
Extras	b 4, lb 16, w 1, nb 2	23
Total (76.3 ov)		320

82, 127, 164, 172, 236, 236, 237, 242, 312

M.P. Bicknell	16	1	69	0
Feltham	13	4	35	1
Murphy	24.3	6	97	6
Frost	10	1	50	1
Medlycott	5	0	34	0
Greig	8	3	15	2

Surrey 1st Innings

G.S. Clinton	b Malcolm	0
D.J. Bicknell	lbw b Malcolm	9
R.I. Alikhan	c Sharma b Mortensen	2
†A.J. Stewart	lbw b Malcolm	0
G.P. Thorpe	c Maher b Warner	44
*I.A. Greig	c Bowler b Warner	43
K.T. Medlycott	lbw b Bishop	1
M.A. Feltham	b Bishop	0
M.P. Bicknell	b Bishop	6
A.J. Murphy	not out	0
M. Frost	b Bishop	0
Extras	b 1, lb 2, w 1, nb 1	5
Total (42.5 ov)		110

7, 12, 12, 14, 96, 99, 99, 108, 110

Bishop	12.5	2	31	4
Mortensen	7	1	13	1
Malcolm	8	3	19	3
Newman	6	1	18	0
Warner	9	1	26	2

Surrey 2nd Innings

G.S. Clinton	lbw b Mortensen	60
D.J. Bicknell	c Maher b Warner	16
†A.J. Stewart	c Barnett b Warner	0
R.I. Alikhan	lbw b Warner	11
G.P. Thorpe	not out	53
*I.A. Greig	b Mortensen	9
K.T. Medlycott	c Newman b Bishop	35
M.A. Feltham	c Bowler b Malcolm	21
M.P. Bicknell	c Maher b Malcolm	0
A.J. Murphy	c Sharma b Malcolm	0
M. Frost	c Bowler b Mortensen	0
Extras	b 1, lb 10, w 1	12
Total		217

45, 45, 65, 121, 137, 189, 215, 216, 216

Bishop	11	3	27	1
Mortensen	18.3	5	39	3
Malcolm	9	0	24	3
Warner	16	2	45	3
Newman	20	3	68	0
Barnett	1	0	3	0

Derbyshire 2nd Innings

P.D. Bowler	c Stewart b M.P. Bicknell	0
R. Sharma	not out	4
T.J.G. O'Gorman	not out	6
Extras		0
Total (1 wkt)		10

0

M.P. Bicknell	3	2	1	1
Murphy	2.4	1	9	0

Umpires: J.D. Bond and D.J. Constant
Toss: Derbyshire

Derbyshire had the game under their control at the end of the first day, with Surrey reeling at 76–4 off 30 overs in reply to 320 off 76.3 overs. Thorpe and Greig continued their unbroken stand on Monday, but once they were gone the innings folded. The follow on was enforced and Surrey owed their second innings fortunes to a series of dropped catches. Even so they only had a lead of two runs with four wickets left when the last day began. Just five runs and 30 balls later they were all out and well before lunch Derbyshire won the game.

v HAMPSHIRE (Derby)

August 5, 7, 8

Drawn. Hants 7pts, Derbys 2pts

Derbyshire 1st Innings

*K.J. Barnett	c Maru b Bakker	33
P.D. Bowler	lbw b Bakker	0
J.E. Morris	b Connor	20
R. Sharma	c Parks b Connor	5
T.J.G. O'Gorman	c Parks b Bakker	43
†B.J.M. Maher	c Parks b Connor	15
A.E. Warner	b Bakker	0
F.A. Griffith	b Connor	2
P.G. Newman	c Terry b Marshall	6
M.A. Holding	b Connor	34
O.H. Mortensen	not out	0
Extras	lb 10, w 1, nb 9	20
Total (62.1 ov)		178

4, 60, 60, 72, 132, 134, 134, 134, 178

Marshall	10	1	41	1
Bakker	19	5	53	4
Connor	20.1	3	50	5
Maru	8	2	12	0
James	5	1	12	0

Hampshire 1st Innings

V.P. Terry	c Griffith b Sharma	180
C.L. Smith	c Newman b Holding	52
K.D. James	c and b Holding	1
R.A. Smith	c and b Griffith	40
*M.C.J. Nicholas	c Newman b Griffith	121
J.R. Wood	c Holding b Sharma	21
M.D. Marshall	not out	27
†R.J. Parks	not out	4
R.J. Maru		
C.A. Connor		
P.J. Bakker		
Extras	b 7, lb 7, w 2, nb 10	26
Total (100 ov: 254–3) (6 wkts dec)		472

115, 119, 195, 343, 416, 464

Holding	30	9	76	2
Mortensen	12	4	21	0
Newman	31	8	107	0
Warner	31	9	78	0
Griffith	18	1	81	2
Sharma	11	3	44	2
Barnett	6	0	35	0
Bowler	3	0	16	0

Derbyshire 2nd Innings

*K.J. Barnett	b Marshall	106
P.D. Bowler	c Nicholas b Marshall	0
J.E. Morris	b Marshall	65
R. Sharma	c Parks b Marshall	2
T.J.G. O'Gorman	c Parks b James	15
†B.J.M. Maher	not out	56
F.A. Griffith	b Maru	13
A.E. Warner	c Nicholas b Marshall	23
P.G. Newman	lbw b Bakker	12
M.A. Holding	lbw b Marshall	10
O.H. Mortensen	not out	0
Extras	lb 18, w 1, nb 5	24
Total (9 wkts)		326

5, 180, 183, 186, 216, 246, 274, 308, 324

Marshall	30	9	69	6
Bakker	25	7	60	1
Connor	15	1	57	0
Maru	24	7	58	1
James	18	6	35	1
C.L. Smith	11	8	10	0
Nicholas	6	1	19	0

Umpires: J.H. Hampshire and N.T. Plews
Toss: Derbyshire

Deciding to bat, Derbyshire found runs difficult to acquire and Connor and Bakker dismissed the home side for 178. Hampshire were 105 without loss at Saturday's close, but had batted 49 overs. Terry reached his 100 on Monday in 4½ hours and Hampshire eventually declared at 472–6, Nicholas having made 121 off 188 balls. Derbyshire began the final day at 72–1. Barnett completed his 27th 100 for Derbyshire, though it was the obdurate Maher who saved the match, batting through 60 overs for his 56.

v LANCASHIRE (Chesterfield)

August 9, 10, 11

Drawn. Derbys 8pts, Lancs 8pts

Lancashire 1st Innings		
G.D. Lloyd	c Maher b Bishop	1
N.J. Speak	c Sharma b Newman	1
G. Fowler	c Adams b Jean-Jacques	83
N.H. Fairbrother	c Base b Jean-Jacques	161
T.E. Jesty	c Maher b Bishop	12
M. Watkinson	b Bishop	2
Wasim Akram	c Maher b Newman	16
†W.K. Hegg	c Barnett b Jean-Jacques	15
P.A.J. DeFreitas	c Base b Jean-Jacques	28
I.D. Austin	not out	13
J.D. Fitton	c Newman b Sharma	8
Extras	b 5, lb 13, w 2, nb 12	32
Total (75.2 ov)		372

2, 14, 270, 279, 285, 294, 312, 351, 355

Bishop	16	3	39	3
Newman	18	1	88	2
Base	15	1	88	0
Jean-Jacques	16	0	93	4
Sharma	10.2	2	46	1

Derbyshire 1st Innings		
*K.J. Barnett	c Hegg b DeFreitas	42
P.D. Bowler	c Hegg b Wasim Akram	4
J.E. Morris	c Speak b DeFreitas	16
R. Sharma	c Hegg b DeFreitas	7
T.J.G. O'Gorman	lbw b Wasim Akram	39
C.J. Adams	c Hegg b Wasim Akram	79
†B.J.M. Maher	c Hegg b Wasim Akram	36
P.G. Newman	not out	86
I.R. Bishop	c Hegg b DeFreitas	8
M. Jean-Jacques	c Hegg b DeFreitas	1
S.J. Base	lbw b DeFreitas	6
Extras	lb 13, w 1, nb 16	30
Total (89.3 ov)		354

4, 63, 68, 83, 194, 203, 310, 328, 332

Wasim Akram	28	0	103	4
DeFreitas	29.3	5	116	6
Austin	17	5	53	0
Watkinson	7	2	39	0
Fitton	8	1	30	0

Lancashire 2nd Innings		
G.D. Lloyd	c Adams b Bishop	5
N.J. Speak	c Adams b Base	8
G. Fowler	c Adams b Newman	58
N.H. Fairbrother	b Base	17
T.E. Jesty	not out	5
I.D. Austin	c Maher b Jean-Jacques	2
Wasim Akram	run out	42
M. Watkinson	lbw b Base	22
†W.K. Hegg	c Maher b Bishop	9
P.A.J. DeFreitas	run out	1
J.D. Fitton	b Base	12
Extras	b 6, lb 5, w 4, nb 5	20
Total		201

13, 17, 51, 71, 151, 156, 175, 179, 200

Bishop	22	9	41	2
Base	22.3	5	80	4
Jean-Jacques	10	3	33	1
Newman	9	1	36	1

Derbyshire 2nd Innings		
*K.J. Barnett	c Hegg b Austin	29
P.D. Bowler	c Hegg b DeFreitas	63
J.E. Morris	c Fowler b Austin	28
R. Sharma	lbw b Austin	0
T.J.G. O'Gorman	c Hegg b DeFreitas	29
C.J. Adams	run out	4
†B.J.M. Maher	b Wasim Akram	0
P.G. Newman	not out	6
I.R. Bishop	c Hegg b DeFreitas	0
M. Jean-Jacques	not out	16
Extras	lb 5, w 2, nb 11	18
Total (8 wkts)		193

58, 95, 95, 159, 169, 169, 169, 169

Wasim Akram	15	4	50	1
DeFreitas	18	2	63	3
Watkinson	6	0	30	0
Austin	13.5	2	45	3

Umpires: K.E. Palmer and D.S. Thompsett

Toss: Derbyshire

Fairbrother hit 161 off 124 balls to produce a Lancashire total of 372 off 75.2 overs. Derby replied with 60–1 off 10 overs when rain ended play on the first day. The home side fought back on the second day with a 7th wicket stand of 107 in 34 overs. Lancashire were 64–3 at the close. On the final afternoon Derbyshire needed 201 in 53 overs, but were handicapped by poor light and collapsed from 159–3 to 169–8. Hegg equalled the world record with 11 catches in the match.

v YORKSHIRE (Chesterfield)

August 24, 25, 26, 28

Won by 3 wkts. Derbys 20pts, Yorks 4pts

Yorkshire 1st Innings		
M.D Moxon	lbw b Base	14
A.A. Metcalfe	b Bishop	0
†R.J. Blakey	lbw b Base	6
K. Sharp	b Base	9
P.E. Robinson	b Base	34
D. Byas	c Sharma b Base	0
*P. Carrick	c Maher b Base	3
C.S. Pickles	c Barnett b Base	24
A. Sidebottom	c Maher b Jean-Jacques	13
P.W. Jarvis	c Maher b Bishop	0
P.A. Booth	not out	5
Extras	b 6, lb 11, nb 11	28
Total (39.5 ov)		136

6, 20, 34, 50, 58, 80, 85, 122, 122

Bishop	12	4	24	2
Base	19.5	5	60	7
Jean-Jacques	8	1	35	1

Derbyshire 1st Innings		
*K.J. Barnett	c Blakey b Jarvis	0
P.D. Bowler	lbw b Jarvis	1
J.E. Morris	c Blakey b Jarvis	7
R. Sharma	c Booth b Sidebottom	6
T.J.G. O'Gorman	c Blakey b Jarvis	44
C.J. Adams	lbw b Sidebottom	24
†B.J.M. Maher	c Booth b Sidebottom	6
F.A. Griffith	c Byas b Sidebottom	1
I.R. Bishop	lbw b Jarvis	7
M. Jean-Jacques	lbw b Jarvis	0
S.J. Base	not out	0
Extras	lb 4, nb 2	6
Total (35 ov)		102

0, 1, 8, 22, 75, 87, 89, 89, 95

Jarvis	13	4	27	6
Sidebottom	14	2	47	4
Pickles	5	1	16	0
Carrick	3	1	8	0

Yorkshire 2nd Innings		
M.D. Moxon	c Griffith b Jean-Jacques	27
A.A. Metcalfe	c Adams b Base	3
†R.J. Blakey	c Maher b Base	27
K. Sharp	retired hurt	15
P.E. Robinson	c Bowler b Base	23
D. Byas	b Base	40
C.S. Pickles	c O'Gorman b Bishop	0
*P. Carrick	c Bowler b Bishop	5
A. Sidebottom	b Base	6
P.W. Jarvis	c Bowler b Bishop	12
P.A. Booth	not out	8
Extras	lb 6, w 3, nb 9	18
Total		184

4, 39, 78, 124, 125, 135, 150, 163

Bishop	19	5	47	3
Base	18	2	93	5
Griffith	7	1	23	0
Jean-Jacques	7	1	15	1

Derbyshire 2nd Innings		
*K.J. Barnett	c Blakey b Sidebottom	74
P.D. Bowler	lbw b Sidebottom	0
J.E. Morris	lbw b Jarvis	16
R. Sharma	b Sidebottom	43
T.J.G. O'Gorman	c Sidebottom b Booth	1
C.J. Adams	not out	38
†B.J. M. Maher	c Blakey b Sidebottom	0
F.A. Griffith	c Blakey b Sidebottom	5
I.R. Bishop	not out	28
Extras	lb 8, nb 6	14
Total (7 wkts)		219

8, 42, 134, 135, 152, 157, 169

Jarvis	18	1	66	1
Sidebottom	27	4	92	5
Moxon	1	0	4	0
Pickles	6	1	28	0
Booth	12	5	21	1
Carrick	1	1	0	0

Umpires: K.J. Lyons and R.A. White

Toss: Derbyshire

21 wickets fell on the first day as the seam bowlers made the best of a helpful wicket. Bad light ended play 21 overs early with Yorkshire in their second innings 39–1. Friday's play was washed out and on Saturday there was little progress, Yorkshire advancing to 117–3. On Monday after Base had returned a career best 12–153, Derbyshire needed 219 in 84 overs. Barnett held the batting together, but it needed an unbroken 8th wicket stand of 50 to win the match.

v NOTTINGHAMSHIRE (Derby)

Sept 8, 9, 10, 11

Won by 1 wkt. Derbys 23pts, Notts 8pts

Nottinghamshire 1st Innings		
B.C. Broad	c Holding b Jean-Jacques	13
P.R. Pollard	run out	26
*R.T. Robinson	c Maher b Warner	30
P. Johnson	lbw b Warner	6
D.W. Randall	b Base	70
F.D. Stephenson	c Maher b Warner	11
†C.W. Scott	b Jean-Jacques	51
E.E. Hemmings	b Jean-Jacques	47
K.E. Cooper	b Base	12
R.A. Pick	c Maher b Jean-Jacques	7
J.A. Afford	not out	3
Extras	b 9, lb 19, w 2, nb 24	54
Total (83.2 ov)		330

52, 53, 75, 98, 126, 206, 284, 301, 330

Base	24	2	106	2
Jean-Jacques	24.2	4	84	4
Warner	18	4	53	3
Holding	17	1	59	0

Derbyshire 1st Innings		
*K.J. Barnett	c Scott b Cooper	5
P.D. Bowler	lbw b Stephenson	11
J.E. Morris	run out	156
A.M. Brown	c Scott b Cooper	65
B. Roberts	c Scott b Cooper	4
S.C. Goldsmith	b Hemmings	30
†B.J.M. Maher	c Johnson b Hemmings	2
A.E. Warner	c and b Pick	0
M. Jean-Jacques	run out	1
M.A. Holding	not out	0
S.J. Base	b Pick	0
Extras	lb 13, nb 6	19
Total (92.2 ov)		293

12, 18, 191, 207, 287, 289, 291, 293, 293

Stephenson	19	2	75	1
Cooper	19	4	53	3
Afford	24	8	85	0
Pick	15.2	1	50	2
Hemmings	15	7	17	2

Nottinghamshire 2nd Innings		
B.C. Broad	c Maher b Jean-Jacques	17
P.R. Pollard	c Roberts b Jean-Jacques	7
*R.T. Robinson	c Maher b Base	2
P. Johnson	c Maher b Warner	24
D.W. Randall	b Holding	27
F.D. Stephenson	c Barnett b Warner	6
†C.W. Scott	b Warner	14
E.E. Hemmings	c Brown b Holding	2
K.E. Cooper	b Warner	2
R.A. Pick	c Maher b Holding	4
J.A. Afford	not out	0
Extras	b 1, w 1, nb 12	14
Total		119

27, 31, 31, 80, 84, 96, 107, 110, 119

Base	7	1	34	1
Jean-Jacques	7	0	33	2
Warner	9.4	1	18	4
Holding	10	1	33	3

Derbyshire 2nd Innings		
*K.J. Barnett	c Robinson b Cooper	14
P.D. Bowler	c Pollard b Afford	58
J.E. Morris	c Johnson b Pick	21
A.M. Brown	c Scott b Pick	2
B. Roberts	b Pick	12
S.C. Goldsmith	c Scott b Afford	17
†B.J.M. Maher	b Hemmings	1
A.E. Warner	c Robinson b Afford	2
M. Jean-Jacques	b Pick	2
M.A. Holding	not out	13
S.J. Base	not out	8
Extras	b 1, lb 7, nb 2	10
Total (9 wkts)		160

23, 68, 74, 93, 119, 126, 129, 138, 139

Stephenson	8	0	34	0
Cooper	4	0	23	1
Afford	12	5	25	3
Pick	12	1	41	4
Hemmings	19	8	29	1

Umpires: J.C. Balderstone and P.J. Eele

Toss: Derbyshire

Play began at 4.15 after rain delayed the start on the first day and after 16 overs with Notts 53–2 bad light ended play for the day. Notts hit out on the second day to gain full batting points, but Morris and Brown fought back the home side nearly matching their opponents. In bad light on the second evening Notts collapsed to 96–6. There was no play on the third day. A stout innings by Bowler – eighth man out – gave Derbyshire victory.

Essex

President: T.N. Pearce
Chairman: D.J. Insole
Secretary: P.J. Edwards, County Ground, New Writtle Street, Chelmsford, CM2 0PG *Tel:* 0245 354533
Coach: R. Richards
Captain: G.A. Gooch
Foundation of Present Club: January 1876, Chelmsford
First First-Class Match: Essex v Leicestershire (Leyton) May 1894
County Champions: 1979, 1983, 1984, 1986
Gillette/NatWest Trophy: Winners 1985
Benson & Hedges Cup: Winners 1979
Sunday League Champions: 1981, 1984, 1985
Refuge Cup: Winners 1989

Summary of Results in 1989
Britannic Assurance County Championship: Played 22, Won 13, Lost 2, Drawn 7, Position 2nd
NatWest Bank Trophy: Lost in first round
Benson & Hedges Cup: Lost in final
Refuge Assurance Sunday League: Played 16, Won 11, Lost 4, No Result 1, Position 2nd
Refuge Assurance Cup: Winners

From left, back: *Paul Prichard, Mark Ilott, Kevin Thomas, Adam Seymour, Alan van Lint, Nadeem Shahid, Nick Knight, Keigh Butler.* Centre: *Ray Cole (Physiotherapist), Mike Garnham, Geoff Miller, Don Topley, John Stephenson, Alan Lilley, John Childs, Mark Waugh, Robert Pook.* Front: *Keith Fletcher, Neil Foster, Derek Pringle, Graham Gooch (Captain), John Lever, Brian Hardie, David East.*
Allsport/Adrian Murrell

Having won the Championship title in 1983, 1984 and 1986, Essex seemed determined to recapture the crown in 1989. Few would argue that, day in day out, the county is the strongest on the circuit over the last decade. The first half of 1989 proved one of almost uninterrupted success. Mark Waugh, now had a secure place in the side and made one appreciate the batting strength of Australia, that they were able to reject this talented and attractive batsmen. Statisticians were rewarded with a pleasing curiosity when the Waugh brothers both hit hundreds in the Essex v Australians match.

Gooch was away with England for much of the summer, appearing in only 13 first-class matches for the county and failed to reach 1,000 runs in the Championship, but, when present, he remained the side's best batsman. The most pleasing feature of the batting was the development of the youngsters. Hussain joined the county after the University season and did so well that not only was he elected 'Young Cricketer of the Year', but he gained a place on the West Indian tour; Stephenson found himself opening for England as Dexter juggled inadequately with his resources.

Turning to the bowling, Pringle, who captained the team in Gooch's absence, had the best summer of his career – his first-class wicket total of 94 was the highest in the country and of the regular bowlers qualified for England, his was the best record. Pringle was well supported by Foster and the left-arm spin of Childs. The latter seems to have come to life in Essex, having been rather unsuccessful in his previous existence, he was unlucky not to be in the England side. The old warhorse, Lever, in his farewell summer, still bowled with accuracy, even if he did fail in the last gasp of the Benson and Hedges Cup Final. Though Essex were losing finalists at Lord's, they later beat their opponents, Notts, in the Refuge Assurance Cup in the Edgbaston Final.

The controversial point of the season was the 25-point penalty which deprived Essex of the Championship. With the Worcester wickets causing much comment during the first half of the year, Essex were unfortunate to say the least.

ONE DAY AWAY MATCHES

The full scorecard of each of Essex's away matches will be found in the sections for the respective home teams.

Refuge Assurance League

Canterbury: April 23
Kent 135 (40 ov) lost to Essex 136–4 (35.4 ov) by 6 wkts. Essex 4pts, Kent 0pts.

Bristol: May 21
Gloucs 167–7 (40 ov) lost to Essex 168–1 (39.1 ov) by 9 wkts. Essex4 pts, Gloucs 0pts.

The Oval: June 11
Surrey 192 (40 ov) beat Essex 160 (38.2 ov) by 32 runs. Surrey 4pts, Essex 0pts.

Horsham: July 2
Sussex 154–7 (40 ov) lost to Essex 157–4 (36 ov) by 6 wkts. Essex 4pts, Sussex 0pts.

Neath: July 9
Essex 205–3 (40 ov) (M.E. Waugh 112*) beat Glamorgan 158 (36.5 ov) by 47 runs. Essex 4pts, Glam 0pts.

Trent Bridge: July 30
Notts 197–4 (37 ov) beat Essex 113 (22.4 ov) K. Saxelby 5–36) on faster scoring rate. Notts 4pts, Essex 0pts.

Old Trafford: August 13
Lancs 135–9 (28 ov) drew with Essex 53–0 (10.4 ov). Essex 2pts, Lancs 2pts.

Northampton: August 27
Essex 144–9 (40 ov) lost to Northants 145–7 (39.4 ov) by 3 wkts. Northants 4pts, Essex 0pts.

Benson and Hedges Cup

Hove: April 25, 26
Essex 232–7 (55 ov) beat Sussex 169 (50.4 ov) by 63 runs. Essex 2pts, Sussex 0pts.

Canterbury: May 9
Kent 192–7 (55 ov) lost to Essex 196–6 (53.3 ov) by 4 wkts. Essex 2pts, Kent 0pts.

Taunton: June 14 (Semi Final)
Essex 293–5 (55 ov) beat Somerset 289 (55 ov) (C.J. Tavare 104*) by 4 runs.

Lord's: July 15 (Final)
Essex 243–7 (55 ov) lost to Notts 244–7 (55 ov) by 3 wkts.

NatWest Bank Trophy

Taunton: June 28
Somerset 276–6 (60 ov) (P.M. Roebuck 102, C.J. Tavaré 101) beat Essex 221 (54.5 ov) by 55 runs.

Refuge Assurance Cup

Worcester: September 6
Essex 211–7 (40 ov) beat Worcs 110 (34.1 ov) by 101 runs.

REFUGE ASSURANCE LEAGUE

v MIDDLESEX (Chelmsford)

April 30
Won by 8 wkts. Essex 4pts, Middx 0pts

Middlesex				
J.D. Carr	b Topley			12
†P.R. Downton	c Pringle b Gooch			7
*M.W. Gatting	lbw b Stephenson			25
M.R. Ramprakash	c Garnham b Stephenson			8
J.E. Emburey	run out			1
R.O. Butcher	b Topley			29
K.R. Brown	c Stephenson b Topley			4
J.F. Sykes	b Stephenson			13
S.P. Hughes	b Foster			5
A.R.C. Fraser	not out			11
N.G. Cowans	c Garnham b Foster			4
Extras	lb 6, w 4, nb 1			11
Total (40 ov)				130
11, 27, 54, 55, 76, 94, 100, 113, 118				
Foster	8	2	12	2
Pringle	8	0	33	0
Gooch	8	1	20	1
Topley	8	0	32	3
Stephenson	8	0	27	3

Essex				
*G.A. Gooch	not out			76
B.R. Hardie	c Downton b Fraser			18
P.J. Prichard	c Cowans b Fraser			11
M.E. Waugh	not out			16
A.W. Lilley				
J.P. Stephenson				
D.R. Pringle				
G. Miller				
†M.A. Garnham				
N.A. Foster				
T.D. Topley				
Extras	lb 10, w 1, nb 2			13
Total (2 wkts. 36.4 ov)				134
58, 88				
Cowans	6	4	3	0
Hughes	6.4	1	29	0
Carr	8	1	28	0
Fraser	8	0	35	2
Emburey	8	1	29	0

Umpires: J.D. Bond and N.T. Plews
Toss: Essex
Excellent seam bowling by Foster meant that Middlesex's batsmen never looked comfortable and the side were dismissed for a very modest 130. Gooch in reply hit a well judged 76 off 102 balls with a six and 10 fours, bringing Essex their second Sunday win of 1989.

v DERBYSHIRE (Chelmsford)

May 7
Won by 1 run. Essex 4pts, Derbys 0pts

Essex				
*G.A. Gooch	c and b Base			22
B.R. Hardie	b Mortensen			36
P.J. Prichard	b Sharma			1
M.E. Waugh	c Roberts b Sharma			6
D.R. Pringle	b Roberts			13
J.P. Stephenson	b Newman			25
A.W. Lilley	b Newman			13
G. Miller	run out			4
†M.A. Garnham	not out			8
T.D. Topley	not out			7
J.K. Lever				
Extras	b 2, lb 13, w 3, nb 1			19
Total (8 wkts, 40 ov)				154
40, 45, 53, 85, 93, 125, 136, 136				
Newman	8	0	22	2
Mortensen	8	1	38	1
Base	8	1	20	1
Holding	8	0	30	0
Sharma	6	0	17	2
Roberts	2	0	12	1

Derbyshire				
*K.J. Barnett	b Pringle			2
P.D. Bowler	c Gooch b Topley			58
J.E. Morris	b Pringle			1
B. Roberts	run out			5
R. Sharma	c Prichard b Topley			10
S.C. Goldsmith	not out			37
†B.J.M. Maher	c Topley b Pringle			17
M.A. Holding	b Gooch			2
P.G. Newman	run out			3
S.J. Base				
O.H. Mortensen				
Extras	b 4, lb 8, w 5, nb 1			18
Total (8 wkts, 40 ov)				153
13, 15, 31, 54, 105, 143, 146, 153				
Lever	8	1	17	0
Pringle	8	1	23	3
Gooch	8	1	37	1
Miller	8	1	22	0
Topley	8	0	42	2

Umpires: D.O. Oslear and R. Palmer
Toss: Derbyshire
In a game where bowlers dominated the proceedings, Essex managed to win by one run, when Newman was run out off the last ball. The victory meant that Essex retained the lead in the table.

PLAYERS

Keith Andrew BUTLER *b* 20.1.1971 Camden Town; Promising right hand batsman; played for Essex v Cambridge Univ in 1989

John Henry CHILDS *b* 15.8.1951 Plymouth; talented slow left arm bowler; left hand batsman; debut 1985; previously played for Gloucs 1975 to 1984; 2 Tests for England in 1988

David Edward EAST *b* 27.7.1959 Clapton; wicketkeeper; right hand batsman; debut 1981; broke a finger in April 1989 and missed almost all the season

Neil Alan FOSTER *b* 6.5.1963 Colchester; right arm fast medium bowler; lower order right hand batsman; debut 1980; 28 Tests for England, including three in 1989; chosen to tour South Africa 1989–90

Michael Anthony GARNHAM *b* 20.8.1960 Johannesburg; wicketkeeper; right hand batsman; joined Essex staff in 1989 and made debut following injury to East; previously played for Gloucs, Leics and Cambs

Graham Alan GOOCH *b* 23.7.1953 Leytonstone; hard hitting right hand batsman; right arm medium pace bowler; debut 1973; 73 Tests for England including 5 in 1989; headed Essex batting averages in 1989; but not so successful for England; chosen as captain of England team to West Indies 1989–90

Brian Ross HARDIE *b* 14.1.1950 Stenhousemuir; sound right hand batsman; debut 1973; previously played for Scotland

Nasser HUSSAIN *b* 28.3.1968 Madras; very promising right hand batsman; debut 1987; capped by county August 19 1989; chosen to tour West Indies 1989–90

Mark Christopher ILOTT *b* 27.8.1970 Watford; Left arm medium fast bowler; left hand batsman; debut 1988 in one Championship match; played in four Championship games in 1989

John Stephenson, one of Essex's Test debutants of 1989.

Allsport

John Kenneth LEVER *b* 24.2.1949 Stepney; Accurate left arm fast medium bowler; lower order right hand batsman; debut 1967; announced his retirement at end of 1989 season; played 21 Tests for England between 1976 and 1986

Alan William LILLEY *b* 8.5.1959 Ilford; Middle order right hand batsman; debut 1978; scoring 100 in first match

Geoffrey MILLER *b* 8.9.1952 Chesterfield; off break bowler; right hand batsman; debut 1987; previously played for Derbyshire 1973 to 1986 and is returning to Derbys for 1990; played 34 Tests for England 1976 to 1984

Paul John PRICHARD *b* 7.1.1965 Billericay; Middle order right hand batsman; debut 1984

Derek Raymond PRINGLE *b* 18.9.1958 Nairobi; very competitive all rounder; right hand batsman; right arm medium fats bowler; debut 1978; played for Cambridge Univ 1979–82; 21 Tests for England including 2 in 1989; went to India for Nehru Cup and is selected for England A to Zimbabwe

Nadeem SHAHID *b* 23.4.1969 Karachi; promising right hand batsman; debut for Essex v Leics 1989

John Patrick STEPHENSON *b* 14.3.1965 Stebbing; right hand batsman; occasional right arm medium pace bowler; debut 1985

Thomas Donald TOPLEY *b* 25.2.1964 Canterbury; right arm medium fast bowler; right hand batsman; debut 1985 (also played one match for Surrey in same year); took 3 wickets in 4 balls v Glamorgan (Swansea) 1989

Mark Edward WAUGH *b* 2.6.1965 Canterbury, NSW; attractive right hand batsman; right arm medium pace change bowler; debut 1988; also plays for New South Wales; twin brother of S.R. Waugh (Austr) and in the Essex v Australians match of 1989, both brothers scored 100s, but for opposing sides

REFUGE ASSURANCE LEAGUE

v HAMPSHIRE (Chelmsford)

May 14

Won by 3 wkts. Essex 4pts, Hants 0pts

Hampshire		
*M.C.J. Nicholas	c Lilley b Lever	7
V.P. Terry	c Garnham b Foster	3
D.R. Turner	c Gooch b Pringle	66
R.J. Scott	run out	10
R.A. Smith	c Prichard b Topley	21
K.D. James	run out	4
S.T. Jefferies	b Pringle	20
†R.J. Parks	run out	0
N.G. Cowley	c Foster b Pringle	7
C.A. Connor	not out	3
P.J. Bakker	not out	1
Extras	lb 10, w 4	14
Total (9 wkts, 40 ov)		156

8, 11, 35, 81, 107, 135, 136, 151, 151

Lever	8	2	17	1
Foster	8	1	16	1
Gooch	8	0	36	0
Pringle	8	2	30	3
Topley	8	0	47	1

Essex		
*G.A. Gooch	b Bakker	63
B.R. Hardie	lbw b Cowley	12
J.P. Stephenson	c Turner b Cowley	12
M.E. Waugh	b Jefferies	22
P.J. Prichard	c Connor b Jefferies	18
D.R. Pringle	b Jefferies	3
A.W. Lilley	not out	14
†M.A. Garnham	c Cowley b Jefferies	3
N.A. Foster	not out	2
T.D. Topley		
J.K. Lever		
Extras	lb 5, w 2, nb 1	8
Total (7 wkts, 40 ov)		157

48, 81, 96, 126, 135, 136, 152

Jefferies	8	0	39	4
Connor	8	1	32	0
Bakker	8	1	31	1
Cowley	8	0	33	2
James	8	0	17	0

Umpires: P.J. Eele and R. Julian
Toss: Essex

On a wicket helping the bowlers, Hampshire prospered due to a sound innings by Turner, who hit 7 fours and a six. Essex, growing fat on victory, then took matters rather easily and some competitive cricket by Hampshire nearly upset the leaders. As it was a single off the last ball brought victory.

v SOMERSET (Chelmsford)

May 28

Won by 47 runs. Essex 4pts, Somerset 0pts

Essex		
*B.R. Hardie	c Bartlett b Roebuck	49
J.P. Stephenson	b Jones	16
A.W. Lilley	c Burns b Palmer	21
M.E. Waugh	not out	81
P.J. Prichard	c Bartlett b Palmer	1
†M.A. Garnham	c Bartlett b Mallender	3
G. Miller	not out	29
K.A. Butler		
T.D. Topley		
J.K. Lever		
J.H. Childs		
Extras	b 8, lb 10	18
Total (5 wkts, 40 ov)		218

44, 96, 100, 103, 121

Mallender	8	0	51	1
Foster	4	0	17	0
Marks	8	1	21	0
Jones	7	0	44	1
Palmer	7	1	40	2
Roebuck	6	0	27	1

Somerset		
S.J. Cook	run out	20
P.M. Roebuck	c Hardie b Stephenson	58
R.J. Bartlett	run out	8
C.J. Tavare	run out	6
R.J. Harden	b Miller	14
*V.J. Marks	b Lever	20
†N.D. Burns	not out	22
G.V. Palmer	b Lever	3
N.A. Mallender	not out	13
A.N. Jones		
D.J. Foster		
Extras	lb 3, w 1, nb 3	7
Total (7 wkts, 40 ov)		171

38, 64, 75, 98, 124, 142, 148

Topley	8	0	38	0
Lever	7	1	22	2
Childs	8	0	28	0
Miller	8	0	45	1
Stephenson	8	0	30	1
Butler	1	0	5	0

Umpires: P.B. Wight and D.S. Thompsett
Toss: Essex

Essex continued their run of success by recording their sixth Sunday win out of six matches, despite the absence of their three England players. Waugh hit 81 off 55 balls to produce a total which Somerset never looked like matching.

v LEICESTESHIRE (Chelmsford)

June 18

Won by 9 wkts. Essex 4pts, Leics 0pts

Leicestershire 1st Innings		
L. Potter	c Garnham b Lever	0
*N.E. Briers	c Waugh b Foster	10
J.J. Whitaker	b Gooch	46
P. Willey	c Prichard b Gooch	25
J.D.R. Benson	c Pringle b Foster	13
†P. Whitticase	c Stephenson b Foster	10
C.C. Lewis	not out	32
W.K.M. Benjamin	not out	41
P.M. Such		
G.J. Parsons		
J.P. Agnew		
Extras	lb 11, w 3, nb 1	15
Total (6 wkts, 40 ov)		192

0, 22, 80, 90, 110, 120

Lever	8	3	36	1
Foster	8	0	30	3
Childs	4	0	22	0
Pringle	8	1	52	0
Gooch	8	1	19	2
Stephenson	4	0	22	0

Essex		
*G.A. Gooch	not out	111
B.R. Hardie	b Potter	67
M.E. Waugh	not	2
N. Hussain		
P.J. Prichard		
J.P. Stephenson		
D.R. Pringle		
†M.A. Garnham		
N.A. Foster		
J.H. Childs		
J.K. Lever		
Extras	b 1, lb 6, w 4, nb 2	13
Total (1 wkt, 37 ov)		193

178

Benjamin	7	0	32	0
Agnew	7	1	26	0
Parsons	8	0	32	0
Such	5	0	34	0
Willey	5	0	30	0
Lewis	3	0	16	0
Potter	2	0	16	1

Umpires: J.W. Holder and K.J. Lyons
Toss: Leicestershire

After being beaten at The Oval on the previous Sunday, Essex returned to success at home. Leicestershire were thoroughly outplayed, with Gooch hitting 111 off 111 balls and 15 fours.

Far left: *Graham Gooch, Essex skipper and leader in the county's Championship batting averages in 1989.* Left: *All-rounder Derek Pringle, leader in the bowling averages.*

Allsport/Adrian Murrell

REFUGE ASSURANCE LEAGUE

v WARWICKSHIRE (Ilford)

June 25

Won by 4 wkts. Essex 4pts, Warwicks 0pts

Warwickshire		
*T.A. Lloyd	c Garnham b Lever	24
G.W. Humpage	st Garnham b Childs	26
Asif Din	c Garnham b Childs	3
P.A. Smith	c Stephenson b Miller	23
D.A. Reeve	not out	70
A.J. Moles	run out	19
N.M.K. Smith	run out	14
G.C. Small	c Hussain b Lever	2
A.A. Donald	not out	17
†K.J. Piper		
T.A. Munton		
Extras	lb 12, w 5, nb 1	18
Total (7 wkts, 40 ov)		216

45, 56, 59, 105, 149, 171, 192

Pringle	8	0	53	0
Lever	8	0	44	2
Stephenson	8	1	40	0
Childs	8	0	23	2
Miller	7	0	35	1
Waugh	1	0	9	0

Essex		
B.R. Hardie	b Small	28
A.W. Lilley	c Reeve b Munton	18
M.E. Waugh	c and b Reeve	48
P.J. Prichard	b Asif Din	5
N. Hussain	not out	63
J.P. Stephenson	b Donald	30
*D.R. Pringle	c Humpage b Donald	0
G. Miller	not out	0
†M.A. Garnham		
J.H. Childs		
J.K. Lever		
Extras	b 6, lb 13, w 5, nb 2	26
Total (6 wkts, 37.3 ov)		218

33,73, 79, 149, 209, 209

Munton	6.3	0	22	1
Donald	7	0	32	2
Asif Din	8	0	60	1
Small	8	0	34	1
N.M.K. Smith	3	0	27	0
Reeve	5	0	24	1

Umpires: J.H. Hampshire and A.A. Jones
Toss: Warwickshire
Essex maintained their lead in the table by beating Warwickshire due to 63 off 54 deliveries by Hussain. Earlier Reeve had hit 70 off 76 balls, after Warwickshire's early batsmen had struggled.

v YORKSHIRE (Southend)

July 23

Won by 8 wkts. Essex 4pts, Yorks 0pts

Yorkshire		
K. Sharp	b Miller	50
A.A. Metcalfe	c Prichard b Miller	29
†R.J. Blakey	not out	66
D. Byas	c Prichard b Foster	25
P.E. Robinson	c and b Stephenson	0
M.D. Moxon	b Lever	30
*P. Carrick	c Hussain b Lever	3
P.W. Jarvis	not out	0
A. Sidebottom		
I.G. Swallow		
S.D. Fletcher		
Extras	b 1, lb 7, w 1, nb 1	10
Total (6 wkts, 40 ov)		213

74, 94, 154, 155, 209, 213

Foster	8	0	44	1
Lever	8	2	35	2
Gooch	5	0	21	0
Miller	7	1	41	2
Pringle	8	0	36	0
Stephenson	4	0	28	1

Essex		
*G.A. Gooch	not out	106
B.R. Hardie	c Carrick b Fletcher	13
M.E. Waugh	b Fletcher	62
P.J. Prichard	not out	27
N. Hussain		
J.P. Stephenson		
D.R. Pringle		
G. Miller		
†M.A. Garnham		
N.A. Foster		
J.K. Lever		
Extras	b 2, lb 6, nb 1	9
Total (2 wkts, 38.5 ov)		217

Jarvis	8	0	45	0
Sidebottom	8	0	40	0
Fletcher	8	0	29	2
Moxon	7.5	0	47	0
Carrick	7	0	48	0

Umpires: K.E. Palmer and N.T. Plews
Toss: Yorkshire
About 7,000 turned up to see Essex win with 7 balls left and Gooch hit a splendid unbeaten 100. Essex remain two points ahead of Lancashire each with four matches to play.

v WORCESTERSHIRE (Colchester)

August 6

Lost by 6 wkts. Worcs 4pts, Essex 0pts

Essex		
*G.A. Gooch	c Botham b Weston	24
B.R. Hardie	b Weston	5
M.E. Waugh	b Weston	2
P.J. Prichard	b Illingworth	27
N. Hussain	b Botham	21
J.P. Stephenson	c Rhodes b Lampitt	5
D.R. Pringle	not out	46
†M.A. Garnham	b Lampitt	1
N.A. Foster	c Lampitt b Botham	44
T.D. Topley	run out	3
J.K. Lever		
Extras	lb 8, w 5, nb 2	15
Total (9 wkts, 40 ov)		193

35, 38, 39, 72, 85, 99, 108, 181, 193

Weston	8	1	21	3
McEwan	8	0	53	0
Botham	8	0	39	2
Illingworth	8	0	29	1
Lampitt	8	0	43	2

Worcestershire		
T.S. Curtis	lbw b Gooch	34
I.T. Botham	c Waugh b Lever	11
G.A. Hick	c Waugh b Topley	54
D.B. d'Oliveira	not out	60
*P.A. Neale	c Garnham b Pringle	6
M.J. Weston	not out	18
†S.J. Rhodes		
S.R. Lampitt		
R.K. Illingworth		
S.M. McEwan		
D.A. Leatherdale		
Extras	b 1, lb 4, w 9	14
Total (4 wkts, 38.4 ov)		197

23, 88, 122, 145

Foster	8	0	31	0
Lever	7	0	28	1
Pringle	6.4	0	45	1
Stephenson	3	0	15	0
Topley	8	0	43	1
Gooch	6	0	30	1

Umpires: H.D. Bird and M.J. Kitchen
Toss: Worcestershire
An eighth wicket stand of 73 in 10 overs by Pringle and Foster saved Essex from total ruin, but Hick's 50 off 50 balls meant that Worcester had little difficulty in achieving the 194 required. This Essex defeat allowed Lancashire to move to the top of the Sunday League table, two points ahead of Essex.

BRITANNIC ASSURANCE COUNTY CHAMPIONSHIP AVERAGES 1989

Batting	*M*	*I*	*NO*	*Runs*	*HS*	*Avge*	*100*	*50*
G.A. Gooch	12	20	1	994	158	52.32	3	6
N. Hussain	14	22	3	945	141	49.74	3	3
N. Shahid	6	7	2	245	52	49.00	–	1
J.P. Stephenson	20	34	3	1249	171	40.29	4	3
M.E. Waugh	22	36	3	1288	165	39.03	3	6
B.R. Hardie	15	24	2	775	142*	35.22	2	2
G. Miller	9	13	3	341	61	34.10	–	3
M.A. Garnham	20	29	7	646	91	29.36	–	3
N.A. Foster	14	15	8	178	50*	25.43	–	1
P.J. Prichard	21	33	4	723	128	24.93	1	4
A.W. Lilley	15	26	2	597	113*	24.88	1	2
D.R. Pringle	17	20	4	388	81*	24.25	–	1
T.D. Topley	22	25	4	268	49	12.76	–	–
J.H. Childs	22	22	10	85	24	7.08	–	–
J.K. Lever	7	9	–	56	27	6.22	–	–

Also batted: D.E. East (2 matches) 0, 2; M.C. Ilott (4 matches) 13*, 2* 0*, 7*.

Bowling	*O*	*M*	*R*	*W*	*Avge*	*BB*	*5i*	*10m*
D.R. Pringle	582	152	1447	89	16.26	7-18	5	2
N.A. Foster	546.2	144	1415	73	19.38	7-105	1	–
T.D. Topley	583	140	1763	77	22.90	5-30	2	–
J.H. Childs	610.5	240	1340	57	23.51	7-38	5	1
J.K. Lever	212.1	42	606	23	26.35	7-48	1	–
M.E. Waugh	70.2	8	270	9	30.00	2-9	–	–
N. Shahid	58	10	190	5	38.00	2-40	–	–
J.P. Stephenson	57	10	220	5	44.00	2-41	–	–
M.C. Ilott	91	18	314	6	52.33	2-29	–	–
G. Miller	165	46	422	8	52.75	2-9	–	–

Also bowled: G.A. Gooch 30-6-124-0; N. Hussain 1-0-1-0; A.W. Lilley 6-0-53-1; P.J. Prichard 16-1-128-0.

Centuries

4 J.P. Stephenson: 109* v Kent (Canterbury); 102 v Somerset (Chelmsford); 114 v Surrey (Oval); 171 v Lancs (Lytham).

3 G.A. Gooch: 148 v Derbys (Chelmsford); 124* v Leics (Chelmsford); 158 v Leics (Chelmsford). N. Hussain: 141 v Warwicks (Ilford); 127 v Kent (Southend); 105* v Lancs (Lytham). M.E. Waugh: 109 v Hants (Ilford); 110 v Middlesex (Uxbridge); 165 v Leics (Leicester).

2 B.R. Hardie: 142* v Surrey (Oval); 101* v Glamorgan (Swansea).

1 A.W. Lilley: 113* v Derbys (Chelmsford). P.J. Prichard: 128 v Northants (Colchester).

BENSON AND HEDGES CUP

v HAMPSHIRE (Chelmsford)
May 2
Won by 7 wkts. Essex 2pts, Hants 0pts

Hampshire		
V.P. Terry	c Gooch b Pringle	73
C.L. Smith	c Waugh b Pringle	4
*M.C.J. Nicholas	lbw b Topley	0
R.A. Smith	c Miller b Gooch	21
D.R. Turner	c Garnham b Gooch	0
K.D. James	b Foster	45
S.T. Jefferies	not out	3
N.G. Cowley	not out	4
†R.J. Parks		
C.A. Connor		
P.J. Bakker		
Extras	b 1, lb 14, w 5, nb 3	23
Total (6 wkts, 55 ov)		173

11, 20, 62, 67, 164, 168

Pringle	11	0	39	2
Foster	11	2	34	1
Topley	11	4	23	1
Gooch	11	2	22	2
Stephenson	7	0	24	0
Miller	4	0	16	0

Essex		
*G.A. Gooch	not out	100
B.R. Hardie	c Parks b Jefferies	20
A.W. Lilley	lbw b Bakker	3
M.E. Waugh	b Nicholas	20
P.J. Prichard	not out	12
J.P. Stephenson		
D.R. Pringle		
G. Miller		
†M.A. Garnham		
N.A. Foster		
T.D. Topley		
Extras	lb 11, w 3, nb 6	20
Total (3 wkts, 46.1 ov)		175

55, 58, 113

James	8	2	23	0
Connor	6	1	24	0
Jefferies	7.1	0	34	1
Bakker	11	1	29	1
Cowley	6	0	24	0
Nicholas	8	1	30	1

Umpires: J.D. Bond and N.T. Plews
Toss: Essex. Gold G.A. Gooch
A steady innings by Terry, and some salvage work by James, helped Hampshire to 173, a total which Gooch quickly proved was inadequate. Gooch faced 142 balls and hit 15 fours.

v GLAMORGAN (Chelmsford)
May 11
Won by 10 wkts. Essex 2pts, Glamorgan 0pts

Glamorgan		
A.R. Butcher	c Gooch b Pringle	22
*H. Morris	c Garnham b Lever	3
P.A. Cottey	b Foster	0
M.P. Maynard	c Lever b Gooch	22
R.J. Shastri	c Lever b Topley	9
M.J. Cann	not out	10
†C.P. Metson	c Garnham b Topley	1
S.J. Dennis	b Foster	1
S.L. Watkin	lbw b Pringle	1
S.R. Barwick	c Hardie b Pringle	0
S. Bastien	c Hardie b Foster	7
Extras	b 1, lb 8, w 10, nb 3	22
Total (44.3 ov)		98

13, 18, 48, 59, 73, 80, 86, 87, 91

Foster	10.3	6	5	3
Lever	8	2	19	1
Pringle	10	3	22	3
Gooch	9	0	28	1
Topley	7	2	15	2

Essex		
*G.A. Gooch	not out	69
B.R. Hardie	not out	20
A.W. Lilley		
M.E. Waugh		
P.J. Prichard		
J.P. Stephenson		
D.R. Pringle		
†M.A. Garnham		
N.A. Foster		
T.D. Topley		
J.K. Lever		
Extras	lb 4, w 5, nb 1	10
Total (0 wkt, 23.2 ov)		99

Watkin	5	0	31	0
Dennis	9	1	20	0
Barwick	4.2	0	23	0
Bastien	5	1	21	0

Umpires: J.H. Hampshire and M.J. Kitchen
Toss: Essex. Gold: G.A. Gooch
Essex completed their four B&H matches by recording their fourth victory and one that totally overwhelmed the opposition. Foster returned a remarkable analysis, being almost unplayable. Gooch then reached 50 off 56 balls and the match ended at 4 pm.

v LANCASHIRE (Chelmsford)
May 31
Won by 3 wkts.

Lancashire		
G.D. Mendis	b Stephenson	23
G. Fowler	c Gooch b Stephenson	28
†W.K. Hegg	c Garnham b Gooch	13
N.H. Fairbrother	lbw b Lever	47
T.E. Jesty	b Pringle	22
M. Watkinson	b Stephenson	2
Wasim Akram	c Garnham b Pringle	39
*D.P. Hughes	c Gooch b Pringle	12
P.A.J. DeFreitas	not out	29
P.J.W. Allott	run out	1
J. Simmons		
Extras	lb 27, w 2, nb 1	30
Total (9 wkts, 55 ov)		246

52, 63, 87, 143, 150, 179, 201, 229, 246

Lever	11	2	35	1
Foster	11	0	67	0
Pringle	11	2	43	3
Stephenson	11	0	37	3
Gooch	9	0	29	1
Miller	2	0	8	0

Essex		
*G.A. Gooch	c Mendis b DeFreitas	1
B.R. Hardie	c Hegg b Watkinson	65
A.W. Lilley	c Hegg b DeFreitas	10
M.E. Waugh	b Wasim Akram	93
P.J. Prichard	not out	35
J.P. Stephenson	c Mendis b Wasim Akram	28
D.R. Pringle	lbw b Wasim Akram	1
†M.A. Garnham	b Wasim Akram	0
G. Miller	not out	0
N.A. Foster		
J.K. Lever		
Extras	lb 9, w 4, nb 4	17
Total (7 wkts, 52.1 ov)		250

3, 13, 171, 191, 238, 246, 246

DeFreitas	10.1	1	35	2
Wasim Akram	11	0	54	4
Allott	11	1	33	0
Simmons	11	0	51	0
Watkinson	9	0	68	1

Umpires: J.H. Hampshire and D.O. Oslear
Toss: Essex. Gold: M.E. Waugh
Lancashire, through Fairbrother's 47 off 76 balls and some late hitting by Akram, reached the satisfactory total of 246, with Foster suffering badly. Waugh however replied with 93 off 101 balls and Essex galloped home with overs in hand.

Away Matches

The full scorecard of each of Essex's away matches will be found in the sections for the respective home teams.

Canterbury: April 20, 21, 22, 24
Essex 203 and 224–3d (J.P. Stephenson 109*) drew with Kent 119 and 133–8. Essex 6pts, Kent 4pts.

Bristol: May 20, 22
Essex 178 and 108 beat Gloucs 80 and 90 by 116 runs. Essex 21pts, Gloucs 4pts.

The Oval: June 10, 12, 13
Surrey 395–5d (A.J. Stewart 206*) and 186–1d (D.J. Bicknell 105*) lost to Essex 303–9d (J.P. Stephenson 114) and 279–2 (B.R. Hardie 142*) by 8 wkts. Essex 21 pts, Surrey 7pts.

Horsham: July 1, 3, 4
Essex 185 and 350–6d drew with Sussex 285 and 240–9 (J.H. Childs 5–84). Sussex 7 pts, Essex 3pts.

Derby: July 5, 6, 7
Derbys 191 (J.H. Childs 5–47) and 174–5 drew with Essex 293 (R. Sharma 5–60). Essex 7pts, Derbys 5pts.

Swansea: July 8, 10, 11
Essex 174 (S.R. Barwick 5–59) and 213–2d (B.R. Hardie 101*) beat Glamorgan 65 (D.R. Pringle 7–18) and 134 by 188 runs. Essex 21pts, Glam 4pts.

Uxbridge: July 26, 27, 28
Essex 390 (M.E. Waugh 110) drew with Middx 195 and 341–2d (M.W. Gatting 158*, D.L. Haynes 143*). Essex 7pts, Middx 4pts.

Trent Bridge: July 30, 31, August 1
Notts 308 and 165–6d beat Essex 210 (F.D. Stephenson 7–59) and 148 (F.D. Stephenson 8–47) by 115 runs. Notts 24pts, Essex 6pts.

Lytham: August 12, 14, 15
Lancs 95 and 381 (G.D. Lloyd 11C) lost to Essex 400–4d (J.P. Stephenson 171, N. Hussain 105*) and 79–3 by 7 wkts. Essex 23pts, Lancs 1pt.

Northampton: August 24, 25, 26, 27
Essex 324 (J.G. Thomas 5–74) and 116–7d lost to Northants 227 (N.A. Foster 7–105) and 264–6 by 4 wkts. Northants 22pts, Essex 8pts.

Leicester: September 8, 9, 10, 11
Essex 415 (M.E. Waugh 165, G.A. Gooch 158, J.P. Agnew 5–89) and 8–0 beat Leics 145 and 274 (D.I. Gower 109, J.H. Childs 5–84) by 10 wkts. Essex 24pts, Leics 2pts.

v MIDDLESEX (Chelmsford)

April 27, 28, 29
Won by 9 wkts. Essex 20pts, Middx 4pts

Middlesex 1st Innings

J.D. Carr	b Pringle	6
†P.R. Downton	c Gooch b Pringle	2
*M.W. Gatting	b Topley	26
M.R. Ramprakash	c and b Topley	22
R.O. Butcher	c Waugh b Pringle	17
K.R. Brown	b Pringle	4
J.E. Emburey	run out	9
S.P. Hughes	c Stephenson b Pringle	21
N.F. Williams	lbw b Foster	0
A.R.C. Fraser	run out	2
N.G. Cowans	not out	5
Extras	b 1, lb 12, nb 2	15
Total (65.5 ov)		129

20, 25, 37, 37, 47, 48, 68, 99, 104

Foster	22	9	28	1
Pringle	22.5	5	42	5
Topley	18	6	40	2
Gooch	3	1	6	0

Essex 1st Innings

*G.A. Gooch	lbw b Hughes	65
J.P. Stephenson	c Gatting b Fraser	0
A.W. Lilley	lbw b Cowans	0
M.E. Waugh	c Downton b Fraser	39
T.D. Topley	c Downton b Cowans	6
P.J. Prichard	c Ramprakash b Hughes	9
D.R. Pringle	c Butcher b Hughes	15
G. Miller	lbw b Cowans	0
†D.E. East	c Downton b Cowans	2
N.A. Foster	lbw b Cowans	3
J.H. Childs	not out	0
Extras	lb 5, nb 5	10
Total (50.3 ov)		149

2, 11, 113, 115, 126, 140, 144, 144, 148

Cowans	17.3	7	34	5
Fraser	13	2	53	2
Williams	8	0	37	0
Hughes	12	3	20	3

Middlesex 2nd Innings

J.D. Carr	lbw b Pringle	7
†P.R. Downton	c Gooch b Foster	23
*M.W. Gatting	c Gooch b Foster	0
M.R. Ramprakash	b Pringle	3
R.O. Butcher	lbw b Pringle	6
K.R. Brown	c Gooch b Foster	15
J.E. Emburey	lbw b Pringle	15
S.P. Hughes	not out	1
N.F. Williams	run out	1
A.R.C. Fraser	lbw b Foster	0
N.G. Cowans	c Topley b Pringle	7
Extras	b 1, lb 3, nb 3	7
Total		85

18, 18, 35, 42, 42, 72, 74, 75, 75

Foster	14	3	42	4
Pringle	13.3	1	38	5
Topley	1	0	1	0

Essex 2nd Innings

*G.A. Gooch	c Brown b Cowans	0
J.P. Stephenson	not out	49
A.W. Lilley	not out	19
Extras	nb 1	1
Total (1 wkt)		69

0

Cowans	5	1	12	1
Fraser	4	0	14	0
Hughes	2.5	1	11	0
Williams	2	0	32	0

Umpires: N.T. Plews and J.D. Bond
Toss: Middlesex

Although there was no play on the first day of this match, the four day fixture was still completed with a day to spare. Middlesex were dismissed on the second day for 129, due to some good bowling by Pringle and by the close Essex had reached 138–5 off 41 overs. On the third morning Essex could only add 11 runs to their total, but Middlesex again fell to Pringle and Stephenson then hit out to end the match.

v DERBYSHIRE (Chelmsford)

May 4, 5, 6
Won by an innings and 212 runs. Essex 24pts, Derbys 0pts

Derbyshire 1st Innings

P.D. Bowler	lbw b Foster	16
†B.J.M. Maher	c Topley b Pringle	0
J.E. Morris	c Foster b Topley	10
B. Roberts	c Gooch b Foster	0
S.C. Goldsmith	c Waugh b Foster	18
R. Sharma	c Garnham b Topley	10
C.J. Adams	c Foster b Topley	5
P.G. Newman	not out	26
*M. A. Holding	b Foster	1
S.J Base	b Topley	1
O.H. Mortensen	b Topley	8
Extras	b 2, lb 15, nb 1	18
Total (45.5 ov)		113

22, 22, 25, 51, 53, 68, 75, 84, 85

Foster	18	5	39	4
Pringle	12	2	27	1
Topley	15.5	6	30	5

Essex 1st Innings

*G.A. Gooch	c Bowler b Newman	148
J.P. Stephenson	b Newman	94
A.W. Lilley	not out	113
M.E. Waugh	b Holding	77
P.J. Prichard	not out	54
B.R. Hardie		
D.R. Pringle		
†M.A. Garnham		
N.A. Foster		
T.D. Topley		
J.H. Childs		
Extras	b 2, lb 24, w 2, nb 8	36
Total (100 ov: 314–2) (3 wkts dec)		522

254, 266, 404

Holding	26	4	96	1
Mortensen	28	4	75	0
Newman	31	5	92	2
Base	27	3	92	0
Sharma	21	3	62	0
Roberts	5	0	22	0
Bowler	10	1	57	0

Derbyshire 2nd Innings

P.D. Bowler	c Topley b Foster	20
†B.J.M. Maher	b Pringle	0
J.E. Morris	b Pringle	2
B. Roberts	c Garnham b Pringle	63
R. Sharma	c Prichard b Foster	4
C.J. Adams	lbw b Childs	22
S.C. Goldsmith	b Topley	4
P.G. Newman	b Childs	57
*M.A. Holding	c Garnham b Foster	3
S.J. Base	lbw b Pringle	10
O.H. Mortensen	not out	0
Extras	b 4, lb 8	12
Total		197

5, 13, 37, 41, 88, 105, 155, 170, 191

Pringle	28.5	10	63	4
Foster	28	9	72	3
Topley	12	5	23	1
Childs	24	17	27	2

Umpires: D.O. Oslear and R. Palmer
Toss: Derbyshire

Essex won this four day game just before tea on the third afternoon. The visitors were completely outplayed from the moment they decided to bat. Morris survived for an hour, but generally there was little resistance to Foster and Topley, though Derbyshire did suffer the inconvenience of Barnett being absent injured. Essex's openers enjoyed themselves and by the close, Gooch was 111* and Stephenson 79*, the total being 204 off 61 overs. Runs continued to flow on the second day, with Lilley making a career best 113* and Derbyshire failed to obtain any bonus points. In the evening Essex declared and took two quick wickets at a cost of 28 runs. On the last day Roberts and Newman made fifties, but otherwise Essex strode uninterrupted to victory.

v SOMERSET (Chelmsford)
May 27, 29, 30
Drawn. Somerset 5pts, Essex 4pts

Essex 1st Innings

*B.R. Hardie	lbw b Marks	46
J.P. Stephenson	c Burns b Roebuck	102
A.W. Lilley	lbw b Mallender	9
M.E. Waugh	run out	26
P.J. Prichard	lbw b Roebuck	40
†M.A. Garnham	lbw b Trump	41
G. Miller	not out	41
T.D. Topley	b Jones	8
J.K. Lever	b Mallender	0
J.H. Childs	not out	0
M.C. Ilott		
Extras	lb 10, nb 4	14
Total (100 ov: 260–5) (8 wkts dec)		327

101, 115, 171, 230, 235, 302, 326, 327

Mallender	17	5	48	2
Jones	14	3	45	1
Foster	10	2	34	0
Marks	40	12	86	1
Trump	29	4	79	1
Roebuck	9	1	25	2

Somerset 1st Innings

S.J. Cook	not out	147
P.M. Roebuck	c Miller b Childs	20
R.J. Bartlett	c Waugh b Childs	0
C.J. Tavare	lbw b Topley	1
R.J. Harden	not out	101
†N.D. Burns		
*V.J. Marks		
G.D. Rose		
H.R.J. Trump		
N.A. Mallender		
A.N. Jones		
Extras	b 5, lb 5, w 1	11
Total (100 ov: 252–3) (3 wkts dec)		280

40, 46, 51

Lever	17.5	5	25	0
Ilott	14	0	57	0
Childs	40	11	86	2
Topley	9	1	30	1
Miller	28	6	72	0

Essex 2nd Innings

*B.R. Hardie	c Marks b Trump	80
J.P. Stephenson	not out	34
A.W. Lilley	c Trump b Foster	9
M.E. Waugh	b Trump	79
G. Miller	not out	4
Extras	b 1, lb 6, w 1, nb 3	11
Total (3 wkts dec)		217

65, 172, 195

Mallender	8	0	35	0
Marks	16	1	80	0
Jones	6	1	20	0
Foster	8	0	36	1
Trump	13	2	39	2

Somerset 2nd Innings

S.J. Cook	b Ilott	10
P.M. Roebuck	not out	65
R.J. Bartlett	lbw b Ilott	4
C.J. Tavare	b Waugh	18
R.J. Harden	run out	8
†N.D. Burns	not out	6
Extras	b 2, nb 3	5
Total (4 wkts)		116

21, 27, 96, 109

Lever	6	0	21	0
Ilott	10	3	29	2
Childs	16	8	14	0
Miller	14	8	25	0
Waugh	5	1	25	1

Umpires: P.B. Wight and D.S. Thompsett
Toss: Essex

Without Gooch, Pringle and Foster, Essex still managed to start the match in excellent form – Stephenson making a well constructed 100. At the close Essex were 327–8. They declared over the weekend and then suffered from Cook, who became the first batsman to reach 1,000 runs in 1989. Harden assisted in a stand worth 229 before Marks declared. On the last day Somerset were set 265, but when Cook and Bartlett failed, the visitors settled for a draw.

v LEICESTERSHIRE (Chelmsford)
June 17, 19, 20
Drawn. Essex 5pts, Leics 4pts

Leicestershire 1st Innings

R.A. Cobb	lbw b Foster	13
*N.E. Briers	lbw b Foster	0
T.J. Boon	c Gooch b Topley	20
P. Willey	c Waugh b Childs	58
J.J. Whitaker	b Pringle	138
L. Potter	c Prichard b Shahid	71
G.J. Parsons	c Stephenson b Childs	13
†P. Whitticase	not out	16
W.K.M. Benjamin	b Shahid	1
J.P. Agnew	not out	8
P.M. Such		
Extras	b 4, lb 21, w 4, nb 10	39
Total (100 ov: 324–5) (8 wkts dec)		377

1, 30, 52, 158, 315, 348, 362, 365

Foster	26	6	77	2
Pringle	21	7	62	1
Topley	13	4	49	1
Waugh	4	0	24	0
Childs	34	8	97	2
Nadeem Shahid	15	2	40	2
Stephenson	2	0	3	0

Essex 1st Innings

*G.A. Gooch	not out	124
J.P. Stephenson	c Potter b Parsons	35
A.W. Lilley	b Agnew	1
M.E. Waugh	not out	89
P.J. Prichard		
D.R. Pringle		
Nadeem Shahid		
†M.A. Garnham		
N.A. Foster		
T.D. Topley		
J.H. Childs		
Extras	lb 8, nb 5	13
Total (2 wkts dec, 76 ov)		262

69, 70

Benjamin	16	3	52	0
Agnew	18	5	60	1
Parsons	19	4	59	1
Such	7	0	32	0
Potter	8	1	31	0
Willey	8	0	20	0

Leicestershire 2nd Innings

R.A. Cobb	c Lilley b Foster	47
*N.E. Briers	c and b Shahid	23
T.J. Boon	b Waugh	72
P. Willey	c Garnham b Topley	2
J.J. Whitaker	not out	92
L. Potter	b Waugh	1
Extras	b 1, lb 8, w 2, nb 3	14
Total (5 wkts dec)		251

54, 102, 105, 229, 151

Foster	20	5	35	1
Topley	14	3	38	1
Stephenson	2	0	8	0
Shahid	20	3	69	1
Childs	16	6	41	0
Prichard	4	1	16	0
Gooch	4	0	26	0
Waugh	4.2	0	9	2

Essex 2nd Innings

*G.A. Gooch	b Benjamin	42
J.P. Stephenson	c Parsons b Agnew	10
M.E. Waugh	lbw b Benjamin	15
A.W. Lilley	b Parsons	48
P.J. Prichard	not out	80
†M.A. Garnham	not out	9
Extras	b 1, lb 9, w 1, nb 1	12
Total (4 wkts)		216

54, 56, 77, 181

Benjamin	11	1	46	2
Agnew	12	0	69	1
Parsons	10	1	45	1
Such	7	2	25	0
Willey	6	0	21	0

Umpires: K.J. Lyons and J.W. Holder
Toss: Leicestershire

In a match of declarations on an easy wicket, the visitors finally set Essex 367 off 52 overs. Gooch set off in pursuit with 50 coming up in the 7th over, but when both the captain and Stephenson departed the run chase became impossible and Prichard was content to bat out time. On Saturday Leicestershire had made 377–8, with Whitaker hitting 138. On Monday Essex declared in arrears as soon as they had gained a third batting point and at the close Leicester were 95–1.

v HAMPSHIRE (Ilford)
June 21, 22, 23
Won by 102 runs. Essex 23pts, Hants 6pts

Essex 1st Innings

*B.R. Hardie	b Maru	33
J.P. Stephenson	c Terry b Maru	20
A.W. Lilley	c Parks b Bakker	7
M.E. Waugh	c Parks b Marshall	20
P.R. Prichard	c Terry b Bakker	0
G. Miller	run out	51
Nadeem Shahid	b Cowley	40
†M.A. Garnham	c Parks b James	54
T.D. Topley	c Parks b James	25
J.H. Childs	c Turner b Maru	0
M.C. Ilott	not out	2
Extras	b 8, lb 15, nb 2	25
Total (93 ov)		277

52, 59, 65, 65, 96, 185, 198, 270, 271

Bakker	21	4	51	2
Marshall	21	8	49	1
James	11	4	28	2
Maru	26	5	73	3
Cowley	13	0	52	1
Nicholas	1	0	1	0

Hampshire 1st Innings

V.P. Terry	st Garnham b Childs	41
C.L. Smith	c Garnham b Ilott	25
K.D. James	c Hardie b Childs	48
*M.C.J. Nicholas	c Garnham b Stephenson	9
R.J. Scott	c Prichard b Childs	0
D.R. Turner	c Prichard b Miller	45
M.D. Marshall	c Prichard b Childs	0
N.G. Cowley	c Garnham b Stephenson	26
†R.J. Parks	c Hardie b Miller	9
R.J. Maru	b Childs	7
P.J. Bakker	not out	0
Extras	b 4, lb 14, w 1, nb 15,	34
Total (90.5 ov)		244

43, 112, 140, 140, 146, 149, 182, 208, 244

Ilott	11	2	50	1
Topley	21	3	74	0
Childs	34.5	17	36	5
Stephenson	13	3	46	2
Miller	11	2	20	2

Essex 2nd Innings

B.R. Hardie	c Nicholas b Marshall	30
J.P. Stephenson	c Terry b Bakker	3
A.W. Lilley	lbw b Marshall	1
M.E. Waugh	c Terry b Cowley	109
P.J. Prichard	c Terry b Marshall	3
G. Miller	c Parks b James	50
†M.A. Garnham	c Parks b James	0
Nadeem Shahid	not out	27
T.D. Topley	b Maru	0
J.H. Childs	c Nicholas b Bakker	2
M.C. Ilott	not out	0
Extras	lb 8, nb 1	9
Total (9 wkts dec)		234

21, 36, 39, 43, 204, 204, 210, 226, 233

Bakker	13	2	45	2
Marshall	15	3	39	3
Maru	15	2	41	1
James	19	5	51	2
Cowley	14	1	50	1
Smith	1	1	0	0

Hampshire 2nd Innings

V.P. Terry	c Prichard b Childs	20
C.L. Smith	c Garnham b Topley	0
K.D. James	c Prichard b Topley	20
*M.C.J. Nicholas	c Lilley b Childs	4
R.J. Scott	c Miller b Childs	27
D.R. Turner	c Hardie b Childs	6
M.D. Marshall	c Lilley b Shahid	6
N.G. Cowley	c and b Childs	42
†R.J. Parks	c Miller b Childs	26
R.J. Maru	not out	0
P.J. Bakker	c Shahid b Childs	0
Extras	b 8, lb 2, nb 4	14
Total		165

0, 36, 44, 52, 68, 77, 107, 164, 165

Topley	11	2	34	2
Ilott	4	0	20	0
Childs	29.1	16	38	7
Miller	21	8	33	0
Shahid	6	2	30	1
Waugh	1	1	0	0

Umpires: J.H. Hampshire and A.A. Jones
Toss: Essex

Waugh reached a maiden Championship 100 and his effort meant Hampshire needed 268 off 63 overs. Good bowling meant Essex won in the final hour.

v WARWICKSHIRE (Ilford)

June 24, 26, 27

Won by 5 wkts. Essex 24pts, Warwicks 8pts

Warwickshire 1st Innings

A.J. Moles	c Garnham b Topley	42
J.D. Radcliffe	c Pringle b Topley	72
*T.A. Lloyd	c Hussain b Childs	14
G.W. Humpage	c Garnham b Childs	18
Asif Din	lbw b Pringle	10
P.A. Smith	c Garnham b Miller	37
D.A. Reeve	not out	97
†K.J. Piper	c Hardie b Miller	1
N.M.K. Smith	c Miller b Childs	8
A.A. Donald	c Hussain b Childs	1
A.R.K. Pierson	b Pringle	13
Extras	b 4, lb 10, nb 11	25
Total (98.4 ov)		338

118, 123, 147, 172, 172, 249, 267, 285, 289

Pringle	22.4	2	73	2
Topley	28	4	92	2
Childs	28	4	96	4
Miller	13	1	42	2
Stephenson	5	1	13	0
Waugh	2	0	8	0

Essex 1st Innings

B.R. Hardie	c Piper b Donald	56
J.P. Stephenson	c Humpage b Donald	27
A.W. Lilley	c Moles b Donald	6
M.E. Waugh	b Pierson	1
P.J. Prichard	c Humpage b Pierson	0
N. Hussain	b Pierson	141
G. Miller	c Piper b Donald	7
*D.R. Pringle	c Asif Din b Pierson	14
†M.A. Garnham	c and b Pierson	19
T.D. Topley	not out	35
J.H. Childs	b Donald	8
Extras	b 8, lb 8, w 1, nb 4	21
Total (79.5 ov)		335

81, 89, 92, 92, 102, 120, 159, 186, 322

Donald	30.5	2	103	5
P.A. Smith	3	0	13	0
Asif Din	9	1	42	0
Pierson	29	4	129	5
Reeve	3	1	3	0
N.M.K. Smith	5	1	29	0

Warwickshire 2nd Innings

A.J. Moles	c Hardie b Pringle	2
J.D. Ratcliffe	c Hardie b Pringle	1
*T.A. Lloyd	c Hardie b Pringle	23
G.W. Humpage	lbw b Pringle	7
Asif Din	c Waugh b Pringle	32
D.A. Reeve	c Stephenson b Topley	42
P.A. Smith	lbw b Pringle	2
†K.J. Piper	c Garnham b Topley	8
N.M.K. Smith	lbw b Pringle	4
A.A. Donald	not out	7
A.R.K. Pierson	c and b Topley	1
Extras	b 10, lb 6	16
Total		145

2, 3, 29, 50, 109, 113, 130, 133, 140

Pringle	30	13	44	7
Topley	24.4	6	44	3
Childs	11	5	31	0
Miller	2	0	10	0

Essex 2nd Innings

B.R. Hardie	c and b Pierson	17
J.P. Stephenson	c Piper b Donald	43
A.W. Lilley	b Donald	49
M.E. Waugh	c Moles b Donald	2
P.J. Prichard	c Reeve b Pierson	2
N. Hussain	not out	16
*D.R. Pringle	not out	9
Extras	b 9, lb 2	11
Total (5 wkts)		149

35, 116, 121, 124, 124

Donald	17	4	52	3
Ratcliffe	3	0	22	0
Pierson	12	2	49	2
Asif Din	2	0	15	0

Umpires: J.H. Hampshire and A.A. Jones
Toss: Warwickshire

Essex maintained their lead in the county championship, when Pringle took seven second innings wickets and thus gave his side 34 overs in which to make 149. The task was completed with 3 overs unbowled. On the first day an unbeaten 97 by Reeve gave Warwickshire full batting points. Essex began Monday at 34–0 off 8 overs. A brilliant hundred by Hussain, after a minor collapse, enabled Essex to hit 335 off 79.5 overs. Warwickshire were 107–4 by the close.

v KENT (Southend)

July 19, 20

Won by an innings and 6 runs. Essex 24pts, Kent 3pts

Kent 1st Innings

N.R. Taylor	c Hussain b Foster	3
M.R. Benson	c Garnham b Foster	0
T.R. Ward	run out	16
J.I. Longley	c Waugh b Pringle	9
*C.S. Cowdrey	b Pringle	8
†S.A. Marsh	c Garnham b Pringle	27
M.C. Dobson	lbw b Pringle	0
R.M. Ellison	not out	39
R.P. Davis	c Gooch b Topley	1
A.P. Igglesden	b Pringle	0
H.L. Alleyne	c Garnham b Pringle	2
Extras	lb 5, w 1, nb 1	7
Total (38.2 ov)		112

3, 9, 26, 37, 45, 49, 94, 103, 104

Foster	15	3	38	2
Pringle	16.2	3	42	6
Topley	7	2	27	1

Essex 1st Innings

*G.A. Gooch	b Alleyne	7
J.P. Stephenson	lbw b Igglesden	16
P.J. Pritchard	c sub b Ellison	40
M.E. Waugh	c Marsh b Igglesden	29
N. Hussain	c Ellison b Alleyne	127
†M.A. Garnham	c Marsh b Igglesden	37
T.D. Topley	lbw b Alleyne	15
D.R. Pringle	run out	15
G. Miller	b Alleyne	24
N.A. Foster	not out	6
J.H. Childs	b Igglesden	2
Extras	b 4, lb 9, w 3, nb 13	29
Total (100 ov: 304–7)		347

12, 41, 87, 108, 177, 264, 286, 339, 340

Igglesden	26	8	66	4
Alleyne	25	0	92	4
Cowdrey	7	2	21	0
Ellison	20	5	50	1
Davis	20	3	68	0
Dobson	9	3	37	0

Kent 2nd Innings

N.R. Taylor	c Hussain b Pringle	0
M.C. Dobson	c Garnham b Pringle	8
T.R. Ward	c Miller b Childs	91
J.I. Longley	b Topley	17
*C.S. Cowdrey	lbw b Foster	27
†S.A. Marsh	b Pringle	4
M.R. Benson	c Prichard b Topley	21
R.M. Ellison	c Hussain b Miller	12
R.P. Davis	c sub b Miller	2
A.P. Igglesden	not out	10
H.L. Alleyne	b Pringle	28
Extras	b 5, lb 3, nb 1	9
Total		229

0, 29, 53, 113, 118, 159, 183, 185, 191

Pringle	17.4	6	60	4
Foster	20	6	53	1
Topley	16	2	68	2
Childs	10	2	31	1
Miller	5	1	9	2

Umpires: K.E. Palmer and N.T. Plews
Toss: Kent

A two-day victory increased Essex's lead at the top of the Championship table to 36 points. Kent were completely outplayed on the first day. The seam bowling of Pringle proved too much for a side which contained too many inexperienced batsmen. Essex were 188–5 off 68 overs at the close. On Thursday Hussain scored an assured hundred off 194 balls with 11 fours. Apart from Ward, Kent collapsed a second time and Pringle brought his match tally to 10. The umpires called for the TCCB inspector of pitches because of the poor quality of the wicket on the first day but Mr Brind found that the wicket's problems were caused by the very dry weather, and no action was taken against Essex.

v YORKSHIRE (Southend)

July 22, 24, 25

Won by 3 wkts. Essex 22pts, Yorks 4pts

Yorkshire 1st Innings

M.D. Moxon	c Foster b Pringle	27
A.A. Metcalfe	c Gooch b Foster	9
†R.J. Blakey	c Foster b Pringle	12
D. Byas	c Gooch b Foster	15
P.E. Robinson	c Garnham b Topley	8
K. Sharp	b Topley	0
*P. Carrick	c Hardie b Topley	0
A. Sidebottom	c and b Foster	21
P.W. Jarvis	c Prichard b Topley	2
C.S. Pickles	not out	13
S.D. Fletcher	c Gooch b Topley	0
Extras	b 6, nb 2	8
Total (41.4 ov)		115

17, 49, 54, 73, 74, 74, 82, 86, 110

Foster	15	5	30	3
Pringle	13	5	33	2
Topley	13.4	0	46	5

Essex 1st Innings

*G.A. Gooch	c Moxon b Jarvis	11
J.P. Stephenson	c Sidebottom b Carrick	85
P.J. Prichard	lbw b Jarvis	0
M.E. Waugh	c Blakey b Sidebottom	27
N. Hussain	lbw b Jarvis	21
B.R. Hardie	b Jarvis	5
†M.A. Garnham	b Jarvis	13
D.R. Pringle	c Fletcher b Carrick	37
N.A. Foster	c Sidebottom b Jarvis	0
T.D. Topley	not out	25
J.H. Childs	c Sidebottom b Carrick	7
Extras	lb 5, w 1, nb 11	17
Total (82.4 ov)		248

18, 23, 120, 151, 161, 163, 182, 188, 228

Jarvis	26	8	76	6
Sidebottom	11	2	40	1
Fletcher	10	0	43	0
Pickles	5	0	22	0
Carrick	30.4	13	62	3

Yorkshire 1st Innings

M.D. Moxon	c Gooch b Foster	37
A.A. Metcalfe	c Topley b Foster	30
†R.J. Blakey	c Waugh b Foster	1
D. Byas	c Hardie b Pringle	20
P.E. Robinson	c Garnham b Topley	47
K. Sharp	c Hardie b Childs	16
*P. Carrick	c Hussain b Pringle	35
A. Sidebottom	c Prichard b Topley	0
P.W. Jarvis	c Garnham b Foster	5
C.S. Pickles	not out	27
S.D. Fletcher	c Prichard b Pringle	7
Extras	b 7, lb 4, nb 3	14
Total		239

56, 62, 76, 106, 146, 175, 175, 182, 217

Foster	36	10	94	4
Pringle	24.1	5	67	3
Topley	19	7	43	2
Childs	23	13	24	1

Essex 2nd Innings

*G.A. Gooch	lbw b Stephenson	1
J.P. Stephenson	c Moxon b Jarvis	0
P.J. Prichard	c Blakey b Sidebottom	13
M.E. Waugh	b Jarvis	0
N. Hussain	b Sidebottom	45
B.R. Hardie	b Jarvis	11
†M.A. Garnham	c Pickles b Sidebottom	0
D.R. Pringle	not out	16
N.A. Foster	not out	4
Extras	b 4, lb 9, nb 4	17
Total (7 wkts)		107

1, 1, 6, 29, 56, 61, 103

Jarvis	11	0	35	3
Sidebottom	10.2	1	48	4
Fletcher	1	0	8	0
Carrick	1	0	3	0

Umpires: K.E. Palmer and N.T. Plews
Toss: Yorkshire

Although Essex continued on their winning way, the County Pitches Committee, under D.B. Carr, penalised the county for producing a sub-standard pitch and Essex had 25 points deducted, cutting their lead at the head of the table to 27 points. It was the first time this penalty had been invoked. Essex took command on Saturday by dismissing Yorkshire for 115 and reaching 205–8 in reply. On Monday Yorkshire reached 209–8, but the umpires reported the wicket and sent for Harry Brind. Hussain was the hero of the last day, scoring 45 out of the 107 Essex required for victory.

v WORCESTERSHIRE (Colchester)

August 5, 7, 8

Drawn. Worcs 7pts, Essex 3pts

Essex 1st Innings		
*G.A. Gooch	c Rhodes b Botham	51
J.P. Stephenson	c Curtis b Dilley	8
P.J. Prichard	c Rhodes b Illingworth	28
M.E. Waugh	c Leatherdale b Illingworth	12
N. Hussain	c and b Hick	47
†M.A. Garnham	b Hick	2
D.R. Pringle	c Neale b Hick	19
G. Miller	c Leatherdale b Hick	1
N.A. Foster	c Curtis b Hick	27
T.D. Topley	c Leatherdale b Illingworth	6
J.H. Childs	not out	0
Extras	lb 4, w 1, nb 2	7
Total (67.4 ov)		208

17, 89, 95, 104, 109, 149, 165, 201, 202

Dilley	7	2	14	1
Botham	16	4	42	1
Lampitt	8	2	39	0
Illingworth	19.4	7	57	3
Hick	17	5	52	5

Worcestershire 1st Innings		
T.S. Curtis	c Foster b Pringle	156
P. Bent	b Topley	55
R.K. Illingworth	c Topley	11
G.A. Hick	c and b Foster	72
B.D. d'Oliveira	lbw b Topley	55
*P.A. Neale	run out	7
I.T. Botham	b Pringle	7
D.A. Leatherdale	lbw b Miller	25
†S.J. Rhodes	c Gooch b Topley	27
S.R. Lampitt	not out	6
G.R. Dilley	not out	9
Extras	b 1, lb 6, w 4, nb 6	17
Total (100 ov: 269–3) (9 wkts dec)		447

98, 121, 234, 336, 349, 367, 388, 430, 434

Foster	31	10	94	1
Pringle	28	6	50	2
Childs	34	11	115	0
Miller	27	7	85	1
Topley	23	5	76	4
Gooch	4	1	20	0

Essex 2nd Innings		
*G.A. Gooch	b Hick	17
J.P. Stephenson	c Rhodes b Hick	20
T.D. Topley	c Curtis b Illingworth	1
P.J. Prichard	c Botham b Illingworth	0
M.E. Waugh	c Leatherdale b Hick	76
N. Hussain	c Lampitt b Illingworth	17
†M.A. Garnham	lbw b Hick	20
D.R. Pringle	c Lampitt b Hick	42
G. Miller	c Leatherdale b Illingworth	46
N.A. Foster	not out	50
J.H. Childs	not out	3
Extras	b 10, lb 16, nb 5	31
Total (9 wkts)		323

20, 21, 21, 93, 116, 159, 166, 242, 295

Dilley	16.2	3	47	0
Botham	2	1	4	0
Illingworth	52	21	115	4
Hick	52	15	131	5

Umpires: H.D. Bird and M.J. Kitchen

Toss: Essex

This vital match was staged with Worcestershire seven points ahead of Essex at the top of the Championship table. On Saturday after Essex's big guns failed, the latter batsmen were bemused by the occasional off-spin of Hick, who returned his career best analysis. The visitors were well placed by the close, being 113–1 off 48 overs. Curtis was 42 not out. On the second day Curtis went on to 156 in about 450 minutes, which provided his side with an unbeatable 447. Essex began the last day at 21–2 and a dropped catch saved Essex from defeat – the escaping batsman being Foster early in his innings of 50.

v NORTHAMPTONSHIRE (Colchester)

August 9, 10, 11

Won by 120 runs. Essex 20pts, Northants 2pts

Essex 1st Innings		
*G.A. Gooch	c Ripley b Davis	75
J.P. Stephenson	c Ripley b Davis	41
P.J. Prichard	st Ripley b Roberts	128
M.E. Waugh	c Capel	24
N. Hussain	c Bailey b Capel	5
Nadeem Shahid	c Ripley b Davis	28
†M.A. Garnham	not out	26
D.R. Pringle	not out	25
N.A. Foster		
T.D. Topley		
J.H. Childs		
Extras	b 4, lb 13, w 3, nb 19	39
Total (100 ov: 371–6) (6 wkts dec)		391

134, 144, 224, 234, 316, 353

Davis	23	4	81	3
Walker	22	3	90	0
Capel	27	3	59	2
Roberts	24	1	110	1
Bailey	7	0	34	0

Northamptonshire 1st Innings		
G. Cook	not out	36
A. Walker	c Garnham b Foster	7
*W. Larkins	not out	76
A. Fordham		
R.J. Bailey		
D.J. Capel		
D.J. Wild		
N.A. Felton		
A. Roberts		
†D. Ripley		
W.W. Davis		
Extras	b 1, lb 10, nb 1	12
Total (1 wkt dec, 23 ov)		131

17

Foster	6	2	13	1
Pringle	6	0	20	0
Gooch	6	0	41	0
Prichard	5	0	46	0

Essex 2nd Innings

Innings forfeited.

Northamptonshire 2nd Innings		
G. Cook	c Prichard b Pringle	2
*W. Larkins	c Prichard b Foster	14
A. Fordham	c Hussain b Pringle	1
R.J. Bailey	c Gooch b Foster	36
D.J. Capel	run out	0
N.A. Felton	c Garnham b Topley	53
D.J. Wild	c Hussain b Foster	8
†D. Ripley	b Pringle	3
A. Roberts	c Garnham b Foster	7
W.W. Davis	c Stephenson b Pringle	0
A. Walker	not out	11
Extras	nb 5	5
Total		140

8, 11, 18, 18, 67, 89, 120, 122, 122

Foster	20.5	5	46	4
Pringle	17	6	49	4
Topley	8	2	24	1
Gooch	5	1	21	0

Umpires: R. Palmer and M.J. Kitchen

Toss: Essex

Essex batted most effectively on the first day. Gooch and Stephenson began with a stand of 134 and this was followed by Prichard's 128 off 182 balls with 21 fours. Northants were 12–0 off 4 overs at stumps. Only eight overs were possible on Thursday, in which time Northants moved to 42–1. Some juggling on Friday left Northants 48 overs in which to score 261 runs – play did not start until 2.55 pm. Foster and Pringle completely wrecked the midland county's hopes and Essex won with 10 overs to spare. This victory meant that Essex were now 15 points behind Worcestershire at the top of the table, each having four matches to play.

v SURREY (Chelmsford)

August 29, 30, 31, Sept 1

Won by 2 wkts. Essex 22pts, Surrey 7pts

Surrey 1st Innings		
D.J. Bicknell	lbw b Foster	0
G.S. Clinton	lbw b Lever	0
†A.J. Stewart	c Garnham b Waugh	120
G.P. Thorpe	c Hussain b Foster	5
M.A. Lynch	c Waugh b Childs	40
*I.A. Greig	lbw b Waugh	8
K.T. Medlycott	lbw b Topley	3
M.A. Feltham	c Hussain b Foster	11
M.P. Bicknell	c Hussain b Lever	32
J. Boiling	not out	6
A.J. Murphy	c Garnham b Foster	4
Extras	b 6, lb 12, w 1, nb 2	21
Total (96.4 ov)		250

0, 6, 40, 133, 180, 193, 193, 213, 241

Foster	28.4	12	50	4
Lever	19	3	64	2
Topley	23	6	60	1
Waugh	12	2	34	2
Childs	14	10	24	1

Essex 1st Innings		
*B.R. Hardie	lbw b Feltham	23
A.W. Lilley	lbw b M.P. Bicknell	21
P.J. Prichard	c Greig b M.P. Bicknell	2
M.E. Waugh	c Clinton b Murphy	40
N. Hussain	lbw b Murphy	19
Nadeem Shahid	lbw b M.P. Bicknell	52
†M.A. Garnham	c Lynch b M.P. Bicknell	16
N.A. Foster	not out	12
T.D. Topley	lbw b M.P. Bicknell	2
J.K. Lever	b Murphy	0
J.H Childs	c Clinton b M.P. Bicknell	0
Extras	b 1, lb 11, nb 8	20
Total (69.5 ov)		207

46, 50, 52, 96, 133, 179, 191, 195, 207

M.P. Bicknell	20.5	6	55	6
Murphy	23	5	70	3
Feltham	14	1	39	1
Medlycott	9	3	25	0
Greig	3	1	6	0

Surrey 2nd Innings		
G.S. Clinton	c Shahid b Foster	15
D.J. Bicknell	b Lever	10
†A.J. Stewart	c Garnham b Lever	8
G.P. Thorpe	c Garnham b Waugh	55
M.A. Lynch	b Lever	12
*I.A. Greig	c Shahid b Foster	32
K.T. Medlycott	c Hardie b Lever	11
M.A. Feltham	b Lever	16
M.P. Bicknell	lbw b Lever	0
J. Boiling	not out	2
A.J. Murphy	b Lever	10
Extras	lb 7, w 1, nb 4	12
Total		183

15, 23, 36, 87, 141, 141, 170, 170, 171

Foster	24	8	41	2
Lever	23.2	8	48	7
Childs	8	4	11	0
Topley	17	5	58	0
Waugh	8	2	18	1

Essex 2nd Innings		
*B.R. Hardie	lbw b Feltham	48
A.W. Lilley	lbw b M.P. Bicknell	18
P.J. Prichard	lbw b M.P. Bicknell	0
M.E. Waugh	c Lynch b Murphy	8
N. Hussain	c Stewart b Medlycott	70
T.D. Topley	c and b Feltham	17
Nadeem Shahid	lbw b Medlycott	31
†M.A. Garnham	not out	22
J.K. Lever	c Thorpe b Medlycott	0
N.A. Foster	not out	0
Extras	lb 7, w 1, nb 5	13
Total (8 wkts)		227

28, 28, 39, 136, 166, 175, 226, 226

M.P. Bicknell	25	5	74	2
Murphy	23	5	51	1
Feltham	16	3	50	2
Greig	5	0	23	0
Medlycott	6	1	13	3
Boiling	1	0	9	0

Umpires: M.J. Kitchen and B.J. Meyer

Toss: Surrey

Victory by Worcester on August 31 meant that Essex could no longer secure the title. Surrey began the third day 79 runs ahead with eight wickets in hand, but Lever playing in his final home match made certain that the lead did not extend too far and on Friday Essex struggled to victory with 2 wickets left.

Glamorgan

President: His Honour Rowe Harding
Chairman: A.R. Lewis
Chief Executive: P.G. Carling, Sophia Gardens, Cardiff CF1 9XR *Tel:* 0222 343478
Coach: A. Jones
Captain: From July 1989: A.R. Butcher
Foundation of Present Club: July 1888 in Cardiff
First First-Class Match: Glamorgan v Sussex (Cardiff Arms Park) May 1921
County Champions: 1948, 1969
Gillette/NatWest Trophy: Losing finalists 1977
Benson & Hedges Cup: Losing semi-finalists 1988
Sunday League Champions: Nil (best position 5th in 1988)
Refuge Cup: Nil

Summary of Results in 1989
Britannic Assurance County Championship: Played 22, Won 3, Lost 6, Drawn 13, Position 17th
NatWest Bank Trophy: Lost in second round
Benson & Hedges Cup: Did not qualify for knock-out section
Refuge Assurance Sunday League: Played 16, Won 2, Lost 12, No Result 2, Position 16th
Refuge Assurance Cup: Did not qualify

Alan Butcher, who joined Glamorgan after a successful career with Surrey and topped the 1989 county batting averages.
Allsport/Mike Powell

ONE DAY AWAY MATCHES

The full scorecard of each of Glamorgan's away matches will be found in the sections for the respective home teams.

Refuge Assurance League

Leicester: April 23
No play. Leics 2 pts, Glamorgan 2pts.

Worcester: June 4
Worcs 262–4 (40 ov) beat Glamorgan 119 (27.2 ov) by 143 runs. Worcs 4pts, Glamorgan 0pts.

Blackpool: June 18
Lancs 244–5 (40 ov) (N.H. Fairbrother 100*) beat Glamorgan 110 (31.4 ov) by 134 runs. Lancs 4pts, Glamorgan 0pts.

Hull: June 25
Yorks 211–7 (40 ov) beat Glamorgan 162 (36.5 ov) by 49 runs. Yorks 4pts, Glamorgan 0pts.

Taunton: July 16
Somerset 249–6 (40 ov) (S.J. Cook 114) beat Glamorgan 168–8 (40 ov) by 81 runs. Somerset 4pts, Glamorgan 0pts.

Heanor: July 23
Glamorgan 243–3 (40 ov) lost to Derbys 245–1 (36 ov) K.J. Barnett 100*, J.E. Morris 100*) by 9 wkts. Derbys 4pts, Glamorgan 0pts.

The Oval: August 6
Surrey 254–8 (40 ov) (A.J. Stewart 119) beat Glamorgan 157 (35 ov) by 97 runs. Surrey 4pts, Glamorgan 0pts.

Canterbury: August 20.
Kent 245–6 (40 ov) (R.F. Pienaar 119) beat Glamorgan 187–7 (40 ov) by 58 runs. Kent 4pts, Glamorgan 0pts.

Benson & Hedges Cup

Southampton: May 9
Hants 286–3 (55 ov) R.A. Smith 155*) lost to Glamorgan 290–2 (53.1 ov) (H. Morris 143*) by 8 wkts. Glamorgan 2pts, Hants 0pts.

Chelmsford: May 11
Glamorgan 98 lost to Essex 99–0 by 10 wkts. Essex 2pts, Glamorgan 0pts.

From left, back: *Adrian Dale, Robert Croft, Michael Cann, Martin Roberts, Simon Moorcroft, Ian Smith, Simon Dennis, Steven Bastien, Mark Davies, David Hemp.* Centre: *Byron Denning (Scorer), Don Shepherd (Assistant Coach), Anthony Cottey, Steven Watkin, Steve Barwick, John Derrick, Colin Metson, Philip North, Dean Conway (Physiotherapist), Gordon Lewis (2nd XI Scorer).* Front: *Geoff Holmes, Rodney Ontong, Alan Jones (Senior Coach), Philip Carling (Chief Executive), Hugh Morris (Captain), Tony Dilloway (Secretary), Alan Butcher, John Steele (2nd XI Captain), Matthew Maynard.*

Allsport/Ben Radford

REFUGE ASSURANCE LEAGUE

v GLOUCESTERSHIRE (Newport)
May 7
Lost by 3 wkts. Gloucs 4pts, Glamorgan 0pts

Glamorgan		
A.R. Butcher	b Pooley	52
*H. Morris	c Jarvis b Pooley	25
M.P. Maynard	c Russell b Pooley	5
R.C. Ontong	c Russell b Greene	15
P.A. Cottey	not out	34
J. Derrick	b Curran	3
M.J. Cann	run out	1
†C.P. Metson	not out	1
S.L. Watkin		
S.J. Dennis		
S. Bastien		
Extras	lb 20, w 14, nb 1	35
Total (6 wkts, 40 ov)		171

86, 97, 104, 128, 144, 153

Jarvis	8	1	27	0
Alleyne	8	1	24	0
Pooley	8	0	37	3
Greene	8	1	26	1
Curran	8	0	37	1

Gloucestershire		
A.J. Wright	c Maynard b Derrick	35
*C.W.J. Athey	lbw b Dennis	21
P. Bainbridge	run out	24
K.M. Curran	c Metson b Watkin	27
P.W. Romaines	c Cann b Watkin	13
M.W. Alleyne	b Derrick	4
V.S. Greene	not out	32
J.W. Lloyds	lbw b Watkin	2
†R.C. Russell	not out	6
M.W. Pooley		
K.B.S. Jarvis		
Extras	lb 5, w 2, nb 2	9
Total (7 wkts, 39.1 ov)		173

56, 78, 92, 128, 128, 133, 162

Ontong	8	0	34	0
Bastien	8	0	28	0
Derrick	8	1	48	2
Watkin	8	1	30	3
Dennis	7.1	0	28	1

Umpires: R. Julian and A.G.T. Whitehead
Toss: Glamorgan
Greene hit two sixes and two fours off 13 deliveries to bring Gloucestershire victory with 5 balls unbowled. Until he struck out it seemed as if Glamorgan would win the game.

v NORTHAMPTONSHIRE (Cardiff)
May 21
Lost by 6 wkts. Northants 4pts, Glamorgan 0pts

Glamorgan		
A.R. Butcher	b N.G.B. Cook	16
*H. Morris	c Ripley b Thomas	3
M.P. Maynard	b Capel	42
P.A. Cottey	b N.G.B. Cook	16
R.J. Shastri	c Ripley b Robinson	1
R.C. Ontong	c sub b Thomas	33
J. Derrick	c Larkins b Thomas	15
†C.P. Metson	not out	21
S.L. Watkin	not out	1
S.J. Dennis		
S.R. Barwick		
Extras	b 2, lb 3, w 6, nb 3	14
Total (7 wkts, 40 ov)		162

14, 29, 61, 64, 86, 112, 154

N.G.B. Cook	8	0	35	2
Robinson	8	0	28	1
Ambrose	8	0	34	0
Thomas	8	1	41	3
Capel	8	0	19	1

Northamptonshire		
G. Cook	c Ontong b Watkin	53
*W. Larkins	c Dennis b Watkin	11
R.J. Bailey	c Ontong b Dennis	0
D.J. Capel	c Watkin b Ontong	25
D.J. Wild	not out	52
N.A. Felton	not out	15
†D. Ripley		
J.G. Thomas		
C.E.L. Ambrose		
M.A. Robinson		
N.G.B. Cook		
Extras	lb 3, w 4	7
Total (4 wkts, 38.1 ov)		163

20, 25, 70, 134

Shastri	7	1	24	0
Barwick	8	0	18	0
Watkin	7.1	1	33	2
Dennis	7	1	32	1
Derrick	5	0	25	0
Ontong	4	0	28	1

Umpires: D.G.L. Evans and P.B. Wight
Toss: Northamptonshire
Put in on a slow pitch, Maynard was the only home batsman to master the spin of Cook. In reply Glamorgan obtained two quick wickets but afterwards Northants found few problems.

v NOTTINGHAMSHIRE (Llanelli)
May 29
Lost by 6 wkts. Notts 4pts, Glamorgan 0pts

Glamorgan		
*A.R. Butcher	c Scott b Pick	8
G.C. Holmes	not out	63
M.P. Maynard	b Pick	4
R.J. Shastri	lbw b Cooper	13
R.C. Ontong	lbw b Hemmings	44
I. Smith	c Robinson b Stephenson	16
J. Derrick	not out	8
†C.P. Metson		
S.J. Dennis		
S.L. Watkin		
S.R. Barwick		
Extras	b 4, lb 4, w 6, nb 2	16
Total (5 wkts, 40 ov)		172

12, 17, 49, 122, 142

Stephenson	8	2	25	1
Pick	8	0	51	2
Cooper	8	0	30	1
Evans	8	0	31	0
Hemmings	8	1	27	1

Nottinghamshire		
B.C. Broad	c Metson b Watkin	4
M. Newell	c Ontong b Barwick	15
D.W. Randall	c Metson b Dennis	1
*R.T. Robinson	not out	76
P. Johnson	c Dennis b Barwick	33
F.D. Stephenson	not out	37
R.A. Pick		
†C.W. Scott		
E.E. Hemmings		
K.E. Cooper		
K.P. Evans		
Extras	lb 4, w 4	8
Total (4 wkts, 38.1 ov)		174

7, 12, 42, 112

Watkin	8	0	36	1
Dennis	7.1	1	22	1
Barwick	7	1	24	2
Ontong	7	0	34	0
Shastri	2	0	19	0
Derrick	7	0	35	0

Umpires: M.J. Kitchen and N.T. Plews
Toss: Glamorgan
Although deciding to bat first, Glamorgan made a poor start and only a stout innings from Holmes produced a reasonable total. Notts also began feebly, but Robinson flourished and enabled his side to win comfortably.

In the 1920s the Welsh County was the Cinderella of the Championship. The famous season of 1948 removed that image. In the last few summers it has returned. While Essex and Notts both celebrated 'double crowns' in the 1980s, Glamorgan ended 1989 with 'double wooden spoons' and they also came bottom of their section in the Benson and Hedges competition. The seriousness of the situation can be gauged by the statistic that the county have not ended in the top half of the Championship since 1970. No other county can match this sad state of affairs.

The strain of captaincy affected the batting of Morris and in mid-season he was replaced by Butcher. Morris' run-getting improved almost overnight. Butcher batted well, but apart from Shastri and latterly Morris, he lacked any consistent support. Ontong, who was forced into retirement by a road accident, was missed, and Maynard, the bright star of 1988, fell right away, his average owing a great deal to his unbeaten 191; it would seem that the opposition bowlers have found the chink in his armour. James and Dale, products of Swansea University, may eventually fill the void, but they will still be at their desks in 1990.

The bright spot of the season was the bowling of Watkin. In 1988 his 44 wickets cost 30 runs each; twelve months later he took 89 Championship wickets at 23 runs each. There was some suggestion that he should go to the West Indies, but mindful of the young talent that has gone to the Caribbean before and disappeared, Dexter has sent him to Zimbabwe instead. Barwick proved to be Watkin's most useful, indeed almost his only, ally, but he could not fill the gap left by Thomas' departure and on the slower front, Shastri's bowling appears to have deserted him.

It cannot be said that the prospects for Glamorgan in 1990 are much brighter. Their period of misery has broadly coincided with the days of instant-overseas-registration and too often the stars selected by the county have lost their glitter in Sophia Gardens.

REFUGE ASSURANCE LEAGUE

v MIDDLESEX (Merthyr Tydfil)

June 11

Won by 37 runs. Glamorgan 4pts, Middx 0pts

Glamorgan		
A.R. Butcher	b Emburey	27
*H. Morris	c Downton b Cowans	4
M.P. Maynard	run out	18
G.C. Holmes	run out	9
R.J. Shastri	c Carr b Emburey	92
R.C. Ontong	not out	34
I. Smith	c Roseberry b Cowans	8
†C.P. Metson	not out	0
S. Bastien		
S.L. Watkin		
S.R. Barwick		
Extras	lb 6, w 11	17
Total (6 wkts, 40 ov)		209

5, 49, 52, 125, 190, 201

Cowans	8	2	45	2
Fraser	8	0	22	0
Tufnell	4	0	19	0
Emburey	8	0	62	2
Carr	8	0	23	0
Sykes	1	0	13	0
Haynes	3	0	19	0

Middlesex		
J.D. Carr	c Maynard b Shastri	41
D.L. Haynes	c Smith b Watkin	2
R.O. Butcher	b Holmes	32
M.A. Roseberry	c Watkin b Ontong	7
*J.E. Emburey	c Metson b Ontong	3
M.R. Ramprakash	b Shastri	14
J.F. Sykes	st Metson b Ontong	18
†P.R. Downton	c Smith b Shastri	0
A.R.C. Fraser	c Maynard b Barwick	25
P.C.R. Tufnell	not out	13
N.G. Cowans	c Metson b Barwick	0
Extras	lb 5, w 11, nb 1	17
Total (37.5 ov)		172

11, 73, 94, 95, 102, 131, 131, 133, 172

Watkin	7	1	37	1
Bastien	4	0	23	0
Barwick	6.5	2	10	2
Shastri	8	1	33	3
Holmes	3	0	20	1
Smith	2	0	12	0
Ontong	7	0	32	3

Umpires: K.E. Palmer and R.A. White
Toss: Middlesex
Shastri hit 6 sixes and 6 fours in his 92 and he then took 3 for 33 to bring the home county a splendid victory on a bowler's wicket.

v ESSEX (Neath)

July 9

Lost by 47 runs. Essex 4pts, Glamorgan 0pts

Essex		
B.R. Hardie	b Holmes	58
A.W. Lilley	b Barwick	3
M.E. Waugh	not out	112
P.J. Prichard	c Metson b Smith	4
N. Hussein	not out	15
J.P. Stephenson		
*D.R. Pringle		
G. Miller		
†M.A. Garnham		
T.D. Topley		
J.K. Lever		
Extras	lb 11, w 2	13
Total (3 wkts, 40 ov)		205

9, 126, 133

Barwick	8	0	35	1
Dennis	8	0	36	0
Shastri	4	0	19	0
Dale	8	0	35	0
Derrick	3	0	16	0
Holmes	5	0	33	1
Smith	4	1	20	1

Glamorgan		
A.R. Butcher	c Garnham b Pringle	10
M.P. Maynard	c Pringle b Stephenson	35
G.C. Holmes	c Hussain b Lever	9
R.J. Shastri	c Pringle b Lever	57
*H. Morris	c Hardie b Topley	7
I. Smith	st Garnham b Stephenson	11
A. Dale	c Lilley b Pringle	5
†C.P. Metson	b Lever	7
S.R. Barwick	not out	2
S.J. Dennis	b Pringle	4
J. Derrick	absent ill	
Extras	lb 9, w 2	11
Total (36.5 ov)		158

17, 26, 92, 106, 121, 131, 152, 153

Lever	6	2	16	3
Pringle	6.5	0	27	3
Topley	6	0	29	1
Miller	6	0	32	0
Stephenson	8	0	27	2
Waugh	4	0	18	0

Umpires: K.J. Lyons and J.H Harris
Toss: Glamorgan
This win by Essex enabled them to gain a clear lead of six points at the head of the Refuge table. Waugh hit his highest score in the competition.

v HAMPSHIRE (Swansea)

July 30

Won by 37 runs. Glamorgan 4pts, Hants 0pts

Glamorgan		
*A.R. Butcher	b Connor	0
S.P. James	c Wood b Marshall	13
A. Dale	b Bakker	14
M.P. Maynard	c Turner b James	17
R.J. Shastri	run out	60
H. Morris	lbw b Bakker	49
I. Smith	c Parks b Bakker	3
†C.P. Metson	not out	5
S.J. Dennis	c Smith b Connor	8
S.L. Watkin	b Marshall	0
S.R. Barwick	not out	2
Extras	lb 10, w 11, nb 1	22
Total (9 wkts, 39 ov)		193

Bakker	8	1	31	3
Connor	7	0	27	2
Marshall	8	0	28	2
James	8	0	40	1
Cowley	7	0	42	0
Nicholas	1	0	15	0

Hampshire		
V.P. Terry	c Morris b Barwick	5
K.D. James	c Smith b Shastri	12
*M.C.J. Nicholas	b Smith	52
D.R. Turner	b Dale	24
M.D. Marshall	b Watkin	24
C.L. Smith	c Dennis b Barwick	17
J.R. Wood	c Metson b Smith	0
N.G. Cowley	c Watkin b Dennis	2
†R.J. Parks	c James b Smith	4
C.A. Connor	b Watkin	8
P.J. Bakker	not out	2
Extras	lb 2, w 4	6
Total (35.3 ov)		156

16, 21, 73, 107, 134, 134, 140, 145, 146

Dennis	7	0	36	1
Watkin	6.3	0	16	2
Barwick	7	1	24	2
Dale	4	0	27	1
Smith	3	0	22	3
Shastri	8	0	29	1

Umpires: H.D. Bird and B. Dudleston
Toss: Hampshire
Glamorgan beat Hampshire at home in the Sunday League for the first time since 1969. Shastri hit 60 off 62 balls and Nicholas conceded 15 off one over. Accurate bowling by Watkin prevented Hampshire's batsmen breaking loose.

PLAYERS

Stephen Royston BARWICK *b* 6.9.1960 Neath; right arm medium fast bowler; tail end right hand batsman; debut 1981
Steven BASTIEN *b* 13.3.1963 Stepney; right arm medium fast bowler; right hand batsman; debut 1988; played in 4 Championship matches in 1989
Alan Raymond BUTCHER *b* 7.1.1954 Croydon; debut 1987; previously played for Surrey 1972 to 1986; brothers played for Leics/Gloucs and Surrey; played in one Test for England in 1979; took over as county captain during 1989
Michael James CANN *b* 4.7.1965 Cardiff; Middle order left hand batsman; off break bowler; debut 1986
Phillip Anthony COTTEY *b* 2.6.1966 Swansea; Diminutive middle order right hand batsman; debut 1986
Richard Damien Bale CROFT *b* 25.5.1970 Morriston; right hand batsman; off break bowler; debut for Glamorgan August 5 1989
Adrian DALE *b* 24.10.1968 Germiston, South Africa; right hand batsman; right arm medium pace bowler; debut for Glamorgan 1989; also played for Combined Universities in B&H Cup 1989
Simon John DENNIS *b* 18.10.1960 Scarborough; left arm fast medium bowler; lower order right hand batsman; debut for Glamorgan in 1989; previously appeared for Yorkshire 1980 to 1988
John DERRICK *b* 15.1.1963 Cwmaman; all rounder; right hand batsman; right arm pace bowler; debut 1983
Geoffrey Clark HOLMES *b* 16.9.1958 Newcastle-upon-Tyne; right hand batsman; debut 1978
Stephen Peter JAMES *b* 7.9.1967 Lydney, Gloucs; promising right hand batsman; debut 1985; debut for Cambridge Univ 1989

Steve Watkin, Glamorgan's leading bowler.
Allsport/Tom Jenkins

Matthew Peter MAYNARD *b* 21.3.1966 Oldham; fast scoring right hand batsman; debut 1985; scoring 100 in first match; chosen to tour South Africa 1989–90; one Test for England in 1988
Colin Peter METSON *b* 2.7.1963 Goffs Oak, Herts; right hand batsman; wicketkeeper; debut 1987; previously played for Middlesex 1981 to 1986
Hugh MORRIS *b* 5.10.1963 Cardiff; left hand batsman; debut 1981; captain 1986; but resigned mid way through 1989 season
Philip David NORTH *b* 16.5.1965 Newport, Mon; slow left arm bowler; right hand batsman; debut 1985
Rodney Craig ONTONG *b* 9.9.1955 Johannesburg; all rounder; right hand batsman; off break bowler; debut 1975; captain 1984–86; returned after serious road accident in Aug 1988; but has now retired; also plays for Northern Transvaal
Martin Leonard ROBERTS *b* 12.4.1966 Mullion; right hand batsman; wicketkeeper; only appeared in limited overs matches in 1989; debut 1985
Ravishankar Jayadritha SHASTRI *b* 27.5.1962 Bombay; attacking right hand batsman; slow left arm bowler; debut 1987; also plays for Bombay; hit six sixes off single over and scored 200 in 113 minutes in Ranji Trophy; played Tests for India since 1980–81
Ian SMITH *b* 11.3.1967 Chopwell, Durham; All rounder; right hand batsman; right arm medium pace bowler; debut 1985
K. A. SOMAIA *b* slow left arm bowler; debut for Glamorgan July 1989
Steven Llewellyn WATKIN *b* 15.9.1964 Maesteg; right arm medium fast bowler; right hand batsman; debut 1986; England 'A' to Zimbabwe 1989

REFUGE ASSURANCE LEAGUE

v SUSSEX (Ebbw Vale)
August 13
Abandoned. Sussex 2pts, Glamorgan 2pts

Glamorgan		
*A.R. Butcher	c Moores b Dodemaide	6
G.C. Holmes	b Hansford	29
M.P. Maynard	c Gould b Hansford	15
R.J. Shastri	b Pigott	28
I. Smith	c A.P. Wells b Pigott	9
H. Morris	not out	16
†M.L. Roberts	not out	1
A. Dale		
S.J. Dennis		
J. Derrick		
S.R. Barwick		
Extras	lb 7, w 15, nb 1	13
Total (5 wkts, 22.3 ov)		117

11, 43, 72, 85, 103

C.M. Wells	6	0	32	0
Dodemaide	3	0	7	1
Babington	3	0	8	0
Hansford	5.3	0	42	2
Pigott	5	0	21	2

Sussex
*P.W.G. Parker
N.J. Lenham
A.P. Wells
C.M. Wells
M.P. Speight
I.J. Gould
A.C.S. Pigott
A.I.C. Dodemaide
†P. Moores
A.M. Babington
A.R. Hansford

Umpires: P.J. Eele and D.O. Oslear
Toss: Sussex
With Glamorgan at the foot of the table and Sussex 12th, both sides needed four points to improve their final 1989 positions, but rain prevented any further play after Glamorgan had reached 117–5.

v WARWICKSHIRE (Aberystwyth)
August 27
Lost by 6 wkts. Warwicks 4pts, Glamorgan 0pts

Glamorgan		
*A.R. Butcher	c Humpage b Munton	17
G.C. Holmes	run out	21
M.P. Maynard	b Twose	2
H. Morris	run out	83
I. Smith	not out	56
S.J. Dennis	not out	2
J. Derrick		
S.L. Watkin		
S.R. Barwick		
A. Dale		
†C.P. Metson		
Extras	b 8, lb 7, w 7	22
Total (4 wkts, 40 ov)		203

22, 35, 51, 186

Twose	8	0	25	1
Benjamin	8	0	34	0
N.M.K. Smith	8	0	54	0
Munton	8	2	18	1
Ratcliffe	5	0	29	0
P.A. Smith	3	0	28	0

Warwickshire		
A.I. Kallicharran	b Smith	32
P.A. Smith	c Dale b Watkin	23
G.W. Humpage	c Holmes b Barwick	19
Asif Din	c Dennis b Derrick	4
*T.A. Lloyd	not out	56
D.A. Reeve	not out	56
R.G. Twose		
J.E. Benjamin		
N.M.K. Smith		
T.A. Munton		
J.D. Ratcliffe		
Extras	lb 9, w 8	17
Total (4 wkts, 39.5 ov)		207

40, 64, 77, 91

Derrick	8	0	32	1
Watkin	8	1	40	1
Dennis	6.5	0	61	0
Barwick	7	1	23	1
Smith	4	0	14	1
Dale	6	1	28	0

Umpires: N.T. Plews and B. Leadbeater
Toss: Warwickshire
The only concern of this match was the battle of the wooden spoon between Glamorgan and Gloucestershire, both anchored at the foot of the table before the game with 12 points each. Both teams lost and thus tied for the award.

BENSON AND HEDGES CUP

v KENT (Cardiff)
April 25
Lost by 6 wkts. Kent 2pts, Glamorgan 0pts

Glamorgan		
A.R. Butcher	c G.R. Cowdrey b Penn	5
*H. Morris	c Taylor b Ellison	8
P.A. Cottey	b Igglesden	4
M.P. Maynard	c Marsh b Alleyne	3
M.J. Cann	run out	15
I. Smith	lbw b C.S. Cowdrey	9
J. Derrick	c Alleyne b G.R. Cowdrey	0
†C.P. Metson	b Alleyne	6
S.J. Dennis	c C.S. Cowdrey b Penn	0
S.L. Watkin	not out	3
S.R. Barwick	b Alleyne	4
Extras	b 4, w 10, nb 11	25
Total (45.3 ov)		82

10, 21, 24, 24, 47, 55, 64, 65, 78

Igglesden	10	2	15	1
Penn	9	3	14	2
Ellison	3	0	4	1
Alleyne	9.3	0	23	3
C.S. Cowdrey	9	2	14	1
G.R. Cowdrey	5	2	8	1

Kent		
M.R. Benson	b Derrick	19
S.G. Hinks	lbw b Barwick	28
N.R. Taylor	lbw b Watkin	15
*C.S. Cowdrey	c Metson b Watkin	4
G.R. Cowdrey	not out	6
T.R. Ward	not out	3
†S.A. Marsh		
R.M. Ellison		
C. Penn		
A.P. Igglesden		
H.L. Alleyne		
Extras	lb 5, w 1, nb 2	8
Total (4 wkts, 32.3 ov)		83

44, 56, 73, 74

Watkin	9.3	2	29	2
Barwick	9	2	16	1
Dennis	5	0	19	0
Derrick	9	2	14	1

Umpires: A.A. Jones and P.B. Wight
Toss: Kent. Gold: H.L. Alleyne
On a damp wicket, the visitors quickly removed the Welsh batsmen and the Glamorgan total owed a great deal to wides and no balls. Despite a stoppage of 25 minutes through rain, the game was at an end by 5.30.

BRITANNIC ASSURANCE COUNTY CHAMPIONSHIP AVERAGES 1989

Batting	*M*	*I*	*NO*	*Runs*	*HS*	*Avge*	*100*	*50*
A.R. Butcher	21	37	5	1527	171*	47.72	3	10
R.J. Shastri	15	24	4	910	127	45.50	2	5
H. Morris	22	38	2	1098	133	30.50	2	6
I. Smith	16	25	2	676	116	29.39	2	2
S.P. James	7	12	–	347	53	28.92	–	1
M.J. Cann	18	31	2	829	109	28.59	1	4
M.P. Maynard	22	37	3	963	191*	28.32	1	3
J. Derrick	5	6	1	135	67	27.090	–	1
R.D.B. Croft	5	8	2	129	45	21.50	–	–
A. Dale	4	8	1	134	44	19.14	–	–
G.C. Holmes	12	19	2	311	38	18.29	–	–
C.P. Metson	22	32	8	399	47	16.63	–	–
R.C. Ontong	5	5	–	54	48	10.80	–	–
S.J. Dennis	14	19	1	187	38	10.39	–	–
K.A. Somaia	3	6	–	50	15	8.33	–	–
P.D. North	3	4	–	32	17	8.00	–	–
P.A. Cottey	3	5	–	32	12	6.40	–	–
S.L. Watkin	21	26	5	131	31	6.24	–	–
S.R. Barwick	20	26	12	59	23	4.21	–	–

Also batted: S. Bastien (4 matches) 1*, 0*.

Bowling	*O*	*M*	*R*	*W*	*Avge*	*BB*	*5i*	*10m*
S.L. Watkin	703	149	2101	89	23.61	7-65	8	3
K.A. Somaia	78.4	19	245	8	30.63	5-87	1	–
S.R. Barwick	745.2	219	1884	61	30.89	7-47	3	1
S.J. Dennis	365.3	98	1062	33	32.18	5-83	1	–
M.J. Cann	69	13	267	7	38.14	3-30	–	–
I. Smith	217	21	936	23	40.70	3-48	–	–
P.D. North	102.3	31	213	5	42.60	3-54	–	–
J. Derrick	131.5	30	398	8	49.75	3-61	–	–
R.C. Ontong	133.5	22	361	6	60.17	2-55	–	–
R.J. Shastri	270.2	66	708	9	78.67	3-77	–	–

Also bowled: S. Bastien 59-12-202-4; A.R. Butcher 41-6-177-4; P.A. Cottey 1-0-6-0; R.D.B. Croft 94-21-312-1; A. Dale 39-10-129-2; G.C. Holmes 45.4-10-125-4; M.P. Maynard 23-4-64-0; H. Morris 8.5-0-33-0.

Centuries

3 A.R. Butcher: 107* v Notts (Cardiff); 101 v Middlesex (Abergavenny); 171* v Warwicks (Edgbaston).

2 H. Morris: 133 v Warwicks (Edgbaston); 108 v Warwicks (Swansea). I. Smith: 105 v Warwicks (Edgbaston); 116 v Kent (Canterbury). R.J. Shastri: 127 & 101* v Middlesex (Abergavenny).

1 M.J. Cann: 109 v Somerset (Cardiff). M.P. Maynard: 191* v Glos (Cardiff).

BENSON AND HEDGES CUP

v SUSSEX (Swansea)

May 13, 14

Lost by 47 runs. Sussex 2pts, Glamorgan 0pts

Sussex		
N.J. Falkner	c Maynard b Watkin	1
D.M. Smith	c Watkin b Butcher	41
I.J. Gould	run out	0
A.P. Wells	c Cann b Barwick	14
*C.M. Wells	c Shastri b Barwick	117
K. Greenfield	lbw b Butcher	0
A.I.C. Dodemaide	c Ontong b Butcher	6
A.C.S. Pigott	not out	9
†P. Moores	not out	0
A.M. Babington		
A.R. Clarke		
Extras	lb 13, w 6	19
Total (7 wkts, 55 ov)		207

2, 2, 20, 144, 148, 165, 206

Watkin	10	3	28	1
Dennis	11	3	28	0
Barwick	11	2	33	2
Ontong	6	0	36	0
Shastri	11	0	37	0
Butcher	6	0	32	3

Glamorgan		
A.R. Butcher	b Babington	41
*H. Morris	lbw b Dodemaide	0
P.A. Cottey	c A.P. Wells b C.M. Wells	4
M.P. Maynard	lbw b Dodemaide	12
R.J. Shastri	st Moores b Clarke	25
R.C. Ontong	c Moores b Babington	40
M.J. Cann	b Pigott	12
†C.P. Metson	b Dodemaide	12
S.J. Dennis	lbw b Babington	0
S.L. Watkin	not out	1
S.R. Barwick	run out	0
Extras	b 1, lb 9, w 3	13
Total (48.2 ov)		160

1, 14, 38, 89, 93, 120, 143, 144, 159

Dodemaide	11	3	26	3
Pigott	8	1	14	1
C.M. Wells	9	0	57	1
Babington	10.2	2	36	3
Clarke	10	2	17	1

Umpires: J.H. Harris and K.E. Palmer

Toss: Glamorgan. Gold: C.M. Wells

Glamorgan needed to win this game to obtain a place in the quarter finals. Owing to rain only the Sussex innings could be completed on the first day and Glamorgan began the second at 13–1 off 6.4 overs. They had to get 208 off 34.1 overs to beat Kent's run rate and qualify. This never really appeared likely.

NATWEST BANK TROPHY

v STAFFORDSHIRE (Cardiff)

June 28, 29

Won by 167 runs.

Glamorgan		
A.R. Butcher	c Dean b McArdle	42
*H. Morris	not out	154
M.P. Maynard	b Blank	56
R.J. Shastri	c Monkhouse b Cartledge	13
G.C. Holmes	b Blank	25
M.J. Cann	not out	2
A. Dale		
†C.P. Metson		
S.L Watkin		
S.R. Barwick		
S.J. Dennis		
Extras	lb 5, w 17, nb 4	26
Total (4 wkts, 60 ov)		318

123, 204, 224, 289

Taylor	12	1	56	0
Monkhouse	12	0	66	0
Grant	12	4	53	0
Blank	12	0	66	2
McArdle	7	0	40	1
Cartledge	5	0	32	1

Staffordshire		
S.J. Dean	b Watkin	12
D. Cartledge	c Cann b Barwick	26
H. Patel	c Holmes b Cann	63
P.R. Oliver	b Shastri	12
B. McArdle	c Holmes b Shastri	1
N.J. Archer	c Morris b Shastri	0
A. Mackelworth	c Morris b Dale	2
P. Taylor	c Barwick b Cann	9
S. Monkhouse	b Cann	11
D.C. Blank	lbw b Dale	5
R. Grant	not out	0
Extras	b 1, lb 2, w 7	10
Total (53.4 ov)		151

18, 49, 73, 84, 84, 96, 115, 135, 148

Shastri	12	3	16	3
Watkin	6	3	10	1
Dennis	6	1	22	0
Barwick	8	1	28	1
Dale	10.4	1	32	2
Cann	11	2	40	3

Umpires: D.J. Dennis and D.R. Shepherd

Toss: Staffordshire. MofM: H. Morris

No play was possible on the first day, but on the second the Welsh side proved much too good for Staffordshire. Morris created a new record individual Glamorgan One-Day score and the county total was another record.

v HAMPSHIRE (Cardiff)

July 12

Lost by 7 wkts.

Glamorgan		
A.R. Butcher	b Connor	11
*H. Morris	c Maru b Bakker	53
M.J. Cann	lbw b Bakker	2
M.P. Maynard	c R.A. Smith b Maru	12
R.J. Shastri	b James	4
G.C. Holmes	c Maru b Marshall	26
I. Smith	b Connor	33
A. Dale	b James	10
S.J. Dennis	run out	1
†C.P. Metson	lbw b Connor	6
S.L. Watkin	not out	2
Extras	lb 20, w 4, nb 5	29
Total (59.4 ov)		189

23, 26, 45, 65, 129, 155, 178, 180, 181

Maru	12	1	19	1
Bakker	12	3	30	2
Marshall	12	3	31	1
James	12	3	46	2
Connor	11.4	1	43	3

Hampshire		
V.P. Terry	b Watkin	2
C.L. Smith	c Metson b Dale	20
K.D. James	c Dennis b Holmes	42
R.A. Smith	not out	69
*M.C.J. Nicholas	not out	46
J.R. Wood		
M.D. Marshall		
†R.J. Parks		
R.J. Maru		
C.A. Connor		
P.J. Bakker		
Extras	lb 1, nb 3, w 7	11
Total (3 wkts, 57 ov)		190

2, 41, 88

Shastri	12	2	40	0
Watkin	12	2	30	1
Dale	9	0	38	1
Dennis	12	5	34	0
Holmes	4	0	22	1
Smith	8	0	25	0

Umpires: J.D. Bond and B.J. Meyer

Toss: Hampshire. MofM: R.A. Smith

Glamorgan's batsmen found the wicket difficult and though Morris survived 3 hours for 53, the total was none too impressive. Watkin dismissed Terry cheaply, but the visiting batsmen then got the measure of the bowling and Smith batted with authority.

Away Matches

The full scorecard of each of Glamorgan's away matches will be found in the sections for the respective home teams.

Leicester: April 20, 21, 22, 24
Leics 190 (S.L. Watkin 6–53) and 415–9d (D.I Gower 228) drew with Glamorgan 167 and 166–4. Leics 5pts, Glamorgan 5pts.

Taunton: April 28, 29, 30, May 1
Glamorgan 118 (V.J. Marks 5–38) and 260–9d drew with Somerset 186 (S.R. Barwick 7–47) and 152–6. Somerset 5pts, Glamorgan 4pts.

Worcester: June 3, 5, 6
Worcs 127 (S.R. Barwick 6–40) and 246–3d (T.S. Curtis 140*) drew with Glamorgan 134 and 20–0. Worcs 4pts, Glamorgan 4pts.

Old Trafford: June 17, 19, 20
Glamorgan 297–9d (Wasim Akram 5–45) and 252–6d beat Lancs 196 (S.L. Watkin 7–65) and 344 (S.L. Watkin 6–94) by 9 runs. Glamorgan 23pts, Lancs 5pts.

Edgbaston: June 21, 22, 23
Glamorgan 290 (I. Smith 105) and 378–2d (A.R. Butcher 171*, H. Morris 133) drew with Warwicks 365–4d (A.J. Moles 130*, G.W. Humpage 183) and 84–0. Warwicks 8pts, Glamorgan 4pts.

Headingley: June 24, 26, 27
Yorks 308–9d (A.A. Metcalfe 113, S.L. Watkin 5–53) drew with Glamorgan 214–2. Yorks 3pts, Glamorgan 3pts.

Bristol: July 19, 20, 21
Glamorgan 89 (K.B.S. Jarvis 5–15) and 171 (V.S. Greene 6–101) lost to Gloucs 383–9d by an innings and 123 runs. Gloucs 23pts, Glamorgan 3pts.

Derby: July 22, 24, 25
Glamorgan 191 (M.A. Holding 6–57) and 241 lost to Derbys 338 (J.E. Morris 134) and 97–1 by 9 wkts. Derbys 23pts, Glamorgan 4pts.

The Oval: August 5, 7, 8
Surrey 357 and 232–4d drew with Glamorgan 227 (K.T. Medlycott 7–68) and 205–3. Surrey 8pts, Glamorgan 5pts.

Canterbury: August 19, 21, 22
Kent 372–9d (R.F. Pienaar 132, S.J. Dennis 5–83) and 218–4d beat Glamorgan 311 (I. Smith 116) and 178 by 101 runs. Kent 24pts, Glamorgan 6pts.

Southampton: September 8, 9, 10, 11
Glamorgan 247 (M.D. Marshall 5–68) and 133 beat Hants 201 (S.L. Watkin 6–73) and 149 (S.L. Watkin 5–46) by 30 runs. Glamorgan 22pts, Hants 4pts.

v GLOUCESTERSHIRE (Cardiff)

May 4, 5, 6,8

Drawn. Glamorgan 4pts, Gloucs 4pts

Gloucestershire 1st Innings

A.J. Wright	c Metson b Watkin	4
A.W. Stovold	c Maynard b Dennis	0
P.W. Romaines	b Watkin	22
*C.W.J. Athey	lbw b Dennis	30
P. Bainbridge	b Ontong	56
K.M. Curran	c Maynard b Dennis	93
J.W. Lloyds	c Metson b Dennis	27
†R.C. Russell	b Derrick	26
V.S. Greene	c Butcher b Derrick	3
D.V. Lawrence	b Derrick	8
D.A. Graveney	not out	3
Extras	b 1, lb 5, w 1, nb 3	10
Total (100 ov: 202–6)		282

5, 7, 60, 67, 138, 202, 265, 271, 271

Watkin	30	15	56	2
Dennis	31	8	56	4
Derrick	36.1	18	61	3
North	20	8	33	0
Ontong	21	6	53	1
Butcher	4	0	17	0

Glamorgan 1st Innings

A.R. Butcher	c Russell b Lloyds	69
*H. Morris	c Wright b Graveney	90
P.A. Cottey	c Athey b Graveney	0
M.P. Maynard	not out	191
R.C. Ontong	lbw b Graveney	2
†C.P. Metson	c Athey b Graveney	0
M.J. Cann	c Greene b Graveney	34
J. Derrick	c Russell b Graveney	0
P.D. North	c Athey b Greene	15
S.L. Watkin	b Greene	0
S.J. Dennis	lbw b Lawrence	0
Extras	b 1, lb 19, w 1, nb 13	34
Total (100 ov: 227–5)		435

168, 168, 186, 199, 213, 372, 376, 432, 432

Lawrence	22	6	41	1
Greene	20	5	68	2
Graveney	50	13	128	6
Lloyds	35	10	91	1
Curran	18	5	49	0
Bainbridge	10	1	38	0

Gloucestershire 2nd Innings

A.W. Stovold	c Cottey b Ontong	24
A.J. Wright	st Metson b Ontong	100
P.W. Romaines	c Cann b Butcher	77
*C.W.J. Athey	not out	93
P. Bainbridge	c Maynard b North	7
K.M. Curran	c Ontong b North	27
J.W. Lloyds	not out	24
Extras	b 10, lb 13, w 1, nb 5	29
Total (5 wkts dec)		381

39, 205, 225, 234, 276

Watkin	17	4	31	0
Dennis	10	6	14	0
Derrick	12	2	35	0
North	37	13	63	2
Ontong	46	5	128	2
Butcher	9	2	30	1
Maynard	11	3	20	0
Cann	8	0	30	0
Morris	1	0	1	0
Cottey	1	0	6	0

Umpires: R. Julian and A.G.T. Whitehead
Toss: Gloucestershire
In this match the experiment of four day games was a total failure. Only 241 runs were scored on the first for the loss of 6 wickets. On the second the crawl continued. At the end of the third day Gloucestershire had reached 102–1 in their second innings. On the last day the visitors were happy to bat on until a declaration allowed the weary spectators and officials to go home.

v NORTHAMPTONSHIRE (Swansea)

May 20, 22, 23

Won by 244 runs. Glamorgan 23pts, Northants 6pts

Glamorgan 1st Innings

A.R. Butcher	c Ripley b Ambrose	0
*H. Morris	c Ripley b Capel	35
R.J. Shastri	c and b N.G.B. Cook	50
M.P. Maynard	lbw b N.G.B. Cook	38
R.C. Ontong	b Thomas	0
M.J. Cann	not out	75
J. Derrick	c Larkins b Capel	23
†C.P. Metson	c Ripley b Ambrose	15
S.J. Dennis	c Wild b N.G.B. Cook	13
S.L. Watkin	c Bailey b Capel	0
S.R. Barwick	c Wild b N.G.B. Cook	1
Extras	b 12, lb 5, w 4, nb 19	40
Total (90.4 ov)		290

0, 63, 127, 133, 142, 197, 245, 281, 281

Ambrose	26	2	72	2
Thomas	19	3	52	1
Capel	18	1	76	3
N.G.B. Cook	23.4	10	62	4
Roberts	3	0	7	0
Bailey	1	0	4	0

Northamptonshire 1st Innings

G. Cook	c Metson b Waktin	21
W. Larkins	hit wkt b Dennis	22
R.J. Bailey	lbw b Barwick	45
*A.J. Lamb	c Shastri b Barwick	15
D.J. Wild	c Watkin b Cann	17
D.J. Capel	c Watkin b Shastri	13
†D. Ripley	c Derrick b Ontong	19
J.G. Thomas	c Metson b Barwick	28
A. Roberts	not out	8
C.E.L. Ambrose	c and b Barwick	0
N.G.B. Cook	c Metson b Shastri	0
Extras	lb 6, nb 6	12
Total (99.3 ov)		200

39, 45, 78, 115, 135, 157, 163, 197, 199

Watkin	13	2	37	1
Dennis	14	2	40	1
Shastri	32.3	9	61	2
Barwick	24	10	31	4
Ontong	15	5	23	1
Cann	1	0	2	1

Glamorgan 2nd Innings

A.R. Butcher	c Larkins b Thomas	10
*H. Morris	c Larkins b Bailey	45
M.J. Cann	not out	45
M.P. Maynard	st Ripley b Roberts	39
R.J. Shastri	c Roberts b Ambrose	48
Extras	b 6, lb 7, w 3, nb 11	27
Total (4 wkts dec)		214

35, 88, 146, 214

Ambrose	8.2	1	25	1
Thomas	10	0	46	1
N.G.B Cook	20	5	49	0
Capel	5	1	16	0
Bailey	7	1	25	1
Roberts	7	1	40	1

Northamptonshire 2nd Innings

W. Larkins	c Metson b Watkin	0
*A.J. Lamb	c Derrick b Dennis	1
R.J. Bailey	c Derrick b Watkin	0
D.J. Wild	c Metson b Watkin	0
D.J. Capel	c Metson b Watkin	1
†D. Ripley	c Morris b Watkin	7
J.G. Thomas	c Maynard b Shastri	22
A. Roberts	c Morris b Watkin	7
C.E.L. Ambrose	st Metson b Shastri	15
N.G.B. Cook	not out	7
G. Cook	absent injured	—
Extras		0
Total		60

1, 1, 1, 1, 6, 31, 31, 50, 60

Watkin	11	3	42	6
Dennis	6	4	7	1
Shastri	4	0	11	2

Umpires: D.G.L. Evans and P.B. Wight
Toss: Glamorgan
Northants were set 305 off 75 overs on the last day, with G. Cook unable to bat. The visitors unbeaten up to this point this season collapsed in an astonishing manner, all out in 77 minutes, with Watkin's seamers proving fatal. He bowled unchanged. There was nothing remarkable about the first day's play, when Northants were 33–0 off 15 overs at stumps. On Monday, Larkins was unfortunately out when his helmet fell on the wicket and by the close Glamorgan were in a strong position.

v NOTTINGHAMSHIRE (Cardiff)
May 27, 29, 30
Drawn. Glamorgan 5pts, Notts 4pts

Nottinghamshire 1st Innings

B.C. Broad	c Metson b Barwick	132
M. Newell	b Watkin	31
P. Johnson	c Barwick b Derrick	52
*R.T. Robinson	c Maynard b Ontong	37
D.W. Randall	lbw b Watkin	8
C.L. Cairns	b Ontong	26
†C.W. Scott	not out	1
E.E. Hemmings	not out	2
K.E. Cooper		
R.A. Pick		
J.A. Afford		
Extras	lb 8, nb 3	11
Total (6 wkts dec, 97.5 ov)		300

124, 224, 224, 235, 296, 297

Watkin	17	2	49	2
Dennis	15	2	34	0
Barwick	26	5	71	1
Derrick	12	1	53	1
Shastri	6	0	20	0
Ontong	20.5	4	55	2
Cann	1	0	10	0

Glamorgan 1st Innings

A.R. Butcher	not out	107
M.J. Cann	c Hemmings b Pick	26
M.P. Maynard	c Robinson b Hemmings	49
R.J. Shastri	not out	54
*H. Morris		
R.C. Ontong		
J. Derrick		
†C.P. Metson		
S.J. Dennis		
S.L. Watkin		
S.R. Barwick		
Extras	lb 5, w 1, nb 8	14
Total (2 wkts dec, 67 ov)		250

73, 147

Pick	12	2	39	1
Cooper	11	1	40	0
Hemmings	17.3	3	59	1
Cairns	8	1	52	0
Afford	19	4	55	0

Nottinghamshire 2nd Innings

B.C. Broad	lbw b Dennis	113
M. Newell	c Metson b Watkin	4
P. Johnson	c Ontong b Dennis	87
*R.T. Robinson	not out	63
D.W. Randall	not out	24
Extras	b 4, lb 2, w 1, nb 4	11
Total (3 wkts dec)		302

21, 200, 233

Watkin	12	2	47	1
Dennis	16	1	65	2
Barwick	19	4	47	0
Derrick	14.4	1	63	0
Ontong	17	0	64	0
Butcher	1	0	10	0

Glamorgan 2nd Innings

A.R. Butcher	c sub b Pick	10
*H. Morris	c Scott b Cairns	7
M.J. Cann	run out	34
M.P. Maynard	c Broad b Hemmings	65
R.J. Shastri	b Hemmings	80
R.C. Ontong	c sub b Afford	48
J. Derrick	not out	22
†C.P. Metson	not out	0
Extras	b 8, lb 3, w 2, nb 7	20
Total (6 wkts)		286

12, 32, 114, 136, 246, 273

Pick	15	2	32	1
Cairns	8	1	17	1
Hemmings	29	1	145	2
Afford	23	4	81	1

Umpires: M.J. Kitchen and N.T. Plews
Toss: Nottinghamshire
Due to two century partnerships, Notts obtained full batting points and at the close of Saturday's play, the home side were 27–0 off 9 overs. On Monday the Welsh batsmen flourished but Morris took the bold step of declaring when the 3rd batting point was gathered in. Notts then hit out, with Broad completing his second 100 of the match. With Cooper injured and Stephenson absent, Robinson delayed his declaration on the last day and Glamorgan found 353 off 77 overs too tall an order.

v SOMERSET (Cardiff)
June 7, 8, 9
Drawn. Glamorgan 3pts, Somerset 3pts

Somerset 1st Innings

P.M. Roebuck	b Barwick	26
S.J. Cook	b Watkin	61
R.J. Bartlett	c Morris b Barwick	0
C.J. Tavare	c Ontong b Watkin	70
R.J. Harden	c Butcher b Watkin	10
†N.D. Burns	not out	86
*V.J. Marks	c Morris b Barwick	17
G.D. Rose	run out	16
N.A. Mallender	c Morris b Bastien	2
H.R.J. Trump	not out	31
A.N. Jones		
Extras	b 1, lb 9, w 1	11
Total (100 ov: 259–7) (8 wkts dec)		330

57, 59, 114, 130, 208, 229, 252, 266

Watkin	33	7	90	3
Barwick	31	14	73	3
Bastien	20	7	52	1
Shastri	10	2	29	0
Ontong	14	2	38	0
Holmes	2	0	4	0
Morris	3.5	0	16	0
Maynard	3	0	18	0

Glamorgan 1st Innings

A.R. Butcher	
*H. Morris	
M.J. Cann	
M.P. Maynard	
R.J. Shastri	did not bat
G.C. Holmes	innings forfeited
R.C. Ontong	
†C.P. Metson	
S.R. Barwick	
S.L. Watkin	
S. Bastien	

Somerset 2nd Innings

did not bat
innings forfeited

Glamorgan 2nd Innings

A.R. Butcher	c Burns b Jones	46
*H. Morris	lbw b Jones	12
M.J. Cann	b Mallender	109
M.P. Maynard	c sub b Jones	22
R.J. Shastri	c Trump b Marks	44
G.C. Holmes	c Bartlett b Marks	7
R.C. Ontong	c and b Marks	4
†C.P. Metson	not out	7
S.R. Barwick	lbw b Marks	0
S.L. Watkin	b Rose	9
S. Bastien	not out	1
Extras	b 1, lb 10, nb 5	16
Total (9 wkts)		277

17, 128, 167, 231, 251, 255, 256, 260, 269

Mallender	20	7	35	1
Jones	16	1	42	3
Rose	20	4	57	1
Trump	17	2	59	0
Marks	21	2	73	4

Umpires: K.J. Lyons and R.A. White
Toss: Somerset
On Wednesday Somerset, despite a good innings by Cook, spent the whole day making 296. Due to rain there was no play at all on the second day and thus on the final day Somerset batted on until they reached 330–8 thanks to the use of the joke bowlers. Both sides then forfeited an innings each which left Glamorgan needing 331 of 94 overs. Butcher was painfully slow, but Cann hit out and whilst he remained Glamorgan had a chance. In the end the last pair survived 7 overs and obtained a draw.

v MIDDLESEX (Abergavenny)
June 10, 12, 13
Drawn. Middx 5pts, Glamorgan 4pts

Glamorgan 1st Innings

A.R. Butcher	c and b Emburey	101
*H. Morris	lbw c Cowans	7
M.J. Cann	b Fraser	2
M.P. Maynard	lbw b Cowans	5
R.J. Shastri	c Downton b Fraser	127
G.C. Holmes	not out	28
I. Smith	c Downton b Tufnell	0
†C.P. Metson	b Tufnell	14
S.R. Barwick	not out	0
S.L. Watkin		
S. Bastien		
Extras	lb 5, nb 13	18
Total (100 ov: 277–6) (7 wkts dec)		302

15, 22, 30, 246, 275, 276, 296

Cowans	12	5	29	2
Fraser	25	3	76	2
Hughes	10	0	31	0
Emburey	29.3	9	84	1
Tufnell	30	4	77	2

Middlesex 1st Innings

J.D. Carr	c Maynard b Bastien	23
D.L. Haynes	b Cann	85
M.A. Roseberry	c Morris b Cann	51
R.O. Butcher	st Metson b Cann	14
M.R. Ramprakash	not out	32
†P.R. Downton	not out	34
*J.E. Emburey		
P.C.R. Tufnell		
S.P. Hughes		
A.R.C. Fraser		
N.G. Cowans		
Extras	b 4, lb 11, nb 9	24
Total (4 wkts dec, 78 ov)		263

41, 154, 181, 190

Watkin	16	2	42	0
Barwick	26	7	68	0
Bastien	13	2	41	1
Smith	8	0	44	0
Shastri	7	2	23	0
Cann	8	1	30	3

Glamorgan 2nd Innings

A.R. Butcher	c Downton b Hughes	51
*H. Morris	c Carr b Fraser	0
M.J. Cann	c Cowans	1
M.P. Maynard	c Emburey b Tufnell	43
G.C. Holmes	c Downton b Fraser	33
I. Smith	c Fraser b Emburey	47
R.J. Shastri	not out	101
†C.P. Metson	not out	22
Extras	b 1, lb 4, nb 8	13
Total (6 wkts dec)		311

1, 8, 78, 132, 140, 223

Cowans	6	1	17	1
Fraser	18	4	64	2
Hughes	8	1	25	1
Emburey	20	6	70	1
Tufnell	22	4	79	1
Ramprakash	3	0	29	0
Roseberry	2.5	0	22	0

Middlesex 2nd Innings

J.D. Carr	c Maynard b Bastien	23
D.L. Haynes	c and b Watkin	4
M.A. Roseberry	c Watkin b Barwick	61
R.O. Butcher	c Smith b Barwick	9
M.R. Ramprakash	lbw b Bastien	62
†P.R. Downton	c and b Barwick	100
N.G. Cowans	lbw b Barwick	10
*J.E. Emburey	lbw b Barwick	5
A.R.C. Fraser	not out	43
S.P. Hughes	not out	5
Extras	b 1, lb 15, w 3, nb 4	23
Total (8 wkts)		345

22, 47, 62, 150, 211, 247, 262, 337

Watkin	18	1	92	2
Barwick	28	3	144	4
Bastien	16	1	70	2
Shastri	6	0	23	0

Umpires: K.E. Palmer and R.A. White
Toss: Glamorgan
Middlesex were set the daunting task of making 351 off 68 overs to win the match. When the final 20 overs began 167 were still needed. Some hard hitting by Downton and Fraser added 75 in 7.3 overs, but they ended 6 runs short of their target. The first day was dominated by a stand of 216 between Butcher and Shastri. Shastri went on to complete two hundreds in the match, the second off 117 balls.

v ESSEX (Swansea)

July 8, 10, 11

Lost by 188 runs. Essex 21pts, Glamorgan 4pts

Essex 1st Innings

B.R. Hardie	lbw b Watkin	13
J.P. Stephenson	lbw b Watkin	0
A.W. Lilley	b Watkin	1
M.E. Waugh	c Metson b Smith	21
P.J. Prichard	not out	81
N. Hussain	c Metson b Barwick	8
T.D. Topley	b Watkin	1
†N.A. Garnham	c Metson b Barwick	0
*D.R. Pringle	lbw b Barwick	2
J.K. Lever	c Metson b Barwick	10
J.H. Childs	b Barwick	24
Extras	lb 11, w 1, nb 1	13
Total (64.2 ov)		174

13, 16, 19, 67, 80, 87, 88, 94, 112

Watkin	25	7	59	4
Dennis	13	6	17	0
Barwick	19.2	2	59	5
Smith	5	1	18	1
Shastri	2	0	10	0

Glamorgan 1st Innings

A.R. Butcher	c Waugh b Pringle	5
*H. Morris	c Prichard b Pringle	0
M.J. Cann	c Waugh b Pringle	19
M.P. Maynard	c Hardie b Pringle	0
R.J. Shastri	b Lever	11
G.C. Holmes	c sub b Lever	3
I. Smith	c and b Lever	16
†C.P. Metson	lbw b Pringle	0
S.J. Dennis	c Lilley b Pringle	0
S.L. Watkin	not out	11
S.R. Barwick	c Garnham b Pringle	0
Extras		0
Total (31.3 ov)		65

4, 9, 13, 26, 35, 51, 52, 52, 54

Lever	16	2	47	3
Pringle	15.3	8	18	7

Essex 2nd Innings

B.R. Hardie	not out	101
J.P. Stephenson	c Smith b Dennis	30
P.J. Prichard	c Holmes b Cann	26
†M.A. Garnham	not out	48
Extras	lb 6, w 1, nb 1	8
Total (2 wkts dec)		213

69, 123

Watkin	13	1	59	0
Dennis	21	2	76	1
Barwick	1	0	5	0
Smith	8	1	37	0
Shastri	14	4	23	0
Cann	3	1	7	1

Glamorgan 2nd Innings

A.R. Butcher	c Hardie b Lever	2
*H. Morris	c Lever b Pringle	19
M.J. Cann	c Prichard b Lever	0
M.P. Maynard	c Waugh b Pringle	13
G.C. Holmes	c Waugh b Topley	31
I. Smith	c Stephenson b Childs	31
R.J. Shastri	b Childs	20
†C.P. Metson	not out	6
S.J. Dennis	c Garnham b Topley	1
S.L. Watkin	c Garnham b Topley	0
S.R. Barwick	lbw b Topley	0
Extras	b 8, lb 3	11
Total		134

2, 2, 39, 58, 101, 109, 127, 134, 134

Lever	6	0	17	2
Pringle	3	2	29	2
Childs	17	6	55	2
Topley	9.1	4	22	4

Umpires: J.H. Harris and K.J Lyons
Toss: Glamorgan

Essex took a clear lead of 33 points at the head of the Championship with this emphatic win. The feature of the game was the bowling of Pringle, who returned a career best of 7 for 18, when the Welsh county was dismissed for 65 on the second day. Rain allowed only 41 overs on the Saturday during which Essex struggled to 101–8 and were saved from utter rout by Prichard who ended the day at 46 not out – unfortunately for the home team he was dropped twice.

v LEICESTERSHIRE (Cardiff)

July 26, 27, 28

Lost by 9 wkts. Leics 22pts, Glamorgan 6pts

Glamorgan 1st Innings

A.R. Butcher	c and b Willey	24
*H. Morris	c Whitaker b Agnew	2
G.C. Holmes	c Boon b Such	38
M.P. Maynard	c and b Willey	14
R.J. Shastri	c Hepworth b Willey	67
A. Dale	b Such	2
I. Smith	c Taylor b Such	9
†C.P. Metson	b Potter	28
K.A. Somaia	c Briers b Willey	11
S.L. Watkin	not out	2
S.R. Barwick	c Nixon b Willey	0
Extras	b 17, lb 11, w 3	31
Total (77.5 ov)		228

12, 73, 91, 95, 97, 107, 206, 206, 228

Agnew	6	1	34	1
Ferris	10	4	20	0
Taylor	6	1	10	0
Such	22	8	54	3
Willey	28.5	8	45	5
Potter	5	3	37	1

Leicestershire 1st Innings

N.E. Briers	b Watkin	2
T.J. Boon	c Maynard b Barwick	45
J.J. Whitaker	c Metson b Somaia	99
P. Willey	c Morris b Somaia	38
L. Potter	c Maynard b Shastri	10
P.N. Hepworth	c Somaia b Shastri	4
†P.A. Nixon	c Maynard b Somaia	10
J.P. Agnew	c Smith b Shastri	9
G.J.F. Ferris	b Somaia	10
L.B. Taylor	not out	0
P.M. Such	b Somaia	14
Extras	lb 3, nb 3	6
Total (98 ov)		247

13, 85, 173, 195, 202, 209, 221, 223, 233

Watkin	8	1	35	1
Barwick	26	11	45	1
Shastri	38	11	77	3
Somaia	26	5	87	5

Glamorgan 2nd Innings

A.R. Butcher	lbw b Ferris	1
A. Dale	c Whitaker b Willey	2
*H. Morris	c Nixon b Willey	20
M.P. Maynard	b Such	1
R.J. Shastri	c and b Potter	44
I. Smith	c Boon b Such	15
G.C. Holmes	c Whitaker b Willey	12
†C.P. Metson	lbw b Such	0
K.A. Somaia	lbw b Such	1
S.L. Watkin	not out	15
S.R. Barwick	c Boon b Willey	0
Extras	b 5, lb 2	7
Total		118

8, 25, 30, 30, 90, 90, 90, 103, 103

Agnew	1	0	3	0
Ferris	5	3	12	1
Such	19	9	28	3
Willey	15.3	5	48	4
Potter	16	7	20	2

Leicestershire 2nd Innings

*N.E. Briers	c Metson b Barwick	25
T.J. Boon	not out	60
J.J. Whitaker	not out	9
Extras	lb 2, nb 4	6
Total (1 wkt)		100

83

Watkin	2	0	12	0
Barwick	10	3	26	1
Shastri	8	1	22	0
Somaia	10.4	1	38	0

Umpires: H.D. Bird and B. Dudleston
Toss: Glamorgan

At lunchtime on the first day, the umpires pronounced the wicket unsatisfactory and summoned Harry Brind, but later in the day Leics managed to reach 125–2 off 39 overs, in reply to Glamorgan's 228. Brind found the pitch fit for first-class cricket, though on the second day 18 wickets fell, so that Leics required 100 on the final day, a total they managed for the loss of Briers. Glamorgan had now lost four successive Britannic matches.

v HAMPSHIRE (Cardiff)

July 29, 31, Aug 1

Drawn. Hants 8pts, Glamorgan 3pts

Glamorgan 1st Innings

A.R. Butcher	c Parks b Connor	7
*H. Morris	c Smith b Connor	6
S.P. James	c Middleton b Bakker	3
M.J. Cann	b Jefferies	70
R.J. Shastri	c Maru b Connor	46
M.P. Maynard	b Connor	11
I. Smith	c Parks b Jefferies	38
A. Dale	lbw b Jefferies	0
†C.P. Metson	c Maru b Jefferies	2
S.J. Dennis	c Parks b Bakker	5
S.R. Barwick	not out	0
Extras	b 4, lb 5, w 1, nb 10	20
Total (67.3 ov)		208

13, 15, 30, 105, 123, 175, 175, 187, 204

Bakker	22	3	68	2
Connor	19	0	40	4
Jefferies	14.3	3	61	4
Maru	7	3	17	0
James	5	0	13	0

Hampshire 1st Innings

V.P. Terry	c James b Dennis	20
C.L. Smith	c Metson b Dale	26
K.D. James	c James b Smith	162
T.C. Middleton	run out	69
*M.C.J. Nicholas	c James b Butcher	0
J.R. Wood	c James b Dennis	42
S.T. Jefferies	not out	7
†R.J. Parks	not out	10
R.J. Maru		
C.A. Connor		
P.J. Bakker		
Extras	b 12, lb 16, nb 6	34
Total (100 ov: 341–4) (6 wkts dec)		370

42, 62, 265, 266, 348, 354

Dennis	27	9	80	2
Barwick	27	8	76	0
Smith	20	3	64	1
Dale	12	4	41	1
Shastri	9	1	36	0
Butcher	11	1	45	1

Glamorgan 2nd Innings

C.P. Metson	lbw b Bakker	4
*H. Morris	c Maru b Connor	1
A.R. Butcher	c Parks b Connor	30
S.P. James	c Terry b James	45
M.J. Cann	c Parks b Connor	12
R.J. Shastri	c Terry b James	35
M.P. Maynard	c Jefferies b Connor	0
I. Smith	c Parks b Jefferies	67
A. Dale	b Maru	37
S.J. Dennis	c Jefferies b Connor	7
S.R. Barwick	not out	0
Extras	b 5, lb 2, w 3, nb 6	16
Total		254

5, 11, 76, 94, 103, 103, 148, 227, 254

Connor	20	4	74	5
Bakker	21	6	58	1
Jefferies	15	3	50	1
Maru	22.3	7	45	1
James	6	1	15	2
Nicholas	4	1	5	0
Smith	1	1	0	0

Hampshire 2nd Innings

V.P. Terry	c Shastri b Smith	4
C.L. Smith	c Maynard b Smith	4
K.D. James	b Smith	35
*M.C.J. Nicholas	c Cann b Dennis	10
J.R. Wood	b Dennis	16
S.T. Jefferies	not out	7
†R.J. Parks	run out	2
C.A. Connor	c and b Dennis	1
R.J. Maru	not out	0
Extras	lb 3, nb 4	7
Total (7 wkts)		86

11, 17, 48, 73, 79, 81, 85

Smith	8	0	48	3
Dennis	8	0	35	3

Umpires: H.D. Bird and B. Dudleston
Toss: Hampshire

The first day was restricted to 69.3 overs due to rain. Glamorgan started badly, but a stand of 75 between Cann and Shastri gave some substance to the innings. James reached a career best of 162 on the second day, but owing to a family bereavement Glamorgan lacked the services of Watkin. An unexpected 8th wicket partnership on the last day meant that Hampshire needed 93 off 16 overs, a target they just failed to reach.

v SUSSEX (Swansea)

August 12, 14, 15

Drawn. Glamorgan 7pts, Sussex 4pts

Sussex 1st Innings		
N.J. Lenham	c Dennis b Watkin	7
M.P. Speight	c Metson b Dennis	69
†P. Moores	c Metson b Barwick	25
A.P. Wells	c Cann b Dennis	33
*P.W.G. Parker	c Metson b Dennis	0
C.M. Wells	not out	57
I.J. Gould	c Cann b Barwick	1
A.I.C. Dodemaide	c Morris b Smith	18
A.C.S. Pigott	c Butcher b Smith	10
B.T.P. Donelan	c Metson b Barwick	3
I.D.K. Salisbury	lbw b Watkin	4
Extras	lb 6, nb 7	13
Total (75 ov)		240

19, 58, 140, 140, 141, 142, 174, 222, 231

Watkin	19	2	52	2
Dennis	16	3	54	3
Barwick	18	7	47	3
Butcher	3	0	15	0
Shastri	6	1	21	0
Smith	13	2	45	2

Glamorgan 1st Innings		
A.R. Butcher	c Parker b Donelan	67
*H. Morris	c Pigott b Dodemaide	0
M.P. Maynard	c Pigott b Dodemaide	65
M.J. Cann	c Parker b C.M. Wells	37
R.J. Shastri	lbw b C.M. Wells	9
S.P. James	run out	42
I. Smith	c C.M. Wells b Salisbury	1
†C.P. Metson	b C.M. Wells	26
S.J. Dennis	c A.P. Wells b Dodemaide	35
S.L. Watkin	run out	3
S.R. Barwick	not out	0
Extras	b 6, lb 9, w 3, nb 5	23
Total (100 ov:253–6)		308

4, 115, 155, 168, 216, 221, 266, 283, 303

Pigott	29	7	69	0
Dodemaide	26.2	4	75	3
C.M. Wells	35	10	69	3
Donelan	11	0	47	1
Lenham	3	0	15	0
Salisbury	7	1	18	1

Sussex 2nd Innings		
N.J. Lenham	c Shastri b Watkin	14
M.P. Speight	c Metson b Dennis	48
*P.W.G. Parker	c Barwick b Cann	63
A.P. Wells	not out	72
C.M. Wells	not out	19
Extras	lb 2, w 4, nb 1	7
Total (3 wkts)		223

23, 92, 170

Watkin	12	4	49	1
Barwick	11	2	36	0
Dennis	7	1	19	1
Smith	6	1	9	0
Cann	16	2	74	1
Morris	4	0	16	0
Maynard	3	0	10	0
Shastri	13	9	8	0

Umpires: P.J. Eele and D.O. Oslear
Toss: Sussex

After an interesting first day, when Glamorgan reached 81–1 in reply to the visitors 240, the second and third days were an anti-climax. Glamorgan made 181 runs on the Monday before rain in the afternoon ended play. They batted on for the final morning and thus Sussex had nothing but a draw to play for when they began their second innings, which soon developed into little more than batting practice.

v WARWICKSHIRE (Swansea)

August 24, 25, 26, 28

Lost by 8 wkts. Warwicks 24pts, Glamorgan 1pt

Warwickshire 1st Innings		
*T.A. Lloyd	c Shastri b Barwick	183
J.D. Ratcliffe	c Metson b Watkin	1
A.I. Kallicharran	c Butcher b Barwick	119
†G.W. Humpage	c Metson b Watkin	19
P.A. Smith	c Maynard b Smith	35
D.A. Reeve	c Shastri b Watkin	1
R.G. Twose	c Metson b Barwick	25
N.M.K. Smith	c Maynard b Watkin	6
A.A. Donald	c Metson b Watkin	6
J.E. Benjamin	c Metson b Watkin	5
T.A. Munton	not out	5
Extras	lb 11, w 2, nb 1	14
Total (100 ov: 362–3)		430

29, 270, 309, 370, 370, 371, 384, 420, 420

Watkin	32.5	8	106	6
Dennis	24	7	69	0
Barwick	33	6	82	3
Smith	8	0	50	1
Shastri	11	1	41	0
Croft	17	3	71	0

Glamorgan 1st Innings		
*A.R. Butcher	lbw b Benjamin	1
H. Morris	lbw b Donald	2
M.P. Maynard	c Humpage b Benjamin	16
S.P. James	lbw b Reeve	31
I. Smith	b Reeve	26
R.J. Shastri	c Humpage b Munton	27
†C.P. Metson	c Humpage b Munton	0
R.D.B. Croft	c P.A. Smith b Munton	11
S.J. Dennis	b Munton	0
S.L. Watkin	c Munton b Reeve	4
S.R. Barwick	not out	0
Extras	lb 8, nb 5	13
Total (56.1 ov)		131

3, 3, 26, 75, 100, 107, 122, 129, 129

Donald	11	3	26	1
Benjamin	15	3	34	2
P.A. Smith	2	0	3	0
Munton	15.1	2	33	4
Reeve	13	2	27	3

Glamorgan 2nd Innings		
*A.R. Butcher	c Reeve b P.A. Smith	34
H. Morris	c Twose b Munton	108
†C.P. Metson	c sub b P.A. Smith	5
M.P. Maynard	c Kallicharran b N.M.K. Smith	15
R.J. Shastri	run out	56
S.P. James	c Benjamin b Munton	38
I. Smith	c Reeve b Benjamin	33
R.D.B. Croft	c sub b Munton	1
S.J. Dennis	not out	9
S.L. Watkin	c Reeve b P.A. Smith	0
S.R. Barwick	b Reeve	12
Extras	lb 9, w 3, nb 6	18
Total		329

122, 130, 155, 205, 252, 299, 300, 310, 310

Munton	36	11	76	3
Benjamin	14	1	33	1
N.M.K. Smith	29	5	74	1
P.A. Smith	24	4	78	3
Reeve	18.1	7	26	1
Twose	8	0	33	0

Warwickshire 2nd Innings		
*T.A. Lloyd	c Shastri b Watkin	1
J.D. Ratcliffe	not out	24
A.I. Kallicharran	c Shastri b Butcher	1
†G.W. Humpage	not out	3
Extras	b 1, nb 1	2
Total (2 wkts)		31

16, 19

Watkin	3	0	11	1
Butcher	2.1	0	19	1

Umpires: B. Leadbeater and N.T. Plews
Toss: Warwickshire

Warwickshire took a firm grip on this match during the first day. Lloyd and Kallicharran added 241 for the 2nd wicket, with the former scoring runs as will – 91* at lunch and 100 out of 134 in 150 minutes. In contrast Kallicharran spent 300 minutes over his 100. 384 for 7 at the close, Warwickshire continued on the second morning and then Glamorgan collapsed to reach 100 for 5 at stumps. The follow on was enforced on Saturday and though Morris batted soundly for 108, Warwickshire won by 8 wickets.

v WORCESTERSHIRE (Pontypridd)

Sept 13, 14, 15, 16

Drawn. Worcs 4pts, Glamorgan 2pts

Glamorgan 1st Innings		
*A.R. Butcher	c Weston b Botham	43
H. Morris	c Dilley b McEwan	7
S.P. James	c Hick b Botham	3
M.P. Maynard	c d'Oliveira b McEwan	44
R.J. Shastri	b Lampitt	22
I. Smith	b Lampitt	0
R.D.B. Croft	lbw b McEwan	45
†C.P. Metson	lbw b Hick	47
S.J. Dennis	c Weston b McEwan	5
S.L. Watkin	not out	2
S. Bastien	not out	0
Extras	lb 11, w 1	12
Total (9 wkts, 78.2 ov)		230

19, 57, 58, 125, 125, 133, 217, 223, 230

Dilley	10	1	40	0
McEwan	15.2	2	38	4
Lampitt	17	3	46	2
Botham	13.3	2	50	2
Weston	2.3	0	12	0
Illingworth	12	6	21	0
Hick	8	2	12	1

Worcestershire – did not bat
T.S. Curtis
M.J. Weston
G.A. Hick
D.B. d'Oliveira
*P.A. Neale
I.T. Botham
†S.J. Rhodes
S.R. Lampitt
R.K. Illingworth
G.R. Dilley
S.M. McEwan

Umpires: J.H. Harris and B.J. Meyer
Toss: Worcestershire.

The brilliant summer came to a watery close. On the first day 76.1 overs were bowled. Worcestershire who had already claimed the Championship title restricted Glamorgan to 221–7 even though both Botham and Dilley had to retire to the pavilion with minor injuries. Only 13 balls could be bowled on the second day, but even that was an improvement on days three and four, when no cricket at all was possible. The rain denied Watkin the chance of reaching 100 wickets in the season – he remained on 94.

Gloucestershire

President: R.J. Bereley
Chairman: D.N. Perry
Secretary: P.G.M. August, Phoenix County Ground, Nevil Road, Bristol BS7 9EJ. *Tel:* 0272 245216
Coach: J.N. Shepherd
Captain: C.W.J. Athey
Foundation of Present Club: In or about 1871
First First-Class Match: Gloucestershire v Surrey (Durdham Downs) June 1870
County Champions: 1873, 1874, 1876, 1877
Gillette/NatWest Trophy: Winners 1973
Benson & Hedges Cup: Winners 1977
Sunday League Champions: Nil (runners-up in 1988)
Refuge Cup: Nil

Summary of Results in 1989
Britannic Assurance County Championship: Played 22, Won 6, Lost 5, Drawn 11, Position 9th
NatWest Bank Trophy: Lost in second round
Benson & Hedges Cup: Lost in quarter-final
Refuge Assurance Sunday League: Played 16, Won 3, Lost 13, Position 16th equal
Refuge Assurance Cup: Did not qualify

Front left, back: *G.A. Tedstone, M.W. Alleyne, P.W. Romaines, M.C.J. Ball, R.C. Russell, K.B.K. Ibadulla.* Centre: *G.G. Wiltshire (Coach), I.P. Butcher, J.W. Lloyds, K.M. Curran, D.V. Lawrence, K.B.S. Jarvis, M.W. Pooley, V.S. Greene, P. Bainbridge.* Front: *A.W. Stovold, P.G.M. August (Secretary), A.J. Wright, C.W.J. Athey, D.N. Perry (Chairman), D.A. Graveney.*
Allsport

All was not well with the county in 1989. On paper their resources seemed adequate, but injuries and an atmosphere of unease in the dressing room, which had been made worse by the way Graveney was dispossessed of the captaincy after the 1988 season, sapped the determination of the players. Athey led the 1989 side, but 1990 will see Wright in charge.

The West Indian fast bowler, Walsh, took over the spot occupied by Alderman in 1988 and the former proved up to the standard of the latter, so the weakness of 1989 did not stem from the overseas connection. Lawrence, who gained an England cap in 1988, was beset by injury and his wicket tally dropped from 77 to 33 – he appeared in only about half the fixtures. Jarvis, who had played in only one Championship game in 1988 – he left Kent at the close of 1987 – was pressed into service, but at the age of 36 he had lost much of his zest for three-day cricket.

Greene, the reserve overseas player, proved useful when Walsh was rested. Ball's off spin took 18 wickets at a reasonable cost and he is regarded as a player who might add to the county's illustrous line of slow bowlers.

The batting was not so pleasant a picture. Curran headed the averages and he is one of the leading all-rounders in county cricket, but not a single Gloucester name could be found in the top 60 of the 1989 batting averages and this speaks for itself. The opening partnership – Butcher replaced Stovold – rarely managed to give the team a sound start. Athey averaged 74 in 1988 a figure which dropped to 29 in 1989. Stovold plunged from 35 to 13 and Russell, who made a famous hundred for England, could only register a high of 41 in Championship cricket. Tedstone was signed from Warwickshire, in case Russell was needed for England and the signing proved a wise move, but Tedstone did not score many runs. It will be interesting to see if Wright can get more out of the players, as a team, than Athey managed to do.

ONE DAY AWAY MATCHES

The full scorecard of each of Gloucestershire's away matches will be found in the sections for the respective home teams.

Refuge Assurance League

The Oval: April 23
Surrey 164–5 (38 ov) beat Gloucs 81 (19.1 ov) on faster scoring rate. Surrey 4pts, Gloucs 0pts.

Cardiff: May 7
Glamorgan 171–6 (40 ov) lost to Gloucs 173–7 (39.1 ov) by 3 wkts. Gloucs 4pts, Glamorgan 0pts.

Leicester: June 11
Gloucs 214–6 (40 ov) beat Leics 155 (35.3 ov) by 59 runs. Gloucs 4pts, Leics 0pts.

Sheffield: June 18
Yorks 196–7 (40 ov) beat Gloucs 184–8 (40 ov) by 12 runs. Yorks 4pts, Gloucs 0pts.

Bath: June 15
Somerset 226–5 (40 ov) (S.J. Cook 124*) beat Gloucs 128 (35.5 ov) by 98 runs. Somerset 4pts, Gloucs 0pts.

Maidstone: July 9
Gloucs 85 (31.2 ov) lost to Kent 86–4 (25.5 ov) by 6 wkts. Kent 4pts, Gloucs 0pts.

Edgbaston: July 30
Warwicks 162–5 (24 ov) beat Gloucs 144–8 (24 ov) by 18 runs. Warwicks 4pts, Gloucs 0pts.

Hove: August 27
Sussex 279–7 (40 ov) beat Gloucs 172–8 (40 ov) (A.R. Hansford 5–32) by 107 runs. Sussex 4pts, Gloucs 0pts.

Benson and Hedges Cup

Worcester: May 9
Gloucs 200–7 (55 ov) beat Worcs 152 (51.1 ov) by 48 runs. Gloucs 2pts, Worcs 0pts.

The Oval: May 11
Gloucs 286–7 (55 ov) beat Surrey 142 (37 ov) by144 runs. Gloucs 2pts, Surrey 0pts.

NatWest Bank Trophy

Oxford: June 28
Gloucs 269–3 (60 ov) beat Oxon 226 (59.4 ov) (K.B.S. Jarvis 5–32) by 43 runs.

REFUGE ASSURANCE LEAGUE

v MIDDLESEX (Bristol)

May 14
Lost by 14 runs. Middx 4pts, Gloucs 0pts

Middlesex		
D.L. Haynes	c Russell b Lawrence	14
*M.W. Gatting	run out	32
R.O. Butcher	c Romaines b Pooley	44
M.R. Ramprakash	b Bainbridge	26
J.F. Sykes	c Athey b Bainbridge	38
†P.R. Downton	c Romaines b Bainbridge	7
K.R. Brown	not out	20
J.E. Emburey	not out	6
N.F. Williams		
S.P. Hughes		
A.R.C. Fraser		
Extras	lb 14, w 1	15
Total (6 wkts, 40 ov)		202

42, 84, 111, 152, 170, 180

Lawrence	8	0	37	1
Greene	8	0	42	0
Curran	8	0	30	0
Pooley	4	0	20	1
Bainbridge	8	0	39	3
Alleyne	4	0	20	0

Gloucestershire		
A.J. Wright	c sub b Emburey	66
*C.W.J. Athey	c Haynes b Gatting	36
P. Bainbridge	b Williams	17
K.M. Curran	b Gatting	0
P.W. Romaines	c Haynes b Gatting	2
V.S. Greene	b Gatting	10
M.W. Alleyne	st Downton b Emburey	15
†R.C. Russell	not out	15
K.B.K. Ibadulla	not out	9
M.W. Pooley		
D.V. Lawrence		
Extras	b 3, lb 10, w 3, nb 2	18
Total (7 wkts, 40 ov)		188

86, 113, 114, 120, 131, 159, 170

Williams	8	0	18	1
Hughes	7	0	27	0
Gatting	9	1	30	4
Sykes	1	0	8	0
Emburey	8	0	60	2
Fraser	8	0	32	0

Umpires: D.G.L. Evans and R. Palmer
Toss: Gloucestershire
All round cricket by Gatting enabled Middlesex to win this game. He returned a career best 4–30 and was unfortunate to be run out by Butcher when batting well. Wright and Athey, for the home side, added 86 in 22 overs, but Middlesex soon sighted victory.

v ESSEX (Bristol)

May 21
Lost by 9 wkts. Essex 4pts, Gloucs 0pts

Gloucestershire		
A.J. Wright	c Stephenson b Lever	2
*C.W.J. Athey	b Topley	16
P. Bainbridge	lbw b Gooch	26
K.M. Curran	b Pringle	34
P.W. Romaines	b Gooch	11
V.S. Greene	not out	10
M.W. Alleyne	c Waugh b Pringle	33
†R.C. Russell	c Hardie b Foster	2
K.B.K. Ibadulla	not out	8
M.W. Pooley		
K.B.S. Jarvis		
Extras	b 5, lb 10, w 9, nb 1	25
Total (7 wkts, 40 ov)		167

4, 10, 45, 68, 86, 148, 149

Lever	7	3	21	1
Foster	8	3	28	1
Pringle	8	0	34	2
Gooch	8	0	33	2
Topley	2	0	14	1
Stephenson	7	0	22	0

Essex		
*G.A. Gooch	b Pooley	76
B.R. Hardie	not out	73
M.E. Waugh	not out	6
P.J. Prichard		
A.W. Lilley		
J.P. Stephenson		
D.R. Pringle		
J.K. Lever		
†M.A. Garnham		
N.A. Foster		
T.D. Topley		
Extras	lb 10, w 2, nb 1	13
Total (1 wkt, 39.1 ov)		168

146

Jarvis	8	0	26	0
Greene	8	0	31	0
Curran	8	0	33	0
Pooley	8	0	32	1
Ibadulla	4	1	14	0
Bainbridge	3.1	0	22	0

Umpires: D.R. Shepherd and R.A. White
Toss: Essex
Gooch hit 76 off 91 deliveries and though Essex only won off the 40th over, they were well in control of the match from an early stage. Athey had the misfortune to break a thumb while batting, but did not retire hurt, though he later went to hospital and did not field.

Kevin Curran, Gloucestershire's Zimbabwean all-rounder, who headed the batting aggregates and averages.

Allsport/Adrian Murrell

PLAYERS

Mark Wayne ALLEYNE *b* 23.5.1968 Tottenham; right hand batsman; right arm medium pace bowler; debut 1986; improved on his 1988 record and played some good innings

Charles William Jeffrey ATHEY *b* 27.9.1957 Middlesbrough; middle order right hand batsman; debut 1984; previously appeared for Yorkshire 1976–1983; captained Gloucs in 1989, but his batting record fell away and has not been re-appointed for 1990; 23 Tests for England 1980 to 1988. Chosen to tour South Africa 1989–90

Philip BAINBRIDGE *b* 16.4.1958 Sneyd Green, Staffs; All-rounder; right hand batsman; right arm medium pace bowler; debut 1977

Martyn Charles John BALL *b* 26.4.1970 Bristol; off break bowler; lower order right hand batsman; debut 1988, when he played in 2 fc matches

S N BARNES made his debut for the county in Sunday League matches in 1989, but has yet to play in fc cricket

Ian Paul BUTCHER *b* 1.7.1962 Farnborough, Kent; right hand batsman; debut 1988; previously played for Leics 1980–87; brother of A.R. (Glamorgan) and M.S. (ex-Surrey)

Kevin Malcolm CURRAN *b* 7.9.1959 Rusape, S. Rhodesia; talented all-rounder; middle order right hand batsham; right arm medium fast bowler; debut 1985; also plays for Zimbabwe

David Anthony GRAVENEY *b* 2.1.1953 Bristol; slow left arm bowler; right arm bowler; right hand batsman; debut 1972; captain 1981–88; son of J.K. (Gloucs); chosen as manager of English Team to South Africa 1989–90

Victor Sylvester GREENE *b* 24.9.1960 Christ Church, Barbados; right arm medium fast bowler; lower order right hand batsman; debut 1987; also plays for Barbados

Geoffrey Dean HODGSON *b* 22.10.1966 Carlisle; right hand batsman; made fc debut for Gloucs in August 1989; previously played in one-day matches for Warwickshire

REFUGE ASSURANCE LEAGUE

v WORCESTERSHIRE (Bristol)

May 28

Lost by 6 wkts. Worcs 4pts, Gloucs 0pts

Gloucestershire		
†R.C. Russell	b Radford	39
A.W. Stovold	c Bevins b Pridgeon	24
K.M. Curran	b Radford	26
P. Bainbridge	c Neale b Newport	24
*A.J. Wright	not out	49
P.W. Romaines	b Pridgeon	31
C.A. Walsh	not out	13
I.P. Butcher		
D.A. Graveney		
M.W. Pooley		
K.B.S. Jarvis		
Extras	b 2, lb 6, w 4, nb 3	15
Total (5 wkts, 40 ov)		221

56, 95, 104, 145, 208

Weston	8	0	32	0
Newport	8	0	26	1
Pridgeon	8	0	57	2
Radford	8	0	31	2
Lampitt	6	0	46	0
Illingworth	2	0	21	0

Worcestershire		
T.S. Curtis	c Russell b Graveney	50
M.J. Weston	b Curran	16
G.A. Hick	c Wright b Curran	84
D.B. d'Oliveira	b Walsh	29
N.V. Radford	not out	25
*P.A. Neale	not out	3
S.R. Lampitt		
†S.R. Bevins		
P.J. Newport		
R.K. Illingworth		
A.P. Pridgeon		
Extras	b 1, lb 8, w 5, nb 1	15
Total (4 wkts, 38.5 ov)		222

30, 119, 179, 201

Jarvis	8	1	36	0
Walsh	7	0	36	1
Curran	7.5	0	64	2
Graveney	8	0	34	1
Bainbridge	8	0	43	0

Umpires: P.J. Eele and D.O. Oslear

Toss: Worcestershire

Hick hit 84 off 77 balls to bring Worcs victory with 7 deliveries remaining. He was aided by Radford who was promoted and made 25 off 11 balls, so Gloucestershire, whose batsmen had all made runs, were beaten despite a total of 221–5.

v NOTTINGHAMSHIRE (Gloucester)

July 2

Lost by 2 wkts. Notts 4pts, Gloucs 0pts

Gloucestershire		
J.W. Lloyds	b Cooper	14
*C.W.J. Athey	lbw b Saxelby	21
K.M. Curran	c French b Stephenson	46
P. Bainbridge	run out	13
A.J. Wright	lbw b Hemmings	9
P.W. Romaines	st French b Hemmings	7
M.W. Alleyne	c Martindale b Stephenson	8
V.S. Greene	not out	18
†R.C. Russell	c and b Stephenson	4
M.W. Pooley	not out	6
K.B.S. Jarvis		
Extras	lb 7, w 1	8
Total (8 wkts, 40 ov)		154

21, 41, 53, 91, 113, 126, 127, 131

Stephenson	8	1	26	3
Cooper	6	0	19	1
Evans	8	1	31	0
Saxelby	6	0	29	1
Hemmings	8	0	26	2
Mike	4	0	16	0

Nottinghamshire		
B.C. Broad	c Wright b Bainbridge	44
*R.T. Robinson	c Russell b Curran	29
D.W. Randall	c Athey b Curran	1
D.J.R. Martindale	b Curran	7
G.W. Mike	c Russell b Curran	0
F.D. Stephenson	lbw b Greene	11
K.P. Evans	c Russell b Pooley	4
†B.N. French	c Wright b Greene	3
E.E. Hemmings	not out	19
K. Saxelby	not out	28
K.E. Cooper		
Extras	lb 8, w 3	11
Total (8 wkts, 37 ov)		157

56, 60, 84, 84, 96, 102, 102, 114

Greene	8	3	29	2
Jarvis	6	0	30	0
Pooley	7	1	50	1
Curran	8	1	27	4
Bainbridge	8	2	13	1

Umpires: J.H. Hampshire and K.E. Palmer

Toss: Gloucestershire

Gloucs began very slowly, Athey batting 15 overs for 21, but Curran made more progress and the total was a reasonable one. Notts added 56 for the 1st wicket and then faltered. Hemmings and Cooper won the match with a Notts record 9th wicket stand of 43 in 5 overs.

v HAMPSHIRE (Trowbridge)

July 16

Won by 21 runs. Gloucs 4pts, Hants 0pts

Gloucestershire		
I.P. Butcher	c sub b Maru	26
*C.W.J. Athey	c Terry b Nicholas	39
P. Bainbridge	c Terry b Nicholas	26
J.W. Lloyds	run out	12
K.M. Curran	run out	3
A.J. Wright	not out	41
M.W. Alleyne	c R.A. Smith b Nicholas	3
V.S. Greene	c R.A. Smith b Nicholas	10
†R.C. Russell	b Connor	8
P.W. Romaines	not out	8
M.W. Pooley		
Extras	lb 7, w 1	8
Total (8 wkts, 40 ov)		184

56, 81, 108, 109, 114, 126, 145, 176

James	6	1	22	0
Bakker	4	1	5	0
Maru	6	1	32	1
Connor	8	0	48	1
Marshall	8	0	40	0
Nicholas	8	1	30	4

Hampshire		
V.P. Terry	st Russell b Alleyne	12
*M.C.J. Nicholas	b Pooley	2
R.A. Smith	c Russell b Greene	3
J.R. Wood	b Bainbridge	19
C.L. Smith	c Greene b Alleyne	8
K.D. James	b Greene	66
M.D. Marshall	c Alleyne b Pooley	14
†R.J. Parks	b Athey	10
R.J. Maru	c Pooley b Bainbridge	1
C.A. Connor	c Butcher b Bainbridge	19
P.J. Bakker	not out	0
Extras	lb 7, w 2	9
Total (38.1 ov)		163

13, 18, 40, 52, 63, 88, 106, 119, 163

Pooley	8	1	29	2
Greene	7	3	17	2
Alleyne	8	0	36	2
Bainbridge	7.1	1	38	3
Athey	8	0	36	1

Umpires: D.J. Constant and K.J. Lyons

Toss: Hampshire

Despite lacking the services of Walsh and Lawrence, the home side defeated Hampshire with relative ease. James however produced the best batting of the day. his 66 coming off 63 balls with 9 fours.

Kassem Ben Khalid IBADULLA *b* 13.10.1964 Birmingham; right hand batsman; debut 1987; also plays for Otago; son of K. Ibadulla (ex-Warwicks)
Kevin Bertram Sidney JARVIS *b* 23.4.1953 Dartford; right arm fast medium bowler; right hand batsman; debut 1988; previously appeared for Kent 1975–87
David Valentine LAWRENCE *b* 28.1.1964 Gloucester; right arm fast bowler; right hand batsman; debut 1981; one Test for England 1988
Jeremy William LLOYDS *b* 17.11.1954 Penang, Malaya; middle order left hand batsman; off break bowler; debut 1985; previously appeared with Somerset 1979–84.
Malcolm William POOLEY *b* 27.7.1969 Truro; right hand batsman; right arm medium pace bowler; debut 1988
Neil M. PRITCHARD debut for Gloucs in one-day matches only in 1989
Paul William ROMAINES *b* 25.12.1955 Bishop Auckland; right hand batsman; debut 1982; previously appeared for Northants 1975–76
Robert Charles (Jack) RUSSELL *b* 15.8.63 Stroud; wicketkeeper; left hand batsman; debut 1981; 7 Tests for England, including all six v Australia last season; selected to tour West Indies 1989–90
Andrew Willis STOVOLD *b* 19.3.1953 Bristol; Opening right hand batsman; wicketkeeper; debut 1973; brother of Martin (ex-Gloucs)
Geoffrey Alan TEDSTONE *b* 19.1.1961 Southport; right hand batsman; wicketkeeper; debut June 1989; previously appeared for Warwicks 1982–88
Courtney Andrew WALSH *b* 30.10.1962 Kingston, Jamaica; right arm fast bowler; lower order right hand batsman; debut 1984; also plays for Jamaica; 34 Tests for the West Indies
Anthony John WRIGHT *b* 27.6.1962 Stevenage; opening right hand batsman; debut 1982; appointed captain for 1990

Courtney Walsh, from Barbados, Gloucestershire's international fast bowler who was easily the county's most effective wicket-taker.
Allsport/Adrian Murrell

REFUGE ASSURANCE LEAGUE

v LANCASHIRE (Cheltenham)
August 6
Lost by 6 wkts. Lancs 4pts, Gloucs 0pts

Gloucestershire		
I.P. Butcher	c Hegg b DeFreitas	0
J.W. Lloyds	lbw b Allott	0
*C.W.J. Athey	lbw b Watkinson	14
P. Bainbridge	c and b Allott	15
K.M. Curran	b Watkinson	14
A.J. Wright	not out	52
M.W. Alleyne	c and b Watkinson	7
†R.C. Russell	c Hegg b Watkinson	4
C.A. Walsh	c Simmons b Austin	4
D.V. Lawrence	b Wasim Akram	16
K.B.S. Jarvis	b Austin	1
Extras	lb 9, w 6, nb 1	16
Total (39.5 ov)		143

0, 5, 25, 34, 56, 64, 70, 81, 136

DeFreitas	8	0	32	1
Allott	8	3	20	2
Watkinson	8	1	29	4
Wasim Akram	8	1	23	1
Austin	7.5	0	30	2

Lancashire		
G.D. Mendis	c Russell b Jarvis	48
G. Fowler	c and b Walsh	0
*D.P. Hughes	c Butcher b Walsh	2
N.H. Fairbrother	hit wkt b Lawrence	45
M. Watkinson	not out	13
Wasim Akram	not out	23
†W.K. Hegg		
P.A.J. DeFreitas		
I.D. Austin		
P.J.W. Allott		
J. Simmons		
Extras	lb 6, w 5, nb 2	13
Total (4 wkts, 27.4 ov)		144

5, 20, 93, 114

Walsh	8	0	21	2
Lawrence	8	1	48	1
Jarvis	5.4	1	29	1
Curran	4	0	30	0
Bainbridge	2	1	10	0

Umpires: K.J. Lyons and D.O. Oslear
Toss: Lancashire
This emphatic victory by Lancashire took that county to the top of the Sunday League table. A ninth wicket stand by Wright and Lawrence meant that the home side did survive into the 40th over, but the Lancashire batsmen had no difficulty in passing the target with 12 overs to spare.

v DERBYSHIRE (Cheltenham)
August 13
Lost by 4 wkts. Derbys 4pts, Gloucs 0pts

Gloucestershire		
I.P. Butcher	c Maher b Newman	14
G.D. Hodgson	c Sharma b Holding	16
*C.W.J. Athey	b Base	5
P. Bainbridge	c Barnett b Holding	6
K.M. Curran	c Maher b Sharma	6
A.J. Wright	c and b Barnett	5
M.W. Alleyne	b Barnett	29
†G.A. Tedstone	run out	12
C.A. Walsh	not out	18
M.W. Pooley	c Sharma b Holding	5
K.B.S. Jarvis	run out	6
Extras	lb 3, w 2	5
Total (40 ov)		127

19, 28, 39, 50, 50, 62, 95, 98, 109

Newman	8	3	17	1
Base	8	0	35	1
Sharma	8	3	24	1
Holding	8	2	21	3
Barnett	7	1	20	2
Jean-Jacques	1	0	7	0

Derbyshire		
*K.J. Barnett	c Tedstone b Curran	6
P.D. Bowler	b Walsh	3
J.E. Morris	c Jarvis b Pooley	35
R. Sharma	c Alleyne b Walsh	3
T.J.G. O'Gorman	b Curran	2
C.J. Adams	not out	46
M.A. Holding	b Walsh	22
†B.J.M. Maher	not out	9
M. Jean-Jacques		
S.J. Base		
P.G. Newman		
Extras	lb 3, w 1	4
Total (6 wkts, 28.2 ov)		130

9, 9, 17, 20, 68, 111

Walsh	8	1	20	3
Curran	8	1	34	2
Jarvis	4	0	22	0
Bainbridge	3	0	26	0
Pooley	5	1	21	1
Wright	0.2	0	4	0

Umpires: B.J. Meyer and A.G.T. Whitehead
Toss: Derbyshire
Gloucestershire's first five wickets went down in 19 overs and only a minor improvement later enabled the side to top 100. Derbyshire found few problems in reaching the modest target.

v NORTHAMPTONSHIRE (Moreton-in-Marsh)
August 20
Lost by 7 wkts. Northans 4pts, Gloucs 0pts

Gloucestershire		
J.W. Lloyds	lbw b Robinson	32
G.D. Hodgson	run out	39
*C.W.J. Athey	c Robinson b Thomas	65
P. Bainbridge	c Cook b Capel	0
K.M. Curran	c Ripley b Ambrose	36
M.W. Alleyne	not out	5
A.J. Wright	not out	1
†R.C. Russell		
C.A. Walsh		
M.W. Pooley		
K.B.S. Jarvis		
Extras	b 2, lb 12, w 2, nb 1	17
Total (5 wkts, 40 ov)		195

63, 90, 92, 190, 193

Robinson	8	1	22	1
Ambrose	8	0	48	1
Cook	8	0	40	0
Larkins	1	0	6	0
Capel	8	1	33	1
Thomas	7	1	32	1

Northamptonshire		
*W. Larkins	c Athey b Curran	101
A. Fordham	c Russell b Curran	10
R.J. Bailey	c Wright b Bainbridge	46
D.J. Capel	not out	25
N.A. Felton	not out	5
D.J. Wild		
J.G. Thomas		
†D. Ripley		
C.E.L. Ambrose		
N.G.B. Cook		
M.A. Robinson		
Extras	lb 4, w 5, nb 2	11
Total (3 wkts, 36.2 ov)		198

42, 144, 185

Walsh	6.2	0	36	0
Curran	8	0	35	2
Jarvis	6	1	36	0
Pooley	8	0	33	0
Bainbridge	5	0	36	1
Lloyds	3	0	18	0

Umpires: J.W. Holder and B. Leadbeater
Toss: Gloucestershire
Athey reached 5,000 Sunday League runs, and the home side totalled a useful 195–5, but with Larkins in great form this proved insufficient and Northants won comfortably. Larkins' 101 came off 82 balls.

BRITANNIC ASSURANCE COUNTY CHAMPIONSHIP AVERAGES 1989

Batting	*M*	*I*	*NO*	*Runs*	*HS*	*Avge*	*100*	*50*
K.M. Curran	22	36	4	1186	128	37.06	4	2
M.W. Alleyne	18	26	4	699	111	31.77	1	5
P. Bainbridge	21	32	3	858	128	29.59	2	4
A.J. Wright	22	38	1	1083	130	29.27	3	5
C.W.J. Athey	21	33	2	900	108	29.03	1	6
J.W. Lloyds	21	36	3	941	71	28.52	–	6
I.P. Butcher	13	21	3	429	105*	23.83	1	1
C.A. Walsh	18	25	5	360	47	18.00	–	–
R.C. Russell	10	15	3	188	41*	15.67	–	–
P.W. Romaines	5	10	–	156	77	15.60	–	1
G.D. Hodgson	3	4	–	60	25	15.00	–	–
D.V. Lawrence	12	17	5	173	45	14.42	–	–
G.A. Tedstone	12	17	2	206	50	13.73	–	1
A.W. Stovold	6	12	–	157	36	13.08	–	–
D.A. Graveney	13	19	5	150	27*	10.71	–	–
M.C.J. Ball	7	6	3	23	17*	7.67	–	–
K.B.S. Jarvis	11	12	3	65	32	7.22	–	–
V.S. Greene	4	6	–	25	13	4.17	–	–
M.W. Pooley	3	3	1	6	3	3.00	–	–

Bowling	*O*	*M*	*R*	*W*	*Avge*	*BB*	*5i*	*10m*
C.A. Walsh	627.4	134	1675	81	20.68	7-19	5	1
M.C.J. Ball	140	25	440	17	25.88	4-53	–	–
D.A. Graveney	452.2	158	960	37	25.95	6-128	1	–
K.M. Curran	408.5	82	1251	47	26.62	7-69	2	–
K.B.S. Jarvis	260.4	56	829	30	27.63	5-15	1	–
V.S. Greene	125.1	30	420	15	28.00	6-101	1	1
P. Bainbridge	271.1	61	723	24	30.13	4-39	–	–
D.V. Lawrence	303.1	52	1059	33	32.09	4-61	–	–
J.W. Lloyds	236	54	659	20	32.95	7-134	1	–

Also bowled: M.W. Alleyne 32.5-5-127-3; C.W.J. Athey 29.4-10-85-2; I.P. Butcher 4-1-15-0; M.W. Pooley 35-6-113-0; A.J. Wright 6-2-16-1.

Centuries

4 K.M. Curran: 116* v Worcs (Bristol); 101* v Somerset (Bath); 117* v Sussex (Hove); 128 v Somerset (Bristol).

3 A.J. Wright: 130 v Northants (Bristol); 100 v Glamorgan (Bristol); 118 v Kent (Maidstone).

2 M.W. Alleyne: 111 v Lancs (Cheltenham). C.W.J. Athey: 109 v Somerset (Bath). I.P. Butcher: 105* v Kent (Maidstone).

BENSON AND HEDGES CUP

v MIDDLESEX (Bristol)

May 2

Won by 6 wkts. Gloucs 2pts, Middx 0pts

Middlesex

J.D. Carr	b Bainbridge	43
†P.R. Downton	lbw b Greene	0
*M.W. Gatting	c Russell b Curran	30
M.R. Ramprakash	run out	2
R.O. Butcher	c Lloyds b Pooley	5
J.F. Sykes	b Greene	38
J.E. Emburey	c Bainbridge b Alleyne	5
N.F. Williams	c Lloyds b Alleyne	2
S.P. Hughes	c Russell b Lawrence	4
A.R.C. Fraser	not out	3
N.G. Cowans	run out	1
Extras	lb 4, w 8, nb 4	16
Total (53.4 ov)		149

2, 59, 68, 83, 94, 109, 115, 137, 147

Lawrence	8	0	42	1
Greene	9.4	1	27	2
Curran	8	0	16	1
Pooley	11	1	33	1
Bainbridge	11	4	12	1
Lloyds	1	0	3	0
Alleyne	5	1	12	2

Gloucestershire

A.W. Stovold	b Hughes	15
A.J. Wright	lbw b Fraser	49
P. Bainbridge	c and b Fraser	47
*C.W.J. Athey	lbw b Hughes	0
K.M. Curran	not out	10
J.W. Lloyds	not out	9
M.W. Alleyne		
R.C. Russell		
V.S. Greene		
D.V. Lawrence		
M.W. Pooley		
Extras	lb 11, w 8, nb 1	20
Total (4 wkts, 47.2 ov)		150

19, 125, 130, 130

Cowans	11	4	28	0
Hughes	8	0	20	2
Fraser	11	2	17	2
Emburey	3	1	16	0
Carr	5	0	15	0
Gatting	2	0	10	0
Williams	7.2	2	33	0

Umpires: K.E. Palmer and P.B. Wight
Toss: Gloucestershire. Gold: P. Bainbridge
Middlesex were always struggling for runs. In the afternoon Wright and Bainbridge addd 106 for the 2nd wicket and virtually won the match on their own.

v COMBINED UNIVERSITIES (Bristol)

May 13

Won by 3 wkts. Gloucs 2pts, Combined Univ 0pts

Combined Universities

S.P. James	c Romaines b Walsh	15
M.A. Crawley	run out	54
*M.A. Atherton	lbw b Lawrence	34
N. Hussain	c Bainbridge b Alleyne	25
†M.P. Speight	b Lawrence	19
J.I. Longley	b Walsh	36
J.C.M. Atkinson	c Wright b Alleyne	7
A. Dale	not out	21
C.M. Tolley	not out	1
A.R. Hansford		
J. Boiling		
Extras	b 2, lb 4, w 3, nb 2	11
Total (7 wkts, 55 ov)		223

17, 99, 113, 155, 155, 170, 222

Walsh	11	2	40	2
Lawrence	11	2	36	2
Pooley	11	0	51	0
Curran	11	1	41	0
Alleyne	11	0	49	2

Gloucestershire

A.W. Stovold	run out	45
A.J. Wright	c Tolley b Dale	27
P.W. Romaines	c Atherton b Crawley	0
*C.W.J. Athey	c Atherton b Tolley	40
P. Bainbridge	c Dale b Boiling	38
K.M. Curran	not out	27
M.W. Alleyne	run out	7
C.A. Walsh	c Atherton b Hansford	28
†R.C. Russell	not out	6
M.W. Pooley		
D.V. Lawrence		
Extras	lb 5, w 3, nb 1	9
Total (7 wkts, 54.5 ov)		227

48, 49, 94, 153, 159, 171, 218

Hansford	11	2	41	1
Tolley	11	0	61	1
Dale	11	0	35	1
Crawley	11	3	18	1
Boiling	10.5	0	67	1

Umpires: R. Palmer and D.G.L. Evans
Toss: Gloucestershire. Gold: M.A. Crawley
With everyone making a contribution, the Universities made a good score and Gloucestershire had to fight all the way to match it, Russell hitting a four off the 4th ball of the last over to win the game. Crawley's all-round success won him the Man of the Match award.

NATWEST BANK TROPHY

v LANCASHIRE (Bristol)

July 12

Lost by one wkt.

Gloucestershire

A.J. Wright	c Hegg b Allott	1
I.P. Butcher	c Allott b DeFreitas	2
J.W. Lloyds	lbw b Allott	5
*C.W.J. Athey	c and b Simmons	25
K.M. Curran	c Wasim Akram b DeFreitas	47
P. Bainbridge	lbw b Allott	13
M.W. Alleyne	b Allott	0
†R.C. Russell	not out	42
C.A. Walsh	not out	9
M.C.J. Ball		
K.B.S. Jarvis		
Extras	b 3, lb 14, w 6, nb 7	30
Total (7 wkts, 60 ov)		174

2, 8, 10, 50, 92, 92, 149

Allott	12	5	31	4
DeFreitas	12	1	35	2
Wasim Akram	12	2	42	0
Watkinson	12	1	36	0
Simmons	12	5	13	1

Lancashire

G.D. Mendis	c Alleyne b Ball	46
G. Fowler	c Alleyne b Walsh	22
†W.K. Hegg	c Curran b Ball	29
P.A.J. DeFreitas	c Alleyne b Ball	0
N.H. Fairbrother	c and b Jarvis	31
T.E. Jesty	lbw b Jarvis	6
M. Watkinson	c Athey b Jarvis	4
Wasim Akram	c Russell b Bainbridge	15
*D.P. Hughes	c Athey b Curran	6
P.J.W. Allott	not out	11
J. Simmons	not out	2
Extras	lb 2, w 5	7
Total (9 wkts, 60 ov)		179

46, 89, 89, 123, 134, 144, 147, 162, 169

Walsh	12	2	27	1
Curran	12	2	41	1
Jarvis	12	2	25	3
Ball	12	1	42	3
Lloyds	7	1	24	0
Bainbridge	5	0	18	0

Umpires: J.H. Harris and N.T. Plews
Toss: Lancashire. MofM: P.J.W. Allott
Lancashire required two off the last ball to win this match with the final pair at the crease. Allott obliged with a six and went through to the quarter-final. Gloucestershire were put to bat and lost 3 for 10, but were allowed to recover somewhat through a very defiant 47 by Curran.

Away Matches

The full scorecard of each of Gloucestershire's away matches will be found in the sections for the respective home teams.

Cardiff: May 4, 5, 6, 8
Gloucs 282 and 381–5d (A.J. Wright 100) drew with Glam 435 (M.P. Maynard 191*, D.A. Graveney 6–128). Gloucs 4pts, Glamorgan 4pts.

Northampton: June 7, 8, 9
Gloucs 118 and 186 lost to Northants 236 (K.M. Curran 7–69) and 69–1 by 9 wkts. Northants 22pts, Gloucs 4pts.

Leicester: June 10, 12, 13
Leics 145 and 238 lost to Gloucs 306 and 78–1 by 9 wkts. Gloucs 24pts, Leics 4pts.

Harrogate: June 17, 19, 20
Yorks 220 (C.A. Walsh 5–86) and 312–6d drew with Gloucs 279 and 163–8. Gloucs 7pts, Yorks 6pts.

Bath: June 21, 22, 23
Somerset 73 (C.A. Walsh 7–19) and 364 (S.J. Cook 147, J.W. Lloyds 7–134) lost to Gloucs 402–4d (C.W.J. Athey 108, K.M. Curran 101*) and 36–2 by 8 wkts. Gloucs 22pts, Somerset 1pt.

The Oval: June 24, 26, 27
Surrey 275 (C.A. Walsh 5–83) and 128–2 beat Gloucs 113 (M.P. Bicknell 6–47) and 289 by 8 wkts. Surrey 23pts, Gloucs 4pts.

Maidstone: July 8, 10,11
Gloucs 251–1d (A.J. Wright 118, I.P. Butcher 105*) and 207–6d beat Kent 209–1d (M.R. Benson 102*) and 202 by 47 runs. Gloucs 19pts, Kent 2pts.

Portsmouth: July 26, 27, 28
Gloucs 240 and 48 (C.A. Connor 7–31) lost to Hants 406–9d (C.L. Smith 107, M.C.J. Nicholas 101) by an innings and 118 runs. Hants 24pts, Gloucs 3pts.

Edgbaston: July 29, 31, Aug 1
Gloucs 279 (P. Bainbridge 101, A.A. Donald 5–67) and 188–4d lost to Warwicks 218–8d and 250–7 by 3 wkts. Warwicks 22pts, Gloucs 6pts.

Hove: August 24, 25, 26, 27
Gloucs 133 and 363 (K.M. Curran 117*) lost to Sussex 323 (D.M. Smith 115) and 175–7 by 3 wkts. Sussex 23pts, Gloucs 3pts.

Worcester: August 29, 30, 21
Worcs 248 and 213 beat Gloucs 206 (S.M. McEwan 5–61) and 124 by 131 runs. Worcs 22pts, Gloucs 6pts.

v NORTHAMPTONSHIRE (Bristol)

April 27, 28, 29, 30
Lost by 10 wkts. Northants 23pts, Gloucs 4pts

Gloucestershire 1st Innings

A.W. Stovold	c Ripley b Thomas	16
A.J. Wright	b Thomas	10
P.W. Romaines	c Lamb b Robinson	13
*C.W.J. Athey	c Wild b Thomas	2
P. Bainbridge	c Bailey b Robinson	59
K.M. Curran	b Robinson	65
J.W. Lloyds	lbw b Thomas	61
†R.C. Russell	c Davis b Robinson	0
V.S. Greene	c G. Cook b Davis	13
D.A. Graveney	c Larkins b Thomas	9
D.V. Lawrence	not out	4
Extras	lb 7, nb 6	13
Total (85.3 ov)		265

24, 28, 47, 47, 171, 175, 179, 221, 252

Davis	18	3	62	1
Thomas	26.3	6	87	5
Robinson	25	5	60	4
Capel	16	2	49	0

Northamptonshire 1st Innings

G. Cook	b Lloyds	76
W. Larkins	c Wright b Lawrence	4
R.J. Bailey	b Lawrence	100
*A.J. Lamb	c Curran b Greene	16
D.J. Wild	c Russell b Lawrence	45
D.J. Capel	c Russell b Graveney	81
R.G. Williams	c and b Lloyds	71
†D. Ripley	c Lawrence b Graveney	22
J.G. Thomas	st Russell b Lloyds	19
W.W. Davis	b Graveney	11
M.A. Robinson	not out	0
Extras	b 3, lb 36, w 1, nb 20	60
Total (100 ov: 250–4)(197.1 ov)		505

27, 194, 214, 226, 330, 417, 451, 490, 499

Lawrence	34	7	101	3
Greene	37	9	93	1
Curran	27	7	71	0
Graveney	47.1	18	78	3
Bainbridge	25	6	72	0
Lloyds	27	7	51	3

Gloucestershire 2nd Innings

A.W. Stovold	c Ripley b Thomas	36
A.J. Wright	c Williams b Capel	130
P.W. Romaines	c Ripley b Thomas	0
*C.W.J. Athey	c Lamb b Robinson	63
P. Bainbridge	c Wild b Davis	0
K.M. Curran	c Wild b Robinson	1
J.W. Lloyds	c Larkins b Capel	14
†R.C. Russell	c Ripley b Capel	0
V.S. Greene	c Ripley b Robinson	4
D.A. Graveney	c Williams b Capel	0
D.V. Lawrence	not out	1
Extras	b 13, lb 13, nb 16	42
Total		291

62, 72, 218, 220, 224, 278, 282, 287, 287

Davis	26	2	96	1
Thomas	19	3	68	2
Capel	23	3	67	4
Robinson	17.4	6	29	3
Williams	3	1	5	0

Northamptonshire 2nd Innings

G. Cook	not out	10
W. Larkins	not out	38
Extras	b 4, lb 1	5
Total (0 wkts)		53

Lawrence	3.5	0	11	0
Greene	3	0	37	0

Umpires: K.E. Palmer and P.J. Eele
Toss: Northamptonshire
On a very chilly first day, Thomas produced some lively bowling to dismiss the home side for 265, with Curran 65 in 125 minutes the best batsman. Northants began Friday at 32–1. The bowling was rather off line and the batsmen gradually built up the Northants total which had reached 324–4 by stumps. Graveney and Lloyds kept down the run rate on the third day, then Gloucester ended at 90–2. At tea on the last day a draw seemed certain, but the last 5 Gloucester wickets fell for 13 and Northants knocked off the runs in less than 7 overs.

v ESSEX (Bristol)

May 20, 22
Lost by 116 runs. Essex 21pts, Gloucs 4pts

Essex 1st Innings

*G.A. Gooch	c Stovold b Lawrence	63
J.P. Stephenson	c Walsh b Lawrence	9
A.W Lilley	c Russell b Walsh	23
M.E. Waugh	c Bainbridge b Walsh	11
P.J. Prichard	c Walsh b Bainbridge	18
B.R. Hardie	b Lawrence	0
D.R. Pringle	c Athey b Lawrence	4
†M.A. Garnham	c Romaines b Bainbridge	0
T.D. Topley	c Athey b Bainbridge	2
N.A. Foster	not out	22
J.H. Childs	c Russell b Walsh	16
Extras	lb 3, nb 7	10
Total (56.1 ov)		178

21, 66, 85, 110, 114, 135, 136, 136, 138

Walsh	17.1	2	57	3
Lawrence	17	4	61	4
Curran	9	2	15	0
Pooley	3	0	24	0
Graveney	1	0	1	0
Bainbridge	9	1	17	3

Gloucestershire 1st Innings

P.W. Romaines	c Garnham b Pringle	20
A.J. Wright	b Foster	8
*C.W.J. Athey	c Hardie b Foster	3
P. Bainbridge	c Foster b Topley	3
K.M. Curran	c Gooch b Pringle	11
†R.C. Russell	c Gooch b Pringle	15
A.W. Stovold	c Prichard b Topley	5
M.W. Pooley	c Hardie b Foster	1
D.A. Graveney	c Foster b Topley	0
D.V. Lawrence	c Waugh b Foster	4
C.A. Walsh	not out	0
Extras	lb 5, nb 5	10
Total (40.4 ov)		80

15, 21, 39, 49, 50, 67, 72, 73, 79

Foster	11.4	5	14	4
Pringle	14	6	22	2
Topley	15	4	39	4

Essex 2nd Innings

*G.A. Gooch	lbw b Lawrence	3
J.P. Stephenson	c Stovold b Bainbridge	0
†M.A. Garnham	c Graveney b Bainbridge	1
A.W. Lilley	b Lawrence	0
M.E. Waugh	c Lawrence b Walsh	9
P.J. Prichard	c sub b Bainbridge	32
B.R. Hardie	c Stovold b Curran	24
D.R. Pringle	lbw b Walsh	2
N.A. Foster	c Russell b Curran	5
T.D. Topley	b Lawrence	10
J.H. Childs	not out	2
Extras	b 4, lb 4, nb 12	20
Total		108

2, 9, 9, 9, 34, 75, 86, 86, 104

Lawrence	12.1	3	23	3
Bainbridge	11	4	23	3
Walsh	13	1	31	2
Curran	10	4	23	2

Gloucestershire 2nd Innings

A.W. Stovold	c Hardie b Pringle	15
A.J. Wright	c Hardie b Foster	4
P.W. Romaines	c and b Topley	10
P. Bainbridge	c Waugh b Foster	2
K.M. Curran	c Garnham b Foster	5
†R.C. Russell	c Garnham b Foster	14
M.W. Pooley	b Waugh	3
D.A. Graveney	lbw b Topley	11
D.V. Lawrence	not out	11
C.A. Walsh	c Lilley b Topley	4
*C.W.J. Athey	absent hurt	0
Extras	lb 3, nb 8	11
Total		90

19, 19, 21, 27, 49, 51, 62, 86

Foster	12	1	35	4
Pringle	12	5	13	1
Topley	8	1	28	3
Waugh	3	0	11	1

Umpires: D.R. Shepherd and R.A. White
Toss: Gloucestershire
24 wickets fell on the first day, with only Gooch reaching an individual fifty. Essex were 18–4 at the close. The visitors just reached three figures on the second morning, and wickets continued to fall as Gloucester were 62–6 at tea. The first ball after tea saw the dismissal of Pooley and at 5.10 pm the game was completed in Essex favour.

v WORCESTERSHIRE (Bristol)

May 27, 29, 30

Lost by 79 runs. Worcs 22pts, Gloucs 4pts

Worcestershire 1st Innings

T.S. Curtis	c Russell b Curran	23
P. Bent	c Russell b Lawrence	0
G.A. Hick	b Lawrence	8
D.B. d'Oliveira	c Russell b Curran	6
*P.A. Neale	c Lawrence b Curran	70
M.J. Weston	c Curran b Lawrence	14
P.J. Newport	c and b Lawrence	6
N.V. Radford	c Wright b Curran	28
R.K. Illingworth	c Wright b Curran	0
†S.R. Bevins	c Russell b Curran	5
A.P. Pridgeon	not out	19
Extras	b 2, lb 5, w 1, nb 14	22
Total (70.5 ov)		201

19, 30, 40, 45, 88, 94, 131, 134, 144

Lawrence	19	5	62	4
Walsh	19	2	42	0
Curran	18.5	4	53	6
Bainbridge	6	2	16	0
Graveney	8	2	21	0

Gloucestershire 1st Innings

A.W. Stovold	c Hick b Radford	5
*A.J. Wright	b Weston	46
P.W. Romaines	c Bevins b Pridgeon	2
M.W. Alleyne	c Hick b Newport	21
†R.C. Russell	c Radford b Newport	0
P. Bainbridge	b Radford	20
K.M. Curran	b Radford	6
J.W. Lloyds	c Bevins b Radford	31
D.A. Graveney	c Hick b Newport	8
C.A. Walsh	lbw b Radford	3
D.V. Lawrence	not out	1
Extras	lb 3, w 1, nb 1	5
Total (62.5 ov)		148

6, 32, 78, 78, 78, 88, 127, 138, 142

Radford	22	8	57	5
Pridgeon	10	3	18	1
Newport	22.5	5	52	3
Weston	8	4	18	1

Worcestershire 2nd Innings

T.S. Curtis	lbw b Curran	102
P. Bent	c Wright b Lawrence	0
G.A. Hick	b Graveney	53
D.B. d'Oliveria	c Russell b Graveney	22
*P.A. Neale	c Stovold b Graveney	34
M.J. Weston	not out	26
N.V. Radford	c Alleyne b Walsh	9
P.J. Newport	not out	10
Extras	b 5, lb 12, b 10	27
Total (6 wkts dec)		283

2, 101, 168, 214, 246, 264

Lawrence	11	0	58	1
Walsh	20	6	47	1
Curran	20	2	75	1
Bainbridge	3	0	10	0
Graveney	35	12	66	3
Lloyds	3	0	10	0

Gloucestershire 2nd Innings

A.W. Stovold	c Bevins b Radford	23
*A.J. Wright	c Illingworth b Radford	0
P.W. Romaines	c Bevins b Newport	10
M.W. Alleyne	c Radford b Newport	9
P. Bainbridge	c Curtis b Newport	12
K.M. Curran	not out	116
J.W. Lloyds	c Radford b Illingworth	19
†R.C. Russell	c Hick b Pridgeon	0
D.A. Graveney	b Newport	15
C.A. Walsh	lbw b Newport	19
D.V. Lawrence	c Curtis b Illingworth	12
Extras	b 2, lb 7, w 6, nb 7	22
Total		257

9, 36, 44, 49, 82, 115, 116, 154, 204

Radford	27	6	88	2
Newport	26	8	73	5
Illingworth	13.4	2	53	2
Pridgeon	13	5	30	1
Weston	1	0	4	0

Umpires: P.J. Eele and D.O. Oslear
Toss: Worcestershire

A last wicket stand of 57 – the highest of the innings – enabled Worcs to obtain a further batting point. Gloucs began Monday at 71–2 off 25 overs, but the remaining 8 wickets scarcely doubled the total. Curtis then hit an excellent 100 and Worcs were 231–4 at the close. Gloucs were set 337 off 87 overs. The score fell to 49–4, before Curran, aided by the tail made a great attempt to save the game – there were 38 balls left when the final wicket fell.

v NOTTINGHAMSHIRE (Gloucester)

July 1, 3

Lost by an innings and 4 runs. Notts 23pts, Gloucs 4pts

Gloucestershire 1st Innings

A.W. Stovold	b Stephenson	0
A.J. Wright	b Stephenson	4
J.W. Lloyds	c Broad b Cooper	12
*C.W.J. Athey	c French b Cooper	8
P. Bainbridge	c French b Stephenson	35
K.M. Curran	b Stephenson	17
M.W. Alleyne	c French b Evans	4
†R.C. Russell	c Pollard b Stephenson	10
V.S. Greene	c French b Cooper	5
M.C.J. Ball	not out	0
K.B.S. Jarvis	b Cooper	0
Extras	b 2, lb 2, w 1, nb 1	6
Total (51.3 ov)		101

0, 9, 19, 39, 76, 81, 83, 101, 101

Stephenson	20	9	32	5
Cooper	18.3	8	28	4
Saxelby	6	1	26	0
Evans	7	4	11	1

Nottinghamshire 1st Innings

B.C. Broad	lbw b Curran	30
P.R. Pollard	c Russell b Curran	7
*R.T. Robinson	b Jarvis	11
D.J.R. Martindale	b Greene	7
D.W. Randall	c Russell b Jarvis	76
F.D. Stephenson	c Lloyds b Curran	81
K.P. Evans	c Russell b Jarvis	0
†B.N. French	lbw b Curran	5
E.E. Hemmings	c Stovold b Greene	4
K.E. Cooper	c Curran b Greene	4
K. Saxelby	not out	0
Extras	lb 22, w 2, nb 3	27
Total (73.1 ov)		252

41, 42, 51, 209, 209, 209, 233, 238, 252

Greene	23.1	4	85	2
Jarvis	19	2	69	4
Curran	20	3	51	4
Bainbridge	9	2	24	0
Ball	2	1	1	0

Gloucestershire 2nd Innings

A.W. Stovold	b Stephenson	10
A.J. Wright	lbw b Cooper	4
J.W. Lloyds	c Broad b Cooper	1
*C.W.J. Athey	lbw b Stephenson	52
P. Bainbridge	c Robinson b Cooper	8
K.M. Curran	c Cooper b Hemmings	34
M.W. Alleyne	c Broad b Stephenson	5
†R.C. Russell	not out	24
V.S. Greene	c Broad b Cooper	0
M.C.J. Ball	c Robinson b Cooper	0
K.B.S. Jarvis	b Cooper	0
Extras	lb 9	9
Total		147

16, 27, 43, 110, 118, 129, 129, 137, 145

Stephenson	15	4	44	3
Cooper	15.1	7	37	6
Saxelby	9	4	27	0
Evans	3	0	11	0
Hemmings	9	4	19	1

Umpires: K.E. Palmer and J.H. Hampshire
Toss: Nottinghamshire

Having been put in to bat, the home county found themsleves quickly demolished by Cooper and Stephenson. Notts on the other hand, after a hesitant start, batted well with Randall and Stephenson taking the score to 192–4 by the Saturday close. The stand was broken quickly on Monday and the remaining wickets fell for 43 runs. Cooper again bowled well in the Gloucester second innings and apart from Athey the batting collapsed. Notts won inside two days.

v SUSSEX (Gloucester)

July 5, 6, 7,

Drawn. Gloucs 7pts, Sussex 3pts

Gloucestershire 1st Innings

A.J. Wright	c C.M. Wells b Green	80
I.P Butcher	b Babington	26
J.W. Lloyds	c Moores b C.M. Wells	59
*C.W.J. Athey	c Gould b Green	50
P. Bainbridge	b Green	69
K.M. Curran	c Gould b Dodemaide	30
M.W. Alleyne	c Green b Babington	27
†G.A. Tedstone	c Moores b Dodemaide	9
C.A. Walsh	c Gould b Salisbury	21
M.W. Pooley	not out	2
M.C.J. Ball		
Extras	b 10, lb 12, w 1, nb 3	26
Total (100 ov: 256–3) (9 wkts dec)		399

55, 173, 183, 295, 306, 359, 368, 393, 399

Dodemaide	16	3	39	2
Babington	30	11	63	2
Pigott	11	1	22	0
C.M. Wells	16	5	43	1
Lenham	7	1	25	0
Salisbury	27.3	5	92	1
Green	34	5	93	3

Sussex 1st Innings

N.J. Lenham	c Tedstone b Ball	50
D.M. Smith	lbw b Walsh	4
A.M. Green	lbw b Walsh	4
A.P. Wells	c Lloyds b Walsh	31
*C.M. Wells	st Tedstone b Ball	28
I.J. Gould	not out	58
A.I.C. Dodemaide	b Ball	24
†P. Moores	c Lloyds b Ball	2
A.C.S. Pigott	st Tedstone b Lloyds	9
I.D.K. Salisbury	lbw b Walsh	1
A.M. Babington	b Walsh	0
Extras	b 3, lb 16, nb 2	21
Total (78.2 ov)		232

9, 15, 72, 125, 134, 193, 205, 231, 232

Walsh	17.2	4	44	5
Curran	16	3	38	0
Pooley	15	3	46	0
Ball	29	2	84	4
Lloyds	1	0	1	1

Sussex 2nd Innings

N.J. Lenham	not out	9
D.M. Smith	not out	9
Extras	lb 2, w 1	3
Total (0 wkts)		21

Walsh	6	3	6	0
Curran	5.3	3	13	0

Umpires: K.E. Palmer and J.H. Hampshire
Toss: Gloucestershire

Although the home side made only 256–3 off the first 100 overs on the opening day, runs came relatively quickly due to the speed at which Sussex bowled their overs the 100 being delivered before 5.00. At the close Gloucester were 366–6. The innings continued for 40 minutes on the second day, then Walsh gave Sussex a jolt. Lenham however, lasted nearly 3 hours for 50 and later Gould hit 58 in 99 minutes. The follow on was enforced and Sussex ended at 9–0. Owing to rain only 38 balls were bowled on the third day.

v GLAMORGAN (Bristol)

July 19, 20, 21

Won by an innings and 123 runs. Gloucs 23pts Glamorgan 3pts

Glamorgan 1st Innings

S.P. James	c Russell b Jarvis	9
*H. Morris	c Russell b Greene	4
M.J. Cann	b Jarvis	6
M.P. Maynard	c Butcher b Jarvis	1
A. Dale	c Russell b Greene	4
G.C. Holmes	not out	37
I. Smith	b Jarvis	1
K. Somaia	b Ball	11
†C.P. Metson	b Greene	2
S.L. Watkin	b Greene	0
S.R. Barwick	c Russell b Jarvis	5
Extras	lb 6, nb 3	9
Total (39.2 ov)		89

11, 19, 20, 27, 29, 32, 63, 69, 77

Greene	16	4	36	4
Jarvis	10.2	3	15	5
Bainbridge	6	0	18	0
Athey	2	0	3	0
Ball	5	2	11	1

Gloucestershire 1st Innings

A.J. Wright	b Watkin	85
I.P. Butcher	b Watkin	10
J.W. Lloyds	c James b Smith	44
*C.W.J. Athey	c and b Barwick	6
K.M. Curran	lbw b Barwick	0
P. Bainbridge	st Metson b Dale	98
M.C.J. Ball	b Watkin	2
M.W. Alleyne	st Metston b Somaia	88
†R.C. Russell	not out	41
V.S. Greene	c Smith b Barwick	0
K.B.S. Jarvis		
Extras	lb 7, w 2	9
Total (100 ov: 270–7) (9 wkts dec)		383

29, 118, 135, 135, 180, 204, 265, 382, 383

Watkin	33	9	84	3
Barwick	35.3	9	85	3
Smith	16	0	93	1
Somaia	22	7	51	1
Dale	20	5	62	1
Cann	1	0	1	0

Glamorgan 2nd Innings

S.P. James	b Greene	16
*H. Morris	b Ball	29
M.J. Cann	c Russell b Greene	1
M.P. Maynard	lbw b Greene	0
A. Dale	c Alleyne b Greene	44
G.C. Holmes	c Butcher b Ball	8
I. Smith	run out	1
K. Somaia	c Wright b Greene	15
†C.P. Metson	not out	27
S.L. Watkin	b Greene	0
S.R. Barwick	b Bainbridge	23
Extras	b 2, lb 3, nb 2	7
Total		171

24, 30, 40, 59, 74, 77, 120, 123, 123

Greene	26	8	101	6
Jarvis	15	6	29	0
Ball	13	5	23	2
Bainbridge	7.2	1	13	1
Alleyne	1	1	0	0
Wright	2	2	0	0

Umpires: J.C. Balderstone and D.J. Constant

Toss: Glamorgan

Despite lacking Lawrence and Walsh, the home side soon disposed of Glamorgan and by the close of the first day Gloucester were 190–5 off 67 overs. Bainbridge and Alleyne added 117 for the 8th wicket on Thursday to give their side a lead of almost 300. Dale, making his debut, prevented a 2 day win and was 33 not out, with Glamorgan 104–6 at stumps. The match was soon over on Friday. Morris announced that he was resigning as Glamorgan's captain and Butcher was appointed to replace him.

v LANCASHIRE (Cheltenham)

August 5, 7, 8

Won by an innings and 23 runs. Gloucs 24pts, Lancs 2pts

Lancashire 1st Innings

G.D. Mendis	c Alleyne b Jarvis	8
G. Fowler	c Curran b Walsh	0
M.A. Atherton	c Curran b Walsh	21
N.H. Fairbrother	not out	30
T.E. Jesty	c Russell b Walsh	17
M. Watkinson	c Wright b Walsh	0
†W.K. Hegg	c Athey b Jarvis	0
*D.P. Hughes	c Alleyne b Walsh	7
P.A.J. DeFreitas	c Wright b Jarvis	4
J.D. Fitton	b Jarvis	0
P.J.W. Allott	c Athey b Walsh	5
Extras	nb 1	1
Total (24.5 ov)		93

1, 29, 29, 63, 63, 68, 79, 84, 85

Walsh	12.5]	2	40	6
Curran	3	1	16	0
Jarvis	9	1	37	4

Gloucestershire 1st Innings

A.J. Wright	c Hegg b Allott	12
I.P. Butcher	c Allott b DeFreitas	40
J.W. Lloyds	c Atherton b Allott	26
*C.W.J. Athey	c Hegg b DeFreitas	13
K.M. Curran	b Watkinson	9
P. Bainbridge	lbw b Watkinson	128
M.W. Alleyne	c Hegg b DeFreitas	111
†R.C. Russell	c Mendis b DeFreitas	4
C.A. Walsh	c Fowler b DeFreitas	4
D.A. Graveney	not out	15
K.B.S. Jarvis	c Fowler b Watkinson	14
Extras	b 1, lb 5, nb 12	18
Total (100 ov: 335–5)		394

18, 72, 90, 102, 104, 349, 361, 363, 365

DeFreitas	29	2	123	5
Allott	27	4	73	2
Watkinson	20.4	4	78	3
Fitton	24	6	81	0
Atherton	12	3	33	0

Lancashire 2nd Innings

G.D. Mendis	retired hurt	30
G. Fowler	c Alleyne b Walsh	12
M.A. Atherton	c Russell b Curran	36
N.H. Fairbrother	c Athey b Walsh	14
T.E. Jesty	lbw b Walsh	68
M. Watkinson	c Lloyds b Graveney	43
†W.K. Hegg	c Russell b Walsh	9
*D.P. Hughes	c Russell b Graveney	2
P.A.J. DeFreitas	c and b Graveney	0
J.D. Fitton	not out	18
P.J.W. Allott	c and b Graveney	28
Extras	lb 7, w 4, nb 7	18
Total		278

38, 82, 123, 193, 226, 229, 231, 231, 278

Walsh	19	3	64	4
Curran	16	3	67	1
Jarvis	11	2	44	0
Graveney	21	7	51	4
Bainbridge	4	0	14	0
Athey	4	1	10	0
Lloyds	6	1	21	0

Umpires: K.J. Lyons and D.O. Oslear

Toss: Lancashire

Walsh and Jarvis bowled out Lancashire on the first morning for 93, then Gloucester replied by making 282–5 off 82 overs, Bainbridge and Alleyne being not out on 85 and 80. The stand was worth 245 before it was broken. Being 301 behind on first innings, Lancashire managed to reach 193–3 in their second, but five wickets went down cheaply and the injured Mendis came in to prevent a two-day defeat, when the extra half hour was claimed. However on the third morning the doctors advised Mendis not to resume and so Gloucester won by an innings.

v MIDDLESEX (Cheltenham)

August 9, 10, 11

Lost by 188 runs. Middx 22pts, Gloucs 4pts

Middlesex 1st Innings

J.D. Carr	c Tedstone b Bainbridge	22
D.L. Haynes	c Butcher b Curran	20
*M.W. Gatting	not out	110
M.R. Ramprakash	c Alleyne b Walsh	0
M.A. Roseberry	b Walsh	21
†P.R. Downton	c Alleyne b Jarvis	6
J.E. Emburey	b Jarvis	5
N.F. Williams	st Tedstone b Graveney	6
S.P. Hughes	c Athey b Graveney	0
R.M. Ellcock	b Walsh	9
N.G. Cowans	b Jarvis	0
Extras	b 4, lb 12, nb 7	23
Total (78 ov)		222

33, 84, 85, 115, 134, 148, 179, 179, 221

Walsh	20	5	50	3
Curran	16	4	36	1
Jarvis	18	2	51	3
Graveney	14	1	44	2
Bainbridge	10	1	25	1

Gloucestershire 1st Innings

A.J. Wright	c Roseberry b Ellcock	2
I.P. Butcher	c Carr b Emburey	21
J.W. Lloyds	c Williams b Emburey	19
†G.A Tedstone	c Ramprakash b Emburey	12
*C.W.J. Athey	c Gatting b Williams	2
K.M. Curran	c Williams b Emburey	0
P. Bainbridge	c Roseberry b Emburey	24
M.W. Alleyne	c Hughes b Emburey	29
C.A. Walsh	c Ramprakash b Emburey	3
D.A. Graveney	c and b Ellcock	0
K.B.S. Jarvis	not out	4
Extras	nb 6	6
Total (39.3 ov)		122

8, 42, 43, 51, 54, 69, 114, 117, 118

Ellcock	11	1	42	2
Cowans	7	1	26	0
Emburey	14.3	2	27	7
Williams	6	0	17	1
Hughes	1	0	10	0

Middlesex 2nd Innings

J.D. Carr	c Jarvis b Lloyds	22
D.L. Haynes	b Lloyds	24
*M.W. Gatting	c Lloyds b Graveney	35
M.R. Ramprakash	c Athey b Graveney	21
M.A. Roseberry	c Bainbridge b Walsh	51
†P.R. Downton	b Lloyds	10
J.E. Emburey	b Walsh	16
N.F. Williams	not out	8
S.P. Hughes	not out	3
Extras	b 10, lb 4, w 1, nb 1	16
Total (7 wkts dec)		206

46, 47, 111, 120, 166, 190, 193

Walsh	14	3	44	2
Curran	3	1	6	0
Graveney	25	5	63	2
Jarvis	3	0	19	0
Lloyds	25	7	60	3

Gloucestershire 2nd Innings

A.J. Wright	c Carr b Williams	11
*C.W.J. Athey	c Downton b Williams	14
J.W. Lloyds	b Hughes	3
K.M. Curran	lbw b Emburey	29
P. Bainbridge	c Gatting b Hughes	3
M.W. Alleyne	b Emburey	9
I.P. Butcher	st Downton b Emburey	19
†G.A. Tedstone	not out	10
C.A. Walsh	c Downton b Emburey	2
D.A. Graveney	c Roseberry b Emburey	0
K.B.S. Jarvis	c Emburey b Williams	1
Extras	b 1, lb 10, nb 6	17
Total		118

27, 29, 50, 56, 74, 88, 112, 116, 117

Ellcock	11	4	37	0
Cowans	3	1	5	0
Emburey	26	8	39	5
Williams	13.2	7	19	3
Hughes	5	3	7	2

Umpires: D.O. Oslear and A.G.T. Whitehead

Toss: Gloucestershire

An excellent captain's innings by Gatting put his colleagues to shame, as the visitors were dismissed for 220. In reply Gloucester were 42–2 off 12 overs after a rain-interrupted day. A career-best 7–27 by Emburey gave his side a lead of 98 and some consistent batting meant that Middlesex were in a strong position. They declared overnight and Emburey took a further 5 wickets to bring the match to an early conclusion.

v DERBYSHIRE (Cheltenham)
August 12, 14, 15
Drawn. Derbys 6pts, Gloucs 2pts

Derbyshire 1st Innings

*K.J. Barnett	c Wright b Walsh	9
P.D. Bowler	c Tedstone b Lawrence	57
J.E. Morris	c Tedstone b Ball	121
R. Sharma	c and b Alleyne	77
T.J.G. O'Gorman	b Walsh	124
C.J. Adams	c Tedstone b Lawrence	5
M. Jean-Jacques	lbw b Alleyne	0
†B.J.M. Maher	b Walsh	5
P.G. Newman	c Tedstone b Walsh	2
M.A. Holding	not out	4
S.J. Base		
Extras	b 6, lb 27, w 5, nb 6	44
Total (100 ov: 383–3) (9 wkts dec)		448

11, 191, 217, 397, 414, 416, 441, 443, 448

Walsh	25.3	6	62	4
Lawrence	21	3	68	2
Ball	20	2	91	1
Curran	14	1	64	0
Lloyds	11	2	30	0
Bainbridge	17	5	49	0
Athey	1	0	10	0
Alleyne	11	0	41	2

Gloucestershire 1st Innings

I.P. Butcher	c Maher b Jean-Jacques	21
†G.A. Tedstone	lbw b Barnett	19
J.W. Lloyds	c Maher b Sharma	30
A.J. Wright	c Barnett b Newman	23
*C.W.J. Athey	b Sharma	10
K.M. Curran	c and b Holding	30
P. Bainbridge	not out	24
M.W. Alleyne	not out	2
C.A. Walsh		
D.V. Lawrence		
M.C.J. Ball		
Extras	b 1, lb 5, w 1, nb 9	16
Total (6 wkts, 64.2 ov)		175

41, 47, 104, 112, 119, 166

Holding	23.1	8	62	1
Base	4	0	18	0
Newman	9	3	26	1
Barnett	9	3	23	1
Sharma	12	4	23	2
Jean-Jacques	7	1	17	1

Umpires: B.J. Meyer and A.G.T. Whitehead
Toss: Derbyshire
Hundreds from O'Gorman and Morris meant that Derbyshire made 422–6 on Saturday. Barnett continued the innings on Monday and the home county were 111–3 off 44.5 overs when a thunderstorm ended play. Gloucester lost three more wickets on the last morning before the rain returned to end the match.

v SOMERSET (Bristol)
Sept 8, 9, 10, 11
Won by 141 runs. Gloucs 23pts, Somerset 5pts

Gloucestershire 1st Innings

A.J. Wright	c Cook b Mallender	7
G.D. Hodgson	c Burns b Rose	15
*C.W.J. Athey	b Jones	22
M.W. Alleyne	c Burns b Jones	14
K.M. Curran	b Jones	0
P. Bainbridge	b Rose	16
J.W. Lloyds	c Cook b Rose	58
†R.C. Russell	c Harden b Marks	15
C.A. Walsh	b Mallender	10
D.A. Graveney	not out	27
D.V. Lawrence	c Burns b Jones	45
Extras	b 9, lb 12, w 5, nb 4	30
Total (94.1 ov)		259

10, 30, 70, 70, 71, 103, 145, 173, 189

Jones	23.1	5	66	4
Mallender	27	5	69	2
Rose	24	7	48	3
Atkinson	2	0	12	0
Marks	18	5	43	1

Somerset 1st Innings

S.J. Cook	b Walsh	18
P.M. Roebuck	c Russell b Walsh	0
J.J. E. Hardy	c Russell b Walsh	40
C.J. Tavare	c Lawrence b Walsh	39
R.J. Harden	lbw b Curran	23
J.C.M. Atkinson	c and b Graveney	17
†N.D. Burns	b Curran	5
*V.J. Marks	c Lloyds b Graveney	15
G.D. Rose	c Athey b Graveney	0
N.A. Mallender	not out	0
A.N. Jones	c Wright b Graveney	0
Extras	lb 3, w 1, nb 4	8
Total (69.3 ov)		165

8, 25, 101, 104, 129, 136, 165, 165, 165

Lawrence	11	0	48	0
Walsh	18	7	33	4
Curran	14	3	37	2
Graveney	23.3	10	37	4
Bainbridge	3	1	7	0

Gloucestershire 2nd Innings

A.J. Wright	c Tavare b Rose	17
G.D. Hodgson	b Rose	25
*C.W.J. Athey	b Rose	1
M.W. Alleyne	c and b Mallender	56
K.M. Curran	b Rose	128
P. Bainbridge	c Burns b Mallender	0
J.W. Lloyds	run out	37
†R.C. Russell	not out	27
C.A. Walsh	not out	10
Extras	lb 8, w 1	9
Total (7 wkts dec)		310

35, 44, 47, 163, 163, 242, 289

Jones	19	2	71	0
Mallender	23	4	59	2
Rose	18	4	82	4
Marks	34	8	90	0

Somerset 2nd Innings

S.J. Cook	c Graveney b Walsh	35
P.M. Roebuck	c Russell b Walsh	117
J.J. E. Hardy	c Russell b Walsh	0
C.J. Tavare	c sub b Bainbridge	36
R.J. Harden	c Athey b Lawrence	10
J.C.M. Atkinson	c Alleyne b Walsh	5
†N.D. Burns	c Wright b Curran	9
*V.J. Marks	retired hurt	18
G.D. Rose	lbw b Graveney	15
N.A. Mallender	c Lawrence b Graveney	9
A.N. Jones	not out	1
Extras	lb 6, nb 2	8
Total		263

62, 62, 151, 172, 189, 210, 243, 262, 263

Lawrence	14	0	81	1
Walsh	20	6	68	4
Curran	17	5	59	1
Graveney	23.4	14	25	2
Bainbridge	9	4	16	1
Lloyds	6	4	8	0

Umpires: H.D. Bird and D.J. Constant
Toss: Somerset
A mundane first day resulted in Somerset starting the second morning at 8–0. Play on Saturday was restricted to 68 overs during which the visitors were dismissed for 165. Curran made his best score of the season on Sunday and enabled the home side to build up a commanding lead. On the last day Gloucester made rather heavy weather of bowling out Somerset and Roebuck survived 281 minutes for his 117 with 19 fours.

v HAMPSHIRE (Bristol)
Sept 13, 14, 15, 16
Drawn. Gloucs 3pts, Hants 3pts

Hampshire 1st Innings

T.C. Middleton	lbw b Lawrence	0
R.J. Scott	st Russell b Lloyds	34
K.D. James	b Graveney	60
R.A. Smith	c Russell b Curran	68
*M.C.J. Nicholas	c Alleyne b Graveney	0
V.P. Terry	run out	17
M.D. Marshall	not out	68
†R.J. Parks	c Russell b Walsh	18
R.J. Maru	not out	0
C.A. Connor		
P.J. Bakker		
Extras	lb 12, nb 10	22
Total (7 wkts, 89.4 ov)		287

0, 70, 175, 175, 175, 228, 287

Lawrence	15	4	48	1
Walsh	18.4	5	49	1
Curran	17	1	64	1
Graveney	21	8	45	2
Lloyds	18	2	69	1

Gloucestershire – did not bat
A.J. Wright
G.D. Hodgson
*C.W.J. Athey
P. Bainbridge
K.M. Curran
J.W. Lloyds
M.W. Alleyne
†R.C. Russell
C.A. Walsh
D.A. Graveney
D.V. Lawrence

Umpires: H.D. Bird and D.S. Thompsett
Toss: Hampshire
Rain virtually washed away this final game. 80 overs were bowled on the first day, then 9.4 on the second, but no play at all took place on the third or fourth days. Hampshire had had hopes of finishing fifth in the table. They had, however, to settle for sixth place.

Hampshire

President: C.G.A. Paris
Chairman: D. Rich
Secretary: A.F. Baker, Northlands Road, Southampton SO9 2TY. *Tel:* 0703 333788.
Coach: P.J. Sainsbury
Captain: M.C.J. Nicholas
Foundation of Present Club: August 1863 in Southampton
First First-Class Match: MCC v Hampshire (Lord's) July 1861
County Champions: 1961, 1973
Gillette/NatWest Trophy: Semi-finalists in 1966, 1976, 1983, 1985, 1988, 1989
Benson & Hedges Cup: Winners 1988
Sunday League Champions: 1975, 1978, 1986
Refuge Cup: Nil

Summary of Results in 1989
Britannic Assurance County Championship: Played 22, Won 6, Lost 8, Drawn 8, Position 6th equal
NatWest Bank Trophy: Lost in semi-final
Benson & Hedges Cup: Did not qualify for knock-out section
Refuge Assurance Sunday League: Played 16, Won 8, Lost 6, Tied 1, No Result 1, Position 6th
Refuge Assurance Cup: Did not qualify

From left, back: *R.J. Maru, R.J. Scott, S. Udal, A.N. Aymes, K. Shine, I. Turner, J. Wood.* Centre: *R. Cox, T.C. Middleton, K.D. James, J.R. Ayling, S.J.W. Andrew, P.J. Bakker, C.A. Connor, P.J. Sainsbury (Coach).* Front: *R.J. Parks, C.L. Smith, D.R. Turner, M.C.J. Nicholas (Captain), V.P. Terry (Vice-Captain), N.G. Cowley, T.M. Tremlett, R.A. Smith.* Allsport/Ben Radford

Up to a certain point the county had a good summer, but the eleven seemed to fall apart in August. The return of the fearsome Marshall – in 1988 he had been destroying England – provided a vital spark to the attack. From 15th in 1988, the county shot up to 6th and as can be inferred from the opening remark the improvement would have been even greater if the form of the early months had continued. Indeed third place might well have been obtained. The Dutchman, Bakker, who had suffered from injury in 1988, played throughout the summer and more than doubled his wicket haul, at the same time keeping the runs down. As in the previous year little was seen of Tremlett, though, from the ring, he appeared to be a most useful all-rounder. Jefferies had few opportunities due to the presence of Marshall, and the South African has been released.

The brothers Smith dominated the batting. Robin was in great form and apart from his county runs, he saved England from humiliation. Chris had to be content with second place in the averages, but he also was most reliable. Wood, a 20-year-old left-hand batsman, unknown at the start of the season, built himself a sound reputation as the summer wore on, having hit 58 on his debut. Another left-hander who won praise from the critics was James, the former Middlesex player, though his average owes a lot to his 162 against Glamorgan. Terry and the captain both played some good innings, but might have been more consistent.

In the one-day competitions Hampshire lost an exciting NatWest semi-final to Middlesex – Chris Smith batting quite admirably. Though little progress was made in the Benson and Hedges competition, the county was always among the front runners in the Sunday league and were unfortunate not to qualify for the Refuge Cup.

ONE DAY AWAY MATCHES

The full scorecard of each of Hampshire's away matches will be found in the sections for the respective home teams.

Refuge Assurance League

The Oval: April 30
Hants 114–9 (40 ov) lost to Surrey 115–5 (39.1 ov) by 5 wkts. Surrey 4pts, Hants 0pts.

Chelmsford: May 14
Hants 156–9 (40 ov) lost to Essex 157–7 (40 ov) by 3 wkts. Essex 4pts, Hants 0pts.

Lord's: June 6
Hants 138 (38.4 ov) tied with Middx 138–8 (40 ov). Middx 2pts, Hants 2pts.

Northampton: July 9
Northants 135–1 drew with Hants did not bat. Hants 2pts, Northants 2pts.

Trowbridge: July 16
Gloucs 184–8 (40 ov) beat Hants 163 (38.1 ov) by 21 runs. Gloucs 4pts, Hants 0pts.

Cardiff: July 30
Glamorgan 193–9 (39 ov) beat Hants 156 (35.3 ov) by 37 runs. Glam 4pts, Hants 0pts.

Derby: August 6
Derbys 148 (40 ov) (P.J. Bakker 5–17) lost to Hants 149–6 (39.2 ov) by 4 wkts. Hants 4pts, Derbys 0pts.

Trent Bridge: August 20
Hants 254–4 (40 ov) (R.A. Smith 131) beat Notts 222 (37.3 ov) by 32 runs. Hants 4pts, Notts 0pts.

Benson and Hedges Cup

Chelmsford: May 2
Hants 173–6 (55 ov) lost to Essex 175–3 (46.1 ov) by 7 wkts. Essex 2pts, Hants 0pts.

Hove: May 11
Hants 242–5 (55 ov) beat Sussex 177 (49.5 ov) by 65 runs. Hants 2pts, Sussex 0pts.

NatWest Bank Trophy

Chester: June 28, 29
Hants 306–2 (60 ov) (C.L. Smith 159) beat Cheshire 159 (47.1 ov) by 147 runs.

Cardiff: July 12
Glamorgan 189 (59.4 ov) lost to Hants 190–3 (57 ov) by 7 wkts.

The Oval: August 2
Surrey 228–8 (60 ov) lost to Hants 229–5 (58 ov) (R.A. Smith 125*) by 5 wkts.

REFUGE ASSURANCE LEAGUE

v SOMERSET (Southampton)

April 23
Won by 5 wkts. Hants 4pts, Somerset 0pts

Somerset		
S.J. Cook	c Connor	2
P.M. Roebuck	c Jefferies b Connor	6
J.J.E. Hardy	c Nicholas b James	1
C.J. Tavare	not out	120
R.J. Bartlett	c Terry b Cowley	32
*V.J. Marks	run out	31
G.D. Rose	lbw b Jefferies	0
†N.D. Burns	run out	6
N.A. Mallender	run out	0
A.N. Jones	not out	0
D.J. Foster		
Extras	lb 16, w 2, nb 4	22
Total (8 wkts, 40 ov)		220

13, 16, 19, 109, 183, 183, 206, 217

James	8	3	10	1
Connor	8	3	28	2
Andrew	6	0	35	0
Jefferies	8	0	59	1
Nicholas	3	0	24	0
Cowley	7	0	48	1

Hampshire		
*M.C.J. Nicholas	c Burns b Mallender	57
V.P. Terry	c Burns b Rose	45
R.A. Smith	c Bartlett b Rose	14
C.L. Smith	not out	41
R.J. Scott	b Jones	31
S.T. Jefferies	run out	26
†R.J. Parks	not out	2
K.D. James		
N.G. Cowley		
S.J.W. Andrew		
C.A. Connor		
Extras	lb 3, w 1, nb 1	5
Total (5 wkts, 39.2 ov)		221

100, 120, 120, 189, 219

Mallender	8	0	33	1
Foster	8	0	48	0
Rose	8	0	29	2
Jones	7.2	0	53	1
Marks	8	0	55	0

Umpires J.H. Harris and D.G.L. Evans
Toss: Hampshire
Tavare hit a century on his Sunday League debut for Somerset, but his effort was insufficient to prevent a Hampshire victory with four balls in hand; the win being due to very consistent batting.

v KENT (Southampton)

May 7
Won by 9 wkts. Hants 4pts, Kent 0pts

Kent		
S.G. Hinks	c Nicholas b Jefferies	44
M.R. Benson	run out	11
N.R. Taylor	c Parks b Jefferies	34
T.R. Ward	c Jefferies b Cowley	1
*C.S.Cowdrey	b Connor	21
G.R. Cowdrey	lbw b Cowley	6
R.M. Ellison	not out	9
†S.A. Marsh	lbw b Tremlett	1
D.J.M. Kelleher	c James b Tremlett	10
R.P. Davis	run out	2
H.L. Alleyne	b Connor	0
Extras	lb 12, w 5	17
Total (38 ov)		156

24, 90, 93, 97, 112, 131, 132, 148, 156

James	8	1	26	0
Connor	7	0	18	2
Tremlett	8	1	29	2
Jefferies	7	0	28	2
Cowley	8	1	43	2

Hampshire		
V.P. Terry	not out	79
*M.C.J. Nicholas	c G.R. Cowdrey b Alleyne	52
R.A. Smith	not out	14
D.R. Turner		
R.J. Scott		
K.D. James		
†R.J. Parks		
S.T. Jefferies		
T.M. Tremlett		
N.G. Cowley		
C.A. Connor		
Extras	lb 4, w 6, nb 3	13
Total (1 wkt, 35.3 ov)		158

133

Kelleher	6	0	17	0
Alleyne	8	2	32	1
Ellison	5.3	0	29	0
Davis	6	0	32	0
C.S. Cowdrey	4	1	20	0
G.R. Cowdrey	6	0	24	0

Umpires: S.B. Hassan and K.E. Palmer
Toss: Hampshire
Kent began batting in a promising manner, but they slid alarmingly from 90 for 1 to 156 all out. In contrast Hampshire virtually won the match before their first wicket fell.

PLAYERS

Stephen Jon Walter ANDREW *b* 27.1.1966 London; right arm medium fast bowler; tail end right hand batsman. Debut 1984

Adrian Nigel AYMES *b* 4.7.1964 Southampton; right hand batsman, wicketkeeper; debut 1987; did not appear in any Championship matches in 1989

Paul-Jan BAKKER *b* 19.8.1957 Vlaardingen, Holland; right arm medium fast bowler; tail end right hand batsmam; debut 1986; capped in Sept 1989

Cardigan Adolphus CONNOR *b* 24.3.1961 The Valley, Anguilla; right arm fast medium bowler; lower order right hand batsman; debut 1984

Nigel Geoffrey COWLEY *b* 1.3.1953 Shaftesbury; right hand batsman; off break bowler; debut 1974; only played in one Championship match 1989

Kevan David JAMES *b* 18.3.1961 Lambeth, S London; left hand batsman; left arm medium fast bowler; debut 1985, previously appeared for Middlesex 1980–84. Capped for Hants July 1989

Stephen Thomas JEFFERIES *b* 8.12.1959 Cape Town; left arm fast medium bowler; left hand batsman; debut 1988; also plays for Western Province; previously appeared for Derbys (1982) and Lancs (1983–85)

Malcolm Denzil MARSHALL *b* 18.4.1958 St Michael, Barbados; right arm fast bowler; hard hitting right hand batsman; debut 1979; also plays for Barbados; 66 Tests for the West Indies and 97 One-Day Internationals; has taken more Test wickets for West Indies than any other bowler

Rajesh Jamandass MARU *b* 28.10.1962 Nairobi; slow left arm bowler; right hand batsman; debut 1984; previously appeared for Middx 1980–82

Tony Charles MIDDLETON *b* 1.2.1964 Winchester; right hand batsman; slow left arm bowler; debut 1984

Mark Charles Jefford NICHOLAS *b* 29.9.1957 London; middle order right hand batsman; right arm medium pace bowler; debut 1978; captain since 1985; selected to captain England 'A' side to Zimbabwe 1989/90

Malcolm Marshall, Hampshire's West Indian fast bowler, who finished top of the county's averages.

Allsport/Gary Mortimore

REFUGE ASSURANCE LEAGUE

v LEICESTERSHIRE (Bournemouth)

May 28

Won by 7 wkts. Hants 4pts, Leics 0pts

Leicestershire		
L. Potter	c Scott b Connor	16
*N.E. Briers	b Connor	20
P. Willey	lbw b Marshall	2
J.J. Whitaker	c Marshall b Cowley	22
T.J. Boon	lbw b Connor	3
J.D.R. Benson	b Cowley	5
C.C. Lewis	b Marshall	21
†P. Whitticase	c James b Cowley	5
G.J. Parsons	c Parks b Bakker	0
J.P. Agnew	not out	0
G.J.F. Ferris	c Parks b Marshall	0
Extras	lb 6, w 3, nb 4	13
Total (31.5 ov)		107

39, 42, 62, 66, 78, 81, 101, 107, 107

James	3	0	17	0
Bakker	6	0	20	1
Connor	6	2	18	3
Marshall	4.5	0	13	3
Cowley	8	1	22	3
Nicholas	4	0	11	0

Hampshire		
*M.C.J. Nicholas	not out	40
V.P. Terry	lbw b Ferris	15
D.R. Turner	c Benson b Lewis	15
R.J. Scott	c Lewis b Willey	13
C.L. Smith	not out	11
K.D. James		
M.D. Marshall		
N.G. Cowley		
†R.J. Parks		
C.A. Connor		
P.J. Bakker		
Extras	lb 2, w 7, nb 7	16
Total (3 wkts, 27.4 ov)		110

16, 48, 84

Agnew	6.4	2	32	0
Ferris	5	1	18	1
Lewis	5	0	19	1
Parsons	7	0	30	0
Willey	4	1	9	1

Umpires: R. Palmer and A.G.T. Whitehead

Toss: Hampshire

Leicestershire lost their third successive Sunday match, when their batting collapsed yet again. Hampshire had no difficulty in passing the modest target required.

v WARWICKSHIRE (Basingstoke)

June 11

Won by 6 wkts. Hants 4pts, Warwicks 0pts

Warwickshire		
*T.A. Lloyd	run out	2
†G.W. Humpage	c Parks b James	6
A.I. Kallicharran	c Marshall b James	55
P.A. Smith	c Marshall b Cowley	41
Asif Din	run out	6
D.A. Reeve	c Connor b James	4
R.G. Twose	b Bakker	9
N.M.K. Smith	c Marshall b Bakker	6
G.C. Small	run out	9
A.A. Donald	not out	14
T.A. Munton	not out	1
Extras	lb 3, w 2	5
Total (9 wkts 39 ov)		158

8, 10, 95, 106, 113, 125, 126, 133, 151

James	8	1	23	3
Bakker	8	0	29	2
Connor	6	1	35	0
Marshall	8	0	29	0
Cowley	8	0	30	1
Nicholas	1	0	9	0

Hampshire		
*M.C.J. Nicholas	b Twose	49
V.P. Terry	run out	53
D.R. Turner	run out	34
R.J. Scott	c Small b Munton	7
C.L. Smith	not out	9
K.D. James	not out	2
M.D. Marshall		
†R.J. Parks		
N.G. Cowley		
C.A. Connor		
P.J. Bakker		
Extras	b 2, lb 2, w 1, nb 1	6
Total (4 wkts 38.1 ov)		160

85, 138, 149, 149

Donald	8	1	18	0
Munton	8	1	33	1
Small	4	0	18	0
P.A. Smith	3.1	0	18	0
Twose	5	0	18	1
N.M.K. Smith	8	0	37	0
Reeve	2	0	14	0

Umpires: D.J. Constant and B. Dudleston

Toss: Warwickshire

Hampshire kept up in their race for the title by this emphatic victory. They reached 138 for 1 in reply to 158–9, but then lost three further wickets securing the last 21 runs.

v SUSSEX (Southampton)

June 25

Won by 3 wkts, Hants 4pts, Sussex 0pts

Sussex		
K. Greenfield	c Scott b James	0
D.M. Smith	b Marshall	56
A.P. Wells	b Connor	27
*C.M. Wells	c Turner b Cowley	32
I.J. Gould	not out	49
A.I.C. Dodemaide	c Turner b Connor	17
A.C.S. Pigott		
†P. Moores		
A.R. Hansford		
A.R. Clarke		
A.M. Babington		
Extras	b 4, lb 7	11
Total (5 wkts, 40 ov)		192

0, 43, 94, 155, 192

James	8	0	39	1
Bakker	8	1	28	0
Connor	8	2	38	2
Marshall	8	0	27	1
Cowley	8	0	49	1

Hampshire		
*M.C.J. Nicholas	b Dodemaide	11
V.P. Terry	b Babington	6
D.R. Turner	c Moores b Hansford	13
C.L. Smith	run out	14
R.J. Scott	c Babington b Clarke	46
K. D. James	not out	48
M.D. Marshall	c Babington b Pigott	31
N.G. Cowley	run out	3
†R.J. Parks	not out	0
C.A. Connor		
P.J. Bakker		
Extras	b 3, lb 17, w 1	21
Total (7 wkts 40 ov)		193

16, 23, 39, 50, 129, 180, 184

Dodemaide	6	0	34	1
Hansford	8	1	19	1
Babington	8	1	14	1
Clarke	8	0	44	1
Pigott	8	0	49	1
C.M. Wells	2	0	13	0

Umpires: B. Hassan and D.R. Shepherd

Toss: Hampshire.

James hit a single off the last possible ball to bring Hampshire victory in this exciting game. Initially however Sussex dominated the game with some good batting and then reducing the home side to 50–4. Scott and Marshall then hit to good effect.

Robert James PARKS *b* 15.6.1959 Cuckfield, Sussex; wicketkeeper; lower order right hand batsman; debut 1980; son of J.M. (ex-Sussex/Som)
Kevin James SHINE *b* 22.2.1969 Bracknell; right hand batsman; right arm medium pace bowler; debut for Hants in May 1989
Richard John SCOTT *b* 2.11.1963 Bournemouth; left hand batsman, right arm medium pace bowler; debut 1988
Christopher Lyall SMITH *b* 15.10.1958 Durban; Attacking right hand batsman; debut 1980; 8 Tests for England 1983–1986; brother of R.A. (Hants)
Robin Arnold SMITH *b* 13.9.1963 Durban; attractive middle order right hand batsman; debut 1982; 8 Tests for England, including 5 v Australia last summer. Selected to tour West Indies 1989/90; brother of C.L. (Hants)
Vivian Paul TERRY *b* 14.1.1959 Osnabruck, West Germany; opening right hand batsman; debut 1978; 2 tests for England in 1984
Timothy Maurice TREMLETT *b* 26.7.1956 Wellington, Som; right arm medium fast bowler; right hand batsman; debut 1976; son of M.F. (ex-Somerset)
Ian John TURNER *b* 18.7.1968 Denmead, Hants; right hand batsman; slow left arm bowler; debut for Hants in Sept 1989
David Roy TURNER *b* 5.2.1949 Chippenham; left hand batsman; debut 1966; scored 1,000 runs in season nine times
Shaun David UDAL *b* 18.3.1969 Cove, Hants; right hand batsman; off break bowler; debut for Hants in June 1989
Julian Ross WOOD *b* 21.11.1968 Winchester; left hand batsman; debut 1989

Chris Smith, second to his brother in the Hampshire batting averages.

Allsport/Adrian Murrell

REFUGE ASSURANCE LEAGUE

v YORKSHIRE (Southampton)
July 2
Won by 6 wkts. Hants 4pts, Yorks 0pts

Yorkshire				
M.D. Moxon	c Parks b James			10
A.A. Metcalfe	lbw b James			22
†R.J. Blakey	b Bakker			43
P.E. Robinson	c and b Cowley			22
J.D. Love	c Connor b Cowley			2
D. Byas	not out			47
*P. Carrick	b Connor			11
P.W. Jarvis	c James b Connor			7
A. Sidebottom	not out			4
C.S. Pickles				
S.D. Fletcher				
Extras	b 4, lb 6, w 1			11
Total (7 wkts, 40 ov)				179
32, 33, 75, 79, 130, 152, 166				
James	8	1	23	2
Bakker	8	1	40	1
Marshall	8	1	37	0
Connor	8	0	32	2
Cowley	8	0	37	2

Hampshire				
*M.C.J. Nicholas	c Blakey b Pickles			13
V.P. Terry	b Sidebottom			2
D.R. Turner	c Love b Sidebottom			1
R.J. Scott	not out			116
C.L. Smith	lbw b Jarvis			45
K. D. James	not out			0
M.D. Marshall				
N.G. Cowley				
†R.J. Parks				
C.A. Connor				
P.J. Bakker				
Extras	lb 5, w 1			6
Total (4 wkts 36.3 ov)				183
10, 18, 24, 174				
Jarvis	7.3	1	38	1
Sidebottom	8	2	29	2
Pickles	6	0	35	1
Fletcher	8	0	41	0
Carrick	7	0	35	0

Umpires: R. Julian and R.A. White
Toss: Hampshire.
Nine sixes and six fours in an innings which lasted 86 balls and produced 116 runs from the bat of Scott won the match for Hampshire, after three wickets had fallen very cheaply.

v LANCASHIRE (Portsmouth)
July 23
Lost by 6 wkts. Lancs 4pts, Hants 0pts

Hampshire				
V.P. Terry	lbw b Allott			20
J.R. Wood	c Fairbrother b Watkinson			5
R.A. Smith	c Hegg b Wasim Akram			20
*M.C.J. Nicholas	c and b Allott			50
C.L. Smith	lbw b Wasim Akram			0
K.D. James	b Simmons			14
M.D. Marshall	c Hughes b Simmons			14
†R.J. Parks	b Wasim Akram			1
R.J. Maru	not out			8
C.A. Connor	c Austin b Allott			8
P.J. Bakker				
Extras	b 1, lb 12, w 11, nb 2			26
Total (9 wkts 40 ov)				166
17, 43, 65, 65, 96, 112, 118, 156, 166				
Watkinson	8	0	30	1
Allott	8	0	41	3
Austin	8	0	23	0
Wasim Akram	8	0	30	3
Simmons	8	0	29	2

Lancashire				
G.D Mendis	lbw b Bakker			8
G. Fowler	lbw b Marshall			29
*D.P. Hughes	b Marshall			21
T.E. Jesty	b Maru			51
N.H. Fairbrother	not out			40
M. Watkinson	not out			3
†W.K. Hegg				
Wasim Akram				
I.D. Austin				
P.J.W. Allott				
J. Simmons				
Extras	b 1, lb 13, w 2			16
Total (4 wkts, 36.1 ov)				168
33, 48, 91, 155				
Bakker	8	2	15	1
James	8	0	53	0
Marshall	8	2	17	2
Connor	5	0	28	0
Nicholas	1	0	8	0
Maru	6.1	1	33	1

Umpires: M.J. Kitchen and P.B. Wight
Toss: Hampshire.
By beating Hampshire, Lancashire held on to second place in the League table, only two points separating them from the leaders. Hampshire batted first but struggled on a lively wicket, which the visitors found much easier later on.

v WORCESTERSHIRE (Bournemouth)
August 13
Lost by 2 runs. Worcs 4pts, Hants 0pts

Worcestershire				
P. Bent	b Connor			2
M.J. Weston	b Connor			2
G.A. Hick	c Middleton b Jefferies			30
D.B. d'Oliveira	c Scott b Cowley			14
*P.A. Neale	c Jefferies b Cowley			3
D.A. Leatherdale	c and b Tremlett			6
†S.J. Rhodes	c Cowley b Connor			33
S.R. Lampitt	c Parks b James			21
N.V. Radford	run out			13
R.K. Illingworth	run out			11
S.R. McEwan	not out			0
Extras	lb 10, w 4			14
Total (39.4 ov)				149
2, 7, 46, 52, 56, 71, 124, 126, 148				
Connor	8	2	26	3
James	8	2	19	1
Tremlett	8	0	43	1
Jefferies	7.4	0	34	1
Cowley	8	2	17	2

Hampshire				
*M.C.J. Nicholas	b McEwan			12
V.P. Terry	c and b Lampitt			37
R.J. Scott	st Rhodes b Hick			18
†R.J. Parks	b Radford			25
C.L. Smith	c Hick b Lampitt			6
K.D. James	c Rhodes b Lampitt			1
S.T. Jefferies	c and b Radford			9
N.G. Cowley	lbw b Radford			0
T.M. Tremlett	not out			7
C.A. Connor	b Lampitt			14
T.C. Middleton	not out			4
Extras	b 1, lb 8, w 3, nb 2			14
Total (9 wkts, 40 ov)				147
18, 46, 101, 101, 104, 119, 119, 120, 141				
Radford	8	1	14	3
Weston	6	0	18	0
McEwan	4	0	15	1
Hick	8	0	24	1
Illingworth	8	1	37	0
Lampitt	6	0	30	4

Umpires: R.A. White and J.D. Bond
Toss: Hampshire.
The two weekend matches at Bournemouth proved disastrous for Hampshire. In this Sunday game their defeat meant that they had no hope of finishing in the top four of the Refuge League. The home side reached 101 for 2 but still failed to reach the 150 required for victory.

BRITANNIC ASSURANCE COUNTY CHAMPIONSHIP AVERAGES 1989

Batting	*M*	*I*	*NO*	*Runs*	*HS*	*Avge*	*100*	*50*
R.A. Smith	11	17	1	959	182	59.94	4	1
C.L. Smith	17	30	2	1006	107	35.93	1	6
J.R. Wood	11	17	2	523	96	34.87	–	3
M.C.J. Nicholas	22	38	4	1130	140	33.24	4	3
V.P. Terry	22	39	1	1198	180	31.53	1	8
S.T. Jefferies	7	12	5	217	42	31.00	–	–
K.D. James	20	34	3	953	162	30.74	1	5
D.R. Turner	10	17	4	364	65*	28.00	–	3
T.M. Tremlett	6	8	4	110	40*	27.50	–	–
R.J. Parks	22	28	12	427	76*	26.69	–	2
M.D. Marshall	15	21	5	412	68*	25.75	–	2
T.C. Middleton	6	9	–	199	69	22.11	–	1
R.J. Scott	11	18	1	375	77	22.06	–	2
C.A. Connor	13	14	2	129	24	10.75	–	–
R.J. Maru	21	24	7	165	29	9.71	–	–
P.J. Bakker	21	18	3	96	22	6.40	–	–
S.J.W. Andrew	4	5	–	21	14	4.20	–	–

Also batted: N.G. Cowley (1 match) 26, 42; K.J. Shine (1 match) 26*, 3; I.J. Turner (1 match) 9*, 0.

Bowling	*O*	*M*	*R*	*W*	*Avge*	*BB*	*5i*	*10m*
M.D. Marshall	428.3	115	1067	64	16.67	6-69	4	–
C.A. Connor	374.1	77	1075	49	21.94	7-31	4	1
T.M. Tremlett	160	49	356	16	22.25	4-67	–	–
P.J. Bakker	629.4	157	1732	77	22.49	6-81	4	–
M.C.J. Nicholas	113.4	16	345	14	24.64	6-37	1	–
R.J. Maru	528.4	145	1344	38	35.37	8-41	1	1
K.D. James	361.5	76	1078	29	37.17	4-24	–	–
S.J.W. Andrew	120	18	345	6	57.50	3-70	–	–
S.T. Jefferies	173.4	27	617	10	61.70	4-61	–	–

Also bowled: N.G. Cowley 27-1-102-2; T.C. Middleton 3-0-26-1; R.J. Scott 7-1-26-0; K.J. Shine 26-6-81-2; C.L. Smith 33-13-69-2; R.A. Smith 15-3-72-0; D.R. Turner 4.2-1-11-0; I.J. Turner 35-21-48-4; J.R. Wood 4.3-0-21-1.

Centuries

4 M.C.J. Nicholas: 140 v Northants (Northampton); 101 v Glos (Portsmouth); 121 v Derbys (Derby); 121* v Somerset (Taunton). R.A. Smith: 127 v Somerset (Southampton); 182 v Kent (Southampton); 148 v Notts (Trent Bridge); 119* v Lancs (Portsmouth).

1 K.D. James: 162 v Glamorgan (Cardiff). C.L. Smith: 107 v Glos (Portsmouth). V.P. Terry: 180 v Derbys (Derby).

BENSON AND HEDGES CUP

v GLAMORGAN (Southampton)

May 9

Lost by 8 wkts. Glamorgan 2pts, Hants 0pts

Hampshire		
V.P. Terry	run out	76
R.J. Scott	b Dennis	0
*M.C.J. Nicholas	b Dennis	2
R.A. Smith	not out	155
D.R. Turner	not out	40
K.D. James		
S.T. Jefferies		
†R.J. Parks		
N.G. Cowley		
C.A. Connor		
P.J. Bakker	lb 5, w 7, nb 1	13
Extras		
Total (3 wkts, 55 ov)		286

0, 6, 191

Watkin	11	5	33	0
Dennis	11	1	37	2
Barwick	11	0	68	0
Shastri	11	0	45	0
Bastien	6	0	43	0
Butcher	3	0	29	0
Maynard	2	0	26	0

Glamorgan		
A.R. Butcher	c Terry b Cowley	24
*H. Morris	not out	143
P.A. Cottey	b Connor	68
M.P. Maynard	not out	43
R.J. Shastri		
M.J. Cann		
S. Bastien		
†C.P. Metson		
S.L. Watkin		
S.J. Dennis		
S.R. Barwick		
Extras	lb 6, w 4, nb 2	12
Total (2 wkts 53.1 ov)		290

79, 224

Connor	9.1	0	66	1
Bakker	11	1	60	0
James	10	1	44	0
Jefferies	11	0	53	0
Cowley	10	0	45	1
Nicholas	2	0	16	0

Umpires: K.E. Palmer and S.B. Hassan
Toss: Glamorgan. Gold: H. Morris
In a game dominated by the batsmen, Robin Smith hit a brilliant 155 with 2 sixes and 13 fours, but Morris responded with 143, with 3 sixes and 15 fours, reaching his 100 off 128 deliveries.

v KENT (Southampton)

May 13

Lost by 4 wkts. Kent 2pts, Hants 0pts

Hampshire		
V.P. Terry	c Cowdrey b Ellison	31
R.J. Scott	b Igglesden	54
R.A. Smith	c Marsh b Fleming	20
D.R. Turner	c Marsh b Kelleher	21
*M.C.J. Nicholas	b Igglesden	32
K.D. James	run out	31
S.T. Jefferies	c Igglesden b Cowdrey	4
N.G. Cowley	b Igglesden	6
†R.J.Parks	not out	4
C.A. Connor	not out	4
P.J. Bakker		
Extras	lb 17, w 11	28
Total (8 wkts, 55 ov)		235

96, 109, 142, 148, 212, 219 225, 230

Igglesden	11	1	43	3
Kelleher	11	0	42	1
Ellison	3	0	15	1
Penn	10	0	36	0
Cowdrey	11	0	46	1
Fleming	9	0	36	1

Kent		
M.R. Benson	c Jefferies b Bakker	48
S.G. Hinks	c Connor b Jefferies	0
N.R. Taylor	c Smith b Connor	64
T.R. Ward	b Nicholas	37
*C.S. Cowdrey	c Parks b Connor	2
M.V. Fleming	c Parks b Jefferies	28
†S.A. Marsh	not out	15
R.M. Ellison	not out	16
C. Penn		
D.J.M. Kelleher		
A.P. Igglesden		
Extras	lb 16, w 10, nb 1	27
Total (6 wkts, 54.3 ov)		237

0, 117, 137, 144, 199, 206

Jefferies	11	0	47	2
Bakker	11	3	37	1
Connor	11	1	46	2
James	9.3	2	48	0
Nicholas	8	0	26	1
Cowley	4	0	17	0

Umpires: H.D. Bird and D.J. Constant
Toss: Kent. Gold: N.R. Taylor
Hampshire, the holders of the Cup, needed to win this match to go through to the knock-out section. In an exciting finish they just failed, despite an excellent total.

NATWEST BANK TROPHY

Semi-Final v MIDDLESEX (Southampton)

August 16

Lost by 3 runs

Middlesex		
J.D. Carr	st Parks b Cowley	83
D.L. Haynes	c Nicholas b Connor	80
*M.W. Gatting	run out	29
M.R. Ramprakash	c Terry b Connor	43
J.E. Emburey	run out	0
M.A. Roseberry	run out	21
†P.R. Downton	c R.A. Smith b Marshall	0
S.P.Hughes	not out	5
A.R.C. Fraser	not out	0
R.M. Ellcock		
N.G. Cowans		
Extras	lb 3, w 2, nb 1	6
Total (7 wkts 60 ov)		267

165, 175, 205, 212, 243, 244, 266

Marshall	12	2	25	1
Bakker	12	3	42	0
James	10	0	56	0
Connor	12	0	62	2
Cowley	12	0	62	1
Nicholas	2	0	17	0

Hampshire		
V.P. Terry	lbw b Cowans	3
C.L. Smith	c Ellcock b Fraser	114
K.D. James	c Carr b Ellcock	18
R.A. Smith	b Emburey	46
*M.C.J. Nicholas	c Downton b Ellcock	24
R.J. Scott	c Cowans b Emburey	22
M.D. Marshall	not out	17
†R.J. Parks	c Haynes b Hughes	0
N.G. Cowley	not out	8
C.A. Connor		
P.J. Bakker		
Extras	b 2, lb 3, w 4, nb 3	12
Total (7 wkts, 60 ov)		264

10, 39, 117, 170, 222, 248, 250

Ellcock	12	0	62	2
Cowans	12	2	48	1
Fraser	12	4	56	1
Hughes	12	1	55	1
Emburey	12	2	38	2

Umpires: B. Dudleston and A.G.T. Whitehead
Toss: Hampshire. MofM: C.L.Smith
Middlesex opened with a partnership of 165 but then three needless run outs meant that the visitors did not reach quite the total expected. Chris Smith played a brilliant innings for Hampshire and when he was dismissed 20 runs were needed off 13 balls. Parks failed, and Marshall needed a six off the final ball – he hit two.

Away Matches

The full scorecard of each of Hampshire's away matches will be found in the sections for the respective home teams.

The Oval: April 27, 28, 29, May 1.
Hants 198 and 215–1d drew with Surrey 217–9d (P.J. Bakker 6–81) and 128–6. Surrey 6pts, Hants 5pts.

Lord's: May 17, 18, 19
Hants 217 and 176 lost to Middx 290 (P.J. Bakker 5–52) and 106–6 by 4 wkts. Middx 23pts, Hants 5pts.

Trent Bridge: May 20, 21, 22
Notts 303–6d and 214–4d drew with Hants 300–6d (R.A. Smith 148) and 172–6. Hants 6pts, Notts 5pts.

Tunbridge Wells: June 3, 5, 6
Hants 213 drew with Kent 276–3 (M.R. Benson 114, N.R. Taylor 104*). Kents 7pts, Hants 3pts.

Ilford: June 21, 22, 23
Essex 277 and 234–9d (M.E. Waugh 109) beat Hants 244 (J.H. Childs 5–36) and 165 (J.H. Childs 7–38) by 102 runs. Essex 23pts, Hants 6pts.

Northampton: July 8, 10, 11
Northants 166 and 253 (M.D. Marshall 5–36) lost to Hants 366–6d (M.C.J. Nicholas 140) and 57–1 by 9 wkts. Hants 24pts, Northants 2pts.

Cardiff: July 29, 31, Aug 1
Glamorgan 208 and 254 (C.A. Connor 5–74) drew with Hants 370–6d (K.D. James 162) and 86–7. Hants 8pts, Glamorgan 3pts.

Derby: August 5, 7, 8
Derbys 178 (C.A. Connor 5–50) and 326–9 (K.J. Barnett 106, M.D. Marshall 6–69) drew with Hants 472–6d (V.P. Terry 180, M.C.J. Nicholas 121). Hants 7pts, Derbys 2pts.

Taunton: August 19, 21, 22
Hants 257 (M.C.J. Nicholas 121*, A.N. Jones 6–37) and 138 (N.A. Mallender 5–55) lost to Somerset 303–8d and 93–2 by 8 wkts. Somerset 24pts, Hants 6 pts.

Hove: August 29, 30, 31
Sussex 430 (I.J. Gould 125, P.J. Bakker 5–83) and 45–1 beat Hants 233 (A.R. Hansford 5–79) and 241 by 9 wkts. Sussex 24pts, Hants 5pts.

Bristol: September 13, 14, 15, 16
Hants 287–7 drew with Gloucs did not bat. Gloucs 3pts, Hants 3pts.

v SOMERSET (Southampton)

April 20, 21, 22, 24
Drawn. Somerset 6pts, Hants 4pts

Somerset 1st Innings		
S.J. Cook	c Maru b Bakker	85
P.M. Roebuck	c Jefferies b Nicholas	149
J.J.E. Hardy	c Scott b Jefferies	1
J.G. Wyatt	lbw b Jefferies	2
R.J. Bartlett	c Parks b Maru	5
†N.D. Burns	lbw b Nicholas	62
*V.J. Marks	c Parks b Nicholas	35
G.D. Rose	c Parks b Nicholas	0
N.A. Mallender	c Parks b Nicholas	31
A.N. Jones	c Maru b Nicholas	0
D.J. Foster	not out	11
Extras	lb 21, w 3, nb 8	32
Total (100 ov: 262–4)		413

143, 152, 156, 175, 326, 341, 341, 397, 398

Andrew	28	6	73	0
Jefferies	34	6	92	2
Bakker	23	8	81	1
James	25	5	58	0
Maru	24	56	51	1
Nicholas	15	2	37	6

Hampshire 1st Innings		
V.P. Terry	c Burns b Jones	0
C.L. Smith	b Foster	45
*M.C.J. Nicholas	b Mallender	0
R.A. Smith	b Rose	127
R.J. Scott	lbw b Rose	0
K.D. James	c Cook b Mallender	2
†R.J. Parks	not out	76
S.T. Jefferies	st Burns b Roebuck	42
R.J. Maru	b Jones	1
S.J.W. Andrew	c Bartlett b Mallender	6
P.J. Bakker	b Mallender	0
Extras	b 4, lb 6, nb 9	19
Total (100 ov: 287–8)		318

0, 3, 136, 139, 156, 210, 286, 287, 312

Jones	23	4	87	2
Mallender	26	4	58	4
Rose	19	3	37	2
Foster	20	4	75	1
Marks	23	8	50	0
Roebuck	1	0	1	1

Somerset 2nd Innings		
S.J. Cook	not out	44
P.M. Roebuck	lbw b Jefferies	26
J.J.E. Hardy	not out	0
Extras	nb 1	1
Total (1 wkt)		71

70

Andrew	6	0	28	0
Bakker	3	0	17	0
Jefferies	9.1	1	20	1
Maru	6	1	6	0

Umpires: D.G.L. Evans and J.H. Harris
Toss: Somerset
Cook hit 85 on his Somerset debut, helping Roebuck to add 143 for the first wicket, but Somerset were only 250–4 off 94.4 overs at the close of the first day. Nicholas surprised his friends on the second day by a career best 6–37, but the scoring rate remained pedestrian and Hants were 90–2 off 35 overs at stumps. On Saturday R.A. Smith and Parks fought successfully to save the follow on, but even before rain came to wash out the last day it appeared the four day game was heading for a draw.

v KENT (Southampton)

May 4, 5, 6, 8
Won by 133 runs. Hants 22pts, Kent 5pts

Hampshire 1st Innings		
V.P. Terry	c Ward b Igglesden	3
R.J.Scott	lbw b Ellison	19
*M.C.J. Nicholas	c C.S. Cowdrey b Igglesden	43
R.A. Smith	run out	182
D.R. Turner	lbw b Penn	12
T.M. Tremlett	lbw b Ellison	12
S.T. Jefferies	b Penn	41
†R.J. Parks	c Marsh b Ellison	12
R.J. Maru	not out	6
S.J.W. Andrew	c C.S. Cowdrey b Ellison	0
P.J. Bakker	c Marsh b Ellison	5
Extras	lb 8, nb 15	23
Total (100 ov: 251–5)		358

10, 35, 124, 152, 201, 306, 341, 344, 345

Igglesden	34	6	88	2
Penn	35	9	96	2
Ellison	34.3	4	98	5
Davis	11	3	32	0
C.S. Cowdrey	23	9	36	0

Kent 1st Innings		
S.G. Hinks	c Parks b Bakker	9
N.R. Taylor	c Nicholas b Maru	78
T.R. Ward	c Smith b Tremlett	91
G.R. Cowdrey	b Tremlett	2
*C.S. Cowdrey	c Smith b Maru	9
†S.A. Marsh	st Parks b Maru	0
R.M. Ellison	b Bakker	10
C. Penn	b Tremlett	24
M.R. Benson	c Maru b Andrew	53
R.P. Davis	c Scott b Maru	67
A.P. Igglesden	not out	11
Extras	lb 8, nb 7	15
Total (100 ov: 257–8)		369

13, 185, 187, 187, 187, 197, 218, 253, 305

Andrew	32	7	76	1
Bakker	23	7	75	2
Smith	1	1	0	0
Tremlett	25	7	60	3
Jefferies	18	1	81	0
Maru	29.3	11	64	4
Nicholas	2	0	5	0

Hampshire 2nd Innings		
V.P. Terry	c Marsh b Ellison	96
R.J. Scott	b Penn	21
*M.C.J. Nicholas	c C.S. Cowdrey b Davis	1
R.A. Smith	c Marsh b Ellison	29
R.J. Maru	c Hinks b Ellison	0
D.R. Turner	not out	65
T.M. Tremlett	retired hurt	40
S.T. Jefferies	not out	8
Extras	b 5, lb 6, nb 9	20
Total (5 wkts dec)		280

89, 99, 147, 151, 160

Penn	26	4	71	1
Igglesden	9	1	28	0
Ellison	21	9	49	3
C.S. Cowdrey	7	0	34	0
Davis	37	12	87	1

Kent 2nd Innings		
S.G. Hinks	b Maru	14
N.R. Taylor	c Andrew b Maru	43
M.R. Benson	lbw b Maru	4
T.R. Ward	c Parks b Bakker	4
*C.S. Cowdrey	c Jefferies b Bakker	38
G.R. Cowdrey	c Nicholas b Maru	4
†S.A. Marsh	not out	13
R.M. Ellison	c Terry b Maru	0
R. P. Davis	c Parks b Maru	8
C. Penn	c Smith b Maru	0
A.P. Igglesden	c Smith b Maru	0
Extras	w 1, nb 7	8
Total		136

32, 36, 41, 91, 111, 111, 114, 126, 131

Andrew	12	2	25	0
Bakker	16	6	40	2
Maru	23.4	8	41	8
Smith	1	1	0	0
Jefferies	4	0	30	0

Umpires: S.B. Hassan and K.E. Palmer
Toss: Hampshire
Robin Smith held Hampshire together on the opening day, batting 254 minutes to reach his 100. The home side were 267–5 at the close. Kent were struggling at 204–6 off 79 overs at stumps on Friday. The last two Kent wickets added 156. Nicholas set Kent 270 off 50 overs on the last day, but Maru's spin took Hampshire to victory with a career best 8 for 41.

v LEICESTERSHIRE (Bournemouth)
May 27, 29, 30
Won by 119 runs. Hants 23pts, Leics 6pts

Hampshire 1st Innings

V.P. Terry	c Lewis b Ferris	5
C.L. Smith	b Agnew	7
K.D. James	c Whitticase b Parsons	68
*M.C.J. Nicholas	b Lewis	32
R.J. Scott	c Potter b Ferris	77
D.R. Turner	c Willey b Parsons	15
M.D. Marshall	c Briers b Lewis	25
†R.J. Parks	c Whitticase b Agnew	26
T.M. Tremlett	c Boon b Ferris	2
R.J. Maru	c Lewis b Parsons	6
P.J. Bakker	not out	4
Extras	lb 9, w 4, nb 8	21
Total (100 ov: 273–8)		288

13, 30, 92, 170, 186, 224, 253, 261, 281

Ferris	20	4	76	3
Agnew	24.2	6	71	2
Lewis	21	8	50	2
Parsons	17	4	42	3
Willey	19	6	40	0

Leicestershire 1st Innings

T.J. Boon	c Smith b Tremlett	35
*N.E. Briers	c Scott b Tremlett	49
P. Willey	c Parks b Bakker	52
J.J. Whitaker	c Smith b Tremlett	48
L. Potter	c Smith b Maru	41
J.R.D. Benson	c Parks b Tremlett	1
C.C. Lewis	c Smith b Maru	4
†P. Whitticase	not out	32
G.J. Parsons	lbw b Bakker	3
J.P. Agnew	c Parks b Bakker	2
G.J.F. Ferris	b Marshall	14
Extras	b 3, lb 4, nb 5	12
Total (98.3 ov)		293

86, 89, 170, 208, 220, 241, 248, 251, 259

Marshall	16.3	7	38	1
Bakker	24	4	63	3
Tremlett	19	5	67	4
James	16	5	42	0
Maru	20	4	73	2
Nicholas	3	2	3	0

Hampshire 2nd Innings

V.P. Terry	c Agnew b Potter	68
C.L. Smith	c Whitticase b Lewis	38
K.D. James	b Boon	40
*M.C.J. Nicholas	c Ferris b Benson	43
R.J. Scott	not out	32
D.R. Turner	not out	1
Extras	b 1, lb 3, w 1, nb 12	17
Total (4 wkts dec)		239

106, 139, 189, 223

Agnew	12	2	38	0
Ferris	3	0	20	0
Potter	10	1	20	1
Lewis	10	0	38	1
Parsons	9	1	34	0
Benson	9.3	0	44	1
Boon	7	0	41	1

Leicestershire 2nd Innings

T.J. Boon	c Parks b Marshall	23
*N.E. Briers	b Bakker	0
P. Willey	c Smith b Bakker	0
J.J. Whitaker	c Parks b James	31
L. Potter	c Parks b Marshall	15
J.D.R. Benson	b James	6
C.C. Lewis	c Nicholas b James	8
†P. Whitticase	c Marshall b James	0
G.J. Parsons	c Parks b Marshall	21
J.P. Agnew	b Marshall	0
G.J.F. Ferris	not out	9
Extras	lb 1, nb 1	2
Total		115

4, 4, 33, 63, 73, 81, 81, 96, 96

Marshall	11.1	4	33	4
Bakker	8	1	27	2
Maru	8	3	25	0
Tremlett	8	4	5	0
James	8	1	24	4

Umpires: R. Palmer and A.G.T. Whitehead
Toss: Hampshire

After the first day the match seemed evenly balanced with Leicester 6–0 in the reply to the home side's 288. This state of affairs continued on Monday, Leicester gaining a modest first innings lead. Nicholas set the visitors 235 to win in 57 overs, but Bakker removed Briers and Willey in the second over and Hampshire took control as Leicester slipped to 96 for 7 with 20 overs to go. James had a very surprising analysis.

v SURREY (Basingstoke)
June 7, 8, 9
Won by 8 wkts. Hants 23pts, Surrey 3pts

Surrey 1st Innings

D.J. Bicknell	c Nicholas b Tremlett	37
G.S. Clinton	c Parks b Bakker	1
A.J. Stewart	c Parks b Bakker	0
G.P. Thorpe	c James b Tremlett	115
†D.M. Ward	run out	23
J.D. Robinson	c Parks b Bakker	9
*I.A. Greig	not out	90
K.T. Medlycott	c Scott b Tremlett	3
C.K. Bullen	lbw b Marshall	3
A.J. Murphy	c Nicholas b Bakker	1
M. Frost	b Marshall	0
Extras	b 1, lb 4, w 1, nb 3	9
Total (100 ov: 235–7)		291

14, 22, 56, 121, 167, 214, 228, 259, 286

Bakker	26	10	55	4
Marshall	20	4	67	2
James	17	4	31	0
Tremlett	21	4	51	3
Maru	18	3	63	0
Nicholas	8	2	19	0

Hampshire 1st Innings

V.P. Terry	c Ward b Murphy	1
C.L. Smith	b Frost	25
K.D. James	not out	83
*M.C.J. Nicholas	c Stewart b Greig	51
R.J. Scott	c Clinton b Greig	5
D.R. Turner	not out	56
M.D. Marshall		
T.M. Tremlett		
†R.J. Parks		
R.J. Maru		
P.J. Bakker		
Extras	b 13, lb 13, w4	30
Total (4 wkts dec, 76.4 ov)		251

9, 42, 132, 144

Frost	19.4	5	48	1
Murphy	23	8	62	1
Greig	20	5	61	2
Medlycott	6	0	20	0
Thorpe	6	0	17	0
Bullen	2	0	17	0

Surrey 2nd Innings

D.J. Bicknell	c Smith b Marshall	6
G.S. Clinton	c Terry b Bakker	6
A.J. Stewart	c Maru b Bakker	29
G.P. Thorpe	b Marshall	22
†D.J. Ward	c Terry b Marshall	8
J.D. Robinson	c Maru b Bakker	4
*I.A. Greig	b Marshall	11
K.T. Medlycott	c Parks b Bakker	0
C.K. Bullen	not out	19
A.J. Murphy	c Parks b Bakker	0
M. Frost	c Terry b Marshall	4
Extras	b 4, lb 3	7
Total		116

7, 31, 66, 77, 82, 84, 84, 84, 105

Bakker	15	2	48	5
Marshall	13.2	1	39	5
James	6	3	18	0
Tremlett	1	0	4	0

Hampshire 2nd Innings

V.P. Terry	c Bullen b Murphy	18
C.L. Smith	c Ward b Frost	29
K.D. James	not out	30
M.C.J. Nicholas	not out	76
Extras	lb 2, nb 2	4
Total (2 wkts)		157

40, 56

Frost	11	0	45	1
Murphy	16	5	34	1
Medlycott	7.2	2	17	0
Robinson	8	3	29	0
Greig	5	0	24	0
Bullen	4	0	6	0

Umpires: B. Dudleston and J.H. Harris
Toss: Hampshire

Thorpe spent about 5 hours on the first day saving Surrey, until Greig came to his help and hit 90 off 87 balls. The close of play came at the end of the Surrey innings. Nicholas declared the Hampshire innings closed as soon as the third batting point had been obtained on the second day and at stumps Surrey were 66–2 in their second innings. On the final morning Surrey collapsed, Bakker and Marshall sharing the wickets and then Nicholas hit an unbeaten 76 to bring victory at a gallop. Hampshire moved up to second place in the table.

v SUSSEX (Southampton)
June 24, 26, 27
Drawn. Hants 8pts, Sussex 4pts

Hampshire 1st Innings

V.P. Terry	c Moores b Salisbury	91
C.L. Smith	c Moores b Pigott	83
K.D. James	c and b Pigott	45
*M.C.J. Nicholas	b Dodemaide	40
J.R. Wood	c Smith b Pigott	58
D.R. Turner	c Moores b Pigott	8
M.D. Marshall	c Pigott b Babington	0
†R.J. Parks	not out	2
R.J. Maru	b Babington	8
C.A. Connor	not out	4
P.J. Bakker		
Extras	lb 14, nb 3	17
Total (100 ov: 321–3) (8 wkts dec)		356

130, 217, 241, 323, 339, 342, 342, 352

Pigott	22	3	63	4
Dodemaide	20	1	97	1
Babington	26	6	66	2
C.M. Wells	19	2	47	0
Salisbury	23	6	69	1

Sussex 1st Innings

N.J. Lenham	c Parks b Bakker	14
D.M. Smith	c Terry b Bakker	24
K. Greenfield	b James	2
A.P. Wells	c Maru b Wood	153
*C.M. Wells	c Parks b Marshall	10
†P. Moores	c Terry b Connor	6
I.J. Gould	b Marshall	11
A.I.C. Dodemaide	b Bakker	1
A.C.S. Pigott	c Nicholas b James	26
I.D.K. Salisbury	c Parks b Connor	2
A.M. Babington	not out	18
Extras	b 8, lb 10, nb 2	20
Total (93.4 ov)		287

33, 40, 46, 72, 87, 127, 132, 167, 185

Marshall	15	3	53	2
Bakker	25	8	74	3
Connor	24	5	65	2
James	15	2	44	2
Maru	9	2	21	0
Nicholas	4	1	7	0
Wood	1.4	0	5	1

Hampshire 2nd Innings

V.P. Terry	c A.P. Wells b C.M. Wells	39
C.L. Smith	c Moores b Dodemaide	35
K.D. James	c Moores b Dodemaide	14
*M.C.J. Nicholas	not out	41
D.R. Turner	not out	38
Extras	lb 3, nb 1	4
Total (3 wkts dec)		171

54, 79, 88

Pigott	7	0	28	0
Babington	15	4	45	0
C.M. Wells	12	2	40	1
Dodemaide	13.5	2	41	2
Salisbury	4	0	14	0

Sussex 2nd Innings

N.J. Lenham	c Parks b Bakker	2
D.M. Smith	c Parks b Connor	14
K. Greenfield	c Smith b Maru	24
A.P. Wells	not out	53
*C.M. Wells	c Parks b Maru	4
I.J. Gould	c Nicholas b Maru	12
A.I.C. Dodemaide	not out	2
Extras	lb 3, nb 2	5
Total (5 wkts)		116

11, 22, 70, 74, 96

Bakker	12	5	15	1
Connor	14	2	40	1
Marshall	6	1	23	0
Maru	13.3	6	26	3
James	3	1	9	0

Umpires: B. Hassan and D.R. Shepherd
Toss: Hampshire

On a marvellous batting strip, the home county's batsmen enjoyed themselves on the first day, helped by some wayward bowling. The declaration came over the weekend and Sussex, several of whose players were struck down by a tummy bug, relied on a last wicket stand of 103 between A.P. Wells and Babington to save the follow on. A.P. Wells batted 286 minutes with 23 fours. Hampshire began the final day at 39–0, then set Sussex 241 off 55 overs. A.P. Wells again batted in fine style. He was now leading the fc averages with 75.90.

v YORKSHIRE (Southampton)

July 1, 3

Lost by 3 wkts. Yorks 20pts, Hants 4pts

Hampshire 1st Innings

V.P. Terry	c Blakey b Sidebottom	35
C.L. Smith	run out	14
K.D. James	c Blakey b Sidebottom	4
*M.C.J. Nicholas	c Blakey b Sidebottom	7
J.R. Wood	c Love b Fletcher	1
D.R. Turner	c Byas b Sidebottom	2
M.D. Marshall	c Byas b Sidebottom	2
†R.J. Parks	lbw b Jarvis	44
R.J. Maru	c Love b Jarvis	9
C.A. Connor	c Byas b Fletcher	11
P.J. Bakker	not out	0
Extras	lb 3, w 3, nb 9	15
Total (47.3 ov)		144

23, 31, 49, 57, 66, 69, 75, 121, 140

Jarvis	17	2	73	2
Sidebottom	18	4	35	5
Fletcher	12.3	4	33	2

Yorkshire 1st Innings

M.D. Moxon	b Connor	35
A.A. Metcalfe	c Parks b Bakker	1
†R.J. Blakey	c Terry b Connor	17
D. Byas	c Parks b Connor	7
J.D. Love	b Connor	0
S.A. Kellett	c Parks b Connor	0
*I.G. Swallow	c Terry b Bakker	20
P. Carrick	b Marshall	10
A. Sidebottom	lbw b Marshall	0
P.W. Jarvis	c Parks b Bakker	7
S.D. Fletcher	not out	1
Extras	lb 9	9
Total (39.1 ov)		107

2, 43, 61, 65, 65, 66, 92, 94, 98

Marshall	9	2	16	2
Bakker	11.1	3	39	3
Connor	12	3	20	5
James	7	0	23	0

Hampshire 2nd Innings

V.P. Terry	lbw b Sidebottom	0
C.L. Smith	c Blakey b Jarvis	7
R.J. Maru	c Blakey b Sidebottom	12
K.D. James	c Blakey b Jarvis	0
C.A. Connor	c Blakey b Sidebottom	19
*M.C.J. Nicholas	b Moxon	25
J.R. Wood	b Sidebottom	45
D.R. Turner	c and b Moxon	1
M.D. Marshall	b Moxon	0
†R.J. Parks	not out	12
P.J. Bakker	c Blakey b Jarvis	22
Extras	lb 6, nb 4	10
Total		153

11, 11, 11, 37, 52, 112, 118, 118, 120

Jarvis	13.5	4	51	3
Sidebottom	14	3	41	4
Fletcher	7	0	31	0
Moxon	6	3	24	3

Yorkshire 2nd Innings

M.D. Moxon	b Bakker	10
A.A. Metcalfe	c James b Bakker	1
†R.J. Blakey	c Parks b Marshall	53
D. Byas	b James	15
J.D. Love	c Terry b James	2
S. A. Kellett	c Wood b Connor	5
I.G. Swallow	c Parks b James	18
*P. Carrick	not out	22
A. Sidebottom	not out	45
Extras	b 6, lb 10, nb 4	20
Total (7 wkts)		191

4, 35, 89, 95, 97, 117, 121

Marshall	17	1	45	1
Bakker	13	4	49	2
Connor	16	3	46	1
Maru	4	0	16	0
James	10	4	19	3

Umpires: R. Julian and R.A. White
Toss: Yorkshire

23 wickets fell on the first day. Sidebottom dismissed the home side after Yorkshire had decided to field, but in their turn Yorkshire's batting collapsed and at stumps Hampshire were 12–3 in their second innings. Yorkshire required 191 in the final innings and at 121 for 7 looked defeated; Carrick and Sidebottom however hit 70 in 12 overs to win the game.

v LANCASHIRE (Portsmouth)

July 22, 24, 25

Won by 3 wkts. Hants 21pts, Lancs 5pts

Lancashire 1st Innings

G.D. Mendis	c Maru b James	34
G. Fowler	c Parks b Marshall	130
M.A. Atherton	c Maru b Marshall	37
N.H. Fairbrother	b Nicholas	159
T.E. Jesty	not out	71
M. Watkinson	not out	25
*D.P. Hughes		
†W.K. Hegg		
J.D. Fitton		
I.D. Austin		
P.J. Martin		
Extras	lb 15, w 2, nb 2	19
Total (100 ov: 423–4) (4 wkts dec)		475

65, 151, 295, 423

Marshall	18	1	63	2
Bakker	14	5	50	0
Connor	19	4	80	0
Maru	25	1	100	0
James	18	3	85	1
C.L. Smith	1	0	1	0
Nicholas	15	0	81	1

Hampshire 1st Innings

V.P. Terry	lbw b Austin	25
C.L. Smith	c Hegg b Watkinson	66
K.D. James	c Fowler b Fitton	47
R.A. Smith	not out	119
*M.C.J. Nicholas	b Fitton	22
M.D. Marshall	not out	41
J.R. Wood		
†R.J. Parks		
R.J. Maru		
C.A. Connor		
P.J. Bakker		
Extras	b 4, lb 10, w 1, nb 1	16
Total (100 ov: 318–4) (4 wkts dec)		336

51, 126, 168, 228

Martin	17	3	51	0
Watkinson	20	5	70	1
Austin	17	6	29	1
Fitton	28	5	99	2
Atherton	22	7	73	0

Lancashire 2nd Innings

G.D. Mendis	b Bakker	5
G. Fowler	c Nicholas b Connor	16
J.D. Fitton	c C.L. Smith b Marshall	2
M.A. Atherton	c Terry b Connor	2
T.E. Jesty	not out	73
M. Watkinson	c Wood b Maru	8
†W.K. Hegg	c Terry b Maru	9
I.D. Austin	not out	20
Extras	b 4, lb 5, nb 3	12
Total (6 wkts dec)		147

17, 25, 34, 35, 66, 96

Marshall	9	3	18	1
Bakker	13	7	14	1
Connor	8	1	40	2
Maru	8	1	23	2
Smith	5	1	36	0
Wood	0.5	0	7	0

Hampshire 2nd Innings

V.P. Terry	c Hegg b Austin	95
C.L. Smith	c Watkinson b Hughes	97
K.D. James	c Hegg b Austin	0
R.A. Smith	c Watkinson b Hughes	10
*M.C.J. Nicholas	c Fowler b Austin	9
J.R. Wood	run out	11
M.D. Marshall	c Hughes b Austin	48
†R.J. Parks	not out	8
R.J. Maru	not out	1
Extras	b 4, lb 4	8
Total (7 wkts)		287

188, 194, 194, 217, 217, 261, 286

Watkinson	16	1	67	0
Martin	5	0	21	0
Austin	18	1	60	4
Fitton	3	0	14	0
Atherton	3	0	24	0
Hughes	18.1	1	93	2

Umpires: M.J. Kitchen and P.B. Wight
Toss: Lancashire

Hampshire won with 11 balls in hand, after being set 287 off 63 overs. Terry and C.L. Smith gave the southern county a splendid opening partnership, but a sudden loss of five wickets put the pressure back on the batsmen. Hampshire began batting first thing on Monday and also enjoyed themselves, which left the final day for a declaration and a tempting target.

v GLOUCESTERSHIRE (Portsmouth)

July 26, 27, 29

Won by an innings and 118 runs. Hants 24pts, Gloucs 3pts

Gloucestershire 1st Innings

A.J. Wright	c Terry b James	8
I.P. Butcher	b Bakker	0
J.W. Lloyds	b Connor	36
*C.W.J. Athey	b Marshall	67
K.M. Curran	c Maru b Marshall	8
P. Bainbridge	c Parks b Connor	5
M.W. Alleyne	lbw b Maru	12
†G.A. Tedstone	c Terry b Marshall	11
C.A. Walsh	b Connor	27
M.C.J. Ball	not out	17
K.B.S. Jarvis	b Bakker	32
Extras	b 4, lb 9, w 2, nb 2	17
Total (92 ov)		240

0, 37, 68, 86, 99, 127, 158, 167, 203

Marshall	28	7	64	3
Bakker	18	5	37	2
James	9	2	30	1
Connor	22	5	52	3
Maru	15	6	44	1

Hampshire 1st Innings

V.P. Terry	c Tedstone b Jarvis	1
C.L. Smith	c Tedstone b Lloyds	107
K.D. James	c Athey b Ball	56
T.C. Middleton	c Wright b Bainbridge	33
*M.C.J. Nicholas	c Ball b Walsh	101
J.R. Wood	c Lloyds b Alleyne	36
M.D. Marshall	c and b Jarvis	21
†R.J. Parks	not out	18
R.J. Maru	c Jarvis b Walsh	3
C.A. Connor	b Bainbridge	17
P.J. Bakker		
Extras	b 2, lb 6, w 1, nb 4	13
Total (100 ov: 311–4) (9 wkts dec)		406

13, 144, 185, 238, 318, 362, 366, 379, 406

Walsh	31	4	91	2
Jarvis	27	7	105	2
Ball	23	6	60	1
Bainbridge	14.5	0	59	2
Curran	6	2	19	0
Lloyds	6	0	24	1
Alleyne	8	0	40	1

Gloucester 2nd Innings

I.P. Butcher	c Middleton b Connor	3
A.J. Wright	c Maru b Marshall	5
†G.A. Tedstone	b Connor	2
M.C.J. Ball	c Middleton b Marshall	0
J.W. Lloyds	c Connor	4
*C.W.J. Athey	c Nicholas b Marshall	14
K.M. Curran	c Terry b Connor	2
P. Bainbridge	not out	6
M.W. Alleyne	b Connor	3
C.A. Walsh	c Marshall b Connor	6
K.B.S. Jarvis	c Connor	0
Extras	lb 3	3
Total		48

3, 5, 10, 11, 15, 31, 31, 34, 48

Marshall	12	3	14	3
Bakker	1	1	0	0
Connor	10.5	3	31	7

Umpires: M.J. Kitchen and P.B. Wight
Toss: Gloucestershire

The game ended before lunch on the third day, when Connor returned his best analysis for the county and dismissed Gloucester for just 48. The victory moved Hampshire up to third place in the Championship. On the first day the Gloucester batsmen struggled but were saved by the tail, the last five wickets doubling the total. Hampshire were 41-1 at the close. C. L. Smith hit a hundred on the second day — his brother was scoring a hundred for England at the same time. With Nicholas also completing three figures and then Gloucester losing two wickets for 10 in the closing minutes of Thursday, Hampshire were well on the way to success when Friday dawned.

v WARWICKSHIRE (Bournemouth)

August 9, 10, 11

Lost by 60 runs. Warwicks 20pts, Hants 4pts

Warwickshire 1st Innings

A.J. Moles	c Middleton b James	23
*T.A. Lloyd	c Terry b Bakker	12
A.I. Kallicharran	c Terry b Connor	0
G.W. Humpage	lbw b Nicholas	51
Asif Din	c Terry b Marshall	57
R.G. Twose	c Terry b Marshall	14
N.M.K. Smith	c Wood b James	19
†K.J. Piper	lbw b Maru	22
A.A. Donald	c Terry b Bakker	13
J.E. Benjamin	c Parks b Maru	5
T.A. Munton	not out	0
Extras	lb 12, nb 1	13
Total (93.3 ov)		229

12, 30, 44, 129, 161, 178, 198, 224, 224

Marshall	17	8	26	2
Bakker	13	4	32	2
Connor	19	4	38	1
James	17	2	61	2
Maru	22.3	7	49	2
Nicholas	5	0	11	1

Hampshire 1st Innings

V.P. Terry	c Piper b Donald	13
C.L. Smith	c Piper b Benjamin	4
K.D. James	lbw b Munton	19
T.C. Middleton	c Piper b Donald	0
*M.C.J. Nicholas	c Benjamin b Smith	28
J.R. Wood	not out	25
M.D. Marshall	not out	8
P.J. Bakker		
C.A. Connor		
R.J. Maru		
†R.J. Parks		
Extras	lb 3, w 1, nb 2	6
Total (5 wkts dec, 51.2 ov)		103

4, 30, 32, 60, 91

Donald	12	4	21	2
Benjamin	16	7	21	1
Munton	15.2	2	43	1
Smith	8	3	15	1

Warwickshire 2nd Innings

A.J. Moles	st Parks b Smith	35
R.G. Twose	b Middleton	37
A.I. Kallicharran	not out	12
G.W. Humpage	not out	13
Extras	b 4, lb 8, nb 1	13
Total (2 wkts dec)		110

65, 83

Marshall	3	3	0	0
Connor	2	0	10	0
James	11	5	20	0
Nicholas	8	3	17	0
Smith	9	3	23	1
Maru	1	0	2	0
Middleton	3	0	26	1

Hampshire 2nd Innings

V.P. Terry	lbw b Donald	7
C.L. Smith	c Piper b Donald	12
K.D. James	c Asif Din b Munton	12
T.C. Middleton	lbw b Donald	14
*M.C.J. Nicholas	c Asif Din b Munton	0
J.R. Wood	b Benjamin	11
M.D. Marshall	c Donald b Smith	46
†R.J. Parks	not out	52
R.J. Maru	c Munton b Benjamin	7
C.A. Connor	run out	0
P.J. Bakker	b Donald	1
Extras	b1, lb 9, nb 4	14
Total		176

16, 21, 40, 40, 61, 78, 120, 137, 137

Donald	17.1	4	47	4
Benjamin	14	3	46	2
Munton	17	4	44	2
Smith	7	1	29	1

Umpires: J.D. Bond and R.A. White

Toss: Warwickshire

Set 72 overs in which to score 237, Hampshire fell far short of their target, only Marshall, with 46 and Parks, 52, responding to the challenge. This loss seriously affected Hampshire's aspirations at the head of the Championship and they were now 55 points behind the leaders, though having a game in hand. On the first day runs came very slowly, Moles taking 2 hours over 23. The home side began the second day on 27–1, but when 56 overs were lost to rain, Nicholas tried to solve the lack of time by declaring at 103–5. In the end the absence of Robin Smith, playing for England, was an important factor in the result.

v WORCESTERSHIRE (Bournemouth)

August 12, 14, 15

Lost by an innings and 91 runs. Worcs 22pts, Hants 3pts

Worcestershire 1st Innings

P. Bent	run out	28
C.M. Tolley	lbw b Marshall	9
G.A. Hick	c Smith b James	44
D.B. d'Oliveira	c Terry b Marshall	4
*P.A. Neale	b Smith	98
D.A. Leatherdale	c Parks b Connor	20
†S.J. Rhodes	c Scott b Maru	1
S.R. Lampitt	c and b James	3
R.K. Illingworth	c Terry b Bakker	71
S.M. McEwan	c Smith b Connor	28
G.R. Dilley	not out	4
Extras	b1, lb 8, w 2, nb 4	15
Total (100 ov: 234–7)		325

18, 91, 93, 104, 146, 149, 158, 264, 311

Bakker	29	7	73	1
Marshall	29	7	67	2
Maru	32	11	63	1
Connor	25.1	4	64	2
James	15	3	38	2
Smith	2	0	4	1
Nicholas	1	0	7	0

Hampshire 1st Innings

V.P. Terry	b Dilley	8
C.L. Smith	b McEwan	38
K.D. James	lbw b Dilley	0
*M.C.J. Nicholas	c Hick b Dilley	17
R.J. Scott	c Leatherdale b Hick	25
J.R. Wood	c Rhodes b Lampitt	13
M.D. Marshall	c McEwan b Lampitt	11
†R.J. Parks	c Rhodes b Lampitt	9
R.J. Maru	c Hick b Lampitt	5
C.A. Connor	not out	5
P.J. Bakker	c d'Oliveira b Lampitt	0
Extras	lb 2, w 1, nb 3	6
Total (48.4 ov)		137

24, 24, 61, 71, 102, 106, 118, 127, 134

Dilley	11	3	32	3
McEwan	15	3	46	1
Lampitt	11.4	1	38	5
Hick	11	4	19	1

Hampshire 2nd Innings

V.P. Terry	c Rhodes b McEwan	8
C.L. Smith	st Rhodes b Illingworth	18
C.A. Connor	b McEwan	0
K.D. James	c Lampitt b McEwan	0
R.J. Scott	lbw b McEwan	0
R.J. Maru	c Leatherdale b Illingworth	23
*M.C.J. Nicholas	c Leatherdale b Illingworth	12
J.R. Wood	st Rhodes b Hick	2
M.D. Marshall	c Bent b Illingworth	23
†R.J. Parks	not out	1
P.J. Bakker	lbw b Illingworth	0
Extras	b 3, lb 7	10
Total		97

13, 13, 13, 17, 46, 67, 70, 90, 96

Dilley	7	2	18	0
McEwan	16	4	32	4
Lampitt	10	4	8	0
Illingworth	17	10	23	5
Hick	7	4	6	1

Umpires: J.D. Bond and R.A. White

Toss: Worcestershire

Hampshire's title hopes were completely dashed by Worcestershire, whose spin bowlers removed the home batsmen for just 97 on the last day. Worcestershire thus increased their lead to 14 points over Essex in second place. Hampshire remained fourth but, 74 points adrift, had virtually no chance of either first or second place. On the first day Worcester batted slowly, reaching just 266–8 in the day, but Hampshire batted poorly on the Monday and the follow on was enforced, the match being more or less lost by the close of the second day, when Hampshire were 28 for 4.

v GLAMORGAN (Southampton)

Sept 8, 9, 10, 11

Lost by 30 runs. Glamorgan 22pts, Hants 4pts

Glamorgan 1st Innings

*A.R. Butcher	lbw b Connor	65
H. Morris	c Middleton b Connor	40
S.P. James	c Connor	40
M.P. Maynard	b Marshall	0
G.C. Holmes	c Nicholas b Turner	7
I. Smith	lbw b Marshall	40
R.D.B. Croft	lbw b Bakker	22
†C.P. Metson	not out	14
S.J. Dennis	c Smith b Marshall	0
S.L. Watkin	b Marshall	7
S.R. Barwick	b Marshall	0
Extras	b 2, lb 7, nb 3	12
Total (100 ov: 230–6)		247

106, 115, 116, 156, 180, 214, 236, 236, 245

Marshall	25.2	6	68	5
Bakker	20	9	33	1
Connor	27	6	68	3
James	14	5	27	0
Turner	18	8	28	1
Smith	2	0	5	0
Scott	5	1	9	0

Hampshire 1st Innings

V.P. Terry	c James b Watkin	11
T.C. Middleton	c Metson b Watkin	33
K.D. James	c Morris b Dennis	13
R.A. Smith	b Dennis	47
*M.C.J. Nicholas	c Metson b Watkin	0
R.J. Scott	lbw b Barwick	15
M.D. Marshall	lbw b Watkin	13
†R.J. Parks	c Morris b Barwick	14
C.A. Connor	c Holmes b Watkin	24
I.J. Turner	not out	9
P.J. Bakker	c Morris b Watkin	10
Extras	lb 9, w 2, nb 1	12
Total (86.1 ov)		201

14, 35, 53, 86, 90, 116, 150, 164, 183

Watkin	27.1	8	73	6
Barwick	39	14	75	2
Dennis	16	7	34	2
Smith	3	0	8	0
Croft	1	0	2	0

Glamorgan 2nd Innings

*A.R. Butcher	b Bakker	1
H. Morris	c Parks b Connor	4
S.P. James	b Marshall	46
M.P. Maynard	b James	20
G.C. Holmes	c Middleton b Turner	22
I. Smith	st Parks b Turner	14
R.D.B. Croft	c Bakker b James	5
†C.P. Metson	not out	12
S.J. Dennis	c Smith b Turner	0
S.L. Watkin	c James b Marshall	0
S.R. Barwick	c James b Marshall	0
Extras	b 1, lb 4, nb 4	9
Total		133

3, 12, 55, 86, 108, 115, 115, 120, 133

Marshall	15.5	5	22	3
Bakker	10	2	27	1
Connor	11	4	25	1
Turner	17	13	20	3
James	9	0	34	2

Hampshire 2nd Innings

V.P. Terry	lbw b Watkin	0
T.C. Middleton	b Barwick	26
K.D. James	c James b Barwick	4
R.A. Smith	c Metson b Smith	47
C.A. Connor	c and b Watkin	0
*M.C.J. Nicholas	c Metson b Smith	15
R.J. Scott	c Croft b Barwick	52
M.D. Marshall	lbw b Watkin	0
†R.J. Parks	not out	0
I.J. Turner	c James b Watkin	0
P.J. Bakker	c Holmes b Watkin	4
Extras	b1	1
Total		149

0, 7, 65, 66, 87, 138, 139, 145, 145

Watkin	16.5	4	46	5
Barwick	14	3	49	3
Dennis	8	3	28	0
Smith	6	1	25	2

Umpires: R. Julian and D.S. Thompsett

Toss: Glamorgan

Glamorgan gained a first innings lead of 48, they then lost their advantage by being dismissed cheaply. Hampshire set about their final innings in disastrous fashion losing both Terry and James. Hampshire started the fourth day at 65–3. Scott hit out briefly but in vain.

Kent

President: H.J. Pocock
Chairman: P.H. Edgley
Secretary: D.B. Dalby, St Lawrence Ground, Old Dover Road, Canterbury CT1 3NZ. *Tel:* 0227 456886.
Cricket Administrator: B.W. Luckhurst
Captain: C.S. Cowdrey
Foundation of Present Club: August 1842 in Canterbury
First First-Class Match: Kent have been considered one of the principal cricketing counties since the middle of the 18th century
County Champions (since 1864): 1906, 1909, 1910, 1913, 1970, 1977 (joint), 1978
Gillette/NatWest Trophy: Winners 1967, 1974
Benson & Hedges Cup: Winners 1973, 1976, 1978
Sunday League Champions: 1972, 1973, 1976
Refuge Cup: Nil

Summary of Results in 1989
Britannic Assurance County Championship: Played 22, Won 3, Lost 8, Drawn 11, Position 15th
NatWest Bank Trophy: Lost in second round
Benson & Hedges Cup: Lost in Semi-Final
Refuge Assurance Sunday League: Played 16, Won 7, Lost 9, Position 11th equal
Refuge Assurance Cup: Did not qualify

Alan Igglesden, Kent's tall fast bowler who was called up into the England Test team during the summer. His 53 wickets headed the county aggregates.
Allsport/Chris Cole

ONE DAY AWAY MATCHES

The full scorecard of each of Kent's away matches will be found in the sections for the respective home teams.

Refuge Assurance League

Hove: April 30
Sussex 110 (35 ov) (A.P. Igglesden 5–13) lost to Kent 114–3 (37.1 ov) by 7 wkts. Kent 4pts, Sussex 0pts.

Southampton: May 7
Kent 156 (38 ov) lost to Hants 158–1 (35.3 ov) by 9 wkts. Hants 4pts, Kent 0pts.

Trent Bridge: June 11
Kent 206 (39.3 ov) lost to Notts 207–7 (39.5 ov) (P.R. Pollard 100) by 3 wkts. Notts 4pts, Kent 0pts.

Bath: June 18
Somerset 249–8 (40 ov) (C.J. Tavare 110, R.P. Davis 5–52) beat Kent 169 by 80 runs. Somerset 4pts, Kent 0pts.

Old Trafford: June 25
Kent 172–9 (39 ov) lost to Lancs 174–2 (36.1 ov) by 8 wkts. Lancs 4pts, Kent 0pts.

Lord's: July 23
Kent 211–7 (40 ov) beat Middx 205–7 (40 ov) by 6 runs. Kent 4pts, Middx 0pts.

Worcester: July 30
Kent 123–8 (22 ov) lost to Worcs 126–3 (20.4 ov) by 7 wkts. Worcs 4pts, Kent 0pts.

Scarborough: August 13
Kent 225–7 (39 ov) lost to Yorks 228–6 (38.1 ov) by 4 wkts. Yorks 4pts, Kent 0pts.

Benson & Hedges Cup

Cardiff: April 25
Glamorgan 82 (45.3 ov) lost to Kent 83–4 (32.2 ov) by 6 wkts. Kent 2pts, Glam 0pts.

Southampton: May 13
Hants 235–8 (55 ov) lost to Kent 237–6 (54.3 ov) by 4 wkts. Kent 2pts, Hants 0pts.

Northampton: May 31 (Quarter Final)
Kent 208–8 (55 ov) beat Northants 187–9 (55 ov) by 21 runs.

Trent Bridge: June 14 (Semi Final)
Notts 296–6 (55 ov) beat Kent 227 (48.4 ov) by 69 runs.

From left, back: *A.G.E. Ealham, P. Farbrace, J.I. Longley, M.A. Ealham, V.J. Wells, M.V. Fleming, D.J. Sabine, M.C. Dobson.* Centre: *J. Folley, T.R. Ward, M.D. Harman, D.J.M. Kelleher, A.P. Igglesden, R.P. Davies, H.L. Alleyne, G. Popplewell, C. Page.* Front: *G.R. Cowdrey, S.G. Hinks, R.M. Ellison, C.S. Cowdrey, M.R. Benson, N.R. Taylor, S.A. Marsh, C. Penn.* Allsport

REFUGE ASSURANCE LEAGUE

v ESSEX (Canterbury)
April 23
Lost by 6 wkts. Essex 4pts, Kent 0pts

Kent		
S.G. Hinks	lbw b Foster	7
M.R. Benson	b Topley	13
N.R. Taylor	b Topley	27
*C.S. Cowdrey	b Gooch	29
G.R. Cowdrey	b Lever	5
T.R. Ward	c Prichard b Pringle	22
†S.A. Marsh	c Prichard b Gooch	9
R.M. Ellison	c Gooch b Foster	5
D.J.M. Kelleher	lbw b Pringle	4
A.P. Igglesden	b Foster	1
H.L. Alleyne	not out	2
Extras	lb 9, nb 2	11
Total (40 ov)		135

7, 43, 82, 90, 92, 116, 125, 132, 132

Lever	8	1	16	1
Foster	8	0	25	3
Pringle	8	1	28	2
Topley	8	0	24	2
Gooch	8	0	33	2

Essex		
*G.A. Gooch	c Benson b Igglesden	34
B.R. Hardie	b Alleyne	31
P.J. Prichard	lbw b Alleyne	6
M.E. Waugh	not out	40
D.R. Pringle	c Marsh b Ellison	10
J.P. Stephenson	not out	0
A.W. Lilley		
J.K. Lever		
†D.E. East		
N.A. Foster		
T.D. Topley		
Extras	lb 8, w 4, nb 3	15
Total (4 wkts, 35.4 ov)		136

54, 64, 94, 132

Igglesden	8	2	21	1
Kelleher	8	0	24	0
Alleyne	8	0	35	2
Ellison	5.4	1	22	1
C.S. Cowdrey	6	0	26	0

Umpires: B. Dudleston and B.J. Meyer
Toss: Essex
On a slow, damp wicket Kent gave an inept batting display, so that, despite very poor light, Essex had few hiccups in making the 136 required for victory – Waugh batted particularly well for his 40.

v SURREY (Canterbury)
May 15
Won by 4 wkts. Kent 4pts, Surrey 0pts

Surrey		
G.S. Clinton	c Hinks b Igglesden	4
M.A. Feltham	b Cowdrey	14
Z.A. Sadiq	run out	10
A.J. Stewart	c Benson b Ellison	43
†D.M. Ward	not out	62
*I.A. Greig	b Kelleher	8
G.P. Thorpe	c Hinks b Ellison	3
K.T. Medlycott	b Igglesden	33
C.K. Bullen	not out	0
M.P. Bicknell		
A.J. Murphy		
Extras	b 2, lb 10, w 5, nb 1	18
Total (7 wkts, 40 ov)		195

9, 33, 34, 109, 123, 131, 184

Igglesden	8	0	32	2
Kelleher	8	0	34	1
Penn	7	2	18	0
Cowdrey	5	0	50	1
Fleming	4	0	30	0
Ellison	8	0	19	2

Kent		
S.G. Hinks	c Ward b Bicknell	6
M.R. Benson	run out	8
N.R. Taylor	c Sadiq b Bullen	38
T.R. Ward	c Feltham b Bullen	47
M.V. Fleming	b Murphy	30
*C.S. Cowdrey	not out	34
†S.A. Marsh	c Ward b Bicknell	17
R.M. Ellison	not out	4
C. Penn		
D.J. M. Kelleher		
A.P. Igglesden		
Extras	lb 12, w 1	13
Total (6 wkts, 39 ov)		197

14, 17, 98, 119, 157, 193

Bicknell	8	1	26	2
Murphy	8	0	30	1
Greig	4	0	22	0
Feltham	7	1	31	0
Bullen	7	0	50	2
Thorpe	5	0	26	0

Umpires: H.D. Bird and D.J. Constant
Toss: Surrey
Stewart and D.M. Ward put some heart into Surrey after three wickets had gone, but their partnership was not enough to defeat Kent. The home side batted solidly in the middle order and a bright 34 from Cowdrey produced victory.

v NORTHAMPTONSHIRE (Canterbury)
May 28
Lost by 8 wkts. Northants 4pts, Kent 0pts

Kent		
T.R. Ward	c Feltham b N.G.B. Cook	34
R.F. Pienaar	c Bailey b Davis	7
N.R. Taylor	c G. Cook b N.G.B. Cook	20
*C.S. Cowdrey	b N.G.B. Cook	12
G.R. Cowdrey	b Capel	40
M.V. Fleming	c Ripley b Davis	37
†S.A. Marsh	c N.G.B. Cook b Davis	15
R.M. Ellison	c and b Davis	3
C. Penn	not out	2
D.J.M. Kelleher	not out	2
A.P. Igglesden		
Extras	b 6, lb 17, w 5, nb 1	29
Total (8 wkts, 40 ov)		201

46, 55, 75, 88, 172, 184, 185, 199

Thomas	8	0	50	0
Davis	8	0	38	4
Robinson	8	1	28	0
N.G.B. Cook	8	1	20	3
Capel	8	0	42	1

Northamptonshire		
G. Cook	not out	66
*W. Larkins	b Igglesden	6
R.J. Bailey	c Penn b Igglesden	96
D.J. Capel	not out	16
D.J. Wild		
N.A. Felton		
†D. Ripley		
J.G. Thomas		
N.G.B. Cook		
W.W. Davis		
M.A. Robinson		
Extras	lb 13, w 7, nb 1	21
Total (2 wkts, 39.3 ov)		205

7, 183

Igglesden	8	0	37	2
Penn	7.3	0	25	0
C.S. Cowdrey	3	0	14	0
Kelleher	3	0	15	0
Fleming	5	0	26	0
Ellison	8	0	44	0
Ward	4	0	20	0
G.R. Cowdrey	1	0	11	0

Umpires: B. Hassan and K.J. Lyons
Toss: Northamptonshire
Kent commenced with 55 off the first 12 overs, then N.G.B. Cook's spin not only slowed the run rate but removed three batsmen. 96 by Bailey dominated the Northants' reply and victory came easily.

The disappearance of Tavaré to Somerset, which had followed closely on the heels of Alderman and Dilley's departures for new pastures, was bound to have an effect on the county's fortunes. The balance of the team in 1989 was further disturbed by the inability of Pienaar to bowl, due to a knee injury. Injury also kept Ellison out of the side and the old England player found his wicket haul halved.

This tale of doom meant that Kent plunged headlong down the Championship, from second to 15th, and the results in the Sunday League were only a little more encouraging. The bowling averages quickly reveal the source of the problem – three fairly regular performers – Kelleher, Penn and Davis – all took wickets at more than 40 runs apiece and Igglesden, though he won an England cap, took 53 wickets at 34.09 each. The captain's bowling appears a thing of the past – up to the beginning of 1989 he had 182 first-class wickets to his name at 37 runs each; in 1989 his dozen victims cost 60 runs each. Hartley Alleyne, when he appeared, was no better and he, together with Harman and Sabine, was released at the end of the summer. The county batting presented a much more pleasant aspect. The attractive Pienaar was not far behind his fellow-countryman, Cook, in the national averages; Benson had a good summer and Taylor was very consistent. Ward, the 21-year-old from Swanley, not only hit his maiden hundred, but went on to complete over 1,000 runs for the first time, establishing himself as a member of the eleven – in 1988 he had appeared in nine Championship matches. Hinks also reached 1,000 runs, but he did not approach his best season of 1985.

After some confused changes of wicket-keeper during the 1980s, Marsh now seems settled in behind the stumps, and if not in Ames' class as a batsman, can score some useful runs.

Off the field, the administration of the club caused some heartburn with the result that Jim Woodhouse, the Chief Executive, resigned at the end of the season.

REFUGE ASSURANCE LEAGUE

v GLOUCESTERSHIRE (Maidstone)

July 9

Won by 6 wkts. Kent 4pts, Gloucs 0pts

Gloucestershire 1st Innings		
J.W. Lloyds	b Penn	31
*C.W.J. Athey	c and b Igglesden	11
K.M. Curran	b Igglesden	0
A.J. Wright	c Marsh b Igglesden	1
M.W. Alleyne	c Dobson b Penn	14
P.W. Romaines	lbw b C.S. Cowdrey	11
I.P. Butcher	b Ellison	3
†G.A. Tedstone	c Marsh b Penn	0
C.A. Walsh	b Penn	0
M.W. Pooley	not out	6
K.B.S. Jarvis	b Alleyne	1
Extras	b 1, lb 4, w 1, nb 1	7
Total (31.2 ov)		85

21, 21, 30, 61, 72, 76, 79, 79, 80

Igglesden	8	3	13	3
Alleyne	7.2	1	20	1
Penn	8	1	15	4
Ellison	6	1	18	1
C.S. Cowdrey	2	0	14	1

Kent		
N.R. Taylor	b Jarvis	1
M.C. Dobson	b Walsh	21
J.I. Longley	run out	19
*C.S. Cowdrey	b Jarvis	11
G.R. Cowdrey	not out	5
M.V. Fleming	not out	22
†S.A. Marsh		
R.M. Ellison		
C. Penn		
H.L. Alleyne		
A.P. Igglesden		
Extras	lb 6, nb 1	7
Total (4 wkts, 25.5 ov)		86

1, 34, 54, 54

Walsh	8	2	9	1
Jarvis	8	3	23	2
Pooley	3.5	0	22	0
Alleyne	6	1	26	0

Umpires: P.J. Eele and B. Leadbeater
Toss: Kent
On a dull day with a damp wicket the batsmen of both sides found run-making difficult. Both Igglesden and Penn took wickets with successive balls and Gloucestershire's innings fell apart. Kent showed more steel and the victory put them in a slightly more respectable place in the table – 14th from 16th. Gloucestershire replaced them in 16th position.

v DERBYSHIRE (Canterbury)

July 16

Lost by 25 runs. Derbys 4pts, Kent 0pts

Derbyshire		
*K.J. Barnett	b Ealham	27
P.D. Bowler	c and b Fleming	17
J.E. Morris	b Ealham	41
R.J. Sharma	c Taylor b Fleming	17
B. Roberts	c G.R. Cowdrey b C.S. Cowdrey	31
†B.J.M. Maher	b Ealham	3
M.A. Holding	c Marsh b Alleyne	4
F.A. Griffith	b Igglesden	1
P.G. Newman	not out	0
S.J. Base	lbw b Alleyne	0
O.H. Mortensen	c Marsh b Alleyne	2
Extras	b 2, lb 12, w 6, nb 1	21
Total (37.4 ov)		164

40, 60, 88, 142, 148, 148, 156, 160, 160

Igglesden	7	0	17	1
Alleyne	6.4	0	25	3
Fleming	8	0	33	2
Davis	6	0	29	0
Ealham	6	0	26	3
C.S. Cowdrey	4	0	20	1

Kent		
N.R. Taylor	b Griffith	56
T.R. Ward	c Maher b Mortensen	9
J.I. Longley	c Morris b Holding	12
*C.S. Cowdrey	c Maher b Holding	10
G.R. Cowdrey	b Griffith	17
†S.A. Marsh	c and b Newman	9
M.V. Fleming	not out	14
M.A. Ealham	c and b Newman	2
H.L. Alleyne	b Holding	2
R.P. Davis	b Holding	1
A.P. Igglesden	b Newman	0
Extras	lb 4, w 1, nb 2	7
Total (38.3 ov)		139

12, 41, 54, 97, 113, 124, 130, 134, 136

Newman	7.3	0	27	3
Mortensen	8	2	23	1
Base	8	0	30	0
Holding	7	1	18	4
Sharma	4	0	23	0
Griffith	4	0	14	2

Umpires: K.E. Palmer and D.S. Thompsett
Toss: Derbyshire
Derbyshire began well, but the last seven wickets disappeared for just 22 runs in six overs. The Kent innings was almost a repeat, but with only Taylor among the top batsmen succeeding, Derbyshire won.

v WARWICKSHIRE (Canterbury)

August 6

Won by 7 wkts. Kent 4pts, Warwicks 0pts

Warwickshire		
*T.A. Lloyd	c Marsh b Igglesden	0
A.I. Kallicharran	c Hinks b Davis	26
Asif Din	c and b Davis	89
D.A. Reeve	c Ealham b C.S. Cowdrey	27
R.G. Twose	lbw b Igglesden	28
N.M.K. Smith	not out	9
J.D. Ratcliffe	not out	5
†K.J. Piper		
A.A. Donald		
G.C. Small		
T.A. Munton		
Extras	lb 10, w 2, nb 5	17
Total (5 wkts, 40 ov)		201

3, 68, 133, 163, 187

Igglesden	8	0	43	2
Penn	8	2	34	0
Fleming	6	1	32	0
Ealham	4	0	16	0
Davis	8	0	41	2
Ward	5	0	21	0
C.S. Cowdrey	1	0	4	1

Kent		
S.G. Hinks	not out	80
R.F. Pienaar	b Donald	24
T.R. Ward	c Reeve b Donald	54
*C.S. Cowdrey	c and b Ratcliffe	22
G.R. Cowdrey	not out	10
C. Penn		
M.V. Fleming		
M.A. Ealham		
†S.A. Marsh		
R.P. Davis		
A.P. Igglesden		
Extras	lb 4, w 6, nb 2	12
Total (3 wkts, 35.1 ov)		202

59, 152, 190

Small	8	0	32	0
Munton	7	0	51	0
Smith	7	0	37	0
Donald	8	0	33	2
Kallicharran	2	0	18	0
Twose	2	0	19	0
Ratcliffe	1.1	0	8	1

Umpires: J.H Harris and B. Hassan
Toss: Warwickshire
Replying to the large Warwickshire total, Kent's batsmen responded in style. Hinks hit 80 off 104 balls in 140 minutes and Ward reached 50 off 40 balls.

PLAYERS

Hartley Leroy ALLEYNE *b* 27.2.1957 Bridgetown, Barbados; right arm fast medium bowler; right hand batsman; debut 1988, also plays for Natal, previously appeared for Worcs 1980–82
Mark Richard BENSON *b* 6.7.1958 Shoreham-by-Sea; left hand batsman; off break bowler;debut 1980; one Test for England 1986
Christopher Stuart COWDREY *b* 20.10.1957 Farnborough, Kent; right hand batsman; right arm medium pace bowler; debut 1977; captain since 1985; 6 Tests for England 1984–88; selected to tour South Africa 1989/90; son of M.C. (ex-Kent) and brother of G.R. (Kent)
Graham Robert COWDREY *b* 27.6.1964 Farnborough, Kent; right hand batsman; right arm medium pace bowler; debut 1984; son of M.C. (ex-Kent) and brother of C.S. (Kent)
Richard Peter DAVIS *b* 18.3.1966 Westbrook, Kent; right hand batsman; slow left arm bowler; debut 1986
Mark Christopher DOBSON *b* 24.10.1967 Canterbury; right hand batsman; slow left arm bowler; debut for Kent July 1989
Mark Alan EALHAM *b* 27.8.1969 Willesborough, Kent; right hand batsman, right arm medium pace bowler; debut for Kent June 1989; son of A.E.G. (ex-Kent)
Richard Mark ELLISON *b* 21.9.1959 Ashford, Kent; right arm medium fast bowler; left hand batsman; debut 1981; 11 Tests for England 1984–86; selected to tour South Africa 1989/90
Paul FARBRACE *b* 7.7.1967 Ash; wicketkeeper; right hand batsman; debut 1987
Matthew Valentine FLEMING *b* 12.12.1964 Macclesfield; right hand batsman; played in one-day matches for county 1988, fc debut 1989
Mark David HARMAN *b* 30.6.1964 Aylesbury; right hand batsman; off break bowler; debut 1988, previously appeared for Somerset 1986–87
Simon Graham HINKS *b* 12,10.1960 Northfleet; left hand batsman; right arm medium pace bowler; debut 1982
Alan Paul IGGLESDEN *b* 8.10.1964 Farnborough, Kent; right arm fast medium bowler; right hand batsman; debut for England in 1989 — one Test; selected to tour Zimbabwe 1989/90
Daniel John Michael KELLEHER *b* 5.5.1966 Southwark, S London. Right hand batsman. Right arm medium fast bowler. Debut 1987
Nigel James LLONG *b* 11.2.1969 Ashford, Kent; Left hand batsman; off break bowler; debut in one-day matches for county in 1989
Jonathan Ian LONGLEY *b* 12.4.1969 New Bruswick, USA. Right hand batsman; fc debut for county July 1989
Steven Andrew MARSH *b* 27.1.1961 London; wicketkeeper; right hand batsman; debut 1982
Kevin David MASTERS *b* 19.5.1961 Chatham; left hand batsman; right arm medium pace bowler; debut 1983; re-appeared in 1989 in one-day matches
Minal Mahesh PATEL *b* 7.7.1970 Bombay; right hand batsman; slow left arm bowler; debut for county in 1989
Christopher PENN *b* 19.6.1963 Dover; left hand batsman; right arm fast medium bowler; debut 1982
Roy Francis PIENAAR b 17.7.1961 Johannesburg; right hand batsman; right arm medium fast bowler; debut 1987; also plays for Northern Transvaal.
Neil Royston TAYLOR *b* 21.7.1959 Orpington; right hand batsman; debut 1979; scored 100 in first match
Trevor Robert WARD *b* 19.1.1968 Farningham; right hand batsman; right arm medium pace bowler; debut 1986
Vincent John Wells *b* 6.8.1965 Dartford; wicketkeeper; right hand batsman; debut 1988
Timothy Neil WREN *b* 26.3.1970 Folkestone; right hand batsman; left arm medium pace bowler; debut for county in Sunday League matches in 1989

Roy Pienaar, who scored 1,321 runs for Kent at an average of over 50. Allsport/Adrian Murrell

REFUGE ASSURANCE LEAGUE

v GLAMORGAN (Canterbury)
August 20
Won by 58 runs. Kent 4pts, Glamorgan 0pts

Kent		
S.G. Hinks	c Metson b Dennis	5
R.F. Pienaar	b Dennis	119
T.R. Ward	c Smith b Dale	29
*C.S. Cowdrey	c Croft b Dale	25
G.R. Cowdrey	b Barwick	38
†S.A. Marsh	not out	20
M.V. Fleming	c Butcher b Dennis	5
M.A. Ealham	not out	1
D.J.M. Kelleher		
A.P. Igglesden		
R.P. Davis		
Extras	w 3	3
Total (6 wkts, 40 ov)		245
15, 72, 133, 199, 229, 241		

Smith	8	0	47	0
Dennis	8	0	44	3
Barwick	8	0	44	1
Croft	5	0	28	0
Dale	8	0	58	2
Butcher	3	0	24	0

Glamorgan		
*A.R. Butcher	c Pienaar b Ward	34
G.C. Holmes	b Davis	18
A. Dale	st Marsh b Ward	9
M.P. Maynard	c Fleming b Ward	10
I. Smith	c Marsh b Fleming	17
H. Morris	not out	62
S.P. James	lbw b Ealham	8
†C.P. Metson	b Ealham	9
R.D.B. Croft	not out	3
S.J. Dennis		
S.R. Barwick		
Extras	b 3, lb 12, w 2	17
Total (7 wkts, 40 ov)		187
50, 68, 77, 84, 104, 134, 172		

Kelleher	6	0	28	0
Igglesden	5	0	11	0
Ward	8	0	20	3
Davis	8	0	29	1
Fleming	7	0	43	1
Ealham	6	0	41	2

Umpires: J.C. Balderstone and D.J. Constant
Toss: Kent
A second hundred in successive days by Pienaar gave Kent a match winning total and Ward then surprised himself by picking up three important wickets.

v LEICESTERSHIRE (Folkestone)
August 27
Won by 52 runs. Kent 4pts, Leics 0pts

Kent		
S.G. Hinks	b Benjamin	7
R.F. Pienaar	c Whitticase b Parsons	30
T.R. Ward	lbw b Benjamin	0
*C.S. Cowdrey	b Benjamin	5
G.R. Cowdrey	not out	102
†S.A. Marsh	run out	29
M.V. Fleming	b Such	16
M.A. Ealham	not out	1
D.J.M. Kelleher		
R.P. Davis		
T.N. Wren		
Extras	b 7, w 2	9
Total (6 wkts, 37 ov)		199
21, 21, 37, 56, 118, 175		

Edmunds	7	0	55	0
Benjamin	6	2	14	3
Parsons	7	0	41	1
Such	5	0	26	1
Lewis	4	1	34	0
Agnew	8	2	22	0

Leicestershire		
L. Potter	c Marsh b Fleming	22
*N.E. Briers	c and b Fleming	24
J.J. Whitaker	run out	38
C.C. Lewis	c C.S. Cowdrey b Ealham	10
T.J. Boon	c Marsh b Fleming	1
W.K.M. Benjamin	c Marsh b Ealham	2
†P. Whitticase	b Davis	2
G.J. Parsons	c Marsh b Ealham	7
J.P. Agnew	c Kelleher b Davis	17
R.H. Edmunds	c C.S. Cowdrey b Wren	9
P.M. Such	not out	8
Extras	lb 4, w 3	7
Total (36.3 ov)		147
48, 59, 86, 89, 92, 103, 110, 117, 131		

Wren	7.3	0	41	1
Kelleher	8	1	20	0
Fleming	8	1	26	3
Ealham	8	1	40	3
Davis	5	0	16	2

Umpires: A.A. Jones and D.S. Thompsett
Toss: Kent
After a disappointing Sunday League season, Kent's victory in their final game meant that they moved into the middle of the League table.

BENSON AND HEDGES CUP

v SUSSEX (Canterbury)
May 2
Lost by 5 wkts. Sussex 2pts, Kent 0pts

Kent		
S.G. Hinks	c Moores b C.M. Wells	25
M.R. Benson	c Smith b Babington	41
N.R. Taylor	lbw b Babington	0
T.R. Ward	b Clarke	22
*C.S Cowdrey	c and b Dodemaide	9
G.R. Cowdrey	c Smith b Dodemaide	37
†S.A. Marsh	lbw b C.M. Wells	4
R.M. Ellison	b C.M. Wells	2
C. Penn	b Pigott	11
D.J.M. Kelleher	not out	4
A.P. Igglesden	not out	2
Extras	b 1, lb 8, w 6, nb 1	16
Total (9 wkts, 55 ov)		173
54, 65, 79, 100, 114, 135, 144, 163, 169		

Pigott	11	0	35	1
Dodemaide	11	0	34	2
C.M. Wells	11	1	45	3
Babington	11	4	21	2
Clarke	11	1	29	1

Sussex		
A.M. Green	b Kelleher	5
D.M. Smith	c G.R. Cowdrey b Igglesden	0
*P.W.G. Parker	not out	85
A.P. Wells	c C.S. Cowdrey b Igglesden	4
C.M. Wells	c Marsh b Igglesden	40
I.J. Gould	c Marsh b C.S. Cowdrey	0
A.I.C. Dodemaide	not out	31
A.C.S. Pigott		
†P. Moores		
A.R. Clarke		
A.M. Babington		
Extras	b 1, lb 3, w 2, nb 5	11
Total (5 wkts, 46.4 ov)		176
5, 5, 10, 100, 115		

Igglesden	9	1	45	3
Kelleher	11	4	23	1
Penn	9	3	27	0
Ellison	8	1	38	0
C.S. Cowdrey	7	1	25	1
G.R. Cowdrey	2.4	0	14	0

Umpires: J.C. Balderstone and R.A. White
Toss: Sussex. Gold: P.W.G. Parker
Kent began with an excellent partnership of 54 by Hinks and Benson, but they failed to build on this and treated the legbreaks of Clarke and Babington with surprising caution. Sussex in contrast began badly, then Parker and C.M. Wells took control adding a decisive 90 for the fourth wicket.

BRITANNIC ASSURANCE COUNTY CHAMPIONSHIP AVERAGES 1989

Batting	*M*	*I*	*NO*	*Runs*	*HS*	*Avge*	*100*	*50*
R.F. Pienaar	15	25	4	1239	134*	59.00	4	6
M.R. Benson	14	27	5	1190	157	54.09	4	6
N.R. Taylor	21	41	6	1495	118	42.71	3	7
C.S. Cowdrey	22	31	2	1093	146*	37.69	2	7
T.R. Ward	21	36	5	1105	104	35.65	1	8
M.V. Fleming	6	9	3	195	45	32.50	–	–
S.G. Hinks	17	33	4	841	104*	29.00	1	6
S.A. Marsh	21	30	6	606	90*	25.25	–	5
R.M. Ellison	11	15	2	257	39*	19.77	–	–
G.R. Cowdrey	8	10	2	153	108*	19.13	1	–
D.J.M. Kelleher	9	10	2	150	53*	18.75	–	1
C. Penn	19	21	4	317	60	18.65	–	1
R.P. Davis	19	20	5	238	67	15.87	–	1
M.C. Dobson	6	8	1	102	52	14.57	–	1
V.J. Wells	2	4	1	37	22	12.33	–	–
H.L. Alleyne	5	8	3	48	28	9.60	–	–
A.P. Igglesden	19	21	8	115	32*	8.85	–	–
J.I. Longley	3	6	0	32	17	5.33	–	–

Also batted: M.A. Ealham (1 match) 45; P. Farbrace (1 match) 8; M.M. Patel (1 match) 3. M.D. Harman played in one match but did not bat.

Bowling	*O*	*M*	*R*	*W*	*Avge*	*BB*	*5i*	*10m*
R.M. Ellison	267.1	66	681	28	24.32	6-43	2	–
A.P. Igglesden	547.5	98	1807	53	34.09	6-73	1	–
C. Penn	567	102	1792	41	43.71	4-57	–	–
D.J.M. Kelleher	233.4	48	840	18	46.67	3-43	–	–
H.L. Alleyne	117.4	12	434	9	48.22	4-92	–	–
R.P. Davis	630	162	1816	35	51.89	4-57	–	–
C.S. Cowdrey	212.3	31	744	12	62.00	4-33	–	–
M.C. Dobson	106.3	22	373	6	62.17	2-20	–	–

Also bowled: M.R. Benson 8-0-66-0; G.R. Cowdrey 6-0-29-1; M.A. Ealham 5-0-26-0; M.V. Fleming 105-23-332-4; M.D. Harman 34-11-112-1; S.G. Hinks 4-0-18-2; S.A. Marsh 4-0-37-0; M.M. Patel 10-2-34-1; P.F. Pienaar 11-3-43-0; N.R. Taylor 2-0-13-0; T.R. Ward 41.5-8-157-1; V.J. Wells 14-2-61-1.

Centuries

4 M.R. Benson: 114 v Hants (Tunbridge Wells); 157 v Somerset (Bath); 102* v Glos (Maidstone); 149 v Surrey (Oval). R.F. Pienaar: 119 v Notts (Trent Bridge); 125 v Yorks (Scarborough); 132 v Glamorgan (Canterbury); 134* v Leics (Folkestone).

3 N.R. Taylor: 104* v Hants (Tunbridge Wells); 118 v Surrey (Canterbury); 111 v Yorks (Scarborough).

2 C.S. Cowdrey: 101* v Notts (Trent Bridge); 146* v Surrey (Oval).

1 G.R. Cowdrey: 108* v Leics (Leicester). S.G. Hinks: 104* v Surrey (Canterbury). T.R. Ward: 104 v Somerset (Bath).

BENSON AND HEDGES CUP

v ESSEX (Canterbury)

May 9

Lost by 4 wkts. Essex 2 pts, Kent 0pts

Kent		
S.G. Hinks	c Hardie b Foster	0
M.R. Benson	b Lever	9
N.R. Taylor	b Pringle	46
T.R. Ward	c Topley b Stephenson	37
*C.S. Cowdrey	c Gooch b Topley	0
M.V. Fleming	c Gooch b Foster	14
†S.A. Marsh	not out	41
R.M. Ellison	c Hardie b Pringle	29
C. Penn	not out	0
A.P. Igglesden		
R.P. Davis		
Extras	lb 4, w 12	16
Total (7 wkts, 55 ov)		192

7, 20, 80, 80, 104, 134, 191

Lever	11	5	23	1
Foster	11	2	44	2
Pringle	11	1	44	2
Gooch	6	2	24	0
Topley	11	3	37	1
Stephenson	5	1	16	1

Essex		
*G.A. Gooch	lbw b Penn	8
B.R. Hardie	b Ellison	24
A.W. Lilley	b Penn	3
M.E. Waugh	b Ellison	22
P.J. Prichard	lbw b Davis	22
J.P. Stephenson	not out	63
D.R. Pringle	c Fleming b Igglesden	6
†M.A. Garnham	not out	27
J.K. Lever		
N.A. Foster		
T.D. Topley		
Extras	b 1, lb 13, w 2, nb 5	21
Total (6 wkts, 53.3 ov)		196

16, 22, 63, 65, 113, 141

Igglesden	10	1	30	1
Penn	10.3	1	39	2
C.S. Cowdrey	7	0	40	0
Ellison	11	2	28	2
Fleming	10	2	24	0
Davis	5	0	21	1

Umpires: P.J. Eele and D.S. Thompsett
Toss: Essex Gold: J.P. Stephenson
Essex made certain of a place in the quarter-finals, having won all three of their matches, while Kent, suffering their second defeat, needed to win their fourth and final match to win a similar place. Kent in fact seemed to be in control of this game until Stephenson grabbed the initiative.

NATWEST BANK TROPHY

v DORSET (Canterbury)

June 28

Won by 198 runs.

Kent		
S.G. Hinks	b Sawney	62
N.R. Taylor	run out	13
R.F. Pienaar	c Ridley b Taylor	90
T.R. Ward	c Sawney b Calway	83
*C.S. Cowdrey	not out	69
G.R. Cowdrey	not out	34
†S.A. Marsh		
R.M. Ellison		
C. Penn		
R.P. Davis		
A.P. Igglesden		
Extras	b 1, lb 3, w 3, nb 1	8
Total (4 wkts, 60 ov)		359

32, 103, 252, 257

Taylor	12	3	65	1
Wingfield-Digby	11	2	83	0
Calway	11	3	66	1
Stone	12	1	31	0
Sawney	12	1	71	1
Hall	2	0	39	0

Dorset		
G.S. Calway	c C.S. Cowdrey b Igglesden	1
A.J. Foot	c Hinks b Penn	0
J.A. Claughton	c Davis b Ward	35
C. Stone	lbw b Penn	1
S.J. Legg	c and b Taylor	66
S.W.D. Rintoul	c Igglesden b Davis	8
J.R. Hall	c Penn b Taylor	17
†D.R. Ridley	c Hinks b Pienaar	10
S. Sawney	c Taylor b Pienaar	2
*A.R. Wingfield-Digby	not out	4
N.R. Taylor	c and b Taylor	0
Extras	b 3, lb 4, w 2, nb 8	17
Total (50.5 ov)		161

0, 8, 10, 57, 68, 118, 153, 157, 161

Igglesden	7	1	17	1
Penn	6	1	8	2
Ellison	2	0	5	0
Davis	12	4	21	1
Ward	12	0	58	1
Taylor	6.5	0	29	3
Pienaar	5	1	16	2

Umpires: A.A. Jones and A.G.T. Whitehead
Toss: Dorset. MofM: T.R. Ward
Kent produced their highest NatWest total in the course of which C.S. Cowdrey hit 69 off 28 balls and with his brother added 102 in 6.2 overs.

v WARWICKSHIRE (Canterbury)

July 12

Lost by 49 runs.

Warwickshire		
A.J. Moles	c Marsh b Ellison	26
*T.A. Lloyd	c Marsh b Ellison	21
A.I. Kallicharran	not out	93
†G.W. Humpage	c and b Fleming	65
P.A. Smith	b Davis	5
D.A. Reeve	c Cowdrey b Igglesden	45
D.A. Thorne	not out	2
G.C. Small		
A.R.K. Pierson		
A.A. Donald		
P.A. Munton		
Extras	b 11, w 3, nb 1	15
Total (5 wkts, 60 ov)		272

33, 59, 168, 187, 264

Igglesden	10	0	50	1
Penn	12	0	61	0
Davis	12	3	43	1
Ellison	12	1	55	2
Fleming	12	2	37	1
Cowdrey	2	0	15	0

Kent		
N.R. Taylor	lbw b Reeve	29
M.R. Benson	b Munton	64
R.F. Pienaar	lbw b Munton	10
T.R. Ward	c Thorne b Smith	18
*C.S. Cowdrey	c Humpage b Donald	52
†S.A. Marsh	b Smith	6
M.V. Fleming	st Humpage b Pierson	12
R.M. Ellison	b Donald	14
C. Penn	b Munton	3
A.P. Igglesden	b Donald	2
R.P. Davis	not out	1
Extras	lb 7, w 4, nb 1	12
Total (57.4 ov)		223

71, 100, 125, 128, 136, 193, 214, 219, 222

Small	12	1	26	0
Donald	10.4	0	41	3
Munton	11	1	36	3
Pierson	9	0	35	1
Reeve	5	0	23	1
Smith	10	0	55	2

Umpires: D.J. Constant and K.E. Palmer
Toss: Kent
Put in to bat Warwickshire produced the highest total in the quarter finals. Kallicharran scored a very cultured 93 and with Humpage added 109 in 25 overs. Kent began well but the innings dissolved when three wickets went for 11 runs and despite some heroics from Cowdrey, Warwickshire marched on to victory.

Away Matches

The full scorecard of each of Kent's away matches will be found in the sections for the respective home teams.

Hove: April 17, 28, 29, 30
Kent 234 (C.M. Wells 7–65) and 252–2d drew with Sussex 261. Sussex 7pts, Kent 5pts.

Southampton: May 4, 5, 6, 8
Hants 358 (R.A. Smith 182, R.M. Ellison 5–98) and 280–5d beat Kent 369 and 136 (R.J. Maru 8–41 by 133 runs. Hants 22pts, Kent 5pts.

Leicester: May 24, 25, 26
Kent 307 (G.R. Cowdrey 108*) and 133–1d drew with Leics 201–7d and 184–7. Kent 5pts, Leics 4pts.

Trent Bridge: June 10, 12, 13
Notts 377–7d (R.T. Robinson 128) and 287–2d (R.T. Robinson 146*, P.R. Pollard 131) lost to Kent 354–7d (R.F. Pienaar 119, C.S. Cowdrey 101*) and 311–6 by 4 wkts. Kent 21pts, Notts 6pts.

Bath: June 17, 19, 20
Kent 526–7d (M.R. Benson 157, T.R. Ward 104) and 108–0d drew with Somerset 274–5d (R.J. Harden 102*) and 276–6 (P.M. Roebuck 107). Kent 6pts, Somerset 4pts.

Old Trafford: June 24, 26, 27
Kent 296 and 42–3 drew with Lancs 298 (A.P. Igglesden 6–73). Kent 7pts, Lancs 6pts.

Southend: July 19, 20
Kent 112 (D.R. Pringle 6–42) and 229 lost to Essex 347 (N. Hussain 127) by an inns and 6 runs.

Uxbridge: July 22, 24, 25
Middx 458–1d (D.L. Haynes 206*, I.J.F. Hutchinson 177) drew with Kent 164 and 231–9. Middx 8pts, Kent 1pt.

Worcester: July 29, 31, Aug 1
Worcs 402–6d (G.A. Hick 147, P. Bent 144) and 27–0 beat Kent 232 and 196 (S.R. Lampitt 5–32) by 10 wkts. Worcs 24pts, Kent 4pts.

Scarborough: August 12, 14, 15
Yorks 400–5d (P.E. Robinson 147, D. Byas 117) and 147–2d lost to Kent 271–6d (N.R. Taylor 111) and 277–5 (R.F. Pienaar 129) by 5 wkts. Kent 20pts, Yorks 5pts.

The Oval: September 8, 9, 10, 11
Surrey 477–6d (G.P. Thorpe 154, M.A. Lynch 172*) and 56–0d drew with Kent 269–3d (M.R. Benson 149) and 228–6 (C.S. Cowdrey 146*). Kent 5pts, Surrey 5pts.

v ESSEX (Canterbury)

April 20, 21, 22, 24
Drawn. Essex 6pts, Kent 4pts

Essex 1st Innings

*G.A. Gooch	c C.S. Cowdrey b Kelleher	32
J.P. Stephenson	c Marsh b Alleyne	0
A.W. Lilley	lbw b Kelleher	65
M.E. Waugh	lbw b Ellison	4
P.J. Prichard	lbw b Penn	11
T.D. Topley	c Marsh b Penn	4
B.R. Hardie	b Alleyne	26
D.R. Pringle	b Penn	20
†D.E. East	b Kelleher	0
N.A. Foster	not out	20
J.H. Childs	c Ward b Penn	0
Extras	lb 8, w 4, nb 9	21
Total (74.4 ov)		203

0, 60, 73, 97, 111, 157, 159, 159, 201

Penn	20.4	7	57	4
Alleyne	18	2	71	2
Ellison	14	4	24	1
Kelleher	22	7	43	3

Kent 1st Innings

S.G. Hinks	c East b Foster	12
M.R. Benson	c Waugh b Foster	3
N.R. Taylor	lbw b Topley	47
*C.S. Cowdrey	c East b Foster	1
D.J.M. Kelleher	c Topley b Pringle	0
G.R. Cowdrey	c Hardie b Topley	1
T.R. Ward	b Pringle	12
†S.A. Marsh	c Pringle b Topley	7
R.M. Ellison	c Gooch b Topley	0
C. Penn	b Foster	16
H.L. Alleyne	not out	10
Extras	lb 4, nb 6	10
Total (52.3 ov)		119

11, 17, 26, 33, 54, 83, 83, 83, 90

Foster	19.3	6	38	4
Pringle	21	4	38	2
Topley	12	3	39	4

Essex 2nd Innings

*G.A. Gooch	c Marsh b Ellison	55
J.P. Stephenson	not out	109
A.W. Lilley	lbw b Kelleher	14
M.E. Waugh	lbw b Kelleher	17
P.J. Prichard	not out	12
Extras	lb 7, w 5, nb 5	17
Total (3 wkts dec)		224

114, 144, 184

Ellison	20	7	34	1
Penn	17	7	45	0
Alleyne	12	1	52	0
Kelleher	18	6	51	2
C.S. Cowdrey	5	0	28	0
G.R. Cowdrey	2	0	7	0

Kent 2nd Innings

S.G. Hinks	lbw b Topley	6
M.R. Benson	c Waugh b Topley	8
N.R. Taylor	c Foster b Waugh	63
*C.S. Cowdrey	c Lilley b Pringle	1
G.R. Cowdrey	b Topley	3
T.R. Ward	lbw b Pringle	25
†S.A. Marsh	c Gooch b Pringle	6
R.M. Ellison	b Pringle	11
D.J.M. Kelleher	not out	4
C. Penn	not out	2
Extras	w 2, nb 2	4
Total (8 wkts)		133

14, 23, 26, 39, 110, 110, 120, 131

Foster	11	3	29	0
Pringle	16.3	3	36	4
Topley	12	1	40	3
Waugh	8	1	28	1

Umpires: B.J. Meyer and B. Dudleston
Toss: Kent
Only 32 overs could be bowled on the first day, during which Essex progressed to 98–4. The second day was miserably cold and again interrupted by the elements. Kent were 30–3 off 20 overs at the close. Topley and Foster dismissed the home side cheaply on Saturday and then Stephenson compiled a maiden first-class hundred to take Essex to 224–3, a lead of 308. Essex declared overnight, but Kent never looked like achieving the target and were only saved from defeat by rain which arrived with 39 overs still to be bowled.

v DERBYSHIRE (Dartford)

May 20, 21, 22,
Lost by 8 wkts. Derbys 24pts, Kent 5pts

Derbyshire 1st Innings

*K.J. Barnett	c Marsh b Penn	36
P.D. Bowler	c Cowdrey b Igglesden	0
†B.J.M. Maher	c Cowdrey b Igglesden	0
J.E. Morris	c Hinks b Igglesden	55
B. Roberts	c Marsh b Davis	102
S.C. Goldsmith	c Marsh b Kelleher	88
R.J. Sharma	c Igglesden b Kelleher	45
P.G. Newman	b Igglesden	13
A.E. Warner	lbw b Kelleher	46
M.A. Holding	not out	5
D.E. Malcolm	c Cowdrey b Davis	2
Extras	lb 13, w 1, nb 10	24
Total (100 ov: 387–7)		416

1, 26, 56, 139, 292, 302, 336, 403, 414

Igglesden	21	1	90	4
Penn	20	1	93	1
Kelleher	16	2	67	3
Davis	39	11	90	2
Wells	9	0	50	0
Cowdrey	3	0	13	0

Kent 1st Innings

S.G. Hinks	retired hurt	1
M.R. Benson	lbw b Malcolm	3
N.R. Taylor	b Malcolm	74
T.R. Ward	c Newman b Holding	27
*C.S. Cowdrey	c Goldsmith b Holding	2
V.J. Wells	b Warner	2
†S.A. Marsh	lbw b Holding	52
D.J.M. Kelleher	c Barnett b Holding	0
C.Penn	c Maher b Malcolm	29
R.P. Davis	not out	1
A.P. Igglesden	c Sharma b Malcolm	6
Extras	b 1, lb 2, w 2, nb 8	13
Total (56.2 ov)		210

13, 63, 67, 79, 160, 172, 172, 204, 210

Malcolm	16.2	2	69	4
Holding	18	3	71	4
Warner	11	2	27	1
Newman	10	0	35	0
Barnett	1	0	5	0

Kent 2nd Innings

T.R. Ward	c Bowler b Sharma	57
M.R. Benson	c Roberts b Warner	16
N.R. Taylor	c Maher b Newman	23
*C.S. Cowdrey	lbw b Newman	0
V.J. Wells	b Newman	1
†S.A. Marsh	st Maher b Sharma	23
D.J.M. Kelleher	not out	53
C. Penn	c Barnett b Malcolm	60
R.P. Davis	c Maher b Malcolm	14
A.P. Igglesden	b Warner	17
S.G. Hinks	absent hurt	0
Extras	b 7, lb 13, nb 8	28
Total		292

53, 83, 83, 87, 123, 131, 215, 240, 292

Malcolm	16	0	61	2
Holding	12	1	53	0
Warner	10.3	1	30	2
Newman	11	2	44	3
Barnett	6	2	18	0
Sharma	18	6	54	2
Bowler	2	0	12	0

Derbyshire 2nd Innings

*K.J. Barnett	c Marsh b Igglesden	8
P.D. Bowler	c Marsh b Wells	31
†B.J.M. Maher	not out	25
J.E. Morris	not out	15
Extras	b 1, lb 1, nb 6	8
Total (2 wkts)		87

13, 66

Penn	10	2	31	0
Igglesden	7	2	24	1
Davis	1	0	9	0
Wells	5	2	11	1
Benson	1	0	6	0
Ward	0.3	0	4	0

Umpires: A.A. Jones and A.G.T. Whitehead
Toss: Derbyshire
13 fours and a six were among the scoring strokes in a sparkling 102 by Roberts and with 88 off 84 deliveries by Goldsmith, Derbyshire reached 416 on Saturday. On Sunday Kent were bowled out by Holding and Malcolm for 210. The follow on was enforced and only bad light prevented Barnett claiming a two-day victory. Starting Monday at 185–6, Kent fought back due to effective batting from Kelleher and Penn. Derbyshire however still won by 8 wkts.

v HAMPSHIRE (Tunbridge Wells)

June 3, 5, 6

Drawn. Kent 7pts, Hants 3pts

Hampshire 1st Innings

V.P. Terry	c Marsh b Penn	9
C.L. Smith	c Marsh b Igglesden	30
K.D James	c C.S. Cowdrey b Ellison	19
R.A. Smith	b Ellison	8
*M.C.J. Nicholas	c Marsh b Penn	12
D.R. Turner	c Davis b Ellison	5
M.D. Marshall	c Igglesden b C.S. Cowdrey	61
†R.J. Parks	c Taylor b Ellison	2
T.M. Tremlett	not out	32
R.J. Maru	c Marsh b Igglesden	4
P.J. Bakker	b Igglesden	1
Extras	lb 7, w 11, nb 12	30
Total (75.2 ov)		213

17, 52, 61, 92, 92, 117, 130, 203, 208

Igglesden	23.2	2	83	3
Penn	25	6	53	2
Ellison	20	5	45	4
Davis	4	0	15	0
C.S. Cowdrey	3	0	10	1

Kent 1st Innings

M.R. Benson	c Parks b Marshall	114
T.R. Ward	c C.L. Smith b James	28
N.R. Taylor	not out	104
R.F. Pienaar	c Nicholas b Marshall	0
G.R. Cowdrey	not out	17
*C.S. Cowdrey		
†S.A. Marsh		
R.M. Ellison		
C. Penn		
R.P. Davis		
A.P. Igglesden		
Extras	b 2, lb 5, nb 6	13
Total (3 wkts, 87 ov)		276

49, 244, 245

Marshall	21	3	64	2
Bakker	17	1	48	0
Maru	13	3	51	0
James	18	1	44	1
Tremlett	16	4	45	0
Nicholas	2	0	17	0

Umpires: J.C. Balderstone and P.B. Wight

Toss: Hampshire

Stoppages for rain and bad light meant that only 53 overs were bowled on Saturday and Hampshire suffered at the hands of Ellison and Penn. The score was 139–7 at the close. Marshall hit out on Monday, then Benson and Taylor enjoyed themselves. Benson batted 4 hours with 13 fours, Taylor was undefeated with 102. Only three overs were possible on the last day, Kent scoring six runs, then a thunderstorm flooded the ground.

v SUSSEX (Tunbridge Wells)

June 7, 8, 9

Lost by 3 wkts. Sussex 20pts, Kent 2pts

Kent 1st Innings

T.R. Ward	c Moores b Pigott	4
M.R. Benson	c Pigott b Salisbury	57
N.R. Taylor	c and b Dodemaide	48
R.F. Pienaar	c Lenham b Salisbury	11
G.R. Cowdrey	c Gould b Babington	4
*C.S. Cowdrey	c Smith b Dodemaide	46
†S.A. Marsh	c Moores b Dodemaide	33
R.M. Ellison	c Dodemaide b C.M. Wells	5
C. Penn	c A.P. Wells b C.M. Wells	15
R.P. Davis	not out	6
A.P. Igglesden	c Salisbury b C.M. Wells	0
Extras	b 3, lb 7, w 2, nb 2	14
Total (86 ov)		243

6, 96, 119, 126, 138, 195, 220, 220, 243

Pigott	20	7	39	1
Dodemaide	24	5	74	3
Babington	16	2	58	1
C.M. Wells	15	5	31	3
Salisbury	11	2	31	2

Sussex 1st Innings

N.J. Lenham	c Taylor b Penn	1
D.M. Smith	not out	44
K. Greenfield	c Benson b Penn	30
A.P. Wells	not out	16
*C.M. Wells		
I.J. Gould		
A.I.C. Dodemaide		
†P. Moores		
A.C.S. Pigott		
I.D.K. Salisbury		
A.M. Babington		
Extras	b 1, lb 1, nb 6	8
Total (2 wkts dec, 41 ov)		99

Igglesden	8	1	24	0
Penn	11	3	23	2
Ellison	13	5	34	0
Davis	7	4	11	0
C.S. Cowdrey	2	0	5	0

Kent 2nd Innings

T.R. Ward	c and b Lenham	2
M.R. Benson	not out	45
N.R. Taylor	not out	32
Extras	lb 2, w 1	3
Total (1 wkt dec)		82

2

Lenham	5	1	25	1
A.P. Wells	5	1	14	0
Gould	4	0	27	0
Greenfield	3	0	11	0
Smith	1	0	3	0

Sussex 2nd Innings

N.J. Lenham	c and b Ellison	7
D.M. Smith	c Marsh b Penn	67
K. Greenfield	c Marsh b Igglesden	11
A.P. Wells	b Igglesden	46
*C.M. Wells	c and b Davis	15
I.J. Gould	c C.S. Cowdrey b Igglesden	5
A.I.C. Dodemaide	not out	14
†P. Moores	c Pienaar b Davis	0
A.C.S. Pigott	not out	54
Extras	b 3, lb 3, w 1, nb 2	9
Total (7 wkts)		228

30, 45, 135, 141, 160, 160, 160

Igglesden	17.2	2	76	3
Penn	14	2	48	1
Ellison	5	0	11	1
Davis	23	9	61	2
C.S. Cowdrey	8	1	26	0

Umpires: J.C. Balderstone and P.B. Wight

Toss: Sussex

Rain which had ruined the previous match at Tunbridge Wells continued to disrupt cricket on the first day of this match. Only 11.3 overs were bowled and Kent finished at 15–1. The second day ended the game evenly balanced. Sussex were 40–1 off 24 overs. Wells declared after 17 more overs on Friday morning, then the batsmen were put on to bowl as Kent hit 82–1. Sussex were invited to score 227 off 64 overs and made rather a mess of the challenge until Pigott arrived. When all seemed lost he hit a quick 54 and won the match with a six, there being ten deliveries remaining.

v NORTHAMPTONSHIRE (Maidstone)

July 5, 6, 7

Drawn. Northants 8pts, Kent 4pts

Kent 1st Innings

S.G. Hinks	c Felton b Davis	35
N.R. Taylor	c Ripley b Davis	10
R.F. Pienaar	c Felton b Capel	30
T.R. Ward	c N.G.B. Cook b Capel	7
G.R. Cowdrey	lbw b Capel	9
*C.S. Cowdrey	b Capel	9
†S.A. Marsh	not out	18
R.M. Ellison	c Ripley b Davis	0
C. Penn	c N.G.B Cook b Robinson	1
R.P. Davis	c Fordham b Davis	18
A.P. Igglesden	b Davis	4
Extras	lb 2, w 1, nb 12	15
Total (42.4 ov)		156

43, 53, 70, 98, 104, 111, 113, 114, 142

Davis	14.4	2	55	5
Brown	4	1	27	0
Capel	11	2	32	4
Robinson	13	0	40	1

Northamptonshire 1st Innings

G. Cook	c G.R. Cowdrey b Igglesden	15
*W. Larkins	b Igglesden	116
N.A. Felton	c Taylor b Penn	46
R.J. Bailey	lbw b Penn	35
D.J. Capel	c Marsh b Penn	105
A. Fordham	c Marsh b Ellison	30
†D. Ripley	c Taylor b C.S. Cowdrey	7
N.G.B. Cook	c Taylor b C.S. Cowdrey	1
W.W. Davis	c Ward b Penn	9
S.J. Brown	not out	5
M.A. Robinson	b Igglesden	1
Extras	lb 2, w 1, nb 5	8
Total (100 ov–366–7)		378

19, 139, 200, 247, 321, 350, 351, 366, 375

Igglesden	26.5	3	131	3
Penn	31	3	109	4
Ellison	22	5	77	1
C.S. Cowdrey	21	3	58	2
Ward	5	4	1	0

Kent 2nd Innings

S.G. Hinks	lbw b Davis	0
N.R. Taylor	b N.G.B. Cook	98
R.F. Pienaar	not out	77
†S.A. Marsh	not out	0
Extras	lb 2, nb 14	16
Total (2 wkts)		191

0, 189

Davis	13	2	43	1
Brown	15	2	62	0
Capel	7	1	26	0
N.G.B. Cook	16	8	25	1
Robinson	7	1	23	0
Bailey	7	3	10	0

Umpires: P.J. Eele and B. Leadbeater

Toss: Northants

Kent were thoroughly outplayed on the first day. Davis wrecked the home batting and Larkins followed this up with a dazzling 116, his 100 coming off 136 balls with 17 fours. Northants were 246–3 off 64 overs at the start of Thursday's play. Capel hit a fast 100, but Kent counter-attacked through Taylor and Pienaar, who put on 189 in 58 overs. Unfortunately rain washed out the last day and the match was thus unfinished.

v GLOUCESTERSHIRE (Maidstone)

July 8, 10, 11

Lost by 47 runs. Gloucs 19pts, Kent 2pts

Gloucestershire 1st Innings

A.J. Wright	c Igglesden b Ellison	118
I.P. Butcher	not out	105
J.W. Lloyds	not out	9
*C.W.J. Athey		
K.M. Curran		
M.W. Alleyne		
†G.A. Tedstone		
C.A. Walsh		
M.W. Pooley		
M.C.J. Ball		
K.B.S. Jarvis		
Extras	b 2, lb 8, w 5, nb 4	19
Total (1 wkt dec, 96 ov)		251

236

Igglesden	27	6	62	0
Penn	22	3	60	0
Ellison	20	4	49	1
C.S. Cowdrey	5	2	15	0
Davis	22	7	55	0

Kent 1st Innings

N.R. Taylor	c Wright b Ball	47
M.R. Benson	not out	102
R.F. Pienaar	not out	47
T.R. Ward		
*C.S. Cowdrey		
G.R. Cowdrey		
†S.A. Marsh		
R.M. Ellison		
C. Penn		
A.P. Igglesden		
R.P. Davis		
Extras	b 4, lb 7, w 1, nb 1	13
Total (1 wkt dec, 72.1 ov)		209

99

Walsh	15	4	38	0
Curran	11	3	33	0
Jarvis	12.1	2	39	0
Ball	13	2	45	1
Pooley	14	3	32	0
Athey	7	3	11	0

Gloucestershire 2nd Innings

A.J. Wright	c Marsh b Penn	7
I.P. Butcher	retired hurt	0
J.W. Lloyds	c Davis b Igglesden	2
†G.A. Tedstone	c Marsh b Igglesden	2
*C.W.J. Athey	c and b Davis	39
K.M. Curran	c Ward b Davis	47
M.W. Alleyne	not out	60
C.A. Walsh	b Davis	47
Extras	lb 3	3
Total (6 wkts dec)		207

8, 12, 12, 82, 139, 207

Igglesden	11	4	18	2
Penn	11	4	19	1
Ellison	5	3	15	0
Davis	20.5	4	67	3
Pienaar	22	3	43	0
Benson	4	0	42	0

Kent 2nd Innings

N.R. Taylor	c Tedstone b Walsh	0
M.R. Benson	c Alleyne b Curran	8
R.F. Pienaar	c Lloyds b Jarvis	8
T.R. Ward	lbw b Jarvis	1
G.R. Cowdrey	c Tedstone b Curran	0
*C.S. Cowdrey	c Tedstone b Ball	43
†S.A. Marsh	not out	90
R.M. Ellison	c and b Ball	30
C. Penn	c Wright b Ball	9
R.P. Davis	c and b Ball	7
A.P. Igglesden	run out	0
Extras	b 1, lb 4, nb 1	6
Total,		

0, 20, 20, 21, 23, 116, 170, 188, 201

Walsh	14.3	3	59	1
Jarvis	14	3	37	2
Curran	7	0	37	2
Pooley	3	1	11	0
Ball	12	1	53	4

Umpires: P.J. Eele and B. Leadbeater

Toss: Kent

More rain marred Kent's home fixtures on the first day of this match. The home bowlers toiled in vain as Gloucestershire reached 187 without loss. The first two innings amassed 460 runs for only two wickets. Gloucestershire began the final day at 12–2, with Butcher retired hurt. Kent were set 250 off 47 overs, but lost Taylor first ball. Ball returned a career best 4–53.

v WARWICKSHIRE (Canterbury)

August 5, 7, 8

Lost by 10 wkts. Warwicks 21pts, Kent 6pts

Kent 1st Innings

S.G. Hinks	c Kallicharran b Smith	53
N.R. Taylor	b Humpage	20
R.F. Pienaar	lbw b Munton	33
T.R. Ward	c Lloyd b Munton	8
*C.S. Cowdrey	b Humpage	56
†S.A. Marsh	lbw b Donald	53
M.V. Fleming	b Donald	45
C. Penn	b Donald	0
R.P. Davis	not out	5
D.J.M. Kelleher	c Piper b Donald	0
A.P. Igglesden	b Donald	4
Extras	b 2, lb 5, w 1, nb 2	10
Total (100 ov: 268–5)		287

60, 104, 115, 128, 197, 276, 276, 278, 287

Donald	21.5	4	57	5
Small	21	7	55	0
Munton	32	9	80	2
Smith	18	3	60	1
Humpage	16	5	28	2

Warwickshire 1st Innings

A.J. Moles	b Penn	12
*T.A. Lloyd	lbw b Fleming	48
A.I. Kallicharran	c Fleming b Penn	38
G.W. Humpage	c Hinks b Kelleher	39
Asif Din	c Pienaar b Igglesden	18
D.A. Reeve	lbw b Penn	18
N.M.K. Smith	lbw b Fleming	11
†K.J. Piper	b Davis	14
G.C. Small	not out	23
A.A. Donald	not out	11
T.A. Munton		
Extras	lb 4, w 1, nb 13	18
Total (8 wkts dec, 90.2 ov)		250

34, 102, 120, 168, 171, 200, 214, 214

Igglesden	22.2	3	92	1
Penn	26	6	61	3
Kelleher	22.4	6	57	1
Fleming	14.2	5	34	2
Davis	5	3	2	1

Kent 2nd Innings

S.G. Hinks	lbw b Munton	16
N.R. Taylor	lbw b Donald	5
R.F. Pienaar	lbw b Reeve	53
T.R. Ward	c sub b Smith	1
M.V. Fleming	b Smith	6
†S.A. Marsh	b Donald	6
*C.S. Cowdrey	c Piper b Reeve	22
C. Penn	c Lloyd b Donald	7
R.P. Davis	lbw b Reeve	4
D.J.M. Kelleher	b Donald	0
A.P. Igglesden	not out	0
Extras	b 5, lb 9, nb 7	21
Total		141

18, 44, 61, 77, 87, 112, 130, 132, 132

Donald	22	6	41	4
Small	3.2	3	3	0
Munton	10.4	3	27	1
Smith	9	1	27	2
Reeve	16.2	7	29	3

Warwickshire 2nd Innings

A.J. Moles	not out	64
*T.A. Lloyd	not out	109
Extras	b 3, lb 5	8
Total (0 wkt)		181

Penn	12.4	3	53	0
Igglesden	8	1	20	0
Fleming	7	1	16	0
Kelleher	4	0	24	0
Davis	4	0	29	0
Cowdrey	7	0	31	0

Umpires: J.H. Harris and B. Hassan

Toss: Kent

This battle between two teams at the bottom end of the table resulted in an overwhelming victory for Warwickshire who thus climbed out of the lowest depths, but it left Kent 20 points adrift at the foot of the Championship. After two indecisive days, the visitors took all ten Kent second innings wickets on the last day for 127 runs, leaving 45 overs in which to make 179. The Kent fielders then gave lives to both Lloyd and Moles in the early stages of their innings before the pair pressed on to a partnership worth 181 and victory.

v SURREY (Canterbury)

August 9, 10, 11

Lost by 7 wkts. Surrey 24pts, Kent 8pts

Kent 1st Innings

S.G. Hinks	c Lynch b Murphy	33
N.R. Taylor	c Medlycott b M.P. Bicknell	118
R.F. Pienaar	lbw b Peters	51
T.R. Ward	st Stewart b Medlycott	3
*C.S. Cowdrey	c D.J. Bicknell b M.P. Bicknell	1
†S.A. Marsh	c Stewart b Murphy	31
M.V. Fleming	c Stewart b Peters	23
M.C. Dobson	lbw b Murphy	0
C. Penn	lbw b Murphy	13
D.J.M. Kelleher	c Thorpe b Murphy	30
A.P. Igglesden	not out	32
Extras	b 5, lb 5, w 1	11
Total (100 ov: 318–9)		346

89, 167, 180, 181, 226, 268, 268, 268, 290

Murphy	27.4	7	94	5
M.P. Bicknell	31	9	81	2
Robinson	5	0	18	0
Peters	19	2	57	2
Greig	7	2	20	0
Medlycott	19	4	66	1

Surrey 1st Innings

D.J. Bicknell	b Igglesden	6
R.I. Alikhan	c Marsh b Penn	23
†A.J. Stewart	lbw b Kelleher	87
G.P. Thorpe	c Hinks b Penn	4
M.A. Lynch	lbw b Igglesden	27
*I.A. Greig	c Penn b Fleming	69
J.D. Robinson	c Marsh b Kelleher	10
K.T. Medlycott	lbw b Penn	17
N.H. Peters	b Dobson	15
M.P. Bicknell	not out	18
A.J. Murphy	not out	5
Extras	b 4, lb 5, nb 12	21
Total (9 wkts dec, 96.3 ov)		302

20, 62, 70, 110, 208, 226, 249, 259, 294

Igglesden	25	3	74	2
Penn	24	3	85	3
Kelleher	21	5	61	2
Fleming	14	6	27	1
Dobson	6.3	2	21	1
Cowdrey	6	1	25	0

Kent 2nd Innings

S.G. Hinks	not out	104
N.R. Taylor	b D.J. Bicknell	45
R.F. Pienaar	lbw b Stewart	16
T.R. Ward	not out	10
Extras	b 5, lb 2, w 2	9
Total (2 wkts dec)		184

126, 161

M.P. Bicknell	2	0	6	0
Murphy	2	0	10	0
Stewart	16	0	88	1
D.J. Bicknell	15.4	1	73	1

Surrey 2nd Innings

D.J. Bicknell	b Kelleher	20
R.I. Alikhan	c Kelleher b Penn	8
†A.J. Stewart	c Pienaar b Kelleher	45
G.P. Thorpe	not out	85
M.A. Lynch	not out	63
Extras	b 1, lb 5, nb 3	9
Total (3 wkts)		230

18, 66, 91

Igglesden	4	0	24	0
Penn	10.4	2	50	1
Fleming	12	1	59	0
Kelleher	8	1	46	2
Dobson	5	0	34	0
Ward	2	0	11	0

Umpires: J.H. Harris and B. Hassan

Toss: Kent

Taylor batted 282 minutes on the first day enabling Kent to gain full batting points. Surrey's innings commenced on the second morning and Stewart and Greig saw the visitors past the 300 mark. Rain prevented any play on the last morning, which meant that Surrey bowled their casual trundlers while Kent knocked up quick runs and Surrey then were given 42 overs in which to make 229, a task they managed with two deliveries to spare. This kept Kent still at the foot of the table, now 22 points adrift, Surrey did however move up two notches to 11th place.

v GLAMORGAN (Canterbury)

August 19, 21, 22

Won by 101 runs. Kent 24pts, Glam 6pts

Kent 1st Innings		
S.G. Hinks	c Morris b Watkin	5
N.R. Taylor	b Barwick	42
R.F. Pienaar	c Morris b Dennis	132
T.R. Ward	c Metson b Dennis	36
*C.S. Cowdrey	c Metson b Smith	57
†P. Farbrace	c Metson b Dennis	8
M.C. Dobson	c Morris b Dennis	52
D.J.M. Kelleher	b Watkin	25
C. Penn	c Metson b Dennis	0
R.P. Davis	not out	0
A.P. Igglesden	not out	7
Extras	lb 8	8
Total (100 ov: 316–6) (9 wkts dec)		372

14, 145, 214, 233, 255, 297, 363, 363, 365

Watkin	23	6	92	2
Dennis	23	3	83	5
Barwick	22	6	55	1
Croft	27	8	81	0
Smith	11	0	46	1
Butcher	4	1	7	0

Glamorgan 1st Innings		
*A.R. Butcher	c Taylor b Penn	7
H. Morris	c Farbrace b Davis	56
M.P. Maynard	b Penn	0
M.J. Cann	c Taylor b Igglesden	9
G.C. Holmes	c Cowdrey b Penn	8
I. Smith	b Kelleher	116
†C.P. Metson	c Farbrace b Dobson	28
R.D.B. Croft	b Igglesden	16
S.J. Dennis	b Igglesden	36
S.L. Watkin	b Kelleher	6
S.R. Barwick	not out	0
Extras	b 9, lb 10, w 1, nb 12	32
Total (92.5 ov)		311

12, 12, 21, 27, 130, 204, 240, 269, 307

Igglesden	22.5	3	75	3
Penn	18	3	51	3
Cowdrey	6	0	43	0
Kelleher	13	3	43	2
Davis	23	7	53	1
Dobson	10	2	27	1

Kent 2nd Innings		
S.G. Hinks	c Metson b Watkin	13
N.R. Taylor	c Metson b Barwick	32
R.F Pienaar	c Metson b Watkin	35
T.R. Ward	not out	78
*C.S. Cowdrey	c and b Dennis	53
Extras	b 2, lb 2, w 2	7
Total (4 wkts dec)		218

17, 79, 106, 218

Watkin	16	1	47	2
Dennis	12	1	47	1
Barwick	12	0	50	1
Croft	11	1	51	0
Smith	2	0	19	0

Glamorgan 2nd Innings		
*A.R. Butcher	c Ward b Davis	46
H. Morris	c Farbrace b Dobson	68
M.P. Maynard	c Cowdrey b Igglesden	21
G.C. Holmes	lbw b Igglesden	1
I. Smith	st Farbrace b Davis	7
M.J. Cann	c Cowdrey b Davis	0
†C.P. Metson	b Davis	0
R.D.B. Croft	not out	24
S.J. Dennis	lbw b Dobson	1
S.L. Watkin	b Igglesden	2
S.R. Barwick	b Igglesden	0
Extras	lb 5, w 1, nb 2	8
Total		178

84, 112, 130, 145, 145, 145, 149, 161, 174

Igglesden	14.3	3	58	4
Kelleher	7	2	23	0
Penn	6	1	15	0
Davis	24	10	57	4
Dobson	13	7	20	2

Umpires: J.C. Balderstone and D.J. Constant
Toss: Kent

Pienaar hit 19 fours and a six in a brilliant innings on Saturday. Helped by 50 off 59 balls by C.S. Cowdrey and a maiden fifty by Dobson, he enabled Kent to reach 372–9 in the day. On Monday Kent declared and Glamorgan crashed to 27–4. Smith arrived and went on to score 116 with 16 fours. Kent ended at 44–1. Kent set Glamorgan 280 in 65 overs. The Welsh side set off at a gallop and 50 came off 13 overs, but Davis then came on to slow down the run getting and soon the wickets began to fall. Kent won with three deliveries remaining.

v LEICESTERSHIRE (Folkestone)

August 24, 25, 26, 28

Drawn. Leics 8pts, Kent 4pts

Leicestershire 1st Innings		
L. Potter	lbw b Penn	96
*N.E. Briers	c Marsh b Penn	28
J.J. Whitaker	c sub b Dobson	116
P. Willey	c Pienaar b Cowdrey	99
C.C. Lewis	c Ward b Penn	69
†P. Whitticase	c Ward b Cowdrey	61
W.K.M. Benjamin	c and b Penn	2
G.J. Parsons	c Kelleher b Davis	10
J.P. Agnew	not out	4
R.H. Edmunds	lbw b Cowdrey	0
P.M. Such	c Marsh b Cowdrey	0
Extras	b 1, lb 5, nb 7	13
Total (100 ov: 349–3)		498

62, 238, 269, 396, 433, 444, 492, 498, 498

Penn	36	6	116	4
Kelleher	33	5	123	0
Davis	40	4	129	1
Dobson	25	3	87	1
Ward	1	0	4	0
Cowdrey	14.5	1	33	4

Kent 1st Innings		
S.G. Hinks	c Whitticase b Agnew	9
M.R. Benson	c Whitticase b Benjamin	42
N.R. Taylor	b Agnew	4
R.F Pienaar	lbw b Edmunds	72
T.R. Ward	run out	78
*C.S. Cowdrey	lbw b Parsons	7
†S.A. Marsh	c Briers b Lewis	4
M.C. Dobson	lbw b Lewis	1
D.J.M. Kelleher	c Potter b Parsons	0
C. Penn	not out	24
R.P. Davis	lbw b Benjamin	0
Extras	lb 10, nb 13	23
Total (75 ov)		264

20, 25, 106, 170, 199, 204, 216, 219, 263

Benjamin	18	7	37	2
Agnew	19	3	72	2
Edmunds	15	2	48	1
Parsons	12	1	52	2
Such	1	1	0	0
Lewis	10	2	45	2

Kent 2nd Innings		
S.G. Hinks	lbw b Benjamin	23
M.R. Benson	c Lewis b Willey	31
N.R. Taylor	not out	63
R.F. Pienaar	not out	134
Extras	b 1, lb 8, w 2, nb 2	16
Total (2 wkts)		267

61, 61

Benjamin	18	10	33	1
Agnew	18	4	59	0
Such	16	5	36	0
Willey	17	7	28	1
Edmunds	11	3	27	0
Parsons	12	3	40	0
Potter	19	7	35	0

Umpires: A.A. Jones and D.S. Thompsett
Toss: Leicestershire

Without Igglesden and Ellison, Kent's attack wore a disjointed air and the visiting batsmen, including the ex-Kent player, Potter, enjoyed themselves. He and Whitaker added 176 in 47 overs and the total at the close was 421–4. On the second day 53 overs were lost to rain and bad light, so Kent closed at 97–2 off 28 overs. Saturday saw the home side forced to follow on and when stumps were drawn the score in their second innings was 32–0. On the final day, when Kent had only a draw to play for, Pienaar hit a hundred in 190 minutes with 2 sixes and 13 fours.

v MIDDLESEX (Canterbury)

September 13, 14, 15, 16,

Drawn. Middx 7pts, Kent 6pts

Kent 1st Innings		
S.G. Hinks	c Brown b Fraser	7
N.R. Taylor	c Gatting b Fraser	5
R.F. Pienaar	c Gatting b Fraser	20
T.R. Ward	c Fraser	21
*C.S. Cowdrey	c Brown b Fraser	69
M.V. Fleming	c sub b Emburey	29
†S.A. Marsh	c Brown b Cowans	3
R.M. Ellison	c Brown b Cowans	0
C. Penn	b Fraser	43
M.M. Patel	b Fraser	3
A.P. Igglesden	not out	9
Extras	b 8, lb 11, nb 13	32
Total (92.2 ov)		241

13, 27, 61, 63, 130, 141, 141, 218, 227

Fraser	34.2	10	77	7
Cowans	28	9	66	2
Hughes	11	1	41	0
Tufnell	3	0	10	0
Emburey	12	5	24	1
Gatting	4	3	4	0

Middlesex 1st Innings		
D.L. Haynes	c Cowdrey b Ellison	17
M.A. Roseberry	c Penn b Ellison	17
*M.W. Gatting	run out	4
M.R. Ramprakash	lbw b Ellison	64
†K.R. Brown	c Patel b Igglesden	76
J.C. Pooley	b Patel	14
J.E. Emburey	c Marsh b Igglesden	5
A.R.C. Fraser	b Ellison	4
S.P. Hughes	lbw b Ellison	6
P.C.R. Tufnell	c and b Ellison	0
N.G. Cowans	not out	10
Extras	b 3, lb 11, w 1, nb 19	34
Total (76.4 ov)		251

37, 41, 54, 160, 194, 209, 226, 237, 237

Penn	15	3	49	0
Igglesden	23	4	99	2
Ellison	24.4	11	43	6
Fleming	4	0	12	0
Patel	10	2	34	1

Kent 2nd Innings		
S.G. Hinks	not out	67
N.R. Taylor	not out	49
Extras	b 3, w 1	4
Total (0 wkt)		120

Fraser	3	2	4	0
Hughes	4	2	11	0
Haynes	6	3	13	0
Tufnell	10	4	25	0
Emburey	6	2	8	0
Roseberry	12	6	25	0
Ramprakash	11	1	31	0

Umpires: M.J. Kitchen and P.J. Eele
Toss: Kent

When the match began Kent were in danger of finishing bottom of the Championship for the first time this century, but six bonus points and the fact that Yorkshire and Glamorgan failed to win their matches meant that Kent finished in 15th position. The first day was cut short by bad light, Kent making 204–7 off 75.3 overs. On Thursday rain ended play at 3.15 with Middlesex 124–3 off 31 overs. Friday was also an abbreviated day, Middlesex moving on to 237–9 off 71.5 overs. The final day was rather pointless, with the two Kent openers filling in time. Middlesex were happy to settle for third place in the Championship, due to their share of bonus points and the failure of fourth placed Lancashire to win against Derbyshire.

Lancashire

President: C. Washbrook
Chairman: R. Bennett
Secretary: C.D. Hassell, County Cricket Ground, Old Trafford, Manchester M16 0PX. *Tel:* 061-848-7021.
Coach: J.A. Ormrod
Captain: D.P. Hughes
Foundation of Present Club: January 1864 in Manchester
First First-Class Match: Lancashire v Middlesex (Old Trafford) July 1865
County Champions: 1879, 1881, 1882, 1889, 1897, 1904, 1926, 1927, 1928, 1930, 1934, 1950 (joint)
Gillette/NatWest Trophy: Winners 1970, 1971, 1972, 1975
Benson & Hedges Cup: Winners 1984
Sunday League Champions: 1969, 1970, 1989
Refuge Cup: Winners 1988

Summary of Results in 1989
Britannic Assurance County Championship: Played 22, Won 8, Lost 5, Drawn 9, Position 4
NatWest Bank Trophy: Lost in quarter-final
Benson & Hedges Cup: Lost in quarter-final
Refuge Assurance Sunday League: Played 16, Won 12, Lost 2, No Result 2, (League winners)
Refuge Assurance Cup: Lost in semi-final

From left, back: *I. Folley, P.A.J. DeFreitas, B.P. Patterson, M. Watkinson, J.D. Fitton, G.D. Mendis.* Front: *W.K. Hegg, T.E. Jesty, D.P. Hughes (Captain), P.J.W. Allott, N.G. Fairbrother.* Inset: *G. Fowler, J. Simmons, Wasim Akram, G. Lloyd, M.A. Atherton.* Bill Smith

The county took the Refuge Assurance title and moved up from ninth to fourth place in the Championship. The doubters, who had criticised the Committee for retaining Hughes as captain, were sent home in confusion. In Mendis and Fowler Lancashire possess one of the best opening partnerships in the country and with neither required by England – Lancastrians wondered why the selectors ignored Mendis – they missed very few matches. Fairbrother was also very busy hitting the ball, and with youngsters Lloyd and Atherton coming into the side, the middle order batting was quite formidable. Lloyd – son of David – celebrated his 20th birthday during the summer and after a cheap hundred at the expense of Oxford, proved himself capable of higher things with two more centuries against Notts and Essex. Atherton, the Cambridge captain, was recognised at the top level, gaining a place in the England side for the last two Tests and survived a duck in his first innings to make England's highest score in the second.

The two overseas stars, Patterson and Wasim Akram, headed the bowling, the Pakistan all-rounder playing more often, and with them appeared DeFreitas, just registered from Leicestershire. Allott and Watkinson acted as first change bowlers, though the former's record was not as impressive as it had been in 1988, both his average and wicket haul being worse. Watkinson continued to put a string in the later batting.

With Hughes reappointed for 1990, Lancashire should begin this summer with come confidence and the fact that the membership lists have been closed with 12,000 on the books is a healthy indication of the club's present position.

Philip DeFreitas, Lancashire's England bowler, who took most wickets for the county in 1989.

Allsport/Ben Radford

ONE DAY AWAY MATCHES

The full scorecard of each of Lancashire's away matches will be found in the sections for the respective home teams.

Refuge Assurance League

Edgbaston: April 23
No play. Lancs 2pts, Warwicks 2pts.

Worcester: May 7
Lancs 202–8 (40 ov) beat Worcs 188–9 (40 ov) by 14 runs. Lancs 4pts, Worcs 0pts.

Leek: May 14
Lancs 176–8 (40 ov) beat Derbys 153–9 (40 ov) by 23 runs. Lancs 4pts, Derbys 0pts.

Taunton: May 21
Somerset 244–7 (39 ov) S.J. Cook 123) lost to Lancs 245–6 (38.2 ov) by 4 wkts. Lancs 4pts, Somerset 0pts.

Leicester: June 4
Lancs 149–9 (40 ov) lost to Leics 152–3 (38.2 ov) by 7 wkts. Leics 4 pts, Lancs 0pts.

Lord's: July 2
Middx 136–8 (40 ov) lost to Lancs 139–6 (38.4 ov) by 4 wkts. Lancs 4pts, Middx 0pts.

Portsmouth: July 23
Hants 166–9 (40 ov) lost to Lancs 168–4 (36.1 ov) by 6 wkts. Lancs 4pts, Hants 0pts.

Cheltenham: August 6
Gloucs 143 lost to Lancs 144–4 (27.4 ov) by 6 wkts. Lancs 4pts, Gloucs 0pts.

Benson and Hedges Cup

Perth: May 2
Scotland 111–9 (55 ov) (Wasim Akram 5–27) lost to Lancs 114–3 (35.2 ov) by 7 wkts. Lancs 2pts, Scotland 0pts.

Northampton: May 9
Northants 235–5 (55 ov) beat Lancs 197 (51.1 ov) by 38 runs. Northants 2pts, Lancs 0pts.

Chelmsford: May 31
Lancs 246–9 (55 ov) lost to Essex 250–7 (52.1 ov) by 3 wkts.

NatWest Bank Trophy

Kendal: June 28, 29
Cumberland 84 (44.5 ov) lost to Lancs 86–6 (33.4 ov) by 4 wkts.

Bristol: July 12
Gloucs 174–7 (60 ov) lost to Lancs 179–9 (60 ov) by 1 wkt.

Worcester: August 2
Lancs 237–9 (60 ov (I.T. Botham 5–51) lost to Worcs 241–3 (52.2 ov) by 7 wkts.

REFUGE ASSURANCE LEAGUE

v NOTTINGHAMSHIRE (Old Trafford)

April 30

Won by 7 wkts. Lancs 4pts, Notts 0pts.

Nottinghamshire		
B.C. Broad	b DeFreitas	54
*R.T. Robinson	run out	8
D.W. Randall	b Simmons	18
P. Johnson	c Hegg b Watkinson	34
F.D. Stephenson	not out	35
M.G. Field-Buss	b Wasim Akram	5
K.P. Evans	not out	4
†B.N. French		
G.W. Mike		
K.E. Cooper		
K. Saxelby		
Extras	b 1, lb 13, w 11, nb 1	26
Total (5 wkts, 40 ov)		184

19, 61, 124, 156, 168

Watkinson	8	1	21	1
DeFreitas	8	0	44	1
Wasim Akram	8	0	35	1
Austin	8	0	26	0
Simmons	7	0	37	1
Hayhurst	1	0	7	0

Lancashire		
A.N. Hayhurst	c Johnson b Evans	29
G. Fowler	c French b Evans	26
N.H. Fairbrother	c and b Cooper	53
T.E. Jesty	not out	45
Wasim Akram	not out	14
M. Watkinson		
*D.P. Hughes		
P.A.J. DeFreitas		
I.D. Austin		
†W.K. Hegg		
J. Simmons		
Extras	b 1, lb 10, w 8	19
Total (3 wkts, 37.4 ov)		186

61, 66, 169

Saxelby	7	0	35	0
Stephenson	6	1	16	0
Cooper	7.4	0	37	1
Evans	8	0	38	2
Field-Buss	6	0	26	0
Mike	3	0	23	0

Umpires: H.D. Bird and D.R. Shepherd
Toss: Lancashire
Broad held the Notts' batting together, but the runs came at a sedate pace until Stephenson hit out, using Randall as his runner. Fairbrother and Jesty put Lancashire on top with a stand worth 103. Victory was virtually certain when Cooper removed the former.

Gehan Mendis sweeps to leg. Mendis was top of the Lancashire averages for 1989. Allsport/Pascal Rondeau

REFUGE ASSURANCE LEAGUE

v SUSSEX (Old Trafford)

May 28

Won by 3 wkts. Lancs 4pts, Suxxex 0pts

Sussex

N.J.Lenham	b Wasim Akram	8
†P. Moores	b Wasim Akram	21
A.P. Wells	c Allott b Austin	19
C.M. Wells	c Austin b Simmons	7
*P.W.G. Parker	c Hughes b Simmons	12
I.J. Gould	c Hughes b Simmons	16
A.I.C. Dodemaide	lbw b Wasim Akram	1
A.C.S. Pigott	lbw b Wasim Akram	27
I.D.K. Salisbury	not out	12
A.R. Clarke	c Wasim Akram b Allott	0
A.M. Babington	not out	1
Extras	b 1, lb 9, w 8, nb 3	21
Total (9 wkts, 40 ov)		145

11, 52, 55, 68, 98, 99, 112, 133, 139

Watkinson	8	0	15	0
Allott	8	0	33	2
Austin	8	1	17	1
Wasim Akram	8	1	32	3
Simmons	8	0	38	3

Lancashire

G.D. Mendis	b Salisbury	46
G. Fowler	c Moores b Pigott	6
N.H. Fairbrother	c Moores b Babington	25
T.E. Jesty	lbw b Clarke	6
M. Watkinson	b Clarke	1
Wasim Akram	not out	44
*D.P. Hughes	c and b Dodemaide	6
I.D. Austin	b Dodemaide	3
†W.K. Hegg	not out	0
P.J.W. Allott		
J. Simmons		
Extras	b 1, lb 7, w 1	9
Total (7 wkts, 36.1 ov)		146

7, 55, 62, 64, 112, 121, 137

Clarke	8	3	27	2
Salisbury	8	0	25	1
Pigott	6	1	25	1
Dodemaide	8	0	31	2
C.M. Wells	2	0	13	0
Babington	4.1	0	17	1

Umpires: J.W. Holder and B. Leadbeater
Toss: Lancashire
Sussex caused some surprise by including both Clarke and Salisbury in their side – two leg spinners, the latter making his Sunday League debut. As it was Wasim Akram, whose batting won the match for Lancashire, was dropped off Salisbury.

v GLAMORGAN (Blackpool)

June 18

Won by 134 runs. Lancs 4pts, Glamorgan 0pts

Lancashire

G.D. Mendis	c and b Shastri	40
G. Fowler	run out	36
N.H. Fairbrother	not out	100
M. Watkinson	c Metson b Barwick	5
Wasim Akram	b Holmes	29
P.A.J. DeFreitas	c Morris b Barwick	12
A.N. Hayhurst	not out	9
†W.K. Hegg		
I.D. Austin		
*P.J.W. Allott		
J. Simmons		
Extras	lb 7, w 5, nb 1	13
Total (5 wkts, 40 ov)		244

70, 95, 115, 169, 194

Shastri	8	0	40	1
Holmes	8	0	55	1
Barwick	8	0	54	2
Watkin	8	0	53	0
Dennis	8	1	35	0

Glamorgan

A.R. Butcher	c Hegg b DeFreitas	6
*H.Morris	c Simmons b Austin	44
M.P. Maynard	c Fairbrother b DeFreitas	10
G.C. Holmes	st Hegg b Simmons	7
R.J. Shastri	c Wasim Akram b Simmons	2
I. Smith	c Fowler b Watkinson	21
M.J. Cann	b Austin	0
†C.P. Metson	run out	4
S.J. Dennis	c Hegg b Wasim Akram	1
S.L. Watkin	not out	0
S.R. Barwick	b Watkinson	0
Extras	lb 11, w 3, nb 1	15
Total (31.4 ov)		110

14, 28, 47, 79, 79, 80, 100, 107, 109

Allott	6	0	16	0
Wasim Akram	5	0	12	1
DeFreitas	5	0	15	2
Simmons	8	1	21	2
Austin	6	0	28	2
Watkinson	1.4	0	7	2

Umpires: R. Palmer and P.J. Eele
Toss: Glamorgan
Fairbrother hit 100 in 73 balls enabling Lancashire to set the Welshmen a large target. They managed to keep up with the required scoring rate for the first 10 overs but with wickets falling then meekly surrendered.

v KENT (Old Trafford)

June 25

Won by 8 wkts. Lancs 4pts, Kent 0pts

Kent

S.G. Hinks	c Fowler b Allott	3
N.R. Taylor	c Austin b Simmons	23
T.R. Ward	c Wasim Akram b Allott	26
*C.S. Cowdrey	c DeFreitas b Austin	39
G.R. Cowdrey	run out	15
†S.A. Marsh	b Austin	14
M.A. Ealham	b Wasim Akram	24
D.J.M. Kelleher	b DeFreitas	7
R.P. Davis	b DeFreitas	0
H.L. Alleyne	not out	1
A.P. Igglesden	not out	1
Extras	b 4, lb 10, nb 3, w2	19
Total (9 wkts, 39 ov)		172

10, 40, 78, 115, 122, 138, 163, 163, 171

Allott	6	1	25	2
DeFreitas	7	1	24	2
Watkinson	8	0	24	0
Wasim Akram	6	0	26	1
Simmons	8	0	34	1
Austin	4	0	25	2

Lancashire

G.D. Mendis	b Alleyne	19
G. Fowler	c G.R. Cowdrey b C.S. Cowdrey	68
N.H. Fairbrother	not out	82
M. Watkinson	not out	0
†W.K. Hegg		
I.D. Austin		
Wasim Akram		
*D.P. Hughes		
P.A.J. DeFreitas		
P.J.W. Allott		
J. Simmons		
Extras	lb 3, w2	5
Total (2 wkts, 36.1 ov)		174

44,169

Igglesden	8	0	29	0
Kelleher	5	0	18	0
Alleyne	5	0	37	1
Ealham	6	1	25	0
C.S. Cowdrey	5.1	0	23	1
Davis	7	0	39	0

Umpires: D.O. Oslear and B.J. Meyer
Toss: Lancashire
The Kent innings never really got going and progressed in fits and starts to a moderate 172. The only worthy note was Simmons claiming his 300th Sunday League wicket. Lancashire won with no alarms or excursions.

PLAYERS

Paul John Walter ALLOTT *b* 14.9.1956 Altrincham; right-arm fast-medium bowler; lower order right-hand batsman; debut 1978; 13 Tests for England 1981–85
Michael Andrew ATHERTON *b* 23.3.1968 Manchester; right-hand batsman; leg-break bowler; debut 1987; Cambridge University 1987–89; two Tests for England in 1989; selected to tour Zimbabwe 1989–90
Ian David AUSTIN *b* 30.5.1966 Haslingden; left-hand batsman; right-arm medium pace bowler; debut 1987
Phillip Anthony Jason DEFREITAS *b* 18.2.1966 Dominica; right-arm fast-medium bowler; right-hand batsman; debut 1989, previously appeared for Leics 1985–88; 13 Tests for England including one in 1989; selected to tour West Indies 1989–90
Neil Harvey FAIRBROTHER *b* 9.9.1963 Warrington; left-hand batsman; left-arm medium pace bowler; debut 1982; four Tests for England 1987–88
John Dexter FITTON *b* 24.8.1965 Littleborough; off-break bowler; left-hand batsman; debut 1987
Ian FOLLEY *b* 9.1.1963 Burnley; right-hand batsman; slow left-arm bowler; debut 1982
Graeme FOWLER *b* 20.4.1957 Accrington; opening left-hand batsman; debut 1979; 21 Tests for England 1982–85
Andrew Neil HAYHURST *b* 23.11.1962 Davyhulme; right-hand batsman; right-arm medium pace bowler; debut 1985
Warren Kevin HEGG *b* 23.2.1968 Whitefield; wicket-keeper; right hand batsman; debut 1986; capped by county 1989
David Paul HUGHES *b* 13.5.1947 Newton-le-Willows; right-hand batsman; slow left-arm bowler; debut 1967; captain 1987–89
Trevor Edward JESTY *b* 2.6.1949 Gosport; right-hand batsman; right-arm medium pace bowler; debut 1988, previously appeared for Hants (1966–1984) and Surrey (1985–87); 10 One-day Internationals for England; capped by Lancs in 1989, thus being capped by all three of his counties
Graham David LLOYD *b* 1.7.1969 Accrington; right-hand batsman; debut 1988; son of David (ex-Lancs)
Peter James MARTIN *b* 15.11.1968 Accrington; right-hand batsman; right-arm fast-medium bowler; fc debut for county in June 1989
Gehan Dixon MENDIS *b* 24.4.1955 Colombo; opening right-hand batsman; debut 1986, previously appeared for Sussex 1974–85
Balfour Patrick PATTERSON *b* 15.9.1961 Portland, Jamaica; right-arm fast bowler; right-hand batsman; debut 1984, also plays for Jamaica; 17 Tests for West Indies
Jack SIMMONS *b* 28.3.1941 Clayton-le-Moors; off-break bowler; right-hand batsman; oldest player in fc cricket in 1989, but announced retirement during season; debut 1968
Nicholas Jason SPEAK *b* 21.11.1966 Manchester; right-hand batsman; off-break bowler; debut 1986–87 with Lancs in Jamaica
John STANWORTH *b* 30.9.1960; wicket-keeper; right-hand batsman; debut 1983
WASIM AKRAM *b* 3.6.1966 Lahore; left-arm fast medium bowler; attacking left-hand batsman; debut 1988, also plays for Lahore; 30 Tests for Pakistan, including playing for Pakistan *v* India 1989–90
Michael WATKINSON *b* 1.8.1961 Westhoughton; right-hand batsman; right-arm medium-fast bowler; debut 1982

Michael Watkinson, Lancashire's all-rounder, who took 55 wickets and scored 733 runs.
Allsport/Adrian Murrell

REFUGE ASSURANCE LEAGUE

v NORTHAMPTONSHIRE (Old Trafford)
July 16
Won by 3 wkts. Lancs 4pts, Northants 0pts

Northamptonshire		
R.J. Bailey	c Hegg b DeFreitas	5
G. Cook	run out	22
D.J. Capel	c Austin b Simmons	48
*A.J. Lamb	c Hegg b Wasim Akram	10
N.A. Felton	c Hegg b Austin	5
D.J. Wild	c Mendis b Simmons	19
†D. Ripley	lbw b Simmons	5
A. Walker	not out	4
C.E.L. Ambrose	c Hegg b DeFreitas	3
N.G.B. Cook	run out	1
M.A. Robinson	lbw b Wasim Akram	0
Extras	b 2, lb 6, w 1, nb 2	11
Total (38.3 ov)		133

12, 53, 69, 81, 103, 119, 124, 131, 132

Allott	6	0	18	0
DeFreitas	7	1	18	2
Watkinson	6	1	26	0
Wasim Akram	5.3	2	16	2
Austin	6	0	16	1
Simmons	8	0	31	3

Lancashire		
G.D. Mendis	c Felton b Ambrose	0
G. Fowler	not out	53
†W.K. Hegg	c Ripley b Ambrose	8
N.H. Fairbrother	c Walker b Capel	31
M. Watkinson	c Wild b Capel	9
Wasim Akram	c Ambrose b Capel	3
P.A.J. DeFreitas	b N.G.B. Cook	11
*D.P. Hughes	c Felton b N.G.B. Cook	0
I.D Austin	not out	5
P.J.W. Allott		
J. Simmons		
Extras	b 5, lb 7, w 3, nb 1	16
Total (7 wkts, 35 ov)		136

0, 15, 65, 84, 90, 112, 114

Ambrose	8	0	15	2
Robinson	5	0	30	0
Capel	8	0	33	3
Walker	7	1	24	0
N.G.B. Cook	7	2	22	2

Umpires: J.C. Balderstone and N.T. Plews
Toss: Lancashire
Some excellent bowling by the veteran Simmons confined Northants to a very modest total and then Fowler batted with great determination to take his side to victory.

v ESSEX (Old Trafford)
August 13
Abandoned. Lancs 2pts, Essex 2pts

Lancashire		
G.D. Mendis	c Stephenson b Miller	8
G. Fowler	c and b Pringle	30
N.H. Fairbrother	c Miller b Pringle	0
M. Watkinson	c Garnham b Pringle	11
Wasim Akram	c Miller b Gooch	33
P.A.J. DeFreitas	b Miller	3
†W.K. Hegg	c Pringle b Foster	3
*D.P. Hughes	not out	14
I.D. Austin	c Miller b Pringle	13
P.J.W. Allott	b Foster	9
J. Simmons		
Extras	lb 6, w 5	11
Total (9 wkts, 28 ov)		135

38, 40, 49, 68, 79, 95, 95, 121, 135

Lever	6	0	28	0
Foster	7	0	33	2
Miller	7	0	26	2
Pringle	6	1	31	4
Gooch	2	0	11	1

Essex		
*G.A. Gooch	not out	21
B.R. Hardie	not out	27
M.E. Waugh		
P.J. Prichard		
N. Hussain		
J.P. Stephenson		
D.R. Pringle		
†M.A. Garnham		
N.A. Foster		
G. Miller		
J.K. Lever		
Extras	lb 3, w 2	5
Total (0 wkt, 10.4 ov)		53

Allott	5	0	15	0
DeFreitas	4	0	20	0
Wasim Akram	1	0	8	0
Watkinson	0.4	0	7	0

Umpires: B. Leadbeater and D.S. Thompsett
Toss: Essex
A late start meant the match being reduced to 28 overs, but when Essex batted the rain returned at 5.30 and the game had to be abandoned. It was a crucial match for both sides, since they stood first and second in the League table, both with 11 wins when the match began.

v YORKSHIRE (Old Trafford)
August 20
Lost by 42 runs. Yorks 4pts, Lancs 0pts

Yorkshire		
K. Sharp	run out	76
A.A. Metcalfe	c Mendis b DeFreitas	2
†R.J. Blakey	c Hegg b Allott	1
J.D. Love	st Hegg b Simmons	32
P.E. Robinson	not out	51
D. Byas	b Wasim Akram	12
N.G. Nicholson	not out	1
*P. Carrick		
C.S. Pickles		
P.W. Jarvis		
S.D. Fletcher		
Extras	b 4, lb 16, w 5, nb 1	26
Total (5 wkts, 40 ov)		201

10, 11, 85, 149, 200

Allott	6	1	9	1
DeFreitas	6	0	21	1
Watkinson	6	0	34	0
Wasim Akram	8	0	51	1
Austin	8	0	28	0
Simmons	6	0	38	1

Lancashire		
G.D. Mendis	run out	18
G. Fowler	c Love b Byas	32
N.H. Fairbrother	c Robinson b Pickles	7
M. Watkinson	c Love b Carrick	9
Wasim Akram	c Nicholson b Pickles	21
P.A.J. DeFreitas	c Robinson b Pickles	15
*D.P. Hughes	b Fletcher	27
I.D. Austin	b Fletcher	10
†W.K. Hegg	c Love b Jarvis	4
P.J.W. Allott	c Nicholson b Fletcher	1
J. Simmons	not out	1
Extras	b 4, lb 14, w6	24
Total (37.5 ov)		169

50, 59, 70, 82, 116, 119, 140, 167, 168

Jarvis	7	2	21	1
Fletcher	6.5	0	20	3
Pickles	8	0	46	3
Byas	8	0	34	1
Carrick	8	2	30	1

Umpires: P.J. Eele and M.J. Kitchen
Toss: Lancashire
Yorkshire produced a surprise by beating Lancashire, who with one match to go, were leading the League Table. About 13,000 watched the visitors outplay the Red Rose at every turn.

BRITANNIC ASSURANCE COUNTY CHAMPIONSHIP AVERAGES 1989

Batting	*M*	*I*	*NO*	*Runs*	*HS*	*Avge*	*100*	*50*
G.D. Mendis	18	32	3	1314	118	45.31	2	10
N.H. Fairbrother	20	35	3	1336	161	41.75	3	7
T.E. Jesty	19	33	7	1018	93*	39.15	–	8
M.A. Atherton	7	14	2	451	115*	37.58	1	2
G. Fowler	20	36	–	1258	130	34.94	2	9
G.D. Lloyd	6	11	1	334	117	33.40	2	–
P.A.J. DeFreitas	16	26	2	558	78	23.25	–	5
Wasim Akram	11	17	2	334	49	22.27	–	–
M. Watkinson	22	39	6	733	70	22.21	–	4
D.P. Hughes	17	24	5	413	50*	21.74	–	1
N.J. Speak	4	8	1	148	64	21.14	–	1
W.K. Hegg	22	37	4	671	86	20.33	–	5
A.N. Hayhurst	7	12	1	175	34	15.91	–	–
J.D. Fitton	16	22	5	262	43	15.41	–	–
I.D. Austin	8	12	3	133	29	14.78	–	–
J. Simmons	6	9	5	56	16	14.00	–	–
P.J.W. Allott	16	23	5	215	28	11.94	–	–
B.P. Patterson	6	7	3	10	4	2.50	–	–

P.J. Martin played in one match but did not bat.

Bowling	*O*	*M*	*R*	*W*	*Avge*	*BB*	*5i*	*10m*
Wasim Akram	413	88	993	50	19.86	6-70	6	1
B.P. Patterson	173.3	37	517	26	19.88	5-48	1	–
I.D. Austin	163.5	42	449	19	23.63	4-60	–	–
P.A.J. DeFreitas	551.2	115	1602	65	24.65	7-21	4	1
D.P. Hughes	102.1	27	303	12	25.25	3-30	–	–
P.J.W. Allott	442.4	115	10521	41	25.66	5-24	1	–
M. Watkinson	485.5	106	1496	52	28.77	7-69	3	–
J.D. Fitton	429	95	1345	33	40.76	5-53	2	–

Also bowled: M.A. Atherton 100.5-22-22-326-4; N.H. Fairbrother 12-1-71-1; G. Fowler 13-1-61-0; A.N. Hayhurst 47-11-152-4; W.K. Hegg 1-0-7-0; T.E. Jesty 12.5-2-43-0; G.D. Lloyd 5-0-55-0; P.J. Martin 22-3-72-0; G.D. Mendis 2-0-5-0; J. Simmons 100-17-309-3.

Centuries

3 N.H. Fairbrother: 159 v Hants (Portsmouth); 161 v Derbys (Chesterfield); 161 v Yorks (Scarborough).

2 G. Fowler: 130 v Hants (Portsmouth); 123 v Yorks (Scarborough). G.D. Lloyd: 117 v Notts (Worksop); 100 v Essex (Lytham). G.D. Mendis: 118 v Notts (Old Trafford); 103* v Yorks (Old Trafford).

1 M.A. Atherton: 115* v Yorks (Old Trafford).

REFUGE ASSURANCE LEAGUE

v SURREY (Old Trafford)
August 27
Won by 3 wkts. Lancs 4pts, Surrey 0pts

Surrey		
G.S. Clinton	c Hegg b Wasim Akram	33
D.J. Bicknell	run out	8
†A.J. Stewart	b Simmons	56
G.P. Thorpe	c and b Wasim Akram	39
D.M. Ward	b Wasim Akram	3
*I.A. Greig	lbw b Wasim Akram	0
J.D. Robinson	c Fowler b Watkinson	9
K.T. Medlycott	run out	6
C.K. Bullen	not out	13
M.P. Bicknell	run out	4
A.J. Murphy	b Austin	0
Extras	lb 10, w 5	15
Total (40 ov)		186

19, 62, 127, 132, 132, 154, 172, 174, 186

Allott	8	1	25	0
Watkinson	8	0	41	1
Wasim Akram	8	0	30	4
Austin	8	0	41	1
Simmons	8	0	39	1

Lancashire		
G.D. Mendis	c Clinton b Murphy	66
G. Fowler	lbw b Bullen	26
N.H. Fairbrother	lbw b Medlycott	5
T.E. Jesty	run out	10
M. Watkinson	lbw b Bullen	3
Wasim Akram	c Stewart b Robinson	13
*D.P. Hughes	b M.P. Bicknell	20
I.D. Austin	not out	19
P.J.W. Allott	not out	12
J. Simmons		
†W.K. Hegg		
Extras	b 1, lb 10, w 3	14
Total (7 wkts, 39.1 ov)		188

68, 85, 112, 121, 122, 142, 170

Murphy	8	0	35	1
M.P. Bicknell	7.1	0	27	1
Robinson	7	0	40	1
Greig	3	0	16	0
Medlycott	6	0	28	1
Bullen	8	0	31	2

Umpires: B. Hassan and R. Julian
Toss: Surrey
A six off the first ball of the 40th over gave Lancashire the 1989 Refuge League, the batsman being Allott. After appearing in a strong position the home side lost the middle order cheaply. It was announced that this would be the final Sunday League appearance for both Simmons and Hughes.

BENSON AND HEDGES CUP

v LEICESTERSHIRE (Old Trafford)
April 25
Won by 7 wkts. Lancs 2pts, Leics 0pts

Leicestershire		
T.J. Boon	c Mendis b Wasim Akram	11
N.E. Briers	c Hegg b Allott	4
*D.I. Gower	b Allott	19
P. Willey	c Fairbrother b Wasim Akram	23
J.J. Whitaker	c Watkinson b Hayhurst	33
L. Potter	b Simmons	21
C.C. Lewis	not out	23
†P. Whitticase	not out	36
G.J. Parsons		
J.P. Agnew		
G.J.F. Ferris		
Extras	b 2, lb 8, nb 6	16
Total (6 wkts, 55 ov)		186

12, 32, 48, 64, 117, 129

DeFreitas	11	1	44	0
Allott	9.1	2	24	2
Wasim Akram	11	2	36	2
Watkinson	10	2	38	0
Simmons	11	3	23	1
Hayhurst	2.5	0	11	1

Lancashire		
G.D. Mendis	not out	82
G. Fowler	c and b Parsons	78
A.N. Hayhurst	c Whitticase b Agnew	1
N.H. Fairbrother	c Boon b Lewis	11
Wasim Akram	not out	5
M. Watkinson		
*D.P. Hughes		
P.A.J. De Freitas		
†W.K. Hegg		
P.J.W. Allott		
J. Simmons		
Extras	lb 3, w 2, nb 5	10
Total (3 wkts, 52.3 ov)		187

156, 159, 182

Ferris	10	1	26	0
Agnew	11	1	47	1
Lewis	9.3	0	47	1
Parsons	11	4	26	1
Willey	11	1	38	0

Umpires: D.O. Oslear and N.T. Plews
Toss: Leicestershire. Gold: G.D. Mendis
Mendis and Fowler ensured victory for Lancs with a 1st wicket stand worth 156. Fowler played a scratchy innings and was dropped twice, but Mendis played a very sound knock. Leicestershire never really recovered from the early loss of Gower and the tail was always fighting a rearguard action.

v WARWICKSHIRE (Old Trafford)
May 13
Won by 5 wkts. Lancs 2pts, Warwicks 0pts

Warwickshire		
*T.A. Lloyd	lbw b Allott	9
A.J. Moles	b Wasim Akram	65
Asif Din	c Fairbrother b Wasim Akram	27
A.I. Kallicharran	c and b DeFreitas	32
D.A. Thorne	not out	24
P.A. Smith	c Allott b Watkinson	10
†G.W. Humpage	lbw b Simmons	7
G.C. Small	b DeFreitas	11
A.R.K. Pierson	run out	1
A.A. Donald	not out	2
T.A. Munton		
Extras	lb 9, nb 2	11
Total (8 wkts, 55 ov)		199

15, 62, 138, 143, 166, 175, 190, 193

DeFreitas	11	3	40	2
Allott	11	1	33	1
Wasim Akram	11	2	40	2
Watkinson	11	2	38	1
Simmons	11	2	39	1

Lancashire		
G.D. Mendis	lbw b Donald	0
G. Fowler	c and b Pierson	41
†W.K. Hegg	retired hurt	10
N.H. Fairbrother	not out	69
T.E. Jesty	c Thorne b Munton	34
M. Watkinson	c Humpage b Smith	1
Wasim Akram	c Humpage b Small	30
*D.P. Hughes	not out	3
P.A.J. DeFreitas		
P.J.W. Allott		
J. Simmons		
Extras	lb 10, w 3, nb 2	15
Total (5 wkts, 47.5 ov)		203

0, 66, 131, 132, 195

Donald	10	2	28	1
Small	10	2	44	1
Smith	7.5	0	53	1
Pierson	11	3	28	1
Munton	9	1	40	1

Umpires: K.J. Lyons and A.G.T. Whitehead
Toss: Lancashire. Gold: N.H. Fairbrother
Moles hit 9 boundaries in reaching 50 and Kallicharran played some useful shots, but Warwickshire were unable to score fast enough. They then fatally dropped Fairbrother and his innings took Lancashire to victory.

Away Matches

The full scorecard of each of Lancashire's away matches will be found in the sections for the respective home teams.

Edgbaston: April 20, 21, 22, 24
Lancs 259 and 171 (G.C. Small 5–55) drew with Warwicks 210 and 81–4. Lancs 7pts, Warwicks 6pts.

Worcester: May 4, 5, 6
Lancs 171 and 231 beat Worcs 166 (Wasim Akram 5–52) and 170 (M. Watkinson 5–44) by 66 runs. Lancs 21pts, Worcs 5pts.

Taunton: May 20, 22, 23
Somerset 399–4d (S.J. Cook 156, C.J. Tavare 153) and 203–4d lost to Lancs 303–8d and 302–4 by 6 wkts. Lancs 21pts, Somerset 7pts.

The Oval: May 24, 25, 26
Lancs 257 and 232–4d drew with Surrey 200–3d (D.J. Bicknell 100*) and 119–3. Surrey 6pts, Lancs 4pts.

Lord's July 1, 3, 4
Lancs 161 and 96 beat Middx 96 (B.P. Patterson 5–48) and 43 (P.A.J. DeFreitas 7–21) by 218 runs. Lancs 21pts, Middx 4pts.

Leicester: July 5, 6, 7
Lancs 411–9d drew with Leics 187 (P.J.W. Allott 5–24) and 91–2. Lancs 8pts, Leics 5pts.

Portsmouth: July 22, 24, 25
Lancs 475–4d (N.H. Fairbrother 159, G. Fowler 130) and 147–6d lost to Hants 336–4d (R.A. Smith 119*) and 287–7 by 3 wkts. Hants 21pts, Lancs 5pts.

Worksop: July 26, 27, 28
Notts 327–8d (D.W. Randall 130) and 211 lost to Lancs 230 and 309–4 (G.D. Lloyd 117) by 6wkts. Lancs 21pts, Notts 8pts.

Cheltenham: August 5, 7, 8
Lancs 93 (C.A Walsh 6–40) and 278 lost to Gloucs 394 (P. Bainbridge 128, M.W. Alleyne 111, P.A.J. DeFreitas 5–123) by an innings and 23 runs. Gloucs 24pts, Lancs 2pts.

Chesterfield: August 9, 10, 11
Lancs 372 (N.H. Fairbrother 161) and 201 drew with Derbys 354 (P.A.J. DeFreitas 6–116) and 193–8. Lancs 8pts, Derbys 8pts.

Scarborough: Sept 8, 9, 10, 11
Lancs 347 (N.H. Fairbrother 161) and 369–8d (G. Fowler 123, J. Batty 5–118) beat Yorks 237 (J.D. Fitton 5–53) and 295 (P.E. Robinson 117) by 184 runs. Lancs 24pts, Yorks 6pts.

v NOTTINGHAMSHIRE (Old Trafford)

April 27, 28, 29 May 1
Drawn. Lancs 7pts, Notts 5 pts

Lancashire 1st Innings

G. Fowler	c Newell b Saxelby	4
G.D. Mendis	lbw b Hemmings	118
A.N. Hayhurst	c Robinson b Hemmings	22
†W.K. Hegg	b Evans	13
T.E. Jesty	b Evans	44
M. Watkinson	not out	61
*D.P. Hughes	b Hemmings	13
Wasim Akram	not out	9
P.A.J. DeFreitas		
J.D. Fitton		
J. Simmons		
Extras	lb 13, nb 3	16
Total (6 wkts dec, 92.1 ov)		300

10, 72, 115, 179, 238, 286

Stephenson	21	5	80	0
Saxelby	15	1	68	1
Cooper	21.1	7	46	0
Hemmings	22	5	57	3
Evans	13	2	36	2

Nottinghamshire 1st Innings

B.C. Broad	c Hegg b DeFreitas	1
*R.T. Robinson	c Hegg b Wasim Akram	66
M. Newell	b DeFreitas	99
P. Johnson	c Fowler b Wasim Akram	2
D.W. Randall	b Wasim Akram	0
F.D. Stephenson	lbw b Wasim Akram	0
†B.N. French	c Fowler b Wasim Akram	5
K.P. Evans	lbw b Simmons	55
E.E. Hemmings	c Fitton b Wasim Akram	3
K. Saxelby	not out	7
K.E. Cooper	not out	23
Extras	lb 4, w 1, nb 17	22
Total (100 ov: 251–7) (9 wkts dec)		283

10, 107, 117, 119, 120, 137, 242, 252, 253

Wasim Akram	29	3	70	6
DeFreitas	32	5	81	2
Watkinson	18	1	40	0
Simmons	24	7	58	1
Fitton	6	1	30	0

Lancashire 2nd Innings

G. Fowler	b Stephenson	4
G.D. Mendis	not out	81
A.N. Hayhurst	c French b Evans	33
T.E. Jesty	c Randall b Stephenson	4
†W.K. Hegg	b Saxelby	50
M. Watkinson	lbw b Saxelby	1
*D.P. Hughes	c Saxelby b Hemmings	23
Wasim Akram	c Broad b Cooper	24
P.A.J. DeFreitas	not out	11
Extras	b 4, lb 12, nb 3	19
Total (7 wkts dec)		250

7, 42, 96, 134, 136, 183, 227

Stephenson	11	4	21	2
Saxelby	13	4	39	2
Cooper	6.3	4	13	1
Hemmings	28	7	94	1
Evans	9	1	23	1
Newell	8	0	44	0

Nottinghamshire 2nd Innings

B.C. Broad	not out	56
*R.T. Robinson	not out	77
Extras	b 1, lb 4, w 3, nb 6	14
Total (0 wkt)		147

Wasim Akram	13	3	21	0
DeFreitas	11	1	39	0
Watkinson	6	1	27	0
Simmons	9	1	34	0
Hughes	4	0	21	0

Umpires: H.D. Bird and D.R. Shepherd
Toss: Lancashire

The first day's play was reduced to 30 overs due to rain, the home side reaching 74–2. Mendis 47 not out overnight went on to 118 in 275 minutes on the second day and Hughes declared as soon as full batting points were gained. Notts were 106–1 at the close. Newell held the side together on the third day occupying the crease for 348 minutes, but poor light aided Akram and the rest of the attack. On the last afternoon Notts were set 268 off 55 overs, but did not attempt to chase the runs.

v WARWICKSHIRE (Old Trafford)

May 17, 18, 19
Won by 62 runs. Lancs 23pts, Warwicks 5pts

Lancashire 1st Innings

G. Fowler	b Smith	30
A.N. Hayhurst	b Small	2
N.J. Speak	c Asif Din b Small	39
N.H. Fairbrother	c Lloyd b Munton	23
T.E. Jesty	c Humpage b Small	1
M. Watkinson	lbw b Munton	7
Wasim Akram	retired hurt	21
†W.K. Hegg	c Thorne b Munton	4
P.A.J. DeFreitas	c Humpage b Smith	78
*P.J.W. Allott	c Pierson b Donald	26
J. Simmons	not out	5
Extras	b 8, lb 12, w 1, nb 4	25
Total (82.4 ov)		261

8, 50, 99, 102, 117, 120, 125, 251, 261

Donald	20.4	4	58	1
Small	21	10	39	3
Munton	22	3	74	3
Smith	16	5	43	2
Pierson	3	0	27	0

Warwickshire 1st Innings

*T.A. Lloyd	c Hegg b DeFreitas	4
A.J. Moles	c sub b Allott	0
Asif Din	c Hegg b Watkinson	67
A.I. Kallicharran	lbw b Watkinson	29
D.A. Thorne	b Watkinson	6
P.A. Smith	c Jesty b Watkinson	19
†G.W. Humpage	lbw b DeFreitas	9
G.C. Small	c Hegg b DeFreitas	2
A.A. Donald	c Hegg b Watkinson	0
A.R.K. Pierson	c Allott b DeFreitas	8
T.A. Munton	not out	6
Extras	b 3, lb 3, w 1, nb 1	8
Total (69 ov)		158

1, 19, 97, 109, 114, 128, 142, 142, 142

DeFreitas	30	10	65	4
Allott	17	2	42	1
Watkinson	22	3	45	5

Lancashire 2nd Innings

A.N. Hayhurst	c Humpage b Smith	9
G. Fowler	c Moles b Donald	4
N.J. Speak	not out	6
N.H. Fairbrother	c Humpage b Donald	62
T.E. Jesty	c Thorne b Donald	7
M. Watkinson	c Humpage b Small	1
P.A.J. DeFreitas	c Lloyd b Small	0
†W.K. Hegg	c Thorne b Small	13
Wasim Akram	lbw b Smith	2
*P.J.W. Allott	c Kallicharran b Donald	0
J. Simmons	b Smith	13
Extras	b 11, lb 2, nb 3	16
Total		133

9, 35, 44, 44, 87, 107, 110, 110, 110

Donald	17	8	23	4
Small	18	2	52	3
Munton	6	1	16	0
Smith	10	2	29	3

Warwickshire 2nd Innings

*T.A. Lloyd	c Hegg b DeFreitas	3
A.R.K. Pierson	c Allott b Watkinson	18
A.J. Moles	b Wasim Akrim	10
Asif Din	c Hegg b Wasim Akram	15
A.I. Kallicharran	lbw b Wasim Akram	5
D.A. Thorne	c Hegg b DeFreitas	1
P.A. Smith	c Wasim Akram b DeFreitas	24
†G.W. Humpage	b DeFreitas	42
G.C. Small	lbw b Allott	10
A.A. Donald	c and b Allott	9
T.A. Munton	not out	0
Extras	b 3, lb 20, w 1, nb 13	37
Total		174

6, 36, 46, 60, 63, 70, 130, 163, 174

DeFreitas	27	7	47	4
Allott	14.2	3	24	2
Watkinson	16	8	22	1
Wasim Akram	26	7	58	3

Umpires: J.H. Hampshire & J.C. Balderstone
Toss: Warwickshire

DeFreitas, aided first by Wasim, who retired struck on the face by Donald, and then Allott, added 126 for the 8th wicket and thus provided Lancashire with a reasonable total. Warwickshire were 50–2 off 24 overs at stumps. Donald did more damage on the second day, forcing two batsmen to retire temporarily for repairs. Warwickshire began the final day needing 237 to win, but only Humpage in the later stages held up Lancashire for long.

v SUSSEX (Liverpool)

May 27, 29, 30

Drawn. Sussex 7pts, Lancs 4pts

Sussex 1st Innings

D.M. Smith	c Allott b Fitton	101
N.J. Lenham	c Hughes b Patterson	8
*P.W.G. Parker	c Allott b Austin	9
A.P. Wells	c Patterson b Fitton	52
C.M. Wells	lbw b Austin	66
I.J. Gould	c Hegg b Austin	20
A.I.C. Dodemaide	b Fitton	1
†P. Moores	not out	38
A.C.S. Pigott	not out	22
I. Salisbury		
A.M. Babington		
Extras	b 4, lb 11, nb 2	17
Total (100 ov: 273–8) (7 wkts dec)		334

29, 50, 145, 248, 254, 259, 283

Patterson	26	2	91	1
Allott	16	5	54	0
Austin	28	7	59	3
Watkinson	13	3	28	0
Fitton	38	11	87	3

Lancashire 1st Innings

G.D. Mendis	run out	10
G. Fowler	c Moores b Babington	7
†W.K. Hegg	lbw b Pigott	19
N.H. Fairbrother	c Moores b Babington	10
M. Watkinson	b Pigott	35
*D.P. Hughes	lbw b Babington	13
I.D. Austin	lbw b Salisbury	29
T.E. Jesty	b Babington	48
J.D. Fitton	c Smith b Salisbury	16
P.J.W. Allott	not out	2
B.P. Patterson	b Babington	4
Extras	lb 10, nb 1	11
Total (72.3 ov)		204

16, 39, 49, 49, 73, 120, 150, 192, 199

Pigott	12	3	45	2
Salisbury	23	6	72	2
Babington	18.3	5	37	5
Dodemaide	12	3	28	0
C.M. Wells	7	2	12	0

Sussex 2nd Innings

N.J. Lenham	lbw b Fitton	25
D.M. Smith	c Hegg b Allott	10
*P.W.G. Parker	c Fitton b Watkinson	17
A.P. Wells	not out	63
C.M. Wells	c Hegg b Watkinson	46
I.J. Gould	not out	16
Extras	lb 5, nb 3	8
Total (4 wkts dec)		185

16, 50, 58, 147

Patterson	9	0	42	0
Allott	11	0	36	1
Austin	3	0	8	0
Watkinson	11	2	29	2
Fitton	23	4	65	1

Lancashire 2nd Innings

G.D. Mendis	c Moores b Pigott	84
G. Fowler	c Moores b Pigott	49
N.H. Fairbrother	c Moores b Babington	24
†W.K. Hegg	b Pigott	0
T.E. Jesty	b Babington	50
M. Watkinson	c Lenham b Babington	4
D.P. Hughes	lbw b Babington	1
I.D. Austin	b Salisbury	1
P.J.W. Allott	not out	18
J.D. Fitton	not out	14
Extras	b 2, lb 17, nb 2	21
Total (8 wkts)		266

132, 147, 155, 221, 228, 229, 230

Dodemaide	17	1	31	0
Pigott	18	1	63	3
Babington	9	2	23	4
Salisbury	25.5	4	109	1
C.M. Wells	8	2	21	0

Umpires: J.W. Holder and B. Leadbeater
Toss: Sussex

On the first day runs came slowly and at the close Sussex were 288–7. On Monday a further 46 were added in 40 minutes before the declaration. Babington returned a career best 5–37 on a slow dry pitch and Salisbury, making his debut took 2 wickets. Sussex began the last day on 54–2 and later set Lancashire 316 off 68 overs. Jesty hit 50 in 37 minutes, mainly off Salisbury, but with wickets falling, Lancashire were happy to hold out for a draw.

v GLAMORGAN (Old Trafford)

June 17, 19, 20

Lost by 9 runs. Glamorgan 23pts, Lancs 5pts

Glamorgan 1st Innings

A.P. Butcher	lbw b Wasim Akram	68
*H. Morris	c DeFreitas b Allott	69
M.J. Cann	c Hegg b Wasim Akram	39
M.P. Maynard	c Hegg b Allott	24
R.J. Shastri	lbw b Wasim Akram	0
G.C. Holmes	lbw b Wasim Akram	1
I. Smith	not out	25
†C.P. Metson	b Watkinson	19
S.J. Dennis	b Wasim Akram	4
S.L Watkin	run out	1
S.R. Barwick	not out	0
Extras	b 9, lb 18, w 3, nb 17	47
Total (9 wkts dec, 100 ov)		297

133, 189, 226, 229, 236, 238, 285, 291, 296

Wasim Akram	28	8	45	5
DeFreitas	21	4	52	0
Watkinson	19	2	79	1
Allott	22	3	69	2
Hayhurst	10	4	25	0

Lancashire 1st Innings

G. Fowler	c Metson b Dennis	0
G.D. Mendis	lbw b Watkin	1
*D.P. Hughes	c Metson b Watkin	0
A.N. Hayhurst	c Metson b Watkin	7
N.H. Fairbrother	c Metson b Watkin	2
T.E. Jesty	c Shastri b Watkin	21
M. Watkinson	c Smith b Barwick	4
Wasim Akram	c Barwick b Watkin	18
†W.K. Hegg	c Shastri b Watkin	73
P.A.J. DeFreitas	c Watkin b Dennis	59
P.J.W. Allott	not out	2
Extras	b 6, lb 3	9
Total (47.2 ov)		196

0, 6, 9, 11, 26, 41, 47, 59, 192

Watkin	22	5	65	7
Dennis	12.2	2	64	2
Barwick	12	1	58	1
Shastri	1	1	0	0

Glamorgan 2nd Innings

A.R. Butcher	c Hegg b Allott	69
*H. Morris	c Hegg b Allott	16
M.J. Cann	lbw b Allott	1
R.J. Shastri	c Hegg b DeFreitas	11
G.C. Holmes	c Mendis b Hayhurst	28
M.P. Maynard	c and b Hughes	52
I. Smith	not out	51
†C.P. Metson	not out	1
Extras	lb 2, w 6, nb 15	23
Total (6 wkts dec)		252

32, 39, 89, 149, 159, 238

Wasim Akram	17	2	50	0
DeFreitas	17	3	57	1
Allott	17	5	33	3
Watkinson	13	4	33	0
Hayhurst	12	2	57	1
Hughes	3	0	6	1
Jesty	0.5	0	14	0

Lancashire 2nd Innings

G. Fowler	c Metson b Watkin	19
G.D. Mendis	run out	67
A.N. Hayhurst	c Metson b Shastri	34
N.H. Fairbrother	run out	65
T.E. Jesty	c Maynard b Watkin	4
M. Watkinson	lbw b Watkin	0
Wasim Akram	c Metson b Watkin	37
†W.K. Hegg	lbw b Watkin	0
P.A.J. DeFreitas	c Butcher b Watkin	59
*D.P. Hughes	not out	26
P.J.W. Allott	c Butcher b Shastri	20
Extras	lb 10, w 2, nb 1	13
Total		344

40, 126, 135, 144, 144, 194, 194, 286, 298

Watkin	24	3	94	6
Dennis	17	2	29	0
Barwick	23	3	83	0
Shastri	32.5	4	128	2

Umpires: P.J. Eele and R. Palmer
Toss: Lancashire

Watkin, who was awarded his county cap immediately after the match, took 13 wickets and enabled Glamorgan to win off the penultimate ball – their first victory at Old Trafford in 28 years. On the first day Watkin reduced Lancashire to 11–4 in reply to 297–9 dec. The home side then made a splendid late recovery with 133 added for the 9th wicket by Hegg and DeFreitas. Glamorgan however had the last laugh.

v NORTHAMPTONSHIRE (Southport)

June 21, 22, 23

Drawn. Lancs 8pts, Northants 3pts

Lancashire 1st Innings

G. Fowler	c and b N.G.B. Cook	92
G.D. Mendis	c N.G.B. Cook b Davis	27
†W.K. Hegg	c Ripley b Robinson	31
N.H. Fairbrother	run out	81
T.E. Jesty	c Ripley b N.G.B. Cook	31
M. Watkinson	c Thomas b N.G.B. Cook	18
Wasim Akram	lbw b N.G.B. Cook	3
*D.P. Hughes	c Larkins b Robinson	28
P.A.J. DeFreitas	c Thomas b N.G.B. Cook	13
J.D. Fitton	b N.G.B. Cook	1
P.J.W. Allott	not out	1
Extras	lb 1, w 1, nb 8	10
Total (100 ov: 316–7)		336

61, 105, 221, 251, 281, 292, 293, 333, 334

Davis	23	1	91	1
Thomas	13	3	46	0
N.G.B. Cook	27.1	8	56	6
Bailey	7	0	23	0
Robinson	20	6	72	2
Capel	14	2	47	0

Northamptonshire 1st Innings

G. Cook	c Allott b DeFreitas	4
N.G.B. Cook	c Jesty b DeFreitas	2
*W. Larkins	lbw b DeFreitas	12
N.A. Felton	c Hughes b Watkinson	37
R.J. Bailey	c Hegg b Wasim Akram	15
D.J. Capel	c Hegg b DeFreitas	34
A. Fordham	c Allott b Watkinson	0
†D. Ripley	b Watkinson	0
J.G. Thomas	c Allott b DeFreitas	4
W.W. Davis	c Wasim Akram b Watkinson	19
M.A. Robinson	not out	0
Extras	lb 4, w 2, nb 11	17
Total (57 ov)		144

8, 16, 27, 48, 116, 120, 120, 122, 140

Wasim Akram	15	3	40	1
DeFreitas	21	7	46	5
Allott	5	2	16	0
Watkinson	14	6	30	4
Fitton	2	0	8	0

Northamptonshire 2nd Innings

G. Cook	c Hegg b Watkinson	128
W. Larkins	c Hughes b Wasim Akram	5
N.A. Felton	c Fairbrother b Fitton	26
R.J. Bailey	c Fowler b Hughes	134
D.J. Capel	lbw b Fitton	22
A. Fordham	not out	37
†D. Ripley	c Allott b Hughes	16
J.G. Thomas	c Watkinson b Hughes	0
N.G.B. Cook	not out	7
Extras	lb 12, w 1, nb 19	32
Total (7 wkts dec)		407

22, 68, 269, 339, 353, 381, 381

Wasim Akram	31	5	95	1
DeFreitas	11	1	43	0
Allott	24	9	37	0
Watkinson	19	4	61	1
Fitton	42	8	125	2
Hughes	19	6	34	3
Fairbrother	1	1	0	0

Umpires: B.J. Meyer and R. Palmer
Toss: Lancashire

A steady innings by Fowler – 92 in 280 minutes – combined with brilliant strokeplay by Fairbrother – 81 in 115 minutes – gave Lancashire the advantage on the first day. Northants, who were 8–1 overnight, were dismissed for 144 and Hughes enforced the follow on. The visitors responded with a much more workmanlike effort and at tea the match was saved. What happened in the last session of play was academic.

v KENT (Old Trafford)

June 24, 26, 27

Drawn. Kent 7pts, Lancs 6pts

Kent 1st Innings		
N.R. Taylor	lbw b Patterson	13
S.G. Hinks	c Fowler b Patterson	4
R.F Pienaar	b Patterson	23
T.R. Ward	c Hughes b Patterson	24
*C.S. Cowdrey	c Allott b Fitton	13
V.J. Wells	c Hughes b Fitton	22
†S.A. Marsh	c Fairbrother b Watkinson	59
M.A. Ealham	c Jesty b Watkinson	45
D.J.M. Kelleher	c Fitton b Watkinson	38
R.P. Davis	c Allott b Fitton	34
A.P. Igglesden	not out	0
Extras	b 2, lb 18, w 1	21
Total (100 ovL: 251–8)		296

16, 17, 52, 79, 87, 133, 207, 224, 296

Patterson	28	9	65	4
Allott	19	1	67	0
Fitton	40	11	98	3
Watkinson	13.1	7	32	3
Hughes	8	2	14	0

Lancashire 1st Innings		
G.D. Mendis	c Wells b Davis	75
G. Fowler	b Davis	65
A.N. Hayhurst	c Cowdrey b Davis	11
N.H. Fairbrother	c Davis b Igglesden	16
T.E. Jesty	not out	55
M. Watkinson	c Igglesden b Kelleher	15
†W.K. Hegg	lbw b Igglesden	11
*D.P. Hughes	c Cowdrey b Igglesden	0
J.D. Fitton	b Igglesden	0
P.J.W. Allott	c Cowdrey b Igglesden	26
B.P. Patterson	c Marsh b Igglesden	0
Extras	b 11, lb 5, nb 8	24
Total (95 ov)		298

143, 162, 171, 183, 213, 251, 251, 257, 292

Igglesden	28	7	73	6
Kelleher	16	2	70	1
Davis	41	13	105	3
Ealham	5	0	26	0
Cowdrey	4	1	8	0
Ward	1	1	0	0

Kent 2nd Innings		
N.R. Taylor	lbw b Hayhurst	10
S.G. Hinks	c Allott b Fitton	7
R.F. Pienaar	c Fowler b Fitton	0
T.R. Ward	not out	10
V.J. Wells	not out	12
Extras	lb 3	3
Total (3 wkts)		42

17, 17, 22

Allott	4	2	6	0
Fitton	6	4	5	2
Watkinson	4	0	6	0
Hegg	1	0	7	0
Jesty	3	1	6	0
Hughes	7	5	4	0
Hayhurst	4	2	5	1

Umpires: B.J. Meyer and D.O. Oslear
Toss: Kent

Kent found runs coming slowly on Saturday and only managed 3 batting points by a very narrow margin. It was however an improvement on the prospect at lunch and this was due to a fine 45 on his debut by Ealham, son of the old captain. On Monday Lancashire also found scoring difficult and they were 247–5 off 81 overs at the close, rain having reduced the playing time. Rain prevented play until 2.40 on the last day and thus the only objective was bonus points. Igglesden in a spell which included 5 for 10 managed to dismiss Lancashire 2 runs short of their target.

v WORCESTERSHIRE (Old Trafford)

July 19, 20, 21

Lost by 36 runs. Worcs 21pts, Lancs 4pts

Worcestershire 1st Innings		
T.S. Curtis	c Atherton b Patterson	0
G.J. Lord	c Hegg b Patterson	13
G.A. Hick	c Fowler b Allott	21
B.D. d'Oliveira	retired hurt	11
P.A. Neale	c Hegg b Patterson	62
I.T. Botham	c and b Allott	1
†S.J. Rhodes	b Allott	8
M.J. Weston	c Atherton b Patterson	12
N.V. Radford	c Hegg b DeFreitas	14
R.K. Illingworth	c Allott b DeFreitas	0
G.R. Dilley	c Fairbrother b Watkinson	31
Extras	lb 7, w 1, nb 10	18
Total (67.3 ov)		191

0, 38, 48, 54, 62, 90, 124, 124, 168

Patterson	19	4	61	4
DeFreitas	18	3	46	2
Allott	18	4	51	3
Watkinson	11.3	3	25	1
Atherton	1	0	1	0

Lancashire 1st Innings		
G.D. Mendis	c Rhodes b Dilley	0
G. Fowler	c Radford b Botham	30
M.A. Atherton	c Rhodes b Dilley	0
N.H Fairbrother	c Illingworth b Dilley	0
T.E. Jesty	retired hurt	32
†W.K. Hegg	lbw b Radford	0
M. Watkinson	c Weston b Dilley	18
*D.P. Hughes	c Rhodes b Botham	10
P.A.J. DeFreitas	c Neale b Botham	14
P.J.W. Allott	b Dilley	0
B.P. Patterson	not out	0
Extras	b 4, lb 11, w 1, nb 5	21
Total (40.2 ov)		125

0, 5, 5, 70, 72, 99, 123, 125, 125

Dilley	12.2	0	30	5
Radford	13	4	41	1
Botham	15	1	39	3

Worcestershire 2nd Innings		
T.S. Curtis	c Hegg b Patterson	21
G.J. Lord	c Hughes b Patterson	3
G.A. Hick	c Mendis b Watkinson	16
†S.J. Rhodes	c Atherton b Patterson	13
*P.A. Neale	c Hegg b Watkinson	14
I.T. Botham	c Hegg b Watkinson	73
M.J. Weston	c Jesty b Watkinson	22
B.D. d'Oliveira	c Hegg b Watkinson	10
N.V. Radford	c Hegg b Watkinson	0
R.K. Illingworth	lbw b Watkinson	10
G.R. Dilley	not out	0
Extras	b 4, lb 5, w 1, nb 7	17
Total		199

30, 37, 59, 65, 138, 155, 181, 184, 190

Patterson	12.1	3	28	3
DeFreitas	2	0	13	0
Allott	20	4	55	0
Watkinson	25	7	69	7
Atherton	9.5	2	25	0

Lancashire 2nd Innings		
G.D. Mendis	c Hick b Botham	70
G. Fowler	c sub b Radford	12
M.A. Atherton	c Hick b Botham	59
N.H. Fairbrother	c Rhodes b Radford	39
T.E. Jesty	c Hick b Dilley	7
M. Watkinson	c Hick b Dilley	7
†W.K. Hegg	c Hick b Dilley	9
*D.P. Hughes	not out	7
P.A.J. DeFreitas	c Rhodes b Dilley	0
P.J.W. Allott	b Botham	5
B.P. Patterson	c Rhodes b Dilley	1
Extras	lb 5, nb 8	13
Total		229

31, 111, 168, 182, 205, 205, 216, 216, 224

Dilley	27.1	4	94	5
Radford	17	1	63	2
Botham	19	4	55	3
Weston	4	0	12	0

Umpires: R. Julian and K.J. Lyons
Toss: Lancashire

On a wicket assisting the faster bowlers, 19 wickets fell on the first day. Neale, 200 minutes for 62, was the only batsman to survive for long. Jesty, retired hurt, hit on the head. At the close of the second day Lancashire appeared on the verge of victory needing 106 to win with 8 wickets standing, Atherton 33*, Fairbrother 37*. On Friday Dilley destroyed this hope – the remaining 8 wickets went down for 61 runs. Hick took 4 slip catches.

v ESSEX (Lytham)

August 12, 14, 15

Lost by 7 wkts. Essex 23pts, Lancs 1pt

Lancashire 1st Innings		
G.D. Lloyd	lbw b Pringle	3
G.D. Mendis	lbw b Topley	24
G. Fowler	c Topley b Pringle	23
*N.H. Fairbrother	c Stephenson b Topley	0
N.J. Speak	lbw b Foster	8
M. Watkinson	c Pringle b Foster	16
†W.K. Hegg	lbw b Foster	0
P.A.J. DeFreitas	c Prichard b Topley	15
I.D. Austin	c Garnham b Foster	0
J.D. Fitton	c Stephenson b Topley	0
J. Simmons	not out	2
Extras	lb 2, nb 2	4
Total (39.5 ov)		95

8, 50, 50, 53, 76, 76, 77, 83, 84

Foster	15	5	31	4
Pringle	11	2	27	2
Childs	3	1	2	0
Topley	10.5	2	33	4

Essex 1st Innings		
*G.A. Gooch	lbw b DeFreitas	68
J.P. Stephenson	c Hegg b DeFreitas	171
P.J. Prichard	c Hegg b Watkinson	19
M.E. Waugh	lbw b Austin	24
N. Hussain	not out	105
†M.A. Garnham	not out	3
Nadim Shahid		
D.R. Pringle		
N.A. Foster		
T.D. Topley		
J.H. Childs		
Extras	b 2, lb 2, nb 6	10
Total (100 ov: 272–3) (4 wkts dec)		400

120, 155, 215, 377

DeFreitas	26	5	94	2
Watkinson	29	5	103	1
Austin	25	5	56	1
Fitton	25	4	76	0
Simmons	25	3	67	0

Lancashire 2nd Innings		
G.D. Lloyd	c Gooch b Foster	100
G.D. Mendis	c Gooch b Foster	10
N.J. Speak	lbw b Childs	64
*N.H. Fairbrother	c Gooch b Shahid	60
G. Fowler	c Prichard b Childs	8
M. Watkinson	c Garnham b Pringle	21
†W.K. Hegg	lbw b Pringle	1
P.A.J. DeFreitas	lbw b Topley	50
I.D. Austin	c Hussain b Childs	14
J.D. Fitton	not out	32
J. Simmons	lbw b Foster	2
Extras	b 10, lb 5, w 1, nb 3	19
Total		381

15, 161, 211, 249, 254, 275, 278, 299, 378

Foster	34	5	134	2
Pringle	22	2	75	2
Childs	43	15	80	4
Topley	12	2	23	1
Shahid	17	3	51	1
Gooch	2	1	3	0

Essex 2nd Innings		
*G.A. Gooch	run out	20
J.P. Stephenson	c Hegg b Watkinson	7
M.E. Waugh	not out	23
P.J. Prichard	run out	10
N. Hussain	not out	14
Extras	lb 4, w 1	5
Total (3 wkts)		79

25, 27, 45

DeFreitas	6	0	44	0
Watkinson	5.5	0	31	1

Umpires: B. Leadbeater and D.S. Thompsett
Toss: Lancashire

The match was more or less decided on the first day, when very feeble batting saw Lancashire dismissed for 95 and without Patterson, Allott or Akram, Essex then scored freely, being 191–2 at stumps. On Monday they declared as soon as Hussain had reached 100 off 159 balls. Lancashire began the last day at 91–1. Lloyd, Speak and Fairbrother batted well and Essex had 14 overs in which to make 79. Some wayward bowling by DeFreitas enabled them to achieve their target without too much heartburn.

v YORKSHIRE (Old Trafford)

August 19, 21, 22

Won by 181 runs. Lancs 23 pts, Yorks 5pts

Lancashire 1st Innings

G. Fowler	c Robinson c Carrick	25
G.D. Mendis	c Swallow b Carrick	28
M.A. Atherton	not out	115
N.H. Fairbrother	c Robinson b Swallow	1
M. Watkinson	c Blakey b Jarvis	48
Wasim Akram	lbw b Carrick	4
†W.K. Hegg	lbw b Jarvis	4
*D.P. Hughes	c Moxon b Carrick	15
P.A.J. DeFreitas	st Blakey b Swallow	12
J.D. Fitton	run out	16
P.W.J. Allott	b Jarvis	7
Extras	b 2, lb 7, w 4, nb 5	18
Total (100 ov: 288–9)		293

52, 62, 69, 129, 134, 145, 212, 251, 275

Jarvis	23.5	5	61	3
Fletcher	15	5	38	0
Pickles	5	2	4	0
Carrick	39	17	85	4
Swallow	20	3	96	2

Yorkshire 1st Innings

M.D. Moxon	lbw b Fitton	21
A.A. Metcalfe	c and b Atherton	44
†R.J. Blakey	b Wasim Akram	56
K. Sharp	c and b Hughes	20
P.E. Robinson	b Wasim Akram	2
D. Byas	c Hegg b Wasim Akram	3
*P. Carrick	b Hughes	1
I.G. Swallow	not out	18
C.S. Pickles	b Wasim Akram	0
P.W. Jarvis	c sub b Hughes	4
S.D. Fletcher	b Wasim Akram	1
Extras	b 5, lb 10, w 1, nb 6	22
Total (88.5 ov)		192

55, 104, 139, 159, 160, 163, 174, 175, 182

Wasim Akram	26.5	9	44	5
DeFreitas	8	1	29	0
Fitton	20	5	48	1
Atherton	13	3	26	1
Hughes	21	10	30	3

Lancashire 2nd Innings

G.D. Mendis	not out	103
M.A. Atherton	b Pickles	16
N.H. Fairbrother	c Blakey b Jarvis	40
J.D. Fitton	c Moxon b Pickles	6
M. Watkinson	not out	51
Extras	b 2, lb 10	12
Total (3 wkts dec)		228

46, 121, 144

Jarvis	11	2	35	1
Fletcher	2	1	5	0
Pickles	14	3	47	1
Carrick	5	5	39	0
Swallow	9	1	44	1
Sharp	1	0	6	0
Byas	4.4	0	40	0

Yorkshire 2nd Innings

M.D. Moxon	c Hughes b DeFreitas	11
A.A. Metcalfe	lbw b Allott	4
†R.J. Blakey	c Allott b Atherton	62
K. Sharp	c Hegg b Allott	0
P.E. Robinson	b Allott	2
D. Byas	lbw b Akram	7
*P. Carrick	b Akram	11
I.G. Swallow	c Fairbrother b Wasim Akram	18
C.S. Pickles	b Wasim Akram	5
P.W. Jarvis	lbw b Wasim Akram	1
S.D. Fletcher	not out	0
Extras	b 5, lb 10, w 4, nb 8	27
Total		148

14, 19, 20, 32, 46, 64, 135, 144, 147

Wasim Akram	22	6	51	5
Allott	15	8	24	3
DeFreitas	4	0	10	1
Watkinson	5	0	17	0
Fitton	4	0	20	0
Hughes	5	3	6	0
Atherton	4	1	5	1

Umpires: P.J. Eele and M.J. Kitchen
Toss: Lancashire
A good century by Atherton provided Lancashire with 3 bonus points on the first day and Yorkshire began Monday at 46–0 off 11 overs. However, the visitors then failed rather miserably, Akram picking up five cheap wickets. Lancashire were 238 runs ahead with eight second innings wickets in hand at the close. Hughes set Yorkshire 330 off 81 overs on the last day but apart from Blakey they failed to fathom Akram and Allott.

v SURREY (Old Trafford)

August 24, 25, 26, 28

Won by 97 runs. Lancs 20pts, Surrey 4pts

Lancashire 1st Innings

G.D. Mendis	lbw b Medlycott	38
G.D. Lloyd	c Stewart b Medlycott	41
I.D. Austin	c Stewart b Murphy	13
N.H. Fairbrother	b Medlycott	0
T.E. Jesty	run out	47
M. Watkinson	c Stewart b M.P. Bicknell	1
Wasim Akram	c Lynch b Frost	34
†W.K. Hegg	c Medlycott b Boiling	28
*D.P. Hughes	not out	40
J.D. Fitton	c Thorpe b Boiling	43
P.J. W. Allott	lbw b Boiling	2
Extras	b 1, lb 13, nb 4	18
Total (93.4 ov)		305

78, 85, 85, 105, 123, 167, 187, 227, 302

Murphy	18	5	62	1
M.P. Bicknell	24	3	64	1
Frost	11	2	31	1
Medlycott	28	4	94	3
Boiling	12.4	2	40	3

Surrey 1st Innings

G.S. Clinton	not out	9
D.J. Bicknell	lbw b Wasim Akram	5
M.P. Bicknell	not out	4
†A.J. Stewart		
G.P. Thorpe		
M.A. Lynch		
*I.A. Greig		
K.T. Medlycott		
J. Boiling		
A.J. Murphy		
M. Frost		
Extras	b 1, lb 5	6
Total (1 wkt dec)		24

12

Wasim Akram	7	4	9	1
Allott	4	1	7	0
Fitton	2	1	2	0

Lancashire 2nd Innings

G.D. Lloyd	not out	8
†W.K. Hegg	c Boiling b Stewart	11
I.D. Austin	not out	1
Extras		0
Total (1 wkt dec)		20

12

Stewart	2.4	0	7	1
Medlycott	2	0	13	0

Surrey 2nd Innings

G.S. Clinton	c Fairbrother b Wasim Akram	2
D.J. Bicknell	b Wasim Akram	3
†A.J. Stewart	c Hegg b Wasim Akram	35
G.P. Thorpe	lbw b Fitton	44
M.A. Lynch	b Fitton	50
*I.A. Greig	b Fitton	19
K.T. Medlycott	not out	24
M.P. Bicknell	c Hughes b Fitton	0
J. Boiling	c Hughes b Fitton	6
A.J. Murphy	b Wasim Akram	0
M. Frost	b Wasim Akram	0
Extras	b 8, lb 4, w 2, nb 7	21
Total		204

6, 7, 66, 126, 155, 169, 169, 203, 204

Wasim Akram	24.4	3	52	5
Allott	15	6	35	0
Fitton	26	7	72	5
Watkinson	8	3	26	0
Austin	3	1	7	0

Umpires: B. Hassan and R. Julian
Toss: Surrey
Lancashire made a brisk start, until Medlycott came on to bowl and took 3–6 in 21 balls. Later Hughes made certain of full batting points and Surrey struggled to 24–1 off 13 overs by the close. There was no play on the second and third days. On Monday Surrey immediately declared, Lancashire had a brief second innings before leaving the visitors 302 in 94 overs. Akram and Fitton prevented the Surrey batsmen becoming established and Lancashire's victory kept them in fifth place in the table.

v DERBYSHIRE (Old Trafford)

September 13, 14, 15, 16

Drawn. Lancs 7pts, Derbys 7pts

Derbyshire 1st Innings

*K.J. Barnett	c Hegg b DeFreitas	3
†P.D. Bowler	b Wasim Akram	81
J.E. Morris	c Hegg d DeFreitas	12
A. Brown	c Fairbrother b DeFreitas	23
C.J. Adams	st Hegg b Atherton	38
B. Roberts	c Austin b Fitton	15
S.C. Goldsmith	c Lloyd b DeFreitas	16
A.E. Warner	c Jesty b Fitton	0
I.R. Bishop	c Watkinson b Fitton	14
S.J. Base	not out	32
O.H. Mortensen	c Hegg b Wasim Akram	8
Extras	b 14, lb 11, w 3, nb 22	50
Total (86.3 ov)		292

5, 36, 75, 147, 186, 210, 210, 238, 250

Wasim Akram	26.3	3	57	2
DeFreitas	28	6	76	4
Watkinson	8	1	32	0
Fitton	21	4	89	3
Atherton	3	0	13	1

Lancashire 1st Innings

G. Fowler	b Warner	24
G.D. Lloyd	c Base b Bishop	2
M.A. Atherton	c Base b Mortensen	0
*N.H. Fairbrother	c Adams b Warner	28
T.E. Jesty	c Morris b Barnett	66
M. Watkinson	c Bishop b Base	17
Wasim Akram	b Barnett	49
†W.K. Hegg	st Bowler b Base	11
P.A.J. DeFreitas	not out	15
I.D. Austin	lbw b Barnett	17
J.D. Fitton	not out	4
Extras	b 11, lb 4, w 1, nb 2	18
Total (9 wkts dec, 85 ov)		251

9, 14, 54, 59, 90, 168, 213, 217, 247

Bishop	17	5	32	1
Mortensen	14	3	46	1
Warner	11	0	50	2
Base	24	8	75	2
Barnett	19	6	33	3

Derbyshire 2nd Innings

†P.D. Bowler	lbw b Watkinson	4
S.C. Goldsmith	c Fairbrother b Austin	6
A. Brown	lbw b Fitton	19
C.J. Adams	lbw b Austin	0
B. Roberts	b DeFreitas	75
J.E. Morris	c Wasim Akram b Fairbrother	66
S.J. Base	not out	19
A.E. Warner	not out	5
Extras	b 10, lb 3, nb 2	15
Total (6 wkts dec, 42 ov)		209

11, 11, 11, 53, 182, 188

DeFreitas	2	0	10	1
Watkinson	6	3	9	1
Fitton	5	1	18	1
Austin	7	3	12	2
Fowler	8	1	36	0
Fairbrother	6	0	42	1
Atherton	3	0	14	0
Lloyd	5	0	55	0

Lancashire 2nd Innings

G. Fowler	c Bowler b Warner	12
G.D. Lloyd	lbw b Barnett	15
M.A. Atherton	not out	12
*N.H. Fairbrother	not out	6
Extras	b 5, lb 2, nb 1	8
Total (2 wkts)		53

29, 33

Bishop	7	0	18	0
Mortensen	6	3	9	0
Warner	4.2	0	17	1
Barnett	4	2	2	1

Umpires: B. Hassan and D.O. Oslear
Toss: Derbyshire
Half a day's play was possible on Wednesday when Derbyshire progressed to 167–4 off 52.3 overs. The feature was Bowler's very careful undefeated 55. Derbyshire had a good day on Thursday, building their total to 292 and then reducing Lancashire to 94–5. On the third day the batting was painfully slow, just over 100 runs coming off 48 overs. The contrivances of the final day failed to produce a definite result and Lancashire who had hoped for third place in the table settled for fourth.

Leicestershire

President: C.H. Palmer
Chairman: C.H. Palmer
Chief Executive: F.M. Turner, County Cricket Ground, Grace Road, Leicester, LE2 8AD. *Tel:* 0533 831880.
Coach: K. Higgs
Captain: in 1989 D.I. Gower
Foundation of Present Club: March 1879 in Leicester
First First-Class Match: Leicestershire v Essex (Leyton) May 1894
County Champions: 1975
Gillette/NatWest Trophy: Semi-finalists in 1977 and 1987
Benson & Hedges Cup: Winners 1972, 1975, 1985
Sunday League Champions: 1974, 1977
Refuge Cup: Nil

Summary of Results in 1989
Britannic Assurance County Championship: Played 22, Won 4, Lost 8, Drawn 10, Position 13th equal
NatWest Bank Trophy: Lost in second round
Benson & Hedges Cup: Did not qualify for knock-out section
Refuge Assurance Sunday League: Played 16, Won 5, Lost 10, No Result 1, Position 14th equal
Refuge Assurance Cup: Did not qualify

From left, back: *P. Whitticase, B. Smith, M. Gidley, P. Nixon, J. Benson, C. Lewis, A. Roseberry, I. Tennant.* Middle: *R. Stenner (Physiotherapist), G. Parsons, T. Boon, P. Such (now with Essex), R. Cobb, G. Ferris, R. Edmunds (Deceased), L. Potter, P. Hepworth, G. Blackburn (Scorer).* Front: *K. Higgs (Coach), J. Whitaker, L. Taylor, C.H. Palmer (President), D. Gower (now with Hampshire), F.M. Turner (Chief Executive), N. Briers (Captain), J. Agnew, P. Willey.* Allsport/Russell Cheyne

The various internal squabbles that have beset the club over the last few years cannot be best resolved when the captain misses so many matches due to Test calls – this of course is not a problem unique to Leicestershire. The loss of DeFreitas to Lancashire – he had topped the county bowling in 1988 – and the decline in effectiveness of Agnew – each of his wickets cost six runs more than in 1988 – clearly put a strain on the rest of the bowlers. The young spinner, Such, remained unable to command a regular place and has moved to Essex for 1990. Easily the most effective bowler was the Antiguan seamer, Benjamin, who had been with the West Indians in 1988. His fellow countryman, Ferris, was handicapped by a knee injury and appeared in only five first-class games; Ferris and Benjamin could not of course appear in the eleven together. The third West Indian seamer, Lewis, has an England qualification, but he also missed many matches, though his average did improve on 1988. Willey had the best record of the slower bowlers. Taylor appears to have come to the end of his career, his record being even more modest than in the previous summer. The promising young bowler, Edmunds, who appeared in a couple of games at the end of the season, tragically died as the result of a road accident in December.

Five batsmen exceeded 1,000 first-class runs, but, apart from Gower, only Whitaker can be said to have had a really satisfactory summer. Briers, the regular opener, averaged 25, which is not good enough for a player in his position and he failed to hit a single hundred, as did Willey. Potter was fairly reliable and has a better record than in 1988. Whitticase, the wicket-keeper, scored runs low down the order and the county introduced another wicket-keeper in Nixon from Cumberland – Garnham, who had been with the county, went to Essex for 1989.

Gower has now given up the captaincy and perhaps the combination of a new leader, as well as a new manager, will improve the returns for 1990.

Farewell to Gower. Leicestershire's skipper decided at the end of the season to switch to Hampshire.

Allsport/Adrian Murrell

ONE DAY AWAY MATCHES

The full scorecard of each of Leicestershire's away matches will be found in the sections for the respective home teams.

Refuge Assurance League

Hove: May 21
Sussex 208–4 (40 ov) beat Leics 131 (38.1 ov) by 77 runs. Sussex 4pts, Leics 0pts.

Bournemouth: May 28
Leics 107 (31.5 ov) lost to Hants 110–3 (27.4 ov) by 7 wkts. Hants 4pts, Leics 0pts.

Chelmsford: June 18
Leics 192–6 (40 ov) lost to Essex 193–1 (37 ov) (G.A. Gooch 111*) by 9 wkts. Essex 4pts, Leics 0pts.

Luton: June 25
Northants 81 (34 ov) (L.B. Taylor 5–20) lost to Leics 82–2 (25.3 ov) by 8 wkts. Leics 4pts, Northants 0pts.

Worcester: July 9
Leics 159–9 (40 ov) lost to Worcs 157–4 (37.3 ov) by 6 wkts. Worcs 4pts, Leics 0pts.

Taunton: July 23
Leics 183 (40 ov) lost to Somerset 186–3 (36.2 ov) by 7 wkts. Somerset 4pts, Leics 0pts.

Lord's July 30
Leics 95–6 (28 ov) lost to Middx 96–4 (26 ov) by 6 wkts. Middx 4pts, Leics 0pts.

Folkestone: August 27
Kent 199–6 (37 ov) beat Leics 147 (36.3 ov) by 52 runs. Kent 4pts, Leics 0pts.

Benson and Hedges Cup

Old Trafford: April 25
Leics 186–6 (55 ov) lost to Lancs 187–3 (52.3 ov) by 7 wkts. Lancs 2pts, Leics 0pts.

Northampton: May 11, 12
Northants 204–6 (55 ov) drew with Leics 11–1 (5.2 ov). Leics 1pt, Northants 1pt.

NatWest Bank Trophy

Telford: June 28
Salop 220–7 (60 ov) lost to Leics 221–4 (54.2 ov) (D.I. Gower 101*) by 6 wkts.

Hove: July 12
Sussex 300–2 (60 ov) beat Leics 232 (55.4 ov) by 68 runs.

REFUGE ASSURANCE LEAGUE

v GLAMORGAN (Leicester)
April 23
Match Abandoned. No play. Leics 2pts, Glam 2pts

Winston Benjamin, Leicestershire's West Indian, who was top of the county's bowling averages.

Allsport

REFUGE ASSURANCE LEAGUE

v DERBYSHIRE (Leicester)

April 30

Lost by 82 runs. Derbys 4pts, Leics 0pts

Derbyshire		
*K.J. Barnett	c Briers b Potter	77
P.D. Bowler	c Potter b Ferris	4
†B.J.M. Maher	c Whitticase b Willey	39
M.A. Holding	c and b Willey	0
B. Roberts	not out	35
S.C. Goldsmith	b Ferris	15
R. Sharma	run out	1
P.G. Newman		
O.H. Mortensen		
S.J. Base		
A.E. Warner		
Extras	b 1, lb 12, nb 3	16
Total (6 wkts, 40 ov)		187

20, 127, 127, 135, 186, 187

Agnew	5	1	23	0
Ferris	7	1	19	2
Parsons	8	0	39	0
Lewis	8	0	36	0
Willey	8	0	31	2
Potter	4	0	26	1

Leicestershire		
L. Potter	c Maher b Mortensen	12
N.E. Briers	c Warner b Mortensen	7
*D.I. Gower	b Base	42
P. Willey	c Sharma b Mortensen	1
J.J. Whitaker	b Holding	0
T.J. Boon	b Base	6
C.C. Lewis	c Holding b Sharma	7
†P. Whitticase	c Maher b Sharma	0
G.J. Parsons	not out	7
J.P. Agnew	b Newman	4
G.J.F. Ferris	c Roberts b Newman	6
Extras	b 5, lb 7, w 1	13
Total (31.5 overs)		105

19, 32, 46, 47, 79, 80, 81, 88, 93

Mortensen	8	0	23	3
Newman	7.5	1	20	2
Holding	4	0	14	1
Base	5	0	14	2
Sharma	4	1	12	2
Warner	3	0	10	0

Umpires: B. Leadbeater and D.S. Thompsett
Toss: Leicestershire

Barnett who hit 6 fours from 98 balls scored an excellent 77 on a slow pitch and only Gower matched him for Leics, but as the England captain's innings only realised 42 runs, the visitors won with little difficulty.

v YORKSHIRE (Leicester)

May 14

Won by 7 wkts. Leics 4pts, Yorks 0pts

Yorkshire		
R.J. Blakey	c Whitticase b Benjamin	5
A.A. Metcalfe	lbw b Benjamin	0
P.E. Robinson	b Agnew	11
†D.L. Bairstow	b Lewis	8
J.D. Love	b Potter	12
D. Byas	b Lewis	2
S.N. Hartley	b Willey	13
*P. Carrick	c Whitaker b Willey	1
P.W. Jarvis	not out	15
C.S. Pickles	b Lewis	2
S. Oldham	not out	4
Extras	lb 7, w 3, nb 6	16
Total (9 wkts, 40 ov)		89

2, 8, 30, 30, 35, 61, 63, 63, 74

Agnew	8	2	15	1
Benjamin	8	1	28	2
Lewis	8	3	9	3
Parsons	8	3	13	0
Willey	6	2	15	2
Potter	2	1	2	1

Leicestershire		
L. Potter	c Oldham b Pickles	34
N.E. Briers	b Jarvis	5
*D.I. Gower	not out	35
P. Willey	lbw b Pickles	8
J.J. Whitaker	not out	3
T.J. Boon		
C.C. Lewis		
G.J. Parsons		
†P. Whitticase		
W.K.M. Benjamin		
J.P. Agnew		
	lb 5, w 2	7
Total (3 wkts, 31.4 ov)		92

17, 73, 83

Jarvis	8	3	11	1
Pickles	7.4	0	32	2
Oldham	8	2	25	0
Byas	2	0	7	0
Carrick	6	1	12	0

Umpires: M.J. Kitchen and D.O. Oslear
Toss: Yorkshire

On a chilly day when the ball swung nicely for the seamers, Yorkshire provided a poor show and were in danger of their lowest Sunday total until Jarvis hit out. Leicestershire had no difficulty knocking off the runs.

v LANCASHIRE (Leicester)

June 4

Won by 7 wkts. Leics 4pts, Lancs 0pts

Lancashire		
G.D. Mendis	b Lewis	28
G. Fowler	b Agnew	6
N.H. Fairbrother	c Briers b Agnew	2
T.E. Jesty	c Nixon b Lewis	23
M. Watkinson	c Benson b Parsons	25
Wasim Akram	b Lewis	0
*D.P. Hughes	b Benjamin	32
P.A.J. DeFreitas	b Parsons	9
†W.K. Hegg	c Willey b Agnew	8
P.J.W. Allott	not out	6
J. Simmons		
Extras	lb 8, nb 2	10
Total (9 wkts, 40 ov)		149

6, 13, 39, 78, 78, 89, 101, 119, 149

Benjamin	8	1	24	1
Agnew	8	2	31	3
Lewis	8	1	38	3
Parsons	8	2	26	2
Willey	8	1	22	0

Leicestershire		
L. Potter	c Hegg b Allott	14
N.E. Briers	retired hurt	6
*D.I. Gower	c Simmons b Wasim Akram	10
P. Willey	b Wasim Akram	31
J.J. Whitaker	not out	48
J.D.R. Benson	not out	25
C.C. Lewis		
†P.A. Nixon		
G.J. Parsons		
W.K.M. Benjamin		
J.P. Agnew		
Extras	b2, lb 8, w 6, nb 2	18
Total (3 wkts, 38.2 ov)		152

27, 45, 110

Allott	8	2	20	1
DeFreitas	7	1	19	0
Watkinson	6.2	0	29	0
Wasim Akram	8	0	38	2
Simmons	8	1	27	0
Jesty	1	0	9	0

Umpires: B.J. Meyer and R.A. White
Toss: Leicestershire.

Put in to bat, Lancashire lost their first Sunday match of the season. Leics opener Briers was struck on the head by a bouncer from DeFreitas but Whitaker batted well to reach 48* when the game ended.

PLAYERS

Jonathan Philip AGNEW *b* 4.4.1960 Macclesfield; right-arm fast-medium bowler; right-hand batsman; debut 1978; three Tests for England 1984–85
Winston Keithroy Matthew BENJAMIN *b* 31.12.1964 St John's Antigua; right-arm fast-medium bowler; right-hand batsman; debut 1986, also plays for Leeward Is; eight Tests for West Indies
Justin David Ramsay BENSON *b* 1.3.1967 Dublin; right-hand batsman; right-arm medium pace bowler; debut 1988
Timothy James BOON *b* 1.11.1961 Doncaster; right-hand batsman; right-arm medium pace bowler; debut 1980
Nigel Edwin BRIERS *b* 15.1 1955 Leicester; right-hand batsman; right-arm medium pace bowler; debut 1971 (aged 16)
Russell Alan COBB *b* 18.5.1961 Leicester; right-hand batsman; slow left-arm bowler; debut 1980
Richard Harold EDMUNDS *b* 27.5.1970 Oakham; right-hand batsman; left-arm fast medium bowler; debut June 1989. He died in December1989 after a road accident.
George John Fitzgerald FERRIS *b* 18.10.1964 Urlings Village, Antigua; right-arm fast bowler, right-hand batsman; debut 1983, also plays for Leeward Is.
Martyn Ian GIDLEY *b* 30.9.1968 Leicester; left-hand batsman; off-break bowler; debut 1989
David Ivon GOWER *b* 1.4.1957 Tunbridge Wells; stylish left-hand batsman; debut 1975; captain 1984–86 and 1988–89; 106 Tests for England including six *v* Australia in 1989 as captain; reached 20,000 f-c runs during 1989; surprise omission from England team to West Indies 1989–90
Peter Nash HEPWORTH *b* 4.5.1967 Achworth; right-hand batsman; off-break bowler; debut 1988
Clairmonte Christopher LEWIS *b* 14.2.1968 Georgetown, Guyana; right-arm medium-fast bowler; right-hand batsman; debut 1987

Paul Andrew NIXON *b* 31.10.1970 Carlisle; wicket-keeper; left-hand batsman; debut July 1989
Gordon James PARSONS *b* 17.10.1959 Slough; left-hand batsman; right-arm medium pace bowler; debut 1978, but played for Warwickshire 1986 to 1988
Laurie POTTER *b* 7.11.1962 Bexleyheath; right-hand batsman; slow left-arm bowler; debut 1986, previously played for Kent 1981–85
Peter Mark SUCH *b* 12.6.1964 Helensburgh; off-break bowler; tail-end right hand batsman; debut 1987, previously played for Notts 1982–86; signed for Essex in 1990.
Leslie Brian TAYLOR *b* 25.10.1953 Earl Shilton; right-arm fast-medium bowler; right-hand batsman; debut 1977; two Tests for England in 1985
Lloyd TENNANT *b* 9.4.1968 Walsall; right-hand batsman; right-arm medium pace bowler; debut 1986
John James WHITAKER *b* 5.5.1962 Skipton, Yorks; middle-order right-hand batsman; debut 1983; one test for England 1986–87; selected to tour Zimbabwe 1989–90.
Philip WHITTICASE *b* 15.3.1965 Marston Green, Birmingham; wicketkeeper; right-hand batsman; debut 1984; missed several matches in 1989 due to broken finger
Peter WILLEY *b* 6.12.1949 Sedgefield, Durham; right-hand batsman; off-break bowler; debut 1984; captain 1987; previously appeared for Northants 1966–83; 26 Tests for England 1976–86

James Whitaker, second to Gower in the batting averages, but with the highest aggregate.
Allsport/Adrian Murrell

REFUGE ASSURANCE LEAGUE

v GLOUCESTERSHIRE (Leicester)
June 11
Lost by 59 runs. Gloucs 4pts, Leics 0pts

Gloucestershire		
A.W. Stovold	c Whitticase b Parsons	29
J.W. Lloyds	c Whitaker b Agnew	8
*C.W.J. Athey	c Benson b Agnew	1
P. Bainbridge	c Briers b Agnew	72
A.J. Wright	b Agnew	81
M.W. Alleyne	not out	5
P.W. Romaines	run out	1
†G.A. Tedstone		
C.A. Walsh		
K.B.S. Jarvis		
D.V. Lawrence		
Extras	b 8, w 9	17
Total (6 wkts, 40 ov)		214

17, 21, 57, 213, 214

Benjamin	8	0	31	0
Agnew	8	1	25	4
Edmunds	8	0	36	0
Parsons	8	0	59	1
Willey	8	0	55	0

Leicestershire		
*N.E. Briers	c Romaines b Jarvis	9
L. Potter	c Lloyds b Lawrence	5
P. Willey	c Tedstone b Alleyne	6
J.J. Whitaker	b Lawrence	23
J.D.R. Benson	c and b Bainbridge	41
†P. Whitticase	c Athey b Bainbridge	4
C.C. Lewis	b Walsh	19
W.K.M. Benjamin	b Jarvis	9
G.J. Parsons	b Walsh	14
J.P. Agnew	not out	11
R.H. Edmunds	lbw b Walsh	0
Extras	b 1, lb 9, w 3, nb 1	14
Total (35.3 ov)		155

11, 23, 23, 78, 88, 106, 127, 142, 155

Lawrence	6	0	15	2
Walsh	5.3	1	16	3
Jarvis	8	1	38	2
Alleyne	8	0	34	1
Bainbridge	8	0	42	2

Umpires: D.G.L. Evans and B. Hassan
Toss: Gloucestershire
A 4th wicket stand of 133 in 19 overs between Bainbridge and Wright enabled the visitors to set a large target. Leicestershire lost their first five batsmen with less than 100 on the board and never looked like approaching the 215 required.

v WARWICKSHIRE (Leicester)
July 2
Won by 21 runs. Leics 4pts, Warwicks 0pts

Leicestershire		
L. Potter	lbw b Munton	4
N.E. Briers	c Humpage b Donald	4
*D.I. Gower	c Humpage b Pierson	82
J.J. Whitaker	b Donald	81
P. Willey	b Pierson	9
C.C. Lewis	not out	17
W.K.M. Benjamin	b Munton	2
G.J. Parsons	not out	1
†P.A Nixon		
J.P. Agnew		
L.B. Taylor		
Extras	b 1, lb 3, w 9, nb 2	15
Total (6 wkts, 40 ov)		215

9, 9, 161, 179, 198, 202

Donald	8	2	30	2
Munton	8	2	27	2
Reeve	8	0	39	0
Pierson	8	0	53	2
Small	8	0	62	0

Warwickshire		
G.W. Humpage	c Potter b Benjamin	1
*T.A. Lloyd	c Lewis b Willey	29
A.I. Kallicharran	b Taylor	38
D.A. Thorne	c Whitaker b Willey	28
D.A. Reeve	c Parsons b Agnew	64
Asif Din	c Potter b Willey	0
A.J. Moles	c Potter b Parsons	7
A.A. Donald	b Benjamin	8
A.R.K. Pierson	b Benjamin	9
T.A. Munton	not out	0
G.C. Small	absent hurt	–
Extras	b 2, lb 4, w 3, nb 1	10
Total (39.1 ov)		194

3, 71, 73, 128, 129, 144, 167, 193, 194

Agnew	7	2	25	1
Benjamin	7.1	1	32	3
Parsons	7	0	45	1
Taylor	8	1	37	1
Willey	8	0	31	3
Lewis	2	0	18	0

Umpires: J.W. Holder and M.J. Kitchen
Toss: Warwickshire
Gower, 82 of 85 balls, and Whitaker, 81 off 87, added 152 for the 3rd wicket and this was the heart of the Leicestershire innings. Despite 64 from Reeve, the visitors were unable to match this and with Small absent, their innings ended with the first ball of the final over.

v NOTTINGHAMSHIRE (Leicester)
July 16
Lost by 36 runs. Notts 4pts, Leics 0pts

Nottinghamshire		
B.C. Broad	c Briers b Willey	71
P.R. Pollard	b Agnew	1
*R.T. Robinson	c Whitticase b Edmunds	1
P. Johnson	b Edmunds	0
D.J.R. Martindale	c and b Potter	24
F.D. Stephenson	b Taylor	37
K.P. Evans	run out	2
†B.N. French	c Lewis b Agnew	2
K.E. Cooper	b Taylor	8
K. Saxelby	not out	6
J.A. Afford	not out	0
Extras	lb 14, w 13, nb 3	30
Total (9 wkts, 38 ov)		182

3, 4, 8, 101, 129, 141, 164, 175, 182

Agnew	6	0	24	2
Edmunds	7	3	27	2
Tennant	5	0	34	0
Taylor	7	0	29	2
Willey	7	1	36	1
Potter	6	1	18	1

Leicestershire		
L. Potter	c Cooper b Saxelby	19
N.E. Briers	c and b Saxelby	13
*D.I. Gower	c Robinson b Evans	5
J.J. Whitaker	b Afford	19
P. Willey	b Cooper	8
C.C. Lewis	b Saxelby	22
†P. Whitticase	c Broad b Saxelby	21
J.P. Agnew	c French b Stephenson	1
L. Tennant	c Robinson b Saxelby	13
R.H. Edmunds	not out	5
L.B. Taylor	b Saxelby	2
Extras	lb 14, w 4	18
Total (36 ov)		146

31, 34, 43, 64, 72, 110, 112, 132, 139

Stephenson	7	0	18	1
Cooper	8	0	28	1
Saxelby	7	0	30	6
Evans	7	1	28	1
Afford	7	1	28	1

Umpires: J.D. Bond and D.O. Oslear
Toss: Nottinghamshire
Broad held the Notts batting together, after three wickets had gone for 8. Saxelby then produced the best Sunday figures of his career and Leicestershire were easily defeated.

BRITANNIC ASSURANCE COUNTY CHAMPIONSHIP AVERAGES 1989

Batting	*M*	*I*	*NO*	*Runs*	*HS*	*Avge*	*100*	*50*
D.I. Gower	9	17	1	664	228	41.50	2	2
J.J. Whitaker	21	36	3	1252	138	37.94	3	5
L. Potter	22	36	5	1006	121*	32.45	1	6
T.J. Boon	19	36	5	972	80*	31.35	–	6
P. Whitticase	17	28	6	654	61	29.73	–	2
P. Willey	22	37	2	1013	99	28.94	–	7
N.E. Briers	22	41	3	951	73	25.03	–	5
G.J. Parsons	17	25	7	445	69	24.72	–	1
P.A. Nixon	5	5	3	46	24	23.00	–	–
R.A. Cobb	5	9	–	157	47	17.44	–	–
W.K.M. Benjamin	14	17	2	259	41	17.27	–	–
J.D.R. Benson	4	8	–	110	45	13.75	–	–
G.J.F. Ferris	5	9	3	80	30	13.33	–	–
C.C. Lewis	11	18	1	223	69	13.12	–	1
J.P. Agnew	21	28	8	196	25	9.80	–	–
P.N. Hepworth	4	6	–	48	17	8.00	–	–
L.B. Taylor	12	15	7	59	27	7.38	–	–
R.H. Edmunds	2	3	–	17	17	5.67	–	–
P.M. Such	9	6	1	15	14	3.00	–	–

Also batted: M.I. Gidley (1 match) 15.

Bowling	*O*	*M*	*R*	*W*	*Avge*	*BB*	*5i*	*10m*
W.K.M. Benjamin	455.1	136	1177	62	18.98	6-26	6	1
G.J.F. Ferris	124.1	39	327	17	19.24	4-44	–	2
C.C. Lewis	286.3	54	966	45	21.47	5-40	3	–
P. Willey	422	131	968	35	27.66	5-45	1	–
L. Potter	141.5	32	393	14	28.07	3-50	–	–
J.P. Agnew	657.3	118	2086	66	31.61	6-56	3	1
P.M. Such	214.2	64	530	15	35.33	3-28	–	–
G.J. Parsons	320.1	72	1086	30	36.20	5-48	1	–
L.B. Taylor	237.4	46	747	19	39.32	4-55	–	–

Also bowled: J.D.R. Benson 9.3-0-44-1; T.J. Boon 7-0-41-1; R.H. Edmunds 37-5-113-3; M.I. Gidley 8-0-23-1; P. Whitticase 0.5-0-7-0.

Centuries

3 J.J. Whitaker: 138 v Essex (Chelmsford); 138 v Warwicks (Hinckley); 116 v Kent (Folkestone).

2 D.I. Gower: 228 v Glamorgan (Leicester); 109 v Essex (Leicester).

1 L. Potter: 121* v Notts (Leicester).

REFUGE ASSURANCE LEAGUE

v SURREY (Leicester)

August 20

Won by 4 runs. Leics 4pts, Surrey 0pts

Leicestershire		
*D.I. Gower	b Greig	32
N.E. Briers	c Murphy b Greig	37
J.J. Whitaker	c Greig b Murphy	55
C.C. Lewis	run out	40
W.K.M. Benjamin	not out	27
L. Potter	not out	11
†P. Whitticase		
G.J. Parsons		
J.P. Agnew		
L.B. Taylor		
P.M. Such		
Extras	b 4, lb 11, w 2	17
Total (4 wkts, 40 ov)		219

72, 96, 179, 184

Murphy	8	1	45	1
M.P. Bicknell	6	0	42	0
Greig	8	1	29	2
Robinson	8	0	35	0
Medlycott	4	0	24	0
Bullen	6	1	29	0

Surrey		
G.S. Clinton	b Parsons	15
D.J. Bicknell	run out	56
†A.J. Stewart	c Whitticase b Such	18
G.P. Thorpe	c Whitaker b Such	11
D. M. Ward	c Gower b Agnew	36
*I.A. Greig	not out	40
K.T. Medlycott	c Potter b Agnew	0
J.D. Robinson	not out	18
C.K. Bullen		
M.P. Bicknell		
A.J. Murphy		
Extras	b 2, lb 14, w 5	21
Total (6 wkts, 40 ov)		215

61, 93, 106, 122, 171, 171

Agnew	8	0	34	2
Benjamin	8	1	41	0
Parsons	8	1	42	1
Taylor	8	0	37	0
Such	8	0	45	2

Umpires: D.R. Shepherd and R.A. White
Toss: Leicestershire
This was a crucial match for Surrey, who needed to win in order to secure a place in the knock-out Cup. Chasing 220, six wickets went down for 171, but Robinson joined Greig and the pair added 44 runs — unfortunately five runs too few for victory.

BENSON AND HEDGES CUP

v WARWICKSHIRE (Leicester)

May 2

Won by 31 runs. Leics 2pts, Warwicks 0pts

Leicestershire		
T.J. Boon	c Humpage b Smith	12
N.E. Briers	c Humpage b Smith	71
*D.I. Gower	c Thorne b Small	36
P. Willey	lbw b Small	41
J.J. Whitaker	c Thorne b Donald	26
L. Potter	not out	22
C.C. Lewis	not out	8
†P. Whitticase		
G.J. Parsons		
J.P. Agnew		
G.J.F. Ferris		
Extras	lb 7, w 5, nb 8	20
Total (5 wkts, 55 ov)		236

31, 115, 140, 192, 208

Small	11	1	61	2
Donald	11	2	44	1
Munton	11	1	41	0
Smith	8	0	36	2
Pierson	11	2	29	0
Moles	3	0	18	0

Warwickshire		
*T.A. Lloyd	b Ferris	7
A.J. Moles	c Briers b Agnew	14
S.J. Green	b Ferris	0
A.I. Kallicharran	b Agnew	62
D.A. Thorne	b Willey	37
P.A. Smith	c Ferris b Lewis	20
†G. W. Humpage	b Lewis	13
G.C. Small	lbw b Parsons	5
A.A. Donald	not out	23
A.R.K. Pierson	b Lewis	0
T.A. Munton	b Ferris	13
Extras	lb 3, w 4, nb 4	11
Total (55 ov)		205

22, 22, 22, 97, 144, 150, 157, 180, 180

Ferris	11	1	42	3
Agnew	10	4	19	2
Lewis	11	1	49	3
Parsons	10	0	41	1
Willey	11	2	42	1
Potter	2	0	9	0

Umpires: A.A. Jones and B.J. Meyer
Toss: Leicestershire. Gold: N.E. Briers
The backbone of the Leics innings was a fine 71 by Briers, whilst Willey hit out to good effect late in the innings. Warwickshire made a bad start and despite Kallicharran's 62, the home side proved superior.

v SCOTLAND (Leicester)

May 9

Won by 111 runs. Leics 2pts, Scotland 0pts

Leicestershire		
T.J. Boon	c Phillip b Morton	40
N.E. Briers	b Bee	5
*D.I. Gower	c Morton b Smith	11
J.J. Whitaker	c Haggo b Morton	48
G.J. Parsons	not out	63
L. Potter	c McGurk b Smith	23
C.C. Lewis	c Haggo b Burnett	17
†P. Whitticase	not out	14
W.K.M. Benjamin		
J.P. Agnew		
P.M. Such		
Extras	b 2, lb 6, w 8, nb 2	18
Total (6 wkts, 55 ov)		239

16, 29, 101, 130, 182, 223

Rice	11	3	39	0
Bee	11	4	21	1
Smith	9	0	74	2
Morton	11	1	42	2
Burnett	9	1	33	1
Henry	4	0	22	0

Scotland		
I.L. Philip	c Lewis b Benjamin	62
G.B.J. McGurk	c Whitticase b Benjamin	5
R.G. Swan	lbw b Agnew	1
*C.E.B. Rice	c Whitticase b Parsons	0
A.C. Storie	st Whitticase b Potter	4
M.J. Smith	b Such	12
O. Henry	c and b Lewis	21
N.W. Burnett	b Parsons	3
W. Morton	not out	0
†D.J. Haggo	lbw b Parsons	0
A.W. Bee	b Parsons	0
Extras	lb 10, w 3, nb 7	20
Total (49 ov)		128

17, 20, 26, 43, 78, 115, 127, 127 127

Agnew	6	0	11	1
Benjamin	9	1	29	2
Lewis	9	0	18	1
Parsons	8	3	12	4
Such	11	2	35	1
Potter	6	3	13	1

Umpires: D.G.L. Evans and N.T. Plews
Toss: Leicestershire. Gold: G.J. Parsons
A bare pitch made runs difficult to find until Parsons used the long handle and with his lower order colleagues took Leics to a safe total. Philip batted well for his 62, but found no one to support him.

Away Matches

The full scorecard of each of Leicestershire's away matches will be found in the sections for the respective home teams.

Northampton: May 4, 5, 6
Leics 208 (J.G. Thomas 6–53) and 250 lost to Northants 185 and 276–9 (A.J. Lamb 148) by one wkt. Northants 21pts, Leics 6pts.

Chesterfield: May 17, 18, 19
Leics 274 and 12–1 beat Derbys 57 (W.K.M. Benjamin 6–26) and 228 (C.C. Lewis 5–69) by 9 wkts. Leics 23pts, Derbys 4pts.

Bournemouth: May 27, 29, 30
Hants 288 and 239–4d beat Leics 293 and 115 by 119 runs. Hants 23pts, Leics 6pts.

Chelmsford: June 17, 19, 20
Leics 377–8d (J.J. Whitaker 138) and 251–5d drew with Essex 262–2d (G.A. Gooch 124*) and 216–4. Essex 5pts, Leics 4pts.

Kidderminster: July 8, 10, 11
Leics 180 and 80 (S.M. McEwan 6–34) lost to Worcs 245 and 16–0 by 10 wkts. Worcs 22pts, Leics 5pts.

Taunton: July 22, 24, 25
Somerset 449 (S.J. Cook 148) beat Leics 250 and 152 by an inns and 47 runs. Somerset 23pts, Leics 3pts.

Cardiff: July 26, 27, 28
Glamorgan 228 (P. Willey 5–45) and 118 lost to Leics 247 (K.A. Somaia 5–87) and 100–1 by 9 wkts. Leics 22pts, Glamorgan 6pts.

Lord's: July 29, 31, Aug 1
Middx 287 and 127–1d drew with Leics 203–6d and 184–8 (P.C.R. Tufnell 5–68). Middx 5pts, Leics 4pts.

Eastbourne: August 9, 10, 11
Sussex 258 and 191–6d drew with Leics 167 (A.I.C. Dodemaide 5–77) and 134–0. Sussex 7pts, Leics 5pts.

Folkestone: August 24, 25, 26, 28
Leics 498 (J.J. Whitaker 116) drew with Kent 264 and 267–2 (R.F. Pienaar 134*). Leics 8pts, Kent 4pts.

Trent Bridge: Sept 13, 14, 15, 16
Notts 121 (W.K.M Benjamin 6–42) and 278 drew with Leics 166 (F.D. Stephenson 7–65) and 125–5. Leics 5pts, Notts 4pts.

v GLAMORGAN (Leicester)

April 20, 21, 22, 24
Drawn. Leics 5pts, Glamorgan 5pts

Leicestershire 1st Innings

T.J. Boon	c Morris b Watkin	11
N.E. Briers	c Metson b Smith	30
*D.I. Gower	lbw b Watkin	4
P. Willey	b Watkin	46
J.J. Whitaker	b Derrick	39
L. Potter	c Derrick b Watkin	29
C.C. Lewis	b Derrick	4
†P. Whitticase	c Cottey b Barwick	21
G.J. Parsons	c Metson b Watkin	1
J.P. Agnew	not out	0
G.J.F. Ferris	c Metson b Watkin	0
Extras	lb 2, nb 3	5
Total (86.3 ov)		190

16, 25, 69, 116, 142, 158, 189, 189, 190

Watkin	27.3	7	53	6
Barwick	24	12	30	1
Derrick	21	4	47	2
Smith	13	2	49	1
North	1	0	9	0

Glamorgan 1st Innings

A.R. Butcher	c Whitticase b Lewis	19
*H. Morris	c Willey b Ferris	0
P.A. Cottey	c Gower b Agnew	2
M.P. Maynard	c Ferris b Lewis	18
M.J. Cann	b Lewis	0
I. Smith	c Whitticase b Ferris	11
J. Derrick	c Potter b Willey	67
†C.P. Metson	c Whitticase b Ferris	6
P.D. North	c Whitticase b Ferris	0
S.L. Watkin	b Willey	31
S.R. Barwick	not out	0
Extras	lb 4, nb 9	13
Total (71.2 ov)		167

3, 22, 38, 42, 49, 79, 95, 95, 154

Ferris	23	6	44	4
Agnew	19	2	57	1
Lewis	16	8	35	3
Willey	5.2	1	7	2
Parsons	6	2	14	0
Potter	2	0	6	0

Leicestershire 2nd Innings

T.J. Boon	c Butcher b Watkin	37
N.E. Briers	c Maynard b Smith	20
*D.I. Gower	c Maynard b Smith	228
P. Willey	c Morris b Watkin	8
J.J. Whitaker	b Watkin	6
L. Potter	c North b Barwick	37
C.C. Lewis	c North b Watkin	7
†P. Whitticase	b Derrick	37
G.J. Parsons	not out	14
J.P. Agnew	c North b Derrick	13
G.J.F. Ferris	not out	1
Extras	lb 7	7
Total (9 wkts dec)		415

43, 72, 112, 130, 272, 314, 387, 387, 414

Watkin	38	7	130	4
Barwick	35	8	101	1
Smith	19	2	57	2
Derrick	26	3	95	2
North	9	1	25	0

Glamorgan 2nd Innings

A.R. Butcher	not out	84
*H. Morris	c Whitticase b Parsons	30
P.A. Cottey	c Whitticase b Agnew	12
M.P. Maynard	lbw b Parsons	14
M.J. Cann	b Ferris	3
Extras	lb 8, w 1, nb 14	23
Total (4 wkts)		166

70, 115, 145, 166

Ferris	12.1	4	29	1
Agnew	19	6	42	1
Lewis	19	4	41	0
Parsons	16	7	44	2
Willey	4	3	2	0

Umpires: A.A. Jones and J.D. Bond
Toss: Leicestershire

Gower's 228 which lasted nearly 6 hours with 317 balls, 2 sixes and 24 fours, was the outstanding feature of this match. Glamorgan required 357 with 9 wickets in hand at the start of the final day, but rain allowed only 83 runs to be scored and the match was therefore drawn. Good bowling on the first day by medium pace Watkin dismissed Leics for 190, then by the close Glamorgan lost 3 for 38. The score slumped to 95–8, before Derrick and Watkin added 59 for the 9th wicket. When play ended on Friday, Gower was well in command being 80 not out and the total 157–4.

v KENT (Leicester)

May 24, 25, 26
Drawn. Leics 4pts, Kent 5pts

Kent 1st Innings

M.R. Benson	b Such	75
T.R. Ward	c Whitticase b Benjamin	11
N.R. Taylor	lbw b Benjamin	4
R.F. Pienaar	b Lewis	35
G.R. Cowdrey	not out	108
*C.S. Cowdrey	c Potter b Lewis	9
†S.A. Marsh	lbw b Willey	12
R.M. Ellison	c Potter b Such	24
C.Penn	c Potter b Such	0
R.P. Davis	run out	6
A.P. Igglesden	b Potter	5
Extras	b 2, lb 9, nb 7	18
Total (100 ov 226–6)		307

14, 19, 74, 165, 183, 205, 266, 266, 288

Benjamin	14	5	28	2
Agnew	29	1	101	0
Lewis	29	5	79	2
Such	28	11	40	3
Willey	18	5	31	1
Potter	5.4	1	17	1

Leicestershire 1st Innings

T.J. Boon	lbw b Igglesden	2
*N.E. Briers	c Ward b Ellison	26
P. Willey	c and b Davis	38
J.J. Whitaker	c Ellison b C.S. Cowdrey	8
L. Potter	b Davis	56
J.D.R. Benson	c C.S. Cowdrey b Davis	45
C.C.Lewis	run out	0
†P. Whitticase	not out	7
J.P. Agnew	not out	0
W.K.M. Benjamin		
J.P. Agnew		
Extras	b 2, lb 9, w 1, nb 7	19
Total (7 wkts dec, 78.4 ov)		201

13, 64, 77, 97, 193, 194, 195

Igglesden	13	5	16	1
Penn	15	1	35	0
Ellison	13	1	41	1
Davis	26	10	47	3
C.S. Cowdrey	8	2	31	1
Taylor	2	0	13	0
Ward	1.4	0	7	0

Kent 2nd Innings

M.R. Benson	not out	37
T.R. Ward	run out	69
N.R. Taylor	not out	18
Extras	lb 6, nb 3	9
Total (1 wkt dec)		133

88

Benjamin	3	0	19	0
Agnew	7	1	40	0
Lewis	3	0	8	0
Such	15	4	29	0
Willey	14	1	31	0

Leicestershire 2nd Innings

T.J. Boon	c Davis b Ellison	25
*N.E. Briers	lbw b Ellison	32
P. Willey	c Taylor b Penn	18
J.J. Whitaker	lbw b Igglesden	36
L. Potter	not out	28
J.D.R. Benson	b Igglesden	16
C.C. Lewis	c Marsh b Igglesden	0
†P. Whitticase	b Ellison	6
W.K.M. Benjamin	not out	14
Extras	lb 8, nb 1	9
Total (7 wkts)		184

57, 70, 109, 124, 146, 152, 166

Igglesden	12.4	5	33	3
Penn	11	1	39	1
Davis	26	6	90	0
Ellison	9	3	14	3

Umpires: J.H. Harris and B. Leadbeater
Toss: Kent

A thunderstorm ended play 80 minutes early on the first day, Kent being 199–5 off 86 overs, with Graham Cowdrey 44*. It took a total of 5 hours for Cowdrey to reach his 100, the scoring being very pedestrian. Leics began the last day at 193–5 with Potter 55*. Briers declared as soon as 200 was reached and later the home side had a maximum of 59 overs to make 240, but wickets fell too quickly for them to maintain the chase to the end.

v YORKSHIRE (Leicester)

June 7, 8, 9

Lost by 49 runs. Yorks 20pts, Leics 4pts

Yorkshire 1st Innings

A.A. Metcalfe	lbw b Agnew	2
M.D. Moxon	c Potter b Parsons	54
R.J. Blakey	c Whitticase b Agnew	26
P.E. Robinson	c Whitticase b Parsons	10
J.D. Love	c Whitticase b Parsons	17
D. Byas	c Benson b Parsons	67
†D.L. Bairstow	c Whitticase b Parsons	0
*P. Carrick	lbw b Lewis	8
A. Sidebottom	c Whitticase b Lewis	3
P.W. Jarvis	c Willey b Lewis	5
C.S. Pickles	not out	34
Extras	lb 4, nb 16	20
Total (82.2 ov)		246

12, 85, 91, 110, 123, 138, 160, 167, 191

Benjamin	20	8	47	0
Agnew	24	4	82	2
Lewis	18	1	65	3
Parsons	20.2	7	48	5

Leicestershire 1st Innings

T.J. Boon	c Bairstow b Jarvis	0
*N.E. Briers	c Blakey b Sidebottom	0
P. Willey	not out	45
J.J. Whitaker	b Jarvis	10
L. Potter	c Blakey b Sidebottom	0
J.D.R. Benson	c Bairstow b Jarvis	2
C.C. Lewis	lbw b Moxon	42
†P. Whitticase	not out	0
G.J. Parsons		
W.K.M. Benjamin		
J.P. Agnew		
Extras	b 2, lb 2, nb 5	9
Total (6 wkts dec, 50 ov)		108

0, 10, 31, 32, 39, 102

Jarvis	16	3	33	3
Sidebottom	16	5	37	2
Pickles	6	3	13	0
Carrick	7	1	11	0
Moxon	5	1	10	1

Yorkshire 2nd Innings

A.A. Metcalfe	c Whitticase b Parsons	41
M.D. Moxon	c Whitticase b Benjamin	8
R.J. Blakey	not out	48
P.E. Robinson	not out	7
Extras	lb 5, nb 3	8
Total (2 wkts dec)		112

13, 81

Benjamin	11	5	20	1
Agnew	9	1	38	0
Lewis	1	0	8	0
Parsons	6	1	22	1
Willey	6	1	19	0

Leicestershire 2nd Innings

T.J. Boon	c Bairstow b Sidebottom	19
*N.E. Briers	b Carrick	57
P. Willey	c Bairstow b Sidebottom	3
J.J. Whitaker	lbw b Pickles	4
L. Potter	lbw b Jarvis	2
J.D.R. Benson	c Byas b Jarvis	2
C.C. Lewis	c Love b Jarvis	7
†P. Whitticase	b Carrick	49
W.K.M. Benjamin	c Pickles b Carrick	10
G.J. Parsons	not out	30
J.P. Agnew	b Jarvis	0
Extras	lb 11, nb 7	18
Total		201

28, 46, 62, 85, 87, 101, 111, 136, 194

Jarvis	23.3	1	86	4
Sidebottom	17	4	44	2
Pickles	8	5	8	1
Carrick	18	7	52	3

Umpires: D.G.L. Evans and N.T. Plews
Toss: Leicestershire

Good batting by Moxon and Byas saved Yorkshire from collapse on the opening day, then Jarvis and Sidebottom reduced the home side to 60–5 off 23 overs by stumps. Only 90 minutes play took place on the second day. Leics declared first thing on Friday, then Yorkshire set them 251 to make in 69 overs. Until a 9th wicket stand of 58 by Whitticase and Parsons, Yorkshire's bowlers were in command. As it was the visitors won with 15 balls remaining.

v GLOUCESTERSHIRE (Leicester)

June 10, 12, 13

Lost by 9 wkts. Gloucs 24pts, Leics 4pts

Leicestershire 1st Innings

R.A. Cobb	c Athey b Walsh	2
*N.E. Briers	c Alleyne b Curran	48
T.J. Boon	c Alleyne b Jarvis	15
P. Willey	c Wright b Lawrence	8
J.J. Whitaker	c Wright b Walsh	12
L. Potter	c Athey b Curran	0
†P. Whitticase	lbw b Curran	8
W.K.M. Benjamin	b Walsh	30
G.J. Parsons	b Walsh	13
J.P. Agnew	not out	5
R.H. Edmunds	c Tedstone b Jarvis	0
Extras	lb 2, w 1, nb 1	4
Total (57.4 ov)		145

2, 31, 45, 88, 89, 96, 101, 139, 140

Walsh	23	9	37	4
Lawrence	10	1	32	1
Jarvis	11.4	1	39	2
Curran	13	4	35	3

Gloucestershire 1st Innings

I.P. Butcher	c Whitticase b Benjamin	7
A.J. Wright	lbw b Edmunds	32
J.W. Lloyds	c Whitaker b Agnew	43
*C.W.J. Athey	c Agnew b Benjamin	17
P. Bainbridge	c Whitticase b Agnew	33
K.M. Curran	c Whitticase b Agnew	43
M.W. Alleyne	c Whitticase b Agnew	26
†G.A. Tedstone	c Benjamin b Edmunds	30
D.V. Lawrence	b Benjamin	20
C.A. Walsh	not out	30
K.B.S. Jarvis	b Potter	10
Extras	b 1, lb 9, nb 5	15
Total (95.5 ov)		306

25, 83, 98, 132, 171, 210, 215, 249, 293

Benjamin	27	6	75	3
Agnew	36	5	101	4
Parsons	18	2	70	0
Edmunds	11	0	38	2
Willey	1	0	3	0
Potter	2.5	0	9	1

Leicestershire 2nd Innings

R.A. Cobb	c Wright b Walsh	7
*N.E. Briers	c Tedstone b Walsh	1
T.J. Boon	b Walsh	11
P. Willey	b Jarvis	9
J.J. Whitaker	c Athey b Curran	11
L. Potter	not out	52
†P. Whitticase	c Lawrence b Curran	46
W.K.M. Benjamin	c Bainbridge b Lawrence	4
G.J. Parsons	c Lloyds b Walsh	69
J.P. Agnew	b Curran	0
R.H. Edmunds	c Alleyne b Curran	17
Extras	b 1, lb 2, nb 8	11
Total		238

5, 20, 23, 42, 46, 98, 105, 219, 220

Walsh	30	6	63	4
Lawrence	16	8	26	1
Jarvis	15	2	57	1
Lloyds	1	0	6	0
Curran	19.1	3	78	4
Alleyne	2	1	5	0

Gloucestershire 2nd Innings

I.P. Butcher	not out	21
A.J. Wright	c Cobb b Agnew	2
J.W. Lloyds	not out	52
Extras	lb 2, nb 1	3
Total (1 wkt)		78

4

Agnew	8	1	39	1
Parsons	5	1	13	0
Willey	5	1	10	0
Potter	2.4	1	14	0

Umpires: D.G.L. Evans and B. Hassan
Toss: Leicestershire

On a difficult wicket only Briers, who batted 158 minutes for 48, survived long against some effective seam bowling. The pitch eased when Gloucester batted and they were within 16 of their opponents' total when play ended – at 7.07 pm. With a large deficit on first innings Leicester collapsed on their second attempt, being 46 for 5, before Whitticase and Parsons raised the total to 150 for 7 by stumps. Potter and Parsons added 114 for the 8th wkt, Potter batting nearly 4 hours for 52*, but Gloucester had no trouble hitting off the winning runs.

v NOTTINGHAMSHIRE (Leicester)

June 24, 26

Won by an innings and 101 runs. Leics 23pts, Notts 1pt

Leicestershire 1st Innings

R.A. Cobb	c Stephenson b Afford	33
*N.E. Briers	c Stephenson b Cooper	3
T.J. Boon	c Newell b Hemmings	57
P. Willey	c Stephenson b Afford	85
L. Potter	not out	121
C.C. Lewis	c Pollard b Hemmings	12
†P. Whitticase	c French b Stephenson	26
W.K.M. Benjamin	not out	4
G.J. Parsons		
J.P. Agnew		
P.M. Such		
Extras	b 2, lb 8, nb 1	11
Total (100 ov: 250–4) (6 wkts dec)		352

14, 80, 103, 245, 270, 342

Stephenson	22	6	66	1
Cooper	32	8	69	1
Saxelby	16	7	51	0
Afford	31	10	90	2
Hemmings	32	9	66	2

Nottinghamshire 1st Innings

P.R. Pollard	c Cobb b Agnew	1
*R.T. Robinson	c Willey b Agnew	8
M. Newell	c Potter b Agnew	4
D.J.R. Martindale	c Such b Lewis	33
D.W. Randall	c Willey b Agnew	12
F.D. Stephenson	c Cobb b Agnew	5
†B.N. French	c and b Lewis	12
E.E. Hemmings	b Lewis	9
K.E. Cooper	b Lewis	13
K. Saxelby	not out	11
J.A. Afford	lbw b Lewis	2
Extras	lb 2, nb 4	6
Total (37 overs)		116

1, 12, 15, 33, 52, 74, 89, 90, 113

Benjamin	10	2	26	0
Agnew	18	6	37	5
Lewis	9	0	51	5

Nottinghamshire 2nd Innings

P.R. Pollard	lbw b Lewis	24
* R. T. Robinson	c Cobb b Agnew	0
M. Newell	c Whitticase b Agnew	0
D.J.R. Martindale	lbw b Benjamin	7
D. W. Randall	c Cobb b Agnew	36
F.D. Stephenson	c Parsons b Agnew	24
†B.N. French	b Lewis	0
E.E. Hemmings	c Parsons b Lewis	4
K.E. Cooper	not out	24
K. Saxelby	lbw b Agnew	4
J.A. Afford	b Agnew	1
Extras	lb 10, w 1	11
Total		135

4, 4, 12, 71, 93, 97, 101, 105, 127

Benjamin	11	4	40	1
Agnew	17.5	5	56	6
Lewis	7	0	29	3

Umpires: B. Leadbeater and K.E. Palmer
Toss: Leicestershire

Leicestershire spent Saturday scoring 310–5 and continued their innings for a further 13 overs on Monday before declaring. Notts were then shot out twice by Agnew and the match was completed within two days. Agnew bowled unchanged through both innings and though he had a certain amount of assistance from the wicket, he owed much of his success to his length and direction.

v WARWICKSHIRE (Hinckley)

July 1, 3, 4

Drawn. Leics 8pts, Warwicks 3pts

Warwickshire 1st Innings

J.D. Ratcliffe	c Nixon b Benjamin	36
A.J. Moles	b Taylor	38
*T.A. Lloyd	lbw b Agnew	6
G.W. Humpage	c Taylor b Parsons	31
Asif Din	b Benjamin	0
D.A. Reeve	c and b Benjamin	55
†K.J. Piper	c Nixon b Parsons	0
G.C. Small	lbw b Benjamin	13
A.A. Donald	b Benjamin	5
A.R.K. Pierson	not out	3
T.A. Munton	c Nixon b Benjamin	0
Extras	lb 5, nb 4	9
Total (81.4 ov)		196

63, 70, 88, 88, 164, 164, 188, 189, 196

Benjamin	25.4	3	70	6
Agnew	26	5	62	1
Taylor	15	2	30	1
Parsons	13	3	29	2
Willey	2	2	0	0

Leicestershire 1st Innings

T.J. Boon	not out	33
N.E. Briers	b Small	25
*D.I. Gower	c Piper b Munton	27
P. Willey	c Piper b Small	96
J.J. Whitaker	b Small	138
L. Potter	c Ratcliffe b Small	0
W.K.M. Benjamin	c Humpage b Pierson	8
G.J. Parsons	not out	21
†P.A. Nixon		
J.P. Agnew		
L.B. Taylor		
Extras	b 2, lb 18, nb 3	23
Total (100 ov: 325–5) (6 wkts dec)		371

49, 82, 264, 323, 323, 332

Donald	14	2	50	0
Small	36	6	95	4
Munton	32	9	97	1
Pierson	36	6	109	1

Warwickshire 2nd Innings

J.D. Ratcliffe	c Nixon b Agnew	32
A.J. Moles	c Nixon b Agnew	0
*T.A. Lloyd	c Agnew b Willey	28
G.W. Humpage	c Parsons b Willey	55
Asif Din	c Boon b Taylor	17
D.A. Reeve	c Nixon b Willey	19
†K.J. Piper	not out	20
G.C. Small	b Benjamin	5
A.R.K. Pierson	c Nixon b Benjamin	0
T.A. Munton	not out	1
A.A. Donald		
Extras	b 5, lb 4, nb 7	16
Total (8 wkts)		193

3, 54, 75, 112, 160, 169, 186, 190

Benjamin	25	13	28	2
Agnew	16	4	50	2
Willey	34	16	63	3
Taylor	12	2	32	1
Parsons	12	7	11	0
Potter	3	3	0	0

Umpires: J.W. Holder and M.J. Kitchen
Toss: Warwickshire
Leicester held the initiative after the first day, Benjamin having dismissed the visitors for 196 and Leicester being 26-0 in reply. Whitaker batted 4 hours on Monday to reach 138. Willey made 96, but Warwickshire suffered from a depleted side, Donald, Munton, Reeve, Asif Din and Small all being less than fully fit. Leicester declared first thing on Tuesday. Humpage however held out for 200 minutes for 55 and the game was drawn.

v LANCASHIRE (Leicester)

July 5, 6, 7

Drawn. Lancs 8pts, Leics 5pts

Lancashire 1st Innings

G.D. Mendis	c Potter b Agnew	80
G.D. Lloyd	c Nixon b Agnew	11
*D.P. Hughes	lbw b Agnew	0
N.H. Fairbrother	st Nixon b Willey	65
T.E. Jesty	b Benjamin	15
M. Watkinson	c and b Willey	27
†W.K. Hegg	run out	86
P.A.J. DeFreitas	c Benjamin b Willey	69
J.D. Fitton	not out	23
P.J.W. Allott	b Parsons	14
B.P. Patterson		
Extras	b 5, lb 15, nb 1	21
Total (99.3 ov, 9 wkts dec)		411

20, 20, 153, 176, 176, 217, 363, 376, 411

Benjamin	19	7	61	1
Agnew	22	5	75	3
Parsons	15.3	0	83	1
Taylor	17	1	78	0
Willey	22	7	73	3
Potter	4	0	21	0

Leicestershire 1st Innings

R.A. Cobb	lbw b Allott	14
*N.E. Briers	b Patterson	1
G.J. Parsons	c DeFreitas b Patterson	30
T.J. Boon	b DeFreitas	28
P. Willey	c and b Allott	85
J.J. Whitaker	b DeFreitas	2
L. Potter	c Hegg b Watkinson	1
W.K.M. Benjamin	lbw b Allott	13
†P.A. Nixon	lbw b Allott	0
J.P. Agnew	not out	0
L.B. Taylor	c Lloyd b Allott	0
Extras	b 1, lb 8, nb 4	13
Total (71.4 ov)		187

5, 48, 48, 143, 153, 173, 187, 187, 187

Patterson	17	5	45	2
De Freitas	20	5	49	2
Allott	17.4	6	24	5
Watkinson	6	2	12	1
Fitton	11	2	48	0

Leicestershire 2nd Innings

R.A. Cobb	lbw b Allott	5
*N.E. Briers	c Hegg b Patterson	33
T.J. Boon	not out	44
P. Willey	not out	8
Extras	w 1	1
Total (2 wkts)		91

14, 78

DeFreitas	14	4	41	0
Allott	14	4	23	1
Patterson	7	1	22	1
Watkinson	1	0	5	0

Umpires: K.J. Lyons and R. Palmer
Toss: Lancashire
Mendis and Fairbrother added 133 in 98 minutes, the score reaching 150 before lunch on the first morning. In the afternoon DeFreitas and Hegg added a further 146 in 105 minutes, so that the 300 arrived off 81 overs. Leics were 25-1 off 7 overs at stumps. A thunderstorm removed 31 overs from the second day, but Leicestershire were all out and reached 24-1 in the second innings when the follow on was enforced. Further rain on the third day ruined the match, only 22 overs being bowled.

v NORTHAMPTONSHIRE (Leicester)

July 19, 20, 21

Drawn. Leics 6pts, Northants 3pts

Northamptonshire 1st Innings

G. Cook	c Whitticase b Agnew	0
N.A. Felton	b Taylor	25
R.J. Bailey	lbw b Agnew	9
*A.J. Lamb	c Willey b Parsons	31
D.J. Capel	c and b Parsons	4
N.A. Stanley	c Boon b Parsons	75
A.L. Penberthy	b Agnew	14
†D. Ripley	b Taylor	12
J.G. Thomas	b Taylor	5
C.E.L. Ambrose	b Parsons	13
N.G.B. Cook	not out	0
Extras	b 1, lb 6, w 1, nb 2	10
Total (69.4 ov)		198

0, 12, 66, 68, 71, 107, 145, 165, 191

Agnew	19	5	50	3
Taylor	19	5	56	3
Parsons	18.4	4	56	4
Willey	1	1	0	0
Such	12	4	29	0

Leicestershire 1st Innings

T.J. Boon	lbw b Thomas	4
N.E. Briers	c Bailey b N.G.B. Cook	46
*D.I. Gower	c Lamb b Ambrose	50
G.J. Parsons	lbw b Ambrose	0
P. Willey	c Bailey b N.G. B. Cook	12
J.J. Whitaker	c Ripley b Thomas	99
L. Potter	c Ripley b Thomas	49
†P. Whitticase	c Ripley b Ambrose	0
J.P. Agnew	b Ambrose	25
L.B. Taylor	not out	4
P.M. Such	b Ambrose	0
Extras	lb 11	11
Total (100 ov: 243–5)		300

27, 100, 101, 106, 126, 270, 271, 279, 300

Ambrose	30.3	10	52	5
Thomas	24	5	89	3
Capel	18	3	58	0
Penberthy	7	2	21	0
N.G.B. Cook	33	13	63	2
Bailey	2	0	6	0

Northamptonshire 2nd Innings

G. Cook	st Whitticase b Potter	105
N.A. Felton	lbw b Agnew	0
R.J. Bailey	lbw b Agnew	52
D.J. Capel	c Whitaker b Willey	77
N.A. Stanley	b Potter	43
A.L. Penberthy	c Gower b Potter	7
†D. Ripley	c Gower b Such	6
J.G. Thomas	not out	13
C.E.L. Ambrose	not out	2
Extras	b 4, lb 3	7
Total (7 wkts dec)		312

1, 83, 211, 279, 284, 297, 297

Agnew	20	3	39	2
Taylor	11	1	32	0
Such	26	8	71	1
Parsons	4	0	9	0
Potter	21.2	3	88	3
Willey	27	10	66	1

Leicestershire 2nd Innings

T.J. Boon	c Capel b Thomas	15
N.E. Briers	run out	1
*D.I. Gower	c Felton b Bailey	91
P. Willey	c Thomas b N.G.B. Cook	20
J.J. Whitaker	c Penberthy b N.G.B. Cook	7
L. Potter	b N.G.B. Cook	5
†P. Whitticase	c Capel b N.G.B. Cook	5
G.J. Parsons	not out	41
J.P. Agnew	not out	5
Extras	b 5, lb 10, w 1	16
Total (7 wkts)		206

15, 49, 93, 106, 114, 122, 169

Ambrose	8	3	17	0
Thomas	7	1	31	1
N.G.B. Cook	14	1	54	4
Capel	7	0	47	0
Bailey	6	0	42	1

Umpires: D.G.L. Evans and B. Leadbeater
Toss: Northants
Stanley, on his first appearance of the summer, held Northants together with a career best 75. Leics were 104–3 off 40 overs at stumps. Whitaker batted 219 minutes for 99, providing his team with a lead of 102, but Northants had replied making 76–1 by Thursday's close. Leics were set 211 in 42 overs, but in spite of 91 by Gower, they failed at the last fence, being 5 runs short, when the overs ran out.

v SURREY (Leicester)

August 19, 21, 22

Lost by 4 wkts. Surrey 21pts, Leics 7pts

Leicestershire 1st Innings

T.J. Boon	c Stewart b Frost	29
N.E. Briers	c Stewart b Murphy	63
*D.I. Gower	c Stewart b Murphy	13
J.J. Whitaker	c Stewart b Murphy	0
P. Willey	c D.J. Bicknell b Medlycott	15
L. Potter	c Stewart b Frost	55
†P. Whitticase	lbw b Medlycott	32
W.K.M. Benjamin	c Stewart b Murphy	41
G.J. Parsons	c D.J. Bicknell b Robinson	9
J.P. Agnew	c Greig b Robinson	21
L.B. Taylor	not out	11
Extras	b 2, lb 4, nb 2	8
Total (99.2 ov)		297

88, 98, 98, 109, 142, 193, 254, 254, 278

M.P. Bicknell	27	11	79	0
Murphy	26	86	66	4
Frost	21	0	61	2
Robinson	7.2	8	37	2
Medlycott	17	0	47	2
D.J. Bicknell	1	0	1	0

Surrey 1st Innings

G.S. Clinton	c Benjamin b Taylor	28
D.J. Bicknell	lbw b Benjamin	29
†A.J. Stewart	b Benjamin	21
G.P. Thorpe	c Gower b Benjamin	34
M.A. Lynch	lbw b Willey	13
*I.A. Greig	b Benjamin	3
J.D. Robinson	retired hurt	14
K.T. Medlycott	st Whitticase b Willey	12
M.P. Bicknell	not out	18
A.J. Murphy	c Parsons b Benjamin	0
M. Frost	b Agnew	3
Extras	b 1, lb 4, w 1, nb 3	9
Total (63 ov)		184

54, 83, 93, 114, 119, 150, 167, 170

Benjamin	24	6	83	5
Agnew	15	1	45	1
Parsons	6	2	19	0
Taylor	4	1	10	1
Willey	14	5	22	2

Leicestershire 2nd Innings

T.J. Boon	lbw b Frost	30
N.E. Briers	lbw b M.P. Bicknell	13
*D.I. Gower	c and b Frost	4
J.J. Whitaker	c Stewart b Murphy	28
P. Willey	c Stewart b M.P. Bicknell	39
L. Potter	run out	2
†P. Whitticase	c Stewart b Frost	47
W.K.M. Benjamin	c Stewart b Frost	5
G.J. Parsons	c Stewart b Frost	2
J.P. Agnew	c Clinton b M.P. Bicknell	3
L.B. Taylor	not out	0
Extras	lb 4, w 2, nb 3	9
Total		182

32, 37, 55, 87, 107, 156, 174, 178, 182

Murphy	10	2	33	1
M.P. Bicknell	18.1	1	55	3
Medlycott	16	5	50	0
Frost	13	2	40	5

Surrey 2nd Innings

G.S. Clinton	c Gower b Willey	84
D.J. Bicknell	lbw b Agnew	22
†A.J. Stewart	c Potter b Agnew	77
G.P. Thorpe	c Potter b Willey	43
M.A. Lynch	run out	3
*I.A. Greig	b Willey	2
K.T. Medlycott	not out	26
M.P. Bicknell	not out	10
Extras	b 12, lb 13, nb 4	29
Total (6 wkts)		296

63, 196, 205, 209, 235, 268

Benjamin	21.5	5	60	0
Agnew	21	3	52	2
Taylor	5	1	21	0
Willey	32	5	91	3
Potter	6	1	21	0
Parsons	5	1	26	0

Umpires: D.R. Shepherd and R.A. White

Toss: Leicestershire

The chief feature of the first day was six catches taken by wicketkeeper Stewart. Some effective pace bowling by Benjamin gained his side a substantial lead on the second day. Stewart equalled the world catching record on the last day and Surrey needed 296 off 92 overs. The Leicester bowling was somewhat erratic and despite a difficult pitch, Surrey won with seven balls to spare.

v DERBYSHIRE (Leicester)

August 29, 30, 31

Won by 10 wkts. Leics 22pts, Derbys 6pts

Derbyshire 1st Innings

*K.J. Barnett	b Benjamin	3
P.D. Bowler	c Lewis b Agnew	17
J.E. Morris	c Parsons b Benjamin	3
R. Sharma	c Whitticase b Taylor	22
T.J.G. O'Gorman	c Whitticase b Taylor	29
B. Roberts	c Whitticase b Taylor	15
†K.M. Krikken	c Potter b Agnew	37
F.A. Griffith	c Lewis b Parsons	5
I.R. Bishop	c Whitticase b Benjamin	27
M. Jean-Jacques	c Parsons b Benjamin	11
S.J. Base	not out	8
Extras	b 4, lb 14, w 1, nb 8	27
Total (79.1 ov)		204

3, 7, 33, 78, 93, 124, 129, 169, 190

Agnew	22	3	58	2
Benjamin	23.1	6	51	5
Taylor	16	3	43	2
Lewis	6	1	17	0
Willey	2	2	0	0
Parsons	10	4	17	1

Leicestershire 1st Innings

T.J. Boon	c Krikken b Base	31
*N.E. Briers	c O'Gorman b Bishop	4
J.J. Whitaker	c Krikken b Bishop	7
P. Willey	c Bowler b Bishop	96
L. Potter	c Krikken b Jean-Jacques	14
C.C. Lewis	st Krikken b Barnett	18
†P. Whitticase	c sub b Griffith	5
W.K.M. Benjamin	c Bowler b Bishop	40
G.J. Parsons	b Bishop	3
J.P. Agnew	not out	3
L.B. Taylor	b Bishop	0
Extras	b 6, lb 2, w 1, nb 11	20
Total (70.3 ov)		241

27, 48, 48, 80, 158, 185, 197, 228, 241

Bishop	22.3	6	67	6
Base	23	4	53	1
Jean-Jacques	10	0	49	1
Sharma	6	1	22	0
Barnett	3	0	12	1
Griffith	6	1	30	1

Derbyshire 2nd Innings

*K.J. Barnett	b Lewis	36
P.D. Bowler	lbw b Benjamin	4
J.E. Morris	c Parsons b Lewis	1
M. Jean-Jacques	c Lewis b Benjamin	3
R. Sharma	lbw b Lewis	3
T.J.G. O'Gorman	c Potter b Lewis	6
B. Roberts	lbw b Lewis	7
F.A. Griffith	lbw b Benjamin	8
I.R. Bishop	c Boon b Benjamin	4
†K.M. Krikken	not out	1
S.J. Base	b Benjamin	0
Extras	lb 1, nb 4	5
Total		78

19, 22, 36, 41, 53, 62, 72, 76, 78

Benjamin	13.5	4	25	5
Agnew	3	0	12	0
Lewis	10	0	40	5

Leicestershire 2nd Innings

T.J. Boon	not out	12
N.E. Briers	not out	23
Extras	b 4, lb 1, nb 2	7
Total (0 wkt)		42

Bishop	6.4	0	17	0
Base	6	1	20	0
Jean-Jacques	1	1	0	0

Umpires: J.W. Holder and R. Palmer

Toss: Leicestershire

This four day game was ended by lunch time on the third day, the Derbyshire batting in their second innings simply collapsing. Then in contrast, the home county found little difficulty in scoring the 42 needed for victory, the Derbyshire bowlers bowling much too short. The only noteworthy batting of a rather dull match was Willey's 96 which he made in 150 minutes with 15 fours.

v ESSEX (Leicester)

Sept 8, 9, 10, 11

Lost by 10 wkts. Essex 24pts, Leics 2pts

Essex 1st Innings

*G.A. Gooch	b Agnew	158
J.P. Stephenson	c Potter b Benjamin	2
P.J. Prichard	lbw b Agnew	2
M.E. Waugh	b Agnew	165
N. Hussain	b Agnew	0
B.R. Hardie	b Agnew	0
†M.A. Garnham	c Gower b Lewis	32
N.A. Foster	b Benjamin	5
D.R. Pringle	c Lewis b Willey	22
T.D. Topley	c and b Lewis	6
J.H. Childs	not out	0
Extras	b 4, lb 10, nb 9	23
Total (100 ov: 356–6)		415

19, 26, 298, 298, 306, 351, 372, 392, 400

Benjamin	29	7	72	2
Agnew	33	10	89	5
Lewis	28	3	137	2
Taylor	13	0	50	0
Willey	16.2	2	53	1

Leicestershire 1st Innings

N.E. Briers	c Childs b Foster	5
T.J. Boon	b Childs	26
*D.I. Gower	lbw b Pringle	0
J.J. Whitaker	lbw b Foster	6
J.P. Agnew	b Topley	10
P. Willey	c Hussain b Childs	4
L. Potter	not out	29
C.C. Lewis	lbw b Pringle	16
†P. Whitticase	c Stephenson b Childs	16
W.K.M. Benjamin	lbw b Topley	23
L.B. Taylor	b Topley	2
Extras	b 1, lb 7	8
Total (57 ov)		145

21, 21, 30, 48, 48, 54, 79, 98, 141

Foster	8	1	29	2
Pringle	12	4	28	2
Topley	17	6	35	3
Childs	20	10	45	3

Leicestershire 2nd Innings

*D.I. Gower	c Hardie b Foster	109
N.E. Briers	c Hussain b Childs	4
J.J. Whitaker	c Stephenson b Foster	44
P. Willey	lbw b Pringle	14
L. Potter	lbw b Pringle	7
C.C. Lewis	c and b Childs	6
†P. Whitticase	c Topley b Lloyds	17
W.K.M. Benjamin	c Foster b Childs	26
J.P. Agnew	b Foster	24
T.J. Boon	c Hussain b Childs	7
L.B. Taylor	not out	0
Extras	b 4, lb 8, nb 4	16
Total		274

25, 161, 178, 190, 197, 197, 239, 244, 260

Foster	25.5	4	98	3
Pringle	18	2	57	2
Childs	32	12	84	5
Topley	5	1	23	0

Essex 2nd Innings

T.D. Topley	not out	4
†M.A. Garnham	not out	3
Extras	lb 1	1
Total (0 wkt)		8

Whitticase	0.5	0	7	0

Umpires: A.A. Jones and D.R. Shepherd

Toss: Essex

Although the first day was limited to just 29 overs and Essex made 84-2 with Gooch 51 not out, the visitors still managed to win this game with time to spare. On Saturday the overnight pair of Gooch and Waugh took their partnership to 272 and Essex raced to 415 off 119.2 overs. Leicester began Monday at 48-3. 55 overs were lost, but Essex still managed to enforce the follow on and Leicester needed 236 to avoid an innings defeat. Gower hit a charming hundred on the last day, in vain however, and Essex collected 24 points and second place in the table.

Middlesex

President: F.G. Mann
Chairman: M.P. Murray
Secretary: J. Hardstaff, Lord's Cricket Ground, St John's Wood, London, NW8 8QN. *Tel:* 01-289 1300.
Coach: D. Bennett
Captain: M.W. Gatting
Foundation of Present Club: December 1863, in London
First First-Class Match: Middlesex v Surrey (Lord's) May 1850
County Champions: 1866, 1903, 1920, 1921, 1947, 1949 (joint), 1976, 1977 (joint), 1980, 1982
Gillette/NatWest Trophy: Winners 1977, 1980, 1984, 1988
Benson & Hedges Cup: Winners 1983, 1986
Sunday League Champions: Nil (runners-up in 1982)
Refuge Cup: Nil

Summary of Results in 1989
Britannic Assurance County Championship: Played 22, Won 9, Lost 2, Drawn 11, Position 3rd
NatWest Bank Trophy: Lost in final
Benson & Hedges Cup: Did not qualify for knock-out section
Refuge Assurance Sunday League: Played 16, Won 8, Lost 7, Tied 1, Position 9th
Refuge Assurance Cup: Did not qualify

Desmond Haynes, Middlesex's recruit from the West Indies, who in his first season for the county scored 1,446 runs.

Allsport/Adrian Murrell

ONE DAY AWAY MATCHES

The full scorecard of each of Middlesex's away matches will be found in the sections for the respective home teams.

Refuge Assurance Matches

Chelmsford: April 30
Middx 130 (40 ov) lost to Essex 134–2 by 8 wkts. Essex 4pts, Middx 0pts.

Bristol: May 14
Middx 202–6 (40 ov) beat Gloucs 187–7 (40 ov) by 15 runs. Middx 4pts, Gloucs 0pts.

Edgbaston: May 28
Warwicks 196–4 beat Middx 167–8 (39 ov) by 29 runs. Warwicks 4pts, Middx 0pts.

Merthyr Tydfil: June 11
Glamorgan 209–6 (40 ov) beat Middx 172 (37.5 ov) by 37 runs. Glam 4pts, Middx 0pts.

Worcester: June 25
Worcs 143 (39.2 ov) (S.P. Hughes 5–23) lost to Middx 144–5 by 5 wkts. Middx 4pts, Worcs 0pts.

Weston-super-Mare: August 6
Somerset 205–8 (40 ov) beat Middx 108 (32.2 ov) by 97 runs. Somerset 4pts, Middx 0pts.

Hastings: August 20
Sussex 170–9 (40 ov) lost to Middx 172–6 (39.3 ov) by 4 wkts. Middx 4pts, Sussex 0pts.

Trent Bridge: August 7
Middx 167 (39.5 ov) lost to Notts 168–2 (34.2 ov) by 8 wkts. Notts 4pts, Middx 0pts.

Benson and Hedges Cup

Bristol: May 2
Middx 149 (53.4 ov) lost to Gloucs 150–4 (47.2 ov) by 6 wkts. Gloucs 2pts, Middx 0pts.

The Parks: May 9
Comb Univ 190–9 (55 ov) lost to Middx 194–2 (53.4 ov) (M.W. Gatting 123*) by 9 wkts. Middx 2pts, Comb Univ 0pts.

NatWest Bank Trophy

Darlington: June 28
Middx 215–7 (60 ov) beat Durham 161 (56.2 ov) by 54 runs.

Southampton: August 16 (semi-final)
Middx 267–7 (60 ov) beat Hants 264–7 (60 ov) (C.L. Smith 114) by 3 runs.

Lord's: September 2 (Final)
Middx 210–5 (60 ov) lost to Warwicks 211–6 (59.4 ov) by 4 wkts.

From left, back: *K.R. Brown, M.R. Ramprakash, R.M. Ellcock, I.J. F. Hutchinson, A. Barnett, P. Weekes, J.C. Pooley, Aftab Habib.* Centre: *D. Bennett (Coach), H.P.H. Sharp (Scorer), M. Roseberry, P.C.R. Tufnell, A.R.C. Fraser, J.F. Sykes, A.G.J. Fraser, C.T. Radley (Assistant Coach), J. Davis (Physiotherapist), A.P. Jones (2nd XI Scorer).* Front: *J.D. Carr, N.G. Cowans, P.R. Downton, J.E. Emburey, M.W. Gatting (Captain), R.O. Butcher, S.P. Hughes, N.F. Williams.* Allsport/Russell Cheyne

REFUGE ASSURANCE LEAGUE

v YORKSHIRE (Lord's)

April 23

Won on faster scoring rate. Middx 4pts, Yorks 0pts

Yorkshire		
D. Byas	b Carr	9
A.A. Metcalfe	run out	76
P.E. Robinson	c Cowans b Sykes	55
†D.L. Bairstow	c Ramprakash b Fraser	5
J.D. Love	b Hughes	14
R.J. Blakey	b Hughes	1
S.N. Hartley	st Downton b Emburey	0
*P. Carrick	c Butcher b Emburey	0
P.W. Jarvis	b Emburey	0
C.S. Pickles	not out	1
P.A. Booth		
Extras	lb 5, w 4	9
Total (9 wkts, 40 ov)		170

19, 100, 129, 156, 164, 169, 169, 169, 170

Cowans	8	2	16	0
Fraser	8	0	28	1
Carr	6	0	26	1
Hughes	8	0	51	2
Emburey	8	0	37	3
Sykes	2	1	7	1

Middlesex		
J.D. Carr	c Blakey b Jarvis	23
†P.R. Downton	c Bairstow b Byas	16
*M.W. Gatting	not out	81
M.R. Rampraskash	not out	29
R.O. Butcher		
K.R. Brown		
J.E. Emburey		
S.P. Hughes		
J.F. Sykes		
A.R.C. Fraser		
N.G. Cowans		
Extras	b 2, lb 6, w 5	13
Total (2 wkts, 34.1 ov)		162

31, 55

Pickles	7	0	49	0
Hartley	7	0	23	0
Jarvis	7.1	0	38	1
Byas	5	0	18	1
Carrick	5	0	16	0
Booth	3	0	10	0

Umpires: D.J. Constant and J.H. Hampshire
Toss: Middlesex

Cowans opened the Middlesex bowling with six overs for just seven runs, but Robinson later hit out to complete 50 off 50 balls. In the final over, four wickets fell. Gatting's innings included 9 fours and 2 sixes.

v SURREY (Lord's)

May 7

Won by 60 runs. Middx 4pts, Surrey 0pts

Middlesex		
J.D. Carr	lbw b Bicknell	86
*M.W. Gatting	c Feltham b Greig	80
R.O. Butcher	b Thorpe	16
M.R. Ramprakash	c Stewart b Feltham	13
J.E. Emburey	c Bullen b Bicknell	5
J.F. Sykes	not out	0
†P.R. Downton		
K.R. Brown		
S.P. Hughes		
N.F. Williams		
A.R.C. Fraser		
Extras	b 4, lb 11, w 5, nb 1	21
Total (5 wkts, 40 ov)		221

147, 173, 208, 220, 221

Bicknell	8	0	43	2
Murphy	8	0	39	0
Feltham	8	0	34	1
Greig	8	0	29	1
Bullen	8	0	20	0
Thorpe	8	0	41	1

Surrey		
K.T. Medlycott	c Butcher b Williams	4
G.S. Clinton	b Carr	35
†A.J. Stewart	c Sykes b Williams	17
D.M. Ward	lbw b Fraser	1
*I.A. Greig	c Emburey b Carr	11
Z.A. Sadiq	b Carr	2
G.P. Thorpe	st Downton b Carr	10
M.A. Feltham	c Downton b Sykes	35
C.K. Bullen	not out	28
M.P. Bicknell	st Downton b Sykes	1
A.J. Murphy	run out	3
Extras	b 4, lb 9, nb 1	14
Total (38.3 ov)		161

9, 33, 48, 65, 71, 90, 97, 149, 156

Williams	8	0	24	2
Hughes	4	0	10	0
Fraser	7.3	0	34	1
Carr	8	2	21	4
Emburey	7	0	29	0
Sykes	4	0	30	2

Umpires: P.B. Wight and R.A. White
Toss: Surrey

An opening stand of 147 by Carr and Gatting established Middlesex as the dominant party in this game. Carr went on to pick up 4 cheap wickets when Surrey batted and Middlesex won the game by a substantial margin.

v HAMPSHIRE (Lord's)

June 4

Tied. Middx 2pts, Hants 2pts

Hampshire		
*M.C.J. Nicholas	c and b Hughes	13
V.P. Terry	b Cowans	2
R.A. Smith	lbw b Cowans	1
D.R. Turner	c Gatting b Fraser	28
C.L. Smith	c Gatting b Cowans	0
K.D. James	b Emburey	31
M.D Marshall	c Carr b Hughes	36
N.G. Cowley	c Emburey b Hughes	9
†R.J. Parks	st Downton b Emburey	3
C.A. Connor	c Downton b Hughes	0
P.J. Bakker	not out	1
Extras	lb 5, w 5, nb 4	14
Total (38.4 ov)		138

16, 16, 17, 26, 78, 123, 123, 130, 131

Cowans	8	5	6	3
Hughes	7.4	0	20	4
Fraser	7	1	23	1
Carr	6	0	46	0
Emburey	8	1	29	2
Gatting	2	0	9	0

Middlesex		
J.D. Carr	b Bakker	2
D.L. Haynes	c Marshall b Bakker	52
M.A. Roseberry	c Bakker b James	20
R.O. Butcher	b Bakker	8
K.R. Brown	c Parks b Marshall	8
†P.R. Downton	c Parks b Connor	11
J.E. Emburey	c Parks b James	10
S.P. Hughes	c Parks b Marshall	3
A.R.C. Fraser	not out	2
*M.W. Gatting	not out	3
N.G. Cowans		
Extras	b 1, lb 10, w 8	19
Total (8 wkts, 40 ov)		138

6, 35, 59, 81, 102, 119, 126, 128

Marshall	8	1	18	2
Bakker	8	0	35	3
James	8	1	22	2
Connor	8	0	19	1
Cowley	7	0	31	0
Nicholas	1	0	2	0

Umpires: J.C. Balderstone and P.B. Wight
Toss: Middlesex

Gatting took a brilliant catch to dismiss Turner and fractured his thumb, then he had to come in to bat with ten runs required. Haynes hit his 52 off 75 balls.

Winners of the NatWest Trophy in 1988, Middlesex failed to gain any trophies last year, but they again reached the NatWest Final and they came third in the Championship, which was pleasing after the poor results in 1987 and 1988 – that is poor by recent Middlesex standards.

Unlike many counties, Middlesex decided to use their overseas 'ticket' to employ a batsman and opted for the long established Test opener, Haynes. This proved an astute move, not only because Haynes scored many runs, but also because young Carr, who had opened the Middlesex batting with some panache over the last year or two, seemed to give up the ghost – he announced his retirement at the end of the summer.

Carr is a disappointment, but the county were lucky enough to possess three other young batsmen, all of whom did well. Ramprakash, who reached his 21st year in the final week of the season, hit 1,000 runs; Hutchinson, the Welshman from Shrewsbury School, scored a double hundred against Oxford; Roseberry also reached three figures at the expense of the University bowlers. Gatting, whose decision to captain England in South Africa caused some controversy, batted just as well as in the past. Downton, not required by England by 1989, played more often than in 1988, but his run aggregate did not reflect this.

The continued progress of Angus Fraser was the most pleasing feature of the bowling – he now causing problems for the best batsmen. Cowans was slightly more expensive than in 1988 and the fast attack was bolstered by Ellcock, the Barbados-born cricketer who had previously been in the Worcestershire ranks. Williams, another recruit from the Caribbean, had a strange change of fortune. Having been top of the averages in 1988, he managed the same total of wickets last year, but ended at the foot of the table. Hughes, on the other hand, had a good summer, having been very expensive in 1988. The spin department was in the hands of the experienced Emburey and the 23-year-old, Tufnell. The latter had more opportunities and picked up 50 first-class wickets. With such a promising band of young players allied to the old heads, Gatting, Haynes and Emburey, Middlesex should do well in 1990. All was not so bright in the club house. The secretary unexpectedly resigned and a name to evoke memories of the past took his place – Joe Hardstaff.

REFUGE ASSURANCE LEAGUE

v LANCASHIRE (Lord's)

July 2

Lost by 4 wkts. Lancs 4pts, Middx 0pts

Middlesex		
I.J.F. Hutchingson	c Jesty b Allott	7
D.L. Haynes	c Jesty b Watkinson	35
*M.W. Gatting	b Allott	1
R.O. Butcher	b DeFreitas	0
M.R. Ramprakash	lbw b Wasim Akram	6
J.D. Carr	c Hegg b Austin	7
†P.R. Downton	not out	31
J.E. Emburey	b Austin	13
A.R.C. Fraser	b Wasim Akram	12
S.P. Hughes	not out	0
N.G. Cowans		
Extras	b 2, lb 18, w 2, nb 2	24
Total (8 wkts, 40 ov)		136

19, 21, 22, 52, 74, 74, 103, 133

DeFreitas	8	0	25	1
Allott	8	2	19	2
Watkinson	8	0	27	1
Wasim Akram	8	1	20	2
Austin	8	1	25	2

Lancashire		
G.D. Mendis	lbw b Emburey	19
†W.K. Hegg	c Emburey b Fraser	1
*D.P. Hughes	b Gatting	5
N.H. Fairbrother	not out	59
T.E. Jesty	c Downton b Cowans	4
M. Watkinson	lbw b Emburey	31
Wasim Akram	c Downton b Hughes	3
P.A.J. DeFreitas	not out	0
I.D. Austin		
P.W.J. Allott		
J. Simmons		
Extras	lb 10, w 5, nb 2	17
Total (6 wkts, 38.4 ov)		139

8, 31, 53, 73, 126, 131

Cowans	8	4	18	1
Fraser	8	3	25	1
Carr	5	0	32	0
Gatting	2	0	8	1
Hughes	7.4	0	28	1
Emburey	8	0	18	2

Umpires: B. Dudleston and B. Hassan
Toss: Lancashire
Haynes held Middlesex together, but his 35 stretched for 25 overs and a total of 136 never looked adequate. Fairbrother batted decisively for Lancashire who won with 8 balls unbowled.

v DERBYSHIRE (Lord's)

July 9

Won on faster scoring rate. Middx 4pts, Derbys 0pts

Derbyshire		
P.D. Bowler	c Williams b Cowans	1
J.E. Morris	b Ellcock	35
C. Gladwin	b Ellcock	20
R. Sharma	c Butcher b Carr	0
I. Redpath	c Downton b Hughes	9
K.M. Krikken	c Hughes b Williams	16
†B.J.M. Maher	not out	49
A.E. Warner	c Ramprakash b Williams	5
*P.G. Newman	not out	0
S.J. Base		
O.H. Mortensen		
Extras	lb 11, w 2	13
Total (7 wkts, 40 ov)		148

4, 56, 67, 65, 81, 112, 132

Cowans	8	1	30	1
Williams	8	1	46	2
Hughes	8	0	33	1
Carr	8	1	19	1
Ellcock	8	1	9	2

Middlesex		
I.J.F. Hutchinson	lbw b Newman	0
D.L. Haynes	c Maher b Mortensen	3
M.A. Roseberry	run out	7
M.R. Ramprakash	b Mortensen	21
J.D. Carr	not out	40
*†P.R. Downton	not out	10
R.O. Butcher		
N.F. Williams		
S.P. Hughes		
R.M. Ellcock		
N.G. Cowans		
Extras	lb 6, nb 2	8
Total (4 wkts, 23.4 ov)		89

0, 8, 23, 52

Newman	4	0	18	1
Mortensen	8	2	19	2
Base	8	0	23	0
Warner	3.4	0	23	0

Umpires: A.A. Jones and R. Julian
Toss: Middlesex
The weather reduced the playing time after Derbyshire had batted out their 40 overs and this meant Middlesex needed 89 off 24 overs – they reached the target in the final over due to Carr's intelligent batting.

v KENT (Lord's)

July 23

Lost by 6 runs. Kent 4pts, Middx 0pts

Kent		
S.G. Hinks	b Cowans	0
N.R. Taylor	c Downton b Fraser	1
T.R. Ward	c Haynes b Cowans	0
J.I. Longley	c Carr	57
*C.S. Cowdrey	c Haynes b Emburey	78
†S.A. Marsh	c Carr b Emburey	53
M.V. Fleming	run out	1
M.A. Ealham	not out	9
N.J. Llong	not out	0
H.L. Alleyne		
A.P. Igglesden		
Extras	lb 9, nb 3	12
Total (7 wkts, 40 ov)		211

1, 1, 4, 118, 168, 184, 209

Fraser	8	4	16	1
Cowans	8	2	18	2
Ellcock	8	0	50	0
Emburey	7	0	43	2
Hughes	4	0	43	0
Carr	5	0	32	1

Middlesex		
I.J.F. Hutchinson	run out	11
D.L. Haynes	c Longley b Fleming	56
*M.W. Gatting	c Igglesden b Llong	54
M.R. Ramprakash	c Cowdrey b Fleming	11
J.D. Carr	b Igglesden	20
†P.R. Downton	not out	17
J.E. Emburey	b Alleyne	0
A.R.C. Fraser	c Marsh b Alleyne	3
S.P. Hughes	not out	4
R.M. Ellcock		
N.G. Cowans		
Extras	b 5, lb 13, w 7, nb 4	29
Total (7 wkts, 40 ov)		205

23, 123, 146, 152, 184, 190

Igglesden	8	0	19	1
Alleyne	7	1	35	2
Ealham	8	1	30	0
Fleming	7	0	33	2
Cowdrey	3	0	28	0
Llong	3	0	20	1
Ward	4	0	22	0

Umpires: K.J. Lyons and R. Palmer
Toss: Kent
Lowly Kent's victory over Middlesex meant that the latter's chances of gaining a place in the Refuge Cup became almost invisible.

PLAYERS

David BODEN *b* 1961; right-arm medium-fast bowler; county debut v Oxford Univ in May 1989
Keith Robert BROWN *b* 18.3.1963 Edmonton; right-hand batsman; wicketkeeper; debut 1984
Roland Orlando BUTCHER *b* 14.10.1953 East Point, Barbados; right-hand batsman; debut 1974; 3 Tests for England 1980–81
John Donald CARR *b* 15.6.1963 St John's Wood; opening right-hand batsman; right-arm off-break bowler; debut 1983; Oxford Univ Blue 1983–85; son of D.B. (ex-Derbys)
Norman George COWANS *b* 17.4.1961 Enfield St Mary, Jamaica; right-arm fast bowler; lower order right-hand batsman; debut 1980; 19 Tests for England 1982–85
Paul Robert DOWNTON *b* 4.4.1957 Farnborough, Kent; wicketkeeper; middle order right-hand batsman; debut 1980; previously appeared for Kent 1977–79; 30 Tests for England 1980–88; son of G.C. (ex-Kent)
Ricardo McDonald ELLCOCK *b* 17.6.1965 Bridgetown, Barbados; right-arm fast bowler; tail end right-hand batsman; debut 1989; previously appeared for Worcs 1982–88; selected to tour West Indies 1989–90
John Ernest EMBUREY *b* 20.8.1952 Peckham, S London; off-break bowler; effective lower order right-hand batsman; debut 1973; 60 Tests for England including three in 1989; captained England in two Tests; selected to tour South Africa 1989–90
Alastair Gregory James FRASER *b* 17.10.1967 Edgware; right-arm fast-medium bowler; lower order right-hand batsman; debut 1986; brother of A.R.C. (Middx)
Angus Robert Charles FRASER *b* 8.8.1965 Billinge, Lancs; right-arm fast-medium bowler; right-hand batsman; debut 1984; Test debut for England 1989, three matches; selected to tour West Indies 1989–90; brother of A.G.J. (Middx)

Michael William GATTING *b* 6.6.1957 Kingsbury; middle order right-hand batsman; right-arm medium pace bowler; debut 1975; captain since 1983; 68 Tests for England; captained England in 23 Tests; selected to captain English Team to South Africa 1989–90
Desmond Leo HAYNES *b* 15.2.1956 Holders Hill, Barbados; attractive opening right-hand batsman; occasional leg-break bowler; debut and cap for Middx in 1989; has played for Barbados since 1977; 85 Tests for West Indies
Simon Peter HUGHES *b* 20.12.1959 Kingston-on-Thames; right-arm fast-medium bowler; right-hand batsman; debut 1980
Ian James Frederick HUTCHINSON *b* 31.10.1964 Welshpool; very promising right-hand batsman; debut 1988
Jason Calvin POOLEY *b* 8.8.1969 Hammersmith; left-hand batsman; off-break bowler; FC debut for county in 1989; but did not play in Championship
Mark Ravin RAMPRAKASH *b* 5.9.1969 Bushey, Herts; talented right-hand batsman; debut 1987
Michael Anthony ROSEBERRY *b* 28.11.1966 Houghton-le-Spring, Durham; middle order right-hand batsman; debut 1986
James Frederick SYKES *b* 30.12.1965 Shoreditch; right-hand batsman; off-break bowler; debut 1983
Philip Clive Roderick TUFNELL *b* 29.4.1966 Barnet; slow left-arm bowler; right-hand batsman; debut 1986
Neil Fitzgerald WILLIAMS *b* 2.7.1962 Hope Well, St Vincent; right-hand batsman; right-arm fast-medium bowler; debut 1982

Ricardo Ellcock, second in Middlesex's bowling averages and picked for the winter tour to West Indies.
Allsport/Russell Cheyne

REFUGE ASSURANCE LEAGUE

v LEICESTERSHIRE (Lord's)

July 30
Won by 6 wkts. Middx 4pts, Leics 0pts

Leicestershire		
L. Potter	st Downton b Tufnell	19
*N.E. Briers	lbw b Cowans	0
J.J. Whitaker	c Downton b Williams	16
P. Willey	lbw b Williams	3
T.J. Boon	b Hughes	20
C.C. Lewis	b Williams	0
G.J. Parsons	c Downton b Hughes	17
J.P. Agnew	c Cowans b Carr	4
†P.A. Nixon	c Hutchinson b Carr	1
L. Tennant	not out	1
L.B. Taylor	not out	1
Extras	lb 2, w 8, nb 3	13
Total (9 wkts, 28 ov)		95

1, 25, 39, 39, 40, 77, 91, 91, 93

Cowans	5	2	14	1
Hughes	7	1	21	2
Williams	7	2	19	3
Tufnell	6	0	25	1
Carr	3	0	14	2

Middlesex		
I.J.F. Hutchinson	c Tennant b Taylor	7
D.L. Haynes	lbw b Taylor	8
J.D. Carr	b Willey	0
M.R. Ramprakash	not out	29
M.A. Roseberry	run out	2
*M.W. Gatting	not out	34
†P.R. Downton		
N.F. Williams		
S.P. Hughes		
P.C.R. Tufnell		
N.G. Cowans		
Extras	lb 5, w 7, nb 4	16
Total (4 wkts, 26 ov)		96

12, 18, 30, 44

Agnew	7	1	18	0
Taylor	6	1	25	2
Tennant	1	0	5	0
Willey	7	0	18	1
Parsons	5	0	25	0

Umpires: D.G.L. Evans and B. Hassan
Toss: Middlesex
On a difficult wicket Leicestershire could only manage 95 off 28 overs and Middlesex did not look much happier, but had the benefit of an erratic over from Tennant which gave away 9 extras. Gatting hit out with 34 off 30 balls and won the match with 2 overs in hand.

v NORTHAMPTONSHIRE'S (Lord's)

August 13
Won by 6 wkts. Middx 4pts, Northants 0pts

Northamptonshire		
G. Cook	c Downton b Fraser	0
*W. Larkins	c Cowans b Fraser	6
R.J. Bailey	run out	46
D.J. Capel	b Emburey	30
N.A. Felton	c Hutchinson b Hughes	17
D.J. Wild	c Ramprakash b Williams	30
J.G. Thomas	c Gatting b Hughes	11
†D. Ripley	not out	1
C.E.L. Ambrose	b Hughes	0
A. Walker	not out	1
M.A. Robinson		
Extras	b 4, lb 8, nb 3	15
Total (8 wkts, 40 ov)		157

3, 19, 75, 99, 140, 145, 154, 156

Fraser	8	0	35	2
Cowans	8	1	17	0
Williams	8	1	24	1
Emburey	8	0	31	1
Hughes	8	2	38	3

Middlesex		
J.D. Carr	b Capel	23
I.J.F. Hutchinson	lbw b Robinson	13
*M.W. Gatting	c Cook b Larkins	40
M.R. Ramprakash	b Robinson	44
M.A. Roseberry	not out	15
†P.R. Downton	not out	9
J.E. Emburey		
N.F. Williams		
A.G.J. Fraser		
S.P. Hughes		
N.G. Cowans		
Extras	b 1, lb 10, w 5	16
Total (4 wkts, 38.5 ov)		160

38, 52, 134, 139

Walker	4.5	1	12	0
Ambrose	6.5	1	26	0
Robinson	8	1	30	2
Thomas	8	1	19	0
Capel	5	0	24	1
Bailey	3.1	0	26	0
Larkins	3	0	12	1

Umpires: R. Julian and P.B. Wight
Toss: Middlesex
Gatting and Ramprakash added 82 in 11 overs after Middlesex's scoring rate had been very much below par, and this stand virtually made certain of victory. Mathematically Middlesex could still gain a place in the Refuge Cup but their chances were remote.

BENSON AND HEDGES CUP

v WORCESTERSHIRE (Lord's)

April 25, 26
Lost by 1 run. Worcs 2pts, Middx 0pts

Worcestershire		
T.S. Curtis	lbw b Cowans	6
I.T. Botham	c Carr b Hughes	10
G.A. Hick	c Gatting b Hughes	21
D.B. d'Oliveira	run out	28
*P.A. Neale	c Downton b Sykes	3
M.J. Weston	not out	19
†S.J. Rhodes	c Downton b Hughes	10
N.C. Radford	not out	9
P.J. Newport		
G.R. Dilley		
A.P. Pridgeon		
Extras	lb 2, w 3, nb 4	9
Total (6 wkts, 31 ov)		115

17, 42, 47, 65, 86, 102

Fraser	6	0	19	0
Cowans	7	2	20	1
Emburey	6	2	14	0
Hughes	6	0	38	3
Sykes	4	0	18	1
Carr	2	0	4	0

Middlesex		
J.D. Carr	b Dilley	16
†P.R. Downton	lbw b Radford	13
*M.W. Gatting	c Hick b Newport	15
M.R. Ramprakash	c Dilley b Botham	19
R.O. Butcher	c d'Oliveira b Botham	7
K.R. Brown	c Botham b Weston	12
J.E. Emburey	c and b Botham	4
J.F. Sykes	not out	16
S.P. Hughes	not out	1
A.R.C. Fraser		
N.G. Cowans		
Extras	lb 6, w 5	11
Total (7 wkts, 31 ov)		114

26, 34, 66, 70, 83, 92, 108

Dilley	6	0	23	1
Radford	6	1	21	1
Pridgeon	6	1	16	0
newport	7	1	20	1
Botham	5	0	17	3
Weston	1	0	11	1

Umpires: J.H. Hampshire and R. Julian
Toss: Middlesex. Gold. I.T. Botham
Rain prevented any play on the first day and on the second the match was reduced to 31 overs. Middlesex ended by requiring 13 off the last over bowled by Weston. Brown was caught on the boundary off the third ball and thus the home team failed by two runs to win.

BRITANNIC ASSURANCE COUNTY CHAMPIONSHIP AVERAGES 1989

Batting	*M*	*I*	*NO*	*Runs*	*HS*	*Avge*	*100*	*50*
M.W. Gatting	17	29	6	1337	158*	58.13	4	6
K.R. Brown	7	11	3	431	90	53.88	–	3
D.L. Haynes	19	35	5	1421	206*	47.37	3	8
I.J.F. Hutchinson	9	17	2	530	177	35.33	2	–
M.R. Ramprakash	19	31	4	952	128	35.26	1	7
M.A. Roseberry	17	28	4	701	79	29.21	–	5
R.O. Butcher	10	18	2	467	126	29.19	1	1
J.D. Carr	16	30	3	617	153*	22.85	1	1
N.F. Williams	13	17	4	253	69*	19.46	–	1
P.R. Downton	21	31	3	519	100	18.54	1	–
J.E. Emburey	16	23	4	329	77*	17.32	–	1
A.R.C. Fraser	16	21	7	214	43*	15.29	–	–
S.P. Hughes	19	26	7	216	31	11.37	–	–
J.F. Sykes	2	3	–	27	19	9.00	–	–
N.G. Cowans	19	22	7	110	21*	7.33	–	–
P.C.R. Tufnell	13	11	3	54	12	6.75	–	–
R.M. Ellcock	8	6	1	27	9	5.40	–	–

Also batted: J.C. Pooley (1 match) 14.

Bowling	*O*	*M*	*R*	*W*	*Avge*	*BB*	*5i*	*10m*
A.R.C. Fraser	567.2	154	1343	78	17.22	7-77	4	–
R.M. Ellcock	182.1	36	615	32	19.22	5-35	1	–
N.G. Cowans	465.3	112	1246	61	20.43	5-34	1	–
S.P. Hughes	435.2	108	1176	56	21.00	4-23	–	–
J.E. Emburey	594.1	218	1183	45	26.29	7-27	3	1
P.C.R. Tufnell	562.1	148	1482	51	29.06	5-60	3	–
N.F. Williams	291.2	51	862	29	29.72	4-39	–	–

Also bowled: J.D. Carr 67-17-139-2; M.W. Gatting 22-12-51-0; D.L. Haynes 6-3-13-0; M.R. Ramprakash 14-1-60-0; M.A. Roseberry 14.5-5-47-0.

Centuries

4 M.W. Gatting: 158* v Essex (Uxbridge); 110* v Glos (Cheltenham); 121 v Sussex (Hastings); 139* v Sussex (Lord's).

3 D.L. Haynes: 102 v Surrey (Oval); 206* v Kent (Uxbridge); 143* v Essex (Uxbridge).

2 I.J.F. Hutchinson: 106 v Derbys (Lord's); 177 v Kent (Uxbridge).

1 R.O. Butcher: 126 v Surrey (Lord's). J.D. Carr: 153* v Northants (Lord's). P.R. Downton: 100 v Glamorgan (Abergavenny). M.R. Ramprakash: 128 v Yorks (Headingley).

BENSON AND HEDGES CUP

v SURREY (Lord's)

May 13

Won by 76 runs. Middx 2pts, Surrey 0pts

Middlesex		
J.D. Carr	lbw b Thorpe	29
D.L. Haynes	c Feltham b Thorpe	59
*M.W. Gatting	c Stewart b Greig	30
R.O. Butcher	c Thorpe b Greig	25
M.R. Ramprakash	c Stewart b Thorpe	3
†P.R. Downton	b M.P. Bicknell	34
J.E. Emburey	b Feltham	18
N.F. Williams	run out	4
N.G. Cowans	c Ward b Feltham	0
S.P. Hughes	not out	15
A.R.C. Fraser		
Extras	lb 12, w 3	15
Total (9 wkts, 55 ov)		232

75, 97, 136, 151, 153, 209, 213, 213, 232

Bicknell	11	1	44	1
Murphy	11	1	52	0
Feltham	11	1	37	2
Greig	11	1	52	2
Thorpe	11	2	35	3

Surrey		
D.J. Bicknell	lbw b Cowans	13
G.S. Clinton	c Gatting b Cowans	27
P.D. Atkins	c Downton b Fraser	6
†A.J. Stewart	b Williams	23
D.M. Ward	b Hughes	3
G.P. Thorpe	c Downton b Hughes	22
*I.A. Greig	b Hughes	9
M.A. Feltham	c Ramprakash b Emburey	29
C.K. Bullen	b Emburey	5
M.P. Bicknell	not out	11
A.J. Murphy	c Downton b Fraser	0
Extras	lb 4, w 1, nb 3	8
Total (38.1 ov)		156

23, 47, 53, 59, 86, 103, 116, 132, 156

Fraser	10.1	0	39	2
Cowans	7	1	23	2
Hughes	6	0	32	3
Williams	7	0	42	1
Emburey	8	3	16	2

Umpires: P.J. Eele and R. Julian

Toss: Middlesex. Gold: D.L. Haynes

With neither side having a chance of obtaining a place in the Knock-Out Section this game was of little interest, save for the successful appearance of the West Indian, Haynes.

NATWEST BANK TROPHY

v NOTTINGHAMSHIRE (Uxbridge)

July 12

Won by 36 runs

Middlesex		
I.J.F. Hutchinson	c Broad b Cooper	1
D.L. Haynes	lbw b Stephenson	0
*M.W. Gatting	c Cooper b Evans	16
M.R. Ramprakash	lbw b Saxelby	11
J.D. Carr	c French b Afford	44
†P.R. Downton	b Saxelby	69
J.E. Emburey	c French b Saxelby	36
A.R.C. Fraser	not out	8
S.P. Hughes	not out	9
R.M. Ellcock		
N.G. Cowans		
Extras	lb 7, w 1, nb 1	9
Total (7 wkts, 60 ov)		203

1, 1, 28, 36, 106, 185, 188

Stephenson	12	2	22	1
Cooper	12	4	31	1
Saxelby	12	0	70	3
Evans	12	1	45	1
Afford	12	2	28	1

Nottinghamshire		
B.C. Broad	lbw b Ellcock	4
P.R. Pollard	c Gatting b Fraser	23
*R.T. Robinson	b Ellcock	9
P. Johnson	c Downton b Fraser	47
D.W. Randall	c Downton b Hughes	29
F.D. Stephenson	lbw b Fraser	22
K.P. Evans	c Downton b Hughes	8
†B.N. French	c Downton b Ellcock	5
K.E. Cooper	b Ellcock	6
K. Saxelby	b Cowans	1
J.A. Afford	not out	0
Extras	lb 4, w 4, nb 5	13
Total (54.4 ov)		167

12, 33, 48, 117, 132, 144, 155, 163, 167

Cowans	7.4	0	24	1
Ellcock	10	2	43	4
Hughes	10	4	25	2
Fraser	12	1	27	3
Carr	3	0	8	0
Emburey	12	1	36	0

Umpires: M.J. Kitchen and D.R. Shepherd

Toss: Middlesex. MofM: P.R. Downton

Although deciding to bat first, Middlesex made a poor start and their total owed much to the batting of Downton who hit 8 fours in his 69. Apart from the stand between Randall and Johnson Nottinghamshire never really challenged the home side's total and Middlesex won with relative ease as the Notts tail collapsed.

v SUSSEX (Lord's)

August 2

Won by 78 runs

Middlesex		
J.D. Carr	c and b Pigott	3
D.L. Haynes	c Moores b Hansford	88
*M.W. Gatting	not out	132
M.R. Ramprakash	st Moores b Hansford	2
J.E. Emburey	not out	20
I.J. F. Hutchinson		
†P.R. Downton		
A.R.C. Fraser		
S.P. Hughes		
P.C.R. Tufnell		
N.G. Cowans		
Extras	b 1, lb 16, w 3, nb 1	21
Total (3 wkts, 60 ov)		266

7, 208, 215

Pigott	12	2	54	1
Dodemaide	12	2	41	0
Hansford	12	0	48	2
Wells	12	0	41	0
Clarke	12	2	65	0

Sussex		
D.M. Smith	c Cowans b Hughes	17
M.P. Speight	run out	7
*P.W.G. Parker	c Downton b Hughes	54
A.P. Wells	c Tufnell b Hughes	58
C.M. Wells	c Hutchinson b Emburey	8
I.J. Gould	c Hutchinson b Tufnell	5
A.C.S. Pigott	c Hutchinson b Emburey	5
A.I.C. Dodemaide	lbw b Fraser	7
†P. Moores	run out	5
A.R. Clarke	st Downton b Emburey	3
A.R. Hansford	not out	5
Extras	lb 9, w 1, nb 4	14
Total (57 ov)		188

23, 42, 142, 153, 158, 168, 168, 174, 182

Cowans	12	1	49	0
Fraser	11	1	32	1
Emburey	12	6	11	3
Hughes	10	0	37	3
Tufnell	12	1	50	1

Umpires: D.G.L. Evans and A.G.T. Whitehead

Toss: Middlesex. MofM: M.W. Gatting

A second wicket partnership of 201 between Haynes and Gatting provided Middlesex with a good position from which to snipe at the visiting batsmen. Gatting made 132 off 157 deliveries and the stand lasted 47 overs. Alan Wells and Parker fought back, but when they left the remaining Sussex batsmen failed completely.

Away Matches

The full scorecard of each of Middlesex's away matches will be found in the sections for the respective home teams.

Chelmsford: April 27, 28, 29
Middx 129 (D.R. Pringle 5–42) and 85 (D.R. Pringle 5–38) lost to Essex 149 (N.G. Cowans 5–34) and 69–1 by 9 wkts. Essex 20pts, Middx 4pts.

Edgbaston: May 27, 29, 30
Warwicks 194 and 112 (A.R.C. Fraser 5–20) lost to Middx 199 (A.A. Donald 7–66) and 108–2 by 8 wkts. Middx 21pts, Warwicks 5pts.

Abergavenny: June 10, 12, 13
Glamorgan 302–7d (R.J. Shastri 127, A.R. Butcher 101) and 311–6d (R.J. Shastri 101*) drew with Middx 263–4d and 345–8 (P.R. Downton 100). Middx 5pts, Glam 4pts.

The Oval: June 17, 19, 20
Surrey 226 and 305–6d (A.J. Stewart 148*) drew with Middx 225 (K.T. Medlycott 5–93) and 243–9 (D.L. Haynes 102). Surrey 6pts, Middx 6pts.

Worcester: June 24, 26
Worcs 142 and 172 lost to Middx 221 and 96–1 by 9 wkts. Middx 22pts, Worcs 4pts.

Headingley: July 19, 20, 21
Yorks 179 (R.M. Ellcock 5–35) and 189 (A.R.C. Fraser 5–47) lost to Middx 294 (M.R. Ramprakash 128, A. Sidebottom 6–79) and 75–7 by 3 wkts. Middx 23pts, Yorks 4pts.

Weston-super-Mare: August 5, 7, 8
Somerset 212 (J.E. Emburey 6–38) and 254–6d drew with Middx 116 and 223–7. Somerset 6pts Middx 4pts.

Cheltenham: August 9, 10, 11
Middx 222 (M.W. Gatting 110*) and 206–7d beat Glouces 122 (J.E. Emburey 7–27) and 118 (J.E. Emburey 5–39) by 188 runs. Middx 22pts, Gloucs 4pts.

Hastings: August 19, 21, 22
Sussex 249 and 216 lost to Middx 370 (M.W. Gatting 121) and 97–1 by 9 wkts. Middx 24pts, Sussex 5pts.

Trent Bridge: August 24, 25, 26, 27
Notts 308 (B.C. Broad 144) and 136 drew with Middx 204–2d and 160–6. Middx 4pts, Notts 3pts.

Canterbury: September 13, 14, 15, 16
Kent 241 (A.R.C. Fraser 7–77) and 120–0 drew with Middx 251 (R.M. Ellison 6–43). Middx 7pts, Kent 6pts.

v YORKSHIRE (Lord's)

April 20, 21, 22, 24
Drawn. Middx 7pts, Yorks 3pts

Middlesex 1st Innings		
J.D. Carr	c Sidebottom b Jarvis	0
†P.R. Downton	c Sidebottom b Gough	17
*M.W. Gatting	c Bairstow b Jarvis	72
M.R. Ramprakash	b Jarvis	34
R.O. Butcher	c Carrick b Pickles	22
K.R. Brown	c Bairstow b Gough	47
J.E. Emburey	c Robinson b Pickles	10
S.P. Hughes	c Bairstow b Jarvis	14
N.F. Williams	c Bairstow b Jarvis	13
A.R.C. Fraser	not out	8
N.G. Cowans	c Bairstow b Gough	4
Extras	b 4, lb 14, nb 1	19
Total (100 ov: 256–8)		260

0, 29, 110, 147, 157, 184, 199, 241, 256

Jarvis	32	12	77	5
Sidebottom	15.2	5	38	0
Gough	15	4	44	3
Pickles	28.4	9	67	2
Carrick	9	3	16	0

Yorkshire 1st Innings		
D. Byas	c Downton b Hughes	30
A.A. Metcalfe	c Butcher b Fraser	0
R.J. Blakey	lbw b Williams	24
P.E. Robinson	lbw b Cowans	31
J.D. Love	b Cowans	1
†D.L. Bairstow	c Downton b Hughes	0
*P. Carrick	run out	13
C.S. Pickles	c Downton b Fraser	5
A. Sidebottom	b Fraser	8
P.W. Jarvis	c Downton b Fraser	0
D. Gough	not out	2
Extras	b 5, lb 10, nb 1	16
Total (50.3 ov)		130

4, 43, 92, 94, 95, 104, 119, 119, 123

Cowans	14	5	31	2
Fraser	14.3	6	28	4
Williams	11	2	40	1
Hughes	11	5	16	2

Middlesex 2nd Innings		
J.D. Carr	b Byas b Gough	31
†P.R. Downton	c Metcalfe b Carrick	40
*M.W. Gatting	c Blakey b Gough	4
M.R. Ramprakash	c Bairstow b Carrick	14
R.O. Butcher	not out	17
K.R. Brown	not out	9
Extras	lb 4	4
Total (4 wkts)		119

49, 53, 83, 104

Jarvis	6	2	16	0
Gough	13	0	47	2
Pickles	11	3	22	0
Carrick	8	2	24	2
Byas	5	2	6	0

Umpires: D.J. Constant and J.H. Hampshire
Toss: Middlesex
Rain preventing any play on the fourth day, this match was consequently left drawn. The weather had already seriously affected the first day, when only 20.4 overs were bowled and on the second day play was restricted to 67.2 overs, with Middlesex ending at 224–7. Injury-hit Yorkshire included Gough in their team and he took his first first-class wicket. Further problems for the visitors emerged when Sidebottom had to retire from the game with a strain.

v SURREY (Lord's)

May 4, 5, 6, 8
Wob by 125 runs. Middx 22pts, Surrey 5pts

Middlesex 1st Innings		
J.D. Carr	b Fletham	19
†P.R. Downton	c D.J. Bicknell b M.P. Bicknell	5
*M.W. Gatting	c Ward b Feltham	54
M.R. Ramprakash	c Feltham b Greig	69
R.O. Butcher	c Greig b M.P. Bicknell	14
K.R. Brown	b Medlycott	37
J.E. Emburey	c Stewart b M.P. Bicknell	3
S.P. Hughes	c and b Medlycott	2
A.R.C. Fraser	c Atkins b Medlycott	3
N.G. Cowans	not out	21
P.C.R. Tufnell	c Stewart b Feltham	3
Extras	lb 1, w 4, nb 12	17
Total (88.2 ov)		247

25, 44, 119, 141, 197, 217, 217, 222, 231

Tazelaar	9.4	1	34	0
M.P. Bicknell	24	6	68	3
Feltham	18.2	2	64	3
Greig	10	2	31	1
Medlycott	26.2	7	49	3

Surrey 1st Innings		
D.J. Bicknell	lbw b Cowans	12
G.S. Clinton	c Downton b Fraser	0
P.D. Atkins	lbw b Cowans	26
†A.J. Stewart	b Cowans	0
D.M. Ward	c Ramprakash b Hughes	31
Z.A. Sadiq	c Downton b Hughes	20
*I.A. Greig	b Fraser	26
K.T. Medlycott	c Butcher b Tufnell	22
M.A. Feltham	c Ramprakash b Emburey	3
D. Tazelaar	not out	18
M.P. Bicknell	c Downton b Tufnell	7
Extras	b 7, lb 8, w 1, nb 9	25
Total (87.4 ov)		190

3, 13, 18, 59, 98, 107, 115, 157, 169

Fraser	22	8	42	2
Cowans	16	8	24	3
Tufnell	22.4	5	48	2
Emburey	17	8	36	1
Hughes	10	3	25	2

Middlsex 2nd Innings		
J.D. Carr	c Stewart b M.P. Bicknell	1
†P.R. Downton	c Feltham b Tazelaar	15
*M.W. Gatting	c Atkins b Medlycott	83
M.R. Ramprakash	b M.P. Bicknell	12
R.O. Butcher	c Stewart b Tazelaar	126
K.R. Brown	c Stewart b M.P. Bicknell	38
J.E. Emburey	not out	21
N.G. Cowans	c Stewart b Tazelaar	0
S.P. Hughes	c Feltham b M.P. Bicknell	6
A.R.C. Fraser	lbw b M.P. Bicknell	2
P.C.R. Tufnell	not out	7
Extras	b 6, lb 15, nb 16	37
Total (9 wkts dec)		348

5, 19, 57, 212, 308, 315, 316, 332, 339

Tazelaar	26	5	88	3
M.P. Bicknell	39	10	99	5
Feltham	18	8	45	0
Medlycott	31	12	79	1
Greig	3	0	16	0

Surrey 2nd Innings		
D.J. Bicknell	c and b Tufnell	93
G.S. Clinton	lbw b Cowans	3
P.D. Atkins	not out	30
A.J. Stewart	c Emburey b Cowans	1
D.M. Ward	run out	9
Z.A. Sadiq	b Hughes	4
*I.A. Greig	b Hughes	4
K.T. Medlycott	b Tufnell	77
M.A. Feltham	c Carr b Tufnell	0
D. Tazelaar	b Cowas	29
M.P. Bicknell	b Fraser	13
Extras	lb 9, w 1, nb 7	17
Total		280

5, 17, 40, 47, 51, 198, 233, 233, 265

Cowans	14	1	45	3
Fraser	21.2	2	87	1
Hughes	13	3	33	2
Emburey	35	19	45	0
Tufnell	22	4	61	3

Umpires: R.A. White and P.B. Wight
Toss: Middlesex
The controversial feature of the first day was the banning of the Australian fast bowler, Tazelaar, when his follow through repeatedly damaged the pitch. Surrey ended the first day 25–3 off 18 overs in reply to Middlesex's 247. At the close on Saturday, Surrey were in great difficulty at 64–5, with D.J. Bicknell 29*.

v HAMPSHIRE (Lord's)

May 17, 18, 19

Won by 4 wkts. Middx 23pts, Hants 5pts

Hampshire 1st Innings

V.P. Terry	lbw b Hughes	30
C.L. Smith	c Butcher b Cowans	2
†M.C.J. Nicholas	b Cowans	0
R.A. Smith	c Gatting b Fraser	31
D.R. Turner	b Hughes	13
T.M. Tremlett	c Downton b Fraser	5
S.T. Jefferies	c Downton b Williams	33
†R.J. Parks	c Emburey b Fraser	18
R.J. Maru	b Fraser	29
P.J. Bakker	b Cowans	20
K.J. Shine	not out	26
Extras	b 2, lb 7, nb 1	10
Total (66.4 ov)		217

11, 11, 51, 80, 85, 109, 134, 138, 177

Cowans	15	3	49	3
Fraser	23.4	12	49	4
Williams	12	2	53	1
Hughes	14	0	52	2
Emburey	1	0	1	0
Carr	1	0	4	0

Middlesex 1st Innings

J.D. Carr	b Shine	4
D.L. Haynes	c Maru b Tremlett	67
*M.W. Gatting	c Parks b Bakker	30
R.O. Butcher	b Bakker	39
M.R. Ramprakash	c Parks b Bakker	6
†P.R. Downton	c Terry b Tremlett	17
J.E. Emburey	b Tremlett	7
N.F. Williams	not out	69
S.P. Hughes	b Maru	1
A.R.C. Fraser	c Terry b Bakker	26
N.G. Cowans	b Bakker	1
Extras	b 5, lb 15, w 2, nb 1	23
Total (100 ov: 274–8)		290

15, 79, 148, 148, 159, 186, 187, 189, 274

Bakker	20.1	3	52	5
Shine	20	3	75	1
Tremlett	34	16	51	3
Jefferies	8	0	52	0
Maru	20	10	27	1
Nicholas	2	0	13	0

Hampshire 2nd Innings

V.P. Terry	c Gatting b Hughes	11
C.L. Smith	lbw b Hughes	30
*M.C.J. Nicholas	b Hughes	5
R.A. Smith	c Butcher b Fraser	46
D.R. Turner	c Gatting b Williams	53
R.J. Maru	b Cowans	0
T.M. Tremlett	b Fraser	5
S.T. Jefferies	b Fraser	7
†R.J. Parks	not out	3
P.J. Bakker	c Emburey b Williams	7
K.J. Shine	c Downton b Cowans	3
Extras	lb 6	6
Total		176

32, 50, 51, 121, 123, 136, 162, 162, 172

Fraser	23	9	62	3
Cowans	14.2	3	33	2
Hughes	16	6	29	3
Williams	12	2	25	2
Emburey	10	4	21	0

Middlesex 2nd Innings

J.D. Carr	c Terry b Bakker	4
D.L. Haynes	run out	22
*M.W. Gatting	b Shine	19
R.O. Butcher	lbw b Bakker	2
M.R. Ramprakash	st Parks b Tremlett	3
†P.R. Downton	b Bakker	6
J.E. Emburey	not out	20
N.F. Williams	not out	19
Extras	b 1, lb 7, w 2, nb 1	11
Total (6 wkts)		106

4, 40, 42, 47, 64, 79

Bakker	16	3	52	3
Jefferies	6	2	9	0
Tremlett	16	7	22	1
Maru	2	0	9	0
Shine	6	3	6	1

Umpires: H.D. Bird and B.J. Meyer
Toss: Hampshire

Victory by Middlesex pushed the county into third place in the table. In their first innings Hampshire's total was due to some hard hitting by the tail end, after Terry had spent nearly three hours over 30. Middlesex began the second day at 117–2, but the middle order failed and it was left to Williams and Fraser to obtain a lead. Middlesex struggled to make the modest 106 required.

v NOTTINGHAMSHIRE (Lord's)

June 7, 8, 9

Drawn. Middx 7pts, Notts 3pts

Middlesex 1st Innings

J.D. Carr	b Evans	37
D.L. Haynes	c and b Hemmings	84
M.A. Roseberry	c Randall b Evans	48
R.O. Butcher	c Randall b Evans	8
M.R. Ramprakash	run out	48
J.F. Sykes	c Evans b Millns	6
*†P.R. Downton	lbw b Cairns	13
N.F. Williams	b Hemmings	9
S.P. Hughes	b Cairns	13
A.R.C. Fraser	not out	2
N.G. Cowans	c sub b Cairns	4
Extras	b 5, b 12, nb 7	24
Total (100 ov: 252–6)		296

69, 158, 173, 188, 216, 237, 255, 289, 292

Millns	20	2	69	1
Cairns	24.2	7	79	3
Cooper	15.3	5	25	0
Evans	21.3	5	51	3
Hemmings	31	14	55	2

Nottinghamshire 1st Innings

P.R. Pollard	c Downton b Williams	24
M. Newell	c Carr b Fraser	3
P. Johnson	c Cowans b Fraser	0
*R.T. Robinson	c Haynes b Fraser	32
D.W. Randall	c Downton b Hughes	17
K.P. Evans	b Cowans	39
C.L. Cairns	b Fraser	0
†C.W. Scott	c Roseberry b Fraser	7
E.E. Hemmings	not out	29
K.E. Cooper	b Hughes	12
D.J. Millns	b Hughes	0
Extras	lb 7, w 1, nb 8	16
Total (65.1 ov)		179

Cowans	16	3	45	1
Fraser	21	6	37	5
Williams	13	2	45	1
Hughes	15.1	3	45	3

Middlesex 2nd Innings

J.D. Carr	c Millns b Cairns	13
D.L. Haynes	c sub b Hemmings	34
M.A. Roseberry	c Johnson b Cairns	4
R.O. Butcher	c Newell b Evans	27
M.R. Ramprakash	lbw b Hemmings	2
J.F. Sykes	b Evans	2
*†P.R. Downton	not out	17
N.F. Williams	c Robinson b Hemmings	0
S.P. Hughes	not out	2
Extras	lb 5, nb 1	6
Total (7 wkts dec)		107

22, 35, 72, 85, 87, 89, 90

Cairns	7	2	17	2
Evans	13	2	60	2
Hemmings	6.3	1	25	3

Nottinghamshire 1st Innings

P.R. Pollard	c Downton b Cowans	28
M. Newell	lbw b Fraser	9
D.W. Randall	c Butcher b Fraser	25
*R.T. Robinson	b Hughes	5
P. Johnson	not out	11
C.L. Cairns	c Carr b Hughes	3
K.P. Evans	not out	6
Extras	lb 7, w 1, nb 2	10
Total (5 wkts)		97

15, 59, 74, 76, 79

Cowans	9	3	29	1
Fraser	14	1	26	2
Williams	7	0	18	0
Hughes	8	3	14	2
Carr	2	1	3	0

Umpires: D.S. Thompsett and A.G.T. Whitehead
Toss: Nottinghamshire

On a slow first day, the home side reached 279–7, but Nottinghamshire fared worse on the second, when with rain curtailing play they made 116–6 off 43 overs. On the final day Nottinghamshire were set 225 off 43 overs, but after Pollard and Newell could only make 15 off the first 13 overs the game meandered to a draw.

v LANCASHIRE (Lord's)

July 1, 3, 4

Lost by 218 runs. Lancs 21pts, Middx 4pts

Lancashire 1st Innings

G.D. Mendis	c Gatting b Fraser	0
G. Fowler	lbw b Cowans	6
†W.K. Hegg	c Downton b Hughes	18
N.H. Fairbrother	lbw b Cowans	0
T.E. Jesty	c Hutchinson b Fraser	4
M. Watkinson	b Cowans	47
*D.P. Hughes	c Downton b Ellock	38
P.A.J. DeFreitas	lbw b Cowans	5
J.D. Fitton	b Ellcock	24
P.J.W. Allott	c Fraser b Hughes	1
B.P. Patterson	not out	0
Extras	lb 12, nb 6	18
Total (61.2 ov)		161

0, 18, 19, 34, 55, 106, 114, 148, 159

Fraser	18	4	38	2
Cowans	15	1	29	4
Hughes	15	4	38	2
Ellcock	10.2	2	32	2
Emburey	3	1	12	0

Middlesex 1st Innings

D.L Haynes	b DeFreitas	0
I.J.F. Hutchinson	c Mendis b Patterson	5
*M.W. Gatting	c Watkinson b Patterson	19
M.A. Roseberry	lbw b DeFreitas	3
M.R. Ramprakash	c Watkinson b Patterson	9
†P.R. Downton	c Hughes b Patterson	5
J.E. Emburey	c Fowler b Allott	16
S.P. Hughes	not out	22
A.R.C. Fraser	lbw b Allott	0
R.M. Ellcock	b DeFreitas	5
N.G. Cowans	c Hegg b Patterson	7
Extras	lb 3, nb 2	5
Total (38.2 ov)		96

0, 10, 25, 33, 39, 48, 66, 66, 79

Patterson	16.2	4	48	5
DeFreitas	16	3	41	3
Allott	3	2	3	2
Watkinson	3	2	1	0

Lancashire 2nd Innings

G.D. Mendis	lbw b Cowans	50
†W.K. Hegg	c Downton b Ellcock	15
*D.P. Hughes	b Fraser	15
N.H. Fairbrother	b Ellcock	24
T.E. Jesty	c Downton b Hughes	17
M. Watkinson	c Hutchinson b Emburey	22
P.A.J. DeFreitas	lbw b Emburey	15
J.D. Fitton	c Hutchinson b Ellcock	15
P.J.W. Allott	c Roseberry b Emburey	17
B.P. Patterson	not out	1
G. Fowler	absent injured	0
Extras	lb 3, nb 2	5
Total		196

28, 81, 84, 116, 137, 160, 165, 189, 196

Fraser	16	3	31	1
Cowans	9	1	32	1
Ellcock	16	4	62	3
Hughes	11	0	20	1
Gatting	2	2	0	0
Emburey	32.1	12	48	3

Middlesex 2nd Innings

I.J.F. Hutchinson	lbw n DeFreitas	13
D.L. Haynes	lbw b DeFreitas	0
*M.W. Gatting	lbw b DeFreitas	0
M.A. Roseberry	b Patterson	0
A.R.C. Fraser	c Hegg b Patterson	0
M.R. Ramprakash	c Hughes b DeFreitas	7
†P.R. Downton	c Hughes b DeFreitas	0
J.E. Emburey	c Allott b Patterson	2
S.P. Hughes	c Hegg b DeFreitas	4
R.M. Ellcock	not out	4
N.G. Cowans	b DeFreitas	7
Extras	lb 2, nb 4	6
Total		43

0, 0, 6, 6, 20, 20, 25, 28, 33

Patterson	11	2	20	3
DeFreitas	10.2	4	21	7

Umpires: B. Dudleston and B. Hassan
Toss: Middlesex

On a damp wicket which assisted the seam bowlers, batsmen found runs hard to acquire. On Saturday, Middlesex ended 66–8 in reply to Lancashire's 161 and by Monday's close matters seemed even more bleak for the home side, who needed 250 to win with 6 second innings wickets in hand. The match finished after just 65 minutes play on the last morning, DeFreitas having match figures of 10 for 62.

v DERBYSHIRE (Lord's)

July 8, 10, 11

Won by 70 runs. Middx 20pts, Derbys 5pts

Middlesex 1st Innings

I.J.F. Hutchinson	lbw b Mortensen	28
D.L. Haynes	c Morris b Malcolm	0
M.A. Roseberry	lbw b Warner	49
R.O. Butcher	c Sharma b Mortensen	34
M.R. Ramprakash	c Maher b Warner	65
J.D. Carr	c Holding b Warner	0
*†P.R. Downton	c Bowler b Malcolm	20
S.P. Hughes	b Malcolm	2
R.M. Ellcock	b Mortensen	1
N.G. Cowans	b Malcolm	0
P.C.R. Tufnell	not out	9
Extras	b 4, lb 5, w 1, nb 5	15
Total (69.1 ov)		223

5, 47, 103, 130, 130, 161, 167, 168, 171

Malcolm	28	3	111	4
Mortensen	26	10	47	3
Holding	8	0	43	0
Warner	8.1	3	13	3

Derbyshire 1st Innings

P.D. Bowler	c Carr b Cowans	6
†B.J.M. Maher	b Ellcock	18
J.E. Morris	c Ellcock b Tufnell	50
R. Sharma	lbw b Hughes	13
C. Gladwin	c Roseberry b Tufnell	6
I. Redpath	not out	41
K.M. Krikken	not out	36
A.E. Warner		
*M.A. Holding		
O.H. Mortensen		
D.E. Malcolm		
Extras	lb 7	7
Total (5 wkts dec, 85 ov)		177

11, 78, 78, 92, 98

Cowans	11	4	20	1
Ellcock	14	3	27	1
Hughes	15	3	47	1
Tufnell	34	14	54	2
Carr	11	2	22	0

Middlesex 2nd Innings

I.J.F. Hutchinson	c Krikken b Bowler	106
D.L. Haynes	b Maher	80
M.A. Roseberry	not out	13
M.R. Ramprakash	not out	1
Extras	b 2, lb 5, w 5, nb 3	15
Total (2 wkts dec)		215

174, 208

Morris	9	2	24	0
Krikken	6	0	40	0
Maher	12	0	81	1
Bowler	15	3	52	1
Redpath	5	2	11	0

Derbyshire 2nd Innings

P.D. Bowler	c and b Tufnell	62
†B.J.M. Maher	c Carr b Cowans	10
J.E. Morris	c Downton b Hughes	15
R. Sharma	lbw b Cowans	15
C. Gladwin	b Ellcock	28
I. Redpath	lbw b Tufnell	0
K.M. Krikken	c and b Tufnell	1
A.E. Warner	c Hutchinson b Tufnell	32
*M.A. Holding	lbw b Ellcock	2
O.H. Mortensen	c Roseberry b Tufnell	0
D.E. Malcolm	not out	12
Extras	b 4, lb 9, w 1	14
Total		191

27, 65, 100, 138, 138, 140, 151, 157, 172

Cowans	10	1	30	2
Ellcock	10	2	26	2
Tufnell	26.3	7	78	5
Hughes	13	7	29	1
Carr	5	0	15	0

Umpires: A.A. Jones and R. Julian
Toss: Derbyshire

Only 45 overs were possible on Saturday, with Middlesex making 152–5. Ramprakash, 13 not out over the weekend, helped the tail to reach 223 on Monday, then Derbyshire's main batting failed until Krikken and Redpath came together. Holding declared first thing on Tuesday morning and then put on his joke bowlers to give away runs. Hutchinson took the opportunity to score a maiden first-class hundred. Derbyshire were set 262 in 220 minutes but the home bowlers kept the upper hand and Middlesex won on the third ball of the last possible over.

v KENT (Uxbridge)

July 22, 24, 25

Drawn. Middx 8pts, Kent 1pt

Middlesex 1st Innings

I.J.F. Hutchinson	c Hinks b Davis	177
D.L. Haynes	not out	206
M.A. Roseberry	not out	48
*M.W. Gatting		
M.R. Ramprakash		
†P.R. Downton		
J.E. Emburey		
S.P. Hughes		
A.R.C. Fraser		
R.M. Ellcock		
P.C.R. Tufnell		
Extras	b 7, b 1, w 6, nb 13	27
Total (100 ov: 368–1) (1 wkt dec)		458

361

Igglesden	24	6	72	0
Alleyne	18	2	69	0
Cowdrey	9	0	56	0
Ellison	15	0	47	0
Davis	30	3	121	1
Dobson	19	3	62	0
Ward	9	2	23	0

Kent 1st Innings

S.G. Hinks	lbw b Fraser	8
N.R. Taylor	c Gatting b Ellcock	10
T.R. Ward	c Downton b Ellcock	0
J.I. Longley	c Downton b Ellcock	1
*C.S. Cowdrey	lbw b Emburey	38
†S.A. Marsh	b Hughes	16
M.C. Dobson	c Downton b Fraser	28
R.M. Ellison	c Hutchinson b Emburey	34
R.P. Davis	c Haynes b Tufnell	12
A.P. Igglesden	c Gatting b Emburey	0
H.L. Alleyne	not out	0
Extras	b 6, lb 5, nb 6	17
Total (68.4 ov)		164

20, 21, 21, 29, 83, 83, 144, 164, 164

Fraser	18	4	46	2
Ellcock	7	3	19	3
Hughes	8	2	28	1
Emburey	23.4	15	23	3
Tufnell	11	3	37	1
Gatting	1	1	0	0

Kent 2nd Innings

S.G. Hinks	lbw b Emburey	10
N.R. Taylor	b Fraser	99
T.R. Ward	c and b Tufnell	15
J.I. Longley	c Downton b Tufnell	1
*C.S. Cowdrey	c Downton b Tufnell	5
†S.A. Marsh	c Gatting b Emburey	20
M.C. Dobson	b Fraser	13
R.M. Ellison	not out	26
R.P. Davis	lbw b Fraser	16
A.P. Igglesden	c Tufnell b Fraser	4
H.L. Alleyne	not out	0
Extras	b 8, lb 5, w 1, nb 8	22
Total (9 wkts)		231

4, 56, 59, 65, 113, 140, 196, 226, 230

Hughes	17	7	26	0
Fraser	18	7	23	4
Emburey	48	27	62	2
Tufnell	46	19	77	3
Ellcock	10	3	30	0

Umpires: R. Palmer and K.J. Lyons
Toss: Middlesex

At the start of the final day Middlesex appeared to hold all the cards, but a very stubborn 99 from Taylor, which lasted 325 minutes together with Ellison's 180 minutes at the crease saved Kent and prevented Middlesex from moving into second place in the Championship. Earlier play was dominated by Hutchinson and Haynes. Their partnership was only six short of the Middlesex record. Haynes batted 337 balls with 29 fours for his double hundred. Hutchinson was dismissed with the final ball on Saturday for his 177. The Kent first innings lacked any positive response to Middlesex's enormous score and Emburey returned a very impressive bowling analysis.

v ESSEX (Uxbridge)

July 26, 27, 28

Drawn. Essex 7pts, Middx 4pts

Essex 1st Innings

B.R. Hardie	c Ramprakash b Hughes	26
J.P. Stephenson	c Hutchinson b Cowans	2
A.W. Lilley	c Hutchinson b Tufnell	40
M.E. Waugh	c Carr b Williams	110
N. Hussain	b Tufnell	23
†M.A. Garnham	lbw b Hughes	21
*D.R. Pringle	c Downton b Cowans	26
G. Miller	c Roseberry b Tufnell	61
T.D. Topley	c Haynes b Hughes	49
J.H. Childs	run out	2
M.C. Ilott	not out	7
Extras	b 3, lb 13, nb 7	23
Total (100 ov: 284–7)		390

9, 53, 76, 145, 208, 246, 281, 377, 381

Cowans	25	2	74	2
Williams	30	5	77	1
Hughes	39.4	7	74	3
Tufnell	38	9	122	3
Carr	12	3	22	0
Gatting	4	3	5	0

Middlesex 1st Innings

I.J.F. Hutchinson	c Waugh b Pringle	2
D.L Haynes	c Hardie b Ilott	4
*M.W. Gatting	b Pringle	25
M.R. Ramprakash	c Ilott b Childs	35
M.A. Roseberry	b Childs	55
J.D. Carr	c Garnham b Pringle	11
†P.R. Downton	lbw b Childs	0
N.F. Williams	c Waugh b Childs	20
S.P. Hughes	not out	22
P.C.R. Tufnell	c and b Topley	8
N.G. Cowans	c Waugh b Topley	4
Extras	b 2, lb 6, w 1	9
Total (73.2 ov)		195

10, 30, 41, 93, 118, 133, 142, 179, 191

Ilott	9	2	21	1
Pringle	22	10	42	3
Topley	13.2	7	35	2
Childs	24	7	78	4
Miller	5	1	11	0

Middlesex 2nd Innings

S.P. Hughes	b Pringle	11
I.J.F. Hutchinson	c Waugh b Ilott	7
D.L. Haynes	not out	143
*M.W. Gatting	not out	158
Extras	b 13, lb 5, w 1, nb 3	22
Total (2 wkts dec)		341

22, 22

Pringle	13	5	45	1
Ilott	14	4	48	1
Childs	24	9	53	0
Topley	15	3	46	0
Miller	10	3	31	0
Waugh	8	0	42	0
Stephenson	10	2	57	0
Hussain	1	0	1	0

Umpires: K.J. Lyons and R. Palmer
Toss: Essex

The Uxbridge ground witnessed a second triple hundred partnership within a week, when Haynes and Gatting batted out the last day to add 319 for the 3rd wicket. Haynes batted 292 minutes with 23 fours, Gatting lasted 290 minutes and hit 30 fours, Middlesex having begun the last day at 4–0. On the first day, Waugh batted 262 minutes, hitting a six and 14 fours as Essex made 301—7. Essex continued to bat out their innings on Thursday, then the spin of Childs removed Middlesex and Pringle enforced the follow on. Essex's failure to win meant that they remained 11 points ahead of Worcestershire at the top of the Championship. Middlesex on the other hand fell to 4th place.

v LEICESTERSHIRE (Lord's)

July 29, 31, August 1

Drawn. Middx 5pts, Leics 4pts

Middlesex 1st Innings

I.J.F. Hutchinson	c Whitaker b Parsons	29
D.L. Haynes	c Such b Agnew	2
*M.W. Gatting	b Such	80
M.R. Ramprakash	b Willey	58
M.A. Roseberry	c Boon b Such	0
J.D. Carr	b Willey	33
†P.R. Downton	c Hepworth b Willey	38
N.F. Williams	c Whitaker b Potter	10
S.P. Hughes	st Nixon b Potter	4
P.C.R. Tufnell	c and b Potter	5
N.G. Cowans	not out	8
Extras	b 1, lb 10, nb 9	20
Total (100 ov: 216–6)		287

3, 77, 158, 158, 192, 238, 265, 273, 274

Agnew	12	0	45	1
Taylor	18	7	33	0
Parsons	17	5	66	1
Willey	30	16	40	3
Potter	16.2	1	50	3
Such	18	5	42	2

Lancashire 1st Innings

T.J. Boon	c Gatting b Williams	1
*N.E. Briers	c Carr b Williams	50
J.J. Whitaker	b Tufnell	46
P. Willey	lbw b Williams	16
L. Potter	c Downton b Williams	20
P.M. Hepworth	c Downton b Tufnell	10
G.J. Parsons	not out	31
†P.A. Nixon	not out	10
J.P. Agnew		
L.B. Taylor		
P.M. Such		
Extras	b 8, lb 2, w 1, nb 8	19
Total (6 wkts dec, 99.5 ov)		203

3, 82, 121, 125, 159, 163

Cowans	12	6	23	0
Williams	24	9	39	4
Hughes	18.5	7	53	0
Tufnell	38	19	71	2
Carr	7	3	7	0

Middlesex 2nd Innings

I.J.F. Hutchinson	c Potter b Such	39
J.D. Carr	not out	68
M.A. Roseberry	not out	16
Extras	nb 4	4
Total (1 wkt dec)		127

78

Agnew	9	1	27	0
Taylor	4	1	7	0
Parsons	11	1	47	0
Such	9	0	33	1
Potter	3	0	13	0

Leicestershire 2nd Innings

T.J. Boon	c Hughes b Tufnell	60
*N.E. Briers	c and b Tufnell	31
J.J. Whitaker	lbw b Cowans	0
P. Willey	c Williams b Hughes	30
G.J. Parsons	c Carr b Tufnell	19
L. Potter	c Hughes b Tufnell	13
P.M. Hepworth	b Tufnell	10
J.P. Agnew	b Hughes	2
†P.A. Nixon	not out	2
L.B. Taylor	not out	0
Extras	b 4, lb 8, nb 5	17
Total (8 wkts)		184

84, 91, 116, 151, 166, 166, 172, 180

Williams	7	0	43	0
Hughes	12	3	44	2
Tufnell	19	2	68	5
Cowans	7	1	17	1

Umpires: B. Hassan and D.G.L. Evans

Toss: Middlesex

Runs came slowly on the first day, with Middlesex restricted to 261 off 100 overs and play ending when the last Middlesex wicket fell. On Monday bad light ended play at 4.43 pm with the visitors 163–5 off 83.1 overs – another slow day. On the last day the news broke concerning Gatting's captaincy of the English team to South Africa and this overshadowed the cricket at Lord's. Leicestershire were invited to score 212 off 44 overs, following a quick 68 by Carr. The game was finely balanced when stumps were drawn.

v NORTHAMPTONSHIRE (Lord's)

August 12, 14, 15

Won by 7 wkts. Middx 22pts, Northants 4pts

Northamptonshire 1st Innings

G. Cook	b Cowans	5
*W. Larkins	c Emburey b Williams	80
A. Fordham	b Williams	29
R.J. Bailey	c Ramprakash b Williams	65
D.J. Capel	c Haynes b Tufnell	90
N.A. Felton	b EMburey	43
J.G. Thomas	c Haynes b Tufnell	2
W.W. Davis	c Roseberry b Tufnell	0
†D. Ripley	b Emburey	24
J.W. Govan	st Downton b Emburey	0
A. Walker	not out	7
Extras	b 4, lb 10, nb 4	18
Total (100 ov: 328–5)		363

5, 68, 187, 190, 321, 331, 331, 333, 338

Ellcock	11	1	60	0
Cowans	19	5	60	1
Emburey	34.5	9	88	3
Carr	6	2	19	0
Williams	19	3	45	3
Tufnell	21	4	77	3

Middlesex 1st Innings

J.D. Carr	not out	153
D.L. Haynes	c Ripley b Davis	76
M.R. Ramprakash	not out	53
*M.W. Gatting		
M.A. Roseberry		
†P.R. Downton		
J.E. Emburey		
N.F. Williams		
R.M. Ellcock		
P.C.R. Tufnell		
N.G. Cowans		
Extras	lb 9, nb 11	20
Total (1 wkt dec, 86.2 ov)		302

181

Davis	19	0	65	1
Thomas	13	1	68	0
Capel	6	1	21	0
Govan	27.2	8	55	0
Larkins	10	1	38	0
Cook	1	0	5	0
Bailey	10	1	41	0

Northamptonshire 2nd Innings

G. Cook	b Emburey	12
*W. Larkins	st Downton b Tufnell	28
A. Fordham	c Ellcock b Tufnell	12
R.J. Bailey	c Roseberry b Tufnell	5
D.J. Capel	b Tufnell	9
N.A. Felton	c Gatting b Emburey	41
J.G. Thomas	b Tufnell	4
†D. Ripley	lbw b Emburey	5
J.W. Govan	c Carr b Ellcock	7
W.W. Davis	not out	6
A. Walker	b Ellcock	1
Extras	b 1, lb 10, nb 1	12
Total		142

29, 52, 61, 69, 94, 120, 120, 125, 138

Gatting	4	0	16	0
Carr	3	0	12	0
Emburey	26	10	39	3
Tufnell	28	6	60	5
Ellcock	12.5	1	4	2

Middlesex 2nd Innings

J.D. Carr	lbw b Thomas	11
D.L. Haynes	c Ripley b Davis	21
*M.W. Gatting	not out	83
M.R. Ramprakash	c and b Govan	43
M.A. Roseberry	not out	14
Extras	b 8, lb 17, nb 7	32
Total (3 wkts)		204

27, 61, 155

Davis	10	1	40	1
Thomas	9	0	39	1
Govan	13	0	55	1
Capel	5	1	26	0
Bailey	1.3	0	9	0
Cook	1	0	10	0

Umpires: R. Julian and P.B. Wight

Toss: Northamptonshire

After two days of stalemate, Tufnell and Emburey made the ball bounce and turn on the third morning and Northants, instead of setting a target, found themselves all out for 142 and Middlesex had 165 minutes in which to make 204, a task they accomplished with 5.3 overs in hand. The Northants first innings occupied Saturday and on Monday Middlesex reached 298–1 off 86 overs, rain lopping 30 overs off the day.

v SUSSEX (Lord's)

September 8, 9, 10, 11

Drawn. Sussex 6pts, Middx 3pts

Sussex 1st Innings

N.J. Lenham	c Downton b Fraser	17
D.M. Smith	c Tufnell b Emburey	129
*P.W.G. Parker	c Gatting b Cowans	136
A.P. Wells	c Fraser b Ellcock	27
†P. Moores	b Ellcock	0
B.T.P. Donelan	c Downton b Cowans	5
C.M. Wells	lbw b Fraser	7
I.J. Gould	b Cowans	4
A.I.C. Dodemaide	c Gatting b Tufnell	46
A.C.S. Pigott	c Brown b Tufnell	32
A.R. Hansford	not out	14
Extras	b 3, lb 16, nb 2	21
Total (100 ov: 265–2)		438

193, 228, 311, 311, 323, 326, 330, 342, 407

Ellcock	23	4	98	2
Cowans	20	3	60	3
Fraser	29	9	60	2
Emburey	47	14	95	1
Tufnell	36	7	106	2

Middlesex 1st Innings

D.L. Haynes	c Smith b Hansford	13
J.D. Carr	b Hansford	12
*M.W. Gatting	not out	139
M.A. Roseberry	c Pigott b Dodemaide	0
K.R. Brown	lbw b Pigott	30
†P.R. Downton	c Pigott b Lenham	25
J.E. Emburey	c Pigott b Lenham	21
A.R.C. Fraser	c Donelan b Pigott	27
R.M. Ellcock	c Moores b Pigott	0
P.C.R. Tufnell	b Pigott	12
N.G. Cowans	b Dodemaide	0
Extras	b 12, lb 9, nb 2	23
Total (100 ov: 288–8)		302

21, 37, 38, 106, 188, 288, 261, 261, 295

Pigott	24	7	71	4
Dodemaide	21	4	51	2
Hansford	24	5	83	2
C.M. Wells	22	6	48	0
Doneland	3	0	12	0
Lenham	10	3	16	2

Sussex 2nd Innings

N.J. Lenham	c Downton b Fraser	8
D.M. Smith	not out	51
*P.W.G. Parker	c Downton b Fraser	0
A.P. Wells	lbw b Cowans	0
C.M. Wells	c Carr b Ellcock	15
I.J. Gould	not out	51
Extras	b 7, lb 4, nb 1	12
Total (4 wkts dec)		137

8, 10, 11, 33

Fraser	10	2	38	2
Cowans	7	4	3	1
Ellcock	4	0	23	1
Emburey	10.4	2	27	0
Carr	1	1	0	0
Tufnell	8	1	35	0

Middlesex 2nd Innings

D.L. Haynes	b Hansford	51
J.D. Carr	run out	8
*M.W. Gatting	c Dodemaide b Hansford	45
M.A. Roseberry	c Lenham b Pigott	16
K.R. Brown	not out	53
†P.R. Downton	b Pigott	8
J.E. Emburey	not out	12
Extras	b 1, b 7, nb 1	9
Total (5 wkts)		202

19, 100, 117, 134, 164

Pigott	14	0	46	2
Dodemaide	7	4	13	0
C.M. Wells	8	1	25	0
Hansford	11.5	2	69	2
Donelan	7	0	34	0
Lenham	1	0	3	0
Gould	1	0	4	0

Umpires: B. Leadbeater and K.J. Lyons

Toss: Sussex

The first day was one of unspectacular progress by Smith and Parker, both of whom occupied the crease for more than five hours and Middlesex failed to obtain any bowling bonus points. On Saturday rain restricted play and Sussex progressed from 313–4 to 438 all out. Gatting spent 5¾ hours on his 139 not out on Sunday and Middlesex just avoided the follow on. The final day's play seemed to lack any enthusiasm after Sussex lost their first three wickets for only 11. Middlesex remained in third place in the table.

Northamptonshire

President: D.C. Lucas
Chairman: W.R.F. Chamberlain
Secretary and Manager: S.P. Coverdale, County Ground, Wantage Road, Northampton NN1 4TJ. *Tel:* 0604 32917.
Coach: R.M. Carter
Captain: A.J.Lamb
Foundation of Present Club: July 1878 in Kettering
First First-Class Match: Northamptonshire v Hampshire (Southampton) May 1905
County Champions: Nil (second in 1912, 1957, 1965, 1976)
Gillette/NatWest Trophy: Winners 1976
Benson & Hedges Cup: Winners 1980
Sunday League Champions: Nil (best position 4th in 1974)
Refuge Cup: Nil

Summary of Results in 1989
Britannic Assurance County Championship: Played 22, Won 7, Lost 8, Drawn 7, Position 5th
NatWest Bank Trophy: Lost in quarter-final
Benson & Hedges Cup: Lost in quarter-final
Refuge Assurance Sunday League: Played 16, Won 8, Lost 6, No Result 2, Position 6th equal
Refuge Assurance Cup: Did not qualify

From left, back: *C. Newton, N. Stanley, G. Smith, S. Brown, G. Thomas, M. Robinson, A. Penberthy.* Middle: *R. Norman (Physiotherapist), A. Fordham, N. Felton, D. Wild, W. Davis, A. Walker, D. Ripley, W. Noon, A. Roberts, R. Carter (Chief Coach).* Front: *D. Capel, R. Williams, W. Larkins, A. Lamb (Captain), N. Cook, G. Cook, R. Bailey.*
Allsport

With the importation of the gangling Antiguan, Ambrose, as well as the Welshman, Thomas, the county's attack ought to have been immeasurably strengthened in 1989, but neither bowler proved quite the force hoped for and the player who actually topped the bowling table was Nick Cook – the only spin bowler with fifty or more wickets to head his county's averages. Robinson and Walker, the two Yorkshire seam bowlers, had disappointing seasons and Davis' wickets each cost five more runs than they had in 1988. However Capel had a better year and gained an England cap.

Lamb missed many matches through injury and then when fit was recruited for England – this continual absence of the captain did not help the county's cause. The critics blamed poor fielding on the fact that Northants failed to win any trophies in 1989 and this is one branch of the game that can be rectified by a captain's hand.

After a poor summer in 1988, Larkins returned to his best form and was the leading run scorer – his efforts were rewarded with a place in the England team for West Indies. Capel remained a very useful batsman, his record being similar to that obtained in 1988, while Geoff Cook, the former captain, had a good summer and Fordham played some good innings. Felton arrived from Somerset, but was not consistent and the lower order batsmen were unreliable, Cook, Robinson and Ambrose forming a very weak tail.

In the first half of the season the county looked as if it would put up a good challenge for the Championship title, but results in the second half were not so impressive. Despite that, Northants finished in fifth place which was a great improvement on 1988. In the Refuge League they won twice as many games as in 1988 and showed a similar rise. They reached the quarter-finals of both the NatWest Trophy and the Benson and Hedges Cup, which again was an improvement on the summer before. In 1990 the county is strong enough to win trophies – all depends on the regular presence of key players and holding on to catches.

ONE DAY AWAY MATCHES

The full scorecard of each of Northamptonshire's away matches will be found in the sections for the respective home teams.

Refuge Assurance Championship

Derby: April 23
No play. Northants 2pts, Derbys 2pts

Cardiff: May 21
Glamorgan 162–7 (40 ov) lost to Northants 163–4 (38.1 ov) by 6 wkts. Northants 4pts, Glamorgan 0pts.

Canterbury: May 28
Kent 201–8 (40 ov) lost to Northants 205–2 (39.3 ov) by 8 wkts. Northants 4pts, Kent 0pts.

Hove: June 11
Northants 189–6 (39 ov) lost to Sussex 190–7 (38.1) by 3 wkts. Sussex 4pts, Northants 0pts.

Old Trafford: July 16
Northants 133 (38.3 ov) lost to Lancs 136–7 (35 ov) by 3 wkts. Lancs 4pts, Northants 0pts

Sheffield: August 6
Northants 198–4 (40 ov) beat Yorks 186 (38.3 ov) by 12 runs. Northants 4pts, Yorks 0pts.

Lord's: August 13
Northants 157–8 (40 ov) lost to Middx 160–4 (38.5 ov) by 6 wkts. Middx 4 pts, Northants 0pts.

Moreton-in-Marsh: August 20
Gloucs 195–5 (40 ov) lost to Northants 198–3 (36.2 ov) (W. Larkins 101) by 7 wkts. Northants 4pts, Gloucs 0pts.

Benson and Hedges Cup

Edgbaston: April 25, 26
Warwicks 221–7 (55 ov) lost to Northants 225–6 (53.5 ov) by 4 wkts. Northants 2 pts, Warwicks 0pts.

Glasgow: May 13
Scotland 207–7 (55 ov) lost to Northants 210–1 (44.4 ov) by 9 wkts. Northants 2pts, Scotland 0pts.

NatWest Bank Trophy

Bury St Edmunds: June 28
Northants 256–6 (60 ov) (A.J. Lamb 103) beat Suffolk 224 (59.5 ov) by 32 runs.

Taunton: July 12
Somerset 210 (55.4 ov) lost to Northants 211–5 (57 ov) by 5 wkts.

REFUGE ASSURANCE LEAGUE

v WARWICKSHIRE (Northampton)

May 7
Won by 7 wkts. Northants 4pts, Warwicks 0pts

Warwickshire		
*T.A. Lloyd	b Williams	25
A.J. Moles	run out	8
D.A. Thorne	c Larkins b Williams	22
A.I. Kallicharran	run out	30
D.A Banks	lbw b Walker	1
P.A. Smith	lbw b Thomas	30
†G.W. Humpage	c and b Thomas	14
G.C. Small	st Ripley b Cook	10
T.A. Munton	not out	4
A.A. Donald	c Ripley b Thomas	7
A.R.K. Pierson	not out	2
Extras	b 1, lb 13, w 3, nb 1	18
Total (9 wkts, 40 ov)		171

19, 46, 81, 82, 112, 137, 137, 158, 168

Davis	8	0	32	0
Thomas	8	0	34	3
Williams	8	0	33	2
Walker	5	2	14	1
Cook	8	0	24	1
Capel	3	0	20	0

Northamptonshire		
D.J. Wild	c Humpage b Munton	3
W. Larkins	b Munton	6
R.J. Bailey	c Munton b Pierson	27
*A.J. Lamb	not out	80
D.J. Capel	not out	40
R.G. Williams		
†D. Ripley		
J.G. Thomas		
N.G.B. Cook		
W.W. Davis		
A. Walker		
Extras	lb 5, w 9, nb 2	16
Total (3 wkts, 38 ov)		172

10, 12, 89

Donald	8	1	23	0
Munton	7	1	17	2
Small	8	0	29	0
Pierson	8	0	49	1
Smith	7	0	49	0

Umpires: J.H. Hampshire and B. Dudleston
Toss: Northamptonshire
A moderate batting performance by the visitors, with no one managing more than 30, looked enough when Munton removed both Northants openers cheaply, but Lamb was in good form and a stand of 77 for the 3rd wicket was followed with an unbroken 83 for the 4th as Northants coasted to victory.

v SURREY (Northampton)

June 4
Won by 42 runs. Northants 4pts, Surrey 0pts

Northamptonshire		
G. Cook	c Ward b Arnold	3
W. Larkins	c Thorpe b Medlycott	63
R.J. Bailey	not out	106
*A.J. Lamb	c Robinson b Greig	21
D.J. Capel	c Thorpe b Murphy	2
D.J. Wild	not out	0
†D. Ripley		
J.G. Thomas		
N.G.B. Cook		
W.W. Davis		
M.A. Robinson		
Extras	b 1, lb 5	6
Total (4 wkts, 40 ov)		201

7, 109, 160, 198

Murphy	8	0	36	1
Arnold	6	3	7	1
Greig	7	0	42	1
Thorpe	4	0	20	0
Bullen	8	0	48	0
Medlycott	7	0	42	1

Surrey		
K.T. Medlycott	c Capel b Davis	3
G.S. Clinton	c Robinson b Davis	56
†D.M. Ward	c Larkins b Capel	14
A.J. Stewart	c Ripley b Robinson	27
Z.A. Sadiq	b Robinson	13
*I.A. Greig	run out	7
G.P. Thorpe	c G. Cook b Capel	14
J.D. Robinson	not out	8
C.K. Bullen	c Ripley b Thomas	0
A.J. Murphy	b Thomas	0
G.G. Arnold	not out	4
Extras	b 1, lb 10, w 2	13
Total (9 wkts, 40 ov)		159

5, 32, 77, 109, 120, 141, 152, 152, 152

Thomas	8	0	28	2
Davis	8	0	18	2
N.G.B. Cook	8	0	31	0
Capel	8	0	40	2
Robinson	8	0	31	2

Umpires: D.J. Constant and A.A. Jones
Toss: Northamptonshire
With M.P. Bicknell and Feltham both injured, G.G. Arnold, aged 44, reappeared for Surrey after an absence of 12 years. Arnold bowled very capably, but Larkins and Bailey added 102 for the 2nd wicket and later Surrey never looked likely to reach their target.

Right: *Wayne Larkins, easily Northants' heaviest scorer in the Championship, a feat which won him a place in the winter touring party.*

Allsport/Adrian Murrell

Far right: *David Capel, Northant's international all-rounder who scored 1,290 runs and took 55 wickets.*

Allsport/Pascal Rondeau

REFUGE ASSURANCE LEAGUE

v LEICESTERSHIRE (Luton)

June 25

Lost by 8 wkts. Leics 4pts, Northants 0pts

Northamptonshire		
G. Cook	b Lewis	8
W. Larkins	c Potter b Agnew	0
R.J. Bailey	c Whitticase b Taylor	20
*A.J. Lamb	b Taylor	0
D.J. Capel	c Lewis b Taylor	0
N.A. Felton	lbw b Taylor	7
D. Ripley	retired hurt	18
J.G. Thomas	c Boon b Taylor	5
C.E.L. Ambrose	c Whitticase b Parsons	1
N.G.B. Cook	not out	13
M.A. Robinson	c Whitticase b Lewis	2
Extras	lb 5, w 2	7
Total (34 ov)		81

1, 29, 29, 31, 34, 45, 53, 61, 81

Benjamin	7	1	13	0
Agnew	6	1	14	1
Lewis	8	0	16	2
Taylor	8	0	20	5
Parsons	5	0	13	1

Leicestershire		
L. Potter	c sub (Noon) b Thomas	0
*N.E. Briers	c Larkins b Thomas	13
T.J. Boon	not out	39
P.N. Hepworth	not out	20
J.D.R. Benson		
C.C. Lewis		
†P. Whitticase		
W.K.M. Benjamin		
G.J. Parsons		
J.P. Agnew		
L.B. Taylor		
Extras	lb 1, w 7, nb 2	10
Total (2 wkts, 25.3 ov)		82

11, 30

Ambrose	8	0	24	0
Thomas	5	0	15	2
Robinson	4	0	10	0
Capel	6.3	1	25	0
N.G.B Cook	2	1	7	0

Umpires: D.S. Thompsett and P.B. Wight
Toss: Northampton
Taylor dismissed Bailey and Lamb with the first two deliveries he bowled and that knocked the heart out of Northants. Leicestershire hit off the runs with no difficulty. Ripley was injured while batting and took no further park in the match, Briers allowed the county deputy wicketkeeper to come on as substitute.

v WORCESTERSHIRE (Tring)

July 2

Lost by 6 wkts. Worcs 4pts, Northants 0pts

Northamptonshire		
N.A. Felton	c Curtis b Weston	18
W. Larkins	c O'Shaughnessy b Weston	17
R.J. Bailey	c Rhodes b Illingworth	32
*A.J. Lamb	c O'Shaughnessy	10
D.J. Capel	b Illingworth	32
D.J. Wild	c Curtis b Botham	25
†D. Ripley	b Radford	5
J.G. Thomas	lbw b Radford	0
C.E.L. Ambrose	lbw b Radford	2
N.G.M. Cook	not out	10
M.A. Robinson	b Illingworth	0
Extras	b 3, lb 10, w 4	17
Total (39.4 ov)		168

33, 49, 69, 123, 124, 139, 139, 147, 163

Weston	8	2	20	2
Botham	8	0	33	1
Radford	8	1	30	3
O'Shaughnessy	8	0	44	1
Illingworth	7.4	0	28	3

Worcestershire		
T.S. Curtis	c Robinson b Cook	63
I.T. Botham	b Ambrose	39
G.A. Hick	c and b Cook	4
D.B. d'Oliveira	c Capel b Thomas	27
*P.A. Neale	not out	23
M.J. Weston	not out	2
S.J. O'Shaughnessy		
†S.J. Rhodes		
N.V. Radford		
R.K. Illingworth		
S.R. Lampitt		
Extras	lb 9, w 2	11
Total (4 wkts, 39.4 ov)		169

82, 93, 136, 157

Ambrose	8	1	38	1
Thomas	7.4	0	32	1
Robinson	8	0	32	0
Capel	8	0	30	0
Cook	8	0	28	2

Umpires: R. Palmer and J.D. Bond
Toss: Northamptonshire
On a slow wicket, Northants found batting difficult, whereas Curtis and Botham got almost halfway to their objective even before a wicket fell and though Hick failed, d'Oliveira and Neale ensured victory.

v HAMPSHIRE (Northampton)

July 9

Abandoned. Northants 2pts, Hants 2pts

Northamptonshire		
R.J. Bailey	not out	53
*W. Larkins	b Nicholas	10
N.A. Felton	not out	58
D.J. Capel		
D.J. Wild		
A. Fordham		
†D. Ripley		
J.G. Thomas		
C.E.L. Ambrose		
A. Walker		
N.G.B. Cook		
	b 2, lb 8, w 4	14
Total (1 wkts, 23.2 ov)		135

21

Marshall	6	1	15	0
Bakker	6	0	37	0
Nicholas	6	0	39	1
Connor	4	0	18	0
Cowley	1.2	0	16	0

Hampshire
V.P. Terry
*M.C.J. Nicholas
D.R. Turner
J.R. Wood
C.L. Smith
R.J. Maru
M.D. Marshall
N.G. Cowley
†R.J. Parks
C.A. Connor
P.J. Bakker

Umpires: N.T. Plews and D.G.L. Evans
Toss: Hampshire
Rain delayed the start and then there were several interruptions due to the weather, before the rain returned in earnest and the match was abandoned.

PLAYERS

Curtly Elconn Lynwall AMBROSE *b* 21.9.1963 Swetes Village, Antigua; right-arm fast bowler; left-hand batsman; debut for Northants in May 1989; also plays for Leeward Is; 17 Tests for West Indies

Robert John BAILEY *b* 28.10.1963 Biddulph, Staffs; right-hand batsman; off-break bowler; debut 1982; one Test for England in 1988; selected to tour West Indies 1989/90

Simon John BROWN *b* 29.6.1969 Cleadon, Durham; left-arm fast medium bowler; right-hand batsman; debut 1987

David John CAPEL *b* 6.2.1963 Northampton; all-rounder; middle order right-hand batsman; right-arm medium-fast bowler; debut 1981; 11 Tests for England, including one in 1989; selected to tour West Indies 1989–90

Geoffrey COOK *b* 9.10.1951 Middlesbrough; opening right-hand batsman; occasional slow left-arm bowler; debut 1971; captain 1981–88; seven Tests for England 1981–83

Nicholas Grant Billson COOK *b* 17.6.1956 Leicester; slow left-arm bowler; lower order right-hand batsman; debut 1986; previously appeared for Leics 1978–85; 15 Tests for England including 3 in 1989; went to India with England for Nehru Cup 1989/90

Winston Walter DAVIS *b* 18.9.1958 Sion Hill, St Vincent; right-arm fast bowler; right-hand batsman; debut 1987; has also played for Windward Is since 1980; played for Glamorgan 1982–84; 15 Tests for West Indies

Nigel Alfred FELTON *b* 24.10.1960 Guildford; left-hand batsman; debut 1989; previously played for Somerset 1982–88

Alan FORDHAM *b* 9.11.1964 Bedford; right-hand batsman; right-arm medium pace bowler; debut 1986

James Walter GOWAN *b* 6.5.1966 Dunfermline; right-hand batsman; off-break bowler; FC debut for Northants in August 1989; previously played for Scotland

Allan Joseph LAMB *b* 20.6.1954 Langebaanweg, S Africa; very talented right-hand batsman; debut 1978; also plays for Organge Free State; 57 Tests for England including 1 in 1989; Captain of county 1989; selected as vice-captain of England to West Indies 1989–90

Greg Thomas, Northants' fast bowling acquisition from Glamorgan, who took 67 wickets for his new county.

Allsport/Pascal Rondeau

Wayne LARKINS *b* 22.11.1953 Roxton, Beds; right-hand batsman; right-arm medium pace bowler; debut 1972; six Tests for England; selected to tour West Indies 1989–90

Wayne Michael NOON *b* 5.2.1971 Grimsby; wicketkeeper; right-hand batsman; FC debut for Northants in June 1989, but appeared in Sunday League in 1988; in one match last year he came on as substitute and kept wicket

Anthony PENBERTHY *b* 1.9.1969 Redruth; left-hand batsman; right-arm medium pace bowler; FC debut for Northants in June 1989, taking wicket with first delivery

David RIPLEY *b* 13.9.1966 Leeds; wicketkeeper; right-hand batsman; debut 1984

Andrew ROBERTS *b* 16.4.1971; leg-break bowler; right-hand batsman; debut for Northants in May 1989

Mark Andrew ROBINSON *b* 23.11.1966 Hull; right-hand batsman; right-arm fast-medium bowler; debut 1987

Gareth SMITH *b* 20.7.1966 Jarrow; right-hand batsman; left-arm medium bowler; debut 1986

Neil Alan STANLEY *b* 16.5.1968 Bedford; right-hand batsman; right-arm medium pace bowler; debut 1988

John Gregory THOMAS *b* 12.8.1960 Trebanos, S Wales; right-arm fast bowler; right-hand batsman; debut for Northants in 1989; previously appeared for Glamorgan 1979–88; also plays for Eastern Province; Five Tests for England; selected to tour South Africa 1989–90

Alan WALKER *b* 7.7.1962 Emley, Yorks; all-rounder; left-hand batsman; right-arm fast medium bowler; debut 1983

Duncan James WILD *b* 28.11.1962 Northampton; left-hand batsman; right-arm medium pace bowler; debut 1974; son of John (ex-Northants)

Richard Grenville WILLIAMS *b* 10.8.1957 Bangor, N Wales; all-rounder; right-hand batsman; off-break bowler; debut 1974

REFUGE ASSURANCE LEAGUE

v NOTTINGHAMSHIRE (Finedon)

July 23

Won by 24 runs. Northants 4pts, Notts 0pts

Northamptonshire		
R.J. Bailey	c and b Evans	25
A. Fordham	c Saxelby b Stephenson	10
D.J. Capel	b Saxelby	40
N.A. Felton	b Saxelby	2
†D. Ripley	c Stephenson b Evans	4
*N.G.B Cook	c French b Saxelby	4
M.A. Robinson	run out	0
N.A. Stanley	c Pollard b Cooper	13
A.L. Penberthy	c Robinson c Saxelby	35
J.G. Thomas	not out	18
C.E.L. Ambrose	lbw b Saxelby	4
Extras	b 1, lb 10, w 4, nb 3	18
Total (40 ov)		173

23, 38, 48, 73, 120, 138, 151, 155, 172

Stephenson	8	0	37	1
Cooper	8	2	27	1
Evans	8	0	33	2
Saxelby	8	0	45	5
Afford	8	1	20	0

Nottinghamshire		
B.C. Broad	b Robinson	38
P.R. Pollard	c Ripley b Ambrose	4
*R.T. Robinson	c Fordham b Capel	13
P. Johnson	c Penberthy b Capel	0
D.J.R. Martindale	b Capel	53
F.D. Stephenson	lbw b Cook	10
K.P. Evans	c Capel b Robinson	5
†B.N. French	b Ambrose	6
K.E. Cooper	b Ambrose	9
K. Saxelby	not out	4
J.A. Afford	b Thomas	0
Extras	lb 3, w 4	7
Total (39.2 ov)		149

8, 28, 28, 84, 121, 128, 130, 140, 147

Ambrose	8	2	15	3
Thomas	7.2	0	31	1
Capel	8	0	28	3
Robinson	8	1	40	2
Cook	8	0	32	1

Umpires: J.H. Harris and J.W. Holder

Toss: Northamptonshire

Saxelby took another five wickets — his third such feat in successive matches — and Notts kept Northants' total down to measureable proportions. The early Notts batsmen however failed to make much headway and only Martindale gave the innings a look of respectability.

v SOMERSET (Northampton)

July 30

Lost by 3 wkts. Somerset 4pts, Northants 0pts

Northamptonshire		
*W. Larkins	c Burns b Jones	1
A. Fordham	lbw b Mallender	12
R.J. Bailey	c Burns b Mallender	22
D.J. Capel	run out	1
D.J. Wild	b Jones	54
N.A. Felton	c Bartlett b Jones	29
A.L. Penberthy	c Bartlett b Rose	7
†D. Ripley	lbw b Marks	1
J.G. Thomas	b Rose	10
W.W. Davis	c Burns b Rose	2
A. Walker	not out	0
Extras	b 2, lb 7, w 1, nb 1	11
Total (39.1 ov)		150

3, 34, 35, 44, 115, 134, 138, 144, 148

Jones	8	1	37	3
Rose	7.1	1	21	3
Mallender	8	1	15	2
Trump	8	0	33	0
Marks	8	0	35	1

Somerset		
S.J. Cook	c Ripley b Walker	18
J.G. Wyatt	b Davis	0
R.J. Bartlett	c Ripley b Capel	12
C.J. Tavare	lbw b Capel	7
R. J. Harden	b Capel	9
*V.J. Marks	lbw b Walker	0
†N.D. Burns	c Wild b Davis	8
G.D. Rose	not out	61
N.A. Mallender	not out	21
H.R.J. Trump		
A.N. Jones		
Extras	lb 8, w 3, nb 5	16
Total (7 wkts, 37.5 ov)		152

3, 28, 37, 51, 52, 58, 82

Davis	7	0	20	2
Thomas	8	0	31	0
Capel	8	0	20	3
Walker	7.5	1	20	2
Penberthy	4	0	24	0
Wild	3	0	29	0

Umpires: K.J. Lyons and A.G.T. Whitehead

Toss: Somerset

This match belonged to Rose, whose bowling was most economical, enabling Somerset to dismiss Northants relatively cheaply. Rose then turned the match by hitting 61 and with Mallender adding an unbroken 70 for the 8th wicket.

v ESSEX (Northampton)

August 27

Won by 3 wkts. Northants 4pts, Essex 0pts

Essex		
*B.R. Hardie	c Ripley b Thomas	8
A.W. Lilley	b Penberthy	33
M.E. Waugh	c Larkins b Govan	31
P.J. Prichard	lbw b Govan	1
N. Hussain	b Penberthy	0
N. Shahid	c Larkins b Penberthy	11
†M.A. Garnham	b Govan	14
N.A. Foster	run out	9
G. Miller	c Ripley b Thomas	3
T.D. Topley	not out	12
J.K. Lever	not out	5
Extras	lb 10, w 6, nb 1	17
Total (9 wkts, 40 ov)		144

29, 69, 81, 81, 82, 110, 112, 123, 127

Robinson	8	0	24	0
Ambrose	8	3	25	0
Thomas	8	0	36	2
Penberthy	8	1	26	3
Govan	8	2	23	3

Northamptonshire		
*W.Larkins	c Waugh b Lever	1
A. Fordham	c Topley b Waugh	31
R.J. Bailey	run out	3
N.A. Felton	c and b Miller	24
D.J. Wild	run out	22
A.L. Penberthy	b Waugh	4
J.G. Thomas	run out	23
†D. Ripley	not out	16
J.W. Govan	not out	9
C.E.L. Ambrose		
M.A. Robinson		
Extras	lb 5, w 7	12
Total (7 wkts, 39.4 ov)		145

8, 17, 53, 66, 75, 118, 119

Lever	8	4	16	1
Foster	7.4	0	34	0
Miller	8	0	24	1
Topley	8	1	33	0
Waugh	8	0	33	2

Umpires: J.C. Balderstone and D.O. Oslear

Toss: Essex had to win this match to make certain of second place in the League, but their batsmen rather let them down and Northants won with two deliveries unbowled. Essex of course were without Gooch, which was a severe handicap in the circumstances.

BRITANNIC ASSURANCE COUNTY CHAMPIONSHIP AVERAGES 1989

Batting	*M*	*I*	*NO*	*Runs*	*HS*	*Avge*	*100*	*50*
A.J. Lamb	8	12	–	537	171	44.75	2	1
W. Larkins	21	40	3	1419	116	38.35	1	12
D.J. Capel	21	36	3	1260	126	38.18	3	9
G. Cook	19	35	3	1158	138	36.19	4	4
A. Fordham	12	21	3	643	199	35.72	1	4
R.J. Bailey	22	39	2	1271	134	34.35	4	6
N.A. Stanley	3	6	–	187	75	31.17	–	1
N.A. Felton	13	24	3	552	60*	26.29	–	4
D. Ripley	22	35	8	590	123	21.85	1	–
R.G. Williams	4	7	1	118	71	19.67	–	1
D.J. Wild	10	14	–	255	121	18.21	1	–
C.E.L. Ambrose	9	14	5	127	23*	14.11	–	–
A.L. Penberthy	3	6	–	75	27	12.50	–	–
J.G. Thomas	19	31	2	333	35	11.48	–	–
A. Roberts	2	3	1	22	8*	11.00	–	–
W.W. Davis	13	17	4	142	40*	10.92	–	–
A. Walker	3	5	2	32	11*	10.67	–	–
N.G.B. Cook	17	24	5	109	21	5.74	–	–
J.W. Govan	2	3	–	11	7	3.67	–	–
G. Smith	2	3	1	6	6	3.00	–	–
M.A. Robinson	16	21	10	16	9	1.45	–	–

Also batted: S.J. Brown (1 match) 5*.

Bowling	*O*	*M*	*R*	*W*	*Avge*	*BB*	*5i*	*10m*
N.G.B. Cook	426.1	161	909	49	18.55	6-56	2	–
W.W. Davis	420	67	1370	50	27.40	5-55	1	–
C.E.L. Ambrose	281	70	795	28	28.39	6-22	2	–
J.G. Thomas	523.2	77	1906	66	28.88	6-53	3	–
M.A. Robinson	373.1	77	1032	34	30.35	4-60	–	–
D.J. Capel	481.2	88	1559	51	30.57	5-53	1	–
R.J. Bailey	115.5	13	483	8	60.38	3-70	–	–

Also bowled: S.J. Brown 19-3-89-0; G. Cook 2-0-15-0; N.A. Felton 7-0-58-1; J.W. Govan 54.2-10-159-3; W. Larkins 14-2-47-0; A.L. Penberthy 23-6-78-0; A. Roberts 34-2-157-2; G. Smith 31-5-112-2; A. Walker 47-12-153-4; R.G. Williams 15.5-4-41-1.

Centuries

4 R.J. Bailey: 100 v Glos (Bristol); 134 v Lancs (Southport); 100 v Somerset (Luton); 116 v Derbys (Northampton). G. Cook: 138 v Sussex (Hove); 128 v Lancs (Southport); 126 v Somerset (Luton); 105 v Leics (Leicester).

3 D.J. Capel: 102 & 126 v Sussex (Hove); 105 v Kent (Maidstone).

2 A.J. Lamb: 148 v Leics (Northampton); 171 v Surrey (Northampton).

1 A. Fordham: 199 v Yorks (Sheffield). W. Larkins: 116 v Kent (Maidstone). D. Ripley: 123 v Yorks (Northampton). D.J. Wild: 121 v Yorks (Northampton).

BENSON AND HEDGES CUP

v LANCASHIRE (Northampton)

May 9

Won by 38 runs. Nothants 2pts, Lancs 0pts

Northamptonshire		
G. Cook	run out	66
W. Larkins	b Simmons	49
R.J. Bailey	run out	39
*A.J. Lamb	run out	38
D.J. Capel	not out	15
J.G. Thomas	c Mendis b DeFreitas	2
R.G. Williams	not out	2
†D. Ripley		
N.G.B Cook		
W.W. Davis		
M.A Robinson		
Extras	b 5, lb 7, w 7, nb 5	24
Total (5 wkts, 55 ov)		235

100, 138, 202, 220, 225

DeFreitas	11	0	56	1
Allott	10	3	25	1
Wasim Akram	11	0	60	0
Watkinson	11	2	49	0
Simmons	11	0	29	1
Jesty	1	0	4	0

Lancashire		
G.D. Mendis	c Capel b Robinson	26
A.N. Hayhurst	c Ripley b Thomas	6
T.E. Jesty	b Capel	20
N.H. Fairbrother	lbw b Thomas	3
M. Watkinson	c Bailey b Williams	7
P.A.J. DeFreitas	c Robinson b Capel	30
*D.P. Hughes	lbw b Capel	2
Wasim Akram	c Ripley b Thomas	52
†W.K. Hegg	run out	5
P.J.W. Allott	b N.G.B. Cook	22
J. Simmons	not out	7
Extras	b 1, lb 10, w 6	17
Total (51.1 ov)		197

35, 39, 46, 65, 77, 97, 110, 141, 182

Davis	8	2	11	0
Thomas	9	0	36	3
Robinson	11	1	19	1
Williams	10	2	66	1
Capel	11	0	47	3
N.G.B. Cook	2.1	0	7	1

Umpires: B. Dudleston and J.H. Hampshire
Toss: Lancashire. Gold: J.G. Thomas
G. Cook and Larkins gave the home county a sound start and the total reched a satisfactory 235–5. Lancashire never looked likely to achieve the target, but Wasim Akram hit 52 off 37 balls to bring a little cheer to visitors.

v LEICESTERSHIRE (Northampton)

May 11, 12

Abandoned. Northants 1pt, Leics 1pt

Northamptonshire		
G. Cook	c Agnew b Willey	25
W. Larkins	lbw b Benjamin	2
R.J. Bailey	run out	30
*A.J. Lamb	not out	87
D.J. Capel	run out	5
R.G. Williams	b Lewis	30
J.G. Thomas	run out	3
†D. Ripley	not out	1
N.G.B. Cook		
W.W. Davis		
M.A. Robinson		
Extras	lb 15, w 3, nb 3	21
Total (6 wkts, 55 ov)		204

11, 50, 92, 100, 181, 190

Benjamin	11	4	28	1
Agnew	11	3	22	0
Lewis	11	1	48	1
Parsons	11	1	67	0
Willey	11	1	24	1

Leicestershire		
T.J. Boon	not out	4
N.E. Briers	c Ripley b Thomas	0
*D.I. Gower	not out	2
P. Willey		
J.J. Whitaker		
L. Potter		
C.C. Lewis		
†P. Whitticase		
G.J. Parsons		
W.K.M. Benjamin		
J.P. Agnew		
Extras	lb 4, w 1	5
Total (1 wkts, 5.2 ov)		11

7

Davis	3	1	5	0
Thomas	2.2	1	2	1

Umpires: J.H. Harris and R.A. White
Toss: Northamptonshire. Gold: Nil
The run outs of Bailey and Capel prevented Northants reaching a very high total, but Lamb, though pulling a muscle and needing a runner for most of his innings, hit a brilliant 87*. Rain reduced the playing time and the match continued on the second day, but only 32 balls were bowled before further rain ended the proceedings.

NATWEST BANK TROPHY

QUARTER FINAL v WARWICKSHIRE (Northampton)

Aug 2

Lost by 3 wkts.

Northamptonshire		
G. Cook	b Smith	45
*W. Larkins	c Lloyd b Donald	0
N.A. Felton	c Humpage b Reeve	6
R.J. Bailey	c Humpage b Twose	30
D.J. Capel	c Lloyd b Donald	54
D.J. Wild	b Donald	38
J.G. Thomas	c Reeve b Small	1
†D. Ripley	b Donald	3
N.G.B. Cook	not out	0
C.E.L. Ambrose		
A. Walker		
Extras	b 1, lb 9, w 4	14
Total (8 wkts, 60 ov)		191

2, 27, 79, 97, 184, 186, 188, 191

Small	12	0	44	1
Donald	12	1	26	4
Munton	12	1	42	0
Reeve	12	2	32	1
Twose	10	0	31	1
Smith	2	0	6	1

Warwickshire		
A.J. Moles	c and b Ambrose	8
*T.A. Lloyd	c Larkins b Thomas	57
A.I. Kallicharran	lbw b Walker	48
G.W. Humpage	c Ripley b Thomas	5
†D.A. Reeve	c Ripley b Capel	15
Asif Din	c Felton b Ambrose	17
R.G. Twose	c Bailey b Thomas	9
N.M.K. Smith	not out	16
G.C. Small	not out	4
A.A. Donald		
T.A. Munton		
Extras	lb 10, w 5	15
Total (7 wkts, 59.4 ov)		194

26, 108, 118, 132, 160, 165, 188

Ambrose	12	4	24	2
Thomas	11	0	54	3
Walker	12	4	29	1
Cook	12	1	29	0
Capel	10.4	1	42	1
Bailey	2	0	6	0

Umpires: J.W. Holder and R.A. White
Toss: Warwickshire. MofM: T.A. Lloyd
Lloyd and Kallicharran were both in form. Bad light however began to cause problems and twice the players left the field. In the end Small hit a four to bring victory with two deliveries to spare.

Away Matches

The full scorecard of each of Northamptonshire's away matches will be found in the sections for the respective home teams.

Derby: April 20, 21, 22, 24
Derbys 183 and 216 (D.J. Capel 5–53) drew with Northants 161 (P.G. Newman 5–45) and 177–9. Derbys 5pts, Northants 5pts.

Bristol: April 27, 28, 29, 30
Gloucs 265 (J.G. Thomas 5–87) and 291 (A.J. Wright 130) lost to Northants 505 (R.J. Bailey 100) and 53–0 by 10 wkts. Northants 23pts, Gloucs 4pts.

Swansea: May 20, 22, 23
Glamorgan 290 and 214–4d beat Northants 200 and 60 (S.L. Watkin 6–42) by 244 runs. Glamorgan 23pts, Northants 6pts.

Hove: June 10, 12, 13
Northants 223 (D.J. Capel 102, A.C.S Pigott 5–52) and 355–5d (G. Cook 138, D.J. Capel 126) drew with Sussex 350–5d and 158–8d. Sussex 8pts, Northants 4pts.

Southport: June 21, 22, 23
Lancs 336 (N.G.B. Cook 6–56) drew with Northants 144 (P.A.J. DeFreitas 5–46) and 407–7d (G. Cook 128, R.J. Bailey 134). Lancs 8pts, Northants 3pts.

Maidstone: July 5, 6, 7
Kent 156 (W.W. Davis 5–55) and 191–2 drew with Northants 378 (W. Larkins 116, D.J. Capel 105). Northants 8pts, Kent 4pts.

Leicester: July 19, 20, 21
Northants 198 and 312–7d (G. Cook 105) drew with Leics 300 (C.E.L. Ambrose 5–52) and 206–7. Leics 6pts, Northants 3pts.

Sheffield: August 5, 7, 8
Northants 379 (A. Fordham 199) and 147–3d beat Yorks 259–3d and 225 by 42 runs. Northants 21pts, Yorks 3pts.

Colchester: August 9, 10, 11
Essex 391–6d (P.J. Prichard 128) and forfeited 2nd inns beat Northants 131–1d and 140 by 120 runs. Essex 20pts, Northants 2pts.

Lord's: August 12, 14, 15
Northants 363 and 142 (P.C.R. Tufnell 5–60) lost to Middx 302–1d (J.D. Carr 153*) and 204–3 by 7 wkts. Middx 22pts, Northants 4pts.

Edgbaston: September 8, 9, 10, 11
Northants 179 and 79–1d drew with Warwicks 0–0d and 217–8. Warwicks 4pts. Northants 1pt.

v LEICESTERSHIRE (Northampton)
May 4, 5, 6
Won by 1 wkt, Northants 21pts, Leics 6 pts

Leicestershire 1st Innings

T.J. Boon	b Thomas	1
N.E. Briers	b Thomas	5
*D.I. Gower	c and b Davis	26
P. Willey	b Thomas	0
J.J. Whitaker	not out	92
L. Potter	lbw b Davis	8
C.C. Lewis	c Ripley b Capel	0
†P. Whitticase	c Bailey b Thomas	16
G.J. Parsons	c Lamb b Thomas	0
J.P. Agnew	c Larkins b Thomas	25
G.J.F. Ferris	c Lamb b Williams	30
Extras	nb 5	5
Total (66.5 ov)		208

1, 28, 32, 34, 53, 98, 98, 132

Davis	19	2	71	2
Thomas	15	2	53	6
Capel	13	2	45	1
Robinson	9	1	22	0
Cook	10	4	12	0
Williams	0.5	0	5	1

Northamptonshire 1st Innings

D.J. Wild	b Ferris	6
W. Larkins	c Whitticase b Parsons	50
R.J. Bailey	c Boon b Agnew	16
*A.J. Lamb	c Gower b Lewis	16
D.J. Capel	c and b Parsons	1
R.G. Williams	lbw Ferris	7
†D. Ripley	c Willey b Ferris	40
J.G. Thomas	b Lewis	35
N.G.B. Cook	c Whitticase b Lewis	1
W.W. Davis	b Lewis	2
M.A. Robinson	not out	0
Extras	b1, lb 3, nb 7	11
Total (68.3 ov)		185

17, 45, 67, 92, 100, 102, 164, 178, 185

Ferris	16	7	30	3
Agnew	21	3	58	1
Lewis	19.3	4	47	4
Parsons	12	3	46	2

Leicester 2nd Innings

T.J. Boon	c Ripley b Capel	14
N.E. Briers	b Cook	41
*D.I. Gower	lbw b Capel	2
P. Willey	b Robinson	0
J.J. Whitaker	c Lamb b Thomas	4
L. Potter	c Ripley b Davis	23
C.C. Lewis	c Ripley b Davis	27
†P. Whitticase	not out	56
G.J. Parsons	c Ripley b Thomas	35
J.P. Agnew	b Thomas	8
G.J.F. Ferris	c Ripley b Cook	15
Extras	b4, lb 6, nb 15	25
Total		250

40, 44, 45, 84, 118, 126, 198, 212, 225

Davis	18	3	51	2
Thomas	22	3	79	3
Capel	14	6	32	2
Robinson	19	5	52	1
Cook	12.1	8	10	2
Williams	6	1	16	0

Northamptonshire 2nd Innings

D.J. Wild	c Whitticase b Agnew	17
W. Larkins	lbw b Ferris	6
R.J. Bailey	b Ferris	8
*A.J. Lamb	b Agnew	148
D.J. Capel	lbw b Parsons	39
R.G. Williams	run out	2
†D. Ripley	b Agnew	18
J.G. Thomas	lbw b Agnew	11
N.G.B. Cook	lbw b Lewis	3
W.W. Davis	not out	7
M.A. Robinson	not out	0
Extras	b1, lb 6, nb 10	17
Total (9 wkts)		276

7, 26, 80, 195, 209, 233, 256, 262, 272

Ferris	17	6	42	2
Agnew	22	7	80	4
Lewis	20.5	4	58	1
Parsons	12	1	61	1
Willey	9	1	28	0

Umpires: B. Dudleston and J.H. Hampshire
Toss: Northamptonshire
The feature of the match was a brilliant innings of 148 by Lamb, who reached his 100 off 81 balls. Lamb came to the wicket at 26-2 and left at 233-6, having hit a six and 21 fours. The tailenders then almost threw away the match. On the first day 16 wickets fell for 340 runs.

v YORKSHIRE (Northampton)
May 16, 17, 18, 19
Won by 6 wkts. Northants 22pts, Yorks 3 pts

Yorkshire 1st Innings

R.J. Blakey	lbw b Davis	13
A.A. Metcalfe	lbw b Davis	49
K. Sharp	lbw b Davis	6
P.E. Robinson	b Thomas	46
D. Byas	c N.G.B. Cook b Davis	1
†D.L. Bairstow	b Capel	9
I.G. Swallow	b N.G.B. Cook	26
*P. Carrick	c Larkins b Thomas	3
P.W. Jarvis	c Ripley b N.G.B. Cook	19
C.S. Pickles	c Ripley b Robinson	4
I.M. Priestley	not out	2
Extras	b2, lb 7, nb 4	13
Total (52.1 ov)		191

47, 70, 75, 87, 104, 148, 154, 183, 184

Davis	13	2	48	4
Thomas	13	1	59	2
Capel	17	1	59	1
Robinson	5.1	1	15	1
Cook	4	3	1	2

Northamptonshire 1st Innings

G. Cook	c Bairstow b Pickles	83
*W. Larkins	lbw b Jarvis	32
R.J. Bailey	b Carrick	15
D.J. Wild	c Sharp b Carrick	121
D.J. Capel	c and b Pickles	2
R.G. Williams	lbw b Jarvis	1
†D. Ripley	c Blakey b Jarvis	123
J.G. Thomas	c Sharp b Pickles	11
N.G.B. Cook	c Robinson b Carrick	14
W.W. Davis	c Byas b Pickles	4
M.A. Robinson	not out	0
Extras	b1, lb 7, w3, nb 1	12
Total (100 ov 235-5)		418

63, 106, 142, 144, 145, 388, 388, 409, 413

Jarvis	46	12	104	3
Pickles	34.3	8	92	4
Carrick	53	22	75	3
Priestley	14	1	73	0
Swallow	26	10	45	0
Byas	9	3	21	0

Yorkshire 2nd Innings

R.J. Blakey	lbw b Davis	12
A.A. Metcalfe	lbw b Davis	10
K. Sharp	c N.G.B. Cook b Capel	39
P.E. Robinson	lbw b Robinson	15
D. Byas	b N.G.B. Cook	50
†D.L. Bairstow	c Ripley b Thomas	44
I.G. Swallow	c Ripley b Thomas	1
*P. Carrick	c Bailey b N.G.B. Cook	10
P.W. Jarvis	c G. Cook b N.G.B. Cook	0
C.S. Pickles	not out	20
I.M. Priestley	b Thomas	23
Extras	b3, lb 13, nb 11	27
Total		251

23, 43, 87, 89, 167, 169, 194, 196, 203

Davis	20	1	73	2
Thomas	20.3	5	58	3
Robinson	17	9	25	1
Capel	16	3	50	1
Williams	6	2	15	0
N.G.B. Cook	19	9	14	3

Northamptonshire 2nd Innings

G. Cook	c Bairstow b Jarvis	4
*W. Larkins	b Pickles	10
R.J. Bailey	c Bairstow b Jarvis	0
D.J. Wild	c Blakey b Pickles	2
D.J. Capel	not out	9
R.G. Williams	not out	1
Extras		0
Total (4 wkts)		26

4, 14, 14, 16

Jarvis	5.2	4	12	2
Pickles	5	1	14	2

Umpires: B. Leadbeater and D.R. Shepherd
Toss: Northamptonshire
The home side took a firm grip on the game during the first day. Davis removed the main Yorkshire batsmen and by the close the Northants total was 113-2 (G. Cook 62*). On the second day runs came slowly, but Wild and Ripley added 241 in an unbroken 6th wkt stand, both batsmen being 121* at the end of play. The stand was soon broken on the 3rd morning and the tail added little. Yorkshire struggled a second time and Northants claimed the extra ½ hour but failed to dislodge the last pair, the total being 222-9 at the end. Pickles and Priestley continued to score runs on the last morning and Northants made a meal out of the final innings.

v SURREY (Northampton)

June 3, 5, 6

Drawn. Northants 8pts, Leics 3 pts

Surrey 1st Innings

D.J. Bicknell	lbw b Davis	0
G.S. Clinton	c N.G.B. Cook b Thomas	15
R.I. Alikhan	lbw b Davis	2
*A.J. Stewart	c Larkins b Davis	0
†D.M. Ward	c Bailey b Capel	37
G.P. Thorpe	c G. Cook b Thomas	21
K.T. Medlycott	c Wild b Capel	69
M.A. Feltham	c Larkins b Davis	0
M.P. Bicknell	c Ripley b Robinson	8
A.J. Murphy	not out	3
M. Frost	c Bailey b Robinson	0
Extras	b4, lb7, w1, nb8	20
Total (50 ov)		175

1, 14, 14, 22, 73, 140, 141, 170, 170

Davis	17	3	40	4
Thomas	15	1	69	2
Capel	9	1	27	2
Robinson	9	1	28	2

Northamptonshire 1st Innings

G. Cook	lbw b M.P. Bicknell	23
W. Larkins	c Alikhan b Murphy	89
R.J. Bailey	c Feltham b Murphy	27
*A.J. Lamb	c D.J. Bicknell b Frost	171
D.J. Capel	not out	76
D.J. Wild	c Thorpe b Murphy	13
†D. Ripley	not out	5
J.G. Thomas		
N.G.B. Cook		
W.W. Davis		
M.A. Robinson		
Extras	b11, lb6, w3, nb1	21
Total (5 wkts, 100 ov)		425

46, 117, 231, 374, 408

M.P. Bicknell	15	4	24	1
Murphy	30	5	116	3
Frost	20	4	94	1
Feltham	5	1	31	0
Thorpe	7	0	37	0
Medlycott	23	1	106	0

Surrey 2nd Innings

D.J. Bicknell	run out	74
G.S. Clinton	c Lamb b Capel	15
R.I. Alikhan	c Davis b Capel	0
*A.J. Stewart	c Ripley b Thomas	30
†D.M. Ward	lbw b Capel	15
G.P. Thorpe	c Capel b Thomas	11
K.T. Medlycott	c Ripley b Davis	11
M.A. Feltham	b Thomas	2
M.P. Bicknell	b Davis	24
A.J. Murphy	not out	0
M. Frost	not out	0
Extras	b2, lb8, nb15	25
Total (9 wkts)		207

52, 52, 95, 135, 147, 152, 160, 202, 207

Davis	27	9	66	2
Thomas	23	2	64	3
Capel	16	5	33	3
Robinson	12	5	21	0
N.G.B. Cook	9	6	13	0

Umpires: D.J. Constant and A.A. Jones
Toss: Northamptonshire
A fast wicket enabled Davis to remove the early Surrey batsmen cheaply and by stumps on Saturday the home side were well placed being 202-2 off 52.1 overs, Larkins 89*. Larkins was out directly on Monday, but Lamb hit 171 in 171 minutes with 20 fours and a six. Surrey began the last morning at 178-7, but heavy overnight rain prevented a start until 5 pm and they managed to bat out the 19 overs available.

v GLOUCESTERSHIRE (Northampton)

June 7, 8, 9

Won by 9 wkts. Northants 22pts, Gloucs 4 pts

Gloucestershire 1st Innings

A.W. Stovold	c Ripley b Thomas	16
A.J. Wright	c Fordham b Davis	0
P.W. Romaines	b Thomas	2
*C.W.J. Athey	c Ripley b Davis	5
P. Bainbridge	c Ripley b Davis	5
K.M. Curran	c Capel	46
J.W. Lloyds	b Davis	0
†G.A. Tedstone	lbw b Capel	5
D.A. Graveney	lbw b Capel	0
D.V. Lawrence	c Larkins b Capel	13
C.A. Walsh	not out	13
Extras	lb7, nb6	13
Total (36.1 ov)		118

14, 18, 23, 26, 39, 39, 86, 86, 99

Davis	13	6	31	4
Thomas	11	4	45	2
Robinson	7	1	21	0
Capel	5.1	2	14	4

Northamptonshire 1st Innings

G. Cook	b Walsh	17
*W. Larkins	lbw b Curran	74
R.J. Bailey	c Athey b Curran	11
D.J. Wild	c Tedstone b Curran	0
D.J. Capel	c Athey b Lawrence	84
A. Fordham	c Tedstone b Curran	0
†D. Ripley	not out	25
J.G. Thomas	b Curran	10
N.G.B. Cook	c Tedstone b Curran	0
W.W. Davis	c Lloyds b Curran	6
M.A. Robinson	c Athey b Walsh	0
Extras	b2, lb6, w1,	9
Total (84.1 ov)		236

28, 55, 65, 170, 170, 203, 224, 224, 236

Walsh	27.1	4	57	2
Lawrence	14	3	46	1
Curran	26	6	69	7
Graveney	5	3	17	0
Bainbridge	12	1	39	0

Gloucestershire 2nd Innings

A.W. Stovold	c and b Davis	7
A.J. Wright	b Davis	21
P.W. Romaines	b Davis	0
*C.W.J. Athey	b Thomas	10
P. Bainbridge	c G. Cook b Thomas	5
K.M. Curran	st Ripley b N.G.B. Cook	33
J.W. Lloyds	lbw b Robinson	37
†G.A. Tedstone	c and b Capel	30
D.A. Graveney	c N.G.B. Cook b Capel	16
D.V. Lawrence	not out	6
C.A. Walsh	b N.G.B. Cook	6
Extras	lb13, nb2	15
Total		186

8, 8, 39, 39, 53, 119, 119, 170, 179

Davis	23	8	53	3
Thomas	14	2	46	2
Capel	17	3	64	2
Robinson	8	5	6	1
N.G.B. Cook	4.5	3	4	2

Northamptonshire 2nd Innings

G. Cook	not out	17
W. Larkins	c Romaines b Bainbridge	42
R.J. Bailey	not out	8
Extras	b1, w1	2
Total (1 wkt)		69

Walsh	7	1	14	0
Lawrence	7	0	35	0
Bainbridge	6	3	11	1
Lloyds	5	3	8	0

Umpires: D.J. Constant and A.A. Jones
Toss: Northamptonshire
The first day belonged to Capel, who finished off the Gloucester tail with 4 for 14 and then joined in a 4th wicket stand of 105 with Larkins when the home side were struggling. On a rain-affected second day, Curran took 7 for 69 and Gloucester were 31-2 when play ended. Good outcricket enabled Northants to win early and thus increase their lead at the top of the Championship table to 17 points.

v SOMERSET (Luton)

June 24, 26, 27

Lost by 12 runs. Somerset 21pts, Northants 8 pts

Somerset 1st Innings

S.J. Cook	b Thomas	25
P.M. Roebuck	lbw b N.G. Cook	70
J.J.E. Hardy	c Felton b Thomas	0
C.J. Tavare	c Ambrose b Thomas	59
R.J. Harden	c Larkins b N.G.B. Cook	16
†N.D. Burns	b Thomas	33
*V.J. Marks	c Felton b Ambrose	19
H.R.J. Trump	b N.G.B. Cook	14
N.A. Mallender	b N.G.B. Cook	6
A.N. Jones	not out	19
D.J. Foster	c Thomas b N.G.B. Cook	0
Extras	lb8, w1, nb4	13
Total (85.2 ov)		274

31, 31, 151, 175, 176, 207, 240, 253, 274

Ambrose	23	3	94	1
Thomas	19	3	76	4
Robinson	13	5	27	0
Capel	13	5	27	0
N.G.B. Cook	15.2	7	28	5
Bailey	2	0	14	0

Northamptonshire 1st Innings

G. Cook	c Burns b Foster	126
W. Larkins	lbw b Mallender	21
R.J. Bailey	c Burns b Jones	20
*A.J. Lamb	c Mallender b Foster	32
D.J. Capel	lbw b Marks	21
N. A. Felton	not out	60
J.G. Thomas	not out	10
†D. Ripley		
N.G.B. Cook		
E.L.C. Ambrose		
M.A. Robinson		
Extras	lb4, w1, nb5	10
Total (5 wkts dec, 88.3 ov)		300

36, 76, 132, 159, 273

Mallender	•6	2	58	1
Jones	17	3	83	1
Foster	17	3	48	2
Trump	14	3	37	0
Marks	24.3	8	70	1

Somerset 2nd Innings

S.J. Cook	c and b N.G.B. Cook	46
J.J.E. Hardy	b Bailey	65
C.J. Tavare	c Capel b Felton	89
R.J. Harden	not out	115
†N.D. Burns	st Ripley b N.G.B. Cook	20
*V.J. Marks	run out	5
H.R.J. Trump	lbw b Bailey	2
N.A. Mallender	st Ripley b N.G.B. Cook	0
A.N. Jones	not out	2
Extras	lb1, nb1	2
Total (7 wkts dec)		346

92, 161, 213, 298, 312, 323, 336

Ambrose	11	3	41	0
Thomas	8	2	27	0
Robinson	6	1	19	0
N.G.B. Cook	26	8	67	3
Capel	6	1	20	0
Bailey	21.5	3	104	2
Larkins	4	1	9	0
Felton	7	0	58	1

Northamptonshire 2nd Innings

G. Cook	c Tavare b Mallender	18
W. Larkins	c sub b Foster	50
R.J. Bailey	c Harden b Trump	100
*A.J. Lamb	st Burns b Marks	24
D.J. Capel	c Jones b Foster	58
N.A. Felton	b Trump	23
†D. Ripley	c Burns b Jones	3
J.G. Thomas	c Marks b Jones	11
C.E.L. Ambrose	c Marks b Trump	0
N.G.B. Cook	not out	6
M.A. Robinson	run out	2
Extras	b5, lb7, nb1	13
Total		308

59, 76, 133, 248, 281, 287, 299, 299, 301

Jones	13.1	0	71	2
Mallender	5	0	27	1
Foster	10	0	43	2
Marks	20	1	95	1
Trump	12	0	60	3

Umpires: D.S. Thompsett and P.B. Wight
Toss: Somerset
Northants innings closed as soon as maximum bonus points had been gathered. Set 321 to win off 61 overs, Northants looked in full control at 248-3, but Somerset won with the first ball of the last possible over.

v WORCESTERSHIRE (Northampton)

July 1, 3, 4

Lost by an innings and 19 runs. Worcs 24pts, Northants 4pts

Northamptonshire 1st Innings

G. Cook	c d'Oliveira b Botham	42
W. Larkins	lbw b Radford	45
R.J. Bailey	lbw b Radford	17
*A.J. Lamb	lbw b Botham	55
D.J. Capel	c Hick b Botham	1
N.A. Felton	not out	52
†D. Ripley	b Dilley	3
J.G. Thomas	b Botham	1
C.E.L. Ambrose	c Rhodes b Botham	22
N.G.B. Cook	c Rhodes b Radford	5
M.A. Robinson	lbw b Botham	2
Extras	b4, lb 2, w 1, nb 4	11
Total (65.5 ov)		256

95, 95, 137, 138, 183, 188, 192, 236, 247

Dilley	19	1	90	1
Radford	18	2	61	3
Botham	28.5	7	99	6

Worcestershire 1st Innings

T.S. Curtis	b Capel	80
G.J. Lord	st Ripley b N.G.B. Cook	54
R.K. Illingworth	b Ambrose	14
G.A. Hick	c Ripley b N.G.B. Cook	111
D.B. d'Oliveira	c Bailey b Robinson	26
*P.A. Neale	c sub b Capel	62
I.T. Botham	run out	0
M.J. Weston	c Ripley b Capel	31
†S.J. Rhodes	lbw b Thomas	4
N.V. Radford	lbw b Capel	13
G.R. Dilley	not out	1
Extras	lb 29, nb 8	37
Total (100 ov 345-4)		433

121, 160, 170, 241, 353, 355, 388, 396, 428

Ambrose	24	4	84	1
Thomas	18	2	100	1
Robinson	24	2	59	1
N.G.B. Cook	29	9	79	2
Capel	23.2	3	82	4

Northamptonshire 2nd Innings

G. Cook	lbw b Botham	1
W. Larkins	lbw b Botham	56
R.J. Bailey	c Weston b Botham	13
N.A.Felton	b Dilley	0
D.J. Capel	c Neale b Botham	53
†D. Ripley	b Dilley	4
J.G. Thomas	c Lord b Botham	10
C.E.L. Ambrose	b Dilley	11
N.G.B. Cook	c Rhodes b Dilley	0
M.A. Robinson	not out	0
*A.J. Lamb	absent injured	—
Extras	lb 4, nb 6	10
Total		158

5, 35, 36, 122, 131, 131, 148, 148, 158

Dilley	16	3	66	4
Botham	19	5	76	5
Weston	5	2	12	0
Illingworth	1	1	0	0

Umpires: R. Palmer and J.D. Bond
Toss: Northamptonshire

Botham took 6 for 99 and by the close of Saturday's play, Northants were in trouble, the visiting openers having replied with a century partnership. Worcester started Monday at 131-1 and batted on past the 300 mark to take a commanding lead. With Lamb having an injured shoulder, the home side were 87-3 at stumps on Monday and only 62 minutes were required on Tuesday to finish off the one-sided affair.

v HAMPSHIRE (Northampton)

July 8, 10, 11

Lost by 9 wkts. Hants 24pts, Northants 2 pts

Northamptonshire 1st Innings

G. Cook	c Parks b Connor	53
*W. Larkins	lbw b Marshall	1
N.A. Felton	c Wood b Marshall	12
R.J. Bailey	c Parks b James	11
D.J. Capel	c Turner b Bakker	4
A. Fordham	b Maru	14
†D. Ripley	c Wood b Connor	0
J.G. Thomas	c Connor	5
W.W. Davis	not out	40
N.G.B. Cook	c Smith b Marshall	10
M.A. Robinson	lbw b Marshall	0
Extras	b5, lb 3, nb 6, w 2	16
Total (68.2 ov)		166

1, 21, 39, 50, 92, 96, 107, 116, 143

Marshall	14.2	6	20	4
Bakker	13	2	34	1
Connor	20	5	59	3
James	10	4	28	1
Nicholas	2	0	7	0
Maru	9	5	10	1

Hampshire 1st Innings

V.P. Terry	c Fordham b Davis	1
C.L. Smith	c Ripley b Thomas	56
K.D. James	b Thomas	6
*M.C.J. Nicholas	c Fordham b Davis	140
D.R. Turner	c Robinson b N.G.B. Cook	20
J.R. Wood	c G. Cook b Davis	96
M.D. Marshall	not out	10
†R.J. Parks	not out	0
R.J. Maru		
C.A. Connor		
P-J. Bakker		
Extras	b 5, lb 7, w 2, nb 23	37
Total (100 ov 321-4) (6 wkts dec)		366

6, 29, 118, 152, 335, 336

Davis	23.5	4	82	3
Thomas	29	5	87	2
Capel	17	1	67	0
Robinson	18	2	69	0
N.G.B. Cook	20	10	35	1
Bailey	3	0	14	0

Northamptonshire 2nd Innings

G. Cook	c Parks b Bakker	5
W. Larkins	lbw b Nicholas	97
N.A. Felton	lbw b Bakker	11
R.J. Bailey	c Parks b Marshall	78
D.J. Capel	lbw b Marshall	16
A. Fordham	c Parks b Marshall	0
†D. Ripley	b Bakker	18
J.G. Thomas	c Parks b Marshall	1
W.W. Davis	c Terry b Marshall	2
N.G.B. Cook	c Smith b Bakker	8
M.A. Robinson	not out	0
Extras	b6, lb 8, nb 3	17
Total		253

21, 39, 202, 207, 207, 232, 234, 240, 248

Marshall	25	11	36	5
Bakker	20.1	5	66	4
Connor	17	3	40	0
James	10	1	47	0
Wood	2	0	9	0
Maru	13	2	35	0
Nicholas	4	1	6	1

Hampshire 2nd Innings

V.P. Terry	c Ripley b Thomas	5
C.L. Smith	not out	13
K.D. James	not out	35
Extras	lb 4	4
Total (1 wkt)		57

7

Davis	4	0	17	0
Thomas	4.5	1	31	1
N.G.B. Cook	1	0	5	0

Umpires: N.T. Plews and D.G.L. Evans
Toss: Hampshire

Third in the Championship at the start of this match, Northants were out of their class against some splendid bowling by Marshall. They were dismissed on the first day for 166, with Hampshire being 83-2 off 24.1 overs on Monday morning. Then Wood, in his third fc match, and Nicholas added 183 in 50 overs for the 5th wicket and Hampshire declared just before the close. Northants were held together by Larkins — 97 in 4 hours — in their second innings, but Hampshire won with three overs to spare.

v NOTTINGHAMSHIRE (Northampton)

July 22, 24, 25

Won by 60 runs. Northants 23pts, Notts 6 pts

Northamptonshire 1st Innings

*W. Larkins	c Broad b Stephenson	78
A. Fordham	b Afford	84
N.A. Felton	c Pollard b Stephenson	1
R.J. Bailey	c Robinson b Evans	9
D.J. Capel	st French b Afford	23
N.A. Stanley	c Johnson b Afford	15
A.L. Penberthy	b Stephenson	27
†D. Ripley	c Robinson b Evans	32
J.G. Thomas	c Pick b Evans	16
C.E.L. Ambrose	not out	23
N.G.B. Cook	c Cooper b Afford	1
Extras	b 4, lb 8, nb 1	13
Total (100 ov 295-8)		322

108, 110, 123, 181, 214, 221, 263, 282, 309

Stephenson	24	5	59	3
Cooper	17	3	64	0
Pick	16	2	44	0
Evans	16	4	64	3
Afford	35.3	7	79	4

Nottinghamshire 1st Innings

B.C. Broad	run out	76
P.R. Pollard	c Bailey b Cook	10
*R.T. Robinson	c Ripley b Ambrose	68
P. Johnson	c Bailey b Ambrose	6
D.W. Randall	c Fordham b Cook	25
F.D. Stephenson	c Bailey b Thomas	15
K.P. Evans	lbw b Cook	1
†B. N. French	not out	51
K.E. Cooper	b Capel	4
R.A. Pick	lbw b Capel	0
J.A. Afford	lbw b Thomas	18
Extras	b 4, lb 7, w 3, nb 1	15
Total (95.5 ov)		289

29, 164, 172, 172, 198, 199, 221, 230, 230

Ambrose	23	10	38	2
Thomas	16.5	1	57	2
N.G.B. Cook	29	9	95	3
Capel	21	3	66	2
Penberthy	3	0	15	0
Bailey	3	1	7	0

Northamptonshire 2nd Innings

*W. Larkins	c Broad b Stephenson	4
A. Fordham	lbw b Stephenson	16
N.A. Felton	c Broad b Stephenson	28
R.J. Bailey	c Broad b Cooper	10
D.J. Capel	c Johnson b Stephenson	51
N.A. Stanley	c Evans b Afford	15
A.L. Penberthy	c Pollard b Afford	8
†D. Ripley	c Robinson b Afford	22
J.G. Thomas	c Randall b Afford	1
C.E.L. Ambrose	not out	2
N.G.B. Cook	not out	2
Extras	b 4, lb 8, w 1, nb 2	15
Total (9 wkts dec)		174

7, 57, 64, 80, 121, 140, 162, 169, 170

Stephenson	22	4	52	4
Cooper	18	9	33	1
Pick	7	1	34	0
Evans	6	0	13	0
Afford	12	5	30	4

Nottinghamshire 2nd Innings

B.C. Broad	lbw b Capel	19
P.R. Pollard	c Ripley b Ambrose	12
*R.T. Robinson	c Bailey b Thomas	30
P. Johnson	b N.G.B. Cook	4
D.W. Randall	lbw b Capel	3
†B. N. French	c Bailey b Ambrose	32
F.D. Stephenson	c Penberthy b Thomas	23
K.P. Evans	lbw b Cook	1
K.E. Cooper	c Penberthy b Thomas	15
R.A. Pick	c Cook b Ambrose	0
J.A. Afford	not out	0
Extras	lb 5, w 2, nb 1	8
Total		147

23, 45, 52, 55, 79, 113, 119, 143, 143

Ambrose	9	2	16	3
Thomas	14.4	1	73	3
Cook	15	6	28	2
Capel	6	0	25	2

Umpires: J.H. Harris and J.W. Holder
Toss: Nottinghamshire

Northants got off to a good start and though three wickets fell in rapid succession, the lower order made runs and the innings ended at Saturday's close of play. Notts also made a good beginning, but then failed. Notts were set 208 off 48 overs and rather unexpectedly Northants won.

v DERBYSHIRE (Northampton)

July 26, 27, 28

Lost by 8 wkts. Derbys 24pts, Northants 6pts

Northamptonshire 1st Innings		
G. Cook	c Adams b Mortensen	23
*W. Larkins	c Morris b Malcolm	21
N.A. Felton	b Malcolm	0
R.J. Bailey	c Maher b Mortensen	116
D.J. Capel	c Morris b Mortensen	60
N.A. Stanley	c Sharma b Mortensen	27
A.L. Penberthy	c Maher b Mortensen	9
†D. Ripley	c Adams b Mortensen	12
J.G. Thomas	c Barnett b Base	3
W.W. Davis	lbw b Base	0
M.A. Robinson	not out	0
Extras	b 1, lb 8, nb 3	12
Total (69.2 ov)		283

37, 37, 65, 205, 262, 263, 274, 283, 283

Bishop	16	0	54	0
Malcolm	14	0	81	2
Base	14	4	34	2
Mortensen	25.2	2	105	6

Derbyshire 1st Innings		
*K.J. Barnett	c Ripley b Capel	30
P.D. Bowler	b Davis	71
J.E. Morris	lbw b Capel	22
R. Sharma	lbw b Thomas	8
S.J. Base	c Bailey b Thomas	25
C.J. Adams	c Ripley b Robinson	21
T.J.G. O'Gorman	not out	113
†B.J.M. Maher	lbw b Bailey	46
I.R. Bishop	lbw b Capel	4
D.E. Malcolm	run out	30
O.H. Mortensen	lbw b Robinson	9
Extras	b 3, lb 18, w 2, nb 18	41
Total (100 ov 349-8)		420

50, 87, 108, 159, 200, 200, 327, 336, 393

Davis	28	2	101	1
Thomas	21	3	86	2
Capel	27	5	99	3
Robinson	20.3	3	59	2
Penberthy	10	3	26	0
Bailey	7	1	28	1

Northamptonshire 2nd Innings		
G. Cook	c Bowler b Bishop	0
*W. Larkins	not out	73
N.A. Felton	lbw b Base	0
R.J. Bailey	c Adams b Bishop	17
D.J. Capel	c Morris b Bishop	11
N.A. Stanley	b Base	12
A.L. Penberthy	c Adams b Malcolm	10
†D. Ripley	c Bowler b Mortensen	0
J.G. Thomas	c Barnett b Malcolm	28
W.W. Davis	c Morris b Malcolm	5
M.A. Robinson	c Bowler b Mortensen	0
Extras	b 2, lb 4, w 1, nb 2	9
Total		165

1, 2, 47, 67, 86, 119, 120, 155, 161

Bishop	9	1	36	3
Base	10	0	54	2
Malcolm	10	1	46	3
Mortensen	8.3	1	23	2

Derbyshire 2nd Innings		
*K.J. Barnett	c Bailey b Thomas	2
P.D. Bowler	lbw b Davis	3
J.E. Morris	not out	11
R. Sharma	not out	10
Extras	nb 3	3
Total (2 wkts)		29

4, 15

Davis	5	2	11	1
Thomas	2	0	2	1
Penberthy	3	1	16	0

Umpires: J.W. Holder and J.D. Bond

The partnership of 140 in 31 overs between Bailey and Capel was the basis of Northants total on the first day. Bailey reached his 100 off 145 balls before Mortensen destroyed the latecomers. Derbyshire were 139-3 off 40 overs at the close. O'Gorman completed a maiden 100 on the second day off 139 balls which gave his side a substantial lead, then Northants fell apart. Derbyshire needed 22 runs on the last day to win the game, a task which occupied 20 minutes.

v WARWICKSHIRE (Northampton)

August 19, 21, 22

Lost by an innings and 31 runs. Warwicks 21pts, Northants 4pts

Northamptonshire 1st Innings		
G. Cook	b Small	4
*W. Larkins	c Reeve b Donald	15
A. Fordham	lbw b Munton	5
R.J. Bailey	c Donald b Reeve	15
D.J. Capel	lbw b Reeve	3
N.A. Felton	b Munton	0
J.G. Thomas	c Ratcliffe b Munton	0
†D. Ripley	b Munton	2
N.G.B. Cook	b Reeve	6
C.E.L. Ambrose	c P.A. Smith b Munton	1
M.A. Robinson	not out	0
Extras		0
Total (33.3 ov)		51

17, 19, 39, 39, 40, 40, 44, 46, 51

Donald	6	4	4	1
Small	9	1	31	1
Munton	11	4	13	5
Reeve	7.3	6	3	3

Warwickshire 1st Innings		
J.D Ratcliffe	c Bailey b Ambrose	0
*T.A. Lloyd	c Felton b Ambrose	2
A.I. Kallicharran	c Ripley b Ambrose	100
G.W. Humpage	b Thomas	10
D.A. Reeve	lbw b Thomas	15
N.M.K. Smith	b N.G.B. Cook	18
†K.J. Piper	c Feltham b Ambrose	28
G.C. Small	c Ripley b Ambrose	0
A.A. Donald	c Fordham b N.G.B. Cook	1
P.A. Smith	b Ambrose	0
T.A. Munton	not out	0
Extras	b 4, lb 8, w 1, nb 4	17
Total (55.1 ov)		191

0, 3, 14, 40, 81, 168, 168, 183, 186

Ambrose	13.1	4	22	6
Thomas	12	3	26	2
Robinson	14	1	51	0
N.G.B. Cook	8	1	40	2
Capel	8	2	40	0

Northamptonshire 2nd innings		
G. Cook	c Piper b Donald	11
*W. Larkins	b Small	3
A. Fordham	c Piper b Small	13
R.J. Bailey	lbw b Donald	26
D.J. Capel	b Donald	2
N.A. Felton	c Piper b P.A. Smith	16
J.G. Thomas	lbw b Munton	14
†D. Ripley	not out	5
N.G.B. Cook	c and b P.A. Smith	7
C.E.L. Ambrose	c Small b P.A. Smith	0
M.A. Robinson	c N.M.K. Smith b P.A. Smith	0
Extras	lb 11, nb 1	12
Total		109

12, 16, 61, 63, 73, 95, 101, 109, 109

Donald	16	4	37	3
Small	18	7	45	2
Munton	6	4	7	1
P.A. Smith	3.4	0	9	4

Umpires: R. Julian and D.S. Thompsett

Toss: Northants

The match was completed by lunch on the second day, with P.A. Smith dismissing the last three batsmen in successive balls, to produce his first hat-trick. The only batsman to score runs on this pitch was Kallicharran, the bowlers otherwise totally dominating this match and by the end of the first day Northants were 27-2, twenty-two wickets having gone down in the day.

v ESSEX (Northampton)

August 24, 25, 26, 28

Won by 4 wkts. Northants 22pts, Essex 8 pts

Essex 1st Innings		
*B.R. Hardie	c Bailey b Thomas	29
A.W. Lilley	c Ripley b Thomas	20
P.J. Prichard	c Ripley b Robinson	1
M.E. Waugh	lbw b Thomas	53
N. Shahid	b Thomas	33
N. Hussain	c Govan b Ambrose	42
†M.A. Garnham	b Thomas	91
N.A. Foster	c Robinson b Govan	11
T.D. Topley	lbw b Govan	1
J.K. Lever	b Robinson	10
J.H. Childs	not out	5
Extras	lb 11, nb 17	28
Total (88.2 ov)		324

48, 53, 57, 145, 170, 229, 248, 267, 317

Ambrose	24	8	94	1
Thomas	20	1	74	5
Robinson	16.2	1	52	2
Smith	14	4	44	0
Govan	14	2	49	2

Northamptonshire 1st Innings		
G. Cook	c Garnham b Foster	18
*W. Larkins	c Shahid b Foster	9
A. Fordham	c Hussain b Foster	75
R.J. Bailey	lbw b Lever	5
N.A. Felton	b Foster	15
J.G. Thomas	c Shahid b Foster	20
†D. Ripley	not out	49
J.W. Govan	b Foster	4
G. Smith	c Garnham b Topley	6
C.E.L. Ambrose	c Waugh b Topley	15
M.A. Robinson	c Waugh b Foster	2
Extras	b 1, lb 5, w 2, nb 1	9
Total (69 ov)		227

13, 65, 77, 112, 129, 154, 164, 197, 215

Foster	35	7	105	7
Lever	17	5	54	1
Topley	17	6	62	2

Essex 2nd Innings		
*B.R. Hardie	b Robinson	41
A.W. Lilley	c and b Ambrose	1
P.J. Prichard	c Felton b Ambrose	3
M.E. Waugh	c Felton b Thomas	1
N. Hussain	c Bailey b Robinson	64
N. Shahid	not out	34
†M.A. Garnham	c Felton b Robinson	3
N.A. Foster	c sub b Thomas	0
T.D. Topley	not out	5
Extras	b 2, lb 6, nb 6	14
Total (7 wkts dec)		166

9, 15, 22, 88, 139, 146, 146

Ambrose	13	2	40	2
Thomas	15	5	38	2
Robinson	10	0	47	3
Smith	7	0	33	0

Northamptonshire 2nd Innings		
G. Cook	lbw b Topley	40
*W. Larkins	c Lilley b Topley	73
A. Fordham	c Hardie b Childs	0
R.J. Bailey	c Prichard b Lever	50
N.A. Felton	run out	55
J.G. Thomas	b Foster	11
†D. Ripley	not out	16
G. Smith	not out	0
Extras	b 5, lb 12, w 1, nb 1	19
Total (6 wkts)		264

101, 112, 124, 209, 242, 256

Foster	17	0	68	1
Lever	14	4	34	1
Topley	19	4	81	2
Childs	22	5	64	1

Umpires: J.C. Balderstone and D.O. Oslear

Toss: Essex

This vital match for Essex was lost when Hardie gambled on a generous declaration and then saw Larkins and Bailey bat sensibly, thus taking Northants to victory. Hardie's cause was not helped by two dropped catches, one of which came early in Larkins' innings. Like most of the four day matches in the same period, following a full first day, the second and third days were ruined by rain, which was the cause of the fourth day declaration.

Nottinghamshire

President: J.W. Baddiley
Chairman: C.W. Gillott
Secretary: B. Robson, County Cricket Ground, Trent Bridge, Nottingham NG2 6AG. *Tel:* 0602 821525.
Cricket Manager: K.A. Taylor
Captain: R.T. Robinson
Foundation of Present Club: April 1841 in Nottingham
First First-Class Match: Sussex v Nottinghamshire (Brighton) August 1835
County Champions: 1865, 1868, 1869, 1871, 1872, 1873, 1875, 1879, 1880, 1882, 1883, 1884, 1885, 1886, 1889, 1907, 1929, 1981, 1987
Gillette/NatWest Trophy: Winners 1987
Benson & Hedges Cup: Winners 1989
Sunday League Champions: Nil (runners-up in 1984, 1987)
Refuge Cup: Nil (losing finalists in 1989)

Summary of Results in 1989
Britannic Assurance County Championship: Played 22, Won 6, Lost 6, Drawn 10, Position 11th
NatWest Bank Trophy: Lost in second round
Benson & Hedges Cup: Winners
Refuge Assurance Sunday League: Played 16, Won 9, Lost 6, No Result 1, Position 4th
Refuge Assurance Cup: Losing finalists

From left, back: *P. Pollard, R.J. Evans, M. Saxelby, C.L. Cairns, J.A. Afford, G.W. Mike.* Centre: *C.W. Scott, D.J.R. Martindale, R.A. Pick, K.P. Evans, K. Saxelby, D.J. Millns, M. Newell, M. Field-Buss.* Front: *K.E. Cooper, F.D. Stephenson, E.E. Hemmings, D.W. Randall, R.T. Robinson, K.A. Taylor (Manager), B.N. French, B.C. Broad, J.D. Birch, P. Johnson.*
Allsport/Russell Cheyne

Right: *Notts skipper Tim Robinson scored over 1,500 runs and headed the batting averages.* Far right: *Franklyn Stephenson, Notts' West Indian all-rounder, was effectively top of the bowling with 92 wickets.*
Allsport/Simon Bruty

ONE DAY AWAY MATCHES

The full scorecard of each of Nottinghamshire's away matches will be found in the sections for the respective home teams.

Refuge Assurance League

Old Trafford: April 30
Notts 184–5 (40 ov) lost to Lancs 185–3 (37.4 ov) by 7 wkts. Lancs 4pts, Notts 0pts.

Headingley: May 7
Yorks 201–4 (40 ov) beat Notts 141 (36.4 ov) by 60 runs. Yorks 4pts, Notts 0pts.

Llanelli: May 29
Glamorgan 172–5 (40 ov) lost to Notts 174–4 (38.1 ov) by 6 wkts. Notts 4pts, Glamorgan 0pts.

Gloucester: July 2
Gloucs 154–8 (40 ov) lost to Notts 157–8 (37 ov) by 2 wkts. Notts 4pts, Gloucs 0pts.

Leicester: July 16
Notts 182–9 (38 ov) beat Leics 146 (36 ov) (K. Saxelby 6–30) by 36 runs. Notts 4pts, Leics 0pts.

Finedon: July 23
Northants 173 (40 ov) (K. Saxelby 5–45) beat Notts 149 (39.2 ov) by 24 runs. Northants 4pts, Notts 0pts.

Eastbourne: August 6
Notts 169–9 (40 ov) lost to Sussex 170–3 (36.4 ov) by 7 wkts. Sussex 4pts, Notts 0pts.

The Oval: August 13
Surrey 233–5 (39 ov) lost to Notts 234–1 (38.2 ov) (P.R. Pollard 123*) by 9 wkts. Notts 4pts, Surrey 0pts.

Refuge Assurance Cup

Old Trafford: September 6
Lancs 187–9 (40 ov) lost to Notts 188–5 (39.2 ov) by 5 wkts

Edgbaston: September 17 Final
Essex 160–5 (40 ov) beat Notts 155 (39.4 ov) by 5 runs.

Benson and Hedges Cup

Oxton: May 9
Minor Counties 172 (52.5 ov) lost to Notts 175–5 (47.2 ov) by 5 wkts. Notts 2pts, Minor Counties 0pts.

Taunton: May 13
Notts 202–9 (55 ov) (A.N. Jones 5–53) lost to Somerset 203–3 (52.5 ov) by 7 wkts. Somerset 2pts, Notts 0pts.

Bristol: May 31
Notts 222–6 (55 ov) (B.C. Broad 106) beat Gloucs 217 (54.3 ov) by 5 runs.

Lord's: July 15 Final
Essex 243–7 (55 ov) lost to Notts 244–7 (55 ov) by 3 wkts.

NatWest Bank Trophy

Hitchin: June 28
Herts 154–7 (60 ov) lost to Notts 155–5 (45.3 ov) by 5 wkts

Uxbridge: July 12
Middx 203–7 (60 ov) beat Notts 167 (54.4 ov) by 36 runs.

REFUGE ASSURANCE LEAGUE

v WORCESTERSHIRE (Trent Bridge)
April 23
Abandoned. No play. Notts 2pts, Worcs 2pts

v SOMERSET (Trent Bridge)
June 4
Lost by 3 wkts. Som 4pts, Notts 0pts

Nottinghamshire		
B.C Broad	c Burns b Mallender	2
M. Newell	c Tavare b Rose	13
D.W. Randall	b Marks	63
*R.T. Robinson	c Burns b Rose	11
P. Johnson	b Mallender	41
C.L. Cairns	b Marks	4
K.P. Evans	not out	19
E.E. Hemmings	c Burns b Jones	2
†C.W. Scott	not out	11
R.A. Pick		
K.E. Cooper		
Extras	lb 6, w 11	17
Total (7 wkts, 40 ov)		183

3, 33, 52, 116, 142, 146, 157

Jones	8	3	34	1
Mallender	8	0	18	2
Palmer	7	0	41	0
Rose	8	1	20	2
Marks	8	0	52	2
Roebuck	1	0	12	0

Somerset		
S.J. Cook	lbw b Evans	28
P.M. Roebuck	c Scott b Cairns	2
R.J. Bartlett	b Hemmings	26
C.J. Tavare	c Johnson b Cairns	20
R.J. Harden	b Evans	20
*V.J. Marks	c Johnson b Hemmings	5
†N.D. Burns	not out	34
G.D. Rose	c Evans b Cooper	30
G.V. Palmer	not out	8
N.A. Mallender		
A.N. Jones		
Extras	b 2, lb 3, w 5, nb 1	11
Total (7 wkts, 40 ov)		184

15, 46, 78, 86, 92, 116, 171

Pick	8	1	38	0
Cairns	8	0	38	2
Cooper	8	0	36	1
Evans	8	1	31	2
Hemmings	8	1	36	2

Umpires: J.H. Harris and R. Julian
Toss: Nottinghamshire
Notts appeared to have the game in hand when Somerset needed 47 off the last 4 overs, but the visitors won by dint of a bye off the final delivery.

Winning the Benson and Hedges Cup – Hemmings hitting the last ball for four – was the highlight of a satisfactory summer, in which the county also reached the final of the Refuge Cup. In this latter game however, Essex had their revenge!

To the casual observer, the county appeared to fail rather badly in the 1989 Championship, dropping from fifth to eleventh, but only 27 points separated them from fifth place and few people need reminding that Notts suffered a 25-point penalty for preparing an unsatisfactory wicket for the game at Trent Bridge against Derbyshire.

Of the individual players, Franklyn Stephenson has become almost as popular with Trent Bridge fans as Derek Randall. The languid West Indian just missed his hundred first-class wickets, but he appeared in only 18 of the county's 25 first-class fixtures. Kevin Cooper, Stephenson's new ball partner, seemed to bowl as accurately as ever, but his wicket haul fell appreciably. Of the other seamers, Kevin Saxelby bemused his admirers with an incredible Sunday League record – five wickets in a match on four successive occasions – Kevin Evans, following a good first half, missed many of the later games through injury and neither Pick nor Cairns showed much improvement on previous efforts.

Eddie Hemmings found favour with Mr Dexter and remains one of England's best off-break bowlers and Andy Afford captured fifty first-class wickets for the first time.

Early runs from Pollard found this young batsman quickly installed as Broad's opening partner. Tim Robinson moved down to number 3 and this trio all had very successful summers, even if two of them failed when recalled to help England. Ignored by the Test selectors, the Trent Bridge imp – Derek Randall – had one of the best seasons of his long career. Certainly his fielding would not have disgraced England. The biggest disappointment was the failure of Paul Johnson to make the most of his natural talent – perhaps 1990 will see more runs from this attacking batsman. Mike Newell and Duncan Martindale were squeezed out of the first eleven, but remain very useful men to have in reserve. Bruce French is still believed by many to be the best wicket-keeper in England and his deputy, Chris Scott, is most capable, when needed.

With all the players, except Millns, retained for 1990, the county ought to be capable of challenging for all the trophies. It is hoped that by the start of the season the new William Clarke stand will be ready to receive visitors.

REFUGE ASSURANCE LEAGUE

v KENT (Trent Bridge)

June 11

Won by 3 wkts. Notts 4pts, Kent 0pts

Kent		
S.G. Hinks	c Stephenson b Hemmings	54
M.R. Benson	b Evans	11
N.R. Taylor	b Mike b Saxelby	37
R.F. Pienaar	b Afford	15
T.R. Ward	lbw b Stephenson	14
*C.S. Cowdrey	c Robinson b Mike	21
M.V. Fleming	c Robinson b Evans	10
†S.A. Marsh	run out	1
C. Penn	run out	12
R.P. Davis	b Saxelby	16
A.P. Igglesden	not out	0
Extras	lb 11, w 4	15
Total (39.3 ov)		206

63, 84, 121, 127, 154, 172, 173, 175, 204

Stephenson	8	0	52	1
Saxelby	7.3	0	38	2
Hemmings	8	1	30	1
Evans	8	0	27	2
Afford	6	1	36	1
Mike	2	0	12	1

Nottinghamshire		
*R.T. Robinson	b Davis	24
P.R. Pollard	b Igglesden	100
D.W. Randall	c Marsh b Igglesden	24
P. Johnson	retired hurt	12
F.D. Stephenson	c Benson b Fleming	1
K.P. Evans	b Igglesden	9
G.W. Mike	not out	25
E.E. Hemmings	c and b Igglesden	4
†C.W. Scott	c Benson b Penn	0
K. Saxelby	not out	0
J.A. Afford		
Extras	lb 5, w 2, nb 1	8
Total (7 wkts, 39.5 ov)		207

72, 121, 140, 174, 183, 199, 200

Igglesden	8	0	41	4
Penn	7.5	0	48	1
Cowdrey	8	0	45	0
Davis	8	0	36	1
Fleming	8	0	32	1

Umpires: J.D. Bond and J.H. Hampshire
Toss: Nottinghamshire

Kent began with a flourish, 63 coming off the first 9 overs, but Stephenson's bowling was hampered by a leg injury. Pollard, in excellent form, hit 100 off 102 balls, but Johnson broke his ankle turning for a second run and it needed a six by young Mike off the last over to win the game.

v DERBYSHIRE (Trent Bridge)

June 25

Won by 42 runs. Notts 4pts, Derbys 0pts

Nottinghamshire		
P.R. Pollard	c Morris b Newman	12
*R.T. Robinson	c Newman b Holding	29
D.W. Randall	c Maher b Mortensen	5
D.J.R. Martindale	not out	49
G.W. Mike	lbw b Base	0
F.D. Stephenson	c Holding b Griffith	18
K.P. Evans	lbw b Griffith	5
†B.N. French	c Bowler b Newman	15
E.E. Hemmings	lbw b Holding	8
K.E. Cooper	not out	9
K. Saxelby		
Extras	lb 9, w 8, nb 3	20
Total (8 wkts, 39 ov)		170

20, 50, 51, 53, 95, 114, 139, 159

Newman	8	0	37	2
Mortensen	8	1	26	1
Holding	7	0	32	2
Griffith	8	2	32	2
Base	8	0	34	1

Derbyshire		
P.D. Bowler	lbw b Cooper	11
J.E. Morris	b Hemmings	45
R. Sharma	lbw b Cooper	0
C. Gladwin	run out	3
B. Roberts	c Hemmings b Evans	24
†B.J.M. Maher	lbw b Hemmings	1
F.A. Griffith	lbw b Evans	5
M.A. Holding	c Stephenson b Evans	11
*P.G. Newman	c Evans b Mike	18
S.J. Base	b Evans	1
O.H. Mortensen	not out	4
Extras	lb 2, w 1, nb 2	5
Total (35.3 ov)		128

22, 28, 31, 80, 88, 88, 101, 106, 119

Cooper	6	0	17	2
Stephenson	5	0	21	0
Saxelby	3	0	19	0
Evans	8	1	28	4
Mike	5.3	0	23	1
Hemmings	8	1	18	2

Umpires: B. Leadbeater and K.E. Palmer
Toss: Derbyshire

A sound innings by Martindale enabled Notts to reach a modest 170 considering the very pleasant conditions. Morris got Derbyshire off to a good start, but he had little support and Notts won with ease.

v WARWICKSHIRE (Trent Bridge)

July 9

Won by 8 wkts. Notts 4pts, Warwicks 0pts

Warwickshire		
*T.A. Lloyd	c Pollard b Saxelby	30
D.A. Thorne	c Broad b Cooper	4
A.I. Kallicharran	run out	19
P.A. Smith	run out	33
D.A. Reeve	c Martindale b Pick	15
G.W. Humpage	c Martindale b Saxelby	11
N.M.K. Smith	b Pick	0
†K.J. Piper	c and b Saxelby	11
G.C. Small	c Johnson b Saxelby	4
A.A. Donald	b Saxelby	0
T.A. Munton	not out	1
Extras	lb 5, w 6	11
Total (40 ov)		139

14, 46, 68, 106, 109, 109, 129, 138, 138

Stephenson	8	0	26	0
Cooper	8	1	28	1
Pick	8	0	30	2
Evans	8	0	26	0
Saxelby	8	0	24	5

Nottinghamshire		
B.C. Broad	c Kallicharran b Small	34
P.R. Pollard	b N.M.K. Smith	36
*R.T. Robinson	not out	42
P. Johnson	not out	18
D.J.R. Martindale		
F.D. Stephenson		
K.P. Evans		
†B.N. French		
R.A. Pick		
K.E. Cooper		
K. Saxelby		
Extras	b 4, lb 2, w 5	11
Total (2 wkts, 35.4 ov)		141

62, 98

Donald	8	1	28	0
Munton	6	1	22	0
N.M.K. Smith	8	1	20	1
Small	8	1	33	1
Kallicharran	2	0	16	0
Reeve	3.4	0	16	0

Umpires: M.J. Kitchen and A.G.T. Whithead
Toss: Nottinghamshire

Warwickshire never looked very happy, only P.A. Smith looking confident and Saxelby returned impressive figures. On the other hand the Notts batsmen found few problems and the match was won with ease.

PLAYERS

John Andrew AFFORD *b* 12.5.1964 Crowland, Lincs; Lower order right-hand batsman; promising slow left arm bowler; debut 1984; selected for England 'B' tour 1989–90

Brian Christopher BROAD *b* 29.9.1957 Bristol; very sound opening left-hand batsman; occasional right-arm medium pace bowler; debut 1984; previously played for Gloucs 1979–83; also Orange Free State 1985–86; England Test debut 1984; appeared in 2 Tests 1989

Christopher Lance CAIRNS *b* 13.6.1970 Picton, New Zealand; hard hitting middle order right-hand batsman; promising right-arm fast-medium bowler; debut 1988; son of B.L. Carins (New Zealand Test player)

Kevin Edwin COOPER *b* 17.12.1957 Sutton-in-Ashfield; lower order left-hand batsman; accurate right-arm fast-medium bowler; debut 1976; took 101 wkts in 1988; benefit 1990

Kevin Paul EVANS *b* 10.9.1963 Calverton; useful all-rounder; right-hand batsman; right-arm medium pace bowler; debut 1984

Russell John EVANS *b* 1.10.1965 Calverton; opening right-hand batsman; occasional right-arm medium pace bowler; debut 1987; brother of K.P.; could not play in 1989 owing to injury

Michael Gwyn FIELD-BUSS *b* 23.9.1964 Mtarfa, Malta; lower order right-hand batsman; off break bowler; devbut 1989; previously played for Essex 1987

Bruce Nicholas FRENCH *b* 13.8.1959 Warsop; attractive middle order right-hand batsman; wicketkeeper; debut 1976 (youngest player for the county); England debut 1986; missed out of 1988 due to injury; but played regularly in 1989

Edward Ernest HEMMINGS *b* 20.2.1949 Leampton Spa, Warwicks; useful lower order right-hand batsman; very effective off break bowler; debut 1979; previously played for Warwicks 1966–78; England Test debut 1982; appeared in one Test in 1989; selected for England tours to India and West Indies 1989–90; took record 10–175 in innings in International XI v West Indies (Kingston) 1982–83

Paul JOHNSON *b* 24.4.1965 Newark; talented middle order right-hand batsman; very good range of strokes; very occasional right-arm medium pace bowler; debut 1982

Duncan John Richardson MARTINDALE *b* 13.12.1963 Harrogate; attractive middle order right-hand batsman; debut 1985

Gregory Wentworth MIKE *b* 14.7.1966 Nottingham; robust right-hand batsman; right-arm medium-fast bowler; debut 1989 (friendly first-class only); has also played in Sunday League

David James MILLNS *b* 27.2.1965 Clipstone; lower order left hand batsmen; finely built right-arm fast-medium bowler; debut 1988. Moved to Leics for 1990

Michael NEWELL *b* 25.2.1965 Blackburn; very obdurate opening right-hand batsman; occasional leg-break bowler; fine close field; debut 1984

Robert Andrew PICK *b* 19.11.1963 Nottingham; lower order left-hand batsman; promising right-arm fast-medium bowler; debut 1983; missed many matches in 1988 through injury; opportunities limited in 1989

Paul Raymond POLLARD *b* 24.9.1968 Carlton, Nottingham; opening left-hand batsman who gained a regular first team place in 1989; debut 1987

Derek William RANDALL *b* 24.2.1951 Retford; middle order right-hand batsman; brilliant cover field; debut 1972; England Test debut 1976–77; has appeared in 47 Tests and is one of the most popular figures in the cricket field; scored 2,151 runs in 1985

Robert Timothy ROBINSON *b* 21.11.1958 Sutton-in-Ashfield; Usually opening right-hand batsman, but often went in at no 3 in 1989; debut in 1978; Notts captain since 1988; England Test debut 1984; appeared in one Test 1989; scored 2,032 runs in 1984

Kevin SAXELBY *b* 23.2.1959 Worksop; lower right-hand batsman; tall right-arm medium fast bowler; debut 1978; returned some remarkable Sunday League analyses in 1989

Mark SAXELBY *b* 4.1.1969 Newark; middle order left-hand batsman; right-arm medium pace bowler; brother of Kevin; debut 1989 (friendly first-class only)

Christopher Wilmot SCOTT *b* 23.1.1964 Thorpe-on-the-Hill, Lincs; useful right-hand batsman; wicketkeeper; debut 1981; opportunties restricted as he acts as French's deputy

Franklyn DaCosta STEPHENSON *b* 8.4.1959 St James, Barbados; attacking right-hand batsman; right-arm fast medium bowler with well disguised slower delivery; debut 1988; performed 'double' in first season; previously played for Tasmania 1981–82, Barbados 1981–82, Gloucs 1982–83; 125 wickets in 1988

REFUGE ASSURANCE LEAGUE

v ESSEX (Trent Bridge)

July 30

Won by 9 runs. Notts 4pts, Essex 0pts

Nottinghamshire		
P.R. Pollard	c Lilley b Lever	16
M. Newell]	b Waugh	47
P. Johnson	c Miller b Stephenson	9
D.J.R. Martindale	c Garnham b Waugh	11
D.W. Randall	not out	70
F.D. Stephenson	not out	20
*†B.N. French		
K.P. Evans		
K.E. Cooper		
K. Saxelby		
J.A. Afford		
Extras	lb 13, w 8, nb 3	24
Total (4 wkts, 37 ov)		197

33, 52, 87, 116

Pringle	8	0	40	0
Lever	8	2	36	1
Topley	7	0	26	0
Stephenson	5	0	18	1
Miller	3	0	20	0
Waugh	6	0	44	2

Essex		
B.R. Hardie	lbw b Stephenson	7
A.W. Lilley	c French b Saxelby	10
M.E. Waugh	c French b Cooper	14
P.J. Prichard	c Johnson b Saxelby	2
N. Hussain	b Stephenson	41
J.P. Stephenson	c Pollard b Saxelby	4
*D.R. Pringle	c and b Stephenson	16
†M.A. Garnham	run out	2
G. Miller	c Stephenson b Saxelby	10
T.D. Topley	b Saxelby	2
J.K. Lever	not out	0
Extras	lb 3, w 1, nb 1	5
Total (22.4 ov)		113

12, 23, 31, 36, 41, 95, 98, 104, 113

Stephenson	8	0	38	3
Cooper	8	0	36	1
Saxelby	6.4	0	36	5

Umpires: R. Palmer and R.A. White
Toss: Essex

Rain delayed the start, reducing the match to 37 overs per side. Notts made a very slow start, but Randall hit 70 off 37 deliveries to produce a useful total. Further breaks for rain meant that Essex needed 123 off 23 overs. In poor light, Stephenson's bowling proved tricky and Saxelby created a new Sunday League record with 5 wickets in his 4th successive match.

v HAMPSHIRE (Trent Bridge)

August 20

Lost by 32 runs. Hants 4pts, Notts 0pts

Hampshire		
R.J. Scott	run out	6
R.A. Smith	run out	131
*M.C.J. Nicholas	c French b Saxelby	16
J.R. Wood	b Cooper	66
K.D. James	not out	14
S.T. Jefferies	not out	10
V.P. Terry		
†R.J. Parks		
S.D. Udal		
R.J. Maru		
C.A. Connor		
Extras	lb 7, w 3, nb 1	11
Total (4 wkts, 40 ov)		254

18, 61, 213, 236

Cooper	8	0	31	1
Stephenson	8	0	51	0
Pick	8	0	61	0
Saxelby	8	0	57	1
Hemmings	8	0	47	0

Nottinghamshire		
M. Newell	run out	7
P.R. Pollard	c Parks b Connor	12
*R.T. Robinson	lbw b Nicholas	0
D.W. Randall	c Terry b Udal	23
D.J.R. Martindale	b Connor	47
F.D. Stephenson	b Connor	69
†B.N. French	c Wood b Jefferies	12
E.E. Hemmings	c Terry b Jefferies	5
K.E. Cooper	b James	25
K. Saxelby	c Connor b James	2
R.A. Pick	not out	0
Extras	b 4, lb 10, w 4, nb 2	20
Total (37.3 ov)		222

16, 20, 22, 62, 173, 180, 191, 195, 222

Connor	8	1	42	3
James	7.3	0	33	2
Nicholas	8	1	30	1
Udal	5	0	36	1
Maru	2	0	15	0
Jefferies	7	0	52	2

Umpires: B.J. Meyer and P.B. Wight
Toss: Hants

Despite fielding a rather weak side, the visitors had all the best of this match. Smith batted splendidly for his 131 and after a poor start, Notts were never in contention, though Martindale and Stephenson saved the country's face.

v MIDDLESEX (Trent Bridge)

August 27

Won by 8 wkts. Notts 4pts, Middx 0pts

Middlesex		
*M.W. Gatting	c French b Pick	26
J.D. Carr	b Pick	8
M.A. Roseberry	b Saxelby	24
R.O. Butcher	b Stephenson	67
K.R. Brown	c French b Cooper	5
†P.R. Downton	c Randall b Pick	8
J.E. Emburey	b Saxelby	13
N.F. Williams	lbw b Stephenson	0
S.P. Hughes	not out	4
R.M. Ellcock	c Martindale b Stephenson	5
N.G. Cowans	b Stephenson	0
Extras	lb 5, w 2	7
Total (39.5 ov)		167

26, 42, 75, 95, 131, 157, 157, 160, 166

Cooper	8	0	25	1
Pick	8	1	29	3
Saxelby	8	0	27	2
Stephenson	7.5	0	33	4
Hemmings	8	0	48	0

Nottinghamshire		
P.R. Pollard	c Downton b Cowans	17
*R.T. Robinson	not out	97
D.W. Randall	c Butcher b Ellcock	26
P. Johnson	not out	20
D.J.R. Martindale		
F.D. Stephenson		
†B.N. French		
R.A. Pick		
E.E. Hemmings		
K.E. Cooper		
K. Saxelby		
Extras	lb 4, w 1, nb 3	8
Total (2 wkts, 34.2 ov)		168

54, 116

Cowans	8	3	17	1
Ellcock	6	0	41	1
Williams	7	0	38	0
Hughes	6	0	26	0
Emburey	7	0	36	0
Brown	0.2	0	6	0

Umpires: B. Dudleston and P.J. Eele
Toss: Nottinghamshire

This was a vital game for the home club, for they had to win it to obtain a place in the Knock-Out Cup. Middlesex's innings never really took off, with only Butcher looking happy. In contrast Robinson played quite splendidly and hit 9 fours and 4 sixes in his unbeaten 97.

BRITANNIC ASSURANCE COUNTY CHAMPIONSHIP AVERAGES 1989

Batting	*M*	*I*	*NO*	*Runs*	*HS*	*Avge*	*100*	*50*
R.T. Robinson	20	36	6	1412	146*	47.06	4	8
B.C. Broad	19	35	2	1376	144	41.69	3	10
D.W. Randall	22	38	5	1327	130	40.21	2	8
K.P. Evans	13	19	6	377	58	29.00	–	3
P.R. Pollard	15	27	–	766	131	28.37	1	3
P. Johnson	18	32	2	810	87	27.00	–	5
B.N. French	15	24	5	502	55*	26.42	–	2
C.L. Cairns	5	6	–	139	58	23.16	–	1
M. Newell	11	20	2	394	99	21.88	–	2
F.D. Stephenson	17	28	3	537	81	21.48	–	4
E.E. Hemmings	18	24	6	320	58*	17.77	–	1
D.J.R. Martindale	6	9	–	159	78	17.67	–	1
C.W. Scott	7	9	2	123	51	17.57	–	1
K. Saxelby	8	10	5	73	19	14.60	–	–
K.E. Cooper	20	25	6	232	33*	12.21	–	–
J.A. Afford	15	14	6	48	22*	6.00	–	–
M.G. Field-Buss	2	3	1	12	6*	6.00	–	–
R.A. Pick	9	13	2	64	17	5.81	–	–

Also batted: D.J. Millns (2 matches) 0.

Bowling	*O*	*M*	*R*	*W*	*Avge*	*BB*	*5i*	*10m*
M.G. Field-Buss	48	15	128	7	18.29	4-33	–	–
F.D. Stephenson	572.3	128	1699	91	18.67	8-47	7	2
K.E. Cooper	582.3	168	1481	55	26.93	6-37	2	1
E.E. Hemmings	540	145	1350	50	27.00	6-87	2	–
K.P. Evans	243.5	56	732	26	28.15	3-20	–	–
J.A. Afford	449.3	125	1318	43	30.65	5-63	2	–
C.L. Cairns	101.2	20	433	13	33.31	3-50	–	–
K. Saxelby	190.4	48	662	15	44.13	4-66	–	–
R.A. Pick	181.4	26	665	13	51.15	4-41	–	–

Also bowled: P. Johnson 4.2-0-64-0; D.J. Millns 46-8-153-3; M. Newell 8-0-44-0; D.W. Randall 1-0-3-0; R.T. Robinson 6-0-46-0.

Centuries

4 R.T. Robinson: 128 & 146* v Kent (Trent Bridge); 136 v Surrey (Guildford); 128 v Somerset (Trent Bridge).

3 B.C. Broad: 132 & 113 v Glamorgan (Cardiff); 144 v Middlesex (Trent Bridge).

2 D.W. Randall: 101 v Surrey (Guildford); 130 v Lancs (Worksop).

1 P.R. Pollard: 131 v Kent (Trent Bridge).

BENSON AND HEDGES CUP

v DERBYSHIRE (Trent Bridge)

May 2

Won by 5 wkts. Notts 2pts, Derbys 0pts

Derbyshire		
*K.J. Barnett	c French b Evans	50
P.D. Bowler	c Broad b Stephenson	6
†B.J.M. Maher	lbw b Hemmings	21
B. Roberts	c French b Cooper	30
S.C. Goldsmith	c Randall b Cooper	32
R. Sharma	b Stephenson	5
F.A. Griffith	b Stephenson	10
M.A. Holding	c Newell b Saxelby	5
P.G. Newman	c Randall b Stephenson	3
S.J. Base	not out	6
O.H. Mortensen	not out	0
Extras	lb 7, w 2, nb 1	10
Total (9 wkst, 55 ov)		178

9, 59, 91, 138, 147, 154, 164, 171, 172

Stephenson	11	1	34	4
Cooper	11	2	23	2
Evans	11	2	39	1
Saxelby	11	0	50	1
Hemmings	11	2	25	1

Nottinghamshire		
*R.T. Robinson	c Maher b Mortensen	15
B.C. Broad	run out	4
M. Newell	c Maher b Holding	7
P. Johnson	b Mortensen	7
D.W. Randall	not out	57
F.D. Stephenson	b Holding	54
†B.N. French	not out	25
K.P. Evans		
E.E. Hemmings		
K. Saxelby		
K.E. Cooper		
Extras	lb 8, w 2	10
Total (5 wkts, 51.1 ov)		179

5, 12, 35, 36, 126

Newman	11	2	25	0
Holding	11	2	31	2
Base	11	1	37	0
Mortensen	11	0	35	2
Sharma	4	0	15	0
Roberts	3.1	0	28	0

Umpires: B. Dudleston and D.R. Shepherd

Toss: Derbyshire. Gold: F.D. Stephenson.

Barnett batted 115 minutes for his 50, but accurate bowling by Cooper and Hemmings kept the scoring rate down. Notts lost 4 cheap wickets before Randall and Stephenson took control and Notts won with 3.5 overs in hand.

v YORKSHIRE (Trent Bridge)

May 11, 12

Won by 33 runs. Notts 2pts, Yorks 0pts

Nottinghamshire		
B.C. Broad	b Oldham	53
*R.T. Robinson	b Jarvis	8
M. Newell	c Bairstow b Oldham	3
D.W. Randall	b Byas b Oldham	22
P.R. Pollard	lbw b Jarvis	12
F.D. Stephenson	b Oldham	0
†B.N. French	run out	6
K.P. Evans	lbw b Byas	13
E.E. Hemmings	c Bairstow b Hartley	4
R.A. Pick	b Jarvis	1
K.E. Cooper	not out	17
Extras	lb 4, w 1	5
Total (52.1 ov)		144

21, 38, 83, 98, 98, 102, 117, 122, 123

Jarvis	11	4	21	3
Pickles	8	0	27	0
Oldham	11	5	13	4
Byas	4.1	0	18	1
Carrick	11	2	32	0
Hartley	7	0	29	1

Yorkshire		
A.A. Metcalfe	c Pollard b Pick	14
R.J. Blakey	c and b Stephenson	16
D. Byas	c Broad b Stephenson	5
J.D. Love	c French b Cooper	30
P.E. Robinson	b Evans	12
†D.L. Bairstow	c Randall b Pick	7
S.N. Hartley	not out	13
*P. Carrick	c Robinson b Evans	1
P.W. Jarvis	lbw c Cooper	0
C.S. Pickles	b Cooper	4
S. Oldham	lbw b Cooper	0
Extras	lb 4, w 3, nb 2	9
Total (49.5 ov)		111

23, 35, 38, 66, 88, 97, 100, 101, 111

Stephenson	10	3	25	2
Cooper	9.5	3	9	4
Pick	9	1	29	2
Hemmings	11	4	16	0
Evans	10	1	28	2

Umpires: A.A. Jones and N.T. Plews

Toss: Yorkshire. Gold: K.E. Cooper

The start being delayed and bad light ending the first day early, this game was extended into a second. Broad batted 122 minutes for 53 and only Randall gave much support. Yorks were 73–4 off 38.5 overs at the close. The game resumed at 1.30 on the second day and Cooper soon finished the visitors off.

Semi Final v KENT (Trent Bridge)

June 15

Won by 69 runs.

Nottinghamshire		
B.C. Broad	b Fleming	66
P.R. Pollard	c Cowdrey b Kelleher	77
*R.T. Robinson	run out	80
D.W. Randall	c Marsh b Fleming	0
G.W. Mike	c Hinks b Cowdrey	29
K.P. Evans	c Pienaar b Cowdrey	1
†B.N. French	not out	22
E.E. Hemmings	not out	2
K.E. Cooper		
K. Saxelby		
J.A. Afford		
Extras	lb 13, w 1, nb 5	19
Total (6 wkts, 55 ov)		296

141, 167, 167, 226, 234, 294

Igglesden	11	1	68	0
Kelleher	10	0	48	1
Fleming	10	1	58	2
Penn	11	0	54	0
Cowdrey	11	1	45	2
Ward	2	0	10	0

Kent		
S.G. Hinks	c French b Evans	49
M.R. Benson	b Afford	65
N.R. Taylor	c Evans b Afford	19
R.F. Pienaar	c and b Afford	7
*C.S. Cowdrey	c Pollard b Afford	3
T.R. Ward	c Evans b Cooper	11
M.V. Fleming	c Robinson b Evans	24
†S.A. Marsh	b Saxelby	12
C. Penn	run out	8
D.J.M. Kelleher	not out	11
A.P. Igglesden	b Saxelby	1
Extras	lb 11, w 6	17
Total (48.4 ov)		227

65, 135, 149, 153, 153, 184, 188, 209, 212

Saxelby	8.4	1	46	2
Cooper	10	0	42	1
Evans	9	0	51	2
Hemmings	10	0	39	0
Afford	11	2	38	4

Umpires: R. Palmer and M. J. Kitchen

Toss: Kent. Gold: J.A. Afford

Broad and Pollard gave Notts a good start with 141 in 110 minutes. Robinson hit out brightly and Notts obtained a substantial total. Kent also began well, but having reached 135–1, they then lost 4 wicktets for 18 due to some good bowling from Afford and Notts dismissed Kent with 6.2 overs to spare.

Away Matches

The full scorecard of each of Nottinghamshire's away matches will be found in the sections for the respective home teams.

Old Trafford: April 27, 28, 29, May 1
Lancs 300–6d (G.D. Mendis 118) and 250–7d drew with Notts 283–9d (Wasim Akram 6–70) and 147–0. Lancs 7pts, Notts 5pts.

Headingley: May 4, 5
Yorks 92 (F.D Stephenson 7–38) and 109 (F.D. Stephenson 6–37) lost to Notts 86 and 119–0 by 10 wkts. Notts 20pts, Yorks 4pts.

Worcester: May 24, 25, 26
Worcs 209 and 180–3d drew with Notts 150–3d and 238–9. Notts 5pts, Worcs 3pts.

Cardiff: May 27, 29, 30
Notts 300–6d (B.C. Broad 132) and 302–3d (B.C. Broad 113) drew with Glamorgan 250–2d (A.R. Butcher 107*) and 286–6. Glamorgan 5pts, Notts 4pts.

Lord's June 7, 8, 9
Middx 296 and 107–7d drew with Notts 179 (A.R.C. Fraser 5–37) and 97–5. Middx 7pts, Notts 3pts.

Leicester: June 24, 26
Leics 352–6d (L. Potter 121*) beat Notts 116 (J.P. Agnew 5–37, C.C. Lewis 5–51) and 135 (J.P. Agnew 6–56) by an inns and 101 runs. Leics 23pts, Notts 1pt.

Gloucester: July 1, 3
Gloucs 101 (F.D. Stephenson 5–32) and 147 (K.E. Cooper 6–37) lost to Notts 252 by an inns and 4 runs. Notts 23pts, Gloucs 4pts.

Guildford: July 5, 6, 7
Notts 475–8d (R.T. Robinson 136, D.W. Randall 101) drew with Surrey 275 (E.E. Hemmings 6–87) and 146–1. Notts 8pts, Surrey 5pts.

Northampton: July 22, 24, 25
Northants 322 and 174 beat Notts 289 and 147 by 60 runs. Northants 23pts, Notts 6pts.

Eastbourne: August 5, 7, 8
Sussex 325–6d (D.M. Smith 184) and 264 (F.D. Stephenson 5–86) lost to Notts 303 and 287–7 by 3 wkts. Notts 22pts, Sussex 7pts.

Derby: September 8, 9, 10, 11
Notts 330 and 119 lost to Derbys 293 (J.E. Morris 156) and 160–9 by one wkt. Derbys 23pts, Notts 8 pts.

v WORCESTERSHIRE (Trent Bridge)

April 20, 21, 22, 24
Lost by 7 wkts. Worcs 22pts, Notts 5pts

Nottinghamshire 1st Innings		
B.C. Broad	b Dilley	30
*R.T. Robinson	c Botham b Dilley	6
M. Newell	c Hick b Botham	35
P. Johnson	c Rhodes b Dilley	38
D.W. Randall	not out	73
F.D. Stephenson	lbw b Botham	1
†B.N. French	c Hick b Dilley	2
K.P. Evans	lbw b Radford	13
E.E. Hemmings	lbw b Newport	0
K. Saxelby	c Lord b Newport	4
K.E. Cooper	b Dilley	0
Extras	lb 13, nb 3	16
Total (85.3 ov)		218

9, 63, 104, 130, 133, 140, 186, 189, 217

Dilley	20.3	0	42	5
Radford	22	5	56	1
Newport	24	2	64	2
Botham	16	7	37	2
Illingworth	3	0	6	0

Worcestershire 1st Innings		
T.S. Curtis	lbw b Cooper	68
G.J. Lord	b Saxelby	6
R.K. Illingworth	b Stephenson	6
G.A. Hick	lbw b Cooper	56
D.B. d'Oliveira	lbw b Cooper	1
*P.A. Neale	c French b Evans	14
I.T. Botham	c and b Saxelby	8
†S.J. Rhodes	not out	40
P.J. Newport	c Randall b Stephenson	16
N.V. Radford	c Stephenson b Hemmings	47
G.R. Dilley	c Broad b Saxelby	4
Extras	lb 19, nb 6	25
Total (100 ov 235–8)		291

22, 47, 135, 137, 159, 175, 175, 199, 285

Stephenson	29.1	5	71	2
Cooper	31.2	12	67	3
Saxelby	25	4	72	3
Hemmings	9.4	3	16	1
Evans	20.5	6	46	1

Nottinghamshire 2nd Innings		
B.C. Broad	c Botham b Newport	61
*R.T. Robinson	c Hick b Dilley	4
M. Newell	lbw b Radford	0
P. Johnson	c DeFreitas b Newport	35
D.W. Randall	b Radford	32
F.D. Stephenson	c Rhodes b Newport	1
†B.N. French	b Radford	27
K.P. Evans	c d'Oliveira b Botham	11
E.E. Hemmings	c Hick b Radford	4
K. Saxelby	not out	6
K.E. Cooper	b Dilley	1
Extras	lb 6, w 1, nb 9	16
Total		198

5, 6, 84, 116, 122, 148, 172, 181, 190

Dilley	14.4	4	40	2
Radford	17	0	56	4
Newport	15	2	47	3
Botham	13	0	49	1

Worcestershire 2nd Innings		
T.S. Curtis	c French b Stephenson	24
G.J. Lord	c Hemmings b Cooper	8
G.A. Hick	not out	55
D.B. d'Oliveira	lbw b Stephenson	8
*P.A. Neale	not out	24
Extras	b 8, w 1, nb 1	10
Total (3 wkts)		129

17, 46, 84

Stephenson	14.2	0	77	2
Cooper	12	4	33	1
Evans	2	0	11	0

Umpires: J.C. Balderstone and B. Leadbeater
Toss: Worcestershire.
On a cold first day, Notts relied on Randall for their modest total and Worcs were 22–1 off 16 overs at the close. The weather failed to improve on the second day, 12 overs being lost ro rain. The Worcs 9th wicket added a crucial 85. Some runs from Broad were all Notts could cheer on the Saturday and on the final day a very wet wicket delayed the start by 85 minutes. At lunch Worcs were 35 for one, but after the interval Hick attacked the bowling and with the rain resuming brought victory for his side. Few matches at Nottingham have been played under such miserable, cold and wet conditions.

v HAMPSHIRE (Trent Bridge)

May 20, 21, 22,
Drawn. Notts 5pts, Hants 6pts

Nottinghamshire 1st Innings		
B.C. Broad	c C.L. Smith b Tremlett	64
M. Newell	c C.L. Smith b Bakker	41
P. Johnson	lbw b Nicholas	43
*R.T. Robinson	lbw b Nicholas	36
D.W. Randall	c Bakker b Tremlett	45
F.D. Stephenson	c R.A. Smith b Nicholas	12
†B.N. French	not out	43
E.E. Hemmings	not out	24
R.A. Pick		
K.E. Cooper		
J.A. Afford		
Extras	lb 13, w 4, nb 6	23
Total (100 ov: 279–6) (6 wkts dec)		331

101, 125, 192, 201, 221, 271

Jefferies	21	4	65	0
Bakker	18	3	61	1
Tremlett	17	2	39	2
James	9	1	40	0
Maru	31	10	76	0
Nicholas	15	2	37	3

Hampshire 1st Innings		
V.P. Terry	c French b Stephenson	12
C.L. Smith	b Stephenson	22
K.D. James	c Broad b Stephenson	0
R.A. Smith	run out	148
D.R. Turner	c Afford b Stephenson	24
*M.C.J. Nicholas	c Randall b Hemmings	71
S.T. Jefferies	not out	4
T.M. Tremlett	not out	5
†R.J. Parks		
R.J. Maru		
P.J. Bakker		
	lb 11, nb 3	14
Total (6 wkts dec, 89.2 ov)		300

16, 16, 61, 137, 280, 295

Stephenson	21	2	84	4
Pick	16	2	62	0
Cooper	16	3	56	0
Hemmings	21.2	1	59	1
Afford	15	6	28	0

Nottinghamshire 2nd Innings		
B.C. Broad	c Nicholas b Maru	15
M. Newell	lbw b Bakker	1
P. Johnson	b Nicholas	69
R.A. Pick	c C.L. Smith b Bakker	4
*R.T. Robinson	not out	73
D.W. Randall	not out	46
Extras	lb 5, w 1	6
Total (4 wkts dec)		214

4, 41, 54, 103

Jefferies	8	1	26	0
Bakker	13	6	25	2
Tremlett	3	0	12	0
James	6	2	11	0
Maru	19	6	46	1
Nicholas	6	1	16	1
R.A. Smith	6	0	31	0
C.L. Smith	8	1	31	0
Turner	4.2	1	11	0

Hampshire 2nd Innings		
V.P. Terry	not out	82
C.L. Smith	lbw b Stephenson	13
K.D. James	c Johnson b Cooper	36
R.A. Smith	c Randall b Pick	20
D.R. Turner	run out	0
*M.C.J. Nicholas	b Pick	0
S.T. Jefferies	c Robinson b Pick	0
T.M. Tremlett	not out	10
Extras	b 2, lb 7, nb 2	11
Total (6 wkts)		172

25, 104, 131, 132, 132, 132

Stephenson	9.3	4	20	1
Pick	10	1	43	3
Cooper	9	1	26	1
Hemmings	14	3	37	0
Afford	12	2	37	0

Umpires: J.H. Hampshire and N.T. Plews
Toss: Nottinghamshire
Although the Notts total reached 99–0 by lunch, the runs came no faster in the afternoon and thus Notts failed to obtain full batting points. Robinson declared overnight and Hants after losing two quick wickets forged ahead with Robin Smith hitting 148 in 289 mins with 19 fours. Notts were 45–2 off 16 overs when play ended. Robinson and Randall picked up cheap runs, before Hants were set 246 in 186 minutes. The total reached 131–2, but then four wickets fell for 1 run and the game petered out.

v YORKSHIRE (Trent Bridge)

June 3, 5, 6

Drawn. Notts 6pts, Yorks 6pts

Yorkshire 1st Innings

A.A. Metcalfe	lbw b Cairns	31
M.D. Moxon	c Randall b Afford	37
R.J. Blakey	lbw b Cooper	10
P.E. Robinson	b Cairns	57
J.D. Love	c Scott b Pick	53
†D.L. Bairstow	c and b Cairns	0
I.G. Swallow	c Broad b Cooper	1
*P. Carrick	c Broad b Cooper	9
A. Sidebottom	c Scott b Cooper	4
P.W. Jarvis	not out	11
C.S. Pickles	b Cooper	0
Extras	lb 6, w 1, nb 3	10
Total (65 ov)		223

40, 60, 113, 182, 182, 191, 202, 207, 223

Pick	12	1	56	1
Cooper	26	7	72	5
Cairns	15	3	50	3
Hemmings	5	1	10	0
Afford	7	2	29	1

Nottinghamshire 1st Innings

B.C. Broad	c Moxon b Jarvis	29
M. Newell	lbw b Jarvis	0
P. Johnson	lbw b Jarvis	0
*R.T. Robinson	b Jarvis	24
D.W. Randall	c Bairstow b Sidebottom	13
C.L. Cairns	c Bairstow b Swallow	41
†C.W. Scott	c Moxon b Carrick	15
E.E. Hemmings	not out	58
K.E. Cooper	c Pickles b Jarvis	21
R.A. Pick	c Bairstow b Jarvis	0
J.A. Afford	b Jarvis	0
Extras	lb 5, nb 8	13
Total (64.4 ov)		214

1, 1, 47, 70, 70, 121, 132, 192, 214

Jarvis	23.4	5	74	7
Sidebottom	25	3	77	1
Carrick	10	3	26	1
Pickles	3	0	15	0
Swallow	3	0	17	1

Yorkshire 2nd Innings

M.D. Moxon	c Robinson b Afford	39
A.A. Metcalfe	c Randall b Cairns	18
R.J. Blakey	c Randall c Afford	1
P.E. Robinson	b Cooper	18
J.D. Love	b Afford	7
†D.L. Bairstow	c Robinson b Afford	7
I.G. Swallow	lbw b Afford	0
*P. Carrick	c Robinson b Cooper	30
A. Sidebottom	b Hemmings	21
P.W. Jarvis	not out	59
C.S. Pickles	not out	28
Extras	b 8, lb 11, w 2, nb 1	22
Total (9 wkts dec)		250

61, 61, 69, 77, 89, 89, 129, 158, 158

Pick	6	1	14	0
Cooper	22	11	42	2
Cairns	8	1	50	1
Hemmings	21	2	62	1
Afford	28.5	11	63	5

Nottinghamshire 2nd Innings

B.C. Broad	b Carrick	31
M. Newell	not out	24
P. Johnson	not out	29
Extras		0
Total (1 wkt)		84

46

Jarvis	9	2	28	0
Sidebottom	9	0	24	0
Carrick	12	6	17	1
Swallow	6	1	15	0

Umpires: J.H.Harris and R. Julian

Toss: Yorkshire.

Yorks relied on fifties from Robinson and Love for the modest 223. Rain then cut 20 overs off the play before Notts reached 47–3 off 20 overs. On the second day, the home county were in trouble until Hemmings and Cooper added 60 for the 8th wicket. Afford bowled particularly well to reduce Yorks to 130–7 at 6.10 pm, when bad light ended play. Jarvis and Pickles put on 92 for the 9th wicket, which allowed Carrick to declare and set Notts 260 in 64 overs. Notts were not interested in chasing the runs and it was a relief when rain ended play at 4.45 pm.

v KENT (Trent Bridge)

June 10, 12, 13

Lost by 4 wkts. Kent 21pts, Notts 6pts

Nottinghamshire 1st Innings

*R.T Robinson	c Ward b Cowdrey	128
P.R. Pollard	b Davis	83
P. Johnson	c Hinks b Igglesden	17
D.W. Randall	C Pienaar b Hinks	56
D.J.R. Martindale	st Marsh b Davis	11
C.L. Cairns	c Cowdrey b Hinks	58
K.P. Evans	c Hinks b Cowdrey	8
†C.W. Scott	not out	1
E.E. Hemmings		
K. Saxelby		
J.A. Afford		
Extras	b 4, lb 6, w 2, nb 3	15
Total (100 ov 364–4) (7 wkts dec)		377

222, 237, 250, 277, 364, 369, 377

Igglesden	18	3	64	1
Penn	16	3	74	0
Cowdrey	13.4	1	44	2
Fleming	12	4	47	0
Davis	36	9	109	2
Ward	4	0	11	0
Hinks	4	0	18	2

Kent 1st Innings

S.G. Hinks	c Pollard b Evans	37
M.R. Benson	c Robinson b Saxelby	17
N.R. Taylor	c and b Evans	2
R.F. Pienaar	c Saxelby b Hemmings	119
T.R. Ward	c sub (Pick) b Afford	35
*C.S Cowdrey	not out	101
M.V. Fleming	c and b Afford	6
†S.A. Marsh	st Scott b Afford	26
C. Penn		
R.P. Davis		
A.P. Igglesden		
Extras	b 2, lb 5, w 1, nb 3	11
Total (100 ov: 354–6) (7 wkts dec)		354

58, 58, 70, 119, 301, 314, 354

Saxelby	19	7	54	1
Cairns	15	4	78	0
Hemmings	29	7	71	1
Evans	13	2	45	2
Afford	24.2	7	99	3

Nottinghamshire 2nd Innings

P.R. Pollard	b Davis	131
*R.T. Robinson	not out	146
D.W. Randall	c Penn b Ward	0
Extras	b 2, lb 5, nb 3	10
Total (2 wkts dec)		287

282, 287

Igglesden	6	0	24	0
Penn	10	1	42	0
Fleming	9	2	29	0
Davis	26	4	101	1
Ward	13.4	0	84	1

Kent 2nd Innings

M.R. Benson	c Evans b Carins	1
S.G. Hinks	run out	70
N.R. Taylor	st Scott b Afford	78
R.F. Pienaar	lbw b Saxelby	40
T.R. Ward	c Martindale b Cairns	18
*C.S. Cowdrey	c Hemmings b Afford	46
M.V. Fleming	not out	36
S.A. Marsh	not out	7
Extras	lb 11, w 2, nb 2	15
Total (6 wkts)		311

7, 143, 162, 211, 262, 278

Saxelby	12.4	0	82	1
Cairns	9	0	53	2
Hemmings	11	1	70	0
Evans	6	1	22	0
Afford	14	1	73	2

Umpires: J.D. Bond and J.H. Hampshire

Toss: Kent.

Pollard and Robinson created a new Notts record by scoring over 200 runs together in both innings for the 1st wicket, 222 and 282. The match was played in gloriously hot weather, with the bat totally dominant. Kent were 23–0 off 8 overs at the close on Saturday. Pienaar and Cowdrey both hit 100s to bring Kent full batting points. Robinson completed his second 100 of the match, in each innings he hit 16 fours. Kent were set 311 in 54 overs. Nearly all the batsmen made runs and the target was reached with 8 deliveries unbowled.

v WARWICKSHIRE (Trent Bridge)

July 8, 10, 11

Drawn. Warwicks 7pts, Notts 4pts

Nottinghamshire 1st Innings

B.C. Broad	c Piper b Small	5
P.R. Pollard	c Humpage b Munton	7
*R.T. Robinson	c Moles b Small	6
D.J.R. Martindale	c Ratcliffe b Munton	8
D.W. Randall	lbw b Munton	10
F.D. Stephenson	b Small	28
K.P. Evans	c Piper b Merrick	18
†B.N. French	c Moles b Merrick	28
E.E. Hemmings	b Merrick	21
K.E. Cooper	b Merrick	4
J.A. Afford	not out	1
Extras	lb 4, w 5, nb 2	11
Total (58.4 ov)		147

15, 22, 22, 34, 41, 75, 116, 127, 141

Small	26	8	50	3
Merrick	15.4	3	38	4
Munton	17	5	55	3

Warwickshire 1st Innings

A.J. Moles	c Pollard b Cooper	6
J.D. Ratcliffe	c Stephenson b Evans	23
*T.A. Lloyd	b Stephenson	100
G.W. Humpage	c Pollard b Cooper	13
D.A. Reeve	c Afford b Stephenson	15
P.A. Smith	c Robinson b Afford	68
T.A. Merrick	c Martindale b Afford	9
G.C. Small	c sub b Afford	17
†K.J. Piper	c Martindale b Stephenson	10
A.R.K. Pierson	not out	7
T.A. Munton	c Pollard b Afford	6
Extras	b 6, lb 11, w 1	18
Total (82.2 ov)		292

11, 52, 89, 113, 216, 231, 261, 269, 283

Stephenson	26	7	66	3
Cooper	23	7	79	2
Evans	12	1	43	1
Hemmings	5	1	13	0
Afford	16.2	1	74	4

Nottinghamshire 2nd Innings

B.C. Broad	c Piper b Munton	63
P.R. Pollard	c Reeve b Munton	25
*R.T. Robinson	c Humpage b Pierson	11
D.J.R. Martindale	c Reeve b Pierson	11
D.W. Randall	not out	56
F.D. Stephenson	c Piper b Munton	8
K.P. Evans	run out	14
†B.N. French	not out	2
Extras	lb 3, w 2, nb 1	6
Total (6 wkts)		196

60, 73, 95, 143, 151, 193

Small	11	2	28	0
Merrick	14	6	30	0
Munton	15	2	37	3
Pierson	24	4	98	2

Umpires: M.J. Kitchen and A.G.T. Whitehead

Toss: Warwickshire.

On a day of heavy cloud, the players assembled on the field promptly at 11.00 am on the first day, but retired before a ball could be bowled. A second start was made 3 hours later. Notts reached 52–5 off 29.3 overs when bad light ended play for the day. The second day was also rain interrupted and though Notts tailenders improved the total, Warwickshire had no difficulty in gaining a substantial lead, and were 216–4 off 59 overs with Lloyd 100*. The last day was one of brilliant sunshine and was used for batting practice once Warwickshire failed to obtain a 4th batting point.

v SOMERSET (Trent Bridge)

July 19, 20, 21

Won and innings and 67 runs. Notts 24pts, Som 2pts

Somerset 1st Innings

S.J. Cook	not out	120
P.M. Roebuck	b Cooper	0
J.J.E Hardy	b Stephenson	6
C.J. Tavare	c French b Evans	21
R.J. Harden	lbw b Cooper	14
†N.D. Burns	b Field-Buss	4
*V.J. Marks	c Johnson b Evans	6
M.W. Cleal	c and b Field-Buss	0
H.R.J. Trump	c Johnson b Field-Buss	1
A.N. Jones	lbw b Field-Buss	4
D.J. Foster	lbw b Stephenson	6
Extras	lb 4	4
Total (67.3 ov)		186

4, 15, 77, 112, 129, 146, 149, 157, 165

Stephenson	9.3	1	29	2
Cooper	17	5	42	2
Evans	16	1	48	2
Afford	9	2	30	0
Field-Buss	16	6	33	4

Nottinghamshire 1st Innings

B.C. Broad	b Trump	70
P.R. Pollard	c Trump b Jones	91
*R.T. Robinson	b Trump	128
P. Johnson	c Burns b Jones	0
D.W. Randall	b Trump	44
F.D. Stephenson	lbw b Marks	7
K.P. Evans	not out	51
M.G. Field-Buss	b Trump	5
†B.N. French	not out	55
K.E. Cooper		
J.A. Afford		
Extras	b 1, lb 14, w 1, nb 4	20
Total (7 wkts dec) (100 ov: 302–3)		471

159, 175, 175, 305, 338, 354, 364

Jones	19	4	64	2
Foster	13	3	60	0
Marks	52.1	19	136	1
Trump	32	5	130	4
Roebuck	4	1	13	0
Cleal	13	3	53	0

Somerset 2nd Innings

S.J. Cook	not out	131
P.M. Roebuck	c Pollard b Afford	50
J.J.E Hardy	lbw b Field-Buss	13
C.J. Tavare	c Robinson b Afford	11
R.J. Harden	c Robinson b Stephenson	1
†N.D. Burns	b Stephenson	0
*V.J. Marks	b Stephenson	0
M.W. Cleal	lbw b Stephenson	0
H.R.J. Trump	c Randall b Afford	2
A.N. Jones	b Afford	0
D.J. Foster	st French b Afford	0
Extras	b 3, lb 6, w 1	10
Total		218

127, 154, 179, 193, 193, 211, 215, 218, 218

Stephenson	20	4	60	4
Cooper	9	4	20	0
Afford	37.3	11	90	5
Field-Buss	20	8	39	1

Umpires: D.G.L. Evans and B. Leadbeater

Toss: Somerset

The most remarkable feature of this match was the batting of Cook, who carried his bat through both completed innings for unbeaten 100s. The feat had only been performed once before – in 1911 – in English fc cricket. Notts otherwise dominated play from the first day, when they were 107–0 in reply to Somerset's 186 all out. Field-Buss made an impressive debut for his adopted county.

v LANCASHIRE (Worksop)

July 26, 27, 28

Lost by 6 wkts. Lancs 21pts, Notts 8pts

Nottinghamshire 1st Innings

B.C. Broad	c Watkinson b Allott	11
P.R. Pollard	c Atherton b Watkinson	7
D.J.R. Martindale	b Watkinson	0
P. Johnson	c Fowler b Atherton	51
D.W. Randall	c Speak b Watkinson	130
*†B.N. French	b Allott	14
F.D. Stephenson	c and b Watkinson	37
K.P. Evans	lbw b Allott	58
M.G. Field-Buss	not out	6
K. Saxelby	not out	5
J.A. Afford		
Extras	b 1, lb 6, nb 1	8
Total (8 wkts dec, 95 ov)		327

16, 18, 18, 108, 139, 207, 290, 314

Allott	27	8	66	3
Watkinson	24	4	99	4
Austin	15	4	43	0
Fitton	14	3	53	0
Atherton	15	0	59	1

Lancashire 1st Innings

G. Fowler	c Johnson b Stephenson	8
G.D. Lloyd	lbw b Afford	31
J.D. Fitton	c Pollard b Afford	0
M.A. Atherton	c Evans b Saxelby	21
N.J. Speak	b Stephenson	15
T.E. Jesty	c French b Saxelby	2
M. Watkinson	c Johnson b Field-Buss	70
†W.K. Hegg	c French b Saxelby	0
*D.P. Hughes	b Saxelby	37
I.D. Austin	lbw b Evans	23
P.J.W. Allott	not out	14
Extras	lb 9	9
Total (71.2 ov)		230

42, 43, 50, 80, 80, 83, 83, 167, 212

Stephenson	23	2	71	2
Saxelby	26	10	66	4
Afford	14	3	39	2
Evans	5.2	1	17	1
Field-Buss	3	0	28	1

Nottinghamshire 2nd Innings

B.C. Broad	b Allott	3
P.R. Pollard	c Allott b Austin	45
D.J.R. Martindale	c Speak b Allott	4
P. Johnson	c and b Flitton	43
D.W. Randall	b Austin	29
*†B.N. French	c Hegg b Austin	40
F.D. Stephenson	c Atherton b Austin	17
K.P. Evans	not out	20
M.G. Field-Buss	c Hegg b Watkinson	1
K. Saxelby	c Hegg b Watkinson	5
J.A. Afford	lbw b Watkinson	0
Extras	b 2, lb 2	4
Total		211

20, 26, 83, 109, 143, 168, 197, 199, 211

Allott	11	3	25	2
Watkinson	15.5	4	59	3
Austin	17	2	60	4
Fitton	13	3	57	1
Atherton	1	0	6	0

Lancashire 2nd Innings

G. Fowler	c Evans b Saxelby	25
G.D. Lloyd	c French b Stephenson	117
M.A. Atherton	c Martindale b Field-Buss	90
N.J. Speak	c French b Stephenson	7
T.E. Jesty	not out	59
M. Watkinson	not out	4
Extras	lb 7	7
Total (4 wkts)		309

51, 190, 204, 296

Stephenson	20	3	69	2
Saxelby	12	2	49	1
Afford	24	4	98	0
Evans	17	4	58	0
Field-Buss	9	1	28	1

Umpires: N.T. Plews and D.J. Constant

Toss: Nottinghamshire.

In this match fortunes ebbed and flowed in an unexpected manner. Notts fell to 18 for 3 on the first morning, but were rescued by Randall. The home side then gained a substantial first innings lead, but lost the advantage by careless batting in their second innings. A maiden century, in 3 hours, by Lloyd, brought victory for Lancashire with half an hour to spare.

v ESSEX (Trent Bridge)

July 29, 31, Aug 1

Won by 115 runs. Notts 24pts, Essex 6pts.

Nottinghamshire 1st Innings

B.C. Broad	c Stephenson b Pringle	53
P.R. Pollard	lbw b Topley	33
M. Newell	c Hardie b Topley	11
P. Johnson	c Pringle b Lever	25
D.W. Randall	lbw b Stephenson	76
*†B.N. French	c Lilley b Pringle	0
F.D. Stephenson	lbw b Topley	23
K.P. Evans	c Waugh b Pringle	26
K.E. Cooper	not out	33
K. Saxelby	b Topley b Waugh	19
J.A. Afford	lbw b Pringle	0
Extras	lb 2, w 1, nb 6	9
Total (94 ov)		308

61, 101, 107, 154, 161, 219, 239, 267, 307

Lever	22	4	72	1
Pringle	27	6	79	4
Topley	27	3	91	3
Childs	6	1	13	0
Stephenson	10	1	40	1
Waugh	2	0	11	1

Essex 1st Innings

B.R. Hardie	c Broad b Stephenson	0
J.P. Stephenson	b Saxelby	26
T.D. Topley	c Johnson b Stephenson	9
A.W. Lilley	c Johnson b Cooper	9
M.E. Waugh	b Stephenson	46
P.J. Prichard	c Newell b Stephenson	14
N. Hussain	b Stephenson	61
†M.A. Garnham	c Newell b Stephenson	33
*D.R. Pringle	c Broad b Evans	0
J.K. Lever	c Newell b Stephenson	3
J.H. Childs	not out	0
Extras	b 1, lb 8	9
Total (79.1 ov)		210

0, 17, 28, 68, 98, 127, 202, 207, 207

Stephenson	25.1	12	59	7
Cooper	21	5	59	1
Afford	4	2	6	0
Saxelby	16	4	46	1
Evans	13	4	31	1

Nottinghamshire 2nd Innings

B.C. Broad	c Waugh b Lever	0
P.R. Pollard	c Prichard b Pringle	0
M. Newell	lbw b Lever	0
P. Johnson	c Garnham b Lever	36
D.W. Randall	c and b Pringle	60
*†B.N. French	lbw b Topley	25
F.D. Stephenson	not out	22
K.P. Evans	not out	14
Extras	b 1, lb 3, nb 4	8
Total (6 wkts dec)		165

0, 0, 0, 50, 125, 126

Lever	17	2	65	3
Pringle	14	3	56	2
Topley	10	1	35	1
Waugh	1	0	5	0

Essex 2nd Innings

B.R. Hardie	c Evans b Stephenson	2
J.P. Stephenson	c Newell b Stephenson	29
A.W. Lilley	c French b Stephenson	10
M.E. Waugh	b Stephenson	26
P.J. Prichard	b Stephenson	12
N. Hussain	c Stephenson b Saxelby	37
†M.A. Garnham	c Evans b Stephenson	0
*D.R. Pringle	lbw b Cooper	9
T.D. Topley	c French b Stephenson	16
J.K. Lever	lbw b Stephenson	1
J.H. Childs	not out	2
Extras	lb 4	4
Total		148

10, 42, 51, 65, 92, 92, 116, 114, 146

Stephenson	18.5	5	47	8
Cooper	10	2	34	1
Saxelby	9	1	42	1
Evans	7	3	21	0

Umpires: R.Palmer and R.A. White

Toss: Essex.

After the middle order failed, Randall and the bowlers hit out to bring Notts full batting points and the first day ended with Essex 14–1. Stephenson demolished Essex on Monday, but in dreadful light Notts lost 3 wickets without scoring a run, then rain ended play. More bright batting from Randall enabled Notts to declare and Stephenson then took his match tally to 15 wickets, the best for Notts since 1954.

v DERBYSHIRE (Trent Bridge)

August 19, 21,

Won by 70 runs. Notts 21pts, Derbys 5pts

Nottinghamshire 1st Innings

B.C. Broad	c Maher b Sharma	57
P.R. Pollard	c Holding b Base	39
M. Newell	c and b Malcolm	12
*R.T. Robinson	c Maher b Base	0
D.W. Randall	lbw b Base	0
P. Johnson	b Sharma	5
F.D. Stephenson	c Barnett b Malcolm	30
†B.N. French	b Sharma	1
E.E. Hemmings	not out	8
K.E. Cooper	lbw b Sharma	21
R.A. Pick	b Base	1
Extras	lb 11	11
Total (56.5 ov)		185

87, 105, 105, 107, 114, 152, 155, 155, 184

Malcolm	12	2	50	2
Mortensen	10	2	29	0
Holding	9	0	31	0
Sharma	18	6	31	4
Base	7.5	1	33	4

Derbyshire 1st Innings

*K.J. Barnett	c French b Cooper	80
P.D. Bowler	c French b Stephenson	14
J.E. Morris	c Newell b Hemmings	1
R. Sharma	c Pollard b Hemmings	4
B. Roberts	b Stephenson	24
T.J.G. O'Gorman	c Pollard b Hemmings	2
†B.J.M. Maher	c Broad b Stephenson	3
M.A. Holding	b Stephenson	6
S.J. Base	c Johnson b Hemmings	17
O.H. Mortensen	not out	1
D.E. Malcolm	absent hurt	—
Extras	b 6, lb 6, nb 1	13
Total (47 ov)		165

58, 63, 93, 111, 129, 136, 143, 162, 165

Stephenson	15	2	59	4
Pick	4	0	21	0
Hemmings	19	6	57	4
Cooper	9	1	16	1

Nottinghamshire 2nd Innings

B.C. Broad	c sub b Holding	11
P.R. Pollard	b Mortensen	10
D.W. Randall	lbw b Mortensen	0
*R.T. Robinson	c Maher b Barnett	8
M. Newell	c and b Barnett	18
P. Johnson	lbw b Barnett	16
F.D. Stephenson	lbw b Barnett	2
†B.N. French	c Barnett b Mortensen	20
E.E. Hemmings	c sub b Mortensen	15
K.E. Cooper	lbw b Base	1
R.A. Pick	not out	1
Extras	b 1, lb 9, nb 2	12
Total		114

20, 21, 28, 36, 66, 74, 77, 104, 106

Holding	4.4	0	12	1
Mortensen	11.5	2	21	4
Sharma	8	0	18	0
Barnett	17.2	5	36	4
Roberts	4	0	8	0
Base	2	0	9	1

Derbyshire 2nd Innings

*K.J. Barnett	c Robinson b Stephenson	0
P.D. Bowler	b Stephenson	0
J.E. Morris	b Hemmings	24
R. Sharma	b Cooper	0
T.J.G. O'Gorman	c Robinson b Stephenson	7
B. Roberts	not out	18
†B.J.M. Maher	lbw b Hemmings	0
S.J. Base	st French b Hemmings	0
O.H. Mortensen	c Broad b Hemmings	11
D.E. Malcolm	c Pollard b Hemmings	1
M.A. Holding	refused to bat	0
Extras	lb 2, w 1	3
Total		64

0, 3, 4, 34, 34, 34, 36, 58, 64

Stephenson	15	5	23	3
Cooper	6	1	19	1
Hemmings	8.1	2	20	5

Umpires: B.J. Meyer and P.B. Wight
Toss: Nottinghamshire

The most controversial match of the season saw the first two innings completed on Saturday. On Monday after 40 minutes batting, Broad was dismissed by Holding, at which point one of the umpires left the field to telephone Lord's because in his opinion the pitch was unfit. After a two hour delay and the consent of both captains the match resumed on the Test Match pitch. Notts were fined 25 points for providing an unsuitable wicket.

v MIDDLESEX (Trent Bridge)

August 24, 25, 26, 28

Drawn. Middx 4pts, Notts 3pts

Nottinghamshire 1st Innings

B.C. Broad	c Gatting b Ellcock	144
P.R. Pollard	c Carr b Hughes	5
*R.T. Robinson	c Downton b Tufnell	26
P. Johnson	c Emburey b Tufnell	4
D.W. Randall	c Ramprakash b Ellcock	78
F.D. Stephenson	c and b Tufnell	1
†B.N. French	b Tufnell	9
E.E. Hemmings	c Ramprakash b Williams	9
K.E. Cooper	c Ramprakash b Ellcock	0
R.A. Pick	c Downton b Ellcock	0
J.A. Afford	not out	0
Extras	b 2, lb 16, w 1, nb 13	32
Total (100 ov: 288–6)		308

41, 81, 85, 245, 250, 284, 307, 307, 307

Ellcock	17	3	63	4
Williams	17.1	4	33	1
Hughes	15	4	42	1
Emburey	33	11	70	0
Tufnell	24	2	72	4
Gatting	1	0	10	0

Middlesex 1st Innings

J.D. Carr	c Johnson b Cooper	13
D.L. Haynes	not out	75
*M.W Gatting	b Cooper	83
M.R. Ramprakash	not out	26
K.R. Brown		
†P.R. Downton		
J.E. Emburey		
N.F. Williams		
S.P. Hughes		
R.M. Ellcock		
P.C.R. Tufnell		
Extras	b 1, lb 1, nb 5	7
Total (2 wkts dec, 66.1 ov)		204

43, 160

Stephenson	14	3	33	0
Cooper	24.1	3	81	2
Pick	16	3	66	0
Hemmings	9	2	20	0
Afford	3	1	2	0

Nottinghamshire 2nd Innings

P.R. Pollard	lbw b Hughes	1
B.C. Broad	c Emburey b Ellcock	5
*R.T. Robinson	st Downton b Tufnell	39
P. Johnson	c Downton b Hughes	9
D.W. Randall	st Downton b Tufnell	8
F.D. Stephenson	c Brown b Emburey	7
†B.N. French	not out	42
E.E. Hemmings	c Haynes b Ellcock	0
K.E. Cooper	c Gatting b Ellcock	0
R.A. Pick	lbw b Hughes	14
J.A. Afford	c Gatting b Ellcock	1
Extras	lb 5, w 1, nb 4	10
Total		136

6, 11, 29, 45, 60, 96, 97, 97, 127

Ellcock	13	3	23	4
Hughes	14	5	24	3
Emburey	13	3	29	1
Tufnell	22	7	55	2

Middlesex 2nd Innings

J.D. Carr	c Robinson b Cooper	27
D.L. Haynes	c Robinson b Afford	36
*M.W Gatting	b Afford	46
M.R. Ramprakash	lbw b Stephenson	1
K.R. Brown	not out	32
†P.R. Downton	st French b Hemmings	0
J.E. Emburey	c Broad b Hemmings	4
N.F. Williams	not out	4
Extras	lb 7, nb 3	10
Total (6 wkts)		160

35, 109, 116, 124, 125, 141

Stephenson	12	2	39	1
Cooper	8	1	33	1
Pick	4	0	26	0
Hemmings	4	0	10	2
Afford	11	3	45	2

Umpires: B. Dudleston and P.J. Eele
Toss: Nottinghamshire

Broad batted through the first day, being 141* out of 297–6 at the close. Pollard reached 1,000 runs for the season, at 20 the youngest Notts player to do so. Rain badly affected both Friday and Saturday's cricket. Gatting declared his first innings closed first thing on the last morning, but when the Notts batting collapsed, rather than hit up quick runs to set a target, the game headed for a draw. Gatting scored a fast 46 though in vain.

v LEICESTERSHIRE (Trent Bridge)

Sept 13, 14, 15, 16

Drawn. Leics 5pts, Notts 4pts

Nottinghamshire 1st Innings

B.C. Broad	c Whitaker b Benjamin	0
P.R. Pollard	c Benjamin b Lewis	10
*R.T. Robinson	c Whitticase b Benjamin	2
P. Johnson	b Benjamin	11
D.W. Randall	c Whitaker b Benjamin	22
F.D. Stephenson	c Whitaker b Benjamin	0
†C.W. Scott	lbw b Lewis	4
E.E. Hemmings	c Gidley b Benjamin	16
K.E. Cooper	c Potter b Lewis	8
R.A. Pick	c and b Lewis	15
J.A. Afford	not out	22
Extras	lb 10, nb 1	11
Total (33.4 ov)		121

0, 10, 16, 43, 43, 52, 72, 78, 83

Benjamin	17	5	42	6
Lewis	16.4	2	69	4

Leicestershire 1st Innings

*D.I. Gower	lbw b Stephenson	27
N.E. Briers	c Johnson b Stephenson	4
J.J. Whitaker	b Stephenson	15
P. Willey	b Stephenson	0
L. Potter	c Scott b Stephenson	19
J.D.R. Benson	lbw b Stephenson	31
C.C. Lewis	c Robinson c Cooper	3
†P. Whitticase	not out	46
W.K.M. Benjamin	b Stephenson	0
M. Gidley	b Cooper	15
L.B. Taylor	c Scott b Cooper	1
Extras	lb 2, nb 3	5
Total (55.1 ov)		166

15, 43, 46, 47, 96, 99, 101, 101, 150

Stephenson	19	2	65	7
Pick	11	0	65	0
Cooper	19.1	5	32	3
Hemmings	4	2	2	0
Afford	2	2	0	0

Nottinghamshire 2nd Innings

B.C. Broad	c and b Taylor	11
P.R. Pollard	c Benjamin b Taylor	18
*R.T. Robinson	lbw b Taylor	2
P. Johnson	c Whitaker b Benjamin	79
D.W. Randall	lbw b Benjamin	9
†C.W. Scott	lbw b Lewis	23
F.D. Stephenson	not out	72
E.E. Hemmings	c Potter b Lewis	14
K.E. Cooper	b Gidley	23
R.A. Pick	lbw b Willey	17
J.A. Afford	lbw b Lewis	0
Extras	lb 8, nb 2	10
Total		278

13, 21, 58, 81, 124, 160, 179, 227, 260

Benjamin	23	4	69	2
Lewis	21.4	6	80	3
Taylor	21	4	69	3
Willey	9	1	29	1
Gidley	8	0	23	1

Leicestershire 2nd Innings

L. Potter	not out	59
N.E. Briers	lbw b Stephenson	26
*D.I. Gower	c Scott b Hemmings	2
J.J. Whitaker	b Hemmings	6
P. Willey	c Johnson b Cooper	10
J.D.R. Benson	lbw b Cooper	7
C.C. Lewis	not out	0
Extras	b 5, lb 8, w 1, nb 1	15
Total (5 wkts)		125

65, 70, 96, 109, 125

Stephenson	15	5	29	1
Pick	5	1	17	0
Cooper	20	6	46	2
Hemmings	13	4	20	2

Umpires: J.W. Holder and R. Palmer
Toss: Leicestershire

On an overcast morning Notts were overwhelmed by Benjamin and Lewis, but Stephenson had his revenge and by the close of the first day Leicester were 96–4 off 38 overs. On a rain interrupted second day Leicester gained a first innings lead and Notts after a poor start made a recovery thanks to Johnson and Stephenson. Rain bit into Friday and on the last day Leicester needed 227 to win. Unfortunately the rain returned with the game poised very evenly.

Somerset

President: C.R.M. Atkinson
Chairman: J. Gardner
Chief Executive: P.W. Anderson, The County Ground, St James's Street, Taunton TA1 1JT. *Tel:* 0823 272946.
Coach: P.J. Robinson
Captain: (1989) V.J. Marks
Foundation of Present Club: August 1875 in Sidmouth
First First-Class Match: Somerset v Lancashire (Old Trafford) June 1882
County Champions: Nil (third in 1892, 1958, 1963, 1966, 1981)
Gillette/NatWest Trophy: Winners 1979, 1983
Benson & Hedges Cup: Winners 1981, 1982
Sunday League Champions: 1979
Refuge Cup: Nil

Summary of Results in 1989
Britannic Assurance County Championship: Played 22, Won 4, Lost 6, Drawn 12, Position 14th
NatWest Bank Trophy: Lost in second round
Benson & Hedges Cup: Lost in semi-final
Refuge Assurance Sunday League: Played 16, Won 7, Lost 8, Tied 1, Position 10th
Refuge Assurance Cup: Did not qualify

ONE DAY AWAY MATCHES

The full scorecard of each of Somerset's away matches will be found in the sections for the respective home teams.

Refuge Assurance League

Southampton: April 23
Somerset 220–8 (40 ov) (C.J. Tavare 120*) lost to Hants 221–5 (39.2 ov) by 5 wkts. Hants 4pts, Somerset 0pts.

Chelmsford: May 28
Essex 218–5 (40 ov) beat Somerset 171–7 (40 ov) by 47 runs. Essex 4pts, Somerset 0pts.

Trent Bridge: June 4
Notts 183–7 (40 ov) lost to Somerset 184–7 (40 ov) by 3 wkts. Somerset 4pts, Notts 0pts.

Derby: July 2
Somerset 155–6 (40 ov) lost to Derbys 161–5 (38.5 ov) by 5 wkts. Derbys 4pts, Somerset 0pts.

The Oval: July 9
Surrey 258–7 (40 ov) beat Somerset 137 (28.5 ov) on faster scoring rate. Surrey 4pts, Somerset 0pts.

Northampton: July 30
Northants 150 (39.1 ov) lost to Somerset 152–7 (37.5 ov) by 3 wkts. Somerset 4pts, Northants 0pts.

Edgbaston: August 13
Somerset 207–8 (40 ov) lost to Warwicks 187–7 (35.4 ov) on faster scoring rate. Warwicks 4pts, Somerset 0pts.

Worcester: August 20
Worcs 202–5 (40 ov) beat Somerset 190–7 (40 ov) by 12 runs. Worcs 4pts, Somerset 0pts.

Benson & Hedges Cup

Derby: April 25, 26
Derbys 141 (54.2 ov) lost to Somerset 142–3 (51.2 ov) by 7 wkts. Somerset 2pts, Derbys 0pts.

Headingley: May 9
Somerset 243–5 (55 ov) beat Yorks 181 (50.3) by 62 runs. Somerset 2pts, Yorks 0pts.

REFUGE ASSURANCE LEAGUE

v SUSSEX (Taunton)
May 7
Tied. Somerset 2pts, Sussex 2pts

Somerset		
S.J. Cook	c Smith b Pigott	0
P.M. Roebuck	lbw b Babington	52
R.J. Bartlett	run out	0
C.J. Tavare	c Pigott b Babington	19
R.J. Harden	c Clarke b Dodemaide	61
*V.J. Marks	c Parker b Pigott	28
G.D. Rose	run out	0
†N.D. Burns	run out	1
G.V. Palmer	not out	2
A.N. Jones	lbw b Pigott	0
D.J. Foster	not out	0
Extras	lb 13, w 3, nb 3	19
Total (9 wkts, 40 ov)		182

0, 1, 43, 105, 175, 175, 177, 180, 180

Pigott	8	1	41	3
Dodemaide	8	0	35	1
Babington	8	0	38	2
C.M. Wells	8	1	22	0
Clarke	8	0	33	0

Sussex		
*P.W.G. Parker	b Marks	32
D.M. Smith	b Marks	35
C.M. Wells	c Burns b Palmer	28
A.P. Wells	c Burns b Roebuck	20
I.J. Gould	not out	26
A.M. Green	c Cook b Roebuck	15
A.C.S. Pigott	b Jones	3
A.I.C. Dodemaide	run out	10
†P. Moores		
A.R. Clarke		
A.M. Babington		
Extras	lb 10, w 2, nb 1	13
Total (7 wkts, 40 ov)		182

58, 93, 117, 123, 165, 169, 182

Jones	7	0	43	1
Foster	5	1	20	0
Palmer	5	0	30	1
Rose	8	1	33	0
Marks	8	3	12	2
Roebuck	7	0	34	2

Umpires: J.C. Balderstone and N.T. Plews
Toss: Somerset
With ten runs needed off the final over bowled by Roebuck, Sussex scored five off the first four balls, then Dodemaide struck the fifth for three, but Gould could only manage a single from the final delivery. A rather dull game had an exciting finish.

v LANCASHIRE (Taunton)
May 21
Lost by 4 wkts. Lancs 4pts, Somerset 0pts

Somerset		
S.J. Cook	b Allott	123
P.M. Roebuck	b Wasim Akram	22
R.J. Bartlett	b Wasim Akram	26
C.J. Tavare	c Hegg b DeFreitas	13
R.J. Harden	c Jesty b Watkinson	15
*V.J. Marks	c Hughes b Simmons	5
†N.D. Burns	not out	12
G.D. Rose	run out	7
N.A. Mallender	not out	0
A.N. Jones		
D.J. Foster		
Extras	lb 9, w 10, nb 2	21
Total (7 wkts, 39 ov)		244

58, 157, 186, 211, 218, 229, 241

Allott	8	0	31	1
DeFreitas	8	0	56	1
Wasim Akram	7	1	32	2
Simmons	8	0	50	1
Watkinson	6	0	44	1
Jesty	2	0	22	0

Lancashire		
G. Fowler	run out	74
A.N. Hayhurst	b Rose	17
P.A.J. DeFreitas	c Roebuck b Rose	0
N.H. Fairbrother	run out	38
T.E. Jesty	st Burns b Marks	7
M. Watkinson	lbw b Mallender	57
Wasim Akram	not out	24
*D.P. Hughes	not out	11
†W.K. Hegg		
P.J.W. Allott		
J. Simmons		
Extras	b 2, lb 10, w 2, nb 3	17
Total (6 wkts, 38.2 ov)		245

56, 56, 118, 134, 189, 222

Jones	7.2	0	57	0
Mallender	8	0	28	1
Rose	8	1	43	2
Foster	7	0	58	0
Marks	8	0	47	1

Umpires: D.J. Constant and M.J. Kitchen
Toss: Lancashire
Watkinson hit four sixes and three fours in his 57 which was off 38 balls to bring victory to Lancashire. Cook reached 123 off 97 balls and was awarded his county cap.

From left, back: *D.J. Foster, N.J. Pringle, P. Rendell, R.J. Bartlett, A. Robinson.* Centre: *G. Townsend, G.V. Palmer, M.W. Cleal, A. Phillips, S.J. Cook, J.J.E. Hardy, P.J. Harden, P. Unwin.* Front: *N.D. Burns, C.J. Tavaré, P.M. Roebuck, J. Birkenshaw (Coach), R. Parsons (Chairman), V.J. Marks (Captain), A.N. Jones, G.D. Rose, T. Gard, P.J. Robinson (Coach).*

Allsport/Ben Radford

REFUGE ASSURANCE LEAGUE

v YORKSHIRE (Taunton)

June 11

Lost by 19 runs.

Yorkshire		
M.D. Moxon	lbw b Jones	2
A.A. Metcalfe	c Burns b Jones	0
R.J. Blakey	c Mallender b Rose	78
P.E. Robinson	c Tavare b Mallender	5
†D.L. Bairstow	c Bartlett b Rose	13
D. Byas	b Marks	19
S.N. Hartley	c Roebuck b Foster	5
*P. Carrick	c Cook b Jones	31
A. Sidebottom	not out	9
P.W. Jarvis	b Mallender	2
C.S. Pickles	not out	1
Extras	b 3, lb 10, w 1, nb 5	19
Total (9 wkts, 40 ov)		184

2, 7, 21, 42, 92, 122, 145, 178, 182

Jones	8	0	33	3
Mallender	8	0	28	2
Foster	8	0	36	1
Rose	8	2	36	2
Marks	8	0	38	1

Somerset		
S.J. Cook	st Bairstow b Carrick	30
P.M. Roebuck	c Sidebottom b Jarvis	3
R.J. Harden	run out	36
C.J. Tavare	c Robinson b Byas	11
R.J. Bartlett	b Jarvis	26
*V.J. Marks	b Jarvis	9
†N.D. Burns	b Pickles	6
G.D. Rose	not out	19
N.A. Mallender	b Jarvis	1
A.N. Jones	b Jarvis	2
D.J. Foster	b Jarvis	0
Extras	b 1, lb 16, w 3, nb 2	22
Total (38.4 ov)		165

10, 63, 92, 92, 116, 123, 159, 161, 165

Jarvis	7.4	1	27	6
Sidebottom	7	0	21	0
Pickles	8	0	41	1
Byas	8	1	25	1
Carrick	8	0	34	1

Umpires: M.J. Kitchen and D.S. Thompsett
Toss: Yorkshire

A good innings by Blakey provided Yorkshire with a reasonable total; in contrast none of the Somerset batsmen flourished and Jarvis made certain the tail had no sting, at the same time returning an impressive analysis.

v KENT (Bath)

June 18

Won by 80 runs. Somerset 4pts, Kent 0pts

Somerset		
S.J. Cook	c Marsh b Kelleher	2
P.M. Roebuck	c Marsh b Igglesden	14
C.J. Tavare	c Fleming b Davis	110
J.G. Wyatt	c Marsh b Fleming	40
R.J. Harden	c Kelleher b Davis	49
*V.J. Marks	c Hinks b Davis	5
A.N. Jones	st Marsh b Davis	6
G.V. Palmer	not out	9
H.R.J. Trump	lbw b Davis	0
N.A. Mallender	not out	3
†T. Gard		
Extras	b 1, lb 5, w 4, nb 1	11
Total (8 wkts, 40 ov)		249

8, 29, 98, 215, 230, 232, 242, 242

Igglesden	8	0	32	1
Kelleher	8	0	49	1
Penn	7	0	40	0
Fleming	2	0	12	1
Davis	8	0	52	5
C.S. Cowdrey	7	0	58	0

Kent		
S.G. Hinks	run out	9
M.R. Benson	c Tavare b Marks	45
R.F. Pienaar	b Mallender	6
T.R. Ward	c Palmer b Trump	3
*C.S. Cowdrey	c Roebuck b Trump	10
M.V. Fleming	b Jones	7
†S.A. Marsh	c and b Marks	40
C. Penn	lbw b Marks	18
D.J.M. Kelleher	c Tavare b Marks	4
R.P. Davis	b Roebuck	9
A.P. Igglesden	not out	0
Extras	lb 7, w 9, nb 2	18
Total (34.4 ov)		169

12, 35, 52, 70, 90, 91, 124, 130, 166

Jones	5	0	27	1
Mallender	5	0	12	1
Trump	8	0	23	2
Palmer	4	0	26	0
Marks	8	1	48	4
Roebuck	4.4	0	26	1

Umpires: D.R. Shepherd and A.G.T. Whitehead
Toss: Somerset

Tavare scored a century against his former colleagues and provided Somerset with a substantial total, Kent on the other hand slumped to 91–6 and only some half-hearted hitting by the tail produced a respectable total.

v GLOUCESTERSHIRE (Bath)

June 25

Won by 98 runs. Somerset 4pts, Gloucs 0pts

Somerset		
S.J. Cook	not out	124
R.J. Bartlett	c Wright b Jarvis	21
C.J. Tavare	c Jarvis b Bainbridge	20
J.G. Wyatt	c Jarvis b Pooley	6
R.J. Harden	b Greene	30
*V.J. Marks	c Alleyne b Bainbridge	11
†N.D. Burns	not out	4
H.R.J. Trump		
M.W. Cleal		
A.N. Jones		
D.J. Foster		
Extras	b 1, lb 8, w 1	10
Total (5 wkts, 40 ov)		226

45, 99, 124, 181, 198

Jarvis	8	0	38	1
Greene	8	0	27	1
Pooley	8	0	34	1
Bainbridge	8	1	57	2
Alleyne	2	0	25	0
Lloyds	6	0	36	0

Gloucestershire		
A.W. Stovold	c Marks b Foster	1
J.W. Lloyds	c Tavare b Jones	13
*C.W.J. Athey	c and b Foster	6
K.M. Curran	b Foster	3
P. Bainbridge	b Marks	21
A.J. Wright	lbw b Marks	17
M.W. Alleyne	c Burns b Jones	17
V.S. Greene	c Cook b Trump	13
M.W. Pooley	c Trump b Marks	8
†G.A. Tedstone	not out	5
K.B.S. Jarvis	b Foster	11
Extras	b 4, lb 8, w 1	13
Total (35.5 ov)		128

8, 24, 25, 30, 70, 77, 96, 112, 116

Jones	6	0	23	2
Foster	7.5	2	26	4
Cleal	6	1	16	0
Trump	8	0	27	1
Marks	8	1	24	3

Umpires: D.J. Constant and R. Palmer
Toss: Gloucestershire

Somerset took revenge for their Britannic defeat with a convincing victory due to Cook's 124 off 112 balls, but Gloucestershire's attack lacked both Walsh and Lawrence. The visitors began their reply badly when Foster took three cheap wickets and never recovered.

The season was dominated by the outstanding achievements of Jimmy Cook. Taking the place of Waugh, who was a member of the Australian touring side, and who had led the Somerset batting averages in 1988, Cook was the first batsman in England to reach both 1,000 and then 2,000 runs. A 36-year-old South African, he was an unknown quantity when he arrived in England but he soon hit the headlines. He made eight centuries and his feat of scoring two centuries in a match and carrying his bat through both innings has only been accomplished once before in first-class cricket.

Tavaré, the old Kent player, joined the county and was very reliable, though the selectors seemed to be clutching at straws when they reinstated him in the England team. Roebuck captained the England team to Holland with an embarrassing result, but he left the leadership of Somerset to Marks. As a batsman of the stubborn variety, Roebuck had another good year, as did Harden who in all first-class matches completed 1,000 runs. Hardy and Bartlett however did not prosper.

The bowling was the weak part of the eleven. Marks bowled 200 overs more than anyone else, but his wickets were obtained at a frightful cost, and the other off-break bowler, the young student, Trump, was just as expensive. The seam bowlers were less generous, but none of them put much fear into the leading opposition batsmen – the days of Garner and Botham are a memory. It would seem that Somerset cannot hope to win any crowns until the attack is bolstered, though it must be stated that both Mallender and Rose were hampered by injury. At the end of the summer, Marks announced his retirement and has taken up an appointment with the *Observer* newspaper.

Vic Marks captained Somerset in 1989, but retired at the end of the season for journalism.

Allsport/Jon Nicholson

REFUGE ASSURANCE LEAGUE

v GLAMORGAN (Taunton)

July 16

Won by 81 runs. Somerset 4pts, Glamorgan 0pts

Somerset		
S.J. Cook	b Butcher	114
P.M. Roebuck	not out	63
C.J. Tavare	st Metson b Somaia	9
J.G. Wyatt	b Dale	11
R.J. Harden	b Dennis	4
*V.J. Marks	c Holmes b Dennis	18
M.W. Cleal	not out	8
A.N. Jones	not out	0
†N.D. Burns		
H.R.J. Trump		
D.J. Foster		
Extras	lb 13, w 7, nb 2	22
Total (6 wkts, 40 ov)		249

176, 194, 211, 217, 232, 245

Watkins	8	2	27	0
Dennis	8	0	32	2
Somaia	8	0	52	1
Smith	5	0	49	0
Dale	6	0	45	2
Butcher	5	0	31	1

Glamorgan		
A.R. Butcher	c Roebuck b Trump	35
*H. Morris	b Jones	0
M.P. Maynard	c Cook b Jones	15
G.C. Holmes	c Cook b Trump	17
P.A. Cottey	lbw b Marks	15
I. Smith	b Marks	16
A. Dale	not out	9
†C.P. Metson	st Burns b Marks	6
K.A. Somaia	c Harden b Marks	0
S.L. Watkin	not out	28
S.J. Dennis		
Extras	b 4, lb 10, w 8, nb 5	27
Total (8 wkts, 40 ov)		168

2, 27, 69, 81, 111, 116, 122, 122

Jones	5	2	11	2
Foster	8	2	40	0
Trump	8	0	27	2
Cleal	7	1	35	0
Marks	8	1	27	4
Roebuck	4	0	14	0

Umpires: J.H. Harris and A.A. Jones
Toss: Somerset
Cook and Roebuck established a new Sunday League record for the county by scoring 176 for the 1st wicket. From then Glamorgan stood little chance of gaining control of the match.

v LEICESTERSHIRE (Taunton)

July 23

Won by 7 wkts. Somerset 4pts, Leics 0pts

Leicestershire		
L. Potter	c Burns b Jones	0
N.E. Briers	c Bartlett b Marks	45
J.J. Whitaker	b Trump	50
*D.I. Gower	b Rose	14
C.C. Lewis	run out	17
†P. Whitticase	c Roebuck b Rose	22
G.J. Parsons	st Burns b Roebuck	20
J.P. Agnew	run out	2
G.J.F. Ferris	not out	1
L.B. Taylor	st Burns b Roebuck	0
P.M. Such	b Roebuck	0
Extras	lb 5, w 7	12
Total (40 ov)		183

0, 91, 116, 118, 139, 179, 181, 183, 183

Jones	7	0	40	1
Rose	7	1	27	2
Trump	8	1	33	1
Cleal	4	0	16	0
Marks	8	0	36	1
Roebuck	6	0	26	3

Somerset		
S.J. Cook	b Taylor	37
P.M. Roebuck	retired hurt	40
C.J. Tavare	b Taylor	0
R.J. Bartlett	c Parsons b Agnew	36
R.J. Harden	not out	49
*V.J. Marks	not out	5
†N.D. Burns		
G.D. Rose		
M.W. Cleal		
H.R.J. Trump		
A.N. Jones		
Extras	lb 10, w 7, nb 2	19
Total (3 wkts, 36.2 ov)		186

80, 80, 161

Agnew	8	0	35	1
Ferris	7	0	38	0
Taylor	6	0	18	2
Parsons	8	0	52	0
Such	7	1	29	0
Potter	0.2	0	4	0

Umpires: H.D. Bird and J.H Hampshire
Toss: Leicestershire
Although Briers and Whitaker added 91 for the second wicket, the visiting batsmen afterwards failed to capitalise. Roebuck unfortunately injured his hand and was unable to play in the following days.

v MIDDLESEX (Weston-super-Mare)

August 6

Won by 97 runs. Somerset 4pts, Middx 0pts

Somerset		
S.J. Cook	b Cowans	16
P.M. Roebuck	b Ellcock	0
R.J. Bartlett	c Downton b Ellcock	47
C.J. Tavare	c Hutchinson b Hughes	65
R.J. Harden	c Ellcock b Fraser	17
G.D. Rose	c Hutchinson b Hughes	14
*V.J. Marks	b Hughes	6
†N.D. Burns	not out	8
N.A. Mallender	c Ellcock b Hughes	1
A.N. Jones	not out	4
H.R.J. Trump		
Extras	lb 14, w 10, nb 3	27
Total (8 wkts, 40 ov)		205

2, 36, 113, 170, 180, 192, 192, 200

Cowans	8	0	17	1
Ellcock	8	0	39	2
Hughes	8	0	50	3
Fraser	8	0	38	2
Emburey	8	0	47	0

Middlesex		
J.D. Carr	c Burns b Rose	2
D.L. Haynes	b Jones	7
M.A. Roseberry	b Trump	34
I.J.F. Hutchinson	c Burns b Jones	0
*M.W. Gatting	c Cook b Rose	0
†P.R. Downton	c Burns b Trump	6
J.E. Emburey	b Marks	17
S.P. Hughes	lbw b Marks	8
A.R.C. Fraser	c Rose b Mallender	10
R.M. Ellcock	b Marks	13
N.G. Cowans	not out	1
Extras	lb 8, nb 2	10
Total (32.2 ov)		108

9, 9, 9, 16, 27, 56, 80, 82, 104

Jones	5	3	8	2
Rose	5	1	9	2
Mallender	7	0	17	1
Trump	8	1	31	2
Marks	7.2	0	35	3

Umpires: B. Dudleston and A.A. Jones
Toss: Middlesex
Tavare hit 65 off 71 balls and none of the visiting batsmen could match this performance, so Somerset won their fourth consecutive Sunday game and thus challenged for a place in the Refuge Cup.

PLAYERS

Jonathon Colin Mark ATKINSON *b* 10.7.1968 Butleigh; right-hand batsman; right-arm medium-fast bowler; debut 1985; Cambridge Univ 1988 and 1989; son of C.R.M (ex-Somerset)
Richard James BARTLETT *b* 8.10.1966 Ash Priors; right-hand batsman; debut 1986; scored 100 runs in debut match
Neil David BURNS *b* 19.9.1965 Chelmsford; wicketkeeper; left-hand batsman; debut 1987; previously appeated for Essex 1986
Matthew William CLEAL *b* 23.7.1969 Yeovil; right-hand batsman; right-arm medium-fast bowler; debut 1988
Stephen James (Jimmy) COOK *b* 31.7.1953 Johannesburg; opening right-hand batsman; debut 1989; when he had an astonishing first season in English cricket; being the first batsman to reach 1,000 and 2,000 runs; also plays for Transvaal; appeared for South Africa in every 'unofficial' Test since 1981
Daren Joseph FOSTER *b* 14.3.1966 Tottenham, N London; right-hand batsman; right-arm fast-medium bowler; debut 1986
Trevor GARD *b* 2.6.1957 West Lambrook; wicketkeeper; right-hand batsman; debut 1976
Richard John HARDEN *b* 16.8.1965 Bridgewater; right-hand batsman; left-arm medium pace bowler; debut 1985
Jonathan James Ean HARDY *b* 2.10.1960 Nakaru, Kenya; debut 1986; previously played for Hants 1984–85
Adrian Nicholas JONES *b* 22.7.1961 Woking; right-arm fats medium bowler; left-hand batsman; debut 1987; previously appeared for Sussex 1981–86
Neil Alan MALLENDER *b* 13.8.1961 Kirk Sandall, Yorks; right-arm fast-medium bowler; right-hand batsman; debut 1987; previously appeared for Northants 1980–86; also plays for Otago

Victor James MARKS *b* 25.6.1955 Middle Chinnock; off-break bowler; right-hand batsman; debut 1975; Oxford Univ 1975–78; captained county 1988–89; six Tests for England 1982–84; in the Middlesex match of August 1989; Marks bowled both right and left-arm
Gary Vincent PALMER *b* 1.11.1965 Taunton; right-arm medium-fast bowler; right-hand batsman; debut 1982; only played in one-day matches in 1989
Nicholas John PRINGLE *b* 20.9.1966; right-hand batsman; right-arm medium pace bowler; debut 1986
Peter Nicholas ROEBUCK *b* 6.3.1956 Oxford; sound right-hand batsman; debut 1974; captain 1986–88; Cambridge Univ 1975–77; brother of P.G.P. (ex-Glam)
Graham David ROSE *b* 12.4.1964 Tottenham, N London; right-hand batsman; debut 1987; previously with Middx 1985–96
Timothy John Adam SCRIVEN *b* 15.12.1965 High Wycombe; right-hand batsman; slow left arm bowler; debut 1988
Christopher James TAVARE *b* 27.10.1954 Orpington; sounds right-hand batsman; debut 1989; previously appeared for Kent 1984–88; Oxford Univ 1975–77; 31 Tests for England including one in 1989
Harvey Russell John TRUMP *b* 11.10.1968 Taunton; right-hand batsman; off-break bowler; debut 1988
Paul David UNWIN *b* 9.6.1967 Waipawa, NZ; off-break bowler; right-hand batsman; Somerset debut v Australians in May 1989; also plays for Central Districts
Julian George WYATT *b* 19.6.1963 Paulton; right-hand batsman; debut 1983

Graham Rose, top of Somerset's bowling in 1989, apart from Peter Unwin, who played in one match.
Allsport/Adrian Murrell

BENSON AND HEDGES CUP

v MINOR COUNTIES (Taunton)
May 2
Won by 35 runs. Somerset 2pts, Minor Counties 0pts

Somerset		
S.J. Cook	b Taylor	55
P.M. Roebuck	b Wingfield-Digby	10
J.J.E. Hardy	st Priestley b Evans	7
C.J. Tavare	b Plumb	78
R.J. Bartlett	c Priestley b Taylor	11
*V.J. Marks	c Folland b Taylor	13
†N.D. Burns	b Plumb	8
G.D. Rose	not out	7
N.A. Mallender	not out	1
A.N. Jones		
D.J. Foster		
Extras	b 9, lb 6	15
Total (7 wkts, 55 ov)		205

32, 45, 115, 159, 186, 196, 200

Taylor	11	2	38	3
Wingfield-Digby	11	3	22	1
Conn	8	1	32	0
Evans	11	2	26	1
Greensword	6	1	24	0
Plumb	8	0	48	2

Minor Counties		
G.K. Brown	c Mallender b Marks	34
C.J. Stockdale	c Burns b Mallender	1
†N. Priestley	run out	32
N.A. Folland	c Burns b Jones	25
P.R. Oliver	c Tavare b Foster	24
*S.G. Plumb	b Jones	15
S. Greensword	not out	13
R.A. Evans	not out	13
I.E. Conn		
N.R. Taylor		
A.R. Wingfield-Digby		
Extras	lb 5, w 5, nb 3	13
Total (6 wkts, 55 ov)		170

4, 50, 92, 111, 134, 149

Mallender	11	2	22	1
Jones	11	4	33	2
Rose	11	1	35	0
Foster	11	3	51	1
Marks	11	3	24	1

Umpires: B. Hassan and R. Julian
Toss: Minor Counties. Gold: C.J. Tavare
The Minors did well to restrict Somerset to 205, but only Priestley in the visitors' innings looked like scoring at the required run rate and he was unfortunately run out.

v NOTTINGHAMSHIRE (Taunton)
May 13
Won by 7 wkts. Somerset 2pts, Notts 0pts

Nottingham		
B.C. Broad	c Tavare b Jones	78
P.R. Pollard	run out	4
M. Newell	c Burns b Mallender	39
F.D. Stephenson	lbw b Marks	3
*R.T. Robinson	c Rose b Jones	30
D.W. Randall	c Rose b Jones	18
†B.N. French	c Tavare b Jones	13
E.E. Hemmings	c and b Mallender	0
K.E. Cooper	c Burns b Jones	1
R.A. Pick	not out	2
J.A. Afford	not out	1
Extras	lb 9, w 2, nb 2	13
Total (9 wkts, 55 ov)		202

33, 115, 120, 156, 171, 193, 193, 199, 199

Jones	11	1	53	5
Mallender	11	2	36	2
Rose	11	1	43	0
Foster	11	1	27	0
Marks	11	1	34	1

Somerset		
S.J. Cook	b Pick	79
P.M. Roebuck	c Robinson b Hemmings	11
R.J. Bartlett	b Afford	10
C.J. Tavare	not out	59
R.J. Harden	not out	17
*V.J. Marks		
†N.D. Burns		
G.D. Rose		
N.A. Mallender		
A.N. Jones		
D.J. Foster		
Extras	b 16, w 4, nb 7	27
Total (3 wkts, 52.2 ov)		203

51, 85, 151

Stephenson	11	2	35	0
Pick	10	1	46	1
Cooper	9.2	0	43	0
Afford	11	1	32	1
Hemmings	11	2	31	1

Umpires: J.D. Bond and P.B. Wight
Toss: Nottinghamshire. Gold: A.N. Jones
Broad held the Notts batting together, making 78 off 152 balls, but the visitors never really got into their stride and good innings by Cook and Tavare made certain Somerset ended with four victories out of four matches.

v COMBINED UNIVERSITIES (Taunton)
May 31
Won by 3 runs.

Somerset		
S.J. Cook	lbw b Atherton	61
P.M. Roebuck	b Atherton	102
C.J. Tavare	c and b Tolley	23
R.J. Bartlett	st Speight b Atherton	36
R.J. Harden	c Hansford b Atherton	7
*V.J. Marks	not out	13
†N.D. Burns	run out	6
G.D. Rose		
N.A. Mallender		
A.N. Jones		
D.J. Foster		
Extras	lb 3, w 1	4
Total (6 wkts, 55 ov)		252

109, 165, 208, 222, 245, 252

Hansford	11	0	50	0
Tolley	9	1	40	1
Boiling	11	2	28	0
Crawley	8	0	43	0
Dale	7	0	46	0
Atherton	9	0	42	4

Combined Universities		
M.A. Crawley	run out	13
T.J. O'Gorman	c Harden b Mallender	9
*M.A. Atherton	c Jones b Marks	26
N. Hussain	c Bartlett b Roebuck	118
†M.P. Speight	st Burns b Marks	12
J.I. Longley	c Roebuck b Jones	49
J.C.M. Atkinson	c Burns b Jones	1
A. Dale	run out	0
C.M. Tolley	st Burns b Roebuck	6
A.R. Hansford	not out	1
J. Boiling	not out	2
Extras	b 2, lb 6, w 2, nb 2	12
Total (9 wkts, 55 ov)		249

17, 78, 109, 223, 225, 226, 244, 245, 246

Mallender	11	1	56	1
Jones	11	1	36	2
Foster	7	1	28	0
Rose	11	1	50	0
Marks	11	0	52	2
Roebuck	4	0	19	2

Umpires: R. Julian and B. Dudleston
Toss: Combined University. Gold: N. Hussain
Having surprised the cricket public by obtaining a place in the quarter finals, the students came very close to beating Somerset. Hussain hit 118 off 145 balls. The Universities required nine off the final over.

BRITANNIC ASSURANCE COUNTY CHAMPIONSHIP AVERAGES 1989

Batting	*M*	*I*	*NO*	*Runs*	*HS*	*Avge*	*100*	*50*
S.J. Cook	22	39	4	2173	156	62.09	8	7
V.J. Marks	20	32	12	822	89*	41.10	–	4
P.M. Roebuck	21	35	2	1286	149	38.97	4	6
C.J. Tavaré	20	36	2	1292	153	38.00	1	9
R.J. Harden	19	32	5	920	115*	34.07	3	2
N.D. Burns	20	30	5	733	90	29.32	–	4
J.C.M. Atkinson	4	7	–	184	53	26.29	–	1
J.J.E. Hardy	13	23	4	435	65	22.89	–	2
G.D. Rose	15	19	7	258	50*	21.50	–	1
N.A. Mallender	17	17	4	186	48*	14.31	–	–
A.N. Jones	22	22	10	171	43*	14.25	–	–
R.J. Bartlett	10	17	–	210	54	12.35	–	1
J.G. Wyatt	3	4	–	46	23	11.50	–	–
M.W. Cleal	6	7	–	68	30	9.71	–	–
H.R.J. Trump	14	15	2	94	31*	7.23	–	–
N.J. Pringle	5	9	1	50	12*	6.25	–	–
D.J. Foster	8	7	1	23	11*	3.83	–	–

Also batted: T. Gard (2 matches) 0, 40. T.J.A. Scriven played in one match but did not bat.

Bowling	*O*	*M*	*R*	*W*	*Avge*	*BB*	*5i*	*10m*
G.D. Rose	396.2	98	1080	46	23.48	4-12	–	–
N.A. Mallender	488.5	115	1309	48	27.27	7-62	3	1
A.N. Jones	577.2	116	1916	69	27.77	6-37	2	–
H.R.J. Trump	416	93	1125	25	45.00	4-80	–	–
P.M. Roebuck	130	33	305	10	30.50	2-22	–	–
V.J. Marks	843.5	246	2252	47	47.91	5-38	1	–
M.W. Cleal	95.4	19	327	6	54.50	2-40	–	–
D.J. Foster	159	19	581	8	72.63	2-43	–	–

Also bowled: J.C.M. Atkinson 13-3-46-0; R.J. Harden 23.3-4-89-0; J.J.E. Hardy 1.4-0-6-0; N.J. Pringle 26-2-122-0; T.J.A. Scriven 43.1-8-155-4.

Centuries

8 S.J. Cook: 156 v Lancs (Taunton); 147* v Essex (Chelmsford); 147 v Glos (Bath); 105 v Surrey (Guildford); 120* & 131* v Notts (Trent Bridge); 148 v Leics (Taunton); 130 v Sussex (Hove).

4 P.M. Roebuck: 149 v Hants (Southampton); 103 v Yorks (Taunton); 107 v Kent (Bath); 117 v Glos (Bristol).

3 R.J. Harden: 101* v Essex (Chelmsford); 102* v Kent (Bath); 115* v Northants (Luton).

1 C.J. Tavaré: 153 v Lancs (Taunton).

BENSON AND HEDGES CUP

Semi-Final v ESSEX (Taunton)

June 14

Lost by 4 runs.

Essex		
*G.A. Gooch	lbw b Jones	20
B.R. Hardie	b Roebuck	41
A.W. Lilley	b Roebuck	43
M.E. Waugh	c Roebuck b Mallender	36
P.J. Prichard	not out	73
J.P. Stephenson	c Mallender b Jones	31
D.R. Pringle	not out	15
†M.A. Garnham		
N.A. Foster		
J.K. Lever		
J.H. Childs		
Extras	b 2, lb 20, w 10, nb 2	34
Total (5 wkts, 55 ov)		293

23, 105, 130, 184, 271

Mallender	11	0	73	1
Jones	9	1	56	2
Foster	8	1	42	0
Rose	5	1	25	0
Marks	11	2	33	0
Roebuck	11	2	42	2

Somerset		
S.J. Cook	b Gooch	28
P.M. Roebuck	c and b Childs	53
C.J. Tavare	not out	104
†N.D. Burns	b Childs	5
R.J. Bartlett	c Lever b Gooch	15
R.J. Harden	c Garnham b Pringle	13
*V.J. Marks	c Hardie b Foster	15
G.D Rose	b Foster	4
N.A. Mallender	lbw b Foster	1
A.N. Jones	run out	25
D.J. Foster	b Lever	0
Extras	lb 18, w 8	26
Total (55 overs)		289

87, 91, 97, 138, 170, 214, 231, 233, 288

Foster	11	1	56	3
Pringle	11	0	58	1
Lever	11	1	55	1
Gooch	11	0	56	2
Childs	11	0	46	2

Umpires: D.J. Constant and K.J. Lyons
Toss: Essex. Gold: C.J. Tavare
Good batting by the Essex players produced a large total, with Prichard and Stephenson really accelerating in the last few overs. Their partnership of 87 came in 9 overs. Tavare replied in splendid fashion. Ten runs were needed off the last over and six off the last ball, which demolished Foster's wicket.

NATWEST BANK TROPHY

v ESSEX (Taunton)

June 29

Won by 55 runs.

Somerset		
S.J. Cook	c Pringle b Foster	1
P.M. Roebuck	run out	102
J.J.E. Hardy	c Prichard b Foster	1
C.J. Tavare	st Garnham b Miller	101
R.J. Harden	c Garnham b Gooch	0
*V.J. Marks	not out	36
A.N. Jones	c Hardy b Pringle	7
M.W. Cleal	not out	3
†N.D. Burns		
H.R.J. Trump		
D.J. Foster		
Extras	b 1, lb 14, w 8, nb 2	25
Total (6 wkts, 60 ov)		276

3, 14, 209, 210, 246, 262

Lever	12	1	42	0
Foster	12	1	50	2
Pringle	12	1	53	1
Gooch	11	1	42	1
Stephenson	4	1	22	0
Miller	9	0	52	1

Essex		
*G.A. Gooch	c Jones b Marks	94
B.R. Hardie	c Marks b Jones	7
M.E. Waugh	c Cook b Jones	0
P.J. Prichard	c Hardy b Cleal	17
N. Hussain	lbw b Marks	24
J.P. Stephenson	c Harden b Roebuck	6
D.R. Pringle	c Trump b Marks	4
G. Miller	st Burns b Trump	15
M.A. Garnham	c Burns b Trump	18
N.A. Foster	lbw b Jones	7
J.K. Lever	not out	3
Extras	b 5, lb 9, w 10, nb 2	26
Total (54.5 ov)		221

21, 24, 84, 130, 162, 168, 176, 210, 210

Jones	9.5	1	32	3
Foster	7	0	17	0
Cleal	8	0	42	1
Trump	12	0	44	2
Marks	12	0	38	3
Roebuck	6	0	34	1

Umpires: D.G.L. Evans and D.J. Halfyard
Toss: Essex. MofM P.M. Roebuck
Somerset caused a major upset by defeating Essex, who had had a remarkable run of success in 1989. On the first day only 40 minutes play took place with Somerset 24–2, but Roebuck and Tavare added 195 for the 3rd wicket. The Essex reply folded when Gooch was dismissed.

v NORTHAMPTONSHIRE (Taunton)

July 12

Lost by 5 wkts.

Somerset		
S.J. Cook	c Ripley b Capel	33
P.M. Roebuck	c N.G.B. Cook b Robinson	18
J.G. Wyatt	lbw b Thomas	9
C.J. Tavare	not out	79
R.J. Harden	c G. Cook b Capel	14
*V.J. Marks	c Larkins b Thomas	19
†N.D. Burns	c Ripley b Thomas	3
M.W. Cleal	c Bailey b Robinson	25
A.N. Jones	b Robinson	2
H.R.J. Trump	c Ripley b Ambrose	0
D.J. Foster	lbw b Robinson	0
Extras	lb 1, w 6, nb 1	8
Total (55.4 ov)		210

40, 59, 63, 98, 141, 150, 203, 205, 209

Ambrose	10	0	36	1
Thomas	10	0	36	3
Robinson	11.4	2	32	4
Capel	12	1	52	2
N.G.B. Cook	12	1	53	0

Northamptonshire		
G. Cook	c Tavare b Jones	4
W. Larkins	c and b Foster	19
N.A. Felton	c Burns b Roebuck	41
R.J. Bailey	not out	86
*A.J. Lamb	lbw b Marks	4
D.J. Capel	c Cook b Cleal	31
†D. Ripley	not out	21
J.G. Thomas		
N.G.B. Cook		
C.E.L. Ambrose		
M.A. Robinson		
Extras	lb 2, w 2, nb 1	5
Total (5 wkts, 57 ov)		211

4, 29, 120, 175, 177

Jones	12	1	62	1
Foster	8	3	15	1
Trump	9	0	29	0
Cleal	12	0	44	1
Marks	12	1	38	1
Roebuck	4	0	21	1

Umpires: J.C. Balderstone and R. Julian
Toss: Somerset. MofM: R.J. Bailey
With Cook, for once, failing, Somerset were held together by Tavare, but Bailey later outscored him, taking Northants to a comfortable win.

Away Matches

The full scorecard of each of Somerset's away matches will be found in the sections for the respective home teams.

Southampton: April 20, 21, 22, 24
Somerset 413 (P.M. Roebuck 149, M.C.J. Nicholas 6–37) and 71–1 drew with Hants 318 (R.A. Smith 127). Somerset 6pts, Hants 4pts.

Chelmsford: May 27, 29, 30
Essex 327–8d (J.P. Stephenson 102) and 217–3d drew with Somerset 280–3d (S.J. Cook 147*, R.J. Harden 101*) and 116–4. Somerset 5pts, Essex 4pts.

Cardiff: June 7, 8, 9
Somerset 330–8d and 2nd inns forfeited drew with Glamorgan 1st inns forfeited and 277–9 (M.J. Cann 109). Glamorgan 3pts, Somerset 3pts.

Luton: June 24, 26, 27
Somerset 274 (N.G.B. Cook 5–28) and 346–7d (R.J. Harden 115*) beat Northants 300–5d (G. Cook 126) and 308 (R.J. Bailey 100) by 12 runs. Somerset 21pts, Northants 8pts.

Derby: July 1, 3, 4
Derbys 444–9d (K.J. Barnett 118, J.E. Morris 127) and 87–2d drew with Somerset 231–5d and 240–7. Derbys 6pts, Somerset 2pts.

Guildford: July 8, 10, 11
Surrey 177 (A.N. Jones 5–62) and 143–6 drew with Somerset 297 (S.J. Cook 105). Somerset 6pts, Surrey 3pts.

Trent Bridge: July 19, 21, 22
Somerset 186 (S.J. Cook 120*) and 218 (S.J. Cook 131*, J.A. Afford 5–90) lost to Notts 471–7d (R.T. Robinson 128) by an inns and 67 runs. Notts 24pts, Somerset 2pts. Cook carried his bat through both completed innings.

Hove: July 26, 27, 28
Sussex 316–9d (P.W.G. Parker 110) and 245–4d (P. Moores 116) drew with Somerset 266–7d and 292–6 (S.J. Cook 130). Somerset 7pts, Sussex 6pts.

Edgbaston: August 12, 14, 15
Somerset 316–8d and 170–7d drew with Warwicks 250–7d and 107–3. Warwicks 6pts, Somerset 6pts.

Worcester: August 24, 25, 26, 27
Somerset 338 and 161–6d lost to Worcs 200–5d and 302–5 (G.A. Hick 136*) by 5 wkts. Worcs 20pts, Somerset 4pts.

Bristol: Sept 8, 9, 10, 11
Gloucs 259 and 310–7d (K.M. Curran 128) beat Somerset 165 and 263 (P.M. Roebuck 117) by 141 runs. Gloucs 23pts, Somerset 5pts.

v GLAMORGAN (Taunton)

April 28, 29, 30, May 1
Drawn. Somerset 5pts, Glamorgan 4pts

Glamorgan 1st Innings

A.R. Butcher	c Hardy b Rose	14
*H. Morris	c Roebuck b Rose	7
P.A. Cottey	c Hardy b Marks	8
M.P. Maynard	c Cook b Rose	5
M.J. Cann	c Hardy b Marks	13
I. Smith	lbw b Marks	3
J. Derrick	b Rose	1
†C.P. Metson	c Tavare b Marks	29
P.D. North	c Jones b Marks	17
S.L. Watkin	b Mallender	4
S.R. Barwick	not out	10
Extras	b 1, lb 4, nb 2	7
Total (70.2 ov)		118

20, 25, 37, 37, 47, 48, 68, 99, 104

Jones	13	4	27	0
Mallender	16	5	36	1
Rose	14	8	12	4
Marks	27.2	13	38	5

Somerset 1st Innings

S.J. Cook	lbw b Cann	42
P.M. Roebuck	c Maynard b Watkin	19
J.J. E. Hardy	lbw b Barwick	51
C.J. Tavare	c Metson b Barwick	5
R.J. Bartlett	c Derrick b Barwick	18
†N.D. Burns	lbw b Watkin	12
*V.J. Marks	c Derrick b Barwick	1
G.D. Rose	lbw b Barwick	13
N.A. Mallender	b Barwick	6
A.N. Jones	not out	6
D.J. Foster	c Cann b Barwick	0
Extras	b 8, lb 4, nb 1	13
Total (93.1 ov)		186

26, 110, 116, 127, 146, 154, 154, 166, 177

Watkin	29	2	50	2
Barwick	25.1	16	47	7
Derrick	5	0	24	0
North	17	5	29	0
Smith	5	3	12	0
Cann	11	6	12	1

Glamorgan 2nd Innings

A.R. Butcher	c Hardy b Rose	10
*H. Morris	c Tavare b Roebuck	96
P.A. Cottey	b Rose	10
M.P. Maynard	st Burns b Marks	22
I. Smith	c Tavare b Mallender	1
M.J. Cann	b Rose	65
J. Derrick	c Bartlett b Jones	22
†C.P. Metson	c Marks b Rose	16
P.D. North	c Mallender b Roebuck	0
S.L. Watkin	not out	2
Extras	b 5, lb 9, w 1, nb 1	16
Total (9 wkts dec)		260

23, 39, 86, 87, 185, 228, 251, 254, 260

Jones	18	4	33	1
Mallender	19	9	31	1
Marks	55	24	96	1
Rose	26.2	9	46	4
Foster	6	0	18	0
Roebuck	14	7	22	2

Somerset 2nd Innings

S.J. Cook	lbw b North	79
P.M. Roebuck	c Morris b North	12
J.J.E. Hardy	b Barwick	0
C.J. Tavare	c Metson b Barwick	22
R.J. Bartlett	b North	0
†N.D. Burns	c Derrick b Barwick	17
*V.J. Marks	not out	11
G.D. Rose	not out	5
Extras	lb 5, nb 1	6
Total (6 wkts)		152

45, 46, 92, 93, 136, 136

Watkin	7	0	29	0
Barwick	31	16	40	3
North	18.3	4	54	3
Cann	1	0	4	0
Derrick	5	1	20	0
Butcher	1	1	0	0

Umpires: B. Hassan and R. Julian
Toss: Glamorgan
Good spin bowling by Marks dismissed Glamorgan for 118 on the opening day and Somerset ended at 85–1. Barwick retaliated on the second day and Somerset's lead was restricted to 87. The Welsh county had wiped off the deficit by the close for the loss of 2 wickets. 96 by Morris put Glamorgan 120 ahead with five wickets in hand. On the last day Somerset were set 193 in 56 overs but only Cook responded.

v SUSSEX (Taunton)

May 4, 5, 6, 8
Won by 5 wkts. Somerset 22pts, Sussex 6pts

Sussex 1st Innings

A.M. Green	c Roebuck b Mallender	5
D.M. Smith	c and b Jones	14
*P.W.G. Parker	c Tavare b Mallender	1
A.P. Wells	c Tavare b Mallender	48
I.J. Gould	c and b Foster	84
C.M. Wells	lbw b Mallender	9
A.I.C. Dodemaide	c Burns b Jones	32
†P. Moores	c Tavare b Foster	6
A.C.S. Pigott	c Tavare b Jones	2
A.R. Clarke	b Mallender	13
A.M. Babington	not out	1
Extras	b 2, lb 6, nb 11	19
Total (84.2 ov)		234

16, 20, 21, 121, 137, 203, 209, 216, 220

Jones	17	3	51	3
Mallender	16.2	6	30	5
Rose	16	4	40	0
Foster	17	2	57	2
Marks	15	2	44	0
Roebuck	3	0	4	0

Somerset 1st Innings

S.J. Cook	lbw b Pigott	91
P.M. Roebuck	b Pigott	18
J.J.E. Hardy	lbw b C.M. Wells	12
C.J. Tavare	run out	3
R.J. Bartlett	b Dodemaide	0
†N.D. Burns	b Dodemaide	4
*V.J. Marks	not out	59
G.D. Rose	c Gould b Clarke	14
N.A. Mallender	run out	7
A.N. Jones	c Moores b Clarke	4
D.J. Foster	b Pigott	1
Extras	lb 9, nb 7	16
Total (100 ov:228–9)		229

41, 74, 100, 100, 110, 165, 191, 217, 222

Pigott	29.4	3	68	3
Dodemaide	24.	6	50	2
Babington	16	2	52	0
C.M. Wells	23	10	39	1
Clarke	8	2	11	2

Sussex 2nd Innings

A.M. Green	lbw b Mallender	7
*P.W.G. Parker	lbw b Mallender	39
A.P. Wells	c Tavare b Mallender	58
A.R. Clarke	c Cook b Mallender	0
D.M. Smith	c Burns b Rose	5
C.M. Wells	c Tavare b Jones	50
I.J. Gould	c Tavare b Jones	24
A.I.C. Dodemaide	c and b Mallender	13
†P. Moores	b Mallender	21
A.C.S. Pigott	c Burns b Mallender	0
A.M. Babington	not out	3
Extras	lb 3, nb 9	12
Total		232

10, 77, 77, 90, 145, 186, 191, 221, 223

Jones	17	4	53	2
Mallender	21.5	4	62	7
Rose	19	2	51	1
Foster	11	1	50	0
Marks	10	5	13	0

Somerset 2nd Innings

S.J. Cook	c Parker b Babington	36
P.M. Roebuck	c Dodemaide b Pigott	36
J.J.E. Hardy	b Dodemaide	34
C.J. Tavare	not out	90
R.J. Bartlett	c Green b Clarke	5
†N.D. Burns	b Clarke	1
*V.J. Marks	not out	25
Extras	b 5, lb 4, w 1, nb 1	11
Total (5 wkts)		238

52, 95, 143, 168, 198

Pigott	18.5	2	46	1
Dodemaide	22	4	61	1
C.M. Wells	22	7	37	0
Babington	15	2	32	1
Clarke	23	7	53	2

Umpired: J.C. Balderstone and N.T. Plews
Toss: Somerset
Gould spent 4½ hours on the first day scoring 84 and this rate of progress seemed to set the standard of the rest of the match. Somerset on the first evening actually reached 37–0 off 22 overs. On the second day, Cook remained four hours for 91, his only real support coming from Marks. Sussex began Saturday at 79–3 and Colin Wells at last cheered up spectators with 50 off 86 balls. Mallender returned a career best bowling analysis and Tavare created a new Somerset fielding record.

v LANCASHIRE (Taunton)

May 20, 22, 23

Lost by 6 wkts. Lancs 21pts, Somerset 7pts

Somerset 1st Innings

S.J. Cook	c and b Simmons	156
P.M. Roebuck	c Hegg b Hayhurst	20
R.J. Bartlett	lbw b Watkinson	20
*C.J. Tavare	c Watkinson b Hughes	153
R.J. Harden	not out	23
J.J.E. Hardy	not out	8
†N.D. Burns		
G.D. Rose		
N.A. Mallender		
A.N. Jones		
T.J.A. Scriven		
Extras	b 5, lb 11, nb 3	19
Total (100 ov: 363–3) (4 wkts dec)		399

33, 77, 353, 379

DeFreitas	17	2	51	0
Allott	17	6	42	0
Watkinson	15	0	46	1
Hayhurst	16	3	52	1
Simmons	33	4	122	1
Hughes	12	0	70	1

Lancashire 1st Innings

G.D. Mendis	b Rose	35
G. Fowler	lbw b Jones	96
†W.K. Hegg	c Burns b Jones	58
N.H. Fairbrother	c Roebuck b Mallender	1
T.E. Jesty	c Roebuck c Scriven	28
*D.P. Hughes	not out	42
P.A.J. DeFreitas	c Bartlett b Roebuck	10
A.N. Hayhurst	retired hurt	0
M. Watkinson	c Mallender b Scriven	1
P.J.W. Allott	c Mallender b Jones	0
J. Simmons	not out	5
Extras	b 13, lb 8, w 1, nb 5	27
Total (8 wkts dec, 99.4 ov)		303

73, 202, 209, 211, 260, 274, 285, 287

Jones	23	1	97	3
Mallender	20	9	34	1
Harden	8.3	1	25	0
Rose	7	2	24	1
Scriven	27.1	5	67	2
Roebuck	14	5	35	1

Somerset 2nd Innings

S.J. Cook	lbw b Allott	17
P.M. Roebuck	c Hegg b Hughes	66
R.J. Bartlett	c Hughes b Simmons	48
*C.J. Tavare	st Hegg b Hughes	1
J.J.E. Hardy	not out	24
†N.D. Burns	not out	38
Extras	b 4, lb 1, nb 2, w 2	9
Total (4 wkts dec)		203

36, 136, 140, 141

DeFreitas	10	2	24	0
Allott	9	2	23	1
Jesty	9	1	23	0
Watkinson	4	0	17	0
Simmons	9	2	28	1
Hughes	5	0	25	2
Fowler	4	0	24	0
Fairbrother	5	0	29	0
Mendis	2	0	5	0

Lancashire 2nd Innings

G.D. Mendis	st Burns b Scriven	59
G. Fowler	c Burns b Mallender	20
†W.K. Hegg	b Scriven	2
N.H. Fairbrother	c Tavare b Jones	47
T.E. Jesty	not out	93
M. Watkinson	not out	59
Extras	b 3, lb 16, nb 3	22
Total (4 wkts)		302

56, 61, 128, 161

Jones	14.5	2	73	1
Mallender	13	0	70	1
Scriven	16	3	88	2
Roebuck	11	1	52	0

Umpires: D.J. Constant and M.J. Kitchen
Toss: Somerset
A third wicket partnership of 276 between Cook and Tavare, both of whom made maiden 100s for their adopted county, dominated the first day. Tavare hit 20 fours and batted 215 minutes, Cook batted 375 minutes and hit 14 fours. Somerset declared over the weekend and Lancashire batted through most of Monday to collect four bonus points. Tavare set Lancashire 300 in 58 overs and a brilliant innings for Jesty – 93 in 110 minutes – produced victory for the visitors with 19 balls to spare.

v YORKSHIRE (Taunton)

June 10, 12, 13

Drawn. Somerset 6pts, Yorks 4pts

Yorkshire 1st Innings

M.D. Moxon	c Jones b Rose	51
A.A. Metcalfe	c Burns b Mallender	0
R.J. Blakey	c Mallender b Rose	7
P.E. Robinson	b Mallender	28
J.D. Love	c Burns b Jones	39
†D.L. Bairstow	lbw b Marks	28
I.G. Swallow	c Cook b Mallender	21
*P. Carrick	c Cook b Roebuck	25
A. Sidebottom	not out	6
P.W. Jarvis	c and b Jones	25
C.S. Pickles	lbw b Rose	1
Extras	lb 4, nb 4	8
Total (85.2 ov)		239

15, 37, 88, 89, 145, 157, 204, 204, 234

Jones	15	3	57	2
Mallender	19	4	60	3
Rose	20.2	6	51	3
Marks	15	6	29	1
Trump	10	3	28	0
Roebuck	6	1	10	1

Somerset 1st Innings

S.J. Cook	b Jarvis	34
P.M. Roebuck	b Carrick	103
J.J.E. Hardy	c Swallow b Jarvis	0
C.J. Tavare	c and b Swallow	42
R.J. Harden	c sub b Carrick	25
†N.D. Burns	lbw b Carrick	4
*V.J. Marks	lbw b Sidebottom	31
G.D. Rose	c Robinson b Sidebottom	4
H.R.J. Trump	st Bairstow b Carrick	23
N.A. Mallender	c sub b Carrick	0
A.M. Jones	not out	20
Extras	lb 8, w 1, nb 4	13
Total (100 ov: 228–5)		299

53, 53, 139, 174, 183, 241, 250, 261, 261

Jarvis	13	4	31	2
Sidebottom	23	6	53	2
Carrick	29.2	14	53	5
Swallow	26	5	83	1
Pickles	18	5	55	0
Moxon	9	2	16	0

Yorkshire 2nd Innings

M.D. Moxon	c Burns b Jones	17
A.A. Metcalfe	run out	7
C.S. Pickles	c Harden b Trump	66
R.J. Blakey	b Trump	51
P.E. Robinson	c Burns b Marks	15
†D.L. Bairstow	not out	51
J.D. Love	not out	39
Extras	b 15, lb 6, w 7, nb 1	29
Total (5 wkts dec)		275

20, 44, 122, 163, 167

Jones	13	0	48	1
Mallender	18	6	34	0
Trump	34	11	50	2
Rose	5	2	4	0
Marks	31	5	75	1
Roebuck	13	3	33	0
Harden	1	0	10	0

Umpires: M.J. Kitchen and D.S. Thompsett
Toss: Yorkshire
Yorkshire, deciding to bat first, performed in a very haphazard manner and at the close Somerset were 22-0 off 16 overs. Roebuck lasted 325 minutes for his 103 which dwarfed the rest of Monday. Tuesday was a painfully dull affair as Yorkshire had nothing to play for but a draw, a task which occupied the whole day.

v KENT (Bath)

June 17, 19, 20,

Drawn. Kent 6pts, Somerset 4pts

Kent 1st Innings

S.G. Hinks	c Harden b Marks	43
M.R. Benson	c Cook b Marks	157
R.F. Pienaar	c Gard b Jones	87
T.R. Ward	run out	104
*C.S. Cowdrey	b Marks	65
M.V. Fleming	b Marks	35
†S.A. Marsh	c Pringle b Jones	1
C. Penn	not out	0
A.P. Igglesden		
R.P. Davis		
M.D. Harman		
Extras	b 7, lb 13, nb 14	34
Total (100 ov: 348–3) (7 wkts dec)		526

99, 272, 348, 472, 525, 526, 526

Jones	17	3	94	2
Mallender	24	2	93	0
Marks	38.1	5	146	4
Pringle	10	0	54	0
Trump	35	6	119	0

Somerset 1st Innings

S.J. Cook	b Igglesden	49
P.M. Roebuck	b Davis	19
J.J.E. Hardy	c Marsh b Harman	1
C.J. Tavare	c Marsh b Igglesden	1
R.J. Harden	not out	102
N.J. Pringle	b Igglesden	0
*V.J. Marks	not out	89
N.A. Mallender		
H.R.J. Trump		
A.N. Jones		
†T. Gard		
Extras	b 5, lb 6, nb 2	13
Total (5 wkts dec, 96 ov)		274

60, 71, 71, 73, 73

Penn	20	2	79	0
Igglesden	23	8	70	3
Davis	26	9	46	1
Harman	22	9	54	1
Cowdrey	5	1	14	0

Kent 2nd Innings

S.G. Hinks	not out	52
M.R. Benson	not out	50
Extras	lb 4, nb 2	6
Total (0 wkt dec)		108

Jones	3	1	9	0
Mallender	3	1	7	0
Pringle	8	2	33	0
Trump	14	2	40	0
Marks	11	6	15	0

Somerset 2nd Innings

S.J. Cook	b Davis	72
P.M. Roebuck	run out	107
J.J.E. Hardy	run out	12
C.J. Tavare	b Davis	23
R.J. Harden	c and b Davis	22
*V.J. Marks	c and b Davis	17
N.J. Pringle	not out	12
A.N. Jones	not out	6
Extras	b 1, lb 4	5
Total (6 wkts)		276

126, 153, 211, 239, 256, 260

Cowdrey	11	0	54	0
Igglesden	15	2	63	0
Davis	30	5	96	4
Harman	12	2	58	0

Umpires: D.R. Shepherd and A.G.T. Whitehead
Toss: Kent
An easy pitch on a sunny Saturday produced 459 runs for the loss of three wickets, with Ward hitting 101* off 115 balls, while Benson's 100 came off 184 balls. Kent continued on Monday to reach 526–7 before declaring. Somerset made a poor start, collapsing to 73–5. Harden and Marks then added 201* for the 6th wicket in 65 overs. Cowdrey, lacking Fleming, set Somerset 361 off 70 overs. Cook and Roebuck made a fine opening stand, but when Cook was dismissed the momentum went out of the innings and the match faded to a draw.

v GLOUCESTERSHIRE (Bath)

June 21, 22, 23

Lost by 8 wkts. Gloucs 22pts, Somerset 1pt

Somerset 1st Innings

S.J. Cook	lbw b Jarvis	12
P.M. Roebuck	c Alleyne b Walsh	4
J.J.E. Hardy	c Bainbridge b Walsh	3
C.J. Tavare	c Curran b Walsh	5
R.J. Harden	b Walsh	25
N.J. Pringle	b Athey	7
*V.J. Marks	c Tedstone b Walsh	6
H.R.J. Trump	b Walsh	0
†T. Gard	b Walsh	0
N.A. Mallender	b Jarvis	5
A.N. Jones	not out	0
Extras	lb 3, w 1, nb 2	6
Total (43.3 ov)		73

13, 18, 23, 30, 53, 66, 67, 67, 73

Walsh	16	4	19	7
Jarvis	16.3	6	27	2
Bainbridge	5	3	9	0
Athey	2	0	9	1
Graveney	3	2	1	0
Lloyds	1	0	5	0

Gloucestershire 1st Innings

A.J. Wright	c Pringle b Marks	68
I.P. Butcher	lbw b Mallender	2
J.W. Lloyds	c Gard b Jones	30
*C.W.J. Athey	c Jones b Roebuck	108
K.M. Curran	not out	101
M.W. Alleyne	not out	58
P. Bainbridge		
†G.A. Tedstone		
D.A. Graveney		
C.A. Walsh		
K.B.S. Jarvis		
Extras	b 4, lb 19, w 1, nb 11	35
Total (100 ov: 245–3)(4 wkts dec)		402

15, 67, 126, 307

Jones	20	6	49	1
Mallender	24	5	47	1
Marks	50	14	149	1
Trump	38.3	9	82	0
Roebuck	16	4	27	1
Pringle	5	0	23	0
Harden	1	0	2	0

Somerset 2nd Innings

S.J. Cook	b Lloyds	147
P.M. Roebuck	b Walsh	25
J.J.E. Hardy	c Athey b Lloyds	31
C.J. Tavare	b Lloyds	25
R.J. Harden	b Graveney	5
N.J. Pringle	b Lloyds	3
*V.J. Marks	b Lloyds	3
H.R.J. Trump	c Alleyne b Lloyds	0
†T. Gard	b Lloyds	40
N.A. Mallender	not out	48
A.N. Jones	c Alleyne b Graveney	8
Extras	b 10, lb 13, nb 6	29
Total		364

86, 176, 222, 231, 245, 253, 253, 268, 348

Walsh	28	6	88	1
Jarvis	7	2	18	0
Graveney	47	13	96	2
Lloyds	45	6	134	7
Athey	1	0	5	0

Gloucestershire 2nd Innings

A.J. Wright	not out	12
J.W. Lloyds	run out	1
K.M. Curran	b Jones	7
*C.W.J. Athey	not out	13
Extras	lb 3	3
Total (2 wkts)		36

7, 16

Jones	3	0	16	1
Marks	1.1	0	9	0
Mallender	1	0	8	0

Umpires: D.R. Shepherd and A.G.T. Whitehead
Toss: Somerset

Cook reached his 1,000 runs, the first batsman to do so in 1989, but that was the extent of Somerset's joy on the first day. By stumps Gloucestershire had reached 142–3 off 63 overs. On the second day Athey and Curran had a partnership of 181 in 74 overs. Curran faced 286 balls and Athey 301. Cook batted splendidly on the last day and survived until 15 minutes after tea, being at the crease 335 minutes. The visitors then seemed on the verge of victory, but Gard and Mallender both survived dropped catches to make the tail wag. Gloucestershire managed to scramble home in the last possible over.

v LEICESTERSHIRE (Taunton)

July 22, 24, 25

Won by an inns and 47 runs. Somerset 23pts, Leics 3pts

Somerset 1st Innings

S.J. Cook	c Briers b Such	148
P.M. Roebuck	lbw b Willey	36
R.J. Bartlett	lbw b Willey	54
C.J. Tavare	c Boon b Willey	9
G.D. Rose	c Briers b Taylor	33
R.J. Harden	b Agnew	30
†N.D. Burns	b Agnew	13
*V.J. Marks	b Taylor	18
M.W. Cleal	c Parsons b Such	30
H.R.J. Trump	c Whitticase b Taylor	0
A.N. Jones	not out	43
Extras	b 9, lb 11, w 1, nb 14	35
Total (100 ov: 305–4)		449

163, 201, 259, 279, 317, 347, 354, 379, 379

Agnew	31	2	105	2
Taylor	32	9	120	3
Parsons	5	1	37	0
Willey	43	9	96	3
Such	23.2	5	71	2

Leicestershire 1st Innings

T.J. Boon	c Barlett b Trump	51
N.E. Briers	lbw b Marks	16
*D.I. Gower	c sub b Jones	48
P. Willey	b Jones	10
J.J. Whitaker	c Harden b Jones	0
L. Potter	c Trump b Cleal	42
†P. Whitticase	c Cook b Trump	19
G.J. Parsons	c Barlett b Marks	24
J.P. Agnew	c Burns b Jones	4
L.B. Taylor	c Cleal	27
P.M. Such	not out	0
Extras	b 1, lb 7, nb 1	9
Total (100 ov: 247–8)		250

25, 115, 119, 121, 126, 162, 200, 208, 247

Jones	25	13	38	3
Rose	18	7	41	1
Marks	28	5	85	2
Cleal	11.4	4	40	2
Trump	23	7	38	2

Leicestershire 2nd Innings

L. Potter	lbw b Jones	22
N.E. Briers	c Burns b Jones	25
T.J. Boon	b Trump	2
*D.I. Gower	b Marks	19
J.J. Whitaker	lbw b Rose	12
P. Willey	c Trump b Rose	4
†P. Whitticase	c Bartlett b Trump	29
G.J. Parsons	not out	23
J.P. Agnew	b Trump	0
L.B. Taylor	c Burns b Rose	14
P.M. Such	lbw b Rose	0
Extras	b 2	2
Total		152

42, 49, 49, 76, 84, 88, 122, 122, 152

Rose	10.4	1	35	4
Cleal	5	1	21	0
Trump	14	3	39	3
Jones	8	1	30	2
Marks	12	3	25	1

Umpires: H.D. Bird and J.H. Hampshire
Toss: Somerset

Cook, easily the top scoring batsman of the season so far, helped himself to 148 runs on Saturday and Somerset ended at 335–5. It was Cook's fourth consecutive 100. On Monday Cleal and Jones had the audacity to add 70 for Somerset's last wicket, then Leicester gave a rather ordinary exhibition of batting to close at 212–8. Apart from Potter's 42 in 3½ hours and some defiance from Taylor, Somerset had it all their own way and achieved victory by an innings on the last afternoon.

v MIDDLESEX (Weston-super-Mare)

August 5, 7, 8

Drawn. Somerset 6pts, Middx 4pts

Somerset 1st Innings

S.J. Cook	c Downton b Williams	25
P.M. Roebuck	lbw b Fraser	18
R.J. Bartlett	lbw b Fraser	0
C.J. Tavare	c Cowans b Emburey	24
R.J. Harden	not out	76
†N.D. Burns	c Hutchinson b Emburey	0
*V.J. Marks	c Hutchinson b Emburey	16
G.D. Rose	c Downton b Cowans	3
N.A. Mallender	c Downton b Emburery	23
H.R. Trump	b Emburey	0
A.N. Jones	c Wiliams b Emburey	13
Extras	lb 5, nb 9	14
Total (84.5 ov)		212

19, 45, 45, 79, 85, 121, 124, 180, 180

Cowans	15	4	43	1
Fraser	21	6	55	2
Williams	16	2	48	1
Emburey	20.5	9	38	6
Carr	6	1	10	0
Tufnell	6	2	13	0

Middlesex 1st Innings

D.L. Haynes	lbw b Jones	17
J.D. Carr	b Rose	11
*M.W. Gatting	lbw b Jones	4
M.A. Roseberry	lbw b Mallender	41
I.J.F. Hutchinson	c Burns b Rose	7
†P.R. Downton	c Burns b Rose	0
J.E. Emburey	c Rose b Marks	9
N.F. Williams	b Mallender	0
A.R.C. Fraser	not out	15
P.C.R. Tufnell	c Burns b Jones	1
N.G. Cowans	b Jones	0
Extras	b 4, lb 2, nb 5	11
Total (46.2 ov)		116

22, 27, 38, 69, 71, 90, 90, 107, 116

Jones	13.2	4	30	4
Mallender	14	2	42	2
Rose	15	4	33	3
Marks	4	2	5	1

Somerset 2nd Innings

S.J. Cook	c Carr b Tufnell	50
P.M. Roebuck	b Cowans	0
R.J. Bartlett	c Carr b Cowans	0
C.J. Tavare	lbw b Taylor	81
R.J. Harden	c Tufnell b Emburey	28
†N.D. Burns	b Fraser	32
*V.J. Marks	not out	26
G.D. Rose	not out	21
Extras	b 1, lb 5, w 1, nb 9	16
Total (6 wkts dec)		254

14, 21, 78, 162, 175, 221

Fraser	19	1	71	2
Cowans	17	2	56	2
Williams	7	1	24	0
Emburey	19	8	38	1
Tufnell	30	8	59	1

Middlesex 2nd Innings

J.D. Carr	lbw b Jones	4
D.L. Haynes	lbw b Rose	38
*M.W. Gatting	b Rose	8
M.A. Roseberry	lbw b Rose	9
I.J.F. Hutchinson	b Marks	1
†P.R. Downton	b Roebuck	18
J.E. Emburey	not out	77
N.F. Williams	lbw b Rose	30
A.R.C. Fraser	not out	12
Extras	b 8, lb 10, nb 8	26
Total (7 wkts)		223

9, 40, 60, 61, 67, 130, 198

Jones	14.4	0	64	1
Mallender	14	5	32	0
Marks	23	9	48	1
Rose	20	10	22	4
Trump	7	1	16	0
Roebuck	13	3	23	1

Umpires: B. Dudleston and A.A. Jones
Toss: Somerset

Somerset decided to bat but were undone by Emburey, with Harden left stranded. Middlesex began the second day at 56–3 off 22 overs; the home pace bowlers quickly removed the remaining seven batsmen and Somerset consolidated their position with Cook and Tavare batting well. A very determined innings by Emburey, who lasted 233 minutes saved Middlesex on the last day, but Somerset did not help themselves by dropping several vital catches. Cook, on the Saturday, reached 2,000 first-class runs.

v WORCESTERSHIRE (Weston-super-Mare)

August 9, 10, 11,
Lost by 9 wkts. Worcs 24pts, Somerset 4pts

Somerset 1st Innings

P.M. Roebuck	c Rhodes b Lampitt	99
S.J. Cook	c d'Oliveira b McEwan	9
R.J. Bartlett	c d'Oliveira b Lampitt	12
C.J. Tavare	c d'Oliveira b McEwan	18
R.J. Harden	c Rhodes b McEwan	59
†N.D. Burns	b Dilley	3
*V.J. Marks	c Rhodes b Lampitt	0
G.D. Rose	lbw b Lampitt	6
N.A. Mallender	b Dilley	5
H.R.J. Trump	c Rhodes b Dilley	12
A.N. Jones	not out	6
Extras	lb 4, w 2, nb 5	11
Total (79.3 ov)		240

23, 78, 123, 159, 164, 172, 182, 189, 211

Dilley	25	5	101	3
McEwan	23.3	5	57	3
Lampitt	23	2	60	4
Illingworth	1	1	0	0
Tolley	7	0	18	0

Worcestershire 1st Innings

P. Bent	lbw b Rose	30
C.M. Tolley	c Roebuck b Rose	23
S.M. McEwan	lbw b Mallender	25
G.A. Hick	lbw b Marks	72
D.B. d'Oliveira	lbw b Mallender	52
*P.A. Neale	not out	44
D.A. Leatherdale	b Roebuck	12
†S.J. Rhodes	not out	30
S.R. Lampitt		
R.K. Illingworth		
G.R. Dilley		
Extras	lb 8, nb 6	14
Total (6 wkts dec, 96.5 ov)		302

42, 55, 125, 185, 229, 248

Jones	14	2	57	0
Mallender	21	2	62	2
Marks	25	4	81	1
Rose	14	3	42	2
Trump	15.5	4	38	0
Roebuck	7	2	14	1

Somerset 2nd Innings

S.J. Cook	c Hick b Illingworth	44
P.M. Roebuck	b McEwan	6
R.J. Harden	c d'Oliveira b Lampitt	15
C.J. Tavare	b Hick	1
H.R.J. Trump	b Hick	0
†N.D. Burns	c Illingworth b Hick	23
*V.J. Marks	c Rhodes b McEwan	20
G.D. Rose	not out	14
R.J. Bartlett	lbw b McEwan	0
N.A. Mallender	b McEwan	3
A.N. Jones	c Rhodes b McEwan	0
Extras	b 6, lb 4, w 1, nb 8	19
Total		145

17, 47, 50, 55, 96, 106, 141, 141, 145

Dilley	14	2	44	0
McEwan	11.2	2	28	5
Lampitt	7	3	10	1
Hick	27	11	40	3
Illingworth	23	14	13	1

Worcestershire 2nd Innings

P. Bent	b Mallender	18
C.M. Tolley	not out	26
G.A. Hick	not out	39
Extras	lb 1, nb 3	4
Total (1 wkt)		87

24

Jones	4	0	15	0
Mallender	7	2	13	1
Marks	8	3	21	0
Rose	6	1	25	0
Trump	3.2	0	12	0

Umpires: B. Dudleston and A.A. Jones
Toss: Somerset

Cook and Roebuck reversed their normal roles on the first day, the latter batting in sparkling style, while Cook defended. At the close Worcester were 51–1 off 15 overs. On Thursday consistent batting produced full bonus points for the visitors and then Somerset lost their way being 55–3 at stumps. McEwan cleared away the tail on the last day, after removing the obdurate Marks. Worcester were now 15 points in the lead in the Championship table with Essex second, both having played 18 matches.

v HAMPSHIRE (Taunton)

August 19, 21, 22
Won by 8 wkts. Somerset 23pts, Hants 5pts

Hampshire 1st Innings

V.P. Terry	c Tavare b Jones	4
R.J. Scott	b Jones	1
K.D. James	st Burns b Marks	56
R.A. Smith	b Jones	4
*M.C.J. Nicholas	not out	121
J.R. Wood	c Harden b Jones	20
M.D. Marshall	run out	2
†R.J. Parks	b Jones	26
R.J. Maru	c Tavare b Jones	0
C.A. Connor	b Rose	13
S.J.W. Andrew	c Harden b Mallender	0
Extras	lb 3, nb 7	10
Total (100 ov: 240–8)		257

4, 5, 14, 114, 159, 162, 211, 211, 252

Jones	17	5	37	6
Mallender	19.1	6	54	1
Rose	24	5	57	1
Atkinson	9	3	31	0
Marks	35	18	68	1
Roebuck	2	0	7	0

Somerset 1st Innings

S.J. Cook	c Maru b Andrew	25
P.M. Roebuck	c Wood b Marshall	14
R.J. Harden	lbw b James	8
C.J. Tavare	b Marshall	11
N.J. Pringle	c Maru b James	10
J.C.M. Atkinson	c Maru b Andrew	40
†N.D. Burns	c Nicholas b Andrew	78
*V.J. Marks	not out	89
G.D. Rose	b Maru	8
A.N. Jones	not out	4
N.A. Mallender		
Extras	lb 8, w 1, nb 7	16
Total (8 wkts dec, 88.3 ov)		303

25, 50, 66, 70, 94, 148, 257, 298

Nicholas	1	0	1	0
Marshall	18	5	60	2
Connor	18	4	53	0
James	13	5	44	2
Andrew	19.3	1	70	3
Maru	19	3	67	1

Hampshire 2nd Innings

V.P. Terry	lbw b Jones	2
R.J. Scott	b Mallender	1
K.D. James	c Cook b Rose	19
R.A. Smith	run out	17
R.J. Maru	lbw b Mallender	6
*M.C.J. Nicholas	c Tavare b Jones	0
J.R. Wood	not out	55
M.D. Marshall	c Mallender b Jones	0
†R.J. Parks	lbw b Mallender	2
C.A. Connor	c Marks b Mallender	17
S.J.W. Andrew	b Mallender	1
Extras	b 4, lb 12, nb 2	18
Total		138

4, 4, 41, 41, 43, 89, 90, 93, 133

Jones	14	4	53	3
Mallender	19.3	6	55	5
Rose	6	3	14	1

Somerset 2nd Innings

S.J. Cook	b Marshall	3
P.M. Roebuck	not out	32
R.J. Harden	c Smith b Marshall	8
C.J. Tavare	not out	46
Extras	lb 1, w 1, nb 2	4
Total (2 wkts)		93

13, 27

Marshall	9	3	33	2
Connor	9	0	33	0
James	1.5	0	16	0
Andrew	2	0	10	0

Umpires: J.W. Holder and B. Leadbeater
Toss: Hampshire

Hampshire relied on the batting of their captain for the first day's modest total of 257. Somerset seemed to do little better on Monday until Burns and Marks rescued them witha 7th wicket stand of 109. Marks hit 12 fours in his two hours batting. By the close Hampshire were 41–4 in their second innings. Wood reached fifty in 69 minutes on the last day, but that was really the sum total of Hampshire's defiance. Marshall dismissed Cook and Harden cheaply, but Roebuck and Tavare quickly dispelled any vision of a dramatic collapse. The defeat dealt a serious blow to Hampshire's hopes of ending in the top three in the Championship.

v WARWICKSHIRE (Taunton)

September 13, 14, 15, 16
Drawn. Warwicks 4pts, Somerset 0pts

Someset 1st Innings

S.J. Cook	c Humpage b Small	9
P.M. Roebuck	b Donald	21
J.J.E. Hardy	c Lloyd b Munton	35
*C.J. Tavare	lbw b Small	2
R.J. Harden	b Munton	5
†N.D. Burns	c Munton b Donald	36
G.D. Rose	c Humpage b Donald	7
M.W. Cleal	b Donald	2
H.R.J. Trump	b Donald	0
N.A. Mallender	not out	9
A.N. Jones	c P.A. Smith b N.M.K. Smith	9
Extras	nb 6	6
Total (48.4 ov)		141

19, 39, 44, 75, 88, 108, 110, 110, 123

Donald	13	1	40	5
Small	10	1	40	2
P.A. Smith	9	2	31	0
Munton	8	3	11	2
N.M.K. Smith	8.4	4	19	1

Warwickshire 1st Innings

A.J. Moles	b Trump	50
*T.A. Lloyd	not out	58
A.I. Kallicharran	not ot	7
†G.W. Humpage		
Asif Din		
D.A. Reeve		
P.A. Smith		
N.M.K. Smith		
A.A. Donald		
G.C. Small		
T.A. Munton		
Extras	w 2, nb 2	4
Total (1 wkt, 35.4 ov)		119

99

Jones	7	1	29	0
Mallender	7	1	18	0
Rose	7.4	1	30	0
Cleal	7	1	22	0
Trump	7	1	20	1

Umpires: D.J. Constant and R.A. White
Toss: Warwickshire

On a damp wicket Donald, Munton and Small bundled out Somerset in 48.4 overts, then the Warwickshire batsmen added 99 before the first wicket fell, with Moles and Lloyd being untroubled by either the pitch or the bowlers. Warwickshire were 119–1 at the close. Rain prevented any play on the following three days, which was very unfortunate for Warwickshire, since full points in this match would have moved them into 5th place in the table.

Surrey

President: C.G. Howard
Chairman: D.H. Newton
Secretary: D.G. Seward, Kennington Oval, London SE11 5SS. *Tel:* 01-582 6660
Coaches: G.G. Arnold and C.E. Waller
Captain: I.A. Greig
Foundation of Present Club: August 1845 in Kennington
First First-Class Match: Surrey have been regarded as one of the principal cricketing counties since the middle of the 18th century
County Champions: 1864, 1887, 1888, 1889, 1890, 1891, 1892, 1894, 1895, 1899, 1914, 1950 (joint), 1952, 1953, 1954, 1955, 1956, 1957, 1958, 1971
Gillette/NatWest Trophy: Winners 1982
Benson & Hedges Cup: Winners 1974
Sunday League Champions: Nil (best position 5th in 1969, 1980)
Refuge Cup: Nil

Summary of Results in 1989

Britannic Assurance County Championship: Played 22, Won 4, Lost 7, Drawn 11, Position 12th
NatWest Bank Trophy: Lost in quarter-final
Benson & Hedges Cup: Did not qualify for knock-out section
Refuge Assurance Sunday League: Played 16, Won 9, Lost 7, Position 6th equal
Refuge Assurance Cup: Did not qualify

Surrey's vice-captain Alec Stewart, who equalled a world record with 11 catches in a match against Leicestershire in 1989, and also scored 1,637 runs. Allsport/Adrian Murrell

ONE DAY AWAY MATCHES

The full scorecard of each of Surrey's away matches will be found in the sections for the respective home teams.

Refuge Assurance Matches

Lord's: May 7
Middx 221–5 (40 ov) beat Surrey 161 (38.3 ov) by 60 runs. Middx 4pts, Surrey 0pts.

Canterbury: May 14
Surrey 195–7 (40 ov) lost to Kent 197–6 (39 ov) by 4 wkts. Surrey 0pts, Kent 4pts.

Worcester: May 21
Surrey 221–5 (40 ov) beat Worcs 216–8 (40 ov) by 5 runs. Surrey 4pts, Worcs 0pts.

Northampton: June 4
Northants 201–4 (40 ov) (R.J. Bailey 106*) beat Surrey 159–9 (40 ov) by 42 runs. Northants 4pts, Surrey 0pts.

Edgbaston: July 23
Surrey 175–7 (40 ov) beat Warwicks 156–9 (40 ov) by 19 runs. Surrey 4pts, Warwicks 0pts.

Derby: July 30
Surrey 125 (39.4 ov) lost to Derbys 127–6 (32.5 ov) by 4 wkts. Derbys 4pts, Surrey 0pts.

Leicester: August 20
Leics 219–4 (40 ov) beat Surrey 215–6 (40 ov) by 4 runs. Leics 4pts, Surrey 0pts.

Old Trafford: August 27
Surrey 186 (40 ov) lost to Lancs 188–7 (39.1 ov) by 3 wkts. Lancs 4pts, Surrey 0pts.

Benson & Hedges Cup

Fenner's: April 25, 26
Combined Univ 116 (36.3 ov) (M.A. Feltham 5–28) beat Surrey 107–9 (37 ov) by 9 runs. Combined Univ 2pts, Surrey 0pts.

Lord's: May 13
Middx 232–9 (55 ov) beat Surrey 156 (38.1 ov) by 76 runs. Middx 2pts, Surrey 0pts.

NatWest Trophy Matches

Jesmond: June 28, 29
Surrey 313–5 (60 ov) beat Northumberland 245–6 (60 ov) by 68 runs.

From left, back: *Graham Brown, Graham Thorpe, James Robinson, Tony Murphy, Mark Frost, Nick Peters, Neil Kendrick, Alistair Brown, Andy Smith.* Centre: *John Deary (Physiotherapist), Chris Mays, David Ward, Rehan Alikhan, James Boiling, Martin Bicknell, Darren Bicknell, Mark Feltham, Paul Atkins, Zahid Sadiq.* Front: *Geoff Arnold (Coach), Chris Bullen, Dirk Tazelaar, Alec Stewart, Ian Greig (Captain), Grahame Clinton, Keith Medlycott, Chris Waller (Cricket Development Manager).* Allsport/Dan Smith

REFUGE ASSURANCE LEAGUE

v GLOUCESTERSHIRE (The Oval)

April 23

Won on faster scoring rate. Surrey 4pts, Goucs 0pts

Surrey		
G.S. Clinton	c Athey b Alleyne	23
J.D. Robinson	b Pooley	10
†A.J. Stewart	c Russell b Pooley	8
D.M. Ward	c Graveney b Greene	57
Z.A. Sadiq	b Lawrence	34
*I.A. Greig	not out	1
K.T. Medlycott		
M.A. Feltham		
C.K. Bullen		
A.J. Murphy		
M.P. Bicknell		
Extras	lb 16, w 14, nb 1	31
Total (5 wkts, 38 ov)		164

38, 48, 54, 156, 164

Lawrence	7	1	23	1
Greene	7	0	23	1
Curran	8	0	43	0
Pooley	8	1	18	2
Alleyne	8	0	41	1

Gloucestershire		
*C.W.J. Athey	c Clinton b Murphy	4
A.J. Wright	c Stewart b Murphy	11
K.M. Curran	c Bicknell b Feltham	13
P. Bainbridge	lbw b Murphy	8
J.W. Lloyds	b Murphy	0
†R.C. Russell	run out	14
M.W. Alleyne	c Stewart b Feltham	6
V.S. Greene	c Bullen b Feltham	14
D.V. Lawrence	run out	0
M.W. Pooley	not out	2
D.A. Graveney	c Stewart b Bicknell	0
Extras	lb 5, w 1, nb 3	9
Total (19.1 ov)		81

11, 29, 32, 32, 47, 56, 63, 68, 81

Bicknell	5.1	0	31	1
Murphy	8	0	22	4
Feltham	6	0	23	3

Umpires: M.J. Kitchen and K.E. Palmer
Toss: Gloucestershire
After Surrey had batted, the weather reduced Gloucestershire's target to 87 off 20 overs. Murphy, the ex-Lancs bowler, picked up 4–22 for his new county.

v HAMPSHIRE (The Oval)

April 30

Won by 5 wkts. Surrey 4pts, Hants 0pts

Hampshire		
V.P. Terry	c Medlycott b Greig	6
*M.C.J. Nicholas	c Stewart b Bicknell	1
R.A. Smith	c Bullen b Feltham	9
D.R. Turner	b Bullen	26
R.J. Scott	b Feltham	2
K.D. James	c Stewart b Robinson	12
N.G. Cowley	b Murphy	6
†R.J. Parks	b Murphy	4
S.T. Jefferies	not out	24
C.A. Connor	c Medlycott b Feltham	6
P.J. Bakker	not out	1
Extras	lb 6, w 7, nb 4	17
Total (9 wkts, 40 ov)		114

4, 16, 29, 33, 68, 71, 78, 81, 112

Bicknell	8	2	18	1
Greig	8	1	19	1
Murphy	8	2	26	2
Feltham	8	3	16	3
Robinson	2	0	13	1
Bullen	6	0	16	1

Surrey		
G.S. Clinton	c Nicholas b Connor	45
K.T. Medlycott	c and b Bakker	7
†A.J. Stewart	c Parks b Jefferies	12
D.M. Ward	lbw b James	15
Z.A. Sadiq	c Terry b Nicholas	16
J.D. Robinson	not out	3
*I.A. Greig	not out	4
M.A. Feltham		
C.K. Bullen		
A.J. Murphy		
M.P. Bicknell		
Extras	lb 10, w 2, nb 1	13
Total (5 wkts, 39.1 ov)		115

27, 47, 82, 107, 107

James	7	0	18	1
Connor	8	1	25	1
Bakker	8	1	11	1
Jefferies	8	2	31	1
Cowley	6	0	17	0
Nicholas	2.1	1	3	1

Umpires: D.O. Oslear and A.G.T. Whitehead
Toss: Surrey
Poor batting on a firm wicket saw Hampshire score only 114 off 40 overs. Surrey timed their reply to a nicety.

v YORKSHIRE (The Oval)

May 28

Won by 32 runs. Surrey 4pts, Yorks 0pts

Surrey		
G.S. Clinton	c Carrick b Sidebottom	76
M.A. Feltham	c Moxon b Sidebottom	31
Z.A. Sadiq	b Fletcher	3
A.J. Stewart	c Pickles b Carrick	15
†D.M. Ward	c Hartley b Carrick	22
*I.A. Greig	not out	61
G.P. Thorpe	not out	13
K.T. Medlycott		
C.K. Bullen		
M.P. Bicknell		
A.J. Murphy		
Extras	b 2, lb 9, w 4, nb 2	17
Total (5 wkts, 40 ov)		238

48, 54, 96, 132, 179

Pickles	8	0	56	0
Fletcher	8	0	71	1
Sidebottom	8	0	33	2
Hartley	8	0	34	0
Carrick	8	0	33	2

Yorkshire		
M.D. Moxon	b Bullen	23
A.A. Metcalfe	c Stewart b Murphy	12
R.J. Blakey	c Sadiq b Buellen	50
K. Sharp	c and b Bullen	12
†D.L. Bairstow	c Ward b Bicknell	3
S.N. Hartley	c Sadiq b Bullen	3
D. Byas	b Feltham	47
*P. Carrick	c and b Bullen	0
A. Sidebottom	b Feltham	20
C.S. Pickles	c Ward b Bicknell	19
S.D. Fletcher	not out	2
Extras	b 1, lb 7, w 7	15
Total (39.2 ov)		206

19, 73, 98, 110, 114, 121, 122, 178, 193

Bicknell	7.2	0	37	2
Murphy	8	0	46	1
Feltham	8	0	54	2
Medlycott	8	0	30	0
Bullen	8	0	31	5

Umpires: J.C. Balderstone and D.G.L. Evans
Toss: Surrey
Surrey made the highest total of the day and with Bullen picking up five wickets moved into third place in the table with four wins from six matches.

On paper Surrey's record in 1989 was undistinguished, but they suffered more than their fair share of bad luck. Lynch was absent for most of the year with a broken leg; Tazelaar, the new signing from Queensland, retired with back trouble and made only four first-class appearances; Clarke, the old West Indian bowler and the outstanding figure in the attack of 1988, was sacked for a breach of discipline.

The authorities were unaware of these difficulties when they dispensed with the services of Gray, the other West Indian fast bowler, Richards, the wicket-keeper and Smith the wandering batsman. What was created were great opportunities for the younger members of the staff and several colts seized their chances. Notable among them were the Bicknell brothers. Darren, the elder, whose talents were as a batsman, saw his record transformed from 363 runs, average 19.05, to 1,392 runs, average 35.69. Martin's fast bowling saw him leap from the most expensive Surrey bowler in 1988 to the leading one of 1989. Almost as dramatic was the apparent transformation of Murphy. In 1988 he was little more than a struggling Lancashire second eleven bowler; for Surrey last year he captured 65 wickets, about double the number he had taken in four seasons with his former county.

Thorpe, the left-hand batsman from Farnham, in his first season of regular county cricket, completed 1,000 runs, which total included two good hundreds. Medlycott found favour with the England selectors, though his figures were not quite up to 1988; another to achieve selectorial aknowledgement was Stewart, son of the England manager. The leading runmaker for the county, he hit four Championship hundreds and also kept wicket when needed – there was a minor hiccup behind the stumps and the local club cricketer Sargeant was co-opted for three games.

One of the major factors in the new spirit at the Oval is the captaincy of Ian Greig. There was some talk of him leading England, but the powers in charge invented some obscure rule which put him out of contention – the ghost of his brother still haunts the corridors of Lord's.

REFUGE ASSURANCE LEAGUE

v ESSEX (The Oval)

June 11

Won by 32 runs. Surrey 4pts, Essex 0pts

Surrey

G.S. Clinton	run out	57
Z.A. Sadiq	c Hussain b Lever	2
A.J. Stewart	c Lever b Miller	50
†D.M. Ward	c Lever b Stephenson	3
*I.A. Greig	c Hussain b Lever	11
G.P. Thorpe	b Topley	40
K.T. Medlycott	b Lever	4
J.D. Robinson	b Lever	4
C.K. Bullen	c Garnham b Topley	4
N.H. Peters	not out	1
A.J. Murphy	b Topley	0
Extras	b 2, lb 7, w 5, nb 2	16
Total (40 ov)		192

8, 117, 124, 128, 166, 178, 186, 188, 192

Lever	8	1	29	4
Ilott	8	0	27	0
Topley	8	1	44	3
Miller	8	0	37	1
Stephenson	8	0	46	1

Essex

*B.R. Hardie	c Ward b Peters	10
J.P. Stephenson	c Stewart b Murphy	4
N. Hussain	lbw b Bullen	23
M.E. Waugh	run out	20
P.J. Prichard	c Ward b Murphy	19
A.W. Lilley	run out	0
†M.A. Garnham	c Bullen b Medlycott	10
G. Miller	not out	44
T.D. Topley	b Greig	9
J.K. Lever	b Murphy	2
M.C. Ilott	run out	4
Extras	b 2, lb 4, w 8, nb 1	15
Total (38.2 ov)		160

15, 17, 53, 62, 63, 85, 95, 126, 129

Peters	7	0	44	1
Murphy	8	0	26	3
Greig	7.2	0	34	1
Medlycott	8	1	32	1
Bullen	8	3	18	1

Umpires: R. Julian and D.O. Oslear
Toss: Surrey
Essex suffered their first Sunday League defeat of 1989 at the hands of Surrey; the visitors however lacked three key players all appearing for England. Surrey reached 117–1, but their batting then collapsed. Essex fared even worse and never looked like winning.

v SOMERSET (The Oval)

July 9

Won on faster scoring rate. Surrey 4pts, Somerset 0pts

Surrey

G.S. Clinton	c Jones b Foster	9
M.A. Feltham	c Marks b Jones	1
A.J. Stewart	run out	72
G.P. Thorpe	c Marks b Foster	56
†D.M. Ward	c Harden b Roebuck	40
*I.A. Greig	c Burns b Jones	25
K.T. Medlycott	c Hardy b Roebuck	12
D.J. Bicknell	not out	22
C.K. Bullen	not out	8
N.H. Peters		
A.J. Murphy		
Extras	b 2, lb 4, w 6, nb 1	13
Total (7 wkts, 40 ov)		258

8, 16, 146, 151, 206, 220, 240

Jones	8	0	49	2
Foster	8	0	45	2
Mallender	8	1	33	0
Trump	6	0	54	0
Marks	8	0	47	0
Roebuck	2	0	24	2

Somerset

P.M. Roebuck	c Ward b Feltham	9
S.J. Cook	c Thorne b Medlycott	18
R.J. Harden	b Bullen	13
J.J.E. Hardy	c Greig b Bullen	0
J.G. Wyatt	c Thorpe b Medlycott	12
*V.J. Marks	c Murphy b Medlycott	4
A.N. Jones	c Bullen b Murphy	37
†N.D. Burns	b Medlycott	13
H.R.J. Trump	c Bicknell b Bullen	2
D.J. Foster	not out	8
N.A. Mallender	c Bullen b Feltham	1
Extras	b 3, lb 7, w 10	20
Total (28.5 ov)		137

26, 45, 47, 56, 73, 73, 124, 125, 134

Peters	3	0	7	0
Murphy	5	0	21	1
Feltham	3.5	1	5	2
Greig	1	0	5	0
Bullen	8	0	44	3
Medlycott	8	0	45	4

Umpires: D.R. Shepherd and P.B. Wight
Toss: Somerset
Surrey made an impressive total, so that even when Somerset were set a reduced target owing to rain, the home county had little difficulty in gaining the points and moved to 5th place in the table.

v SUSSEX (The Oval)

July 16

Won by 24 runs. Surrey 4pts, Sussex 0pts

Surrey

G.S. Clinton	c Moores b Babington	47
M.A. Feltham	run out	17
†A.J. Stewart	not out	100
G.P. Thorpe	st Moores b Clarke	29
D.M. Ward	b Clarke	11
*I.A. Greig	not out	4
D.J. Bicknell		
K.T. Medlycott		
C.K. Bullen		
M.P. Bicknell		
A.J. Murphy		
Extras	b 4, lb 7, w 4, nb 2	17
Total (4 wkts, 40 ov)		225

33, 115, 195, 217

Dodemaide	8	1	41	0
Hansford	7	0	41	0
Babington	8	0	56	1
C.M. Wells	8	2	17	0
Clarke	8	0	48	2
Lenham	1	0	11	0

Sussex

D.M. Smith	b M.P. Bicknell	1
M.P. Speight	run out	35
A.P. Wells	c and b Greig	12
*C.M. Wells	c Bullen b Medlycott	28
I.J. Gould	not out	84
A.I.C. Dodemaide	c Greig b Medlycott	18
†P. Moores	b Bullen	0
N.J. Lenham	st Stewart b Medlycott	8
A.R. Clarke	b Murphy	3
A.R. Hansford	not out	2
A.M. Babington		
Extras	lb 1, lb 4, w 5	10
Total (8 wkts, 40 ov)		201

3, 30, 78, 91, 139, 139, 165, 195

Murphy	5	0	17	1
M.P. Bicknell	6	1	21	1
Greig	5	0	23	1
Feltham	8	0	43	0
Bullen	8	0	38	1
Medlycott	8	0	54	3

Umpires: B. Dudleston and A.G.T. Whitehead
Toss: Surrey
After a slow start, Surrey hit 126 off the final 12 overs. Sussex managed to keep up the required scoring rate for the first 30 overs, but then lost two wickets and their momentum.

PLAYERS

Rehan Iqbal ALIKHAN *b* 28.12.1961 Westminster; right-hand batsman; off-break bowler; debut for Surrey in 1989; previously played for Sussex 1986–88

Geoffrey Graham ARNOLD *b* 3.9.1944 Earlsfield; right-arm medium pace bowler; right-hand batsman; debut 1963; left county after 1977 season and joined Sussex 1978, playing until 1982; re-appeared for Surrey in one-day match in 1989; 34 Tests for England 1967–75

Paul David ATKINS *b* 11.6.1966 Aylesbury; right-hand batsman; off-break bowler; debut 1988; scoring 100 in first match

Darren John BICKNELL *b* 24.6.1967 Guildford; left-hand batsman; left-arm medium pace bowler; debut 1977; selected to tour Zimbabwe 1989–90

Martin Paul BICKNELL *b* 14.1.1969 Guildford; right-arm fast-medium bowler; right-hand batsman; debut 1986; brother of D.J. (Surrey); selected to tour Zimbabwe 1989–90

James BOILING *b* 8.4.1968 New Delhi; right-hand batsman; off-break bowler; debut 1988

Graham Elliott BROWN *b* 11.10.1966 Balham, S London; Wicketkeeper; right-hand batsman; debut 1986

Christopher Keith BULLEN *b* 5.11.1962 Clapham; right-hand batsman; off-break bowler; debut 1982

Sylvester Theophilus CLARKE *b* 11.12.1954 Christ Church, Barbados; right-arm fast bowler; right-hand batsman; debut 1979; his contract with Surrey was terminated early in 1989 season; also plays for Orange Free State; 11 Tests for West Indies

Grahame Selvey CLINTON *b* 5.5.1953 Sidcup; left-hand batsman; debut 1979; previously played for Kent 1974–78

Mark Andrew FELTHAM *b* 26.6.1963 St John's Wood; right-hand batsman; right-arm medium pace bowler; debut 1983

Mark FROST *b* 21.10.1962 Barking; right-hand batsman; right-arm medium-fast bowler; debut 1988

Martin Bicknell, who came top of Surrey's bowling averages with 65 wickets.

Allsport/Adrian Murrell

Ian Alexander GREIG *b* 8.12.1955 Queenstown, S Africa; right-hand batsman; right-arm medium pace bowler; debut 1987 as captain; previously appeared for Sussex 1980–85 and Cambridge Univ 1977–79; two Tests for England 1982

Neil Michael KENDRICK *b* 11.11.1967 Bromley, Kent; right-hand batsman; slow left-arm bowler; debut 1988

Monte Alan LYNCH *b* 21.5.1958 Georgetown; right-hand batsman; right-arm medium or spin bowler; debut 1977

Keith Thomas MEDLYCOTT *b* 12.5.1965 Whitechapel, E London; slow left-arm bowler; right-hand batsman; debut 1984 scoring 100 on debut; selected to tour West Indiess 1989–90

Anthony John MURPHY *b* 6.8.1963 Manchester; right-arm medium fast bowler; right-hand batsman; debut 1989; previously played for Lancashire 1985–88

Nicholas Howard PETERS *b* 21.2.1968 Guildford; right-hand batsman; right-arm fast-medium bowler; debut 1988

Jonathan David ROBINSON *b* 3.8.1966 Epsom; left-hand batsman; right-arm medium pace bowler; debut 1988

Zahid Asa SADIQ *b* 6.5.1965 Nairobi; right-hand batsman; debut 1988

Neil Frederick SARGEANT *b* 8.11.1965 Hammersmith; wicketkeeper; right-hand batsman; debut for Surrey v Gloucs in June 1989

Alec James STEWART *b* 8.4.1963 Merton; right-hand batsman; wicketkeeper; debut 1981; son of M.J. (ex-Surrey); took 11 dismissals in match v Leics in 1989; selected to tour West Indies 1989–90

Dirk TAZELAAR *b* 13.1.1963 Ipswich, Austr; left-arm fast-medium bowler; right-hand batsman; debut 1989; also plays for Queensland

Graham Paul THORPE *b* 1.8.1969 Farnham; left-hand batsman; right-arm medium-pace bowler; debut 1988

David Mark WARD *b* 10.2.1961 Croydon; right-hand batsman; off-break bowler

REFUGE ASSURANCE LEAGUE

v GLAMORGAN (The Oval)

August 6

Won by 97 runs. Surrey 4pts, Glamorgan 0pt

Surrey		
G.S. Clinton	run out	9
D.J. Bicknell	b Dennis	25
†A.J. Stewart	b Smith	119
G.P. Thorpe	lb Barwick	80
D.M. Ward	c Watkin b Dennis	2
*I.A. Greig	c Morris b Barwick	3
K.T. Medlycott	run out	4
J.D. Robinson	c Butcher b Barwick	2
C.K. Bullen	not out	0
M.P. Bicknell	not out	1
A.J. Murphy		
Extras	b 1, lb 1, w7	9
Total (8 wkts, 40 ov)		254
34, 35, 235, 241, 245, 250, 253, 253		

Watkin	8	0	63	0
Dennis	7	0	39	2
Shastri	8	0	44	0
Barwick	8	0	34	3
Dale	4	0	28	0
Smith	5	0	44	1

Glamorgan		
*A.R. Butcher	run out	5
S.P. James	c Stewart b Murphy	9
A. Dale	c Stewart b Murphy	1
M.P. Maynard	run out	4
R.J. Shastri	st Stewart b Greig	39
H. Morris	c Thorpe b Medlycott	40
I. Smith	b Medlycott	4
†C.P. Metson	c and b Medlycott	15
S.J. Dennis	c Robinson b Bullen	8
S.L. Watkin	b Medlycott	5
S.R. Barwick	not out	8
Extras	b 2, lb 11, w 6	19
Total (35 ov)		157
14, 20, 21, 27, 91, 105, 132, 134, 146		

M.P. Bicknell	4	0	10	0
Murphy	4	0	9	2
Greig	8	0	41	1
Robinson	8	0	34	0
Medlycott	6	1	20	4
Bullen	5	0	30	1

Umpires: A.G.T. Whitehead and P.B. Wight
Toss: Surrey

Surrey gained their 7th successive victory at home in the Sunday league and retained fourth place in the table, two points behind Worcestershire, but with a match in hand.

v NOTTINGHAMSHIRE (The Oval)

August 13

Lost by 9 wkts. Notts 4pts, Surrey 0pts

Surrey		
G.S. Clinton	c Afford b Cooper	60
D.J. Bicknell	run out	4
†A.J. Stewart	b Saxelby	77
G.P. Thorpe	run out	51
D.M. Ward	not out	19
*I.A. Greig	b Stephenson	4
K.T. Medlycott	not out	0
J.D. Robinson		
C.K. Bullen		
M.A. Feltham		
M.P. Bicknell		
Extras	b 4, lb 6, w 8	18
Total (5wkts, 39 ov)		233
6, 134, 185, 218, 230		

Stephenson	8	1	31	1
Saxelby	8	0	60	1
Cooper	8	0	48	1
Evans	7	0	26	0
Afford	8	0	58	0

Nottinghamshire		
P.R. Pollard	not out	123
*R.T. Robinson	c Ward b Medlycott	50
D.W. Randall	not out	43
D.J.R. Martindale		
P. Johnson		
F.D. Stephenson		
†B.N. French		
K.P. Evans		
K. Saxelby		
K.E. Cooper		
J.A. Afford		
Extras	lb 11, w 6, nb 1	18
Total (1 wkt, 38.2 ov)		234
119		

M.P. Bicknell	7.2	0	46	0
Feltham	8	0	47	0
Greig	3	0	20	0
Robinson	4	0	17	0
Bullen	8	0	41	0
Medlycott	8	0	52	1

Umpires: J.C. Balderstone and A.A. Jones
Toss: Surrey

Surrey suffered a severe setback in their hopes of qualifying for the Refuge Cup when Nottinghamshire outplayed them completely.

BENSON AND HEDGES CUP

v WORCESTERSHIRE (The Oval)

May 2

Won by 1 wkt. Surrey 2pts, Worcs 0pts

Worcestershire		
T.S. Curtis	lbw b Feltham	38
G.J. Lord	b Clarke	0
G.A. Hick	c Stewart b Greig	24
D.B. d'Oliveira	c Greig b Bullen	12
*I.T. Botham	c Bullen b M.P. Bicknell	31
M.J. Weston	c Bullen b M.P. Bicknell	15
†S.J. Rhodes	not out	42
P.J.N. Newport	c M.P. Bicknell b Feltham	1
R.K. Illingworth	not out	7
G.R. Dilley		
A.P. Pridgeon		
Extras	b 3, lb 14, w 2, nb 1	20
Total (7 wkts, 55 ov)		190
3, 63, 76, 92, 130, 138, 146		

M.P. Bicknell	11	4	33	2
Clarke	11	2	29	1
Feltham	11	3	36	2
Greig	11	0	44	1
Bullen	11	1	31	1

Surrey		
G.S. Clinton	c Newport b Botham	74
D.J. Bicknell	c Rhodes b Pridgeon	11
P.D. Atkins	lbw b Botham	9
†A.J. Stewart	c Illingworth b Dilley	44
Z.A. Sadiq	c Illingworth b Newport	1
D.M. Ward	lbw b Botham	9
*I.A. Greig	c Weston b Botham	5
M.A. Feltham	c Botham b Dilley	1
C.K. Bullen	not out	7
M.P. Bicknell	c Botham b Dilley	6
S.T. Clarke	not out	2
Extras	b 1, lb 6, w 14, nb 1	22
Total (9 wkts, 55 ov)		191
13, 37, 120, 126, 167, 168, 173, 175, 189		

Dilley	11	1	28	3
Pridgeon	11	2	31	1
Newport	11	1	39	1
Botham	11	0	44	4
Illingworth	9	1	27	0
Hick	2	0	15	0

Umpires: A.G.T. Whitehead and D.O. Oslear
Toss: Surrey. Gold: G.S. Clinton

Clarke scored two off the last possible delivery to bring victory for Surrey, but Botham did his side's cause no good by delivering 9 wides. Clinton played the innings of the match.

BRITANNIC ASSURANCE COUNTY CHAMPIONSHIP AVERAGES 1989

Batting	*M*	*I*	*NO*	*Runs*	*HS*	*Avge*	*100*	*50*
M.A. Lynch	6	9	2	383	172*	54.71	1	2
A.J. Stewart	22	41	5	1633	206*	45.36	4	5
G.P. Thorpe	18	30	5	1132	154	45.28	2	8
I.A. Greig	21	33	9	906	90*	37.75	–	8
D.J. Bicknell	22	44	6	1310	119	34.47	4	5
K.T. Medlycott	22	36	6	861	86*	28.70	–	6
C.K. Bullen	2	3	1	53	31	26.50	–	–
G.S. Clinton	21	39	3	854	90*	23.72	–	5
R.I. Alikhan	9	17	2	351	84*	23.40	–	3
P.D. Atkins	3	5	1	91	30*	22.75	–	–
D. Tazelaar	3	4	1	65	29	21.67	–	–
D.M. Ward	14	25	2	463	45	20.13	–	–
M.A. Feltham	13	20	2	342	64	19.00	–	1
J. Boiling	3	4	2	29	15	14.50	–	–
J.D. Robinson	6	9	1	108	29	13.50	–	–
M.P. Bicknell	18	24	6	234	40*	13.00	–	–
N.F. Sargeant	3	3	1	26	16	13.00	–	–
Zahid Sadiq	2	4	–	42	20	10.50	–	–
N.M. Kendrick	3	3	1	17	11*	8.50	–	–
A.J. Murphy	19	21	8	78	38	6.00	–	–
N.H. Peters	4	3	–	16	15	5.33	–	–
M. Frost	8	9	1	11	4	1.38	–	–

Bowling	*O*	*M*	*R*	*W*	*Avge*	*BB*	*5i*	*10m*
N.M. Kendrick	62	21	139	6	23.17	3-50	–	–
M.P. Bicknell	622.3	136	1717	65	26.42	6-47	4	–
A.J. Murphy	623	127	2008	65	30.89	6-97	2	–
K.T. Medlycott	663.4	165	1974	62	31.84	7-68	2	–
J. Boiling	66.4	26	162	5	32.40	3-40	–	–
M.A. Feltham	364.3	76	1070	31	34.52	4-68	–	–
D. Tazelaar	98.4	19	338	7	48.29	3-88	–	–
N.H. Peters	82.1	11	292	6	48.67	2-46	–	–
M. Frost	163.4	28	618	12	51.50	5-40	1	–
I.A. Greig	161	28	536	10	53.60	2-15	–	–

Also bowled: R.I. Alikhan 5.1-0-24-1; D.J. Bicknell 16.4-1-74-1; C.K. Bullen 12-1-46-0; M.A. Lynch 1-1-0-0; J.D. Robinson 28.2-5-117-3; A.J. Stewart 21.4-0-120-2; G.P. Thorpe 55-5-205-4.

Centuries

4 D.J. Bicknell: 101 v Sussex (Hove); 100* v Lancs (Oval); 119 v Yorks (Oval); 105* v Essex (Oval). A.J. Stewart: 206* v Essex (Oval); 148* v Middlesex (Oval); 120 v Essex (Chelmsford); 199* v Sussex (Oval).

2 G.P. Thorpe: 115 v Hants (Basingstoke); 154 v Kent (Oval).

1 M.A. Lynch: 172* v Kent (Oval).

BENSON AND HEDGES CUP

v GLOUCESTERSHIRE (The Oval)

May 11

Lost by 144 runs. Gloucs 2pts, Surrey 0pts

Gloucestershire		
A.W. Stovold	c and b Bullen	90
A.J. Wright	c Stewart b Greig	48
P.W. Romaines	c D.J. Bicknell b Feltham	76
*C.W.J. Athey	run out	15
K.M. Curran	run out	0
P. Bainbridge	run out	7
M.W. Alleyne	not out	17
C.A. Walsh	c Bullen b M.P. Bicknell	0
†R.C. Russell	not out	6
M.W. Pooley		
D.V. Lawrence		
Extras	b 7, b 11, w 5, nb 4	27
Total (7 wkts, 55 ov)		286

113, 196, 246, 246, 252, 267, 267

M.P. Bicknell	11	1	54	1
Murphy	11	0	34	0
Greig	9	0	52	1
Feltham	11	0	50	1
Bullen	11	2	52	1
Medlycott	2	0	26	0

Surrey		
G.S. Clinton	c Russell b Lawrence	6
D.J. Bicknell	c Russell b Lawrence	8
P.D. Atkins	retired hurt	0
†A.J. Stewart	b Pooley	4
D.M. Ward	b Curran	14
*I.A. Greig	c Russell b Pooley	33
K.T. Medlycott	b Alleyne	11
M.A. Feltham	b Bainbridge	26
C.K. Bullen	not out	20
M.P. Bicknell	run out	9
A.J. Murphy	lbw b Bainbridge	0
Extras	lb 8, w 1, nb 2	11
Total (37 ov)		142

12, 17, 27, 71, 81, 97, 127, 142, 142

Walsh	7	3	12	0
Lawrence	5	1	12	2
Pooley	8	1	30	2
Curran	6	0	25	1
Alleyne	5	0	40	1
Bainbridge	6	1	15	2

Umpires: B. Dudleston and P.J. Eele
Toss: Surrey. Gold: A.W. Stovold
Without Clarke the Surrey attack looked rather thin and Stovold, Wright and Romaines took full advantage. Surrey's first batsmen were quickly disposed of by Lawrence and after a dozen overs the match was virtually decided.

NATWEST BANK TROPHY

v YORKSHIRE (The Oval)

July 12

Won by one run

Surrey		
D.J. Bicknell	not out	135
G.S. Clinton	retired ill	1
A.J. Stewart	run out	5
G.P. Thorpe	c Jarvis b Moxon	8
†D.M. Ward	b Moxon	80
*I.A. Greig	c and b Jarvis	15
K.T. Medlycott	not out	2
M.A. Feltham		
C.K. Bullen		
M.P. Bicknell		
A.J. Murphy		
Extras	lb 7, w 3	10
Total (4 wkts, 60 ov)		256

27, 61, 202, 248

Jarvis	12	1	50	1
Sidebottom	12	2	39	0
Fletcher	9	1	63	0
Swallow	4	0	16	0
Moxon	11	4	34	2
Carrick	12	0	47	0

Yorkshire		
M.D. Moxon	b M.P. Bicknell	59
A.A. Metcalfe	c and b M.P. Bicknell	40
†R.J. Blakey	run out	22
D. Byas	b Medlycott	17
K. Sharp	b Feltham	15
S.N. Hartley	c Stewart b M.P. Bicknell	20
*P. Carrick	c Medlycott b M.P. Bicknell	17
I.G. Swallow	not out	17
A. Sidebottom	c Greig b Murphy	8
P.W. Jarvis	b Feltham	6
S.D. Fletcher	not out	16
Extras	b 1, lb 16, w 1	18
Total (9 wkts, 60 ov)		255

106, 107, 142, 157, 166, 205, 206, 220, 228

Murphy	12	2	51	1
M.P. Bicknell	12	0	49	4
Feltham	12	2	46	2
Medlycott	12	3	45	1
Bullen	12	0	47	0

Umpires: R. Palmer and D.S. Thompsett
Toss: Surrey. MofM: D.J. Bicknell
D.J. Bicknell saw his fellow opener, Clinton, collapse at the crease, then Stewart ran himself out. However Bicknell carried his bat through the innings and reached 135. Yorkshire required eight off the final over bowled by Murphy. Three were still needed off the final ball, Swallow could only manage a single.

v HAMPSHIRE (The Oval)

August 2

Lost by 5 wkts.

Surrey		
G.S. Clinton	c Terry b Marshall	1
D.J. Bicknell	c Parks b James	43
†A.J. Stewart	b Connor	20
G.P. Thorpe	c Maru b Connor	1
D.M. Ward	c Maru b Connor	21
*I.A. Greig	run out	75
K.T. Medlycott	b Bakker	18
M.A. Feltham	not out	19
C.K. Bullen	c R.A. Smith b James	8
M.P. Bicknell		
A.J. Murphy		
Extras	lb 9, w 8, nb 5	22
Total (8 wkts, 60 ov)		228

17, 42, 46, 84, 106, 173, 206, 228

Bakker	12	2	44	1
Marshall	12	3	40	1
Connor	12	3	61	3
James	12	2	39	2
Maru	12	0	35	0

Hampshire		
C.L. Smith	lbw b Murphy	0
V.P. Terry	lbw b M.P. Bicknell	6
K.D. James	c Medlycott b Greig	10
R.A. Smith	not out	125
*M.C.J. Nicholas	c Stewart b Murphy	71
M.D. Marshall	c and b M.P. Bicknell	3
J.R. Wood	not out	3
†R.J. Parks		
R.J. Maru		
C.A. Connor		
P.J. Bakker		
Extras	lb 4, w 4, nb 3	11
Total (5 wkts, 58 ov)		229

8, 14, 23, 199, 208

Murphy	11	1	34	2
M.P. Bicknell	12	3	32	2
Greig	5	0	37	1
Feltham	6	0	45	0
Bullen	12	1	36	0
Medlycott	12	2	41	0

Umpires: D.O. Oslear and P.B. Wight
Toss: Surrey. MofM: R.A. Smith
Surrey's batsmen failed to make the most of an ideal batting wicket and their total owed a great deal to a cavalier 75 off 73 balls by the captain. The visitors began in disastrous fashion, but a commanding knock by Robin Smith took them to victory with two overs in hand.

Away Matches

The full scorecard of each of Surrey's away matches will be found in the sections for the respective home teams.

Lord's: May 4, 5, 6
Middx 247 and 348–9d (R.O. Butcher 126, M.P. Bicknell 5–99) beat Surrey 190 and 280 by 125 runs. Middx 22pts, Surrey 5pts.

Hove: May 17, 18, 19
Sussex 300–7d (N.J. Lenham 116, A.P. Wells 103) and 233–6d drew with Surrey 259 and 204–5 (D.J. Bicknell 101). Sussex 7pts, Surrey 5pts.

Edgbaston: May 20, 22, 23
Surrey 293 (P.A. Smith 5–82) and 108 (A.A. Donald 5–18) beat Warwicks 190 (M.P. Bicknell 6–64) and 207 by 4 runs. Surrey 23pts, Warwicks 5pts.

Northampton: June 3, 5, 6
Surrey 175 and 207–9 drew with Northants 425–5d (A.J. Lamb 171). Northants 8pts, Surrey 3pts.

Basingstoke: June 7, 8, 9
Surrey 291 (G.P. Thorpe 115) and 116 (P.J. Bakker 5–48, M.D. Marshall 5–39) lost to Hants 251–4d and 157–2 by 8 wkts. Hants 22pts, Surrey 3pts.

Worcester: July 26, 27, 28
Worcs 284 and 256–6d beat Surrey 153 and 285 by 102 runs. Worcs 23pts, Surrey 5pts.

Derby: July 29, 31, Aug 1
Derbys 320 (P.D. Bowler 106, A.J. Murphy 6–97) and 10–1 beat Surrey 110 and 217 by 9 wkts. Derbys 24pts, Surrey 4pts.

Canterbury: Aug 9, 10, 11
Kent 346 (N.R. Taylor 118, A.J. Murphy 5–94) and 184–2d (S.G. Hinks 104*) lost to Surrey 302–9d and 230–3 by 7 wkts. Surrey 24pts, Kent 8pts.

Leicester: August 19, 21, 22
Leics 297 and 182 (M. Frost 5–40) lost to Surrey 184 (W.K.M. Benjamin 5–83) and 296–6 by 4 wkts. Surrey 21pts, Leics 7pts.

Old Trafford: August 24, 25, 26, 27
Lancs 305 and 20–1d beat Surrey 24–1d and 204 (Wasim Akram 5–52, J.D. Fitton 5–72) by 97 runs. Lancs 20pts, Surrey 4pts.

Chelmsford: August 29, 30, 31, Sept 1
Surrey 250 (A.J. Stewart 120) and 183 (J.K. Lever 7–48) lost to Essex 207 (M.P. Bicknell 6–55) and 227–8 by 2 wkts. Essex 22pts, Surrey 7pts.

v HAMPSHIRE (The Oval)

April 27, 28, 29, May 1
Drawn. Surrey 6pts, Hants 5pts

Hampshire 1st Innings		
V.P. Terry	lbw b Tazelaar	63
C.L. Smith	b M.P. Bicknell	14
*M.C.J. Nicholas	c Robinson b Feltham	2
R.A. Smith	c D.J. Bicknell b Feltham	16
R.J. Scott	c Sadiq b Medlycott	30
K.D. James	c Ward b Medlycott	10
†R.J. Parks	lbw b Greig	2
S.T. Jefferies	c Medlycott b M.P. Bicknell	12
R.J. Maru	not out	11
S.J.W. Andrew	c Stewart b M.P. Bicknell	14
P.J. Bakker	c Sadiq b Medlycott	1
Extras	lb 7, w 2, nb 14	23
Total (69.3 ov)		198

35, 47, 77, 120, 149, 152, 165, 175, 195

Tazelaar	15	4	43	1
M.P. Bicknell	22	7	66	3
Feltham	11	0	34	2
Greig	9	2	24	1
Medlycott	12.3	3	24	3

Surrey 1st Innings		
G.S. Clinton	c Andrew b Bakker	6
D.J. Bicknell	c Terry b Bakker	2
J.D. Robinson	c Parks b Bakker	3
†A.J. Stewart	b James	46
D.M. Ward	b Maru	0
M.A. Feltham	c Jefferies b Bakker	64
Z.A. Sadiq	c Terry b Bakker	6
*I.A. Greig	not out	69
K.T. Medlycott	lbw b Bakker	1
D. Tazelaar	c Terry b Andrew	4
M.P. Bicknell	b Nicholas	4
Extras	b 2, lb 3, w 2, nb 7	14
Total (73.4 ov)		219

8, 15, 16, 31, 124, 131, 138, 157, 174

Jefferies	13	4	24	0
Bakker	26	3	81	6
Andrew	10	1	34	1
Maru	7	3	8	1
James	13	0	55	1
Nicholas	4.4	0	12	1

Hampshire 2nd Innings		
V.P. Terry	c M.P. Bicknell b Greig	88
C.L. Smith	not out	94
*M.C.J. Nicholas	not out	14
Extras	b 4, lb 7, nb 8	19
Total (1 wkt)		215

168

M.P. Bicknell	12	3	39	0
Tazelaar	15	3	44	0
Feltham	17	2	67	0
Greig	11	2	41	1
Medlycott	3	1	13	0

Surrey 2nd Innings		
G.S. Clinton	lbw b Andrew	14
D.J. Bicknell	b Maru	34
J.D. Robinson	c Parks b Jefferies	1
†A.J. Stewart	b Bakker	13
D.M. Ward	c Scott b Maru	1
Z.A. Sadiq	c Jefferies b Maru	12
*I.A. Greig	not out	9
K.T. Medlycott	not out	21
Extras	b 4, lb 13, nb 6	23
Total (6 wkts)		128

31, 35, 66, 77, 82, 93

Bakker	11	3	26	1
Andrew	10.3	1	29	1
Maru	11	2	18	3
Jefferies	4	0	18	1
James	6	0	20	0

Umpires: D.O. Oslear and A.G.T. Whitehead
Toss: Hampshire
After play was delayed for an hour due to the damp outfield, the visitors were dismissed for 198, then Surrey fell to 32–4 off 20 overs. Terry survived 150 minutes for 63, this after the first day had been washed out. Rain again restricted activities on the Saturday, though some hitting by Greig gave Surrey a lead. On the last day Hampshire began at 3–0; Terry and Smith put on 168 for the 1st wicket before a declaration set Surrey 195 in 42 overs, but Maru captured three cheap wickets and it was then more a matter of Surrey's survival.

v LANCASHIRE (The Oval)

May 24, 25, 26
Drawn. Surrey 6pts, Lancs 4pts

Lancashire 1st Innings		
G.D. Mendis	c Medlycott b Murphy	11
G. Fowler	c Ward b Feltham	20
†W.K. Hegg	c Ward b Medlycott	59
N.H. Fairbrother	c Ward b Greig	26
T.E. Jesty	c Ward b Feltham	38
M. Watkinson	c D.J. Bicknell b Medlycott	2
Wasim Akram	c M.P. Bicknell b Medlycott	2
*D.P. Hughes	not out	50
I.D. Austin	c Stewart b Medlycott	0
J.D. Fitton	b Murphy	19
P.J.W. Allott	c Alikhan b M.P. Bicknell	9
Extras	b 13, lb 5, w 1, nb 2	21
Total (91.1 ov)		257

19, 51, 112, 126, 136, 140, 109, 194, 232

M.P. Bicknell	27.1	6	67	1
Murphy	20	3	62	2
Feltham	17	5	33	2
Thorpe	2	0	17	0
Greig	2	0	18	1
Medlycott	23	9	42	4

Surrey 1st Innings		
G.S. Clinton	c Mendis b Austin	15
D.J. Bicknell	not out	100
R.I. Alikhan	c Austin b Watkinson	16
A.J. Stewart	c Hughes b Fitton	31
†D.M. Ward	not out	24
G.P. Thorpe		
*I.A. Greig		
K.T. Medlycott		
M.A. Feltham		
A.J. Murphy		
M.P. Bicknell		
Extras	b 1, lb 5, nb 8	14
Total (3 wkts dec, 60 ov)		200

61, 86, 143

Wasim Akram	14	2	33	0
Allott	16	6	43	0
Watkinson	10	2	45	1
Austin	7	4	15	1
Fitton	13	2	58	1

Lancashire 2nd Innings		
G.D. Mendis	b Medlycott	40
G. Fowler	c Thorne b Murphy	52
†W.K. Hegg	b Medlycott	28
N.H. Fairbrother	not out	62
T.E. Jesty	c Ward b Medlycott	23
M. Watkinson	not out	10
Extras	b 2, lb 12, w 2, nb 1	17
Total (4 wkts dec)		232

71, 110, 134, 186

M.P. Bicknell	14	3	44	0
Murphy	15	1	76	1
Medlycott	14	1	59	3
Feltham	3	0	8	0
Thorpe	4	0	10	0
Alikhan	1.1	0	17	0
Stewart	1	0	4	0

Surrey 2nd Innings		
G.S. Clinton	c Allott b Wasim Akram	8
D.J. Bicknell	c Hegg b Wasim Akram	2
R.I. Alikhan	not out	30
A.J. Stewart	c Allott b Fitton	29
†D.M. Ward	not out	26
Extras	b 8, lb 3, w 1, nb 12	24
Total (3 wkts)		119

7, 14, 60

Wasim Akram	13	2	31	2
Allott	10	2	14	0
Austin	3	1	2	0
Watkinson	10	0	21	0
Fitton	13	5	39	1
Fowler	1	0	1	0

Umpires: D.G.L. Evans and J.C. Balderstone
Toss: Lancashire
Bad light ended play at 3.25 on the first day, by which time Lancashire had made 196–8 off 60 overs. Hughes hit 50 on the second morning to produce a reasonable total, then Bicknell batted 210 minutes to complete an unbeaten 100. Greig declared and Lancashire were 39–0 at the close. On the last day Surrey had 59 overs to make 290. After losing two quick wickets, the home side were content to bat out time. The last day was in fact overshadowed by the announcement that Surrey had dismissed Clarke for persistent breaches of his contract.

v YORKSHIRE (The Oval)

May 27, 29, 30

Drawn. Surrey 6pts, Yorks 6pts

Surrey 1st Innings		
G.S. Clinton	b Pickles	30
D.J. Bicknell	c Metcalfe b Swallow	119
R.I. Alikhan	c Bairstow b Fletcher	51
A.J. Stewart	b Carrick	39
†D.M. Ward	b Byas b Swallow	1
G.P. Thorpe	not out	64
K.T. Medlycott	c Byas b Pickles	71
*I.A. Greig	not out	4
M.A. Feltham		
A.J. Murphy		
M.P. Bicknell		
Extras	lb 10, w 5, nb 6	21
Total (100 ov: 280–5) (6 wkts dec)		400

54, 168, 231, 232, 253, 384

Sidebottom	26	3	89	0
Fletcher	21	5	75	1
Pickles	17.2	2	60	2
Carrick	30	7	75	1
Moxon	2	0	10	0
Swallow	27	4	81	2

Yorshire 1st Innings		
M.D. Moxon	not out	162
A.A. Metcalfe	c Feltham b M.P. Bicknell	4
R.J. Blakey	b Murphy	13
K. Sharp	b Feltham	4
D. Byas	c Ward b Murphy	10
†D.L. Bairstow	c Medlyott b Murphy	2
I.G. Swallow	run out	2
*P. Carrick	b Medlycott	51
A. Sidebottom	c Ward b Feltham	7
C.S. Pickles	not out	19
S.D. Fletcher		
Extras	b 16, lb 6, nb 7	29
Total (8 wkts dec) (95.5 ov)		303

26, 65, 79, 100, 109, 111, 216, 227

Murphy	24	5	84	3
M.P. Bicknell	6	0	16	1
Feltham	26	8	46	2
Medlycott	25.5	6	74	1
Thorpe	10	1	33	0
Greig	3	0	15	0
Stewart	1	0	13	0

Surrey 2nd Innings		
G.S. Clinton	c Sidebottom b Pickles	27
D.J. Bicknell	c Bairstow b Pickles	26
R.I. Alikhan	c Sharp b Moxon	9
A.J. Stewart	run out	42
†D.M. Ward	c Moxon b Byas	10
G.P. Thorpe	c Blakey b Pickles	17
K.T. Medlycott	c Bairstow b Byas	7
M.A. Feltham	not out	32
*I.A. Greig	not out	2
Extras	lb 2, nb 3	5
Total (7 wkts dec)		177

43, 61, 90, 118, 120, 128, 158

Sidebottom	9	2	37	0
Pickles	11	1	49	3
Moxon	8	0	31	1
Byas	7	0	39	2
Sharp	1	0	15	0
Metcalfe	0.4	0	4	0

Yorkshire 2nd Innings		
M.D. Moxon	c D.J. Bicknell b Murphy	0
A.A. Metcalfe	lbw b Thorpe	12
R.J. Blakey	b Murphy	40
K. Sharp	retired hurt	3
D. Byas	c D.J. Bicknell b Thorpe	11
†D.L. Bairstow	not out	101
I.G. Swallow	b Alikhan	9
*P. Carrick	b Medlycott	15
A. Sidebottom	ot out	12
Extras	b 6, lb 8	14
Total (6 wkts)		217

0, 34, 54, 110, 143, 177

Murphy	24	2	73	2
Feltham	12	2	21	0
Thorpe	10	1	34	2
Medlycott	19	4	72	1
Alikhan	2	0	3	1

Umpires: J.C. Balderstone and D.G.L. Evans
Toss: Surrey
D.J. Bicknell hit a career best 119 to take Surrey to three batting points and 330–5 on the first day. The home side continued on Monday to reach 400 with Yorkshire replying with 303–8. Yorkshire declared first thing on Tuesday and later they were set 275 in 4 hours. Bairstow's 100 came off the last ball.

v ESSEX (The Oval)

June 10, 12, 13

Lost by 8 wkts. Essex 21pts, Surrey 7pts

Surrey 1st Innings		
D.J. Bicknell	c Waugh b Lever	0
G.S. Clinton	c Waugh b Stephenson	70
†A.J. Stewart	not out	206
G.P. Thorpe	lbw b Stephenson	0
D.M. Ward	c Garnham b Ilott	38
J.D. Robinson	c Waugh b Lever	29
K.T. Medlycott	not out	37
*I.A. Greig		
N.H. Peters		
A.J. Murphy		
M. Frost		
Extras	lb 11, w 1, nb 3	15
Total (100: 292–4) (5 wkts dec)		395

0, 186, 186, 259, 339

Lever	32	5	99	2
Ilott	26	7	74	1
Topley	26	6	74	0
Waugh	12	1	55	0
Childs	11	5	15	0
Stephenson	11	3	41	2
Miller	9	2	26	0

Essex 1st Innings		
*B.R. Hardie	run out	21
J.P. Stephenson	b Medlycott	114
A.W. Lilley	c Peters b Medlycott	67
M.E. Waugh	lbw b Thorpe	13
P.J. Prichard	c Peters b Thorpe	13
G. Miller	not out	24
†M.A. Garnham	c Thorpe b Medlycott	1
T.D. Topley	b Murphy	18
J.H. Childs	c Bicknell b Murphy	1
J.K. Lever	c Bicknell b Medlycott	5
M.C. Ilott	not out	13
Extras	b 3, lb 7, w 1, nb 2	13
Total (9 wkts dec, 99.3 ov)		303

65, 199, 224, 224, 242, 243, 263, 274, 285

Murphy	15.3	1	51	2
Frost	13	2	45	0
Peters	13	3	36	0
Medlycott	39	14	95	4
Thorpe	13	3	31	2
Robinson	2	0	12	0
Greig	4	0	23	0

Surrey 2nd Innings		
D.J. Bicknell	not out	105
K.T. Medlycott	c Waugh b Lilley	61
†A.J. Stewart	not out	12
Extras	b 1, lb 5, w 2	8
Total (1 wkt dec)		186

123

Lever	4	0	9	0
Ilott	3	0	15	0
Prichard	7	0	66	0
Lilley	6	0	53	1
Topley	3	0	37	0

Essex 2nd Innings		
B.R. Hardie	not out	142
J.P. Stephenson	c Ward b Peters	36
A.W. Lilley	c Murphy b Medlycott	35
M.E. Waugh	not out	58
Extras	b 4, lb 4	8
Total (2 wkts)		279

75, 174,

Murphy	11	0	56	0
Frost	13	2	53	0
Peters	16.1	3	59	1
Medlycott	27	0	92	1
Thorpe	1	0	11	0

Umpires: R. Julian and D.O. Oslear
Toss: Surrey
Without Foster and Pringle, the Essex bowling was attacked by Stewart, who, on a perfect batting strip, reached 178 not out on Saturday, Surrey being 324–4. On Monday Greig allowed Stewart to complete his 200 before declaring and then Stephenson hit a career best 114 as Essex were 260–6 off 91 overs at stumps. The last day was one of declarations; Essex ended by needing 279 off 71 overs. A commanding 142 by Hardie gave Essex victory.

v MIDDLESEX (The Oval)

June 17, 19, 20

Drawn. Middx 6pts, Surrey 6pts

Surrey 1st Innings		
G.S. Clinton	c Butcher b Fraser	19
D.J. Bicknell	c Butcher b Fraser	5
†A.J. Stewart	lbw b Emburey	33
G.P. Thorpe	c Downton b Hughes	0
D.M. Ward	c Emburey b Fraser	23
*I.A. Greig	lbw b Cowans	5
K.T. Medlycott	not out	86
C.K. Bullen	c Downton b Hughes	31
N.H. Peters	c Roseberry b Tufnell	1
M.P. Bicknell	b Tufnell	10
A.J. Murphy	run out	0
Extras	lb 6, nb 7	13
Total (98 ov)		226

23, 34, 43, 66, 82, 91, 187, 198, 216

Cowans	19	5	61	1
Fraser	22	5	40	3
Hughes	18	3	47	2
Emburey	20	10	29	1
Tufnell	13	3	27	2
Gatting	6	3	16	0

Middlesex 1st Innings		
D.L. Haynes	b Murphy	64
M.A. Roseberry	b Murphy	2
S.P. Hughes	b Medlycott	31
*M.W. Gatting	c Thorpe b Medlycott	0
R.O. Butcher	c Ward b Peters	6
M.R. Ramprakash	c Stewart b M.P. Bicknell	35
†P.R. Downton	c Clinton b Medlycott	15
A.R.C. Fraser	c Stewart b Medlycott	29
J.E. Emburey	c Ward b Medlycott	9
N.G. Cowans	c Ward b Peters	12
P.C.R. Tufnell	not out	3
Extras	lb 13, w 1, nb 5	19
Total (78 ov)		225

15, 82, 83, 94, 126, 165, 171, 188, 213

M.P. Bicknell	19	5	38	1
Murphy	17	6	35	2
Peters	14	2	46	2
Medlycott	28	9	93	5

Surrey 2nd Innings		
D.J. Bicknell	c Downton b Cowans	10
G.S. Clinton	c Hughes b Fraser	7
†A.J. Stewart	not out	148
G.P. Thorpe	run out	7
D.M. Ward	c Roseberry b Emburey	43
*I.A. Greig	b Emburey	67
K.T. Medlycott	c Haynes b Tufnell	11
Extras	lb 5, nb 7	12
Total (6 wkts dec)		305

11, 22, 47, 130, 275, 305

Fraser	14	3	30	1
Cowans	12	2	33	1
Hughes	5	0	19	0
Emburey	39	8	103	2
Tufnell	27	4	115	1

Middlesex 2nd Innings		
D.L. Haynes	lbw b Medlycott	102
M.A. Roseberry	c and b Medlycott	79
*M.W. Gatting	b Murphy	1
R.O. Butcher	b Medlycott	16
M.R. Ramprakash	c Bullen b M.P. Bicknell	13
†P.R. Downton	not out	11
A.R.C. Fraser	c Stewart b M.P. Bicknell	2
J.E. Emburey	c Stewart b M.P. Bicknell	1
S.P. Hughes	c Peters b M.P. Bicknell	0
P.C.R. Tufnell	run out	2
N.G. Cowans	not out	0
Extras	b 6, lb 5, nb 5	16
Total (9 wkts)		243

155, 156, 199, 221, 227, 231, 232, 233, 239

M.P. Bicknell	16	1	63	4
Murphy	10	1	60	1
Medlycott	22	4	86	3
Bullen	6	1	23	0

Umpires: B.J. Meyer and N.T. Plews
Toss: Surrey
Middlesex were set 307 off 54 overs on the last afternoon and responded with a first wicket stand of 155 off 28 overs by Haynes and Roseberry. Then nine wickets disappeared for 88 runs and Cowans, the last man, had to bat out the last over to save the game. On the first day Surrey's batsmen gave a moderate display and gained only 2 points. Middlesex began Monday at 20–1 off 9 overs and were spun out by Medlycott, which meant that on Tuesday morning Surrey were 106 runs ahead with seven wickets standing.

v GLOUCESTERSHIRE (The Oval)

June 24, 26, 27

Won by 8 wkts. Surrey 23pts, Gloucs 4pts

Surrey 1st Innings

G.S. Clinton	c Athey b Bainbridge	26
D.J. Bicknell	c Alleyne b Lawrence	32
A.J. Stewart	c Wright b Bainbridge	3
G.P. Thorpe	lbw b Bainbridge	29
D.M. Ward	c Athey b Walsh	0
*I.A. Greig	c Athey b Walsh	61
K.T. Medlycott	b Walsh	12
†N.F. Sargeant	c Tedstone b Walsh	16
N.M. Kendrick	c Lloyds b Bainbridge	4
M.P. Bicknell	not out	40
A.J. Murphy	c Alleyne b Walsh	38
Extras	b 10, lb 3, nb 1	14
Total (71.2 ov)		275

55, 68, 85, 98, 100, 132, 174, 179, 199

Walsh	23.2	2	83	5
Lawrence	14	0	61	1
Jarvis	16	1	53	0
Bainbridge	14	1	39	4
Lloyds	2	1	6	0
Alleyne	2	0	20	0

Gloucestershire 1st Innings

A.J. Wright	c Thorpe b M.P. Bicknell	4
I.P. Butcher	c Medlycott b Murphy	13
J.W. Lloyds	c and b Greig	23
*C.W.J. Athey	b Greig	11
K.M. Curran	lbw b M.P. Bicknell	19
P. Bainbridge	c Sargeant b M.P. Bicknell	15
M.W. Alleyne	b M.P. Bicknell	12
†G.A. Tedstone	not out	6
C.A. Walsh	c Stewart b Murphy	4
D.V. Lawrence	c Sargeant b M.P. Bicknell	0
K.B.S. Jarvis	b M.P. Bicknell	0
Extras	b 4, nb 2	6
Total (43.2 ov)		113

4, 41, 53, 65, 82, 100, 105, 110, 111

M.P. Bicknell	16.2	3	47	6
Murphy	17	4	31	2
Greig	10	2	31	2

Gloucestershire 2nd Innings

A.J. Wright	c Kendrick b Murphy	55
I.P. Butcher	c Medlycott b Kendrick	68
J.W. Lloyds	b Kendrick	7
*C.W.J. Athey	run out	37
K.M. Curran	c M.P. Bicknell b Medlycott	4
P. Bainbridge	b Kendrick	29
M.W. Alleyne	c and b Medlycott	0
†G.A. Tedstone	c Medlycott b M.P. Bicknell	50
C.A. Walsh	b Murphy	0
D.V. Lawrence	c Kendrick b Murphy	20
K.B.S. Jarvis	not out	0
Extras	b 11, lb 5, nb 3	19
Total		289

57, 136, 145, 156, 156, 199, 269, 269, 275

Murphy	19.5	5	45	3
M.P. Bicknell	24	7	40	1
Greig	16	4	44	0
Medlycott	35	11	74	2
Kendrick	22	5	70	3

Surrey 2nd Innings

G.S. Clinton	c Alleyne b Jarvis	0
D.J. Bicknell	not out	58
A.J. Stewart	c Lloyds b Jarvis	6
G.P. Thorpe	not out	54
Extras	b 5, lb 3, w 1, nb 1	10
Total (2 wkts)		128

2, 10

Walsh	12	4	20	0
Jarvis	16	5	54	2
Bainbridge	5	1	12	0
Lloyds	2	0	14	0
Alleyne	4.5	0	20	0
Butcher	1	1	0	0

Umpires: J.W. H older and K.J. Lyons
Toss: Surrey
After Saturday's play Surrey had this match well in hand, having reduced Gloucestershire to 104–6 off 36 overs in reply to the home side's 275. On Monday the remaining 4 wickets disappeared in 7.2 overs and Greig enforced the follow on. Butcher then remained 220 minutes for 68 and late in the day Tedstone hit an undefeated 50 to make sure the match went into the third day. On the final morning Gloucestershire only managed 20 more runs for their last three wickets, leaving Surrey most of the day to make 128. The win pushed Surrey into 7th place in the Championship at the halfway stage.

v NOTTINGHAMSHIRE (Guildford)

July 5, 6, 7

Drawn. Notts 8pts, Surrey 5pts

Nottinghamshire 1st Innings

B.C. Broad	c Sargeant b Murphy	7
P.R. Pollard	b Medlycott	36
*R.T. Robinson	c Ward b Medlycott	136
D.J.R. Martindale	st Sargeant b Medlycott	78
D.W. Randall	c Medlycott b Murphy	101
F.D. Stephenson	c Stewart b Peters	56
K.P. Evans	not out	17
†B.N. French	c Clinton b Medlycott	14
E.E. Hemmings	b Murphy	18
K.E. Cooper	not out	1
J.A. Afford		
Extras	lb 7, w 1, nb 3	11
Total (100 ov: 428–5) (8 wickets dec)		475

7, 102, 236, 286, 393, 431, 452, 474

Peters	20	1	94	1
Murphy	25	1	104	3
Greig	4	0	20	0
Feltham	18	1	81	0
Medlycott	43	5	169	4

Surrey 1st Innings

D.J. Bicknell	c French b Hemmings	70
G.S. Clinton	st French b Afford	42
A.J. Stewart	b Afford	26
G.P. Thorpe	c Pollard b Hemmings	62
D.M. Ward	c and b Hemmings	22
*I.A. Greig	c Cooper b Hemmings	13
K.T. Medlycott	b Afford	6
M.A. Feltham	b Afford	13
†N.F. Sargeant	not out	9
N.H. Peters	b Hemmings	0
A.J. Murphy	c Martindale b Hemmings	2
Extras	lb 7, nb 3	10
Total (100 ov: 274–9)		275

118, 118, 166, 225, 243, 249, 251, 268, 273

Stephenson	17	3	63	0
Cooper	12	1	44	0
Hemmings	38.5	9	87	6
Evans	14	7	35	0
Afford	20	6	39	4

Surrey 2nd Innings

D.J. Bicknell	not out	59
G.S. Clinton	c Cooper b Stephenson	65
A.J. Stewart	not out	16
Extras	b 2, lb 3, nb 1	6
Total (1 wkt)		146

101

Stephenson	13	2	34	1
Cooper	5	2	11	0
Evans	3	0	20	0
Hemmings	27	10	32	0
Afford	26	11	41	0
Randall	1	0	3	0

Umpires: D.R. Shepherd and P.B. Wight
Toss: Nottinghamshire
There was a complete contrast on each of the three days of this match. On Wednesday Nottinghamshire hit up 475, with scintillating innings from Robinson and Randall and 56 of 49 balls by Stephenson. On Thursday Surrey spent all day over 275, then on the last day Surrey followed on and between intervals for rain and bad light made 146–1.

v SOMERSET (Guildford)

July 8, 10, 11

Drawn. Somerset 6pts, Surrey 3pts

Surrey 1st Innings

D.J. Bicknell	c Burns b Jones	9
G.S. Clinton	lbw b Marks	16
A.J. Stewart	c Burns b Jones	1
G.P. Thorpe	b Jones	2
D.M. Ward	c Hardy b Jones	27
*I.A. Greig	not out	85
K.T. Medlycott	c Hardy b Marks	2
M.A. Feltham	c Cook b Marks	17
†N.F. Sargeant	b Cleal	1
N.M. Kendrick	c Burns b Marks	2
A.J. Murphy	c Burns b Jones	8
Extras	lb 4, nb 3	7
Total (77 ov)		177

14, 16, 22, 23, 90, 104, 132, 141, 160

Jones	18	5	62	5
Foster	10	2	22	0
Marks	27	10	44	4
Cleal	10	3	23	1
Trump	11	4	21	0
Roebuck	1	0	1	0

Somerset 1st Innings

S.J. Cook	b Kendrick	105
P.M. Roebuck	lbw b Medlycott	13
J.J.E. Hardy	retired hurt	35
J.G. Wyatt	b Kendrick	2
R.J. Harden	b Feltham	41
†N.D. Burns	c Medlycott b Kendrick	15
*V.J. Marks	b Feltham	49
M.W. Cleal	b Murphy	0
A.N. Jones	c Thorpe b Feltham	12
H.R.J. Trump	c Sargeant b Murphy	9
D.J. Foster	b Feltham	5
Extras	lb 10, nb 1	11
Total (100 ov: 226–5)		297

38, 135, 189, 217, 225, 235, 264, 291, 297

Murphy	37	8	98	2
Feltham	43.5	9	108	4
Thorpe	2	0	15	0
Medlycott	14	5	16	1
Kendrick	31	13	50	3

Surrey 2nd Innings

D.J. Bicknell	b Trump	29
G.S. Clinton	c Burns b Marks	19
A.J. Stewart	c Harden b Marks	0
G.P. Thorpe	c Cook b Trump	0
D.M. Ward	b Jones	28
K.T. Medlycott	c Burns b Marks	4
M.A. Feltham	not out	22
*I.A. Greig	not out	20
Extras	b 11, lb 7, nb 3	21
Total (6 wkts)		143

53, 53, 62, 73, 82, 108

Jones	11	4	22	1
Foster	10	1	31	0
Marks	26	12	31	3
Trump	22	8	31	2
Roebuck	14	0	10	0

Umpires: D.R. Shephard and P.B. Wight
Toss: Surrey
Rain in the afternoon meant that Surrey scored 143–8 off 69 overs on the first day. Greig took his score to an unbeaten 85 on the second morning, after which Cook presided. His 105 lasted 5 hours and Somerset were 226–5 at stumps. On the last day Somerset needed to bowl out Surrey cheaply, but the home county batted out time, with Greig again playing an important role.

v GLAMORGAN (The Oval)

August 5, 7, 8

Drawn. Surrey 8pts, Glamorgan 5pts

Surrey 1st Innings		
G.S. Clinton	c Smith b Watkin	47
D.J. Bicknell	run out	25
†A.J. Stewart	c James b Smith	68
R.I. Alikhan	c Maynard b Watkin	6
G.P. Thorpe	st Metson b Butcher	82
*I.A. Greig	c Butcher b Smith	8
J.D. Robinson	c Smith b Barwick	23
K.T. Medlycott	b Barwick	53
M.P. Bicknell	run out	5
J. Boiling	c Cann b Smith	15
A.J. Murphy	not out	1
Extras	b 3, lb 10, w 10, nb 1	24
Total (100 ov: 315–8)		357

72, 78, 106, 190, 223, 275, 275, 301, 344

Watkin	25	3	96	2
Barwick	21.3	6	50	2
Smith	30	2	86	3
Croft	31	9	72	0
Shastri	5	0	33	0
Cann	1	0	4	0
Butcher	2	1	3	1

Glamorgan 1st Innings		
†C.P. Metson	b Robinson	12
H. Morris	c Stewart b M.P. Bicknell	25
*A.R. Butcher	st Stewart b Boiling	61
S.P. James	c Stewart b Medlycott	53
M.J. Cann	c Alikhan b Medlycott	1
R.J. Shastri	b Medlycott	15
M.P. Maynard	c D.J. Bicknell b Medlycott	25
I. Smith	b Medlycott	18
R.D.B. Croft	not out	5
S.L. Watkin	c Thorpe b Medlycott	0
S.R. Barwick	c Robinson b Medlycott	8
Extras	lb 3, nb 1	4
Total (84.4 ov)		227

35, 39, 139, 146, 168, 185, 204, 217, 217

M.P. Bicknell	15	1	41	1
Murphy	8	1	28	0
Robinson	6	2	21	1
Medlycott	30.4	8	68	7
Boiling	25	8	66	1

Glamorgan 2nd Innings		
D.J. Bicknell	b Watkin	13
R.I. Alikhan	not out	84
G.P. Thorpe	c Butcher b Croft	12
†A.J. Stewart	c James b Smith	99
J.D. Robinson	b Smith	15
*I.A. Greig	not out	2
Extras	lb 5, w 2	7
Total (4 wkts dec)		232

22, 49, 199, 219

Watkin	11	0	41	1
Smith	12	0	56	2
Croft	7	0	35	1
barwick	11	0	50	0
Shastri	5	1	14	0
Butcher	4	0	31	0

Glamorgan 2nd Innings		
*A.R. Butcher	not out	88
H. Morris	c Medlycott b Boiling	50
S.P. James	b Medlycott	21
M.J. Cann	c Stewart b M.P. Bicknell	22
R.J. Shastri	not out	14
Extras	b 7, lb 2, nb 1	10
Total (3 wkts)		205

62, 95, 172

M.P. Bicknell	15	3	46	1
Murphy	6	0	32	0
Boiling	28	17	47	1
Medlycott	34	12	69	1
Alikhan	1	0	2	0

Umpires: A.G.T. Whitehead and P.B. Wight
Toss: Surrey

Surrey had an excellent Saturday achieving full batting points and Glamorgan began Monday at 4–0. Butcher and James shared in a stand of 100 and Glamorgan looked happy at 139–2, but the remaining eight wickets could only muster 88 and by the close Surrey with 115–2 were 245 ahead. Surrey were very cautious on the final day and when Glamorgan were invited to make 363 the match took on the appearance of a draw – an image which hardened as Butcher held firm.

v KENT (The Oval)

September 8, 9, 10, 11

Drawn. Surrey 5pts, Kent 5pts

Surrey 1st Innings		
G.S. Clinton	b Kelleher	30
D.J. Bicknell	c Ward b Igglesden	5
†A.J. Stewart	c Pienaar b Igglesden	13
G.P. Thorpe	b Igglesden	154
M.A. Lynch	not out	172
*I.A. Greig	c and b Davis	7
K.T. Medlycott	b Igglesden	45
N.M. Kendrick	not out	11
M.P. Bicknell		
M. Frost		
A.J. Murphy		
Extras	b 1, lb 9, w 2, nb 28	40
Total (100 ov: 395–5) (6 wkts dec)		477

16, 34, 98, 314, 326, 449

Kelleher	16	3	88	1
Igglesden	33	7	100	4
Penn	31	3	138	0
Cowdrey	14	4	57	0
Davis	24	4	84	1

Kent 1st Innings		
M.R. Benson	c Kendrick b Mledlycott	149
S.G. Hinks	b Medlycott	16
N.R. Taylor	c Lynch b Medlycott	10
R.F. Pienaar	not out	53
T.R. Ward	not out	22
*C.S. Cowdrey		
†S.A. Marsh		
D.J.M. Kelleher		
C. Penn		
A.P. Igglesden		
R.P. Davis		
Extras	b 8, lb 6, nb 5	19
Total (3 wkts dec, 85.3 ov)		269

93, 139, 225

Murphy	14	3	45	0
M.P. Bicknell	19.3	5	37	0
Frost	18	3	85	0
Greig	2	0	15	0
Medlycott	25	6	63	3
Kendrick	6	3	10	0
Lynch	1	1	0	0

Surrey 2nd Innings		
G.S. Clinton	not out	34
D.J. Bicknell	not out	19
Extras	lb 1, w 2	3
Total (0 wkt dec)		56

Marsh	14	0	37	0
Benson	14	0	18	0

Kent 2nd Innings		
M.R. Benson	c Stewart b Murphy	56
S.G. Hinks	c Medlycott b M.P. Bicknell	6
N.R. Taylor	lbw b Murphy	0
R.F. Pienaar	c Stewart b M.P. Bicknell	0
T.R. Ward	c Thorpe b M.P. Bicknell	4
*C.S. Cowdrey	not out	146
†S.A. Marsh	b M.P. Bicknell	8
C. Penn	not out	0
Extras	b 4, lb 1, nb 3	8
Total (6 wkts)		228

7, 8, 9, 22, 173, 224

Murphy	16.1	1	65	2
M.P. Bicknell	18	3	64	4
Frost	3	0	21	0
Medlycott	12	2	64	0
Kendrick	3	0	9	0

Umpires: J.H. Harris and K.E. Palmer
Toss: Surrey

Thorpe hit 29 fours in the highest score of his career and Surrey were 395–5 at the close of the first day. Rain more or less removed Saturday's play, so the county began Sunday at 404–5. A century from Benson meant that Kent were 237–3 off 7 overs by Sunday night and this four day game degenerated into more declarations on Monday. The captains agreed to ignore the follow on possibility when Cowdrey declared and the rest of the game belonged to the Kent captain who hit 146 off 152 balls and nearly produced a surprise victory.

v SUSSEX (The Oval)

September 13, 14, 15, 16

Drawn. Surrey 4pts, Surrey 3pts

Surrey 1st Innings		
G.S. Clinton	lbw b Babington	1
D.J. Bicknell	c Moores b C.M. Wells	38
†A.J. Stewart	not out	199
G.P. Thorpe	b Pigott	4
M.A. Lynch	c and b C.M. Wells	3
*I.A. Greig	c Pigott and C.M. Wells	71
K.T. Medlycott	c Moores b Pigott	14
M.A. Feltham	lbw b C.M. Wells	26
M.P. Bicknell	c Pigott b C.M. Wells	1
A.J. Murphy	lbw b C.M. Wells	0
M. Frost	c Gould b C.M. Wells	4
Extras	b 1, lb 18, w 1, nb 4	24
Total (100 ov: 329–6)		385

12, 79, 86, 93, 274, 306, 363, 365, 367

Pigott	35	6	95	2
Babington	16	1	62	1
Hansford	17	1	71	0
C.M. Wells	34.4	7	82	7
Lenham	3	0	14	0
Donelan	11	1	42	0

Sussex 1st Innings		
D.M. Smith	c Stewart b Murphy	62
N.J. Lenham	not out	81
*P.W.G. Parker	c Stewart b Murphy	3
A.P. Wells	not out	0
C.M. Wells		
I.J. Gould		
A.C.S. Pigott		
†P. Moores		
B. Donelan		
A.M. Babington		
A.R. Hansford		
Extras	lb 3, nb 4	7
Total (2 wkts dec, 43.4 ov)		153

110, 126

M.P. Bicknell	17	2	48	0
Murphy	11.4	1	54	2
Frost	10	1	37	0
Feltham	4	0	10	0
Greig	1	0	1	0

Surrey 2nd Innings		
D.J. Bicknell	not out	23
M.P. Bicknell	b Gould	9
K.T. Medlycott	c Babington b Gould	0
*I.A. Greig	c Hansford b Gould	11
G.P. Thorpe	not out	8
Extras	lb 2	2
Total (3 wkts dec)		53

21, 21, 37

C.M. Wells	2	0	3	0
Donelan	4	1	26	0
Gould	4	1	10	3
Smith	2	0	12	0

Sussex 2nd Innings		
D.M. Smith	retired hurt	4
N.J. Lenham	c Greig b Murphy	2
*P.W.G. Parker	not out	74
A.P. Wells	lbw b M.P. Bicknell	22
C.M. Wells	c Lynch b Murphy	1
I.J. Gould	c Clinton b Murphy	6
†P. Moores	not out	16
Extras	lb 2, nb 1	3
Total (4 wkts)		128

6, 44, 47, 61

Murphy	11	1	43	3
M.P. Bicknell	8	0	19	1
Feltham	2	0	16	0
Medlycott	7	3	23	0
Greig	6	2	17	0
Frost	1	0	8	0

Umpires: J.H. Hampshire and K.E. Palmer
Toss: Sussex

Poor light marred the first day, when Surrey made 332–6. Stewart was 171 not out at the close. Stewart remained unbeaten at the end, having hit 33 fours in his 199. Rain stopped play on the secon d day with Sussex 64–0 off 20 overs. Rain continued on Friday and just 18.4 overs were bowled, the score rising to 126–2, Lenham 56 not out. Two declarations on Saturday still could not produce a definite result and Surrey ended the season in 12th place, a substantial drop on 1988.

Sussex

President: The Marquess of Abergavenny
Chairman: R.M. Leadley
Secretary: N. Bett, County Ground, Eaton Road, Hove BN3 3AN
Tel: 0273 732161.
Coach: N. Gifford
Captain: P.W.G. Parker
Foundation of Present Club: March 1839 in Brighton
First First-Class Match: The county has been regarded as one of the principal cricketing counties since the 18th century
County Champions: Before 1864 Sussex was regarded as 'Champion County' in several seasons, but since that year the county's best position has been second in 1902, 1903, 1932, 1933, 1934, 1953, 1981
Gillette/NatWest Trophy: Winners 1963, 1964, 1978, 1986
Benson & Hedges Cup: Semi-finalists in 1982
Sunday League Champions: 1982
Refuge Cup: Nil

Summary of Results in 1989
Britannic Assurance County Championship: Played 22, Won 4, Lost 4, Drawn 14, Position 10th
NatWest Bank Trophy: Lost in quarter-final
Benson & Hedges Cup: Did not qualify for knock-out section
Refuge Assurance Sunday League: Played 16, Won 6, Lost 8, Tied 1, No Result 1, Position 11th
Refuge Assurance Cup: Did not qualify

Allan Wells, who averaged over 50 to top the Sussex batting averages.

Allsport/Adrian Murrell

ONE DAY AWAY MATCHES

The full scorecard of each of Sussex's away matches will be found in the sections for the respective home teams.

Refuge Assurance Matches

Taunton: May 7
Somerset 182–9 (40 ov) tied with Sussex 182–7 (40 ov). Sussex 2pts, Somerset 2pts.

Old Trafford: May 28
Sussex 145–9 (40 ov) lost to Lancs 146–7 (36.1 ov) by 3 wkts. Lancs 4pts, Sussex 0pts.

Edgbaston: June 4
Sussex 165–5 (40 ov) lost to Warwicks 169–4 (38.3 ov) by 6 wkts. Warwicks 4pts, Sussex 0pts.

Derby: June 18
Sussex 130 (37.4 ov) lost to Derbys 134–7 (39 ov) by 3 wkts. Derbys 4pts, Sussex 0pts.

Southampton: June 25
Sussex 192–5 (40 ov) lost to Hants 193–7 (40 ov) by 3 wkts. Hants 4pts, Sussex 0pts.

Middlesbrough: July 9
Sussex 161–5 (20 ov) beat Yorks 151–8 (20 ov) by 10 runs. Sussex 4pts, Yorks 0pts.

The Oval: July 16
Surrey 225–4 (40 ov) (A.J. Stewart 100*) beat Sussex 201–8 (40 ov) by 24 runs. Surrey 4pts, Sussex 0pts.

Ebbw Vale: August 13
Glamorgan 117–5 (22.3 ov) drew with Sussex did not bat. Sussex 2pts, Glamorgan 2pts.

Benson & Hedges Cup

Canterbury: May 2
Kent 173–9 (55 ov) lost to Sussex 176–5 (46.4 ov) by 5 wkts. Sussex 2pts, Kent 0pts.

Swansea: May 13, 14
Sussex 207–7 (55 ov) (C.M. Wells 117) beat Glamorgan 160 (48.2 ov) by 47 runs. Sussex 2pts, Glamorgan 0pts.

NatWest Trophy Matches

Lord's: August 2
Middx 266–3 (60 ov) (M.W. Gatting 132*) beat Sussex 188 (57 ov) by 78 runs.

REFUGE ASSURANCE LEAGUE

v KENT (Hove)
April 30
Lost by 7 wkts. Kent 4pts, Sussex 0pts

Sussex		
*P.W.G. Parker	c Marsh b Igglesden	10
D.M. Smith	b C.S. Cowdrey	17
C.M. Wells	c Marsh b Igglesden	1
A.P. Wells	b Igglesden	0
I.J. Gould	run out	5
A.M. Green	b C.S. Cowdrey	28
A.I.C. Dodemaide	b Davis	21
†P. Moores	c Hinks b C.S. Cowdrey	10
A.C.S. Pigott	not out	3
A.R. Clarke	b Igglesden	0
A.M. Babington	b Igglesden	0
Extras	lb 9, w 4, nb 2	15
Total (35 ov)		110

19, 21, 21, 38, 49, 95, 107, 107, 110

Iggleden	8	3	13	5
Kelleher	8	4	11	0
Davis	7	1	19	1
Alleyne	5	0	28	0
C.S. Cowdrey	5	0	18	3
G.R. Cowdrey	2	0	12	0

Kent		
S.G. Hinks	c Moores b C.M. Wells	27
M.R. Benson	c Parker b Babington	27
N.R. Taylor	not out	27
T.R. Ward	c Green b Clarke	10
*C.S. Cowdrey	not out	20
G.R. Cowdrey		
†S.A. Marsh		
D.J.M. Kelleher		
R.P. Davis		
A.P. Igglesden		
H.L. Alleyne		
	b 1, lb 2	3
Total (3 wkts, 37.1 ov)		114

41, 63, 79

Pigott	8	0	35	0
Dodemaide	8	1	20	0
Clarke	8	1	24	1
C.M. Wells	6	2	12	1
Babington	7.1	0	20	1

Umpires: M.J. Kitchen and R.A. White
Toss: Kent
With Igglesden taking five for 13, Sussex were dismissed in 35 overs and the Kent batsmen had little difficulty in reaching a very modest target.

From left, back: *Alan Hansford, Paul Boarer, Philip Threlfall, James Hall, Andy Babington, Simon Kimber, Ian Salisbury, Carlos Remy.* Centre: *Norman Gifford, John North, Keith Greenfield, Rodney Bunting, Neil Lenham, David Smith, Nick Faulkner, Peter Morres, Andy Clarke, Martin Speight, Ian Waring.* Front: *Alan Wells, Alan Green, Tony Pigott, Paul Parker, Colin Wells, Ian Gould.* Allsport/Ben Radford

REFUGE ASSURANCE LEAGUE

v LEICESTERSHIRE (Hove)

May 21

Won by 77 runs. Sussex 4pts, Leics 0pts

Sussex		
N.J. Lenham	lbw b Lewis	26
D.M. Smith	c Agnew b Parsons	43
A.P. Wells	c Gower b Lewis	69
C.M. Wells	c Whitticase b Agnew	10
*P.W.G. Parker	not out	24
I.J. Gould	not out	12
A.I.C. Dodemaide		
A.C.S. Pigott		
†P. Moores		
A.R. Clarke		
A.M. Babington		
Extras	b 6, lb 11, w 5, nb 2	24
Total (4 wkts, 40 ov)		208

57, 117, 150, 177

Agnew	8	0	41	1
Benhamin	8	1	30	0
Willey	8	1	24	0
Lewis	8	1	45	2
Taylor	4	0	24	0
Parsons	4	0	27	1

Leicestershire		
L. Potter	b C.M. Wells	16
N.E. Briers	b Clarke	28
*D.I. Gower	b Babington	5
P. Willey	c Clarke b Babington	20
J.J. Whitaker	b C.M. Wells	10
C.C. Lewis	c A.P. Wells b Clarke	3
†P. Whitticase	b Babington	11
W.K.M. Benjamin	run out	5
G.J. Parsons	b Pigott	8
J.P. Agnew	c Moores b Dodemaide	14
L.B. Taylor	not out	3
Extras	b 1, lb 6, w 1	8
Total (38.1 ov)		131

38, 55, 59, 87, 88, 96, 105, 107, 119

Pigott	8	0	33	1
Dodemaide	7.1	1	20	1
C.M. Wells	8	2	19	2
Babington	8	1	26	3
Clarke	7	0	26	2

Umpires: B. Dudleston and P.J. Eele
Toss: Sussex
A hard hit 69, including a six into the pavilion, by Alan Wells produced a total of 208–4. Accurate bowling by Colin Wells and the best Sunday analysis of his career by Babington made certain of the home county's victory.

v NORTHAMPTONSHIRE (Hove)

June 11

Won by 3 wkts. Sussex 4pts, Northants 0pts

Northamptonshire		
G. Cook	b Babington	20
*W. Larkins	c C.M. Wells b Babington	44
R.J. Bailey	c Moores b Babington	7
D.J. Capel	run out	63
D.J. Wild	b Clarke	0
A. Fordham	lbw b Clarke	23
C.E.L. Ambrose	not out	13
†D. Ripley	not out	5
G. Smith		
N.G.B. Cook		
M.A. Robinson		
Extras	lb 4, w 7, nb 3	14
Total (6 wkts, 39 ov)		189

40, 48, 89, 90, 157, 180

Pigott	7	0	33	0
Dodemaide	8	1	21	0
Babington	8	0	33	3
C.M. Wells	8	0	46	0
Clarke	8	0	52	2

Sussex		
K. Greenfield	b Cook	22
†P. Moores	c Ripley b Ambrose	4
A.P. Wells	b Ambrose	48
*P.W.G. Parker	b Cook	5
C.M.Wells	run out	19
I.J. Gould	run out	1
A.I.C. Dodemaide	c Ripley b Capel	9
A.C.S. Pigott	not out	51
D.M. Smith	not out	22
A.R. Clarke		
A.M. Babington		
Extras	b 1, lb 4, nb 4	9
Total (7 wkts, 38.1 ov)		190

12, 59, 71, 97, 98, 111, 115

Ambrose	7.1	1	17	2
Capel	8	0	44	1
Robinson	8	0	34	0
Smith	7	0	63	0
N.G.B. Cook	8	0	27	2

Umpires: B.J. Meyer and A.G.T. Whitehead
Toss: Sussex
An attacking innings by Pigott, who hit 51 off 23 balls with 7 fours and 2 sixes, took victory from the jaws of defeat, after Sussex had collapsed to 115–7, requiring 190 to win.

v ESSEX (Horsham)

July 2

Lost by 6 wkts. Essex 4pts, Sussex 0pts

Sussex		
M.P. Speight	b Foster	0
A.M. Green	c Waugh b Lever	3
A.P. Wells	c Waugh b Foster	5
*C.M. Wells	c Waugh b Topley	4
I.J. Gould	run out	63
N.J. Lenham	c Waugh b Topley	3
A.I.C. Dodemaide	not out	38
†P. Moores	lbw b Foster	5
A.R. Clarke	not out	9
A.R. Hansford		
A.M. Babington		
Extras	b 1, lb 13, w 10	24
Total (7 wkts, 40 ov)		154

0, 11, 11, 29, 46, 104, 141

Foster	8	2	24	3
Lever	8	1	28	1
Topley	8	0	11	2
Gooch	8	2	27	0
Stephenson	4	0	30	0
Miller	4	0	20	0

Essex		
*G.A. Gooch	c Dodemaide b Hansford	41
B.R. Hardie	c Green b Babington	38
M.E. Waugh	c Gould b Clarke	32
P.J. Prichard	not out	37
N. Hussain	lbw b Clarke	0
J.P. Stephenson	not out	2
T.D. Topley		
G. Miller		
†M.A. Garnham		
N.A. Foster		
J.K. Lever		
Extras	lb 7	7
Total (4 wkts, 36 ov)		157

64, 110, 135, 135

Dodemaide	7	0	43	0
C.M. Wells	7	0	21	0
Hansford	8	0	30	1
Babington	8	0	38	1
Clarke	6	1	18	2

Umpires: D.J. Constant and D.R. Shepherd
Toss: Essex
This victory kept Essex at the top of the Refuge League, with nine wins from ten matches. Lever and Foster commanded the respect of the home batsmen from the beginning and Essex were never in danger of defeat.

The results in all four major competitions were marginally better than in 1988. Sussex created something of a splash by pronouncing their faith in leg-break bowling. Yorkshire, of course, always tried to avoid the leg-break bowler if possible, but Sussex have been out on a limb before – they insisted on using a lob bowler, Humpreys, years after such under-arm rubbish had had its day, and for several seasons he was successful. It is still early days in the great new leg-break experiment. At the present time the bowling as a whole is not strong. Dodemaide, the Tasmanian in his first year, and Pigott took their wickets at about 30 runs each and were the only two to top 50 Championship wickets.

Alan Wells had a splendid summer with the bat and his thirteen scores between 50 and 99, showed just how reliable he was. David Smith from Surrey made four hundreds in his debut season for his adopted county. Gould, who now plays only as a batsman, was another consistent scorer. The captain, Parker, missed many early matches through injury, but returned a respectable average. Colin Wells was the side's principal all-rounder and just reached 1,000 runs in all matches, he also had some good spells with the ball.

Green, the opening batsman, who had played fairly often in 1988, did little on the occasions when he was required and decided to leave the county at the end of the summer. Lenham, who has been dogged by injury over the last few summers, began well, but then lost his place in the side; his record was similar to that of 1988. Moores, the wicket-keeper had the satisfaction of hitting a maiden first-class hundred against Somerset at Hove and his batting certainly strengthens the lower order.

Sussex really need an improvement in the attack if they are to add any trophies to the NatWest, which they last won in 1986.

REFUGE ASSURANCE LEAGUE

v WORCESTERSHIRE (Hove)
July 23
Won by 14 runs. Sussex 4pts, Worcs 0pts

Sussex		
*P.W.G. Parker	c McEwan b Botham	26
M.P. Speight	c Radford b Hick	74
A.P. Wells	c and b McEwan	20
C.M. Wells	not out	56
I.J. Gould	st Rhodes b Hick	17
A.C.S. Pigottt	c O'Shaughnessy b Radford	18
A.I.C. Dodemaide	not out	3
†P. Moores		
A.R. Clarke		
B.T.P. Donelan		
A.M. Babington		
Extras	lb 17, w 7, nb 1	25
Total (5 wkts, 40 ov)		239

59, 106, 149, 185, 230

McEwan	8	0	34	1
Weston	5	0	24	0
Botham	7	1	27	1
Radford	8	1	59	1
Illingworth	6	0	41	0
O'Shaughnessy	2	0	13	0
Hick	4	0	24	2

Worcestershire		
T.S. Curtis	c Moores b Dodemaide	16
I.T. Botham	c Pigott b C.M. Wells	3
G.A. Hick	c Moores b Pigott	35
D.B. D'Oliveira	c Pigott b Babington	31
*P.A. Neale	b Babington	43
M.J. Weston	b Dodemaide	13
†S.J. Rhodes	c Parker b Babington	2
N.V. Radford	st Moores b Babington	11
S.J. O'Shaughnessy	b C.M. Wells	24
R.K. Illingworth	b Babington	22
S.M. McEwan	not out	7
Extras	lb 13, w 5	18
Total (39.4 ov)		225

17, 29, 75, 120, 154, 154, 163, 170, 202

Dodemaide	8	0	32	2
C.M. Wells	8	0	43	2
Donelan	1	0	14	0
Babington	6.4	0	48	4
Pigott	8	0	27	1
Clarke	8	0	48	1

Umpires: B. Hassan and A.A. Jones
Toss: Worcestershire
Radford was unusually erratic in his bowling spell and the extra 20 runs he conceded cost the visitors the match. Sussex's win in the Championship game the following Tuesday was a second blow to Worcestershire.

v NOTTINGHAMSHIRE (Eastbourne)
August 6
Won by 7 wkts. Sussex 4pts, Notts 0pts

Nottinghamshire		
B.C. Broad	run out	2
P.R. Pollard	run out	29
*R.T. Robinson	c Babington b Dodemaide	55
D.W Randall	c Moores b Dodemaide	13
P. Johnson	c Dodemaide b Pigott	11
F.D. Stephenson	b Dodemaide	12
†B.N. French	c Speight b Hansford	4
E.E. Hemmings	not out	20
K.E. Cooper	run out	0
K. Saxelby	b Hansford	0
D.J. Millns	not out	0
Extras	b 4, lb 19	23
Total (9 wkts, 40 ov)		169

12, 60, 109, 113, 134, 138, 161, 165, 167

Dodemaide	8	1	19	3
C.M. Wells	8	1	24	0
Hansford	8	0	32	2
Babington	8	0	27	0
Pigott	8	0	44	1

Sussex		
*P.W.G. Parker	c Saxelby b Stephenson	0
D.M. Smith	b Stephenson	49
A.P. Wells	c French b Saxelby	26
C.M. Wells	not out	46
M.P. Speight	not out	28
I.J. Gould		
A.I.C. Dodemaide		
A.C.S. Pigott		
†P. Moore		
A.R. Hansford		
A.M. Babington		
Extras	b 1, lb 8, w 12	21
Total (3 wkts, 36.4 ov)		170

0, 71, 105

Stephenson	8	1	16	2
Cooper	8	1	36	0
Saxelby	6.4	0	33	1
Millns	6	0	34	0
Hemmings	8	1	42	0

Umpires: D.J. Constant and R. Julian
Toss: Sussex
Sussex had a surprisingly easy win, which dimmed Notts' hopes of a place in the Refuge Cup. Only Stephenson of the visiting bowlers commanded much respect as Sussex won with 3.2 overs in hand.

v MIDDLESEX (Hastings)
August 20
Lost by 4 wkts. Middx 4pts, Sussex 0pts

Sussex		
*P.W.G. Parker	b Ellcock	7
D.M. Smith	lbw b Ellcock	2
A.P. Wells	c Carr b Emburey	72
C.M. Wells	c Downton b Fraser	2
M.P. Speight	b Williams	8
I.J. Gould	b Hughes	30
A.C.S. Pigott	lbw b Emburey	18
A.I.C. Dodemaide	not out	14
†P. Moores	b Moores	4
A.R. Hansford	c Carr b Emburey	1
A.M. Babington	not out	0
Extras	lb 5, w 5, nb 2	12
Total (9 wkts, 40 ov)		170

8, 25, 32, 44, 114, 151, 152, 165, 167

Ellcock	8	2	19	2
Fraser	5	0	22	1
Williams	8	1	36	1
Hughes	8	0	48	1
Emburey	8	0	28	4
Carr	3	0	12	0

Middlesex		
*M.W. Gatting	c Parker b Dodemaide	3
J.D. Carr	b Pigott	27
M.A. Roseberry	not out	83
R.O. Butcher	lbw b Pigott	15
K.R. Brown	c C.M. Wells b Pigott	20
†P.R. Downton	b Dodemaide	5
N.F. Williams	b Dodemaide	0
J.E. Emburey	not out	6
R.M. Ellcock		
S.P. Hughes		
A.G.J. Fraser		
Extras	lb 5, w 2, nb 6	13
Total (6 wkts, 39.3 ov)		172

5, 61, 91, 150, 165, 165

Dodemaide	8	1	34	3
C.M. Wells	8	0	31	0
babington	8	0	45	0
Hansford	7.3	0	24	0
Pigott	8	1	33	3

Umpires: J.H. Harris and R. Palmer
Toss: Sussex
A six off the third ball of the 40th over brought victory for Middlesex and kept them in contention for a place in the Refuge Cup.

BRITANNIC ASSURANCE COUNTY CHAMPIONSHIP AVERAGES 1989

Batting	*M*	*I*	*NO*	*Runs*	*HS*	*Avge*	*100*	*50*
A.P. Wells	22	38	7	1629	153	52.55	2	13
D.M. Smith	19	35	6	1305	184	45.00	4	6
P.W.G. Parker	15	28	3	972	136	38.88	2	5
C.M. Wells	21	35	4	1021	84*	32.94	–	8
A.I.C. Dodemaide	20	30	9	683	80	32.52	–	4
I.J. Gould	21	32	4	869	125	31.04	1	7
M.P. Speight	9	17	1	425	88	26.56	–	3
N.J. Lenham	14	26	3	608	116	26.43	1	3
P. Moores	22	30	6	629	116	26.21	1	2
A.C.S. Pigott	21	27	5	556	91	25.27	–	3
A.R. Hansford	4	3	1	48	18	24.00	–	–
A.R. Clarke	4	4	1	57	36*	19.00	–	–
A.M. Green	4	6	–	104	39	17.33	–	–
K. Greenfield	4	7	–	84	30	12.00	–	–
I.D.K. Salisbury	11	10	4	62	37	10.33	–	–
N.J. Falkner	2	3	–	28	17	9.33	–	–
A.M. Babington	17	14	8	49	18*	8.17	–	–
B.T.P. Donelan	9	9	3	41	10*	6.83	–	–

Also batted: R.A. Bunting (1 match) 6*; S.J.S. Kimber (1 match) 25; C.C. Remy (1 match) 0.

Bowling	*O*	*M*	*R*	*W*	*Avge*	*BB*	*5i*	*10m*
A.R. Clarke	68	18	189	8	23.63	2-11	–	–
C.M. Wells	562	151	1345	47	28.62	7-65	2	–
A.I.C. Dodemaide	672.1	133	1971	65	30.32	5-77	2	–
A.C. S. Pigott	679.1	130	2084	66	31.58	5-52	1	–
A.R. Hansford	134.3	31	414	12	34.50	5-79	1	–
A.M. Babington	485.4	87	1493	43	34.72	5-37	2	–
B.T.P. Donelan	193	42	633	14	45.21	3-51	–	–
I.D.K. Salisbury	277.4	61	932	15	62.13	3-75	–	–

Also bowled: R.A. Bunting 17-1-90-1; I.J. Gould 9-1-41-3; A.M. Green 34-5-93-3; K. Greenfield 3-0-11-0; S.J.S. Kimber 19-3-59-2; N.J. Lenham 35-5-120-4; P. Moores 1-0-10-0; P.W.G. Parker 7-2-17-0; C.C. Remy 15-3-33-1; D.M. Smith 4.1-0-21-0; A.P. Wells 11.1-2-54-0.

Centuries

4 D.M. Smith: 101 v Lancs (Liverpool); 184 v Notts (Eastbourne); 115 v Glos (Hove); 129 v Middlesex (Lord's).

2 P.W.G. Parker: 110 v Somerset (Hove); 136 v Middlesex (Lord's). A.P. Wells: 103 v Surrey (Hove); 153 v Hants (Southampton).

1 I.J. Gould: 125 v Hants (Hove). N.J. Lenham: 116 v Surrey (Hove). P. Moores: 116 v Somerset (Hove).

REFUGE ASSURANCE LEAGUE

v GLOUCESTERSHIRE (Hove)

August 27

Won by 107 runs. Sussex 4pts, Gloucs 0pts

Sussex		
N.J. Lenham	b Pooley	4
M.P. Speight	c Wright b Alleyne	31
A.P. Wells	c Lloyds b Alleyne	38
C.M. Wells	c Hodgson b Jarvis	63
*P.W.G. Parker	c Athey b Jarvis	67
I.J. Gould	b Pooley	47
A.C.S. Pigott	c and b Jarvis	19
†P. Moores	not out	0
A.M. Babington		
A.R. Clarke		
A.R. Hansford		
Extras	lb 7, w 3	10
Total (7 wkts, 40 ov)		279

7, 68, 92, 186, 241, 261, 279

Barnes	8	0	54	0
Pooley	8	0	45	2
Alleyne	8	1	39	2
Ball	8	0	49	0
Jarvis	8	0	85	3

Gloucestershire		
J.W. Lloyds	st Moores b Hansford	46
G.D. Hodgson	lbw b C.M. Wells	8
*C.W.J. Athey	st Moores b Hansford	19
A.J. Wright	st Mooers b Hansford	46
M.W. Alleyne	c Moores b Hansford	1
M.M. Pritchard	b Lenham	9
†G.A. Tedstone	not out	11
M.W. Pooley	c A.P. Wells b Hansford	0
M.C.J. Ball	b Lenham	4
S.N. Barnes	not out	11
K.B.S. Jarvis		
Extras	b 1, lb 13, w 1, nb 2	17
Total (8 wkts, 40 ov)		172

15, 59, 100, 110, 138, 144, 145, 158

C.M. Wells	8	1	21	1
Babington	8	0	28	0
Hansford	8	1	32	5
Clarke	8	0	36	0
Pigott	4	0	12	0
Lenham	3	0	19	2
Parker	1	0	10	0

Umpires: J.D. Bond and P.B. Wight
Toss: Sussex
Fielding a weak side, Gloucestershire were completely outplayed by the home county, for whom Hansford took five inexpensive wickets.

BENSON AND HEDGES CUP

v ESSEX (Hove)

April 25, 26

Lost by 63 runs. Essex 2pts, Sussex 0pts

Essex		
*G.A. Gooch	c Moores b C.M. Wells	18
B.R. Hardie	c Moores b Pigott	5
A.W. Lilley	c Moores b C.M. Wells	20
M.E. Waugh	c Pigott b C.M. Wells	0
P.J. Prichard	c Clarke	73
J.P. Stephenson	c Gould b Pigott	38
D.R. Pringle	not out	44
G. Miller	c Gould b Babington	20
†D.E. East	not out	1
N.A. Foster		
T.D. Topley		
Extras	lb 8, w 1, nb 4	13
Total (7 wkts, 55 ov)		232

19, 43, 43, 54, 144, 173, 210

Pigott	11	2	60	2
Dodemaide	9	1	45	0
C.M. Wells	11	3	24	3
Babington	11	2	41	1
Clarke	11	2	46	1
Green	2	0	8	0

Sussex		
D.M. Smith	c East b Pringle	1
A.M. Green	c East b Pringle	4
*P.W.G. Parker	b Foster	3
A.P. Wells	c Gooch b Topley	17
C.M. Wells	c East b Stephenson	11
I.J. Gould	b Gooch	16
A.I.C. Dodemaide	c Lilley b Topley	38
†P. Moores	lbw b Stephenson	3
A.C.S. Pigott	not out	49
A.R. Clarke	c Gooch b Pringle	1
A.M. Babington	c Pringle b Foster	9
Extras	lb 6, w 4, nb 8	17
Total (50.4 ov)		169

1, 4, 10, 35, 56, 62, 65, 142, 155

Foster	8.4	0	25	2
Pringle	10	3	35	3
Topley	11	3	26	2
Gooch	9	3	19	1
Stephenson	6	2	18	2
Waugh	2	0	20	0
Miller	4	0	20	0

Umpires: A.G.T. Whitehead and R. Palmer
Toss: Sussex. Gold: P.J. Prichard
A good innings by Prichard and some powerful blows by Pringle provided Essex with 232–7 and when bad light ended play Sussex had stumbled to 72–7 off 31 overs in reply. Pigott could not prevent an Essex victory.

v HAMPSHIRE (Hove)

May 11

Lost by 65 runs. Hants 2pts, Sussex 0pts

Hampshire		
V.P. Terry	lbw b Dodemaide	4
R.J. Scott	c C.M. Wells b Dodemaide	69
*M.C.J. Nicholas	c A.P. Wells v C.M. Wells	15
R.A. Smith	not out	96
D.R. Turner	b Clarke	20
S.T. Jefferies	c Clarke b Pigott	7
K.D. James	not out	18
†R.J. Parks		
N.G. Cowley		
P.J. Bakker		
C.A. Connor		
Extras	b 4, lb 6, w 2, nb 1	13
Total (5 wkts, 55 ov)		242

5, 51, 129, 178, 210

Pigott	11	3	43	1
Dodemaide	11	2	18	2
Babington	11	2	52	0
C.M. Wells	11	1	56	1
Clarke	11	0	63	1

Sussex		
N.J. Falkner	c and b Jefferies	4
D.M. Smith	c and b Bakker	13
A.P. Wells	b Connor	20
*P.W.G. Parker	lbw b James	57
C.M. Wells	c Parks b Connor	20
I.J. Gould	c Smith b Connor	3
A.I.C. Dodemaide	c Smith b Jefferies	32
A.C.S. Pigott	b Connor	6
†P. Moores	b James	1
A.R. Clarke	b James	0
A.M. Babington	not out	1
Extras	lb 17, w 3	20
Total (49.5 ov)		177

6, 23, 56, 60, 65, 167, 173, 176, 176

Jefferies	9	0	37	2
Bakker	11	3	20	1
James	7.5	0	34	3
Connor	8	2	19	4
Cowley	11	2	33	0
Nicholas	3	0	17	0

Umpires: D.G.L. Evans and D.S. Thompsett
Toss: Sussex. Gold: R.A. Smith
Robin Smith hit 96 off 99 balls, which gave the visitors a sound total and the only worthwhile response by Sussex was 57 from Parker, who retired hurt, but returned to help Dodemaide add 102 for the 6th wicket. Hampshire ended as comfortable winners.

PLAYERS

Andrew Mark BABINGTON *b* 22.7.1963 London; left-hand batsman; right-arm fast medium bowler; debut 1986

Rodney Alan BUNTING *b* 25.4.1965 East Winch, Norfolk; right-hand batsman; right-arm fast-medium bowler; debut 1988

Andrew Russell CLARKE *b* 23.12.1961 Patcham; right-hand batsman; leg-break bowler; debut 1988

Anthony Ian Christopher DODEMAIDE *b* 5.10.1963 Williamstown, Austr; right-arm fast-medium bowler; right-hand batsman; debut 1989; also plays for Victoria; three Tests for Australia; capped by Sussex 1989

Bradleigh Thomas DONELAN *b* 3.1.89 Park Royal, Middlx; right-hand batsman; off-break bowler; debut v Worcs in July 1989

Ian James GOULD *b* 19.8.1957 Slough; left-hand batsman; wicketkeeper; debut 1981; previously appeared for Middx 1975–80; Sussex captain 1987

Nicholas James FALKNER *b* 30.9.1962 Redhill; right-hand batsman; right-arm medium-pace bowler; debut 1988; previously played for Surrey 1984–87

Allan Michael GREEN *b* 28.5. 1960 Pulborough; right-hand batsman; debut 1980

Keith GREENFIELD *b* 6.12.1968 Brighton; right-hand batsman; right-arm medium pace bowler; debut 1987

Alan Roderick HANSFORD *b* 1.10.1968 Cuckfield; right-arm medium-fast bowler; right-hand batsman; FC debut v Cambridge Univ in June 1989

Simon Julian Spencer KIMBER *b* 6.10.1963; right-arm medium fast bowler; right-hand batsman; debut 1977; previously played for Worcs 1985

Neil John LENHAM *b* 17.12.1965 Worthing; right-hand batsman; right-arm medium bowler; debut 1984; son of L.J. (ex-Sussex)

Peter MOORES *b* 18.12.1962 Macclesfield; wicketkeeper; right-hand batsman – scored maiden fc hundred in 1989; debut 1985; previously played for Worcs 1983–84

Paul William Giles PARKER *b* 15.1.1956 Bulawayo, S Rhodesia; right-hand batsman; debut 1976; captain since 1988; Cambridge Univ 1976–78; one Test for England in 1981

Anthony Charles Shackleton PIGOTT *b* 4.6.1958 London; right-arm fast-medium bowler; right-hand batsman; debut 1978; one Test for England, in emergency in 1983–84

Carlos C. REMY *b* 24.7.1968 St Lucia, WI; right-hand batsman; FC debut for Sussex v Hants August 1989; he had the misfortune to be dismissed first ball he received when opening the batting

Ian David Kenneth SALISBURY *b* 21.1.1970 Northampton; leg-break bowler; right-hand batsman; FC debut for Sussex in May 1989

David Mark SMITH *b* 9.1.1956 Balham, S London; opening left-hand batsman; debut 1989; capped June 1989; previously appeared for Surrey 1973–83, Worcs 1984–86 and Surrey again 1987–88; has now received caps from three counties; two Tests for England 1985–86

Martin Peter SPEIGHT *b* 24.10.1967 Walsall; wicketkeeper; right-hand batsman; debut 1986

Alan Peter WELLS *b* 2.10.1961 Newhaven; right-hand batsman; occasional right-arm medium pace bowler; debut 1981; brother of C.M. (Sussex)

Colin Mark WELLS *b* 3.3.1960 Newhaven; all-rounder; right-hand batsman; right-arm medium-pace bowler; debut 1979

NATWEST BANK TROPHY

v BERKSHIRE (Hove)

June 28, 29

Won by 35 runs.

Sussex

N.J. Lenham	c Stevens b Jackson	17
D.M. Smith	not out	99
A.M. Green	c Heseltine b Dodd	18
A.P. Wells	c Mercer b Dodd	30
*C.M. Wells	lbw b Hartley	2
I.J. Gould	c and b Jones	14
A.I.C. Dodemaide	run out	1
A.C.S. Pigott	lbw b Jackson	13
†P. Moores	b Jackson	20
A.R. Clarke	not out	2
A.M. Babington		
Extras	b 1, lb 5, w 8, nb 5	19
Total (8 wkts, 60 ov)		235

35, 78, 139, 148, 183, 185, 203, 233

Jones	12	1	72	1
Jackson	12	1	38	3
Dodd	12	1	37	2
Stear	12	0	38	0
Hartley	12	1	44	1

Berkshire

M.G. Lickley	c C.M. Wells b Clarke	22
G.E. Loveday	run out	26
P.J. Heseltine	c A.P. Wells b Babington	30
*M.L. Simmons	c Babington b Pigott	34
D.J.M. Mercer	lbw b Clarke	45
B. Jackson	c C.M. Wells b Clarke	3
M.G. Stear	not out	2
T.P.J. Dodd	not out	4
†M.E. Stevens		
J.H. Jones		
D. Hartley		
Extras	b 1, lb 14, w 18, nb 1	34
Total (6 wkts, 60 ov)		200

46, 73, 106, 190, 190, 195

Pigott	12	1	37	1
Dodemaide	12	2	24	0
C.M. Wells	12	1	51	0
Babington	12	1	32	1
Clarke	12	3	41	3

Umpires: B. Hassan and R. Palmer

Toss: Berkshire. MofM: D.M. Smith

On the first day Sussex made 235, with Smith carrying out his bat, but rain prevented Berkshire beginning their reply. Play began at 10.30 on the second day but after 15 minutes rain caused a six hour break and the match finally ended at 8.15. Berkshire never really looked likely to reach the 236 required.

v LEICESTERSHIRE (Hove)

July 12

Won by 68 runs

Sussex

D.M. Smith	c Potter b Willey	59
M.P. Speight	c Briers b Taylor	48
*P.W.G. Parker	not out	87
A.P. Wells	not out	86
C.M. Wells		
I.J. Gould		
A.I.C. Dodemaide		
A.C.S. Pigott		
†P. Moores		
A.R. Clarke		
A.M. Babington		
Extras	b 5, lb 12, w 2, nb 1	20
Total (2 wkts, 60 ov)		300

93, 145

Agnew	12	2	49	0
Benjamin	12	4	39	0
Parsons	8	0	64	0
Taylor	11	0	67	1
Willey	12	2	31	1
Potter	5	0	33	0

Leicestershire

*D.I. Gower	b Dodemaide	23
N.E. Briers	b Dodemaide	8
P. Willey	run out	89
J.J. Whitaker	c C.M. Wells b Dodemaide	36
L. Potter	c Moores b Babington	17
C.C. Lewis	c and b Babington	5
†P. Whitticase	c Gould b Pigott	0
W.K.M. Benjamin	b Babington	17
G.J. Parsons	not out	16
J.P. Agnew	lbw b Dodemaide	6
L.B. Taylor	absent hurt	0
Extras	b 1, w 12, nb 2	15
Total (55.4 ov)		232

22, 37, 99, 147, 159, 159, 188, 220, 232

Piggot	12	1	71	1
Dodemaide	10.4	1	37	4
C.M. Wells	10	0	29	0
Babington	11	0	53	3
Clarke	12	1	41	0

Umpires: A.A. Jones and P.J. Eele

Toss: Sussex. MofM: P.W.G. Parker

The Sussex openers put on 93 in 25 overs and with substantial innings from Parker and Alan Wells Sussex reached their highest ever NatWest total. In reply Willey was defiant, but no one gave him much support and Sussex won by a large margin.

OTHER FIRST CLASS MATCH

v CAMBRIDGE UNIVERSITY (Hove)

June 21, 22, 23

Won by an Innings and 75 runs

Cambridge University 1st Innings

S.P. James	c Gould b Babington	3
R. Heap	b Hansford	0
*M.A. Atherton	lbw b Hansford	27
J.M.G. Willatt	c Greenfield b Clarke	45
J.C.M. Atkinson	lbw b Babington	1
M.T. Alban	c and b Babington	36
†R.J. Turner	lbw b Hansford	43
R.A. Pyman	run out	55
D.J. Bush	c Gould b Babington	5
A.J. Buzza	not out	1
B.C. Cotton	b Hansford	0
Extras	b 6, lb 5, w 1, nb 1	13
Total		229

3, 7, 37, 38, 116, 118, 196, 229, 229

Hansford	18.5	5	46	4
Babington	21	7	45	4
Bunting	10	2	45	0
Kimber	8	2	24	0
Clarke	12	3	33	1
Lenham	3	0	7	0
Green	4	1	18	0

Sussex 1st Innings

N.J. Lenham	c Atherton b Pyman	25
K. Greenfield	b Buzza	48
R.A. Bunting	c Heap b Pyman	73
A.M. Green	c Atkinson b Buzza	94
N.J. Falkner	c Atherton	48
*C.M. Wells	lbw b Pyman	33
†I.J. Gould	c and b Buzza	1
S.J.S. Kimber	c Atherton b Cotton	21
A.R. Clarke	c Atkinson b Pyman	12
A.R. Hansford	not out	5
A.M. Babington	not out	1
Extras	b 5, lb 4, w 1	10
Total (9 wkts dec)		371

43, 116, 196, 292, 296, 297, 341, 363, 363

Bush	20	4	51	0
Cotton	14	3	48	1
Pyman	27	4	81	4
Atherton	31	9	74	1
Buzza	35	5	108	3

Cambridge University 2nd Innings

S.P. James	lbw b Hansford	16
R. Heap	c Gould b Bunting	6
*M.A. Atherton	c sub b Hansford	2
J.M. G. Willatt	c Lenham b Bunting	4
J.C.M. Atkinson	c Green b Hansford	0
M.T. Alban	lbw b Hansford	2
†R.J. Turner	c Greenfield b Bunting	6
R.A. Pyman	c Hansford b C.M. Wells	18
D.J. Bush	lbw b Bunting	0
A.J. Buzza	b C.M. Wells	3
B.C. Cotton	not out	0
Extras	b 4, lb 3, w 1, nb 2	10
Total		67

24, 28, 28, 28, 38, 42, 52, 52, 67

Hansford	14	3	25	4
Babington	5	3	3	0
Bunting	9	3	18	4
Clarke	1	1	0	0
Kimber	3	1	8	0
C.M. Wells	2.5	0	6	2

Umpires: R. Julian and D.S. Thompsett

Toss: Cambridge University

Hansford from Surrey University, took his first wicket in first class cricket on the opening day and ended the match with eight, as the students fell apart twice. The only bright spot in the University batting was Pyman's 55. Sussex began the second day at 43–1 and then Bunting made maiden a 50, when acting as nightwatchman. Green scored 94 in 3 hours. Sussex declared their innings overnight and swept quickly to success on the last day.

Away Matches

The full scorecard of each of Sussex's away matches will be found in the sections for the respective home teams.

Britannic Assurance Championship

Taunton: May 4, 5, 6
Sussex 234 (N.A. Mallender 5–30) and 232 (N.A. Mallender 7–62) lost to Somerset 229 and 238–5 by 5 wkts. Somerset 22pts, Sussex 6pts.

Liverpool: May 27, 29, 30
Sussex 334–7 (D.M. Smith 101) and 185–4d drew with Lancs 204 (A.M. Babington 5–37) and 266–8. Sussex 7pts, Lancs 4pts.

Edgbaston: June 3, 5, 6
Sussex 259 and 85–0 drew with Warwicks 277 (A.M. Babington 5–59). Sussex 7pts, Warwicks 7pts.

Tunbridge Wells: June 7, 8, 9
Kent 243 and 82–1d lost to Sussex 99–2d and 228–7 by 3 wkts. Sussex 20pts, Kent 2pts.

Derby: June 17, 19, 20
Derbys 342 (A.I.C. Dodemaide 5–112) and 223–9d drew with Sussex 417. Derbys 6pts, Sussex 6pts.

Southampton: June 24, 26, 27
Hants 356–8d and 171–3d drew with Sussex 287 (A.P. Wells 153) and 116–5. Hants 8pts, Sussex 4pts.

Gloucester: July 5, 6, 7
Gloucs 399–9d drew with Sussex 232 (C.A. Walsh 5–44) and 21–0. Gloucs 7pts, Sussex 3pts.

Middlesbrough: July 8, 10, 11
Yorks 260–8d and forfeited 2nd inns beat Sussex forfeited 1st inns and 252 (A. Sidebottom 5–56) by 8 runs. Yorks 19pts, Sussex 3pts.

Swansea: August 12, 14, 15
Sussex 240 and 223–3 drew with Glamorgan 308. Glamorgan 7pts, Sussex 4pts.

Lord's: Sept 8, 9, 10, 11
Sussex 438 (P.W.G. Parker 136, D.M. Smith 129) and 137–4d drew with Middx 302 (M.W. Gatting 139*) and 202–5. Sussex 6pts, Middx 3pts.

The Oval: Sept 13, 14, 15, 16
Surrey 385 (A.J. Stewart 199*, C.M. Wells 7–82) and 53–3d drew with Sussex 153–2d and 128–4. Surrey 4pts, Sussex 3pts.

v KENT (Hove)

April 27, 28, 29, May 1
Drawn. Sussex 7pts, Kent 5pts

Kent 1st Innings

S.G. Hinks	c Gould b C.M. Wells	30
M.R. Benson	b C.M. Wells	45
N.R. Taylor	c Moores b C.M. Wells	1
T.R. Ward	lbw b C.M. Wells	64
*C.S. Cowdrey	b C.M. Wells	40
G.R. Cowdrey	c Moores b Dodemaide	5
†S.A. Marsh	c Parker b Dodemaide	0
C. Penn	c Moore b Babington	21
R.P. Davis	not out	12
A.P. Igglesden	lbw b C.M. Wells	0
H.L. Alleyne	c and b C.M. Wells	2
Extras	b 1, lb 3, nb 10	14
Total (83.4 ov)		234

47, 49, 138, 153, 162, 168, 210, 228, 232

Pigott	16	5	36	0
Dodemaide	22	8	44	2
C.M. Wells	20.4	6	65	7
Clarke	4	1	7	0
Babington	21	1	78	1

Sussex 1st Innings

A.M. Green	c C.S. Cowdrey b Penn	34
D.M. Smith	b Davis	68
*P.W.G. Parker	b Penn	16
A.P. Wells	lbw b Davis	7
C.M. Wells	b C.S. Cowdrey	25
I.J. Gould	c Marsh b G.R. Cowdrey	49
A.I.C. Dodemaide	c Marsh b C.S. Cowdrey	10
†P. Moores	lbw b Alleyne	10
A.C.S. Pigott	c Marsh b Igglesden	64
A.R. Clarke	not out	36
A.M. Babington	b Alleyne	3
Extras	b 4, lb 11, w 3, nb 21	39
Total (100 ov: 299–8)		361

65, 123, 152, 153, 188, 206, 220, 286, 352

Igglesden	25	2	78	1
Alleyne	28.4	3	101	2
Penn	27	4	62	2
C.S. Cowdrey	17	3	46	2
Davis	17	5	37	2
G.R. Cowdrey	4	0	22	1

Kent 2nd Innings

S.G. Hinks	c Moores b Pigott	56
M.R. Benson	not out	74
N.R. Taylor	c Parker b Pigott	23
T.R. Ward	not out	87
Extras	lb 6, nb 6	12
Total (2 wkts dec)		252

99, 135

Pigott	20	5	72	2
Dodemaide	23	5	53	0
C.M. Wells	18	4	48	0
Babington	10	3	34	0
A.P. Wells	6	1	34	0
Parker	5	2	5	0

Umpires: M.J. Kitchen and R.A. White
Toss: Sussex
Colin Wells achieved the best bowling analysis of his career on the first day, when he dismissed Kent for 234, but Dodemaide, on his Championship debut, also bowled impressively. The Sussex innings began at start of play on Friday, with D.M. Smith making 68 on his Sussex Championship debut, but it was an eighth wicket stand of 66 by Gould and Pigott that ensured a reasonable lead for the home side, the total being 332–8 at the close. Rain restricted play on Saturday during which Kent moved to 80–0 in their second innings. On Monday playing time was again reduced and a draw became inevitable.

v SURREY (Hove)

May 17, 18, 19
Drawn. Sussex 7pts, Surrey 5pts

Sussex 1st Innings

N.J. Falkner	c D.J. Bicknell b Tazelaar	10
D.M. Smith	c Ward b M.P. Bicknell	4
N.J. Lenham	c Atkins b Medlycott	116
A.P. Wells	c Greig b Tazelaar	103
*C.M. Wells	c M.P. Bicknell b Feltham	8
I.J. Gould	lbw b Feltham	4
A.I.C. Dodemaide	not out	29
A.C.S. Pigott	c Talezaar b M.P. Bicknell	4
†P. Moores	not out	1
A.R. Clarke		
A.M. Babington		
Extras	b 6, nb 15	21
Total (100 ov: 298–6) (7 wkts dec)		300

13, 23, 214, 230, 242, 271, 289

Tazelaar	21	4	89	2
M.P. Bicknell	24	10	51	2
Feltham	25	6	62	2
Greig	18	2	43	0
Medlycott	13	3	47	1
Alikhan	1	0	2	0

Surrey 1st Innings

D.J. Bicknell	c Gould b Dodemaide	10
G.S. Clinton	c Gould b Pigott	0
M.A. Feltham	c Moores b Dodemaide	40
R.I. Alikhan	c and b Pigott	4
†A.J. Stewart	lbw b Pigott	26
P.D. Atkins	c Gould b Babington	2
D.M. Ward	c Moores b C.M. Wells	45
*I.A. Greig	not out	87
K.T. Medlycott	c Smith b Clarke	5
D. Tazelaar	lbw b Dodemaide	14
M.P. Bicknell	c A.P. Wells b Pigott	16
Extras	b 3, lb 7	10
Total (92.4 ov)		259

1, 37, 44, 56, 59, 100, 168, 177, 210

Pigott	23.4	2	91	4
Dodemaide	29	5	61	3
Babington	14	4	35	1
C.M. Wells	14	3	28	1
Clarke	12	5	34	1

Sussex 2nd Innings

N.J. Falkner	b Feltham	17
D.M. Smith	lbw b Tazelaar	1
N.J. Lenham	b Medlycott	48
†P. Moores	c Ward b M.P. Bicknell	44
A.P. Wells	not out	54
*C.M. Wells	c Stewart b Medlycott	36
I.J. Gould	c Ward b Feltham	3
A.I.C. Dodemaide	not out	0
Extras	b 14, lb 4, nb 12	30
Total (6 wkts dec)		233

6, 27, 128, 128, 215, 228

Tazelaar	12	2	40	1
M.P. Bicknell	18	4	44	1
Feltham	18	3	67	2
Medlycott	19	4	56	2
Stewart	1	0	8	0

Surrey 2nd Innings

D.J. Bicknell	b Dodemaide	101
G.S. Clinton	not out	90
*I.A. Greig	c Pigott b Clarke	10
M.A. Feltham	run out	1
D.M. Ward	b Dodemaide	3
†A.J. Stewart	b Clarke	13
K.T. Medlycott	not out	6
Extras	b 3, lb 6, w 2	11
Total (5 wkts)		235

178, 195, 197, 206, 227

Pigott	4	1	18	0
Dodemaide	17	2	65	2
Babington	10	0	36	0
C.M. Wells	6	0	39	0
Clarke	14	0	68	2

Umpires: B. Dudleston and D.S. Thompsett
Toss: Surrey
Surrey were set 275 in 52 overs and began in brilliant style, Bicknell and Clinton putting on 178. The former hit 101 off 153 balls. Four wickets fell in nine overs however and Surrey gave up the chase when 40 runs were required with one over remaining. The first day was mainly devoted to a partnership between Lenham and Alan Wells, which realised 191 runs. Surrey started Thursday with 11–1 off 5 overs, and the main batting then failed until Greig arrived to score a chanceless 87. Sussex were 77 ahead with eight wickets in hand when play commenced on the last morning.

v NORTHAMPTONSHIRE (Hove)

June 10, 12, 13

Drawn. Sussex 8pts, Northants 4pts

Northamptonshire 1st Innings		
G. Cook	c and b Pigott	6
*W. Larkins	lbw b Babington	16
R.J. Bailey	c Moores b Babington	11
D.J. Wild	c Moores b Pigott	13
D.J. Capel	b Dodemaide	102
A. Fordham	c Moores b Babington	3
†D. Ripley	c C.M. Wells b Pigott	12
G. Smith	lbw b Dodemaide	0
N.G.B. Cook	c Lenham b Pigott	21
C.E.L. Ambrose	not out	16
M.A. Robinson	c Dodemaide b Pigott	9
Extras	lb 4, w 4, nb 6	14
Total (93 ov)		223

14, 32, 37, 98, 145, 162, 162, 196, 201

Pigott	18	3	52	5
Dodemaide	23	3	55	2
Babington	23	4	65	3
C.M. Wells	17	6	37	0
Salisbury	12	8	10	0

Sussex 1st Innings		
N.J. Lenham	c Larkins b Ambrose	14
D.M. Smith	retired hurt	22
K. Greenfield	b Ambrose	13
A.P. Wells	b Robinson	89
*P.W.G. Parker	b Robinson	45
C.M. Wells	not out	84
A.I.C. Dodemaide	run out	54
†P. Moores	not out	8
A.C.S. Pigott		
I.D.K. Salisbury		
A.M. Babington		
Extras	lb 13, nb 8	21
Total (5 wkts dec, 100 ov)		350

59, 60, 195, 200, 331

Ambrose	28	5	106	2
Capel	17	4	60	0
Smith	6	1	27	0
Robinson	22	4	78	2
N.G.B. Cook	25	7	57	0
Bailey	2	0	9	0

Northamptonshire 2nd Innings		
G. Cook	c Moores b Salisbury	138
*W. Larkins	c Parker b Dodemaide	13
R.J. Bailey	b Babington	25
D.J. Wild	b Babington	5
D.J. Capel	st Moores b Lenham	126
A. Fordham	not out	20
†D. Ripley	not out	4
Extras	lb 12, w 1, nb 11	24
Total (5 wkts dec)		355

27, 81, 87, 313, 343

Pigott	11	0	53	0
Dodemaide	9	1	45	1
Babington	19.1	3	52	2
C.M. Wells	6	1	15	0
Salisbury	35	3	147	1
Parker	2	0	12	0
Lenham	4	0	19	1

Sussex 2nd Innings		
N.J. Lenham	lbw b Robinson	17
D.M. Smith	c N.G.B. Cook b Ambrose	12
K. Greenfield	c Ripley b Ambrose	4
A.P. Wells	c Ripley b Robinson	4
C.M. Wells	c Fordham b Robinson	2
A.I.C. Dodemaide	c G. Cook b Smith	13
†P. Moores	c N.G.B. Cook b Capel	60
A.C.S. Pigott	b Smith	0
*P.W.G. Parker	not out	28
I.D.K. Salisbury	not out	4
Extras	b 4, lb 6, nb 4	14
Total (8 wkts)		158

20, 33, 40, 42, 42, 84, 84, 154

Ambrose	14	5	43	2
Robinson	12	0	49	3
Smith	4	0	8	2
Capel	5.5	0	48	1

Umpires: A.G.T. Whitehead and J.H Harris
Toss: Sussex
Sussex appeared to have control of this match, having dismissed Northants for 223 on the first day and replied with 350–5 on the second. Alan Wells hit 89 off 125 balls and his brother 84 off 135 balls. On the final morning Northants were then reduced to 87–3, but Capel then joined Geoff Cook and the pair added 226 in 50 overs, Capel completing his second 100 of the match. Sussex were set 229 off 36 overs. They collapsed to 42–5 and were saved from an unexpected defeat by Moores.

v ESSEX (Horsham)

July 1, 3, 4

Drawn. Sussex 7pts, Essex 3pts

Essex 1st Innings		
*G.A. Gooch	b C.M. Wells	29
J.P. Stephenson	c Smith b C.M. Wells	34
G. Miller	c Pigott b C.M. Wells	11
M.E. Waugh	run out	0
P.J. Prichard	b Pigott	9
N. Hussain	lbw b Dodemaide	32
D.R. Pringle	c Moores b Dodemaide	13
†M.A. Garnham	c Moores b Dodemaide	18
N.A. Foster	not out	13
T.D. Topley	c Moores b Dodemaide	3
J.H. Childs	c Smith b C.M. Wells	4
Extras	b 4, b 11, w 2, nb 2	19
Total (70.4 ov)		185

54, 78, 79, 86, 102, 139, 154, 161, 175

Dodemaide	19.4	4	58	4
Pigott	15.2	4	34	1
Babington	21	2	45	0
C.M. Wells	14.4	4	33	4

Sussex 1st Innings		
N.J. Lenham	c Gooch b Foster	4
D.M. Smith	c Hussain b Foster	46
A.M. Green	c Garnham b Pringle	39
A.P. Wells	lbw b Foster	1
*C.M. Wells	lbw b Pringle	20
I.J. Gould	c Topley b Childs	58
I.D.K. Salisbury	c Foster b Childs	37
A.I.C. Dodemaide	c Hussain b Topley	35
†P. Moores	not out	5
A.C.S. Pigott	c Garnham b Topley	0
A.M. Babington	b Foster	5
Extras	b 6, lb 25, w 1, nb 3	35
Total (100 ov: 256–6)		285

4, 39, 75, 86, 180, 203, 274, 274, 274}

Foster	28.5	8	53	4
Pringle	21	5	46	2
Topley	20	7	63	2
Stephenson	4	0	12	0
Childs	16	7	38	2
Miller	17	7	35	0
Gooch	6	2	7	0

Essex 2nd Innings		
*G.A. Gooch	b C.M. Wells	25
J.P. Stephenson	c Moores b Babington	0
G. Miller	c sub b C.M. Wells	21
M.E. Waugh	c and b Dodemaide	8
P.J. Prichard	c Smith b Babington	60
N. Hussain	c Moores b Dodemaide	23
†M.A. Garnham	not out	90
D.R. Pringle	not out	81
Extras	b 18, lb 21, nb 3	42
Total (6 wkts dec)		350

2, 43, 52, 76, 133, 176

Dodemaide	31	6	108	2
Babington	20	1	54	2
C.M. Wells	23	6	62	2
Salisbury	9	0	52	0
Pigott	7	0	35	0

Sussex 2nd Innings		
N.J. Lenham	c Garnham b Foster	0
D.M. Smith	c Miller b Childs	71
A.M. Green	c and b Childs	15
A.P. Wells	c Gooch b Pringle	49
I.J. Gould	c Foster b Pringle	20
*C.M. Wells	c Stephenson b Childs	27
A.C.S. Pigott	c Hussain b Childs	32
A.I.C. Dodemaide	b Childs	0
†P. Moores	c Hussain b Miller	4
I.D.K. Salisbury	not out	3
A.M. Babington	not out	0
Extras	b 4, lb 13, nb 2	19
Total (9 wkts)		240

0, 79, 106, 143, 176, 225, 230, 235, 240

Foster	4	1	29	1
Pringle	17	1	62	2
Childs	20	3	84	5
Topley	7	1	25	0
Miller	3	0	23	1

Umpires: D.J. Constant and D.R. Shepherd
Toss: Sussex
Having gained a first innings lead of 100, Sussex found the match slipping away from them on the final day. Garnham and Pringle hit 174 in 35 overs and thus were able to set Sussex 251 in 51 overs. At the start of the last hour, the Wells brothers might have won the match, but when both fell after having briefly attacked the bowling, the home county were forced on the defensive and just saved the game.

v WORCESTERSHIRE (Hove)

July 22, 24, 25

Won by 4 wkts. Sussex 22pts, Worcs 6pts

Worcestershire 1st Innings		
T.S. Curtis	c Moores b Pigott	102
G.J. Lord	retired hurt	4
G.A. Hick	c Smith b Dodemaide	0
D.B. d'Oliveira	c Moores b Pigott	2
*P.A. Neale	run out	16
I.T. Botham	b Donelan	8
†S.J. Rhodes	c Smith b Donelan	11
M.J. Weston	b Donelan	70
N.V. Radford	not out	66
R.K. Illingworth	c Moores b Dodemaide	8
G.R. Dilley	b Dodemaide	6
Extras	b 4, lb 18, nb 5	27
Total (100 ov: 239–6)		320

14, 19, 75, 93, 113, 215, 278, 310, 320

Pigott	26	7	77	2
Dodemaide	26.3	7	56	3
Babington	20	5	66	0
C.M. Wells	22	6	48	0
Donelan	28	11	51	3

Sussex 1st Innings		
*P.W.G. Parker	lbw b Botham	66
M.P. Speight	c Curtis b Botham	7
†P. Moores	c sub b Botham	12
A.P. Wells	b Botham	15
C.M. Wells	c Weston b Botham	81
I.J. Gould	lbw b Botham	4
D.M. Smith	lbw b Botham	12
A.I.C. Dodemaide	c Weston b Hick	36
A.C.S. Pigott	b Hick	32
B.T.P. Donelan	not out	10
A.M. Babington	c d'Oliveira b Hick	6
Extras	b 8, lb 3, w 1, nb 8	20
Total (94 ov)		301

25, 56, 106, 107, 113, 143, 229, 261, 284

Dilley	9	0	62	0
Botham	40	10	85	7
Radford	5	1	18	0
Illingworth	10	5	56	0
Weston	6	0	34	0
Hick	14	4	35	3

Worcestershire 2nd Innings		
T.S. Curtis	c Gould b Pigott	12
M.J. Weston	c C.M. Wells b Dodemaide	4
G.A. Hick	not out	110
D.B. D'Oliveira	b Donelan	55
I.T. Botham	c C.M. Wells b Donelan	4
*P.A. Neale	not out	33
Extras	b 4, lb 7, w 1	12
Total (4 wkts dec)		230

16, 16, 160, 168

Pigott	15	2	69	1
Dodemaide	13	3	51	1
Donelan	17	3	78	2
Babington	6	0	21	0

Sussex 2nd Innings		
D.M. Smith	run out	24
M.P. Speight	c Hick b Illingworth	26
*P.W.G. Parker	lbw b Botham	86
A.P. Wells	c Hick b Botham	40
C.M. Wells	c Radford b Hick	26
A.C.S. Pigott	not out	27
I.J. Gould	st Rhodes b Hick	6
A.I.C. Dodemaide	not out	7
Extras	b 2, lb 5, nb 1	8
Total (6 wkts)		250

46, 78, 142, 205, 208, 227

Radford	6	0	26	0
Botham	25	4	92	2
Illingworth	9	1	42	1
Hick	11	0	83	2

Umpires: B. Hassan and A.A. Jones
Toss: Worcestershire
In an exciting finish Sussex required two runs off the final ball of the match and Pigott duly obliged, thus giving Sussex a valuable victory, which moved them from 14th to 11th in the table and at the same time damaging Worcester's hopes of the Championship, as Essex now had a lead of 27 points over the Midland county in second place. In the final stages of the game, the visitors were handicapped due to an injury to Dilley. Sussex had 48 overs in which to make their runs and were well served by their captain.

v SOMERSET (Hove)

July 26, 27, 28

Drawn. Somerset 7pts, Sussex 6pts

Sussex 1st Innings

D.M. Smith	c Cook b Jones	6
M.P. Speight	c Burns b Jones	1
†P. Moores	b Marks	29
A.P. Wells	c Burns b Jones	37
*P.W.G. Parker	c Burns b Marks	110
C.M. Wells	c Harden b Cleal	44
I.J. Gould	c Jones b Marks	53
A.I.C. Dodemaide	c Rose b Cleal	21
B.T.P. Donelan	c Bartlett b Marks	2
I.D.K. Salisbury	not out	0
A.M. Babington		
Extras	lb 11, nb 2	13
Total (9 wkts dec, 90.1 ov)		316

7, 8, 44, 96, 222, 247, 313, 315, 316

Jones	15	5	48	3
Rose	19	3	74	0
Marks	23.1	6	65	4
Cleal	17	1	62	2
Trump	11	4	42	0
Harden	5	2	14	0

Somerset 1st Innings

S.J. Cook	c Spaight b Dodemaide	6
J.G. Wyatt	c Moores b C.M. Wells	23
M.W. Cleal	b C.M. Wells	20
R.J. Bartlett	c Moores b Dodemaide	7
C.J. Tavare	c and b Salisbury	83
R.J. Harden	c Moores b Salisbury	39
†N.D. Burns	not out	38
*V.J. Marks	st Moores b Salisbury	33
G.D. Rose		
H.R.J. Trump		
A.N. Jones		
Extras	b 4, lb 6, nb 7	17
Total (100 ov: 260–6) (7 wkts dec)		266

18, 49, 57, 63, 174, 208, 266

Dodemaide	24	7	55	2
Babington	18	2	64	0
C.M. Wells	18	5	44	2
Donelan	12	5	18	0
Salisbury	31.2	9	75	3

Sussex 2nd Innings

D.M. Smith	b Rose	24
M.P. Speight	c Burns b Rose	6
*P.W.G. Parker	c and b Rose	4
A.P. Wells	not out	78
†P. Moores	Marks b Trump	116
C.M. Wells	not out	9
Extras	lb 6, nb 2	8
Total (4 wkts dec)		245

6, 18, 46, 228

Jones	10	5	23	0
Rose	14	1	69	3
Cleal	10	3	33	0
Marks	14	4	45	0
Trump	8	0	37	1
Harden	6	1	32	0

Somerset 2nd Innings

S.J. Cook	c A.P. Wells b C.M. Wells	130
J.G. Wyatt	c Parker b Dodemaide	19
R.J. Bartlett	c Speight b Babington	37
C.J. Tavare	b Donelan	25
R.J. Harden	run out	39
*V.J. Marks	not out	32
A.N. Jones	b Dodemaide	1
G.D. Rose	not out	3
Extras	lb 3, w 1, nb 2	6
Total (6 wkts)		292

44, 132, 180, 238, 276, 278

Dodemaide	18	1	79	2
C.M. Wells	9	4	13	1
Salisbury	19	2	113	0
Babington	6	0	25	1
Donelan	11	0	59	1

Umpires: B. Hassan and R.A. White

Toss: Sussex

Somerset required 296 off 63 overs to win the match and with Cook making 130 off 146 balls, this target reduced to 14 off the last over. Marks then needed to hit six off the last ball, but failed by a few yards. Earlier Moores had hit a maiden century in 108 balls, allowing Sussex to declare. On the first day Sussex made 316 and Somerset were 33–1 in reply. The play was marred by some offensive language by Jones, who had been previously fined during the season for the same oaths. Somerset batted slowly on the second day, but Marks declared 50 runs in arrears and when Sussex fell to 52–3 by stumps the game was interestingly poised.

v NOTTINGHAMSHIRE (Eastbourne)

August 5, 7, 8

Lost by 3 wkts. Notts 22pts, Sussex 7pts

Sussex 1st Innings

D.M. Smith	lbw b Hemmings	184
M.P. Speight	lbw b Millns	1
*P.W.G. Parker	lbw b Cooper	24
A.P. Wells	lbw b Millns	17
C.M. Wells	lbw b Hemmings	65
I.J. Gould	lbw b Hemmings	3
A.I.C. Dodemaide	not out	16
A.C.S. Pigott	not out	9
†P. Moores		
B.T.P. Donelan		
A.M. Babington		
Extras	lb 6	6
Total (100 ov: 313–6) (6 wkts dec)		325

6, 49, 99, 286, 299, 300

Stephenson	15	1	77	0
Millns	15	3	45	2
Cooper	22	5	62	1
Hemmings	33	12	75	3
Afford	17	4	60	0

Nottinghamshire 1st Innings

B.C. Broad	c Moores b Dodemaide	16
P.R. Pollard	b Pigott	82
*R.T. Robinson	c Speight b C.M. Wells	22
P. Johnson	lbw b Babington	47
D.W. Randall	c Parker b C.M. Wells	24
F.D. Stephenson	not out	64
†B.N. French	b Pigott	26
E.E. Hemmings	b Pigott	8
K.E. Cooper	not out	8
D.J. Millns		
J.A. Afford		
Extras	lb 6	6
Total (7 wkts dec, 74 ov)		303

39, 69, 144, 173, 206, 264, 278

Dodemaide	16	2	97	1
Pigott	23	2	92	3
Babington	15	3	56	1
C.M. Wells	18	5	38	2
Donelan	2	0	14	0

Sussex 2nd Innings

D.M. Smith	b Stephenson	26
M.P. Speight	c French b Stephenson	0
†P. Moores	c French b Stephenson	1
A.P. Wells	b Cooper	20
*P.W.G. Parker	st French b Afford	72
C.M. Wells	c Hemmings b Cooper	79
I.J. Gould	lbw b Stephenson	7
A.I.C. Dodemaide	c Cooper b Stephenson	26
A.C.S. Pigott	c Broad b Hemmings	15
B.T.P. Donelan	not out	3
A.M. Babington	not out	0
Extras	b 4, lb 7, w 2, nb 2	15
Total (9 wkts dec)		264

5, 9, 38, 50, 171, 180, 229, 259, 262

Stephenson	27	7	86	5
Cooper	24	5	68	2
Millns	11	3	39	0
Hemmings	13	2	40	1
Afford	8	3	20	1

Nottinghamshire 2nd Innings

B.C. Broad	run out	90
P.R. Pollard	lbw b Pigott	4
*R.T. Robinson	c C.M. Wells b Babington	57
P. Johnson	c and b Donelan	37
D.W. Randall	c Donelan b Pigott	38
F.D. Stephenson	b Pigott	1
†B.N. French	c Babington b Donelan	19
E.E. Hemmings	not out	9
K.E. Cooper	not out	0
Extras	b 14, lb 18	32
Total (7 wkts)		287

11, 129, 192, 247, 255, 266, 286

Pigott	19	3	73	3
Dodemaide	7	1	21	0
Donelan	19	2	95	3
C.M. Wells	10	0	33	0
Babington	4	0	33	1

Umpires: D.J. Constant and R. Julian

Toss: Sussex

For the second Sussex home match in succession the result depended on the last possible ball. This time Hemmings ran a leg bye to win the game for Nottinghamshire, his six earlier in the final over really delivered the coup de grace. Smith hit a commanding 184 on the first day, during which every dismissed batsman was adjudged lbw. Sussex later declared to set Notts 287 in 59 overs.

v LEICESTERSHIRE (Eastbourne)

August 9, 10, 11

Drawn. Sussex 7pts, Leics 5pts

Sussex 1st Innings

D.M. Smith	b Agnew	5
M.P. Speight	lbw b Willey	88
*P.W.G. Parker	lbw b Benjamin	45
A.P. Wells	c Taylor b Benjain	47
C.M. Wells	c Briers b Willey	35
I.J. Gould	lbw b Agnew	13
A.I.C. Dodemaide	b Agnew	0
A.C.S. Pigott	c Whitaker b Benjamin	3
†P. Moores	lbw b Agnew	11
B.T.P. Donelan	not out	4
I.D.K. Salisbury	lbw b Benjamin	2
Extras	b 3, lb 2	5
Total (87.4 ov)		258

23, 116, 154, 199, 222, 222, 229, 250, 252

Benjamin	23.4	7	63	4
Agnew	22	2	84	4
Taylor	9	1	30	0
Willey	28	12	60	2
Such	5	1	16	0

Leicestershire 1st Innings

T.J. Boon	lbw b Dodemaide	36
*N.E. Briers	c A.P. Wells b C.M. Wells	13
J.J. Whitaker	c Pigott b Donelan	53
P. Willey	c Speight b C.M. Wells	2
L. Potter	c A.P. Wells b C.M. Wells	4
P.N. Hepworth	lbw b Dodemaide	17
†P.A. Nixon	not out	24
W.K.M. Benjamin	c Dodemaide b Donelan	1
J.P. Agnew	c Salisbury b Dodemaide	10
L.B. Taylor	b Dodemaide	0
P.M. Such	c Moores b Dodemaide	1
Extras	lb 4, nb 2	6
Total (79.2 ov)		167

45, 63, 74, 100, 117, 141, 142, 161, 161

Pigott	18	6	30	0
Dodemaide	26.2	5	77	5
Wells	17	7	29	3
Salisbury	2	1	8	0
Donelan	16	9	19	2

Sussex 2nd Innings

†P. Moores	b Benjamin	8
M.P. Speight	b Potter	43
*P.W.G. Parker	c Potter b Benjamin	0
A.P. Wells	b Benjamin	56
C.M. Wells	c Hepworth b Potter	15
A.C.S. Pigott	c Potter b Taylor	9
I.J. Gould	not out	26
A.I.C. Dodemaide	not out	27
Extras	b 4, lb 3	7
Total (6 wkts dec)		191

8, 16, 106, 128, 128, 138

Benjamin	17	4	55	3
Taylor	13.5	2	61	1
Willey	11	2	33	0
Such	6	1	24	0
Potter	6	2	11	2

Leicestershire 2nd Innings

T.J. Boon	not out	80
*N.E. Briers	not out	48
Extras	b 4, lb 2	6
Total (0 wkt)		134

Pigott	8	1	32	0
Dodemaide	6	1	20	0
C.M. Wells	8	2	14	0
Salisbury	13	4	32	0
Donelan	11	1	30	0

Umpires: D.J. Constant and R. Julian

Toss: Sussex

This match was dead by lunch time on the last day, but the players continued with the last rites until 5.30, both Boon and Briers improving their batting averages. On the first day Speight hit 88 before lunch, though his innings contained two blemishes. Leicestershire were 44–0 off 20 overs at the close. The Midland county struggled on Thursday and Dodemaide produced his best analysis for Sussex. By the close Sussex had a lead of 224 with five wickets standing. Rain on the last morning delayed the start and dampened the players' enthusiasm, both being in the lower reaches of the Championship there was little to be achieved.

v MIDDLESEX (Hastings)

August 19, 21, 22

Lost by 9 wkts. Middx 23pts, Sussex 5pts

Sussex 1st Innings		
D.M. Smith	lbw b Emburey	13
M.P. Speight	c Downton b Hughes	35
*P.W.G. Parker	c Gatting b Hughes	5
A.P. Wells	c Gatting b Williams	66
C.M. Wells	c Haynes b Tufnell	11
I.J. Gould	c Haynes b Carr	30
A.I.C. Dodemaide	not out	61
A.C.S. Pigott	c Emburey b Williams	3
†P. Moores	c Gatting b Williams	1
B.T.P. Donelan	run out	4
A.M. Babington	c Gatting b Fraser	3
Extras	b 5, lb 4, w 1, nb 7	17
Total (100 ov: 230–8)		249

36, 56, 57, 77, 129, 200, 213, 217, 234

Williams	21	4	48	3
Fraser	26	9	52	1
Emburey	18	11	34	1
Hughes	20	4	58	2
Tufnell	19	8	40	1
Carr	4	1	8	1

Middlesex 1st Innings		
J.D. Carr	b Pigott	0
D.L. Haynes	lbw b Dodemaide	0
P.C.R. Tufnell	b Pigott	4
N.F. Williams	c Smith b C.M. Wells	36
*M.W. Gatting	c Moores b Babington	121
M.A. Roseberry	b Babington	32
K.R. Brown	c Parker b Dodemaide	90
†P.R. Downton	c Moores b Babington	42
J.E. Emburey	c Donelan b Babington	14
S.P. Hughes	b Dodemaide	5
A.R.C. Fraser	not out	0
Extras	b 3, lb 11, w 1, nb 11	26
Total (100 ov: 345–7)		370

0, 4, 4, 123, 195, 218, 345, 350, 369

Pigott	21	2	93	2
Dodemaide	23.1	4	78	3
Babington	27	7	94	4
C.M. Wells	24	4	69	1
Donelan	11	4	22	0

Sussex 2nd Innings		
B.T.P. Donelan	c Emburey b Hughes	0
M.P. Speight	c Brown b Fraser	6
D.M. Smith	c Brown b Hughes	3
*P.W.G. Parker	b Williams	24
A.P. Wells	c Brown b Emburey	51
C.M. Wells	c Emburey b Williams	12
I.J. Gould	lbw b Emburey	38
A.I.C. Dodemaide	lbw b Hughes	6
A.C.S. Pigott	c Carr b Tufnell	11
†P. Moores	c Downton b Williams	50
A.M. Babington	not out	1
Extras	b 4, lb 3, nb 7	14
Total		216

6, 10, 14, 76, 98, 104, 124, 149, 202

Williams	16.5	3	58	3
Hughes	15	2	65	3
Fraser	5	1	19	1
Emburey	14	2	40	2
Carr	5	2	11	0
Tufnell	6	2	16	1

Middlesex 2nd Innings		
J.D. Carr	c Moores b C.M. Wells	26
D.L. Haynes	not out	46
*M.W. Gatting	not out	21
Extras	b 2, lb 1, nb 1	4
Total (1 wkt)		97

59

Pigott	4	0	20	0
Dodemaide	7	1	14	0
Babington	3	0	26	0
C.M. Wells	7	1	21	1
Donelan	3	0	9	0
Smith	0.1	0	4	0

Umpires: J.H. Harris and R. Palmer
Toss: Sussex

This match was billed as the final first-class fixture to be staged at Priory Meadow, Hastings. By the final day however there seemed very few locals interested in the proceedings. Sussex having a deficit of 121 on first innings never put sufficient gumption into their second innings to make the Middlesex players fight for their victory. The home side began the last morning at 5–0 and the only real resistance came from Moores.

v GLOUCESTERSHIRE (Hove)

August 24, 25, 26

Won by 3 wkts. Sussex 23pts, Gloucs 3pts

Gloucestershire 1st Innings		
A.J. Wright	c Moores b Dodemaide	17
I.P. Butcher	b Dodemaide	5
J.W. Lloyds	c Speight b Pigott	0
*C.W.J. Athey	c Pigott b C.M. Wells	36
K.M. Curran	c Parker b C.M. Wells	36
P. Bainbridge	not out	19
M.W. Alleyne	c A.P. Wells b C.M. Wells	0
†G.A. Tedstone	lbw b C.M. Wells	0
C.A. Walsh	lbw b Pigott	6
D.A. Graveney	run out	3
D.V. Lawrence	b Pigott	6
Extras	lb 1, w 1, nb 3	5
Total (44.4 ov)		133

6, 12, 31, 88, 103, 103, 103, 122, 133

Pigott	14.4	3	37	3
Dodemaide	8	1	22	2
Bunting	3	1	20	0
C.M. Wells	14	5	39	4
Hansford	5	1	14	0

Sussex 1st Innings		
D.M. Smith	b Curran	115
M.P. Speight	c Tedstone b Lawrence	1
*P.W.G. Parker	lbw b Lawrence	2
A.P. Wells	lbw b Curran	37
C.M. Wells	c Alleyne b Graveney	5
I.J. Gould	c Lloyds b Graveney	0
A.I.C. Dodemaide	lbw b Walsh	80
†P. Moores	c Tedstone b Bainbridge	29
A.C.S. Pigott	c Lloyds b Walsh	7
R.A. Bunting	not out	6
A.R. Hansford	b Lawrence	18
Extras	b 5, b 11, w 1, nb 6	23
Total (100 ov: 299–7)		323

4, 15, 88, 95, 95, 233, 286, 299, 300

Walsh	26	6	74	2
Lawrence	19.1	4	85	3
Curran	20	5	52	2
Graveney	23	7	48	2
Bainbridge	15	4	29	1
Lloyds	2	1	1	0
Athey	2	0	18	0

Gloucestershire 2nd Innings		
A.J. Wright	c Speight b C.M. Wells	33
I.P. Butcher	b Pigott	9
J.W. Lloyds	b Pigott	43
*C.W.J. Athey	lbw b Dodemaide	11
K.M. Curran	not out	117
P. Bainbridge	run out	3
M.W. Alleyne	b Hansford	41
†G.A. Tedstone	c Speight b Hansford	12
C.A. Walsh	c A.P. Wells b Hansford	29
D.A. Graveney	c Gould b Bunting	25
D.V. Lawrence	b Pigott	14
Extras	b 8, lb 11, w 7	26
Total		363

22, 87, 104, 104, 115, 175, 201, 241, 304

Pigott	37	9	129	3
Dodemaide	12.2	5	30	1
Bunting	14	0	70	1
C.M. Wells	19	9	45	1
Hansford	31.4	8	70	3

Sussex 2nd Innings		
D.M. Smith	lbw b Lawrence	1
M.P. Speight	c Wright b Walsh	0
*P.W.G. Parker	b Walsh	49
A.P. Wells	lbw b Lawrence	4
C.M. Wells	run out	46
I.J. Gould	lbw b Walsh	5
†P. Moores	run out	11
A.I.C. Dodemaide	not out	27
A.C.S. Pigott	not out	14
Extras	lb 13, nb 5	18
Total (7 wkts)		175

1, 3, 12, 106, 113, 122, 140

Walsh	20	3	59	3
Lawrence	11.2	1	41	2
Curran	2	0	14	0
Bainbridge	3	1	15	0
Graveney	13	4	33	0

Umpires: J.D. Bond and D.G.L. Evans
Toss: Gloucestershire

This was one of the few four-day matches which really demonstrated the advantages of having an extra day. Gloucester, who were 190 runs behind on first innings, hit 363 in their second attempt and without the need for false declarations, Sussex had to work hard to win the game.

v HAMPSHIRE (Hove)

August 29, 30, 31

Won by 9 wkts. Sussex 24pts, Hants 5pts

Sussex 1st Innings		
N.J. Lenham	b Connor	28
C.C. Remy	lbw b Bakker	0
*P.W.G. Parker	c Middleton b Bakker	0
A.P. Wells	c Parks b Jefferies	91
M.P. Speight	c Maru b Bakker	20
I.J. Gould	lbw b Connor	125
†P. Moores	c Terry b Connor	17
A.C.S. Pigott	lbw b Connor	91
B.T.P. Donelan	c and b Bakker	10
A.R. Hansford	c Terry b Bakker	16
A.M. Babington	not out	9
Extras	b 1, lb 11, w 4, nb 7	23
Total (100 ov: 403–8)		430

3, 3, 87, 152, 153, 197, 381, 399, 407

Bakker	23.1	2	83	5
Jefferies	16	2	64	1
Connor	26	2	90	4
James	22	0	56	0
Maru	23	5	84	0
Nicholas	5	0	24	0
Scott	2	0	17	0

Hampshire 1st Innings		
V.P. Terry	lbw b Hansford	24
T.C. Middleton	c Moores b Hansford	22
K.D. James	c Speight b Hansford	8
*M.C.J. Nicholas	run out	39
R.J. Scott	c Moores b Babington	9
J.R. Wood	c Pigott b Donelan	36
S.T. Jefferies	b Pigott	15
†R.J. Parks	b Hansford	1
R.J. Maru	not out	24
C.A. Connor	c Moores b Pigott	14
P.J. Bakker	b Hansford	11
Extras	b 4, lb 13, nb 13	30
Total (91 ov)		233

37, 53, 72, 89, 163, 163, 164, 187, 215

Pigott	21	5	53	2
Babington	17	6	39	1
Hansford	32	9	79	5
Remy	8	2	11	0
Lenham	2	0	3	0
Donelan	11	1	31	1

Hampshire 2nd Innings		
V.P. Terry	c Gould b Donelan	61
T.C. Middleton	b Pigott	2
K.D. James	lbw b Babington	1
*M.C.J. Nicholas	c Gould b Pigott	19
R.J. Maru	c Moores b Pigott	3
C.A. Connor	c Remy b Babington	4
R.J. Scott	lbw b Remy	27
J.R. Wood	c A.P. Wells b Pigott	35
S.T. Jefferies	not out	40
†R.J. Parks	b Donelan	30
P.J. Bakker	c Moores b Babington	10
Extras	lb 5, w 1, nb 3	9
Total		241

5, 8, 37, 41, 48, 96, 158, 166, 212

Pigott	22	5	58	4
Babington	22.5	2	82	3
Hansford	13	5	28	0
Remy	7	1	22	1
Donelan	16	4	46	2

Sussex 2nd Innings		
N.J. Lenham	c Middleton b Bakker	4
M.P. Speight	not out	21
*P.W.G. Parker	not out	12
Extras	w 1, nb 7	8
Total (1 wkt)		45

15

Bakker	4	0	20	1
Jefferies	3	0	25	0

Umpires: J.D Bond and P.B. Wright
Toss: Hampshire

This four-day game was completed in three, as Sussex swept to a convincing victory by nine wickets. On the first day Sussex hit 430 runs, due to a brilliant partnership by Gould and Pigott which realised 184 runs. Alan Wells was also in attacking form, making 91 in 133 minutes. Hampshire began very slowly on the second day, only 23 runs coming in the first hour and soon Hansford caused wickets to fall. The follow on was enforced and the visitors were 43–4 at stumps. The tail scored more runs than usual on the third day, but it still left Sussex with a simple task and the win took them 4 places up the table to 9th . Hampshire remained in 6th place.

Warwickshire

President: The Earl of Aylesford
Chairman: R.J. Evans
Secretary: D.M.W. Heath, County Ground, Edgbaston Birmingham B5 7QU. *Tel:* 021-440-4292.
Cricket Manager: R.M.H. Cottam
Captain: T.A. Lloyd
Foundation of Present Club: April 1882 in Coventry
First First-Class Match: Warwickshire v Nottinghamshire (Trent Bridge) May 1894
County Champions: 1911, 1951, 1972
Gillette/NatWest Trophy: Winners 1966, 1968, 1989
Benson & Hedges Cup: Losing finalists 1984
Sunday League Champions: 1980
Refuge Cup: Nil

Summary of Results in 1989
Britannic Assurance County Championship: Played 22, Won 5, Lost 4, Drawn 13, Position 8th
NatWest Bank Trophy: Winners
Benson & Hedges Cup: Did not qualify for knock-out section
Refuge Assurance Sunday League: Played 16, Won 5, Lost 10, No Result 1, Position 14th equal
Refuge Assurance Cup: Did not qualify

Neil Smith hits a six in the final over of the NatWest Bank Trophy final at Lord's, the shot which effectively won the match for Warwickshire. Patrick Eagar

ONE DAY AWAY MATCHES

The full scorecard of each of Warwickshire's away matches will be found in the sections for the respective home teams.

Refuge Assurance League

Northampton: May 7
Warwicks 171–9 (40 ov) lost to Northampton 172–3 (38 ov) by 7 wkts. Northants 4pts, Warwicks 0pts.

Headingley: May 21
Warwicks 191–7 (40 ov) (A.I. Kallicharran 104) lost to Yorks 192–5 (39 ov) by 5 wkts. Yorks 4pts, Warwicks 0pts.

Basingstoke: June 11
Warwicks 158–9 (39 ov) lost to Hants 160–4 (38.1 ov) by 6 wkts. Hants 4pts, Warwicks 0pts.

Ilford: June 25
Warwicks 216–7 (40 ov) lost to Essex 218–6 (37.3 ov) by 4 wkts. Essex 4 pts, Warwicks 0pts.

Leicester: July 2
Leics 215–6 (40 ov) beat Warwicks 194 by 21 runs. Leics 4pts, Warwicks 0pts.

Trent Bridge: July 9
Warwicks 139 (40 ov) (K. Saxelby 5–24) lost to Notts 141–2 (35.4 ov) by 8 wkts. Notts 4pts, Warwicks 0pts.

Canterbury: August 6
Warwicks 201–5 (40 ov) lost to Kent 202–3 (35.1 ov) by 7 wkts. Kent 4pts, Warwicks 0pts.

Aberystwyth: August 27
Glamorgan 203–4 (40 ov) lost to Warwicks 207–4 (37.5 ov) by 6 wkts. Warwicks 4pts, Glamorgan 0pts.

Benson & Hedges Cup

Leicester: May 2
Leics 236–5 (55 ov) beat Warwicks 205 (55 ov) by 31 runs. Leics 2pts, Warwicks 0pts.

Old Trafford: May 13
Warwicks 199–8 (55 ov) lost to Lancs 203–5 (47.4 ov) by 5 wkts. Lancs 2pts, Warwicks 0pts.

NatWest Bank Trophy

Canterbury: July 12
Warwicks 272–5 (60 ov) beat Kent 223 (57.4 ov) by 49 runs.

Northampton: August 2
Northants 191–8 (60 ov) lost to Warwicks 194–7 (59.4 ov) by 3 wkts.

Lord's: September 2: FINAL
Middx 210–5 (60 ov) lost to Warwicks 211–6 (59.4 ov) by 4 wkts.

From left, back: *K.J. Piper, G. Steer, R.G. Twose, G.N.P.B. Williamson, N.M.K. Smith, J.E. Benjamin, S.J. Green, A.J. Moles, O.S. Chagar, G. Welch.* Centre: *D.A. Reeve, A. Merrick, A.R.K. Pierson, D.A. Banks, T.A. Munton, A.A. Donald, J.D. Ratcliffe, R. Earl, D.A. Thorne.* Front: *R.N. Abberley, G.C. Small, G.W. Humpage, R.M.H. Cottam, T.A. Lloyd. A. Kallicharran, A. Din, P.A. Smith.* Allsport

REFUGE ASSURANCE LEAGUE

v LANCASHIRE (Edgbaston)

April 23

Match Abandoned. No Play. Warwicks 2pts, Lancs 2pts

v MIDDLESEX (Edgbaston)

May 28

Won by 29 runs. Warwicks 4pts, Middx 0pts

Warwicks		
*T.A. Lloyd	c Downton b Fraser	28
+G.W. Humpage	c Downton b Fraser	25
A.I. Kallicharran	c Carr b Sykes	0
P.A. Smith	not out	93
Asif Din	lbw b Cowans	33
D.A. Reeve	not out	4
R.G. Twose		
N.M.K. Smith		
G.C. Small		
A.A. Donald		
T.A. Munton		
Extras	b 1, lb 6, w 5, nb 1	13
Total (4 wkts, 39 ov)		196

49, 50, 62, 145

Williams	8	0	36	0
Cowans	8	1	38	1
Carr	3	0	14	0
Fraser	8	0	26	2
Sykes	5	0	27	1
Hughes	7	0	48	0

Middlesex		
J.D. Carr	c Lloyd b Small	39
D.L. Haynes	c Lloyd b Munton	2
R.O. Butcher	b N.M.K. Smith	27
M.R. Ramprakash	c Small b Donald	16
K.R. Brown	c Twose b Donald	2
J.F. Sykes	b Donald	35
*†P.R. Downton	c Donald b N.M.K. Smith	3
N.F. Williams	c Small b Donald	22
S.P. Hughes	not out	4
A.R.C. Fraser	not out	2
N.G. Cowans		
Extras	b 7, lb 2, w 6	15
Total (8 wkts, 39 ov)		167

11, 58, 80, 90, 107, 112, 158, 163

Donald	8	0	32	4
Munton	8	0	26	1
P.A. Smith	7	0	33	0
Small	8	0	32	1
N.M.K. Smith	8	0	35	2

Umpires: J.D. Bond and J.H. Harris
Toss: Warwickshire
Middlesex felt the loss of Gatting and Emburey, who were in the England Test squad, and this gave Warwickshire the opportunity for their first Sunday win of 1989.

v SUSSEX (Edgbaston)

June 4

Won by 6 wkts. Warwicks 4pts, Sussex 0pts

Sussex		
D.M. Smith	c P.A. Smith b Pierson	36
N.J. Falkner	b Donald	1
A.P. Wells	run out	0
*C.M. Wells	run out	15
I.J. Gould	c Humpage b P.A. Smith	10
A.I.C. Dodemaide	not out	40
A.C.S. Pigott	not out	49
I.D.K. Salisbury		
†P. Moores		
A.R. Clarke		
A.M. Babington		
Extras	lb 7, w 6, nb 1	14
Total (5 wkts, 40 ov)		165

1, 1, 47, 66, 68

Munton	8	1	34	0
Donald	8	1	36	1
P.A. Smith	8	0	25	1
Small	8	0	20	0
Pierson	8	1	43	1

Warwickshire		
*T.A. Lloyd	b Salisbury	38
†G.W. Humpage	c Smith b Pigott	0
A.I. Kallicharran	c Dodemaide b Pigott	66
P.A. Smith	run out	28
Asif Din	not out	11
D.A. Reeve	not out	15
R.G. Twose		
A.A. Donald		
G.S. Small		
A.R.K. Pierson		
T.A. Munton		
Extras	lb 4, w 2, nb 5	11
Total (4 wkts, 38.3 ov)		169

1, 78, 140, 144

Pigott	8	0	31	2
Dodemaide	6.3	0	32	0
Clarke	8	1	27	0
C.M. Wells	3	0	13	0
Babington	5	0	25	0
Salisbury	8	0	37	1

Umpires: H.D. Bird and P.J. Eele
Toss: Sussex
Dodemaide and Pigott saved the visitors' faces, but their stand of 95 in 17 overs was insufficient to worry Warwickshire, Kallicharran scoring an excellent 66.

After a very moderate start in the season, Warwickshire made steady progress and at the close had the NatWest Trophy locked up at Edgbaston.

Donald, who had played just a minor role in the events of 1988, played in 19 Championship games in 1989 and his record was even better than that of Malcolm Marshall, a statement which fully expresses Donald's achievements. Merrick, who had been one of the main bowlers of 1988, was seen only rarely and was released by the county at the end of the summer – it is reported that Moody, the Australian, has been signed for 1990.

Gladstone Small provided Donald with his best support, but the England bowler's record was not quite as outstanding as in some previous years, so that Munton came second in terms of wickets taken.

Gifford having finally retired — he now coaches Sussex – the spin department was in the hands of younger cricketers, notably Pierson and Neil Smith, both of whom are rather expensive.

There was not much to choose between the principal batsmen. Humpage, Lloyd, P.A. Smith, Ratcliffe and Moles all batted well on occasion. The first named gave up keeping wicket, his place in the second half of the season being taken by Piper — a 19-year-old from Leicester. The veteran West Indian, now English, Kallicharran, scored two hundreds – against Northants and Glamorgan – but in his other 24 first-class innings could only muster about 400 runs; Asif Din also had a moderate year, both his aggregate and average falling – in 1988 he had been second in the batting table.

Reeve, the former Sussex player, who joined Warwickshire in 1988, was successful as an all-rounder and played a vital role in the famous NatWest Final victory. It is a long time since Warwickshire made a real impact in the Championship – not in the top three since 1972 – perhaps 1990 could see a move forward.

REFUGE ASSURANCE LEAGUE

v WORCESTERSHIRE (Edgbaston)

June 18

Lost by 22 runs. Worcs 4pts, Warwicks 0pts

Worcestershire		
T.S. Curtis	run out	40
M.J. Weston	c Munton b Pierson	63
G.A. Hick	not out	35
D.B. d'Oliveira	b Pierson	15
N.V. Radford	b Donald	4
*P.A. Neale	c Smith b Munton	18
S.J. O'Shaughnessy	not out	1
†S.J. Rhodes		
S.R. Lampitt		
R.K. Illingworth		
G.R. Dilley		
Extras	b 1, lb 13, w 4	18
Total (5 wkts, 40 ov)		194

111, 118, 136, 146, 187

Benjamin	8	0	23	0
Munton	8	1	29	1
Smith	8	1	35	0
Donald	8	0	53	1
Pierson	8	0	40	2

Warwickshire		
*T.A. Lloyd	lbw b Dilley	6
G.W. Humpage	c Rhodes b Dilley	2
Asif Din	run out	44
P.A. Smith	c O'Shaughnessy b Illingworth	45
D.A. Reeve	c Neale b Dilley	24
D.A. Thorne	st Rhodes b Illingworth	8
†K.J. Piper	b Radford	20
A.A. Donald	c Curtis b Radford	0
J.E. Benjamin	not out	9
A.R.K. Pierson	not out	6
T.A. Munton		
Extras	lb 6, w 1, nb 1	8
Total (8 wkts, 40 ov)		172

9, 14, 103, 106, 115, 156, 156, 159

Dilley	8	0	30	3
Weston	8	0	26	0
Radford	7	0	29	2
Illingworth	8	0	32	2
O'Shaughnessy	3	0	19	0
Hick	6	0	30	0

Umpires: R. Julian and K.E. Palmer
Toss: Worcestershire
Hick hit two sixes and a four off the last four balls of the innings and this assault more or less sealed Warwickshire's fate, as Dilley removed both openers cheaply and thus put the home batsmen at a disadvantage from the early stages of their innings.

v SURREY (Egbaston)

July 23

Lost by 19 runs. Surrey 4pts, Warwicks 0pts

Surrey		
G.S. Clinton	c Piper b Smith	37
M.A. Feltham	run out	2
†A.J. Stewart	c Piper b Munton	5
D.M. Ward	c Lloyd b Donald	76
D.J. Bicknell	c Donald b Small	12
*I.A. Greig	c Small b Donald	15
K.T. Medlycott	not out	5
J.D. Robinson	run out	3
C.K. Bullen	not out	3
M.P. Bicknell		
A.J. Murphy		
Extras	b 6, lb 7, w 3, nb 1	17
Total (7 wkts, 40 ov)		175

10, 17, 96, 121, 164, 164, 167

Munton	8	3	33	1
Small	8	1	29	1
Reeve	5	0	18	0
Donald	8	0	31	2
Smith	8	0	36	1
Asif Din	3	0	15	0

Warwickshire		
*T.A. Lloyd	b Bullen	38
J.D. Ratcliffe	b Murphy	0
A.I. Kallicharran	run out	9
P.A. Smith	c and b Feltham	6
D.A. Reeve	lbw b Medlycott	22
Asif Din	not out	49
D.A. Thorne	st Stewart b Medleycott	0
†K.J. Piper	c M.P. Bicknell b Medlycott	0
G.C. Small	c M.P. Bicknell b Medlycott	4
A.A. Donald	b Feltham	17
T.A. Munton	not out	4
Extras	b 1, lb 4, w 2	7
Total (9 wkts, 40 ov)		156

13, 38, 47, 75, 95, 95, 95, 121, 150

Murphy	8	0	52	1
M.P. Bicknell	8	0	30	0
Feltham	8	0	29	2
Bullen	8	2	22	1
Medlycott	8	1	18	4

Umpires: P.J. Eele and D.S. Thompsett
Toss: Surrey
Surrey boosted their chances in the Sunday League by winning this match, when all their immediate rivals were failing. They owed their success to the spin of Medlycott and Bullen who kept the run rate at a trickle only 40 runs off their 16 overs.

v GLOUCESTERSHIRE (Edgbaston)

July 30

Won by 18 runs. Warwicks 4pts, Gloucs 0pts

Warwicks		
*T.A. Lloyd	c and b Pooley	7
A.I. Kallicharran	c Alleyne b Curran	76
P.A. Smith	b Walsh	61
D.A. Reeve	not out	9
Asif Din	b Curran	0
R.G. Twose	lbw b Curran	0
T.A. Merrick	not out	1
N.M.K. Smith		
†K.J. Piper		
G.C. Small		
T.A. Munton		
Extras	lb 6, w 2	8
Total (5 wkts, 24 ov)		162

19, 138, 160, 160, 160

Jarvis	5	0	14	0
Pooley	4	1	28	1
Bainbridge	5	0	30	0
Curran	5	0	33	3
Walsh	5	0	51	1

Gloucestershire		
J.W. Lloyds	c Kallicharran b Small	1
*C.W.J. Athey	b Small	0
P. Bainbridge	c Small b N.M.K. Smith	32
K.M. Curran	b Merrick	54
A.J. Wright	c Twose b N.M.K. Smith	2
M.W. Alleyne	not out	41
P.W. Romaines	b Merrick	0
C.A. Walsh	run out	1
†G.A. Tedstone	c Piper b P.A. Smith	0
M.W. Pooley	not out	1
K.B.S. Jarvis		
Extras	lb 9, w 3	12
Total (8 wkts, 24 ov)		144

2, 4, 60, 62, 130, 130, 140, 140

Small	5	0	25	2
Munton	5	0	26	0
N.M.K. Smith	5	0	17	2
Merrick	5	0	38	2
P.A. Smith	4	0	29	1

Umpires: A.A. Jones and D.R. Shepherd
Toss: Gloucestershire
The partnership of 119 between Kallicharran and Paul Smith proved the decisive factor in this game which was reduced to 24 overs per side by the weather. Curran had the satisfaction of claiming a hat-trick in the final over of Warwickshire's innings.

PLAYERS

Mohammad ASIF DIN *b* 21.9.1960 Kampala, Uganda; right-hand batsman; leg-break bowler; debut 1981

David Andrew BANKS *b* 11.1.1961 Pensnett, Staffs; righit-hand batsman; debut 1988; previously appeared for Worcs 1983–85, then three seasons with his native county

Joseph Emmanuel BENJAMIN *b* 2.2.1961 Christ Church, St Kitts; right-arm medium fast bowler; right-hand batsman; debut 1988

Allan Anthony DONALD *b* 20.10.1966 Bloemfontein; right-arm fast-medium bowler; right-hand batsman; debut 1987; also plays for Orange Free State

Simon James GREEN *b* 19.3.1970 Bloxwich, Staffs; right-hand batsman; left-arm medium pace bowler; debut 1988

Geoffrey William HUMPAGE *b* 24.4.1954 Sparkhill, Birmingham; middle order right-hand batsman; wicketkeeper; debut 1974; three One Day Internationals for England

Alvin Isaac KALLICHARRAN *b* 21.3.1949 Paidema, British Guiana; middle-order left-hand batsman; debut 1971; also plays for Orange Free State; 66 Tests for West Indies 1971/2–1980/1; nine as captain

Timothy Andrew LLOYD *b* 5.11.1956 Oswestry; left-hand batsman; debut 1977; captain since 1988; One Test for England 1984

Tyrone Anthony MERRICK *b* 10.6.1963 St John's, Antigua; right-arm fast-medium bowler; debut 1987; has also played for Leewards Is since 1982

Andrew James MOLES *b* 12.2.1961 Solihull; right-hand batsman; right-arm medium-pace bowler; debut 1986; also plays for Griqualand West

Timothy Alan MUNTON *b* 30.7.1965 Melton Mowbray; right-arm medium fast bowler; right-hand batsman; debut 1985; capped in 1989

Adrian Roger Kirshaw PIERSON *b* 21.7.1963 Enfield, Middx; off-break bowler; right-hand batsman; debut 1985

Keith John PIPER *b* 18.12.1969 Leicester; wicketkeeper; right-hand batsman; FC debut for Warwicks in May 1989; preferred to Humpage as wicketkeeper in some matches

Jason David RATCLIFFE *b* 19.6.1969 Solihull; right-hand batsman; occasional right-arm medium-pace bowler; debut 1988

Dermont Alexander REEVE *b* 2.4.1963 Kowloon, Hong Kong; all-rounder; right-hand batsman; right-arm medium-fast bowler; debut 1988, previously appeared for Sussex 1983–87; played for Hong Kong in ICC Trophy in 1982

Gladstone Cleophas SMALL *b* 18.10.1961 St George, Barbados; right-arm fast-medium bowler; right-hand batsman; debut 1980; five Tests for England including one in 1989; selected to tour West Indies 1989–90

Neil Michael Knight SMITH *b* 27.7.1967 Birmingham; right-hand batsman; off-break bowler; debut 1987; scored maiden FC hundred in 1989; son of M.J.K. (ex-Leics/Warwicks)

Paul Andrew SMITH *b* 15.4.1964 Jesmond; right-hand batsman; right-arm fast-medium bowler; debut 19832; brother of K.D. (ex-Warwicks)

David Anthony THORNE *b* 12.12.1964 Coventry; right-hand batsman; left-arm medium pace bowler; debut 1983; Oxford Univ 1984–86

Roger G. TWOSE *b* 14.4.1968 Torquay; right-hand batsman; leg-break bowler; debut for Warwicks v Australians May 1989

Dermot Reeve in Sussex sweater, but now a Warwickshire player. Although playing only 14 matches, he finished top of the batting list and second in the bowling.

Allsport/Simon Bruty

REFUGE ASSURANCE LEAGUE

v SOMERSET (Edgbaston)

August 13

Won on faster scoring rate. Warwicks 4pts, Somerset 0pts

Somerset		
S.J. Cook	b Merrick	0
P.M. Roebuck	lbw b Munton	2
R.J. Harden	c Smith b Small	11
C.J. Tavare	b Small	51
J.C.M. Atkinson	b Small	69
G.D. Rose	b Ratcliffe	4
*V.J. Marks	b Small	28
†N.D. Burns	c Humpage b Merrick	13
N.A. Mallender	not out	11
A.N. Jones	not out	2
H.R.J. Trump		
Extras	lb 11, w 5	16
Total (8 wkts, 40 ov)		207

0, 4, 34, 134, 141, 177, 180, 196

Merrick	8	2	18	2
Munton	8	0	34	1
Small	8	1	36	4
Smith	8	0	46	0
Twose	5	0	41	0
Ratcliffe	3	0	21	1

Warwickshire		
A.J. Moles	run out	17
J.D. Ratcliffe	b Marks	37
Asif Din	b Mallender	18
*†G.W. Humpage	b Jones	7
D.A. Reeve	c Roebuck b Rose	31
D.A. Banks	c Harden b Jones	1
R.G. Twose	c Burns b Jones	23
N.M.K. Smith	not out	11
T.A. Merrick	not out	21
G.C. Small		
T.A Munton		
Extras	lb 16, w 4, nb 1	21
Total (7 wkts, 35.4 ov)		187

28, 78, 81, 100, 108, 149, 153

Jones	8	1	42	3
Rose	8	0	36	1
Trump	4	0	22	0
Mallender	7.4	0	36	1
Marks	8	0	35	1

Umpires: D.G.L. Evans and J.H. Hampshire
Toss: Warwicks
Although Atkinson hit 69 off 49 balls, Warwickshire scored fast enough to win the match when rain prematurely ended the proceedings.

v DERBYSHIRE (Edgbaston)

August 20

Lost by 5 wkts. Derbys 4pts, Warwicks 0pts

Warwickshire		
*T.A. Lloyd	lbw b Sharma	20
J.D. Ratcliffe	lbw b Newman	5
A.I. Kallicharran	b Mortensen	34
P.A. Smith	lbw b Holding	70
D.A. Reeve	b Sharma	19
T.A. Merrick	b Sharma	0
R.G. Twose	not out	18
N.M.K. Smith	c and b Holding	3
†K.J. Piper	not out	10
G.C. Small		
T.A. Munton		
Extras	b 1, lb 7, w 5	13
Total (7 wkts, 40 ov)		192

15, 35, 84, 151, 151, 160, 168

Newman	3.4	0	16	1
Mortensen	8	1	27	1
Barnett	7.2	0	28	0
Holding	8	0	34	2
Sharma	8	1	44	3
Base	5	0	35	0

Derbyshire		
*K.J. Barnett	b Merrick	3
P.D. Bowler	b N.M.K. Smith	13
J.E. Morris	not out	112
R. Sharma	c Munton b P.A. Smith	15
T.J.G. O'Gorman	c and b Small	3
B. Roberts	run out	0
M.A. Holding	not out	33
P.G. Newman		
†B.J.M. Maher		
O.H. Mortensen		
S.J. Base		
Extras	b 2, lb 9, w 5	16
Total (5 wkts, 37.2 ov)		195

14, 67, 94, 130, 131

Merrick	6.2	0	29	1
Munton	7	2	25	0
Small	8	0	54	1
P.A. Smith	8	0	35	1
N.M.K. Smith	8	1	41	1

Umpires: R. Julian and D.S. Thompsett
Toss: Warwicks
Good bowling by the Derbyshire seamers restricted the Warwickshire run flow and then an unbeaten hundred by Morris produced the necessary runs with overs in hand.

BENSON AND HEDGES CUP

v NORTHAMPTONSHIRE (Edgbaston)

April 25, 26

Lost by 4 wkts. Northants 2pts, Warwicks 0pts

Warwickshire		
*T.A. Lloyd	c Larkins b Williams	37
A.J. Moles	c Thomas b Robinson	2
Asif Din	c Ripley b Capel	10
A.I. Kallicharran	c Lamb b Williams	50
D.A. Thorne	b Capel	3
P.A. Smith	b Thomas	74
†G.W. Humpage	b Davis	17
G.C. Small	not out	3
A.A. Donald	not out	5
A.R.K. Pierson		
T.A. Munton		
Extras	lb 11, w 2, nb 7	20
Total (7 wkts, 55 ov)		221

37, 57, 57, 66, 168, 211, 215

Davis	11	0	65	1
Thomas	11	3	25	1
Robinson	11	1	42	1
Capel	11	0	35	2
Williams	11	3	43	2

Northamptonshire		
G. Cook	run out	57
N.G.B. Cook	c Munton b Smith	14
W. Larkins	b Smith	15
R.J. Bailey	lbw b Munton	0
*A.J. Lamb	not out	84
D.J. Capel	c Thorne b Munton	3
R.G. Williams	c Humpage b Small	8
†D. Ripley	not out	22
J.G. Thomas		
W.W. Davis		
M.A. Robinson		
Extras	lb 19, w 1, nb 2	22
Total (6 wkts, 53.5 ov)		225

23, 46, 49, 140, 154, 174

Small	11	3	36	1
Donald	10.5	1	51	0
Smith	11	3	34	2
Munton	10	0	39	2
Pierson	11	0	46	0

Umpires: D.R. Shepherd and D.S. Thompsett
Toss: Northants. Gold: A.J. Lamb
Warwickshire appeared in serious trouble at 66 for 4, but Kallicharran and Smith added 102 in 22 overs to produce a high score for such a pitch. Northants began the second day at 8–0 off 5 overs. Lamb then played one of his best innings, though critically for Warwickshire, he was given a chance early on.

BRITANNIC ASSURANCE COUNTY CHAMPIONSHIP AVERAGES 1989

Batting	*M*	*I*	*NO*	*Runs*	*HS*	*Avge*	*100*	*50*
D.A. Reeve	14	17	4	581	97*	44.69	–	4
T.A. Lloyd	21	32	2	1116	183	37.20	3	3
G.W. Humpage	21	31	7	878	183	36.58	1	3
A.J. Moles	19	35	5	1049	130*	34.97	2	7
P.A. Smith	18	25	4	701	140	33.38	1	2
J.D. Ratcliffe	9	16	3	391	72	30.08	–	2
M. Asif Din	17	26	3	660	82*	28.70	–	3
N.M.K. Smith	9	11	2	248	161	27.56	1	–
A.I. Kallicharran	16	26	2	610	119	25.42	2	1
R.G. Twose	4	7	2	107	37	21.40	–	–
T.A. Merrick	2	2	–	40	31	20.00	–	–
K.J. Piper	12	15	2	208	41	16.00	–	–
A.A. Donald	19	22	6	215	40	13.44	–	–
G.C. Small	17	22	4	232	34	12.89	–	–
D.A. Thorne	4	8	–	91	32	11.38	–	–
S.J. Green	1	2	–	18	11	9.00	–	–
A.R.K. Pierson	14	19	4	122	18	8.13	–	–
J.E. Benjamin	4	3	–	17	7	5.67	–	–
T.A. Munton	19	19	11	40	7	5.00	–	–
D.A. Banks	2	3	–	10	10	3.33	–	–

Bowling	*O*	*M*	*R*	*W*	*Avge*	*BB*	*5i*	*10m*
T.A. Merrick	57.4	17	135	10	13.50	6-67	1	–
D.A. Reeve	97.4	35	163	11	14.82	3-3	–	–
A.A. Donald	537.1	122	1398	86	16.26	7-66	6	–
G.C. Small	477	122	1202	51	23.57	5-55	1	–
T.A. Munton	557.4	158	1367	56	24.41	5-13	1	–
P.A. Smith	253.1	34	830	31	26.77	5-82	1	–
J.E. Benjamin	126	33	306	11	27.82	3-55	–	–
A.R.K. Pierson	279.5	52	946	27	35.04	6-82	2	–
N.M.K. Smith	130.4	27	427	11	38.82	3-62	–	–
M. Asif Din	84.5	4	366	6	61.00	2-13	–	–

Also bowled: D.A. Banks 5-1-13-0; G.W. Humpage 27-7-56-3; A.I. Kallicharran 28.5-8-55-2; T.A. Lloyd 29-7-111-1; A.J. Moles 24-3-136-1; J.D. Ratcliffe 23-6-75-1; R.G. Twose 35.5-3-120-1.

Centuries

3 T.A. Lloyd: 100 v Notts (Trent Bridge); 109* v Kent (Canterbury); 183 v Glamorgan (Swansea).

2 A.I. Kallicharran: 100 v Northants (Northampton); 119 v Glamorgan (Swansea). A.J. Moles: 100 v Surrey (Edgbaston); 130* v Glamorgan (Edgbaston).

1 G.W. Humpage: 183 v Glamorgan (Edgbaston). N.M.K. Smith: 161 v Yorks (Headingley). P.A. Smith: 140 v Worcs (Worcester).

BENSON AND HEDGES CUP

v SCOTLAND (Edgbaston)

May 11

Won by 6 wkts. Warwicks 2pts, Scotland 0pts

Scotland		
I.L. Philip	lbw b Munton	10
A.C. Storie	c Asif Din b Small	6
R.G. Swan	b Small	40
*C.E.B. Rice	b Munton	2
G.B.J. McGurk	run out	29
O. Henry	lbw b Small	5
M.J. Smith	not out	21
N.W. Burnett	not out	6
W. Morton		
†D.J. Haggo		
A.W. Bee		
Extras	b 1, lb 20, w 18	39
Total (6 wkts, 55 ov)		158

26, 28, 32, 112, 121, 138

Small	11	4	15	3
Donald	11	1	35	0
Munton	11	3	20	2
Smith	11	3	16	0
Moles	4	0	18	0
Pierson	7	0	33	0

Warwickshire		
*T.A. Lloyd	lbw b Rice	8
A.J. Moles	lbw b Rice	10
Asif Din	b Bee	0
A.I. Kallicharran	lbw b Rice	31
D.A. Thorne	not out	57
P.A. Smith	not out	39
†G.W. Humpage		
G.C. Small		
A.A. Donald		
A.R.K. Pierson		
T.A. Munton		
Extras	b 1, lb 4, w 9	14
Total (4 wkts, 36.4 ov)		159

17, 18, 18, 73

Rice	9	0	34	3
Bee	8	1	26	1
Smith	7.4	1	30	0
Burnett	6	0	31	0
Morton	6	1	33	0

Umpires: J.D. Bond and D.J. Constant

Toss: Scotland. Gold: P.A. Smith

Held together by Swan, who lasted 41 overs for 40 runs, Scotland made a very steady 158, helped by Donald bowling wides – 6 in one over. Warwickshire got off to a poor start, but after Kallicharran hit a quick 31, Thorne and Smith moved to within 16 runs of victory. Rain cleared away at 7.20 to allow the game to be completed.

NATWEST BANK TROPHY

v WILTSHIRE (Edgbaston)

June 28, 29

Won by 186 runs

Warwickshire		
A.J. Moles	b Pike	26
J.D. Ratcliffe	lbw b Pike	59
*T.A. Lloyd	b Cooper	57
G.W. Humpage	c sub b Davis	59
Asif Din	not out	41
D.A. Reeve	not out	2
†K.J. Piper		
G.C. Small		
A.A. Donald		
A.R.K. Pierson		
T.A. Munton		
Extras	b 5, lb 12, w 9	26
Total (4 wkts, 60 ov)		270

87, 110, 186, 239

Davis	11	1	53	1
Thompson	11	2	36	0
Pike	12	2	40	2
Holland	12	1	43	0
Mildenhall	7	0	45	0
Cooper	7	0	36	1

Wiltshire		
B.H. White	c Piper b Donald	0
P.A. Bail	b Donald	4
S. Williams	b Donald	0
J.J. Newman	lbw b Pierson	12
D.R. Pike	b Donald	3
*R.C. Cooper	b Donald	0
M. Davis	c Pierson b Small	1
J. Thompson	c Piper b Pierson	34
†W. Johnson	not out	14
A. Mildenhall	lbw b Pierson	2
M. Holland	lbw b Munton	0
Extras	lb 7, w 7	14
Total (30 ov)		84

0, 2, 5, 9, 9, 18, 34, 79, 83

Donald	7	2	12	5
Small	6	3	14	1
Reeve	6	1	25	0
Pierson	8	3	20	3
Munton	3	0	6	1

Umpires: R. Julian and C. Cook

Toss: Wiltshire. MofM: A.A. Donald

Owing to the weather even one innings could not be completed on the first day, but the home side were very comfortably placed at 238-3 off 56 overs when play resumed on the second day. Donald and Pierson overwhelmed Wiltshire to bring victory by a large margin.

SEMI FINAL v WORCESTERSHIRE (Edgbaston) August 16

Won by 100 runs

Warwickshire		
A.J. Moles	b Illingworth	61
*T.A. Lloyd	c d'Oliveira b McEwan	0
A.I. Kallicharran	b McEwan	21
†G.W. Humpage	b Radford	10
Asif Din	not out	94
D.A. Reeve	st Rhodes b Illingworth	7
P.A. Smith	b Lampitt	2
N.M.K. Smith	c Weston b McEwan	0
G.C. Small	c Neale b Lampitt	15
A.A. Donald	run out	0
T.A. Munton	not out	1
Extras	lb 7, w 2	9
Total (9 wkts, 60 ov)		220

4, 21, 125, 137, 176, 179, 182, 212, 212

Radford	12	5	18	1
McEwan	11	3	51	3
Lampitt	8	0	37	2
Illingworth	12	0	45	2
Hick	12	0	43	0
Weston	5	0	19	0

Worcestershire		
T.S. Curtis	lbw b Donald	0
M.J. Weston	b P.A. Smith	26
*S.J. Rhodes	b Small	3
G.A. Hick	c Humpage b Reeve	7
D.B. d'Oliveira	c N.M.K. Smith b P.A. Smith	32
*P.A. Neale	run out	11
D.A. Leatherdale	lbw b P.A. Smith	5
S.R. Lampitt	not out	9
R.K. Illingworth	run out	1
N.V. Radford	lbw b Small	0
S.M. McEwan	b Munton	6
Extras	lb 14, w 6	20
Total (46 ov)		120

0, 7, 26, 52, 84, 92, 102, 108, 109

Donald	6	1	17	1
Small	10	1	15	2
Reeve	12	4	24	1
Munton	7	2	11	1
P.A. Smith	11	0	39	3

Umpires: J.H. Harris and B. Leadbeater

Toss: Worcestershire. MofM: Asif Din

Asif Din batted 138 balls for his undefeated 94 and with Moles added 104 in 31 overs. The total of 220 did not appear formidable, but rain interrupted the Worcestershire reply just after Curtis was dismissed and the visitors never gained any momentum. About 20,000 attended the match, the receipts being £150,000.

Away Matches

The full scorecard of each of Warwickshire's away matches will be found in the sections for the respective home teams.

Old Trafford: May 17, 18, 19
Lancs 261 and 133 beat Warwicks 158 (M. Watkinson 5–45) and 174 by 62 runs. Lancs 23pts, Warwicks 5pts.

Ilford: June 24, 26, 27
Warwicks 338 and 145 (D.R. Pringle 7–44) lost to Essex 335 (A.A. Donald 5–103, A.R.K. Pierson 5–129) and 149–5 by 5 wkts. Essex 24pts, Warwicks 8pts.

Hinckley: July 1, 3, 4
Warwicks 196 (W.K.M. Benjamin 6–70) and 103–8 drew with Leics 371–6d (J.J. Whitaker 138). Leics 8pts, Warwicks 3pts.

Worcester: July 5, 6, 7
Warwicks 265 (P.A. Smith 140) and 47–0 drew with Worcs 232 (T.A. Merrick 6–67). Warwicks 7pts, Worcs 6pts.

Trent Bridge: July 8, 10, 11
Notts 147 and 196–6 drew with Warwicks 292 (T.A. Lloyd 100). Warwicks 7pts, Notts 4pts.

Canterbury: August 5, 7, 8
Kent 287 (A.A. McDonald 5–57) and 141 lost to Warwicks 250–8d and 181–0 (T.A. Lloyd 109*) by 10 wkts. Warwicks 21pts, Kent 6pts.

Bournemouth: August 9, 10, 11
Warwicks 229 and 110–2d beat Hants 103–5d and 176 by 60 runs. Warwicks 20pts, Hants 4pts.

Northampton: August 19, 21
Northants 51 (T.A. Munton 5–13) and 109 lost to Warwicks 191 (C.E.L. Ambrose 6–22) by an inns and 31 runs. Warwicks 21pts, Northants 4pts.

Swansea: Aug 24, 25, 26, 27
Warwicks 430 (T.A. Lloyd 183, A.I. Kallicharran 119, S.L. Watkin 6–106) and 31–2 beat Glamorgan 131 and 329 (H. Morris 108) by 8 wkts. Warwicks 24pts, Glamorgan 1pt.

Headingley: August 29, 30, 31, Sept 1
Yorks 426–9d (A.A. Metcalfe 138) drew with Warwicks 248 (P. Carrick 6–70) and 296–3d (N.M.K. Smith 161). Yorks 5pts, Warwicks 3pts.

Taunton: Sept 13, 14, 15, 16
Somerset 141 drew with Warwicks 119–1. Warwicks 4pts, Somerset 0pts.

v LANCASHIRE (Edgbaston)

April 20, 21, 22, 24
Drawn. Lancs 5pts, Warwicks 6pts

Lancashire 1st Innings

G.D. Mendis	c Humpage b Small	22
G. Fowler	c Smith b Munton	56
A.N. Hayhurst	c Humpage b Munton	10
N.H. Fairbrother	lbw b Smith	4
M. Watkinson	c Humpage b Smith	9
*D.P. Hughes	c Moles b Donald	33
Wasim Akram	c and b Pierson	18
†W.K. Hegg	not out	31
P.A.J. DeFreitas	c Humpage b Donald	11
P.J.W. Allott	c Lloyd b Donald	5
J. Simmons	b Small	16
Extras	b 9, lb 24, w 4, nb 7	44
Total (82.4 ov)		259

62, 86, 91, 105, 154, 180, 180, 205, 212

Donald	21	5	55	3
Small	22.4	3	61	2
Munton	20	5	63	2
Smith	15	0	35	2
Pierson	4	2	12	1

Warwickshire 1st Innings

*T.A. Lloyd	c Simmons b Watkinson	65
A.J. Moles	lbw b Wasim Akram	1
Asif Din	c Allott b Wasim Akram	10
A.I. Kallicharran	c Allott b Wasim Akram	1
D.A. Thorne	c Hegg b DeFreitas	32
P.A. Smith	lbw b Wasim Akram	26
†G.W. Humpage	lbw b Allott	30
G.C. Small	c Hegg b Allott	13
A.A. Donald	c Hegg b Allott	8
A.R.K. Pierson	c Simmons b Allott	8
T.A. Munton	not out	4
Extras	lb 5, w 5, nb 2	12
Total (75.4 ov)		210

26, 39, 42, 104, 120, 167, 175, 189, 199

Wasim Akram	20	7	51	3
DeFreitas	23	6	68	2
Allott	19.4	5	44	4
Watkinson	13	5	42	1

Lancashire 2nd Innings

G.D. Mendis	b Donald	47
G. Fowler	lbw b Donald	22
†W.K. Hegg	lbw b Small	1
A.N. Hayhurst	c Humpage b Small	12
N.H. Fairbrother	c Humpage b Munton	9
M. Watkinson	c Humpage b Donald	2
*D.P. Hughes	c Thorne b Small	5
Wasim Akram	lbw b Small	36
P.A.J. DeFreitas	c Humpage b Pierson	19
P.J.W. Allott	b Small	5
J. Simmons	not out	0
Extras	lb 7, nb 6	13
Total		171

34, 41, 86, 91, 97, 102, 121, 155, 171

Donald	19	4	41	3
Small	25.1	6	55	5
Smith	4	0	22	0
Munton	14	4	32	1
Pierson	4	0	14	1

Warwickshire 2nd Innings

A.J. Moles	lbw b DeFreitas	23
*T.A. Lloyd	c Allott b DeFreitas	36
Asif Din	not out	16
A.I. Kallicharran	c Allott b DeFreitas	2
D.A. Thorne	c Hegg b Allott	1
P.A. Smith	not out	1
Extras	lb 2	2
Total (4 wkts)		81

42, 65, 71, 74

Wasim Akram	5	1	22	0
DeFreitas	16.5	6	37	3
Allott	13	4	20	1

Umpires: D.R. Shepherd and D.S. Thompsett
Toss: Lancashire
Fowler survived for 210 minutes and 56 runs on the first day, which was much too cold and damp for cricket. Warwickshire were 8–0 off 5 overs by the close. Conditions were as poor on the second day, when only Lloyd batted with confidence and Lancs were 37–1 at stumps. About half Saturday was lost to the weather and the last day saw hail, sleet and rain, but only 40 balls delivered and the players thankfully retreated to the warmth of the pavilion.

v WORCESTERSHIRE (Edgbaston)

April 27, 28, 29, 30
Drawn with scores level. Warwicks 12pts, Worcs 4pts

Worcestershire 1st Innings

T.S. Curtis	c Humpage b Donald	8
G.J. Lord	c and b Small	16
G.A. Hick	c Thorne b Munton	7
D.B. d'Oliveira	c Moles b Donald	19
*P.A. Neale	c Green b Donald	11
I.T. Botham	c Humpage b Munton	5
†S.J. Rhodes	lbw b Munton	24
P.J. Newport	b Small	18
R.K. Illingworth	c Humpage b Small	1
N.V. Radford	lbw b Munton	16
G.R. Dilley	not out	2
Extras	lb 10, w 1, nb 5	16
Total (55.3 overs)		143

21, 35, 45, 68, 77, 77, 121, 132, 133

Small	17	7	42	3
Donald	15	1	37	3
Munton	20.3	7	39	4
Smith	3	1	15	0

Warwickshire 1st Innings

A.J. Moles	c Rhodes b Dilley	2
*T.A. Lloyd	c Hick b Radford	11
S.J. Green	c Rhodes b Dilley	7
A.I. Kallicharran	lbw b Radford	3
D.A. Thorne	lbw b Dilley	1
P.A. Smith	c Rhodes b Dilley	4
†G.W. Humpage	not out	31
G.C. Small	c Rhodes b Newport	11
A.A. Donald	c Rhodes b Radford	12
A.R.K. Pierson	c Rhodes b Dilley	3
T.A. Munton	lbw b Radford	0
Extras	lb 7, nb 7	14
Total (36.4 overs)		99

6, 20, 21, 22, 31, 31, 67, 98, 99

Dilley	12	5	28	5
Radford	14.4	1	43	4
Newport	6	1	12	1
Botham	4	0	9	0

Worcestershire 2nd Innings

T.S. Curtis	not out	55
G.J. Lord	lbw b Donald	1
R.K. Illingworth	b Munton	21
G.A. Hick	lbw b Munton	5
D.B. d'Oliveira	c Smith b Donald	2
I.T. Botham	c Lloyd b Munton	7
†S.J. Rhodes	not out	42
Extras	b 1, lb 16, w 5, nb 5	27
Total (5 wkts dec)		160

14, 58, 75, 81, 89

Donald	11	1	37	2
Small	18	4	43	0
Munton	23	4	63	3

Warwickshire 2nd Innings

*T.A. Lloyd	lbw b Botham	21
A.J. Moles	not out	85
S.J. Green	c Botham b Dilley	11
A.I. Kallicharran	run out	19
D.A. Thorne	c sub b Newport	30
P.A. Smith	run out	5
†G.W. Humpage	not out	5
G.C. Small	not out	7
Extras	b 6, lb 13, nb 2	21
Total (6 wkts)		204

43, 92, 133, 181, 187, 199

Dilley	14	2	45	1
Radford	4	2	8	0
Illingworth	6	0	23	1
Newport	12	1	39	1
Botham	16	2	70	1

Umpires: R. Palmer and P.B. Wight
Toss: Warwickshire
After no play on the first day, there were plenty of wickets on a damp grassy wicket on the second. Worcs managed 143, but the home side were 80–7 off 33 ovrs when bad light and rain ended play early. Play did not start until 4.30 pm on the third day and then after 8.4 overs bad light sent the players back to the pavilion, Worcs being 16–1. Worcs declared on the last day setting Warwicks 205 off 52 overs. They finally required 7 off the last, but could only tie, but as they were the side batting last they received an extra 8 points.

v SURREY (Edgbaston)

May 20, 22, 23

Lost by 4 runs. Surrey 23pts, Warwicks 5pts

Surrey 1st Innings

D.J. Bicknell	c Piper b Smith	34
G.S. Clinton	lbw b Smith	38
R.I. Alikhan	lbw b Smith	9
A.J. Stewart	c Pierson b Munton	60
P.D. Atkins	lbw b Small	17
†D.M. Ward	c Asif Din b Donald	14
*I.A. Greig	c Reeve b Smith	35
K.T. Medlycott	c Pierson b Smith	48
M.A. Feltham	b Donald	13
M.P. Bicknell	lbw b Donald	0
A.J. Murphy	not out	1
Extras	lb 4, w 13, nb 7	24
Total (94.5 ov)		293

70, 80, 89, 168, 168, 199, 246, 269, 271

Small	21	4	61	1
Donald	23	5	74	3
Munton	25	8	44	1
Smith	19.5	1	82	5
Pierson	6	1	28	0

Warwickshire 1st Innings

*T.A. Lloyd	c Ward b Murphy	15
A.J. Moles	lbw b M.P. Bicknell	4
Asif Din	c Ward b M.P. Bicknell	6
A.R.K. Pierson	c Alikhan b M.P. Bicknell	0
A.I. Kallicharran	c Ward b Murphy	37
D.A. Reeve	lbw b M.P. Bicknell	8
P.A. Smith	lbw b Feltham	45
†K.J. Piper	lbw b Feltham	41
G.C. Small	c D.J. Bicknell b M.P. Bicknell	3
A.A. Donald	not out	9
T.A. Munton	c Ward b M.P. Bicknell	3
Extras	b 4, lb 9, nb 6	19
Total (57.2 ov)		190

7, 13, 13, 36, 77, 89, 160, 178, 178

M.P. Bicknell	24.2	5	64	6
Murphy	16	5	41	2
Feltham	13	3	56	2
Greig	4	0	16	0

Surrey 2nd Innings

G.S. Clinton	c Moles b Donald	0
D.J. Bicknell	lbw b Donald	1
R.I. Alikhan	b Donald	35
A.J. Stewart	b Small	14
P.D. Atkins	c Asif Din b Pierson	16
D.M. Ward	lbw b Donald	10
*I.A. Greig	c Moles b Donald	0
K.T. Medlycott	b Small	7
M.A. Feltham	lbw b Small	11
M.P. Bicknell	c Kallicharran b Smith	6
A.J. Murphy	not out	4
Extras	lb 3, nb 1	4
Total		108

0, 1, 17, 68, 68, 72, 83, 95, 102

Small	11.4	3	27	3
Donald	16	6	18	5
Munton	19	5	43	0
Pierson	3	1	3	1
Smith	5	0	14	1

Warwickshire 2nd Innings

A.J. Moles	b Feltham	100
*T.A. Lloyd	lbw b M.P. Bicknell	35
Asif Din	c Stewart b M.P. Bicknell	0
A.I. Kallicharran	lbw b M.P. Bicknell	6
D.A. Reeve	c Ward b Feltham	7
P.A. Smith	lbw b Murphy	20
†K.J. Piper	c Feltham b Murphy	13
G.C. Small	lbw b Murphy	10
A.A. Donald	lbw b Feltham	0
A.R.K. Pierson	c Alikhan b Feltham	5
T.A. Munton	not out	0
Extras	b 3, lb 6, nb 2	11
Total		207

60, 69, 81, 102, 127, 164, 187, 188, 206

M.P. Bicknell	29	8	46	3
Murphy	33	9	62	3
Feltham	27.2	7	68	4
Medlycott	15	8	22	0

Umpires: J.W. Holder and R. Julian

Toss: Warwickshire

A hard hit 60 from Stewart allied to three cheap wickets by Martin Bicknell put Surrey on top after the first day's play – Warwicks were 22–3 off 12 overs at the close. The home side started the final day wanting 212 with all wickets in hand. Moles batted nearly 6½ hours but failed to bring Warwickshire victory when he was the last man out, when five runs were needed off the last over.

v MIDDLESEX (Edgbaston)

May 27, 29, 30

Lost by 8 wkts. Middx 21pts, Warwicks 5pts

Warwickshire 1st Innings

*T.A. Lloyd	b Williams	26
A.J. Moles	b Cowans	5
Asif Din	c Butcher b Hughes	36
A.I. Kallicharran	lbw b Cowans	30
P.A. Smith	lbw b Williams	5
†G.W. Humpage	lbw b Hughes	14
D.A. Thorne	c Butcher b Carr	20
G.C. Small	c Hutchinson b Hughes	5
A.R.K. Pierson	c Downton b Williams	11
A.A. Donald	not out	19
T.A. Munton	c Butcher b Cowans	7
Extras	b 2, lb 6, nb 8	16
Total (94.4 ov)		194

23, 35, 93, 107, 107, 139, 151, 152, 181

Cowans	19.4	3	43	3
Fraser	27	13	41	0
Williams	20	4	52	3
Hughes	24	9	44	3
Carr	4	1	6	1

Middlesex 1st Innings

J.D. Carr	c Munton b Donald	9
D.L. Haynes	lbw b Donald	27
I.J.F. Hutchinson	c Humpage b Donald	12
R.O. Butcher	c Humpage b Donald	58
M.A. Roseberry	c Munton b Small	2
M.R. Ramprakash	c Humpage b Donald	32
†P.R. Downton	c Humpage b Donald	1
N.F. Williams	b Smith	12
S.P. Hughes	not out	14
A.R.C. Fraser	c Humpage b Smith	12
N.G. Cowans	c and b Donald	0
Extras	b 4, lb 9, w 2, nb 5	20
Total (59.5 ov)		199

13, 56, 64, 81, 148, 153, 156, 169, 197

Small	18	2	60	1
Donald	23.5	7	66	7
Munton	8	0	29	0
Smith	10	1	31	2

Warwickshire 2nd Innings

A.J. Moles	lbw b Fraser	4
*T.A. Lloyd	b Hughes	7
Asif Din	c Hutchinson b Fraser	39
A.I. Kallicharran	lbw b Hughes	0
P.A. Smith	c Haynes b Fraser	29
†G.W. Humpage	run out	5
D.A. Thorne	b Fraser	0
G.C. Small	not out	5
A.R.K. Pierson	c Downton b Fraser	10
A.A. Donald	c Haynes b Hughes	1
T.A. Munton	not out	5
Extras	lb 1, w 1, nb 5	7
Total		112

8, 26, 34, 81, 90, 90, 91, 103, 104

Fraser	16	6	20	5
Cowans	9	2	28	0
Williams	13	1	40	0
Hughes	9.5	3	23	4

Middlesex 2nd Innings

J.D. Carr	retired hurt	19
D.L. Haynes	lbw b Munton	9
S.P. Hughes	ht wkt b Donald	12
I.J.F. Hutchinson	not out	17
R.O. Butcher	not out	41
Extras	b 4 lb 2, nb 4	10
Total (2 wkts)		108

20, 38

Donald	15	2	43	1
Munton	12	3	35	1
Pierson	2	0	8	0
Smith	2.4	0	16	0

Umpires: J.D. Bond and J.H Harris

Toss: Warwickshire

250 runs were scored on the first day for the loss of 12 wickets, Asif Din's 36 being the highest score. The unpredictable wicket was an aid to Donald and then Fraser on the second day, but the over-rate was so slow that it was 7.20 before play ended with Middlesex 20–1 in their second innings. Donald's 7–66 was his best to date for his county. On the last day Carr retired with a bruised elbow, then Butcher hit 41 off 32 balls to end the match.

v SUSSEX (Edgbaston)

June 3, 5, 6

Drawn. Warwicks 7pts, Sussex 7pts

Sussex 1st Innings

D.M. Smith	lbw b Small	50
N.J. Lenham	c Humpage b Small	12
N.J. Falkner	b Donald	1
A.P. Wells	b Small	29
*C.M. Wells	lbw b Munton	6
I.J. Gould	c Moles b Small	8
A.I.C. Dodemaide	lbw b Donald	52
†P. Moores	c Moles b Pierson	43
A.C.S. Pigott	c and b Pierson	26
I.D.K. Salisbury	c Munton b Pierson	5
A.M. Babington	not out	0
Extras	lb 25, nb 2	27
Total (94.2 ov)		259

27, 34, 104, 112, 115, 125, 218, 252, 259

Donald	17.2	4	49	2
Small	26	4	70	4
Smith	14	1	39	0
Pierson	23	6	52	3
Munton	14	5	24	1

Warwickshire 1st Innings

*T.A. Lloyd	c Pigott b Babington	35
A.J. Moles	lbw b Dodemaide	13
Asif Din	c Smith b Pigott	36
A.I. Kallicharran	c C.M. Wells b Babington	5
D.A. Banks	b Babington	0
P.A. Smith	b Babington b Dodemaide	66
†G.W. Humpage	c Moores b Dodemaide	38
G.C. Small	b Dodemaide	34
A.R.K. Pierson	not out	14
A.A. Donald	c C.M. Wells b Babington	15
T.A. Munton	c Pigott b Babington	0
Extras	b 5, lb 5, nb 11	21
Total (93.1 ov)		277

33, 73, 85, 85, 120, 180, 245, 256, 275

Pigott	29	3	93	1
Dodemaide	31	9	75	4
Babington	21.1	5	59	5
Salisbury	3	1	6	0
C.M. Wells	9	3	34	0

Sussex 2nd Innings

D.M. Smith	not out	46
N.J. Lenham	not out	38
Extras	lb 1	1
Total (0 wkt dec)		85

Lloyd	18	7	29	0
Kallicharran	18	8	25	0
Moles	5	1	17	0
Banks	5	0	13	0

Umpires: H.D. Bird and P.J. Eele

Toss: Sussex

Sussex were in deep trouble with 6 wickets down for 125, only Smith, who batted 130 balls for 50 holding out for long, then Dodemaide and Moores launched a counter-attack and 93 runs were added in 31 overs for the 7th wicket. Warwickshire began Monday at 28–0 off 12 overs and their innings was reminiscent of Sussex, since their 7th wicket added 65 and enabled them to claim a third batting point. The last day was total farce with play starting at 4.05 pm and Smith and Lenham getting some very gentle batting practice against some second rate bowlers.

v DERBYSHIRE (Griff & Coton Ground, Nuneaton)

June 7, 8, 9

Drawn. Warwicks 5pts, Derbys 4pts

Warwickshire 1st Innings

A.J. Moles	c Bowler b Bishop	53
*T.A. Lloyd	c Goldsmith b Mortensen	5
Asif Din	c Sharma b Warner	18
A.I. Kallicharran	c Maher b Mortensen	17
D.A. Banks	lbw b Mortensen	0
P.A. Smith	c Goldsmith b Mortensen	18
†G.W. Humpage	c and b Newman	16
G.C. Small	c Maher b Mortensen	4
A.R.K. Pierson	c Roberts b Mortensen	3
A.A. Donald	b Newman	9
T.A. Munton	not out	1
Extras	lb 10, nb 1	11
Total (73.5 ov)		155

6, 57, 99, 99, 99, 138, 142, 142, 151

Bishop	17	3	48	1
Mortensen	20.5	6	38	6
Newman	20	8	31	2
Warner	16	5	28	1

Derbyshire 1st Innings

*P.G. Newman	lbw b Donald	7
†B.J. M. Maher	c Humpage b Small	1
O.H. Mortensen	c Humpage b Donald	2
P.D.Bowler	c Humpage b Small	6
J.E. Morris	c Munton b Pierson	25
B. Roberts	c Lloyd b Munton	23
S.C. Goldsmith	st Humpage b Pierson	0
R. Sharma	not out	36
F.A. Griffith	c Pierson b Asif Din	12
A.E. Warner	st Humpage b Asif Din	0
I.R. Bishop	lbw b Donald	13
Extras	lb 9, nb 1	10
Total (61.4 ov)		135

5, 9, 16, 23, 72, 72, 76, 109, 109

Small	11	2	24	2
Donald	18.4	5	38	3
Pierson	20	7	40	2
Munton	6	5	4	1
Asif Din	6	0	20	2

Warwickshire 2nd Innings

*T.A. Lloyd	c Roberts b Bishop	5
A.J. Moles	c Maher b Bishop	79
Asif Din	c Griffith b Warner	46
A.I. Kallicharran	c Maher b Newman	23
D.A. Banks	c Morris b Mortensen	10
P.A. Smith	c Goldsmith b Bishop	5
†G.W. Humpage	not out	8
G.C. Small	not out	13
Extras	lb 8, w 1, nb 1	10
Total (6 wkts dec)		199

5, 89, 135, 142, 176, 178

Mortensen	11	1	48	1
Bishop	13	1	54	3
Warner	10	2	24	1
Newman	9	0	51	1
Morris	1	0	14	0

Derbyshire 2nd Innings

P.D. Bowler	c Banks b Pierson	78
S.C. Goldsmith	b Donald	0
J.E. Morris	b Pierson	24
B. Roberts	c Kallicharran b Pierson	12
R. Sharma	c Munton b Pierson	23
†B.J.M. Maher	c Small b Pierson	23
F.A. Griffith	st Humpage b Pierson	22
A.E. Warner	not out	9
*P.G. Newman	lbw b Donald	1
I.R. Bishop	not out	3
Extras	lb 16, nb 1	17
Total (8 wkts)		212

1, 46, 70, 108, 144, 195, 198, 199

Donald	9	2	29	2
Small	5	1	15	0
Pierson	23	1	82	6
Munton	9	1	28	0
Asif Din	10	1	42	0

Umpires: P.J. Eele and B. Hassan
Toss: Derbyshire

Moles batted 3½ hours o the first day to hold Warwickshire's team together. Derbyshire began the second day at 7–1 and with 3 hours lost to rain were all out at the close for 135. On the final day Lloyd set a target of 220 in 56 overs and would have beaten Derbyshire but for three dropped catches. On the other hand, Bowler's batting came close to bringing his team victory and the result was an interesting, if inconclusive, last day.

v GLAMORGAN (Edgbaston)

June 21, 22, 23

Drawn. Warwicks 8pts, Glamorgan 4pts

Glamorgan 1st Innings

A.R. Butcher	c Moles b Small	14
*H. Morris	lbw b Donald	10
M.J. Cann	c Asif Din b Smith	38
M.P. Maynard	lbw b Smith	41
R.J. Shastri	lbw b Donald	8
G.C. Holmes	b Donald	4
I. Smith	b Small	105
†C.P. Metson	lbw b Munton	6
S.J. Dennis	c Piper b Donald	15
S.L. Watkin	c Piper b Small	22
S.R. Barwick	not out	0
Extras	b 8, lb 11, w 4, nb 4	27
Total (98.1 ov)		290

17, 35, 109, 122, 133, 134, 144, 197, 267

Donald	25	8	53	4
Small	18.1	1	49	3
Smith	21	7	55	2
Munton	25	9	61	1
Pierson	6	0	42	0
Asif Din	3	0	11	0

Warwickshire 1st Innings

A.J. Moles	not out	130
J.D. Ratcliffe	c Maynard b Watkin	4
A.R.K. Pierson	lbw b Watkin	3
Asif Din	lbw b Smith	9
G.W. Humpage	c Morris b Smith	183
P.A. Smith	not out	20
*T.A. Lloyd		
†K.J. Piper		
G.C. Small		
A.A. Donald		
T.A. Munton		
Extras	b 1, lb 6, w 1, nb 8	16
Total (100 ov: 328–3) (4 wkts dec)		365

5, 33, 58, 337

Watkin	23	6	57	2
Dennis	12	3	42	0
Shastri	25	5	60	0
Barwick	11	5	11	0
Smith	18	1	94	2
Cann	6	0	36	0
Holmes	13	2	58	0

Glamorgan 2nd Innings

A.R. Butcher	not out	171
*H. Morris	c Humpage b Lloyd	133
M.J. Cann	c Piper b Moles	20
M.P. Maynard	not out	41
Extras	b 6, lb 6, nb 1	13
Total (2 wkts dec)		378

269, 300

Donald	10	1	21	0
Small	10	5	18	0
Pierson	23	6	68	0
Smith	6	0	21	0
Munton	4	1	13	0
Asif Din	15	0	61	0
Moles	14	2	63	1
Lloyd	11	0	82	1
Ratcliffe	4	0	19	0

Warwickshire 2nd Innings

A.J. Moles	not out	46
J.D. Ratcliffe	not out	35
Extras	lb 1, nb 2	3
Total (0 wkt)		84

Watkin	4	0	7	0
Smith	4	0	23	0
Maynard	6	1	16	0
Cann	6	0	37	0

Umpires: J.H Harris and D.O. Oslear
Toss: Glamorgan

There was a run glut at Birmingham, which began with a maiden first-class 100 by Ian Smith, developed into a whirlwind 183 from Humpage, while Moles plodded to 130, then Glamorgan finished off with a record 269 first wicket stand and Butcher's best innings for his new county. In the last rites, Moles put himself in the record books by making 46* and thus being on the field throughout the three day match.

v YORKSHIRE (Edgbaston)

July 26, 27, 28

Drawn. Warwicks 7pts, Yorks 4pts

Warwickshire 1st Innings

*T.A. Lloyd	c Moxon b Fletcher	49
A.J. Moles	lbw b Sidebottom	13
A.I. Kallicharran	c and b Pickles	15
G.W. Humpage	c Blakey b Fletcher	15
P.A. Smith	c Blakey b Carrick	33
Asif Din	lbw b Carrick	39
D.A. Reeve	not out	97
†K.J. Piper	b Carrick	1
G.C. Small	lbw b Fletcher	0
A.A. Donald	c Moxon b Fletcher	40
A.R.K. Pierson	c Moxon b Pickles	12
Extras	b 5, lb 15, w 3, nb 15	38
Total (100 ov – 254–8)		352

48, 76, 110, 124, 172, 237, 245, 246, 335

Fletcher	34	5	88	4
Sidebottom	24	3	58	1
Pickles	27.5	2	90	2
Hartley	12	1	51	0
Carrick	24	9	45	3

Yorkshire 1st Innings

M.D. Moxon	lbw b Smith	10
A.A. Metcalfe	c Reeve b Smith	112
†R.J. Blakey	c Small b Asif Din	88
D. Byas	c Reeve b Smith	0
K. Sharp	not out	51
P.E. Robinson	not out	16
*P. Carrick		
A. Sidebottom		
P.J. Hartley		
C.S. Pickles		
S.D. Fletcher		
Extras	b 1, lb 17, w 2, nb 4	24
Total (4 wkts dec, 86.3 ov)		301

39, 194, 198, 252

Donald	17	2	60	0
Small	18	8	36	0
Smith	17	1	70	3
Pierson	20	2	63	0
Asif Din	7.3	0	35	1
Reeve	7	1	19	0

Warwickshire 2nd Innings

*T.A. Lloyd	c Sharp b Fletcher	46
A.J. Moles	lbw b Pickles	5
A.I. Kallicharran	b Byas	70
G.W. Humpage	not out	66
P.A. Smith	not out	42
Extras	lb 8	8
Total (3 wkts dec)		237

11, 91, 169

Fletcher	11	2	44	1
Pickles	7	1	50	1
Carrick	8	0	51	0
Sharp	8	0	52	0
Byas	6	1	32	1

Yorkshire 2nd Innings

M.D. Moxon	c Kallicharran b Smith	34
A.A. Metcalfe	c Reeve b Pierson	40
†R.J. Blakey	not out	73
D. Byas	not out	18
Extras	lb 5, nb 1	6
Total (2 wkts)		171

54, 99

Donald	7	3	14	0
Small	10	4	26	0
Smith	11	0	43	1
Pierson	16	3	41	1
Asif Din	10	0	42	0

Umpires: D.G.L. Evans and D.O. Oslear
Toss: Yorkshire

The Warwickshire batting on the first day owed much to Reeve, who hit a quick 84 and aided by the tail gained 3 batting points. The home side, 316–8 overnight, batted on on the second day and thus made a draw fairly certain, though Yorkshire reached 300 off 86.3 overs and promptly declared at the close. Yorkshire were invited to make 289 in 220 minutes on the last afternoon and showed little interest.

v GLOUCESTERSHIRE (Edgbaston)

July 29, 31, Aug 1

Won by 3 wkts. Warwicks 22pts, Gloucs 6pts

Glocestershire 1st Innings		
I.P. Butcher	lbw b Donald	5
A.J. Wright	b Donald	4
J.W. Lloyds	b Smith	71
*C.W.J. Athey	c Piper b Small	21
K.M. Curran	b Small	4
P. Bainbridge	lbw b Donald	101
M.W. Alleyne	lbw b Small	17
†G.A. Tedstone	c Asif Din b Donald	1
C.A. Walsh	c Kallicharran b Small	16
M.C.J. Ball	not out	4
K.B.S. Jarvis	b Donald	0
Extras	b 9, lb 18, w 1, nb 7	35
Total (88.5 ov)		279

5, 14, 60, 68, 167, 203, 233, 270, 279

Donald	23.5	6	67	5
Small	22	4	58	4
Smith	18	4	62	1
Pierson	22	7	57	0
Asif Din	3	0	8	0

Warwickshire 1st Innings		
*T.A. Lloyd	b Bainbridge	44
A.J. Moles	c Athey b Curran	76
A.I. Kallicharran	b Curran	16
P.A. Smith	retired hurt	4
Asif Din	c Alleyne b Ball	25
G.W. Humpage	b Ball	16
D.A. Reeve	not out	8
†K.J. Piper	b Bainbridge	1
G.C. Small	b Bainbridge	0
A.A. Donald	b Walsh	4
A.R.K. Pierson	not out	3
Extras	b 8, lb 9, nb 4	21
Total (8 wkts dec, 69.3 ov)		218

120, 137, 152, 187, 196, 197, 197, 211

Walsh	18	3	50	1
Jarvis	12	3	42	0
Bainbridge	15	3	41	3
Curran	13.3	2	45	2
Ball	11	4	23	2

Gloucestershire 2nd Innings		
I.P. Butcher	lbw b Donald	2
A.J. Wright	b Humpage	33
J.W. Lloyds	c Piper b Kallicharran	54
*C.W.J. Athey	st Piper b Kallicharran	49
K.M. Curran	not out	36
Extras	b 4, lb 9, nb 1	14
Total (4 wkts dec)		188

5, 65, 121, 188

Donald	6	0	23	1
Small	4	3	8	0
Asif Din	6	1	39	0
Humpage	11	2	28	1
Kallicharran	10.5	0	30	2
Moles	4	0	47	0

Warwickshire 2nd Innings		
*T.A. Lloyd	c Alleyne b Walsh	12
A.J. Moles	c Tedstone b Curran	10
A.I. Kallicharran	c Alleyne b Curran	1
G.W. Humpage	b Ball	19
Asif Din	not out	32
D.A. Reeve	not out	86
†K.J. Piper	c Curran b Jarvis	30
G.C. Small	lbw b Curran	24
A.A. Donald	run out	15
Extras	b 2, lb 7, w 4, nb 8	21
Total (7 wkts)		250

19, 23, 30, 72, 139, 186, 225

Walsh	21	2	73	1
Curran	18	0	60	3
Bainbridge	7	2	16	0
Jarvis	10	2	43	1
Ball	12	0	49	1

Umpires: A.A. Jones and D.R. Shepherd
Toss: Warwickshire

On the first day, which was restricted to 84 overs, Gloucester reached 268–7, Bainbridge's 98 not out saving his side after a poor start. Bad light cut an hour off the second day, during which the home county struggled to 218–8, with Paul Smith having to retire hurt with a broken nose. Athey set Warwickshire 250 in 69 overs on the last afternoon. Reeve hit a brilliant 86 to bring Warwickshire their first victory in 21 first-class matches.

v SOMERSET (Edgbaston)

August 12, 14, 15

Drawn. Somerset 6pts, Warwicks 6pts

Somerset 1st Innings		
S.J. Cook	lbw b Benjamin	4
P.M. Roebuck	b Benjamin	1
R.J. Harden	b Munton	3
C.J. Tavare	c Moles b Smith	52
N.J. Pringle	b Benjamin	8
J.C.M. Atkinson	b Donald	17
†N.D. Burns	c Moles b Munton	90
*V.J. Marks	c Munton b Asif	75
G.D. Rose	not out	27
N.A. Mallender	not out	12
A.N. Jones		
Extras	b 10, lb 16, nb 1	27
Total (100 ov: 280-8) (8 wkts dec)		316

2, 10, 16, 29, 58, 144, 222, 280

Donald	15	4	45	1
Benjamin	25	7	55	3
Munton	32	14	65	2
Reeve	5	0	9	0
Twose	10	1	33	0
Smith	17	3	57	1
Asif Din	6	1	26	1

Warwickshire 1st Innings		
A.J. Moles	c Roebuck b Rose	18
J.D. Ratcliffe	run out	67
Asif Din	b Rose	37
*G.W. Humpage	c Tavare b Mallender	34
D.A. Reeve	c Pringle b Jones	41
R.G. Twose	b Marks	0
N.M.K. Smith	b Mallender	0
†K.J. Piper	not out	17
A.A. Donald	not out	13
J.E. Benjamin		
T.A. Munton		
Extras	b 6, lb 11, w 1, nb 5	23
Total (7 wkts, 83.2 ov)		250

32, 132, 136, 206, 207, 208, 220

Jones	16	2	42	1
Mallender	18	6	42	2
Rose	19.2	5	47	2
Marks	24	6	91	1
Roebuck	6	2	11	0

Somerset 2nd Innings		
S.J. Cook	run out	16
P.M. Roebuck	lbw b Donald	11
R.J. Harden	c Piper b Benjamin	1
C.J. Tavare	b Munton	42
N.J. Pringle	b Munton	6
J.C.M. Atkinson	c Reeve b Asif Din	53
†N.D. Burns	c Reeve b Asif Din	13
*V.J. Marks	not out	1
Extras	b 10, lb 12, nb 5	27
Total (7 wkts dec)		170

31, 37, 37, 60, 117, 164, 170

Donald	10	2	32	1
Benjamin	10	4	23	1
Munton	12	2	37	2
Ratcliffe	6	2	19	0
Smith	6	2	24	0
Asif Din	4	2	13	2

Warwickshire 2nd Innings		
A.J. Moles	c Atkinson b Jones	16
J.D. Ratcliffe	st Burns b Marks	30
Asif Din	lbw b Jones	1
*G.W. Humpage	not out	29
R.G. Twose	not out	26
Extras	lb 3, w 1, nb 1	5
Total (3 wkts)		107

48, 51, 51

Jones	8	2	21	2
Mallender	8	2	25	0
Rose	4	0	19	0
Marks	12	2	39	1

Umpires: D.G.L. Evans and J.H. Hampshire
Toss: Somerset

After five wickets had gone down for 58 runs, Somerset staged a remarkable recovery. Tavare defied the bowlers early on, then Burns and Marks scored more freely. Somerset declared over the weekend and the home side progressed to 241–7 off 81 overs on a reduced second day. Somerset delayed their second declaration to mid-afternoon on the last day and the game gently subsided into oblivion.

v NORTHANTS (Edgbaston)

Sept 8, 9, 10, 11

Drawn. Warwicks 4pts, Northants 1pt

Northamptonshire 1st Innings		
*W. Larkins	c Humpage b Munton	18
A. Fordham	c Kallicharran b Small	50
N.A. Felton	c Humpage b Munton	0
R.J. Bailey	c Reeve b Donald	1
D.J. Capel	c Lloyd b Donald	46
D.J. Wild	b Munton	8
†D. Ripley	not out	25
J.G. Thomas	lbw b Small	12
N.G.B. Cook	lbw b Small	0
W.W. Davis	c Humpage b Small	0
M.A. Robinson	lbw b Reeve	0
Extras	b 4, lb 13, nb 2	19
Total (73.4 ov)		179

42, 42, 43, 111, 132, 146, 172, 174, 174

Donald	16	4	37	2
Small	20	8	49	4
Munton	20	4	46	3
P.A. Smith	6	2	16	0
Reeve	11.4	5	14	1

Warwickshire 1st Innings		
A.J. Moles	not out	0
N.M.K. Smith	not out	0
*T.A. Lloyd		
A.I. Kallicharran		
†G.W. Humpage		
P.A. Smith		
D.A. Reeve		
Asif Din		
G.C. Small		
A.A. Donald		
T.A. Munton		
Extras		0
Total (0 wkt dec)		0

No balls bowled

Northamptonshire 2nd Innings		
*W. Larkins	c and b Munton	14
A. Fordham	not out	55
N.A. Felton	not out	8
Extras	lb 2	2
Total (1 wkt dec)		79

48

Munton	8	2	37	1
N.M.K. Smith	6	1	31	0
Moles	1	0	9	0

Warwickshire 2nd Innings		
A.J. Moles	b Davis	50
*T.A. Lloyd	c Cook b Thomas	28
A.I. Kallicharran	c Larkins b Capel	31
†G.W. Humpage	c Capel	11
P.A. Smith	c Cook b Robinson	22
D.A. Reeve	lbw b Robinson	6
Asif Din	b Capel	0
N.M. K. Smith	not out	15
G.C. Small	run out	20
A.A. Donald	not out	6
Extras	b 7, lb 13, w 1, nb 7	28
Total (8 wkts)		217

68, 113, 129, 138, 166, 167, 179, 209

Davis	20	3	74	1
Thomas	11	2	27	1
Robinson	13	2	38	2
Capel	16	4	45	3
Cook	6	3	13	0

Umpires: M.J. Kitchen and B. Hassan
Toss: Warwickshire

Two days having been lost through rain, and the Saturday employed by Northants first innings, Warwickshire took the unusual step of declaring their first innings closed before it had started. The final day therefore began with Northants making a token 79–1 in their second innings setting Warwickshire 259 in 65 overs. Northants in fact came close to winning but were foiled by N.M.K. Smith who survived 19 overs for 15 not out.

Worcestershire

President: D. Kenyon
Chairman: C.D. Fearnley
Secretary: M.D. Vockins, County Ground, New Road, Worcester WR2 4QQ. *Tel:* 0905 422694.
Coach: B.L. d'Oliveira
Captain: P.A. Neale
Foundation of Present Club: March 1865 in Worcester
First First-Class Match: Worcestershire v Yorkshire (Worcester) May 1899
County Champions: 1964, 1965, 1974, 1988, 1989
Gillette/NatWest Trophy: Losing finalists in 1963, 1966, 1988
Benson & Hedges Cup: Losing finalists 1973, 1976
Sunday League Champions: 1971, 1987, 1988
Refuge Cup: Losing finalists 1988

Summary of Results in 1989
Britannic Assurance County Championship: Played 22, Won 12, Lost 3, Drawn 7, Winners
NatWest Bank Trophy: Lost in semi-final
Benson & Hedges Cup: Did not qualify for knock-out section
Refuge Assurance Sunday League: Played 16, Won 11, Lost 4, No Result 1, Position 2nd equal
Refuge Assurance Cup: Lost in semi-final

Tim Curtis, Worcestershire's opening batsman, who was second to Hick in the county batting averages.
Allsport/Bob Martin

Phil Neale, the Worcestershire skipper, who led his county to their second successive Championship.
Allsport/Adrian Murrell

ONE DAY AWAY MATCHES

The full scorecard of each of Worcestershire's away matches will be found in the sections for the respective home teams.

Refuge Assurance League

Trent Bridge: April 23
No play. Worcs 2pts, Notts 2pts.

Bristol: May 28
Gloucs 221–5 (40 ov) lost to Worcs 222–4 (38.5 ov) by 6 wkts. Worcs 4pts, Gloucs 0pts.

Edgbaston: June 18
Worcs 194–5 (40 ov) beat Warwicks 172–8 (40 ov) by 22 runs. Worcs 4pts, Warwicks 0pts.

Tring: July 2
Northants 168 (39.4 ov) lost to Worcs 169–4 (39.4 ov) by 6 wkts. Worcs 4pts, Northants 0pts.

Scarborough: July 16
Yorks 204–7 (40 ov) lost to Worcs 208–4 (40 ov) by 6 wkts. Worcs 4pts, Yorks 0pts.

Hove: July 23
Sussex 239–5 (40 ov) beat Worcs 225 (39.4 ov) by 14 runs. Sussex 4pts, Worcs 0pts.

Colchester: August 6
Essex 193–9 (40 ov) lost to Worcs 197–4 (38.4 ov) by 6 wkts. Worcs 4pts, Essex 0pts.

Bournemouth: August 13
Worcs 149 (39.4 ov) beat Hants 147–9 (40 ov) by two runs. Worcs 4pts, Hants 0pts.

Benson and Hedges Cup

Lords: April 25, 26
Worcs 115–6 (31 ov) beat Middx 114–7 (31 ov) by one run. Worcs 2pts, Middx 0pts.

The Oval: May 2
Worcs 190–7 (55 ov) lost to Surrey 191–9 (55 ov) by one wkt. Surrey 2pts, Worcs 0pts.

NatWest Bank Trophy

March: June 28
Cambs 202–4 (60 ov) lost to Worcs 206–1 (48.1 ov) by 9 wkts.

Edgbaston: August 16 semi-final
Warwicks 220–9 (60 ov) beat Worcs 120 (46 ov) by 100 runs.

From left, back: *J.W. Sewter (Scorer), G. Bryant, M.S. Scott, M.P. Briers, S.R. Bevins, S.R. Lampitt, D.A. Leatherdale, S.J. O'Shaughnessy, P. Bent, R.D. Stemp, D.W. Headley, G.R. Haynes, S.M. McEwan, C.M. Tolley, G.J. Lord, D. Roberts.* Front: *B.L. d'Oliveira (Coach), R.K. Illingworth, M.J. Weston, I.T. Botham, G.A. Hick, N.V. Radford, T.S. Curtis, D. Kenyon (President), P.A. Neale (Captain), C.D. Fearnley (Chairman), A.P. Pridgeon, D.B d'Oliveira, P.J.Newport, G.R. Dilley, S.J. Rhodes, M.G. Jones (Chairman, Cricket Committee).*

Allsport/Chris Rapheal

REFUGE ASSURANCE LEAGUE

v LANCASHIRE (Worcester)

May 7

Lost by 14 runs. Lancs 4pts, Worcs 0pts

Lancashire		
G. Fowler	c d'Oliveira b Newport	39
A.N. Hayhurst	c Illingworth b Newport	5
N.H. Fairbrother	st Rhodes b Illingworth	64
T.E. Jesty	b Radford	8
Wasim Akram	c O'Shaughnessy b Illingworth	3
M. Watkinson	b Botham	38
*D.P. Hughes	lbw b Radford	0
P.A.J. DeFreitas	c Curtis b Pridgeon	25
†W.K. Hegg	not out	1
P.W.J. Allott		
J. Simmons		
Extras	b 4, lb 13, nb 2	19
Total (8 wkts, 40 ov)		202

18, 109, 124, 134, 139, 139, 198, 202

Newport	8	0	27	2
Pridgeon	8	1	30	1
Botham	5	0	34	1
Lampitt	5	0	28	0
Radford	8	0	29	2
Illingworth	6	0	37	2

Worcestershire		
T.S. Curtis	b Simmons	22
*I.T. Botham	b DeFreitas	0
G.A. Hick	b DeFreitas	4
D.B. d'Oliveira	c Fairbrother b Allott	6
S.R. Lampitt	lbw b Allott	3
S.J. O'Shaughnessy	c Hughes b Wasim Akram	69
†S.J. Rhodes	lbw b Simmons	14
P.J. Newport	c Hegg b Wasim Akram	1
N.V. Radford	c Hughes b Watkinson	37
R.K. Illingworth	not out	16
A.P. Pridgeon	not out	4
Extras	lb 9, w 1, nb 2	12
Total (9 wkts, 40 ov)		188

1, 5, 20, 26, 55, 81, 86, 158, 169

DeFreitas	8	1	27	2
Allott	8	3	9	2
Wasim Akram	8	0	28	2
Simmons	8	0	54	2
Watkinson	8	0	61	1

Umpires: J.H. Harris and A.A. Jones
Toss: Worcestershire

Fowler and Fairbrother gave the Lancashire innings a sound start. In contrast DeFreitas removed the heart out of Worcs by bowling both Botham and Hick. O'Shaughnessy's innings saved the face of his new colleagues against his old county.

v SURREY (Worcester)

May21

Lost by 5 runs. Surrey 4pts, Worcs 0pts

Surrey		
G.S. Clinton	c Newport b Pridgeon	78
M.A. Feltham	c Neale b Weston	24
Zahid Sadiq	c Rhodes b Botham	7
A.J. Stewart	c Curtis b Newport	55
†D.M. Ward	c Weston b Botham	30
*I.A. Greig	not out	9
K.T. Medlycott	not out	1
G.P. Thorpe		
C.K. Bullen		
M.P. Bicknell		
A.J. Murphy		
Extras	lb 11, w 3, nb 3	17
Total (5 wkts, 40 ov)		221

53, 65, 157, 202, 217

Newport	8	0	38	1
Weston	8	1	37	1
Botham	7	0	33	2
Pridgeon	7	0	46	1
Radford	8	0	41	0
O'Shaughnessy	2	0	15	0

Worcestershire		
T.S. Curtis	c Ward b Greig	43
I.T. Botham	run out	31
G.A. Hick	c Greig b Bullen	1
D.B. d'Oliveira	not out	91
S.J. O'Shaughnessy	b Bicknell	9
†S.J. Rhodes	b Bullen	4
*P.A. Neale	b Murphy	3
M.J. Weston	c Thorpe b Feltham	7
N.V. Radford	b Feltham	2
P.J. Newport	not out	10
A.P. Pridgeon		
Extras	b 4, lb 10, nb 1	15
Total (8 wkts, 40 ov)		216

68, 70, 102, 126, 137, 163, 180, 191

Bicknell	8	0	43	1
Murphy	8	0	41	1
Feltham	8	0	45	2
Greig	8	0	40	1
Bullen	8	0	33	2

Umpires: J.W. Holder and R. Julian
Toss: Worcestershire

Surrey due to a workmanlike 78 from Clinton and a hard hit 55 from Stewart set Worcs 222. Curtis and Botham began with a stand of 68, but after this was broken only d'Oliveira with 91 off 80 balls kept the home side in the match.

v GLAMORGAN (Worcester)

July 4

Won by 143 runs. Worcs 4pts, Glamorgan 0pts

Worcestershire		
T.S. Curtis	b Ontong	47
I.T. Botham	b Derrick	70
G.A. Hick	c Morris b Watkin	50
D.B. d'Oliveira	c Metson b Ontong	1
*P.A. Neale	not out	49
N.V. Radford	not out	29
S.R. Lampitt		
†S.J. Rhodes		
P.J. Newport		
R.K. Illingworth		
A.P. Pridgeon		
Extras	lb 10, w 6	16
Total (4 wkts, 40 ov)		262

123, 135, 136, 219

Watkin	8	0	38	1
Dennis	8	0	52	0
Barwick	8	0	75	0
Derrick	6	0	28	1
Ontong	8	0	49	2
Shastri	2	0	10	0

Glamorgan		
A.R. Butcher	c Neale b Newport	4
*H. Morris	c Rhodes b Newport	6
M.P. Maynard	b Pridgeon	20
R.J. Shastri	b Newport	8
G.C. Holmes	b Botham	9
R.C. Ontong	c Curtis b Botham	1
†C.P. Metson	lbw b Pridgeon	2
S.J. Dennis	c Botham b Pridgeon	0
S.L. Watkin	c Rhodes b Botham	16
S.R. Barwick	not out	48
J. Derrick	c Rhodes b Newport	0
Extras	lb 3, w 2	5
Total (27.2 ov)		119

8, 11, 30, 49, 49, 52, 52, 52, 109

Newport	6.2	0	18	4
Lampitt	5	0	27	0
Botham	8	2	31	3
Pridgeon	8	0	40	3

Umpires: J.W. Holder and R. Palmer
Toss: Glamorgan

An opening stand of 123 by Curtis and Botham was followed by Hick's 50 off 40 balls and Worcs realised the highest Sunday total to date this season. Glamorgan fell cheaply to Newport though Barwick hit a career best and enabled the Welshman to reach three figures.

The county retained the Championship title it had won in 1988, but the rain at the end of the season meant the crown was gained only by dint of Essex's 25 penalty points. Worcestershire came second in the Sunday League – a good effort after they began so feebly, but in the Refuge Cup they were paired against Essex and thoroughly mauled.

All eyes were on Hick after his famous summer of 1988 with its 405 not out against Somerset. He was still head and shoulders above the rest in 1989, but did not quite reach the pinnacle scaled the previous year – yet only Cook of Somerset scored more runs than the Zimbabwean. Hick's bowling proved of more use and against Essex he actually picked up 10 wickets in a match, an achievement not attained by the usual occasional bowler.

Neale and Curtis were splendidly consistent and the wicket-keeper, Rhodes, helped by numerous uncompleted innings, averaged above 30. After playing in less than half the matches in 1988, d'Oliveira turned out in every first-class game, but his record was a modest one. Weston also found runs hard to acquire. Botham brightened up the one-day matches, but an average of 18 in first-class cricket is not one of much merit for a cricketer of his standing, even allowing for his operation in 1988.

The bowling statistics presented a very pleasant surprise. McEwan and Lampitt, also unknown before the summer began, stepped in when the more celebrated trundlers were unavailable and both returned good records. Radford continued to take wickets and maintained his form of 1988, but Newport fell back, though he appeared in the first Test. Botham, bowling in his slower style, was more use with the ball than he was with the bat. A knee operation in May meant Dilley missed about half the season, but he bowled well when fit.

In view of the demands of England on Worcestershire's cricketers and problems through injury, 1989 might be regarded as equal to the best in the county's history.

REFUGE ASSURANCE LEAGUE

v DERBYSHIRE (Worcester)

June 11

Won by 30 runs. Worcs 4pts, Derby 0pts

Worcestershire		
T.S. Curtis	b Warner	18
M.J. Weston	b Warner	72
G.A. Hick	c Maher b Sharma	6
D.B. d'Oliveira	c Goldsmith b Sharma	15
*P.A. Neale	run out	25
N.V. Radford	not out	38
S.J. O'Shaughnessy	c Sharma b Bishop	17
†S.J. Rhodes		
S.R. Lampitt		
R.K. Illingworth		
G.R. Dilley		
Extras	lb 7, w 6, nb 3	16
Total (6 wkts, 40 ov)		207

65, 85, 113, 133, 169, 207

Mortensen	6	0	24	0
Newman	7	1	43	0
Bishop	8	0	51	1
Warner	8	1	35	2
Griffith	4	0	23	0
Sharma	7	0	24	2

Derbyshire		
P.D. Bowler	lbw b Weston	12
R. Sharma	c Rhodes b Weston	6
B. Roberts	b Radford	24
S.C. Goldsmith	st Rhodes b Hick	49
†B.J.M. Maher	b Illingworth	0
F.A. Griffith	lbw b Illingworth	1
*P.G. Newman	c Lampitt b Hick	24
A.E. Warner	c Rhodes b O'Shaughnessy	8
I.R. Bishop	not out	16
O.H. Mortensen	c O'Shaughnessy b Radford	11
J.E. Morris	not out	3
Extras	b 1, lb 17, w 5	23
Total (9 wkts, 40 ov)		177

23, 28, 71, 72, 80, 131, 142, 146, 168

Dilley	5	0	11	0
Weston	8	0	38	2
Illingworth	8	1	21	2
Radford	8	2	15	2
Hick	7	0	44	2
O'Shaughnessy	5	0	30	1

Umpires: H.D. Bird and N.T. Plews
Toss: Worcestershire

Despite the failure of Hick and absence of Botham, Worcestershire reached 200 and Weston, who hit the highest score for his team, then opened the bowling and removed Derbyshire's first two batsmen cheaply. The visitors never recovered.

v MIDDLESEX (Worcester)

June 25

Lost by 5 wkts. Worcs 0pts, Middx 4pts

Worcestershire		
T.S. Curtis	c Downton b Hughes	11
I.T. Botham	b Fraser	8
G.A. Hick	b Cowans	5
D.B. d'Oliveira	b Carr	43
*P.A. Neale	c Hughes b Ellcock	20
M.J. Weston	C Ramprakash b Carr	2
S.J. O'Shaughnessy	c Butcher b Hughes	26
N.V. Radford	c Haynes b Hughes	3
S.R. Lampitt	c Ellcock b Hughes	6
†S.J. Rhodes	c Ellcock b Hughes	7
R.K. Illingworth	not out	0
Extras	b 4, lb 7, w 1	12
Total (39.2 ov)		143

14, 25, 29, 85, 89, 102, 108, 130, 143

Cowans	8	1	36	1
Fraser	8	2	23	1
Hughes	7.2	1	23	5
Ellcock	8	1	26	1
Carr	8	0	24	2

Middlesex		
D.L. Haynes	b Weston	19
M.A. Roseberry	lbw b Botham	7
R.O. Butcher	c Curtis b Radford	28
M.R. Ramprakash	not out	47
J.D. Carr	b Botham	20
J.F. Sykes	c Hick b Radford	8
*†P.R. Downton	not out	7
S.P. Hughes		
A.R.C. Fraser		
R.M. Ellcock		
N.G. Cowans		
Extras	lb 3, w5	8
Total (5 wkts, 38.2 ov)		144

22, 40, 77, 126, 135

Botham	8	0	29	2
Weston	8	0	28	1
Illingworth	8	2	21	0
Radford	7.2	1	21	2
Hick	5	0	29	0
O'Shaughnessy	2	0	13	0

Umpires: P.J. Eele and D.G.L. Evans
Toss: Worcestershire

A capacity crowd of 5,000 saw the home side beaten due to an excellent innings from Ramprakash, after the three top Worcester batsmen had failed. Ellcock, the former Worcester bowler, made his debut for Middlesex.

v LEICESTERSHIRE (Worcester)

July 9

Won by 6 wkts. Worcs 4pts, Leics 0pts

Leicestershire		
L. Potter	c Rhodes b Weston	10
* N.E. Briers	b Lampitt	20
J.J. Whitaker	c Rhodes b Weston	2
P. Willey	lbw b Lampitt	6
J.D.R. Benson	c Neale b Radford	6
C.C. Lewis	c d'Oliveira b Radford	50
†P. Whitticase	run out	23
W.K.M. Benjamin	b Radford	0
G.J. Parsons	not out	5
J.P. Agnew	b Illingworth	0
L.B. Taylor	not out	2
Extras	b 1, lb 14, w 17	32
Total (9 wkts, 40 ov)		156

29, 38, 56, 59, 69, 139, 146, 150, 154

Weston	8	2	21	2
McEwan	5	0	18	0
Lampitt	8	0	21	2
Radford	8	2	16	3
O'Shaughnessy	4	0	29	0
Illingworth	7	0	36	1

Worcestershire		
S.J. O'Shaughnessy	b Willey	15
M.J. Weston	c Whitticase by Parsons	19
G.A. Hick	run out	13
D.B. d'Oliveira	c Potter b Taylor	45
*P.A. Neale	not out	36
D.A. Leatherdale	not out	11
S.R. Lampitt		
†S.J. Rhodes		
N.V. Radford		
R.K. Illingworth		
S.M. McEwan		
Extras	b 4, lb 6, w 8	18
Total (4 wkts, 37.3 ov)		157

39, 49, 68, 139

Benjamin	7	0	20	0
Agnew	6.3	1	19	0
Parsons	8	0	38	1
Willey	8	0	28	1
Taylor	8	0	42	1

Umpires: J.H. Hampshire and B.J. Meyer
Toss: Worcestershire

Put in to bat, Leicester lost their first six wickets for 69 on a lively New Road wicket. Lewis then hit 50 off 58 balls with three sixes. The home side found little difficulty in reaching the modest total required despite losing Hick cheaply.

PLAYERS

Paul BENT *b* 1.5.1965 Worcester; right-hand batsman; off-break bowler; debut 1985

Stuart Roy BEVINS *b* 8.3.1967 Solihull; wicketkeeper; right-hand batsman; FC debut for Worcs in May 1989

Ian Terence BOTHAM *b* 24.11.1955 Heswall, Ches; outstanding all-rounder; hard-hitting middle order right-hand batsman; right-arm medium (formerly fast) bowler; debut 1987; previously appeared for Somerset 1974–86; 97 Tests for England, including 12 as captain; record number of wickets for England 376; missed most of 1988 due to injury, but returned in 1989

Timothy Stephen CURTIS *b* 15.1.1960 Chislehurst; opening right-hand batsman; debut 1979; Cambridge Univ 1983; five Tests for England including three in 1989

Graham Roy DILLEY *b* 18.5.1959 Dartford; right-arm fast bowler; left-hand batsman; debut 1987; previously played for Kent 1977–86; 41 Tests for England including two in 1989; selected to tour South Africa 1989–90

Damien Basil d'OLIVEIRA *b* 19.10.1960 Cape Town; right-hand batsman; off-break bowler; debut 1982; son of B.L. (ex-Worcs)

Graeme Ashley HICK *b* 23.5.1966 Salisbury, Rhodesia; brilliant middle order right-hand batsman; off-break bowler; Debut 1984; also plays for Northern Districts

Richard Keith ILLINGWORTH *b* 23.8.1963 Bradford; slow left-arm bowler; right-hand batsman; debut 1982; selected to tour Zimbabwe 1989–90

Stuart Richard LAMPITT *b* 29.7.1966 Wolverhampton; right-hand batsman; right-arm medium pace bowler; debut 1985

David Anthony LEATHERDALE *b* 26.11.1967 Bradford; right-hand batsman; right-arm medium pace bowler; debut 1988

Gordon John LORD *b* 25.4.1961 Edgbaston; left-hand batsman; slow left-arm bowler; debut 1987; previously appeared for Warwicks 1983–86

Steven Michael McEWAN *b* 5.5.1962 Worcester; right-arm fast medium bowler; right-hand batsman; debut 1985; capped in August 1989

Phillip Anthony NEALE *b* 5.6.1954 Scunthorpe; right-hand batsman; debut 1975; captain since 1982; one of the last FC cricketers to play regular league football

Philip John NEWPORT *b* 11.10.1962 High Wycombe; right-arm fast medium bowler; right-hand batsman; debut 1982; two Tests for England, including on in 1989

Steven Joseph O'SHAUGHNESSY *b* 9.9.1961 Bury; all-rounder; right-hand batsman; right-arm medium pace bowler; debut 1988; previously appeared for Lancs 1980–87; announced retirement in 1989; hit fastest 100 in 35 mins for Lancs in 1983

Alan Paul PRIDGEON *b* 22.2.1954 Wall Heath, Staffs; right-arm medium fast bowler; right-hand batsman; debut 1972

Neal Victor RADFORD *b* 7.6.1957 Luanshya, N Rhodesia; right-arm fast medium bowler; right-hand batsman; debut 1985; also plays for Transvaal; previously appeared for Lancs 1980–84; three Tests for England 1986

Steven John RHODES *b* 17.6.1964 Bradford; wicketkeeper; right-hand batsman; debut 1985; previously appeared for Yorks 1981–84; three One Day Internationals for England in 1989; Selected to tour Zimbabwe 1989–90; son of W.E. (ex-Notts)

Christopher Mark TOLLEY *b* 30.12.1967 Kidderminster; right-hand batsman; left-arm medium pace bowler; FC debut for Worcs in July 1989

Martin John WESTON *b* 8.4.1959 Worcester; opening right-hand batsman; right-arm mediudm page bowler; debut 1979

Stuart Lampitt, Worcestershire's medium-pace bowler who finished top of the county averages.

Bill Smith

REFUGE ASSURANCE LEAGUE

v KENT (Worcester)

July 30

Won by 7 wkts Worcs 4pts, Kent 0pts

Kent		
S.G. Hinks	c d'Oliveira b Illingworth	45
T.R. Ward	c Neale b O'Shaughnessy	41
M.V. Fleming	c d'Oliveira b O'Shaughnessy	2
*C.S. Cowdrey	run out	1
J.I. Longley	c Rhodes b Radford	8
R.M. Ellison	b Illingworth	0
M.A. Ealham	c Neale b Radford	3
N.R. Taylor	not out	7
H.L. Alleyne	b Illingworth	3
†P. Farbrace	not out	1
A.P. Igglesden		
Extras	lb 8, w 4	12
Total (8 wkts, 22 ov)		123

79, 85, 97, 99, 102, 108, 116, 121

Tolley	5	0	19	0
McEwan	3	0	11	0
Radford	5	0	29	2
O'Shaughnessy	4	0	30	2
Lampitt	1	0	8	0
Illingworth	4	0	18	3

Worcestershire		
†S.J. Rhodes	not out	48
S.J. O'Shaughnessy	lbw b Ealham	1
G.A. Hick	b Fleming	15
D.B. d'Oliveira	b Igglesden	32
*P.A. Neale	not out	22
C.M. Tolley		
D.A. Leatherdale		
S.R. Lampitt		
N.V. Radford		
R.K. Illingworth		
S.M. McEwan		
Extras	lb 7, w 1	8
Total (3 wkts, 20.4 ov)		126

3, 26, 78

Ealham	5	0	17	1
Igglesden	5	0	39	1
Fleming	4	0	18	1
Ward	1	0	5	0
Alleyne	3.4	0	27	0
Cowdrey	2	0	13	0

Umpires: J.C. Balderstone and R. Julian

Toss: Worcestershire

Reduced to 22 overs per side, this match began with Kent taking a commanding position, their opening batsmen adding 79 for the 1st wicket in 14.4 overs. Then eight wickets tumbled and Worcestershire had a manageable target.

v SOMERSET (Worcester)

August 20

Won by 12 runs. Worcs 4pts Somerset 0pts

Worcestershire		
T.S. Curtis	lbw b Rose	14
M.J. Weston	c and b Marks	35
G.A. Hick	c Mallender b Jones	81
D.B. d'Oliveira	b Rose	47
*P.A. Neale	not out	22
D.A. Leatherdale	c Tavare b Rose	1
†S.J. Rhodes		
S.R. Lampitt		
C.M. Tolley		
R.K. Illingworth		
S.M. McEwan		
Extras	lb 1, w 1	2
Total (5 wkts, 40 ov)		202

23, 74, 167, 194, 202

Jones	8	2	49	1
Rose	8	2	30	3
Mallender	8	1	31	0
Trump	4	0	32	0
Marks	8	0	29	1
Cleal	4	0	30	0

Somerset		
S.J. Cook	b Tolley	14
G.D. Rose	c Tolley b Illingworth	25
C.J. Tavare	c Rhodes b Illingworth	5
R.J. Harden	c Rhodes b McEwan	4
J.C.M. Atkinson	b McEwan	6
*V.J. Marks	not out	67
†N.D. Burns	b Lampitt	19
M.W. Cleal	st Rhodes b Hick	15
N.A. Mallender	not out	19
A.N. Jones		
H.R.J. Trump		
Extras	b 1, lb 10, w 5	16
Total (7 wkts, 40 ov)		190

46, 46, 54, 64, 66, 104, 142

Tolley	8	1	18	1
Weston	6	0	23	0
Illingworth	8	1	25	2
McEwan	8	0	47	2
Lampitt	4	0	20	1
Hick	6	0	46	1

Umpires: J.D. Bond and K.J. Lyons

Toss: Somerset

Hick hit 81 off 77 balls on a slow pitch and then Somerset's early batsmen failed, so that, despite a hard hit 67 off 62 balls by Marks, Worcestershire won their final Sunday League match.

BENSON AND HEDGES CUP

v GLOUCESTERSHIRE (Worcester)

May 9

Lost by 48 runs. Gloucs 2pts, Worcs 0pts

Gloucester		
A.W. Stovold	b Newport	23
A.J. Wright	lbw b Botham	4
P.W. Romaines	c Botham b Newport	12
*C.W.J. Athey	b Radford	35
P. Bainbridge	c O'Shaughnessy b Dilley	53
K.J. Curran	c Hick b Botham	36
V.S. Greene	c Hick b Dilley	1
M.W. Alleyne	not out	23
†R.C. Russell	not out	0
M.W. Pooley		
D.V. Lawrence		
Extras	b 4, lb 4, w 1, nb 4	13
Total (7 wkts, 55 ov)		200

29, 29, 58, 103, 168, 170, 190

Dilley	10	1	40	2
Radford	11	2	30	1
Botham	10	2	41	2
Newport	11	2	33	2
Weston	11	1	28	0
Illingworth	2	0	20	0

Worcestershire		
T.S. Curtis	lbw b Curran	26
S.J. O'Shaughnessy	b Greene	4
G.A. Hick	c Athey b Curran	16
D.B. d'Oliveira	run out	7
*I.T. Botham	b Greene	37
M.J. Weston	lbw b Curran	0
†S.J. Rhodes	b Alleyne	21
N.V. Radford	c and b Greene	0
P.J. Newport	b Bainbridge	12
R.K. Illingworth	b Greene	11
G.R. Dilley	not out	0
Extras	lb 13, nb 5	18
Total (51.1 ov)		152

11, 51, 62, 66, 67, 120, 125, 130, 152

Lawrence	9	1	31	0
Greene	9.1	2	15	4
Pooley	11	1	42	0
Curran	11	5	15	3
Bainbridge	10	1	34	1
Alleyne	1	0	2	1

Umpires: J.H. Harris and A.A. Jones

Toss: Worcestershire. Gold: K.M. Curran

Gloucester's middle batting performed well enough to enable the country to reach 200. This reasonable total was beyond Worcestershire, Greene and Curran returning impressive analyses. The fitness of Botham was of great interest to the press.

BRITANNIC ASSURANCE COUNTY CHAMPIONSHIP AVERAGES 1989

Batting	*M*	*I*	*NO*	*Runs*	*HS*	*Avge*	*100*	*50*
G.A. Hick	22	35	5	1595	150	53.17	5	8
T.S. Curtis	16	27	2	1213	156	48.52	4	7
P.A. Neale	21	31	7	911	98	37.96	–	7
S.J. Rhodes	20	29	13	589	83	36.81	–	2
C.M. Tolley	5	6	2	120	37	30.00	–	–
M.J. Weston	14	22	3	473	74	24.89	–	2
P. Bent	13	22	–	530	144	24.09	1	2
S.M. McEwan	11	9	3	139	28*	23.17	–	–
G.R. Dilley	12	14	10	88	31	22.00	–	–
D.B. D'Oliveira	22	34	1	723	63	21.91	–	5
S.R. Lampitt	9	7	2	99	46	19.80	–	–
N.V. Radford	16	20	1	319	66*	16.79	–	1
I.T. Botham	12	18	1	276	73	16.24	–	1
G.J. Lord	8	13	2	170	54	15.45	–	1
R.K. Illingworth	22	24	1	321	71	13.96	–	2
D.A. Leatherdale	7	8	1	93	25	13.29	–	–
P.J. Newport	6	8	1	86	27	12.29	–	–
S.R. Bevins	2	2	1	11	6*	11.00	–	–
A.P. Pridgeon	4	4	1	24	19*	8.00	–	–

Bowling	*O*	*M*	*R*	*W*	*Avge*	*BB*	*5i*	*10m*
S.R. Lampitt	219.5	56	526	31	16.97	5-32	2	–
S.M. McEwan	368.3	82	999	52	19.21	6-34	3	–
G.R. Dilley	321.2	58	1062	55	19.31	5-28	5	1
P.J. Newport	181	28	525	27	19.44	5-73	1	–
G.A. Hick	214.4	65	519	26	19.96	5-52	2	1
R.K. Illingworth	429.4	176	857	40	21.43	5-23	1	–
I.T. Botham	386.4	86	1122	51	22.00	7-85	3	1
N.V. Radford	516.2	105	1575	67	23.51	6-59	3	–
M.J. Weston	141.3	44	365	12	30.42	3-21	–	–

Also bowled: T.S. Curtis 4.3-0-10-0; P.A. Neale 1-0-8-0; A.P. Prigeon 47.5-14-95-3; C.M. Tolley 61-16-138-1.

Centuries

5 G.A. Hick: 150 v Yorks (Sheffield); 111 v Northants (Northampton); 110* v Somerset (Hove); 147 v Kent (Worcester); 136* v Somerset (Worcester).

4 T.S. Curtis: 102 v Glos (Bristol); 140* v Glamorgan (Worcester); 102 v Susex (Hove); 156 v Essex (Colchester).

1 P. Bent: 144 v Kent (Worcester).

BENSON AND HEDGES CUP

v COMBINED UNIVERSITIES (Worcester)

May 11

Lost by 5 wkts. Combined Univ 2pts, Worcs 0pts

Worcestershire		
T.S. Curtis	b Hansford	9
G.J. Lord	c O'Gorman b Dale	18
G.A. Hick	c O'Gorman b Hansford	109
D.B. d'Oliveira	c Speight b Dale	15
*I.T. Botham	c Speight b Dale	0
S.J. O'Shaughnessy	c Crawley b Boiling	14
†S.J. Rhodes	c and b Crawley	1
P.J. Newport	c Dale b Crawley	1
N.V. Radford	not out	39
R.K. Illingworth	not out	1
A.P. Pridgeon		
Extras	lb 6, w 3	9
Total (8 wkts, 55 ov)		216

14, 48, 74, 82, 116, 126, 137, 211

Hansford	11	3	39	2
Tolley	11	4	32	0
Crawley	11	1	72	2
Dale	11	2	35	3
Boiling	11	1	32	1

Combined Universities		
S.P. James	b Radford	65
T.J.G. O'Gorman	lbw b Radford	0
*M.A. Atherton	st Rhodes b Illingworth	20
N. Hussain	b Radford	67
†M.P. Speight	b Radford	29
J.I. Longley	not out	14
M.A. Crawley	not out	8
A. Dale		
C.M. Tolley		
A. Hansford		
J. Boiling		
Extras	lb 3, w 7, nb 4	14
Total (5 wkts, 53.1 ov)		217

2, 46, 152, 195, 196

Radford	11	0	38	4
Pridgeon	9.1	0	41	0
Newport	10	0	50	0
Illingworth	11	2	29	1
Botham	4	0	21	0
Hick	8	0	35	0

Umpires: B.J. Meyer and B. Hassan
Toss: Worcestershire. Gold: G.A. Hick
Hick reached his 50 in 79 balls and doubled that in a further 39, when he and Radford added 74 for the 8th wkt. The Universities were up with the run rate due to a fine stand of 106 between James and Hussain and even when that was broken, they continued on course.

NATWEST BANK TROPHY

v DERBYSHIRE (Worcester)

July 12

Won by 38 runs

Worcestershire		
T.S. Curtis	b Maher b Warner	13
M.J. Weston	c Barnett b Newman	43
†S. J. Rhodes	c Barnett b Malcolm	61
G.A. Hick	c Maher b Holding	45
D.B. d'Oliveira	lbw b Holding	1
I.T. Botham	c Mortensen b Newman	53
*P.A. Neale	not out	43
S.R. Lampitt	c Mortensen b Malcolm	0
N.V. Radford	not out	0
R.K. Illingworth		
G.R. Dilley		
Extras	b 5, lb 6, w 6, nb 2	19
Total (7 wkts, 60 ov)		278

46, 69, 137, 141, 224, 275, 275

Malcolm	12	0	62	2
Mortensen	12	0	46	0
Warner	12	2	60	1
Holding	12	3	20	2
Newman	12	1	79	2

Derbyshire		
*K.J. Barnett	c Neale b Illingworth	55
P.D. Bowler	c Hick b Botham	9
J.E. Morris	b Botham	0
R. Sharma	b Dilley	50
B. Roberts	not out	64
†B.J.M. Maher	lbw b Radford	3
P.G. Newman	b Lampitt	25
M.A. Holding	b Botham	6
A.E. Warner	run out	0
O.H. Mortensen	c Dilley b Botham	1
D.E. Malcolm	c Neale b Lampitt	6
Extras	lb 8, w 10, nb 3	21
Total (56 ov)		240

39, 39, 114, 135, 146, 204, 216, 217, 223

Dilley	10	4	38	1
Radford	9	3	23	1
Botham	12	1	62	4
Illingworth	12	2	43	1
Weston	6	0	31	0
Lampitt	7	0	35	2

Umpires: J.H. Hampshire and B. Hassan
Toss: Derbyshire. MofM: I.T. Botham
Worcestershire put in Rhodes at no. 3 and the wicketkeeper played an anchor role, whilst Hick, Botham and Neale kept the runs flowing. However they were helped by dropped catches. Derbyshire's batsmen made a brave attempt, but the target always looked beyond them.

QUARTER FINAL v LANCASHIRE (Worcester) August 2

Won by 7 wkts

Lancashire		
G. Fowler	b Botham	8
G.D. Mendis	c Botham b Illingworth	34
M.A. Atherton	c Weston b Illingworth	35
N.H. Fairbrother	c Curtis b Botham	25
M. Watkinson	b Radford	62
Wasim Akram	run out	4
P.A. J. DeFreitas	c Weston b Botham	25
†W.K. Hegg	c Illingworth b Botham	10
*D.P. Hughes	b Botham	3
P.J.W. Allott	not out	0
J. Simmons	not out	0
Extras	lb 13, w 14, nb 4	31
Total (9 wkts, 60 ov)		237

22, 93, 101, 192, 196, 199, 223, 237, 237

Dilley	12	3	47	0
Radford	12	3	31	1
Botham	12	1	51	5
Weston	8	1	22	0
Lampitt	5	0	18	0
Illingworth	11	0	55	2

Worcestershire		
T.S. Curtis	b Simmons	51
M.J. Weston	c Simmons b Watkinson	50
G.A. Hick	not out	90
D.A. Leatherdale	lbw b Allott	11
*P.A. Neale	not out	20
I.T. Botham		
†S.J. Rhodes		
S.R. Lampitt		
R.K. Illingworth		
N.V. Radford		
G.R. Dilley		
Extras	lb 7, w 9, nb 3	19
Total (3 wkts, 52.2 ov)		241

80, 161, 186

DeFreitas	10	3	22	0
Allott	11.2	0	52	1
Wasim Akram	9	0	52	0
Watkinson	8	0	52	1
Simmons	12	0	44	1
Atherton	2	0	12	0

Umpires: H.D. Bird and M.J. Kitchen
Toss: Worcestershire. MofM: M.J. Weston
Put in to bat, Lancashire found runs very hard to accumulate. After 30 overs ths total had only mounted to 71 and Mendis was almost crease-bound with 21. Worcestershire made light of the 238 runs required. Hick put Lancashire out of their misery.

Away Matches

The full scorecard of each of Worcestershire's away matches will be found in the sections for the respective home teams.

Trent Bridge: April 20, 21, 22, 24
Notts 218 (G.R. Dilley 5–42) and 198 lost to Worcs 291 and 129–3 by 7 wkts. Worcs 22pts, Notts 5pts.

Edgbaston: April 27, 28, 29
Worcs 143 and 160–5d drew with Warwicks 99 (G.R. Dilley 5–28) and 204–6. Warwicks 12pts, Worcs 4pts.

Bristol: May 27, 29, 30
Worcs 201 (K.M. Curran 6–53) and 283–6d (T.S. Curtis 102) beat Gloucs 148 (N.V. Radford 5–57) and 257 (K.M. Curran 116*, P.J. Newport 5–73) by 79 runs. Worcs 22pts, Gloucs 4pts.

Sheffield: June 21, 22, 23
Yorks 249 (N.V. Radford 5–86) and 280–4 drew with Worcs 389–7d (G.A. Hick 150). Worcs 7pts, Yorks 4pts.

Northampton: July 1, 3, 4
Northants 256 (I.T. Botham 6–99) and 158 (I.T. Botham 5–76) lost to Worcs 433 (G.A. Hick 111) by an inns and 19 runs. Worcs 24pts, Northants 4pts.

Old Trafford: July 19, 20, 21
Worcs 191 and 199 (Wilkinson 7–69) beat Lancs 125 (G.R. Dilley 5–30) and 229 (G.R. Dilley 5–94) by 36 runs. Worcs 21pts, Lancs 4pts.

Hove: July 22, 24, 25
Worcs 320 (T.S. Curtis 102) and 230–4d (G.A. Hick 110*) lost to Sussex 301 (I.T. Botham 7–85) and 250–6 by 4 wkts. Sussex 22pts, Worcs 6pts.

Colchester: August 5, 7, 8
Essex 208 (G.A. Hick 5–52) and 323–9 (G.A. Hick 5–131) drew with Worcs 447–9d (T.S. Curtis 156). Worcs 7pts, Essex 3pts.

Weston-super-Mare: August 9, 10, 11
Somerset 240 and 145 (S.M. McEwan 5–28) lost to Worcs 302–6d and 87–1 by 9 wkts. Worcs 24pts, Somerset 4pts.

Bournemouth: August 12, 14, 15
Worcs 325 beat Hants 137 (S.R.Lampitt 5–38) and 97 (R.K. Illingworth 5–23) by an inns and 91 runs. Worcs 22pts, Hants 3pts.

Pontypridd: Sept 13, 14, 15, 16
Glamorgan 230–9 drew with Worcs did not bat. Worcs 4pts, Glam 2pts.

Other First-Class Match

Lords: April 15, 16, 17, 18
Worcs 474–3d (G.A. Hick 173*) drew with MCC 281–4.

v LANCASHIRE (Worcester)

May 4, 5, 6
Lost by 66 runs. Lancs 21pts, Worcs 5pts

Lancashire 1st Innings

G.D. Mendis	lbw b Dilley	0
G. Fowler	c Dilley b Botham	60
A.N. Hayhurst	b Newport	26
N.H. Fairbrother	c Illingworth b Botham	1
T.E. Jesty	c Hick b Dilley	7
M. Watkinson	lbw b Botham	0
*D.P. Hughes	b Botham	6
Wasim Akram	c Hick b Dilley	5
†W.K. Hegg	not out	31
P.A.J. DeFreitas	b Radford	26
J. Simmons	c Hick b Newport	1
Extras	lb 8	8
Total (52.5 ov)		171

0, 59, 72, 83, 86, 96, 109, 117, 162

Dilley	13	2	41	3
Radford	8	2	28	1
Botham	18	4	53	4
Newport	13.5	3	41	2

Worcestershire 1st Innings

T.S. Curtis	c Hegg b DeFreitas	4
G.J. Lord	lbw b DeFreitas	14
G.A. Hick	lbw b Wasim Akram	15
*I.T. Botham	c Fowler b Wasim Akram	33
M.J. Weston	b Wasim Akram	17
†S.J. Rhodes	lbw b Hayhurst	25
†S.J. Rhodes	b Wasim Akram	9
P.J. Newport	lbw b Wasim Akram	2
R.K. Illingworth	d DeFreitas	13
N.V. Radford	c Watkinson b DeFreitas	9
G.R. Dilley	not out	0
Extras	lb 17, w 1, nb 7	25
Total (71.4 ov)		166

5, 36, 40, 73, 106, 135, 137, 140, 159

Wasim Akram	28	10	52	5
DeFreitas	27.4	9	61	4
Watkinson	11	5	23	0
Hayhurst	5	0	13	1

Lancashire 2nd Innings

G.D. Mendis	c d'Oliveira b Botham	69
G. Fowler	c Newport b Radford	5
A.N. Hayhurst	c Hick b Dilley	9
N.H. Fairbrother	lbw b Dilley	31
T.E. Jesty	c d'Oliveira b Botham	8
M. Watkinson	c Weston b Dilley	45
*D.P. Hughes	c d'Oliveira b Dilley	1
Wasim Akram	st Rhodes b Botham	14
†W.K. Hegg	b Botham	1
P.A.J. DeFreitas	b Newport	18
J. Simmons	not out	12
Extras	b 3, lb 10, nb 5	18
Total		231

6, 64, 102, 126, 130, 134, 157, 159, 193

Dilley	16.1	2	62	4
Radford	16	2	50	1
Newport	15	0	45	1
Botham	27	10	61	4

Worcestershire 2nd Innings

T.S. Curtis	c Hegg b DeFreitas	10
G.J. Lord	c Hegg b Wasim Akram	9
G.A. Hick	c Hughes b DeFreitas	2
D.B. d'Oliveira	run out	58
*I.T. Botham	b DeFreitas	0
M.J. Weston	c Fowler b Watkinson	5
†S.J. Rhodes	lbw b Watkinson	43
P.J. Newport	c Hegg b Watkinson	2
R.K. Illingworth	c Simmons b Watkinson	3
N.V. Radford	c Hayhurst b Watkinson	9
G.R. Dilley	not out	5
Extras	lb 14, w 3, nb 7	24
Total		170

24, 26, 28, 32, 54, 139, 151, 153, 158

Wasim Akram	24	5	59	1
DeFreitas	29	6	53	3
Watkinson	22.2	6	44	5

Umpires: J.H. Harris and A.A. Jones
Toss: Worcestershire
At the close on the first day, the two sides looked evenly matched, Worcs being 123–5 off 54 overs. Much interest centred on the fact that Botham took 4 wickets. On the second day the bowlers made the ball swing quite appreciably and only Mendis, 69 off 105 balls, made much impression with the bat.

v NOTTINGHAMSHIRE (Worcester)

May 24, 25, 26
Drawn. Worcs 3pts, Notts 5pts

Worcestershire 1st Innings

T.S. Curtis	c Newell b Hemmings	50
P.Bent	c Newell b Cooper	9
G.A. Hick	c Cooper b Evans	9
D.B. d'Oliveira	c Newell b Cooper	43
*P.A. Neale	c Johnson b Hemmings	0
M.J. Weston	c Cooper	9
P.J. Newport	c Scott b Cairns	27
N.V. Radford	c Robinson b Hemmings	39
R.K. Illingworth	c Johnson b Hemmings	1
S.R. Bevins	not out	6
A.P. Pridgeon	b Pick	2
Extras	b 5, lb 6, nb 3	14
Total (96.2 ov)		209

42, 55, 77, 77, 94, 148, 176, 177, 206

Pick	17.2	8	30	1
Cairns	7	1	37	1
Cooper	28	9	53	3
Evans	10	6	18	1
Hemmings	34	14	60	4

Nottinghamshire 1st Innings

B.C. Broad	b Illingworth	26
M. Newell	c Bevins b Newport	8
P. Johnson	c Hick b Illingworth	18
*R.T. Robinson	not out	54
D.W. Randall	not out	35
C.L. Cairns		
K.P. Evans		
E.E. Hemmings		
K.E. Cooper		
†C.W. Scott		
R.A. Pick		
Extras	b 7, lb 2	9
Total (3 wkts dec, 59 ov)		150

33, 43, 84

Radford	13	2	41	0
Pridgeon	7	4	10	0
Newport	9	2	32	1
Illingworth	23	9	37	2
Hick	7	2	21	0

Worcestershire 2nd Innings

T.S. Curtis	c Broad b Cooper	19
P. Bent	c Johnson b Hemmings	14
G.A. Hick	not out	90
D.B. d'Oliveira	b Cooper	4
*P.A. Neale	not out	51
Extras	lb 2	2
Total (3 wkts dec)		180

33, 45, 54

Pick	3	0	25	0
Cooper	11	4	25	2
Hemmings	10	4	18	1
Robinson	6	0	46	0
Johnson	4.2	0	64	0

Nottinghamshire 2nd Innings

B.C. Broad	c Bevins b Newport	40
M. Newell	c Curtis b Illingworth	62
P. Johnson	c Radford b Newport	6
*R.T. Robinson	c Radford b Newport	19
D.W. Randall	b Newport	18
C.L. Cairns	c Bevins b Illingworth	11
K.P. Evans	not out	25
E.E. Hemmings	b Illingworth	16
K.E. Cooper	c Newport b Radford	2
†C.W. Scott	b Radford	7
R.A. Pick	not out	1
Extras	b 12, lb 12, nb 7	31
Total (9 wkts)		238

74, 84, 122, 148, 173, 177, 207, 213, 237

Radford	14	1	54	2
Pridgeon	5	1	10	0
Illingworth	23	7	68	3
Newport	17	1	64	4
Hick	2	0	18	0

Umpires: K.J. Lyons & B. Hassan
Toss: Worcestershire
The ground was almost flooded by a thunderstorm a few hours before the game was due to start, but a hot sun enabled a commencement after tea. Worcs were 75–2 off 28 overs at the close. With the pitch helping the bowlers, the home side were dismssed for 209 and Notts struggled to 116–3 off 46 overs on the second day. Declarations on the last day left Notts needing 240 off 61 overs. This came down to 2 wickets or 10 runs from the final over, but neither side could force victory.

v GLAMORGAN (Worcester)

June 3, 5, 6

Drawn. Worcs 4pts, Glamorgan 4pts.

Worcestershire 1st Innings		
T.S. Curtis	lbw b Watkin	1
P.Bent	c Metson b Dennis	7
G.A. Hick	lbw b Barwick	43
D.B. d'Oliveira	lbw b Dennis	4
*P.A. Neale	c Watkin b Barwick	22
I.T. Botham	c Holmes b Barwick	0
†S.J. Rhodes	not out	22
N.V. Radford	c Butcher b Barwick	6
P.J. Newport	c Metson b Barwick	5
R.K. Illingworth	c Holmes b Barwick	11
A.P. Pridgeon	c Shastri b Dennis	2
Extras	b 2, lb 1, w 1	4
Total (65.1 ov)		127

8, 8, 27, 73, 80, 80, 88, 98, 110

Watkin	25	11	54	1
Dennis	16.1	10	22	3
Barwick	22	9	40	6
Shastri	2	0	8	0

Glamorgan 1st Innings		
A.R. Butcher	b Pridgeon	32
*H. Morris	lbw b Newport	21
M.J. Cann	lbw b Botham	11
M.P. Maynard	c Newport b Botham	11
R.J. Shastri	c Botham b Radford	11
G.C. Holmes	c Hick b Newport	19
R.C. Ontong	c d'Oliveira b Radford	0
†C.P. Metson	c Neale b Radford	3
S.J. Dennis	c Rhodes b Newport	13
S.L. Watkin	b Newport	0
S.R. Barwick	not out	0
Extras	lb 10, w 1, nb 2	13
Total (55.2 ov)		134

36, 69, 75, 80, 113, 113, 113, 117, 129

Radford	18	3	36	3
Newport	16.2	3	37	4
Pridgeon	11	1	22	1
Botham	10	1	29	2

Worcestershire 2nd Innings		
T.S. Curtis	not out	140
P.Bent	b Watkin	22
G.A. Hick	c Shastri b Watkin	0
D.B. d'Oliveira	lbw b Watkin	33
*P.A. Neale	retired hurt	10
I.T. Botham	retired hurt	10
†S.J. Rhodes	not out	15
Extras	b 6, lb 9, nb 1	16
Total (3 wkts dec)		246

66, 68, 159

Watkin	29	8	75	3
Dennis	20	4	63	0
Barwick	31	10	80	0
Holmes	9	4	12	0
Shastri	1	0	1	0

Glamorgan 2nd Innings		
A.R. Butcher	not out	3
*H. Morris	not out	16
Extras	lb 1	1
Total (0 wkt)		20

Newport	4	0	19	0
Radford	3.4	3	0	0

Umpires: J.W. Holder and R. Palmer
Toss: Worcestershire

Coming on as first change, Barwick took 5 wickets for 6 runs and only some blows from Rhodes spoilt his analysis. The atmosphere and wicket were of great assistance to the bowlers and by Saturday's close 14 wickets had gone, Glamorgan being 105–4 off 43 overs. On Monday both Neale and Botham were hit in the face by the ball and retired hurt, but Curtis completed a workmanlike 100 and was 116* at the close. Curtis in all batted 313 minutes for 140, though rain on the last day prevented any sort of attempt at a definite result.

v DERBYSHIRE (Worcester)

June 10, 12, 13

Won by 145 runs. Worcs 22pts, Derbys 5pts

Worcestershire 1st Innings		
T.S. Curtis	c Maher b Griffith	58
P. Bent	c Maher b Bishop	16
G.A. Hick	c Roberts b Newman	17
D.B. d'Oliveira	b Griffith	26
*P.A. Neale	c and b Warner	22
M.J. Weston	c Roberts b Base	3
†S.J. Rhodes	c Maher b Warner	1
N.V. Radford	b Newman	36
R.K. Illingworth	c Maher b Newman	4
G.R. Dilley	not out	8
A.P. Pridgeon	b Base	1
Extras	b 2, lb 9, w 9, nb 8	28
Total (86.4 ov)		220

35, 76, 132, 147, 154, 155, 193, 201, 216

Bishop	21	0	61	1
Base	21.4	4	63	2
Newman	17	6	30	3
Warner	16	5	32	2
Sharma	1	0	5	0
Griffith	10	3	18	2

Derbyshire 1st Innings		
P.D. Bowler	b Dilley	16
†B.J.M Maher	lbw b Dilley	17
J.E. Morris	c Rhodes b Weston	48
B. Roberts	c Hick b Radford	2
S.C. Goldsmith	c d'Oliveira b Dilley	0
R. Sharma	c Rhodes b Dilley	6
F.A. Griffith	c Radford b Dilley	30
*P.G. Newman	lbw b Radford	10
A.E. Warner	c Curtis b Weston	14
I.R. Bishop	c d'Oliveira b Weston	0
S.J. Base	not out	0
Extras	b 1, lb 10, w 1, nb 2	14
Total (67.2 ov)		157

22, 50, 51, 59, 68, 83, 100, 157, 157

Dilley	21.2	9	42	5
Radford	20	3	51	2
Pridgeon	1.5	0	5	0
Weston	15	7	21	3
Illingworth	9.1	3	27	0

Worcestershire 2nd Innings		
T.S. Curtis	c Sharma b Bishop	14
P. Bent	b Bishop	62
G.A. Hick	c Maher b Bishop	42
D.B. d'Oliveira	b Base	47
*P.A. Neale	c sub b Base	17
N.V. Radford	c Base b Bishop	5
M.J. Weston	b Maher b Base	7
†S.J. Rhodes	b Base	0
R.K. Illingworth	not out	5
G.R. Dilley	not out	11
Extras	lb 15, w 1, nb 1	17
Total (8 wkts dec)		227

18, 72, 154, 171, 194, 208, 210, 211

Bishop	19	6	50	4
Base	18	2	82	4
Warner	10	4	24	0
Newman	10	4	36	0
Sharma	11	4	20	0

Derbyshire 2nd Innings		
P.D. Bowler	run out	26
†B.J.M Maher	lbw b Radford	0
B. Roberts	b Radford	0
S.C. Goldsmith	c Hick b Radford	20
R. Sharma	b Weston	14
F.A. Griffith	c Rhodes b Radford	4
J.E.Morris	not out	47
A.E. Warner	retired hurt	10
*P.G.Newman	b Radford	12
I.R. Bishop	c Hick b Radford	1
S.J. Base	b Dilley	0
Extras	b 4, lb 6, nb 1	11
Total		145

0, 0, 40, 57, 66, 68, 138, 140, 145

Dilley	14.	4	51	1
Radford	25	6	59	6
Weston	13	5	21	1
Illingworth	8	4	4	0

Umpires: H.D. Bird and N.T. Plews
Toss: Derbyshire

On a seamers' wicket, only the patience of Curtis could cope with the Derbyshire attack and Worcestershire struggled to 220 off 86.4 overs. The visitors were 47–1 off 20 overs at the close. The home side began the final day with 172–3. Neale declared but Derbyshire never looked like making the 291 required and Radford returned his best figures so far this season.

v MIDDLESEX (Worcester)

June 24, 26

Lost by 9 wkts. Middx 22pts, Worcs 4pts

Worcestershire 1st Innings		
T.S. Curtis	lbw b Foster	3
P. Bent	b Cowans	9
G.A. Hick	b Fraser	5
D.B. d'Oliveira	c Ramprakash b Fraser	11
*P.A. Neale	c Downton b Fraser	8
I.T Botham	lbw b Cowans	47
M.J. Weston	c Downton b Hughes	45
†S.J. Rhodes	c Downton b Hughes	5
N.V. Radford	lbw b Cowans	0
R.K. Illingworth	run out	0
S.M. McEwan	not out	2
Extras	lb 1, nb 6	7
Total (36 overs)		142

12, 17, 18, 31, 59, 96, 103, 114, 119

Fraser	15	2	34	4
Cowans	15	5	50	3
Williams	5	0	32	0
Hughes	7.5	1	25	2

Middlesex 1st Innings		
D.L. Haynes	lbw b Radford	0
M.A. Roseberry	lbw b Weston	35
I.J.F. Hutchinson	c Rhodes b Botham	42
R.O. Butcher	st Rhodes b Illingworth	11
M.R. Ramprakash	c Rhodes b Hick	54
*†P.R. Downton	c Rhodes b Illingworth	10
N.F. Williams	c d'Oliveira b Illingworth	16
J.F. Skyes	b Botham	19
S.P. Hughes	lbw b Botham	5
A.R.C. Fraser	b Radford	7
N.G. Cowans	not out	10
Extras	b 3, lb 8, nb 1	12
Total (71.2 ov)		221

0, 73, 83, 108, 132, 156, 181, 196, 207

Radford	16.2	5	61	2
McEwan	5	0	18	0
Weston	7	0	26	1
Botham	20	1	59	3
Illingworth	19	10	40	3
Hick	4	2	6	1

Worcestershire 2nd Innings		
T.S. Curtis	c Downton b Williams	16
P. Bent	lbw b Cowans	1
G.A. Hick	b Fraser	6
D.B. d'Oliveira	lbw b Fraser	2
*P.A. Neale	not out	75
I.T Botham	b Fraser	6
M.J. Weston	b Cowans	6
†S.J. Rhodes	b Hughes	13
N.V. Radford	lbw b Hughes	3
R.K. Illingworth	c Butcher b Cowans	18
S.M. McEwan	c Sykes b Fraser	8
Extras	b 4, lb 4, nb 10	18
Total		172

15, 22, 24, 33, 45, 62, 87, 91, 155

Cowans	18	4	49	3
Fraser	19	5	39	4
Williams	11	1	37	1
Hughes	10	0	39	2

Middlesex 2nd Innings		
D.L. Haynes	not out	39
M.A. Roseberry	c Curtis b Radford	13
I.J. F. Hutchinson	not out	40
	lb 1, nb 3	4
Total (1 wkt)		96

30

Radford	11	2	49	1
McEwan	5	0	32	0
Botham	5	1	14	0

Umpires: P.J. Eele and D.G.L. Evans
Toss: Worcestershire

Some excellent bowling form Fraser, who dismissed the redoubtable Hick cheaply twice, won this match for Middlesex inside two days. On Saturday only a powerful innings from Botham – 47 off 58 balls – kept the home side afloat. Middlesex had a lead of 51 with 3 wickets in hand at the close. In Worcester's second innings Neale batted well and a 9th wicket stand of 64 in 17 overs prolonged the match well into the afternoon, but Middlesex knocked off the 96 needed with little trouble.

v WARWICKSHIRE (Worcester)

July 5, 6, 7

Drawn. Warwicks 7pts, Worcs 6pts

Warwickshire 1st Innings		
A.J. Moles	lbw b Radford	0
J.D. Ratcliffe	lbw b McEwan	3
*T.A. Lloyd	lbw b McEwan	24
G.W. Humpage	c Rhodes b McEwan	0
D.A. Reeve	c d'Oliveira b Illingworth	33
P.A. Smith	b Illingworth	140
†K.J. Piper	lbw b Lampitt	2
G.C. Small	lbw b Illingworth	15
T.A. Merrick	c Lampitt b Illingworth	31
A.R.K. Pierson	b McEwan	0
T.A. Munton	not out	2
Extras	lb 14, nb 1	15
Total (87.2 ov)		265

0, 18, 18, 29, 176, 185, 231, 238, 243

Radford	16	2	68	1
McEwan	17	1	62	4
Weston	13	3	36	0
Lampitt	15	4	36	1
Illingworth	22.2	12	33	4
Hick	4	0	16	0

Worcestershire 1st Innings		
M.J. Weston	b Merrick	37
G.J. Lord	c Piper b Small	5
G.A. Hick	b Merrick	4
D.B. d'Oliveira	lbw b Merrick	0
D.A. Leatherdale	b Merrick	5
†S.J. Rhodes	lbw b Merrick	44
*P.A. Neale	c Moles b Pierson	26
S.R. Lampitt	c Ratcliffe b Pierson	46
N.V. Radford	lbw b Merrick	4
R.K. Illingworth	c Pierson b Smith	0
S.M. McEwan	not out	28
Extras	b 3, lb 17, w 6, nb 7	33
Total (82.5 ov)		232

5, 14, 15, 24, 88, 140, 140, 159, 160

Small	26	6	62	1
Merrick	28	8	67	6
Munton	12	6	23	0
Smith	13	0	36	1
Pierson	3.5	0	24	2

Warwickshire 2nd Innings		
A.J. Moles	not out	34
J.D. Ratcliffe	not out	8
Extras	b 3, lb 2	5
Total (0 wkts)		47

Radford	5	0	26	0
McEwan	7	0	12	0
Lampitt	3.2	0	4	0
Weston	1	1	0	0

Umpires: J.D. Bond and B.J. Meyer
Toss: Warwickshire

Moles was dismissed first ball of the match and Warwickshire plunged to 29 for 4 before Paul Smith came to the rescue. With Reeve (33 in 162 minutes) he added 140 for the 5th wicket and hit a six and 24 fours. The home side were 49–4 off 22 overs at stumps. A last wicket stand of 72 by Lampitt and McEwan frustrated Warwickshire on the second day. They reached 47–0 in their second innings when a thunderstorm at 5.00 pm ended play and indeed the match, because further rain prevented a resumption on the third day.

v LEICESTERSHIRE (Kidderminster)

July 8, 10, 11

Won by 10 wickets. Worcs 22pts, Leics 5pts

Leicestershire 1st Innings		
R.A. Cobb	c Rhodes b Radford	2
*N.E. Briers	c Rhodes b McEwan	54
P.N. Hepworth	b McEwan	7
P. Willey	c Rhodes b McEwan	33
J.J. Whitaker	b Weston	6
L. Potter	lbw b Radford	22
†P. Whitticase	c Hick b Radford	40
G.J. Parsons	b Radford	0
J.P. Agnew	c Lampitt b Illingworth	8
G.J.F. Ferris	not out	1
L.B. Taylor	b Illingworth	0
Extras	b 1, lb 4, nb 2	7
Total (67 ov)		180

6, 37, 99, 105, 110, 146, 150, 179, 179

Radford	21	8	57	4
McEwan	20	7	53	3
Lampitt	6	0	25	0
Weston	11	4	31	1
Illingworth	9	5	9	2

Worcestershire 1st Innings		
M.J. Weston	b Ferris	11
G.J. Lord	c Whitticase b Taylor	33
G.A. Hick	b Parsons	41
D.B. d'Oliveira	c Potter b Taylor	0
*P.A. Neale	c Whitticase b Ferris	18
D.A. Leatherdale	b Taylor	0
†S.J. Rhodes	not out	73
S.R. Lampitt	c Parsons b Agnew	5
N.V. Radford	lbw b Agnew	0
R.K. Illingworth	b Ferris	34
S.M. McEwan	b Taylor	9
Extras	b 1, lb 6, w 7, nb 7	21
Total (75.5 ov)		245

18, 83, 84, 98, 98, 125, 130, 130, 209

Agnew	24	5	81	2
Ferris	18	5	54	3
Taylor	19.5	5	55	4
Parsons	14	2	48	1

Leicestershire 2nd Innings		
R.A. Cobb	b McEwan	34
*N.E. Briers	c Rhodes b Radford	0
P.N. Hepworth	b McEwan	0
J.J. Whitaker	c Neale b Weston	23
L. Potter	b Radford	12
†P. Whitticase	c Leatherdale b McEwan	2
P. Willey	c Rhodes b McEwan	0
G.J. Parsons	b McEwan	0
J.P. Agnew	b McEwan	7
G.J.F. Ferris	b Radford	0
L.B. Taylor	not out	0
Extras	w 2	2
Total		80

5, 10, 44, 50, 68, 72, 72, 76, 80

Radford	15.3	7	24	3
McEwan	14	5	34	6
Weston	7	2	14	1
Illingworth	5	1	8	0

Worcestershire 2nd Innings		
M.J. Weston	not out	10
G.J. Lord	not out	4
Extras	lb 1, w 1	2
Total (0 wkts)		16

Taylor	2	0	10	0
Parsons	1.4	0	5	0

Umpires: J.H. Hampshire and B.J. Meyer
Toss: Worcestershire

The medium pace of McEwan, who normally cannot command a regular place in the Worcester side, proved too much for Leicestershire, who were dismissd for 180 on a rain-interrupted first day. On Monday Rhodes propped up the home batting, but on the last day their lead of 65 proved more than adequate as Leicester collapsed, McEwan having a spell of 5 for 10 in 22 deliveries.

v SURREY (Worcester)

July 26, 27, 28

Won by 102 runs. Worcs 23pts, Surrey 5pts

Worcestershire 1st Innings		
P. Bent	c Stewart b Murphy	0
M.J. Weston	lbw b M.P. Bicknell	22
G.A. Hick	lbw b Feltham	9
D.B. d'Oliveria	c Stewart b Feltham	17
*P.A. Neale	c Greig b M.P. Bicknell	29
D.A. Leatherdale	c Stewart b M.P. Bicknell	5
†S.J. Rhodes	b Murphy	83
C.M. Tolley	c Stewart b Feltham	14
N.V. Radford	c Stewart b Murphy	11
R.K. Illingworth	c Medlycott b M.P. Bicknell	70
S.M. McEwan	not out	7
Extras	b 1, lb 11, nb 5	17
Total (87.1 ov)		284

0, 32, 36, 68, 79, 86, 111, 153, 262

Murphy	25	9	53	3
M.P. Bicknell	23.1	3	101	4
Feltham	31	10	85	3
Greig	6	1	16	0
Medlycott	2	0	17	0

Surrey 1st Innings		
D.J. Bicknell	c Weston b Radford	34
G.S. Clinton	lbw b Radford	3
R.I. Alikhan	lbw b McEwan	11
G.P. Thorpe	c Rhodes b McEwan	23
†A.J. Stewart	b McEwan	0
D.M. Ward	b Radford	4
*I.A. Grieg	b Weston	22
K.T. Medlycott	c Leatherdale b Illingworth	29
M.A. Feltham	lbw b Radford	12
M.P. Bicknell	b McEwan	3
A.J. Murphy	not out	1
Extras	b 7, lb 3, w 1	11
Total (64.1 ov)		153

16, 29, 37, 46, 67, 99, 127, 143, 151

Radford	28.1	5	66	4
McEwan	21	8	57	4
Weston	6	1	8	1
Tolley	5	2	8	0
Illingworth	4	3	4	1

Worcestershire 2nd Innings		
P. Bent	c M.P. Bicknell	22
M.J. Weston	c D.J. Bicknell b Feltham	74
G.A. Hick	lbw b Medlycott	85
D.B. d'Oliveria	c Feltham b Murphy	14
*P.A. Neale	c Alikhan b Medlycott	28
D.A. Leatherdale	not out	17
N.V. Radford	c M.P. Bicknell b Medlycott	4
†S.J. Rhodes	not out	5
Extras	lb 6, w 1	7
Total (6 wkts dec)		256

61, 127, 181, 216, 241, 245

Murphy	21	3	106	1
M.P. Bicknell	10	0	61	1
Feltham	13	1	44	1
Greig	4	0	16	0
Medlycott	5	0	23	3

Surrey 2nd Innings		
G.S. Clinton	c d'Oliveira b Radford	9
M.A. Feltham	b McEwan	38
D.J. Bicknell	b McEwan	5
†A.J. Stewart	c Hick b Radford	37
R.I. Alikhan	st Rhodes b Illingworth	50
G.P. Thorpe	c Hick b Illingworth	78
D.M. Ward	c Leatherdale b Hick	21
*I.A. Greig	c sub b Illingworth	2
K.T. Medlycott	c Illingworth b Radford	24
M.P. Bicknell	not out	0
A.J. Murphy	b Radford	0
Extras	b 10, lb 10, nb 1	21
Total		285

34, 53, 60, 123, 161, 218, 226, 277, 285

Radford	28.2	4	108	4
McEwan	25	7	61	2
Illingworth	35	15	53	3
Tolley	6	2	14	0
Hick	16	5	29	1

Umpires: J.C. Balderstone and P.J. Eele
Toss: Worcestershire

A 9th wicket stand of 109 in 22 overs by Rhodes and Illingworth saved Worcester on the first day and Surrey were 37–2 at the close. Their innings ended shortly after lunch on the second day, after which Hick put the home county in a very strong position, his 85 being made off 71 balls. At 18–0, Surrey needed 370 on the last day to win the game. Although victory looked increasingly unlikely, the vistors held out until the last hour and Worcester won with just 8.4 overs in hand.

v KENT (Worcester)

July 29, 31, Aug 1

Won by 10 wkts. Worcs 24pts, Kent 4 pts

Worcestershire 1st Innings		
P.Bent	c Marsh b Penn	144
C.M. Tolley	c Marsh b Penn	37
G.A. Hick	b Penn	147
D.B. d'Oliveira	lbw b Alleyne	19
*P.A. Neale	c Davis b Penn	11
D.A. Leatherdale	c and b Davis	9
†S.J. Rhodes	not out	8
S.R. Lampitt	not out	4
N.V. Radford		
R.K. Illingworth		
S.M. McEwan		
Extras	b 4, lb 16, w 1, nb 2	23
Total (6 wkts dec, 100 ov)		402

113, 248, 320, 361, 374, 390

Igglesden	20	0	82	0
Alleyne	16	4	49	1
Penn	22	6	81	4
Ellison	11	0	50	0
Davis	23	4	93	1
Cowdrey	6	0	26	0
Ward	2	1	1	0

Kent 1st Innings		
S.G. Hinks	b McEwan	0
N.R. Taylor	not out	45
T.R. Ward	lbw b Radford	12
J.I. Longley	run out	4
R.M. Ellison	c and b Radford	30
R.P. Davis	lbw b Lampitt	25
*C.S. Cowdrey	lbw b Lampitt	56
†S.A. Marsh	lbw b Illingworth	5
C. Penn	c McEwan b Radford	42
A.P. Igglesden	lbw b Radford	1
H.L. Alleyne	c Radford b Hick	6
Extras	b 2, lb 4	6
Total (100 ov: 230–9)		232

1, 5, 39, 62, 95, 106, 150, 210, 212

Radford	26	8	73	4
McEwan	28	8	50	1
Tolley	4	1	9	0
Lampitt	15	5	29	2
Illingworth	25	6	58	1
Hick	6.4	2	7	1

Kent 2nd Innings		
S.G. Hinks	c Rhodes b McEwan	13
T.R. Ward	c Hick b Lampitt	30
J.I. Longley	lbw b McEwan	0
N.R. Taylor	c Rhodes b Lampitt	12
*C.S. Cowdrey	b Lampitt	21
†S.A. Marsh	lbw b Lampitt	53
R.M. Ellison	c Leatherdale b Illingworth	36
R.P. Davis	b Lampitt	0
C. Penn	c Leatherdale b Illingworth	11
H.L. Alleyne	c Radford b Illingworth	0
A.P. Igglesden	not out	5
Extras	b 4, lb 10, w 1	15
Total		196

13, 13, 54, 61, 143, 144, 144, 177, 177

Radford	11	1	45	0
McEwan	24	4	73	2
Lampitt	23	13	32	5
Tolley	6	3	9	0
Illingworth	20.5	13	22	3
Hick	2	1	1	0

Worcestershire 2nd Innings		
†S.J. Rhodes	not out	16
C.M. Tolley	not out	11
Extras		0
Total (0 wkt)		27

Davis	2.5	0	16	0
Ward	2	0	11	0

Umpires: J.C. Balderstone and R. Julian
Toss: Worcestershire

This victory enabled Worcestershire to move to the top of the Championship table, displacing Essex, which county had held the lead for much of the season to date. Bent hit a career best 144 on the first day and was aided by the young colt, Tolley, in a first wicket stand of 113. Hick then hit 147 and Worcester were well on top at the end of Saturday. Kent spent the whole of Monday making 232 runs and when the follow on was enforced on Tuesday they just avoided an innings defeat.

v SOMERSET (Worcester)

August 24, 25, 26, 27

Won by 5 wkts. Worcs 20pts, Somerset 4pts.

Somerset 1st Innings		
S.J. Cook	lbw b Lampitt	10
P.M. Roebuck	c Illingworth b Lampitt	22
R.J. Harden	lbw b McEwan	27
C.J. Tavare	c d'Oliveira b McEwan	89
N.J. Pringle	c Rhodes b Weston	4
J.C.M. Atkinson	c and b Hick	46
†N.D. Burns	c Illingworth b Lampitt	5
*V.J. Marks	c Rhodes b McEwan	45
G.D. Rose	not out	50
N.A. Mallender	b McEwan	20
A.N. Jones	b Lampitt	13
Extras	lb 4, nb 3	7
Total (100 ov: 212–6)		338

13, 42, 73, 78, 162, 173, 249, 254, 309

McEwan	38	4	111	4
Lampitt	36.5	5	89	4
Tolley	27	8	59	0
Illingworth	20	11	22	0
Weston	11	4	32	1
Hick	13	5	21	1

Worcestershire 1st Innings		
T.S. Curtis	b Mallender	1
P. Bent	lbw b Mallender	0
G.A. Hick	c Rose b Jones	86
D.B. d'Oliveira	c Burns b Jones	63
*P.A. Neale	c Burns b Jones	4
M.J. Weston	not out	11
†S.J. Rhodes	not out	7
S.R. Lampitt		
C.M. Tolley		
R.K. Illingworth		
S.M. McEwan		
Extras	b 11, lb 8, w 2, nb 7	28
Total (5 wkts dec, 61.2 ov)		200

6, 16, 169, 170, 176

Jones	15	1	55	3
Mallender	15	4	18	2
Rose	15	2	51	0
Atkinson	2	0	3	0
Marks	11.2	2	42	0
Pringle	3	0	12	0

Somerset 2nd Innings		
S.J. Cook	b Lampitt	3
N.J. Pringle	lbw b Lampitt	0
†N.D. Burns	c Rhodes b Tolley	38
R.J. Harden	b McEwan	0
C.J. Tavare	b McEwan	62
J.C.M. Atkinson	c Rhodes b McEwan	6
*V.J. Marks	not out	24
G.D. Rose	not out	19
Extras	lb 7, w 1, nb 1	9
Total (6 wkts dec)		161

3, 8, 11, 84, 116, 117

Mc Ewan	16	5	46	3
Lampitt	16	3	48	2
Tolley	6	0	21	1
Weston	5	0	26	0
Neale	1	0	8	0
Curtis	0.3	0	5	0

Worcestershire 2nd Innings		
T.S. Curtis	b Rose	84
P. Bent	run out	25
G.A. Hick	not out	136
D.B. d'Oliveira	c Pringle b Rose	0
*P.A. Neale	c Pringle b Marks	25
M.J. Weston	c Burns b Jones	8
†S.J. Rhodes	not out	13
Extras	lb 10, w 1	11
Total (5 wkts)		302

51, 179, 179, 254, 287

Jones	14.1	1	77	1
Mallender	9	1	47	0
Rose	15	1	69	2
Marks	18	1	99	1

Umpires: J.W. Holder and A.G.T. Whitehead
Toss: Somerset

Tavare batted 282 minutes on the first day to hold Somerset together, the side reaching 256–8 after a very tedious first day. Less than an hour's play took place ont he second day, during which Worcester were frustrated by a 9th wicket stand of 46. Hick and d'Oliveria hit out on the third day and Neale declared 138 runs in arrears. Somerset were 2–0 at stumps. On the last day the home team were left 300 to make in 57 overs. A brilliant innings of 136 off 168 balls by Hick produced victory with 5 balls left.

v GLOUCESTERSHIRE (Worcester)

August 29, 30, 31

Won by 131 runs. Worcs 22pts, Gloucs 6pts

Worcestershire 1st Innings		
T.S. Curtis	b Walsh	98
P. Bent	c Alleyne b Bainbridge	21
G.A. Hick	lbw b Curran	19
D.B. d'Oliveira	b Graveney	29
*P.A. Neale	c Tedstone b Curran	4
I.T. Botham	c Lloyds b Curran	13
†S.J. Rhodes	c Lloyds b Graveney	9
S.R. Lampitt	b Lawrence	23
R.K. Illingworth	c Tedstone b Graveney	0
S.M. McEwan	c Athey b Walsh	15
G.R. Dilley	not out	6
Extras	lb 6, nb 5	11
Total (98.4 ov)		248

52, 73, 143, 158, 176, 193, 205, 206, 240

Walsh	21	4	60	2
Lawrence	12.4	1	47	1
Bainbridge	15	8	25	1
Curran	17	4	45	3
Graveney	33	15	65	3

Gloucestershire 1st Innings		
A.J. Wright	c Curtis b Illingworth	34
G.D. Hodgson	c Hick b McEwan	4
J.W. Lloyds	c Hick b Dilley	12
*C.W.J. Athey	c Rhodes b McEwan	1
K.M. Curran	b Dilley	40
P. Bainbridge	c Rhodes b Dilley	4
M.W. Alleyne	b McEwan	55
†G.A. Tedstone	lbw b Lampitt	4
C.A. Walsh	c Botham b McEwan	30
D.A. Graveney	not out	11
D.V. Lawrence	lbw b McEwan	4
Extras	lb 5, nb 2	7
Total (66.2 ov)		206

4, 29, 30, 88, 101, 102, 130, 183, 200

Dilley	13	2	51	3
McEwan	20.2	4	61	5
Botham	14	2	47	0
Lampitt	12	2	30	1
Illingworth	7	3	12	1

Worcestershire 2nd Innings		
T.S. Curtis	lbw b Walsh	21
P. Bent	run out	27
S.R. Lampitt	c Tedstone b Lawrence	12
R.K.Illingworth	c Graveney b Curran	26
G.A. Hick	c Curran b Bainbrige	20
D.B. d'Oliveira	b Bainbridge	17
*P.A. Neale	c Graveney b Curran	10
I.T. Botham	c Alleyne b Lawrence	29
†S.J. Rhodes	not out	22
S.M. McEwan	c Wright b Lawrence	7
G.R. Dilley	lbw b Walsh	1
Extras	b 9, lb 5, nb 7	21
Total		213

55, 55, 76, 112, 120, 135, 168, 184, 204

Walsh	21.4	4	45	2
Lawrence	19	2	84	3
Bainbridge	13	2	43	2
Curran	12	1	27	2
Graveney	1	1	0	0

Gloucestershire 2nd Innings		
A.J. Wright	lbw b Botham	27
G.D. Hodgson	b Lampitt	16
J.W. Lloyds	c Hick b Lampitt	5
*C.W.J. Athey	c Illingworth b Botham	11
P. Bainbridge	b Dilley	45
K.M.Curran	c Illingworth b Lampitt	1
M.W. Alleyne	b Lampitt	2
†G.A. Tedstone	b Dilley	3
C.A. Walsh	not out	6
D.A. Graveney	c Rhodes b Dilley	0
D.V. Lawrence	c Illingworth b Dilley	.4
Extras	lb 3, nb 1	4
Total		124

43, 49, 53, 75, 80, 84, 109, 114, 114

Dilley	8.4	2	22	4
McEwan	9	1	28	0
Botham	17	5	39	2
Lampitt	16	6	32	4

Umpires: K.J. Lyons and P.J. Eele
Toss: Worcestershire

Dilley took the last four Gloucestershire wickets in 11 balls to clinch the Championship for Worcestershire with a day plus one more fixture in hand. Curtis batted 330 minutes for 98 on the first day which ended with Worcestershire 240–8 off 95 overs. By the end of the second day they had dismissed Gloucestershire for 206 and had a lead of 104.

Yorkshire

President: The Viscount Mountgarret
Chairman: B. Walsh
Secretary: J. Lister, Headingley Cricket Ground, Leeds, LS6 3BU. *Tel:* 0532 787394.
Cricket Manager: S. Oldham
Captain: P. Carrick
Foundation of Present Club: January 1863 in Sheffield
First First-Class Match: Yorkshire v Norfolk (Sheffield) September 1833
County Champions: 1867, 1869, 1870, 1893, 1896, 1898, 1900, 1901, 1902, 1905, 1908, 1912, 1919, 1922, 1923, 1924, 1925, 1931, 1932, 1933, 1935, 1937, 1938, 1939, 1946, 1949 (joint), 1959, 1960, 1962, 1963, 1966. 1967, 1968
Gillette/NatWest Trophy: Winners 1965, 1969
Benson & Hedges Cup: Winners 1987
Sunday League Champions: Winners 1983
Refuge Cup: Nil

Summary of Results in 1989
Britannic Assurance County Championship: Played 22, Won 3, Lost 9, Drawn 10, Position 15th
NatWest Bank Trophy: Lost in second round
Benson & Hedges Cup: Did not qualify for knock-out section
Refuge Assurance Sunday League: Played 16, Won 7, Lost 9, Position 11th equal
Refuge Assurance Cup: Did not qualify

From left, back: *N. Nicholson, R.J. Blakey, P.J. Hartley, P.J. Berry, P.A. Booth, S.D. Fletcher, C. Shaw, D. Byas, C.S. Pickles, S. Oldham, S.A. Kellett, P.W. Jarvis, P.E. Robinson, G. Swallow.* Front: *W.P. Morton (Physiotherapist), S.W. Hartley, K. Sharpe, A. Sidebottom, D.L. Bairstow, P. Carrick, J.D. Love, M.D. Moxon, A.A. Metcalfe, D.E.V. Padgett (Coach).* Allsport/Dan Smith

The lack of success continues to cause ructions among county members and inside the Committee. The players signed a petition asking that the rule permitting only Yorkshire-born cricketers in the eleven be dropped and this split supporters in the county into two opposing camps, and has had no effect.

Finishing 16th in the Championship meant that 1989 was the second worst season in the county's history – Yorkshire footed the table just once. The main effort to improve playing standards over the last decade has been a change of captaincy and this has now happened yet again. Moxon will replace Carrick for 1990.

Moxon and Metcalfe were the leading batsmen of 1989. The former was selected for one Test during the summer, but neither of these players has yet achieved the potential which they clearly showed when first in the county side. Third in the batting table came Sharpe, but he missed half the season through injury. Blakey proved very reliable and without the aid of any high scores reached 1,000 runs. In contrast Robinson scored two hundreds, but was inconsistent. The 34-year-old Love did not command a regular place in the side and was released at the end of the year – another player whose potential has never fully been realised. The wicket-keeping duties were shared between the veteran Bairstow and young Blakey.

The attack really formed around Jarvis, Sidebottom and the spin of Carrick. Pickles, Swallow and Fletcher were very expensive and the fact that 19 players were called upon to bowl in Championship cricket showed the weakness of that half of the eleven. One or two of the younger players who were given trials look promising, but the danger is overbowling them before they are ready for regular first-class cricket – the call by the players for one overseas fast bowler is not made without cause.

ONE DAY AWAY MATCHES

The full scorecard of each of Yorkshire's away matches will be found in the sections for the respective home teams.

Refuge Assurance Matches

Lord's April 23
Yorks 170–9 (40 ov) lost to Middx 162–2 (33.1 ov) on faster scoring rate. Middx 4pts, Yorks 0pts.

Leicester: May 14
Yorks 89–9 (40 ov) lost to Leics 92–3 (31.4 ov) by 7 wkts. Leics 4pts, Yorks 0pts.

The Oval: May 28
Surrey 238–5 (40 ov) beat Yorks 206 (C.K. Bullen 5–31) by 32 runs. Surrey 4pts, Yorks 0pts.

Taunton: June 11
Yorks 184–9 (40 ov) beat Somerset 165 (38.4 ov) by 19 runs. Yorks 4pts, Somerset 0pts.

Southampton: July 2
Yorks 179–7 (40 ov) lost to Hants 183–4 (36.3 ov) (R.J. Scott 116*) by 6 wkts. Hants 4pts, Yorks 0pts.

Southend: July 23
Yorks 213–6 (40 ov) lost to Essex 217–2 (38.5 ov) (G.A. Gooch 106*) by 8 wkts. Essex 4pts, Yorks 0pts.

Old Trafford: August 20
Yorks 201–5 (40 ov) beat Lancs 169 (37.5 ov) by 32 runs. Yorks 4pts, Lancs 0pts.

Chesterfield: August 27
Yorks 147–8 (40 ov) lost to Derbys 148–3 (38 ov) by 7 wkts. Derbys 4pts, Yorks 0pts.

Benson and Hedges

Jesmond: April 25, 26
Minor Counties 179–6 (55 ov) lost to Yorks 181–5 (53.4 ov) by 5 wkts. Yorks 2pts, Minor Counties 0pts.

Trent Bridge: May 11, 12
Notts 144 (52.1 ov) beat Yorks 111 (49.5 ov) by 33 runs. Notts 2pts, Yorks 0pts.

NatWest Trophy Matches

The Oval: July 12
Surrey 256–4 (60 ov) (D.J. Bicknell 135*) beat Yorks 255–9 (60 ov) by one run.

REFUGE ASSURANCE LEAGUE

v NOTTINGHAMSHIRE (Headingley)
May 7
Won by 60 runs. Yorks 4pts, Notts 0pts

Yorkshire		
D. Byas	c French b Stephenson	6
A.A. Metcalfe	c French b Stephenson	19
P.E. Robinson	c French b Stephenson	0
†D.L. Bairstow	not out	65
R.J. Blakey	c Robinson b Evans	61
J.D. Love	not out	35
*P. Carrick		
C.S. Pickles		
S.N Hartley		
P.W. Jarvis		
S. Oldham		
Extras	lb 10, w 3, nb 2	15
Total (4 wkts, 40 ov)		201
21, 21, 32, 150		

Stephenson	8	3	22	3
Pick	6	0	37	0
Cooper	8	1	20	0
Saxelby	7	1	40	0
Evans	8	0	44	1
Field-Buss	3	1	28	0

Nottinghamshire		
B.C. Broad	c Byas b Oldham	18
*R.T. Robinson	c Bairstow b Pickles	4
D.W. Randall	b Byas	55
P. Johnson	c Oldham b Carrick	2
F.D. Stephenson	b Carrick	14
M.G. Field-Buss	lbw b Byas	0
†B.N. French	run out	21
K.E. Cooper	b Hartley	0
K.P. Evans	b Byas	8
R.A. Pick	c Carrick b Hartley	6
K. Saxelby	not out	3
Extras	b 1, lb 7, w 2	10
Total (36.4 ov)		141
11, 35, 37, 66, 67, 122, 122, 122, 137		

Pickles	5	1	11	1
Jarvis	6	0	20	0
Oldham	8	0	28	1
Carrick	8	2	19	2
Byas	4	0	19	3
Hartley	5.4	0	36	2

Umpires: J.W. Holder and B.J. Meyer
Toss: Nottinghamshire
Stephenson took 3 wickets in 5 balls to give Yorkshire a very shaky start, but Bairstow and Blakey then put on 118 for the 4th wicket and Yorkshire reached 200. Notts never mastered the bowling, only Randall putting up much resistance and Yorkshire won easily.

v WARWICKSHIRE (Headingley)
May 21
Won by 5 wkts. Yorks 4pts, Warwicks 0pts.

Warwickshire		
*T.A. Lloyd	run out	9
R.G. Twose	c Sidebottom b Jarvis	1
A.I. Kallicharran	c Jarvis b Sidebottom	104
P.A. Smith	c and b Carrick	26
D.A. Thorne	c Robinson b Byas	8
D.A. Reeve	lbw b Hartley	15
N.M.K.Smith	b Jarvis	5
G.C. Small	not out	8
†K.J. Piper	not out	5
A.A. Donald		
T.A. Munton		
Extras	lb 7, w 1, nb 2	10
Total (7 wkts, 40 ov)		191
3, 25, 99, 121, 164, 178, 178		

Jarvis	8	1	43	2
Pickles	7	0	22	0
Sidebottom	8	0	38	1
Carrick	8	2	28	1
Hartley	6	0	33	1
Byas	3	0	20	1

Yorkshire		
R.J. Blakey	not out	94
A.A. Metcalfe	b Munton	0
K. Sharp	b P.A. Smith	16
D. Byas	lbw b Small	12
P.E. Robinson	c Small b Twose	24
†D.L. Bairstow	run out	21
S.N. Hartley	not out	5
*P. Carrick		
A. Sidebottom		
P.W. Jarvis		
C.S Pickles		
Extras	b 1, lb 17, w 1, nb 1	20
Total (5 wkts, 39 ov)		192
0, 44, 77, 113, 172		

Donald	8	26	0
Munton	7	32	1
P.A. Smith	4	21	1
Small	8	24	1
N.M.K. Smith	8	46	0
Twose	4	25	1

Umpires: B. Leadbeater and B. Hassan
Toss: Warwickshire
Blakey carried out his bat for an excellent 94 of 130 balls to bring victory for Yorkshire, despite Kallicharran's 104 off 111 balls with 13 fours. Sidebottom was fined on the spot for obscene language, after he was hit for two successive fours by the West Indian.

Paul Jarvis appeals unsuccessfully for lbw against Geoff Marsh in the 1989 Test series. Jarvis' 74 wickets for Yorkshire won him his Test place.

Allsport/Adrian Murrell

REFUGE ASSURANCE LEAGUE

v GLOUCESTERSHIRE (Headingley)

June 18

Won by 12 runs. Yorks 4pts, Gloucs 0pts

Yorkshire		
M.D. Moxon	c Russell b Walsh	0
A.A. Metcalfe	c Russell b Pooley	18
R.J. Blakey	c Pooley b Alleyne	73
P.E. Robinson	c Russell b Alleyne	13
†D.L. Bairstow	run out	52
J.D. Love	st Russell b Bainbridge	6
D. Byas	not out	19
P.W. Jarvis	b Walsh	4
C.S. Pickles	not out	7
S.D. Fletcher		
*P. Carrick		
Extras	lb 4	4
Total (7 wkts, 40 ov)		196

5, 48, 73, 132, 162, 176, 181

Jarvis	8	1	26	0
Walsh	8	0	45	2
Pooley	8	0	32	1
Alleyne	8	0	49	2
Bainbridge	8	1	40	1

Gloucestershire		
A.W. Stovold	c Metcalfe b Carrick	38
J.W. Lloyds	c Pickles b Jarvis	65
K.M. Curran	b Fletcher	25
P. Bainbridge	b Fletcher	24
A.J. Wright	b Byas	1
*C.W.J. Athey	c Bairstow b Jarvis	11
C.A. Walsh	b Fletcher	1
M.W. Alleyne	st Bairstow b Carrick	8
†R.C. Russell	not out	1
M.W. Pooley	not out	1
K.B.S. Jarvis		
Extra	b 2, lb 7	9
Total (8 wkts, 40 ov)		184

93, 126, 144, 147, 165, 173, 174, 182

Fletcher	8	1	29	3
Jarvis	8	1	26	2
Pickles	8	0	39	0
Moxon	8	0	27	0
Byas	2	0	23	1
Carrick	6	0	31	2

Umpires: J.C. Balderstone and B. Leadbeater
Toss: Yorkshire
A rather curious match resulted in the defeat of the visitors. They seemed well in command with 93 on the board before the 1st wicket fell,but with the match almost won, eight wickets fell in the final six overs and the tail were unable to hit out. Yorkshire therefore proved victorious by a narrow margin.

v GLAMORGAN (Hull)

June 25

Won by 49 runs. Yorks 4pts, Glam 0pts

Yorkshire		
M.D. Moxon	lbw b Shastri	40
A.A. Metcalfe	c Shastri b Barwick	22
R.J. Blakey	not out	92
P.E. Robinson	b Shastri	15
†D.L. Bairstow	c Bastien b Watkin	22
J.D. Love	c Morris b Watkin	3
D. Byas	run out	3
*P. Carrick	b Holmes	0
A. Sidebottom		
C.S. Pickles		
S.D. Fletcher	b 3, lb 9, w 2	14
Extras		
Total (7 wkts, 40 ov)		211

65, 69, 100, 160, 166, 208, 211

Watkin	7	0	45	2
Bastien	3	0	14	0
Barwick	8	1	35	1
Shastri	8	0	33	2
Dale	8	0	35	0
Holmes	6	0	37	1

Glamorgan		
*H. Morris	c Bairstow b Byas	4
M.P. Maynard	lbw b Sidebottom	11
G.C. Holmes	b Sidebottom	0
R.J. Shastri	c Bairstow b Pickles	11
A.R. Butcher	not out	76
M.J. Cann	c Bairstow b Fletcher	5
A. Dale	c Blakey b Moxon	34
†C.P. Metson	c Bairstow b Moxon	4
S.L. Watkin	lbw b Moxon	0
S.R. Barwick	b Fletcher	10
S. Bastien	b Sidebottom	1
Extras	lb 3, w 3	6
Total (36.5 ov)		162

11, 11, 24, 36, 72, 140, 147, 147, 161

Sidebottom	6.3	4	4	3
Fletcher	8	0	32	2
Pickles	4	0	26	1
Byas	2	0	22	1
Carrick	8	0	38	0
Moxon	8	1	37	3

Umpires: J.D. Bond and B. Dudleston
Toss: Yorkshire.
Moxon and Metcalfe opened with 50 off 9 overs, then Blakey continued the good work with his fifth successive Sunday 50. In contrast the Welshmen never recovered from a bad start, only Butcher really attacking the bowling.

v SUSSEX (Middlesbrough)

July 9

Lost by 10 runs. Sussex 4pts, Yorks 0pts

Sussex		
D.M. Smith	c Robinson b Fletcher	26
M.P. Speight	c Robinson b Byas	60
*C.M. Wells	c Sharp b Sidebottom	0
A.P. Wells	c Love b Moxon	32
I.J. Gould	b Fletcher	20
A.I.C. Dodemaide	not out	4
†P. Moores	not out	7
N.J. Lenham		
I.D.K. Salisbury		
A.R. Clarke		
A.M. Babington		
Extras	b 2, lb 9, w 1	12
Total (5 wkts, 20 ov)		161

80, 93, 97, 143, 150

Sidebottom	4	0	21	1
Moxon	4	0	22	1
Pickles	4	0	39	0
Carrick	2	0	24	0
Byas	2	0	16	1
Fletcher	4	0	28	2

Yorkshire		
†R.J. Blakey	c and b Babington	46
A.A. Metcalfe	c Speight b Clarke	8
P.E. Robinson	c A.P. Wells b Lenham	4
D. Byas	b Dodemaide	30
K. Sharp	run out	14
J.D. Love	c Moores b Dodemaide	1
M.D. Moxon	c Speight b C.M. Wells	26
*P. Carrick	c Smith b C.M. Wells	16
A. Sidebottom	not out	0
C.S. Pickles		
S.D. Fletcher		
Extras	lb 4, w 2	6
Total (8 wkts, 20 ov)		151

27, 41, 81, 93, 96, 121, 145, 151

Dodemaide	4	0	23	2
Babington	4	0	27	1
Clarke	4	0	30	1
Lenham	4	0	29	1
C.M. Wells	4	0	38	2

Umpires: D.O. Oslear and D.S. Thompsett
Toss: Yorkshire
The match commenced at 3.15 after Saturday's rain. Speight then hit 60 off 35 balls and Yorkshire threw away the game by dropping several catches, including Speight in the first over.

PLAYERS

David Leslie BAIRSTOW *b* 1.9.1951 Bradford; wicketkeeper; right-hand batsman; debut 1970; captain 1984–86; four Tests for England 1979–81; broke county record for most dismissals by wicketkeeper in carrer during 1989

J. BATTY *b* off-break bowler; FC debut for Yorks in September 1989

Philip John BERRY *b* 28.12.1966 Saltburn; right-hand batsman; off-break bowler; debut 1986

Richard John BLAKEY *b* 15.1.1967 Huddersfield; right-hand batsman; wicketkeeper; debut 1985; selected to tour Zimbabwe 1989–90

Paul Antony BOOTH *b* 5.9.1965 Huddersfield; left-hand batsman; slow left-arm bowler; debut 1982

David BYAS *b* 26.8.1963 Kilham; left-hand batsman; right-arm medium pace bowler; debut 1986

Phillip CARRICK *b* 16.7.1952 Armley; slow left-arm bowler; right-hand batsman; debut 1970; captain since 1987

Stuart David FLETCHER *b* 8.6.1964 Keighley; right-arm medium-fast bowler; right-hand batsman; debut 1983

Darren GOUGH *b* 18.9.1970 Barnsley; right-hand batsman; right-arm medium fast bowler; FC debut for Yorks v Middx at Lord's 1989

Peter John HARTLEY *b* 18.4.1960 Keighley; right-hand batsman; right-arm medium-fast bowler; debut 1985; previously played for Warwickshire in 1982; in 1989 he only appeared in one Championship game

Stuart Neil HARTLEY *b* 18.3.1956 Shipley; right-hand batsman; right-arm medium pace bowler; debut 1978; only appeared in One Day matches in 1989

Ian John HOUSEMAN *b* 12.10.1969 Harrogate; right-hand batsman; right-arm fast bowler; FC debut for Yorks v Sussex in July 1989

Martyn Moxon who, apart from Nicholson, who played in three matches, topped the Yorkshire batting.

Allsport/Adrian Murrell

Paul William JARVIS *b* 29.6.1965 Redcar; right-arm fast-medium bowler; right-hand batsman; debut 1981; being the youngest player ever to represent the county in fc cricket; six Tests for England including two in 1989; selected to tour South Africa 1989–90

Simon Andrew KELLETT *b* 16.10.1967 Mirfield; right-hand batsman; debut 1989.

James Derek LOVE *b* 22.4.1955 Leeds; right-hand batsman; debut 1975; released at end of 1989 season.

Ashley Anthony METCALFE *b* 25.12.1963 Horsforth; opening right-hand batsman; debut 1983; scored 100 on first appearance

Martyn Douglas MOXON *b* 4.5.1960 Barnsley; opening right-hand batsman; debut 1981; scored 100 on first appearance; ten Tests for England including one in 1989

Neil George NICHOLSON *b* 17.10.1963 Danby; right-hand batsman; off break or medium pace bowler; debut 1989

Stephen OLDHAM *b* 27.7.1948 High Green, Sheffield; right arm fast medium bowler; right hand batsman; debut 1974; but appeared for Derbyshire 1980–83 then returned to native county; only played in One Day matches in 1989 and appointed Cricket Manager for 1990

Christopher Stephen PICKLES *b* 30.1.1966 Mirfield; right-hand batsman; right-arm medium pace bowler; debut 1985

Ian John PRIESTLEY *b* 25.9.1967; right-hand batsman; right-arm medium pace bowler; debut in May 1989

Phillip Edward ROBINSON *b* 3.8.1963 Keighley; right-hand batsman; left-arm medium pace bowler; debut 1984

Kevin SHARP *b* 6.4.1959 Leeds; Middle order left-hand batsman; off-break bowler; debut 1976

Arnold SIDEBOTTOM *b* 1.4.1954 Barnsley; right-arm medium-fast bowler; right-hand batsman; debut 1973; one Test for England in 1985

Ian Geoffrey SWALLOW *b* 18.12.1962 Barnsley; right-hand batsman; off-break bowler; debut 1983

REFUGE ASSURANCE LEAGUE

v WORCESTERSHIRE (Scarborough)

July 16

Lost by 6 wkts. Worcs 4pts, Yorks 0pts

Yorkshire		
K. Sharp	c Botham b McEwan	80
A.A. Metcalfe	c Illingworth b Weston	11
†R.J. Blakey	c Rhodes b Weston	5
D. Byas	run out	8
P.E. Robinson	c Botham b Ilingworth	16
M.D. Moxon	c Lampitt b Ilingworth	18
S.N. Hartley	b Illingworth	8
*P. Carrick	not out	48
A. Sidebottom	not out	2
P.W. Jarvis		
C.S. Pickles		
Extras	b 1, lb 4, w 3	8
Total (7 wkts, 40 ov)		204

24, 30, 45, 81, 112, 130, 194

Dilley	8	0	45	0
Weston	8	0	25	2
McEwan	7	0	32	1
Botham	7	0	56	0
Illingworth	8	0	28	3
Lampitt	2	0	13	0

Worcestershire		
T.S. Curtis	c Sharp b Pickles	79
I.T. Botham	c Jarvis b Moxon	68
G.A. Hick	c Sharp b Pickles	18
D.B. d'Oliveira	c Jarvis b Pickles	14
*P.A. Neale	not out	12
†S.J. Rhodes	not out	0
M.J. Weston		
R.K. Illingworth		
S.R. Lampitt		
G.R. Dilley		
S.M. McEwan		
Extras	lb 9, w 6, nb 2	17
Total (4 wkts, 40 ov)		208

138, 175, 193, 204

Sidebottom	8	0	29	0
Jarvis	8	0	37	0
Pickles	7	1	40	3
Moxon	8	0	54	1
Carrick	2	1	11	0
Byas	7	0	28	0

Umpires: B. Leadbeater and R.A. White

Toss: Yorkshire.

Record receipts of £23,544 came from a crowd of 10,000. Yorkshire scored a fine 204, but Curtis and Botham replied with 138 for the 1st wicket and Neale had the satisfaction of hiting the winning run off the final possible delivery.

v NORTHAMPTONSHIRE (Sheffield)

August 6

Lost by 12 runs. Northants 4 pts, Yorks 0pts.

Northampton		
G. Cook	b Sidebottom	77
*W. Larkins	lbw b Pickles	19
A. Fordham	c Carrick b Moxon	6
R.J. Bailey	not out	.58
D.J. Capel	b Fletcher	24
D.J. Wild	not out	5
†D. Ripley		
J.G. Thomas		
C.E.L. Ambrose		
N.G.B. Cook		
A. Walker		
Extras	lb 8, w 1	9
Total (4 wkts, 40 ov)		198

42, 61, 131, 176

Jarvis	8	1	34	0
Sidebottom	8	0	26	1
Fletcher	7	0	44	1
Pickles	8	1	46	1
Moxon	4	0	17	1
Carrick	5	0	23	0

Yorkshire		
K. Sharp	c and b Walker	5
A.A. Metcalfe	c Fordham b Walker	75
†R.J. Blakey	c Thomas b N.G.B. Cook	8
D. Byas	run out	11
P.E. Robinson	c Fordham b N.G.B. Cook	0
M.D. Moxon	b Walker	59
*P. Carrick	b Walker	7
A. Sidebottom	b Thomas	3
C.S. Pickles	c G. Cook b Thomas	0
P.W. Jarvis	not out	6
S.D. Fletcher	b Ambrose	0
Extras	lb 5, w 6, nb 1	12
Total (38.3 ov)		186

9, 24, 60, 60, 165, 174, 175, 178, 184

Ambrose	7.3	4	12	1
Walker	8	0	39	4
Thomas	7	0	45	2
N.G.B. Cook	8	2	22	2
Capel	8	0	63	0

Umpires: J.C. Balderstone and K.E. Palmer

Toss: Yorkshire.

After a slow star G. Cook and Bailey built up a useful total for the visitors. Yorkshire slumped to 60 for 4, but their hopes of victory were revived by a fast 59 from Moxon off 43 balls. The last six wickets however went down for just 19 runs and Northants took the points.

KENT (Scarborough)

August 13.

Won by 4 wkts. Yorks 4pts, Kent 0pts.

Kent		
S.G. Hinks	c Sidebottom b Carrick	19
R.F. Pienaar	c Blakey b Pickles	37
T.R. Ward	c Sidebottom b Carrick	11
M.V. Fleming	c Jarvis b Pickles	32
*C.S Cowdrey	not out	68
G.R. Cowdrey	b Jarvis	13
†S.A. Marsh	b Jarvis	9
M.A. Ealham	c Blakey b Jarvis	5
C. Penn	not out	15
D.J.M. Kelleher		
R.P. Davis		
Extras	lb 11, w 5	16
Total (7 wkts, 39 ov)		225

42, 70, 88, 133, 161, 178, 184

Fletcher	7	0	42	0
Jarvis	8	0	37	3
Sidebottom	8	0	48	0
Pickles	6	0	20	2
Carrick	8	1	45	2
Byas	2	0	22	0

Yorkshire		
K. Sharp	c Marsh b Kelleher	3
A.A. Metcalfe	c Marsh b Ealham	73
†R.J. Blakey	lbw b Ealham	15
J.D. Love	c Ealham b C.S. Cowdrey	65
P.E. Robinson	run out	12
D. Byas	c G.R. Cowdrey b C.S. Cowdrey	10
*P. Carrick	not out	11
C.S. Pickles	not out	16
A. Sidebottom		
P.W. Jarvis		
S.D Fletcher		
Extras	b 1, lb 18, w 3, nb 1	23
Total (6 wkts, 38.1 ov)		228

5, 38, 148, 182, 182, 201

Kelleher	8	0	18	1
Penn	7.1	0	47	0
Ealham	7	1	27	2
Fleming	5	0	37	0
Ward	1	0	10	0
Davis	2	0	14	0
C.S. Cowdrey	8	0	56	2

Umpires: H.D. Bird and R. Palmer

Toss: Yorkshire.

A splendid partnership between Metcalfe and Love added 110 for the 3rd wicket and put Yorkshire on a winning course, which was achieved in the final over.

BRITANNIC ASSURANCE COUNTY CHAMPIONSHIP AVERAGES 1989

Batting	*M*	*I*	*NO*	*Runs*	*HS*	*Avge*	*100*	*50*
N.G. Nicholson	3	4	2	87	56*	43.50	–	1
M.D. Moxon	18	32	1	1156	162*	37.29	1	7
A.A. Metcalfe	21	37	1	1230	138	34.17	3	6
K. Sharp	11	19	4	512	78	34.13	–	5
R.J. Blakey	22	39	3	1159	97	32.19	–	8
P.E. Robinson	18	31	4	781	147	28.93	2	1
D. Byas	20	33	2	844	117	27.23	1	5
D.L. Bairstow	10	16	3	299	101*	23.00	1	1
C.S. Pickles	18	24	7	388	66	22.82	–	2
J.D. Love	9	15	2	264	53	20.31	–	1
A. Sidebottom	19	24	5	344	45*	18.11	–	–
P. Carrick	22	31	3	483	65*	17.25	–	2
I.G. Swallow	13	20	2	287	64	15.94	–	1
I.M. Priestley	2	4	2	25	23	12.50	–	–
P.W. Jarvis	16	22	5	203	59*	11.94	–	1
S.D. Fletcher	11	11	4	33	13	4.71	–	–
S.A. Kellett	2	3	–	5	5	1.67	–	–

Also batted: J. Batty (1 match) 4*, 0; P.A. Booth (2 matches) 2*, 5*, 8*; D. Gough (2 matches) 2*, 9; I.J. Houseman (1 match) 18. P.J. Hartley played in one match but did not bat.

Bowling	*O*	*M*	*R*	*W*	*Avge*	*BB*	*5i*	*10m*
P.W. Jarvis	548.1	129	1634	74	22.08	7-74	4	–
A. Sidebottom	576	129	1590	68	23.38	6-79	5	1
J. Batty	64.1	17	193	8	24.13	5-118	1	–
P. Carrick	697.1	242	1603	57	28.12	6-70	2	–
D. Gough	65	13	173	6	28.83	3-44	–	–
D. Byas	41.4	10	176	6	29.33	2-25	–	–
M.D. Moxon	50	9	165	5	33.00	3-24	–	–
C.S. Pickles	347.2	79	1177	29	40.59	4-92	–	–
I.G. Swallow	225	56	728	16	45.50	4-58	–	–
S.D. Fletcher	230	37	772	15	51.47	4-88	–	–

Also bowled: P.A. Booth 26-11-47-1; P.J. Hartley 12-1-51-0; I.J. Houseman 9-1-61-0; J.D. Love 4-1-20-2; A.A. Metcalfe 13.4-2-33-0; N.G. Nicholson 5-0-25-0; I.M. Priestley 30-6-119-4; P.E. Robinson 7-0-22-0; K. Sharp 14-0-85-0.

Centuries

3 A.A. Metcalfe: 113 v Glamorgan (Headingley); 112 v Warwicks (Edgbaston); 138 v Warwicks (Headingley).

2 P.E. Robinson: 147 v Kent (Scarborough); 117 v Lancs (Scarborough).

1 D.L. Bairstow: 101* v Surrey (Oval). D. Byas: 117 v Kent (Scarborough). M.D. Moxon: 162* v Surrey (Oval).

BENSON AND HEDGES CUP

v SOMERSET (Headingley)

May 9

Lost by 62 runs. Somerset 2pts, Yorks 0pts.

Somerset		
S.J. Cook	run out	62
P.M. Roebuck	c Bairstow b Byas	25
J.J.E. Hardy	c Metcalfe b Byas	12
C.J. Tavare	b Jarvis	65
R.J. Harden	c Oldham b Jarvis	44
*V.J. Marks	not out	15
†N. D. Burns	not out	0
G.D. Rose		
N.A. Mallender		
A.N. Jones		
D.J. Foster	b 1, lb 12, w 6, nb 1	20
Extras		
Total (5 wkts 55 ov)		243

83, 95, 121, 209, 241

Jarvis	11	1	35	2
Pickles	8	2	49	0
Oldham	8	0	48	0
Carrick	11	0	36	0
Byas	11	1	38	2
Hartley	6	1	24	0

Yorkshire		
D. Byas	b Jones	0
A.A. Metcalfe	lbw b Rose	35
R.J. Blakey	c Jones b Foster	19
P.E. Robinson	b Foster	7
J.D. Love	run out	2
†D.L. Bairstow	not out	51
S.N. Hartley	c Burns b Jones	39
*P. Carrick	b Marks	1
P.W. Jarvis	c Cook b Rose	4
C.S. Pickles	b Jones	5
S. Oldham	b Jones	0
Extras	lb 8, w 2, nb 8	18
Total (50.3 ov)		181

0, 58, 60, 63, 69, 150, 151, 152, 181

Jones	9.3	1	47	4
Mallender	9	3	31	0
Rose	10	1	38	2
Foster	11	3	26	2
Marks	11	4	31	1

Umpires: B.J. Meyer and J.W. Holder
Toss: Somerset. Gold: C.J. Tavare.
Hit by injuries, Yorkshire never looked like beating Somerset. The visitors found little to worry them in the home attack and facing a target of 244, only Bairstow put up much of a fight.

v DERBYSHIRE (Headingley)

May 13

Won by 7 runs. Yorks 2pts, Derbys 0pts.

Yorkshire		
R.J. Blakey	b Newman	39
A.A. Metcalfe	c Barnett b Warner	77
K. Sharp	c Goldsmith b Warner	5
P.E. Robinson	c Barnett b Mortensen	11
J.D. Love	c Bowler b Mortensen	3
D. Byas	not out	27
†D. L. Bairstow	not out	26
*P. Carrick		
S.N. Hartley		
C.S. Pickles		
S. Oldham		
Extras	b 1, lb 5, w 9, nb 5	20
Total (5 wkts, 55 ov)		208

131, 131, 149, 152, 157

Mortensen	11	2	33	2
Newman	11	1	53	1
Holding	11	1	44	0
Base	11	2	40	0
Warner	11	3	32	2

Derbyshire		
K.J. Barnett	c Robinson b Hartley	101
†P.D. Bowler	c Sharp b Hartley	11
B.J.M Maher	b Carrick	21
J.E. Morris	c Byas b Hartley	13
B. Roberts	not out	26
M.A. Holding	c Sharp b Pickles	6
A.E. Warner	b Hartley	0
S.C. Goldsmith	not out	1
P.G. Newman		
S.J. Base		
O.H. Mortensen		
Extras	lb 14, w 6, nb 2	22
Total (6 wkts, 55 ov)		201

32, 85, 130, 190, 198, 199

Oldham	11	0	49	0
Pickles	11	3	42	1
Byas	11	3	24	0
Hartley	11	2	32	4
Carrick	11	2	40	1

Umpires: D.O. Oslear and M.J. Kitchen
Toss: Derbyshire. Gold K.J. Barnett.
Yorkshire made a confident start, Blakey and Metcalfe hitting 131, but 5 wickets then fell cheaply and only due to the hard hitting of Bairstow was 200 reached. Barnett hit 101 off 158 balls with 9 fours and a six, but this well judged innings failed to bring Derbyshire victory.

NATWEST BANK TROPHY

v SCOTLAND (Headingley)

June 28, 29

Won by 3 wkts

Scotland		
I.L. Phillips	lbw b Pickles	73
B.M.W. Patterson	lbw b Sidebottom	39
R.G. Swan	b Carrick	6
*C.E.B. Rice	not out	29
O. Henry	not out	47
A. Goram		
D.L. Snodgrass		
†D.J. Haggo		
J.D. Moir		
D. Cowan		
J.G. Williamson		
Extras	lb 11, w 2, nb 3	16
Total (3 wkts, 60 ov)		210

67, 93, 130

Jarvis	12	0	48	0
Sidebottom	12	4	27	1
Fletcher	12	0	53	0
Pickles	12	1	41	1
Carrick	12	2	30	1

Yorkshire		
M.D. Moxon	b Cowan	14
A.A. Metcalfe	c Philip b Henry	50
R.J. Blakey	b Goram	17
D. Byas	c Swan b Snodgrass	54
J.D. Love	c Snodgrass b Henry	8
*P. Carrick	not out	33
A. Sidebottom	c and b Snodgrass	0
C.S. Pickles	b Cowan	3
P.W. Jarvis	not out	15
†D.L. Bairstow		
S.D. Fletcher		
Extras	b 1, lb 14, w 2, nb 1	18
Total (7 wkts, 58.5 ov)		212

34, 75, 93, 117, 178, 178, 192

Rice	11	4	27	0
Cowan	11.5	1	47	2
Williamson	3	0	9	0
Moir	12	2	39	0
Goram	7	0	32	1
Henry	12	1	35	2
Snodgrass	2	0	8	2

Umpires: J.D. Bond and K.E. Palmer
Toss: Scotland. MofM: O. Henry.
On a first day restricted to 50 overs, Scotland scored 139 for 3. Rice and Henry, the overnight batsmen put on 80 runs to take the total to 210 and Yorkshire looked in difficulties with 3 overs left and 19 required, but Carrick hit out to save their blushes.

Away Matches

The full scorecard of each of Yorkshire's away matches will be found in the sections for the respective home teams.

Lord's: April 20, 21, 22, 24
Middx 260 (P.W. Jarvis 5–77) and 119–4 drew with Yorks 130 (50.3 ov). Middx 7pts, Yorks 3pts.

Northampton: May 16, 17, 18, 19
Yorks 191 and 251 lost to Northants 418 (D. Ripley 123, D.J. Wild 121) and 26–4 by 6 wkts. Northants 22pts, Yorks 3pts.

The Oval: May 27, 29, 30
Surrey 400–6d (D.J. Bicknell 119) and 177–7d drew with Yorks 303–8d (M.D. Moxon 162* and 217–6 (D.L. Bairstow 101*). Yorks 6pts, Surrey 6pts.

Trent Bridge: June 3, 5, 6
Yorks 223 (K.E. Cooper 5–72) and 250–9d (J.A. Afford 5–63) drew with Notts 214 (P.W. Jarvis 7–74) and 84–1. Yorks 6pts, Notts 6pts.

Leicester: June 7, 8, 9
Yorks 246 (G.J. Parsons 5–84) and 112–2d beat Leics 108–6d and 201 by 49 runs. Yorks 20pts, Leics 4pts.

Taunton: June 10, 12, 13
Yorks 239 and 275–5d drew with Somerset 299 (P.M. Roebuck 103, P. Carrick 5–53). Somerset 6pts, Yorks 4pts.

Southampton: July 1, 3
Hants 144 (A. Sidebottom 5–35) and 153 lost to Yorks 107 (C.A. Connor 5–20) and 191–7 by 3 wkts. Yorks 20pts, Hants 4pts.

Southend: July 22, 24, 25
Yorks 115 (T.D. Topley 5–46) and 239 lost to Essex 248 (P.W. Jarvis 6–76) and 107–7 by 3 wkts. Essex 22pts, Yorks 4pts.

Edgbaston: July 26, 27, 28
Warwicks 352 and 237–3d drew with Yorks 301–4d (A.A. Metcalfe 112) and 171–2. Yorks 7pts, Warwicks 4pts.

Old Trafford: August 19, 21, 22
Lancs 293 (M‹A. Atherton 115*) and 228–3d (G.D. Mendis 103*) beat Yorks 192 (Wasim Akram 5–44) and 148 (Wasim Akram 5–51) by 181 runs. Lancs 23pts, Yorks 5pts.

Chesterfield: August 24, 25, 26, 28
Yorks 136 (S.J. Base 7–60) and 184 (S.J. Base 5–93) lost to Derbys 102 (P.W. Jarvis 6–27) and 219–7 (A. Sidebottom 5–92) by 3 wkts. Derbys 20pts, Yorks 4pts.

v NOTTINGHAMSHIRE (Headingly)

May 4, 5
Lost by 10 wkts. Notts 20pts, Yorks 4pts

Yorkshire

D. Byas	c French b Stephenson	15
A.A. Metcalfe	c Newell b Stephenson	7
R.J. Blakey	c Newell b Stephenson	33
P.E. Robinson	c Newell b Stephenson	13
J.D. Love	c Evans b Stephenson	0
†D.L. Bairstow	c French b Evans	9
*P. Carrick	c Randall b Evans	5
P.W. Jarvis	lbw b Stephenson	0
C.S. Pickles	lbw b Stephenson	7
I.M. Priestley	not out	0
S.D. Fletcher	c Cooper b Evans	1
Extras	lb 2	2
Total (48.1 ov)		92

22, 25, 52, 52, 69, 69, 79, 87, 91

Stephenson	19	11	38	7
Cooper	11	7	11	0
Saxelby	7	2	16	0
Hemmings	2	0	5	0
Evans	9.1	4	20	3

Nottinghamshire

*R.T. Robinson	c Priestley b Jarvis	1
B.C. Broad	c Robinson b Priestly	23
M. Newell	not out	32
P. Johnson	c and b Pickles	0
D.W. Randall	lbw b Priestley	1
F.D. Stephenson	c Jarvis b Pickles	6
†B.N. French	c Metcalfe b Pickles	7
K.P. Evans	c Bairstow b Priestley	0
E.E. Hemmings	lbw b Priestley	0
K. Saxelby	c Byas b Jarvis	12
K.E. Cooper	c Bairstow b Jarvis	0
Extras	lb 2, w 2	4
Total (34.4 ov)		86

12, 32, 37, 44, 58, 66, 69, 69, 86

Jarvis	9.4	3	10	3
Fletcher	6	1	21	0
Priestley	11	4	27	4
Pickles	8	0	26	3

Yorkshire 2nd Innings

D. Byas	lbw b Stephenson	3
A.A. Metcalfe	c French b Cooper	19
R.J. Blakey	c Evans b Stephenson	39
P.E. Robinson	c French b Evans	17
C.S. Pickles	c Newell b Evans	2
J.D Love	c Stephenson b Cooper	14
†D.L. Bairstow	c Evans b Stephenson	0
P. Carrick	c Robinson b Stephenson	10
P.W. Jarvis	b Stephenson	3
I.M. Priestley	c Evans b Stephenson	0
S.D. Fletcher	not out	1
Extras	lb 1	1
Total		109

6, 30, 60, 70, 94, 94, 100, 104, 104

Stephenson	11.1	1	37	6
Cooper	9	1	19	2
Saxelby	5	1	24	0
Evans	7	2	28	2

Nottinghamshire

B.C. Broad	not out	54
*R.T. Robinson	not out	55
Extras	lb 6, w 4	10
Total (0 wkt)		119

Jarvis	10.2	2	44	0
Fletcher	9	2	34	0
Priestley	5	1	19	0
Pickles	3	0	16	0

Umpires: J.W. Holder and B.J. Meyer
Toss: Yorkshire

This fourth day match was completed in two. No less than 23 wickets fell on the opening day. Stephenson picked up a career best 7-38 and then Priestley, making his debut, took 4-27. The low cloud greatly assisted the seam bowlers. The only batsman to survive was Newell, whose unbeaten innings lasted 107 minutes. Yorkshire started the second day at 61-3 and they did not last long, Stephenson claiming another 6 wickets. Notts' final innings was played with no difficulty in bright sunshine and 30 minutes after lunch the game was completed.

v DERBYSHIRE (Headingley)

May 24, 25, 26
Drawn. Yorks 8pts, Derbys 4pts

Derbyshire 1st Innings

P.D. Bowler	c Metcalfe b Carrick	41
C. Gladwin	b Sidebottom	12
†B.J.M. Maher	c Swallow b Carrick	1
J.E. Morris	b Carrick	31
B. Roberts	c Blakey b Carrick	0
S.C. Goldsmith	lbw b Sidebottom	3
R. Sharma	b Pickles	39
P.G. Newman	c Sharp b Sidebottom	13
A.E. Warner	b Sidebottom	20
*M.A. Holding	c and b Sidebottom	0
D.E. Malcolm	not out	8
Extras	b 2, lb 1, w 4, nb 3	10
Total (82.4 ov)		178

35, 40, 88, 88, 92, 92, 140, 169, 169

Sidebottom	24.4	14	40	5
Pickles	15	6	37	1
Carrick	25	6	60	4
Booth	9	2	22	0
Swallow	9	5	16	0

Yorkshire 1st Innings

M.D. Moxon	c and b Warner	50
A.A. Metcalfe	lbw b Holding	60
R.J. Blakey	b Newman	0
K. Sharp	c Roberts b Sharma	51
D. Byas	b Malcolm	30
† D.L. Bairstow	lbw b Sharma	0
I.G. Swallow	b Warner	64
*P. Carrick	lbw b Holding	22
A. Sidebottom	b Malcolm	22
C.S. Pickles	c Sharma b Malcom	4
P.A. Booth	not out	2
Extras	lb 6, w 1, nb 1	8
Total (100 ov: 305–8)		313

94, 99, 127, 181, 181, 206, 268, 305, 311

Malcolm	21	1	94	3
Holding	27	5	79	2
Warner	26.2	10	58	2
Newman	16	4	39	1
Sharma	14	4	37	2

Derbyshire 2nd Innings

P.D. Bowler	lbw b Sidebottom	17
C. Gladwin	c Moxon b Pickles	0
†B.J.M. Maher	c Blakey b Sidebottom	20
J.E. Morris	c Moxon b Carrick	70
B. Roberts	lbw b Sidebottom	4
S.C. Goldsmith	c and b Carrick	7
R. Sharma	not out	53
P.G. Newman	c Moxon b Carrick	0
A.E. Warner	not out	8
Extras	b 1, lb 1, nb 8	10
Total (7 wkts)		189

4, 28, 62, 67, 94, 163, 163

Sidebottom	26	3	71	3
Pickles	19	3	67	1
Carrick	36	27	28	3
Swallow	4	0	17	0
Booth	5	4	4	0

Umpires: J.D. Bond and D.S. Thompsett
Toss: Derbyshire

Derbyshire reached 159–7 off 76 overs before bad light stopped play on the first day. Overnight rain delayed the second day's start, but Yorks managed to obtain a long first innings lead. They batted on for 19 runs and 30 minutes on the last day, after which Derbyshire, with nothing to play for, batted out time.

v GLOUCESTERSHIRE (Harrogate)

June 17, 19, 20

Drawn. Gloucs 7pts, Yorks 6pts

Yorkshire 1st Innings		
M.D. Moxon	c Athey b Graveney	38
R.J. Blakey	b Walsh	15
D. Byas	c Alleyne b Bainbridge	16
P.E. Robinson	b Jarvis	19
J.D. Love	c Russell b Jarvis	18
†D.L. Bairstow	c Russell b Walsh	1
*P. Carrick	c Athey b Walsh	4
I.G. Swallow	c Alleyne b Lloyds	37
A. Sidebottom	b Walsh	39
P.W. Jarvis	not out	20
C.S Pickles	b Walsh	4
Extras	lb 6, nb 3	9
Total (92.3 ov)		220

43, 65, 75, 111, 112, 112, 119, 192, 204

Walsh	24.3	5	86	5
Jarvis	14	7	37	2
Bainbridge	17	4	43	1
Graveney	20	11	30	1
Athey	2	2	0	0
Alleyne	4	3	1	0
Lloyds	11	4	17	1

Gloucestershire 1st Innings		
I.P. Butcher	lbw b Jarvis	49
A.J. Wright	b Jarvis	4
J.W. Lloyds	lbw b Swallow	42
K.M. Curran	lbw b Carrick	10
P. Bainbridge	c Moxon b Swallow	6
*C.W.J. Athey	b Pickles	81
M.W. Alleyne	c Carrick b Swallow	20
†R.C. Russell	c Love b Jarvis	12
C.A. Walsh	c Love b Carrick	38
D.A. Graveney	c Blakey b Sidebottom	6
K.B.S. Jarvis	not out	4
Extras	lb 6, nb 1	7
Total (97.5 ov)		279

4, 74, 93, 106, 135, 164, 181, 227, 241

Jarvis	26	2	84	3
Sidebottom	14	4	44	1
Carrick	36	8	96	2
Swallow	21	7	49	3
Pickles	0.5	0	0	1

Yorkshire 2nd Innings		
M.D. Moxon	c Athey b Wright	95
R.J. Blakey	c Graveney b Lloyds	38
D. Byas	c Alleyne b Graveney	15
P.E. Robinson	b Athey	28
J.D. Love	run out	0
†D.L. Bairstow	not out	42
I.G. Swallow	c and b Lloyds	14
*P. Carrick	not out	65
Extras	b 9, lb 3, nb 3	15
Total (6 wkts dec)		312

69, 134, 180, 185, 203, 222

Walsh	8	4	22	0
Jarvis	4	0	14	0
Graveney	38	12	111	1
Lloyds	29	6	103	2
Athey	8.4	4	19	1
Wright	4	0	16	1
Butcher	3	0	15	0

Gloucestershire 2nd Innings		
I.P. Butcher	c Blakey b Carrick	3
A.J. Wright	c Love b Swallow	52
J.W. Lloyds	lbw b Swallow	5
K.M. Curran	lbw b Carrick	31
P. Bainbridge	b Love	18
*C.W.J. Athey	b Swallow	0
M.W. Alleyne	not out	18
†R.C. Russell	c Robinson b Love	0
C.A. Walsh	c sub b Swallow	26
D.A. Graveney	not out	1
Extras	b 6, lb 3	9
Total (8 wkts)		163

12, 19, 90, 94, 98, 112, 112, 146

Jarvis	8	2	17	0
Sidebottom	2	1	4	0
Carrick	23	10	55	2
Swallow	18	8	58	4
Love	4	1	20	2

Umpires: B. Leadbeater and J.C. Balderstone
Toss: Yorkshire
Deciding to bat first, the home side fell to 119–7, but the tail managed to almost double that total. Gloucester were 74–1 off 19 overs at the start on Monday, but only managed a modest first innings lead. By stumps Yorks had wiped out the deficit and were 98–1. On the last day Alleyne batted 26 overs for 18.

v WORCESTERSHIRE (Sheffield)

June 21, 22, 23

Drawn. Worcs 8pts, Yorks 4pts

Yorkshire 1st Innings		
M.D. Moxon	c Curtis b Botham	69
A.A. Metcalfe	lbw b Radford	0
†R.J. Blakey	c Botham b Weston	26
D.Byas	not out	82
P.E. Robinson	c Rhodes b Botham	4
J.D. Love	lbw b McEwan	2
I.G. Swallow	c McEwan b Weston	17
*P. Carrick	c Curtis b Radford	13
A. Sidebottom	c Hick b Radford	12
C.S. Pickles	lbw b Radford	4
S.D. Fletcher	c and b Radford	13
Extras	b 2, lb 2, w 2, nb 1	7
Total (100 ov: 215–9)		249

7, 69, 99, 109, 112, 147, 176, 199, 207

Radford	31.4	5	86	5
McEwan	25	8	65	1
Botham	24	8	45	2
Weston	20	10	33	2
Illingworth	6	1	16	0

Worcestershire 1st Innings		
R.K. Illingworth	b Sidebottom	4
T.S. Curtis	c Byas b Carrick	43
P. Bent	c Blakey b Fletcher	20
G.A. Hick	c Blakey b Pickles	150
D.B. d'Oliveira	b Fletcher	30
*P.A. Neale	not out	62
I.T. Botham	lbw b Byas	41
M.J. Weston	c Robinson b Byas	21
†S.J. Rhodes	not out	1
N.V. Radford		
S.M. McEwan		
Extras	lb 9, nb 8	17
Total (7 wkts dec)		389

7, 36, 144, 251, 270, 345, 373

Fletcher	28	7	85	2
Sidebottom	26	4	91	1
Pickles	18	4	99	1
Carrick	25	14	39	1
Swallow	5	1	17	0
Moxon	4	0	24	0
Byas	5	0	25	2

Yorkshire 2nd Innings		
M.D. Moxon	c Rhodes b Radford	15
A.A. Metcalfe	c and b Hick	76
†R.J. Blakey	c Rhodes b Botham	16
D. Byas	b Radford	80
P.E. Robinson	not out	32
J.D. Love	not out	40
Extras	b 4, lb 10, w 4, nb 3	21
Total (4 wkts dec)		280

28, 65, 183, 223

Radford	23	6	76	2
Botham	24	7	68	1
McEwan	13	4	35	0
Illingworth	16	4	35	0
Weston	6	1	25	0
Hick	10	3	22	1
Curtis	4	0	5	0

Umpires: B. Leadbeater and B. Dudleston
Toss: Yorkshire
A staunch innings from Byas, who occupied the crease for 270 minutes while making 82 kept Worcester in the field virtually all Wednesday. The visitors began Thursday 0–0 off 1 over and ended 289–7. Hick made a splendid 150 off 156 balls with 2 sixes and 25 fours. Worcester declared overnight and Yorkshire with only a draw to play for managed that objective admirably.

v GLAMORGAN (Headingley)

June 24, 26, 27

Drawn. Yorks 3pts, Glam 3pts

Yorkshire 1st Innings		
M.D. Moxon	c Maynard b Barwick	24
A.A. Metcalfe	c Metson b Watkin	113
R.J. Blakey	b Watkin	97
D. Byas	b Smith	7
P.E. Robinson	lbw b Barwick	1
J.D. Love	b Watkin	32
†D.L. Bairstow	lbw b Watkin	5
*P. Carrick	lbw b Barwick	0
C.S. Pickles	not out	4
A. Sidebottom	b Watkin	4
S.D. Fletcher		
Extras	lb 11, w 1, nb 9	21
Total (9 wkts dec 100 ov: 254–4)		308

62, 86, 94, 160, 255, 299, 300, 300, 308

Watkin	25.4	6	53	5
Bastien	10	2	39	0
Barwick	32	10	72	3
Shastri	32	14	59	0
Smith	12	2	53	1
Holmes	2	1	1	0
Cann	6	2	20	0

Glamorgan 1st Innings		
A.R. Butcher	c and b Pickles	87
*H. Morris	retired hurt	0
M.J. Cann	c Bairstow b Fletcher	95
M.P Maynard	not out	13
R.J. Shastri	not out	10
G.C. Holmes		
I. Smith		
†C.P. Metson		
S. Bastien		
S.L. Watkin		
S.R. Barwick		
Extras	b 4, w 1, nb 4	9
Total (2 wkts, 59.1 ov)		214

184, 192

Sidebottom	15	1	43	0
Fletcher	15	3	50	1
Pickles	13.1	2	63	1
Carrick	13	2	36	0
Moxon	3	1	18	0

Umpires: B.J. Meyer and D.O. Oslear
Toss: Glamorgan
Rain ended the match before tea on the second day, no play at all being possible on the 3rd day. Even this loss of time probably made little difference for the game seemed to be heading for a draw after the first day during which the home county meandered to 295–4.

v SUSSEX (Middlesbrough)

July 8, 10, 11

Won by 8 runs. Yorks 19pts, Sussex 3pts

Yorkshire 1st Innings

M.D. Moxon	c Pigott b Dodemaide	18
A.A. Metcalfe	c Moores b Dodemaide	64
†R.J. Blakey	c Moores b Babington	9
D. Byas	c Parker b Babington	43
K. Sharp	c Parker b Pigott	27
I.J. Houseman	c Speight b Clarke	18
S.A. Kellett	c Lenham b Pigott	0
I.G. Swallow	lbw b C.M. Wells	16
*P. Carrick	not out	47
A. Sidebottom	not out	7
S.D. Fletcher		
Extras	b 2, lb 4, nb 5	11
Total (8 wkts dec, 92.1 ov)		260

25, 52, 133, 163, 168, 168, 189, 244

Dodemaide	27	3	71	2
Babington	26	4	91	2
C.M.Wells	16	2	30	1
Pigott	15	6	30	2
Clarke	7	3	16	1
Moores	1	0	10	0
A.P. Wells	0.1	0	6	0

Sussex 1st Innings: forfeited
Yorkshire 2nd Innings: forfeited
Sussex 2nd Innings

N.J. Lenham	c Blakey b Sidebottom	20
M.P. Speight	c Blakey b Sidebottom	53
*P.W.G. Parker	b Carrick	42
A.P. Wells	c Blakey b Sidebottom	0
C.M. Wells	b Sidebottom	0
I.J. Gould	c Kellett b Carrick	63
A.I.C. Dodemaide	c Blakey b Sidebottom	3
†P. Moores	not out	26
A.C.S. Pigott	lbw b Carrick	24
A.R. Clarke	b Fletcher	8
A.M. Babington	c Blakey b Fletcher	0
Extras	b 1, lb 6, w 5, nb 1	13
Total (62.3 ov)		252

44, 48, 48, 128, 155, 185, 202, 241, 252

Houseman	9	1	61	0
Sidebottom	20	3	56	5
Fletcher	11.3	0	45	2
Carrick	22	3	83	3

Umpires: D.O. Oslear and D.S Thompsett
Toss: Sussex

Rain washed out the first day and allowed only 56 overs on the second, during which Yorkshire made 163–4. On Tuesday Yorkshire declared and then both sides forfeited an innings, which left Sussex wanting 261 off 62 overs. In a tight finish, Yorkshire won with 9 balls to spare – the margin would have been larger if the Yorkshire fielding had been up to scratch. Houseman of Harrogate made his first class debut.

v MIDDLESEX (Headingley)

July 19, 20, 21

Lost by 3 wkts, Middx 23pts, Yorks 4pts

Yorkshire 1st Innings

M.D.Moxon	c Hutchinson b Fraser	21
A.A. Metcalfe	c Downton b Ellcock	10
†R.J. Blakey	lbw b Cowans	47
D. Byas	b Cowans	23
P.E. Robinson	c Haynes b Fraser	9
K. Sharp	c Hutchinson b Ellcock	23
I.G. Swallow	lbw b Fraser	2
*P. Carrick	b Ellcock	19
A. Sidebottom	c Downton b Ellcock	1
P.W. Jarvis	not out	12
S.D. Fletcher	c Emburey b Ellcock	4
Extras	b 2, lb 2, w 2, nb 2	8
Total (60 ov)		179

26, 48, 98, 107, 125, 135, 152, 160, 163

Cowans	12	2	43	2
Fraser	15	2	40	3
Ellcock	12	2	35	5
Hughes	8	2	21	0
Emburey	13	3	36	0

Middlesex 1st Innings

I.J.F. Hutchinson	c and b Sidebottom	5
D.L. Haynes	b Sidebottom	10
M.A. Roseberry	lbw b Jarvis	20
M.R. Ramprakash	lbw b Carrick	128
*M.W. Gatting	c Moxon b Sidebottom	34
†P.R. Downton	c Moxon b Sidebottom	15
J.E. Emburey	c Sharp b Jarvis	47
S.P. Hughes	c Blakey b Sidebottom	5
A.R.C. Fraser	lbw b Sidebottom	4
R.M. Ellcock	b Fletcher	8
N.G. Cowans	not out	0
Extras	lb 4, nb 14	18
Total (100 ov: 274–8)		294

7, 20, 63, 156, 227, 227, 252, 274, 294

Jarvis	28.1	11	77	2
Sidebottom	30	8	79	6
Fletcher	21	2	50	1
Moxon	12	2	28	0
Carrick	11	4	49	1
Swallow	1	0	7	0

Yorkshire 2nd Innings

M.D. Moxon	b Fraser	25
A.A. Metcalfe	c Downton b Fraser	81
†R.J. Blakey	b Fraser	0
D. Byas	c Gatting b Hughes	5
K. Sharp	c Gatting b Cowans	18
P.E. Robinson	b Ellcock	0
I.G. Swallow	lbw b Cowans	1
*P. Carrick	b Fraser	30
A. Sidebottom	b Cowans	5
P.W. Jarvis	not out	12
S.D. Fletcher	lbw b Fraser	5
Extras	lb 4, nb 3	7
Total		189

39, 43, 48, 105, 110, 110, 119, 162, 179

Cowans	17	4	47	3
Ellcock	10	0	34	1
Hughes	8	1	40	1
Fraser	22.3	7	47	5
Emburey	8	1	17	0

Middlesex 2nd Innings

I.J.F. Hutchinson	c Blakey b Sidebottom	0
D.L. Haynes	b Sidebottom	5
M.A. Roseberry	c Byas b Jarvis	1
M.R., Ramprakash	c Robinson b Sidebottom	0
*M.W. Gatting	not out	33
†P.R. Downton	c Byas b Sidebottom	6
J.E. Emburey	b Jarvis	1
S.P. Hughes	Blakey b Jarvis	5
A.R.C. Fraser	not out	16
Extras	lb 4, nb 4	8
Total (7 wkts)		75

1, 6, 6, 6, 18, 22, 34

Jarvis	18	7	29	3
Sidebottom	16.4	5	32	4
Fletcher	1	0	10	0

Umpires: D.O. Oslear and R.A. White
Toss: Yorks

On a pitch covered in cracks from the first morning, the batsmen were always at a disadvantage. Middlesex had made 118–3 off 50 overs on the close of Wednesday, with Ramprakash 50*. He completed a maiden fc century on the second day giving Middlesex a substantial lead. Yorkshire continued to struggle, though Metcalfe, having retired hurt for a period was 80* at stumps. Gatting took Middlesex to victory on the last day, but stated he felt the pitch was unfit for the Championship.

v NORTHAMPTONSHIRE (Sheffield)

August 5, 7, 8

Lost by 42 runs. Northants 21pts, Yorks 3pts

Northamptonshire 1st Innings

G. Cook	b Swallow	35
*W. Larkins	c Metcalfe b Sidebottom	5
A. Fordham	c Metcalfe b Sidebottom	199
R.J. Bailey	c Sharp b Sidebottom	98
D.J. Capel	c Sharp b Fletcher	5
D.J. Wild	c Moxon b Jarvis	0
J.G. Thomas	b Jarvis	10
†D. Ripley	b Jarvis	0
C.E.L. Ambrose	not out	7
N.G.B. Cook	c Swallow b Sidebottom	0
A. Walker	c Metcalfe b Jarvis	6
Extras	lb 8, w 1, nb 5	14
Total (100 ov: 349–4)		379

8, 86, 338, 348, 349, 362, 362, 367, 368

Jarvis	24.3	5	89	4
Sidebottom	27	2	75	4
Carrick	19	5	61	0
Fletcher	21	0	79	1
Swallow	14	3	46	1
Byas	2	1	13	0
Sharp	2	0	8	0

Yorkshire 1st Innings

M.D. Moxon	c N.G.B. Cook b Walker	18
A.A. Metcalfe	c Bailey c Capel	56
†R.J. Blakey	retired hurt	87
D. Byas	c Bailey b N.G.B. Cook	10
K. Sharp	not out	73
P.E. Robinson	not out	9
I.G. Swallow		
*P. Carrick		
A. Sidebottom		
P.W. Jarvis		
S.D. Fletcher		
Extras	lb 5, nb 1	6
Total (100 ov: 212–3) (3 wkts dec)		259

58, 102, 128

Ambrose	21	7	31	0
Thomas	21	2	76	0
N.G.B. Cook	37	16	50	1
Walker	12	4	31	1
Capel	8	1	23	1
Bailey	18	4	43	0

Northamptonshire 2nd Innings

G. Cook	b Jarvis	0
*W. Larkins	c Moxon b Carrick	83
A. Fordham	lbw b Sidebottom	0
R.J. Bailey	not out	59
D.J. Capel	not out	1
Extras	lb 3, nb 1	4
Total (3 wkts dec)		147

0, 1, 139

Jarvis	7	1	25	1
Sidebottom	10	3	28	1
Fletcher	4	0	33	0
Swallow	7	1	29	0
Carrick	8	1	29	1

Yorkshire 2nd Innings

M.D. Moxon	c Larkins b N.G.B. Cook	53
A.A. Metcalfe	c Fordham b Walker	45
†R.J. Blakey	c Ripley b Walker	3
D. Byas	c Larkins b Walker	9
K. Sharp	c Walker b Bailey	78
P.E. Robinson	c Walker b Bailey	16
*P. Carrick	c Capel b N.G.B. Cook	1
I.G. Swallow	c Walker b Bailey	1
A. Sidebottom	c and b N.G.B. Cook	9
P.W. Jarvis	b N.G.B. Cook	4
S.D. Fletcher	not out	0
Extras	b 4, lb 2	6
Total		225

77, 83, 115, 122, 161, 169, 190, 207, 225

Ambrose	5	1	20	0
Thomas	5	0	31	0
Capel	7	2	17	0
Walker	13	5	32	3
N.G.B. Cook	22	7	49	4
Bailey	10.3	0	70	3

Umpires: K.E. Palmer and J.C. Balderstone
Toss: Northants

Fordham's highest score of his career provided Northants with full batting points and the substantial total of 379 on the first day. Yorkshire spent the whole of Monday making 259–3, Moxon taking 29 overs to score 18. An overnight declaration led to Northants hitting out — Larkins made 83 in 105 minutes and Yorkshire were set 268 in 69 overs. Northants dismissed the home side with some overs in hand.

v KENT (Scarborough)

August 12, 14, 15

Lost by 5 wkts. Kent 20pts, Yorks 5pts

Yorkshire 1st Innings

†R.J. Blakey	c and b Davis	33
A.A. Metcalfe	c Taylor b Penn	7
K. Sharp	b Kelleher	53
P.E. Robinson	run out	147
D. Byas	b Penn	117
N.G. Nicholson	not out	24
I.G. Swallow	not out	1
*P. Carrick		
A. Sidebottom		
C.S. Pickles		
P.W. Jarvis		
Extras	b 6, lb 9, nb 3	18
Total (100 ov: 282–3) (5 wkts dec)		400

17, 71, 105, 363, 390

Penn	24	3	57	2
Kelleher	30	3	117	1
Fleming	23	3	75	0
Davis	31.2	11	61	1
Dobson	12	0	45	0
Cowdrey	7	0	30	0

Kent 1st Innings

S.G. Hinks	lbw b Sidebottom	13
M.R. Benson	lbw b Pickles	14
N.R. Taylor	c Nicholson b Swallow	111
R.F. Pienaar	b Pickles	38
*C.S. Cowdrey	c Sharp b Carrick	80
†S.A. Marsh	c Pickles b Carrick	10
M.V. Fleming	not out	0
M.C. Dobson	not out	0
C. Penn		
D.J.M. Kelleher		
R.P. Davis		
Extras	lb 5	5
Total (6 wkts, 98.3 ov)		271

23, 33, 111, 249, 267, 271

Jarvis	13	5	35	0
Sidebottom	12	3	28	1
Pickles	15	4	37	2
Carrick	30.3	3	79	2
Sharp	2	0	4	0
Swallow	26	0	83	1

Yorkshire 2nd Innings

†R.J. Blakey	b Dobson	30
A.A. Metcalfe	not out	87
K. Sharp	b Fleming	26
Extras	b 1, lb 1, w 2	4
Total (2 wkts dec)		147

85, 147

Kelleher	7	3	27	0
Fleming	9.4	1	33	1
Davis	10	2	45	0
Dobson	7	2	40	1

Kent 2nd Innings

S.G. Hinks	c Carrick	69
M.R. Benson	b Jarvis	8
N.R. Taylor	c Nicholson b Sidebottom	6
R.F. Pienaar	lbw b Sidebottom	125
*C.S. Cowdrey	b Sidebottom	24
†S.A. Marsh	not out	19
M.V. Fleming	not out	15
Extras	b 5, lb 4, nb 2	11
Total (5 wkts)		277

19, 29, 184, 223, 250

Jarvis	14.2	2	69	1
Sidebottom	25	5	71	3
Carrick	21	4	73	1
Pickles	7	0	30	0
Swallow	3	0	25	0

Umpires: H.D. Bird and R. Palmer
Toss: Yorks
On a very good batting strip, Yorkshire made 363–4 on Saturday and then continued on Monday, so that Kent spent most of the second afternoon making sure they avoided the follow on. That having been achieved the game went in favour of the visitors. Cowdrey declared overnight; Carrick then set Kent 277 off 72 overs, a task which Pienaar accomplished with 10 deliveries unbowled.

v WARWICKSHIRE (Headingley)

August 29, 30, 31, Sept 1

Drawn. Yorks 6pts, Warwicks 3pts

Yorkshire 1st Innings

M.D. Moxon	b P.A. Smith	41
A.A. Metcalfe	lbw b Benjamin	138
†R.J. Blakey	lbw b Munton	9
P.E. Robinson	c Twose b Munton	0
D. Byas	c Humpage b Ratcliffe	95
N.G. Nicholson	not out	56
C.S. Pickles	b N.M.K. Smith	30
D. Gough	c Munton b N.M.K. Smith	9
*P. Carrick	c Ratcliffe b N.M.K. Smith	1
A. Sidebottom	b Twose	19
P.W. Jarvis		
Extras	b 5, lb 16, w 3, nb 4	28
Total (9 wkts dec) (100 ov: 370–3)		426

82, 97, 101, 299, 308, 349, 361, 363, 426

Benjamin	32	8	94	1
Munton	31	11	68	2
P.A. Smith	20	3	67	1
Reeve	16	6	33	0
Twose	17.5	2	54	1
N.M.K. Smith	17	2	62	3
Ratcliffe	10	3	15	1
Asif Din	3	0	12	0

Warwickshire 1st Innings

J.D. Ratcliffe	b Carrick	14
*T.A. Lloyd	c Jarvis b Gough	61
A.I. Kallicharran	c Nicholson b Carrick	23
†G.W. Humpage	c Carrick b Sidebottom	46
Asif Din	lbw b Sidebottom	12
P.A. Smith	c Blakey b Carrick	31
D.A. Reeve	st Blakey b Carrick	33
R.G. Twose	b Sidebottom	3
N.M.K. Smith	b Carrick	6
J.E. Benjamin	c Moxon b Carrick	7
T.A. Munton	not out	0
Extras	b 3, lb 8, w 1	12
Total (100 ov: 221–5)		248

76, 76, 106, 160, 165, 225, 231, 236, 243

Jarvis	18	7	30	0
Sidebottom	23	10	37	3
Pickles	17	7	54	0
Gough	20	6	46	1
Carrick	42.4	17	70	6

Warwickshire 2nd Innings

T.A. Munton	b Jarvis	0
J.D. Ratcliffe	c Nicholson b Carrick	41
N.M.K. Smith	b Byas	161
Asif Din	not out	82
R.G. Twose	not out	2
Extras	b 2, lb 6, nb 2	10
Total (3 wkts dec)		296

0, 104, 288

Jarvis	16	5	63	1
Sidebottom	16	7	18	0
Carrick	26	11	56	1
Gough	16	3	36	0
Pickles	8	1	39	0
Metcalfe	13	3	29	0
Robinson	7	0	22	0
Nicholson	5	0	25	0
Byas	3	3	0	1

Umpires: B. Dudleston and A.G.T. Whitehead
Toss: Yorks
In murky conditions with the start delayed and several intermediate stoppages, the home county made 178–3 off 67.1 overs on the first day, Metcalfe being 84 not out. In all Metcalfe batted 330 minutes for his 138 and with bad light again reducing the playing time Warwickshire were 9–0 off 4 overs on Wednesday evening. On the third day the batting was very pedestrian, but the visitors failed to avoid the follow on and were 6–1 at the close. Smith reached a maiden hundred on the last day, but the afternoon session was devoid of any real significance.

v LANCASHIRE (Scarborough)

Sept 8, 9, 10, 11

Lost by 184 runs. Lancs 24pts, Yorks 4pts

Lancashire 1st Innings

G.D. Mendis	c Metcalfe b Jarvis	22
G. Fowler	c Pickles b Carrick	58
M.A. Atherton	c Blakey b Pickles	3
N.H. Fairbrother	c Blakey b Batty	161
T.E. Jesty	c Pickles b Carrick	26
M. Watkinson	b Jarvis	0
P.A.J. DeFreitas	c Moxon b Carrick	26
†W.K. Hegg	not out	7
J.D. Fitton	c Nicholson b Carrick	11
*P.J.W. Allott	b Batty	8
B.P. Patterson	c Sidebottom b Batty	4
Extras	b 12, lb 4, nb 5	21
Total (98 ov)		347

25, 46, 188, 231, 233, 291, 317, 334, 343

Jarvis	18	1	74	2
Sidebottom	15	3	56	0
Pickles	11	3	57	1
Batty	26	9	75	3
Carrick	28	9	69	4

Yorkshire 1st Innings

M.D. Moxon	c Atherton b Fitton	54
A.A. Metcalfe	c Fairbrother b Patterson	19
†R.J. Blakey	lbw b Allott	15
P.E. Robinson	b Fitton	10
D. Byas	b Fitton	0
N.G. Nicholson	c Fowler b Fitton	1
C.S. Pickles	b Fitton	62
*P. Carrick	c Fitton b Allott	15
A. Sidebottom	b Patterson	40
P.W. Jarvis	b Watkinson	0
J. Batty	not out	4
Extras	b 5, w 4, nb 8	17
Total (77 ov)		237

23, 72, 91, 91, 105, 112, 163, 206,209

Patterson	16	3	58	2
DeFreitas	10	1	44	0
Allott	17	5	37	2
Fitton	20	2	53	5
Atherton	8	4	22	0
Watkinson	6	0	18	1

Lancashire 2nd Innings

G.D. Mendis	c Carrick b Batty	66
G. Fowler	b Batty	123
M.A. Atherton	c Robinson b Jarvis	39
N.H. Fairbrother	c Robinson b Batty	67
T.E. Jesty	lbw b Jarvis	35
M. Watkinson	c Byas b Batty	10
P.A.J. DeFreitas	lbw b Jarvis	0
†W.K. Hegg	not out	13
J.D. Fitton	b Batty	0
Extras	b 5, lb 8, w 1, nb 2	16
Total (8 wkts dec)		369

143, 225, 261, 338, 350, 350, 356, 369

Jarvis	31	5	103	3
Sidebottom	15	6	57	0
Batty	38.1	8	118	5
Carrick	33	7	78	0

Yorkshire 2nd Innings

M.D. Moxon	b Allott	41
A.A. Metcalfe	lbw b Patterson	30
†R.J. Blakey	b Fitton	22
P.E. Robinson	c Fitton b Watkinson	117
D. Byas	b Fitton	0
N.G. Nicholson	c Watkinson b De Freitas	6
C.S. Pickles	lbw b Allott	25
*P. Carrick	c Watkinson b Allott	0
A. Sidebottom	not out	40
P.W. Jarvis	c Jesty b Watkinson	2
J. Batty	c Atherton b Watkinson	0
Extras	b 4, lb 6, nb 2	12
Total		295

67, 88, 114, 114, 146, 205, 227, 269, 287

Patterson	12	4	37	1
Allott	20	3	59	3
Fitton	22	6	70	2
Atherton	6	2	25	0
DeFreitas	17	5	58	1
Watkinson	6.3	1	36	3

Umpires: N.T. Plews and P.B. Wight
Toss: Lancs
Yorkshire completed their Championship programme with a heavy defeat at the hands of their traditional rivals. The Red Rose controlled the match almost from the start. Fairbrother and Fowler batted well for their side, but the Yorkshire bowling was not too incisive. Robinson hit 117 off 142 balls on the last day with 21 fours, but it was in vain.

Universities

OXFORD FIRST CLASS MATCHES

v NORTHAMPTONSHIRE (The Parks)

April 15, 17, 18

Drawn.

Northamptonshire 1st Innings

G. Cook	b Hampton	16
*W. Larkins	c sub b Hampton	126
R.J. Bailey	b Hester	27
D.J. Capel	b Hampton	30
D.J. Wild	c and b Hampton	38
R.G. Williams	c Chauhan b Hester	48
†D. Ripley	not out	46
J.G. Thomas	not out	13
N.G.B. Thomas		
A. Walker		
M.A. Robinson		
Extras	b 3, lb 7, nb 2	12
Total (6 wkts dec)		356

46, 128, 202, 227, 246, 320

Hester	24	4	66	2
Henderson	4	1	25	0
Hampton	32	9	91	4
Oppenheimer	15	1	58	0
Lunn	24	3	73	0
Chauhan	1	0	1	0
Kilborn	7	1	32	0

Oxford Univ 1st Innings

S.A. Almaer	c Cook b Capel	11
D.A. Hagan	b Capel	33
M.J. Kilborn	c Larkins b Brown	52
R.E. Morris	b Thomas	9
S. Chauhan	c Bailey b Capel	2
P.D. Lunn	c Larkins b Capel	7
A.N.S. Hampton	c Wild b Cook	25
C.W. Timm	lbw b Robinson	5
I.M. Henderson	b Cook	0
E.D. Hester	c Cook b Williams	5
J.M.E. Oppenheimer	not out	0
Extras	b 1, lb 9, w 1, nb 17	28
Total		177

51, 56, 95, 112, 124, 159, 163, 168, 173

Thomas	13	2	40	1
Brown	12	3	38	1
Capel	12	2	33	4
Robinson	14	1	35	1
Cook	13	4	18	2
Williams	6.2	3	3	1

Northants 2nd Innings

R.J. Bailey	not out	19
N.G.B. Cook	not out	18
Extras	b 1, nb 1	2
Total (0 wkts)		39

Hester	6	0	22	0
Oppenheimer	6	0	16	0

Umpires: R. Julian and P.J. Eele

Toss: Northamptonshire

On an easy pitch, Larkins hit the first first-class 100 of 1989 and the county cruised to 356–6 by the close of Saturday's play. No play was possible on Monday, so that the only way to produce a definite result was for Northants to dismiss the University twice very cheaply. Kilborn batted for 159 minutes however and the tailenders, though adding only 14 for the last 4 wickets batted for 13 overs. Northants in the circumstances, did not enforce the follow on and the game was drawn.

v SURREY (The Parks)

April 19, 20, 21

Drawn

Surrey 1st Innings

G.S. Clinton	c Morris b Munro	16
D.J. Bicknell	c Edwards b Toogood	82
J.D. Robinson	c Hampton b Edwards	29
†A.J. Stewart	b Edwards	4
D.M. Ward	lbw b Edwards	145
Z.A. Sadiq	c Hampton b Lunn	36
*I.A. Greig	not out	107
K.T. Medlycott	not out	11
M.A. Feltham		
D. Tazelaar		
M. Frost		
Extras	b 4, lb 4, w 7, nb 2	17
Total (6 wkts dec)		447

33, 84, 95, 177, 258, 383

Oppenheimer	17	5	77	0
Toogood	27	4	107	1
Munro	7	1	15	1
Edwards	28	6	114	3
Lunn	15	1	76	1
Hampton	8	0	50	0

Oxford Univ 1st Innings

S.A. Almaer	c Sadiq b Feltham	18
R.E. Morris	lbw b Feltham	14
*M.J. Kilborn	lbw b Greig	20
G.J. Toogood	b Medlycott	19
P.D. Lunn	c Stewart b Frost	61
S. Chauhan	c Robinson b Medlycott	10
†G.D. Reynolds	c Stewart b Tazelaar	1
A.N.S. Hampton	c Stewart b Tazalaar	10
M. Munro	not out	12
P.G. Edwards	c Medlycott b Frost	1
J.M.E. Oppenheimer	c Medlycott b Frost	0
Extras	b 1, lb 11, nb 23	35
Total		201

38, 56, 61, 108, 123, 124, 172, 193, 201

Tazelaar	22	5	58	2
Frost	12.4	6	27	3
Feltham	10	3	19	2
Greig	14	3	36	1
Medlycott	21	8	46	2
Robinson	2	0	3	0

Surrey 2nd Innings

M.A. Feltham	c Almaer b Kilborn	19
K.T. Medlycott	not out	56
J.D. Robinson	not out	38
Extras	lb 1, w 5	6
Total (1 wkt dec)		119

40

Oppenheimer	10	3	42	0
Munro	1	0	6	0
Kilborn	10	0	62	1
Toogood	2	1	8	0

Oxford Univ 2nd Innings

S.A. Almaer	not out	39
R.E. Morris	c Stewart b Tazelaar	17
*M.J. Kilborn	lbw b Feltham	26
P.D. Lunn	c Stewart b Feltham	7
S. Chauhan	c Stewart b Feltham	0
A.N.S. Hampton	not out	19
Extras	lb 1, nb 11	12
Total (4 wkts)		120

28, 88, 97, 97

Tazelaar	7	0	21	1
Frost	9	2	34	0
Feltham	14	2	35	3
Greig	6	2	24	0
Medlycott	6	3	5	0

Umpires: R. Julian and P.J. Eele

Toss: Surrey

Surrey had an enjoyable first day reaching 447–6 by the close. Ward hit 19 fours and 3 sixes in his 145 and Greig was 107 not out. Following the overnight declaration, play was restricted to 61 overs on the second day, during which Oxford made 147–6. Tazelaar, from Queensland, was given a trial by Surrey but was very erratic. Greig did not enforce the follow on and when Oxford were set 366 in 180 minutes the game lost credibility.

v DERBYSHIRE (The Parks)

April 27, 28, 29

Drawn.

Derbyshire 1st Innings

P.D. Bowler	run out	157
†B.J.M. Maher	lbw b Edwards	25
J.E. Morris	retired hurt	42
B. Roberts	b Edwards	24
S.C. Goldsmith	c Kilborn b Nuttall	46
S.J. Base	c Hampton b Nuttall	0
P.G. Newman	not out	2
D.E. Malcolm	not out	11
*K.J. Barnett		
R. Sharma		
A.E. Warner		
Extras	b 4, lb 8, w 1	13
Total (5 wkts dec)		320

56, 198, 304, 305, 308

Nuttall	21	3	65	2
Oppenheimer	20	7	57	0
Crawley	14	5	27	0
Edwards	25	6	86	2
Hampton	14	3	49	0
Lunn	6	0	24	0

Oxford Univ 1st Innings

S.A. Almaer	b Sharma	22
R.E. Morris	c Goldsmith b Malcolm	17
M.J. Kilborn	c Roberts b Sharma	4
*D.A. Crawley	b Base	60
D.A. Hagan	c Base b Malcolm	45
A.N.S. Hampton	lbw b Base	0
†G.D. Reynolds	lbw b Malcolm	16
J.D. Nuttall	lbw b Base	4
P.G. Edwards	not out	4
J.M.E. Oppenheimer	c Maher b Base	0
P.D. Lunn		
Extras	b 4, lb 5	9
Total (9 wkts dec)		181

42, 44, 50, 153, 153, 159, 166, 181, 181

Malcolm	15	3	49	3
Warner	6	2	15	0
Base	15.4	6	21	4
Sharma	17	7	34	2
Barnett	11	2	27	0
Newman	7	1	26	0

Derbyshire 2nd Innings

†B.J. Maher	not out	53
R. Sharma	c Hampton b Oppenheimer	21
P.G. Newman	lbw b Oppenheimer	1
A.E. Warner	c Nuttall b Oppenheimer	7
S.J. Base	st Reynolds b Edwards	12
D.E. Malcolm	b Edwards	1
S.C. Goldsmith	not out	47
Extras	b 1	1
Total (5 wkts dec)		143

29, 33, 47, 62, 66

Nuttall	9	1	35	0
Oppenheimer	14	1	51	3
Edwards	9	1	36	2
Hampton	4	1	10	0
Kilborn	3	0	10	0

Umpires: B. Leadbeater and D.S. Thompsett

Toss: Derbyshire

Rain held up the start on the first day and then only allowed 3 hours play, during which the county reached 151–1 (Bowler 76*, Morris 42*). Bowler completed his 100 on the second day. Barnett declared and 3 University wickets fell cheaply before Crawley and Morris added an unbroken 100 for the 4th. The partnership was quickly broken on the last morning, but with the follow on avoided, the play lacked any interest.

v NOTTINGHAMSHIRE (The Parks)

May 17, 18, 19

Lost by 240 runs.

Nottinghamshire 1st Innings

*R.T. Robinson	lbw b Hester	26
P.R. Pollard	c Higgo b Hester	72
M. Newell	c Hagen b Hester	43
P. Johnson	c and b Crawley	7
D.W. Randall	not out	100
E.E. Hemmings	c Hampton b Hester	34
K.P. Evans	c Almaer b Nuttall	10
†C.W. Scott	not out	13
R.A. Pick		
K.S. Saxelby		
J.A. Afford		
Extras	b 4, lb 7, w 4	15
Total (6 wkts dec)		320

42, 147, 153, 161, 233, 289

Hester	26	4	100	4
Nuttall	22.5	6	78	1
Crawley	17	4	48	1
Edwards	17	5	46	0
Lunn	7	2	23	0
Hampton	2	0	14	0

Oxford Univ 1st Innings

S.A. Almaer	c Scott b Pick	0
R.E. Morris	b Saxelby	55
P.G. Edwards	c Pollard b Pick	4
*M.A. Crawley	c Robinson b Evans	17
D.A. Hagan	c Scott b Evans	0
P.D. Lunn	b Pick	30
J. Higgo	c Pollard b Pick	2
A.N.S. Hampton	c Evans b Pick	53
†G.J. Reynolds	c Randall b Evans	13
E.D. Hester	b Pick	5
J.D. Nuttall	not out	1
Extras	lb 4, w 2, nb 5	11
Total		191

1, 10, 56, 56, 114, 114, 118, 153, 173

Pick	19.3	6	52	6
Saxelby	21	8	50	1
Evans	15	3	49	3
Afford	15	0	32	0
Hemmings	4	1	4	0

Nottinghamshire 2nd Innings

*R.T. Robinson	c Morris b Nuttall	24
M. Newell	c Hampton b Hester	28
P. Johnson	not out	109
K.P. Evans	c Crawley b Edwards	8
E.E. Hemmings	not out	14
Extras	b 5, lb 3, w 2, nb 1	11
Total (3 wkts dec)		194

36, 112, 153

Hester	23	3	72	1
Nuttall	13	2	51	1
Edwards	14	3	44	1
Crawley	7	0	19	0
Lunn	2	2	0	0

Oxford Univ 2nd Innings

S.A. Almaer	c Newell b Saxelby	5
R.E. Morris	c Robinson b Saxelby	2
*M.A. Crawley	b Pick	4
D.A. Hagan	c Saxelby b Hemmings	26
P.D. Lunn	c Scott b Pick	0
J. Higgo	c Robinson b Hemmings	4
A.N.S. Hampton	c Robinsonn b Afford	4
†G.J. Reynolds	b Afford	20
E.D. Hester	b Afford	0
J.D. Nuttall	lbw b Hemmings	13
P.G. Edwards	not out	0
Extras	lb 5	5
Total		83

3, 12, 12, 12, 43, 44, 52, 56, 81

Pick	4	2	7	2
Saxelby	6	2	18	2
Afford	13	3	35	3
Hemmings	10.4	2	18	3

Umpires: R. Palmer and H.J. Rhodes
Toss: Nottinghamshire

Randall hit a delightful 100 off 135 balls to enliven the first day's play, which ended with the students 10–2. Morris and Hampton, both given chances, made fifties, but the University could not reach 200 and only avoided the follow on by dint of a ninth wicket stand. Notts declared on the last day when Johnson reached his 100 and then skittled out Oxford for 83.

v MIDDLESEX (The Parks)

May 24, 25, 26

Drawn.

Middlesex 1st Innings

J.D. Carr	c Higgo b Edwards	50
I.J.F. Hutchinson	not out	201
M.A. Roseberry	not out	101
M.R. Ramprakash		
†K.R. Brown		
J.F. Sykes		
P.C.R. Tufnell		
*P.R. Downton		
D. Boden		
N.F. Williams		
S.P. Hughes		
Extras	b 4, lb 1, nb 1	6
Total (1 wkt dec)		358

112

Hester	15	2	73	0
Oppenheimer	16	4	78	0
Crawley	22	8	66	0
Edwards	22	0	94	1
Lunn	3	0	25	0
Hampton	4	0	17	0

Oxford Univ 1st Innings

S.A. Almaer	b Boden	0
R.E. Morris	c and b Carr	16
*M.A. Crawley	c Hutchinson b Boden	14
D.A. Hagan	c Downton b Hughes	2
P.D. Lunn	c Ramprakash b Sykes	14
J. Higgo	b Sykes	3
A.N.S. Hampton	c Boden b Tufnell	19
†C.W. Timms	c Brown b Boden	5
E.D. Hester	b Sykes	0
P.G. Edwards	not out	6
J.M.E. Oppenheimer	lbw b Boden	0
Extras	b 9, lb 4	13
Total		92

0, 26, 34, 38, 50, 77, 77, 77, 92

Williams	8	4	13	0
Boden	10.5	6	11	4
Carr	5	2	9	1
Hughes	6	4	3	1
Tufnell	16	7	21	1
Sykes	12	5	22	3

Middlesex 2nd Innings

M.R. Ramprakash	c Hagan b Oppenheimer	21
*P.R. Downton	c Oppenheimer b Edwards	39
K.R. Brown	st Timms b Edwards	91
J.F. Sykes	not out	14
Extras	b 2, lb 6	8
Total (3 wkts dec)		173

41, 108, 173

Hester	15	7	35	0
Oppenheimer	13	2	50	1
Edwards	9.3	1	39	2
Hampton	7	0	32	0
Lunn	1	0	9	0

Oxford Univ 2nd Innings

S.A. Almaer	c Roseberry b Tufnell	62
D.A. Hagan	c Roseberry b Williams	33
*M.A. Crawley	b Sykes	29
R.E. Morris	c Carr b Tufnell	3
P.D. Lunn	not out	20
J. Higgo	b Tufnell	9
A.N.S. Hampton	not out	1
Extras	lb 8, nb 9	17
Total (5 wkts)		174

50, 109, 112, 146, 172

Williams	8	1	37	1
Boden	4	1	15	0
Hughes	11	3	22	0
Tufnell	24	5	61	3
Sykes	18	9	25	1
Carr	2	1	6	0
Ramprakash	1	1	0	0

Umpires: V.A. Holder and A.A. Jones
Toss: Middlesex

Hutchinson hit 102 not out off 127 balls to take Middlesex to 193–1 when rain ended play on the first day. On the second day he hit a further 99 before lunch and directly afterwards completed a maiden 200. Oxford collapsed, with Boden on his first-class debut taking 4-11 and Downton decided not to enforce the follow on. On the last day the students managed to bat out time.

v LANCASHIRE (The Parks)

June 7, 8, 9

Drawn.

Lancashire 1st Innings

*G. Fowler	c Chauhan b Henderson	112
G.D. Lloyd	lbw b Hester	108
I.D. Austin	c Hagan b Henderson	38
J.D. Fitton	not out	28
A.N. Hayhurst		
N.H. Fairbrother		
T.E. Jesty		
M. Watkinson		
I. Folley		
†J. Stanworth		
B.P. Patterson		
Extras	b 1, lb 10, w 4	15
Total (3 wkts dec)		301

219, 241, 301

Henderson	21.5	4	93	2
Hester	20	4	88	1
Edwards	8	1	41	0
Jackson	12	2	64	0
Lunn	1	0	4	0

Oxford Univ 1st Innings

S.A. Almaer	b Patterson	14
R.E. Morris	b Patterson	6
P.D. Lunn	c Stanworth b Austin	45
*D.A. Hagan	b Austin	53
A.N.S. Hampton	c Fowler b Watkinson	55
S. Chauhan	b Fitton	10
†G.D. Reynolds	b Watkinson	13
I.M. Henderson	c Stanworth b Watkinson	0
E.D. Hester	not out	2
P.G. Edwards		
R.M. Jackson		
Extras	lb 10, w 2	12
Total (8 wkts dec)		210

17, 36, 119, 122, 164, 207, 207, 210

Patterson	17	2	37	2
Watkinson	18	3	44	3
Austin	14	4	24	2
Fitton	20	5	58	1
Folley	7	0	37	0

Lancashire 2nd Innings

A.N. Hayhurst	not out	30
N.H. Fairbrother	not out	71
Extras	lb 2	2
Total (0 wkt)		103

Henderson	5	1	11	0
Hester	3	0	17	0
Jackson	9	1	23	0
Edwards	10	3	25	0
Lunn	4	0	25	0

Umpires: V.A. Holder and H.J. Rhodes
Toss: Oxford University

Lloyd hit his maiden first-class hundred in his second match, reaching the landmark on the second day after rain had seriously interfered with the first. Further rain on Thursday meant that the university ended the day at 43–2. There was little point to the third day save for batting practice.

M.A. Crawley, captain of Oxford University.

Bill Smith

OXFORD FIRST CLASS MATCHES

v HAMPSHIRE (The Parks)
June 10, 12, 13
Lost by 127 runs

Hampshire 1st Innings

C.L. Smith	not out	143
T.C. Middleton	c Reynolds b Oppenheimer	20
R.J. Scott	lbw b Henderson	18
*M.C.J. Nicholas	c Hagan b Edwards	37
K.D. James	lbw b Edwards	3
†A.N. Aymes	not out	24
R.J. Maru		
S.D. Udal		
C.A. Connor		
S.J.W. Andrew		
K.J. Shine		
Extras	lb 8, w 1	9
Total (4 wkts dec)		254

45, 106, 170, 178

Henderson	28	9	80	1
Oppenheimer	23	2	102	1
Crocker	20	9	35	0
Hampton	4	1	14	0
Edwards	6	1	15	2

Oxford Univ 1st Innings

*D.A. Hagan	c Maru b Connor	5
S.L. Almaer	c Aymes b Connor	4
R.E. Morris	c Aymes b Shine	4
P.D. Lunn	c Aymes b Andrew	17
J. Higgo	b James	0
A.N.S. Hampton	c Nicholas b Andrew	8
†G.D. Reynolds	not out	37
I.M. Henderson	c Aymes b Connor	6
P.G. Edwards	c Smith b Connor	0
J.M.E. Oppenheimer	c Smith b Connor	0
C. Crocker	b Connor	7
Extras	lb 3, nb 2	5
Total		93

5, 10, 20, 21, 36, 47, 67, 67, 67

Connor	21	14	19	6
Shine	6.2	2	7	1
James	13.4	4	32	1
Andrew	10	3	21	2
Maru	7	3	9	0
Udal	3	1	2	0

Hampshire 2nd Innings

T.C. Middleton	not out	55
R.J. Scott	c Lunn b Henderson	6
K.D. James	c Reynolds b Henderson	21
R.J. Maru	not out	27
Extras	b 1, lb 3	4
Total (2 wkts dec)		113

10, 72

Henderson	13	3	40	2
Crocker	7	4	15	0
Edwards	12	2	42	0
Oppenheimer	7	3	12	0

Oxford Univ 2nd Innings

S.A. Almaer	c Aymes b Andrew	6
*D.A. Hagan	c Aymes b Connor	0
R.E. Morris	c Nicholas b James	19
P.D. Lunn	c Aymes b James	24
J. Higgo	lbw b James	0
A.N.S. Hampton	c Aymes b James	5
†G.D. Reynolds	c Aymes b James	40
I.M. Henderson	c Smith b Connor	26
C. Crocker	c Aymes b Andrew	2
P.G. Edwards	not out	10
J.M.E. Oppenheimer	c Andrew b Maru	7
Extras	b 4, lb 3, w1	8
Total		147

2, 12, 42, 42, 52, 57, 127, 131, 147

Connor	19	5	42	2
Andrew	16	5	29	2
James	17	7	41	5
Udal	8	5	19	0
Maru	6.2	2	9	1

Umpires: B. Dudleston and H.J. Rhodes
Toss: Oxford University
Rain interrupted the first day, but Chris Smith hit an unbeaten 92 with 17 fours as Hampshire reached 178 for 4. Smith was 143* when Nicholas declared on Monday and the students collapsed to Connor, but the follow on was not enforced and the county were 34–1 at stumps. Aymes equalled the Hampshire record with 10 catches as Oxford failed a second time, Hampshire winning by a large margin.

CAMBRIDGE FIRST CLASS MATCHES

v GLAMORGAN (Fenner's)
April 15, 16, 17
Drawn

Glamorgan 1st Innings

A.R. Butcher	c Turner b Mullins	37
*H. Morris	c Bush b Mullins	102
P.A. Cottey	b Atherton	24
M.P. Maynard	lbw b Mullins	4
M.J. Cann	c Turner b Mullins	58
I. Smith	c Morris b Pyman	11
J. Derrick	c Atkinson b Atherton	47
†C.P. Metson	lbw b Mullins	0
P.D. North	lbw b Atherton	0
S.L. Watkin	run out	0
S.R. Barwick	not out	6
Extras	b 6, lb 4, w 4, nb 4	18
Total		307

86, 146, 151, 189, 212, 289, 290, 296, 301

Bush	21	7	66	0
Mullins	29	7	77	5
Atkinson	2	0	24	0
Pyman	21	4	70	1
Atherton	27.5	5	60	3

Cambridge Univ 1st Innings

S.P. James	hit wicket b Watkin	38
J.M.G. Willatt	b Derrick	5
*M.A. Atherton	lbw b Derrick	36
R. Heap	c Metson b Barwick	19
J.C.M. Atkinson	c sub b Derrick	16
M. Morris	not out	6
R. Bate	c Metson b Barwick	0
†R.J. Turner	not out	0
R.A. Pyman		
D.J. Bush		
M.F. Mullins		
Extras	b 6, lb 8, nb 1	15
Total (6 wkts)		135

Watkin	16	7	19	1
Barwick	20	11	23	2
Derrick	24	12	41	3
North	6	2	16	0
Smith	4	2	14	0
Maynard	3	1	8	0

Umpires: B. Hassan and R.A. White
Toss: Glamorgan
On the first day Glamorgan made 307. Morris hit 17 fours in his 102, but the tail failed to take advantage of some friendly bowling. Bad light reduced the playing time on Sunday when only James batted with much authority. No play was possible on the third day.

v GLOUCESTERSHIRE (Fenner's)
April 19, 20, 21
Drawn.

Gloucestershire 1st Innings

A.W. Stovold	c Heap b Mullins	27
A.J. Wright	b Mullins	55
P.W. Romaines	c Mullins b Buzza	64
*C.W.J. Athey	b Mullins	14
P. Bainbridge	c Atkinson b Atherton	97
K.M. Curran	c and b Buzza	0
J.W.Lloyds	c Atkinson b Buzza	9
†R.C. Russell	not out	59
D.A. Graveney	not out	12
D.V. Lawrence		
K.B.S. Jarvis		
Extras	lb 4, nb 4	8
Total (7 wkts dec)		345

59, 97, 129, 203, 209, 225, 312

Bush	19	4	53	1
Mullins	32	11	88	3
Pyman	9	2	43	0
Atherton	23	3	74	1
Buzza	23	3	83	2

Cambridge Univ 1st Innings

S.P. James	c Russell b Jarvis	36
J.M.G. Willatt	lbw b Lawrence	3
*M.A. Atherton	c Graveney b Bainbridge	42
R. Heap	not out	42
J.C.M. Atkinson	c Russell b Jarvis	51
M.J. Morris	lbw b Lloyds	2
†R.J. Turner	c Russell b Jarvis	1
R.A. Pyman	not out	1
A.J. Buzza		
D.J. Bush		
M.F. Mullins		
Extras	lb 6, nb 3	9
Total (6 wkts)		187

17, 48, 93

Lawrence	10	2	45	1
Curran	6	3	7	0
Jarvis	13	6	22	3
Graveney	10	4	23	0
Bainbridge	8	2	39	1
Lloyds	5	1	45	1

Umpires: B. Hassan and R.A. White
Toss: Cambridge University
Rain so badly affected this match that even the first two innings could not be completed. Gloucester were 210–5 at tea on the first day when the rain arrived. The match did not resume until the third day. Athey declared at lunchtime and the students spent the afternoon practising their strokes, Atkinson looking most elegant.

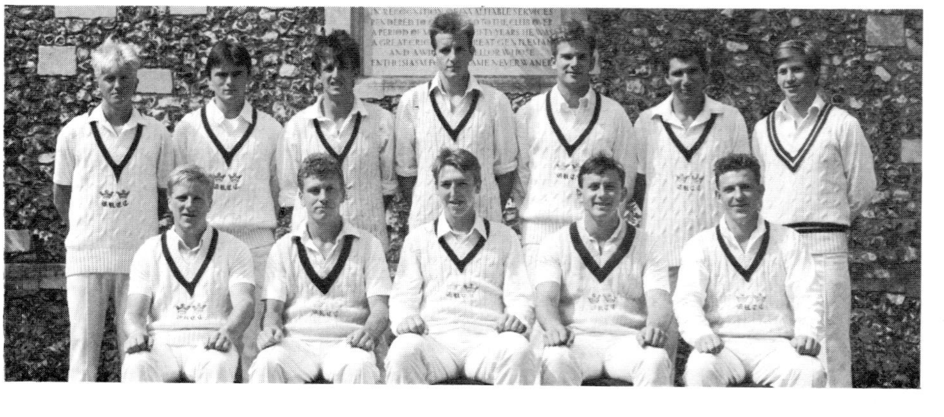

v LEICESTERSHIRE (Fenner's)

April 27, 28, 29
Drawn.

Leicestershire 1st Innings

T.J. Boon	c Bush b Mullins	39
N.E. Briers	c Atkinson b Mullins	54
J.J. Whitaker	c Atherton c Pyman	89
L. Potter	c Heap b Atherton	28
C.C. Lewis	c Willatt b Buzza	54
†P. Whitticase	c Heap b Atherton	30
G.J. Parsons	not out	29
J.P. Agnew	c Buzza b Atherton	14
L.B. Taylor	b Pyman	1
*D.I. Gower		
P. Willey		
Extras	b 3, lb 2, w 1	6
Total (8 wkts dec)		344

76, 119, 210, 222, 279, 313, 343, 344

Bush	23	4	71	0
Mullins	22	6	75	2
Pyman	21.2	8	60	2
Atherton	28	7	67	3
Buzza	15	1	66	1

Cambridge Univ 1st Innings

S.P. James	lbw b Parsons	35
J.M.G. Willatt	c Gower b Taylor	0
*M.A. Atherton	lbw b Taylor	2
R. Heap	c Whitticase b Agnew	0
J.C.M. Atkinson	b Taylor	37
M.J. Morris	c Gower b Potter	33
†R.J. Turner	c Taylor b Willey	36
R.A. Pyman	not out	9
A.J. Buzza	not out	0
D.J. Bush		
M.F. Mullins		
Extras	b 4, lb 2, nb 1	7
Total (8 wkts)		159

2, 4, 7, 56, 92, 117, 155, 159

Agnew	12	2	33	1
Taylor	12	5	44	3
Parsons	14	7	14	1
Lewis	13	5	20	0
Willey	9.1	5	17	2
Potter	9	2	25	1

Umpires: K.J. Lyons and H.J. Rhodes
Toss: Leicestershire
Rain prevented any play on the first day. On the second the county batsmen indulged in some gentle practice helped by dropped catches. A restricted third day produced very little of note.

Cambridge University 1989. From left, back: *R. Heap, D.H. Shufflebotham, M.T. Alban, D.J. Bush, J.M.G. Willatt, R.A. Pyman, M. Morris.* Front: *S.P. James, J.C.M. Atkinson, M.A. Atherton (Captain), R.J. Turner, A.J. Buzza.*

Bill Smith

Oxford University 1989. From left, back: *P. Lunn, A.N.S. Hampton, I. Henderson, J.D. Nuttall, E.D. Hester, A. Almaer, J. Oppenheimer.* Front: *R.E. Morris, D.A. Hagan, M.A. Crawley (Captain), P.G. Edwards, G.D. Reynolds.*

Bill Smith

v WARWICKSHIRE (Fenner's)

May 4, 5, 6
Drawn.

Warwickshire 1st Innings

A.J. Moles	st Turner b Buzza	66
J.D. Ratcliffe	c Turner b Bush	30
D.A. Thorne	st Turner b Buzza	41
*†G.W. Humpage	b Buzza	8
D.A. Banks	not out	60
S.J. Green	c Morris b Atherton	1
P.A. Smith	c Atkinson b Bush	61
A.R.K. Pierson		
T.A. Merrick		
J.E. Benjamin		
T.A. Munton		
Extras	b 1, lb 9, w 5, nb 2	17
Total (6 wkts dec)		284

62, 140, 155, 160, 165, 284

Bush	15.4	4	52	2
Mullins	13	2	48	0
Pyman	19.1	5	41	0
Atherton	18.5	4	50	1
Buzza	25	4	83	3

Cambridge Univ 1st Innings

S.P. James	not out	151
J.M.G. Willatt	lbw b Smith	1
*M.A. Atherton	b Smith	43
R. Heap	lbw b Merrick	4
J.C.M. Atkinson	b Benjamin	36
M.J. Morris	lbw b Pierson	3
†R.J. Turner	not out	15
R.A. Pyman		
A.J. Buzza		
D.J. Bush		
M.F. Mullins		
Extras	b 3, lb 16, nb 4	23
Total (5 wkts dec)		276

35, 123, 140, 211, 226

Merrick	16	6	41	1
Benjamin	20	6	56	1
Pierson	36	8	72	1
Smith	15.3	1	61	2
Munton	9	3	20	0
Ratcliffe	4	1	7	0

Warwickshire 2nd Innings

*†G.W. Humpage	run out	97
J.D. Ratcliffe	not out	127
D.A. Thorne	c Morris b Atherton	2
D.A Banks	not out	32
Extras	lb 5	5
Total (2 wkts dec)		263

177, 187

Bush	10	0	43	0
Mullins	10	1	57	0
Atherton	21	3	59	1
Pyman	5	1	27	0
Buzza	15	0	72	0

Cambridge Univ 2nd Innings

S.P. James	lbw b Benjamin	8
R. Heap	b Munton	35
*M.A. Atherton	c Green b Pierson	24
J.M.G. Willatt	lbw b Pierson	12
J.C.M. Atkinson	c Humpage b Pierson	2
M.J. Morris	not out	18
†R.J. Turner	not out	0
Extras	b 7, lb 6, nb 2	15
Total (5 wkts)		114

23, 72, 76, 84, 105

Merrick	7	2	14	0
Benjamin	10	2	31	1
Pierson	19	7	30	3
Smith	4	2	7	0
Munton	5	4	6	1
Thorne	6	2	13	0

Umpires: J.D. Bond and D.R. Shepherd
Toss: Warwickshire
The county made a moderate start on the first day, but Smith joined Banks in a 6th wicket stand of 119 to enable Humpage to declare. The University, 23–0 overnight, batted well on the second day, with James at the wicket 346 minutes for 151. Warwickshire were 25–0. On Saturday Humpage and Ratcliffe stretched their partnership to 177, the former being run out three short of his century. The University batted out time in the afternoon.

v KENT (Fenner's)

May 17, 18 19
Lost by 7 wkts

Cambridge Univ 1st Innings

S.P. James	c Ward b Ellison	15
R. Heap	c Ward b Harman	46
*M.A. Atherton	lbw b Harman	27
J.M.G. Willatt	b Davis	3
M.J. Morris	c Hinks b Kelleher	57
†R.J. Turner	c Davis b Harman	0
R.A. Pyman	lbw b Fleming	58
D.J. Bush	c Marsh b Davis	3
A.J. Buzza	b Harman	28
M.F. Mullins	lbw b Fleming	0
Extras	not out	0
	b 3, lb 10, w 6, nb 3	22
Total		259

48, 94, 107, 109, 134, 184, 193, 259, 259

Kelleher	15	6	41	1
Ellison	15	2	43	1
Davis	31	17	64	2
Fleming	11	3	42	2
Harman	24.4	6	56	4

Kent 1st Innings

G.R. Cowdrey	b Atherton c Bush	78
S.G. Hinks	c Bush b Buzza	86
R.F. Pienaar	b Pyman	0
*C.S. Cowdrey	c Turner b Buzza	59
M.V. Fleming	c Atherton b Buzza	2
†S.A. Marsh	st Turner b Buzza	8
T.R. Ward	st Turner b Buzza	30
D.J.M. Kelleher	c Heap b Buzza	8
R.M. Ellison	c Turner b Buzza	7
R.P. Davis	c Turner b Atherton	14
M.D. Harman	not out	0
Extras	b 3, lb 2, w 6, nb 1	12
Total		304

132, 141, 232, 235, 235, 247, 257, 271, 302

Bush	12	4	36	0
Mullins	9	2	33	0
Pyman	22	4	51	1
Atherton	36.1	13	77	3
Buzza	36	5	102	6

Cambridge Univ 2nd Innings

S.P. James	lbw b Kelleher	5
R. Heap	c G.R. Cowdrey b Harman	43
R.A. Pyman	c Ward b Harman	37
*M.A. Atherton	b Davis	79
J.M.G. Willatt	c G.R. Cowdrey b Harman	18
J.C .M. Atkinson	b Harman	0
M.J. Morris	b Davis	4
†R.J. Turner	c Pienaar b Harman	5
D.J. Bush	not out	3
A.J. Buzza	c G.R. Cowdrey b Davis	8
M.F. Mullins	c Pienaar b Davis	0
Extras	b 4, lb 6, w 4, nb 4	18
Total		220

13, 82, 143, 189, 189, 199, 206, 206, 220

Ellison	10	3	28	0
Kelleher	9	2	18	1
Davis	34.4	17	68	4
Harman	35	12	80	5
Fleming	5	1	16	0

Kent 2nd Innings

R.F. Pienaar	b Atherton	75
T.R. Ward	b Atherton	54
D.J.M. Kelleher	st Turner b Atherton	16
G.R. Cowdrey	not out	13
*C.S. Cowdrey	not out	5
Extras	b 5, lb 7, w 1	13
Total (3 wkts)		176

102, 155, 168

Pyman	12	2	47	0
Bush	6	0	33	0
Atherton	9	0	58	3
Buzza	3	0	26	0

Umpires: V.A. Holder and D.O. Oslear
Toss: Cambridge University
A dry pitch helping the spinners provided Harman and Fleming with wickets on the first day. Kent began Thursday at 39–0 and the openers took their stand to 132, but the rest of the county batsmen seemed rather worried by Buzza's slow left arm deliveries. The University seemed capable of saving the match on the last day, but with 5 wickets going down for 21, their tail collapsed and Kent won off the last possible ball.

CAMBRIDGE FIRST CLASS MATCHES

v ESSEX (Fenner's)

May 24, 25, 26

Lost by an inns and 30 runs.

Cambridge Univ 1st Innings				
S.P. James	lbw b Ilott			13
R. Heap	c Miller b Waugh			14
*M.A. Atherton	b Ilott			12
J.M.G. Willatt	c Garnham b Lever			10
J.M.C. Atkinson	b Waugh			15
M.J. Morris	b Stephenson			9
†A. Davies	c Lever b Stephenson			16
R.A. Pyman	c Lilley b Ilott			13
D.J. Bush	not out			13
D.C. Cotton	b Illott			4
M.F. Mullins	c and b Waugh			0
Extras	b 3, lb 8, w 3			14
Total				133
20, 39, 43, 68, 70, 100, 101, 128, 132				
Ilott	11	3	26	4
Lever	9	2	23	1
Waugh	12	4	23	3
Stephenson	13	5	18	2
Childs	20	11	24	0
Miller	9	6	8	0

Essex 1st Innings				
*B.R. Hardie	c Davies b Bush			0
J.P. Stephenson	b Cotton			63
A.W. Lilley	c Davies b Bush			16
M.E. Waugh	lbw b Atherton			92
P.J. Prichard	c Davies b Bush			88
G. Miller	c Morris b Atherton			5
†M.A. Garnham	not out			55
K. Butler	not out			10
M.C. Ilott				
J.H. Childs				
J.K. Lever				
Extras	b 4, lb 10, w 1, nb 3			18
Total (6 wkts dec)				347
0, 34, 112, 265, 267, 296				
Bush	19	6	64	3
Pyman	26	4	71	0
Mullins	13	1	60	0
Atherton	25	4	80	2
Cotton	11	0	58	1

Cambridge Univ 2nd Innings				
S.P. James	c Lilley b Childs			60
R. Heap	lbw b Lever			19
*M.A. Atherton	c Garnham b Childs			7
J.M.G. Willatt	b Miller			44
J.M.C. Atkinson	b Garnham b Childs			0
M.J. Morris	c Hardie b Childs			0
†A. Davies	c Lilley b Childs			29
R.A. Pyman	c Garnham b Childs			0
D.J. Bush	not out			8
D.C. Cotton	lbw b Childs			0
M.F. Mullins	lbw b Miller			3
Extras	b 1, lb 12, w 1			14
Total				184
60, 88, 89, 89, 89, 171, 171, 171, 171				
Ilott	7	1	25	0
Lever	12	5	26	1
Stephenson	17	5	37	0
Childs	19	11	35	7
Miller	17.4	8	34	2
Waugh	8	4	14	0

Umpires: B. Dudleston and H.J. Rhodes
Toss: Cambridge University

The University first innings was somewhat of an oddity, totalling 133 but with the highest individual score only 16. Ilott, the left arm pace bowler took 4 for 26. Essex began Thursday at 81–2 and had little difficulty in raising the total to 347. Hardie then declared, the students making 77–1 by the close. Childs bowled two remarkable spells on the last day, taking 4 wickets in 13 balls and later 3 in 7. Essex won with plenty of time to spare.

v NOTTINGHAMSHIRE (Fenner's)

June 17, 19, 20

Drawn.

Nottinghamshire 1st Innings				
B.C. Broad	lbw b Bush			18
P.R. Pollard	c Heap b Bush			153
M. Newell	lbw b Atherton			29
D.J.R. Martindale	b Cotton			60
C.L. Cairns	not out			47
M. Saxelby	lbw b Atherton			4
G.W. Mike	b Buzza			15
*†B.N. French	b Buzza			6
K. Saxelby	not out			8
D.J. Mullins				
J.A. Afford				
Extras	lb 8, w 3			11
Total (7 wkts dec)				351
19, 127, 253, 287, 300, 323, 337				
Bush	13	2	59	2
Pyman	14	2	65	0
Cotton	13	0	52	1
Buzza	21.3	2	98	2
Atherton	22	4	69	2

Cambridge Univ 1st Innings				
S.P. James	b Mike			117
R. Heap	b Millns			6
R.A. Pyman	c Martindale b Afford			69
*M.A. Atherton	c and b Afford			1
J.M.G. Willatt	c French b Mike			11
J.M.C. Atkinson	c Pollard b Afford			9
M.T. Alban	c Millns b Afford			10
†R.J. Turner	not out			32
D.J. Bush	c Pollard b Afford			0
D.C. Cotton	not out			25
M.F. Mullins				
Extras	b 5, lb 14, w 2, nb 7			28
Total (8 wkts dec)				308
17, 177, 183, 217, 230, 234, 265, 268				
Millns	23	4	83	1
K. Saxelby	18	7	28	0
Afford	36	11	91	5
Mike	20	4	62	2
M. Saxelby	7	2	25	0

Nottinghamshire 2nd Innings				
B.C. Broad	b Atherton			36
P.R. Pollard	c Atherton b Buzza			27
M. Newell	c Atherton b Buzza			35
D.J.R. Martindale	lbw b Atherton			2
C.L. Cairns	lbw b Atherton			29
M. Saxelby	not out			32
G.W. Mike	not out			56
Extras	b 10, lb 1, w 1			12
Total (5 wkts dec)				229
66, 66, 87, 137, 147				
Bush	8	2	21	0
Cotton	7	0	30	0
Buzza	26	4	77	2
Atherton	26	5	69	3
Alban	2	0	21	0

Cambridge Univ 2nd Innings				
S.P. James	lbw b M. Saxelby			50
R. Heap	c Broad b M. Saxelby			12
*M.A. Atherton	not out			29
J.M.G. Willatt	not out			0
Extras	b 4, lb 2, w 1, nb 2			9
Total (2 wkts)				100
35, 96				
Mullins	10	3	24	0
Mike	8	1	45	0
M. Saxelby	9	1	25	2

Umpires: J.D. Bond and M.J. Kitchen
Toss: Nottinghamshire

Pollard hit 26 fours and a six in his fine innings on the opening day. On Sunday, Pyman, who had come in as nightwatchman assisted James in a stand worth 160 and Cambridge topped the 300. The county batsmen, apart from a late effort by Mike were unable to score fast enough on the last morning and the game drifted to a draw. Mike and M. Saxelby made their fc debuts.

VARSITY MATCH

OXFORD v CAMBRIDGE (Lord's)

July 5, 6, 7

Drawn.

Cambridge Univ 1st Innings				
S.P. James	c Reynolds b Hester			23
R. Heap	b Henderson			7
*M.A. Atherton	c Crawley b Hester			56
J.M.G. Willatt	lbw b Edwards			16
J.C.M. Atkinson	lbw b Hester			39
M.T. Alban	b Edwards			86
†R.J. Turner	c and b Hampton			57
R.A. Pyman	not out			10
D.H. Shufflebotham	st Reynolds b Edwards			28
A.J. Buzza				
D.J. Bush				
Extras	b 1, lb 7, nb 10			18
Total (8 wkts)				340
17, 53, 99, 137, 152, 301, 301, 340				
Henderson	15	1	64	1
Hester	23	4	95	3
Nuttall	14	3	46	0
Edwards	24.4	5	79	3
Crawley	3	0	10	0
Lunn	7	1	12	0
Hampton	6	0	26	1

Oxford Univ 1st Innings				
D.A. Hagan	b Bush			0
S.A. Almaer	c Turner b Pyman			0
R.E. Morris	lbw b Pyman			76
J.D. Nuttall	lbw b Pyman			74
*M.A. Crawley	b Pyman			5
P.D Lunn	c Pyman b Atherton			22
A.N.S. Hampton	lbw b Shufflebotham			36
†G.D. Reynolds	lbw b Pyman			7
I.M. Henderson	not out			20
E.D. Hester	c Pyman b Buzza			4
P.G Edwards	not out			3
Extras	b 7, lb 5, nb 3			15
Total (9 wkts dec)				192
0, 8, 12, 32, 72, 150, 150, 162, 186				
Bush	14	4	22	1
Pyman	23	7	43	5
Atherton	29	10	40	1
Shufflebotham	15	3	34	1
Buzza	21	7	41	1

Cambridge Univ 2nd Innings				
S.P. James	c Crawley b Henderson			5
R. Heap	not out			25
*M.A. Atherton	c Reynolds b Edwards			30
Extras	w 1, nb 1			2
Total (2 wkts)				62
10, 62				
Henderson	4	1	12	1
Hester	2	1	4	0
Lunn	4	0	20	0
Edwards	1.3	0	5	1
Morris	1	0	5	0
Hampton	2	0	16	0

Umpires: A.A. Jones and R. Julian
Toss: Oxford

Put in to bat, Cambridge found the bowling and the wicket just to their liking. The best innings of the first day came from Alban, who was only a late choice, he made 86 and with Turner added 149 for the 6th wicket. Oxford fell to 24–3 by the close of Wednesday's play. Due only to 76 from Morris, Oxford saved the follow on, Pyman, whose delivery was most alarming, troubled all the batsmen. Cambridge reached 62–2 by the close. Owing to rain there was no play on the last day.

COMBINED UNIVERSITIES BENSON AND HEDGES CUP MATCHES

v SURREY (Fenner's)

April 25, 26

Won by 9 runs. Combined Univ 2pts, Surrey 0pts.

Combined Universities		
S.P. James	c Stewart b Bicknell	9
†M.P. Speight	c Clinton b Feltham	30
*M.A. Atherton	c Greig b Bullen	14
N. Hussain	c Bicknell b Feltham	23
J.C.M. Atkinson	st Stewart b Bullen	1
J. Longley	c Medlycott b Feltham	20
A. Dale	b Feltham	9
C. Tolley	st Stewart b Medlycott	1
A.R. Hansford	c Ward b Medlycott	1
T.R. Parker	c and b Feltham	0
J. Boiling	not out	2
Extras	lb 3, nb 3	6
Total (36.6 ov)		116

23, 49, 64, 72, 92, 106, 109, 114, 114

Murphy	5	1	10	0
Bicknell	8	0	24	1
Feltham	7	0	28	5
Greig	6	1	26	0
Bullen	8	2	14	2
Medlycott	2.3	0	11	2

Surrey		
J.D. Robinson	b Tolley	0
G.S. Clinton	b Boiling	36
†A.J. Stewart	lbw b Hansford	4
D.M. Ward	b Hansford	8
Z.A. Sadiq	b Boiling	9
*I.A. Greig	c James b Boiling	2
K.T. Medlycott	c Speight b Dale	2
M.A. Feltham	c Hussain b Dale	2
C.K. Bullen	not out	35
M.P. Bicknell	c Parker b Dale	2
A.J. Murphy	not out	5
Extras	w 2	2
Total (9 wkts, 37 ov)		107

4, 11, 23, 39, 54, 62, 64, 67, 75

Hansford	8	4	11	2
Tolley	7	1	12	1
Parker	4	0	30	0
Boiling	8	3	9	3
Dale	7	0	24	3
Atherton	3	0	21	0

Umpires: B.J. Meyer and B. Leadbeater

Toss: Combined Universities. Gold: J. Boiling

The first scheduled day having been washed out, the Universities made a modest 116 on a pitch which assisted the bowlers. The county surprised themselves by being unable to reach this total and the students gained their first B&H success for 5 years.

v MIDDLESEX (Oxford)

May 9

Lost by 8 wkts. Middx 2pts, Combined Univ 0pts.

Combined Universities		
S.P James	c Butcher b Williams	16
†M.P. Speight	b Fraser	20
*M.A. Atherton	c Downton b Emburey	66
N. Hussain	c Downton b Hughes	4
J.I. Longley	b Fraser	0
J.C.M. Atkinson	c and b Carr	16
M.A. Crawley	c Carr b Emburey	16
A.Dale	c Cowans b Emburey	15
C.M. Tolley	c Cowans b Hughes	22
A. Hansford	not out	8
J. Boiling	not out	0
Extras	lb 3, w 2, nb 2	7
Total (9 wkts, 55 ov)		190

31, 39, 55, 56, 88, 123, 156, 163, 188

Cowans	9	1	36	0
Williams	9	2	33	1
Hughes	8	1	36	2
Fraser		3	26	2
Carr	7	1	17	1
Emburey	11	1	39	3

Middlesex		
J.D. Carr	c Speight b Dale	26
*M.W Gatting	not out	123
R.O. Butcher	lbw b Tolley	15
M.R. Ramprakash	not out	24
†P.R. Downton		
J.F. Sykes		
J.E. Emburey		
S.P. Hughes		
N.G. Cowans		
A.R.C. Fraser		
N.F. Williams		
Extras	lb 5, w 1	6
Total (2 wkts, 53.4 ov)		194

105, 145

Hansford	11	3	26	0
Tolley	11	2	22	1
Dale	11	2	28	1
Crawley	8	0	37	0
Boiling	8.4	1	53	0
Atherton	4	0	23	0

Umpires: J.C. Balderstone and M.J. Kitchen

Toss: Combined Universities. Gold: M.W. Gatting

Although deciding to bat the Universities slumped to 88 for 5. Atherton however batted well and the total reached 190–9. On an easy pitch this looked an inadequate total and so it proved. Gatting hit 19 fours in his 123 and dominated the second half of the match.

Mike Atherton, the Cambridge skipper who played for England during the season.

Allsport/Adrian Murrell

Away Matches

The full scorecard of each of the Universities' away matches will be found in the sections for the respective home teams.

First Class

Hove: June 21, 22, 23

Camb Univ 229 and 67 lost to Sussex 371–9d by an innings and 75 runs.

Benson and Hedges Cup

Worcester: May 11

Worcs 216–8 (55 ov) (G.A. Hick 109) lost to Combined Univ 217–5 (53.1 ov) by 5 wkts. Combined Univ 2pts, Worcs 0pts.

Bristol: May 13

Combined Univ 223–7 (55 ov) lost to Gloucs 227–7 (54.5 ov) by 3 wkts. Gloucs 2pts, Combined Univ 0pts.

Taunton: May 31

Somerset 252–6 (55 ov) (P.M. Roebuck 102) beat Combined Univ 249–9 (55 ov) (N. Hussain 118) by 3 runs.

Cambridge University

Results: Played 9; lost 3, drawn 6

First-class averages

Batting	M	I	NO	R	HS	Avge
S.P. James†	9	15	1	575	151*	41.07
R.J. Turner†	8	11	4	253	58	36.14
M.T. Alban†	3	4	0	134	86	33.50
R.A. Pyman†	9	10	3	215	69	30.71
M.A. Atherton†	9	15	1	417	79	29.78
R. Heap†	9	15	2	278	46	21.38
J.C.M. Atkinson†	9	13	0	263	57	20.23
J.M.G. Willatt†	9	14	1	172	45	13.23
A.J. Buzza†	7	5	2	37	25*	12.33
D.J. Bush†	9	8	3	57	28	11.40
M.J. Morris	6	9	2	75	33	10.71
D.C. Cotton	3	4	1	4	4	1.33
M.F. Mullins	6	4	1	3	3	1.00

Also batted: R. Bate (1 match) 0; A. Davies (1 match) 16, 29; D.H. Shufflebotham† (1 match) 28.

Hundreds (2)

2 S.P. James: 151* v Warwicks, Cambridge; 117 v Notts, Cambridge.

Bowling	O	M	R	W	Avge	Best
M.A. Atherton	296.5	67	777	24	32.37	3–58
A.J. Buzza	220.3	31	756	20	37.80	6–102
M.F. Mullins	128	30	438	10	43.80	5–77
R.A. Pyman	199.3	43	599	13	46.07	5–43
D.T. Bush	180.4	41	571	9	63.44	3–64

Also bowled: M.T. Alban 2–0–21–0; J.C.M. Atkinson 2–0–24–0; D.C. Cotton 45–3–188–3; D.H. Shufflebotham 15–3–34–1.

Oxford University

Results: Played 8; lost 2, drawn 6

First-class averages

Batting	M	I	NO	R	HS	Avge
M.J. Kilborn	3	4	0	102	52	25.50
P.D. Lunn†	8	11	1	247	61	24.70
A.N.S. Hampton†	8	12	2	235	55	23.50
M.A. Crawley†	4	6	0	129	60	21.50
G.D. Reynolds†	6	8	1	147	40	21.00
R.E. Morris†	8	12	0	238	76	19.83
D.A. Hagan†	7	10	0	197	53	19.70
S.A. Almaer†	8	12	1	181	62	16.45
I.M. Henderson†	4	5	1	52	26	13.00
P.G. Edwards	7	8	5	28	10*	9.33
J.D. Nuttall†	3	4	1	22	13	7.33
S.C. Chauhan	3	4	0	22	10	5.50
E.D. Hester†	5	6	1	16	5	5.50
J. Higgo	3	6		18	9	3.20
J.M.E. Oppenheimer	5	6		7	7	3.00
						1.40

Also batted: C. Crocker (1 match) 7, 2; M. Munro (1 match) 12*; C.W. Timms (2 matches) 5, 5; G.J. Toogood (1 match) 19. R.M. Jackson played one match but did not bat.

Bowling	O	M	R	W	Avge	Best
P.G. Edwards	186.4	34	666	17	39.17	3–79
I.M. Henderson	90.5	20	325	7	46.42	2–40
E.D. Hester	157	29	572	11	52.00	4–100
A.N.S. Hampton	83	14	319	5	63.80	4–91
J.M.E. Oppenheimer	141	28	543	5	108.60	3–51

Also bowled: S.C. Chauhan 1–0–1–0; M.A. Crawley 63–17–170–1; C. Crocker 27–13–50–0; R.M. Jackson 21–3–87–0; M.J. Kilborn 20–1–104–1; P.D. Lunn 74–9–291–1; R.E. Morris 1–0–5–0; M. Munro 8–1–21–1; J.D. Nuttall 79.5–15–275–4; G.J. Toogood 29–5–115–1.

Scotland and Ireland

The match between Scotland and Ireland is considered first-class by the TCCB and therefore the performances in this annual international contest are included in first-class records. However when either Scotland or Ireland oppose any other side which is recognised as first-class, the resulting match is not now regarded as first-class. Ireland first played a first-class match in 1902 and Scotland in 1905, but there has been very little logic involved concerning exactly which matches since those dates have been considered first-class and the position of the two countries in relation to first-class status continues to be muddled.

ONE DAY AWAY MATCHES

The full scorecard of each of Scotland and Ireland's away matches will be found in the sections for the respective home teams.

Benson and Hedges Cup

Leicester: May 9
Leics 239–6 (55 ov) beat Scotland 128 (49 ov) by 111 runs. Leics 2pts, Scotland 0pts.

Edgbaston: May 11
Scotland 158–6 (55 ov) lost to Warwicks 159–4 (36.4 ov) by 6 wkts. Warwicks 2pts, Scotland 0pts.

NatWest Bank Trophy

Derby: June 28, 29
Derbys 145 (56.1 ov) beat Ireland 82 (31.4 ov) (O.H. Mortensen 6–14) by 63 runs.

Headingley: June 28, 29
Scotland 210–3 (60 ov) lost to Yorks 212–7 (58.5 ov) by 3 wkts.

SCOTLAND BENSON AND HEDGES CUP MATCHES

v LANCASHIRE (Perth)

May 2
Lost by 7 wkts. Lancs 2pts, Scotland 0pts.

Scotland		
I.L. Philip	c Fowler d Freitas	0
G.B.J. McGurk	lbw b DeFreitas	5
R.G. Swan	c Hegg b DeFreitas	2
*C.E.B. Rice	c Mendis b DeFreitas	2
B.M.W. Patterson	c Watkinson b Wasim Akram	7
O. Henry	not out	58
D.L. Snodgrass	c Hegg b Wasim Akram	0
W. Morton	c Hegg b Wasim Akram	0
J.W. Govan	c Hegg b Wasim Akram	16
†D.J. Haggo	lbw b Wasim Akram	0
D. Cowan	not out	6
Extras	b1, lb 4, w 9, nb 1	15
Total (9 wkts, 55ov)		111

0, 6, 9, 14, 36, 38, 40, 92, 92

DeFreitas	11	5	13	4
Watkinson	11	2	28	0
Wasim Akram	11	4	27	5
Hayhurst	9	3	16	0
Jesty	4	2	3	0
Simmons	9	4	19	0

Lancashire		
G.D. Mendis	lbw b Snodgrass	27
G. Fowler	b Morton	42
A.N. Hayhurst	b Morton	13
N.H. Fairbrother	not out	18
T.E. Jesty	not out	1
M. Watkinson		
*D.P. Hughes		
Wasim Akram		
†W.K. Hegg		
P.A.J. DeFreitas		
J. Simmons		
Extras	lb 5, w 7, nb 1	13
Total (3 wkts, 35.2 ov)		114

65, 90, 99

Rice	5	1	11	0
Cowan	5	0	18	0
Snodgrass	8	0	25	1
Govan	6	1	24	0
Morton	6.2	1	24	2
Henry	5	2	7	0

Umpires: H.D. Bird and J.W. Holder
Toss: Lancashire. Gold: P.A.J. DeFreitas
Put in to bat the Scottish side could do little with DeFreitas, though Henry, the South African, made certain the total topped 100. The county required only 35.2 overs to knock off the runs.

v NORTHAMPTONSHIRE (Glasgow)

May 13
Lost by 9 wkts. Northants 2pts, Scotland 0pts.

Scotland		
I.L. Philip	c G. Cook b Robinson	21
G.B.J. McGurk	lbw b Thomas	0
R.G. Swan	c Larkins b Robinson	40
*C.E.B. Rice	c Larkins b Robinson	0
M.J. Smith	b N.G.B. Cook	2
O. Henry	c Williams b Capel	42
D.L. Snodgrass	c Larkins b Williams	28
J.W. Govan	not out	38
W.Morton	not out	18
P.G. Duthie		
†D.J. Haggo		
Extras	lb 11, w 6, nb 1	18
Total (7 wkts 55 ov)		207

2, 50, 50, 54, 72, 139, 173

Davis	11	0	48	0
Thomas	10	1	34	1
N.G.B. Cook	11	2	24	1
Robinson	11	1	20	3
Williams	5	0	38	1
Capel	7	0	32	1

Northamptonshire		
G. Cook	not out	72
*W. Larkins	c Snodgrass b Morton	54
R.J. Bailey	not out	69
D.J. Capel		
J.G. Thomas		
D.J. Wild		
R.G. Williams		
†W. Noon		
N.G.B. Cook		
W.W. Davis		
M.A. Robinson		
Extras	lb 12, w 1, nb 2	15
Total (1 wkt, 44.4 ov)		210

Rice	9	0	18	0
Duthie	3	0	21	0
Snodgrass	2	0	21	0
Govan	11	2	38	0
Smith	7.4	0	34	0
Morton	6	0	37	1
Henry	6	1	29	0

Umpires: B. Leadbeater and R.A. White
Toss: Scotland. Gold: R.J. Bailey
Play began 15 minutes late when the Northants players lost their way to the ground. Scotland reached the highest score of the series with 207, but Northants played rings round all but Rice and won with ample overs in hand.

IRELAND v SCOTLAND

v SCOTLAND (Dublin)

July 8,, 9, 10
Drawn.

Scotland 1st Innings		
I.L. Philip	c Cohen b Nelson	0
B.M.W Patterson	lbw b Thompson	89
*R.G. Swan	lbw b Nelson	9
D.L. Snodgrass	b Nelson	9
O. Henry	b Lewis	25
A.L. Goram	c Lewis b Nelson	32
M.J. Smith	c Harrison b Nelson	4
J. Govan	c Jackson b Halliday	2
†D.J. Haggo	lbw b Thompson	18
D.R. Brown	not out	44
J.D. Moir	lbw b Jeffrey	15
Extras	b 1, lb 10, w 2, nb 1	14
Total		261

0, 12, 31, 73, 123, 130, 133, 180, 213

Nelson	21	7	27	5
Jeffrey	12.2	2	39	1
Thompson	27	8	67	2
Lewis	5	1	33	1
Halliday	31	4	83	1
Harrison	2	1	1	0

Ireland 1st Innings		
S.J.S. Warke	c Haggo b Henry	37
M.F. Cohen	c Swan b Moir	25
M.A. Nulty	c Smith b Henry	43
D.A. Lewis	c and b Henry	11
G.D. Harrison	c and b Henry	18
J.D. Garth	c Haggo b Govan	6
N. Thompson	c Govan b Henry	5
*†P.B. Jackson	c Govan b Henry	36
M. Halliday	lbw b Govan	36
A.N. Nelson	b Moir	1
A.S. Jeffrey	not out	12
Extras	b 7, lb 8, w 1, nb 3	19
Total		249

32, 95, 122, 124, 148, 148, 173, 211, 218

Moir	21	7	47	2
Brown	9	2	29	0
Henry	31	5	88	6
Govan	17.5	3	54	2
Goram	3	1	16	0

Scotland 2nd Innings		
I.L. Philip	st Jackson b Harrison	69
B.M.W Patterson	c Jackson b Jeffrey	10
*R.G. Swan	b Jeffrey	3
D.L. Snodgrass	b Jefrrey	13
D.J. Haggo	c Garth b Harrison	9
O. Henry	c Thompson b Harrison	26
A.L. Goram	lbw b Harrison	11
M.J. Smith	b Harrison	22
D.R. Brown	c Garth b Harrison	5
J. Govan	c Jackson b Halliday	17
J.D. Moir	not out	1
Extras	b 2, lb 5	7
Total		193

12, 16, 38, 63, 107, 139, 156, 166, 183

Nelson	12	0	36	0
Jeffrey	7	0	22	3
Harrison	24	5	75	6
Halliday	14.3	2	53	1

Ireland 2nd Innings		
S.J.S. Warke	c Goram b Henry	32
M.F. Cohen	c Philip b Henry	36
M.A. Nulty	b Henry	17
D.A. Lewis	c Goram b Henry	42
G.D. Harrison	c Goram b Henry	10
J.D. Garth	c Snodgrass b Henry	9
N. Thompson	c Patterson b Henry	1
*†P.B. Jackson	c Patterson b Henry	6
M. Halliday	not out	15
A.N. Nelson	not out	6
Extras	b 4, lb 7, nb 1	12
Total (8 wkts)		186

69, 69, 102, 117, 142, 156, 163, 165

Moir	5	1	16	0
Brown	6	1	17	0
Govan	26	9	56	1
Henry	28	4	86	7

Umpires: G.C. Archer and L. Hogan
Toss: Scotland
Patterson held Scotland together with an innings of 89, then the last wicket added 48 to take the total to 261. Nelson returned very creditable figures. Ireland began Sunday at 32–0 and then batted consistently without any outstanding individual performance. Scotland were 171–8 by the close. On the final day Henry thwarted any attempt on the part of the home side to obtain the runs.

First-Class Averages

Batting
(Qualification: 8 innings; avge 10.00)

	M	*I*	*NO*	*Runs*	*HS*	*Avge*	*100*	*50*
D.M. Jones (Aus)	14	20	3	1510	248	88.82	5	8
S.R. Waugh (Aus)	16	24	8	1030	177*	64.37	4	3
S.J. Cook (Som)	23	41	4	2241	156	60.56	8	8
R.A. Smith (Hts)	18	29	2	1577	182	58.40	6	5
K.R. Brown (Mx)	8	12	3	522	91	58.00	–	4
M.A. Taylor (Aus)	17	30	1	1669	219	57.55	3	10
G.A. Hick (Wo)	24	38	6	1824	173*	57.00	6	8
D.C. Boon (Aus)	17	28	5	1306	151	56.78	3	8
M.W. Gatting (Mx)	19	33	6	1503	158*	55.66	4	8
M.A. Lynch (Sy)	6	9	2	383	172*	54.71	1	2
A.R. Border (Aus)	16	22	4	979	135	54.38	1	9
M.R. Benson (Kt)	15	29	5	1299	157	54.12	5	6
R.F. Pienaar (Kt)	17	29	4	1321	134*	52.84	4	7
A.P. Wells (Sx)	22	38	7	1629	153	52.54	2	13
A.J. Lamb (Nrth)	11	15	1	733	171	52.35	3	2
I.J.F. Hutchinson (Mx)	10	18	3	731	201*	48.73	3	–
N. Hussain (Ex)	15	24	3	990	141	47.14	3	3
A.R. Butcher (Glam)	23	40	5	1632	171*	46.62	3	11
R.J. Shastri (Glam)	17	27	5	1004	127	45.63	2	5
G.P. Thorpe (Sy)	18	30	5	1132	154	45.28	2	8
D.L. Haynes (Mx)	20	37	5	1446	206*	45.18	3	8
D.M. Smith (Sx)	19	35	6	1305	184	45.00	4	6
D.A. Reeve (Wa)	14	17	4	581	97*	44.69	–	4
A.J. Stewart (Sy)	23	42	5	1637	206*	44.24	4	5
G.D. Mendis (La)	19	34	3	1367	118	44.09	2	10
M.E. Waugh (Ex)	24	39	4	1537	165	43.91	4	8
T.S. Curtis (Wo)	21	35	2	1430	156	43.33	4	8
J.E. Morris (Dby)	23	43	5	1638	156	43.10	4	8
N.H. Fairbrother (La)	22	38	4	1458	161	42.88	3	8
N.R. Taylor (Kt)	21	41	6	1495	118	42.71	3	7
W. Larkins (Nrth)	24	45	3	1787	126	42.54	3	13
C.L. Smith (Hts)	19	33	4	1230	143*	42.41	2	6
I.A. Grieg (Sy)	22	34	10	1013	107*	42.20	1	8
R.T. Robinson (Notts)	23	42	6	1516	146*	42.11	4	8
M.R.J. Veletta (Aus)	5	8	1	294	134*	42.00	1	1
G.A. Gooch (Ex)	18	31	1	1256	158	41.86	3	9
P.M. Roebuck (Som)	22	37	3	1399	149	41.14	5	6
V.J. Marks (Som)	20	32	12	822	89*	41.10	–	4
G.D. Lloyd (La)	7	12	1	442	117	40.18	3	–
D.W. Randall (Notts)	25	43	6	1485	130	40.13	3	8
P.A. Neale (Wo)	22	32	8	961	98	40.04	–	8
C.S. Cowdrey (Kt)	24	34	4	1169	146*	38.96	2	8
B.C. Broad (Notts)	22	41	2	1512	144	38.76	3	10
G.W. Humpage (La)	23	34	7	1041	183	38.55	1	5
T.J.G. O'Gorman (Dby)	8	14	2	462	124	38.50	2	–
D.I. Gower (Leics)	17	30	1	1102	228	38.00	3	4
J.J. Whitaker (Leics)	23	39	3	1364	138	37.88	3	6
P.W.G. Parker (Sx)	16	29	3	984	136	37.84	2	5
J.P. Stephenson (Ex)	23	39	3	1354	171	37.61	4	4
G. Fowler (La)	21	37	0	1370	130	37.02	3	9
T.E. Jesty (La)	21	35	7	1030	93*	36.78	–	8
J.R. Wood (Hts)	12	18	2	588	96	36.75	–	4
T.A. Lloyd (Wa)	22	33	2	1138	183	36.70	3	3
N. Shahid (Ex)	7	9	2	255	52	36.42	–	1
D.J. Capel (Nrth)	23	39	3	1311	126	36.41	3	9
C.J. Tavaré (Som)	22	39	2	1343	153	36.29	1	9
M.R. Ramprakash (Mx)	21	34	5	1052	128	36.27	1	7
M.C.J. Nicholas (Hts)	24	40	5	1269	140	36.25	5	3
R.J. Turner (CU)	8	11	4	253	58	36.14	–	2
T.R. Ward (Kt)	23	40	5	1257	104	35.91	1	9
D.J. Bicknell (Sy)	23	45	6	1392	119	35.69	4	6
J.D. Ratcliffe (Wa)	11	20	4	571	127*	35.68	1	2
G. Cook (Nrth)	20	36	3	1174	138	35.57	4	4
M.D. Moxon (Yks)	19	34	1	1174	162*	35.57	1	7
K.J. Barnett (Dby)	22	36	1	1244	118	35.54	2	8
S.P. James (Hts)	16	27	1	922	151*	35.46	2	3
K.M. Curran (Glos)	24	39	4	1236	128	35.31	4	2
T.M. Moody (Aus)	12	20	4	564	144*	35.25	1	3
S.T. Jefferies (Hts)	8	13	6	245	42	35.00	–	–
P.A. Smith (Wa)	19	26	4	762	140	34.63	1	3
S.J. Rhodes (Wo)	22	31	13	623	83	34.61	–	2
R.J. Harden (Som)	20	34	6	969	115*	34.60	3	2
A.J. Moles (Wa)	21	38	5	1138	130*	34.48	2	8
A.A. Metcalfe (Yks)	21	37	1	1230	138	34.16	3	6
K. Sharp (Yks)	11	19	4	512	78	34.13	–	5
M.A. Roseberry (Mx)	18	29	5	804	101*	33.50	1	5
R.J. Bailey (Nrth)	25	44	4	1337	134	33.42	4	6
R.P. Pollard (Notts)	18	32	0	1064	153	33.25	2	4
H. Morris (Glam)	15	43	2	1351	133	32.95	3	7
C.M. Wells (Sx)	22	36	4	1054	84*	32.93	–	8
I. Smith (Glam)	18	28	4	786	116	32.75	2	3
A.I.C. Dodemaide (Sx)	20	30	9	683	80	32.52	–	4
A. Fordham (Nrth)	13	23	3	647	199	32.35	1	4
G.R. Marsh (Aus)	18	33	4	934	138	32.20	2	2
R.J. Blakey (Yk)	22	39	5	1159	97	32.19	–	8
L. Potter (Lei)	24	39	3	1093	121*	32.14	1	6
S.G. Hinks (Kt)	19	36	4	1028	104*	32.12	1	8
V.P. Terry (Hts)	23	41	2	1245	180	31.92	1	8
P. Bainbridge (Glos)	22	33	3	955	128	31.83	2	5
B.R. Hardie (Ex)	17	27	2	792	142*	31.68	2	2
G. Miller (Ex)	10	14	3	346	61	31.45	–	3
M.A. Atherton (La)	18	33	3	941	115*	31.36	1	4
K.T. Medlycott (Sy)	24	38	8	928	86*	30.93	–	7
T.J. Boon (Lei)	21	39	5	1045	80*	30.73	–	6
C.L. Cairns (Notts)	6	8	1	215	58	30.71	–	1
R.A. Pyman (OU)	9	10	3	215	69	30.71	–	2
M.A. Garnham (Ex)	22	32	9	703	91	30.56	–	4
N.D. Burns (Som)	22	33	6	818	90	30.29	–	5
M.W. Alleyne (Glos)	19	28	4	721	111	30.04	1	5
I.J. Gould (Sx)	22	33	4	870	125	30.00	1	7
Asif Din (Wa)	18	28	3	748	82*	29.92	–	4
P. Whitticase (Lei)	18	29	6	684	61	29.73	–	2
P.D. Bowler (Dby)	24	46	1	1337	157	29.71	2	10
P.J. Prichard (Ex)	23	36	4	949	128	29.65	1	7
I.A. Healy (Aus)	14	19	4	442	73*	29.46	–	1
A.J. Wright (Glos)	24	41	1	1159	130	28.97	3	6
P. Willey (Lei)	23	37	2	1013	99	28.94	–	7
P.E. Robinson (Yk)	18	31	4	781	147	28.92	2	1
K.D. James (Hts)	22	37	3	982	162	28.88	1	5
R.O. Butcher (Mx)	11	20	2	519	126	28.83	1	1
T.J. Zoehrer (Aus)	7	9	0	259	93	28.77	–	1
P. Johnson (Notts)	20	36	3	949	109*	28.75	1	5
J.W. Lloyds (Glos)	23	39	3	1032	71	28.66	–	6
T.V. Hohns (Aus)	15	18	4	393	95	28.07	–	2
D.R. Turner (Hts)	10	17	4	364	65*	28.00	–	3
M.P. Maynard (Glam)	24	40	3	1035	191*	27.97	1	3
M.J. Cann (Glam)	20	34	2	895	109	27.96	1	5
C.W.J. Athey (Glos)	23	36	2	948	108	27.88	1	6
N.M.K. Smith (Wa)	9	11	2	248	161	27.55	1	–
T.M. Tremlett (Hts)	6	8	4	110	40*	27.50	–	–
T.C. Middleton (Hts)	7	11	1	274	69	27.40	–	2
D. Byas (Yk)	20	33	2	844	117	27.22	1	5
G.R. Cowdrey (Kt)	9	12	3	244	108*	27.11	1	1
R.C. Russell (Glos)	19	29	7	586	128*	26.63	1	2
M.P. Speight (Sx)	9	17	1	425	88	26.56	–	3
N.J. Lenham (Sx)	15	27	3	633	116	26.37	1	3
G.J. Parsons (Lei)	18	26	8	474	69	26.33	–	1
K.P. Evans (Notts)	14	21	6	395	58	26.33	–	3
P. Moores (Sx)	22	30	6	629	116	26.20	1	2
C.J. Adams (Dby)	7	11	1	261	79	26.10	–	1
N.E. Briers (Lei)	24	44	3	1061	73	25.87	–	6
M.D. Marshall (Hts)	15	21	5	412	68*	25.75	–	2
A.I. Kallicharran (Wa)	16	26	2	610	119	25.41	2	1
D.M. Ward (Sy)	15	26	2	608	145	25.33	1	–
A.C.S. Pigott (Sx)	21	27	5	556	91	25.27	–	3
N.A. Felton (Nrth)	14	26	3	579	60*	25.17	–	4
R.J. Parks (Hts)	23	29	12	427	76*	25.11	–	2
M.J. Weston (Wor)	14	22	3	473	74	24.89	–	2
J.D. Carr (Mx)	19	34	3	766	153*	24.70	1	3
P.D. Lunn (OU)	8	11	1	247	61	24.70	–	1
S.A. Marsh (Kt)	22	31	6	614	90*	24.56	–	5
A.W. Lilley (Ex)	16	27	2	613	113*	24.52	1	2
B.N. French (Notts)	17	27	5	537	55*	24.40	–	2
P. Bent (Wor)	13	22	0	530	144	24.09	1	2
R.G. Williams (Nrth)	5	8	1	166	71	23.71	–	1
R. Sharma (Dby)	21	37	5	755	77	23.59	–	3
D. Ripley (Nrth)	23	36	9	636	123	23.55	1	–
G.S. Clinton (Sy)	22	40	3	870	90*	23.51	–	5
A.N.S. Hampton (OU)	8	12	2	235	55	23.50	–	2
R.I. Alikhan (Sy)	9	17	2	351	84*	23.40	–	3
D.L. Bairstow (Yk)	11	17	3	327	101*	23.35	1	1
S.M. McEwan (Wor)	11	9	3	139	28*	23.16	–	–
R.G. Twose (Wa)	5	9	3	139	37	23.16	–	–
J.J.E. Hardy (Som)	13	23	4	435	65	22.89	–	2
C.S. Pickles (Yk)	18	24	7	388	66	22.82	–	2
M. Newell (Notts)	14	26	2	545	99	22.70	–	2
M.V. Fleming (Kt)	8	12	3	204	45	22.66	–	–
N.F. Williams (Mx)	15	19	5	317	69*	22.64	–	1
N.A. Foster (Ex)	17	21	10	246	50*	22.36	–	1
J.C.M. Atkinson (CU)	13	20	0	447	57	22.35	–	3
P.A.J. DeFreitas (La)	17	28	2	580	78	22.30	–	5
M. Watkinson (La)	23	39	6	733	70	22.21	–	4
D.R. Pringle (Ex)	19	23	4	421	81*	22.15	–	1
F.D. Stephenson (Notts)	18	30	3	597	81	22.11	–	4
I.P. Butcher (Glos)	14	23	3	437	105*	21.85	1	1
D.P. Hughes (La)	17	24	5	413	50*	21.73	–	1
G.R. Dilley (Wor)	15	17	11	130	31	21.66	–	–
R.D.B. Croft (Glam)	5	8	2	129	45	21.50	–	–
R. Heap (CU)	9	15	2	278	46	21.38	–	–
D.B. d'Oliveira (Wor)	24	37	1	766	63	21.27	–	5
R.J. Scott (Hts)	12	20	1	399	77	21.00	–	2
G.D. Reynolds (OU)	6	8	1	147	40	21.00	–	–
B. Roberts (Dby)	15	27	1	541	102	20.80	1	2

D.E. Malcolm (Dby)	12	16	7	186	51	20.66	–	1
N.J. Speak (La)	5	10	1	186	64	20.66	–	1
Wasim Akram (La)	13	20	3	350	49	20.58	–	–
M.G. Hughes (Aus)	15	16	4	246	71	20.50	–	1
J.D. Love (Yk)	9	15	2	264	53	20.30	–	1
E.E. Hemmings (Notts)	22	32	7	505	58*	20.20	–	2
D.J.R. Martindale (Notts)	7	11	0	221	78	20.09	–	2
P.W. Romaines (Glos)	6	11	0	220	77	20.00	–	2
A.N. Hayhurst (La)	9	15	2	258	40	19.84	–	–
G.D. Rose (Som)	16	20	7	258	50*	19.84	–	1
R.E. Morris (OU)	8	12	0	238	76	19.83	–	2
W.K. Hegg (La)	23	39	4	694	86	19.82	–	5
D.A. Hagan (OU)	7	10	0	197	53	19.70	–	1
D.J. Wild (Notts)	11	15	0	293	121	19.53	1	–
J.D. Robinson (Sy)	7	11	2	175	38*	19.44	–	–
C.W. Scott (Notts)	8	10	3	136	51	19.42	–	1
A. Dale (Glam)	4	8	1	134	44	19.14	–	–
M.A. Feltham (Sy)	14	21	2	361	64	19.00	–	1
R.M. Ellison (Kt)	12	16	2	264	39*	18.85	–	–
S.C. Goldsmith (Dby)	11	21	1	376	88	18.80	–	1
G.C. Holmes (Glam)	13	21	3	337	38	18.72	–	–
G.L. Lord (Wor)	10	16	2	262	80	18.71	–	2
C. Penn (Kt)	19	21	4	317	60	18.64	–	1
J.E. Emburey (Mx)	20	30	5	464	77*	18.56	–	2
P.R. Downton (Mx)	23	34	3	572	100	18.45	1	–
I.T. Botham (Wor)	17	24	1	419	73	18.21	–	1
A. Sidebottom (Yk)	19	24	5	344	45*	18.10	–	–
C.A. Walsh (Glo)	18	25	5	360	47	18.00	–	–
J.D. Fitton (La)	18	25	6	336	44	17.68	–	–
B.J.M. Maher (Dby)	22	40	6	601	97	17.67	–	3
D.J.M. Kelleher (Kt)	11	14	3	194	53*	17.63	–	1
K.M. Krikken (Dby)	4	8	3	88	37	17.60	–	–
R.A. Cobb (Lei)	5	9	0	157	47	17.44	–	–
G.F. Lawson (Aus)	14	12	2	174	74	17.40	–	1
P. Carrick (Yk)	22	31	3	483	65*	17.25	–	2
N.V. Radford (Wor)	18	21	2	325	66*	17.10	–	1
I.D. Austin (La)	9	13	3	171	38	17.10	–	–
K. Greenfield (Sx)	5	8	0	132	48	16.50	–	–
S.A. Almaer (OU)	8	12	1	181	62	16.45	–	1
K. Saxelby (Notts)	10	11	6	81	19	16.20	–	–
W.K.M. Benjamin (Lei)	15	19	2	273	41	16.05	–	–
K.J. Piper (Wa)	12	15	2	208	41	16.00	–	–
C.P. Metson (Glam)	24	33	8	399	47	15.96	–	–
I.G. Swallow (Yk)	13	20	2	287	64	15.94	–	1
C. Gladwin (Dby)	4	8	0	127	59	15.87	–	1

Derek Randall enjoyed a good season in 1989, scoring 1,485 runs at over 40.

Allsport/Adrian Murrell

Nasser Hussain, wearing his Essex cap. He also played for Durham University and Combined Universities during the season, and was in the England squad for one of the Test matches, reward for his consistent batting which brought him an average of 47.14.

Allsport/Pascal Rondeau

R.P. Davis (Kt)	21	23	6	263	67	15.47	–	1
C.C. Lewis (Lei)	12	19	1	277	69	15.38	–	2
G.C. Small (Wa)	18	23	4	291	59	15.31	–	1
M.C. Dobson (Kt)	7	10	1	137	52	15.22	–	1
A.E. Warner (Dby)	15	23	6	253	46	14.88	–	–
P.G. Newman (Dby)	15	25	4	309	86*	14.71	–	2
D.V. Lawrence (Glos)	14	17	5	173	45	14.41	–	–
A.N. Jones (Som)	23	23	10	186	43*	14.30	–	–
A.W. Stovold (Glos)	7	133	0	184	36	14.15	–	–
C.E.L. Ambrose (Nrth)	9	14	5	127	23*	14.11	–	–
J. Simmons (La)	6	9	5	56	16	14.00	–	–
R.K. Illingworth (Wor)	24	26	2	333	71	13.87	–	2
P.J. Newport (Wor)	9	12	2	138	36	13.80	–	–
J.D.R. Benson (Lei)	4	8	0	110	45	13.75	–	–
G.A. Tedstone (Glo)	12	17	2	206	50	13.73	–	1
A.A. Donald (Wa)	19	22	6	215	40	13.43	–	–
D.A. Thorne (Wa)	5	10	0	134	41	13.40	–	–
G.J.F. Ferris (Lei)	5	9	3	80	30	13.33	–	–
N.A. Mallender (Som)	18	18	4	186	48*	13.28	–	–
D.A. Leatherdale (Wor)	7	8	1	93	25	13.28	–	–
J.M.G. Willatt (CU)	9	14	1	172	45	13.23	–	–
M.P. Bicknell (Sy)	18	24	6	234	40*	13.00	–	–
T.D. Topley (Ex)	23	26	4	277	49	12.59	–	–
A.R.C. Fraser (Mx)	21	28	7	264	43*	12.57	–	–
J.P. Agnew (Lei)	24	31	8	279	39	12.13	–	–
R.J. Bartlett (Som)	11	19	0	228	54	12.00	–	1
K.E. Cooper (Notts)	21	27	6	251	33*	11.95	–	–
P.J.W. Allott (La)	16	23	5	215	28	11.94	–	–
J.G. Thomas (Nrth)	20	32	3	346	35	11.93	–	–
P.W. Jarvis (Yk)	18	25	5	236	59*	11.80	–	1
T.B.A. May (Aus)	10	8	3	59	24	11.80	–	–
D.A. Graveney (Glos)	15	22	8	164	27*	11.71	–	–
D.J. Bush (CU)	9	8	3	57	28	11.40	–	–
R.J. Maru (Hts)	23	25	8	192	29	11.29	–	–
W.W. Davis (Nrth)	14	19	4	166	40*	11.06	–	–
G.D. Campbell (Aus)	11	10	2	87	31	10.87	–	–
C.A. Connor (Hts)	15	14	2	129	24	10.75	–	–
M.J. Morris (CU)	6	9	2	75	33	10.71	–	–
S.P. Hughes (Mx)	21	28	7	221	31	10.52	–	–
S.J. Dennis (Glam)	15	19	1	187	38	10.38	–	–
I.D.K. Salisbury (Sx)	11	10	4	62	37	10.33	–	–
F.A. Griffith (Dby)	5	10	0	102	30	10.20	–	–
I.R. Bishop (Dby)	12	20	2	180	28*	10.00	–	–
M.A. Holding (Dby)	10	13	4	90	34	10.00	–	–

Bowling

(Qualication: 10 wickets in 10 innings)

Alan Donald, Warwickshire's South African bowler, who finished second in the bowling averages to the Australian tourist, Terry Alderman.

Bill Smith

	O	*M*	*R*	*W*	*Avge*	*BB*	*5i*
T.M. Alderman (Aus)	411.2	104	1095	70	15.64	6-128	6
A.A. Donald (Wa)	537.1	122	1398	86	16.25	7-66	6
M.D. Marshall (Hts)	428.3	115	1067	64	16.67	6-69	4
S.R. Lampitt (Wor)	219.5	57	526	31	16.96	5-32	2
Wasim Akram (La)	466.1	103	1117	63	17.73	7-42	7
W.K.M. Benjamin (Lei)	484.1	145	1238	69	17.94	7-54	7
D.R. Pringle (Ex)	668.2	164	1753	94	18.64	7-18	5
F.D. Stephenson (Notts)	592.3	135	1727	92	18.77	8-47	7
S.M. McEwan (Wor)	368.3	80	999	52	19.21	6-34	3
R.M. Ellcock (Mx)	182.1	36	615	32	19.21	5-35	1
B.P. Patterson (La)	210.3	43	618	32	19.31	5-48	1
G.A. Hick (Wor)	214.4	65	519	26	19.96	5-52	2
A.R.C. Fraser (Mx)	797.1	203	1861	92	20.22	7-77	4
O.H. Mortensen (Dby)	334.4	64	878	43	20.41	6-38	2
C.A. Walsh (Glos)	627.4	134	1675	81	20.67	7-19	5
G.F. Lawson (Aus)	522.3	140	1447	69	20.97	6-30	3
C.A. Connor (Hts)	443.2	99	1255	59	21.27	7-31	5
N.G. Cowans (Mx)	492.3	117	1321	62	21.30	5-34	1
S.P. Hughes (Mx)	463.2	120	1242	58	21.41	4-23	–
N.A. Foster (Ex)	713.2	186	1836	85	21.60	7-105	1
N.G.B. Cook (Nrth)	587	200	1328	61	21.77	6-56	3
R.K. Illingworth (Wor)	445.4	179	893	41	21.78	5-23	1
C.C. Lewis (Lei)	300.3	59	986	45	21.91	5-40	3
P.J. Newport (Wor)	279.5	42	902	41	22.00	6-43	3
T.M. Tremlett (Hts)	160	49	356	16	22.25	4-67	–
I.R. Bishop (Dby)	337	66	920	41	22.43	6-67	1
P.J. Bakker (Hts)	629.4	157	1732	77	22.49	6-81	4
I.D. Austin (La)	187.5	46	473	21	22.52	4-60	–
J.H. Childs (Ex)	679.5	265	1521	67	22.70	7-35	6
N.V. Radford (Wor)	572.4	119	1725	75	23.00	6-59	3
C.G. Rackemann (Aus)	223.5	47	747	32	23.34	5-65	1
A. Sidebottom (Yk)	576	129	1590	68	23.38	6-79	5
A.E. Warner (Dby)	331.1	80	821	35	23.45	4-18	–
D.E. Malcolm (Dby)	297.5	40	1122	47	23.87	4-68	–
G.R. Dilley (Wor)	422.2	76	1438	60	23.96	5-28	5
T.D. Topley (Ex)	606	143	1851	77	24.03	5-30	2
S.J. Base (Dby)	417.3	73	1451	60	24.18	7-60	2
G.D. Rose (Som)	418.2	104	1143	47	24.31	4-12	–
S.R. Waugh (Aus)	176.1	39	571	23	24.82	3-10	–
S.L. Watkin (Glam)	792	170	1259	94	25.09	7-65	8
D.P. Hughes (La)	102.1	27	303	12	25.25	3-30	–
I.T. Botham (Wor)	496.4	109	1417	56	25.30	7-85	3
P.W. Jarvis (Yk)	617.3	137	1924	76	25.31	7-74	4
G.C. Small (Wa)	537	134	1400	55	25.45	5-55	1
M.C.J. Nicholas (Hts)	122.4	16	384	15	25.60	6-37	1
P.J.W. Allott (La)	442.4	115	1052	41	25.65	5-24	1
K.B.S. Jarvis (Yk)	298.4	69	928	36	25.77	5-15	1
R.M. Ellison (Kt)	292.1	71	752	29	25.93	6-43	2
T.A. Munton (Wa)	613.4	178	1538	59	26.06	5-13	1
K.E. Cooper (Notts)	609	177	1553	59	26.32	6-37	2
M.P. Bicknell (Sy)	622.3	136	1717	65	26.41	6-47	4
M.G. Hughes (Aus)	399	102	1242	47	26.42	5-37	3
T.B.A. May (Aus)	287.5	86	740	28	26.42	4-43	–
P. Willey (Lei)	431.1	136	985	37	26.62	5-45	1
P.A.J. DeFreitas (La)	614.5	125	1818	68	26.73	7-21	4
K.M. Curran (Glos)	414.5	85	1258	47	26.76	7-69	2
K.P. Evans (Notts)	258.5	59	781	29	26.93	3-20	–
P.A. Smith (Wa)	272.4	37	898	33	27.21	5-82	1
R. Sharma (Dby)	191.5	50	547	20	27.35	5-60	1
G.D. Campbell (Aus)	250.2	50	824	30	27.46	5-54	1
C.M. Wells (Sx)	564.5	152	1351	49	27.57	7-65	2
W.W. Davis (Nrth)	440	68	1444	52	27.76	5-55	1
N.A. Mallender (Som)	514.5	121	1389	50	27.78	7-62	3
M. Watkinson (La)	503.5	109	1540	55	28.00	7-69	3
M.C.J. Ball (Glos)	155	26	504	18	28.00	4-53	–
D.A. Graveney (Glos)	488.2	165	1095	39	28.07	6-128	1
P. Carrick (Yk)	697.1	242	1603	57	28.12	6-70	2
A.N. Jones (Som)	603.2	119	2014	71	28.36	6-37	2
C.E.L. Ambrose (Nrth)	281	70	795	28	28.39	6-22	2
P.C.R. Tufnell (Mx)	602.1	160	1564	55	28.43	5-60	3
K.J. Barnett (Dby)	113.2	24	313	11	28.45	4-36	–
J.K. Lever (Ex)	263.1	54	754	26	29.00	7-48	1
J.G. Thomas (Nrth)	536.2	79	1946	67	29.04	6-53	3
M.E. Waugh (Ex)	117.2	19	415	14	29.64	3-23	–
E.E. Hemmings (Notts)	663.2	172	1720	58	29.65	6-87	2
D.J. Capel (Nrth)	517.2	92	1693	57	29.70	5-53	1
J.E. Emburey (Mx)	787.1	266	1658	55	30.14	7-27	3
A.I.C. Dodemaide (Sx)	672.1	133	1971	65	30.32	5-77	2
M.J. Weston (Wor)	141.3	44	365	12	30.41	3-21	–
S.R. Barwick (Glam)	781.2	232	1948	64	30.43	7-47	3
P. Bainbridge (Glos)	279.1	63	762	25	30.48	4-39	–
J.A. Afford (Notts)	545.3	145	1619	53	30.54	5-63	3
L. Potter (Lei)	160.5	34	460	15	30.66	3-50	–
M.A. Robinson (Nrth)	411.1	81	1139	37	30.78	4-60	–
M.A. Holding (Dby)	258	46	863	28	30.82	6-57	1
A.J. Murphy (Sy)	623	127	2008	65	30.89	6-97	2
T.V. Hohns (Aus)	321.4	108	809	26	31.11	4-87	–
M.A. Feltham (Sy)	388.3	81	1124	36	31.22	4-68	–
N.F. Williams (Mx)	327.2	58	970	31	31.29	4-39	–
P.M. Roebuck (Som)	141	35	347	11	31.54	2-22	–
A.C.S. Pigott (Sx)	679.1	130	2084	66	31.57	5-52	1
A.M. Babington (Sx)	511.4	97	1541	47	32.78	5-37	2
J.W. Lloyds (Glos)	245.2	55	726	22	33.00	7-134	1
K.D. James (Hts)	415.3	91	1222	37	33.02	5-41	1
J.P. Agnew (Lei)	732.3	132	2322	70	33.17	6-56	3
K.T. Medlycott (Sy)	722.4	181	2166	65	33.32	7-68	2
R.J. Maru (Hts)	586	162	1491	44	33.88	8-41	2
S.J. Dennis (Glam)	418.3	110	1196	35	34.17	5-83	1
R.A. Pick (Notts)	205.1	34	724	21	34.47	6-52	1
A.P. Igglesden (Kt)	584.5	101	1953	56	34.87	6-73	1
D.V. Lawrence (Glos)	344.1	60	1186	34	34.88	4-61	–
G.J. Parsons (Lei)	334.1	79	1100	31	35.48	5-48	1
J.E. Benjamin (Wa)	177	44	505	14	36.07	3-55	–
L.B. Taylor (Lei)	270.4	53	871	24	36.29	4-55	–
M.C. Ilott (Ex)	109	22	365	10	36.50	4-26	–
A.R.K. Pierson (Wa)	383.5	79	1197	32	37.40	6-82	2
P.G. Newman (Dby)	333.5	73	1014	27	37.55	5-45	1
A.J. Buzza (CU)	220.3	31	756	20	37.80	6-102	1
N.M.K. Smith (Wa)	130.4	27	427	11	38.81	3-62	–
P.G. Edwards (OU)	186.4	34	666	17	39.17	3-79	–
S.J.W. Andrew (Hts)	170.5	29	523	13	40.23	3-70	–
C.S. Pickles (Yk)	347.2	79	1177	29	40.58	4-92	–
M.A. Atherton (La)	405.4	89	1137	28	40.60	3-58	–
D.J.M. Kelleher (Kt)	283.5	63	981	24	40.87	4-82	–
P.M. Such (Lei)	244.2	70	616	15	41.06	3-28	–
I. Smith (Glam)	257.2	28	1091	26	41.96	3-48	–
K. Saxelby (Notts)	235.4	65	758	18	41.11	4-66	–
J.D. Fitton (La)	470.3	103	1475	35	41.14	5-53	2
C. Penn (Kt)	567	102	1792	41	43.70	4-57	–
H.R.J. Trump (Som)	416	93	1125	25	45.00	4-80	–
B.T.P. Donelan (Sx)	193	42	633	14	45.21	3-51	–
M. Frost (Sy)	185.2	36	679	15	45.26	5-40	1
I.G. Swallow (Yk)	225	56	728	16	45.50	4-58	–
R.A. Pyman (CU)	199.3	43	599	13	46.07	5-43	1
G. Miller (Ex)	191.4	60	464	10	46.40	2-9	–
V.J. Marks (Som)	843.5	246	2252	47	47.91	5-38	1
R.P. Davis (Kt)	716.4	199	2023	42	48.16	4-57	–
S.D. Fletcher (Yk)	230	37	772	15	51.46	4-88	–
E.D. Hester (OU)	157	29	572	11	52.00	4-100	–
I.A. Greig (Sy)	181	33	596	11	54.18	2-15	–
R.J. Bailey (Nrth)	139.1	19	552	10	55.20	3-70	–
S.T. Jefferies (Hts)	199.4	30	702	12	58.50	4-61	–
I.D.K. Salisbury (Sx)	277.4	61	932	15	62.13	3-75	–
C.S. Cowdrey (Kt)	227.3	32	798	12	66.50	4-33	–
R.J. Shastri (Glam)	282.2	66	780	11	70.90	3-77	–

Minor Counties

The first attempt to organise a competition between non-first-class counties was in 1888, when the Editor of Wisden determined to rationalise the position of several counties – notably Hampshire, Derbyshire and Somerset – which were on the fringes of the County Championship. In 1894 the main counties outside the County Championship were raised to first-class status and the following year, other interested counties set up the Minor Counties Cricket Association and from 1895 those counties have run their own Championship. For many years First-Class counties' Second Elevens competed in the Championship but all have now dropped out, Somerset and Lancashire being the last to participate.

Hertfordshire and Oxfordshire, having finished as leaders of the East and West Divisions of the Championship, met in a Championship title decider at Worcester and the title of Minor County Champions of 1989 was taken by Oxfordshire:
Hertfordshire 199–8 (55 overs) (N.R.C. Mac laurin 36, K.A. Arnold 3–38) lost to Oxfordshire 200–3 (53 overs) (S.N.V. Waterton 75 not out, T.A. Lester 46) by 7 wickets.

Hertfordshire also featured in the Holts Knock-Out Cup Final, this time meeting Cumberland at Lord's:
Hertfordshire 188–7 (55 overs) (A.J. Miller 59, D. Halliwell 4–44) lost to Cumberland 191–1 (39.1 overs) (S. Sharp 108 not out,) by 9 wickets.

This was the first time the Final had been staged at Lord's and the first time Cumberland had taken the trophy.

The leading run-scorer in the Championship was Waterton of Oxfordshire and previously of Kent and Northants. He was the only player to exceed 900 runs in the two–day matches. The best average was achieved by Archer from Staffordshire, but he had 6 not outs. The leading wicket-taker was the Ashby-de-la-Zouch cricketer, Taylor, who had previously appeared for Derbyshire.

The season was marred by some juggling to acquire points. The Hertfordshire against Northumberland match at the end of the season provided the former county with victory almost by arrangement, and Wiltshire scored 506 for seven in order to improve their 'average'. The Minor Counties Cricket Association will sooner or later have to face the fact that two-day matches rarely bring what the cricket supporter would describe as a genuine result. Three-day cricket must come.

ONE DAY AWAY MATCHES

The full scorecards of each of the Minor Counties' away matches will be found in the sections for the respective home teams.

Benson & Hedges Cup

Taunton: May 2
Somerset 205–7 (55 ov) beat Minor Counties 170–6 (55 ov) by 35 runs. Somerset 2pts, Minor Counties 0pts.

Derby: May 11
Minor Counties 149 (44.4 ov) lost to Derbys 150–3 (34 ov) by 7 wkts. Derbys 2pts, Minor Counties 0pts.

NatWest Bank Trophy

Cardiff: June 28
Glamorgan 318–4 (60 ov) (H. Morris 154*) beat Staffs 151 (53.4 ov) by 167 runs.

Canterbury: June 28
Kent 359–4 (60 ov) beat Dorset 161 (50.5 ov) by 198 runs.

Hove: June 28
Sussex 235–8 (60 ov) beat Berks 200–6 (60 ov) by 35 runs.

Edgbaston: June 28
Warwicks 270–4 (60 ov) beat Wilts 84 (30 ov) (A.A. Donald 5–12) by 186 runs.

BENSON AND HEDGES CUP

v YORKSHIRE (Jesmond)
April 25, 26
Lost by 5 wkts. Yorks 2pts, Minor Counties 0pts.

Minor Counties		
S.R. Atkinson	c Pickles b Byas	25
G.K. Brown	c Jarvis b Carrick	26
N.A. Folland	b Jarvis	61
P.R. Oliver	lbw b Jarvis	13
*S.G. Plumb	lbw b Carrick	1
S. Greenword	not out	29
†N. Priestley	b Jarvis	0
R.A. Evans	not out	2
I.E. Conn		
R.C. Green		
N.R. Taylor		
Extras	b 2, lb 10, w 10	22
Total (6 wkts, 55 ov)		179

52, 59, 87, 91, 173, 173

Jarvis	11	4	28	3
Pickles	11	3	24	0
Oldham	10	3	38	0
Booth	4	0	19	0
Carrick	11	1	33	2
Byas	8	0	25	1

Yorkshire		
D. Byas	c Priestley b Conn	22
A.A. Metcalfe	c Folland b Conn	18
R.J. Blakey	lbw b Greenwood	7
P.E. Robinson	b Conn	37
J.D. Love	c Priestley b Taylor	9
†D.L. Bairstow	not out	48
*P. Carrick	not out	18
C.S. Pickles		
P.W. Jarvis		
P.W. Booth		
S. Oldham		
Extras	b 4, lb 10, w 8	22
Total (5 wkts, 53.4 ov)		181

48, 49, 75, 106, 119

Green	5	0	17	0
Taylor	10.4	1	33	1
Conn	11	2	27	3
Evans	11	2	26	0
Greenwood	9	0	35	1
Plumb	7	2	29	0

Umpires: J.W. Holder and B. Hassan
Toss: Yorkshire. Gold: D.L. Bairstow.
61 off 88 balls by Folland gave some hope to the Minors, when they were forced to bat first on a green wicket. Heavy rain held up play on the first afternoon and Yorkshire looked in an uncomfortable position at 103–3 off 38 overs at stumps. Two wickets fell quickly on the second morning, but Bairstow hit out and gave Yorkshire victory.

Perhaps the most exciting moment of the domestic season was the final of the Benson and Hedges Cup. Eddie Hemmings (left) hit the last ball for four for victory, and he and partner Bruce French (right) are mobbed by fans.

Allsport/Adrian Murrell

BENSON AND HEDGES CUP

v NOTTINGHAMSHIRE (Oxton)

May 9

Lost by 5 wkts. Notts 2pts, Minor Counties 0pts

Minor Counties		
G.K. Brown	c Broad b Hemmings	29
C.J. Stockdale	c French b Pick	5
N.A. Folland	c French b Hemmings	19
P.R. Oliver	lbw b Cooper	9
*S.G. Plumb	b Pick	43
N.T. O'Brien	c Randall b Hemmings	17
D.A. Hale	c Broad b Evans	11
†A.R. Fothergill	b Stephenson	13
R.A. Evans	b Stephenson	2
I.E. Conn	lbw b Stephenson	0
N.R Taylor	not out	1
Extras	lb 15, w 7, nb 1	23
Total (52.2 ov)		172

26, 58, 72, 84, 134, 144, 158, 167, 167

Stephenson	9.2	3	19	3
Cooper	10	2	20	1
Pick	11	1	30	2
Evans	11	0	52	1
Hemmings	11	2	36	3

Nottinghamshire		
*R.T. Robinson	c Fothergill b Taylor	6
B.C. Broad	b O'Brien	31
P.R. Pollard	b O'Brien	0
M. Newell	c Fothergill b Taylor	30
D.W. Randall	b Hale	52
F.D. Stephenson	not out	33
†B.N. French	not out	4
K.P. Evans		
E.E. Hemmings		
K.E. Cooper		
R.A. Pick		
Extras	b 3, lb 11, w 2, nb 3	19
Total (5 wkts, 47.2 ov)		175

27, 49, 55, 126, 165

Taylor	11	1	35	2
Hale	7.2	1	37	1
Evans	11	3	21	0
O'Brien	8	1	32	2
Conn	7	0	23	0
Plumb	2	0	5	0
Brown	1	0	8	0

Umpires: H.D. Bird and B. Leadbeater
Toss: Minor Counties. Gold: D.W. Randall
The Minor Counties put up a solid display, but were unable to cope with the batting of Randall, who came in with Notts 55 for 3 and aided by Stephenson had no problem reaching the 173 required.

MINOR COUNTIES NATWEST BANK TROPHY FIRST ROUND

CAMBRIDGESHIRE v WORCESTERSHIRE (March)

June 28.

Worcs won by 9 wkts

Cambridgeshire		
I.S. Lawrence	b Botham	74
*N.T. Gadsby	retired hurt	8
P.J. Dicks	lbw b Illingworth	22
†P.A. Redfarn	c Rhodes b Weston	3
N.J. Adams	b Botham	50
D.P. Norman	not out	13
D.S. Hoffman	not out	17
M.G. Stephenson		
D.C. Collard		
A.P.S. Wykes		
C.R.F. Green		
Extras	b 5, lb 4, w 6	15
Total (4 wkts, 60 ov)		202

51, 69, 167, 178

Radford	11	2	33	0
Lampitt	8	1	24	0
Botham	11	1	44	2
Illingworth	12	2	22	1
Weston	11	0	32	1
O'Shaughnessy	4	0	14	0
Hick	3	0	24	0

Worcestershire		
T.S. Curtis	not out	91
M.J. Weston	c Redfarn b Collard	23
G.A. Hick	not out	86
D.B. d'Oliveira		
*P.A. Neale		
I.T. Botham		
†S.J. Rhodes		
N.V. Radford		
R.K. Illingworth		
S.R. Lampitt		
S.J. O'Shaughnessy		
Extras	b 2, lb 4	6
Total (1 wkt, 48.1 ov)		206

36

Hoffman	11	1	61	0
Collard	12	0	29	1
Stephenson	7	0	34	0
Wykes	6.1	0	28	0
Green	10	0	35	0
Adams	2	0	13	0

Umpires: J.C. Balderstone and D.S. Thompsett
Toss: Worcestershire. MofM: I.S. Lawrence
Lawrence played an excellent innings to both hold the side together and earn himself the Man of the Match Award, but the Worcester batsmen proved much too good for the Minors bowling and the first-class side had the game well in hand.

CHESHIRE v HAMPSHIRE (Boughton Hall, Chester)

June 28

Hants won by 147 runs

Hampshire		
V.P. Terry	c Wood b Fox	99
C.L. Smith	b Fox	159
D.R. Turner	not out	22
*M.C.J. Nicholas	not out	14
K.D. James		
R.J. Scott		
M.D. Marshall		
N.G. Cowley		
P.J. Bakker		
†R.J. Parks		
C.A. Connor		
Extras	b 1, lb 6, w 5	12
Total (2 wkts, 60 ov)		306

228, 289

Fox	12	2	48	2
Dyson	8	0	52	0
Wood	12	1	39	0
J.S. Hitchmough	7	0	28	0
J.F.M. O'Brien	9	0	43	0
N.T. O'Brien	12	0	89	0

Cheshire		
B. Wood	c Parks b Marshall	3
D.W. Varey	c Parks b Marshall	4
I. Cockbain	c Cowley b Connor	16
J.J. Hitchmough	c Parks b James	10
S.T. Crawley	c Parks b Connor	38
*N.T. O'Brien	c Turner b James	22
J.S. Hitchmough	b Marshall	34
†N. Smith	run out	0
A. Fox	run out	11
S. Dyson	b Marshall	0
J.F.M. O'Brien	not out	13
Extras	b 1, lb 2, nb 5	8
Total (47.1 ov)		159

6, 15, 34, 60, 92, 100, 100, 128, 128

Bakker	8	2	13	0
Marshall	10.1	1	40	4
Connor	12	3	38	2
James	8	1	26	2
Cowley	9	0	39	0

Umpires: B. Leadbeater and T.G. Wilson
Toss: Hampshire. MofM: C.L. Smith
Rain washed out the first day, but on the second Hampshire swept aside their opponents; they began by creating a new record first wicket stand for the competition and Marshall ended any remote hope Cheshire had of scoring the necessary runs.

FINAL TABLES

Eastern Division

		Outright		1st inns		Points
	P	W	L	W	L	
Hertfordshire	9	4	0	1	4	47
Norfolk	9	3	1	3	2	44
Suffolk	9	3	1	3	2	41
Staffordshire	9	2	0	6	1	39
Durham	9	1	0	4	4	26
Lincolnshire	9	1	4	3	1	26
Cambridgeshire	9	1	2	2	4	26
Bedfordshire	9	1	5	1	2	24
Cumberland	9	0	3	5	1	22
Northumberland	9	1	1	0	7	20

Western Division

	P	W	L	W	L	Points
Oxfordshire	9	4	0	4	1	53
Berkshire	9	4	2	1	2	51
Dorset	9	4	1	2	2	51
Buckinghamshire	9	4	1	2	2	48
Shropshire	9	3	1	3	2	41
Devon	9	2	4	3	0	37
Wiltshire	9	1	1	3	4	26
Cheshire	9	1	4	2	2	18
Wales	9	1	6	1	1	17
Cornwall	9	0	4	0	5	11

Leading Averages

Batting	I	NO	R	HS	Avge
N.J. Archer (Staffs)	12	6	497	107*	82.83
K.N. Foyle (Wiltshire)	12	4	617	183	77.13
J. Foster (Shropshire)	8	3	369	130*	73.80
J. Abrahams (Shropshire)	16	4	796	103*	66.33
C. Gladwin (Suffolk)	8	3	325	79*	65.00
N.R. Gaywood (Devon)	10	0	632	126	63.20
T.A. Lester (Oxfords)	14	5	553	83	61.44
M.J. Roberts (Bucks)	16	2	818	193*	58.43
I. Cockbain (Cheshire)	16	3	743	131*	57.15
S.N.V. Waterton (Oxfords)	18	2	914	146*	57.13
M.S.A. McEvoy (Suffolk)	16	1	851	154	56.73
N.A. Riddell (Durham)	14	5	510	65*	56.67
N.A. Folland (Devon)	16	4	666	106*	55.50
M.E Younger (Northumberland)	11	5	327	74*	54.50
G.E. Loveday (Berkshire)	17	2	806	143	53.73

Bowling	O	M	R	Wkts	Avge
D.R. Thomas (Norfolk)	80	16	221	20	11.05
D. Cork (Staffs)	96.4	13	309	23	13.43
A.J. Mack (Norfolk)	224.1	64	578	38	15.21
S. Greensword (Durham)	117.1	22	362	23	15.74
M.G. Stear (Berkshire)	170.5	39	446	25	17.84
B.W. Reidy (Cumberland)	167.2	40	481	26	18.50
G.R. Black (Bucks)	121.3	26	391	20	19.55
J.P. Taylor (Staffs)	326.4	77	900	46	19.57
R.A. Evans (Oxfords)	157	45	395	20	19.75
R. Kingshott (Norfolk)	240.4	63	702	35	20.06

MINOR COUNTIES NATWEST BANK TROPHY FIRST ROUND

CUMBERLAND v LANCASHIRE (Kendal)
June 28, 29
Lancs won by 4wkts

Cumberland		
S. Sharp	lbw b DeFreitas	0
C. Stockdale	c Fowler b Wasim Akram	17
K. Hayes	b DeFreitas	0
B. Reidy	lbw b Allott	0
G. Clarke	lbw b DeFreitas	0
J.R. Moyes	lbw b Allott	1
S. Dutton	b Watkinson	15
M.D. Woods	b DeFreitas	11
S. Wall	b Wasim Akram	1
D. Halliwell	not out	25
R. Ellwood	b DeFreitas	0
Extras	lb 7, w 2, nb 5	14
Total (44.5 ov)		84

3, 4, 5, 6, 9, 42, 42, 44, 82

De Freitas	10.5	3	13	5
Allott	12	7	7	2
Watkinson	8	1	26	1
Wasim Akram	8	4	20	2
Simmons	6	3	11	0

Lancashire		
G.D. Mendis	b Wall	1
G. Fowler	c Dutton b Halliwell	0
†W.K. Hegg	c and b Reidy	26
N.H. Fairbrother	c Moyes b Wall	7
T.E. Jesty	b Reidy	13
M.W. Watkinson	not out	16
Wasim Akram	lbw b Wall	19
*D.P. Hughes	not out	0
P.A.J. DeFreitas		
P.J.W. Allott		
J. Simmons		
Extras	lb 2, nb 2	4
Total (6 wkts, 33.4 ov)		86

1, 10, 23, 50, 51, 82

Halliwell	8	3	17	1
Wall	9	3	24	3
Reidy	10.4	4	27	2
Wood	6	3	16	0

Umpires: B.J. Meyer and D.B. Harrison
Toss: Lancashire. MofM: P.A.J. DeFreitas
Arranged for Carlisle, this game was moved to Kendal due to the condition of the former wicket. The home side were overwhelmed by DeFreitas and the Lancashire batsmen had an easy task.

DURHAM v MIDDLESEX (Darlington)
June 28
Middlesex won by 54 runs

Middlesex		
D.L. Haynes	lbw b Conn	83
M.A. Roseberry	lbw b Johnston	17
*M.W. Gatting	b Trotter	37
R.O. Butcher	run out	3
N.R. Ramprakash	c Fothergill b Trotter	1
†P.R. Downton	not out	31
A.R.C. Fraser	c Trotter b Johnston	19
S. P. Hughes	b Simmons	11
R. Ellcock	not out	0
J.E. Emburey		
N.G. Cowans		
Extras	b3, lb 3, w 5, nb 2	13
Total (7 wkts, 60 ov)		215

26, 119, 129, 131, 163, 192, 215

Johnson	12	4	33	2
Simmons	12	2	43	1
Conn	12	1	47	1
Greensword	12	2	26	0
Trotter	12	0	60	2

Durham		
G. Brown	c Downton b Cowans	24
P. Simmons	c Downton b Hughes	33
P. Burn	c Gatting b Hughes	43
J. Glendenen	c Ellcock b Cowans	6
A.S. Pastel	c Downton b Fraser	1
*N.A. Riddell	run out	11
S. Greensword	c Ramprakash b Hughes	9
†A. Fothergill	not out	12
I. Conn	c Gatting b Ellcock	3
K. Trotter	c Ramprakash b Ellcock	4
J. Johnston	b Hughes	0
Extras	b 4, lb 7, w 3, nb 1	15
Total (56.2 ov)		161

46, 83, 100, 101, 130, 138, 140, 146, 150

Fraser	12	2	45	1
Cowans	12	3	29	2
Hughes	10.2	2	20	4
Ellcock	12	3	38	2
Emburey	10	5	18	0

Umpires: D.C. Oslear and J. van Geloven
Toss: Durham. MofM: D.L. Haynes
Some good bowling by Greensword and Johnston kept all but Haynes under control after Middlesex decided to bat first. Durham made a sound start in reply but the runs never came fast enough to challenge the first-class county's total.

NORTHUMBERLAND v SURREY (Jesmond)
June 28, 29
Surrey won by 68 runs

Surrey		
C.S. Clinton	b Dalby	40
D.J. Bicknell	b Pont	5
†A.J. Stewart	b Dalby	55
G.P. Thorpe	c Corby b O'Donnell	74
D.M. Ward	c Tiffin b Dalby	97
*I.A. Greig	not out	23
K.T. Medlycott	not out	7
M.A. Feltham		
C.K. Bullen		
N.P. Bicknell		
A.J. Murphy		
Extras	b 1, lb 7, w 4	12
Total (5 wkts, 60 ov)		313

32, 100, 107, 277, 283

O'Donnell	12	4	33	1
Pont	10	0	62	1
Purvis	4	1	22	0
Graham	12	1	38	0
Dalby	10	1	87	3
Dutton	4	0	22	0
Younger	8	1	41	0

Northumberland		
K. Pearson	c Ward b M.P. Bicknell	42
P.G. Cormack	c and b Bullen	36
S.P. O'Donnell	c Thorpe b Feltham	44
I.L. Pont	b M.P. Bicknell	0
*M.E. Younger	c Bullen b Murphy	27
A. Dalby	lbw b Feltham	6
P.N.S. Dutton	not out	26
M.S. Tiffin	not out	49
†K. Corby		
J.R. Purvis		
P.C. Graham		
Extras	b 8, lb 6, w 1	15
Total (6 wkts, 60 ov)		245

67, 107, 115, 158, 166, 166

Murphy	12	1	49	1
M.P. Bicknell	9	2	24	2
Greig	12	0	46	0
Feltham	11	0	61	2
Bullen	12	0	31	1
Medlycott	2	0	8	0
Thorpe	2	0	12	0

Umpires: H.J. Rhodes and R.A. White
Toss: Northmberland. MofM: D.M. Ward
No play was possible on the first day, but on the second Surrey reached their highest one-day total, with 97 runs coming from the last 10 overs.

PLAYERS

Stephen Robert ATKINSON *b* 8.12.1952 Birtley, Durham; opening right-hand batsman; debut for Durham 1972; has represented Minor Counties since 1978

Gary Kevin BROWN *b* 16.6.1965 Welling, Kent; opening right-hand batsman; debut for Durham 1988; previously appeared for Middlesex

Ian Edward CONN *b* 16.4.1962 Sunderland; right-arm medium fast bowler; right-hand batsman; debut for Durham in 1982

Rupert Alfred EVANS *b* 24.2.1954 Kingston, Jamaica; off-break bowler; right-hand batsman; debut for Oxfordshire in 1973

Nicholas Arthur FOLLAND *b* 17.9.1963 Bristol; left-hand batsman; debut for Devon in 1981

Andrew Robert FOTHERGILL *b* 10.2.1962 Newcastle-on-Tyne; wicketkeeper; right-hand batsman; debut for Durham in 1982

Russell Christopher GREEN *b* 10.7.1959 St Albans; right-arm fast medium bowler: right-hand batsman; debut for Suffolk in 1982; has represented Minor Counties since 1987

Stephen GREENSWORD *b* 6.9.1943 Gateshead; right-hand batsman; right-arm medium pace bowler; debut for Durham in 1970; played for Leics 1963–66; has represented Minor Counties since 1973

David Andrew HALE *b* 20.3.1966 Oxford; right-hand batsman; right-arm fast-medium bowler; debut for Oxfordshire in 1984

Neil Terence O'BRIEN *b* 9.3.1945 Heaton Moor; right-hand batsman; slow left-arm bowler; debut for Cheshire in 1970; has represented Minor Counties since 1977

Philip Robert OLIVER *b* 9.5.1956 West Bromwich; right-hand batsman; off-break bowler; debut for Staffordshire in 1987; originally played for Shropshire and then Warwickshire 1975–82.

Stephen George PLUMB *b* 17.1.1954 Wimbush, Essex; right hand batsman; off-break bowler; debut for Norfolk in 1978; previously appeared for Essex 1975–77; represented Minor Counties since 1980; captain in 1989

Neil PRIESTLEY *b* 23.6.1961 Blyborough; left-hand batsman; wicketkeeper; debut for Lincs in 1983; represented Minor Counties since 1986

Christopher James STOCKDALE *b* 15.5.1965 Carlisle; right-hand batsman; right-arm medium pace bowler; debut for Cumberland in 1981

Neil Raymond TAYLOR *b* 9.2.1964 Boscombe; right-arm medium pace bowler; right-hand batsman; debut for Dorset in 1987

Rev. Andrew Richard WINGFIELD-DIGBY *b* 25.7.1950 Sherborne; right-arm medium pace bowler; left-hand batsman; debut for Dorset in 1972; Oxford Univ Blue

David Capel excelled with the bat and took 3–54 in Northants NatWest Bank Trophy win over Suffolk.

Allsport/Adrian Murrell

MINOR COUNTIES NATWEST BANK TROPHY FIRST ROUND

OXFORDSHIRE v GLOUCESTERSHIRE (Christ Church, Oxford)

June 28

Gloucestershire won by 43 runs

Gloucestershire		
I.P. Butcher	c Garner b Hartley	71
A.W. Stovold	c Hale b Curtis	49
J.W. Lloyds	c Waterton b Hartley	28
*C.W.J. Athey	not out	56
K.M. Curran	not out	45
P. Bainbridge		
M.W. Alleyne		
†R.C. Russell		
M.W. Pooley		
V.S. Greene		
K.B.S. Jarvis		
Extras	b 2, lb 13, w 5	20
Total (3 wkts, 60 ov)		269

101, 144, 184

Arnold	12	1	58	0
Hale	12	1	57	0
Savin	12	1	48	0
Hartley	12	1	48	2
Curtis	12	0	43	1

Oxfordshire		
G.C. Ford	lbw b Jarvis	5
†S.N.V. Waterton	c Athey b Jarvis	92
*P.J. Garner	c Athey b Jarvis	1
T.A. Lester	c Athey b Jarvis	19
D.A.J. Wise	b Greene	0
P.M. Jobson	lbw b Bainbridge	1
J. Hartley	c Russell b Alleyne	46
G.P. Savin	b Bainbridge	8
D.A. Hale	b Jarvis	33
K.A. Arnold	b Greene	1
I.J. Curtis	not out	2
Extras	lb 12, w 5, nb 1	18
Total (59.4 ov)		226

5, 11, 39, 40, 62, 123, 136, 219, 224

Greene	12	2	43	2
Jarvis	10.4	0	32	5
Pooley	12	2	35	0
Bainbridge	12	0	46	2
Alleyne	10	2	43	1
Lloyds	3	0	15	0

Umpires: D.J. Constant and V.A Holder
Toss: Oxfordshire. MofM: S.N.V. Waterton

Oxfordshire's bowlers kept some control over the visitors' innings until Athey and Curran added 85 in the final 10 overs, Curran's 45 came off 28 balls. Waterton batted in excellent style, but his only support came from Hartley and Hale; the latter helped to add 83 for the 8th wicket, but the cause was already lost by then.

SHROPSHIRE v LEICESTERSHIRE (Telford)

June 28

Lost by 6 wkts

Shropshire		
J. Foster	c Whitticase b Agnew	4
J.B.R. Jones	b Agnew	3
J.S. Johnson	c Whitticase b Taylor	2
J. Abrahams	c Parsons b Willey	79
M.R. Davies	b Benjamin	89
A. Johnson	run out	12
P.B. Wormald	not out	3
D.J. Ashley	b Benjamin	4
A.S. Barnard		
G. Edmunds		
J.S. Roberts		
Extras	lb 16, w 4, nb 4	24
Total (7 wkts, 60 ov)		220

8, 11, 21, 174, 207, 215, 220

Agnew	12	2	30	2
Benjamin	12	3	39	2
Parsons	12	1	54	0
Taylor	12	0	40	1
Willey	12	1	41	1

Leicestershire		
N.E. Briers	c and b Wormald	15
T.J. Boon	c J.S. Johnson b Edmunds	24
*D.I. Gower	not out	101
P. Willey	c and b Roberts	43
J.J. Whitaker	c A. Johnson b Barnard	6
L. Potter	not out	4
†P. Whitticase		
G.J. Parsons		
W.K.M. Benjamin		
J.P. Agnew		
L.B. Taylor		
Extras	b 4, lb 9, w 14, nb 1	28
Total (4 wkts, 54.2 ov)		221

24, 77, 181, 202

Roberts	12	2	52	1
Wormald	9.2	0	30	1
Edmunds	12	0	41	1
Barnard	12	2	41	1
Abrahams	9	0	44	0

Umpires: P.J. Eele and J.H. Hampshire
Toss: Leicestershire. MofM: M.R. Davies

On an easy wicket, Abrahams and Davies added 153 for the 4th wicket and this provided Shropshire with a fair total. With Gower in brilliant form however, Leicestershire found little difficulty in overcoming the Minors' attack and the match was completed with 34 balls to spare.

SUFFOLK v NORTHAMPTONSHIRE (Bury St Edmunds)

June 28, 29

Lost by 32 runs

Northamptonshire		
G. Cook	b Wright	4
W. Larkins	b Wright	1
R.J. Bailey	b Wright	0
*A.J. Lamb	c Brown b Robinson	103
D.J. Capel	not out	92
N.A. Feltham	run out	23
†D.J. Ripley	not out	4
J.G. Thomas		
N.G.B. Cook		
C.E.L. Ambrose		
M.A. Robinson		
Extras	lb 14, w 13, nb 2	29
Total (5 wkts, 60 ov)		256

2, 2, 16, 183, 252

Green	12	2	38	0
Wright	8	0	29	3
Hayes	6	0	20	0
Bailey	12	1	36	0
Caley	12	0	58	0
Robinson	10	0	61	1

Suffolk		
M.S.A. McEvoy	lbw b Thomas	61
J.W. Edrich	b Capel	7
†A.D. Brown	b Capel	51
S.J. Halliday	c G.Cook b Robinson	1
S.M. Clements	c Capel b N.G.B. Cook	7
P.J. Caley	b Ambrose	22
H.J.W. Wright	b Capel	8
R.J. Robinson	not out	40
P.J. Hayes	c Ripley b Thomas	2
R.C. Green	b Ambrose	1
*M.D. Bailey	b Ambrose	1
Extras	b 1, lb 9, w 5, nb 8	23
Total (59.5 ov)		224

23, 125, 126, 137, 142, 160, 204, 221, 222

Ambrose	11.5	1	31	3
Robinson	12	2	30	1
N.G.B. Cook	11	2	49	1
Capel	12	1	54	3
Larkins	6	0	26	0
Thomas	7	0	24	2

Umpires J.W. Holder and R.H. Duckett
Toss: Northamptonshire. MofM: D.J. Capel

On a rain-affected first day, Wright began by reducing Northants to 16 for 3. Lamb and Capel then took charge and fatally for Suffolk, Lamb was dropped on 30. At the close Suffolk were 133–3 off 42 overs. They were unable to score the necessary 124 on the second day.

The Winter Season 1988–89

England were due to tour India in 1988–89. The tour was cancelled, problems having arisen after the appointment as captain of the touring party of Graham Gooch, who captained England in the last Test of the 1988 season (he was the last of four captains England used during the summer against the West Indies).

Two of the other captains, Mike Gatting and Chris Cowdrey, declared themselves unavailable for the tour. Gatting had been sacked as captain for 'irresponsible behaviour' in inviting a girl back to his room for a drink during the first Test at Edgbaston. After his previous winter's experiences with Shakoor Rana, the Pakistani umpire with whom he had a more or less public row, and a TCCB investigation into the remarks he made about it in a subsequent book (the question was whether he was in breach of contract in writing about it), Gatting probably decided he had had enough of playing for England for the time being.

Chris Cowdrey had been made captain for the fourth Test, but had withdrawn from the fifth with a bruised foot. He was not even picked for the Test against Sri Lanka. Cowdrey was angry with his treatment by the England management, whom he claimed had not bothered to keep him in touch with the Test squad, as promised, but had given him the impression that he was surplus to requirements. Cowdrey complained of his treatment in a newspaper, and declared himself unavailable for the tour to India.

The party to tour under Gooch was announced as follows: J.E. Emburey (vice-captain), R.J. Bailey, K.J. Barnett, J.H. Childs, G.R. Dilley, N.A. Foster, D.I. Gower, E.E. Hemmings, A.J. Lamb, D.V. Lawrence, P.J. Newport, S.J. Rhodes, R.T. Robinson, R.C. Russell, R.A. Smith.

Some of these players had connections with South Africa including Gooch, who withdrew from a winter contract with Western Province to take the job. Gooch was asked if he would have withdrawn had he been selected to tour India as a player only, rather than as captian, and he implied that he would not. This immediately upset the Indian authorities, and the Minister of Sport, Mrs Margaret Alva, suggested that Gooch should not be allowed into the country. The Indian Foreign Ministry confirmed that no player in the party having sporting links with South Africa, or likely to have them, would be allowed to enter the country. The TCCB, of course, would not alter the party to suit the Indian authorities and, although the matter dragged on, there was never any possibility of the tour taking place, and it was officially cancelled on 7 October 1988.

A planned tour of Sri Lanka had earlier been cancelled on the grounds of security (the last tour there, by New Zealand in 1986–87, had ended after the first Test because of rioting).

Without a tour, the England players were paid a substantial proportion of the £12,000 fee and asked to hold themselves in preparation for a substitute tour if one could be arranged. It was later announced that the party picked for India would make a seven-week tour of New Zealand, and two Tests, four matches against the district sides and a one-day international series involving also Pakistan, were arranged. However Pakistan withdrew, and the New Zealand Cricket Council anticipated that a tour would not be viable if England alone came, so this tour was also cancelled. The England team therefore did not play in the winter season at all.

Benson and Hedges World Series Cup

The Benson and Hedges World Series Cup was competed for in 1988–89 by Australia, West Indies and Pakistan, who were to tour New Zealand.

Each team played each of the others four times in a league table to determine two finalists for a three-leg play-off: 15 matches in all. After all this there was much dissatisfaction at the final result, which was rain-affected.

West Indies beat Australia in the first two matches they played, while Australia won the second two. Pakistan beat Australia and West Indies once each. At one stage West Indies were clear, having won their first five matches, while Australia and Pakistan had won two matches each, but Australia won their last four and West Indies lost their last three so that Australia and West Indies finished level at the top of the table.

Haynes (2) and Geoff Marsh were the only centurions. The men of the match in the 12 league games were: Desmond Haynes (three times), Merv Hughes, Curtly Ambrose, Ian Bishop, Aamer Malik, Steve Waugh, Imran Khan, Terry Alderman, Geoff Marsh and Peter Taylor.

The final table was:

	P	W	L	Run Rate	Points
West Indies	8	5	3	4.50	10
Australia	8	5	3	4.48	10
Pakistan	8	2	6	4.24	4

In the first final at Melbourne, Australia decided to bat on winning the toss. Before 73,000 spectators, Border made 78, but Ambrose (five for 26) caused a stutter at the end and the 50 overs yielded 204 for nine. West Indies began badly, but the middle and lower order were mounting a good attack on the target when Marshall was given run out and argued with the umpire. He needed an escort to the dressing room, but TV replays confirmed that keeper Healy had dropped the ball before breaking the wicket. West Indies failed to get the nine needed in Hughes' last over, and at 202 for nine were defeated by two runs.

At Sydney, on a spinning wicket, West Indies decided to bat and Haynes and Greenidge got them off to a good start, despite Haynes being ill by the pitch. West Indies, with four men passing 50, hit a huge 277 for nine. Australia began well but there were run-outs in the chase for runs, and the innings closed after only 40 overs and 185 all out. Brawling on the Hill led to 24 arrests and renewed calls for the famous spectator area to be replaced by a stand. It was decided that a restriction on alcohol and video surveillance would be introduced for the following season.

The deciding match was also at Sydney, where 31,900 began as the attendance, but rain spoiled the match. Australia won the toss and batted in a gloomy light. At 83 for two heavy rain stopped play for two hours, and the match was reduced to one of 38 overs per side. Australia made an assault on the bowling on resuming, and reached 226 for four, with Dean Jones smashing 93 not out from 82 balls, adding 74 in the last seven overs with Steve Waugh. West Indies lost two wickets with the score at four, but Haynes and Richards had rushed to 48 for two from only 6.4 overs when rain again stopped play, this time for 83 minutes. It was a day/night match, and calculations were made to assess West Indies' new target. West Indies' innings was now reduced to 18 overs, and their target, based on Australia's rate of 6.95 per over, was 108 runs. When play resumed at 9.25, therefore, they needed only 61 from an outstanding 11.2 overs. Richards and Haynes knocked them off in 6.4 overs in half-an-hour. It was an unsatisfactory end. So far as spectators went, the 15 one-day internationals had attracted nearly half as many again as the 24 days of the five Tests.

Sharjah Cup

The Sharjah Cup, consisting of a one-day international tournament, was contested by only two countries, Pakistan and Sri Lanka, in 1988–89. Pakistan beat Sri Lanka in both games. Put in in the first, they scored 237 for eight in 50 overs, and then dismissed Sri Lanka for 207. Shoaib Mohammad with 76 was man of the match. Sri Lanka decided to bat in the second match, making 244 for eight in 50 overs, but Pakistan won comfortably by seven wickets, Salim Malik's 100 not out taking the award.

Champion's Trophy

India, Pakistan and West Indies took part in the Champions' Trophy, a one-day tournament, at Sharjah in October 1988.

In the first match, India beat West Indies, after being put in. They made 238 for five in 50 overs, Srikkanth scoring 112 and taking the man of the match award. Vengsarkar made 76 not out. West Indies were bowled out for 215, Sanjeet Sharma taking five for 26 and Hirwani four for 50. Srikkanth's five sixes included three in succession off Harper.

In the second match, West Indies put Pakistan in. Pakistan did even better than India, reaching 294 for six in 50 overs, Javed top-scoring with 79. West Indies reached only 210 for five, Greenidge getting 102 not out. Wasim Akram's three for 37 won the man of the match award.

Pakistan and India met for the first place in the final. India put Pakistan in, and Pakistan made 246 being all out after one ball of the final over. Salim Malik's 101 won the match award. India could reach only 212 for eight.

India now had to play West Indies again to determine Pakistan's final opponents. India won the toss and decided to bat, but could reach only 169 for seven in the 50 overs. Greenidge (77 not out) and Haynes (85), the Man of the Match, put on 165 for the first wicket, and West Indies won by eight wickets.

Pakistan put West Indies in in the final, and West Indies made 235 for six in 50 overs. Pakistan were all out in the last over for 224. Ambrose won the match award with four for 29. Umpire Dickie Bird collapsed with dehydration during the final, and David Shepherd officiated at both ends, a substitute standing at square leg. The series was for the benefit of Indian and Pakistani players, principally for Mohsin Khan and R.J. Shastri, and secondarily for Munir Malik and B.S. Chandrasekhar. West Indies won a peculiar tournament in which they lost two games and won two, while Pakistan won two and lost one.

Asia Cup

An Asia Cup consisting of one-day internationals of 45 overs per side was played in October and November 1988 in Bangladesh. The host country, plus India, Pakistan and Sri Lanka, played each other on a league basis, the top two meeting in the final.

Shoaib Mohammad, who scored two centuries in two Test innings for Pakistan in New Zealand.

Allsport/Adrian Murrell

Sri Lanka beat all three rivals, and Bangladesh lost all three games. The vital game was thus Pakistan versus India, which India won by four wickets. India thus played Sri Lanka in the final, and Sri Lanka were put in. Sri Lanka made 176 in 43.2 overs, and India won the cup by scoring 180 for four in 37.1 overs.

The 'men of the matches' were: R.S. Mahamana (Sri Lanka), N.S. Sidhu (India), P.A. De Silva (Sri Lanka), Moin-ul-Atiq (Pakistan), Arshad Ayub (India), D.S.B.P. Kuruppu (Sri Lanka), and, in the final, N.S. Sidhu (India).

WINTER TEST SERIES

Pakistan v Australia

Australia toured Pakistan, playing three Tests and three other first-class games. Because of flooding in Gujranwala and rioting in Karachi, only one one-day game was possible, won by Pakistan.

The first Test in Karachi, where Pakistan have never been beaten, was dominated by Javed Miandad and umpiring disputes. Imran had declined to play in the 'off-season' series – the first Test started in September – and Javed led a Pakistan side which included three front-line spinners on a wicket suited to them. He won the toss and batted and, although two men were out for 21, he himself added 196 with Shoaib Mohammad, going on to 211 himself. It was his fifth Test double-century, each being made against a different country, the West Indies being the odd one out. Pakistan declared on the third morning at 469 for nine.

Pakistan soon had the spinners operating, and Australia were rapidly in difficulties. The first big umpiring dissent came when Waugh was given lbw for a duck – he and Graeme Wood at the non-striker's end registered amazement and disgust. Wood was playing after a four-year gap, and when he was dismissed he kicked a Pakistani helmet, which had been left behind the wicket keeper, on his way to the pavilion.

Australia reached 165, the last four wickets accounting for over 100, and followed on, where they subsided even quicker, being out for 116 within 90 minutes of the start on the fifth day. The Australians immediately after the game protested strongly over the umpiring, and the team voted to call off the tour (they later changed their minds). The Australian coach, Bobby Simpson, pointed out the six lbw decisions against Australia to one against Pakistan, while captain Border claimed a conspiracy and said Australia were never in with a chance.

Pakistan again won the toss at Faisalabad, and again batted. The side was again packed with spin, but the spinners were less effective and a more even match ensued. Dodemaide soon had the Australians on top, with Pakistan 25 for four, but Javed again halted the rout, and Ijaz Ahmed's century hoisted a reasonable total of 316. Australia began better but, even so, required a gritty 119 not out from Allan Border on the third day to manage 321, a first-innings lead of five. Both Pakistan openers fell at 64, but Javed (107) and Shoaib, who was suffering with what was thought to be appendicitis, added 172. Although four wickets fell for 10 runs at the start of the final day, Salim scored 66 not out and the match was drawn after a token declaration.

Border won the toss in Lahore, and batted. Australia made slow but steady progress, ending the first day at 175 for three. Border took his time over his 75, and Australia took nearly all of two days to make 340. A thunderstorm which washed out the third afternoon seemed to have ruled out any chance of their winning, but Pakistan collapsed on the fourth morning – beginning the day at 165 for three they were all out for 233. However during this period Australian fast bowler Bruce Reid retired with muscle spasms in his back, an injury which was to cost him his place on the forthcoming tour of England. Australia declared after three overs on the last morning had added 29 runs, Pakistan being set the rest of the day (it turned out to be 84 overs) to score 269 to win. Pakistan made no attempt to win – a policy which nearly led to defeat. At 131 for seven, and 16 overs left, Australia appeared to have a good chance to level the series, but Iqbal Qasim and Tauseef Ahmed held out.

Although there were no more unseemly incidents after the first Test, the Australians were highly critical of the umpiring in Pakistan.

In the only one-day international which could be played, Pakistan put Australia in at Lahore, and the visitors made 229 for eight in their 45 overs, Marsh making 89. In reply, Pakistan made 229 for seven, and won the match on the grounds of having lost fewer wickets. Abdul Qadir had the presence of mind to block the last ball, not attempting to score from it. Mudassar Nazar, 76 and two for 40, was man of the match. The match profits were donated to flood relief – floods having prevented the scheduled match at Gujranwala.

India v New Zealand

New Zealand, under the captaincy of John Wright, toured India and played three Tests, three other first-class matches, and five one-day internationals, one of which was abandoned due to flooding.

The first Test was at Bangalore, where several New Zealand players were suffering from a virus infection which made them sick and feverish. Five substitutes took the field for India's second innings, among them former skipper Jeremy Coney, recruited from the press box.

India won the toss and batted. Richard Hadlee began the tour with 373 Test wickets, at which total he had stood level with Ian Botham in the all-time list since the previous season. With Botham on the sidelines with injuries, Hadlee had to wait only until his third over to overtake his rival, having Arun Lal caught by Test debutant seamer Chris Kuggeleijn. Navjot Sidhu (116), recalled after five years, and skipper Vengsarkar (75) rescued India from 10 for two and helped them reach 384 for nine declared.

New Zealand struggled to 145 for six at the close of the third day, and then during the rest day the fever struck Hadlee, not out overnight, who collapsed. But when New Zealand lost their eighth and ninth wickets with two runs still needed to save the follow-on, he was forced to hobble to the wicket to edge the necessary boundary. India rattled up 141 for one declared in 28 overs, setting New Zealand 337 to win. The openers put on 77, but all the wickets fell for another 87, and India won easily.

The New Zealanders had recovered for the second Test at Bombay a week later. Wright won the toss and batted, but the spinners soon had them in trouble. They reached 236, but a record ninth-wicket stand for New Zealand against India of 76 by John Bracewell and Daniel Morrison was needed. Srikkanth (94) and Vengsarkar (25) put on 100 for India's third wicket, but Hadlee's six for 49 ensured they did not overtake the New Zealand total. They finished two behind. Vengsarkar was the seventh player to pass 100 Tests (Viv Richards achieved the feat six days earlier, playing in Australia).

New Zealand collapsed from 149 for two to 181 for eight in the second innings, but again Bracewell came to the rescue, this time helped by Ian Smith. A total of 279 set India 282 to win with plenty of time to score them. But Srikkanth was lbw to Hadlee's first ball, offering no stroke, and India never recovered. Bracewell completed a splendid match with six for 51 and Hadlee took ten wickets in a Test for the ninth time, twice more than anybody else. R.C. Patel, making his debut for India, took nought for 14 and nought for 37, and scored 0 and 0, but he took one catch.

In the third Test at Hyderabad, the first there for 19 years, Wright again won the toss and batted. New Zealand were in trouble against Ayub at 91 for six, but Greatbatch (90 not out) and Smith (79) added 139. New Zealand's 254 was not enough, especially when India's last three wickets added 79 to boost their lead to 104. New Zealand again collapsed against spin, making only 124 after the opening pair had put on 49. Wright (62) batted throughout the innings to get half the runs. India needed only 21 and won by ten wickets.

Four one-day internationals played in eight days were all won by India. At Visakhapatnam, India put New Zealand in and kept them to 196 for nine in the 50 overs, Srikkanth taking five for 27. India made the runs for the loss of six wickets in 46.2 overs, and as Srikkanth made top score of 70, he was automatically the man of the match.

At Cuttack, New Zealand won the toss and batted, scoring 160 for seven in only 45 overs. India needed 41.3 overs to win by five wickets, Sidhu being man of the match for his 67.

Wright put India in on winning the toss at Indore. In 45 overs India scored 222 for six, V.B. Chandrasekhar making 53 in his first one-day series. Sharma's 52 not out, with three sixes and three fours, won the man of the match award. New Zealand made only 169 for nine, to lose by 53 runs.

At Baroda, Wright batted on winning the toss, and New Zealand made an excellent 278 for three, with Greatbatch getting 84 not out after Wright and Jones had scored 140 for the first wicket. However India passed this in 47.1 overs, scoring 282 for eight, with Azharuddin contributing 108 not out and gaining the man of the match award. He hit three sixes and ten fours, the decisive stand being 127 for the sixth wicket with A. Sharma. Azharuddin's century (61 balls) was the fastest in one-day internationals, beating Javed's in 69 balls for Pakistan against India in Lahore in 1982–83.

The fifth and final one-day international, scheduled for Jammu, was abandoned without a ball being bowled because rain flooded the pitch.

Australia v West Indies

Viv Richards' team visited Australia and played five Tests among 11 first-class games and they also took part in the Benson and Hedges World Series Cup one-day tournament with the hosts and Pakistan, a total of 11 one-day games.

The first Test was played at Brisbane, where Border won the toss and batted. Against a battery of four pace bowlers, they struggled all day on a greenish pitch and were shot out for 167, despite Patterson suffering a knee injury and bowling only three overs and one ball. Richards became the sixth player to play in 100 Test matches, and when he caught Dodemaide he took his 100th Test catch. Greenidge and Haynes put on 135 for the first wicket, and West Indies took control, batting on to 394. Australia lost two quick second innings wickets, and at 65 Walsh came on and dismissed Veletta and Wood with his first two balls. Border, who had broken a finger taking a catch, came in at number 6 to avert the hat-trick, but then it was realised that Walsh had taken the last wicket of the first innings, so that in fact he had already completed a hat-trick. Border and Waugh staged a short recovery, but only when McDermott and Matthews added 58 for the ninth wicket did Australia avoid losing by an innings. West Indies needed 63 and won by nine wickets.

At Perth, Border put West Indies in on winning the toss. Only Haynes fell early, but not before he and Greenidge had scored their 5,000th run in Test partnerships, a record. Richards made 146 and West Indies posted 449 runs, the recalled Merv Hughes claiming five for 130. Marsh and Boon got Australia away to a good start, and Graeme Wood and Steve Waugh added 200 for the fifth wicket, but the tail collapsed. At 395 for eight, Lawson had his jaw broken by a delivery from Ambrose, and in falling broke his wicket. However Border declared when Lawson was stretchered off, and the umpires decided Lawson was 'retired hurt', a curious decision.

The first ball of West Indies second innings from the fired-up Hughes trapped Greenidge lbw, giving Hughes a remarkable hat-trick. Not only was it the second of the series, both spread over two innings, but Hughes' was actually spread over three overs, as he dismissed Ambrose with the last bowl of one over and Patterson with the first of the next to end the first innings and Greenidge with the first ball of the second innings.

On the fourth day, however, Haynes made a century and West Indies declared early on the last day at 349 for nine, setting Australia 404 to win. Hughes took eight for 87, easily his best Test figures, as were his match figures of 13 for 217.

Australia made 234 runs at a good rate (Lawson did not bat) but lost by 169 runs.

Border, playing his 100th Test (the eighth to reach this mark), put the West Indies in again in the Christmas Test at Melbourne, which turned out to be an unseasonably acrimonious one. Alderman returned to Test cricket after a three-year ban for playing in South Africa, and on an unreliable wicket helped Australia reduce West Indies to 199 for eight, but West Indies recovered a little on the second day to reach 280. Australia's innings followed a similar erratic course to 242, but the Aussies were annoyed at what they considered to be excessive use of the bouncer. Several players were hit.

In West Indies' second innings Richardson played an innings of class for 122 and Richards made an explosive 63, allowing a declaration at 361 for nine. Australia had the whole of the last day to bat, but lasted only 4½ hours, battered out for 114. Marshall, wicketless in the first innings, claimed Boon lbw for his 300th Test wicket. But Patterson and Ambrose were warned by the umpires for short-pitched bowling, and Patterson was given the cold shoulder by Aussies when he went to the dressing-room to protest about a remark.

West Indies batted at Sydney, having already clinched the Worrell Trophy. Even on a pitch which favoured spin there was no reason for them to be bowled out on the first day for 224. Border, with one wicket in his previous 49 Tests, put himself on and took seven for 46 in a surprising display, the last nine wickets falling for 80. Australia were 200 for three at the end of the second day, and went on to 401. Boon made 148, and Border, determined not to waste the advantage his bowling had gained, scored the slowest 50 by an Australian: 310 minutes (262 balls). He went on to 75. Haynes' 143 was more than half West Indies' second innings total, Border getting four more wickets, and Australia knocked off the 80 needed to win by seven wickets.

At Adelaide, Border decided to bat on an easy wicket, and Dean Jones took the opportunity to make 216. He was assisted by a rapid 72 not out from Hughes at number 10, and Australia reached 515. Haynes and Richardson were not in trouble when West Indies batted, and the visitors scored 369. Border declared at 224 for four, setting a target of 371 with all the last day to get them. Marshall, irked by a decision against him, shouted at the umpire and then bowled a donkey drop to Boon, who patted it back, whereupon Marshall bad temperedly threw down his wicket. West Indies did not seriously attempt the runs, and with 14 overs left at 233 for four, the match was agreed drawn.

The Australian board referred the umpire's report on the match to the West Indies Board. It was critical of the behaviour of some of the West Indian players.

Allan Border and Desmond Haynes shared the 'player of the finals' award. Haynes, Jones, Marsh and Javed Miandad topped the batting averages, and Ambrose, Border, Bishop and Alderman the bowling averages.

New Zealand v Pakistan

Pakistan, under Imran, toured New Zealand in 1988–89, playing six first-class matches including three Tests, and five one-day internationals, including an extra one played when the first Test was washed out. They also played in the one-day competition in Australia.

The Tests were spoiled by umpiring disputes and much negative play. The first, at Dunedin, was completely washed out by heavy rain, only the fourth Test ever to be abandoned without a ball being bowled.

The second Test was at Wellington, New Zealand being put in when Imran won the toss. Imran bowled his first eight overs for one run, after which both opening batsmen were dismissed at 18, the first hour seeing only 13 runs scored. Jones (86) and Martin Crowe (174) staged a recovery, but New Zealand had scored only 229 for four at the end of the first day. After an hour's rain, New Zealand's innings ended at the end of the second day for 447. Pakistan also lost two quick wickets, and recovered, but at an even slower rate. They batted into the final morning before declaring behind at 438 for seven. Shoaib Mohammad (163) batted for 12 hours, the sixth-longest Test innings (his father Hanif has the longest), and the slowest ever Test 150 (624 minutes). Javed made his 20th Test century. New Zealand, having passed 100 with one man out, collapsed to 186 for eight, but it was all academic. Aaqib Javed made his Test debut aged 16 years 189 days, the second youngest Test player behind Mushtaq Mohammad. He might have become the youngest wicket-taker in Tests, but failed to take a wicket in 47 overs. He did not bat or take a catch and was not selected for the remaining Test.

The third and final Test was on a spinners' wicket at Auckland. Pakistan won the toss and batted, and after two wickets had gone for 44, Shoaib and Javed made a big stand, as they had in the previous Test, but at a much faster rate. Shoaib was run out for 112 when the pair had added 248. Javed went on to 271, having scored 1,069 in his last eight Tests. Pakistan finally declared at lunch on the third day at 616 for five. Abdul Qadir was given a long bowl when New Zealand went in, and took six for 160, gradually working through New Zealand until they were out for 403, just failing to avoid the follow-on. The game ended when they reached 99 for three, and both sides, but particularly the visitors, had harsh words to say about the umpiring in the series as a whole.

In the first one-day international, played at Dunedin when the first Test was abandoned, Pakistan made 170 for nine in 48 overs, of which Salim made 83 and Hadlee took five for 38, and New Zealand won easily with 174 for two in 46.3 overs, Jones getting 55 not out.

At Christchurch Pakistan made 170 for seven in 47 overs and New Zealand again won easily with 171 for three in 40.5 overs. Javed injured his back during the practice and was stretchered off. It was a bad-tempered match in which the Pakistan innings contained three five-ball overs. With New Zealand needing five to win Aaqib Javed bowled five consecutive no-balls. Salim was jostled leaving the field.

The third match at Wellington saw a better Pakistan score of 253 for six in 50 overs, Shoaib making 126 not out. New Zealand still reached the target with three overs and six wickets to spare, Martin Crowe (87 not out) and Ian Smith (62 not out) adding 108 in 99 balls.

New Zealand batted first in the fourth match at Auckland, using all but one ball of their 50 overs to make 249 all out. Pakistan scored 251 for three in the 49th over, with Rameez getting 101.

The last match was at Hamilton, and Pakistan made 138 for nine, with Morrison getting four for 33. New Zealand got 139 for three to win easily and take the series by four matches to one.

West Indies v India

After touring England and Australia, West Indies were hosts to India, led by Dilip Vengsarkar. India played eight first-class games, including the four Tests, plus five one-day internationals. They failed to win a match.

The first Test at Georgetown was spoiled by rain, which allowed only two days' play. India put West Indies in, which they probably regretted, as it gave their opponents batting practice, particularly Richardson, who made 194. He was dropped at 46 and had the benefit of an lbw decision at 143, when Kapil Dev, who had just taken two wickets in two balls, argued pointedly with the umpire. India had made 86 for one in reply to West Indies' 437 when the rain came.

The second Test was at Bridgetown, and this time India were invited to bat when Richards won the toss. The first three wickets fell by 27, but Sanjay Manjrekar's 108 helped them to 321, Bishop taking six for 87, his first Test wickets. After passing 200 with only Haynes out, West Indies did not consolidate, being all out 377, Greenidge getting 117 after being dropped on eight. The Indians, however, lost four wickets knocking off the arrears, and it needed 107 from Shastri, and support from Moré in a seventh-wicket stand of 132, to reach 251 and set a target of 196. West Indies had no trouble getting these for the loss of two wickets, Haynes making 112 not out.

Left-hander Raman, who had flown out to replace the injured Srikkanth, took Azharuddin's place in the third Test, where Vengsarkar put West Indies in on a green pitch at Port-of-Spain. Although the pitch took spin, West Indies batted solidly all the way down to score 314. Logie being top scorer with 87 and Ayub getting five for 117. India were in grave trouble against Walsh and Marshall, reaching 150 only after a ninth-wicket stand of 49. The Indians, particularly Sharma, one of the ninth-wicket pair, were annoyed at the West Indian short-pitched bowling, and Sharma's anger lasted long enough for him to claim the West Indian openers quickly in the second innings, but Richardson's 99 steadied the ship, and a total of 266 was too many for India, who needed 431. Kapil Dev, who finally bowled Richardson, had had further words with an umpire, and after the match the Indians complained bitterly about the umpiring. Vengsarkar and Moré offered some resistance in the fourth innings, adding 98 for the seventh wicket, but West Indies won easily by 217, Marshall getting 11 wickets in the match, having been dropped down to second change bowler.

Richards put India in in the final Test at Kingston on a bumpy pitch, but Sidhu, who had made 286 against Jamaica in the previous match, ensured it was not one-way traffic with a stubborn 116, after being forced to retire hurt when one of a number of bouncers from Marshall struck him on the wrist. India made 289, a score which looked better when West Indies were 86 for three, but at this stage Richardson (156) and Richards (110) added 235. Richards was given out caught behind, probably mistakenly, and his gestures to keeper and bowler provoked half-an-hour's stoppage for crowd unrest and bottle-throwing. Richards was given a suspended fine. West Indies made 384, Kapil Dev claiming six for 84, and India went in again 95 behind. In the face of fierce bowling by Bishop and Walsh they made only 152, and West Indies won by seven wickets, rain delaying the coup de grace until the final morning.

West Indies made a clean sweep of the one-day games which preceded the Tests. At Bridgetown they made 248 for four in 48 overs after being put in, Haynes making 117 not out, and India could make only 198 for eight. At Port-of-Spain, India were put in, and could make only 148 in 48 overs, an easy task for West Indies, who made 151 for four to win with over nine overs to spare, Greenidge, with 70, being man of the match.

In the third match, also at Port-of-Spain, India batted and made 192 in all but one ball of their 50 overs. Arthurton, with 76 not out, took the match award as West Indies reached 193 for four in the 48th over. At St John's, India decided to bat and made their best score so far, 237 for eight in 50 overs, Vengsarkar getting 88. West Indies, however, raced to 240 for two in only 43.2 overs, Greenidge clinching the match award with 117, which included eight sixes, a new record for one-day internationals, beating Viv Richards' seven, also against India the previous season.

India put West Indies in in the last match at Georgetown, but the run-spree continued, led by Haynes, who won the match award with 152 not out. He hit six sixes and 12 fours. He and Greenidge (80) put on 185 for the first wicket in a match reduced to 44 overs a side by rain. West Indies made 289 for two in 43.5 overs. India replied with 188 for eight. A ball from Bishop broke the left forearm of Srikkanth, who was forced to fly home and miss the Test matches.

After the tour, some Indian players flew off to play in an 'American Cup' series, in which they were beaten in the final by Pakistan in New York. The tour was unauthorised, and was made against the directive of the Indian board. The fees were about twice those for the tour of the West Indies. Six players, Vengsarkar, Kapil Dev, Moré, Azharuddin, Shastri and Arun Lal, were banned for a year and fined, but the penalties were overruled by the Supreme Court of India. Vengsarkar, however, lost the captaincy of his country, Srikkanth taking over.

PAKISTAN v AUSTRALIA

First Test, Karachi

September 15, 16, 17, 19, 20, 1988

Pakistan won by an innings and 188 runs

Pakistan 1st Innings		
Mudassar Nazar	b Reid	0
Rameez Raja	c Healy b Reid	9
Shoaib Mohammad	b Waugh	94
*Javed Miandad	c Boon b Reid	211
Tauseef Ahmed	c Boon b May	35
Salim Malik	c Boon b May	45
Ijaz Ahmed	c Boon b Reid	12
Aamer Malik	not out	17
†Salim Yousuf	c Wood b May	5
Abdul Qadir	c Marsh b May	8
Iqbal Qasim		
Extras	b 16, lb 12, nb 5	33
Total (9 wkts dec, 169.5 ov)		469

0, 21, 217, 284, 398, 428, 444, 457, 469

Reid	41	10	109	4
Dodemaide	29	13	35	0
Waugh	26	3	94	1
May	40.5	10	97	4
Taylor	16	2	73	0
Border	17	7	33	0

Australia 1st Innings		
G.R. Marsh	b Qasim	8
D.C. Boon	b Qadir	14
D.M. Jones	lbw b Qasim	3
G.M. Wood	c Qasim b Tauseef	23
*A.R. Border	c Aamer b Qasim	4
S.R. Waugh	lbw b Qasim	0
P.L. Taylor	not out	54
†I.A. Healy	c Ijaz b Mudassar	26
A.I.C. Dodemaide	c Ijaz b Salim Malik	8
T.B.A. May	c Yousuf b Quadir	6
B.A. Reid	lbw b Qasim	0
Extras	b 12, l b 7	19
Total (122 ov)		165

19, 23, 40, 48, 54, 64, 106, 139, 162

Mudassar	10	3	15	1
Aamer	2	0	6	0
Qasim	39	24	35	5
Qadir	37	16	54	2
Tauseef	26	15	28	1
Shoaib	2	1	1	0
Salim Malik	6	4	7	1

Australia 2nd Innings		
G.R. Marsh	lbw b Tauseef	16
P.L. Taylor	c Ijaz b Aamer	2
D.C. Boon	b Qasim	4
D.M. Jones	c Ijaz b Qaid	4
G.M. Wood	lbw b Qasim	15
*A.R. Border	b Qasim	18
S.R. Waugh	st Yousuf b Qasim	13
†I.A. Healy	c Shoaib b Qadir	21
A.I.C. Dodemaide	st Yousuf b Tauseef	2
T.B.A. May	lbw b Qadir	0
B.A. Reid	not out	8
Extras	b 6, lb 7	13
Total (64.4 ov)		116

4, 10, 15, 46, 50, 80, 93, 104, 104

Mudassar	3	0	5	0
Aamer	2	2	0	1
Qasim	25	14	49	4
Qadir	13	4	33	3
Tauseef	21.4	13	16	2

Umpires: Khizar Hayat and Mahboon Shah
Toss: Pakistan.
Man of the Match: Javed Miandad

Above left: *Javed Miandad, who made double centuries against both Australia and New Zealand during the 1988–89 season.*

Allsport/Adrian Murrell

Left: *Merv Hughes, who took 13 wickets in a match against West Indies in 1988–89.*

Allsport/Adrian Murrell

Second Test, Faisalabad

September 23, 24, 25, 27, 28, 1988

Drawn

Pakistan 1st Innings		
Mudassar Nazar	c Marsh b Reid	9
Rameez Raja	lbw b Dodemaide	0
Shoaib Mohammad	b Dodemaide	11
*Javed Miandad	c Boon b May	43
Salim Malik	b Dodemaide	0
Ijaz Ahmed	b Reid	122
†Salim Yousuf	c Boon b Dodemaide	62
Abdul Qadir	b Reid	6
Tauseef Ahmed	not out	35
Iqbal Qasim	c and b Sleep	16
Salim Jaffer	lbw b Sleep	0
Extras	b 2, lb6 nb 4	12
Total (106.5 ov)		316

4, 20, 24, 25, 144, 255, 255, 267, 316

Reid	31	8	92	3
Dodemaide	34	6	87	4
Waugh	11	3	36	0
Sleep	5.5	1	24	2
May	19	3	58	1
Border	6	1	11	0

Australia 1st Innings		
D.C. Boon	b Mudassar	13
G.R. Marsh	b Tauseef	51
D.M. Jones	lbw b Qadir	16
G.M. Wood	lbw b Jaffer	32
A.I.C. Dodemaide	c Ijaz b Mudassar	19
*A.R. Border	not out	113
S.R. Waugh	st Yousuf b Tauseef	1
P.R. Sleep	b Tauseef	12
†I.A. Healy	c Qasim b Jaffer	27
T.B.A. May	c sub b Qadir	14
B.A. Reid	c Yousuf b Qasim	1
Extras	b 4, b 15, w 1, nb 2	22
Total (129.5 ov)		321

24, 65, 122, 122, 167, 170, 204 256, 318

Jaffer	29	7	69	2
Mudassar	17	5	39	2
Qadir	34	5	84	2
Tauseef	35	10	73	3
Qasim	14.5	4	37	1

Pakistan 2nd Innings		
Mudassar Nazar	c Border b May	27
Rameez Raja	c Boon b Waugh	32
Shoaib Mohammad	st Healy b May	74
*Javed Miandad	lbw b Reid	107
Salim Malik	c Border b Reid	10
Ijaz Ahmed	c Healy b Reid	0
†Salim Yousuf	not out	66
Tauseef Ahmed	c Waugh b Dodemaide	2
Iqbal Qasim	b Reid	29
Abdul Qadir	c Reid b May	13
Extras	lb 5, nb 13	18
Total (9 wkts dec, 116.4 ov)		378

64, 64, 236, 264, 264, 269, 274, 344, 378

Reid	30	6	100	4
Dodemaide	20	4	49	1
Waugh	18	0	44	1
May	34.4	7	126	3
Sleep	13	4	51	0
Border	1	0	3	0

Australia 2nd Innings		
G.R. Marsh	b Qadir	9
D.C. Boon	c Mudassar b Tauseef	15
D.M. Jones	not out	21
S.R. Waugh	c and b Shoaib	19
G.M. Wood	not out	2
Extras	b1	1
Total (3 wkts, 26 ov)		67

1, 30, 65

Jaffer	2	0	8	0
Mudassar	2	0	5	0
Qadir	10	1	34	1
Tauseef	11	4	17	1
Shoaib	1	0	2	1

Umpires: Mahboon Shah and Tariq Ata
Toss: Pakistan.
Men of the Match: A.R. Border and Ijaz Ahmed

PAKISTAN v AUSTRALIA

Third Test, Lahore
October 7, 8, 9, 10, 11, 1988
Drawn

Australia 1st Innings

D.C. Boon	c Shoaib b Jaffer	43
G.R. Marsh	st Yousuf b Qasim	64
D.M. Jones	lbw b Tauseef	0
*A.R. Border	c Yousuf b Tauseef	75
G.M. Wood	lbw b Mudassar	15
P.L. Taylor	st Yousuf b Qadir	29
S.R. Waugh	c Ijaz b Qasim	59
†I.A. Healy	lbw b Qadir	0
A.I.C. Dodemaide	c Qasim b Qadir	14
T.B.A. May	not out	13
B.A. Reid	c Mudassar b Tauseef	8
Extras	b 4, lb 12, nb 4	20
Total (157.5 ov)		340

87, 88, 155, 200, 231, 241, 241, 294, 331

Jaffer	33	9	82	1
Mudassar	15	6	23	1
Qadir	37	10	88	3
Tauseef	50.5	20	86	3
Qasim	21	6	41	2
Shoaib	1	0	4	0

Pakistan 1st Innings

Mudassar Nazar	c Boon b May	27
Rameez Raja	c Healy b Reid	64
Shoaib Mohammad	run out	13
*Javed Miandad	c Healy b Reid	27
Salim Malik	c and b Dodemaide	26
Ijaz Ahmed	lbw b Dodemaide	23
†Salim Yousuf	c Healy b Reid	1
Abdul Qadir	lbw b Dodemaide	18
Iqbal Qasim	lbw b May	14
Tauseef Ahmed	c Boon b May	3
Salim Jaffer	not out	0
Extras	lb 6, nb 11	17
Total (98.2 ov)		233

80, 104, 118, 172, 172, 173, 206, 228, 232

Reid	23	3	53	3
Waugh	18	4	34	0
Dodemaide	26	6	56	3
May	27.2	6	73	3
Taylor	4	2	11	0

Australia 2nd Innings

G.R. Marsh	not out	84
D.C. Boon	c Miandad b Jaffer	28
D.J. Jones	lbw b Jaffer	0
*A.R. Border	c Yousuf b Tauseef	20
P.L. Taylor	not out	25
Extras	lb 4	4
Total (3 wkts dec, 41 ov)		161

71, 71, 108

Jaffer	14	2	60	2
Mudassar	3	0	8	0
Tauseef	17	2	48	1
Qadir	4	1	26	0
Qasim	3	0	15	0

Pakistan 2nd Innings

Mudassar Nazar	c Border b Taylor	49
Rameez Raja	c Boon b May	21
Shoaib Mohammad	lbw b May	3
*Javed Miandad	c Border b May	24
Salim Malik	c Healy b Taylor	13
Ijaz Ahmed	c Taylor b Dodemaide	15
†Salim Yousuf	c Waugh b Taylor	2
Abdul Qadir	st Healy b Taylor	6
Iqbal Qasim	not out	10
Tauseef Ahmed	not out	1
Extras	b 6, lb 1, nb 2	9
Total (8 wkts, 84 ov)		153

36, 48, 86, 107, 123, 125, 131, 147

Dodemaide	12	5	20	1
Waugh	5	1	8	0
May	35	20	39	3
Taylor	28	9	78	4
Border	4	3	1	0

Umpires: Khizar Hayat and Salim Badar
Toss: Australia
Men of the Series: Javed Miandad and B.A. Reid

INDIA v NEW ZEALAND

First Test, Bangalore
November 12, 13, 14, 15, 16, 17, 1988
India won by 172 runs

India 1st Innings

K. Srikkanth	b Hadlee	1
Arun Lal	c Kuggeleijn b Hadlee	6
N.S. Sidhu	c Jones b Gray	116
*D.B. Vengsarkar	b Hadlee	75
M. Azharuddin	c Smith b Hadlee	42
W.V. Raman	b Hadlee	3
R.J. Shastri	c Rutherford b Gray	54
Kapil Dev	c Jones b Chatfield	24
†K.S. Moré	lbw b Kuggeleijn	46
A. Ayub	not out	2
N. Hirwani	not out	0
Extras	b 4, lb4 nb 7	15
Total (9 wkts dec, 142 ov)		384

9, 10, 236, 244, 254, 258, 294, 378, 384
Vengsarkar retired hurt at 184–2 and resumed at 244–4.

Hadlee	30	10	65	5
Chatfield	30	12	53	1
Kuggeleijn	13	2	50	1
Gray	45	8	128	2
Bracewell	24	1	80	0

New Zealand 1st Innings

T.J. Franklin	c Azharuddin b Ayub	28
*J.G. Wright	c Arun Lal b Ayub	22
A.H. Jones	c Srikkanth b Ayub	45
M.J. Greatbatch	c Srikkanth b Raman	14
K.R. Rutherford	c Arun Lal b Hirwani	14
E.J. Gray	lbw b Hirwani	1
R.J. Hadlee	b Kapil Dev	5
J.G. Bracewell	c Moré b Ayub	3
†I.D.S. Smith	lbw b Kapil Dev	30
E.J. Chatfield	not out	4
C.M. Kuggeleijn	lbw b Kapil Dev	0
Extras	b 6, lb 8, nb 9	23
Total (122.3 ov)		189

58, 62, 118, 128, 135, 140, 149, 183, 183.
Hadlee retired ill at 145–6 and resumed at 183–9.

Kapil Dev	9.3	4	24	3
Ayub	48	21	51	4
Hirwani	31	12	62	2
Shastri	14	8	11	0
Raman	17	8	26	1
Srikkanth	3	2	1	0

India 2nd Innings

K. Srikkanth	not out	58
Arun Lal	c and b Gray	33
N.S. Sidhu	not out	43
	b 5, lb 2	7
Total (1 wkt dec, 28 ov)		141

64

Chatfield	14	0	61	0
Bracewell	8	0	34	0
Gray	6	0	39	1

New Zealand 2nd Innings

T.J. Franklin	b Hirwani	16
J.G. Wright	lbw b Hirwani	58
A.H. Jones	lbw b Hirwani	17
M.J. Greatbatch	c Kapil Dev b Ayub	10
E.J. Gray	c Srikkanth b Hirwani	2
K.R. Rutherford	lbw b Hirwani	0
C.M. Kuggeleijn	c Moré b Ayub	0
R.J. Hadlee	not out	13
†I.D.S. Smith	lbw b Hirwani	25
J.G. Bracewell	c Arun Lal b Ayub	11
E.J. Chatfield	c Vengsarkar b Ayub	0
Extras	b 10, nb 2	12
Total (78.4 ov)		164

77, 92, 107, 113, 113, 113, 113, 143, 164

Kapil Dev	4	0	16	0
Ayub	35.4	12	53	4
Hirwani	30	10	59	6
Shastri	7	1	21	0
Raman	2	0	5	0

Umpires: S.K. Ghosh and P.D. Reporter
Toss: India

Second Test, Bombay
November 24, 25, 26, 27, 29, 1988
New Zealand won by 136 runs

New Zealand 1st Innings

T.J. Franklin	st Moré b Ayub	18
*J.G. Wright	c Moré b Hirwani	33
A.H. Jones	lbw b Kapil Dev	3
M.J. Greatbatch	lbw b Shastri	46
K.R. Rutherford	c Srikkanth b Hirwani	6
T.E. Blain	c Kapil Dev b Shastri	16
R.J. Hadlee	c Patel b Hirwani	10
†I.D.S. Smith	b Shastri	13
J.G. Bracewell	c Moré b Shastri	52
D.K. Morrison	not out	27
E.J. Chatfield	b Kapil Dev	0
Extras	lb 5, nb 7	12
Total (93.3 ov)		236

36, 43, 67, 82, 110, 121, 141, 158, 234

Kapil Dev	15.3	4	48	2
Patel	4	0	14	0
Ayub	25	10	42	1
Hirwani	31	6	82	4
Shastri	18	1	45	4

India 1st Innings

K. Srikkanth	c Franklin b Hadlee	94
Arun Lal	lbw b Hadlee	9
N.S. Sidhu	lbw b Chatfield	6
*D.B. Vengsarkar	c Blain b Bracewell	25
M. Azharuddin	c Greatbatch b Bracewell	9
R.J. Shastri	b Chatfield	32
Kapil Dev	b Hadlee	7
†K.S. Moré	b Hadlee	28
A. Ayub	c Bracewell b Hadlee	10
R.G. Patel	c Rutherford b Hadlee	0
N. Hirwani	not out	2
Extras	lb 5, nb 7	12
Total (75.5 ov)		234

26, 34, 134, 150, 150, 172, 209, 224, 229

Hadlee	20.5	5	49	6
Morrison	16	1	58	0
Chatfield	18	6	41	2
Bracewell	21	6	81	2

New Zealand 2nd Innings

T.J. Franklin	c Moré b Kapil Dev	2
J.G. Wright	lbw b Hirwani	36
A.H. Jones	lbw b Ayub	78
M.J. Greatbatch	b Hirwani	31
K.R. Rutherford	c Arun Lal b Ayub	17
T.E. Blain	lbw b Ayub	5
R.J. Hadlee	c Vengsarkar b Hirwani	1
†I.D.S. Smith	c Vengsarkar b Ayub	54
D.K. Morrison	c Moré b Hirwani	0
J.G. Bracewell	c and b Ayub	32
E.J. Chatfield	not out	2
Extras	b 4, lb 8, w 1, nb 8	21
Total (115 ov)		279

2, 73, 149, 163, 169, 176, 176, 181, 250

Kapil Dev	24	5	52	1
Patel	10	0	37	0
Ayub	33	11	50	5
Hirwani	38	7	93	4
Shastri	10	1	35	0

Indian 2nd Innings

K. Srikkanth	lbw b Hadlee	0
Arun Lal	c Greatbatch b Hadlee	47
N.S. Sidhu	b Bracewell	14
*D.B. Vengsarkar	b Cracewell	0
M. Azharuddin	c Rutherford b Bracewell	21
R.J. Shastri	c Smith b Hadlee	6
Kapil Dev	c Wright b Bracewell	36
†K.S. Moré	b Bracewell	2
A. Ayub	not out	4
R.G. Patel	c Smith b Hadlee	0
N. Hirwani	c Chatfield b Bracewell	3
Extras	b 5, lb 4, nb 3	12
Total (49.4 ov)		145

0, 48, 54, 89, 89, 134, 134, 141, 142

Hadlee	16	3	39	4
Morrison	6	1	27	0
Chatfield	10	1	19	0
Bracewell	17.4	3	51	6

Umpires: R.B. Gupta and K. Ramaswamy
Toss: New Zealand

INDIA v NEW ZEALAND

Third Test, Hyderabad
December 2, 3, 4, 5, 7, 1988
India won by 10 wkts

New Zealand 1st Innings

T.J. Franklin	c Arun Lal b Ayub	7
*J.G. Wright	c and b Ayub	17
A.H. Jones	c Kapil Dev b Ayub	8
M.J. Greatbatch	not out	90
T.E. Blain	b Hirwani	15
C.M. Kuggeleijn	c Vengsarkar b Hirwani	7
R.J. Hadlee	c Azharuddin b Ayub	1
†I.D.S. Smith	c Srikkanth b Kapil Dev	79
J.G. Bracewell	c Vengsarkar b Sharma	3
M.C. Snedden	lbw b Sharma	0
E.J. Chatfield	c Srikkanth b Sharma	0
Extras	b 8, lb 11, w 1, nb 7	27
Total (95 ov)		254

25, 33, 38, 82, 90, 91, 230, 248 248

Kapil Dev	26	6	71	1
Sharma	17	4	37	3
Ayub	30	9	55	4
Shastri	6	2	15	0
Hirwani	15	2	51	2
Srikkanth	1	0	6	0

India 1st Innings

K. Srikkanth	c Bracewell b Snedden	69
Arun Lal	c Greatbatch b Hadlee	8
N.S. Sidhu	c Franklin b Snedden	19
*D.B. Vengsarkar	c Hadlee b Chatfield	32
R.J. Shastri	c Franklin b Chatfield	42
M. Azharuddin	c Smith b Chatfield	81
†K.S. Moré	c Wright b Hadlee	40
A. Ayub	c Bracewell b Sendden	0
S.K.Sharma	c Smith b Hadlee	19
N. Hirwani	not out	18
Extras	c and b Snedden	17
	lb 9, nb 4	13
Total (106.3 ov)		358

17, 48, 116, 150, 217, 279, 281, 310, 322

Hadlee	34	7	99	3
Chatfield	33	6	82	3
Snedden	18.3	3	69	4
Bracewell	18	1	86	0
Kuggeleijn	3	0	13	0

New Zealand 2nd Innings

T.J. Franklin	c Kapil Dev b Hirwani	15
*J.G. Wright	c and b Shastri	62
A.H. Jones	c Vengsarkar b Ayub	5
M.C. Snedden	lbw b Ayub	0
M.J. Greatbatch	lbw b Hirwani	5
T.E. Blain	c Arun Lal b Hirwani	0
C.M. Kuggeleijn	c Sharma b Ayub	0
R.J. Hadlee	c Moré b Kapil Dev	31
†I.D.S. Smith	b Kapil Dev	0
J.G. Bracewell	lbw b Kapil Dev	0
E.J. Chatfield	not out	0
Extras	lb 1, w 5	6
Total (65.3 ov)		124

49, 58, 60, 71, 75, 80, 118, 118, 124

Kapil Dev	10	3	21	3
Sharma	4	0	13	0
Hirwani	23	10	43	3
Ayub	25	12	36	3
Shastri	3.3	1	10	1

India 2nd Innings

K. Srikkanth	not out	18
Arun Lal	not out	0
Extras	nb 4	4
Total (0 wkt, 2.1 ov)		22

Chatfield	1	0	5	0
Snedden	1	0	13	0
Kuggeleijn	0.1	0	4	0

Umpires: S.K. Ghosh and R.B. Gupta
Toss: New Zealand

AUSTRALIA v WEST INDIES

First Test, Brisbane
November 18, 19, 20, 21, 1988
West Indies won by 9 wkts

Australia 1st Innings

G.R. Marsh	c Logie b Ambrose	27
D.C. Boon	lbw b Marshall	10
M.R.J. Veletta	b Hooper	37
G.M. Wood	c Greenidge b Ambrose	6
*A.R. Border	c Dujon b Ambrose	4
S.R. Waugh	lbw b Marshall	4
†I.A. Healy	c Logie b Walsh	27
C.J. McDermott	c Logie b Walsh	2
A.I.C. Dodemaide	c Richards b Walsh	22
C.D. Matthews	c Dujon b Walsh	1
T.B.A. May	not out	4
Extras	b 1, lb 5, w 1, nb 16	23
Total (69.3 ov)		167

19, 52, 64, 76,m 86, 126, 138, 140, 150

Marshall	18	3	39	2
Patterson	3.1	1	5	0
Ambrose	16.5	5	30	3
Walsh	18.3	3	62	4
Hooper	12	2	24	1
Richards	1	0	1	0

West Indies 1st Innings

C.G. Greenidge	b May	80
D.L. Haynes	c Healy b Waugh	40
R.B. Richardson	lbw b Dodemaide	81
C.L. Hooper	c Border b Waugh	1
*I.V.A. Richards	c McDermott b May	68
A.L. Logie	c Border b May	19
†P.J.L. Dujon	c May b McDermott	27
M.D. Marshall	c Border b McDermott	11
C.E.L. Ambrose	not out	19
C.A. Walsh	lbw b McDermott	0
B.P. Patterson	lbw b Dodemaide	0
Extras	b 5, lb 9, w 6, nb 28	48
Total (113.4 ov)		394

135, 156, 162, 270, 307, 359, 361, 389, 393

McDermott	28	3	99	3
Matthews	21	3	62	0
Dodemaide	16.4	2	60	2
May	29	6	90	3
Waugh	18	2	61	2
Border	1	0	8	0

Australia 2nd Innings

D.C. Boon	c Dujon b Marshall	12
G.R. Marsh	lbw b Ambrose	2
M.R.J. Veletta	c Hooper b Walsh	10
S.R. Waugh	c Haynes b Marhsall	90
G.M. Wood	lbw b Walsh	0
*A.R. Border	c Haynes b Ambrose	41
†I.A. Healy	c Ambrose b Marshall	28
A.I.C. Dodemaide	c Richards b Marshall	7
C.J. McDermott	not out	32
C.D. Matthews	c sub b Walsh	32
T.B.A. May	c Hooper b Ambrose	5
Extras	b 4, lb 5, nb 21	30
Total (86.1 ov)		289

14, 16, 65, 65, 157, 199, 212, 212, 270

Marshall	26	2	92	4
Ambrose	26.1	5	78	3
Walsh	19	3	61	3
Richards	11	4	26	0
Hooper	4	0	23	0

West Indies 2nd Innings

C.G. Greenidge	c Healy b Dodemaide	16
D.L. Haynes	not out	30
R.B. Richardson	not out	7
Extras	lb 4, w 3, nb 3	10
Total (1 wkt, 19.1 ov)		63

43

McDermott	4	0	12	0
Matthews	3.5	1	18	0
Dodemaide	5.2	1	15	1
Waugh	6	0	14	0

Umpiers: A.R. Crafter and P.J. McConnell
Toss: Australia
Man of the Match: C.E.L. Ambrose

Second Test, Perth
December 2, 3, 4, 5, 6, 1988
West Indies won by 169 runs

West Indies 1st Innings

C.G. Greenidge	b Lawson	40
D.L. Haynes	lbw b Hughes	11
R.B. Richardson	c Boon b Hughes	66
C.L. Hooper	c Boon b Lawson	26
*I.V.A. Richards	c Dodemaide b Lawson	146
A.L. Logie	c Waugh b May	93
†P.J.L. Dujon	c Valetta b May	32
M.D. Marshall	c Valetta b Hughes	4
C.E.L. Ambrose	c Healy b Hughes	8
C.A. Walsh	not out	0
B.P. Patterson	c Dodemaide b Hughes	1
Extras	b 1, lb 12, nb 9	22
Total (123.1 ov)		449

16, 82, 126, 180, 343, 421, 426, 440, 448

Lawson	32	7	97	3
Hughes	36.1	7	130	5
Dodemaide	17	1	79	0
Waugh	28	3	90	0
May	10	3	40	2

Australia 1st Innings

G.R. Marsh	c Richardson b Walsh	30
D.C. Boon	c Logie b Ambrose	80
M.R.J. Veletta	run out	11
G.M. Wood	c Richardson b Ambrose	111
*A.R. Border	c Dujon b Ambrose	6
S.R. Waugh	c Dujon b Ambrose	91
†I.A. Healy	lbw b Marshall	8
A.I.C. Dodemaide	not out	7
T.B.A. May	c Richards b Ambrose	2
G.F. Lawson	retired hurt	0
M.G. Hughes		
Extras	b 6, lb 8, nb 35	49
Total (8 wkts dec, 100.3 ov)		395

83, 139, 152, 167, 367, 374, 388, 395

Marshall	23	3	84	1
Patterson	16	1	95	0
Walsh	19	3	58	1
Ambrose	23.3	3	72	5
Richards	14	0	43	0
Hooper	5	0	29	0

West Indies 2nd Innings

C.G. Greenidge	lbw b Hughes	0
D.L. Haynes	c Healy b Hughes	100
R.B. Richardson	c Healy b Hughes	48
C.L. Hooper	c Dodemaide b Hughes	64
*I.V.A. Richards	lbw b Hughes	5
A.L. Logie	b Hughes	30
†P.J.L. Dujon	c Dodemaide b Hughes	9
M.D. Marshall	c Healy b Dodemaide	23
C.E.L. Ambrose	c Wood b Hughes	15
C.A. Walsh	not out	17
B.P. Patterson	not out	6
Extras	b 14, lb 9, nb 9	32
Total (9 wkts dec, 98 ov)		349

0, 103, 216, 236, 246, 259, 300, 310, 341

Hughes	37	9	87	8
Dodemaide	24	2	101	1
Waugh	23	1	70	0
May	14	1	68	0

Australia 2nd Innings

D.C. Boon	b Patterson	4
G.R. Marsh	lc Logie b Marshall	6
M.R.J. Veletta	c Dujon b Marshall	13
G.M. Wood	c Greenidge b Walsh	42
*A.R. Border	b Hooper	26
S.R. Waugh	c Hooper b Patterson	26
A.I.C. Dodemaide	lbw b Ambrose	11
†I.A. Healy	c Logie b Ambrose	52
T.B.A. May	not out	8
M.G. Hughes	c Logie b Ambrose	0
G.F. Lawson	absent hurt	0
Extras	b 5, lb 4, nb 37	46
Total (63 ov)		234

14, 14, 46, 93, 138, 140, 190, 232, 234

Marshall	12	0	50	2
Patterson	14	2	58	2
Ambrose	17	1	66	3
Walsh	15	1	46	1
Hooper	5	2	5	1

Umpires: R.C. Bailache and T.A. Prue
Toss: Australia
Man of the Match: M.G. Hughes

Third Test, Melbourne

December 24, 26, 27, 28, 29, 1988

West Indies won by 285 runs

West Indies 1st Innings

C.G. Greenidge	c Healy b Alderman	49
D.L. Haynes	c Boon b McDermott	17
R.B. Richardson	c Taylor b Alderman	26
C.L. Hooper	c Border b McDermott	38
*I.V.A. Richards	c Border b Waugh	12
A.L. Logie	lbw b Alderman	10
†P.J.L. Dujon	c Healy b Waugh	26
M.D. Marshall	c Jones b Waugh	7
C.E.L. Ambrose	lbw b McDermott	44
C.A. Walsh	not out	30
B.P. Patterson	lbw b Alderman	13
Extras	b 1, lb 4, nb 3	8
Total (93.1 ov)		280

68, 68, 114, 137, 147, 166, 185, 199, 256

Hughes	14	3	52	0
Alderman	32.1	9	68	4
McDermott	19	3	62	3
Waugh	21	3	77	3
Taylor	7	3	16	0

Australia 1st Innings

D.C. Boon	run out	23
G.R. Marsh	b Patterson	36
D.M. Jones	b Ambrose	28
G.M. Wood	c Haynes b Patterson	12
*A.R. Border	b Ambrose	0
S.R. Waugh	c Greenidge b Ambrose	42
†I.A. Healy	lbw b Patterson	4
P.L. Taylor	c Greenidge b Ambrose	14
C.J. McDermott	c Marshall b Patterson	28
M.G. Hughes	not out	21
T.M. Alderman	b Walsh	3
Extras	b 2, lb 14, nb 15	31
Total (94.3 ov)		242

40, 103, 117, 117, 155, 161, 186, 190, 234

Marshall	30	8	68	0
Ambrose	27	7	60	4
Walsh	17.3	3	49	1
Patterson	20	2	49	4

West Indies 2nd Innings

C.G. Greenidge	not out	36
D.L. Haynes	lbw b Alderman	23
R.B. Richardson	c and b Waugh	122
C.L. Hooper	lbw b Alderman	4
†P.J.L. Dujon	c Wood b Alderman	46
*I.V.A. Richards	lbw b Waugh	63
M.D. Marshall	c Alderman b Waugh	19
C.E.L. Ambrose	c Marsh b McDermott	5
C.A. Walsh	c Marsh b Waugh	6
A.L. Logie	c Border b Waugh	17
B.P. Patterson	not out	3
Extras	lb 1, nb 16	17
Total (9 wkts dec, 120 ov)		361

38, 92, 191, 284, 317, 324, 324, 335, 356

Greenidge retired hurt at 69–1 and resumed 335–8.

Hughes	24	8	71	0
Alderman	36	12	78	3
Waugh	24	5	92	5
McDermott	26	3	78	1
Border	1	1	0	0
Taylor	9	1	41	0

Australia 2nd Innings

G.R. Marsh	b Patterson	1
D.C. Boon	lbw b Marshall	20
D.M. Jones	c sub b Ambrose	18
G.M. Wood	c Ambrose b Walsh	7
*A.R. Border	c Haynes b Patterson	20
S.R. Waugh	c sub b Ambrose	3
†I.A. Healy	c Hooper b Walsh	8
P.L. Taylor	not out	18
C.J. McDermott	c sub b Patterson	0
M.G. Hughes	c Dujon b Patterson	4
T.M. Alderman	c Dujon b Patterson	0
Extras	b 4, lb 5, nb 6	15
Total (57.1 ov)		114

7, 30, 56, 58, 64, 75, 104, 104, 114

Marshall	9	3	12	1
Patterson	15.1	3	39	5
Ambrose	13	5	21	2
Walsh	16	7	21	2
Richards	4	1	12	0

Umpires: A.R. Crafter and P.J. McConnell
Toss: Australia
Man of the Match: C.E.L. Ambrose

Fourth Test, Sydney

January 26, 27, 28, 29, 30, 1989

Australia won by 7 wkts

West Indies 1st Innings

C.G. Greenidge	c Waugh b P.L. Taylor	56
D.L. Haynes	c Boon b Hohns	75
R.B. Richardson	c P.L. Taylor b Border	28
C.L. Hooper	c Marsh b Border	0
*I.V.A. Richards	c Boon b Border	11
A.L. Logie	b Border	0
†P.J.L. Dujon	c Hughes b Border	18
R.A. Harper	c P.L. Taylor b Border	17
M.D. Marshall	c Marsh b Border	9
C.E.L. Ambrose	c Jones b P.L. Taylor	1
C.A. Walsh	not out	4
Extras	b 1, w 1, nb 3	5
Total (99.2 ov		224

90, 144, 156, 174, 174, 174, 199, 213, 220

Alderman	10	2	17	0
Hughes	10	3	28	0
P.L. Taylor	25.2	2	65	2
Hohns	24	8	49	1
Border	26	10	46	7
Waugh	4	0	18	0

Australia 1st Innings

G.R. Marsh	c Dujon b Marshall	2
M.A. Taylor	b Ambrose	25
D.C. Boon	c Dujon b Walsh	149
D.M. Jones	b Richards	29
*A.R. Border	b Marshall	75
S.R. Waugh	not out	55
†I.A. Healy	c Logie b Marshall	11
P.L. Taylor	lbw b Marshall	0
T.V. Hohns	b Marshall	0
M.G. Hughes	c Dujon b Walsh	12
T.M. Alderman	run out	9
Extras	b 6, lb 14, nb 14	34
Total (191.5 ov)		401

14, 43, 114, 284, 335, 355, 357, 357, 388

Marshall	31	16	29	5
Ambrose	33	5	78	1
Harper	37	9	86	0
Walsh	22.5	5	48	2
Hooper	37	10	72	0
Richards	31	1	68	1

West Indies 2nd Innings

C.G. Greenidge	c and b Hughes	4
D.L. Haynes	c M.A. Taylor b Border	143
R.B. Richardson	c Hughes b P.L. Taylor	22
C.L. Hooper	c Jones b Hohns	35
*I.V.A. Richards	c Jones b Hohns	4
A.L. Logie	c P.L. Taylor b Hohns	6
†P.J.L. Dujon	run out	9
R.A. Harper	lbw b Border	12
M.D. Marshall	c P.L. Taylor b Border	3
C.E.L. Ambrose	c Boon b Border	5
C.A. Walsh	not out	7
Extras	b 1, w 1, nb 4	6
Total (104.4 ov)		256

17, 56, 167, 188, 198, 225, 232, 244, 247

Hughes	18	6	29	1
Alderman	2	0	6	0
Waugh	3	0	10	0
P.L. Taylor	29	4	91	1
Hohns	34	11	69	3
Border	18.4	3	50	4

Australia 1st Innings

M.A. Taylor	c Haynes b Ambrose	3
G.R. Marsh	b Richards	23
D.C. Boon	c Harper b Marshall	10
D.M. Jones	not out	24
*A.R. Border	not out	16
	b 3, lb 1, nb 2	6
Total (3 wkts, 35.3 ov)		82

3, 16, 55

Marshall	8	2	17	1
Ambrose	7	1	16	1
Hooper	10.3	2	24	0
Walsh	3	0	9	0
Richards	7	2	12	1

Umpires: L.J. King and T.A. Prue
Toss: West Indies
Man of the Match: A.R. Border

Fifth Test, Adelaide

February 3, 4, 5, 6, 7, 1989

Drawn

Australia 1st Innings

G.R. Marsh	c Dujon b Ambrose	21
M.A. Taylor	run out	3
D.C. Boon	c Richardson b Ambrose	34
D.M. Jones	run out	216
*A.R. Border	b Marshall	64
S.R. Waugh	c Dujon b Walsh	12
†I.A. Healy	lbw b Walsh	0
T.V. Hohns	c Hooper b Walsh	9
T.B.A. May	c Richardson b Ambrose	24
M.G. Hughes	not out	72
M.R. Whitney	c Dujon b Patterson	2
Extras	lb 18, nb 40	58
Total (140.5 ov)		515

7, 64, 75, 289, 311, 311, 333, 383, 497

Marshall	23	3	67	1
Patterson	30.5	1	130	1
Ambrose	26	4	93	3
Walsh	33	5	120	3
Hooper	3	0	14	0
Richards	25	1	73	0

West Indies 1st Innings

C.G. Greenidge	b Whitney	12
D.L. Haynes	run out	83
R.B. Richardson	c Jones b Whitney	106
C.L. Hooper	c Healy b Whitney	2
*I.V.A. Richards	c Boon b Whitney	69
A.L. Logie	c Healy b Johns	21
†P.J.L. Dujon	b Hohns	28
M.D. Marshall	c Marsh b Whitney	0
C.E.L. Ambrose	c Boon b Whitney	4
C.A. Walsh	c Healy b Whitney	4
B.P. Patterson	not out	9
Extras	b 6, lb 10, nb 10	26
Total (121.4 ov)		369

19, 186, 190, 231, 293, 315, 315, 331, 346

Hughes	15	0	86	0
Whitney	30	6	89	7
May	16	6	42	0
Waugh	3	0	17	0
Hohns	47.4	9	106	2
Border	10	2	13	0

Australia 2nd Innings

G.R. Marsh	c Dujon b Ambrose	79
M.A. Taylor	run out	36
D.C. Boon	not out	55
D.M. Jones	lbw b Richards	6
S.R. Waugh	run out	8
*A.R. Border	not out	6
Extras	b 11, lb 13, nb 10	34
Total (4 wkts dec, 75 ov)		224

98, 176, 187, 213

Marshall	12	2	30	0
Ambrose	15	2	44	1
Walsh	13	2	26	0
Patterson	8	1	29	0
Richards	24	3	64	1
Hooper	3	1	7	0

West Indies 2nd Innings

C.G. Greenidge	c Boon b May	104
D.L. Haynes	c Healy b Whitney	15
R.B. Richardson	c Border b Whitney	22
C.L. Hooper	b May	0
*I.V.A. Richards	not out	68
A.L. Logie	not out	2
Extras	b 3, lb 7, w 1, nb 11	22
Total (4 wkts, 81 ov)		233

21, 87, 89, 212

Hughes	9	5	20	0
Whitney	20	4	60	2
Waugh	9	3	23	0
Hohns	15	3	56	0
May	23	2	60	2
Border	5	3	4	0

Umpires: R.J. Evans and P.J. McConnell
Toss: Australia
Man of the Match: D.M. Jones
Man of the Series: C.E.L. Ambrose

NEW ZEALAND v PAKISTAN

First Test, Dunedin
February 3, 4, 5, 6, 7, 1989
Abandoned on third day without a ball being bowled

Second Test, Wellington
February 10, 11, 12, 13, 14, 1989
Drawn

New Zealand 1st Innings		
R.H. Vance	c Yousuf b Mudassar	5
*J.G. Wright	c Yousuf b Mudassar	7
A.H. Jones	c Shoaib b Jaffer	86
M.D. Crowe	c Miandad b Jaffer	174
D.N. Patel	lbw b Imran	0
J.J. Crowe	b Qadir	39
J.G. Bracewell	b Imran	15
R.J. Hadlee	c Rizwan b Jaffer	32
†I.D.S. Smith	not out	40
D.K. Morrison	lbw b Imran	0
E.J. Chatfield	run out	14
Extras	b 10, lb 14, nb 11	35
Total (169.4 ov)		447

13, 18, 167, 168, 282, 321, 389, 398, 399

Imran	46.4	18	75	3
Jaffer	34	5	94	3
Mudassar	22	5	59	2
Aaqib	34	5	103	0
Qadir	29	4	83	1
Aamer	4	1	9	0

Pakistan 1st Innings		
Mudassar Nazar	c and b Morrison	6
Rizwan-uz-Zaman	lbw b Hadlee	18
Shoaib Mohammad	b Hadlee	163
Javed Miandad	lbw b Hadlee	118
Salim Malik	c Smith b Bracewell	38
*Imran Khan	b Chatfield	71
Aamer Malik	not out	8
†Salim Yousuf	c Jones b Hadlee	4
Abdul Qadir	not out	0
Salim Jaffer		
Aaqib Javed		
	b 1, lb 8, nb 3	12
Total (7 wkts dec, 195 ov)		438

14, 54, 274, 325, 422, 430, 437

Hadlee	54	14	101	4
Morrison	36	10	96	1
Chatfield	53	21	82	1
Bracewell	40	8	123	1
Patel	12	3	27	0

New Zealand 2nd Innings		
R.H. Vance	lbw b Imran	44
*J.G. Wright	c Miandad b Imran	19
A.H. Jones	c sub b Jaffer	39
M.D. Crowe	lbw b Jaffer	0
D.N. Patel	c Yousuf b Jaffer	2
J.J. Crowe	b Jaffer	23
J.G. Bracewell	lbw b Jaffer	0
R.J. Hadlee	c sub b Imran	7
†I.D.S. Smith	not out	29
D.K. Morrison	not out	1
Extras	b 10, lb 6, nb 6	22
Total (8 wkts, 61 ov)		186

36, 107, 108, 117, 128, 132, 140, 180

Imran	17	8	34	3
Aaqib	13	1	57	0
Qadir	14	3	39	0
Jaffer	17	4	40	5

Umpires: R.S. Dunne and S.J. Woodward
Toss: Pakistan
Man of the Match: Imran Khan

Third Test, Auckland
February 24, 25, 26, 27, 28, 1989
Drawn

Pakistan 1st Innings		
Mudassar Nazar	lbw b Hadlee	5
Rizwan-uz-Zaman	c J.J. Crowe b Boock	15
Shoaib Mohammad	run out	112
Javed Miandad	c Smith b Chatfield	271
Aamer Malik	c J.J. Crowe b Bracewell	56
Salim Malik	not out	80
*Imran Khan	not out	69
†Salim Yousuf		
Abdul Qadir		
Tauseef Ahmed		
Salim Jaffer		
Extras	lb 7, nb 1	8
Total (5 wkts dec, 203 ov)		616

10, 44, 292, 439, 480

Hadlee	28	7	68	1
Chatfield	65	14	158	1
Boock	70	10	229	1
Bracewell	37	4	138	1
Jones	3	0	16	0

New Zealand 1st Innings		
R.H. Vance	c Shoaib b Qadir	68
*J.G. Wright	c Rizwan b Tauseef	2
A.H. Jones	run out	47
M.D. Crowe	c Yousuf b Jaffer	78
S.L. Boock	c Mudassar b Qadir	8
M.J. Greatbatch	b Qadir	76
J.J. Crowe	c Miandad b Qadir	33
J.G. Bracewell	b Qadir	0
†I.D.S. Smith	c Mudassar b Imran	58
R.J. Hadlee	not out	14
E.J. Chatfield	c Aamer b Qadir	0
Extras	b 7, lb 2, nb 10	19
Total (184.1 ov)		403

13, 122, 123, 132, 286, 294, 294, 388, 388

Jaffer	18	6	44	1
Imran	34	9	76	1
Tauseef	69	28	106	1
Qadir	58.1	18	160	6
Shoaib	2	1	1	0
Mudassar	3	1	7	0

New Zealand 2nd Innings		
*J.G. Wright	c Yousuf b Qadir	36
R.H. Vance	c Yousuf b Mudassar	31
A.H. Jones	c Yousuf b Mudassar	0
M.D. Crowe	not out	9
M.J. Greatbatch	not out	13
	nb 10	10
Total (3 wkts, 50.4 ov)		99

68, 71, 76

Imran	5.4	1	13	0
Jaffer	8	4	18	0
Tauseef	12	4	23	0
Qadir	16	7	27	1
Shoaib	1	0	5	0
Mudassar	8	2	13	2

Umpires: B.L. Aldridge and S.J. Woodward
Toss: Pakistan
Man of the Match: Javed Miandad

WEST INDIES v INDIA

First Test, Georgetown
March 25, 26, 27, 28, 29, 30, 1989
Drawn

West Indies 1st Innings		
C.G. Greenidge	b Sharma	82
D.L. Haynes	b Ayub	20
R.B. Richardson	c Shastri b Ayub	194
K.L.T. Arthurton	run out	9
*I.V.A. Richards	b Kapil Dev	5
I.R. Bishop	lbw b Kapil Dev	0
A.L. Logie	c and b Hirwani	46
†P.J.L. Dujon	lbw b Ayub	31
C.E.L. Ambrose	not out	13
W.K.M. Benjamin	c Sharma b Ayub	7
C.A. Walsh	b Ayub	6
Extras	lb 5, w 4, nb 15	24
Total (140.5 ov)		437

41, 219, 231, 270, 270, 357, 412, 413, 423

Kapil Dev	28	8	67	2
Sharma	20	2	68	1
Shastri	33	6	87	0
Ayub	30.5	4	104	5
Hirwani	29	2	106	1

India 1st Innings		
Arun Lal	c Richards b Walsh	9
N.S. Sidhu	not out	42
R.J. Shastri	not out	29
*D.B. Vengsarkar		
M. Azharuddin		
S.V. Manjrekar		
Kapil Dev		
†K.S. Moré		
A. Ayub		
C. Sharma		
N.D. Hirwani		
Extras	lb 1, nb 5	6
Total (1 wkt, 39 ov)		86

14

Ambrose	3	2	6	0
Bishop	9	3	16	0
Benjamin	11	2	27	0
Walsh	6	0	12	1
Richards	7	1	17	0
Arthurton	3	0	7	0

Umpires: D.M. Archer & L.H. Barker
Toss: India

Richie Richardson, who scored 1,147 runs in two Test series against Australia and India, averaging nearly 72.
Allsport/Adrian Murrell

Second Test, Bridgetown
April 7, 8, 9, 11, 12, 1989
West Indies won by 8 wkts

India 1st Innings

Arun Lal	c Dujon b Bishop	8
N.S. Sidhu	c Richards b Walsh	9
R.J. Shastri	c Richardson b Bishop	6
*D.B. Vengsarkar	run out	20
M.Azharuddin	c Ambrose b Bishop	61
S.V. Manjrekar	c Greenidge b Bishop	108
Kapil Dev	c Richardson b Bishop	34
†K.S. Moré	c Dujon b Marshall	1
A. Ayub	c Richards b Bishop	32
C. Sharma	not out	12
N.D. Hirwani	c Haynes b Walsh	1
Extras	b 2, lb 5, nb 22	29
Total (105.2 ov)		321

14, 22, 27, 68, 139, 218, 219, 303, 320

Marshall	22	0	56	1
Ambrose	26	5	84	0
Bishop	25	5	87	6
Walsh	23.2	5	69	2
Richards	9	3	18	0

West Indies 1st Innings

D.L. Haynes	c Manjrekar b Shastri	27
C.G. Greenidge	c Hirwani b Sharma	117
R.B. Richardson	c Sidhu b Ayub	93
K.L.T. Arthurton	b Hirwani	0
*I.V.A. Richards	c sub b Hirwani	1
A.L. Logie	c Manjrekar b Shastri	26
†P.J.L. Dujon	c Manjrekar b Shastri	33
M.D. Marshall	not out	40
C.E.L. Ambrose	c Kapil Dev b Shastri	3
I.R. Bishop	lbw b Kapil Dev	8
C.A. Walsh	b Kapil Dev	0
Extras	lb 7, nb 22	29
Total (111.5 ov)		377

84, 201, 201, 203, 246, 325, 325, 354, 377

Kapil Dev	24.5	3	68	2
Sharma	18	1	86	1
Ayub	17	1	55	1
Hirwani	24	1	83	2
Shastri	28	7	78	4

India 2nd Innings

Arun Lal	c Haynes b Walsh	15
N.S. Sidhu	c Logie b Marshall	0
R.J. Shastri	c sub b Ambrose	107
*D.B. Vengsarkar	c Dujon b Bishop	6
M.Azharuddin	c Dujon b Marshall	14
S.V. Manjrekar	c Logie b Ambrose	3
Kapil Dev	c Dujon b Marshall	1
†K.S. Moré	b Marshall	50
A. Ayub	b Marshall	0
C. Sharma	c Dujon b Ambrose	21
N.D. Hirwani	not out	1
Extras	b 16, lb 4, nb 13	33
Total (98.4 ov)		251

0, 23, 32, 53, 62, 63, 195, 195, 245

Marshall	26	5	60	5
Ambrose	21.4	3	66	3
Walsh	20	6	34	1
Bishop	24	7	55	1
Richards	6	0	16	0
Arthurton	1	1	0	0

West Indies 2nd Innings

C.G. Greenidge	lbw b Sharma	6
D.L. Haynes	not out	112
R.B. Richardson	b Ayub	59
K.L.T. Arthurton	not out	11
Extras	lb 5, nb 3	8
Total (2 wkts, 49 ov)		196

Kapil Dev	8	0	42	0
Sharma	4	4	19	1
Ayub	14	0	26	1
Hirwani	11	2	56	0
Shastri	11	0	41	0
Manjrekar	1		7	0

Umpires: D.M. Archer and L.H. Barker
Toss: West Indies
Man of the Match: R.J. Shastri

Third Test, Port-of-Spain
April 15, 16, 17, 19, 20, 1989
West Indies won by 217 runs

West Indies 1st Innings

C.G. Greenidge	c Moré b Kapil Dev	21
D.L. Haynes	c Raman b Shastri	65
R.B. Richardson	c Hirwani b Ayub	15
K.L.T. Arthurton	c sub b Ayub	37
*I.V.A. Richards	b Ayub	19
A.L. Logie	c Moré b Hirwani	87
†P.J.L. Dujon	c Raman b Ayub	5
M.D. Marshall	st Moré b Ayub	18
C.E.L. Ambrose	c Moré b Kapil Dev	12
I.R. Bishop	not out	11
C.A. Walsh	c Arun Lal b Hirwani	6
Extras	b 7, lb 5, nb 6	18
Total (123.3 ov)		314

38, 80, 118, 146, 216, 228, 269, 294, 302

Kapil Dev	19	6	45	2
Sharma	6	1	23	0
Ayub	52	11	117	5
Shastri	27	8	58	1
Hirwani	19.3	1	59	2

India 1st Innings

Arun Lal	c Richards b Marshall	30
N.S. Sidhu	b Marshall	11
R.J. Shastri	c Logie b Marshall	8
*D.B. Vengsarkar	b Richards	2
W.V. Raman	c Dujon b Walsh	17
S.V. Manjrekar	lbw b Marshall	0
Kapil Dev	c Dujon b Marshall	16
†K.S. Moré	b Walsh	2
A. Ayub	b Walsh	29
C. Sharma	not out	19
N.D. Hirwani	lbw b Walsh	0
Extras	b 2, lb 5, w 1, nb 8	16
Total (67 ov)		150

Ambrose	9	1	28	0
Bishop	11	4	16	0
Walsh	18	5	37	4
Marshall	17	7	34	5
Richards	12	3	28	1

West Indies 2nd Innings

C.G. Greenidge	c Moré b Sharma	5
D.L. Haynes	c Shastri b Sharma	6
R.B. Richardson	b Kapil Dev	99
K.L.T. Arthurton	lbw b Kapil Dev	1
*I.V.A. Richards	c Manjrekar b Sharma	0
A.L. Logie	c and b Hirwani	38
†P.J.L. Dujon	b Shastri	3
M.D. Marshall	lbw b Kapil Dev	26
C.E.L. Ambrose	c Moré b Kapil Dev	16
I.R. Bishop	not out	30
C.A. Walsh	b Kapil Dev	4
Extras	b 3, lb 24, w 1, nb 10	38
Total (103 ov)		266

17, 18, 23, 26, 100, 119, 180, 204, 250

Kapil Dev	25	5	58	5
Sharma	20	0	54	3
Ayub	18	1	50	0
Shastri	18	3	32	1
Hirwani	18	4	40	1
Raman	4	1	5	0

India 2nd Innings

N.S. Sidhu	c Dujon b Ambrose	1
Arun Lal	c Dujon b Marshall	18
R.J. Shastri	c Dujon b Bishop	15
W.V. Raman	lbw b Marshall	15
*D.B. Vengsarkar	c Logie b Marshall	62
S.V. Manjrekar	lbw b Marshall	1
Kapil Dev	c Dujon b Bishop	4
†K.S. Moré	lbw b Marshall	42
A. Ayub	c Richards b Bishop	1
C. Sharma	b Marshall	7
N.D. Hirwani	not out	1
Extras	b 7, lb 15, nb 24	46
Total (81.5 ov)		213

20, 60, 64, 66, 76, 92, 190, 194, 212

Ambrose	15	8	23	1
Bishop	25	8	81	3
Walsh	10	4	15	0
Marshall	19.5	2	55	6
Richards	8	0	13	0
Arthurton	4	2	4	0

Umpires: C.E. Cumberbatch and A. Weekes
Toss: India
Man of the Match: M.D. Marshall

Fourth Test, Kingston
April 28, 29 30, May 2, 3, 1989
West Indies won by 7 wkts

India 1st Innings

S.D. Sidhu	c Richards b Walsh	116
Arun Lal	c Richards b Marshall	7
R.J. Shastri	c Richards b Bishop	5
*D.B. Vengsarkar	c Dujon b Bishop	12
M. Azharuddin	c Richards b Walsh	25
S.V. Manjrekar	c Logie b Walsh	47
†K.S. Moré	ht wkt b Walsh	6
Kapil Dev	c Ambrose b Walsh	23
A. Ayub	c Arthurton b Walsh	2
C. Sharma	c Arthurton b Ambrose	6
M. Venkataramana	not out	0
Extras	b 1, lb 7, w 1, nb 31	40
Total (102.2 ov)		289

35, 64, 97, 142, 252, 252, 256, 279, 285

Ambrose	13.2	1	46	1
Bishop	26	8	55	2
Walsh	29	6	62	6
Marshall	19	4	56	1
Richards	9	1	36	0
Arthurton	6	0	26	0

West Indies 1st Innings

C.G. Greenidge	c Arun Lal b Kapil Dev	0
D.L. Haynes	c Shastri b Kapil Dev	15
R.B. Richardson	b Kapil Dev	156
K.L.T. Arthurton	c Azharuddin b Sharma	20
*I.V.A. Richards	c Moré b Kapil Dev	110
A.L. Logie	lbw b Kapil Dev	11
†P.J.L. Dujon	b Ayub	11
M.D. Marshall	b Kapil Dev	0
C.E.L. Ambrose	c Moré b Sharma	10
I.R. Bishop	not out	6
C.A. Walsh	c Venkataramana b Ayub	4
Extras	b 10, lb 9, w 23, nb 19	41
Total (128.5 ov)		384

1, 32, 86, 321, 343, 344, 344, 364, 378

Kapil Dev	38	7	84	6
Sharma	27	2	100	2
Ayub	39.5	12	99	2
Venkataramana	11	1	48	0
Shastri	13	1	34	0

India 2nd 1st Innings

Arun Lal	c Greenidge b Bishop	26
N.S. Sidhu	c Greenidge b Walsh	0
R.J. Shastri	lbw b Bishop	0
S.V. Manjrekar	c Haynes b Walsh	41
*D.B. Vengsarkar	b Bishop	8
M. Azharuddin	b Walsh	13
Kapil Dev	c Richards b Bishop	13
†K.S. Moré	c Dujon b Walsh	2
A. Ayub	run out	14
C. Sharma	b Marshall	21
M. Venkataramana	not out	0
Extras	b 1, lb 2, nb 11	14
Total (48.3 ov)		152

0, 1, 75, 75, 88, 100, 107, 113, 150

Bishop	17	3	61	4
Walsh	17	7	39	4
Marshall	7.3	0	29	1
Ambrose	7	0	20	0

West Indies 2nd Innings

C.G. Greenidge	c Moré b Kapil Dev	12
D.L. Hayes	st Moré b Venkataramana	35
R.B. Richardson	st Moré b Shastri	3
K.L.T. Arthurton	not out	0
A.L. Logie	not out	6
	lb 3, nb 1	4
Total (3 wkts, 18.4 ov)		60

31, 50, 54

Kapil Dev	9	2	22	1
Sharma	2	0	16	0
Shastri	7	2	9	1
Venkataramana	0.4	0	10	1

Umpires: D.M. Archer and S. Bucknor
Toss: West Indies
Man of the Match: C.A. Walsh
Man of the Series: R.B. Richardson

PAKISTAN v AUSTRALIA 1988–89 – Test match averages

PAKISTAN

Batting and fielding	*M*	*I*	*NO*	*Runs*	*HS*	*Avge*	*100*	*50*	*Ct*	*St*
Javed Miandad	3	5	–	412	211	82.40	2	–	1	–
Shoaib Mohammad	3	5	–	195	94	39.00	–	2	3	–
Ijaz Ahmed	3	5	–	172	122	34.40	1	–	6	–
Salim Yousuf	3	5	1	136	66*	34.00	–	2	4	5
Tauseef Ahmed	3	5	2	76	35*	25.33	–	–	–	–
Rameez Raja	3	5	0	126	64	25.20	–	1	–	–
Iqbal Qasim	3	4	1	69	29	23.00	–	–	3	–
Mudassar Nazar	3	5	0	112	49	22.40	–	–	2	–
Salim Malik	3	5	0	94	45	18.80	–	–	–	–
Abdul Qadir	3	5	0	51	18	10.20	–	–	–	–

Played in two matches: Salim Jaffer 0, 0*.
Played in one match: Aamer Malik 17* (1 ct).

Bowling	*O*	*M*	*R*	*W*	*Avge*	*BB*	*5i*	*10m*
Iqbal Qasim	102.5	48	177	12	14.75	5–35	1	–
Mudassar Nazar	50	13	95	4	23.75	2–39	–	–
Tauseef Ahmed	161.3	64	268	11	24.36	3–73	–	–
Abdul Quadir	125	37	319	11	29.00	3–33	–	–
Salim Jaffer	78	18	219	5	43.90	2–60	–	–

Also bowled: Aamer Malik 4-2-6-1, Salim Malik 6-4-7-1, Shoaib Mohammad 4-1-7-1.

AUSTRALIA

Batting and fielding	*M*	*I*	*NO*	*Runs*	*HS*	*Av*	*100*	*50*	*Ct*	*St*
A.R. Border	3	5	1	230	113*	57.50	1	1	4	–
P.L. Taylor	2	4	2	110	54*	55.00	–	1	1	–
G.R. Marsh	3	6	1	232	84*	46.40	–	3	2	–
G.M. Wood	3	5	1	87	32	21.75	–	–	1	–
D.C. Boon	3	6	–	117	43	19.50	–	–	10	–
I.A. Healy	3	4	–	74	27	18.50	–	–	6	2
S.R. Waugh	3	5	–	92	59	18.40	–	1	2	–
T.B.A. May	3	4	1	33	14	11.00	–	–	–	–
A.I.C. Dodemaide	3	4	–	43	19	10.75	–	–	1	–
D.M. Jones	3	6	1	44	21*	8.80	–	–	–	–
B.A. Reid	3	4	1	17	8*	5.67	–	–	1	–

Played in one match: P.R. Sleep 12 (1 ct).

Bowling	*O*	*M*	*R*	*W*	*Avge*	*BB*	*5i*	*10m*
B.A. Reid	125	27	354	14	25.29	4–100	–	–
A.I.C. Dodemaide	121	34	247	9	27.44	4–87	–	–
T.B.A. May	156.5	46	393	14	28.07	4–97	–	–
P.L. Taylor	48	13	162	4	40.50	4–78	–	–

Also bowled: A.R. Border 28-11-48-0, P.R. Sleep 18.5-5-75-2, S.R. Waugh 78-11-216-2.
For Pakistan. Moin-ul-Atiq took one catch as a substitute.

Martin Crowe, who returned to Test cricket after missing the tour to India and made 174 in his first innings against Pakistan.

Allsport/Adrian Murrell

Krish Srikkanth, who missed the Test series in West Indies after breaking his arm in the one-day internationals. He had topped the averages in the earlier series against New Zealand.

Allsport/Adrian Murrell

INDIA v NEW ZEALAND 1988–89 — Test match averages

INDIA

Batting and fielding	*M*	*I*	*NO*	*Runs*	*HS*	*Avge*	*100*	*50*	*Ct*	*St*
K. Srikkanth	3	6	2	240	94	60.00	–	3	6	–
N.S. Sidhu	3	5	1	198	116	49.50	1	–	–	–
M. Azharuddin	3	4	–	153	81	38.25	–	1	2	–
R.J. Shastri	3	4	–	134	54	33.50	–	1	1	–
D.B. Vengsarkar	3	4	–	132	75	33.00	–	1	6	–
Kapil Dev	3	4	–	107	40	26.75	–	–	4	–
Arun Lal	3	6	1	103	47	20.60	–	–	6	–
K.S. Moré	3	4	–	76	46	19.00	–	–	7	1
A. Ayub	3	4	2	35	19	17.50	–	–	2	–
N. Hirwani	3	4	2	22	17	11.00	–	–	–	–

Played in one match: R.G. Patel 0, 0 (1 ct); W.V. Raman 3; S.K. Sharma 18* (1 ct).

Bowling	*O*	*M*	*R*	*W*	*Avge*	*BB*	*5i*	*10m*
A.Ayub	196.4	75	287	21	13.67	5–50	1	–
S.K. Sharma	21	4	50	3	16.67	3–37	–	–
N. Hirwani	168	47	390	20	19.50	6–59	1	–
Kapil Dev	89	22	232	10	23.20	3–21	–	–
R.J. Shastri	58.3	14	137	5	27.40	4–45	–	–

Also bowled: R.G. Patel 14-0-51-0, W.V. Raman 19-8-31-1, K. Srikkanth 4-2-7-0.

NEW ZEALAND

Batting and fielding	*M*	*I*	*NO*	*Runs*	*HS*	*Avge*	*100*	*50*	*Ct*	*St*
M.J. Greatbatch	3	6	1	196	90*	39.20	–	1	3	–
J.G. Wright	3	6	–	228	62	38.00	–	2	2	–
I.D.S. Smith	3	6	–	201	79	33.50	–	2	5	–
A.H. Jones	3	6	–	156	78	26.00	–	1	2	–
J.G. Bracewell	3	6	–	101	52	16.83	–	1	3	–
T.J. Franklin	3	6	–	86	28	14.33	–	–	3	–
R.J. Hadlee	3	6	1	61	31	12.20	–	–	1	–
K.R. Rutherford	2	4	–	37	17	9.25	–	–	3	–
T.E. Blain	2	4	–	36	16	9.00	–	–	1	–
E.J. Chatfield	3	6	3	6	4*	2.00	–	–	1	–
C.M. Kuggeleijn	2	4	–	7	7	1.75	–	–	1	–

Played in one match: E.J. Gray 1, 2 (1 ct); D.K. Morrison 27*, 0; M.C. Snedden 0, 0 (1 ct).

Bowling	*O*	*M*	*R*	*W*	*Avge*	*BB*	*5i*	*10m*
R.J. Hadlee	100.5	25	252	18	14.00	6–49	2	1
M.C. Snedden	19.3	3	82	4	20.50	4–69	–	–
J.G. Bracewell	88.4	11	332	8	41.50	6–51	1	–
E.J. Chatfield	106	25	261	6	43.50	2–82	–	–
E.J. Gray	51	8	167	3	55.67	2–128	–	–

Also bowled: C.M. Kuggeleijn 16.1-2-67-1, D.K. Morrison 22-2-85-0.

AUSTRALIA v WEST INDIES 1988–89 – Test match averages

AUSTRALIA

Batting and fielding	*M*	*I*	*NO*	*Runs*	*HS*	*Avge*	*100*	*50*	*Ct*	*St*
D.M.Jones	3	6	1	321	216	64.20	1	–	5	–
D.C. Boon	4	10	1	397	149	44.11	1	2	9	–
S.R. Waugh	5	9	1	331	91	41.38	–	3	3	–
M.G. Hughes	4	5	2	109	72*	36.33	–	1	3	–
A.R. Border	5	10	2	258	75	32.25	–	2	7	–
G.M. Wood	3	6	–	178	111	29.67	1	–	2	–
G.R. Marsh	5	10	–	227	79	22.70	–	1	5	–
C.J. McDermott	2	4	1	62	32*	20.67	–	–	1	–
M.R.J. Veletta	2	4	–	71	37	17.75	–	–	2	–
I.A. Healy	5	8	–	138	52	17.25	–	1	12	–
M.A. Taylor	2	4	–	67	36	16.75	–	–	1	–
P.L. Taylor	2	3	1	32	18*	16.00	–	–	5	–
A.I.C. Dodemaide	2	4	1	47	22	15.67	–	–	4	–
T.B.A. May	3	5	2	43	24	14.33	–	–	1	–
T.V. Hohns	2	2	–	9	9	4.50	–	–	–	–
T.M. Alderman	2	3	–	12	9	4.00	–	–	1	–

Played in one match: G.F. Lawson 0*; C.D. Matthews 1, 32; M.R. Whitney 2.

Bowling	*O*	*M*	*R*	*W*	*Avge*	*BB*	*5i*	*10m*
A.R. Border	61.4	19	121	11	11.00	7–46	1	1
M.R. Whitney	50.	10	149	9	16.56	7–89	1	–
T.M. Alderman	80.1	23	169	7	24.14	4–68	–	–
G.F. Lawson	32	7	97	3	32.33	3–97	–	–
C.J. McDermott	77	9	251	7	35.86	3–62	–	–
M.G. Hughes	163.1	41	503	14	35.93	8–87	2	1
T.B.A. May	92	18	300	7	42.86	3–90	–	–
T.V. Hohns	120.4	31	280	6	46.67	3–69	–	–
S.R. Waugh	139	17	472	10	47.20	5–92	1	–
A.I.C. Dodemaide	63	6	255	4	63.75	2–60	–	–
P.L. Taylor	70.2	16	213	3	71.00	2–65	–	–

Also bowled: C.D. Matthews 24.5-4-80-0.

WEST INDIES

Batting and fielding	*M*	*I*	*NO*	*Runs*	*HS*	*Avge*	*100*	*50*	*Ct*	*St*
D.L. Haynes	5	10	1	537	143	59.67	2	2	5	–
R.B. Richardson	5	10	1	528	122	58.67	2	2	4	–
I.V.A. Richards	5	9	1	446	146	55.75	1	4	3	–
C.G. Greenidge	5	10	1	397	104	44.11	1	2	4	–
A.L. Logie	5	9	1	198	93	24.75	–	1	8	–
P.J.L. Dujon	5	8	–	195	46	24.38	–	–	15	–
C.A. Walsh	5	8	5	68	30*	22.67	–	–	–	–
C.L. Hooper	5	9	–	170	64	18.89	–	1	5	–
C.E.L. Ambrose	5	8	1	106	44	15.14	–	–	2	–
B.P. Patterson	4	6	3	32	13	10.67	–	–	–	–
M.D. Marshall	5	8	–	76	23	9.50	–	–	1	–

Played in one match: R.A. Harper 17, 12 (1 ct).

Bowling	*O*	*M*	*R*	*W*	*Avge*	*BB*	*5i*	*10m*
C.E.L. Ambrose	204.3	38	558	26	21.46	5–72	1	–
M.D. Marshall	192	42	488	17	28.71	5–29	1	–
C.A. Walsh	176.5	32	500	17	29.41	4–62	–	–
B.P. Patterson	107.1	11	405	12	33.75	5–39	1	–
I.V.A. Richards	117	12	299	3	99.67	1–12	–	–

Also bowled: R.A. Harper 37-9-86-0, C.L. Hooper 79.317-198-2.

K.L.T. Arthurton (2) and R.A. Harper (2) took catches while fielding as substitutes.

NEW ZEALAND v PAKISTAN 1988–89 – Test match averages

NEW ZEALAND

Batting and fielding	*M*	*I*	*NO*	*Runs*	*HS*	*Avge*	*100*	*50*	*Ct*	*St*
I.D.S. Smith	2	3	2	127	58	127.00	–	1	2	–
M.J. Greatbatch	1	2	1	89	76	89.00	–	1	–	–
M.D. Crowe	2	4	1	261	174	87.00	1	1	–	–
A.H. Jones	2	4	–	172	86	43.00	–	1	1	–
R.H. Vance	2	4	–	148	68	37.00	–	1	–	–
J.J. Crowe	2	3	–	95	39	31.66	–	–	2	–
R.J. Hadlee	2	3	1	63	32	26.50	–	–	–	–
J.G. Wright	2	4	–	64	36	16.00	–	–	–	–
E.J. Chatfield	2	2	–	14	14	7.00	–	–	–	–
J.G. Bracewell	2	3	–	15	15	5.00	–	–	–	–
D.N. Patel	1	2	–	2	2	1.00	–	–	–	–
D.K. Morrison	1	2	1	1	1*	1.00	–	–	1	–

Played in one match: S.L. Boock 8

Bowling	*O*	*M*	*R*	*W*	*Avge*	*BB*	*5i*	*10m*
R.J. Hadlee	82	21	169	5	33.80	4–101	–	–

Also bowled: S.L. Boock 70-1--229-1; J.G. Bracewell 77-12-261-2; E.J. Chatfield 118-35-240-2; A.H. Jones 3-0-16-0; D.K. Morrison 36-10-96-1; D.N. Patel 12-3-27-0.

PAKISTAN

Batting and fielding	*M*	*I*	*NO*	*Runs*	*HS*	*Avge*	*100*	*50*	*Ct*	*St*
Javed Miandad	2	2	0	389	271	194.50	2	–	3	–
Imran Khan	2	2	1	140	73	140.00	–	2	–	–
Shoaib Mohammad	2	2	0	275	163	137.50	2	1	2	–
Salim Malik	2	2	1	118	80*	118.00	–	1	–	–
Aamer Malik	2	2	1	64	561	64.00	–	–	1	–
Rizwan-uz-Zaman	2	2	0	33	18	16.50	–	–	2	–
Mudassar Nazar	2	2	0	11	6	5.50	–		2	–

Played in two matches: Abdul Qadir 0*; Salim Yousuf 4 (7 ct); Salim Jaffer did not bat

Played in one match: Aaqib Jaffer and Tausif Ahmed did not bat.

Bowling	*O*	*M*	*R*	*W*	*Avge*	*BB*	*5i*	*10m*
Mudassar Nazar	33	8	79	4	19.75	2–13	–	–
Salim Jaffer	77	19	196	9	21.77	5–40	1	–
Imran Khan	103.2	35	198	7	28.28	3–34	–	–
Abdul Qadir	117.1	31	309	8	38.62	6–160	1	–

Also bowled: Aamer Malik 4-1-9-0; Aaqib Javed 47-6-16-0; Shoaib Mohammad 3-1-6-0; Tausif Ahmed 81-32-129-1.

WEST INDIES v INDIA 1988–89 – Test match averages

WEST INDIES

Batting and fielding	*M*	*I*	*NO*	*Runs*	*HS*	*Avge*	*100*	*50*	*Ct*	*St*
R.B. Richardson	4	7	–	619	194	88.43	2	3	2	–
D.L. Haynes	4	7	1	280	112*	46.67	1	1	3	–
A.L. Logie	4	6	1	214	87	42.80	–	1	5	–
C.G. Greenidge	4	7	–	243	117	34.71	1	1	3	–
M.D. Marshall	3	4	1	84	40*	28.00	–	–	–	–
I.R. Bishop	4	5	3	55	30*	27.50	–	–	–	–
I.V.A. Richards	4	5	–	135	110	27.00	1	–	10	–
P.J.L. Dujon	4	5	–	83	33	16.60	–	–	14	–
K.L.T. Arthurton	4	7	2	78	37	15.60	–	–	2	–
C.E.L. Ambrose	4	5	1	54	16	13.50	–	–	2	–
C.A. Walsh	4	5	–	20	6	4.00	–	–	–	–

Played in one match: W.K.M. Benjamin 7.

Bowling	*O*	*M*	*R*	*W*	*Avge*	*BB*	*5i*	*10m*
C.A. Walsh	123.2	33	268	18	14.89	6–62	1	1
M.D. Marshall	111.2	18	290	19	15.26	6–55	3	1
I.R. Bishop	137	38	371	16	23.19	6–87	1	–
C.E.L. Ambrose	95	20	273	5	54.60	3–66	–	–

Also bowled: K.L.T. Arthurton 14-3-37-0, W.K.M. Benjamin 11-2-27-0, I.V.A. Richards 51-8-128-1.

INDIA

Batting and fielding	*M*	*I*	*NO*	*Runs*	*HS*	*Avge*	*100*	*50*	*Ct*	*St*
S.V. Manjrekar	4	6	–	200	108	33.33	1	–	4	–
N.S. Sidhu	4	7	1	179	116	29.83	1	–	1	–
R.J. Shastri	4	7	1	170	107	28.22	1	–	3	–
M. Azharuddin	3	4	–	113	61	28.25	–	1	1	–
C. Sharma	4	6	2	86	21	21.50	–	–	1	–
D.B. Vengsarkar	4	6	–	110	62	18.33	–	1	–	–
K.S. Moré	4	6	–	103	50	17.17	–	1	8	3
Arun Lal	4	7	–	113	30	16.14	–	–	2	–
Kapil Dev	4	6	–	91	34	15.17	–	–	1	–
A. Ayub	4	6	–	78	32	13.00	–	–	–	–
N.D. Hirwani	3	4	2	3	1*	1.50	–	–	4	–

Played in one match: W.V. Raman 17, 15 (2 ct); M. Venkataramana 0*, 0* (1 ct).

Bowling	*O*	*M*	*R*	*W*	*Avge*	*BB*	*5i*	*10m*
Kapil Dev	151.5	31	386	18	21.44	6–84	2	–
A. Ayub	171.4	33	451	14	32.21	5–104	2	–
C. Sharma	97	6	366	8	45.75	3–54	–	–
R.J. Shastri	137	29	339	7	48.43	4–78	–	–
N.D. Hirwani	102.3	8	344	6	57.33	2–59	–	–

Also bowled: S.V. Manjrekar 1-0-7-0, W.V. Raman 4-1-5-0, M. Venkataramana 11.4-1.58-1.

For India, Rabindra Singh took two catches as a substitute: Winston Herbert (a local player with no first-class experience) took one for West Indies.

Richard Hadlee finally became the most successful bowler in Test history when he passed Ian Botham's total of wickets in 1988–89. He ended the season four wickets short of 400. Allsport/Adrian Murrell

Cricket Books of 1989

In conjunction with Sport-in-Print, of 3 Radcliffe Road, West Bridgford, Nottingham, we list with brief comments the new titles which appeared during the year. Almost 100 volumes come within the scope of this list and we do not include a further 100 county, league or club annuals, or the increasingly elaborate benefit brochures which many county players issue.

Author	*Title*	*Publisher*	*Pages*	*Price*	
R. Adams (ed)	**Famous Writers on Cricket**	**Partridge**	**107**	**£9.95**	Quite a number of the writers are anything but famous and the chief interest lies in the captions to the photographs. The Who's Who is rather inaccurate.
G. Andrew	**Tales from the Tin Tabernacle**	**Darf**	**81**	**£3.95**	A paperback with some amusingly comical lines on village cricket and its characters, drawn more than life size.
J. Bailey	**Conflicts in Cricket**	**Kingswood**	**203**	**£14.99**	Mr Bailey 'resigned' in the controversy when MCC played TCCB – he explains the results of the match and its consequences.
T.E. Bailey	**The Greatest Since My Time**	**Hodder**	**272**	**£12.95**	Son of 'The Greatest of My Time' – essays on 30 cricketers post-1965 and some notes on the changes in the game since Bailey retired.
R. Baker	**Iron and Willow**	**Author**	**124**	**£5.00**	Cyclostated history of Middlesbrough CC 1855–1911.
P. Ball (ed)	**Imran Khan's Cricket Skills**	**Hamlyn**	**127**	**£6.95**	A good coaching manual with excellent colour illustrations.
S. Barnes	**A La Recherche du Cricket Perdu**	**Macmillan**	**144**	**£7.99**	The author writes a series of essays in the style of famous writers frm Proust (hence the title) upwards. Unusual book for the really literary.
N. Barrett (ed)	**The Daily Telegraph Cricket Year 89**	**Pan**	**240**	**£7.95**	Appeared much later with new publisher, which might indicate sales are not very buoyant. Usual format.
H.D. Bird	**That's Out**	**Barker**	**160**	**£4.95**	A paperback of the 1985 book with most of the familiar stories.
P. Baxter	**The Ashes: Highlights since 1948**	**BBC**	**192**	**£12.95**	Series of essays by the Test Match Special team on various incidents they have seen and commentated on
D. Birley	**The Willow Wand**	**Simon and Schuster**	**221**	**£6.95**	Paperback of the book that appeared 10 years ago and caused some comment at the time.
G. Brodribb	**Cricket At Hastings**	**Spellmount**	**128**	**£12.95**	The story of County matches staged on the ground which is scheduled for redevelopment this year.
R.Brooke/ D.Goodyear	**Who's Who of Warwickshire CCC**	**Hale**	**240**	**£14.95**	Photos and potted biographies of the county players; good idea marred by poor photos and layout.
N. Burdett	**Weldon CC 125 Not Out**	**Club**	**16**	**£1.50**	A brief resume of this Northants club, whose present mentor is related to William Clarke.
R. Butcher	**Rising to the Challenge**	**Pelham**	**176**	**£12.95**	The story of the Middlesex cricketer from the West Indies who played for England.
G.H. Chesterton/ G.H.G. Doggart	**Oxford and Cambridge Cricket**	**Collins**	**319**	**£14.95**	An uneven history attached to the scores of the University match – an opportunity not fully taken.
J.P. Coldham	**F.S. Jackson**	**Crowood**	**208**	**£12.95**	From this description Mr Jackson was not as exciting as expected.
G. Cotter	**The Ashes Captains**	**Crowood**	**320**	**£16.95**	The care with which this book was written should have been lavished on something more original.
T. Cozier	**B&H West Indies Cricket Annual 1989**	**Carribean Communications**	**88**	**£3.50**	The standard West Indies Annual with details of the 1988–89 season – an attractive production.
N. Craven	**Waiting for Cheltenham**	**Author**	**58**	**£3.25**	Essays on the author's cricketing trips in 1988 mainly revolving around Gloucestershire.
M. and S. Davie	**The Faber Book of Cricket**	**Faber**	**398**	**£4.99**	Paperback of the anthology of two years ago, with all the familiar pens.
P.H. Edmonds	**100 Greatest Bowlers**	**Macdonald**	**256**	**£16.95**	Companion to Arlott's batsmen – clearly subjective and going back to Hambledon. Better to have done 100 bowlers I have known.
J.M. Eldershaw	**I Zingari in Australia**	**Allen**	**207**	**£20.00**	An expensive history of the Australian IZ.
J.E. Emburey	**Spinning in the Fast Lane**	**Robson**	**160**	**£11.95**	The most interesting piece of this autobiography is the piece with Edmonds. Otherwise the usual format.
N. Ford	**Cricket Widows**	**Angus and Robertson**	**96**	**£3.50**	Cartoons and quips between the sexes.
W.H. Frindall	**England Test Cricketers**	**Collins**	**526**	**£19.95**	Match by match details of every England player with a brief essay and photograph.
W.H. Frindall (ed)	**Playfair Cricket Annual 1989**	**Macdonald**	**256**	**£1.75**	The essential pocket annual but with some confusion at the proof reader's.
J.S. Finch	**Three Men at the Match**	**Macdonald**	**220**	**£11.95**	A sequel to 'Game in Season' – three companions on their trips to watch county matches, mainly in the Midlands.
D. Frith	**England versus Australia**	**Macdonald**	**352**	**£19.95**	New edition of this tome which pops up when the two countries are at war.
N. Garnham	**Copdock CC 150th Anniversary**	**Author**	**52**	**£2.50**	The East Anglian side which once featured Fuller Pilch – a nice brochure
M.W. Gatting	**Leading From The Front**	**Queen Anne Press**	**358**	**£3.99**	Paperback of this best-seller by the ex-England captain.
B. Green	**The Wisden Papers**	**Stanley Paul**	**319**	**£14.95**	A collection of essays which have featured in the Almanack over the last 100 years.
B. Green	**The Wisden Papers of N. Cardus**	**Century-Hutchinson**	**159**	**£15.95**	Another collection of Cardus and much more expensive than the last.
D.M. Griffiths	**200 Not Out: Uxbridge CC**	**Club**	**122**	**£12.95**	The club claims to be founded 200 years ago and this book traces its history since then.
I. Haffenden	**Cricket Menopause**	**Haf**	**99**	**£4.50**	Rather a pedestrian saga of Sidmouth CC – the town that launched Somerset.
L.Hatton	**ACS Second Eleven Annual 1989**	**Association of Cricket Statisticians**	**44**	**£2.25**	Essential guide to first-class counties' lesser players.
S. Hogben	**Mentone CC Centenary Book**	**Club**	**132**	**£5.00**	The Australian Club which produced players such as O'Brien and Meckiff, a nice history.
R. Holt	**Sport and the British**	**OUP**	**410**	**£19.30**	Cricket is just one chapter in this tome; the author tries to explain the influence of sport on the British.
D. Hodgson	**The Official History of Yorkshire CC**	**Crowood**	**346**	**£17.95**	The second history of the county to appear in 1989, much slimmer, but same price. Story well told, but index woolly.
G. Howat	**Crickets Second Golden Age**	**Hodder**	**300**	**£14.95**	Rose-coloured glasses are needed to see Golden Ages and such glasses will hopefully obscure the errors.
M. Hughes	**Cardus on the Ashes**	**Souvenir**	**287**	**£14.95**	Cardus on Tests 1902 to 1970/71, at half the price of Mr Green's effort.
C.L.R. James	**Cricket**	**Allison, Busby**	**331**	**£5.99**	Paperback containing the writings of the best West Indian cricket writer.
B. Johnston	**It's Been a Piece of Cake**	**Methuen**	**288**	**£12.99**	The amiable commentator writes as he broadcasts and it shows.
J. Kemp	**Cheerful Charlie**	**Author**	**160**	**£10.95**	McGahey of Essex – a cheerful cricketer who came to a sad end, written with enthusiasm.
D. Lemmon	**The History of Surrey CCC**	**Helm**	**379**	**£15.95**	A workmanlike history which gives a rounded picture of the county's ups and downs.
D. Lemmon	**The History of Worcestershire CCC**	**Helm**	**296**	**£14.95**	Another history maintaining the high standard of the Helm series.
D. Lemmon	**Benson and Hedges Cricket Year, 8th Ed.**	**Pelham**	**480**	**£16.95**	The first annual covering 1989 came out well before Christmas and is as handsome as ever and as free from error as one can expect.
A. Lee	**Wisden Book of Cricket Heroes**	**Stanley Paul**	**96**	**£4.95**	A slim volume in the Wisden series.
C. Lee	**From The Sea End**	**Partridge**	**336**	**£15.00**	The history of Sussex with emphasis on the early years – the team photographs might have been larger.

L.Lenham **Copybook Cricket** **Robson** **188** **£10.95**
A nice coaching book marred by some poor pictures.

J.K. Lever **A Cricketer's Cricketer** **Unwin Hyman** **192** **£12.95**
Pat Gibson helps the Essex bowler tell his story, coinciding with his final season.

Lord's Taverners **Tales from Around the Wicket** **David and Charles** **126** **£7.50**
A collection of essays as variable as the authors, but all in a good cause.

E. Midwinter **Red Roses Crest The Caps** **Kingswood** **256** **£12.99**
The story of Lancashire cricket placed in its setting and pleasantly told.

H. Milton **F.E. Woolley** **Association of Cricket Statisticians** **84** **£3.50**
A detailed study of all his first-class innings with additional commentary.

A. Miller **Allan's Australian Annual** **Author** **131** **£7.00**
The detailed scorecards and descriptions of all the 1988–89 Australian matches – large size softback.

R. Moorhouse **Armitage Bridge CC 150th Anniversary** **Author** **92** **£3.50**
A brochure on the Yorkshire Club which bred some famous Yorkshire cricketers.

I. Morrison **Play The Game: Cricket** **Ward Lock** **80** **£3.99**
Softback introduction to cricket – one of a long series on games and sports.

D. Mosey **Laker: Portrait of A Legend** **Macdonald** **189** **£12.95**
The author, who knew his subject well, provides an interesting book on this brusque Yorkshireman.

K.H. Moss **Pudsey St Lawrence CC Centenary** **Author** **50** **£2.50**
One of Yorkshire's most famous Clubs celebrates 100 years.

D. Neely **Radio NZ Sport Cricket Annual** **RNZS** **196** **£14.95**
The rival to the Shell Almanack, with not so much statistical details as the older annual.

I. Orr-Ewing **A Celebration of Lords and Commons Cricket, 1850–1988** **Kingswood** **224** **£25.00**
Nicely produced, well illustrated, but more detail on the 19th century would have been appreciated.

M. Patherya **The Penguin Book of Cricket Lists** **Penguin** **240** **£3.99**
Odd tit-bits of information, some more accurate than others.

F. Payne/I. Smith **1989 Shell Cricket Almanack of New Zealand** **Moa** **312** **£11.95**
Well up to the high standard of its predecessors.

P. Pickup **History of the Bradford League** **Author** **128** **£7.00**
A well researched book of one of the strongest leagues; many Test players appear in its pages.

G. Plumptre **Cricket Cartoons and Caricatures** **Collins** **159** **£16.95**
104 cartoons and sketches mainly from Lords's – it should be read in conjunction with 'The Art of Cricket'.

J. Pollard **The Bradman Years** **Angus and Robertson** **422** **£16.95**
Continuing the author's monumental history of Australian cricket, this volumn treats the years from the end of the 1920s to the end of the 1940s – they are aptly titled.

W. Powell **Wisden Guide to Cricket Grounds** **Stanley Paul** **416** **£10.95**
All that the spectator wants to know concerning the grounds currently used by the first-class counties – an improved version of Norman Yardley's 'Homes of Cricket'.

D. Rayvern-Allen **The Essential John Arlott** **Willow** **320** **£14.95**
A fifth collection of Arlott's writings; he will soon be catching Cardus as the favourite of anthologists.

C. Rhys **The Cricketer Book of Cricket Days** **Lennard** **150** **£10.95**
To each day of the year is attached three or four cricketing events – useful for those interested in lists.

T. Rice **Treasures of Lord's** **Collins** **160** **£16.95**
Some very pleasant illustrations but the text is a little pallid.

J. Richards **100 Years of Broadstone Cricket** **Club** **80** **£5.00**
A Dorset cricket club's centenary story – the most notable of their cricketers is R.M. Poore.

M. Ronayne **Test Cricket: Selecting the English Team** **Author** **28** **£2.00**
A detailed analysis of the selectors and their choices.

J. Scott **Caught in Court** **Deutsch** **278** **£12.95**
A selection of legal cases involving cricketers from the famous player hanged for murder downwards.

M. Selvey **The Ashes Surrendered** **Macdonald** **128** **£12.95**
The author's comments from *The Guardian* reprinted in book form with slight adjustments – rather a slim volume, perhaps due to the result.

J. Shawcroft **The History of Derbyshire CCC** **Helm** **335** **£14.95**
A well constructed history of the county with statistics by Frank Peach.

Sport-in-Print **Four Albums of Notts Cricketers** **Sport-in-Print** **64** **£8.00**
Nicely produced cards featuring famous Notts players with brief biographies.

Statisticians, Associaton of Cricket **Cricket Matches 1855–59** **Association of Cricket Statisticians** **170** **£6.50**
The detailed scores of the important matches played during the five years in the title. The series now covers 45 years.

Statisticians, Association of Cricket **Guide to Pakistan first-class matches** **Association of Cricket Statisticians** **40** **£3.50**
List of every first-class match played in Pakistan and where the score can be found – about 30 scores are still missing.

Statisticians, Association of Cricket **Lancashire Cricketers 1865–1988** **Association of Cricket Statisticians** **50** **£2.50**
The now familiar format of brief biographies and career records, both for the county and in all first-class matches.

Statisticians, Association of Cricket **Warwickshire Cricket Grounds** **Association of Cricket Statisticians** **32** **£2.75**
A detailed history of all the grounds in the county used for important matches, well researched by the Warwickshire historian, Robert Brooke.

A. Synge **The Voyage of the Colin Cowdrey** **Weidenfeld** **192** **£10.95**
A piece of fiction which makes a pleasant read.

W.H. Slatter **Recollections of Lord's and MCC** **McKenzie** **40** **£16.75**
Reprint of the book issued in 1914 written by the clerk of works at Lord's.

I. Sproat **The Cricketers' Who's Who 1989** **Collins-Willow** **525** **£8.95**
Standard annual describing current players in their own words, plus mug shots and statistics.

I. Thomson and M. Davies **Cricket Quiz Book** **Sphere** **192** **£2.50**
Paperback with 1,040 questions in groups of ten, the vast majority post-1945.

P. Tinniswood **Hayballs** **Hutchinson** **205** **£11.95**
Winston Hayballs is the hero of this fictional romp, but the plot is rather thin.

S. Thyagarajan **Indian Cricket 1989** **Kasturi and Sons** **800** **£6.00**
The 43rd edition of this standard work, the record section of which still worries many people.

F. Watson **Double Triumph: Worcestershire 1988** **Brewin** **253** **£7.95**
The county's feats of 1988 as recorded by the local Cricketcall correspondent.

P.N. Walker **The Liverpool Competition** **Countywise** **87** **£2.95**
A rather academic study of cricket in the Liverpool area.

T.M.K. Walton **Warwickshire Sunday League Records** **Author** **88** **£4.00**
A carefully compiled record book giving all the information one requires.

T.M.K. Walton **G.A. Headley** **Assocation of Cricket Statisticians** **32** **£2.50**
Detailed analysis of the great batsman's career with commentary.

P. West **Denis Compton** **Stanley Paul** **192** **£12.95**
A well told story of the golden boy of English cricket in the immediate post-war years.

G.D. West **Twelve Days of Grace** **Darf** **232** **£12.95**
A misleading title, but twelve informative essays on 19th-century cricketers whose careers touched that of the Grand Old Man.

A. Woodhouse **The History of Yorkshire CCC** **Helm** **624** **£17.95**
Detailed study of the players and matches that together comprise Yorkshire County Cricket Club.

G.Wright **Wisden Cricketers' Almanack 1989** **Wisden** **1,268** **£16.95**
The bible of English cricket, which remains as detailed and as accurate as ever.

* * *

The compilers of this current annual were involved in three books which appeared in 1989:

An Ashes Anthology **Helm** **256** **£14.95**
Contemporary reports and comments on each Ashes series since the start.

The History of Lancashire CCC **Helm** **296** **£14.95**
A careful study of the county's cricket from its earliest days with statistics by the Rev Malcolm Lorimer.

Cricket Tours at Home and Abroad **Hamlyn** **399** **£14.95**
Comment, averages, potted scores and pictures on all the major tours to and from England since 1859.

Obituaries 1989

Edward Lambert A'BECKETT died in Australia on 2 June, aged 81. His career in first-class cricket was of brief duration, for he retired aged 24 to concentrate on his work in the legal profession. A useful all-rounder A'Beckett toured England with the 1930 Australians, but illness restricted his opportunities on his only overseas tour. He represented Australia in four Tests and played 25 matches for Victoria. His son represented the same State in 1966–67.

Sir George Edmond Brackenbury ABELL, KCIE, OBE, who died on 11 January, aged 84, played for Oxford against Cambridge in 1924, 1926 and 1927. A wicket-keeper-batsman he also appeared intermittently for Worcestershire between 1923 and 1939, when on leave from India. On the sub-continent, where he was later Private Secretary to the Viceroy, he claimed a cricketing record by being the first batsman to score a double century in the Ranji Trophy competition – he captained Northern India. Returning to England after independence. He was a Director of the Bank of England. Two of his sons played occasional games in English first-class cricket, but not in the County Championship.

Sir George Oswald Browning ALLEN, CBE died on 30 November, aged 87. His career in first-class cricket extended over 34 years and he appeared for Middlesex from 1921 to 1950, but he could never be described as a regular county player, since he played in a total of only 146 county games over all that period. He went on three England Test tours, to Australia in 1932–33 and 1936–37 and to West Indies in 1947–48. He captained the side on the last two tours, when both rubbers were lost. Allen was regarded as the best Public School bowler of 1921, when he was in the Eton Eleven and the following year went up to Cambridge, where he was again most successful, but on leaving University he went into the City and appeared for Middlesex literally on his occasional days off. He first appeared for England in 1930 at Lord's, when Larwood was forced to withdraw, but Allen failed to take a wicket, conceded 115 runs and suffered at the hands of young Bradman. In 1931 he had an easier ride against the New Zealanders, hitting a century, as well as taking five for 14 in another match. This form resulted in his selection Jardine's 1932–33 side.

Allen declined to employ bodyline tactics, but

G.O.B. Allen batting for England against Australia in 1934.

had a most successful tour both with the ball and the bat, as well as fielding brilliantly close to the wicket. He captained England against the 1936 Indians and then led the side in the following winter to Australia. After that tour he did not again represent in England until 1947–48, a lapse of 11 years, being brought back when the reigning England captain, Yardley, was not available to tour West Indies.

Off the field of play, Allen was first elected to the MCC Committee in 1935, from 1964 to 1976 he was Treasurer of MCC, and from 1955 to 1961 Chairman of the Test Selectors. In his early Committee days he found the friendship of Lord Harris and Sir Pelham Warner very useful and he succeeded those two gentlemen as the most influential figure in English cricket. As such he transformed the mechanical workings of the MCC and removed those whom he thought unnecessary. An amateur of the old school, he was not everyone's ideal, but he took an enormous amount of trouble over the task of cricket administration and cricket benefitted greatly.

William Harry Russell ANDREWS died on 9 January at Weston-super-Mare, aged 80. A man who held forthright views – it was rumoured that his autobiography had to be drastically cut before the publisher's lawyers would allow it to be printed – Bill Andrews was devoted to Somerset cricket. He appeared 226 times for the county between 1930 and 1947 and achieved the 'double' in 1937 and 1938. His bowling contained a deceptive swing which baffled many opponents and his batting was of the hurricane variety, if not quite equal to his friend, Arthur Wellard. He was sacked and reinstated by Somerset three times and in later years he served as coach – one of the most enthusiastic in the country.

W.H.R. Andrews

Samuel Barclay BECKETT died on 22 December, aged 83. A Nobel Prize winner for literature, his most famous work was the play 'Waiting for Godot'. A left-hand batsman, and right-arm off break bowler, he played in two first-class matches for Dublin University.

Ronald Victor BELL, the Sussex slow left-arm bowler, died of cancer 26 October, aged 58. Born in Chelsea he played five matches for his native county before moving on to Sussex, where he spent eight seasons. He took 392 first-class wickets at 28.34, his best year being 1963. After leaving county cricket he became coach at Sandhurst.

Fred BERRY died on 2 January, aged 78. An all-rounder he played in 47 matches for Surrey between 1934 and 1939 and after the war for Berkshire, when he was engaged as professional at Wellington.

Tom BILLSON, the Surrey scorer since 1984, died on 19 May, aged 69. He had taken up scoring for the County when he retired from the Civil Service; a charming man of diverse interests, he appeared last year on TV's Mastermind, answering questions on music.

Nigel Clement Francis BLOY died at Sherborne on 7 January, aged 66. A useful left-hand batsman, he obtained his blue at Oxford in 1946 and 1947; later he played for Devon and MCC.

Fred Demetrius BEATTIE died on 20 March, aged 79. Educated at Rossall, where he was in the Eleven, he appeared for his native Lancashire in five matches in 1932, but failed to make much impression. He scored plenty of runs for the County Second Eleven however and as a result was chosen to represent the Minor Counties. In 1975–76 he was President of Lancashire CCC.

William Henry BOWLES, BEM, who died in July, aged 89, was the groundsman at Eton College for nearly 50 years and founder of the National Association of Groundsmen (now Institute of Groundsmanship). He acted as advisor to Notts CCC in 1952–53, when the notorious featherbed wickets were excavated and a new square prepared.

Thomas Leslie BRIERLEY, who died in Vancouver on 7 January, aged 78, appeared regularly for Glamorgan in the 1930s and after the war played for three summers for Lancashire prior to taking a coaching post with Vancouver CC. He came back to England as a member of the 1954 Canadian touring side.

James William BROOK played once for Yorkshire in 1923. A right-hand batsman he was a major figure with Ossett CC for many years. Brook died at Selby on 3 March, aged 92.

Henry Butler CAVE, who toured England with the New Zealand sides of 1949 and 1958, died at his home town of Wanganui on 15 September. A right-arm medium-pace bowler he appeared in 19 Tests for New Zealand and captained the side to India and Pakistan in 1955–56. He took 362 wickets at an average of 23.93 in first-class matches, but his record at international level was modest and although he hit two first-class hundreds, he could average only 8.80 in Test matches.

T.L. Brierley attempts a pull shot.

Cosmo Stafford CRAWLEY, who died on 10 February, aged 84, played for Harrow and for Oxford without obtaining his blue. He appeared twice in first-class county cricket, once for Hampshire in 1923 and once for Middlesex in 1929. He was a very useful batsman in club cricket, but not as well known as his brother, Aiden, the politician and Editor of ITN.

Leslie Thomas DEAKINS, MBE, died on 19 October, aged 80. From 1944 to 76 he was the Secretary of Warwickshire CCC and it was due to his hard work and endeavours that Edgbaston was transformed during the first ten years after the Second World War and Warwickshire became one of the most prosperous county clubs. Deakins paid attention to the little points which can so often be overlooked and though relatively unimportant in themselves, when properly administered make the difference between success and failure.

James Hamilton DOGGART died at Guildford on 15 October. A member of the well-known cricketing family, which includes the England player, G.H.G. Doggart, J.H. Doggart's first-class cricket was confined to one match for Cambridge University in 1919. A useful all-rounder, he also appeared occasionally for his native Durham in Minor County matches.

Alan Robert DUFF, who died of cancer on 28 June, aged 51, was a cricketing prodigy in his schooldays, his leg-breaks at Radley being formidable. He went up to Oxford, where he obtained his blue in 1960 and 1961, but he was never much of a force in county cricket, when he appeared in the Worcestershire ranks. He went on many minor MCC overseas tours and his bowling against the weaker opposition remained potent. A master at Malvern, he fully upheld the school's cricketing traditions.

Maurice Edward Frank DUNKLEY who was born in Kettering on February 19, 1914 died at Preston, Rutland, on December 27. An all round sportsman, he played as a middle order right hand batsman for Northants from 1937 to 1939. As a professional footballer he appeared for Manchester City and latterly he was a well known golfer.

Richard Harold EDMUNDS, who made his first-class debut for Leicestershire in June of last year, tragically died as a result of a road accident in December, aged 19. He was a promising left-arm fast bowler.

Commander Heneage EMMET died on 1 November, aged 77. He was Editor of *The Journal of the Cricket Society* from 1965 to 1970 and wrote articles for that magazine as well as the more popular monthlies. He was reported as being the captain of the MI5 cricket team, of which side few details have emerged!

Miles Robert FORMBY, who died in Norwich on 15 June, was a very good medium-pace bowler for Cheltenham, but going up to Cambridge he failed to obtain a blue; he did however play for the University in first-class matches in 1925.

Albert 'Bert' Charles Taylor GEARY died in Jersey in January, aged 88. He played for Surrey from 1922 to 31 as a right-arm medium pace bowler. Much of his cricket was for the Second Eleven, but in 1927 he appeared fairly often in the senior side and took 79 wickets. Leaving the Oval staff he obtained a coaching engagement in the Channel Isles.

Clifford Marshall GRAINGER, who was born in Heckmondwyke on 21 July, 1927, played for Oxford University as a fast bowler for three seasons, but failed to obtain his blue. He also appeared for Yorkshire Second Eleven and after leaving Oxford became a master at Leeds Grammar School. He died in Leeds on 26 May.

Vernon GRIMSHAW died on 21 June, aged 73. A right-hand batsman he appeared 19 times for Worcestershire in the 1930s.

Brian HALL, who died at Doncaster on 27 February, aged 59, represented his native county in one game in 1952, but with little success. His club cricket was mainly for East Bierley.

George Joseph HARRIS, who died at Briton Ferry, aged 84, played once for Glamorgan in 1932. An opening batsman he was on the staff at Trent Bridge for several seasons without representing his native county in first-class matches. His brother was the well-known Charlie Harris, who formed the famous opening partnership with Walter Keeton for Notts.

Reginald Allen HOLLINGDALE, who died in Scotland in September was born at Burgess Hill and played 78 matches for Sussex as a fast-medium bowler between 1925 and 1930. He moved to Scotland in 1931 where he appeared for Greenock and later Grange CC, making his final first-class appearance for Scotland in 1938.

Harold John HUBBLE, who died at Tenterden in January, aged 84, was the nephew of the former Kent wicket-keeper J.C. Hubble. A sound right-hand batsman, H.J. Hubble played a few games for Kent between 1929 and 1931, but became better known as the proprietor of a sports goods shop in Canterbury.

Cyril Lionel Robert JAMES, who died in Brixton on 31 May, aged 88, was best known to the cricketing public from his book 'Beyond A Boundary', which tells the story of life in Trinidad, both political and cricketal. He came to England in 1932 and was a journalist with the *Manchester Guardian* and then the *Glasgow Herald*, but went to America in the late 1930s and remained there until expelled in 1953 for his left-wing political views. Most of his later years were spent in London.

Emrys Closs JONES, who died at Briton Ferry on 14 April, aged 77, played for Glamorgan as an off-spinner in 101 matches between 1934 and 1946 – he originally appeared as an amateur but changed to the professional ranks in 1937. After 1946 he was still a noted figure in various South Wales Leagues.

John Miles LAWRENCE, who died at Toulston on 16 April, was generally known as Miles Lawrence to distinguish him from his famous cricketing father, Johnny Lawrence. Miles appeared in 18 matches for Somerset as an all-rounder between 1959 and 1961 – his father predeceased him by only four months.

James Edward Fryer LINTON died in Mexico on December 21, aged 80. A middle order right hand batsman and medium pace bowler he was educated at Charterhouse and made a couple of appearances for Glamorgan in 1932, but with little success.

Group Captain Gerald Edward LIVOCK, DFC, AFC, who died at his Dorset home on 27 January, aged 91, was a talented wicket-keeper. He was in the Cheltenham Eleven of 1914 and after the war played occasionally for Middlesex and then Cambridgeshire. In 1934 he went with Martineau's side to Egypt. After leaving the RAF he became headmaster of a prep school.

Kenneth McCANLIS died on 3 May, aged 80. A fast bowler, he played for Surrey Second Eleven for three seasons, but became more familiar to cricket watchers as a first-class umpire between

1948 and 1958. His grandfather, William McCanlis, appeared for Kent in the 1860s and 1870s, as did his great-uncle, George.

Percy Alec MACKENZIE, DSO, DFC, died in Winchelsea on 1 January, aged 70. He was a useful right-hand batsman and made 22 appearances for Hampshire immediately before the war. He was later seen in the Berkshire ranks.

Edwin George McLEOD died on 14 September aged 88 and was, prior to his death, the oldest living Test cricketer, though the extent of his international career was just one match for New Zealand in 1929–30. He also played hockey for New Zealand.

William Norman MERCER, a Lancastrian, played twice for Sussex, eight seasons separating the two matches. He was a most useful all-rounder in club cricket. He died at Brighton in April, aged 66.

Laurance William MEYNELL, who died on 4 April, aged 89, was a prolific author with some 170 titles to his credit, many written under a nom de plume. He wrote two well-known cricket books – "Famous Cricket Grounds" and "Plum Warner". At one time he was Chairman of the Authors' Club and a regular player in the annual Authors v Publishers match.

The Reverend Wilfred Ernest Granville PAYTON, CB, appeared briefly for both Notts and Derbyshire, but is more often associated with Cambridge University, winning his blue in 1936, and later the Combined Services. He died in September, aged 75, having risen to the rank of Chaplain-in-Chief in the RAF and then, retiring from the Forces, he became vicar of Abingdon and an Honorary Chaplain to the Queen. His father, W.R.D. Payton, was the noted Notts professional and his uncle also played for the county.

Lancelot Richard PIERRE, who died on 14 April, aged 67, came to England with the 1950 West Indian tourists, but his fast bowling was not employed in that summer's Tests – the West Indian attack being dominated by Ramadhin and Valentine. Born in Woodbrook, Trinidad, he represented his native island from 1940–41 to 1949–50, but only once appeared for the West Indies, when he was asked to bowl just seven overs. He retired after 1950, but acted as team manager for some years for Trinidad.

RAJINDERNATH, who died at Madras on 22 November, 1989, aged 61, had a brief career, but appeared once as a wicket-keeper for India against Pakistan in 1952–53, when he made four stumpings, but did not bat or take a catch.

John REDDISH died on 18 October, aged 85. An all-rounder he was on the Notts staff for five years, but appeared only once in first-class cricket – Notts v Oxford University in 1930. He was better known as a soccer player for Tottenham and Lincoln City and later as sports master at Elizabeth College, Guernsey, before retiring to Buxton.

Stuart Denzil RHODES, who died in Stamford on 7 January, aged 78, was appointed joint-captain of Nottinghamshire in controversial circumstances – the County Committee dismissed Arthur Carr in 1934 and the following winter saw the county members force a vote of confidence in the Committee, the vote was carried and the Committee resigned. Rhodes' county cricket was very limited, but he played regularly for Sir Julien Cahn's side, scoring many runs. After the war he turned out for Berkshire.

Harold RILEY, who died on 24 January in Leicester, was an attacking batsman for his native county, but only in 1929 did he really prove successful. He was later coach at Bradfield College. His father appeared for Leicestershire in 1895.

Andrew Duncan Glenn ROBERTS, who died of a heart attack in Wellington, New Zealnd, on 26 October, aged only 42, appeared in seven Test matches for New Zealand, two against India in 1975–76 and five on the tour of Pakistan and India in 1976–77. He scored 254 Test runs (average 23.09) and took four wickets. In all he scored 5,865 first-class runs at 34.70 and took 84 wickets at 29.88.

Harley James ROBERTS, who died on 19 February, aged 76, at Romsley, appeared in 17 matches for Warwickshire as an all-rounder.

Clayton Graeme Wynne ROBSON, who died at Long Melford on 26 February, aged 87, was a very stylish middle order batsman. Born in India he captained Malvern in 1920 and the following summer turned out for Worcestershire. Five seasons later he made an occasional appearance for Middlesex, but achieved little in first-class cricket.

Edmund John Rowe who died at Bridlington on December 17, joined the staff at Trent Bridge in 1947 and remained with Notts until 1959, but his career in first-class cricket on a regular basis spanned only five seasons, those summers coinciding with the bowling of Bruce Dooland, Rowe becoming an expert at reading the Australian's flipper. In 1960 he was appointed coach at Ellesmere College and while coaching there helped to devise Indoor Cricket in the 1960s. He was 69 at the time of his death, having been born in Netherfield on July 21, 1920.

Kenneth Anderson SELLAR, DSO, DSC, who died in Cape Town on 15 May, was a noted figure in naval sporting circles in the 1920s and 1930s – he represented the Royal Navy on both the cricket and rugby football field. As a cricketer he also played briefly for Sussex, as a rugby footballer he was England's full back. After retiring from the Navy he became a stockbroker and in 1982 moved to South Africa.

Peter SICHEL died in Cape Town on 11 May, aged 64. He took over from Denys Heesom as the editor of the Protea Cricket Annual of South Africa and at the time of his death was regarded as the leading cricket statistician in South Africa.

Wilfred Norris SLACK collapsed and died on 15 January, while batting in a match at Banjul, Gambia. The Middlesex left-hand opening batsman had had several blackouts previously when playing cricket, but despite medical tests, no cause could be found. Born in St Vincent, he emigrated to England in 1966 and his first-class career began with Middlesex in 1977. He appeared in three Tests for England, including one on the 1985–86 tour of the West Indies. With G.D. Barlow he holds the Middlesex first-wicket record partnership of 367 undivided v Kent at Lord's in 1981; in the same summer he hit his highest score of 248 not out v Worcestershire at Lord's.

George Williams Oswald SMITH died in Worthing on November 25. Born in Halstead, Essex in 1906. He failed to obtain his blue while at Cambridge, but played for his native county in ten matches during 1929 and 1930.

James SMURTHWAITE was a bowler who mixed medium pace seamers with off breaks. He played in seven matches for Yorkshire in the years immediately before the war and afterwards made a name for himself in the North Yorkshire and South Durham League. He died in Middlesbrough on October 20, aged 73.

Jeffrey Baxter STOLLMEYER, who died in a Florida hospital, after having been shot in his Port-of-Spain home by intruders, toured England with the 1939 and 1950 West Indies. An elegant opening batsman, he appeared in 32 Tests scoring 2,159 runs at an average of 42.33. He took over the captaincy of the West Indies from John Goddard in 1951–52 and altogether led his country in 13 Tests. He later played an important role as a cricket administrator, being at one time a selector of West Indian teams. He was born in Santa Cruz on 11 April 1921 and one of his brothers, Victor, also played for Trinidad and the West Indies.

John TEMPLE, who died in York, aged 75, on 6 October, was on the County Cricket Club Committee of Yorkshire for 21 years and was Chairman from 1971–78, during a very difficult period in the County's history.

Dr Laurance WARKE died in Belfast on 22 January aged 61. He represented Ireland from 1950 to 1961 as an all-rounder, scoring a century against Scotland in 1954. His son, S.J.S. Warke, is the present Irish cricketer.

Major-General Philip Sidney WHITCOMBE, OBE, CB, died on 9 August, aged 95, having been born in Windsor on 3 October, 1893. A useful all-rounder he made one appearance for Essex in 1922 and, while serving in India, played for the Europeans. His brother also appeared for Essex, while his son played three times for Middlesex in 1948.

Peter WHITELEY collapsed and died while playing golf at Crompton on October 28. A useful all-rounder, he had a trial with his native Lancashire in 1957 and 1958, but most of his cricket was in the Central Lancashire League for Crompton and Milnrow.

Douglas James 'Jim' WOOD, who died at Horsted Keynes on 12 March, aged 74, was a very useful left-arm fast bowler for Sussex in the years straddling the Second World War. His best summer was in 1952 when he took 103 wickets at an average of 24.56. He later became a first-class umpire and then cricket coach at Ardingley College.

Norman Walter Dransfield YARDLEY, who died in October, captained England in 14 Tests and his native Yorkshire from 1948–55. A sound middle order batsman and an under-used medium-pace bowler he first came to prominence in schools cricket for St Peter's, York. Going up to Cambridge he played against Oxford four times and gained his first England cap on the 1938–39 tour to South Africa. He later was an England Test selector and was Chairman 1951–52. An all-round athlete, he was also very successful in the squash court.

Far left: *D.J. Wood*
Left: *N.W.D. Yardley*

Fixtures 1990

Duration of Matches (*including play on Sunday)

Cornhill Insurance Test	5 days
Britannic Assurance County Championship	3 days or as stated
Tourist Matches	3 days or as stated
Universities v Counties	3 days
Texaco Trophy	1 day
Benson & Hedges Cup	1 day
NatWest Bank Trophy	1 day
Refuge Assurance League/Cup	1 day
Other matches	as stated

14 April, Saturday
*Cambridge University v Northamptonshire
Oxford University v Gloucestershire

17 April, Tuesday
MCC v Worcestershire (Lord's, 4 days)

18 April, Wednesday
Cambridge University v Derbyshire
Oxford University v Somerset

22 April, Sunday
Refuge Assurance League
Essex v Kent
Gloucestershire v Glamorgan
Lancashire v Middlesex
Leicestershire v Northamptonshire
Nottinghamshire v Yorkshire
Somerset v Worcestershire
Sussex v Derbyshire

24 April, Tuesday
Benson & Hedges Cup
Gloucestershire v Worcestershire
Warwickshire v Glamorgan
Derbyshire v Sussex
Middlesex v Minor Counties
Hampshire v Yorkshire
Lancashire v Surrey
Essex v Nottinghamshire
Leicestershire v Northamptonshire

26 April, Thursday
Britannic Assurance Championship (4 days)
Glamorgan v Leicestershire
Kent v Hampshire
Lancashire v Worcestershire
Middlesex v Essex
Nottinghamshire v Derbyshire
*Somerset v Gloucestershire
Sussex v Surrey
Yorkshire v Northamptonshire

Other Match
Cambridge University v Warwickshire

29 April, Sunday
Refuge Assurance League
Derbyshire v Worcestershire
Glamorgan v Leicestershire
Kent v Hampshire
Middlesex v Essex
Nottinghamshire v Lancashire
Sussex v Surrey
Warwickshire v Northampton

1 May, Tuesday
Benson & Hedges Cup
Worcestershire v Kent
Glamorgan v Gloucestershire
Minor Counties v Sussex
Somerset v Derbyshire
Combined Universities v Lancashire
Surrey v Hampshire
Scotland v Essex
Nottinghamshire v Leicestershire

3 May, Thursday
Britannic Assurance Championship (4 days)
Essex v Leicestershire
*Glamorgan v Somerset
Kent v Sussex
Northamptonshire v Derbyshire
Surrey v Lancashire
Warwickshire v Yorkshire
Worcestershire v Nottinghamshire

Other Matches
Cambridge University v Middlesex
Oxford University v Hampshire

6 May, Sunday
Refuge Assurance League
Hampshire v Gloucestershire
Kent v Middlesex
Leicestershire v Essex
Northamptonshire v Derbyshire
Surrey v Lancashire
Warwickshire v Yorkshire
Worcestershire v Nottinghamshire

Tourist Match
Lavinia, Dunchess of Norfolk's XI v New Zealand (Arundel, 1 day)

7 May, Monday
Tourist Match
MCC v New Zealand (Lord's 1 day)

8 May, Tuesday
Benson & Hedges Cup
Worcestershire v Glamorgan
Kent v Warwickshire
Sussex v Middlesex
Somerset v Minor Counties
Yorkshire v Combined Universities
Lancashire v Hampshire
Scotland v Nottinghamshire
Northamptonshire v Essex

9 May, Wednesday
Tourist Match
Ireland v New Zealand (1 day)

10 May, Thursday
Benson & Hedges Cup
Kent v Gloucestershire
Warwickshire v Worcestershire
Middlesex v Somerset
Minor Counties v Derbyshire
Yorkshire v Lancashire
Combined Universities v Surrey
Northamptonshire v Scotland
Essex v Leicestershire

Tourist Match
Ireland v New Zealand (1 day)

12 May, Saturday
Benson & Hedges Cup
Gloucestershire v Warwickshire
Glamorgan v Kent
Derbyshire v Middlesex
Sussex v Somerset
Hampshire v Combined Universities
Surrey v Yorkshire
Leicestershire v Scotland (Reserve day Sunday)
Nottinghamshire v Northamptonshire

Tourist Match
*Worcestershire v New Zealand

13 May, Sunday
Refuge Assurance League
Essex v Gloucestershire
Glamorgan v Kent
Middlesex v Nottinghamshire
Somerset v Hampshire
Yorkshire v Derbyshire

Tourist Match
Sussex v Zimbabwe (1 day)

14 May, Monday
Tourist Match
Essex v Zimababwe (1 day)

15 May, Tuesday
Britannic Assurance Championship (4 days)
Derbyshire v Lancashire
Gloucestershire v Glamorgan
Hampshire v Sussex
Leicestershire v Nottinghamshire
Middlesex v Kent
Northamptonshire v Warwickshire

16 May, Wednesday
Tourist Match
Somerset v New Zealand
Yorkshire v Zimbabwe

Other Matches
Cambridge University v Essex
Oxford University v Surrey

19 May, Saturday
Britannic Assurance Championship
Lancashire v Leicestershire
Somerset v Derbyshire
Surrey v Hampshire
Sussex v Glamorgan
Warwickshire v Nottinghamshire
Worcestershire v Essex

Tourist Matches
*Middlesex v New Zealand
Gloucestershire v Zimbabwe

20 May, Sunday
Refuge Assurance Championship
Gloucestershire v Warwickshire
Kent v Yorkshire
Lancashire v Leicestershire
Nottinghamshire v Surrey
Somerset v Derbyshire
Sussex v Glamorgan
Worcestershire v Essex

23 May, Wednesday
Texaco Trophy (1st 1-day International)
England v New Zealand (Headingley)

Britannic Assurance Championship
Derbyshire v Yorkshire
Glamorgan v Kent
Hampshire v Essex
Middlesex v Surrey
Nottinghamshire v Northamptonshire
Somerset v Sussex

Tourist Match
Lancashire v Zimbabwe

Other Matches
Cambridge University v Gloucestershire
Oxford University v Leicestershire

25 May, Friday
Texaco Trophy (2nd 1-day International)
England v New Zealand (Oval)

26 May, Saturday
Britannic Assurance Championship
*Derbyshire v Nottinghamshire
Glamorgan v Lancashire
Leicestershire v Somerset
Middlesex v Gloucestershire
Warwickshire v Worcestershire
Yorkshire v Hampshire

Tourist Match
*Sussex v New Zealand

27 May, Sunday
Refuge Assurance League
Glamorgan v Lancashire
Leicestershire v Somerset
Middlesex v Gloucestershire
Northamptonshire v Kent
Worcestershire v Warwickshire
Yorkshire v Hampshire

30 May, Wednesday
Benson & Hedges Cup
Quarter-Finals

Tourist Match
Warwickshire or Lancashire v New Zealand

2 June, Saturday
Britannic Assurance Championship
Essex v Middlesex
Gloucestershire v Somerset
Kent v Nottinghamshire
Leicestershire v Hampshire
Sussex v Lancashire
Warwickshire v Northamptonshire

Worcestershire v Yorkshire

Tourist Match
*Derbyshire v New Zealand

Other Match
Oxford University v New Zealand

3 June, Sunday
Refuge Assurance League
Essex v Glamorgan
Gloucestershire v Somerset
Leicestershire v Hampshire
Middlesex v Warwickshire
Surrey v Northamptonshire
Sussex v Lancashire
Worcestershire v Yorkshire

6 June, Wednesday
Britannic Assurance Championship
Essex v Gloucestershire
Hampshire v Somerset
Kent v Yorkshire
Middlesex v Warwickshire
Northamptonshire v Leicestershire
Surrey v Derbyshire

Other Match
Oxford University v Nottinghamshire

7 June, Thursday
First Cornhill Test
ENGLAND v NEW ZEALAND (Trent Bridge)

9 June, Saturday
Britannic Assurance Championship
Kent v Somerset
Lancashire v Gloucestershire
Northamptonshire v Glamorgan
Warwickshire v Essex
Yorkshire v Surrey

10 June, Sunday
Refuge Assurance League
Derbyshire v Nottinghamshire
Hampshire v Middlesex
Kent v Somerset
Lancashire v Gloucestershire
Leicestershire v Sussex
Northamptonshire v Glamorgan
Warwickshire v Essex
Yorkshire v Surrey

13 June, Wednesday
Benson & Hedges Cup
Semi-Finals

Tourist Match
Lancashire or Warwickshire v New Zealand

16 June, Saturday
Britannic Assurance Championship
Derbyshire v Warwickshire
Hampshire v Glamorgan
Leicestershire v Middlesex
Somerset v Essex
Surrey v Worcestershire
Sussex v Gloucestershire

Tourist Match
*Northamptonshire v New Zealand

Other Matches
Cambridge University v Nottinghamshire
Oxford University v Lancashire

17 June, Sunday
Refuge Assurance League
Derbyshire v Warwickshire
Hampshire v Glamorgan
Kent v Nottinghamshire
Leicestershire v Middlesex
Somerset v Essex
Surrey v Worcestershire
Sussex v Yorkshire

20 June, Wednesday
Britannic Assurance Championship
Gloucestershire v Hampshire
Lancashire v Middlesex
Leicestershire v Derbyshire
Nottinghamshire v Surrey
Somerset v Glamorgan
Worcestershire v Sussex
Yorkshire v Warwickshire

Other Match
Cambridge University v Kent

21 June, Thursday
Second Cornhill Test
ENGLAND v NEW ZEALAND (Lord's)

23 June, Saturday
Britannic Assurance Championship
Glamorgan v Yorkshire
Gloucestershire v Leicestershire
Lancashire v Hampshire
Northamptonshire v Middlesex
Warwickshire v Kent

24 June, Sunday
Refuge Assurance League
Glamorgan v Yorkshire
Gloucestershire v Leicestershire
Lancashire v Hampshire
Northamptonshire v Middlesex
Somerset v Nottinghamshire
Surrey v Derbyshire
Warwickshire v Kent
Worcestershire v Sussex

27 June, Wednesday
NatWest Bank Trophy
First Round

Tourist Match
Oxbridge v New Zealand

28 June, Thursday
Tourist Match
League Cricket Conference v India (1 day)

30 June, Saturday
Britannic Assurance Championship
Derbyshire v Gloucester
Glamorgan v Surrey
Kent v Lancashire
Middlesex v Worcestershire
Nottinghamshire v Leicestershire
Somerset v Northamptonshire

Tourist Matches
*Essex v New Zealand
*Yorkshire v India

Other Match
Sussex v Cambridge University

1 July, Sunday
Refuge Assurance League
Derbyshire v Gloucestershire
Glamorgan v Surrey
Kent v Lancashire
Middlesex v Worcestershire
Nottinghamshire v Leicestershire
Somerset v Northamptonshire
Sussex v Hampshire

4 July, Wednesday
Britannic Assurance Championship
Glamorgan v Gloucestershire
Kent v Essex
Somerset v Warwickshire
Surrey v Northamptonshire
Sussex v Derbyshire
Yorkshire v Nottinghamshire

Tourist Match
Hampshire v India

Varsity Match
Oxford University v Cambridge University (Lord's)

5 July, Thursday
Third Cornhill Test
ENGLAND v NEW ZEALAND (Edgbaston)

7 July, Saturday
Britannic Assurance Championship
Lancashire v Derbyshire
*Leicestershire v Glamorgan
Northamptonshire v Yorkshire
Nottinghamshire v Sussex
Surrey v Warwickshire
Worcestershire v Gloucesershire

Tourist Match
*Kent v India

8 July, Sunday
Refuge Assurance League
Hampshire v Essex
Lancashire v Derbyshire
Middlesex v Somerset
Northamptonshire v Yorkshire
Nottinghamshire v Sussex
Surrey v Warwickshire
Worcestershire v Gloucestershire

11 July, Wednesday
NatWest Bank Trophy
Second Round

Tourist Match
Minor Counties v India

14 July, Saturday
Benson & Hedges Cup
Final (Lord's)

Tourist Match
Scotland v India (1 day)

15 July, Sunday
Refuge Assurance League
Derbyshire v Leicestershire
Essex v Northamptonshire
Gloucestershire v Sussex
Hampshire v Nottinghamshire
Lancashire v Worcestershire
Surrey v Middlesex
Warwickshire v Glamorgan
Yorkshire v Somerset

16 July, Monday
Tourist Match
Derbyshire (or other county if in B & H Final) v India (1 day)

18 July, Wednesday
Texaco Trophy (1st 1-day International)
England v India (Headingley)

Britannic Assurance Championship
Essex v Derbyshire
Hampshire v Nottinghamshire
Middlesex v Yorkshire
Northamptonshire v Kent
Surrey v Sussex
Warwickshire v Lancashire
Worcestershire v Somerset

20 July, Friday
Texaco Trophy (2nd 1-day International)
England v India (Trent Bridge)

21 July, Saturday
Britannic Assurance Championship
Essex v Lancashire
Glamorgan v Worcestershire
Gloucestershire v Yorkshire
Hampshire v Derbyshire
Middlesex v Somerset
Northamptonshire v Sussex
Surrey v Kent

Tourist Match
*Leicestershire v India

22 July, Sunday
Refuge Assurance League
Essex v Lancashire
Glamorgan v Somerset
Gloucestershire v Yorkshire
Hampshire v Derbyshire
Northampton v Sussex
Surrey v Kent
Warwickshire v Nottinghamshire

25 July, Wednesday
Britannic Assurance Championship
Derbyshire v Worcestershire
Glamorgan v Warwickshire
Gloucestershire v Warwickshire
Kent v Middlesex
Lancashire v Nottinghamshire
Leciestershire v Essex
Sussex v Hampshire
Yorkshire v Somerset

26 July, Thursday
First Cornhill Test
ENGLAND v INDIA (Lord's)

28 July, Saturday
Britannic Assurance Championship
Essex v Sussex
Gloucestershire v Surrey
Kent v Worcestershire
Lancashire v Somerset
Nottinghamshire v Middlesex
Warwickshire v Hampshire
Yorkshire v Leicestershire

29 July, Sunday
Refuge Assurance League
Essex v Sussex
Glamorgan v Derbyshire
Gloucestershire v Surrey

Kent v Worcestershire
Lancashire v Somerset
Nottinghamshire v Northamptonshire
Warwickshire v Hampshire
Yorkshire v Leicestershire

1 August, Wednesday
NatWest Bank Trophy
Quarter-Finals

Tourist Match
Surrey or Nottinghamshire v India

2 August, Thursday
England XI v Rest of World XI (Jesmond, 1 day)

3 August, Friday
England XI v Rest of World XI (Jesmond, 1 day)

4 August, Saturday
Briannic Assurance Championship
Derbyshire v Kent
Essex v Nottinghamshire
Hampshire v Northamptonshire
Leicestershire v Worcestershire
Middlesex v Glamorgan
Somerset v Surrey
Sussex v Warwickshire
Yorkshire v Lancashire

Tourist Match
*Gloucestershire v India

5 August, Sunday
Refuge Assurance League
Derbyshire v Kent
Essex v Nottinghamshire
Hampshire v Northamptonshire
Leicestershire v Worcestershire
Middlesex v Glamorgan
Somerset v Surrey
Sussex v Warwickshire
Yorkshire v Lancashire

8 August, Wednesday
Britannic Assurance Championship
Derbyshire v Northamptonshire
Essex v Glamorgan
Gloucestershire v Warwickshire
Hampshire v Middlesex
Kent v Leicestershire
Somerset v Nottinghamshire
Sussex v Yorkshire
Worcestershire v Lancashire

9 August, Thursday
Second Cornhill Test
ENGLAND v INDIA (Old Trafford)

11 August, Saturday
Britannic Assurance Championship
Gloucestershire v Kent
Middlesex v Sussex
Northamptonshire v Lancashire
Nottinghamshire v Glamorgan
Surrey v Leicestershire
Worcestershire v Hampshire
Yorkshire v Essex

12 August, Sunday
Refuge Assurance League
Gloucestershire v Kent
Middlesex v Sussex
Northamptonshire v Lancashire
Nottinghamshire v Glamorgan
Somerset v Warwickshire
Surrey v Leicestershire
Worcestershire v Hampshire
Yorkshire v Essex

13 or 14 August, Monday or Tuesday
Bain Clarkson Trophy
Semi-Finals (1 day)

15 August, Wednesday
NatWest Bank Trophy
Semi-Finals

Tourist Match
TCCB Under-25 XI v India

18 August, Saturday
Britannic Assurance Championship
Derbyshire v Middlesex
Essex v Surrey
*Lancashire v Yorkshire (4 days)
Nottinghamshire v Gloucestershire
*Somerset v Hampshire (4 days)
Sussex v Kent
Warwickshire v Leicestershire
Worcestershire v Northampton

Tourist Match
*Glamorgan v India

19 August, Sunday
Refuge Assurance League
Derbyshire v Middlesex
Essex v Surrey
Kent v Sussex
Nottinghamshire v Gloucestershire
Warwickshire v Leicestershire
Worcestershire v Northamptonshire

22 August, Wednesday
Tourist Match
Glamorgan v Sri Lanka

23 August, Thursday
Third Cornhill Test
ENGLAND v INDIA (Oval)

Britannic Assurance Championship (4 days)
Derbyshire v Essex
Hampshire v Surrey
Leicestershire v Kent
Northamptonshire v Gloucestershire
Sussex v Somerset
Worcestershire v Warwickshire
Yorkshire v Middlesex

25 August, Saturday
Tourist Match
Nottinghamshire v Sri Lanka

26 August, Sunday
Refuge Assurance League
Derbyshire v Essex
Glamorgan v Worcestershire
Hampshire v Surrey
Lancashire v Warwickshire
Leicestershire v Kent
Northamptonshire v Gloucestershire
Sussex v Somerset
Yorkshire v Middlesex

29 August, Wednesday
Britannic Assurance Championship
Glamorgan v Derbyshire
Hampshire v Kent
Lancashire v Surrey
Leicestershire v Sussex
Northamptonshire v Essex
Nottinghamshire v Worcestershire

Tourist Match
Warwickshire v Sri Lanka

1 September, Saturday
NatWest Bank Trophy
Final (Lord's)

2 September, Sunday
Tourist Match
Surrey v Sri Lanka (1 day)

3 September, Monday
Bain Clarkson Trophy
Final (1 day)

Tourist Match
Somerset v Sri Lanka (1 day)

5 September, Wednesday
Refuge Assurance Cup
Semi-Finals

Tourist Match
Sussex v Sri Lanka

7 September, Friday
Britannic Assurance Championship (4 days)
*Essex v Northamptonshire
*Glamorgan v Hampshire
*Gloucestershire v Worcestershire
*Kent v Surrey
*Middlesex v Nottinghamshire
*Warwickshire v Somerset
*Yorkshire v Derbyshire

8 September, Saturday
Tourist Match
Lancashire v Sri Lanka

12 September, Wednesday
Britannic Assurance Championship (4 days)
Essex v Kent
Gloucestershire v Sussex
Leicestershire v Northamptonshire
Nottinghamshire v Lancashire
Somerset v Worcestershire
Surrey v Middlesex
Warwickshrie v Glamorgan

Tourist Match
Hampshire v Sri Lanka

16 September, Sunday
Refuge Assurance Cup
Final

18 September, Tuesday
Britannic Assurance Championship (4 days)
Derbyshire v Leicestershire
Hampshire v Gloucestershire
Lancashire v Warwickshire
Nottinghamshire v Yorkshire
Surrey v Essex
Sussex v Middlesex
Worcestershire v Glamorgan